CLAUDIO PAVONE was born in Rome in 1920 and, as a young man, took an active part in the Resistance movement. A renowned historian, he worked in the National Archives and was Professor of Contemporary History at the University of Pisa. At present, he is the President of the Historic Institute of the Liberation Movement in Italy, the Vice-President of the Italian Society of Contemporary History and the Director of the journal *Parolechiave*.

A Civil War

A HISTORY OF THE ITALIAN RESISTANCE

CLAUDIO PAVONE

Translated by Peter Levy
with the assistance of David Broder

Edited with an introduction by Stanislao G. Pugliese

VERSO
London • New York

This paperback edition first published by Verso 2014
First published by Verso 2013
Translation © Peter Levy 2013, 2014
Introduction © Stanislao G. Pugliese 2013, 2014

1 3 5 7 9 10 8 6 4 2

Verso
UK: 6 Meard Street, London W1F 0EG
US: 20 Jay Street, Suite 1010, Brooklyn, NY 11201
www.versobooks.com

Verso is the imprint of New Left Books

ISBN-13: 978-1-78168-777-2 (PB)
eISBN-13: 978-1-78168-236-4 (US)
eISBN-13: 978-1-78168-541-9 (UK)

British Library Cataloguing in Publication Data
A catalogue record for this book is available from the British Library

The Library of Congress Has Cataloged the Hardback Edition as Follows:

Pavone, Claudio.
[Guerra civile. English]
 A civil war : a history of the Italian resistance /
Claudio Pavone ; translated by Peter Levy with the
assistance of David Broder; introduced by Stanislao G.
Pugliese.
    page cm
 Originally published as: Guerra civile. Torino : Bollati
Boringhieri, 1991.
 Includes bibliographical references and index.
 ISBN 978-1-84467-750-4 (alk. paper)
 1. Italy–Politics and government–1943–1947.
 2. World War, 1939-1945–Underground movements–
Italy. I. Title.
 DG572.P3513 2013
 940.53'45–dc23
                          2013029227

Typeset in Minion Pro by MJ & N Gavan, Truro, Cornwall

Printed and bound in Great Britain by
Marston Book Services Limited, Oxfordshire

To my daughters
Liberiana, Flaminia and Sabina

Contents

The Italian Resistance: Three Wars and the Eternal Struggle for the Past

'The past is never dead. It's not even past.'
William Faulkner, *Requiem for a Nun*, 1950

Nearly seventy years after the end of the Second World War, the armed Resistance against fascism – in both its Italian and German variants – is still the *caesura* of contemporary Italian politics, society and culture. Historically, psychologically, and culturally, it functions much like the Dreyfus Affair in France or the Civil War in the United States. As in France, the Italian Resistance evolved its own necessary mythology, thereby generating a counter-narrative of rightist revisionism. But from its earliest days, the Resistance, its participants and its chroniclers were aware of the sometimes morally ambiguous nature of the movement.

On its initial publication in 1991 by the Italian publishing house of Bollati Boringhieri in Turin, Claudio Pavone's *Una guerra civile* was generally acknowledged to be the most important work of history in a generation.[1] With 800 pages of text and notes, this was a monumental work of scholarship, maturing after decades of labour in the relevant archives. Two decades later, it can be seen to have altered the terms of debate on the armed Resistance; a true paradigm-shifter in Italian historiography.[2] When first published in France, it was recognised outside Italy's borders as a fundamental work.[3] Now, after a convoluted

---

1 'Pavone's study of the struggle between the Resistance and the Fascist Republican regime, *Una guerra civile*, has provided the broad interpretative framework for much recent scholarship.' Alexander De Grand, *American Historical Review* 106: 2 (April 2001), p. 677.

2 For Pavone's influence on two generations of Italian historians, see Cesare Bermani, et al., *La nuova storia contemporanea in Italia: omaggio a Claudio Pavone*, Turin: Bollati Boringhieri, 2001 and Paolo Pezzino and Gabriele Ranzato, eds, *Laboratorio di storia. Studi in onore di Claudio Pavone*, Milan: Franco Angeli, 1994.

3 *Une guerre civile: Essai historique sur l'éthique de la Résistance italienne*, ed. Bernard Droz and transl. Jérôme Grossman, Paris: Seuil, 2005. 'Un ouvrage fondamental sur l'histoire des années 1940 en Italie', according to Jean Marie Guillon, *Vingtième Siècle. Revue d'histoire* 54 (April–June 1997), p. 155; while Fédéric Attal wrote that 'est le travail le plus accompli jamais écrit sur la Résistance italienne', *Vingtième Siècle. Revue d'histoire* 91 (July–September 2006), p. 180.

and complicated history, the book is finally available to English-language readers.[4]

Its most fundamental contribution to Resistance historiography is in Pavone's delineation of three simultaneous wars: a patriotic war, a civil war and a class war. Pavone had first used the loaded term 'civil war' at a conference in Belluno in October 1988.[5] Previously, only the Fascists and neo- or post-Fascists had used the phrase.[6] Just as only a Nixon could go to China, only an historian with such impeccable anti-Fascist credentials as Pavone could propose looking at the Resistance in this manner. Today, it is almost a commonplace to speak of the civil war in Italy between 1943 and 1945.[7]

This book's genesis might be said to have begun with Pavone's participation in the Resistance as a young man. Its more immediate birth was recounted by the author in his preface to the original Italian edition.[8] Many years earlier, Ferruccio Parri had proposed that Pavone write a history of the Resistance using, as a model, two fundamental works that had been published in France some time before: Henri Michel's *Les courants de pensée de la Résistance*,[9] and, by the same Henri Michel and Boris Mirkine-Guetzévitch, *Les idées politiques et sociales de la Résistance*.[10] When Norberto Bobbio invited Pavone to develop a series of seminars on the relationship between politics and morality at the Centro Gobetti in Turin, the lectures became the nucleus of this book.

Pavone's original intent to focus on the institutions of the Resistance, based on his earlier essay, 'La continuità del Stato',[11] was abandoned when he 'became convinced of the difficulty, in an essay on the Italian Resistance, of separating political, social, and institutional ideas and programmes'. Instead the work

---

4 A collective decision was made to edit the late Peter Edward Levy's translation with a light hand. Levy, who taught in Siena, translated Pavone's erudite, Latinate Italian into a complex, intricately rendered English. My thanks to Charles Maier, Mark Mazower, Victoria De Grazia and the late Tony Judt for their unflagging support in publishing this English translation.

5 Proceedings published as Massimo Legnani, Ferruccio Vendramini, eds, *Guerra, guerra di liberazione, guerra civile*, Milan: Franco Angeli, 1990.

6 See, for example, Giorgio Pisanò, *Storia della guerra civile in Italia (1943–1945)*, Milan: FPE, 1965; and Indro Montanelli, *L'Italia della guerra civile*, vol. 9 of his monumental 12-volume *Storia d'Italia*, Milan: Corriere della Sera, 2003.

7 See Gianni Oliva, *Primavera 1945: Il sangue della guerra civile*, Milan: Giunti, 2011; or, for a more wide-ranging and contested application, Stanley G. Payne, *Civil War in Europe, 1905–1949*, New York: Cambridge University Press, 2011.

8 'Premessa' in Pavone, *Una guerra civile. Saggio storico sulla moralità nella Resistenza*, Turin: Bollati Boringhieri, 1991, ix–xii.

9 Paris: PUF, 1962.

10 Paris: PUF, 1954.

11 The essay now appears in Claudio Pavone, *Alle origini della repubblica: scritti su fascismo, antifascismo e continuità dello stato*, Turin: Bollati Boringhieri, 1995.

refocused on 'analysing the behaviour of the protagonists to understand the ideas that inspired them, even if those ideas were formulated without clarity or coherence'. Hence Pavone's focus on the partisans themselves, without his losing sight of the political and military frameworks in which they acted. Letters, memoirs and diaries are used extensively, as are literary texts, such as those by Beppe Fenoglio and Italo Calvino.

Pavone argues that, from September 1943 to April 1945, Italy was divided by three different wars occurring simultaneously: there was a class war, a civil war and a patriotic war. The book was part of a larger trend in Italian historiography concerning the Resistance, yet it is also the single most influential piece of scholarship in the last generation. In his depiction of the vast social dimension of the Resistance and his sensitive exploration of the moral and ethical problems associated with armed resistance, Pavone has written a work that is often described as a masterpiece of the historian's craft. It demonstrates the evolving and sophisticated nature of Italian historical writing – a reality often not recognised outside Italy. *A Civil War* is not just a standard but a central point of reference in the rapidly growing body of scholarship on history and memory, so that the continued absence of an English-language edition posed a serious obstacle to a fuller understanding of these issues, making one of the finest examples of contemporary Italian historical scholarship inaccessible to Anglophone readers.

While *A Civil War* is universally recognised as the most important work of history and historiography in a generation, it can also be seen as the intellectual and historiographical response to Renzo De Felice's monumental eight-volume biography of Benito Mussolini. Pavone has crafted a more subtle and substantive interpretation of the armed Resistance against Fascism and the Nazi occupation of Italy. Mediating between the hagiography of the left and the dismissive revisionism of the right, he has forged a new reading of the most important event in modern Italian history.

Most influential has been his reading of the Resistance as three interrelated wars. Using this imaginative and innovative framework, Pavone was able to draw together the amazingly complex events, discourses and interpretations into a new narrative. While most scholarly and popular attention has been focused on these three interrelated wars, Pavone also offers a sophisticated and ambitious chapter on the moral and political nature of violence, carefully delineating a profound difference between Fascist violence and partisan violence, thereby avoiding any moral equivalency between the two.

As readers will soon notice, 8 September 1943 looms large in the book. Much of the subsequent historiography and political mythology revolve around this seminal date. Historians and politicians still debate the symbolism and political ramifications of Italy's surrender. The left saw (and sees) the date as the beginning of Italy's attempt to redeem itself, with the armed Resistance as a 'second Risorgimento'. The right offers a very different interpretation. For example, in

1996, Italian historian Ernesto Galli Della Loggia published *La morte della patria*, in which he equated the collapse of Fascism (July 1943) and the Armistice with the Allies (September 1943) with the 'Death of the Fatherland'.[12] Most historians and citizens agree that the events of July–September 1943 engendered a crisis of moral consciousness and national identity, but the larger and longer-term ramifications have been the subject of widely varying interpretations. Historian Elena Aga Rossi offers an overview of the issues in commenting critically on Pavone's book:

> In Claudio Pavone's book *Una guerra civile*, the choice in the days following the Armistice between loyalty to the monarchy and loyalty to Mussolini is for the first time considered a legitimate 'moral' one. Pavone, an intellectual of the left, uses the concept of 'civil war' to explain the struggle between partisans and exponents of the Italian Social Republic, thereby avoiding the usual condemnation of the followers of Mussolini voiced by historians of the Resistance.
>
> ...
>
> In historical studies, the patriotic element has been relegated to second place, while the concepts of the Resistance as a 'civil' and a 'class' war have prevailed – to borrow Claudio Pavone's most useful classification. Pavone's text is a good example of the contradictions that can be found in many histories of that period. It represents a turning-point, since it introduces reflections on the patriotic theme, but at the same time it does not in the least free itself from old assumptions, dedicating to the patriotic war much less space than that devoted to the 'civil' and 'class' aspects of the conflict.[13]

Aga Rossi's critique of *A Civil War* was not unusual, but it failed to recognise how distinctive Pavone's work really was.

The armed Resistance did not appear spontaneously on 8 September 1943. In fact, it had a distinguished if complex political and intellectual genealogy. And considering the involvement of the Italian volunteers in the Spanish Civil War fighting alongside the Loyalists in defending the Republic, it also had a military prehistory as well. What follows is a brief contextualisation of the Resistance for those readers who may not be familiar with the history.

Even before the Second World War came to an end in Italy, the political and intellectual battle over the ultimate meaning and significance of Fascism and the armed Resistance was joined.[14] Had Fascism been a revolution that radi-

---

12 Ernesto Galli Della Loggia, *La morte della patria. La crisi dell'idea di nazione tra Resistenza, antifascismo e Repubblica*, Rome: Laterza, 1996.

13 Elena Aga Rossi, *A Nation Collapses: The Italian Surrender of September 1943*, transl. Harvey Fergusson II, Cambridge: Cambridge University Press, 2000, pp. 134–8.

14 Parts of this Introduction have been adapted from an earlier essay, 'A Past That

cally changed Italy and the Italians, or merely the violent reaction of a morally and politically bankrupt bourgeoisie threatened by socialist revolution? Was the regime a manifestation of deep-rooted historical, economic, and social problems that could be traced back to a failed Risorgimento, the movement for national unification in the nineteenth century? Had Mussolini been a buffoon, a manipulator, an opportunist? Had he been a 'sincere' revolutionary? Had he indeed made the trains run on time and saved Italy from a Bolshevik revolution? Had he committed his 'only' mistake in allying himself with Hitler in the mid 1930s? Was the armed Resistance an illegal movement that betrayed the nation-state, and the Armistice of 8 September 1943 a betrayal of Italy's Axis partner, Nazi Germany? Was the Resistance a second – and truly popular – Risorgimento, bringing the masses into the struggle for a democratic republic founded on the principles of social justice and individual liberty? Had the regime fostered a genuine 'consensus', or was the populace coerced into political silence? Was Fascism an early form of totalitarianism, or was there room for artists, writers, intellectuals and individuals to think and create on their own? Were the Fascist and Nazi massacres of civilians legitimate acts of war or crimes against humanity? Was the Italian Communist Party (PCI) – the largest and most influential of the anti-Fascist forces – a patriotic organisation or the tool of Stalin's Soviet Union? Were the anti-Fascist activities of sabotage, killings and executions of Mussolini and Fascists legitimate acts of war or acts of terrorism? Had the pernicious effects of Fascism ended with 25 April 1945 (the date usually understood to mean the end of the war in Italy), or were they to infect the very foundations of the Italian Republic as it emerged after the war? Has post-war Italy come to terms with and fully acknowledged its Fascist past?

Interpretations and readings of the fascist *ventennio* and the anti-Fascist Resistance have proved extraordinarily contentious for more than half a century. The fiftieth anniversary of the end of the war in 1995 served as a catalyst for a major re-examination of the issues that bore more than a passing resemblance to the infamous *Historikerstreit* (Historians' Debate) over the nature of Nazism in Germany during the 1980s.[15]

Will Not Pass: Fascism, Anti-Fascism and the Resistance in Italy', in *Fascism, Anti-Fascism and the Resistance in Italy*, Lanham, MD: Rowman & Littlefield, 2004, pp. 1–22.

15 The 'Historians' Debate' in West Germany unfolded in the mid-to-late 1980s over the nature of the Holocaust and its relation with the Soviet gulag system. Originally a dispute between historian Ernst Nolte and philosopher Jürgen Habermas, it evolved into a watershed philosophical and historiographical moment. In English, see Rudolf Augstein et al., *Forever in the Shadow of Hitler? Original Documents of the Historikerstreit, The Controversy Concerning the Singularity of the Holocaust*, Atlantic Highlands, NJ: Humanities Press, 1993 (English-language edition of 'Historikerstreit': *Die Dokumentation der Kontroverse um die Einzigartigkeit der nationalsozialistschen Judenvernichtung*, Munich: Piper, 1987); Peter Baldwin, *Hitler, the Holocaust and the Historians Dispute*, Boston, MA: Beacon Press, 1990; Richard Evans, *In Hitler's Shadow:*

Some anti-Fascists, such as Ugo La Malfa, then a member of the Action Party and later a leading figure of the Italian Republican Party (PRI), argued that a broad coalition of anti-Fascist parties would be required to effect the necessary break with the pre-Fascist past. In May 1944, La Malfa charged that 'Italy has never been a real democracy' and called for a 'progressive democracy' that avoided the injustices of both the liberal and the communist state.[16] La Malfa was echoing the heretical ideas first proposed by the liberal socialist Carlo Rosselli in the 1920 and 1930s. This indictment of the status quo ante could not go unchallenged. In a radio broadcast on 1 September 1944, Pope Pius XII offered a religious justification of private property, while Alcide De Gasperi, leader of the Christian Democrats (DC), would write that 'anti-Fascism is a contingent political phenomenon, which will at a certain moment be overturned by other political ideals more in keeping with the ... feelings of Italian public life, for the good and the progress of the nation'.[17] Ada Gobetti of the Action Party spoke for many in this later recollection:

> In a confusing way I sensed, however, that another struggle was beginning: longer, more difficult, more tiring, even if less bloody. It was no longer the question of fighting against arrogance, cruelty and violence ... but ... of not allowing that little flame of solidarity and fraternal humanism, which we had seen born, to die in the calm atmosphere of an apparent return to normal life.[18]

In a famous speech before the National Assembly on 26 September 1945, Prime Minister Parri shocked his audience by echoing Piero Gobetti and Carlo Rosselli: 'I do not believe that the governments we had before Fascism can be called democratic.' For the new prime minister, the legacy of the anti-Fascist Resistance was that it was the only democratic movement in the history of Italy that the masses had supported. With the Resistance, both Fascism and the nineteenth-century liberal state based on formal law had been superseded: 'We can say that in the history of anti-Fascism all the best traditions of the Italian spirit ... are summed up and gathered together and guide it to successive liberating

---

West German Historians and the Attempt to Escape the Nazi Past, New York: Pantheon, 1989; *New German Critique* 44 (special issue on the *Historikerstreit*) (Spring–Summer 1988); Ian Kershaw, *The Nazi Dictatorship: Problems and Perspectives of Interpretations*, London: Arnold, 1989; Charles Maier, *The Unmasterable Past: History, Holocaust and German National Identity*, Cambridge, MA: Harvard University Press, 1988.

16 Domenico Settembrini, 'The Divided Left: After Fascism, What?' in Spencer Di Scala, ed., *Italian Socialism: Between Politics and History* (Amherst, MA: University of Massachusetts Press, 1996), p. 110.

17 Quoted in Giorgio Bocca, *Storia dell'Italia partigiana*, Milan: Mondadori, 1995, p. 416.

18 Ada Gobetti, *Diario partigiano*, Turin: Einaudi, 1956, p. 414.

stages, beginning with the first enlightenment revolution of the eighteenth century.'[19]

The first militant anti-Fascist organisation (1921–22), the Arditi del Popolo, had a troubled history, but managed to cobble together diverse groups in order to combat Fascism in the field. Not averse to combating the violence of the *squadristi* with violence of their own, they were forsaken by the official organs of the state (police, military, judiciary) and even the leaders of the Italian Socialist and Communist parties; consequently, they were left to fend for themselves. With hindsight, most now recognise that the Arditi del Popolo represented a 'lost opportunity' to confront – and perhaps defeat – Fascism in its earliest form.

Originally used by the fascists to express contempt for the anti-Fascist exiles, the term *fuorusciti* (literally: those who have gone outside, outlaws) came to encompass the entire spectrum of anti-Fascism abroad. Paris was the capital of the *fuorusciti*, but there were other centres of activity in London and New York. A major flaw of the *fuorusciti* was their insistence on continuing the old political party divisions while in exile. This problem was fully evident in the most important anti-Fascist organisation abroad, the Concentrazione Antifascista, established in April 1927 with headquarters in Paris. Led by the socialist Pietro Nenni, the Concentrazione Antifascista was composed of the revolutionary PSI and the reformist PSU (which merged in July 1930), the PRI, the Confederazione Generale del Lavoro (CGL), and Lega Internazionale dei Diritti dell'Uomo (LIDU). The CA published a weekly newspaper, *La Libertà*, from May 1927 until May 1934, and managed to gather many of the *fuorusciti* into one organisation. The PCI refused to join, and internal divisions were to cause the CA to dissolve in 1934; it was replaced by a Unity of Action Pact.[20]

A major development in intellectual and political anti-Fascism was the foundation of a new, left-wing movement, Giustizia e Libertà (GL). Born in Paris in the summer of 1929, GL was inspired by Carlo Rosselli, who had managed a sensational escape from *confino* on the penal island of Lipari. Rosselli (1899–1937) was born into a wealthy Jewish family with strong ties to the Risorgimento. Abandoning a promising career as a professor of political economy, he joined the anti-Fascist cause and was instrumental in publishing the first underground anti-Fascist newspaper. Arrested for his activities, he was sentenced to *confino* on the island of Lipari, off the coast of Sicily. After a daring escape, he made his way to Paris where, in August 1929, he founded GL, the largest and most influential non-Marxist leftist movement. From Paris, Rosselli wrote essays, organised the movement, and even plotted Mussolini's assassination. When the Spanish Civil War broke out in 1936, Rosselli was one of the first to arrive in Barcelona in

---

19 Ferruccio Parri, *Scritti 1915–1975*, Milan: Feltrinelli, 1976, p. 179.
20 Alexander De Grand, *The Italian Left in the Twentieth Century*, Bloomington: Indiana University Press, 1989, pp. 68–70.

defence of the Spanish Republic. Rosselli believed that the Spanish Civil War had to be transformed into a European-wide offensive against Fascism and Nazism. That idea, and his speech, 'Oggi in Spagna, domani in Italia' ('Today in Spain, Tomorrow in Italy'), given over Radio Barcelona on 13 November 1936, may have sealed his fate. An anonymous police spy wrote to Rome that Rosselli was 'the most dangerous of the anti-Fascists in exile' and that it was necessary that he be 'suppressed'. While recuperating in the French countryside, Rosselli was assassinated, together with his brother, the noted historian Nello, on 9 June 1937.

While on Lipari, Rosselli clandestinely wrote his major theoretical work, *Socialismo liberale*, in which he argued that twentieth-century socialism was the logical heir to nineteenth-century liberalism. Attacked from both the left and the right, Rosselli insisted on an heretical 'liberal socialism' and was acknowledged as the *enfant terrible* of Italian anti-Fascism.[21] GL attracted some of the most important anti-Fascist intellectuals, and was second in influence only to the PCI.

Another factor in anti-Fascism was Italian anarchism, led by the heroic figure of Errico Malatesta (1853–1932), the tragic figure of Camillo Berneri (1897–1937), assassinated by Stalin's agents during the Spanish Civil War, and the romantic figure of Carlo Tresca (1879–1943), assassinated by still-unknown persons on New York City's Fifth Avenue.

Ignazio Silone, an important member of the PCI until he abandoned Communism and active politics, attempted an analysis of Fascism from his exile in Switzerland. For Silone, Fascism was neither accidental ('Fascism did not fall from the heavens') nor the destiny of Italy ('Fascism was not inevitable'). His novel, *Fontamara* (Bitter Spring), written in exile while Silone thought he was mortally ill with tuberculosis, was the most influential piece of anti-Fascist literature, translated into a dozen languages and selling millions of copies.[22]

The culture of liberal anti-Fascism was embodied in the figure of Benedetto Croce. The philosopher had acquired such international prestige by the 1920s that the regime dared not silence him. In his works of history and historiography, Croce served as a beacon for two generations under Fascism. His work was often openly read as an implicit condemnation of Fascism.

Anti-Fascists, led by the Communists, successfully organised mass strikes in March 1943 protesting against Fascist Italy's continuing participation in a losing war and the dire economic and social conditions on the home front. In the summer of 1943, Rome was bombed by the Allies as they began an invasion of Sicily. Mussolini was deposed on 25 July 1943, but confusion reigned. Marshal Pietro Badoglio was named prime minister, but his radio announcement that

---

21 On the charismatic Rosselli, see Stanislao G. Pugliese, *Carlo Rosselli: Socialist Heretic and Antifascist Exile*. Cambridge, MA: Harvard University Press, 1999.

22 For the first biography of Silone in English, see Stanislao G. Pugliese, *Bitter Spring: A Life of Ignazio Silone*, New York: Farrar, Straus & Giroux, 2009.

'the war continues' was more confusing than inspiring. The *confinati* were released and the *fuorusciti* returned from exile, sparking the armed Resistance.[23] On 8 September 1943, Italy signed an Armistice with the Allies, and the next day the Comitato di Liberazione Nazionale (CLN) was formed. The CLN comprised five political parties, the Liberals (PLI), the DC, the Socialists (PSI), the PCI, and the Partito d'Azione (Actionists). Tensions eventually developed between the CLN and the Allied Military Government over the CLN's role in post-war Italy. Mussolini was rescued by the Nazis and installed in a puppet regime, the Republic of Salò. When Salò issued a decree calling for all able-bodied men to join its army, many fled instead into the hills, countryside and mountains, and joined the Resistance. The PCI was the largest and most influential of the anti-Fascist movements, followed by the Actionists, a movement founded on the legacy of Rosselli's GL. Women played a critical role in the Resistance, often as *staffette*, relaying written or oral communications between partisan groups, conveying arms, and gathering information. They were also permitted, not without considerable dissent and grumbling, a role in military operations. Renata Viganò's *L'Agnese va a morire* and Ada Gobetti's *Diario partigiano* represent the important contribution made by Italian women to the armed Resistance.[24]

Conservatives and neo-Fascists argue that Mussolini and those who joined the fascist Repubblica Sociale Italiana (RSI) were performing a patriotic duty; others see the RSI as the last gasp of a brutal regime. Indeed, one of the RSI's major duties was the repression and execution of Italian partisans. The RSI also tried and executed those Fascists who had voted for the dictator's dismissal on 25 July 1943. Mussolini's own foreign minister and son-in-law, Galeazzo Ciano, was executed despite the pleas of his daughter, Edda Mussolini Ciano. On 14 November 1943 the first congress was held of the Fascist Republican Party, which issued the so-called 'Manifesto of Verona', a confusing mix of Fascism's early radicalism and an attempt to placate the Nazis.

The Italians who rallied to the Salò Republic and their activities remain controversial to this day: Were they defending the honour of Italy from an invading foe (the so-called 'ragazzi di Salò'), or were they fanatical Fascists determined to fight until the end? Prince Junio Valerio Borghese, from a noble Roman

---

23 For an excellent anthology of writings in Italian on the armed Resistance, see Philip Cooke, ed., *The Italian Resistance: An Anthology*, Manchester: Manchester University Press, 1997.

24 Renata Viganò, *L'Agnese va a morire*, Turin: Einaudi, 1949 – winner of the Premio Viareggio and basis of the 1976 film of the same name directed by Giuliano Montaldi; Ada Gobetti, *Diario partigiano*, Turin: Einaudi, 1949 – there is a forthcoming English translation by JoMarie Alano. See also Rosetta D'Angelo and Barbara Zaczek, eds, *Resisting Bodies: Narratives of Italian Partisan Women*, Chapel Hill, NC: Annali d'Italianistica, 2008; and Jane Slaughter, *Women and the Italian Resistance, 1943–1945*, Denver: Arden Press, 1997.

family, was symbolic of this choice. He commanded the notorious Decima Mas (a torpedo boat squadron) and carried out barbaric reprisals against the anti-Fascist partisans. Sentenced to twelve years in prison after the war for his atrocities, Borghese was instead immediately released and became a prominent neo-Fascist politician. In 1971, when his role in a murky right-wing coup d'état was revealed, he fled to Spain.[25] His funeral in Rome three years later was the occasion for a major neo-Fascist demonstration. Borghese's story is recounted here as an indication of how Fascism survived the immediate post-war period and became something of a force in Italian politics, even to this day.[26] Others responsible for anti-Fascist reprisals included the ironically named Mario Carità, who organised the infamous Carità Band and worked with the SS and Gestapo in Florence; Pietro Koch, who committed atrocities in Rome; and Pietro Caruso, involved in the notorious Ardeatine Caves massacre.[27]

Examples of Fascist brutality against the Resistance are legion. One episode has been recounted by Guglielmo Petroni. Born in Lucca, Petroni (1911–93) became a poet and journalist in Florence. In 1943 he joined the Resistance, but was arrested on 3 May 1944. For the next thirty-three days he was interrogated and tortured by the Gestapo in various prisons in Rome. His memoir of those days, *The World is a Prison*, has been almost continuously in print since it first appeared in 1948. In it, he not only chronicles his experiences but meditates on the nature of a precarious existence in which paradox and absurdity abound:

> I had the terrible sensation that seems to become more acute in such circumstances than when one is alone in the darkness of the prison; I felt a sense of infinite solitude, the impression that the whole world had forgotten me, something that even today it occurs to me must be similar to what a shipwrecked person feels when alone and lost in the middle of the ocean. But this feeling was submerged, it lay hidden at the bottom of the soul; on the level of my nerves, never had I felt so alive and secure in an unwavering mood, whatever might happen.[28]

In January 1952, the Turin publishing house Einaudi published a collection of letters by anti-Fascists condemned to death, thereby reigniting the debate over the Resistance. Covering a broad spectrum of Italian society, from aristocratic

---

25 On the persistence of Fascist and neo-Fascist threats to the Italian Republic, see Franco Ferraresi's *Threats to Democracy: The Radical Right in Italy after the War*, Princeton: Princeton University Press, 1996 (original edition published by Feltrinelli in Milan, 1995).

26 Alessandra Mussolini (born 1962), member of the Italian parliament, still defends her grandfather's political legacy.

27 See Robert Katz, *Death in Rome*, New York: Macmillan, 1967.

28 Guglielmo Petroni, transl. John Shepley, *The World Is a Prison*, Evanston, IL: Marlboro Press, 1999, pp. 74–6.

military officers to workers and peasants, from conservative monarchists to liberals and communists, the letters are an eloquent testimony to the sacrifices and ideals of those who fought for the principles of liberty and justice. An excerpt from the letter of Antonio Fossati, a member of the Corpo Volontari Libertà in Milan, to his fiancé Anna:

> On the 2nd they tortured me for the third time: they put flaming candles to my feet and I found myself tied to a chair; my hair turned all grey, but I didn't talk and it passed. On the 4th I was taken to a room where there was a table where I was tied with a rope by the neck and for ten minutes an electric shock passed through me; this went on for three days until the 6th, when at five in the afternoon they said if I was ready to talk but I refused to answered; I wanted to know what my fate was to be so I could write to my dear Anna and they told me of that terrible condemnation: death. I made them see that I was very proud. But when I was brought back to the cell I fell on my knees and wept.[29]

A different kind of letter was penned by Giacomo Ulivi, an anti-Fascist in hiding in Modena, charging his colleagues with the moral and political tasks still to be to addressed:

> Have you ever thought that in the coming months the fate of our country and our own will be decided? What will be the decisive influence of our will if we rely on it? That if we encounter danger it will be our responsibility? There is much to do. Try to ask yourselves, each and every day, what idea you have of the true life: is it well-ordered? Inquire about the objectives. Do you believe in democratic freedom, in which, within the limits of the Constitution, you yourselves may direct public affairs, or rather wait for a new more egalitarian conception of life and property? And if you accept the first solution, do you want the power to elect to be for everyone, so that the elected body is a genuine and direct expression of our country, or do you wish to restrict it to those better prepared today to achieve a progressive programme? This and more you have to ask yourselves. You have to convince yourselves and prepare yourselves to convince others, neither to overpower others, nor to give up. Today we must fight against the oppressor. This is the first duty of us all, but it is good to be prepared to solve those problems in a sustainable manner, and to avoid their resurgence and the repetition of all that has befallen us. I end this long letter a bit confused, I know, but spontaneous, with apologies and wishing you all good luck.[30]

---

29 Piero Malvezzi and Giovanni Pirelli, eds, *Lettere di condannati a morte della Resistenza italiana: 8 settembre 1943–25 aprile 1945*, Turin: Einaudi, 1994, 3–4, transl. Stanislao G. Pugliese.

30 Ibid., pp. 319–20.

Although a High Commission for the Expurgation of Fascism was created after the war, it failed to achieve its goals and was hampered by political conservatives in Italy.[31]

The CNL and the Allies worked together (not without problems), and the war eventually came to an end. On 25 April 1945 Milan revolted, expelling the Fascists and Nazis, and the war soon ended. Mussolini and his mistress Clara Petacci were captured by partisans on 27 April as they were trying to reach Switzerland, and executed the next day. Their battered bodies were hung upside-down at a petrol station in Milan's Piazzale Loreto, where anti-Fascist partisans had been executed months earlier, their bodies left hanging for days for the edification of the local population. Ferruccio Parri of the Action Party was Italy's first post-war prime minister (19 June–24 November 1945). Parri had been active in anti-Fascist circles since the 1920s but was not able to manage the post-war peace. When the Liberals and Christian Democrats refused to follow his reform programme his government collapsed, initiating a four-decade monopoly of power by the Christian Democrats. On 2 June 1946, the Italian people voted 54 percent to 46 percent to abolish the monarchy and create an Italian Republic. A new Constitution, crafted by a constituent assembly, went into effect on the first day of 1948.

After the war, Fascism and anti-Fascism continued to play important roles in Italian politics, culture and society. The Action Party dissolved, and the PCI became the largest communist party in western Europe. Fascism, although outlawed, survived in the *uomo qualunque* movement and the Movimento Sociale Italiano; it survived in the guise of 'post-Fascism' in the Alleanza Nazionale, a political party dissolved in 2009. Anti-Fascism became – at least in official rhetoric and according to the Constitution – the foundation of the Italian Republic. Some have criticised the 'myth' of anti-Fascism, and the last two decades have witnessed a sustained historiographical and political attack on the ideals of the Resistance.

In some ways, Pavone's book can be seen as a reply to the work of Renzo De Felice, the dean of fascist studies in Italy. De Felice (1929–96) was considered one of the foremost historians of Fascism. Professor of contemporary history at the University of Rome, he was also director of the journal *Storia contemporanea* and editor of the *Journal of Contemporary History*. His monumental seven-volume biography of Mussolini (the last volume published posthumously) forced a reconsideration of the Italian dictator. Based on extensive archival research, De Felice claimed it was time to examine Mussolini and Fascism from an 'objective' point of view, but he was criticised by some for 'rehabilitating' the dictator. De Felice argued that the Resistance had generated its own mythology

---

31 See Roy Palmer Domenico, *Italian Fascists on Trial, 1943–1948*, Chappell Hill: University of North Carolina Press, 1992.

and alienated many Italians from the state. More specifically, he argued that there existed a 'Resistance vulgate' censoring any debate and forcing historians, intellectuals and citizens to accept a historiography based on myth. In the place of this mythologised historiography, De Felice argued for one based on a 'scientific' methodology:

> Anti-Fascism cannot constitute the only explanatory principle in understanding the historical significance of the Resistance. Nor does it follow that the anti-Fascist 'label' can replace the democratic 'label' or that the two years 1943–1945 must be interpreted exclusively in the vast riverbed of the collective crisis that conditioned the circumstances since that time and that influences those of today; or that the hierarchy of value of 'anti-Fascist purity' at whose vertex the PCI immediately placed itself finds resonance anymore (if it ever did) among the majority of Italians.
>
> Neither Fascists nor anti-Fascists, neither Communists nor anti-Communists, are legitimised to explain to the people what happened in those two years or how decisive they have been for the history of today's Italy. And, after all, the people no longer trust them anymore, and consider them sellers of myths in which it no longer believes and to whom it attributes a good part of the responsibility for the situation in which Italy finds itself today. What is even more serious, the people extend this negative judgment of the reconstruction of the past done by intellectuals to all of history. The result is that which Rosario Romeo[32] feared, in a less degraded context twenty years ago: that of increasing that crisis of identity among Italians. And that today is more and more difficult to halt.[33]

De Felice's critique is echoed by Aga Rossi:

> The Italian republic emerging from the 1946 referendum was founded on the myths that the Resistance was a popular struggle and that the population adhered to the values of anti-Fascism. To support these myths it was necessary to deny the fact that the majority of the population had accepted the Fascist regime, thus upholding a false interpretation and preventing the country from coming to terms with its Fascist past.[34]

But it has been argued that De Felice's historiography, and what came to be called an anti-anti-Fascism, was permeated by its own mythology. A clear critique of De Felice's historiography was offered by Nicola Tranfaglia in his book

---

32 Editor's note: Rosario Romeo, *Il problema nazionale tra 19° e 20° secolo: idee e realtà*, Roma: Bulzoni, 1977.

33 Renzo De Felice, *Rosso e nero*, Milan: Baldini & Castoldi, 1995, pp. 12–25, transl. Stanislao G. Pugliese.

34 Aga Rossi, *A Nation Collapses*, p. 137.

Un passato scomodo (An Uncomfortable Past).[35] An example of what De Felice derisively called the 'Resistance vulgate' can be seen on the final page of Roberto Battaglia's seminal *Storia della Resistenza italiana*, first published in 1953 and awarded the Premio Viareggio. Battaglia was a partisan in the Action Party, and, after its dissolution in 1946, joined the PCI. In his conclusion he delineates the political and ethical importance of the Resistance both to Italy's domestic and its international politics:

> The historic importance of the part played by the Resistance in the liberation of Italy and the overthrow of National Socialism and Fascism cannot be too strongly emphasised. Of the countless patriots who had flocked to the movement and fight in defence of national independence, many thousands acquired for the first time an understanding of the part they would be called on to play in the future of their country, and, when the war was over, these new protagonists, the workers and the peasants, entered the lists.
>
> On the international plane, the Resistance redeemed the honour of Italy which had been so vilely besmirched by the Fascists. At home, it paved the way for the Republican Constitution which was approved, in 1947, by the Constituent Assembly in an atmosphere of harmony and unity that was due to the fraternity of the struggle for liberation. The political and social principles on which the Republican Constitution was based were those that had inspired the Resistance throughout, the principles that every Italian who cherishes the independence, liberty, and well-being of his fellow countrymen will always have at heart.[36]

Today, the denigration of the Resistance comes not only from Fascist, neo-Fascist or post-Fascist politicians and intellectuals. In 2002, the government of right-wing Prime Minister Silvio Berlusconi proposed a drastic rewriting of the country's history textbooks to purge them of 'left-wing bias'. Berlusconi argued that the nation's history textbooks tended to glorify the Resistance and denigrate those who defended the Salò Republic. In this rewriting of history, Fascists were also victims of the Second World War. A corollary to this proposal recommended the abolition of the many historical institutes dedicated to the study of the armed Resistance. Since 1995 – the fiftieth anniversary of the end of the Second World War – there has been a protracted and often bitter debate over the scale, significance and repercussions of the Resistance. Here, journalist Alexander Stille writes about recent developments in the continuing struggle to define and interpret the past:

---

35 Nicola Tranfaglia, *Un passato scomodo. Fascismo e postfascismo*, Rome and Bari: Laterza, 1996.

36 Roberto Battaglia, *The Story of the Italian Resistance*, trans. P. D. Cummings, London: Odhams Press, 1957, p. 281.

Last summer [2002], the head of the Italian state broadcasting system (RAI), Antonio Baldassarre, addressed the national congress of the National Alliance, the right-wing party led principally by 'post-Fascists', and announced that it was time to 'rewrite history' as it is presented on Italian television. 'The old RAI represented only one culture and not others', he said. 'Often, they didn't tell real history, but told fables, offered one-sided interpretations.' This call to 'rewrite history', before a party many of whose leaders were ardent admirers of Italian Fascism, had a very clear meaning: no more 'one-sided' portrayals of anti-Fascists as noble patriots and Fascists as evil villains.[37]

As this introduction is being drafted, Berlusconi again finds himself in the political spotlight. Considered a dark horse in national elections, he added a new twist to the old 'Mussolini's only mistake was allying himself with Hitler' argument. On Holocaust Remembrance Day 2013 (27 January), he declared that, while the Racial Laws were Mussolini's 'worst mistake', the Duce had done the right thing for Italy in allying with Hitler as it was obvious that Nazi Germany was on its way to victory.[38] At the same time, controversy flares as a public monument in Affile (near Rome), his hometown, is dedicated to General Rodolfo Graziani, accused of war crimes.

In this current climate of anti-anti-Fascism and the denigration of the Resistance, a mysterious transformation (some might say a miracle) occurred in Rome. Over the entrance to the EUR Administration building, designed by Gaetano Minucci, a bas-relief by Publio Morbiducci depicts the history of Rome. The facade, originally constructed during the Fascist era, included an imperious Mussolini astride an impressive steed hailed by men, women and children. With the fall of the Fascist regime in July 1943, the bas-relief was attacked and the face of Mussolini chipped off. Recently, the face has been restored and the facade cleaned.[39]

Yet we should not throw up our hands and conclude that the debate over the political and ethical significance of the Resistance is simply and forever spinning its wheels in mud. As Claudio Pavone made clear in a recent communication, while it is true that the debate continues to this day, its physiognomy

---

37 Alexander Stille, *New York Times*, 28 September 2002.

38 'Il fatto delle leggi razziali è stata la peggiore colpa di un leader, Mussolini, che per tanti altri versi invece aveva fatto bene … certamente il governo di allora per timore che la potenza tedesca vincesse preferì essere alleato alla Germania di Hitler piuttosto che opporvisi.' *La Repubblica*, 27 January 2013, p. 1. 'The fact of the Racial Laws was the worst mistake of a leader, Mussolini, who, for so many other reasons, was good for Italy … certainly the government of the time, fearful that German power would win, preferred to ally itself with Hitler's Germany rather than oppose it.'

39 See Borden W. Painter, Jr, *Mussolini's Rome: Rebuilding the Eternal City*, New York: Palgrave, 2005, p. 160.

has changed (for the better) with the change in the political and cultural climate in Italy.[40]

Looking back over the last two decades, one is struck by how Pavone's *A Civil War* has influenced the debate over the Resistance, both in the academy and in popular culture. Of course, as British historian Philip Cooke has observed, 'Pavone's book is a work that has suffered the fate of being more talked about than read. There is a gulf between what is actually in Pavone's book and what is perceived to be in it.'[41] Perhaps the writing and reception of history is paradoxically and unavoidably both public and personal. As Pavone himself acknowledges in a personal 'last observation':

> great and exceptional events render problematic that which usually appears obvious. This simultaneously promotes the drive towards clear-cut choices and judgments and the love of ambiguity that allow us to comprehend others when they resonate in us. Those who in their youth were involved in these great events have difficulty transmitting all of this wealth to newer generations. And if one tries to do it with historical research, a silent process, mustered over so many years of memory, insinuates itself in the selection of sources. In this sense, my research has also been of an autobiographical nature.[42]

Stanislao G. Pugliese
Hofstra University
April 2013

---

40 Claudio Pavone email message to Stanislao G. Pugliese, 28 March 2013.
41 Philip Cooke, *The Legacy of the Italian Resistance*, New York: Palgrave, 2011, p. 160.
42 Pavone, 'Premessa', pp. xi–xii.

Preface

Many years ago, Ferruccio Parri proposed to me that I write a book using, as a model, two works that sometime before had been published in France: *Les courants de pensée de la Résistance* by Henri Michel and, by the same Michel and Boris Mirkine-Guetzévitch, *Les idées politiques et sociales de la Résistance*. When I began my research I was, at first and above all, attracted to the institutional theme, though it was indeed through the drafting of the essay on *La continuità dello Stato* when I became convinced of the difficulty, in an essay on the Italian Resistance, of separating political, social, and institutional ideas and programmes.

Above all, many of the ideas that circulated during the Resistance were developed earlier, or, if developed at that time, were later on elaborated a great deal and organised in a climate of rapid political change. This not only made the identification of the sources difficult, but also indicated the necessity of analysing the behaviour of the protagonists to understand the ideas that inspired them, even if those ideas were formulated without clarity or coherence. Thus, the objective of my research shifted from programmes to the protagonists themselves – their moral convictions, the cultural structures around the protagonists themselves, their feelings, and the doubts and passions elicited by that brief and intense sequence of events. On what grounds did people base their actions, when institutions – within the frame of which they had been accustomed to operate – vacillated or vanished, to then reassemble themselves and demand new and different loyalties? To this question, years of terrorism added yet another question, illustrated with particular dramatic force: if, how, and why is violence justified when it must be carried out without a clear, institutional legitimacy? In other words: when the state is no longer capable of exercising its monopoly of violence with any certainty? The question appeared particularly difficult to those who refused an answer that denied politics and history. And it was in fact at that moment, during a series of seminars on the relationship between politics and morality initiated by Norberto Bobbio at the Centro studi Piero Gobetti in Turin, that the presentation I made constituted the first nucleus of this book.

The word that seemed to me to best summarise what appeared to become the object of my research was '*moralità*'. Not 'morals', a term that, on the one hand was confined to the individual conscience, while on the other risked sliding into the rhetoric of the Resistance. Not '*mentalità*', a word that in a short time has acquired multiple meanings and generated controversies which I did not intend to get caught up in. When my book was already finished, I found confirmation of my choices in a letter from Giorgio Agosti to Dante Livio Bianco in their recently published correspondence: 'Your correspondence has the interests and the character of an eighteenth-century epistolary exchange – full, as it is, of "*moralità*" and of perspicacious "notations.""[1]

Moralità is a word particularly suited to define the territory on which politics and ethics meet and clash, relying on history as a possible common measure. It was necessary, whenever possible, to immerse oneself in the historical context when dealing with matters that first appeared to be political but which were in reality great moral problems and, reciprocally, to show how these same historical events necessarily influenced those problems.

The 'high' [political] sources – the most noted and studied – have thus ceded much of the field to 'low' [popular] sources. In fact, I propose not to reconstruct once again the history of leading organisations – parties such as CLN, CVL, etc. – but to see how the general directives were received and acted upon at various levels, being adapted by these organisations to a vast array of individual and collective experiences, that just through these adaptations, and even upheavals, left a trace of themselves. That which the political approach and military strategy in this subtle diffusion lost in coherence, it gained in adherence to reality; and this, if not always pleasing to politicians, today it is surely so for historians.

Is it possible, in only so many pages and with only so many examples, to give everyone a say? There are partisans who have never spoken, nor will they ever speak; they have not escaped from the situation, as expressed by a concentration camp survivor, in which: "It is sad to live without letting others know." I would be very happy if they could recognise themselves, even slightly, in what I have written here.

It goes without saying that this book could not have been written if the ground had not been broken by others, starting from the pioneering *Storia della Resistenza italiana* by Roberto Battaglia (the first edition published in 1953), to the vast research promoted by the Istituto Nazionale per la Storia del Movimento di Liberazione in Italia and the network of institutes associated with it. Only these works allowed me to accept certain assessments of facts and analysis of ideologies.

My book presumes a distinction between a Resistance in a real and proper sense, the one fought politically and militarily in the North by a conspicuous minority, and a Resistance in the broader and more literal sense, that assumed with time – even for those who had not participated or who had tried to avoid,

1 Giorgio Agosti and Dante Livio Bianco, *Un'amicizia partigiana, 1943–1945*. Edited by Giovanni De Luna. Turin: Bollati Boringhieri, 2007, p. 17.

manipulate or marginalise its memory – the role of legitimising the entire political system of the Italian Republic and its ruling class (the 'constitutional arch,' heir of the CLN). This book deals with the Resistance in the former sense, but must necessarily emphasise, side by side with the differences, also its connection with the Resistance in the latter, broader, sense.

The three central chapters could be grouped under the title "The Three Wars: Patriotic, Civil and Class." I first used this formula in a work presented at a conference held in Belluno in October of 1998. In this work, civil war emerges from the other two. It, in fact, offers a key reading in a general sense (and above all, denies fascist or pro-fascist apologists with provocative intentions the possibility of manipulating the facts). This interpretation of civil war prevented that separate parts of the book be dedicated to fascists: fascists, as opponents, are present everywhere in this volume.

A last observation: great and exceptional events render problematic that which usually appears obvious, and promotes simultaneously the drive towards clear-cut choices and judgments, and the love of ambiguity that alone allows us to comprehend others when they resonate in us. Those who in their youth were involved in these great events have difficulty transmitting all of this wealth of experience to newer generations, and, if one tries to do it through historical research, a silent process, mustered over so many years of memory, insinuates itself in the selection of sources. In this sense, my research has also been of an autobiographical nature.

CHAPTER 1

The Choice

1. The collapse

On 23 August 1943, as he left the prison of Castelfranco Emilia, Vittorio Foa gave Giambattista Vico's *Scienza Nuova* to his cellmate Bruno Corbi, inscribing these words from Vico's text as a dedication: 'by various and diverse ways, which seemed like hazards and were in fact opportunities.'[1]

Foa was referring to 'the last harrowing years of Fascism', but the situation was such that those words were as apt an interpretation of the recent past as they were prophetic of the immediate future. They divine that 'widening of the field of possibility'[2] which, before long, the 8 September 1943 catastrophe and the Resistance were to offer the Italian people, and which Foa himself, elsewhere in his writings, was to reformulate as follows: 'During the Resistance and, for a brief moment, at the Liberation, all had seemed possible to us.'[3]

In a short article entitled 'Omero antimilitarista' ('Homer the Anti-militarist') in the Turin edition of *L'Unità* for 15 September 1946, Italo Calvino was to write:

> What in fact is *The Odyssey*? It is the myth of the return home, born during the long years of 'naja' [military service] of the soldiers who have gone off to fight in distant places, of their anxiety about how they will manage to get home, when the war is over, of the fear that assails them in their dreams of never managing to make it home, of the strange obstacles that appear on their journey. *The Odyssey* is the story of the eighth of September, of all the eighth of Septembers in History: the need to return home by hook or by crook, through lands fraught with enemies.

---

1 Vittorio Foa's testimony. See B. Corbi, *Scusateci tanto (carceri e Resistenza)*, Milan: La Pietra, 1977, where Foa's dedication is the book's epigraph.

2 The concept was formulated by Sartre in relation to the Vietnam war and 1968: 'The field of the possible is much vaster than the dominant classes have accustomed us to believing'. See 'Il rischio della spontaneità, la logica dell'istituzione', interview given to Rossana Rossanda and published with the title 'Classe e partito' in *Il Manifesto* 4 (1 September 1969), pp. 41–54, at p. 49.

3 V. Foa, 'Carlo Levi "uomo politico"' in Foa, *Per una storia del movimento operaio*, Turin: Einaudi, 1980, p. 50.

Between these two poles – a readiness to consider new possibilities and a run for cover in what was familiar and secure – lies the wide range of reactions provoked in the Italians by the 8 September 1943 Armistice and the collapse of the country's military and civil structures immediately following it. To turn our attention to the Resistance means to give pride of place to the first of these positions – which was the minority position; but the variety of attitudes adopted by the Italians and the common elements linking, often in the most tenuous way, otherwise conflicting positions, creates a complex web of blurred relations between the two types of experience. Thus, the disappointment caused by being denied the chance to return home impelled many to take stock of the other possibilities that the situation had to offer.

As yet we know little about the Italians who fought in the Second World War between 1940 and 1943. The inglorious defeat, the change of sides, the Resistance regarded as the founding moment of the new Italian republic, the memory of the connection between the desire to return home and right-wing subversivism, stressed by Fascism and to all effects assimilated by post-Fascism, the tendency of the protagonists to forget a past charged with sufferings that could not easily be re-processed in memory – all help to account for this lack.[4] What we can say with a fair degree of certainty, however, is that weariness with a long, hard and ill-motivated military life had led the vast majority of the soldiers to the conviction that armistice, the end of the war, and return home amounted to the same thing. It was in these three aspirations that the desire to fight dissipated, experienced as a necessity which would brook no delay.

With emphases and approximations reflecting the character of the document, yet in a singularly prophetic way, a group of Italian and English anti-Fascists had declared in 1941:

> The Italian soldier will fight no more under the orders of Mussolini, either for Hitler or against Hitler, not even for Italy. The Italian soldier will fold his arms and let himself be killed by the enemy in front or by the rifles of the Blackshirts watching over him from behind.[5]

---

4 Among recent studies that have begun to fill the gap, see F. Ferratini Tosi, G. Grassi and M. Legnani, eds, *L' Italia nella seconda guerra mondiale e nella Resistenza*, Milan: Franco Angeli, 1988, and R. De Felice, *Mussolini l'alleato*, Turin: Einaudi, 1990. For the prisoners in British and American hands see F. Conti, *I prigionieri di guerra italiani 1940–45*, Bologna: Il Mulino, 1986; and, in general, G. Rochat, 'I prigionieri di guerra, un problema rimosso' in *Italia contemporanea* 171 (June 1988), pp. 7–14. For the veterans, C. Pavone, 'Appunti sul problema dei reduci', in N. Gallerano ed., *L' altro dopoguerra, Roma e il Sud 1943–45*, Milan: Franco Angeli, 1985, pp. 89–106. An up-to-date survey is G. Rochat, 'Gli studi di storia militare sull'Italia contemporanea', in *Rivista di storia contemporanea* XVIII (1989), pp. 605–27. See also Chapter 2, below.

5 PENTAD, *The Remaking of Italy*, London: Penguin, 1941, immediately printed in Italian as *L' Italia di domani*, Harmondsworth–New York: Edizioni del Pinguino, 1942.

This page concluded by saying that the Italians would take up arms again only if they had something real to hope for.

On 25 July 1943, weariness with the war had found a sort of moral sanction in the all-but-heroic fall of its promoters, guarantors of its political and patriotic significance. As Second Lieutenant Giorgio Chiesura, on garrison duty in Sicily, noted in his diary:

> If they wanted an armistice, the change of government was all right. But it makes no sense if they want to go on with the war, as seems to be the case. We won't pick up as we did after Caporetto. Miracles are no longer possible. The war seems to be completely unjustified after the fall of the government responsible for its beginnings and its presuppositions.[6]

The impossibility of a recovery such as occurred after Caporetto had already been noted in February 1943 by an Italian informer of the Germans (possibly Guido Buffarini Guidi, dismissed from the under-secretaryship for the Ministry of the Interior on 6 February), who did not mince his words in his judgment of the Fascist power system: 'Since Fascism is a totalitarian regime it leaves no room for spontaneous patriotic reactions as in 1917.'[7]

It is historically debatable whether Caporetto had in fact constituted the 'spur to a racehorse';[8] but what is important here is the illusory appeals made to the memory of that event in the aftermath of the Fascist war. Figures as diverse as the federal secretary of Cuneo[9] and the philosopher Giovanni Gentile gave credence to the legitimacy of that appeal. The latter, in a speech to the Italians given at Campidoglio on 24 June 1943, had in fact referred to one of his writings

---

The authors are A. F. Magri, L. Minio, I. Thomas, R.Orlando and P. P. Fano. The passage quoted is from p. 256 of the original edition.

6 G. Chiesura, *Sicilia 1943*, Vicenza: Neri Pozza, 1954, p. 57 (under the date of 8 August). On 27 July Chiesura had recorded that the news of the coup d'état, after being greeted initially with indifference, had quickly generated euphoria 'because it amounts to a declaration that by now the war is lost and finished' (p. 50).

7 Quoted in F. W. Deakin, *The Brutal Friendship*, London: Weidenfeld & Nicolson, 1962, p. 219.

8 Giorgo Rochat, from whom I take the image recorded in the text, has no hesitation in calling it 'una leggenda' ('a legend'): see his book *Gli arditi della grande guerra. Origini, battaglie e miti*, Milan: Feltrinelli, 1981, p. 71. For a detailed judgment on the reactions provoked by the defeat see Giovanni Procacci, 'Aspetti della mentalità collettiva durante la guerra: L'Italia dopo Caporetto', in D. Leoni and C. Zadra, eds, *La grande guerra. Esperienze, memorie, immagini*, Bologna: Il Mulino, 1986, pp. 261–89.

9 See the last article he wrote for *La Provincia Granda*, 19 February 1943, quoted in R. Belmondo, L. Bertello, P. Bologna, M. Calandri, A. Cavaglion and E. Mana, 'La campagna di Russia nella stampa piemontese e in particolare nella provincia di Cuneo', in Istituto Storico della Resistenza in Cuneo e provincia, *Gli italiani sul fronte russo*, Bari: De Donato, 1982, p. 452).

dating from 1917.[10] Paradoxically, greater realism was shown, in their way, by those Fascists, real incunabula of the Italian Social Republic, who, albeit in the deviant form of an obsessive denunciation of traitors whom they saw lurking everywhere, were more fully aware of the oncoming collapse. From Radio Londra, Umberto Calosso had clearly explained that Fascism could not hope to construct 'a space of patriotic passion for defence as on the Piave'.[11] A cavalry captain who, after Stalingrad, El Alamein and the North African landing was going around declaring that the Italian people 'if given a whipping will react overwhelmingly and victoriously', aroused mere pity and a sense of the ridiculous in another officer who had close dealings with the new anti-Fascist recruits, and all the more so since the captain himself had the look of 'a whipped cur'.[12] After 25 July the tangled thread of motivations – Italian war, Fascist war – that had run through all three years of a war conducted in an increasingly subordinate position to Nazi Germany was highlighted with all its contradictions: 'On 25 July – recalls a survivor of deportation – suddenly we were all happy, like a liberation, because we took it to be the end of the war; and then when we realised that this wasn't the case, anger took possession of us, a terrible anger.'[13]

In Venice, a diary records how a sort of 'banditore', or town-crier, went through *calli* and *campi* shouting the announcement of Mussolini's overthrow in a voice that bespoke 'emotion, hilarity and at the same time uncertainty, like somebody experimenting with an unfamiliar language'; and one soldier had 'such a radiant smile on his face that it seems to contain all the joy in his heart, all the words he would like to utter: he's a recalled soldier, he's old, his family's far away, knows no one here, for sure, and hopes now to return home'.[14]

The passage from joy to hope and from hope to disappointment is described in numerous memoirs and testimonies, together with the wish to believe that

---

10 The speech is published in B. Gentile, *Giovanni Gentile. Dal discorso agli Italiani alla morte*, Florence: Sansoni, 1951, pp. 65–81. The reference cited is on pp. 69–70. It is from the article 'Esame di coscienza', published in *Il Resto del Carlino*, 15 December 1917 (then in G. Gentile, *Guerra e fede*, ed. Hervé A. Cavallera, Florence: Le Lettere, 1989, pp. 45–8).

11 See M. Piccialuti Caprioli, *Radio Londra 1940–45. Inventario delle trasmissione per l'Italia*, Rome: Pubblicazioni degli Archivi di Stato, 1976, I, p. 329 (Free Italy Talks, 16 April 1943).

12 M. Tarchi, *Con l'armata italiana in Russia*, Livorno, 1944, p. 36. This book was printed clandestinely in Milan under the editorship of the Partito Italiano del Lavoro [Italian Labour Party]. The author, Giusto Tolloy, republished it in 1947 with De Silva in Turin.

13 Lidia Beccaria Rolfi's testimony in A. Bravo and D. Jalla, eds, *La vita offesa. Storia e memoria dei lager nazisti nei racconti di duecento sopravvissuti*, Milan: Franco Angeli, 1986, p. 79.

14 F. Calamandrei, *La vita indivisibile. Diario 1941–1947*, Rome: Riuniti, 1984, pp. 103–4.

the words of Badoglio's proclamation – 'The war goes on. Italy … will keep its word'[15] – were insincere and dictated by mere tactical prudence. Most Italians took those words 'as being a simulation' and 'from that moment they began not just to dream of the Armistice but to behave as if it had already taken place'.[16] In a climate such as this, attempts to re-dub as 'national' the war that had been wished on the Italians by the now demolished Fascism had not the slightest hope of receiving a hearing.[17]

Much has been written both about the tortuous and clumsily devious route by which the Badoglio government arrived at the drafting and then announcement of the Armistice with the Anglo-Americans,[18] and about the responsibility for the disastrous predicaments that ensued to be attributed to King Victor Emmanuel III, Marshal Pietro Badoglio and his government, and the High Commands. They did not pay serious enough heed to the patently obvious prediction, unambiguously stated by Baron von Mackensen, the German ambassador in Rome, as early as 4 December 1942, that 'A separate peace aimed at keeping the war away from the Italian mainland would automatically make it a theater of war.'[19] Immediately after Mussolini's overthrow, President Roosevelt himself had also stated: 'Fighting between the Germans and the Italian Army and population will probably be a result of the fate of the German troops in Italy and particularly of those south of Rome.'[20]

What also needs emphasising is that the generals and colonels were not sufficiently aware of the state of mind of the men serving under them. The fact that they themselves, in their heart of hearts, shared this state of mind very probably induced them first of all to hide its truth and significance, and then, by their conduct, to set the avalanche on its disastrous descent. The well-known, ambiguous sentence with which Badoglio concluded his proclamation of the

---

15 These words were suggested by Vittorio Emanuele Orlando. See G. Bianchi, *25 luglio, crollo di un regime*, Milan: Mursia, 1966, pp. 416–18.

16 E. Forcella, 'Le trappole di Badoglio', in *Il Messaggero*, 5 September 1983.

17 Attempts in this direction occurred for example among the *paracadutisti* (paratroopers), whose strong *esprit de corps* was called into question by the crisis of the war. On 15 August their newspaper, *Folgore*, published an article, 'Momenti seri', which reaffirmed the possibility of victory if everyone did their duty 'freely, conscientiously, entirely' (I take this information from the degree thesis of Marco Di Giovanni of the University of Pisa, 1988, on the Italian paratroopers in the Second World War).

18 On 29 July a young intellectual wrote: 'It makes no sense trying to be smart with a power [Britain] stronger than us, to which every citizen owes infinite gratitude'. E. Artom, *Diari: gennaio 1940–febbraio 1944*, Milan: Centro di documentazione ebraica contemporanea, 1966, p. 58.

19 See Deakin, *The Brutal Friendship*, p. 145.

20 *Foreign Relations of the United States. Diplomatic Papers 1943*, II, *Europe*, Washington, DC: United States Printing Office, 1964, p. 338; and the reply, of 30 July, to a note on the fall of Mussolini made by Churchill on 26 July (ibid., pp. 332–5).

Armistice – the armed forces 'will repel any possible attacks from any other quarter' – expressed both the hope that Italy would get off lightly and a resigned belief that things should be allowed to run their course.[21] Thus, in the absence of precise and unequivocal directives, morally still more than technically,[22] Italy was heading towards a fate analogous to that vividly recalled in 1942 by Churchill with regard to Bulgaria in 1918:

> When a nation is thoroughly beaten in war it does all sorts of things which no one would imagine beforehand. The sudden, sullen, universal, simultaneous way in which Bulgaria – Government, Army, and people alike – cut out in 1918 remains in my memory. Without caring to make any arrangements for their future or for their safety, the troops simply marched out of the lines and dispersed to their homes, and King Ferdinand fled. A Government headed by a peasant leader remained to await the judgment of the victors.[23]

Weariness with the war and a desire for peace were not phenomena limited to the men-at-arms. 'We are waiting for peace and only peace' – so ran a report on the 'politico-economic situation of the Kingdom on 28 February 1943–XXI'.[24] The violence suffered at first hand with the air-raids, solidarity with relatives of those who had been killed or gone missing, scattered among innumerable theatres of operations, hunger and other material privations, and awareness of the overwhelming superiority of the enemy, vied with each other in making it seem pointless to go on with a war that was irremediably lost.[25] 'We thought our

---

21 Here we are not entering the controversy as to whether that infelicitous sentence was another attempt to play a double game. See R. Zangandi, *1943: l'8 settembre*, Milan: Feltrinelli, 1967. The text of the proclamation is in P. Badoglio, *L'Italia nella seconda guerra mondiale*, Milan: Mondadori, 1948, pp. 106–7.

22 Memoria 44, and promemorias no. 1 and 2 and teletype no. 2402 issued between 5 and 9 September (see them in Zangrandi, *1943*, pp. 364–73).

23 W. Churchill, *The Second World War: Closing the Ring*, London: Cassell, 1952, p. 50 (prime minister's note, 25 November 1942).

24 Roman numerals were used to signify the year of the Fascist regime, starting from the year 1922, and were standard notation at the time. In this case, XXI is the twenty-first year of Fascist rule in Italy (1943). Report quoted in Belmondo et al., *La campagna in Russia*, p. 452.

25 On the collapse of the 'fronte interno' ('home front') see in particular N. Gallerano, 'Il fronte interno attraverso i rapporti delle autorità (1942–1943)', in *Il Movimento di liberazione in Italia* XXIV: 109 (1972), pp. 4–32, and 'La disgregazione delle basi di massa del fascismo nel Mezzogiorno e il ruolo delle masse contadine', in Gianfranco Bertolo, Luigi Ganapini, Massimo Legnani, *Operai e contadini nella crisi italiana del 1943–1944*, Milan: Feltrinelli, 1974, pp. 435–96; R. Giacomini, 'Manifestazioni pacifiste e sovversionismo popolare nei primi anni di guerra', in M. Pacetti, M. Papini and M. Sarcinelli, eds, *La cultura della pace dalla Resistenza al Patto Atlantico*, Bologna: Il Lavoro editoriale, 1988,

sufferings were over', a later testimony of 25 July recalls: 'instead, 8 September came.'[26]

The fact that Mussolini's overthrow and the Armistice did not coincide created the feeling that, if the war was not over, Fascism was not well and truly over either.[27] From Radio Milano Libertà (namely, Radio Moscow) Togliatti warned that 'party hierarchs and followers ... have in no way capitulated and are preparing to take their revenge in a more or less hidden manner': the most dangerous were those who 'have put a mask on'.[28] The BBC Italian Service received instructions to highlight 'the Badoglio Government failure' in the work of de-Fascistisation, which was limited to 'half-measures and palliatives'.[29] This, no doubt, was a way of putting pressure on Badoglio.[30] But the fact that Radio Londra often called the Marshal 'Duke of Addis Ababa' well expressed a grotesque fact that was plain to the Italians and, for that matter, to the Resistance movements of other countries, but not to Badoglio himself, who declared to 'the officers in Agro di San Giorgio Ionico': 'I am still Marshall Badoglio, your general of the Sabotino, of Vittorio Veneto, of Addis Ababa.'[31]

A soldier stationed in the Balkans, finding himself before an 'immense, widespread, host of enemies' ('the Germans, the Bulgarians, the Ustashas, the Cetnics, the Muslims, etc.') had the sensation that everything had come to a standstill in a 'leaden, agonal' climate.[32] And a young man, protagonist of an

pp. 127–69 – in particular the final section, 'Manifestazioni di entusiasmo per una pace ... che tarda a venire'.

26 Albina Caviglione Lusso in A. M. Bruzzone and R. Farina, eds, *La Resistenza taciuta. Dodici vite di partigiane piemontesi*, Milan: La Pietra, 1976, p. 67.

27 See a testimony along these lines in R. Battaglia, *Un uomo, un partigiano*, Rome–Florence–Milan: Edizioni U, 1945, p. 17.

28 P. Togliatti, *Opere*, IV, 2, ed. F. Andreucci and P. Spriano, Rome: Riuniti, 1979, p. 477.

29 *Special Directives* of the Political Warfare Executive of 10 August 1943, in Piccialuti Caprioli, Radio Londra 1940–45, pp. xlvi, xlvii – the citation of two broadcasts in this spirit, by Candidus (John Joseph Marus) and Umberto Calosso.

30 See A. Berselli, 'Il 'Times' di fronte ai governi Badoglio', in *Inghilterra e Italia nel '900: Atti del Convengo di Bagni di Lucca, 193–200*, Florence: La Nuova Italia, 1973, p. 137, where an editorial of 27 July 1943, 'A Dictator's Downfall' is cited.

31 Badoglio's speech on 'La caduta del fascismo e l'armistizio' is cited in an extract by *Agro*, n.d., but shortly after the constitution of the RSI, preserved in ISRT, *Fondo Foscolo Lombardi*, envelope 22, folder IV. For the comments by the French Resistance see, for example, 'Pensée et Action. Organe de l'Union des Intellectuels Patriotes', where Badoglio is spoken of as the 'shameful heir of fascism, who drags like a ball-and-chain his ridiculous title of Duke of Addis Ababa ' (article entitled 'L'Effondrement du fascisme', July–August 1943).

32 Testimony by Ferdinando Pepi, who subsequently became a 'tenente della Garibaldi' ('Garibaldi brigade lieutenant'). See 'La divisione Garibaldi', in R. Bilenchi, *Cronache degli anni neri*, Rome: Riuniti, 1984, p. 101.

autobiographical novel, who would subsequently opt to join the Social Republic, expressed himself thus: 'That lot have lost no time! They've lost no time! ... But what does that leave us with?'[33]

The anti-Fascist parties, which were busy re-establishing themselves during Badoglio's forty-five days of rule, pressed ahead, each with its own nuances, with the request that the war be brought to an end. As early as April, *Riconstruzione: Organo del fronte unico della libertà*, in its 'Appello agli italiani', had asked for 'the passage from the state of war to the state of peace', and the manifesto agreed in Milan on 26 July by the Gruppo di Riconstruzione Liberale, the Democrazia Cristiana (DC), the Partito d'Azione, the Partito Socialista, the Movimento d'Unità Proletaria, and the Partito Communista, numbered among its points 'an armistice for the conclusion of an honourable peace' (this formula, the fruit of mediation between the parties, was in fact confused compared with the victors' clear desire to impose an unconditional surrender – a desire which, it should be repeated, despite historiographical polemics, was correct).[34]

The 4 August 1943 Milan edition of *L'Unità* had this long headline: 'The communists are fighting alongside Italians of all persuasions on the road to peace and freedom in order to save the *patria* from ruin.' A year later, *L'Unità* would again speak of 'the sloth and organic incapacity of a government in which the people did not participate, the betrayal undermining an army'.[35] The paper of the Action Party denounced, 'more than a month after 25 July', the fact that the cardinal error of the coup d'état had been its failure to proclaim explicitly: 'Fascism has fallen. The Fascist war is over.'[36] These comments are quoted not so much because they testify to the different party lines (which were as yet little known to the Italians) and their capacity to exert a widespread and direct influence on the popular will, as to the existence of a state of mind that the parties would necessarily have to take as their point of departure.

The common desire to have done with the war was not enough to create that correspondence of intention and action between the army and the population that was also part of official rhetoric during Badoglio's forty-five days. This failure was due not only to the attitude of the High Commands, described above, but also to the fact that the use of the armed forces for public order immediately put paid to any form of fraternisation; even though, as has been noted, the troops and junior officers frequently showed themselves reluctant to carry out the more drastic orders.[37]

---

33 C. Mazzantini, *A cercar la bella morte*, Milan: Mondadori, 1986, p. 11.

34 For the manifesto, see F. Catalano, *Storia del CLNAI*, Bari: Laterza, 1956, p. 36.

35 Article entitled 'Cammino di un anno', northern edition, 25 July 1944.

36 Article entitled 'Un mese' in *L'Italia Libera*, August 1943.

37 See 'L'Italia dei quarantacinque giorni 1943: 25 luglio–8 settembre', *Quaderni del Movimento di Liberazione in Italia*, Milan, 1969, 4, p. 37. For confirmation of the attitude of subaltern officers see A. Borrini, A. Mignemi and R. Muratore, eds, *Parlare e*

The circular issued by Mario Roatta, chief of the Army General Staff, with orders to proceed against demonstrators 'in combat formation, and to open fire at long range even with mortars and artillery without forewarning of any kind', and the Bari and Reggio Emilia massacres, are among the most glaring . cases in point. Another circular, by General Quirino Armellini, who had been appointed commander of the Fascist militia that Badoglio incorporated into the Royalist Army, provides the most complete – indeed, grotesque – measure of this. Armellini, whose words are worth quoting, recalled the 'merits of which we are all aware' of the MVSN (*Milizia volontaria per la sicurezza nazionale*), 'born of the action squads'; deplored the reaction of the country, 'hostile and often brutal towards the Milizia', as well as 'the ill-advised demonstrations and offences coming from the turbid rabble', and concluded with an enjoinder to oppose the enemy, who were fired 'by inhuman hate and the stern resolution to annihilate' the *patria*, with ourselves, in the name of God, Christianity, Rome and the King and Emperor.[38] Some of the themes that were to form part of the propaganda of the Social Republic are anticipated in this circular, mixed with others that were to be taken up and voiced by the monarchist and reactionary press in the South.

Thus, in its relationship with the people, the army as an institution came to find itself in an ambiguous position, which was starkly evoked, years later, by a Torinese Communist militant: 'Fascism had fallen but it had returned in Badoglio's army; it had ended up inside the army.'[39] It is striking how deeply this remained imprinted in people's memory as a dominant fact, and how this memory coincides, for instance, with the amazement observed by Second Lieutenant Giorgio Chiesura in the people of Fossano at the rigorous mainte-nance of law and order by the troops against a population who had so warmly approved the anti-Fascist coup performed by none other than the armed forces.[40] Amazement becomes contempt in an appeal addressed, in August in Bologna, to the women of Emilia: 'Twenty-three years of oppression and slavery and still we're not satisfied! Still Badoglio, still the generals.'[41]

This small manifesto was certainly Communist-inspired; the line that can be identified in the underground press of the same period, even that of the left, is far more variable, caught as it was between, on the one hand, the need to

scrivere di Ciro, Novara: Cooperativa Bighinzoli, 1987, p. 20 (Ciro was the Garibaldino commander Eraldo Gastone).

38 For Roatta's circular of 26 July, see *L'Italia dei quarantacinque giorni*, pp. 11–12. The circular is attacked by *L'Avanti!*, 22 August, in the article entitled 'La repressione'. A copy of Armellini's circular of 30 July is preserved in ACS, *Carte Casati*, folder H. See *L'Italia dei quarantacinque giorni*, p. 46.

39 Teresa Cirio's testimony, in Bruzzone and Farina, eds, *La Resistenza taciuta*, p.78.

40 Chiesura, *Sicilia 1943*, p.83.

41 *Saggio bibliografico*, no. 3081.

acknowledge popular weariness and suspicion and to use them as a weapon of pressure on the government, and, on the other, the not yet discarded hope that something positive might still be agreed on and projected with those armed forces. On 4 August the Milan edition of *L'Unità* considered it an 'absurd crime' to go on with the war now that Mussolini was no longer in power, and added: 'The popular masses are beginning to ask themselves whether the liquidation of Fascism might not be a tragic swindle.' On 12 August, *L'Unità* ran this headline on all its front pages: 'Ma la musica è sempre la stessa' ('But the music is always the same'), and on the second page: 'Soldiers! Don't fire at the workers. They are fighting to enable your return home', while a subtitle urged: 'People and soldiers! Unite in demanding an immediate peace that will save the nation. Workers! Demand the end of Hitler's war! Save your lives, your houses, your factories!'

Appeals for peace and fraternisation between the civilian population and the soldiers became more pressing after the massive strikes that shook the factories of the North from 17 to 20 August, and which acquired a distinctly political character by virtue of the request for the liberation of political prisoners and arrested workers, for the expulsion from the factories not only of the Fascists but of the troops as well, and for the creation of internal commissions. Dominating all was the manifestation of a clear opposition to the continuance of the war.[42] On 22 August, *Avanti!* denounced the 'absurdity' (a recurrent epithet in the anti-Fascist press that week) of the continuation of the war,[43] and bore the subtitle: 'Peace, peace immediately, peace at all costs.' On the same day *L'Unità* once again urged: 'Soldiers and people unite in the struggle for peace!' As early as 26 July in Cuneo, and on the 27 July in Turin, Duccio Galimberti had launched an appeal to the crowd for war against the Germans. This position would appear explicitly in the article 'Guerra e pace', in the August issue of *Italia Libera*.[44] At the semi-clandestine congress of the Action Party, held in Florence between 2 and 7 September, above all Ferruccio Parri, who had been appointed the party official responsible for military affairs in northern Italy, argued for armed struggle – volunteers fighting alongside the army – against German domination, heralded by the massive influx of forces into Italy after 25 July.[45]

It is well known that the anti-Fascist left-wing parties did not confine

---

42 See Catalano, *Storia del CLNAI*, p. 44, and *L'Italia dei quarantacinque giorni*, Chapter IV.

43 Article entitled, 'Come prima, peggio di prima'.

44 See L. Valiani, 'Il partito d'azione', in L. Valiani, G. Bianchi and E. Ragionieri, *Azionisti, cattolici e comunisti nella Resistenza*, Milan: Franco Angeli, 1971, pp. 57–9.

45 On the Florence conference see G. De Luna, *Storia del Partito d'Azione, 1942–1947*, Milan: Feltrinelli, 1982, pp. 85–8. Cf. 'L'Intervista sulla guerra partigiana', given by Parri on 28 October and 3 November 1966 to Luisa La Malfa Calogero and Maria Vittoria de Filippis, published in *Italia contemporanea* 149 (December 1982), pp. 21–8.

themselves to launching appeals of this kind, but that – winning over, whenever possible, the other parties from the fronts and committees that were being
formed at the time – they also made overtures to the government, or directly to
the military authorities,[46] in order to prepare the ground for the joint actions
they hoped for in anticipation of the day of reckoning with the Germans that
was clearly imminent. The best known of these approaches was that attempted
by Luigi Longo to Badoglio, which was duly formalised in the 'pro memoria',
presented on 30 August, in the name of the Communist Party, to the committee
of opposition[47] The demand for peace was combined, with increasing insistence,
as an indispensable stage with the demand for war against the Germans. Peace
and giving chase to the Germans are the objectives indicated by a Communist
leaflet of 4 September, with its enjoinder to create 'fighting formations'.[48] The
document presented to the Prefect of Turin, during the August strikes, by the
representatives of the 'fronte nazionale' states that the people 'want peace even
at the cost of war against Nazism'.[49] At the eleventh hour by now, on 7 September,
L'Unità, in a headline occupying the entire front page, wrote, with impatience
verging on breathlessness: 'The People and the Army want peace. Peace can be
obtained by chasing the Germans off our territory.' The ensuing article, 'To soldiers and officers for the conquest and defense of peace', enjoined the army to
make ready for its new, imminent tasks by identifying and isolating the Fascist
elements who were ready to capitulate. Another part of the paper read: 'Driving
out the Germans is possible. Italy must dare.'

The army was certainly not lacking in openly Fascist elements; and in
denouncing them, the Communist Party was again attempting to salvage the
others, the good elements, the majority. But the collapse that followed soon
afterwards was too widespread to attribute simply to the deliberate will of a few
diehard Fascists. The fact is that the 'heroes' of 1918, who, as in Bloch's account
of 1940 France, still largely occupied the top echelons of the military hierarchy,

46 For example, in Modena General Negro opposed the offer of the committee of
anti-Fascist parties of a 'possible collaboration by volunteers' with a 'courteous but firm
rejection'. See E. Gorrieri, La Republica di Montefiorino. Per una storia della Resistenza in
Emilia, Bologna: Il Mulino, 1966, p. 21.

47 'Promemoria sulla necessità urgente di organizzare la difesa nazionale contro
l'occupazione e la minaccia di colpi di mano da parte dei tedeschi', in L. Longo, Sulla
via dell'insurrezione nazionale, Rome: Riuniti, 1971, pp. 33–4; republished in Le Brigate
Garibaldi nella Resistenza. Documenti, 3 vols, Milan: Feltrinelli, 1979, vol. I, eds G.
Carocci and G. Grassi, p. 93. For Longo's attempted approaches, see R. Battaglia, Storia
della Resistenza italiana, Turin: Einaudi, 1964, p. 69. As a testimony of the clear perception, on the part of the Communists, of the need immediately after the imminent
armistice to engage in armed struggle, see P. Colajanni, 'I comunisti e l'organizzazione
militare clandestina antifascista', in Quaderni siciliani, 1973, 3–4, pp. 71–94.

48 See L'Italia dei quarantacinque giorni, pp. 337–8.

49 A copy of the document is preserved in IG, Archivio PCI.

had by now 'gone soft after a lifetime of bureaucratic administration and devi-
ousness', and were therefore incapable of coping with emergency situations and
interpreting the state of mind of the great masses of armed citizens who had
been entrusted to their care. And it was the entire army that, in the climate
of tension and also of opaqueness weighing on the country, was about to collapse, corroded by a 'crisis of morality' that was indeed comparable to the crisis
that had demolished the French Army in June 1940.[50] The failure of army and
country to engage each other in the days of the Armistice was to be one of the
first facts with which the resistance forces would have to reckon.

   Badoglio's forty-five days had not, then, 'saved what there was to save', to
quote a formula in fashion at the time that was contemptuously contested by
the youthful intransigence of the new belligerent anti-Fascism.[51] The 'serious
condition of the history of Italy' was in fact preventing Fascism from evading
'its responsibilities by pretending to scuttle itself with a decree by the Grand
Council'.[52] In time of war, Freud had written in 1915, 'the State demands the
maximum obedience and the maximum sacrifice from its citizens, but then
treats them like children, thereby giving birth to a state of mind defenceless
against every unfavourable turn of events'.[53] In Italy the Fascist war and the
8 September collapse generated this type of phenomenon on an immense scale;
but those defenceless children displayed a vast range of reactions which, even
in their contradictions, attested to their determination not to let themselves
go under.

   The collapse following Badoglio's proclamation of the Armistice with the
Anglo-Americans on the evening of 8 September has been described countless
times, especially as regards the conduct of the political and military leaders. I do
not intend here to retrace those events, correcting the odd point, adding the odd
detail and increasing the plethora of literature about the 'failure to defend Rome'.
Two circumstances do, however, need recalling: on the one hand, the objective difficulties that even more competent and better-intentioned Commands
would have come up against; on the other hand, the opportunities still available in the days immediately following the Salerno landing, which proved to
be such hard-going for the Allies, for an initiative by Badoglio and the king.[54]

---

   50 The expressions relating to France are taken from M. Bloch, L'étrange défaite,
Paris: Colin, 1957, pp. 126, 138.

   51 See the 'Bollettini' ('Bulletins') of the Popolo e Libertà movement, July 1943, p. 32,
and August 1943, p. 3 (La sagra della viltà).

   52 I have taken the first expression from C. Casucci's Introduction to Il fascismo.
Antologia di scritti critici, Bologna: Il Mulino, 1982, pp. 13–18, and the second from I.
Calvino, 'Tante storie che abbiamo dimenticato', in La Repubblica, 23 April 1985.

   53 S. Freud, 'Thoughts for the Times on War and Death', 1915, available at
panarchy.org.

   54 Worth quoting, among all the documents that can be invoked on this score, is

Churchill himself, ill-disposed towards Italy though he was, had written in a memorandum prepared for the meeting with Roosevelt at the White House on 9 September: 'Should fighting break out between Italians and Germans, the public prejudices will very rapidly depart, and in a fortnight or so matters may be ripe, if we can so direct events, for an Italian declaration of war against Germany.'[55]

Again, the behaviour of the Italian Commands is comparable to that displayed in France in 1940, as described by Bloch: 'Our Command ... did not limit itself to undergoing the defeat: ... they accepted it ... Deep in their hearts [the chiefs] were inclined to despair of the very country they should have defended and of the common people from whose ranks the soldiers came.'[56]

As the editors of a collection of testimonies by surviving Nazi concentration camp deportees have pointed out, '8 September was the watershed to our memory of things'.[57] There was nothing 'splendid' about the disaster marked by that date:[58] not, obviously, for the Fascists, but neither for the mass of the population, nor the anti-Fascists, who could appeal to it only by taking it as a grievous disaster. The 8 September collapse succeeded in combining the effects of an event that had been too long awaited and of an event that had come unexpectedly. An ancient testamentary formula ran: 'Nihil morte certius et nihil incertus hora eius' ('Nothing is as certain as death and nothing as uncertain as its hour'). For the Italians the hour came at a moment that set two contradictory certainties against each other: the omnipotence of the Allies and the invincibility of the Germans. The Allies – this was the widespread desire – should, by

---

the telegram sent by Eisenhower to Badoglio on 10 September: 'If Italy rises up now as a single man we shall grab every German by the throat. I urge you to make an overwhelming appeal to all Italian patriots. They have already done much locally, but their action seems uncertain and disconnected.' But already on 13 September, writing to the Chief of Staff George Marshall, Eisenhower spoke of 'weak and supine Italians ... of little help and inert'. Badoglio's reply of 11 September had, besides, been unsatisfactory to the point of impertinence: Badoglio had assured the Anglo-American commander-in-chief that he had ordered the armed forces (not at any rate the patriots, as Eisenhower had requested) to 'act vigorously against German aggression' (see M. Toscano, *Dal 25 luglio all'8 settembre*, Florence: Le Monnier, 1966, pp. 216, 218). For the pressure exerted directly on the king and Badoglio by Roosevelt and Churchill to do something for the good of Italy, see N. Kogan, *Italy and the Allies*, Cambridge: Harvard University Press, 1961, pp. 42ff).

55 Churchill, *Second World War: Closing the Ring*, pp. 134–5.

56 Bloch, *L'étrange défaite*, p. 158. See also, on p. 202: 'Our leaders did not only allow themselves to be beaten: they immediately found it natural to have been beaten.'

57 A. Bravo and D. Jalla, Introduction to *La vita offesa*, p. 23.

58 F. T. Marinetti had spoken of a 'disastro splendido' as something desirable in his essay 'Futurismo e Fascismo', published in *La civiltà fascista*, Turin: UTET, 1928 (cf. Casucci, *Il fascismo*, p. 106).

their rapid and total deployment of troops, have prevented the Germans from exercising their uncheckable power, thereby sparing the Italians the agony suffered by so many other European peoples. The false news, at the moment of the Allied air and sea landings and immediately after, of German reactions against Italians still swifter and more fearsome than those actually occurring, was given credence, tallying almost to the letter with the path traced by Bloch in a famous essay, because 'representations collectives qui préexistent' converged with chance misunderstandings: in the course of those few days the whole of Italy became one immense cauldron, which is generally the place where false news is concocted.[59] Witness a top-level example. When, at Chieti late in the evening of 9 September, the king, Badoglio and the other fleeing generals received news that Trieste, Genoa and La Spezia had already been occupied, some of them still believed that the occupiers were the Allies.[60] But during those days the hunger for news was such that 'it was enough for a drunkard to raise his voice a bit and shout disconnected words, for people to come running from every direction to hear him.'[61]

The first major piece of 'false news' that the Italians saw belied by events was that the Armistice meant peace. Far more swiftly than after 25 July, and with infinitely more radical consequences, the immediate reactions were overturned, running the rapid gamut, widely attested by the documents and memoirs, of incredulity–stupor–joy–worry–bewilderment.

'Those who don't understand, those who half-understand. Soldiers embracing, caps flying. The soldiers are in high spirits as if the war really was over': these are the first reactions recorded, in Cuneo, by Nuto Revelli.[62] In Venice, Franco Calamandrei described 'exclamations of delight, joyful singing by children, smiling yelps from babies ... The usual sudden, short-lived optimism [and then] annihilation, silence, confusion.'[63] A corporal stationed at Udine recently recollected that 'the people, out on the streets, were elated and the soldiers rejoiced, [after which] a scramble by the officers, ours included.'[64] Other testimonies concur about there being 'a mixed atmosphere of joy, incredulity and bewilderment', of 'joy and sadness', of people 'partly exulting and partly – above all the older ones – expressing concern about what was going to happen.'[65]

---

59 See M. Bloch, 'Réflexions d'un historien sur les fausses nouvelles de la guerre', in *Mélanges historiques* I, Paris: Écoles des hautes études en sciences sociales, 1983, pp. 41–57 (in particular, p. 54).

60 See Zangrandi, *1943*, p. 181, which refers to a testimony by J. Di Benigno, *Occasioni mancate. Roma in un diario segreto*, Rome: SEI, 1945, p. 137.

61 Thus Calamandrei, *La vita indivisibile*, p. 112 (8 September in Venice).

62 N. Revelli, *La guerra dei poveri*, Turin: Einaudi, 1962, p. 127.

63 Calamandrei, *La vita indivisibile*, pp. 109–10.

64 Testimony by Carlo Barbaglia, from Como, born in 1910.

65 Testimonies by Luigi Airaldi, from Milan, stationed at Pegli; of Tullio Benigni,

The future partisan leader Guido Quazza wrote in his diary of the passage from joy to uncertainty to anxiety, of the desire to flee, of physical exhaustion and moral sorrow suffered in those few days.[66] And another partisan commander *in pectore*, Giovanni Battista Lazagna, recalled that 'after the initial moments of euphoria the more open-eyed began to take stock of the situation'.[67] And soon there was a widespread sense of having been abandoned – the soldiers by their officers, all Italians by every authority which ought in fact to have been protecting them.

'They've betrayed us, the officers have run away, even the King has abandoned us!' cried the soldiers who, in Padua on 9 September, descended into Prato della Valle from a nearby barracks.[68] 'They've all bolted' was the sentry's 'brutal' reply to his interrogators outside the headquarters of the Rome Corps in Piazza della Pilotta.[69] In Turin, 'lying in the fields were bayonets, holster-belts that the soldiers were discarding, saying "make them into shoes". The officers are the first to flee, then the troops, and of course this is useful to Communism, because the bourgeois classes have cut a dreadful figure'.[70] Again in Turin, a sapper recalls, 'after two days, seeing that we weren't receiving orders, we thought the best thing to do was cut and run, because in those conditions the only thing that could happen to us was to get caught in a trap like a lot of mice'.[71] In the 4th Army divisions that, 'each man shifting for himself as best he could', made it to Cuneo from France, the soldiers stood there in amazement, looking at each other 'wide-eyed', until eventually each decided to save himself as best he could.[72] One soldier asked the question, which no one was able to answer: 'But, in short, signor colonello, what, now, are we supposed to do?'[73]

---

from Umbria, stationed in Vicenza; of Aldo Accorsi, from Carpi, a sailor who embarked on one of the ships that managed to reach Malta from Pola (*CU*).

66 G. Quazza, 'Un diario partigiano', in *La Resistenza italiana. Appunti e documenti*, Turin: Giappichelli, 1966, pp. 133–5.

67 G. B. Lazagna, *Ponte rotto*, Quaderni di '*Il Novese*', Nuovi Ligure: 1967, p. 17.

68 Testimony by A. B., from Padova,, who was sixteen years old at the time (*CU*).

69 Testimony of the attorney Adolfo Gatti (*La Repubblica*, 7 September 1983). The same sentry replied to the present author: 'We have orders to hand in our weapons as soon as they arrive – The Anglo-Americans? – No, the Germans.'

70 Artom, *Diari*, p. 76 (10 September). On the first day the diary records (p. 75) the meeting with the captain who, when asked 'What can those who defend the *patria* do?', replies: 'Why are you asking me?' – 'Because you are an officer in the army' – 'I have nothing to do with it', he replies, 'Ask the command of the territorial defence' – 'And how will they greet us?' – 'They won't even listen to you'.

71 Testimony by Uberto Revelli in Bravo and Jalla, eds, *La vita offesa*, p. 80.

72 Testimony by the Tuscan Giuseppe Bandin (*CU*). On the dissolution of the 4th army see Istituto Storico della Resistenza in Cuneo e provincia, *8 settembre. Lo sfacelo della IV armata*, Turin: Book Store, 1979.

73 D. Benelli, *Un Ponte fra due castelli. Fascismo e antifascismo nelle Signe*, Florence:

The growing frustration during the aimless waiting into which the not yet disbanded division had plummeted in the first few hours is well described by a pilot, a lieutenant in the air force, who was shortly to take refuge in Switzerland. After recalling the growing 'nervous tension' that had taken possession of the airmen, he wrote, 'We began to distrust our superiors, whom' – he is quick to add – 'we had always distrusted, all the way through the war': finally, 'on the evening of the 11th the troop staff, who in this delicate moment had maintained a marvellous control, always disciplined and respectful, lost their calm and started sacking the airport, as a reprisal against the lack of orders and initiatives on the part of the airport commander'.[74]

The passage from the general breakup to the material breaking-up of whatever objects were within arm's reach is also recorded, by a naval gunner stationed on an Istrian island: 'Then we smashed up everything; the barracks completely destroyed, the cannon into the sea, everything; everything was smashed up'.[75]

The dissolution of the Royal Army had actually begun earlier, at least as far back as the Sicily landing. On 16 July 1943 the 16th Corps Command found itself compelled to issue draconian orders against the disbanded soldiers who – by way of a general rehearsal, as it were, for what was to happen shortly afterwards – 'especially those born on the island, have abandoned their uniforms, buying civilian clothes, and altered their uniforms in the attempt to make them look like civilian clothes by ripping off insignia, stars and badges denoting rank'. The Corps Command had branded as deserters the soldiers who behaved in that way, ordering that they be shot.[76] What is remarkable about the 8 September catastrophe is that no one, be he officer or soldier, felt that by disguising himself as a civilian he was deserting;[77] nor did it occur to anyone that that mass flight ought to be denounced as an act of desertion. The feelings aroused and the first judgments formulated were of an altogether different nature. Eraldo Gastone, the future Ciro commander of the Garibaldi Brigades in which

---

Istituto Gramsci Sezione Toscana, 1983, cited and appropriated in the testimony of private P (*CU*).

74 'Declaration' of lieutenant Raffaele Sciandone regarding Linate Pozzolo (Gallarate) airport, n.d., attached to a report by the CLNAI delegation in Switzerland, November 1944 (INSMLI, *CLNAI*, envelope 3, folder I. Ib).

75 Testimony by Claudio Locci in A. Portelli, *Biografia di una città. Storia e racconto: Terni (1830–1985)*, Turin: Einaudi, 1985, p. 258.

76 The document, preserved in the Historic Museum of the Folgore Parachute Brigade, is cited in M. Di Giovanni's degree thesis, which also quotes a police report of 20 July 1943 describing the airmen of Ciampino airport who took to the country after an air-raid and who, the following morning, 'were wandering along the via Appia, several kilometres from the field, without their jackets, with a blanket over their shoulders and a flask in their hands'.

77 An observation of this sort is in Zangrandi, *1943*, p. 22.

Cino Moscatelli was to be the commissar, spoke of an 'indecorous, doleful strip-tease'.[78]

'The soldiers went by like a defeated flock of sheep', Primo Levi recalled.[79] Roberto Battaglia, still hot from the scene, spoke of a 'humiliating spectacle'.[80] In one of the finest diaries about partisan life, Pietro Chiodi records: 'It breaks my heart to see groups of soldiers being herded about like animals by the SS'.[81] And another witness writes: 'Like so many sheep we formed up and, escorted by the SS, passed through the streets of Cuneo which were deserted'.[82] To this day a woman dolefully recalls the long file of soldiers who, with just one German at their head and one at the rear, came out of a barracks 'with their rifles lowered like thieves to surrender their weapons'.[83] Dante Livio Bianco speaks of the decomposition of the 4th Army as 'one of the saddest and most humiliating' spectacles, and describes 'the pain that wrung our hearts and the shame that burned us'.[84] Eraldo Gastone commented on a similar episode in these terms: 'That before such meagre forces an entire division should have surrendered with its general at the head seemed to me outrageous'.[85]

The passivity of the soldiers, the dulling in them of every instinct of personal defence, seems to have imprinted itself with particular intensity, and with persistent stupor, on the memories of the women: 'Tempted yet uncertain': this was how the soldiers of the Valdocco di Torino stared back at the women who were urging them to escape.[86] Those who had been interned in the provisional camp of Vitipeno are described by another woman in these words: 'These men have left me dumbfounded: they didn't move, they wept, seemed half-witted, had no spirit left for anything' – though it was still easy to escape from that camp. Indeed, she herself escaped; and an Alpino asked her: 'Ma anduva toi ve?' ('Where do you think you're off to?').[87] In Modena the women urged the soldiers to escape through the sewers of the barracks, but only four decided to make an attempt.[88]

Fits of anger and desperation seized those who witnessed scenes in which very small numbers of Germans overpowered hosts of bewildered, dazed Italians.

---

78 See Borrini, Mignemi and Muratore, *Parlare*, p. 22. Gastone, for the time being, chose to disguise himself as a military chaplain.

79 Testimony in *La Repubblica*, 7 September 1983.

80 Battaglia, *Un uomo*, p. 19.

81 P. Chiodi, *Banditi*, Turin: Einaudi, 1975, p. 15 (9 September).

82 L. Bocci, 'Ricordi di un allievo ufficiale', in Bilenchi, *Cronache degli anni neri*, p. 40.

83 Testimony by Marina Azzoni Soldat (*CU*).

84 D. L. Bianco, *Guerra partigiana*, Turin: Einaudi, 1973, pp. 6–7.

85 Borrini, Mignemi and Muratore, eds, *Parlare*, p. 23.

86 A. Gobetti, *Diario partigiano*, Turin: Einaudi, 1972, p. 23.

87 Testimony by Elsa Oliva in Bruzzone and Farina, *La Resistenza taciuta*, p. 127.

88 Testimony by Olimpio Zuffa (*CU*).

Ada Gobetti writes that she wept with 'unbearable sorrow' at the sight of the Germans, few and undisturbed, taking possession of Turin; and, recording the desperation of her son Paolo, she notes: 'It was his first disappointment in love.'[89] The present author remembers being seized by the shoulders in Via di Roma by a weeping girl imploring him to do something to prevent a lone German, who was shaking his rifle about and yelling, from holding at bay a crowd of civilians and disbanded soldiers. To avoid this anguish, Second Lieutenant Giampiero Carocci placed himself at the head of what remained of his company and gave himself up to the Germans.[90]

The young men who had not ceased to believe in the Fascist war were engulfed by a bewilderment without hope, which was to characterise many of those who would opt for the Italian Social Republic: 'Here they were, all had become small, vulnerable: a sense of misery, of being nothing any longer, at the mercy of what would befall, without so much as a gesture of opposition, a word, anything.'[91]

To complete the picture, there was often the sacking of civilian and above all military depots. The intention of depriving the Germans of those goods or the elementary need for survival were often invoked as a cover for acts that appeared to be 'a blatant manifestation of the general anarchy and confusion'.[92] At times the Germans threatened to have the pillagers shot,[93] at others they themselves urged the pillaging of what they were unable to carry away.[94] It was yet another way for them to get their own back on an ally who had abandoned them, and also a confirmation – which they perfidiously provoked and at times gleefully photographed – that they were dealing with what Dr Goebbels defined, in his diary entries for those very days, as 'a nation of gypsies'.[95] The truth of the matter

---

89 Gobetti, *Diario partigiano*, pp. 26, 21.

90 See G. Carocci, *Il campo degli ufficiali*, Turin: Einaudi, 1954, p. 26. A colleague had said 'let's flee too'; and Carocci writes: 'But it bothered me for the sake of the soldiers' (p. 25).

91 Mazzantini, *A cercar la bella morte*, p. 18.

92 This, for example, is what Gorrieri writes in *La Repubblica di Montefiorino* (p. 28). On the pillaging that took place in Milan, see E. Tortoreto, 'Notizie sul movimento operaio in Milano dal 25 luglio 1943 al marzo 1944', in *Il Movimento di liberazione in Italia*, July 1956, 43, pp. 16–41; on those that occurred in Lazio, V. Tedesco, 'Vita di guerra, Resistenza, dopoguerra in provincia di Roma', in Gallerano, ed., *L'altro dopoguerra*, p. 226.

93 A proclamation of September of the German military command of Modena (*Fondo RSI*, no. 313).

94 On the huge amount of booty captured by the Germans in Italy, see Zangrandi, *1943*, pp. 379–81, and G. Bocca, *La Repubblica di Mussolini*, Bari: Laterza, 1977, p. 67.

95 Mussolini is 'the last Roman, but behind his powerful figure a people of gypsies will end up putrefying' (10 September). The previous day Goebbels had written: 'I presume that the Italians, who put their hands up in every theatre of war, will do the

was that the anonymous crowd was giving itself the satisfaction of demonstrating that, while the population were suffering starvation, 'la roba' ('the stuff') was actually there in the public warehouses; above all it was a collective way of experiencing and endorsing the exceptional nature of events that sanctioned some of the most transgressive forms of conduct. Italo Calvino recounted how this exceptional opportunity to pillage had remained impressed even in the memories of the soldiers of the Social Republic, whose favourite topic of conversation, in the barracks he describes, 'was about the stuff they had made off with on 8 September', and about what they might make off with 'when the next 8 September comes'.[96]

Even those who did not pillage, or flee, or disobey (insofar as nobody was around any longer to give orders) saw that the pillagers, the fugitives, the insubordinate did not, at least for the time being, receive any punishment. Those first few days, therefore, saw a lightning development of acts of demonstrative disobedience, which could, however, easily change into acquiescence before the crudest and most flagrant acts of high-handedness.

At the suggestion of the Ministry of Popular Culture[97] the announcement of the Armistice had been published by the newspapers as an obituary notice. This was an act of hypocrisy both towards the vast majority of the population who wanted, somehow or other, to have done with the war, and towards the Fascists, who wanted to continue it. What was felt to be a new massive Caporetto was not defeat by the British and Americans, but sudden, headlong defeat by the Germans.[98] Victor Emmanuel III turned on its head the appeal that had been made by the Fascist government, and, in an attempt to rally people's spirits, this time against the Germans, once again reverted to the memory of 1917 in his speech broadcast on Radio Bari on 24 September.[99] As we shall see, the sense of defeat was to reappear in the Fascists of the Social Republic as a stimulus to their desire for revenge and, at least in some members of the Resistance, as a need to give a new face, after the two-fold defeat, to national identity.

---

same when they find themselves facing German soldiers' (quoted in E. Ragionieri, *Italia giudicata*, Turin: Einaudi, 1976, pp. 796, 795). In agreement with his minister, the diary of a German soldier in Italy (G. Nebel, *Unter Partisanen und Krezfahrern*, Stuttgart, 1950) describes 'splendidly', according to Schmitt, 'when a large regular army dissolves and, as a mob, is either exterminated by the local population or itself turns to killing and plundering' (C. Schmitt, *Theory of the Partisan*, Chicago: University of Chicago Press, 2004, p. 71).

96 I. Calvino, 'Angoscia in caserma', in *Ultimo viene il corvo*, Turin: Einaudi, 1976, pp. 102–3.

97 See Zangrandi, *1943*, p. 129; E. Forcella, 'Un black-out ante litteram, come e perché giornali e radio non parlano dell'8 settembre', in *Il Manifesto*, 9 September 1983.

98 'Una seconda Caporetto' ('A second Caporetto'), says an elderly station-master of Mestre. See Benelli, *Un ponte fra due castelli*, p. 80.

99 See A. Degli Espinosa, *Il Regno del Sud*, Rome: Migliaresi, 1946, p. 81.

To enrich the picture, we must recall the manifestations of solidarity and help that a large part of the population immediately offered the disbanded and fugitive troops.[100] This solidarity essentially took the form of concrete actions. Alongside the first glimmers of active resistance, the seeds were widely sown, in the course of those days, of 'passive resistance', insofar as a climate and environment were created favouring the former. The railway engineers slowed down the trains and made unscheduled halts to allow the soldiers to escape, or left saws and hammers in the wagons to aid flight.[101] The peasants were 'moved by a confused and powerful sentiment that was at once both heartfelt pity for all those homeless and endangered "figli di mamma", and solidarity for these men from other regions, most of them peasants like themselves'.[102] One witness speaks tearfully to this day of Emilian girls who 'waited for the soldiers, brought them food and then said "if you want to stay here..."'[103] Bewildered soldiers were 'surrounded by people wanting to help them'.[104] Everybody offered the soldiers civilian clothing. Fraternisation between civilians and soldiers, which had failed to occur under the equivocal sign of Badoglio, succeeded under that of common misfortune. No one rallied around the institution of the Royal Army, but everyone came to the aid of Italians who had been plunged into dire peril. In Turin, the few soldiers still in active service whom it had occurred to someone to dispatch to disperse the crowd were applauded and embraced by them;[105] the soldiers interned by the Germans in a barracks at Acqui were set free by the local people.[106] The eruption of a potential *bellum omnium contra omnes* was counterbalanced by the aid total strangers offered each other. The bitterness of civil war and of war against the occupier was beating at the door, and people seemed to have discovered that the only remaining support lay in trusting one's neighbour. Exceptionally powerful fears and acts of exceptional solidarity commingled in the thick of daily living: 'The State is in ruins, the army

---

100 I have had to omit specific references to the situation created after 8 September in the Balkans and the Aegean islands between the Italian occupying troops, where 'those who had a shred of common sense started to cry, because for us the worst was beginning' (testimony by Antonio Paccagnella in Bravo and Jalla, *La vita offesa*, p. 79).

101 See Borrini, Mignemi and Muratore, *Parlare*, p. 21, and the testimonies of Bruno Simioli and Felice Perosino in Bravo and Jalla, *La vita offesa*, pp. 80, 128. On the role played by the railway workers and the Germans' distrust of them, see E. Vallini, *Guerra sulle rotaie: contributo ad una storia della Resistenza*, Milan: Lerici, 1964.

102 This is how it was to be recalled in the article entitled, 'I contadini e la guerra di liberazione', in *L'Italia Libera*, 30 May 1944 (Roman edition).

103 Testimony by Carlo Rameri, in D. Borioli and R. Botta, *I giorni della montagna. Otto saggi sui partigiani della Pinan Cichero*, Alessandria: WR Edizioni, 1990, p. 80.

104 Testimony by Luigi Airaldi.

105 See Artom, *Diari*, p. 74 (9 September).

106 See G. Pesce, *Senza tregua*, Milan: Feltrinelli, 1974, pp. 15–16.

has disintegrated, but the train from Acqui to Alessandria is still running. It seems absurd.'[107]

If on the one hand this 'absurd' normality was an offence against the exceptional character of the situation, on the other hand it responded to a wistful hankering after complete normality and a desire to re-enter the 'womb-like warmth of legality'.[108] Acquiescence to the authority of the RSI, and of that administrative machinery that it somehow or other reactivated, was to have its roots in this desire.

Reluctance to face the fact that institutional legality had completely dissolved helps account for the residual attempts by the anti-Fascist forces to lean on royal, military and civilian authorities, in the hope of involving them in the taking of firm stances in both word and deed. In the case of the moderate left-wing parties, this responded to their fear of losing contact with those authorities and their wish to leave no stone unturned. But one needs to distinguish between attempts made from the ranks by the odd new-born partisan squad to win over those fragments of the defeated Royal Army that were still, for the time being, on their feet,[109] and high-level approaches still made in the name of legality. In Turin the constitutional scruples about poster-sticking and holding assemblies were such that Communists and Actionists had no option but to dissociate themselves from the other parties.[110] In Rome, in a situation whose atypical character was further highlighted by the pretence that it was a '*città aperta*', uncertainty and fear generated in the local press an 'evasive and minimising approach'[111] whose sole concern was the maintenance of public order. Thus, while *Il Lavoro*

---

107 Ibid., p. 19.

108 These are Calvino's words in *Angoscia in caserma*, p. 105.

109 A Garibaldini report reads: 'We went along to the barracks of the 88th infantry and tried to persuade the soldiers not to abandon their posts, or at least to come and swell our ranks. We found a great incomprehension in them, and correspondingly a great yearning to go home, and so we made them give up their weapons. As the days went by the collapse of our army became more and more accentuated' (report on the 'squadra d'azione di Castiglioncello' [Castiglioncello action squad] of the 3rd Garibaldi brigade, signed by the detachment commander, Francesco Pandolfi). The author of the report recalls the 'moral depression' which this behaviour on the part of soldiers generated in his men (IG, *BG*, 012056).

110 'The National Front is warned through the assemblies; it protests (the representatives of the various parties are all infatuated by legality) saying that assemblies should not be held because the prefect does not authorise them, that they could cause incidents, that by doing so the Communist Party breaks with the National Front, et cetera. Only the Action Party representative agrees with us': this is what Giovanni (Remo Scappini) wrote in a 'report from Turin' of 15 September (IG, *Archivio PCI*).

111 E. Forcella, 'L'arte della fuga: il black-out dell'informazione nella crisi italiana dell'8 settembre 1943', in *Movimento operaio e socialista*, n.s., VI, 1983, pp. 481–97. See also Zangrandi, *1943*, pp. 130–1.

appeared, a lone voice, with its headline 'Torna Garibaldi' occupying the entire front page,[112] *Il Piccolo* saw applause for the armed forces as a wish to collaborate 'in the maintenance of order', and *Il Messaggero* praised the common-sense of the Romans, entitling its back-page article for 12 September, 'Calma e fiducia', repeated on the local pages as: 'Fermezza e dignità dell'Urbe' ('Firmness and dignity of the City').

More than a year later, a newspaper of the Giustizia e Libertà (GL) units printed a caustic article against the myth of order that had brought Fascism to power, but added that the people now 'have the arms and the force to impose that minimum of salutary "disorder" which in 1789 heralded a century of liberty for the poor and which has one name alone: REVOLUTION'.[113] Even if we discard that prediction of a revolutionary turning-point, the optimistic interpretation of disorder as an opportunity for liberty and the pessimistic one which, by contrast, generated bewilderment and a desire for the restoration of order, were the two ways in which people reacted against the institutional void that had been created – a void which could indeed produce either exaltation, or dismay and a sense of having been abandoned. If we regard the state, even the Italian state which was the subject of so much atavistic suspicion, as 'the last great form of collective solidarity in which individuals take refuge',[114] this refuge suddenly vanished, and those individuals found themselves compelled to make up for it in other ways. But that void was felt, and has remained in people's memories as a basic fact. Immediately after the Liberation the regional CLN [Committee of National Liberation] would say, of Tuscan public opinion, 'we felt completely isolated and abandoned at the moment of greatest crisis'.[115]

'Nothing was left, there was no established order' – this was how Terni was recalled.[116] The feeling of collapse was widespread: 'When the Italian state collapsed on 10 September', wrote Vittorio Foa a few months later;[117] and as late as 1948 another Actionist, Dante Livio Bianco, would speak of the 'collapse of the

---

112 See *Il Lavoro* (formerly *Il lavoro fascista*, which became the organ of the confederation of workers during the Badoglian period). This title and the entire contents of the newspaper, particularly an article by Mario Alicata, should be considered among the first explicit incitements to armed struggle.

113 Editorial in *Giustizia e Libertà. Notiziario dei patrioti delle Alpi Cozie*, October 1944, quoted in M. Giovana, *Storia di una formazione partigiana*, Turin: Einaudi, 1964, pp. 199–200.

114 M. Fioravanti, 'Stato (Diritto intermedio)', in *Enciclopedia del diritto*, Milan: Giuffré, 1987, p. 41 of the extract.

115 'Relazione sull'attività del CTLN', presented to the Allies, 9 August 1944 (ISRT, *Carte Francesco Berti*, envelope I, folder 3, subfolder CTLN *verbali*).

116 Testimony by Alberto Petrini regarding the abandonment of the city after the bombings that followed 8 September (Portelli, *Biografia di una città*, p. 255).

117 C. Inverni (V. Foa), 'I partiti e la nuova realtà italiana (la politica del CLN)', *Quaderni dell'Italia Libera*, n.s., I, p. 17 (written in Turin in March 1944).

'state' that occurred in the days of September.[118] 'Italians, in Italy there is no longer a government. The king has fled, Badoglio has abandoned his post', declared a socialist leaflet of 12 September.[119] Even a jurist, Costantino Mortati, would then describe the CLNs 'true organs of the state community, having organised themselves after the disintegration of pre-existing state structures'.[120] A French historian has written: 'The collapse of the state and of civil order had consti- tuted, also in France in June 1940, the fact that had most affected the citizens, who were left to fend for themselves.'[121]

I do not intend here to take up the issue of the problem of the character of the CLNs and of state continuity as the guiding thread and goal of the process that began on 25 July.[122] All I wish to do is to highlight the eclipse of the insti- tutions that occurred during those days in September, and to identify, in the reactions triggered by so richly illustrative an event, the seeds of many of the attitudes that the Italians adopted in the months that followed. In the anti- Fascist parties, people were to interrogate themselves, during the struggle, about the exact significance of the rupture that had taken place and about the political value they should attach 'to the instincts and elementary popular reactions to the events that had occurred';[123] they would also tend to emphasise its impor- tance as an epoch-making milestone.[124] The following March, in quite another

118 Speech made in Cuneo on 18 September 1948, in the presence of the president of the republic, Luigi Einaudi, at the award ceremony for valour for seven partisans (see Bianco, *Guerra partigiana*, Appendix, p. 149).

119 *Saggio bibliografico*, no. 2698. Cf. the testimony of the partisan Luigi Gandolfo: 'So, if there is no army, if no government exists, who are we?' (Borioli e Botta, *I giorni della montagna*, p. 73).

120 C. Mortati, *Istituzioni di diritto pubblico* I, Padua: Cedam, 1975, p. 88.

121 H. Rousso, 'Vichy, il grande fossato', with an Introduction by C. Pavone in *Rivista di storia contemporanea* XIV (1985), p. 593 (original edition, 'Vichy, le grand fossé', in *Vingtième siècle* [January–March 1985], 5).

122 On this point see C. Pavone, 'La continuità dello Stato', in R. Paci, ed., *Scritti storici in onore di Enzo Piscitelli*, Padua: Antenore, 1982, pp. 537–68, and C. Pavone, 'Tre governi e due occupazioni', in *L'Italia nella seconda guerra mondiale e nella Resistenza*, pp. 423–52.

123 This is what Mauro Scoccimarro wrote from Rome to the Milan headquarters, 5 October 1943 (in L. Longo, *I Centri dirigenti del PCI nella Resistenza*, Rome: Riuniti, 1974, p. 58). See also 'Per l'unità del popolo italiano nella lotta contro il nazismo e il fas- cismo', in *L'Unità*, Roman edition, 29 September 1943. This article speaks of the 'profound marks' left 'in the mind of the Italians' by the period 25 July–10 September and by the collapse of the ruling class.

124 On 27 September the Milan edition of *L'Avanti!* published an article entitled 'Coraggio', which read: 'A whole civilisation is being wiped out, a whole capitalistic order with its economically costly and morally absurd contradictions is falling and will not raise itself again.' The influence of the ex-members of the Movimento di Unità Proletaria [Movement of Proletarian Unity] (Lelio Basso) on this kind of judgment is stressed

language, Teresio Olivelli, Catholic and former Fascist militant, would write: '8 September is a watershed: here springs and flowers the new life of the nation, which bursts forth in the spirit, is illumined with truth, quivers in action.'[125] And Giaime Pintor, more soberly: 'The soldiers who traversed Italy last September, famished and half-naked, wanted above all to return home, to hear no more talk of war and hardships. They were a defeated people; but they bore within themselves the seed of a dimly-sensed recovery: the sense of offences afflicted and endured, disgust with the injustice in which they had lived.'[126]

It was in fact to be the memory of the abyss that opened wide on 8 September that nourished the Resistance with pride at having succeeded in hauling themselves out of it. 'And they were days of desperate humiliation, but followed by a recovery', L'Italia Libera was to write in January. In November the same newspaper had made this profession of faith: 'We refuse to consider the days of September as a tragic episode in the history of Italy. In the torment of an unprecedented national tragedy we see the travail of a people which will eventually give itself the principles of living.'[127]

One aspect of those September days still needs emphasising. In the dissolution of the military and civil institutions and the emergence of solidarity, the working classes, at least those in the main factories, were the social group who gave the greatest indication of internal cohesion. Officers and soldiers fled and scattered, but the workers tended to stay united and to draw from this unity the impetus to free themselves from passivity and anger at their impotence:

This morning certain workers had the harebrained idea of making an unarmed dash for it to get hold of the Germans' machine-guns; others tried to dissuade them. One man aged around forty, well-dressed, with a gleaming-new bicycle, intervened, explaining that it was impossible to react against the Germans, and everyone insulted him then, saying, 'We're tired of obeying you *borghesi*; twenty years of Fascism is enough.'[128]

To this day a worker from Terni still gets riled when, at a distance of years and superimposing two such diverse episodes, he recalls things as follows: 'What I find hard to swallow is 8 September, because on 8 September we could have

by F. Taddei, *Il socialismo italiano del dopoguerra. Correnti ideologiche e scelte politiche (1943–1947)*, Milan: Franco Angeli, 1984, p. 49.

125 Article entitled 'Ribelli', in *Il Ribelle*, 24 March 1944.

126 G. Pintor, 'Il colpo di Stato del 25 luglio', written in Naples in October 1943 and published in New York's *Quaderni Italiani*, IV, 1944; now in G. Pintor, *Il sangue d'Europa (1939-1943)*, collected writings, ed. V. Gerratana, Turin: Einaudi, 1950, pp. 225–41 (the extract quoted is on p. 241).

127 Articles in *L'Italia Libera*, Roman edition, 'I volontari della libertà' (27 January 1944), and 'Responsabilità (11 November 1943 – then reprinted in Turin as well).

128 Artom, *Diari*, p. 75 (Turin, 9 September).

beaten the hides off the Germans ... we could have done anything. Instead, *calma, calma, calma* ... it was just like the Togliatti business, *calma, calma, calma.*[129]

Here resentment against *i borghesi* is combined with, and possibly predominates over, that against the prudence of the Communist Party cadres. The state authorities are, by contrast, the exclusive target of another accusation: 'We went on strike on 8 September and on that occasion we wanted, all together, to assail the *Distretto*, but the police dispersed us. Together with other workers we held big demonstrations. In the factory a comrade held an assembly urging us to strike.'[130] And here is a Turin partisan's recollection of events:

> The boys immediately went [on the announcement of the Armistice] to storm the barracks ... then we held a big demonstration outside the *Camera del Lavoro*, where the workers asked for weapons: 'Torino like Stalingrad' ... It was nothing less than the army of the working class that was on the march ... Wonderful! We went to the barracks, we took the guns, formed up. You should have seen it: all for the Fronte Nazionale. Voluntary enlistment. It lasted only a few hours, though, because General Adami-Rossi, commander of the Torino fortress, betrayed us.[131]

Again in Turin, after the 10 September assembly the workers asked: 'Where shall we go? What direction should we head in?'[132]

A more complete attempt at analysis, along the lines of the class war – to be examined later – appears in a Communist report, again from Turin, written in December 1943. The worker, it says, 'feels that new events are at hand and knows too that everything that will issue from this fearful struggle will lead him towards the emancipation of his class, and so, though having no clear set of political principles, he feels that only through our programme will he obtain that social justice vainly promised and anxiously awaited.'[133]

2. A CLEAR AND DIFFICULT CHOICE

Great, exceptional, catastrophic events confront peoples and individuals with radical options and, with little or no forewarning, compel them to take stock

---

129 Testimony by Settimio Piemonti, in Portelli, *Biografia di una città*, p. 18.

130 Minutes of the 'meeting of the party representatives' of some Padua factories, 18 March 1945. The episode in the text is recalled by a worker of Breda (IG, *Archivio PCI*; the document is partly published, though excluding the part cited above, in C. Pavone, *Le Brigate Garibaldi* III, pp. 490–4).

131 Testimony by Teresa Cirio, Bruzzone and Farina, eds, *La Resistenza taciuta*, pp. 79–80.

132 See N. Paruta (F. Venturi), 'La crisi italiana (25 luglio–8 settembre)', *Quaderni dell'Italia Libera* (September 4, 1943).

133 'Rapporto sulla situazione nelle fabbriche', by Giovanni (IG, *Archivio PCI*).

of truths that were working away unbeknown to them, or of which full knowledge was the preserve only of a select few. The institutional void created by
8 September gave the predicament in which the Italians found themselves this
character: they were called upon to make choices that many of them had never
for one moment believed that their lives would ever require of them. In the
normal run of things, 'it is not necessary to be taking up positions continually
in favour of the system.'[1] But the need explicitly to agree, or dissent, becomes
impelling when the system totters, the monopoly of state violence shatters, and
one's obligations towards the state no longer constitute a sure reference point for
individual conduct, since the state is no longer in a position to demand those
'sacrifices for love' on which it often relies.[2] A classic page from Hobbes, seems
to sum up Italy as it was in September 1943:

> The Obligation of Subjects to the Sovereign is understood to last as long, and no
> longer, than the power lasteth, by which he is able to protect them. For the right
> men have by Nature to protect themselves, when none else can protect them, can by
> no Covenant be relinquished. The Soveraignty is the Soule of the Commonwealth;
> which once departed from the Body, the members do no more receive their motion
> from it. The end of Obedience is Protection; which, wheresoever a man seeth it,
> either in his own, or in anothers sword, Nature applyeth his obedience to it, and
> his endeavour to maintain it. And though Soveraignty, in the intention of them
> that make it, be immortall; yet is it in its own nature, not only subject to violent
> death, by forreign war; but also through the ignorance, and passions of men, it
> hath in it, from the very institution, many seeds of a naturall mortality, by Intestine
> Discord.[3]

The non-presence of the state might be felt with a sense of disorientation or
as an opportunity to make a bid for freedom. But first of all it might be experienced immediately as an exceptional moment of harmony in a community freed
from the shackles of power.

Perhaps the finest testimony we have of this experience, almost of a blissful,
miraculous and fleeting aurora, is that of an English colonel:

> When a village has been in no-man's land for weeks, between our lines and the
> enemy's, the folk don't rob and kill each other, but help one another to an incred-
> ible degree. All that is absurd and marvellous. Then we come along and set up the

---

1 R. Schnur, *Rivoluzione e guerra civile*, Milan: Giuffrè, 1986, p. 143 (original
edition: *Revolution und Weltbürger Krieg*, Berlin: Dunker & Humblot, 1983).

2 I take this concept from a seminar held at the Department of Modern and
Contemporary History of the University of Pisa by Pietro Costa, author of *Lo Stato
immaginario*, Milan: Giuffrè, 1986.

3 T. Hobbes, *Leviathan*, XXI, ed. C. B. MacPherson, London: Penguin, 1985, p. 272.

indispensable AMG offices and services, and all at once the Italians fall out, bicker, quarrel over trifles, denounce each another. The previous harmony dissolves into feuds and vendettas of every sort. Quite incredible.[4]

Strictly speaking, the situation described here does not typify the Resistance. In the Resistance nobody chooses anything, but interpersonal relationships are lived with self-sufficient spontaneity. It does, however, display some traits shared with the solidarity extended to entire communities above all in the very first days after the collapse, but subsequently in several free zones too, or in territories where the presence of German and Fascist authorities was not strongly felt. Thus, a protagonist who was ten years old at the time recalls the formative value of experiencing the intense altruism shown by one and all, 'without orders' and 'freely chosen', at Borgo Anime in the province of Ravenna.[5]

'We behaved well towards one another, in fact we were fonder of one another', recalls a tradesman from the Terni area speaking of the mass exoduses from the city.[6] No doubt these are transfigurations of memory, filled with nostalgia for the moments when the absence of authoritarian ties did not give rise to the *bellum omnium contra omnes*. But a book of memoirs, still hot from the event, of the Umbrian countryside which generously took in the fugitive Allied prisoners points out that 'for once the eternal rancour of traditional disagreements, which divide and have always divided peasants sharing the boundaries of a field or a wood, had an unexpected outlet of goodness.'[7] Generalising, a sociologist has written: 'Partisan aggregation was favoured by small local communities, by a not hostile or a favourable local community environment.'[8]

When the German occupying troops began to give a minimum of formalisation to their violence, which had flooded the space left vacant by the eclipse

---

4 R. Craveri, *La campagna d'Italia e i servizi segreti. La storia dell'ORI*, Milan: La Pietra, 1980, pp. 38–9.

5 Testimony by Achille Alberani (*CU*).

6 Testimony by A. S., in A. Portelli, 'Assolutamente niente. L'esperienza degli sfollati a Terni', in Gallerano, ed., *L'altro dopoguerra*, p. 137. Regarding this, Portelli speaks of 'the restoration of elementary solidaristic communities', and makes a comparison with some pages from 1930s American literature on the effects of the Great Depression. A comparison could also be made with the description of the effect of feeling liberated from the mutual distrust that several anarchic communities had during the Spanish Civil War. See for example the testimonies collected by A. M. Merlo, 'Gli anarchici e l'esperienza collettivistica durante la guerra civile spagnola', in *Rivista di storia contemporanea* X (1981), pp. 505–47.

7 Battaglia, *Un uomo*, p. 26.

8 A. Ardigò, 'L'insorgenza partigiana come forma di partecipazione sociale nella società civile', in Ardigò, ed., *Società civile e insorgenza partigiana: indagine sociologica sulla diffusione dell'insorgenza partigiana nella provincia di Bologna*, Bologna: Cappelli, 1979, p. 19.

of the Italian authorities, and when, immediately after, the Fascists created the Social Republic – when, that is, the institutional void was somehow or other filled by a different system of authority – the choice became more difficult and more dramatic, because the spontaneous human solidarity of the first days no longer sufficed. Now the choice had to be made between disobedience, for which the price to pay would be ever higher, and the allure of Nazi–Fascist normalisation, grim though it was.

The words with which Sartre begins a famous work – 'Never have we been so free as under the German occupation' – pinpoint this core of Resistance experience: a choice all the more authentic the more one was compelled by events to choose, and the stakes could be summed up in the formula 'rather death than …'. Out of this grew, writes Sartre, 'in shadow and in blood … the strongest of Republics … without institutions, without an army, without police'.[9] Some years later, a text as dry as a library catalogue would reach a conclusion that endorses Sartre's eloquent position: 'On pourrait presque soutenir que les conditions difficiles égalisent les chances et favorisent les plus résolus, jamais presse ne fut plus libre que cette interdite.'[10]

Sergeant Cecco Baroni, who ended up in a POW camp in Germany, puts the same situation simply: 'You see those sentries behind the barbed wire? It's they who are Hitler's prisoners, not us. We say no to Hitler and Mussolini, even when they want to starve us out.'[11]

The first meaning of liberty, acquired by the decision to resist, is implicit in its being an act of disobedience. It was not so much a question of disobeying a legal government, since it was a moot point who possessed legality, as of disobeying those who had the power to make themselves obeyed. In other words, it was a revolt against man's power over man, a reaffirmation of the ancient principle that power should not prevail over virtue.[12] The fact that the power you were revolting against might subsequently be deemed illegal as well as illegitimate in the strong sense of the word simply completes the picture. The Fascists' decision to join the Social Republic – this is a difference that we would do well to highlight from the start – was not enveloped in this light of critical disobedience. As we know, 'I did it because I was ordered to do so' was to be the main argument used by the Fascists and Nazis to defend themselves in the trials instituted

---

9 J.-P. Sartre, 'La République du silence', Les Lettres Françaises, 9 April 1944, p. 1.

10 Bibliothèque nationale, Catalogue des pèriodiques clandestins (1939–1945), Paris, 1954, pp. xiii–xiv. 'One could almost argue that the difficult conditions equalized opportunities and promoted the most resolute, never was the press freer than when it was banned'.

11 Quoted by M. Rigoni Stern in the introductory note to P. Iuso, ed., Soldati italiani dopo il settembre 1943, Rome: FIAP, 1988, p. vi.

12 Franco Venturi held a seminar around this principle in 1988 at the Scuola Normale Superiore of Pisa (see also p. 658, n. 7).

against them after the war.[13] So intrinsic was this to the Nazi–Fascist ethic that it was to relegate to second place, and not just for reasons of courtroom expediency, the independently inspired choices which, as we shall presently see, some Fascists also made.

For the first time in the history of united Italy, the Italians lived, in one form or another, an experience of mass disobedience. This was particularly important for the generation who had been made, at elementary school, to learn by heart these words from the only state textbook: 'What must be the first virtue of a *balilla*? Obedience! and the second? Obedience!' (in gigantic letters).

A second thing to consider is that that the link between necessity and liberty, which it is always so difficult to put one's finger on, appears in the at once problematic and limpid decision to resist. The thorniest aspect of its problematic character lies in the fact that the choice was made in that 'total responsibility in total solitude', which Sartre has called 'the very revelation of our freedom'.[14] So profound was this solitude that not even the Catholics could escape from it, even though they had the backing of the only institutions that had not collapsed; but in those weeks those institutions too had left consciences to dangle in the void.[15] A letter sent on 25 September by Cazzani, bishop of Cremona, to the archbishop of Milan, Schuster, is sincere in registering this attitude. The monsignor wrote to the cardinal that he 'assume[d] no responsibility for advising a definite line of action. I tell them the possible dangers of one or the other path, and that they are to do as they wish.'[16]

One consequence of the choice made in solitude was that, when the spontaneous solidarity of the first days no longer sufficed, the Italians were compelled to size each other up again, to demand new credentials of each other, to establish who was an accomplice and who a victim of persecution.[17] No one any longer

---

13 On this point see P. Levi's reflections in *I sommersi e i salvati*, Turin: Einaudi, 1986, pp. 15, 44.

14 See Sartre, 'La République du silence'. An analogous observation can be found in G. Falaschi, *La Resistenza armata nella narrativa italiana*, Turin: Einaudi, 1976, p. 41. For Sartre, see also the character Mathieu in *La mort dans l'âme*, Paris: Gallimard, 1949.

15 See G. Baget- Bozzo, *Il partito cristiano al potere*, Florence: Vallecchi, 1974, p. 52. The author writes that 'Christian anti-Fascism was a widespread position among Catholics, but was not a position of the Church'. Compare what has been observed about the scant number of Catholics from the Catholic youth formations who joined the Resistance (M. Reineri, 'Per uno studio comparato del movimento cattolico durante la Resistenza: l'esperienza piemontese', in *Società rurale e Resistenza nelle Venezie*, Milan: Feltrinelli, 1978, p. 269).

16 And he went on: 'What will all those who go into hiding do in the approaching season? Will they become bands of thieves and brigands?' (quoted in G. Bianchi, 'I cattolici', in Valiani, Bianchi and Ragionieri, *Azionisti, cattolici e comunisti nella Resistenza*, p. 178).

17 'In this common atmosphere there couldn't help being the inevitable fear that

could predict for certain the behaviour of others according to the old canons. Something similar, if more devastating, had occurred in France after the June 1940 catastrophe. As Léon Blum wrote, 'Friends, meeting each other, never knew beforehand whether they would find themselves in agreement or not.'[18] Earlier still, immediately after the *Anschluss*, there had been 'a terrible solitude. No one could trust anyone any more, no one knew any longer who the other was.'[19] The very opposite of this was to occur in April 1945, when, in the euphoria of victory, everybody seemed certain that they could recognise the sentiments of others. Thus Ada Gobetti:

> 'Well?', I shouted, soft-pedalling my bicycle. And so identical were our feelings and thoughts during those days that they completely understood the meaning of my question and, though they didn't know me any more than I knew them, they answered with a gay wave of the hand: 'They've gone!'[20]

It is as if solitude, that is, full individual responsibility for one's decisions – 'I've done this of my own free will, so you mustn't cry', a man condemned to death was to say[21] – is exalted and at the same time redeemed by the realisation of the unavoidable need to choose between one or other form of behaviour bearing inscribed values, which immediately implies an objective situation, shared by all ('Those who are not with us are against us', a German proclamation threatened).[22] Again, this is not just true of Italy. An Austrian awaiting execution wrote that several times he had asked himself whether he ought not to have behaved differently: 'But I always come to the same conclusion: "I could not have done otherwise".'[23] Of France it was written: 'The defeat puts paid to any possible way out ... and thus the imperative need to make fundamental choices.'[24] 'Desperate necessity' is the expression used by Vittorio Foa.[25] A similar kind of 'desperation' seems to inspire these words of Arturo Jemolo's: 'curious, this

---

everybody in one way or another must be either accomplices or persecuted' (Battaglia, *Un uomo*, pp. 48–9).

18 Cited in H. Michel, *The Shadow War*, London: Deutsch, 1972, p. 102.

19 Bruno Kreisky in an interview given to Vanna Vannuccini, 'Kreisky accusa Waldheim', in *La Repubblica*, 1 March 1988.

20 Gobetti, *Diario partigiano*, p. 363.

21 Letter of the nineteen-year-old lathe-operator, Vito Salmi, a Garibaldino, shot at Bardi on 4 May 1944 (*LRI*, pp. 197–8).

22 Quoted in S. Flamigni and L. Marzocchi, *Resistenza in Romagna*, Milan: La Pietra, 1969, p. 113.

23 Letter written by Franz Mittendorfer, Communist, 10 November 1942 (*LRE*, p. 23).

24 Rousso, *Vichy*, p. 593.

25 V. Foa, 'La crisi della Resistenza prima della liberazione', in *Il Ponte* III: (November–December 1947), 11-12; and *Per una storia del movimento operaio*, pp. 13–24.

terrible *freedom of choice* concerning the most important things, this already marked out path concerning the things of least importance'.[26]

Roberto Battaglia wrote that it was the first time that society 'had put him with his back to the wall'.[27] Franco Venturi evoked the 'sense of necessity lying at the basis of this creation of freedom, a sense of serene acceptance of the fact of being finally outlaws of an impossible world'.[28] When Ada Gobetti notes in a boy the 'fascinating normality' of his being a partisan,[29] she is simply registering a concrete case of the experience illustrated by Franco Venturi, which is also recalled by these other words: 'Today, despite the wreckage, the situation is better ... therefore, despite the collapse, liberty lives today among us'.[30] Immediately after the Liberation, Massimo Mila was to speak of 8 September as a 'self-revelation' of a new possibility of life.[31]

This sense of life 'beginning anew', though it had in many respects assumed the guise of politics, went well beyond that 'politician's risk-taking' which, in Schmittian terms, has been considered the ineluctable consequence of the fact that 'all citizens are obliged to take sides in a civil war'.[32] Rather, there is the 'sudden perception (or illusion) that I am able to act to change society for the better and, what is more, that I am able to unite with other people of like mind' and that all this is 'pleasurable and indeed inebriating'.[33]

This inebriation sprung from a singular fusion – which does not mean that it was felt always and by everyone – between the tragic sense of life and the

26 Jemolo, in a similar spirit to Baget-Bozzzo's in the page quoted above, criticised the evasive behaviour of all the religions before the terrible problems posed by the war, while the Catholic Church continued, for its part, to concern itself with questions like 'how many caresses are permissible between fiancés'. A. C. Jemolo, 'La Tragedia inavvertita', in *Il Ponte* I (1945); then in *Nuova Antologia* CXX: 2153 (January–March 1985), pp. 7–12.

27 Battaglia, *Un uomo*, p. 20.

28 Preface to the 1946 edition of D. L. Bianco's book, cited several times (cited in G. Carocci, *La Resistenza italiana*, Milan: Garzanti, 1963, p. 149).

29 Gobetti, *Diario partigiano*, p. 122 (2 April 1944).

30 T. Ruoti, *La lotta per la libertà*, p. 4. It is an Actionist-inspired pamphlet, written in October 1943.

31 M. Mila, 'Bilancio della guerra partigiana in Piemonte', in *Risorgimento. Rivista mensile*, I, 25 August 1945, 5, pp. 412–19.

32 These words occur in the article 'Dovere di combattere', which appeared in *Risorgimento Liberale* (Roman edition), 23 November 1943, and is built around the theme of 8 September as the reconquest of liberty.

33 Schnur, *Rivoluzione e guerra civile*, pp. 48, 143. Consider, by contrast, this passage by Schmitt: 'In war the adversaries most often confront each other openly: normally they are identifiable by a uniform, and the distinction between friend and enemy is therefore no longer a political problem which the fighting soldier has to solve.' C. Schmitt, *The Concept of the Political*, Chicago: University of Chicago Press, 1996, p. 34.

joy of living.[34] Roberto Battaglia spoke of the 'unbridled joy' that seized him at the moment of the partisan formation's arrival, and evoked the 'blessed days, a new infancy of ourselves and our guerrilla, at the memory of which that dark sense of being survivors that we bore imprinted in us seems to vanish.'[35] When Calvino read Ada Gobetti's diary, he exclaimed: 'My God, what fun you had!' This comment was in line with the 'Ariostesque' character he had given to his novel *The Path to the Nest of Spiders*.[36] In her *Diario partigiano*, Gobetti herself resorts to expressions such as 'as if we were going on vacation', 'a new, free and adventurous infancy', 'gush of sudden joy', 'moments of the most perfect seren-ity' – 'fulfilment, completeness, harmony – felt at the very moment of greatest danger'; and recognises the 'providential' character of the 'absurd, widespread irresponsibility.'[37]

'We went up into the mountains like that … it seemed such a merry thing, so to speak': not even deportation to Mauthausen was enough to cancel the memory of it in this survivor.[38] And a Catholic officer, who described his expe-rience in Venezia Giulia with one of the first mixed Italo-Slovene formations as being 'a joyous rush towards the large dark mountain, the partisans' stronghold', felt, thanks to the 'seriousness, enthusiasm, fervour of life' that he found there, that 'his childhood faith regained a singular virginity, a freshness, and grew more profound.'[39] Again hot from the event, the Tuscan Garibaldino Attilio De Gaudio spoke of 'happy moments – and they were the best in my life – that I lived with my division in that ideal environment, where, to use an apt expression of the railwayman Bonassai, we were all for one, one for all, as in 1919–22, when liberty was no myth but a living, concrete reality.'[40]

Here emerges a thread that we shall encounter again: the recovery of the historical memory of the *biennio rosso*. Another Tuscan, a political commissar

---

34 A. O. Hirschman, *Shifting Involvements: Private Interest and Public Action*, Princeton: Princeton University Press, 1982, p. 101. The same author has written else-where: 'Creativity always comes as a surprise' (*Exit, Voice and Loyalty*, Cambridge, MA: Harvard University Press, 1970, p. 80).

35 Battaglia, *Un uomo*, pp. 50, 104.

36 Testimony by Vittorio Foa to the author.

37 Gobetti, *Diario partigiano*, p. 258 (30 September 1944) and p. 57 (November 1943).

38 Testimony by Antonio Bellina, worker, who had earlier emigrated to France (Bravo and Jalla, *La vita offesa*, p. 84). For 'il divertimento' ('enjoyment') in another emergency situation, see the censored letter quoted by L. Briguglio, 'Clero e contadini nella provincia di Padova dal Fascismo alla Resistenza', in *Società rurale*, p. 334.

39 'Esperienza di un partigiano cattolico', in *Voce Operaia*, newspaper of the Communist Catholics of Rome, 16 December 1943.

40 Report by Del Gaudio on the events at the 'Casone dei ferrovieri' ('Railway workers' house') during the battle for the liberation of Florence (ISRT, *ANPI Firenze*, envelope 3, *XXII bis brigata Garibaldi Sinigaglia*).

of the Potente Garibaldi division (the Arno division that had taken the name of its commander Aligi Barducci, who fell during the battle for the liberation of Florence), was to write in his final report: 'Often, in moments of melancholy solitude, I feel nostalgia for those almost carefree moments, for that was the time when our attention was centred on how to surprise, offend and dodge our enemies' – almost a game that concentrated and absorbed all one's energies.[41] Many years later the Roman Gappist Rosario Bentivegna was to declare to Robert Katz: 'Strangely enough we felt free, close to everyone.'[42]

In agreement on this point are the women's testimonies collected in *La Resistenza taciuta*, where, however, the sense of death is prominent:

> For me it was the best period of my life. It was also tragic for me, because I saw so many lads die when I would have liked to give my life twenty times over to save theirs, and this made me suffer atrociously. We risked death, but there was such joy in living! Every so often I read that my companions were gloomy. That's not true. We were serene. Indeed, we were actually happy, because we knew that we were doing something very important ... That time was fantastic, a wonderful period. I have never lived such a fine life since then. There were sufferings all right, but what an experience![43]

In testimonies of this kind, individual choice has already been transformed into a sense of collective responsibility.

Speaking very generally of the Second World War as a whole, E. P. Thompson remarked that it was an 'extraordinary formative moment in which it was possible to be deeply committed even to the point of life itself in support of a particular political struggle that was at the same time a popular struggle'.[44] In an Italy that had been for so long repressed and alienated by the conviction, 'We all are all of one mind', this process was favoured by the conviction, 'This last-minute opportunity to intervene, once and for all to become participants,

---

41 The report, signed 'Stella', is preserved in ISRT, CVL, *Comando militare toscano*, envelope 5, folder 7. Stella was Alessandro Pieri, a carpenter and long-standing Communist militant, condemned during the regime (see C. Francovich, *La Resistenza a Firenze*, Florence: La Nuova Italia, 1961, p. 369).

42 The English text has the words 'near everything' (p. 39). R. Katz, *Morte a Roma*, Rome: Riuniti, 1973, p. 56 (original edition *Death in Rome*, New York: Macmillan, 1967). The American writer follows with this comment: 'If there was a lack of unity in action and methods, there was nevertheless an intensely felt camaraderie and a naïve faith in the goodness of the coming post-war world. No one, given the circumstances, would fight for anything less' (English edition, p. 39).

43 See Bruzzone and Farina, eds, *La Resistenza taciuta*, pp. 44, 81–2, 85. The testimonies are those of Nelia Benissone Costa and Teresa Cirio.

44 E. P. Thompson, in Henry Abelove, ed., *Visions of History*, Manchester: Manchester University Press, 1983, p. 11.

was not to be missed.' This commitment of Franco Calamandrei's is all the more relevant for being accompanied by the scrupulous admission that 'perhaps it has come looking for me more than I have gone looking for it', and by the awareness of the part played in his choice by the 'taste for danger' and 'escape from a bourgeois upbringing sought in adventure'.[45] A GL women's newspaper wrote, with equal pregnancy: 'It is not just that "finally one can speak without danger" of the forty-five days, but "finally one can do something and one can do it at the cost of sacrifices, dangerously"'.[46]

Beppe Fenoglio succeeded in expressing with poetic force the conjunction of liberty and energy that followed the decision to resist:

> And at the moment when he left, he felt himself invested – *death itself would not have been divestiture* – in the name of the authentic people of Italy, to oppose Fascism in every possible way, to judge and to act, to decide militarily and as a citizen. Such supreme power was intoxicating, but infinitely more intoxicating was the consciousness of the legitimate use he would make of it.
>
> And even physically he had never been so much a man, herculean he bent the wind and the earth.[47]

Natalia Ginzburg, in turn, has lovingly re-evoked the significance of the rapid coming of age that the Resistance experience had for many:

> They were years in which many became different from what they had been before. Different and better. The sensation that people had become better circulated in the streets. Each person felt the need to give the best of his or her self. This spread around an extraordinary well-being, and when we remember those years, we remember the well-being together with the discomfort, the cold, the hunger and the fear, which during those days never left us: and thus one discovered that 'one's neighbour' was different from the 'stupid multitudes yelling lies in the squares'.[48]

---

45 Calamandrei, *La vita indivisibile*, pp. 114, 116, 118, 129 (12 September, October, Autumn 1943, beginning of 1944). On p. 114 Calamandrei quotes these verses from *The Spoon River Anthology*: 'To put meaning to one's life may end in madness / But a life without meaning is the torture / Of restlessness and vague desire / It is a boat longing for the sea and yet afraid'.

46 *La Nuova Realtà. Organo del Movimento femminile 'Giustizia e Libertà'*, Piedmontese edition, n.d. (but 1945), I, 2, article entitled 'Chi siamo'. Compare the dry, tragic tone of this letter by a member of the Greek resistance, tortured and shot by the Italians on 24 February 1943: 'Since because of my age I didn't go to Albania, I too was obliged to risk my life for the *patria*': letter written by the thirty-eight-year-old lawyer Spiros Giavellas (*LRE*, p. 454).

47 B. Fenoglio, *Il partigiano Johnny*, Turin: Einaudi, 1968, p. 40.

48 N. Ginzburg, Preface to *La letteratura partigiana in Italia 1943–1945*, anthology, ed. G. Falaschi, Rome: Riuniti, 1984, p. 8.

'That 8 September I suddenly became an adult ... from that day I made my choice', a protagonist recalls today.[49] This invigorating discovery of oneself and of others included a powerful desire to set things right, a desire to punish oneself for one's own offences and those of one's generation. 'In our confused way we felt that somebody at least had to suffer for what had happened in Italy; at certain moments it seemed to us a personal exercise in mortification, at others a civic commitment. It was as if we had to bear with us the weight of Italy and its misfortunes.'[50] Ferdinando Mautino speaks of the 'sacrifice of the anti-Fascist forces to redeem the crimes committed by Fascism',[51] and Franco Calamandrei of the 'consciousness of all the impurity that remains incorrigible within me'.[52] A forty-year-old who had anticipated the decision to resist by deserting in favour of Tito's partisans was convinced that only 'the hardest personal sacrifices', to the point of 'offering my very life', would liberate him from his atrocious remorse at having behaved in so cowardly a way in 1922, just to obey the 'exhortations of family and friends'.[53]

There is scant evidence of this desire for redemption and self-punishment among the combatants of the South. A paratrooper from the Corpo Italiano di Liberazione (Italian Liberation Corps) writes that he fails to understand why one should be fighting 'to redeem oneself from strange offences which only the day before were considered merits'.[54]

Within the picture traced so far, a wider variety of individual motivations may be identified: the intolerableness of a world that had become a theatre of ferocity;[55] rebellion against abuses of power coming from near and far, at times against the very smallest of abuses;[56] a self-defensive instinct; the desire to avenge a dead relative;[57] the spirit of adventure;[58] love of risk together with a not fully

---

49 Testimony by the Piedmontese Domenico Adriano, who later became a Garibaldino (*CU*).

50 L. Meghello, *I piccoli maestri*, Milan: Feltrinelli, 1964, pp. 58–9.

51 F. Mautino, *Guerra di popolo. Storia delle formazione garibaldine friulane*, Preface by E. Collotti, Padua: Libreria Feltrinelli, 1981, p. 31.

52 Calamandrei, *La vita indivisibile*, p. 130 (February 1944).

53 B. Parri (Spartaco), 'Otto mesi coi partigiani di Tito', in Bilenchi, *Cronache degli anni neri*, pp. 87–8.

54 C. V. Bianchi, *Un'isola che si chiama Sardegna*, Rome: L' Arnia, 1951, quoted in M. Di Giovanni's degree thesis.

55 Chiodi recalls as a decisive moment the sight, when he was arrested by the Italian SS, of 'a street full of blood and a cart with four corpses', while the railway inspector said 'better to die than tolerate this' (Chiodi, *Banditi*, p. 41 [18 August 1944]).

56 Testimony by Renato Fracassi, from a Genoese family of longshoremen (Bravo and Jalla, *La vita offesa*, p. 74).

57 See the case of the fifty-year-old father who was to join a band with the machine gun of his son who had been killed. Chiodi, *Banditi*, p. 32 (5 August 1944).

58 See, for example, Mario Filipponi's testimony (Portelli, *Biografia di una città*,

conscious awareness of it;[59] family traditions; long-standing or more recent anti-Fascism; love of one's country; class hatred.[60] These motivations, of differing cultural weight, often interweave, and we can only grasp how they unfolded in people's consequent behaviour if we bear in mind the entire span of Resistance experience. We shall in fact encounter these various substructures again.

Here all that needs stressing is that the choices, whatever motivated them, belong to a climate of moral enthusiasm that is a far cry from the resigned, gloomy and resentful mood of many combatants in the weary army that the Royal government was attempting to put back on its feet way down in the South. Witness the following letter:

> Today the only reality that exists is our defeat with all its tremendous consequences: hunger, unemployment, moral disorganisation. Don't you too feel what uncertain times we're living in, how impossible it is to reconstruct anything solid? We must await the Armistice, the real one, and ignore the stupid accident of a year ago. Only then will we be able to start again, and there will be a lot of hard work to do.[61]

When, after the Liberation, the magistracy wanted to apply general mitigating circumstances for the crimes committed by the partisans during the Resistance, it was to invoke the climate of 'moral disintegration' in which the combatants had, in its view, acted.[62] The upshot of this was that, out of good intentions, it damagingly assimilated the Resistance spirit with the lowest points reached by the public spirit in those twenty months.

Some clarification is necessary at this point on what we have said so far about the founding value of choice. On the one hand, liberty as a value is attributed to the very act of choosing; on the other, it seems impossible to avoid putting off the choice actually entailed in practical terms. There is no getting around this contradiction. We do, however, need to be clearly aware of it if we wish to recognise the fact that the republican Fascists too (at any rate, the committed, militant ones) also made their choice and, at the same time, to hold fast to the

p. 266). See also the 'bel giovane' who possessed 'molte di quelle doti che possono fare un avventuriero o un eroe' ('many of those qualities that can make an adventurer or a hero'), described by Gobetti, *Diario partigiano*, p. 66 (27 November 1943).

59 'When you're twenty you don't take much account of things', testimony by Giuseppe Seriucano, farmer (Bravo and Jalla, *La vita offesa*, p. 81).

60 See the example of motivation shown in Bianco, *Guerra partigiana*, pp. 11–12.

61 Letter transcribed in 'Sintesi delle relazioni degli uffici militari censura di guerra del mese di settembre 1944'. The document, preserved in ACS, is published in E. Aga-Rossi, 'La situazione politica ed economica nell'Italia nel periodo 1944–45. I governi Bonomi, in *Quaderni dell'Istituto romano per la storia d'Italia del fascismo alla Resistenza*, Rome 1971, vol. 2, p. 129.

62 See G. Neppi Modona, ed., *Giustizia penale e guerra di liberazione*, Milan: Franco Angeli, 1984, pp. 37, 189.

difference between the two choices. Possibly it might help in such a difficult attempt, and one that will become extremely difficult when we get on to the theme of violence, to warn of the quicksands of ambiguity, in its multiple senses: an attempt to shirk the choice; subterranean affinities between opposing forms of behaviour; and the coexistence, in the crisis of the weeks immediately following 8 September, of possibilities of divergent courses of action.

Many episodes bear witness to this tendency to be chosen rather than to choose, to the point of yielding to a resigned and bloodless moralism; to remain up there in the 'house on the hill', rather than choose the partisan mountain or the Fascist city.[63] A significant case in point is that of Second Lieutenant Giorgio Chiesura, to whose diary I have already referred. Chiesura managed to return to his home in Venice possessed by this state of mind: 'All I knew was that for me it was over; let the others do what they wanted.' But he was so tired that even hiding was too much of an effort for him. So when the Germans issued the public summons to present oneself, he gave himself up – and was to be deported to Germany – 'because he did not want to recommence doing what the so-called *patria* orders us', nor, to avoid this, did he want to 'live amid flights, subterfuges, expedients, compromises, shiftings': hitherto his life had consisted of 'serving without any premises for doing so'; now he no longer wanted to collaborate. On 8 September he was prepared to fight against the Germans: if the generals and colonels now wanted to wage their war again in the service of the Germans, let them go ahead and do so. They could count him out. This behaviour, and the motivations adopted in support of it, are certainly a special case, rationalised after the event; but they do express a kind of reaction that is less paradoxical and rare than might at first appear. Indicative too are the attitudes of those nearest and dearest to Chiesura. His girlfriend says: 'But are you crazy?' His parents, on the other hand, advise him to give himself up, because they can't conceive the idea of disobeying an order issued by an authority, of whatever kind it may be. In a state of such extraordinary emergency, all they are able to do is conduct themselves in obeisance to traditional resignation before the fate of their sons called to the hazard of military service.[64]

Evading the choice is at times presented as standing above the contending parties: 'Since there are two governments in Italy, the king's and Mussolini's, I have advised the young peasants to stay at home, work their land and procure bread for all Italians ... Let the Germans and the Allies pass through, the poor Italians have to be fed.' Speaking here is Sandro Scotti, who, during the Resistance, tried to revive the Partito dei contadini d'Italia (The Party of the

---

63 *La casa in collina* (The House on the Hill) is the symbolic title that Cesare Pavese gave to his novel, published in 1949, but the first idea for which came in 1943.

64 For the whole incident see Chiesura, *Sicilia 1943*, pp. 96ff. It is worth remembering the film *Tutti a casa* [1960], in which the father (Eduardo De Filippo) urges his son (Alberto Sordi) to present himself.

Peasants of Italy), which he had founded after the First World War. The 'colonna rurale Monviso', which he organised as an instrument of peasants' self-defence, was to approach first Democrazia Cristiana and then GL, thereby demonstrating the impossibility of remaining well and truly impartial, let alone in a state of indolence.[65]

Resentment against the artificers of the defeat, anger against those responsible for the collapse, contempt for the king, Badoglio and the fleeing generals involved a still more insidious risk than the one described above. They could produce – I am still referring to the weeks immediately following 8 September – a zone of uncertain and oscillating reactions, which still fell short of choosing between the Resistance and the Social Republic.

With pragmatic open-mindedness, Palmiro Togliatti was later to talk in terms of a 'misunderstanding … inadequate though the word might be as a description of so profound a political and social event' – that somehow or other had been created 'between us and some of those who were fighting against us'.[66] More penetratingly, Calvino had put into the mouth of the partisan Kim these words: 'Basta un nulla, un passo falso, un impennamento dell'anima, e ci si trova dall'altra parte' ('Just a trifle, a false step, a tipping of the soul, and we find ourselves on the other side').[67]

This 'nulla' ('trifle'), which was, all the same, capable of generating an abyss, might be, particularly in the case of young men from bourgeois families, a chance encounter with the right person or the wrong person, and could hark back to reactions during the days following 25 July, when haughty spirits viewed the vital explosion of popular joy that 'took possession of the *fait accompli*' as a last-minute *volte-face*,[68] – a camouflage, what is more, for the most opportunistic, and those who had most seriously compromised themselves with the regime.

'The people to whom bootlicking is nothing new are now indulging in cowardly outrage', Emanuele Artom had written in his diary.[69] Nuto Revelli's testimony is candid enough to admit this. On 12 October he noted in his diary:

> If it hadn't been for Russia, on 8 September perhaps I'd have hidden myself like a sick dog. If on the night of 25 July I had let myself be beaten up, today perhaps I'd

---

65 See Reineri, *Per uno studio comparato*, p. 273, which publishes a page from Scotti's diary. On the 'partito dei contadini', see G. De Luna, *Alessandro Scotti e il partito dei contadini (1889–1974)*, Milan: Franco Angeli, 1985.

66 'La crisi morale dei giovani italiani', speech made at the PCI youth conference, Rome, 24 May 1947, now in P. Togliatti, *Opera*, V, ed. L. Gruppi, Rome: Riuniti, 1984, p. 301.

67 I. Calvino, *Il sentiero dei nidi di ragno*, Turin: Einaudi, 1946, p. 146.

68 This fine expression occurs in an article, 'Pacta sunt servanda', *Azione*, organ of the Christian Socialists, 20 October 1943.

69 Artom, *Diari*, p. 57 (28 July 1943).

have been on the other side. Those who say they've always understood everything, who continue to understand everything, give me the willies. It was no easy thing to understand 8 September!

And on 1 February 1944, surer now of his decision to join the Resistance:

> On 26 July you could also make the wrong choice. If they'd hit me, if they'd spat at me, perhaps I'd have joined the other side, with the Fascists, with the victims of that precise moment. Today I'd be with the scoundrels, with the Barabbases, with the Germans' spies. I wouldn't be in the Todt or in a district, that is, I wouldn't at any rate have been among draft dodgers.[70]

There appear to have been a few weeks of uncertainty and crisis in the province of Modena.[71] 'The drama of indecision' is the title of an article that recalled that period about a year later.[72] There were thoughts and second thoughts, as in the case of some Nembo paratroopers who, in Calabria, first followed Captain Eduardo Sala in joining the retreating Germans, then returned to their regiment that was awaiting the Allies.[73] Several paratroopers of the Ciclone battalion, whose commander, Major Giovanni Blotto, fought with the Social Republic, participated in the defence of the Futa pass against the Germans.[74] Officers who had initially been part of the 'apolitical' bands then went over to the Social Republic.[75] This was a sort of prelude to the changes of sides which, in two senses, would later occur on more than one occasion. After several weeks of torment – 'Calosso from London didn't convince me. Alessandro Pavolini from Salò made me ashamed of myself' – a prominent figure like Davide Lajolo,

---

70 Revelli, *La guerra dei poveri*, pp. 143, 168. On 26 July in Cuneo, finding himself in front of a drunken black-marketeer wrapped in the tricolore flag, Revelli had not been able to restrain himself and had shouted: 'Pagiacci!' ('Buffoons!'). An 'ometto' ('little man') behind him had immediately shouted in his turn: 'They are patriots, not buffoons. You are a Fascist, there's a Fascist here. I'm an evacuee from Genoa, I've lost my house in Genoa. He's a Fascist, he's a Fascist' (ibid., p. 125).

71 See Gorrieri, *La Repubblica di Montefiorino*, pp. 696–8.

72 To be found in 'Chiarezza. Quaderni di discussione politica tra giovani', July–August 1944 (typescript).

73 The episode is recorded in M. Di Giovanni's degree thesis. In units gifted with a strong *esprit de corps* like the paratroopers, the choice made by the commanders in favour of the Germans or in favour of the Allies carried great, but not absolute, weight.

74 See M. Di Giovanni's degree thesis. For other cases see G. Pisanò, *Storia della guerra civile in Italia (1943–1945)*, 3 vols, Milan: Edizioni FPE, 1965–66, vol. I, 1965, pp. 68–70.

75 Episodes of this kind are reported, for the province of Belluno, by S. Tramontin, 'Contadini e movimento partigiano nelle relazioni di parroci bellunesi, in *Società rurale*, p. 285.

the future Garibaldi commander Ulisse, but a militant Fascist at the time –
made a choice that was decided by his meeting with an old Socialist uncle.[76]
Thus it is possible to detect genuine regret, alongside the obvious propagandist intent, in these words that appeared a year later in a Fascist newspaper:
'One need only skim the collections of youth weeklies: not only would we
understand why many youths who went unheeded are unfortunately not
with us now, but we would find the same reasons that could be used to argue
our case.'[77]

Of the uncertainties which, in their turn, marked some of the decisions to
join the Social Republic, I here want to recall those manifested by a young man
who enlisted in the fanatically Fascist naval flotilla Decima Mas:

> Perhaps at the crucial moment that we are going through we should no longer speak
> of patriotic sentiment, because nobody knows who the real enemy is. So everyone
> is left to decide for himself; there are those who hate the Germans, there are those
> who hate the Anglo-Americans. I … am one of the latter. I have witnessed so many
> scenes that have made me ashamed to be Italian … They have been apocalyptic
> scenes.[78]

– and others of an eighteen-year-old, who became an Alpino in the Monterosa,
who described to his parents the tempests that had swept through his soul, concluding with a reassuring 'doubt didn't last long'.[79] Worthy of mention is the
exceptional case – though it is that of a former volunteer to Africa and Spain, a
survivor of the massacres perpetrated by the Germans on Cefalonia, who joined
the RSI because, indignant though he was about those massacres, he was 'yet
more indignant against the Italian General Command who had ordered the generous combatants to resist without giving them the slightest help'.[80]

The common features distinguishing initial uncertainties and ambiguities reinforce rather than diminish the significance of the choice. That choice
was indeed made on the basis of what appeared to be the essential, decisive
and all-engaging point. It is this that makes the decision to resist most akin to
that taken in the German internment camps by the soldiers who preferred life
behind barbed wire to fighting back for the Social Republic. Whether or not
to step forward in answer to a Fascist officer's exhortation symbolically distils

76 See D. Lajolo, *Il 'voltagabbana'*, Milan: Il Saggiatore, 1963, Chapter X (the words
quoted are on p. 198).

77 'Divagazioni sulla viltà', in *Il Giornale dell'Emilia*, 21 December 1944, quoted in
T. M. Mazzotosta, 'Educazione e scuola nella Repubblica Sociale Italiana', in *Storia contemporanea* IX (1978), p. 64.

78 Emanuele Frezza's letter to his parents, 20 November 1943 (*LRSI*, p. 44).

79 Letter written by Massimo Moratti, 25 October 1943 (*LRSI*, p. 271).

80 This was Mario Merlini (*LRSI*, pp. 210–11).

individual motivations that might be very different from each other.[81] In short, it was a question, for one and all, of a process of simplification, which took pride of place over whatever those who came down on opposing sides might have in common, particularly at a level of deep and long-standing culture. What was involved, therefore, were not misunderstandings, which it is the historian's business to unmask, but a radical rooting and re-rooting of differences – which were destined to endure, even when the end of the state of emergency saw dormant affinities resurface. It has been said that, in 'modern economies of the emotions', passions do not flare up or flicker out suddenly, but tend to burn slowly and flamelessly, and that the 'time-worn pigeonholing of people as angels or demons gives way to other, psychologically more sophisticated classifications', so that 'all relationships tend to be ambivalent'.[82] The Resistance – indeed, the Second World War as a whole – reignited the flame of conflicting passions, and left indelible burns. At the same time, kindred passions were driven to group together into homogenous blocks, following a pattern that gave rise to 'a system of emotions' tending to take the form of 'an institution' – and that institution eventually regarded those very emotions as undesirable elements.[83] Even Sartre's model of 'the group in a state of fusion', containing the seed of its own disintegration, may usefully be applied to those processes which, during the Resistance, saw ties between different persons form, dissolve, and re-form.[84]

As for the choice made by the Fascists – 'We can no longer compel anyone, let whoever wants to come, come' – was initially the attitude of the most highly motivated of them;[85] we have already seen some examples, and shall see others. Here it should be added that, for the Fascists, the memory of 8 September was

81 The episode I am referring to is recounted by N. Della Santa, 'Oggi più che mai no', in ANEI, *Resistenza senz'armi. Un capitolo di storia italiana (1943–45) dalle testimonianze di militari toscani internati nei Lager nazisti*, Florence: Le Monnier, 1984, quoted in G. Rochat, 'Memorialistica e storiografia sull'internamento', in N. Della Santa, ed., *I militari italiani internati dai tedeschi dopo l'8 settembre 1943*, Florence: Giunti, 1986, p. 34. On the internees in Germany, indispensable reading is Vittorio Emanuele Giuntella's civil and historiographical work; see in particular *Il nazismo e i Lager*, Rome: Studium, 1979. See also C. Schminck-Gustavus, *L'attesa. Cronaca di una prigonia al tempo dei Lager*, Rome: Riuniti, 1989; and A. Bendotti, G. Bertacchi, M. Pelliccioli and E. Valtulina, eds, *Prigionieri in Germania*, Bergamo: Il filo di Arianna, 1990.

82 See the paraphrase of a page of Elis given in M. Eve, 'L'opera storica di Norbert Elias', in *Rivista di storia contemporanea* XII (1983), p. 400.

83 See Lucien Febvre, 'How to Reconstruct the Emotional Life of the Past', in *A New Kind of History and Other Essays*, New York: Harper & Row, 1973, esp. p. 15.

84 For the theory of groups in fusion see J.-P. Sartre, *Critique of Dialectical Reason*, London: Verso, 2004, above all in the section 'The Fused Group. The group – the equivalence of freedom as necessity and of necessity as freedom' (original edition: *Critique de la raison dialectique*, Paris: Gallimard, 1960).

85 Mazzantini, *A cercar la bella morte*, p. 42.

to remain a nightmare throughout. To this day, the view of 8 September as pure tragedy or as the beginning of a process of liberation remains a distinguishing line between the ways in which the event is interpreted by those of opposite persuasions.[86] At the time, only very few Fascists saw the catastrophe as a liberating act of the kind that appears in this letter: 'Amid so many calamities, the betrayal has offered us the chance to let the great truths of Fascism shine forth and to gain mastery over the popular mind in this *Second Revolution*.'[87] In turn, Paratroop Major Mario Rizzati wrote that, following the blow of the capitulation, 'after a moment's meditation, I felt curiously happy: ah, at long last we had emerged from the equivocal situation of a war we didn't want to win, like Cadorna. At long last the clarification which had not come at Caporetto had arrived. Not all evil, I concluded, comes to do harm.'[88]

But very few took the myth of the return to origins so literally as to get much joy from it. The most convinced Fascists, like the others who for one reason or another fought under the flag of the Social Republic, were more or less all, even those who insisted on believing in inevitable victory, shrouded in the black shadow of a grim and incomprehensible catastrophe and of the terror that it might repeat itself.[89] To revert again to an opinion expressed about an altogether different historical experience, the Fascists 'who had once attributed so magnificent a destiny to themselves, just wouldn't resign themselves to recognising the truth, not even in defeat'.[90] On the contrary, the decision to join the Social Republic was often a way of fleeing a moment of truth that would mean necessarily having to think things through to the end – the prospect that the Fascists dreaded most.

What prevailed, therefore, in those who opted for the Social Republic was the fear of losing the identity they had grown accustomed to and the urge to

---

86 See for example A. Del Noce's article, 'La tragedia dell'8 settembre', published by *Il Tempo*, 26 November 1988, with the significant subtitle 'L'inizio di una revisione nell' opera di Bartoli' (the reference being to D. Bartoli, *L'Italia si arrende. La tragedia dell'8 settembre 1943*, Milan: Editoriale Nuova, 1988).

87 Captain Alberto Tombari's letter to Mussolini, 25 October 1944 (ACS, SPD, CR, RSI, envelope 24, folder 167).

88 Memorial letter written to a friend, 18 October 1943, a copy of which was then sent to Mussolini by Rizzati.

89 See for example the essence that G. Pansa drew from the GNR reports in 'L' esercito di Salò nei rapporti riservati alla Guardia nazionale repubblica 1943–44', *Quaderni del Movimento di Liberazione in Italia*, Milan 1969, vol. 3, p. 142. See also G. Pansa, *Il gladio e l'alloro. L' esercito di Salò*, Milan: Mondadori, 1991. This reality is intuited by a Communist leaflet, n.d., which, urging the soldiers of the RSI to desert with their weapons and kit, exhorts them not to allow 'a repetition of 8 September' (ISRT, *Raccolta volantini*, PCI Firenze, clandestini 1943–1944).

90 P. Vidal-Naquet, *Flavius Josèphe ou du bon usage de la trahison*, Paris: Editions de Minuit, 1977.

recover it no matter how, both in its version of reassuring order and in its nihilistic version. These were, after all, the two historic animators of Fascism, which were doomed to be played out, in that final showdown, in the form of sluggish opacity or ferocity. The Fascist author quoted above speaks of the 'sensation of being as it were uprooted', and describes how this turned into 'blind anger', the refusal of 'passive acceptance': 'To accept that defeat meant to accept everything that had led to it: the hypocrisy, the falsehood, the cowardice … And we didn't want that!' These words are all the more notable for the fact that the writer records how, in the months that followed, the reasons for making a choice on the basis of such considerations grew progressively fainter.[91]

A particularly radical choice, at once ideological and belligerent, was that made by the Fascists who placed themselves directly at the service of the Germans, without awaiting Mussolini's resurrection. A case in point is Major Rizzati, mentioned earlier – a protagonist, in Sardinia, with his Nembo division, of one of the first episodes of the civil war, which led to the execution of Colonel Alberto Bechi, who intended to ensure that Badoglio's orders were respected.[92] The 63rd battalion of the Tagliamento division in turn went over to direct service under the Germans,[93] as, immediately, did some hundred paratroopers from the Viterbo school and part of the 10th Arditi unit at Civitavecchia.[94] Already at Salerno, Lieutenant Dante Ciabatti, one of Renato Ricci's orderly officers, placed himself under the orders of the Germans, but, unlike Rizzatti, would not swear the oath of allegiance to the Führer.[95] These, clearly, were men who acted out of quite different motives from those who answered Rodolfo Graziani's call-up. It is no accident that, in a paratrooper formation Command document, Nembo complained that those who answered the Marshal's call-up were 'all those officers, perhaps even the senior ones, who on 9, 10, 11 and 12 September ordered

91 Mazzantini, *A cercar la bella morte*, pp. 20, 22, 200, 112. The decision to join the RSI by a disbanded Belluno soldier who had wandered for three days around the hills above Salò was motivated by the rediscovery of 'that security and that role that he had missed after the armistice'. A. Lotto, 'Obbedienza a rivolta: motivazioni, forme, esiti 1919–1945', in *Protagonisti* IX: 32 (July–September 1988), p. 13.

92 See the file cited in Rizzatti. Another paratrooper stationed in Sardinia has recounted that 'the idea of jumping up into one of the German trucks presented itself with the fascination of rebellion', a fascination to which however he did not yield himself (Bianchi, *Un'isola*, pp. 28–9, quoted in M. Di Giovanni's degree thesis).

93 See C. Dellavalle, *Operai, industriali e partito comunista nel Biellese, 1940–1945*, Milan: Feltrinelli, 1978, p. 98.

94 See M. Di Giovanni's degree thesis, as well as O. Barbieri, *Ponti sull' Arno. La Resistenza a Firenze*, Preface by F. Parri, Rome: Riuniti, 1975, and G. Pisanò, *Gli ultimi in grigioverde. Storia delle forze armate della Repubblica sociale italiana*, Milan: FPG, 1967.

95 See S. Setta, *Renato Ricci. Dallo squadrismo alla Repubblica sociale italiana*, Bologna: Il Mulino, 1986.

their men to shoot at the German armed forces and those who were ostenta-tiously Anglophile'.[96]

Dante Di Nanni, the Gappist who, besieged by Fascists in his house in Turin, put up a heroic defence before succumbing, was given this food for thought by another Gappist, Giovanni Pesce: 'In this war each of us has made his choice. Not one of us has had a gun put in his hands without being told why. He has chosen the side to be on in complete conscience; and the same was true with the Fascist on the balcony. Each pays the debts he has agreed to pay'.[97]

The recognition that, if you were on one side rather than the other, it was because you chose to be, is encountered with the reappearance of that most tradi-tional figure, the volunteer. The political commissar Andrea, from a detachment of the 28th Mario Gordini GAP brigade, gave this proud reply to the question, 'Why are we fighting?': 'We *gappisti* volunteers to this organisation, the spear-head, the backbone of the proletariat, have taken up arms not because a superior force has imposed it on us, nor even because we were ordered to by our party; nobody has imposed it on us; we are volunteers'.[98]

Commander Fulco, another Gappist from the province of Ravenna, put things more bluntly still when he recalled that the Garibaldini, each of whom initially 'refused to call themselves comandante', were not 'all of a sudden to place themselves on the loathsome leash of orders from above'. And he explained:

The distinguishing feature of the Commands of all illegal and volunteer formations, be they of bandits, mutineers or rebels, is that it is always from the breasts of the masses they are leading that they draw that course of action and also those orders which they will then impose on the very people who have dictated them. For those who rebel are the possessors of that will, that powerful sense of justice and injustice, everything, in short, that makes strong-willed *individuality*. It is a mistake to believe that a *volunteer* is more blindly obedient than others: indeed, seeing that he starts the struggle from an act of his *own* will, it is hardly likely that he will accept the progress of the battle however it is imposed on him. Whenever each man's personal sense of justice is violated, he, the volunteer, will again have the courage to impose his own will, on himself, if he is alone, or on the whole rebel organism, if his will is that of the majority of the insurgents.[99]

96 Memorandum to Giovanni Dolfin, Mussolini's secretary, 27 December 1943, cited in M. Di Giovanni's degree thesis.

97 Pesce, *Senza tregua*, p. 139. The navy would number Di Nanni among its gold medal recipients (I thank Giorgio Rochat for this information).

98 See L. Casali, *Il movimento di liberazione a Ravenna*, Ravenna: Istituto Storico della Resistenza, vol. I, n.d., p. 91.

99 Report to the CUMER by the command of the Mario Gordini 28th GAP brigade, 29 August 1944, sent after two punishing Nazi-Fascist reprisals that month (published in Casali, *Il movimento di liberazione a Ravenna* II [1965], pp. 276–8).

The profoundly fundamental nature of the choice whose autonomy these Garibaldini are claiming demanded constant reaffirmation. On the one hand, the choice was felt to be irrevocable, in the sense that 'there is no turning back';[100] on the other hand, it needed continual reconfirmation, implicitly or explicitly, to endorse this irrevocability. Formulae like 'He who chooses has chosen for ever' are thus both statement and exhortation. An article, 'Impegno d'onore' ('Honorable commitment'), which appeared in a Giustizia e Libertà newspaper, vigorously stresses this moral:

> Just as when we took up arms each of us was moved by a purely personal reflection and each of us weighed up clearly the import of what he was doing and took full responsibility for it, so we wish that responsibility, as the struggle goes on, to be forever present in the minds of each of us, like an honourable commitment from which one cannot and must not deflect.[101]

The impossibility of backing out is present in another Action Party document almost as a crude, incontrovertible fact, its purpose being to urge its readers to accept the full political consequences the choice contains *in nuce*, with that identification of moral coherence and intellectual self-consistency which distinguished the political philosophy of the Action Party:

> To all those who have joined the struggle from the tragedy afflicting the country, we say this: have no illusions: breaking with the totalitarian state, not answering the call-up, not taking the oath, resisting in any form or way you can, means taking a path that events themselves will oblige you to follow to the end. The struggle against totalitarianism is totalitarian. 'Normality' can only be reconquered now by passing through a profound revolution.[102]

There was a constant need to make the choice over and over again, at times in conditions yet more difficult than those of the first months, which reduced the space conceded to wavering, second thoughts, abandoning the cause ('We were well aware ... that we couldn't prevent anyone from making off, if they didn't want to stay with us').[103] Under the pressure of new dilemmas there

---

100 Letter by a Milanese engineer, Umberto Fogagnolo, a socialist, to his wife, 31 July 1943, when he had begun the political activity that he pursued after 8 September (*LRI*, pp. 87–8).

101 The article was published in January 1945 in *Giustizia e Libertà. Notiziario dei patrioti delle Alpi Cozie*; it is reproduced in Giovana, *Storia di una formazione partigiana*, p. 202.

102 Mutilated, anonymous document of the northern Italian Action Party, n.d., sent to the party's regional and provincial committees (INSMLI, *CLNAI*, envelope 8, folder 12).

103 Bini (Giovanni Serbandini) spoke in these terms in Lazagna, *Ponte rotto*, p. 50.

grew what we might call the tardy vocations, prompted by the Fascist calls-to-arms and the German labour call-ups,[104] or the fruit of more personal itineraries.[105] The choice should therefore be considered not as a moment of sudden illumination but as a process that at times asserted itself arduously, because the men who had to make it were weary. From the point of view of the intensity of the values called into play, it might be thought of as a set of non-linear and chronologically non-overlapping diagrams.[106] In any case, it is obvious that the choices made in spring 1945, when the end was nigh and there was not the slightest doubt about the outcome, were different from those of September 1943. To jump on the victor's bandwagon is not a choice, at least not in the sense described above. All the same, it is worth getting a few things straight on this score.

There is no doubt that certainty of victory marks off the entire Italian Resistance from the other European resistance movements. While the resistance workers of the other countries, in making their initial choice, took a risk as to both the outcome and duration of the struggle, the only risk the Italian *resistenti* took regarded the duration. True, in the other countries as well – in France and even in Yugoslavia – the resistance got truly under way only towards the end of

---

104 'There were the bands: to go, or not to go ... and I decided'; 'When that moment [the call-up for Germany] came you had to choose which road to follow'; 'They almost obliged us to decide to go'. Testimony by Achille Vignolini, furnace-workman, Giovanni Carretta, Fiat worker, Silvestro Silvio Tedeschi, carpenter, in Bravo and Jalla, *La vita offesa*, pp. 84, 83, 82. It should be borne in mind that deportations from Piedmont reached their peak in the first six months of 1944 (40 percent of the total). Ibid., pp. 55–6. A public draft notice for those born in 1925, and for shares of those born in 1923 and 1924, were issued by Graziani, the defence minister, on 4 November 1943. See E. Piscitelli, 'I bandi tedeschi e fascisti', *Quaderni della Resistenza laziale*, Rome n.d., but 1975, vol. 4, pp. 14–43. See also Pansa, *L'esercito di Salò*, pp. 22–5ff. In Rome notices for officers to present themselves had already been appearing since 29 September (Piscitelli, *I bandi*, p. 133). The proliferation of notices of this kind was to be a characteristic of the RSI.

105 Here I can recall the case of Colonel Giovanni Duca. Commander of the camp of the Military academy of Modena, on 8 September 1943, the best he managed to do was disband the units, though these were in the Modenese Apennines that were to become an epicentre of the partisan struggle. Then Colonel Duca, in another region of the North, participated in the Resistance and was captured, tortured and killed by the SS; one of his sons died in Mauthausen (see Gorrieri, *La Repubblica di Montefiorino*, pp. 24–6).

106 One of the very few sociological research projects devoted to the Resistance makes this process rigid by defining as full-fledged 'innovators' only those who opted for the Resistance in the first months (by 31 December, to be precise). All the others are placed in the categories of 'primi adottanti' ('first adopters'), 'prima maggioranza' ('first majority'), 'ultima maggioranza' ('last majority') and 'marginali', according to the scheme devised by E. M. Rogers (see Ardigò, *L'insorgenza partigiana*, esp. pp. 88–9). For a criticism of this scheme see G. Quazza, 'Fra sociologia e storia: una ricerca sulla Resistenza', in *Rivista di storia contemporanea* X (1981), pp. 619–25.

1942, when Stalingrad, the Anglo-American landing in French North Africa, and El Alamein showed, for those with eyes to see, the turn the military tide had unequivocally taken. Nevertheless, Italy remains a special case in this respect. Not that this turns the Italian *resistenti* into 'cortigiani della vittoria' ('suitors of victory'), as an authoritative philosopher has recently claimed.[107] Rather, it should induce us to focus our attention on the significance acquired by the wish to give destiny a helping hand, to aid her by making oneself worthy of her, and thereby to become what one was.[108] This attitude was the very antipode of that practised by those collaborationists who had reckoned themselves to be cannier than others and more capable of bending destiny to their own Machiavellian ends.[109] In Rome the *resistenti* wanted to be different from the mass of their fellow citizens, who, as one caustic definition has it, were awaiting the liberation as a gift owed to themselves and to the Pontiff.[110]

Even if the Nazi–Fascist defeat was a rationally and authoritatively justified prediction, with the Italian *resistenti* it acquired the force of a self-fulfilling prophecy. This faith in victory was 'the linchpin of the new, as yet poor, symbolic system that was coming about, largely through interpersonal communication and clandestine public opinion'.[111]

On the other hand, chancing one's luck only on the duration of the struggle, even if in the first few months it was reckoned that it would be shorter than it turned out to be, did not mean that you were not putting your life at risk. On the contrary, to die without savouring the fruit of a now imminent victory could be still more heartbreaking. Thus, predicting his fate, Artom wrote: 'It seems to me bitter indeed to have certain victory in sight, but to seem unable to seize it and enjoy it because death makes off with us and takes us far away.'[112]

Many *resistenti* felt the sense of a recovery that was still possible for themselves and for Italy. Foa wrote: 'From a profound and long-term point of view

---

107 See Del Noce, *La tragedia del'8 settembre*. It is a fine example of how political factiousness can blunt the sharpest of minds. However, the author who inspires Del Noce on that page is Curzio Malaparte.

108 Conversation with Vittorio Foa (1985). 'Obedience to destiny' is from G. W. F. Hegel's *Philosophische Propädeutik*. 'It becomes what you are' is a maxim of Goethe's. In 1976 Foa was to write: 'In Fascism, Rossi and Bauer taught us that one needed to be capable of choosing without counting the years ahead; in the Resistance, Leo Valiani and Ferruccio Parri taught us that one needed to fight even if the destiny of the war and of Fascism were in any case marked by the military events, one needed to fight if one wanted the future not to be a continuity with the past, but a break with it.' V. Foa, 'Ernesto Rossi', in *Per una storia del movimento operaio*, pp. 231–2.

109 This is what Claudio Magris wrote of General Vlasov in *Illazione su una sciabola*, Bari: Cariplo-Laterza, n.d.

110 Battaglia, *Un uomo*, p. 47.

111 Ardigò, *L'insorgenza partigiana*, p. 23.

112 Artom, *Diari*, p. 122 (13 December 1943).

the German occupation is a great boon for Italy ... In fact, it has befallen Italy to have the sad privilege not, like the other European peoples, to have lived the full destructive experience of the war.'[113] And the Action Party newspaper: 'We no longer need to sneak out at night and stealthily write: "Long live the heroic Danes": we too are like them, like the French, the Belgians, the Dutch, like the Yugoslavs and the Greeks, like the Czechs and the Poles.'[114] The Garibaldino commander Ferdinando Mautino says much the same when he recalls that he and those like him made their choice in the spirit of the PCI Italian Communist Party (PCI) call-to-arms – 'Only with a gun in our hands against the enemy do we feel that we are still men and that we are reaffirming our humanity and dignity' – but independently of that appeal, 'which we would know only by taking action.'[115]

Dante Livio Bianco recognised in himself 'the great joy of having finally been able to pass from a theoretical position to a practical position.'[116] It was the same joy, Bianco recalls, that the founder of Giustiza e Libertà, Carlo Rosselli, had manifested on arriving in Spain. In the veteran anti-Fascists, the redemption was from humiliations such as had been suffered by the socialist Filippo Turati, old and exiled, when the public prosecutor for the Seine had asked him: 'Mais, expliquez-moi, monsieur le député, comment donc se fait-il que l'Italie ne se révolte pas?'[117] In 1943 the moment seemed well and truly to have come 'to start over again from scratch', as Claudio Treves, another great exile, had said to the young Giorgio Amendola.[118]

The very fact of being the last to get there, with so heavy a burden on one's shoulders, made the Italian *resistenti* particularly sensitive to the problems of a future that was not to limit itself to defeating the Germans. 'Gagner la guerre et gagner la paix' was the formula used by the newspaper founded in France by Silvio Trentin to sum up the problem.[119] In that newspaper, there were contemp-

---

113 Inverni (V. Foa), *I partiti*, pp. 11–12 (cf. p. 59).

114 *L'Italia Libera*, Roman edition, 11 September 1943 (note the early date), article entitled 'L'Europa libera'.

115 Mautino, *Guerra di popolo*, p. 20. Enzo Collotti, in the Preface, underlines the 'naturezza' ('naturalness') of Mautino's choice, its 'elementary' and 'just' but not 'easy' 'simplicity': a form, that is, 'of moral indemnity towards oneself and towards others' (p. 6).

116 See Bianco, *Guerra partigiana*, p. 12.

117 'But tell me, sir, how then is it that Italy does not rebel?' Turati himself recounts the episode, connected with the request by the Fascist government for him to be extradited for the Savona trial, in a letter to Bianca Pittoni of 28 August 1928. See F. Turati, *Lettere dall'esilio*, ed. B. Pittoni, Milan: Pan, 1968, p. 182.

118 'We are defeated men. Don't expect anything from us. You have to start everything again from scratch (G. Amendola's conversation with the author).

119 This is the title of an editorial in *Libérer et Fédérer*, February–March 1943, from which also the quotations that follow are taken.

tuous attacks against 'new fair-weather patriots' against 'last-minute workers', against all those who 'follow the chariot of victory, regardless of the driver, whether Hitler, Churchill, Roosevelt or Stalin'. When he subsequently took part in the Italian Resistance, Trentin certainly did not consider himself to be part of this 'surging and roaring tide that lifts the mounted trophy of Victory'. He probably felt that the short time remaining to Italy to prove herself demanded a still greater commitment, before the star of victory cast its light also on the eleventh-hour apprentices.

3. Betrayal

The problem of political morality that the Italians had to face most immediately was that of betrayal. All the parties involved bandied around accusations of betrayal. In fact, 'no one wants to appear as a traitor' but all 'are firmly convinced that traitors exist and that they must be punished in the most severe way possible: preferably with death'.[1]

In the situation in Italy following 8 September 1943, the accusations of betrayal from opposing sides bounced back and forth, interwove and contaminated one another in various ways, because all of them, or almost all, contained some fragments of truth. On the other hand, everyone seemed to be possessed by a 'need of great treasons' against which to salve themselves.[2] The result of this was that the semantic field of the word was greatly extended. If from the point of view of Italian positive law treason was only a military offence,[3] the events overwhelming Italy and Europe went well beyond the terrain of soldiers and their rules of conduct. The balance in the dialectic of freedom and bonds had dissolved – if indeed it had ever existed – as 'unavoidable dependence' was 'transferred more and more to the periphery, to the externals of life'.[4] Bonds, which the totalitarian regimes and the war had wished to be all-inclusive, either plummeted or became still more exclusive; and, on the other hand, in order to get a hearing, the freedom to appeal only to one's own conscience had to take the form of absolute intransigence. The accusations of treason became both drastic and multivalent; but at the same time 'the good use of treason' once again came to exert its fascination.

---

1 H. M. Enzenberger, 'Sulla teoria del tradimento', in *Menabò di letteratura*, 1964, vol. 7, p. 15 (original title 'Uber die Theorie des Hochverrats').

2 Brissot's words used in the text are quoted by J.-P. Sartre, *Search for a Method*, New York: Vintage, 1968, p. 41.

3 See, for example, the entries 'Tradimento' in *Il Digesto italiano* (1916) and in *Il Nuovo Digesto italiano* (1940), which converge in this evaluation.

4 G. Simmel, 'Fashion', *International Quarterly* 10: 130–55 (1904), p. 148. Besides the example of fashion, Simmel also gives that of law.

Polybius, going over to the Romans, had written that 'those who decide freely to come to terms with kings or dynasties and to cooperate with them' are not traitors, nor is anyone who organises an overturning of alliances. Polybius had difficulty, however, answering the question of 'who should really be considered a traitor'. In the struggle between resistance fighters and collaborationists things, on the contrary, became clear-cut: a group of French Jewish resistance fighters, supporters of Irgun, reopened the trial against Flavius Josephus, and condemned him to death as a collaborationist with the Romans and a traitor.[5] A popular poet from Terni inveighed against 'those who are always traitors! (the bosses, the Fascists, the powerful);[6] a Fascist we have already come across, possibly recalling the song of the Piave' – 'ma in a notte triste si parlò di tradimento' ('but one sad night we spoke of betrayal') – now wrote: 'In this war everything is betrayal, nothing but betrayal.'[7]

The people about whom opinions converged most generally, albeit for different motives, in branding them as traitors were the king and Badoglio. They appeared so to the Germans, the Fascists, the majority of the *resistenti*, and a sizable number of the internees in Germany, wary though the latter were, for understandable reasons, of voicing this opinion openly. To the Allies they appeared at the very least as useful weathervanes, who seemed to be reviving the age-old habit the Savoys had of never concluding a war on the same side they had begun it on – unless, as was also said, they had changed front twice. In its 6 May 1944 Rome edition, *Avanti!* wrote: 'The Savoys can't possibly overturn the alliances as they did in the eighteenth century.' As for the Germans, it was obvious that they should regard the king and Badoglio as traitors. Above all, there had been that rash sentence inserted in the proclamation Badoglio launched immediately after 25 July: 'Italy will keep faith with the word it has given, a jealous custodian of its millenary traditions!' If the intention behind the second part of this sentence had been to hint at a sibylline and almost comic mental reservation, now it appeared only as exacerbating the *volte-face*.

'This is breaking your word', said Rudolf von Rahn, who was in charge of German affairs in Rome, to Foreign Minister Raffaele Guariglia, who, at 7 p.m. on 8 September, came to announce the Armistice to him.[8] 'The more deceived the German troops and leadership were, the harsher the reaction was', General Alfred Jodl later said.[9] On 10 September Josef Goebbels wrote in his diary

---

5 For the references to Polybius and Flavius Josephus, see Vidal-Naquet, *Flavius Josèphe*.

6 See Portelli, *Biografia di una città*, p. 8.

7 Major Rizzati, memorial letter of 18 October 1943.

8 Rahn's report to the German foreign minister, quoted in Pisanò, *Storia della guerra civile*, vol. I, p. 86.

9 Report by Jodl, chief of the General Staff of the Wehrmacht, of 7 November 1943, to the Reich-Gauleiters, and included among the Nuremburg documents, quoted in E.

that the German people, 'abler and more clairvoyant than its government', had always distrusted the Italians.[10] In his verdict of betrayal, Goebbels thus engulfed the whole Italian people; and he then laid it on thick: 'The Italians, through their infidelity and treachery, have lost any right to be a modern national state. They must be punished with the utmost severity, as the laws of history impose.'[11]

It has been rightly observed that the German reaction stemmed from the fact that they expected absolute 'vassalic loyalty' on the part of their Italian ally,[12] who had therefore made themselves guilty of treason ('maresciallo fellone' was indeed one of the phrases used most widely to describe Badoglio). As the war had gradually taken a turn for the worse, Italian protests of 'fidelity' to Germany[13] had been reiterated, without the Germans feeling the slightest need to offer corresponding reassurances. But the arrogance of the master left his vassal no other 'freedom' except to betray him by going over to the enemy. The Germans' reluctance (at least until Kuby's recent book)[14] to consider themselves, essentially, as traitors to the Italians probably lies in this idea: a vassal can betray his master; but that the master can betray the vassal, is, for the master, a nonsensical proposition.

But, in any case, whatever the underlying convictions might have been, the distinction between the treacherous leaders and the Italian people who were themselves the victims of betrayal was too pragmatically useful not to be resorted to by the Germans. And in fact the Germans lost no time in inviting the Italians to disassociate themselves from the traitors; but they did this with a crudity that magnified the contradictions of that invitation and made the chances still scarcer of its finding mass acceptance.

'It is evident what path you must follow', was how one of the first German appeals, broadcast widely by radio, rounded off: 'Leave the traitors, and come along with your German comrades.'[15] It is curious how little aware the Germans

---

Collotti, *L'amministrazione tedesca nell'Italia occupata, 1943–1945*, Milan: Lerici, 1963, p. 80.

10 Quoted in Ragionieri, *Italia giudicata*, pp. 796–7.

11 Quoted in Collotti, *L'amministrazione*, p. 103. The Japanese view was similar: 'Italy belongs to the Italians. From the Japanese point of view, a nation constitutes an inseparable bloc; we therefore think that the entire Italian people is responsible for the betrayal of Italy'. Report to the Mikado, n.d., in *Ragionieri, Italia giudicata*, p. 805.

12 J. Förster, 'Il ruolo dell'8ª armata italiana dal punto di vista tedesco', in Istituto Storico della Resistenza in Cuneo e provincia, *Gli italiani sul fronte russo*, p. 258.

13 On this subject, see E. Collotti, *L'alleanza italo-tedesca 1941–1943*, p. 60.

14 E. Kuby, *Verrat auf deutsch*, Hamburg: Konkret Verlag, 1982. In an interview with Vannuccini, Karl Dietrich Bracher declared that 'the whole thesis of the [Italian] betrayal makes no sense' (*La Repubblica*, 7 September 1983).

15 The text of the appeal can be read in a leaflet dropped by German aircraft on the isle of Elba on 10 September 1943. A photographic copy of it exists in ISRT, *Documenti dei CLN di Livorno e Piombino*.

seemed to be that, if there was one word at that moment that repelled the great majority of Italians, and particularly the officers and soldiers to whom the appeal was primarily addressed, it was 'camarata' ('comrade'); and even if this might have been a hasty translation of a word with less extensive Fascist connotations in German, the fact remains that they ought nonetheless to have realised how it sounded to the ears of the Italians they were addressing. Probably the writers and inspirers of that proclamation were capable only of showing that they seriously believed the thesis whereby the Italians were all honest comrades, whom only betrayal had snatched away from their German allies. Besides, it was true to German tradition to interpret defeats and setbacks as acts of betrayal by many or few. Contempt for the Italians is, in any case, revealed in the passage in the appeal where it was promised that 'like the German soldiers you too will be well fed, paid and treated'.

The Germans themselves and, obviously, the Fascists of the Social Republic were not the only ones to brand the king and Badoglio as traitors of the Germans. Anti-Fascists like Gaetano Salvemini had no doubts on this score: 'The king has committed an act of perfidy and betrayal, even if it has been committed against a bandit like Hitler: a rascal does not become a gentleman when he betrays another rascal.'[16] Even *La Voce Repubblicana* didn't mince words in calling the king's conduct towards Germany betrayal – the last link in a chain begun by Charles Albert when, in 1821, he had betrayed the Carbonari.[17] Then again, more than a year later, in a letter to Piero Calamandrei, Salvemini gave his view of things in political terms that were widely shared by the Resistance:

> My belief is that war against the Germans could not have been declared by a king who had signed the alliance treaty of May 1939, and by Badoglio who had been the military instrument of the Axis from 1936 to December 1940. The two men would have committed a patent act of treachery. And whoever had associated themselves with them would have dishonoured themselves with them and would have dishonoured the Italian people. Italy is already accused (wrongly) of having betrayed the allies in 1914–15. God forbid that she should go down in history with the (just) accusation of having betrayed Hitler in 1943.[18]

---

16 Article entitled 'Chi tradisce?' in the 23 October 1943 issue of *L'Adunata dei refrattari*, the newspaper of the Italian anarchists in America (quoted in Laura Valentini's degree thesis on Italian political emigration and the anti-Fascist press in the United States between 1940 and 1945, discussed at the University of Pisa with Professor Elena Aga-Rossi, academic year 1980–81).

17 Article entitled 'Il Re', in *La Voce Repubblicana*, 6 October 1943. In the same number another article, 'Quattro necessità', spoke in any case of the Germans as the 'ally, traitor'.

18 Salvemini and Calamandrei, 7 December 1944, published in G. Salvemini, *Lettere dall'America 1944–1946*, ed. A. Merola, Bari: Laterza, 1967, pp. 53–4.

It is notable that the ghost of the changing of sides of 1915 – the 'giro di valzer' ('deviation from foreign policy') – which certainly fluttered around the ex-revolutionary interventionist Benito Mussolini in spring 1940, returned to the mind of the ex–democratic interventionist Gaetano Salvemini in 1943–44.

Incapable even of 'betraying well' was Silvio Trentin's verdict on the Savoy family and the 're gaglioffo' ('good-for-nothing king'): 'Now, always, invariably, throughout history, the Savoys have excelled not in the vile shamelessness of their oath-breaking, but rather in their shameful and perfidious cowardice.' Trentin levelled at the monarchy an accusation that bore the clear mark of the Resistance: that of having prevented 8 September from 'being transformed into a triumphal and redemptive day of resurrection'.[19] In the same spirit, the draft of an article for an underground paper accused Badoglio of having given 'that abandonment of Germany the character of a calculated act of treachery when it could have expressed the revolt of an entire people against an alliance that they had never wanted'.[20] This sense of a golden opportunity degraded to base intrigue may help us understand attitudes such as that of a Venetian gentleman who relates how he 'went up to a German and shook his hand, without saying a word, in a fit of disgust at what he saw going on'.[21]

Recognition of – or at least doubts about – the fact that the Germans had some reason to consider themselves betrayed also appears in testimonies given forty years later by people who did not join the RSI: 'This news, naturally, was considered by our German allies to be an act of great treachery'; or, more dramatically: 'Forty years have gone by and I'm still ashamed to have been their allies in war and then betrayed them as Judas did. But it was our leaders, who are always disgusting, who sold us out.'[22]

A guilty conscience towards the Germans had been displayed, in an altogether different context, by the generals heading along the road of the coup d'état and then the Armistice. In a note to Mussolini written just after his appointment as head of the General Staff of the Combined Forces, Arturo Ambrosio put forward the argument that 'the Germans must change their operative intentions and must come to our aid, otherwise we shall not be obliged to follow them in their erroneous conduct of the war'.[23]

---

19 S. Trentin, 'Appello ai veneti, guardia avanzata della nazione italiana', September 1943, published in *Giustizia e Libertà*, organ of the Veneto Action Party, 1 November 1943, also in S. Trentin, *Antifascismo e rivoluzione. Scritti e discorsi 1927–1944*, Venice: Marsilio, 1985, pp. 527–8.

20 IVSR, *Stampa antifascista*.

21 The episode is recounted by Calamandrei, *La vita indivisibile*, p. 110.

22 Testimonies by Giuseppe Bandini, from Cecina, told to Tenda, and of OR, from Gorizia; the second recalls how the Germans, after capturing him and his fellow soldiers, abandoned by their officers, near Frascati, 'left us to our destinies' (*CU*).

23 On 17 February 1943, to be exact. Cited in Deakin, *The Brutal Friendship*, p. 166. In another note that follows soon after (3 March), Ambrosio repeated the same concepts,

It was as if a preventive alibi were being sought, authorising one to consider the Germans traitors because they were dispatching too few troops to the rescue of an Italy threatened at close range now by the Anglo-Americans. On 17 July 1943, just after the Sicily landing (9–10 July) the Supreme Command, still more scared, unwittingly revealed the fragility of the argument: 'And if, say, the Germans wanted to make Italy into their battlefield, I don't rule out the possibility that Italy would fight against these allies who have systematically broken their word.'[24]

On the one hand, then, a greater German military presence in Italy was asked for, and on the other, it was feared that the Germans wanted to make Italy into a battlefield. This was how, in a way that may possibly have been intended to be artful but succeeded only in being tragically grotesque, the illusion-cum-fiction of the 'parallel war' was playing itself out. It had always, as an intelligent German observer pointed out, come up against the contradiction between 'the desire to be as independent as possible from German control' and 'the need to seek German support'.[25]

It was not, then, by the monarchy and the high Commands of the Royal Army that the Germans needed seriously to fear being accused of betrayal, even if this was obviously attempted by those directly concerned. In his Radio Bari broadcast of 24 September 1943, the king praised those who had managed to avoid the 'enemy's betrayal' and 'the flattery of the repudiators of the *patria*'.[26] The rulers of the South, who during the forty-five days could hardly be said to have been hard on the Fascists, could feel themselves to be the object at least of the latter's ingratitude.

As regards betraying the Germans, part of the same underground press is at times threaded with a defensive attitude that echoes the arguments of the High Command, to which a whole class of disappointed nationalists were not insensitive. A case in point is the Roman newspaper *L'Indice dei fatti e delle idee*. On 15 November 1943, in the article actually entitled 'Chi ha tradito' ('The betrayers'), Germany is accused, not altogether without reason, of having failed to pay enough attention to the interests of Italy since the time of the armistice with France, and of having always underrated the Mediterranean theatre of operations.[27]

---

accusing the Germans of not understanding the importance of the Mediterranean front (p. 202).

24 'Appunti' ('Notes') for the Foreign Ministry. See Deakin, p. 376.

25 See General Rintelen's report of late March 1943, quoted in Deakin, pp. 358–9. The formula 'guerra parallela' ('parallel war') is contained in a memorandum by Mussolini to the king of 31 March 1940 (Deakin, p. 11).

26 See Degli Espinosa , *Il Regno del Sud*, p. 81.

27 Analogous arguments were to be put forward on 15 January 1944 in the article entitled 'Un'alleanza sbagliata'.

More directly, and in the style of a court sentence, the Piedmontese paper *Riscossa Italiana* pronounced that 'the accuser is discredited' and 'the accusation [of betrayal] is objectively bereft of any shade of legitimacy'.[28] In October 1943, *Il Risorgimento Liberale* assured its readers that 'propaganda about the joke of betraying the Germans will come to nothing'; but in April 1944, regarding the similar fate that had befallen Hungary, it would still feel the need to repeat that, if betrayal is 'failure to keep one's word', Mussolini's word could not place the Italian people under any obligation.[29] The Partito della Democrazia del Lavoro entitled the entire October 1943 Roman issue of its paper of the same name, 'Dov'è il tradimento?' ('What betrayal?'), concluding that the real traitor was Mussolini.[30] 'Non c'è tradimento' ('There is no betrayal') was the title of an article in *L'Azione*: this too argued that, if betrayal there was, it was Mussolini's betrayal of the Italian people.[31] One could talk in terms of betrayal – writes *Voce Operaia*, organ of the Catholic communists in Rome – if the war against the Germans were being conducted, as a last-minute bid to save themselves, by those who had allied themselves with the Germans.[32] This was an argument analogous to Salvemini's, referred to above, and one which we shall see taken up again in the debate about the declaration of war against Germany.

Perhaps it is no accident that some of the quotations exemplifying this 'defensive' stance are found in resistance journalism that may be called 'minor', in the sense that it cannot be attributed to parties, or to politically prominent and well-defined groups. These publications, wrongly neglected by historiography, are one of the scanty number of sources available for reconstructing the opinion of the middle-ranking, muddled bourgeoisie which was later to carry so much weight in the days following the Liberation, not least in relation to this knotty question of the attitude held in the past and to be held in the future concerning the lost war. Of the above quotations, those of the politically well-defined parties and groups – even if, like La Democrazia del Lavoro, they carried scant weight with the Resistance – nevertheless already introduce the retaliation against Mussolini and, as in the case of *Voce Operaia*, extend it to the king and to the generals of the South. The Action Party newspaper, for example, was to go a long way down this path: in September 1943 it did not hesitate to maintain that 'the Badoglio government and the Crown were betraying one and all, the Germans and the Anglo-Americans. To save Italy? No. To save themselves.' Still

---

28 'La storia del preteso tradimento', 20 October 1943.

29 'In documento d'infamia', 29 October 1943 (Roman edition); 'Il caso dell'Ungheria', April 1944 (Piedmontese edition).

30 The next issue, of November 1943, took a similar line.

31 *L'Azione*, 20 November 1943. On 20 October the Christian Social newspaper had advanced a similar thesis – we are the betrayed, not the betrayers – in the already-cited article bearing the challenging title *Pacta sunt servanda*.

32 'Tutto il potere al CLN', 28 January 1944.

along the lines of a punishable betrayal, the same newspaper affirmed: 'All this is material for a war tribunal … And maybe the people will find a way to abbreviate procedures.'[33] Ferdinando Mautino placed himself more directly on the moral plane when he noted in his diary: 'Had it never by chance befallen the ruling classes, the marshals and the Majesties, to possess a spirit capable of committing themselves to fidelity to any of the numerous sacred principles in whose name millions of Italians have been called upon to give up all their affections, the construction of their own future, life itself.'[34]

As we know, the attitude to the king and Badoglio was to be conditioned in the Resistance press by the way the political situation as a whole was unfolding, and by the change in the parties' positions after the Salerno 'turning-point'. What needs to be stressed here is that including Badoglio and above all the king in the accusation of betrayal meant, on the one hand, shifting the terms of judgment and accusation onto a political and moral plane that transcended the very events following 8 September; and, on the other hand, it made the problem of whether or not to keep the oath a particularly pressing one. If, from a lay point of view, the oath was a 'guarantee against the future' and against the very freedom of the person taking it, it was also an 'inert determination of the future.'[35] The eternal value, essential to the form of the oath, may therefore come into conflict with the need for new and unforeseen acts of liberty. There thus emerges the clause, never openly voiced, that the oath was valid only if the fundamental conditions that determined it did not change. Thus, at the very moment when it should be deploying its whole cogent force, the oath might instead become null.

Every, or nearly every, Italian had taken two oaths: one to the king, the other to the Duce.[36] More or less all those who had been enlisted in the regime's youth organisations had sung: 'Duce! Duce! Chi no saprà morir? Il giuramento chi mai rinnegherà?' ('Duce! Duce! Who will not be prepared to die? Who will ever break the oath?'). Compelled now to choose between one oath or the other, the Resistance simply cut the Gordian knot by choosing neither one nor the other, and thereby freed the solemn matter of being true to oneself from any

---

33 L'Italia Libera, Roman edition, September 1943, articles entitled 'Tradimenti' and 'Per la storia'.

34 Mautino, Guerra di popolo, pp. 31–2.

35 See Sartre, Critique of Dialectical Reason I, pp. 419–20.

36 These were the formulas: 'I swear to be faithful to the king and his royal successors, to loyally observe the Statute and the other laws of the state, to fulfil all the duties of my state, for the sole purpose of the inseparable good of the king and the patria'; 'In the name of God and of Italy, I swear to execute the orders of the Duce and to serve with all my strength and, if necessary, with my blood, the cause of the Fascist Revolution' (Statute of the PNF of 1938, Art. 9). Until the Statute of 1926 betrayal had been closely connected to expulsion from the party. See M. Missori, Gerarchia e statuti del PNF, Rome: Bonacci, 1986.

pre-established institutional encumbrance and personal bond. But even those who felt bound to one oath rather than the other, and branded those of the opposite persuasion as traitors, were, in order to justify their choice, induced to resort to principles that went beyond loyalty to the oath as such. Thus a still predominantly formal criterion might be invoked, such as legitimacy and legality, or else deeper motivations involving the contents synthesised, or simply implicit, in the formula and the very act of taking the oath.

Things became more complicated with the problem of the legitimacy of the Social Republic, particularly when the latter demanded a further oath, thereby reviving the conflict and creating new opportunities to betray (as *L'Italia Libera* wrote: 'Whoever takes the oath is a traitor').[37] It was obvious that the anti-Fascist parties and the CLNs, starting with those of northern Italy,[38] would urge people not to take the oath, thus bestowing legitimacy on the government of the South, and offering visible and easily comprehensible support to undecided consciences.

But the conflict between oaths was not simply a question of two opposing legalities confronting each other. To paraphrase Gramsci's famous remark that, in the West, with the trembling of the state the structures of civil society can be glimpsed with the naked eye,[39] we might say that the conflict that was born around the question of betrayal–oath–loyalty caused cultural structures deeply inscribed in the conscience of the Italians to surface.

The determination not to break one's oath to the king undoubtedly fed the steadfast and dignified behaviour of a large number of the internees in the German concentration camps, where even Badoglio's name figures as a point of reference. 'Hurrah Badoglio!' was how friendly Russian prisoners sometimes greeted their Italian companions.[40] Testimonies of this kind abound.[41] Among the most eloquent worth citing is that of the 245 second lieutenants of the Pinerolo cavalry school, who, not yet having sworn the oath to the king, pronounced it, in the camp of Przemyśl before the oldest officer.[42]

---

37 Title of an article in the Roman edition, 20 January 1944.

38 See the motion to public functionaries of 7 January, the decree of 14 September on the sanctions to apply to the officers and public functionaries who swear, the motions to officers on leave of 24 October 1944, and the decree of 29 March 1945, again on the sanctions (demotion) to apply to officers who swear the oath (*Atti*, CLNAI [Acts of the Committee for National Liberation of Northern Italy], pp. 111–12, 172, 197, 294).

39 The passage from Gramsci reads as follows: 'In the East the state was everything, civil society was primordial and gelatinous; in the West between state and civil society there was a just relationship and in the trembling of the state a robust structure of civil society could be discerned immediately'. A. Gramsci, *Quaderni del carcere*, ed. V. Gerratana, II, Turin: Einaudi, 1975, p. 866.

40 Testimony by Giampiero Carocci to the author.

41 See V. E. Giuntella and G. Rochat's works, cited above.

42 See Rochat, *Memorialistica e storiografia sull'internamento*, p. 37.

An officer shot in Greece by the Germans wrote: 'I have always been loyal to any oaths I have taken and for the oath of loyalty to the King of Italy I give my life.'[43]

It is also a certified fact that the oath to the king carried more weight in the consciences of the officers, especially the older ones, than in those of the soldiers[44] – an indication of the hiatus existing in the country between governing classes and the populace and, in the army, between officers and troops. The Germans tried to make the most of this hiatus, boasting the greater egalitarianism existing in their army.[45] But beyond keeping one's word and appealing to an implicit judgment of constitutional legality, other explanations as to why the oath to the king appeared more binding than that to the Duce ought to be explored.

At work certainly was a stronger, more long-standing and deep-rooted sense of the *patria*–state, in the person of the king, than of the government–regime, in the person of the Duce. For example, it has been noted how, in the memoirs of the ex-military internees, there is a good deal more cursing of the high Commands than of the king and Badoglio himself.[46] The fact that the Fascist national party had lost, along with its entire retinue of organisations, much of its political sting, and that, to the majority of Italians, it seemed by now to be no more than one of the many bureaucratic apparatuses of the state, played against the possibility of the resurrected Republican Fascist Party's competing on an equal footing with the traditional state, however tattered the latter might be. On the contrary, this Fascist pretension was to seem on the one hand devoid of any serious foundation, and on the other hand compromising in a new sense, which went well beyond the ritual request for the bread ration card ('tessera del pane').

One ex-internee offers this testimony:

> Many of us, all of us, had been Fascists, some out of personal interests or compulsion, others (and they were the majority) out of conviction. But the offer that was made to us at that moment [to adhere to the RSI] acquired another meaning and consequently no more than some fifty [in his camp] were those who accepted the proposal.[47]

---

43 Letter to his mother by Giuseppe Di Stefano, reserve lieutenant, philosophy professor, Sicilian, 6 December 1943 (*LRE*, p. 462).

44 See Rochat, *Memorialistica e storiografia sull'internamento*, p. 37.

45 Testimony by Cinzio Violante to the author (1982).

46 See Rochat, *Memorialistica e storiografia sull'internamento*, p. 37.

47 G. Vangelista, *Oltre il filo spinato. Storia e considerazioni di un ex internato militare italiano*, Rome: Stampa d'oggi, n.d., quoted in Rochat, *Memorialistica e storiografia sull'internamento*, p. 48.

The Christian Democrat paper *Il Popolo*, also keen to rebut accusations of betrayal of the Germans,[48] tried to take an explicit look at the thorny question of the two oaths.[49] It is no accident that this was a Catholic paper: the oath to the Duce had in fact constituted one of the polemical objectives of Pius XI's encyclical *Non abbiamo bisogno* of 29 June 1931. The Pope had suggested that the already signed-up Fascists there should make this mental reservation: 'apart from the laws of God and of the Church' or 'apart from the duties of the good Christian', and reserved the right to ask that in future the formula be modified, 'should one not wish to do better, far better, and omit the oath, which is such a religious act, and is certainly not in the place most fitting to it on a party membership card'. To these mental reservations Pius XI had suggested adding this other one: 'with the firm intention to declare such a reservation even overtly, should the need arise'.[50]

That need had now arisen with an urgency and a vengeance that were probably unforeseen by the Pope when he dictated those words. And the Christian Democrat paper strove to argue the different value to be attributed to the two oaths. The oath to the king, it wrote, 'is a promise made freely and voluntarily, calling God to witness one's own words'; by contrast, that to the Duce 'is absurd and illicit, given the aim it commits one to. It was wrung out of the majority of people with violence, since it was imposed as a condition for saving one's life.'

Truth to tell, to 'save one's life' an Italian had to swear to the king as well; and the opening words of the text in question implicit in the reference to 'the aim that [the oath] commits one to' was contradicted when the article denied that the king's conduct might invalidate the oath taken to him. The upshot of this was the invocation of the age-old argument whereby only the oath's addressee, raised to the status of sole independent variable, had the power to release one from it. Mussolini, it said, could not release himself from the oath he had sworn to the king. It would have been all too easy for a Fascist to reply: And how can the king release himself from the oath he swore to Mussolini? A defensive article in *Il Messaggero*, which was not yet fully 'normalised' in the Fascist sense, seems implicitly to accept the adversary's terrain, in recognising the greater weight to

---

48 See the articles 'Il supremo dovere' and 'Gli artefici della guerra civile', both of 23 October 1943 (Roman edition).

49 Article entitled 'Fede a un giuramento', 14 November 1943 (Roman edition), signed 'un ufficiale di Marina' ('a Naval officer').

50 See P. Scoppola, *Chiesa e Stato nella storia d'Italia*, Bari: Laterza, 1967, p. 673. In the agreement with the regime reached on 2 September 1931 the pope was to renounce the modification of the oath. Giovanni Gentile had replied to the pope's stance in his article 'Dopo due anni', published in *Educazione fascista*, 20 July 1931, and later included in *Origini e dottrina del fascismo*, Rome: Istituto nazionale fascista di cultura, 1934, pp. 98–103.

be given to the oath to the king. Shortly after 8 September, the Roman news-paper wrote:

> Let whoever wants to say that an oath is an act of faith, and thus indestructible, and that we can be released from it only by the person who has received it. This is rheto-ric; and even if it were not, it is preparation for an alibi for a neutrality which tallies well with the cowardice of the king and his fleeing lieutenant.[51]

If it had simply been a question of one oath, the criterion adopted by *Il Popolo* might have had some archaic resonance; but it was an altogether inad-equate way of resolving the conflict between the two oaths, from which neither of the two addressees had the slightest intention of releasing those who had sworn it. It was not the will of the addressee, therefore, but his act of betrayal that again became the liberating element. Obviously, this argument was widely used by the Fascists. A manifesto that they addressed to the soldiers said in fact that the King's treachery had released them from any obligation to be loyal to him.[52] Prophetically almost, an RSI journalist, Ezio Maria Gray, had in 1936 absolved Admiral Francesco Caracciolo from the accusation of treason towards his Bourbon king, Ferdinand IV – an accusation in which strictly monarchical writers were indulging, on the grounds that the king had been the first person to betray the nation.[53] Even the most committed *resistenti* argued that the king's betrayal of the people released the latter from any obligation contracted with the oath, the only difference being that they applied the same criterion also to the betrayal committed, *ab antiquo*, by the Duce.

In answer to the oath requested by the Social Republic, the archbishop of Milan resorted to an argument very much along the same lines as that of Pius XI in 1931. In his *Communicazioni al clero ambrosiano* of 1 May 1944, Cardinal Schuster issued the following decree: 'It is legitimate to take an oath to a "de facto government", responsible for maintaining public order: always provided, however, it is in accordance with one's conscience, with divine and ecclesiastical

---

51 'Il giuramento', article in *Il Messaggero*, 28 September 1943. The same article reads: 'The ally could be betrayed, not played with', almost a revealing lapse in the strenu-ous pursuit of the *Realpolitik* model that the Fascists always engaged in. *Il Messaggero* would become the fully fledged organ of the RSI with the appointment to the editorship of Bruno Spampanato on 14 December 1943. See G. Talamo, *Il Messaggero, un giornale durante il fascismo*, Florence: Le Monnier, 1988, pp. 336 ff.

52 *Fondo RSI*, n. 755 (September 1943).

53 In the commemoration of June 1942, Alfredo De Marsico repeated this argu-ment in less clear-cut terms, defending the Neapolitan admiral, however, against the accusation of oath-breaking brought against him in the entry entitled 'Caracciolo, Francesco, duca' in *Enciclopedia italiana* (VIII, 1930, p. 928) by Francesco Lemmi. On this whole affair see L. Canfora, *La sentenza. Concetto Marchesi e Giovanni Gentile*, Palermo: Sellerio, 1985, pp. 41–5.

law and is within the sphere of its own duty and office.'[54] In fact, the subtle casuistry of the Catholic tradition proved incapable of unravelling so intricate and dramatic a knot. Those with uncompromising religious consciences were the first to shun the preventive absolutions offered them by those who advocated long promises with short waits. Witness this episode recounted by Sergio Cotta:

> I remember the case of an internee friend, who told me that he hadn't joined the RSI exclusively out of loyalty to his oath. He was no monarchist, but a Catholic. A field priest had explained to him that an oath given out of official obligation is not binding on one's conscience, since for the believer it is such only when pronounced when his conscience freely and fully adheres to it. Well, despite this he had not felt released from his oath, out of loyalty not so much to the king and to formal commitment, but to his own personal dignity.[55]

A great Catholic jurist, Costantino Mortati, then appealed to natural law as the only possible basis of the 'ethical imperative' capable of resolving 'conflicts of loyalties'.[56]

Distinctions and mental reservations, suggested not only by Catholics, came to be instruments of general reconciliation. To claim that the state of necessity – that very state in which the sacred character of one's obligation to the oath shone forth – on the one hand released one from the oath previously taken, and on the other hand nullified the new, different one, led, even beyond the intentions of those who argued in this manner, to a final indemnity. Hence, the words of the Catholic intellectual Mario Apollonio: 'the moral validity of the oath, if he who takes it does so against his spontaneous will, is null',[57] and those cruder words of a Roman rag which explained to those who swore the oath to the RSI under

---

54 Quoted in G. Rovero, 'Il clero piemontese nella Resistenza', in Giorgio Agosti, ed., *Aspetti della Resistenza in Piemonte*, Turin: ISRP, 1950, p. 44.

55 S. Cotta, replies to the remarks on his report 'Lineamenti di storia della Resistenza italiana nel periodo dell'occupazione', in *Rassegna del Lazio*, XII, 1965, special number with the proceedings of the national conference on the Resistance held in Rome on 23 and 24 October 1964, pp. 124–5.

56 Here is the passage devoted to 'diritto alla resistenza' ('the right to resist'), which 'tends precisely to confer efficacy to natural right, affirming the pre-eminence of this respect to that emanated by the state. If one starts from the opinion that the observation of state law by citizens, independently of its content, is in itself a moral duty, the affirmation of the right to resist in order to make respect for an ethical imperative prevail gives rise to one of those 'conflicts of loyalty' which has already been mentioned; conflicts that are resolved as circumstances present themselves, according the gravity of the conflict, the intensity of the sentiment that feeds the faith in ethical values, the coercive capacity of legal power' (Mortati, *Istituzioni di diritto pubblico*, vol. I, p. 51).

57 'Perché non giuriamo', in *L'Uomo*, 3, quoted in Bianchi, *I cattolici*, pp. 223–4.

coercion that they nevertheless remained 'soldiers of the king',[58] could lead the last liberal Catholic in Italian history, Arturo Carlo Jemolo, to remark bitterly: 'It was hands off everybody, and it was admitted that even a soldier is all right if he changes sides, when he does so in a state of grave coercion.'[59]

To the out-and-out *resistenti*, who made a clean break with past oaths, these must have appeared in the scathing light in which Proudhon placed them when speaking of the post-1789 French as 'intrepid oath-swearers': 'We are all busy swearing and forswearing: we have made an oath sworn reluctantly and mentally retracted into an act of virtue.'[60]

To those who moved in these circles, the decision to oppose the Social Republic in the name of the oath taken to the king appeared as a decision to respect, but slightly clouded when compared with the oath of those who directly and autonomously chose on the basis of a judgment of value, without feeling the need to support today's act with another act performed yesterday in conditions that had been so much less free. In response to the first 'military' bands of Boves, which, on the initiative of Ignazio Via, were made to repeat the oath 'to the king and his royal successors' (but the very need to reconfirm what was in itself an imperishable act already revealed a flawed certainty), a rigorous lay conscience like that of Dante Livio Bianco remarked: 'But really, how often do even the most genuine reactionaries, albeit unwittingly, not make an exterior show of nobility?'[61]

In using the adjective 'exterior' with such severity, Bianco undoubtedly had two things in mind. The first, which was more starkly moral and existential, consisted of placing in default the determining value of behaviour motivated by criteria of heteronymous loyalty to an institutional, though interiorised, fact. The second, which was political in nature, lay in his denunciation of the continuity of the old Italian state, which could take advantage of that 'exterior nobility'.

Military honour, to which the stances taken by men such as Ignazio Vian or Martini Mauri appeal, was not the most important of Resistance values.[62] It might refer not only to the institution of the Royal Army, but cover a professional

---

58 'Appello ai presentatisi', in *L'Italiano*, 15 March 1944. Another article in the same number, however, presents the RSI enrollments as 'La tratta dei minorenni'.

59 A. C. Jemolo, *Anni di prova*, Vicenza: Neri Pozza, 1969, p. 194.

60 P. G. Proudhon, *De la capacité politique des classes ouvrières*, Paris: Dentu, 1865, p. 250.

61 Bianco, *Guerra partigiana*, pp. 20–1. Of Vian, the animator of the Boves bands, it has been written that faith to the oath, religiously motivated, was 'the main reason for his resistance'. V. E. Giuntella, *Ignazio Vian, il difensore di Boves*, edited by his family, Rome 1954, p. 6.

62 Action Party pamphlet 'Che cos'è il CLN' (*Quaderni dell'Italia libera* 3), p. 6, observed that the words of Badoglio's 8 September proclamation – 'Italian troops will respond to attacks wherever they may come from' – reduced everything to 'a question of military honour'.

dignity and lifestyle chosen at some time or other, and not sufficiently under-mined by the disaster of the war. Honour could be appealed to also in this broad, self-legitimising sense, very widespread in the French Resistance not just in its Gaullist variety, and expressed as follows by one of its exponents: 'Many of our comrades did not calculate whether they were within the law ... they have simply obeyed the command to fight for the honour of our country which is the custodian of such precious values.'[63]

The leading article of an underground paper, De l'Honneur, read as follows: 'Crimes against honour are unforgivable. We could accept the French leaders' imbecility, cowardice, senile vanity, political rancour, powerless pretention. Their daily insults to honour are revolting to a people that disgorges them even before it punishes them.'[64]

Presently we shall see that the appeal to honour was to be one of the most widespread motifs among the Fascists of the Social Republic. Unaware of the gaffe, a clandestine Roman paper – one of the minor ones – thought that it was putting those Fascists in difficulty by comparing them to De Gaulle, who had been called a traitor for not having accepted the capitulation of his country,[65] while Risorgimento Liberale preferred to toss back at the Fascists the theme of honour to be defended.[66]

The problem of the oath would reappear within the partisan movement as a consequence of its very development, producing significantly discordant responses. Those who insisted on the free nature of the choice, which was to be constantly repeated to ensure that the commitment that had determined it did not diminish, inevitably had scant sympathy for the introduction of oath-taking in the partisan formations. An outright rejection can be found in Mario Giovana's explanation of how the oath was not introduced in the Damianis' group, in the province of Cuneo: 'because it is considered an act that goes against the genuinely voluntary, and so morally tenser character of the struggle; besides, the experience of Fascism had demonstrated the vanity of these commitments if they were not accompanied by the genuine adhesion of ideal conscience, for which it is repugnant to resuscitate only its formal aspect.'[67]

But not all Justice and Liberty and Action Party members proved so intransi-gent. In the 'Italia Libera' band (again in the province of Cuneo), the request was

63 The words are R. Cassin's, quoted in H. Michel, Les courants de pensée de la Résistance, Paris: PUF, 1962, p. 49. On de Gaulle's and France Libre's self-legitimisation, see again Michel, 'Gli Alleati e la Resistenza in Europa', in INSMLI, La Resistenza europea e gli Alleati, Milan: Lerici, 1962, p. 27.

64 Valmy, typescipt newspaper of the 'Section parisienne du 15ème arrondisse-ment del la Jeunesse Républicaine', May 1941. Accusations against Vichy of betrayal and dishonour are extremely widespread in the French underground press.

65 La Voce del Popolo, 12–19 February 1944.

66 Article entitled 'Onore', March 1944 (northern edition).

67 Giovana, Storia di una formazione partigiana, p. 63.

made to commit oneself 'with the oath of a man of honour' to fight the Germans and the Fascists, and 'pursue ideals of social justice and democratic liberty'. Any betrayal would be punishable by death. And Dante Livio Bianco recalls dealing out the death sentence 'with a completely clear conscience' to three partisans who were preparing to desert in the event of a roundup.[68] And when the Valle Stura Carlo Rosselli brigade, which had crossed the border into France, had to resist pressures aimed at incorporating them into the 74th (foreigners') battalion of the French regular army, Revelli was to point out, in a memorandum to General Alphonse Juin, that 'the proposal was rejected because it ran counter to honour and the freely taken oath'.[69]

The request for the oath needs to be considered in relation to the militarisation and politicisation of the bands, which will be discussed later. It is no accident that in the Garibaldi brigades, which had a more precise ideological point of reference and were particularly committed to nursing the prospect of being incorporated in the future regular army, the provoked fewer doubts, and was used to reunite the formations in times of crisis.[70] On 9 December 1944, Cino (Cino Moscatelli) and Ciro (Eraldo Gastone), in the name of the group command of Garibaldi assault divisions of Valsesia, Ossola, Cusio and Verbano, almost as if they wished to crown a practice followed in the formations for some time now, were to propose this formula to the general Garibaldi brigade Command: 'I swear to fight by every means in my power, to the point of the supreme sacrifice of my life, for the total destruction of Nazi-Fascism, for a free, democratic and popular Italy, to be loyal to the general Command of the Garibaldi assault brigades and not to lay down my arms or the Garibaldi uniform until ordered.'[71]

In the final words there seems to be a pre-emptive stance in relation to the disarmament that the Allies were ordering; but still clearer is the echo of a Third International–type institutional culture. Bearing a yet greater ideological mark, but still starker, is the oath adopted by the Belluno Garibaldi division: 'I swear never to lay down these arms until the principles of progressivist liberty and democracy are established, and to combat any offensive return of Fascism and of anti-democratic and anti-popular reaction that may attempt to wrest power

---

68 Bianco, *Guerra partigiana*, pp. 56–7. The test of the oath pronounced by Bianco himself is published in G. De Luna, *Formazioni GL*, Instituto nazionale per la storia del movimento di liberazione in Italia, Federazione italiana delle associazoni partigiane, Milan: Franco Angeli, 1985, p. 83, where an editor's note warns that 'the numerous conservative formularies of the oath are identical'.

69 Revelli, *La guerra dei poveri*, p. 478.

70 With this line of argument, for example, the 'Proposta di riorganizzazione', no author, undated, relating to the province of Parma, demanded the oath for every patriot (IG, *BG, Emilia-Romagna*, G.IV3.2)

71 IG, *BG*, 07315.

from the representative organs of the people.'⁷²

For their part, the 'autonomous' and 'military' formations had no objection, in principle, to the oath. Major Martini Mauri had his bands repeat the one customarily used in the Royal Army. As has already been said of the first Boves bands, the soldiers should, rather, have considered reviving the oath to be superfluous, given that they saw themselves as operating, in perfect continuity, within the institutions of the Kingdom of Italy. All the same, they were loath to renounce the symbolic value of the oath and of the cohesive force traditionally attributed to it; nor is it by any means sure whether, coexisting with certainty as to the legitimacy of the institutions, there was not some doubt and anxiety as to their ethical value. At times the autonomous bands proposed high-flown formulae, such as this one of the Brescia Green Flames (Fiamme Verdi):

> I swear to fight until Germans and Fascists have been driven once and for all off the soil of the *patria*, until Italy once again has Unity, Liberty, Dignity. I swear to make no truce with cowards, turncoats, spies, to keep the secret and never to fall short of discipline. Should I ever fail to keep my oath, I invoke upon myself the revenge of my Italian brothers and the justice of God.⁷³

In fact, as has already been suggested, various kinds of cultural elements influenced the practice of the oath. The honour appealed to by the military and, in their way, the aforementioned *giellisti* (of Giustizia e Libertà) is certainly of a different feather from what must have been going through sixteen-year-old Walter Atti's mind when, as he was being led out of the prison of Castelfranco Emilia to be shot, he took his leave with these words: 'They are taking me to the wall because I have sworn loyalty to Stalin.'⁷⁴ Here the category of the oath (and, in implicit opposition to it, of treason) has nothing to do with institutions.

Beyond remaining loyal to or abjuring both old oaths and institutions and new commitments, treason came to acquire meanings that no longer, or not only, regarded the power system, however conceived, but also and above all in reference to the system of human solidarity, of people's deepest affections and convictions. On the local scale, 'a whole dense web of ties' had formerly united the partisans not just to one another but also to their Fascist enemies, and all of a sudden 'each, reciprocally, had become a traitor in the other's eyes.'⁷⁵ 'Traitor' was, in short, becoming a label to pin on those who, like the Fascists, refused to collaborate in the reconstruction of a profound system of human solidarity, and indeed were doing their level best to nip it in the bud.

---

72 Ibid., 09447.
73 The text of the oath constitutes point 14 of a 'Regolamento' ('Regulation') in sixteen paragraphs, conserved in INSMLI, *CVL*, envelope 90, folder 12.
74 Memory of the author's.
75 Battaglia, *Un uomo*, p. 242.

But within the Resistance groups themselves, suspicions of betrayal could reappear, contrasting with the idealised compactness of the group itself, reiterated possibly in the very act of oath-taking – suspicions both of those who seemed to deny that compactness and of other groups. As we shall see, this process appeared most evident in the relations between the Communists and the groups to their left, and found classic expression in Pietro Secchia's article 'Il sinistrismo maschera della Gestapo'.[76] But the Third Internationalists were not the only ones to 'paint their adversaries as traitors'.[77] The temptation to do so could nest within the same fraternal bond uniting the *resistenti* as such. Terror may indeed bud from fraternity, and 'the magic power of the taboo of betrayal' spread 'to those who break it'.[78] This helps account for the great fear of betraying, particularly under torture, felt by many *resistenti*. To save himself from this danger, Luciano Bolis cut his throat in prison, thereby succeeding in severing his vocal cords.[79] To this day a Mauthausen deportee recalls: 'In a certain sense I felt freer because at least I no longer had this anxiety' – namely of betraying.[80] It should be added that the Italian Resistance was less afflicted by such degenerative processes than other Resistance movements, such as the Yugoslav, the Greek and the French. In Italy, affinity between certain basic ethical and existential attitudes and unity as a main political line probably managed better to help each other out on this score.

The *resistenti* frequently felt rage against 'those who have betrayed us'. 'Che Dio maledica chi ci ha tradito/portandoci sul Don e poi è fuggito' ('God curse those who betrayed us/leading us to the Don and then escaping'), ran *Pietà l'è morta*, one of the most intense partisan songs. This was one of the ways in which the revolt of a generation was expressed against the regime brought up under and against the ruling class that had dragged them into war. The accusation feeding this revolt cannot be seen exclusively in terms of betrayal; but betrayal does help explain the label 'traitor' when it is attributed not only to the Fascists, but also, as we have seen, to the king, Badoglio and the Germans themselves.

'Betrayal', 'loyalty', 'honour' and the like frequently figure in the propaganda and journalism of the Social Republic, but also in the letters of the fallen Fascists. For many of them, too, the point of departure seems to be the 'apocalyptic

---

76 The article was published in December 1943 in *La nostra lotta* I: 3, pp. 16–19.

77 These words are Merleau-Ponty's, quoted in F. Fortini, *Dieci inverbi 1947–1957*, Bari: De Donato, 1973, p. 247.

78 The disturbing oath–fraternity–terror route is described in Sartre, *Critica*, vol. II, pp. 90–103 ('traitors, in fact, are by definition a minority' – p. 100). Enzensberger, *Sulla teoria del tradimento*, p. 25, continues the passage on the taboo with these words: 'The history of revolutionary conspiracies shows us traces of this infection everywhere'.

79 L. Bolis, *Il mio granello di sabbia*, Turin: Einaudi, 1946.

80 Testimony by Bruno Vasari, functionary of the EIAR, Action Party. Bravo and Jalla, *La vita offesa*, p. 114.

devastation of 8 September',[81] the reaction to the fact that men 'have flung their consciences in the mud and become mere wrecks'.[82] But 8 September, as we have seen, remained in the minds of the Fascists as a nightmare,[83] a baffling offence. The letter of a sixteen-year-old member of the Republican National Guard, written to his mother, expresses this sense of a catastrophe from which one is trying to emerge, only to become more and more ensnared; and it is worth quoting a passage from it at length, where the memory of 8 September serves to reconfirm the boy's reasons for his choice in response to the emotion provoked by the wounded Italian enemy:

> 'Mamma' was the invocation of the partisan whom I myself had to carry in my arms to the dressing station. During the journey, his sole thought was his mother. Over and over again he asked me if we would have harmed his mother too, and incredulous when I said no, spoke to me to remind me of my own mother, wanted to know about you, asked whether I got mail from you, if I had a photograph of you, since he did not have one of his own and that way, he said, he would see his own mother in you. I wish that scene had been witnessed by all those people who discuss and talk so lightly about 8 September, without having the slightest notion of what disaster and ruin it brought to our *patria*. Because, you see, that partisan, the one I had to fire at – otherwise he would have fired first – spoke the same language as me, said 'mamma' as I am saying it now; he was a brother! Believe me, if at that moment I'd had that @#$%! in my hands and those who helped him, I'd have made mincemeat of them.[84]

But who and what, for the Fascist combatants, should not have been betrayed? One might answer, with a pat formula: above all a past with which they could identify only in terms of mechanical continuity. It was a past partly lived at first hand, partly imagined, as seems to be the case with the very young joining up for the first time, often invoking loyalty to their father, 'Italian and Fascist',[85] and to an Italy 'which you older combatants have entrusted to us, to maintain her prestige and her honour'.[86] Loyalty to the oath itself gained force above all in this context; and there is a whole category of Fascists whose oath to the Duce as an institution was unquestionably influenced by the charismatic figure of the Duce, even when, as things now stood, he came across as the object of at least momentary but always affectionate pity: 'Poor Duce, what a change

---

81 Undated letter to his mother by Vinicio Gotti, soon to be sub-lieutenant of the republican National Guard (*LRSI*, p. 200).

82 Letter to his mother by Umberto Scaramelli, inhabitant of Fiume, participant in the March on Rome, detachment commander of the Black Brigades, who was to be shot by the partisans on 12 February 1945, written 28 October 1944 (*LRSI*, p. 168).

83 See, for example, Pansa, *L'esercito di Salò*, particularly pp. 142 and 144.

84 Letter by Roberto Nanni, 21 January 1945 (*LRSI*, p. 183).

85 Many letters collected in *LRSI* are written in this spirit.

86 Undated letter to his father by Attilio Gianoli, of the X Mas (*LRSI*, p. 140).

has come upon him!' wrote a soldier who had had the honour of sitting at table with him, and who immediately continues: 'The Man he was, robust, authoritarian, is no longer recognisable; what he has suffered in these months must have been indescribable for Him who loved Italy so much and had given everything for her. Now, however, he has gathered … new energy and with his will, which is made of iron, is reconstructing our Italy anew.'[87]

A paratrooper of the Folgore Division sent his mother his medallion of the Duce so that she would always wear it on her breast as a reminder of him.[88] We shall be returning to the myth of Mussolini betrayed. Suffice it to record for the time being that Mussolini really did appear, paradoxically and somewhat grotesquely, as the most betrayed of all Italians. 'Pisenti, we've been betrayed by the Germans and by the Italians', was how the Duce summed it up to his minister of justice, on returning from his visit to the archbishop's palace, when the final catastrophe was well and truly under way.[89]

Among the republican Fascists there were also those intent on demonstrating the illegality of the Badoglio government, as a basis for their conduct,[90] and those, by contrast, who wished to vindicate 'the act of will of which all the soldiers of the Italian Social Republic are justly proud'. These words conclude a passage dedicated to admirals Mascherpa and Campioni, who were shot by the Fascists because they had obeyed orders to oppose the Germans: the two admirals 'could have rebelled but there is no juridical thesis that can demonstrate that they were obliged to do so'.[91]

The right to rebel against the order to betray was invoked by Major Mario Rizzatti to justify his own conduct: 'The regulation of discipline establishes that all orders are to be obeyed save one: which is, if one's superior commands one to betray one's country. Often, speaking to the whole assembled battalion, I would illustrate, with imaginary examples, this duty of non-obedience, hinting that sooner or later it would have to be applied.'[92]

According to the Fascists, those who above all were not to be betrayed were the Germans, 'to whom we are tied by a pact, a war fought together. And this out of loyalty and a sense of honour, independently of any sentimentalism and practical interest.'[93] We are united to the Germans, another letter reads, by 'sworn

---

87 Letter to his mother by Filippo Uecher, 31 December 1943 (*LRSI*, p. 49).

88 Letter by Paolino Leone, born in 1928 in Mogadishu, 18 May 1944 (*LRSI*, p. 114).

89 See E. Amicucci, *I seicento giorni di Mussolini*, Rome: Faro, 1949, p. 317.

90 E. Lodolini, *La illegittimità del governo Badoglio*, Milan: Gastaldi, 1953. Mortati, *Istituzioni di diritto pubblico*, vol. I, p. 87, agrees with Lodolini's thesis.

91 See *Repubblica Sociale Italiana (Storia)*, ed. Centro editoriale nazionale, quoted in R. Perrone Capano, *La Resistenza in Roma*, Naples: Macchiaroli, 1963, vol. I, p. 165.

92 Memorial letter of 18 October 1943.

93 Note written immediately after 8 September 1943 by Attilio Bonvicini, lieutenant of the Decima Mas (*LRSI*, p. 34).

faith, friendship cemented by blood in a hundred engagements'.[94] More dryly, another Fascist wrote: 'I started with an enemy, I must finish against the same enemy'.[95]

A Fascist (later a member of the Movimento Sociale Italiano) gave this dignified testimony:

> I found 'la guerra continua' ['the war must go on'] and 8 September ignoble. Therefore I considered it a question of personal coherence to stay on the losing side, knowing that almost certainly I was following the losing side. But I didn't think it right at such a moment to turn your back on your ally, because it was well and truly an act of betrayal.[96]

An interpreter in the employ of the Germans replied to the internees who complained about the treatment being meted out to them, that it was 'good and what you deserve, given that we had betrayed them'.[97]

As the Fascists saw it, the war dead were not to be betrayed.[98] Here mechanical continuity with the past is particularly evident, especially if compared with the effect that insistence on the same need had on so many other fighting men who joined the Resistance. In the Fascists, this need sometimes assumed the guise of a desire for physical and close-range revenge. 'I cannot follow those who have killed a brother whom I must avenge at all costs',[99] one letter reads; and another: 'For what reason did I join up? Because I have a brother asking to be avenged, who was killed by our enemies, by our dear "Liberators".'[100] At times, Fascist fidelity to the war even transcends fidelity to the dead. It might be a question of a 'perennial and metaphysical war', or a war which is 'like a disease'.[101] In these 'combatants of all wars', human solidarity appears to have stiffened into virile camaraderie.

---

94 Letter by Roberto Salvi, of a mobile battalion, to his father 'old soldier of the Carso and the Piave' (*LRSI*, p. 155).

95 Francesco Attimonelli's reply to some of his fellow soldiers, undated (*LRSI*, p. 104).

96 Testimony by Canzio Eupizi, in Portelli, *Biografia di una città*, p. 263.

97 Memoir by Vincenzo Fenudi, carabinieri marshal, non-collaborationist, on the time he spent in the disinfestation bath of Vorlagen (my thanks to his son Mariano for allowing me to read it).

98 Invocation to the war dead are frequent in *LRSI*.

99 Enzo Braschi, airforce lieutenant, to his mother, 21 September 1943 (*LRSI*, p. 39).

100 Francesco Nepoti, born in 1926, of the 'Volontari della Morte' battalion, to the voluntary recruitment and enlistment centre of Bologna, 4 March 1944 (*LRSI*, p. 39).

101 This expression comes from a letter sent to me on 26 September 1986 by Franco Manni about his father's experience. (I shall make use of his father's unpublished memoirs below. My thanks to his son for having allowed me to read them.) The second expression is attributed by Mazzantini, *A cercar la bella morte*, p. 221, to a sergeant who had fought in Africa, Spain and Russia.

At other times the Fascists seem to be banging their heads against the wall, dismayed and furious at what appeared to be a 'war fought in vain … a war of few, betrayed by many [and which all the same] is my whole life'.[102] Indeed, rife among the Fascist combatants too was the sensation of being victims of a profound and obscure swindle, of which the wicked 8 September was but a partial manifestation. They saw the traitor not in Fascism but in those who had betrayed Fascism, all the worse if the latter were Fascists and, as such, unpardonable: 'Betrayed ideas cannot welcome back the traitors with open arms.'[103]

These Fascists thought that the Social Republic was the last opportunity to rediscover the purity that had been sullied by the Fascism of the *ventennio*. A man who had asked to enlist in the republican army wrote from Germany that he wanted to fight 'for the *patria* and the idea', and that he was certain he would find 'real men', who were not 'used only to cheering, flag-waving, uniforms of every ilk, as before, and to which the men of the past regime had accustomed us, but men who said little, but who were ready to take up arms to wash away the dishonour with which we have been stained by the traitors who have sold themselves to the enemy'.[104] 'We are few but healthy', says another letter explaining the reasons for joining the republican Fascist party;[105] and a naval lieutenant declared that 'all in all the party has gained' by ridding itself 'of the dead wood of opportunists'.[106]

Carlo Emanuele Basile, the Genoese provincial chief, boasted to the SS Command that 'the shame of betrayal can only be washed out in the blood of a well-trained minority who show that not all Italians are servile in spirit'.[107] In a private letter, a republican National Guard militiaman rejoiced at the idea of

---

102 See the note quoted in Bonvicini, *LSRI*, 34. On 10 October 1944, in a letter to a friend, Bonvicini was to express himself in a way that sounded almost like Alfieri: 'I believe and I suffer, I feel – I want and I must' (*LRSI*, p. 35).

103 Unsigned article, 'Traditori arrestati e deferiti ai Tribunali Speciali', in *La Stampa*, 20 October 1944, quoted in G. Gabrielli, 'La stampa di Salò e il problema dell'epurazione', in P. P. Poggio, ed., *La repubblica sociale italiana 1943–45*, Conference Proceedings, Brescia, 4–5 October 1985, *Annali della Fondazione Micheletti* 2 (1986), Brescia, p. 170.

104 Letter to his wife by Emanuele De Lorenzo, born in 1909, December 1943 (*LRSI*, p. 139). The fact that it came from Germany accentuates, rather than diminishes, the significance of this testimony, which is eager to speak in terms of the 'past regime'. De Lorenzo was to die fighting against the partisans in Val di Taro with the Monterosa. His contempt for 'uniforms of every shape and kind' sounds pathetic, given that he was to find a much vaster assortment in the RSI.

105 Letter to a friend, November 1943, by Attilio Gianoli, of the X Mas (*LRSI*, p. 40).

106 Dionisio Biondi's declaration, quoted in Perrone Capano, *La Resistenza in Roma*, p. 166.

107 Quoted in A. Gibelli and M. Ilardi, 'Lotte operaie: Genova', in *Operai e contadini*, p. 137.

taking revenge on the traitors with fire and the sword.[108] Major Mario Carità refused to allow a condemned man to be shot in the breast rather than the back: 'No, you are a traitor, you have fought against your country in the ranks of the red militias, and must die as traitors die.'[109] On the same occasion, the brother, also a Fascist officer, of Lieutenant Colonel Gobbi, for whose killing there was a reprisal, abused the victims thus: 'Cowards, let them thank God they died in daylight; my brother was killed last night treacherously, at the street corner on his way home after doing his duty.'[110] Here things seem to come full circle: traitors can only strike 'treacherously'.

Even those who almost boast about pitching Italy – warring Italy – against Fascism seem to be convinced of the need to take revenge on traitors: 'I am a twenty-one-year-old son of Italy. I belong neither to Graziani nor to Badoglio but I am Italian: and I am following the path that will save the honour of Italy.'[111]

But among the republican Fascists there were those who felt the need to reject the accusation that it was they who were the traitors. A republican National Guard militiaman wrote to his children that their father 'has been neither a coward nor a traitor but one of the few who have kept an oath that they swore, without ever having had anything in compensation.'[112] And even a 'Muti' was to implore: 'Look at me, mamma, I'm your son, your Dante: I haven't sold myself, I'm not a turncoat, I'm not a traitor. I'm your son.'[113]

But since this book has referred constantly, though at times only implicitly, to the war waged from 10 June 1940 to 8 September 1943, we would do well, at this point, to take a direct look at that period.

108 'Esame della corrispondenza censurata al 30 giugno 1944' (ACS, SPD, CR, RSI, envelope 9, folder 3).

109 G. B. A., 'Fucilazioni alle Cascine', in Bilenchi, Cronache degli anni neri, p. 70.

110 Ibid., pp. 70–1. Before the firing squad, the five men who were shot had sung 'The Internationale'.

111 'Spiritual testimony' of Giampiero Civati, killed 5 December 1944 (LRSI, p. 180).

112 Letter by Elio Busi, born 1902, of 25 October 1944 (LRSI, p. 216). A 'Multi' is a member of the Fascist paramilitary Black Brigade.

113 Letter to his mother by the seventeen-year-old Dante Natta, 10 January 1945 (LRSI, p. 182).

CHAPTER 2

The Legacy of the Fascist War

1. WISHING FOR AND FEARING DEFEAT

The 'party of the foreigner' has never been viewed kindly, especially when a country is at war. One of anti-Fascism's hardest tasks was to shake off this defamatory judgment, whereby anyone is to be regarded as a traitor if he sees the realisation of his principles as depending on the defeat of his country. It has been justly observed that 'from an ethical point of view, paradoxically, "treason" is less tolerable in a democratic society, which admits diversified political positions, than in a totalitarian state, where it is often the only possible form of opposition'.[1]

This was the pass into which Fascism drove many Italians when, on 10 June 1940, it declared war on France and Great Britain. This was the pass which as early as November 1941 induced a group of young Italians to write: 'We are reduced to attempting by whatever means to flee what at one time we actually regarded as our duties ... to despair of Italy and the Italians, to think in terms of help from outside as the only kind which can liberate us from tyranny'.[2] The situation that had come about was similar to that sketched in 1858 by Fustel de Coulanges in his remarks on Polybius's defection to the Romans: 'That an honest citizen, devoted to his country, should rejoice at the success of the public enemy, that this preference is not treason, but almost a form of patriotism is a fact worthy of attention.'[3] Worthy of attention, certainly, are utterances made on different occasions, like that of the student Emanuele Artom: 'It is in Italy's interest to be defeated'; or another one, overheard in an *osteria*: 'We'd do better to lose the war, that way we'll be able to liberate ourselves from Fascism'; or again that of an intellectual, Pietro Chiodi: 'He who is not free has no *patria*, he who has no *patria* has no military duties'.[4] Some time earlier, an intelligent policeman, Arturo Bocchini, or it might have been Carmine Senise, had put his finger

---

1 T. Todorov , 'La tolleranza e l'intollerabile', in P. C. Bori, ed., *L'intolleranza: uguali e diversi nella storia*, Bologna: Il Mulino, 1986, p. 103.

2 Manifesto 'Agli Italiani', which begins: 'Italiani, cosa sarà di noi?' ('Italians, what will become of us?', in *Bolletino Popolo e Libertà*, June 1943).

3 *Polybe: ou, la Grèce conquise par les Romains*, Paris, 1858, p. 2.

4 Artom, *Diari*, p. 61 (July 31, 1953); police report, relating to Terni, 1943, quoted in Portelli, *Biografia di una città*, p. 243; Chiodi, *Banditi*, p. 7 (10 January 1941).

on the problem: 'One can confidently state that in Italy the only ones who have good reason for desiring the war are the anti-Fascists, because only with the war will they be able to rid themselves of the hated regime.'[5]

. It was in fact since 1789, according to Bloch, that 'Rulers, in a war, place their regime at risk as much as they do the country as a whole':[6]

> Fascism – a common lot of many nationalist movements – had ended up severing and wearing out even the most tenacious fibres of nationalism ... and proposing to the nation the conservation or failure to conserve Fascism as what was truly and decisively at stake in the struggle (whence ... the invincible repugnance for a victory thus conditioned and, given the prevailing revolutionary immaturity, the withdrawal into a sluggish, resigned waiting on events with marked sympathy for the so-called enemy forces and an aversion for the so-called allies, which grew, the more likely and then certain their inferiority appeared).[7]

Of this situation, which saw so many Italians living the first phase of the Second World War in an atmosphere ranging from hope in a defeat to the anxiety which that prospect provoked, by way of various forms of resignation – in the absence to this day of a complete historiographic reconstruction of this situation, two components above all will be traced: the anti-Fascists and the combatants. One of the premises of the encounter in the Resistance between veteran anti-Fascism and some of the new generation who had grown up under Fascism was the positions the respective parties took towards the war.

The positions taken by the various anti-Fascist currents towards Europe's headlong descent into war are well enough known. Likewise for the first phase of the war, which was the most tormented from an ideological point of view, until the attack on the USSR appeared to simplify things. The agony of Italian anti-Fascism needs to be seen in the context of the difficult re-conversion of the European left from pacifism, felt almost as a point of honour after the 1914 catastrophe, to the wholehearted espousal of the war against Nazi Germany and Fascist Italy. Keep the peace or fight against fascism? was the problem that the European left posed itself with increasing apprehension in the second half of the 1930s; and the French trade unionist who put the problem in the above terms answered his question with contradictory baldness: 'We want peace even if this consolidates the different Fascisms. And we know that war would reinforce all

---

5 See C. Senise, *Quando ero capo della polizia, 1940–1943*, Rome: Ruffolo, 1946, p. 38. Senise writes that he inserted the sentence in a report prepared by Bocchini for Mussolini.

6 Quoted in Michel, *Les courants*, p. 150.

7 C. Botti (C. Dionisotti), 'Giovanni Gentile', in *Nuovi Quaderni di Giustizia e Libertà*, vol. I (May–June 1944), p. 94, republished under the title 'La storia che giudica', in *L'Indice dei libri del mese* II: 9 (November 1985), pp. 23–6.

Fascisms, ours included.'[8] 'From pacifism to fascism, what deception!', what 'tragic sophistry!', was, conversely, how a Resistance newspaper responded.[9] The British Labour Party was for a long time held back by fear that a rearmament policy would reinforce the Tories.[10] But an American intellectual was keen to point out, after the war in Spain, that neutrality in the sense of non-belligerence did not mean 'treating the aggressor and his victim alike'.[11]

For the Italian anti-Fascists, who spoke in the name of a nation that already had Fascism in power, the problem had been particularly dramatic. It is to Carlo Rosselli's credit that he put things with precocious lucidity, immediately after Hitler came to power, in his famous article 'La guerra che torna'. 'The struggle between Fascism and anti-Fascism,' wrote Rosselli, 'is heading for the judgment of God … From this moment Mussolini can launch his anathema against the traitors of the Fascist *patria*.'[12]

A fair idea of the difficulty a movement of long-standing pacifist traditions had in following the Giustizia e Libertà leader on a path thought to be too brazen is given by Pietro Nenni's response. Faithful to the position he assumed in July 1930, at the congress of socialist unity, against the hypothesis of war as a means of defeating Fascism,[13] Nenni wrote that an anti-Fascist preventive war would acquire the character of an 'imperialist intervention, dictated by imperialist considerations', whereas 'revolutionary duty is to say no to war, to deny it in whatever form it should present itself, whether under the wing of revolutionary war or war of liberty'.[14] These words certainly bespeak the anti-warmongering

---

8 See an article bearing that title by A. Lavenir, secretary of the teachers' union of the department of Rodano, published in *L'École Libératrice* of 2 April 1938, and quoted in F. Di Palma, 'Il caso dei maestri in Francia tra fronte popolare e moti antirepubblicani', in *Rivista di storia contemporanea* XV (1986), p. 269.

9 *La Pensée française. Organe des intellectuels du Front National du Nord e du Pas-de-Calais*, April–May 1944. An article dedicated to *Herr Déat*, 'Le Père Duchesne', September 1943, heavily criticised the passage from 'objection de conscience' to 'abjection de conscience'.

10 I recommend everyone read G. D. H. Cole, *A History of Socialist Thought*, vol. V, *Socialism and Fascism (1931–1939)*, London: Macmillan, 1960, p. 79ff. See also, in general, A. Salsano, ed., *Antologia del pensiero socialista*, vol. V, *Socialismo e fascismo*, Bari: Laterza 1983, part II, Chapter 5, 'L'IOS di fronte al fascismo e alla guerra'.

11 Emily Balch, cited in W. E. Leuchtenburg, *Franklin D. Roosevelt and the New Deal, 1932–1940*, New York: Harper & Row, 1963, p. 211.

12 Published in November 1933 in *Quaderni di Giustizia e Libertà*, and later in C. Rosselli, *Scritti dall'esilio*, vol. I, *Giustizia e Libertà e la concentrazione antifascista (1929–1934)*, ed. C. Casucci, Turin: Einaudi 1988, pp. 250–8.

13 See G. Arfé, 'La politica del gruppo dirigente socialista nell'esilio', in Istituto Socialista di Studi Storici, *L'emigrazione socialista nella lotta contro il fascismo (1926–1939)*, Florence: Sanzoni 1982, p. 20. Arfé believes that the way indicated by Rosselli was 'for the socialists, and not without good reason, too risky' (p. 22).

14 Leading article, 'Contro l'illusione della guerra rivoluzionaria e per la libertà', in

passion of a former interventionist, which is what Nenni had been, and which induced him to write, in the article just cited, that 'all the illusions, all the errors of 1914–15, are returning'. But the whole of the PSI, in its oscillations and in its contradictions, appeared in those years to be an interesting laboratory of the problems of peace and war, closely interwoven with those of the autonomy to be salvaged for socialism and anti-Fascism in the increasingly acute conflict between the great powers.[15] Even after the unity-of-action pact with the Communists, viewed by the latter primarily as a projection of the drawing together of the USSR and Popular Front France, the autonomist group of the PSI, whose foremost exponent was Giuseppe Emanuele Modigliani, had inserted in the closing motion of the congress held in Paris in June 1937 an appeal to the need for the workers' and socialist movement not to identify 'at all costs with a bloc of anti-Fascist states'.[16]

Distrust of the USSR and the memory of Zimmerwald converged in this position, which, after the German–Soviet pact and the outbreak of the war, came to sound uncannily like the Communist theses about the Second World War as an imperialist war. Indeed, between September 1939 and June 1941 there runs the most tormented phase of the positions of the Italian anti-Fascists concerning the war. The German–Soviet pact had reshuffled all the cards that had been laboriously assembled in the name of international anti-Fascism. Staying out of the war, however it was argued, went against another long-standing tradition – the defence of democracy, bourgeois though it might be. This was, in fact, felt particularly strongly by those, like Nenni, who were deeply nurtured by post-Jacobin political culture. On 31 August 1939 *Nuovo Avanti!* lost no time in headlining its front page 'Gli Italiani sono al fianco della Francia' ('The Italians are at France's side'); and, on the third page, hosting an article by Nenni, 'Il

---

Avanti!, Zurich, 2 December 1933. Foa referred to this very article when, in a projected interview with Nenni that never took place (1975), he asked Nenni this question: 'What weight did a pacifism in principle carry in socialism and in the left in general?' See V. Foa, 'Centoquarantacinque domande a Pietro Nenni', in *Per una storia del movimento operaio*, p. 199. Nenni's article and Rosselli's article in the form of a letter to *Avanti!* of 30 December 1933 can now be read in Rosselli, *Scritti dall'esilio*, pp. 312–16, 259–64. Nenni was simply repeating the positions against the war that he had taken in articles that had previously appeared in *Avanti!*: 'Amsterdam e la guerra rivoluzionaria' (10 September 1932); 'Risposta a tre quesiti' (17 September 1932); ' Condannare la guerra in sé e per sé' (24 September 1932); 'Né guerra rivoluzionaria né guerra per la libertà' (4 March 1933). The articles can now be read in P. Nenni, *La battaglia contro il fascismo*, ed. D. Zucaro, Milan: Mursia 1977, pp. 327–43.

15 See S. Colarizi's recapitulatory article, 'La guerra e i partiti antifascisti', in Pacetti, Papini and Sarcinelli, *La cultura della pace*, pp. 327–43.

16 See A. Landuyt, 'Un tentativo di rinnovamento del socialimo italiano: Silone e il Centro estero di Zurigo', in Istituto Socialista di Studi Storici, *L'emigrazione*, pp. 75–6. The motion concluded with an appeal to the United States of Europe.

voltafaccia della politica sovietica' ('The about-turn of Soviet policy').[17] But the very fact of coming out in favour of the bourgeois democracies at war with Hitler made the PSI all the more eager to stress its own specificity, from a socialist and class point of view, regarding the war. For example, a carefully measured-out dosage of weights and counterweights characterised Nenni's address to the party leadership on 15 December 1939.

Given the way things stand – he said plainly – the progress of Humanity depends above all on the defeat of Fascism. The task of the proletariat is therefore to support, with all the creative energy of which it is capable, the war for the overthrow of Hitler and the Fascist political system; and he added: 'The parallelism of aims between the proletariat, which wants to rid humanity of Fascism, and the bourgeois democracies that are at war with the Third Reich, does not influence the fundamental problems of political direction and the aims of the war ... Neither defeatism, therefore, nor holy union.'

This conclusion of Nenni's was formulated with one eye on Daladier's government and the other on the watchword 'neither adhere nor sabotage' of 1915–18. But, when it came to Italy, Nenni was in no doubt. If Mussolini dragged it into the conflict, one's duty would be to 'sabotage the Fascist war and transform it into the civil war of workers against their oppressors'. It is particularly significant that Nenni regarded this Leninist invitation of his as valid even if Mussolini, enlisted in extremis by France and England 'among the crusaders of democracy', were to enter the war 'in a possible anti-Bolshevik league'.[18]

---

17 See G. Arfé, *Storia dell'Avanti! 1926–1940*, Milan–Rome: Edizioni Avanti! 1958, p. 212. Nenni's article can be read in Nenni, *La battaglia socialista contro il fascismo*, pp. 537–43. But in a figure like Modigliani, pacifism and neutralism were so deeply rooted as to inspire his conduct even after the outbreak of war. See G. Arfé, 'Modigliani Giuseppe Emanuele', in F. Andeucci and T. Detti, eds, *Il Movimento operaio italiano. Dizionario biografico 1853–1943*, vol. III, Rome: Riuniti 1977, pp. 491–503.

18 The text of Nenni's then unpublished report (following his resignation as party secretary with an announcement that appeared in the 7 September issue of *Nuovo Avanti!*) can be found in the Tasca archive, and was published as S. Merli, 'La ricostruzione del movimento socialista in Italia e la lotta contro il fascismo dal 1934 alla seconda guerra mondiale', in *Annali dell'Istituto Giangiacomo Feltrinelli* V (1962), pp. 836–44. The essay was republished, without the documents, in S. Merli, *Fronte antifascista e politica di classe. Socialisti e comunisti in Italia, 1923–1939*, Bari: De Donato 1962, pp. 3–74. From a copy, now in ACS, sent by the Fascist representative from Paris to the Ministry of the Interior, and republished in S. Colarizi, ed., *L'Italia antifascista dal 1922 al 1940. La lotta dei protagonisti*, Bari: Laterza 1976, pp. 154–68. Colarizi notes that Nenni's report was rejected by six votes to two. See also, in general, Leonardo Rapone's paper, 'Guerra e politica. L'emigrazione antifascista agli inizi della seconda guerra mondiale', at the conference 'L'Italia in guerra 1940–43', held at the Fondazione Micheletti of Brescia from 27 to 30 September 1989.

When the USSR was carried completely over into the anti-Nazi camp by the German attack on Russia, the Socialists – above all those who had sponsored the unity-of-action pact – heaved a veritable sigh of relief. But so profound had been the trauma that, as late as 1 May 1944, a PSIUP executive declaration said that, if there had been as strong a Communist party in England as there was in France, that would have favoured Hitler's victory.[19] In the Socialist camp, in any case, there were still those – from Ignazio Silone to Lelio Basso – who were particularly intent on Socialist anti-Fascism's remaining autonomous from the policy of the great powers, including the USSR.[20]

As for the relationship with the desire for Fascist Italy's defeat, the prospect of a third, autonomous anti-Fascist way was undoubtedly a sort of preventive answer to the thesis of the 'foreigner's party', just as the never-to-be-realised creation of a corps of Italian volunteers to fight alongside the Allies would have been.[21] On the eve of the war, Eugenio Curiel, a young Socialist active within the party, had put his finger clearly on the problem.[22] Speaking in the name of 'our Milanese comrades and others', Curiel had declared himself in favour of the creation, in France, of an Italian legion which 'must represent the Italian people in this oncoming war'. With equal clarity, Curiel had affirmed: 'We do not want tomorrow's government to be the government of defeat, the Weimar government', and had therefore argued that one needed to have the courage to assume the role, within Italy, of *disfattista* (defeatist), even if 'tomorrow a handful of scoundrels, in the pay of some residual Fascist, might yell the same old insults at us'. These words can be read as the invitation by a member of the new anti-

19 The document was published by the Rome edition of *Avanti!*, 6 May 1944, under the title 'L'esecutivo del partito definisce la posizione socialista di fronte al nuovo Governo Badoglio ed ai problemi dell' unità d'azione e della unità antifascista'. The Communists replied severely with an article, 'Il partito socialista, il governo nazionale democratico di guerra e il problema dell'unità' in *La nostra lotta* II: 10 (June 1944), pp. 6–9.

20 For Silone, see his 'Tesi del Terzo Fronte', adopted by the Centro Estero (Foreign Center) of the PSI in Zurich, and published in *L'Avvenire dei lavoratori*, 1 August 1944. See Landuyt, *Un tentativo di rinnovamento*, pp. 90–5. For Basso see the whole affair, which is fairly well known, of the MUP and of *Bandiera Rossa*. See in particular M. Salvati, 'Il Psiup Alta Italia nelle carte dell'archivio Basso (1943–1945)', in *Il Movimento di liberazione in Italia*, XXIV: 109 (October–December 1972), pp. 61–88, and Enzo Collotti, ed., *Ripensare il socialismo: la ricerca di Lelio Basso*, Milan: Mazzotta 1988.

21 For the unsuccessful attempts by the Socialists, the Republicans, GL, the Lega Italiana dei Diritti dell'Uomo, and the Unione Popolare immediately after the declaration of war, to create the legion, see Artè, *Storia dell'Avanti!*, p. 218. For the no less fortunate successive attempts, see Emilio Lussu's note, 'Il problema della legione', undated, *Archivi di Giustizia e Libertà. 1915–1945*, inventory edited by C. Casucci, Rome: Publications of the Archivi di Stato, 1968, p. 59; and regarding Randolfo Pacciardi's initiatives, A. Baldini and P. Palma, ed., *Gli antifascisti italiani in America. 1942–1944*, Preface by R. De Felice, Florence: Le Monnier, 1990.

22 Letter to Giuseppe Faravelli, 10 May 1939, in Merli *La ricostruzione*, pp. 831–4.

Fascist generation to a representative of the old guard to profit from the experience of the post–First World War period without allowing himself to be paralysed by it, indeed proudly assuming that epithet *disfattista*, which still troubled many veterans, and legitimising it by participating in the war on the just side.

The Weimar nightmare would continue to weigh heavily on the moderate anti-Fascists, who had not swept it away with Curiel's moral intransigence. From the United States Luigi Sturzo would appear concerned that those 'who will take up the government will be subjected (as happened with the Weimar democrats in Germany) to all the effects of the mutilation and humiliation that the Allies will cause to Italy'.[23] During Badoglio's forty-five days, with an suffocating calculation of costs and benefits, Alcide De Gasperi maintained, in the same spirit, that of the two questions to settle – Mussolini's defeat and the Armistice – while the former, which was active, had already been achieved to the advantage of those who had arranged it, in the case of the latter, which was passive, and thus liable to create 'doleful responsibilities for its negotiators', it was better not to get involved.[24] Unfettered by ties of caution, tradition and obedience, Justice and Liberty and the Action Party were the anti-Fascist groups which, true to the model provided by Rosselli in 1933, unrepentantly and with proud clarity, included, in the passage from pacifism to active intervention against Fascism, the prospect of Italy's defeat. In 1935 Francesco Fancello wrote from prison, with reference to Germany (though what he said could clearly be extended to Italy): 'Only in very exceptional cases may the defeat of one's own country appear a price justified by forecasts of subsequent recoveries.'[25] Nazism and Fascism had created precisely one of those exceptional cases in which the force of arms, even when it appeared triumphant, could only be opposed by faith in principles. Faced with the catastrophe of France, Vittorio Foa wrote to his parents from Regina Coeli prison: 'I know very well that even when in Europe all the institutions in which we found our faith in a tolerable future have collapsed, nothing will be lost again if those institutions remain alive in the consciences of a few thousand Europeans; and against this spiritual tension the German tank divisions have scant influence.'[26]

This spiritual tension was re-evoked by Altiero Spinelli when, shortly before

---

23   L. Sturzo, 'Italy after Mussolini', *Foreign Affairs*, April 1943. For the Weimar syndrome and anti-Fascism's merits for having avoided it, see C. Casucci, 'La guerra di Carlo Rosselli', in *Libera Stampa* (Lugano), 21 June 1990.

24   See I. Bonomi, *Diario di un anno (2 giugno 1943–10 giugno 1944)*, Milan: Garzanti, 1947, p. 35.

25   Letter to his mother, 2 August 1935, in *Lettere di antifascisti dal carcere e dal confino*, ed. L. Cortesi, Rome: Riuniti, 1962, p. 123.

26   Letter of 19 May 1940, not censored as a mark of respect for its non-belligerence. My thanks to Foa for drawing my attention to it.

his death, he testified that in 1940 he and those like him wished for the defeat of Italy, 'even if 100 percent of the Italians were of Italian origin'.[27]

Little more than one month after 8 September, *La Libertà*, the Tuscan organ of the Action Party, wrote:

> Not for a single instant did we hesitate to wish for the defeat of our country, infested by Fascism, for the triumph of the ideal of justice and liberty ... None of this cost us any effort because we were well aware of what was at stake. But this should be taken as being to our credit, because a man does not reach the point of desiring the ruin of all that is immediately closest to him, for the victory of an idea, without having thought at length, meditated sorrowfully, and without encountering the hostility and contempt of his fellow countrymen.

By now on the eve of its final dissolution, the northern edition of *L'Italia Libera* would speak of the 'military defeat suffered in the Fascist war' as a 'defeat that we have wished for and considered rightly as a victory'.[28] The anti-Fascist party which suffered the greatest travail between September 1939 and June 1941 was certainly the Communist Party.[29] But it was a travail frozen by loyalty to the USSR, a drama that involved the consciences of the militants a good deal more than was shown in the official party line. Thus Spinelli describes the Communists imprisoned at Ventotene, on hearing about the signing of the German–Soviet pact, as follows:

> Their whole world trembled fearfully but, like Tertullian, they said *credo quia absurdum*, closed ranks, retreated into themselves, waited, and were rewarded, when the USSR, attacked by Hitler, became the ally of the democracies and freed their souls, imprinting theological authorisation on their profound desire to fight in the front rank and with fervour in the resistance.[30]

In fact, the Communists had never associated the struggle against Fascism with the prospect of a war that would necessarily involve the USSR. In August

---

27 Spinelli polemicised against those who, during the Falklands War, supported the cause of the Argentinian generals on the basis of the argument that about 50 percent of the population of Argentina is of Italian origin (Vittorio Foa's testimony to the author).

28 Articles entitled, respectively, 'Al popolo italiano, agli amici, ai nemici' and 'Nostalgie colonialistiche', in *La Libertà*, 27 October 1943, and *L'Italia Libera*, 18 January 1945.

29 For an account of events during that two-year period see P. Spriano, *Storia del Partito comunista italiano*, vol. IV, *La fine del fascismo. Dalla riscossa operaia alla lotta armata*, Turin: Einaudi, 1973. See also, in vol. III, *I fronti popolari, Stalin, la guerra*, Turin: Einaudi 1970, Chapter XVIII, 'I comunisti e la guerra'.

30 A. Spinelli, *Io Ulisse. Come ho tentato di diventare saggio*, Bologna: Il Mulino 1984, p. 281.

1935, in his report to the 7th Congress of the International, Togliatti had criticised the workers 'who think, who have come to the point of thinking, that only war will be able to give their class the chance of taking up the revolutionary struggle again.'[31] The defence of peace against the new imperialist war beating at the gates, anti-Fascism, the cause of socialism, seemed firmly united, under the guarantee of the USSR, according to the watchword 'struggle against the imperialist war, for peace, for the defence of the Soviet Union' (which is how Togliatti concluded his report to the 7th Congress). The August 1939 pact put paid to these convergences, and peace now came to materialise in the extraneousness of the USSR to the second imperialist war. When Germany attacked the USSR, the German Communist Party was to accuse Hitler of having treacherously violated the pact of friendship between the two peoples.[32]

As we know, it was in France that the 'second imperialist war' thesis had its most tragic consequences. At first the Communists voted for the claims of war, but then immediately came to toe the Comintern line. Togliatti noted with satisfaction 'the French Communists' courageous and sincere criticism' of their initial error of forgetting that 'today the only just policy for the working class and the Communist party is the courageous struggle against the imperialist war, for peace', and then reiterated his denunciation of the disorientation and opportunism generated by those who made 'a sort of sentimental distinction between the two belligerent imperialist blocs'.[33] The watchword became, 'Down with the imperialist war';[34] or again, 'Between Hitler's Germany and capitalist England, the workers choose the French Soviet Republic'.[35] Not that the party line expressed the conscience of the militants without there being residual divergences. In fact, 'What was true for the party was far less so for the individual.'[36]

But we also need to evaluate the weight of the memory, alive not just in France, of the 'Socialist' betrayal of 1914. Again, it was Togliatti who appealed to this, accusing the Socialists of being, as in 1914–18, 'in the direct service of

---

31 The report, entitled 'La preparazione di una nuova guerrra mondiale da parte degli imperialisti e i compiti dell'Internazionale comunista', is in P. Togliatti, *Opere*, vol. III: 2, ed. E. Ragionieri, Rome: Riuniti, 1973, pp. 730–805 (the passage quoted is on p. 765).

32 See the appeal of 24 June 1941 in F. Etnasi, *La Resistenza in Europa*, Rome: Grafica Editoriale, 1970, 1, pp. 275–8. Compare the identical position assumed by the Bulgarian Workers' Party (pp. 87–9).

33 See the 'Lettere di Spartaco', no. 9 of 1–10 March and no. 11 of 1–15 April 1940. Togliatti, *Opere*, vol. IV: 2, pp. 21–3, 26–31. In the second article a passage from Dimitrov is quoted against 'the legend of the reputed anti-Fascist character of the war'.

34 This is the title of a leading article (March 1940) of *Le Réveil des cochers-chauffeurs du Comité pour l'idependance et l'unité des syndicats* (cyclostyled).

35 Motto of *La Bretagne*, cited in Michel, *Les courants*, p. 570.

36 J. J. Becker, 'L'Union Sacrée: l'exception qui confirme la règle?', in *Vingtième Siècle* vol. 5 (January–March 1985), p. 120.

the imperialist, reactionary and warmongering bourgeoisie'.[37] That memory was also recalled by sworn enemies of the Stalinists, such as the Trotskyists and anarchists, convinced in their turn that what was afoot was a new imperialist war.[38] Defeat and German occupation made the viability of this position still more arduous for the French Communists. Alongside the watchword, 'Neither Berlin, nor London,' there appeared the afterword 'nor Vichy';[39] but the fundamental theme remained the peace – 'Only the communists fight against the war!' – to impose on the creators of the imperialist conflict, whom 'the traitors of 1940' had befriended.[40] As for Italy, a country occupied by the French from time immemorial, if on the one hand it was still a tricky business squaring the circle, especially after her entry into the war, on the other hand anti-Fascism had become too intrinsic a part of the Communist movement not to remain, in one form or another, in the foreground of party policy. The PCI thus forced itself to keep together the theoretically non-contradictory objectives of 'revolutionary *disfattismo*' and the overthrow of Fascism.[41] The prestige of the USSR, which had kept out of the imperialist bloodbath, might even prove to grow from this. In a leaflet, confiscated in Trieste by the *carabinieri* on 11 June 1940, the war that had just been declared was defined as being 'like all others, that is serving the interests of the rich and bringing starvation and death to the poor'; and 'Down with the imperialist war, Down with Churchill and Hitler' could be seen scribbled on several walls, flanked however by a number of pro-English ones as well.[42] This coupling, whether occasional or polemical, symbolised a real contradiction in working-class anti-Fascism, to be dissolved or at least placated with the changed nature of the conflict that was reckoned to have derived from it.[43] In fact, as we

37 'Chi è Spartaco', in *Lettere di Spartaco*, 1–10 March 1940 (Togliatti, *Opere*, vol. IV: 2, p. 13).

38 For the Trotskyists, see for example the 'Lettre à un camarade communiste', in *La Vérité. Organe bolchevik-léniniste*, 15 September 1940 (there are notable assonances between Stalinists and Trotskyists in this period, even if unwelcome on both parts). For the anarchists see *Il Martello*, edited by Carlo Tresca in the United States, quoted in L. Valentini, University of Pisa degree thesis.

39 For the former, see for example a document of the 'Section communiste Michelin', published in *Bibendum. Organe de défense des ouvriers et ouvrières*, November 1940; for the integration, *L'Avant-Garde, édité par la Fédération des jeunesses de France* (Montpellier), 1 June 1941 (cyclostyled).

40 See 'L' Appel de Maurice Thorez et Jacques Duclos', in H. Noguères, *Histoire de la Résistance en France de 1940 à 1945*, Paris: Laffont 1967, vol. I, pp. 461–7.

41 See the chapter, entitled 'Il disfattismo rivoluzionario' ('revolutionary defeatism'), of volume IV of P. Spriano, *Storia del partito comunista italiano*.

42 See T. Sala, *Opinione pubblica e lotta politica a Trieste dalla 'non belligeranza' alla 'guerra parallela' (1939–1941)*, Trieste: Libreria Internazionale Italo Svevo, 1968, pp. 26, 50.

43 The difference in nature of the war before and after the attack on the USSR was denied and affirmed, on different occasions, by Stalin himself. See his speech of 9 January

shall see, the problem of the war–revolution nexus was to return in the course of the Resistance; and in the meantime it interwove with that of the defeat of Italy in the Fascist war.

Alessandro Natta has recently recalled a heated discussion between himself and Gillo Pontecorvo, both pupils of the Pisa Scuola Normale Superiore, before the German attack on Russia. In the name of the PCI line, Pontecorvo considered the cause of peace the first priority, whereas Natta was convinced that war was indispensable to bring about the collapse of Fascism.[44] In the Turin workers' circles, on the one hand, there was clear hostility to entering the war alongside the Germans;[45] on the other, according to a Communist leader's testimony, the view was going around that 'for our liberation war is needed'.[46] These two positions were logically contradictory but emotionally convergent. Without mincing words Vittorio Benni, a painter and decorator from Foligno, wrote in a letter: 'I wish a greater war would come about to destroy the three leaders who are commanding Italy', and the Special Tribunal condemned him to five years' imprisonment for having offended the king, the Duce and the Pope.[47]

A PCI document of March 1941 recognised that defeat would put an end to the relationship between Fascism and the country.[48] The 1 May 1942 appeal by

---

1946 (Spriano, *Storia del Partito comunista italiano*, vol. III, p. 321) and his *Economic Problems of Socialism in the USSR*. As an example of the difficulties encountered by Soviet historiography in bringing these different evaluations into a single judgment, consider this passage from the address given by Yevgeny Boltin, in the name of the Moscow Institute for Marxism–Leninism, at the international congress held in Milan in March 1961: 'The Second World War which broke out in the form of a collision between two imperialistic coalitions, began to change character for Germany's adversaries when large popular masses began the anti-Fascist struggle. From that moment the conflict gradually acquired a just, liberating and anti-Fascist character, which was defining and affirmed definitively after the Soviet Union entered the war following the Nazi attack'. 'L'Unione Sovietica e la resistenza in Europa durante la seconda guerra mondiale', in INSMLI, *La Resistenza europea e gli Alleati*, p. 175.

44 Speech given on 25 April 1985 in the main hall of the University of Pisa.

45 See L. Passerini, *Torino operaia e fascismo*, Bari: Laterza 1984, p. 238, where a police report of 11 May 1939 is recorded.

46 Report by 'compagno André sul lavoro di Torino, marzo 1939–gennaio 1940', quoted in Spriano, *Storia del partito comunista italiano*, vol. IV, p. 19.

47 See A. Dal Pont, A. Leonetti, P. Maiello and L. Zocchi, *Aula IV. Tutti i processi del Tribunale speciale fascista*, Milan: La Pietra, 1978, p. 409. In the 1980 edition (A. Dal Pont and S. Carolini, eds), the motivation for the condemnation is omitted. See what was communicated by an informer from Genoa, 3 September 1936, in response to the news that was coming from Spain, where nobles, rich people and priests were being killed: 'Papa, Re o Duce, si dice, dovranno scontare insieme questa tirannia' ('Pope, King or Duce, it is said, will have to pay for this tyranny together'). In A. Aquarone, 'La guerrra di Spagna e l'opinione pubblica italiana', in *Il Cannochiale* 4–6 (1966), p. 29.

48 See G. Amendola, 'Analisi e prospettive politiche in un documento del

now urged desertion in favour of the USSR, the Yugoslav partisans, 'et cetera' (an et cetera which, discreetly, stood for the Anglo-Americans).[49]

Giorgio Amendola attributes to Concetto Marchesi the radical opinion, which he sets alongside that of Lelio Basso, that the catastrophe of the bourgeoisie, the monarchy and Fascism should be allowed to run its course, making way for Socialist revolution.[50] Again, during the forty-five days a Florentine Communist newspaper was to write: 'About eight years ago Mussolini began what from that point on our Russian comrades called the "beginning of the second imperialist war".'[51] In the same period a party leader criticised the error of those comrades who, after 1941, had not concealed the *general* anti-imperialist character of the war at the very moment when the USSR 'was trying, in our view, not to make capitalism anxious and to remain obscure about its own dangerous intentions'.[52]

Togliatti was to give an ambiguously reductive version of this complex and dramatic trajectory when, in his report to the Fifth Party Congress, he claimed that, 'with the outbreak of war, we were never for the defeat ... but for the salvation of the country'. On that occasion, Togliatti's purpose may well have been to reassure the 'unfortunate combatants that we have never despised their sacrifice'; but, through excessive zeal, he impoverished the experience that so many of his comrades and so many Italians had gone through, by adding: 'It is no pleasant thing to have foreseen the evil that befell the country, even if we did everything in our power to avoid it ... This feeling of profound, insuperable bitterness made even the victory of the great democratic nations over Fascism sad for us.'[53]

I have indicated some of the attitudes that the anti-Fascist militants had to the war in order to identify some of the features that the political culture of anti-Fascism would offer to the way *resistenti* would behave and think. However, as the war ran its devastating course, the points of view of the moderate forces who were busy reorganising themselves in the country came into play. The first issue of *Ricostruzione*, which came out in April 1943, read: 'Today, in the firing line, the soldier still feels the fascination of the flag, the solidarity of his unit, and is

1941 riveduto da Togliatti', in *Critica marxista* VI: I (January–February 1968), pp. 75–102.

49 See *Il comunismo italiano nella seconda guerra mondiale*, Introduction by G. Amendola, Rome: Riuniti, 1963, pp. 158–9.

50 G. Amendola, *Lettere a Milano. Ricordi e documenti*, Rome: Riuniti, 1974, p. 103.

51 Article entitled 'Perché la guerra continua', in *Rivoluzione, supplemento de l'Unità* 3 (August 1943).

52 'Relazione politica' ('Political report') from the Marche, which can be dated to the end of August 1943 (IG, *Archivio PCI*). Another part of the document is cited in E. Ragionieri, 'I comunisti', in Valiani, Bianchi and Ragionieri, *Azionisti, cattolici e comunisti nella Resistenza*, p. 338.

53 Togliatti, *Opere*, vol. V, pp. 176–80. For an earlier stance in this regard, see the report to the leadership of the Neapolitan Communist organisation, 11 April 1944.

dying for a cause he knows to be unjust; knowing, at the same time, that defeat is just ... They call us defeatists. But it is they, those responsible for the present ruin, who are the defeatists.'[54]

This was a far cry from the invitation, come what may, to do your duty to your country in arms, which Giorgio Amendola remembers Benedetto Croce as having made,[55] and as Croce himself wrote in a page of his autobiography.[56] Defeat and the accumulation of sufferings that had clustered around it, by now utterly intolerable because patently useless, made it insufficient to take refuge in the widespread and resigned slogan, 'Neither adhere nor sabotage', which distinguished the deep consciousness of so many Italians during the Second World War. The hope of getting through the gigantic conflict with the minimum of moral compromise and material damage had failed to stand the test, yielding almost to an unexpressed *drôle de guerre*, which was humiliating for the regime.

A Fascist Party informer wrote from Milan: 'For many it seems impossible that Italy is at war and they have a job believing it, sunk as they are in the conviction that Germany would have managed things alone or that our intervention would have occurred only to gather the fruits of our political and military support.'[57]

The *questore* of Venice reported that 'the war, though undesired, was accepted by the majority as a necessary evil', in view of its brevity and the advantages that could be obtained from it.[58] Other reports – still in 1940 – speak of

---

54 Article entitled 'Antifascisti perché italiani'. Ivanoe Bonomi, who inspired it, defines *Ricostruzione. Organo del fronte unico della libertà* as follows: 'It was not the expression of a single party or a single current, but, without intransigence and without damaging particularism, it wished to unite all anti-Facism, from the Liberals to the Socialists, from the Democrats to the Catholics, as far as the Communists.' See Bonomi, *Diario*, p. xxx, where the paper is presented as the counter-attraction to the Action Party's *Italia Libera*.

55 Testimony given by Giorgio Amendola in the presentation (Rome, November 1965) of Pasquale Schiano's book, *La Resistenza nel Napoletano*, with a Preface by F. Parri, Naples–Foggia–Bari: CESP, 1965. On the same occasion, Gaetano Arfé recalled in his turn the advice that Croce gave to the young in 1941: Study!

56 'What was particularly anguishing was the impossibility that I felt in the last stages, when there was war, of being wholly on the side of my country, because Germany's victory would have meant Europe's slavery under a degenerate Germany which would not have spared Italy the old German arrogance and contempt. But practically I solved this conflict by exhorting the young, who turned to me for advice, to save Italy's military honour and to remember that the army should reserve politics for politicians.' B. Croce, *Filosofia, Poesia, Storia*, Milan–Naples: Ricciardi, 1951, p. 1173. This was written in 1950.

57 P. Melograni, *Rapporti segreti della polizia fascista 1938–1940*, Bari: Laterza, 1979, p. 94.

58 Report of 23 December 1940 in L. Rizzi, *Lo sguardo del potere*, Milan: Rizzoli, 1984, p. 54.

a 'deaf and opaque mass' and of 'general weariness of a psychological nature';[59] while a combatant in Russia uses this image: 'The Italian army entered the war only little by little, like some poor wretch whose sleeve gets caught in a grinder and is swallowed up by it.'[60]

The Italian masses seemed then to have come to terms with the war – still more 'taciturn and fatalist' than those of the Western democracies, following the definition given to the latter by Stefan Zweig, who compared the 'ecstasy' of 1914 to the 'tough, unemotional determination' of 1939.[61] "How do you win a war without waging it?' may be taken as the essence of the *drôle de guerre* Italian-style.[62] Most Italians would sooner have fought as little as possible, or at least not far from home, leaving their powerful German allies to do the rest. As a July 1940 report by the prefect of Trieste says, registering a real fact, the population praised the Duce for having chosen the opportune moment – the thousand dead needed to sit down at the peace treaty table – 'to assure Italy of the maximum advantage with the minimum necessary sacrifice.'[63] On receiving the news brought by an officer back from the Russian front, where things were going from bad to worse, Roman military circles seem to have reacted by reproaching the Germans for having violated the rules of the game – namely 'that they were to get down to it and win the war.'[64] The Germans, for their part, sustained by their racial arrogance, were convinced that they were dealing with 'jumped-up farm-hands brought in for the harvest', led by officers who were 'too touchy, too full of

---

59 Reports by the prefect of Cremona, 31 October 1940, and summary of the provincial censorship committee of Gorizia, in ibid., pp. 56–7.

60 Tarchi (G. Tolloy), *Con l'armata italiana in Russia*, pp. 90–1.

61 See S. Zweig, *The World of Yesterday: An Autobiography*, Lincoln: University of Nebraska Press, 1964, p. 436 (original edition: *Die Welt von gestern. Erinnerungen eines Europäers*, Stockholm: Bermann-Fischer, 1942). For 'The spirit of 1914', see Chapter VIII of J. Joll, *The Origins of the First World War*, London: Longman, 1984. Regarding the fact that in 1939 'there was a real effort to redo 1914 … but people's hearts weren't in it', see, for France, Becker, *L'Union sacrée*, p. 121. A German historian has wished to trace in Germany as well a difference between the 'enthusiasm' and 'the atmosphere of febrile reawakening' of 1914 and the 'fright and resigned acceptance of an event that seemed ineluctable' of 1939. A. Hillgruber, *Der Zweite Weltkrieg 1939–1945*, Stuttgart–Berlin: Kohlhammer, 1982. For the counterpoint between the spirit of 1914 and the spirit of 1939, see P. Fussell, *Wartime: Understanding and Behaviour in the Second World War*, New York: Oxford University Press, 1989.

62 This is the sense that J. J. Becker, reviewing them, draws from the two volumes of F. Bédarida, *La stratégie secrète de la drôle de guerre*, Paris: Presses de la Fondation Nationale de sciences politiques et Éditions du CNRS, 1979, and from the proceedings of the Franco-British talks of 8–12 December 1975, *Français et Britanniques dans la drôle de guerre*, Paris: Éditions du CNRS, 1979. *Revue d'histoire moderne et contemporaine* XXIX (April–June 1982), pp. 348–50.

63 Quoted in Sala, *Opinione*, p. 229.

64 Tarchi (G. Tolloy), *Con l'armata italiana in Russia*, p. 110.

themselves, too vain'.[65] The Italians were to be compelled, in one way or another, to shake off the 'sad apathy' which, according to a pungent judgment by Radio London, they shared with the 'beaten French',[66] only by defeat, and then by the lash of the occupying Germans. But meanwhile their sense of identity had been worn down – already it had been vulgarised by Fascism, then humiliated by allies and enemies, and reduced more 'to a state of fact than to a self-operating force, more to a condition than a principle'.[67] As we shall see, one of the highest aims of the Resistance would be precisely that of regaining a national identity, even if the outcome of this would be uncertain because, as Ferruccio Parri wrote, part of Italy 'had suffered the misery of war, not the moral jolt of insurrection'.[68]

That considerable part of Italian society represented by the Catholic world participated in the events of the war along mobile and multiple lines, which have not yet been sufficiently investigated, where things specifically Italian and general interests of the Holy See intertwined. It is understandable that research into the incunabula of the Christian Democratic party, which governed Italy after the war, has been the main focus of scholars' attention. The result, though, has been that the field of a potentially far richer investigation has narrowed. For some time now, however, more complex and truly religious phenomena have also begun to be examined[69] – at times too hastily reduced, by Catholic writers,

---

65 See the accounts by O. Groehler and W. Schumann, *La Germania e i suoi alleati*, and by Förster, *Il ruolo dell'8 armata italiana*, in Istituto storico della Resistenza in Cuneo e provincia, *Gli italiani sul fronte russo*, pp. 121, 230, 244. The remark about 'reaper farmhands' (in Italian 'braccianti mietatori') is attributed to Hitler himself. The opinion about the officers is taken from the memoirs of Field Marshal Weichs, on whom the Italian army in Russia depended.

66 Colonel Stevens, the most popular commentator on Radio London's Italian broadcasts, had expressed himself in this way when the moves of the various European Resistance movements appeared to be still uncertain, particularly if seen from the other side of the English Channel: 'The true Europe is personified in the passive resistance of the Poles, the Czechs, the Norwegians, the Dutch, the Belgians and in the same sad apathy of the defeated French and the subservient Italians.' ('Europe looks to England', 8 July 1941, 9.40 p.m.: *Italian New Comment*, no. 342; BBC Written Archives, series I, envelope 6).

67 I take these words from an article by Giovanni Ferrara, 'Italia vostra' (*La Repubblica*, 20 November 1985) – where, however, no mention is made of the resistance experience.

68 F. Parri, 1945–1955, in *Il Ponte* XI: 4–5 (April–May 1955), p. 468. See the long title of the interview granted to Antonio Spinosa for *Il Punto* and published also in *Resistenza*, December 1957: 'Only a part of the country, territorially speaking, has been profoundly touched by the Resistance and only a part of Italian society participates in it or accepts it'. F. Parri, *Scritti 1915–1975*, eds E. Collotti, G. Rochat, G. Solaro Pelazza and P. Speziale, Milan: Feltrinelli, 1976, pp. 232–6.

69 See above all the overall works of F. Traniello, 'Il mondo cattolico italiano nella seconda guerra mondiale', in Francesca Ferratini Tosi, Gaetano Grassi, Massimo Legnani,

to the level of 'pastoral' activity, chiefly of the bishops, where the need for political mediation was in fact already incorporated. The behaviour of those who, in
one way or another – from straight faith to superstition[70] – reacquired religious
attitudes, has remained in the shadows; and this has also happened in the case of
the Catholics during the two Resistance years.

In the great debate about war and peace, the evolution of the Catholic attitude could be said to have followed, by and large, a reverse course to that of the
anti-Fascist lay forces. While the latter questioned an a priori pacifism, among
the Catholics – compromised by pro-Fascism, the anti-Bolshevik crusade and
the desire to 'support the honour of our flag',[71] in order to show, as in 1915–18,
that they were exemplary citizens – raising the question of war and peace meant
having to start rethinking their relations with Fascism and the mission entrusted
to it as a centuries-old weapon in the re-establishment of Christian society. I
am not thinking so much of the Catholic peasant world's traditional aversion
to war[72] – and still less of mannered balancing acts such as the statement that
the Pope wanted peace and that, at the same time, the Catholics, or rather the
priests, 'do not cease among us to be loyal Italian soldiers'.[73] What I mean rather
is the revival of the debate about the 'just war', which obliged one to shake off
the conformism according to which, before the orders of established authority,
one was to refrain from making one's own personal judgment on the reasons for
any conflict taking place.[74] As we shall see, these were tensions that would come
to a head – not for the Holy See, which would already have made its choices,
but for individual consciences – in the war between the Social Republic and the
Resistance.

Meanwhile, faced with the Fascist war, only small minorities of Catholics
– among whom the figure of don Primo Mazzolari, parish priest of Bozzolo,

---

L'Italia nella seconda guerrra mondiale e nella Resistenza, pp. 325–69, and of R. Moro, 'I
cattolici italiani di fronte alla guerra fascista', in Pacetti, Papini and Sarcinelli, eds, *La
cultura della pace*, pp. 75–126.

70 See a hint in this direction by N. Gallerano, 'Gli italiani in guerra 1940–1943.
Appunti per una ricerca', in *L'Italia nella seconda guerra mondiale e nella Resistenza*,
p. 309.

71 The words in quotes are from G. Andreotti, *De Gasperi e il suo tempo*, Milan:
Mondadori 1964, p. 186. Andreotti wrote that De Gasperi 'did not take part in the
macabre glee of those who rejoiced over the adverse fates of the second war'.

72 See F. Malgeri, *La Chiesa italiana e la guerra*, Rome: Studium, 1980.

73 'Estranea la Chiesa alla guerra? Ma chi dice questo è in mala fede, o vive nel
mondo della luna : Lettera pastorale al popolo Ambrosiano di S.E. il Cardinale Ildefonso
Schuster', 21 November 1942, with the title (an unwitting paraphrase of Marc Bloch!)
Contro i propalatori di notizie false sulla guerra (published by the Compagnia di San
Paolo di Milano).

74 See in Moro, *I cattolici italiani*, para. 3, 'Il dibattito sulla guerra giusta', and the
pungent final remarks, a genuine hymn to don Mazzolari's stance.

stands out – proved capable of tackling with radical energy the problem of the relationship between martial violence and the fifth commandment. Let us try a parallel reading of a crass pamphlet signed by don Sergio Pignedoli, circulated by the most enlightened Catholic organisation, the Federazione Universitaria Cattolica Italiana (FUCI), and Primo Mazzolari's vigorous 'Risposta a un avia-tore' ('Reply to an Airman').[75] Pignedoli approvingly cites Mussolini, and even Pétain, who in the 1914–18 war would go to Mass with his officers; he finds that there is 'an appealing beauty in scraping the bottom of a mess-tin with a spoon, when for twenty years we have been eating off a plate'; he reminds a university student that he no longer belongs to himself, but to the *patria*, to society, to the brotherhood of man, to God, to history; he rounds off in the name of 'Christian and Imperial Rome, to whom a few days ago the Pope appealed'.

Mazzolari is replying to a young airman who has bared his conscience to him before the task, to which he has been summoned, of killing and getting himself killed, and who had criticised the Church's silence and ambiguity.[76] The essence of Mazzolari's long reply lies in the maximum emphasis it lays on the terms of inner conflicts. Though not giving straight practical advice, which, in the circumstances, could only have been to rebel or desert, Mazzolari thus managed, undisguisedly, to transform back into a moral problem the practice, which Pignedoli and his ilk took for granted, of obeying the country's authorities when they ordered one to go to war. 'The myth of duty, or on the limits of my loyalty,' was, for example, the heading of one of the sections of Mazzolari's reply. Mazzolari gave full moral, and not simply diplomatic, significance to the 'useless slaughter' of Benedict XV's famous allocution, thereby implicitly raising another question too: Is the war to be condemned because it is useless or because it is unjust?

Was not dying and killing uselessly quite as harrowing a business as dying and killing unjustly? Mazzolari gave no reply, but remarked that the church had condemned war in general, not *this* war. And while Pignedoli, and so many of his kind, were speaking above all of the possibility of being killed, so as to alleviate the fear of it, Mazzolari, resorting even to a quotation from Remarque – 'Tell me at least *why* I have to kill' – baldly recalled that war consisted also of killing. The parish priest of Bozzolo added that a Christian cannot hate anyone, and there-fore not even the enemy; and it is easy to see how distant he was from another

---

75 *A te, universitario soldato*, pamphlet signed by 'Sac. Sergio Pignedoli, tenente cappellano' ('Priest Sergio Pignedoli, lieutenant chaplain'), Rome: Editrice Studium, 1941; *Risposta a un aviatore (I problemi della ricostruzione cristiana)*, dated 10 August 1941, in P. Mazzolari, *La Chiesa, il fascismo e la guerra*, ed. L. Bedeschi, Florence: Vallecchi, 1966, pp. 39–88.

76 Jemolo's work *La tragedia inavvertita*, mentioned earlier, was to say that 'to the fearsome queries raised by the war no religion, to my knowledge, arrogated to itself the fearsome privilege of replying' (p. 10).

priest, don Tullio Calcagno, the future promoter, under the Social Republic, of 'Crociata italica' ('Italian Crusade'), who on the contrary considered it indispensable to hate the enemy.[77] Thus Mazzolari again raised a possibly insoluble question: whether it is therefore preferable to kill in cold blood.[78] 'The soldier who dies without knowing why he is dying takes the kingdom of the servile to its utmost limit', Mazzolari concluded. Inscribed in the knowledge of why you are dying in effect is a conscious judgment of the enemy you have to kill: otherwise you would not be soldiers, but those martyrs who 'inaugurated the kingdom of the sons of God and of truly free man'. This setting of martyrdom and war against each other was essentially Mazzolari's metapolitical and metahistorical answer.

Altogether different in inspiration was the reappearance of that current of Catholic apologetics which, from de Maistre onward, had indicated war as a castigation that God sends men because of their sins. The fearsome scale of the castigation that was taking place could only be proportional to the greatest of sins: the de-Christianisation of society. The war, from whatever angle it was viewed, thus ceased to be a struggle between warring parties and became a scourge sent indiscriminately to all men. From the pulpit in a Roman church, a preacher translated this awesome theological message into petty scolding of 'children who have not listened to their mother', and of mothers 'who have failed to hold their children in check. And vainly does the Madonna implore Jesus to save men. Irritated, Jesus refuses to listen to her.'[79]

The interiorisation of a sense of guilt, to the point of desperation, is to be found in the letters of civilians and soldiers alike: 'This is a castigation by God because we are too bad'; 'Ask the Lord what we have done wrong in this world to be tortured in this way'.[80] This is a far cry from the presentation, found in some Catholic texts, of the current war as a holy war, insofar as it was a 'titanic struggle in defence of European, Roman and Christian civilisation, threatened by the hordes of militant atheism'.[81]

---

77 See Moro, *I cattolici italiani*, p. 100.

78 It would be useful to compare this with the subtle casuistry developed by padre Gemelli during the First World War: one went from killing with 'punctuality and exactness', but without hate, to the inflamed reawakening of aggressive 'ancient spirits'. A. Gemelli, *Il nostro soldato. Saggio di psicologia militare*, Milan: Treves, 1917.

79 This is the paraphrase of the plea that one reads in Calamandrei, *La vita indivisibile*, p. 120, beneath the date 8 December 1943.

80 Letter of a civilian from Mantua to a second lieutenant in Russia, 16 March 1942, and letter of 12 January (with no other indications), in Rizzi, *Lo sguardo del potere*, pp. 103, 118.

81 See, as an example of this position, the Catholic press of the province of Cuneo examined in Belmondo et al., *La campagna di Russia*, pp. 432–9. The quotation in the text is taken (p. 434, note 12) from *La Gazzetta d'Alba*, 26 June 1941 – that is, shortly after the attack on the USSR. On 6 July 1940 a small inter-parish paper, *La Bisalta*, had let fly at

2. The uncertain motivations of the combatants

One thing that many of the surviving testimonies have in common is that the vast majority of the combatants felt they had been thrown into an enterprise whose proportions, intensity and significance it was not only beyond their direct power to control, but even simply to comprehend. As Nuto Revelli wrote: 'We knew nothing. We viewed modern warfare like folk from another age, and were alien to it.'[1]

In fact, not only do General Staffs often face a war with the technical culture of their predecessor (the most glaring example certainly being that of the stolid French General Staff of 1939–40), but the very men who have to fight it have difficulty shaking off the memory that has been transmitted to them by veterans' tales, literature, and myth-making. To many Italian soldiers their German ally – and the British, Soviet and American foes – must have appeared like people from another world and another age. The memory of the Germans, whether in the African desert or in the frozen wastes of Russia, fleeing in automobiles while the Italians fled on foot, has become widely known and consolidated, beyond the real episodes that triggered it, precisely because of the significance it has acquired as an index of how alien the mass of Italian soldiers felt to that technical and ruthless war.

Except for the few convinced Fascists and the very few who were already clearly anti-Fascist, the majority of Italian soldiers cannot be said to have been altogether devoid of motivation: had motivation been totally absent, the desire to survive and the *spirito di corpo*, seen as a factor making for group cohesion, would not always have sufficed to save them from suicidal rebellion or madness. But the motivations involved were uncertain, in the sense that they were unable to give unitary firmness to the men's consciences, and, even when they appeared firmer and rooted in long-standing tradition, such as loyalty to the institutions, the line separating them from resignation remained uncertain and jagged.

A little earlier I recalled the sense of *sub specie* Catholic expiation. But no explicitly religious anchorage was needed to cultivate, in a good many combatants, a sentiment that took the form of the sublimation of sufferings endured for an uncertain and obscure cause, in the name of a duty regarded a priori as unavoidable. It was thus a desire for expiation with tragic overtones, for it lacked hope; whereas the analogous aspiration of the *resistenti*, which we have seen in at least some of them, was to be illuminated and, as it were, sweetened by confident hopes deferred to a future guaranteed by the justice of their cause. Some of the

---

France, heir of 1789, 'field of every sort of libertinism, the country where the most shady and criminal of every kind took refuge, the anarchists, the Communists, the masons, the Jews and conspirators of that ilk'.

1 Revelli, *La guerra dei poveri*, pp. 18–19 (on the campaign in Russia).

Fascists of the Social Republic were also to display this spirit of dedication; but in their case it would be wrapped in the mortuary rhetorical shroud of sacrifice as an end in itself.[2]

The more expiation is detached from the prospect of a feasible and morally certain future, the more – as appears evident even in the noblest of its expressions of 1940–43 – it places all its hope of not being vain in the very fact of laying down one's life. Combatants uncertain of what they are fighting for can thus paradoxically seek it in offering their lives. Perhaps the formula that it is always the best ones who die – used in the most varied contexts, Resistance and post-Resistance included – has a non-rhetorical motivation in this essentially religious substructure, which leaves survivors with an insidious and persistent sense of guilt. Even sacrifice accepted in the name of the *patria* can be experienced as an 'act of divine clemency'. 'I think that the Lord has had pity on us, after our corrupt existence, in having me die for the great, infinite Italian *patria*', wrote a corporal who was to die in Marmarica.[3] More tersely and resolutely, a Catholic who was subsequently to be killed during the Resistance wrote from the front: 'Before God, I am doing my duty to the full as an Italian. But any kind of Fascist ideal is utterly alien to me.'[4]

While in those soldiers who felt the first glimmerings of an anti-Fascist conscience, 'we must expiate everything' was transformed into the commitment to self-redemption by making good the privileges they had enjoyed as officers and students,[5] in others this process took, and seemed to keep, the form of solidarity – come risk, come misfortune – with one's compatriots who had been hurled into the same predicament.

A second lieutenant in the Alpini wrote from Russia of the 'moral and purely moral value of our sacrifice', and of the desire that 'our privileged condition as students should not save us from the common destiny of expiation

---

2 Sacrifice as an end in itself 'is only the supreme expression of what Fascism aims at in all its ramifications: the annihilation of the individual self and its utter submission to a higher power. It is the perversion of true sacrifice'. E. Fromm, *The Fear of Freedom*, New York: Avon, 1941, p. 231. On the Fascist (and Catholic) components of 'sacrifice to the pure state', see an observation by M. Isnenghi, 'Alle origini del 18 aprile. Miti, riti, mass media', in M. Isnenghi and S. Lanaro, eds, *La Democrazia cristiana dal fascismo al 18 aprile. Movimento cattolico e Democrazia cristiana nel Veneto 1945–1948*, Venice: Marsilio, 1978, p. 284.

3 Letter of August 1941 by Gustavo Fragola, of Barra (Naples), to his mother, in B. Ceva, *Cinque anni di storia italiana 1940–1945. Da lettere e diari di caduti*, Milan: Edizioni di Comunità, 1964, p. 21.

4 Letter by Dottor Angelo Coatto, hanged in Veneto by the SS, 2 October 1944 (Bianchi, *I cattolici*, p. 245).

5 'The best, those who have not erred, must', in this perspective, 'be the first to do so, conscious of their duty and right to point the way', Tarchi (G. Tolloy), *Con l'armata italiana in Russia*, p. 190; compare p. 4.

and suffering'.[6] Another officer wrote to his wife, again from the Russian front: 'Marina, I can't abandon my soldiers who are in danger, to return to Rome to work in a ministry.'[7] Or again:

> When I have lost my life in the trenches of the Don, I shall only have done my duty as an Italian. I have no cause at all to hate the wretches who over on the other bank are doing what we are doing; but I am sure that my place as an Italian is this one alone, among my soldiers whom I love ... The politics, responsibility and motives of this war don't count here; Italy is at war and this alone is where I should be.[8]

In another testimony the invitation, in Catholic form, to do what was commanded of one, whatever the circumstances, merges with the duty to participate 'in this great doleful destiny that has befallen our generation'. According to these combatants, the war was 'un grande fatto' ('a great event') transcending the will of those who had decided to wage it, and those who did not go to war 'betray human solidarity, snap the bond linking them to others and basically, out of cowardice, go against fundamental moral law ... possibly regretting that there is not another war instead, against another enemy, in which case, they say, they would become fierce'.[9] The tragic thing here is that the sense, albeit confused, of the existence of a great historic alternative is taken as being a mere matter of personal convenience. This is present in the account of a survivor of the death camps: 'When I was called up to leave Novi for Albania, my father said to me: "Look, those you are off to fight as your enemies aren't enemies: try, if you can, to save your skin and not to hurt anyone." He said that to me at the station and I have held those words sacred.'[10]

Among the reasons for the proverbial passivity of the Italian soldier is also this uncertainty as to the figure of the enemy, who seemed by contrast to be a good deal more highly motivated. An intelligent National Fascist Party (PNF)

---

6 Letter to a friend by Alpini second lieutenant Sandro Bonicelli, born in Brescia in 1921, a law graduate. He was to be killed at Nikolaevka, 5 February 1943 (in Ceva, *Cinque anni*, p. 79).

7 Letter of 6 January 1943 by Alpino engineers captain Gaetano Gabardini, born in 1900, professor at the Politecnico di Milano. He was to die in prison (ibid., p. 99).

8 The letter of 30 October 1944 continued: 'Don't mourn my death ... My tomb will be along a roadside or near the Don, a wooden cross, with my rank, my name, the date, the name of Milan and my helmet'. Emilio De Marchi, Milanese, born in 1913, lawyer, volunteer, second lieutenant of the Alpini who was killed in January 1943 (ibid., pp. 96–7).

9 Letter by Gino Ferroni, of the FUCI, lieutenant of the Alpini who fell on the Russian front.

10 Testimony by Marco Apruzzese, sentenced to twenty years' imprisonment for self-inflicted wounding (Bravo and Jalla, eds, *La vita offesa*, p. 77). His father was a hairdresser and a socialist.

inspector reported from Albania that the 'divisions, large and small alike, seemed to be afflicted by a morbid form of melancholy and resigned fatalism, which grew, the closer they got to the firing line [against] an enemy imbued with a sort of religious mania and ready to die unsparingly'.[11] A censor noted down that, in the troops' letters, 'even when there are encouraging and patriotic words, these spring forth as an act directed *towards* the person one is writing to but reveal the depression of the *man writing*'.[12] Giorgio Rochat has pointed out a paradoxical indicator of the shaky conviction even in those who sacrificed themselves in the name of duty: the low number of executions ordered by the military tribunals compared with those carried out in the Great War. In fact, only a strong faith in the justice of the cause can induce the body of officers to take initiatives of drastic repression on a large scale and with a clear conscience.[13]

Obviously, I am not denying the presence in the Italian armed forces of men with Fascist or para-Fascist motivations. These motivations were at times explicit, at other times attributable to ideological graftings that they had been taught at school. Thus a volunteer who, in Albania, invokes vendetta (not 'rehabilitation') for the Alpini brackets together in the one list – culminating in Mussolini – Mazzini, Gioberti, Cavour, Garibaldi, 'Crispi of the Sicilian revolution', 'two kings of the House of Savoy', D'Annunzio, Carducci and Verdi.[14] One soldier declares that he is fighting 'for the great empire of Rome'; one writes: 'I was born for Mussolini's war and for him I wish to die'; one refuses to take part in singing instruction because he has 'left the shop, my mother and my girl to fight, not to sing'.[15] Even in letters of this kind a distinction needs to be made between propagandist stereotypes, adopted with different degrees of sincerity and self-consolation, which are hard to gauge (and their limited presence in letters from the front is itself indicative),[16] from more personal letters. For

---

11 Report by Inspector Parini, 22 February 1941 (quoted in Rizzi, *Lo sguardo del potere*, p. 65).

12 Note by the censorship commission of Gorizia, 9 December 1940 (quoted in ibid., p. 223).

13 See G. Rochat, 'Lo sforzo bellico 1940–1943. Analisi di una sconfitta', in Francesca Ferratini Tosi, Gaetano Grassi, Massimo Legnani, *L'Italia nella seconda guerra mondiale e nella Resistenza*, pp. 237–8.

14 Letter of 4 March 1941 by second lieutenant Vincenzo Ambrosio, born in Rome in 1913, functionary of the Ministry for Italian Africa, killed in Albania, 10 March 1941 (in Ceva, *Cinque anni*, p. 41).

15 Letters by tank corps lieutenant Giuseppe Locatelli, 9 October 1940, who was to die on the Egyptian front in November 1941; by Blackshirt, and volunteer, Riccardo Bedeschi, Milanese, born 1923, of 9 January 1943, killed in Tunisia; of lieutenant Alessandro Oddi Baglioni, who on 23 February 1943 recounts the episode from North Africa (ibid., pp. 161, 135, 156). The lack of popular songs was frequently noted.

16 This is indicative because if self-censorship led to limiting and expressing in coded form critical expressions about the regime and its war, this did not happen in the

example, a fifty-year-old soldier writes: 'When I was at home I was an ardent Fascist and was always saying we needed to fight this war; now I'd be ashamed to return home.'[17]

Large numbers often participated in the demonstrations of anti-British hatred, inspired by that motto 'Dio stramaledica gli inglesi' ('God curse the English') which figured on a specially minted badge. The English were in fact seen as richer and more successful competitors in imperialism. This point of view had existed for some time in Italian nationalism; but to it the Fascists added a plebeian resentment and racist fear-cum-envy: 'I've seen so many of these curs whom we've taken prisoner and have given them a solemn raspberry.'[18] Writing to a comrade, a Blackshirt savours the prospect of the time when the English will have to 'learn to eat two meals a day and have done with their five traditional ones'; conversely, 'presently it will be our turn to have, for once at least, five meals a day, like the English, and a good pipe of Oriental tobacco.'[19]

Fascist stereotypes were upset by the recognition that a declared nation of shopkeepers should know how to make war.[20] The accent then shifted to denouncing the fact that the English made their subject peoples – and what's more, coloured ones – fight for their own profit. Sometimes sympathy is expressed for the latter: 'It's almost always coloured troops who are put there for the defence of their blond masters and skinny spinsters. Our tank-crews compel these poor Indians to put their hands up.'[21] But more often there are manifestations of racist contempt and fear, which we shall encounter again in the Social

---

case of favourable ones. On censorship, which 'is a trap for the simple, an alarm for the crafty', and on self-censorship, which only accentuates what is 'for many a habit of life', see Nuto Revelli's observations in *L'ultimo fronte*, Turin: Einaudi, 1971, p. xlii.

17 Episode recounted in Paolo Masera's letter from North Africa, 13 February 1942 (in Ceva, *Cinque anni*, p. 150).

18 Letter by artilleryman Gino Lanfranchi, from Omegna, February 1941 (ibid., p. 29).

19 The first letter is quoted in B. Bellomo, *Lettere censurate*, Milan: Longanesi, 1975, pp. 22–3; the second, by a civilian from Gorizia to a sergeant-major, in Rizzi, *Lo sguardo del potere*, p. 98.

20 See the contrast that, already during the First World War, the Germans had drawn between themselves, as a people of heroes, and the British as a people of traders and shopkeepers. See W. Sombart's 'war handbook', *Händler und Helden*, quoted by Hirschman, *Shifting Involvements*, p. 6, ironically in view of the fact that it was precisely in 1914 that the British had by contrast rediscovered the figure of the 'warrior' (Hirschman refers to Eric J. Leed's *No Man's Land: Combat and Identity in World War I*, New York: Cambridge University Press, 1979, and Paul Fussell's *The Great War and Modern Memory*, New York: Oxford University Press, 1975).

21 Page written for *La Tradotta Libica* by engineer corps sergeant-major Carlo Biagioli, *Fronte d'Egitto, 3 novembre 1942/XXI* (in Ceva, *Cinque anni*, p. 126).

Republic, both in the official propaganda[22] and in the newest young recruits: 'The dead must be avenged. Italy needs us young men to prevent the niggers, in the service of England, from contaminating her sacred soil!'[23] In short, hatred of the British could become a 'more than ever supernatural' hate.[24]

Nor were manifestations of openly ideological aversion to the Russians lacking, as was evident when they were dubbed 'reds' or 'Bolsheviks', or when Catholic motivations became intertwined with Fascist ones. 'The pride of those who want to destroy the Roman Catholic Church will certainly pass ... Christ has always won', is the prediction of a soldier who seems to have found in Russia, against the godless, that motivation he had been hard put to discern in Albania.[25] In another letter the Russians are spoken of as 'people without faith'.[26] 'Either Rome or Moscow', the Fascist propaganda slogan, in any case seemed tailor-made to please Fascist and Catholic ears alike, given the centuries-old polysemy of the word 'Rome'.

The Russian campaign, like the occupation of the Balkans, was to offer, by contrast, that contact with the invaded and exploited peoples that was lacking in the war waged in North Africa, and that would provide the first occasion for reflection for many combatants of the Fascist war.[27]

Meanwhile, besides political and ideological motivations, identifiable in the fighting men were attitudes and sympathetic support offered above all to themselves, which, as we have seen, were to be found, in another key, in some *resistenti* as well: the urge for adventure, supported 'by hatred of the humdrum routine of life; the monotony of certain family habits; a certain senselessness of

22 See in Fondo RSI numbers 316, 365, 396, 432, 479, 601, 613, 667, 689, 690, 761, 771, 988, 989, 991. Black soldiers are often presented as rapists of women.

23 Undated letter to his parents by Giorgio Monti, of Macerata Feltria, who was killed at Castel di Decima on 3 June 1944 (*LRSI*, p. 92).

24 Letter to his family, in Mantua, by gunner Valentino Coda, 30 January 1943 (in Rizzo, *Lo sguardo del potere*, p.184). For the Italian combatants in North Africa see, in general, L. Ceva, 'Gli italiani in Africa Settentrionale', in Tosi, et al., *L'Italia nella seconda guerra mondiale e nella Resistenza*, pp. 185–96, and works cited in it.

25 Letter by the tanner Carlo Rolando, 1 November 1942, who later went missing. In Albania Rolando, at Christmas 1940, had taken refuge in the idea that 'Il Re dei Rei' ('The King of Kings') wanted everything that was happening to happen 'in order to give the world perennial justice and order. Let us therefore trust in Him and resign ourselves to His will' (Revelli, *L'ultimo fronte*, pp. 39, 36–7).

26 Letter of 27 December 1941 by second lieutenant Amedeo Rainaldi, student at the Catholic University, killed in December 1942 (in Ceva, *Cinque anni*, p. 67). For Catholic participation, with its own particular accent, in the war against Bolshevik Russia, see M. Isnenghi, 'La campagna di Russia nella stampa e nella pubblicistica fascista', in Istituto storico della Resistenza in Cuneo e provincia, 'Gli italiani sul fronte russo', pp. 404–6.

27 See several observations made by Battaglia, *Storia della Resistenza*, Chapter 1, section entitled 'Gli italiani sul fronte russo', pp. 404–6.

social life'.[28] Some youths from Rutino (in the province of Salerno) asked to be drafted into the paratroop corps because 'here life is no longer tolerable'.[29] 'We were very young; like all young men [we sought] adventure; for us, the war was an adventure, we were thoroughly irresponsible ... And then the war was adventure, something new that might just break the dreary routine'.[30]

Proceeding in a way that was possibly an attempt to resemble Renato Serra's famous *Esame di coscienza*, a Sardinian university student wrote:

> I can't make myself out. I only know this, that finally I've found the only thing that has been able to shake me and exalt me and pull me out of melancholy, by throwing me into a state of complete inebriation, this unquiet spirit of mine which in civilian life has only been able to feel disgust for everything that makes up our paltry everyday existence. And this thing is the war ... This reconnaissance had a real tang of Salgarian adventure.[31]

In his diary Giaime Pintor wrote that 'among sluggard men war seemed to be a way out'.[32] Even a combatant who does not spare his words in describing the horrors of the war and who does the rare thing of calling 'sticking bayonets into others' bellies ... murdering human beings', goes on to say that he finds in 'love of the unknown and of adventures' the only motivation that sustains him – not, certainly, the 'mania for greatness or empires'.[33] Instead of adventure, which is after all always an individual and dynamic experience, a peasant, to reassure his

28 Letter to the author, 6 January 1986, by Enzo Marino, at that time a medical student, who had applied to be enlisted as a volunteer. In a previous letter, of 4 January, Marino writes: 'Perhaps it was already then a certain fear of the unknown, of a possible or presumed insufficiency of our forces which drove us towards "arditistico" decisions, which were certainly always hasty and irrational.'

29 Quoted (by ACS) in M. Di Giovanni's degree thesis. As will be noted, some of the letters that I am quoting are by volunteers, who were possibly more numerous than claimed by F. Chabod, *L'Italia contemporanea 1918–1948*, Turin: Einaudi, 1961, p.103. Nevertheless, I think that the judgment expressed there about the lack of a 'collective movement' that might revive 'a typical phenomenon of Italian history' is still valid. The Fascists must have found this situation such a sore point that, towards the end of the war, all the university students born in 1920 were officially declared 'volunteers'.

30 Testimonies by Settimio Bernaducci and Ferruccio Mauri, in Portelli, *Biografia di una città*, pp. 241, 239.

31 Letter by Nuccio Floris, published in *Intervento* (Sassari), November XIX [1941], and quoted in M. Addis Saba, *Gioventù italiana del Littorio. La stampa dei giovani nella guerra fascista*, Milan: Feltrinelli, 1973, p. 175.

32 G. Pintor, *Doppio diario 1936–1943*, Turin: Einaudi, 1978, p. 84 (23 November 1940).

33 Letter of 15 July 1942 to his fiancée. The soldier warned the girl, who seemed prey to heroic furies, that 'a woman must never speak of certain things that are incomprehensible to her. If she did so, her very essence as a woman would disappear' (in Rizzi, *Lo sguardo del potere*, p. 106).

family and himself – 'we resign ourselves and realise that it is a great party for us youngsters' – equates departure for the front with the traditional and cheerful demeanor of raw recruits.[34]

The spirit of adventure could, in true Fascist style, become expectation of an easy victory. 'They'd like to stab, win, deck themselves with glory, come out of it in one piece and get back to Italy as soon as possible ... greeted as conquerors', a lieutenant colonel wrote from the Russian front.[35] The superficiality denounced by this serious officer on the one hand clashed with the stereotypical idea of the war as a forger of character – 'We need to be men, by God, and here we learn to become so, take my word for it'[36] – and on the other hand with the harsh impact with reality. This was true whether one wished to see this, intellectually, as 'a first step towards possessing something concrete',[37] or described it as 'falling on your back into the mud and drowning your face in the mire', which put paid to any myth of 'dying with a bullet through your heart, kissed by the sun'.[38] The impact with reality did in fact have contradictory results. In the keenest men, it might at first make them stubbornly deny that very reality – 'We shall win because we must win, otherwise it would be too great a disaster'[39] – after which it could induce them to feel betrayed, by men and/or fate – a reaction which can be called proto–Social Republic.[40] In those who were not motivated, or only dimly so, the counterblow was the feeling that they were victims, with

---

34   Letter by the peasant Giovanni Barroero, 27 November 1940, about to leave for Albania (Revelli, L'ultimo fronte, p. 31).

35   Letter of 30 August 1941 to his wife and son by Bersaglieri lieutenant colonel Aminto Carretto, who did not enrol in the PNF out of repugnance at adding a second oath to the one he had taken to the king. He was killed in July 1942 (Ceva, Cinque anni, p. 55).

36   Letter to his family, 11 January 1941, by Silvano Buffa, Triestine, born in 1914, Alpini second lieutenant, killed in Greece in March 1941 (ibid., p. 45).

37   Pintor, Doppio diario, p. 112.

38   Diary of Alpini second lieutenant Antonio Cantore, killed in Greece (in Ceva, Cinque anni, p. 31). This is a clear paraphrase of the Risorgimento notion of falling in a cornfield with a bullet through one's forehead.

39   Undated letter from North Africa by a Blackshirt to a civilian, in Rizzi, Lo sguardo del potere, p. 101, where the editor refers to stereotypes of reassurance and of fears that this would degenerate.

40   Consider this leaflet circulated at Adria soon after Italy entered the war, by youths born in 1922 who were offering themselves as volunteers against shirkers: 'the "revolutionary march is continuing", Our Duce has said and we shall make sure it continues; the cudgel has remained too inactive, the castor-oil has piled up too greatly in the pharmacies; our "ripulisti" ["clean out"] is near'. As a nice example of politico-cultural syncretism that had not yet been dissolved by the 8 September blow, the leaflet ended by proposing this motto: 'Italy and Victor Emmanuel III! Benito Mussolini!' (in ACS, quoted in M. Di Giovanni, laureate thesis). This refers to a report by the prefect of Rovigo to the Ministry of the Interior, 18 June 1944.

a further, successive doubling of results: to cease being so as soon as one could by heaving oneself out of those waters, or by finding in it a cause for reflection and a desire for a positive response. The latter reaction could be called proto-Resistance, while the former is *proto-attesistico* (proto-fence-sitting).[41] Pity for the enemy, confused with pity for oneself, appears as a first and simple way of placing oneself again in a humanly tolerable position. 'There, there'll be Greeks, poor and decent mountain folk perhaps, who'll put out the white flag', wrote an Alpini second lieutenant;[42] and this is how another describes a female literature professor whom he had met in Rostov: 'An eye and a face that struck one for their patient resignation beneath the blows of misfortune'.[43]

There are by now numerous testimonies about the contradictory reactions kindled in the Italians by contact with Russia – its land, people, army and regime. Possibly the most widespread sentiment is that of stupor – both stupor that aroused fear, and stupor that generated admiration in various forms and degrees (for example, for the widespread education and great industrial complexes that prompted one officer to give an elaborate discourse on 'modernisation').[44] One thing that aroused particular surprise was the coexistence in the Russian populations of the occupied territories of a determined Soviet patriotism and a civil and even kindly manner towards the Italians as individuals.[45] There was here a sort of rediscovery of the possibility that human relations might survive the crushing blow that the Germans were ruthlessly dealing them for reasons of war. That this rediscovery was nourished by the Italian soldier's tendency to make another family for himself[46] wherever he might be only made it more persuasive.

---

41 'It has been on the battlefields that we have measured the spiritual dissolution of the Italians and at the same time the responsibility of the ruling class … No, our Fallen, our mutilated, are not the "heroes" of a militarism for its own sake, but rather the "victims" of the atrocious selfishness of the ruling class: their memory cannot and must not be of glory, but of pity.' ('Il dovere compiuto, il dovere da compiere', in *Bollettino Popolo e Libertà*, November–December 1943, 6).

42 Fragment from a diary (19 April 1941) by Valerio Graziola, fallen in action (in Ceva, *Cinque anni*, p. 83).

43 Letter by Sandro Bonicelli, 20 August 1942. On 21 July, before the sight of the 'luckless [Polish] people', Bonicelli had written: 'On these yellow faces and under-nourished faces that have suffered greatly there gleams the mute sadness of those who have been defeated but who have not ceded' (ibid., pp. 83, 80). For Bonicelli, see Ceva, *Cinque anni*, p. 79.

44 Letter of 23 August 1942 by second lieutenant Bonicelli, referred to in the previous note (ibid., p. 84).

45 See Ceva, *Cinque anni di storia italiana*; Tarchi (G. Tolloy), *Con l'armata italiana in Russia*; cf. Revelli, *La guerra dei poveri*; especially the pages devoted to the campaign in Russia.

46 Observation suggested to me by Luca D'Angiolini, Alpini second lieutenant wounded at the battle of Nikolaevka.

However, the event that left the greatest mark on the Italian experience in Russia was the terrible retreat. This was not only 'a major turning-point in the relations between the two countries [Italy and Germany], and indeed the decisive psychological failure in "Fascist" warfare',[47] but for many of those involved it marked the beginning of a radical reappraisal of their own position regarding Fascism and the war, a lesson certainly more incisive than the Soviet appeals to rebel against Mussolini who 'is drinking your blood'.[48] An emblematic figure of this new tendency is certainly Nuto Revelli.[49]

'Che Dio maledica chi ci ha tradito/ Portandoci su Don e poi fuggito' ('God curse him who betrayed us/Taking us to the Don, then escaping'), are lines from 'Pietà l'è morta', the partisan song inspired by Revelli, who wrote in his diary: 'We have christened our formation: la compagnia Rivendicazione caduti. We want to avenge those who fell in Russia. Our oath says: "For every Italian who died in Russia ten Fascists and ten Germans are to be done in".'[50] The memorial tablet in the main square in Boves is a document of this kind of continuity between the Russian retreat and the Resistance: 'died in Russia 95', 'died in the Resistance 134', plus 11 in the German camps (when the figure for each of the other fronts does not exceed thirteen). True, this was an Alpini recruitment zone (of about 20,500 men from the Cuneo division, no more than 3,000 made it home);[51] while in the immediate post-war climate the fate of the prisoners in Russian hands was to unleash passions of an opposite kind to those witnessed by Revelli. But, even steering clear of hasty generalisations, the fact remains that the survivors were, at the very least, vehicles of mistrust and disheartenment – 'horrible things heard, which I don't intend to recount'[52] – that is when they did not transmit acutely, as has been written of one of them, 'a tormenting guilt complex and, together with this, an anxious desire for liberation, mixed with an almost religious sentiment of expiation'.[53]

---

47 Deakin, The Brutal Friendship, p. 206.

48 These were the incitements that came from the loudspeakers on the other bank of the Don. See A. Carracciolo, Teresio Olivelli, Brescia: La Scuola Editrice, 1947, p. 82.

49 See in this regard Aldo Garosci's observations in the introduction to La guerra dei poveri.

50 Revelli, La guerra dei poveri, p. 141. On 5 October 1943, the date of this annotation, Revelli had not yet established relations with the GL formations.

51 I have taken these figures from Belmondo et al., La campagna di Russia, p. 455. In total, out of 229,005 men, Italian losses in Russia amounted to 84,830, plus 26,690 wounded and frozen (General R. Cruccu's report, 'Le operazioni italiane in Russia', in Istituto storico della resistenza in Cuneo e provincia, Gli italiani sul fronte russo, pp. 209–23).

52 Testimony by Eghertone Barbanti, Modenese born in 1924, regarding the 'first impact with the survivors of the Russian campaign' in a Mantua barracks (CU).

53 Anonymous Romagnolo, 1943–45. Storie ai margini della storia, Milan: Ottavio Capriolo, 1984, p. 181, regarding the survivor Gal. (Galeazzo Viganò).

Giorgio Rochat justly writes that the majority of the testimonies (which are by officers) register 'the abandonment or, better to say, the shelving during the retreat of many of the traditional values of society and of the Italian army', but that, 'as soon as they were out of danger', the officers 'once again started demanding observation of that very code of values which they had by their own confession infringed'.[54] But meanwhile the code had shown cracks and reversals that were premonitory of the 8 September collapse and the repudiation of the Royal Army.[55]

Two encounters left their mark, albeit to very different degrees, on the Italians dispatched to occupy the lands of Russia and the Balkans. As is well known, the scant knowledge of the extermination of the Jews that the Germans had begun is a phenomenon regarding not only the Italian soldiers. The failure to see even where things were all too visible and to recount the little, or much, one had seen makes testimonies on this score extremely scarce. The Jews working along the railway, one survivor from Russia and the German concentration camps has written, 'looked thin, exhausted, continually threatened by the Germans. And that was when I began to understand what the Germans were like' – not least because they explained to him that Jews themselves had been made to dig the ditches there alongside them for their own bodies.[56] When he heard a German officer's calm account of the massacre of the Kiev Jews, a chaplain who was a keen supporter of the anti-Bolshevik crusade said: 'I too am beginning to believe that this war can't be won.'[57]

The impact with the partisans, which one was to be on one's guard against, was harder to avoid. In Vorošilovgrad, Revelli encountered some twenty of them, prisoners, in civilian dress, on their way to be shot with their heads held high: 'We were mere wretches with gentlemen's airs and pretensions. I watched those partisans with great admiration. I felt humiliated.'[58] Another Italian, who called them 'Russian partisan bandits', was astonished by the presence of women among the combatants: 'There, three young women driving the tank disarmed me.'[59]

---

54 G. Rochat, 'Memorialistica e storiografia sulla campagna italiana di Russia, 1941–1943', in Istituto storico della resistenza in *Cuneo e provincia, Gli italiani sul fronte russo*, p. 471.

55 Among the first Communist partisans of the Avezzano area (Alpini were recruited in Abruzzo too), there were numerous survivors from Russia ('verbale seduta segretaria 26 novembre 1943': *IG, Archivio PCI*).

56 Testimony by Diego Verardo, born in the province of Treviso in 1914, regular soldier, then partisan (Bravo and Jalla, *La vita offesa*, p. 76).

57 Tarchi (G. Tolloy), *Con l'armata italiana in Russia*, p. 21.

58 Revelli, *La guerra dei poveri*, p. 30.

59 Story told by G. V., ex-prisoner, quoted in Ceva, *Cinque anni*, p.113. In the railway wagon that transported the prisoners there were 'those who wept, those who shouted, those who died'.

The experience of coming suddenly face to face with the partisan war could give rise to troubled consciences, inurement to witnessing and passively practising violence, education in repressive ferocity. 'Lieutenant, if you'd been a rebel you wouldn't have reacted like this, yet a rebel is a man', was how a soldier answered the officer who had reprimanded him for killing a deer. And yet this lieutenant, Falco Marin, who was killed in Slovenia in July 1943, was a sensitive and reflective man. He wrote in a letter:

> I can't make out these Slovenes, these Croats, these Serbs, who are fighting with such ardour for something that baffles me, but which will certainly lead to the death of all of them or else to their liberty ... The game is mortal because we're still strong enough to be able to kill them all; but their strength lies in a strange perplexity we feel ... Off he goes into the wood alone with a rifle, lives heaven knows how, but safer than if he were at home. And we who go in the hundreds to catch him feel his fascination and get ourselves hit without ever managing to catch him.[60]

In the memoirs of the officers interned in Germany, the counter-guerrilla operations in the Balkans are mentioned more than any other wartime episode. Rochat, who has noted this fact, attributes this to the desire to 'underline the change of sides and role brought about by the Armistice':[61] almost as if they were applying to themselves the law of retaliation ...

The deep impression made by the Yugoslav partisans was to have a maturing effect on Aligi Barducci ('Potente') and others like him;[62] and for other partisan chiefs the impression of the guerrilla activity they had been sent to repress acted as a veritable school of partisan warfare. This is what Giulio Nicoletta, commander of the autonomous De Vitis division, has recalled.[63] Mario Gordini was spurred to form the Ravenna battalion in the Apennines around Faenza by a veteran from Yugoslavia.[64] After the initial setbacks,

---

60 Diary (22 February 1943) and letter (2 April 1943), ibid., p. 173–4. For the stupor aroused by the 'imperturbability' of the Croat partisans who were led out to be shot – 'they seemed to be going to a dance party' – see the letter to his family by a soldier from Casaboldo who had witnessed their executions, 12 July 1942 (in Rizzi, *Lo sguardo del potere*, p. 115).

61 Rochat, *Memorialistica e storiografia sull'internamento*, p. 30.

62 See the introductory essay by M. A. and S. Timpanaro and G. and E. Varlecchi, *Potente. Aligi Barducci, comandante della divisione Garibaldi-Arno*, eds M.A. and S. Timpanaro, Florence: Libreria Feltrinelli, 1975, p. 72. Another future partisan chief, Ciro, was to tell of the importance of his first encounter with partisans in Belgium (Borrini, Mignemi and Muratore, *Parlare*, p. 18).

63 See ANED, *Gli scioperi del marzo 1944*, Milan: Franco Angeli, 1986, p. 58.

64 See L. Casali, 'appunti sull'antifascismo e la Resistenza armata nel Ravennate', in *Il Movimento di liberazione in Italia* 77 (October–December 1964), p. 58.

several officers took to reorganising the bands in the light of their experience in the Balkans.[65]

The presence in Italy of Yugoslav partisans who, on 8 September, had escaped from the concentration camps would intersect with these personal experiences of Italians, which at times bore the label, taken precisely from the Slav example, of 'extremism'.[66] It was in paradoxical terms that the Garibaldi commander Primo (Giovanni Rocca), formerly a member of the PNF, who had fought in Croatia for three years, was presented: in the Langhe, Primo 'waged a hard, ferocious war without quarter', following in fact the Yugoslav example, but also because he was 'self-taught, with no guide, under the influence of Fascist propaganda, convincing himself that he was a Communist partisan as the Fascist papers describe the Communist partisans (revolution, extremism, ferocity)'.[67]

As I have already suggested, anti-partisan repression, including the shooting of hostages, practised above all in the Balkans, but also in Venezia Giulia,[68] was a sorry precedent for the Fascists of the Social Republic, more so certainly than a stimulus, for everyone critically to reappraise the myth of the 'goodness of the Italians'. A soldier wrote from Yugoslavia: 'We have orders to kill everyone and to set fire to everything we come across, so we reckon we'll finish things off rapidly'; and another: 'We've destroyed everything from top to bottom without sparing innocents … We're killing entire families, every night, beating them to death or shooting them. If they try to make so much as a move we shoot without pity and whoever dies, dies.'[69]

---

65 'Relazione di massima sull'attività dei partigiani della provincia di Arezzo' (ISRT, *Fondo Berti*, envelope I folder 6).

66 For the sectarianism of Slavs active in Umbria, see the testimony of captain Melis, who describes them, however, as the 'spina dorsale' ('backbone') of the movement (Portelli, *Biografia di una città*, p. 266).

67 Primo, who stood out for 'love of the people, courage, honesty, the spirit of sacrifice', then – according to the author of the document – moved into line: not only did all the Communist symbols disappear, but he also succeeded in having as chaplain-commissar in the brigade an excellent patriot Salesian priest (report by Andreis [Italo Nicoletti], inspector at the 6th Langhe division, to the Piedmont delegation of the General Command of the Garibaldi brigades, 12 October 1944, quoted in *Le Brigate Garibaldi*, vol. II, ed. G. Nisticò, p. 436).

68 In April 1943 anti-partisan paratroopers were sent into the zone between Caporetto and Postumia. Their commander, Captain Edoardo Sala, was to be head of a regiment of RSI paratroopers and sentenced, after the Liberation, for crimes committed in Piedmont (M. Di Giovanni's degree thesis, and Neppi Modona, *Giustizia penale*, p. 76).

69 Letters by Ottavio Luccheto to his wife, February 1942, and by Salvatore Seldi to his family, 1 July 1942, quoted in P. Moraca, 'I crimini commessi da occupanti e collaborazionisti in Jugoslavia durante la seconda guerra mondiale', in E. Collotti, ed., *L'occupazione nazista in Europa*, Rome: Riuniti, 1964, p. 543. According to Yugoslav sources used by the editors of *LRE*, pp. 557–8, the dead caused by the occupation numbered about half a

We know that quotations of this kind can be counterbalanced by those telling a different story, testifying to acts of great humanity.[70] Here, let me make just two points.

The first is that the Resistance press, for understandable enough reasons, was keen to emphasise the differences in the ways the Italians and the Germans behaved in the occupied territories. 'The sons of the *popolo* in grey-green did not fight furiously on any front and did not commit those acts of ferocity against the helpless populations which have disgraced the Hitlerian hordes and the few M battalions'; and again: 'Where they conquered they brought, in contrast with the Germans, kindness and mildness; and in Greece and Croatia they fed the starving, and saved the lives of Jews, and always defended the persecuted, whatever their race and religion.'[71]

It should also be borne in mind that the 'goodness of the Italians' is a largely pre-political fact. At that level, the Italian soldier might very well not have made that much distinction between his friend and his enemy (witness what was observed above in his relations with the Russian population). But this kind of 'goodness', which is extremely difficult to practise in wartime, where it fostered the stereotype of the Italian as incapable of fighting, a songster and buffoon, made him defenceless before orders to commit, and before examples of, indescribable violence, whether those orders came from the Italian commands, the Germans or local collaborationists.[72] The violence practised during the Resistance would, by contrast, be 'political', and its relations with 'bontà' ('goodness') were thus different.

---

million. For Italian repressive measures in Russia (round-ups, reprisals, forced labour, under pain of serious punishment, to report the presence of partisans), see L. Porcari, 'La "Cunneense" sulle fronti di guerra', in Istituto storico della Resistenza in Cuneo e provincia, *Gli italiani sul fronte russo*, pp. 261–89 (which includes as an appendix a circular on this subject by General Nasci, commander of the Alpino corps, dated 2 August 1942).

70   With regard to the protection given to Jews by the Italian troops, especially in southern France, see L. Poliakov, *Bréviaire de la haine. Le III Reich et les Juifs*, Paris: Calman-Lévy, 1951.

71   See *La Riscossa italiana. Organo piemontese del Fronte di liberazione nazionale*, 20 October 1943, article entitled 'La gioventù italiana'; and *L'Azione. Organo del Movimento cristiano sociale*, 20 November 1943, article entitled 'Non c'è tradimento'. The latter, actually, rather than describing an event that really occurred, illustrates the ideal behaviour of a Christian.

72   In his last letter to his mother Tone Tomšic, Triestine by birth, leader of the Slovene Communist party, ordered to be shot in Lubyana 21 May 1942 by the Italian military tribunal, writes that 'the Italians dare to shoot us' only thanks to the help and endorsement given to them by 'the bishop, Ehlich and all the other renegades of our nation' (*LRE*, pp. 568–70). For the stereotype suggested in the text see Fussell, *Tempo di guerra*, pp. 159–63.

In the collection of servicemen's letters that I have drawn on widely, Bianca Ceva observes that one has the sensation of 'finding oneself before human beings, not citizens'.[73] This view is borne out by the subsequent publication of letters and memoirs, and more than any other sums up the failure of the Fascist war. Certainly, Ceva's point of reference are the letters of the First World War combatants collected by Adolfo Omodeo in *Momenti della vita di guerra* – namely the letters of those officers, above all reserve officers, whose quality as 'citizens' heirs of the Risorgimento Omodeo had been especially intent on celebrating.[74] But if one looks at the 'umili' ('the humble') – tucked away by Omodeo in a slim appendix to the second edition of his book, and retrieved for history first by Leo Spitzer[75] and then by more recent studies by Forcella, Isnenghi, Monticone and Rochard (to name but the leaders) – one finds in the trenches of Carso also 'human beings', noble or fragile, more than 'citizens'.[76] In any case, these two qualities tend to converge a good deal more in a defensive war fought on one's own soil – like the war after Caporetto – than in a war of aggression taken into distant and inhospitable lands. What Ceva highlights acquires greater significance in that it referred not only to the 'umili', but, as we have seen, involved the officer corps as well.

On 14 February 1941 a note of the chief of police's secretariat registered the 'lack of a genuine spiritual preparation for the war'; and the following 26 December, the *questore* of Venice touched on a sore point by observing that 'one would have expected men's spirits and resources to be better prepared after twenty years of totalitarian rule'.[77]

Fascism's supreme ambition had indeed been to fuse politics with war – that is, the citizen with the soldier, or better still the warrior. In 1937 Giuseppe Bottai had, incautiously, taken it for granted that this fusion had already come about, on the model of the Fascist assault troops' fighting spirit. The Blackshirts were

---

73 Ceva, *Cinque anni*, p. 10.

74 A. Omodeo, 'Momenti della vita di guerra. Dai diari e dalle lettere dei caduti 1915–1918', published in instalments in *La Critica* from 1929 to 1933, then collected in one volume, Bari: Laterza 1933. The book was republished in 1968 by Einaudi with a long, fine Introduction by Alessandro Galante Garrone, who recommends that readers of the work distinguish between 'storiografico, rievocativo, polemico' ('historiography, reminiscence, and polemic' [p. xxxi]).

75 L. Spitzer, *Lettere di prigionieri di guerra italiani 1915–1918*, Turin: Boringhieri, 1976 (original edition *Italienische Kriegsgefangenbriefe Materialien zu einer Charakteristik der volkstümlichen italienischen Korrespondenza*, Bonn: Peter Hanstein Verlag, 1921). Spitzer is the main source of Omodeo's Appendix, mentioned in the text.

76 In his presentation of Spitzer's book, cited above, Lorenzo notes the affinities of the texts collected by the Austrian scholar with those published by Revelli in *L'Ultimo fronte*, which I have mentioned several times.

77 The two documents, conserved in ACS, are quoted respectively in Belmondo et al., *La campagna di Russia*, p. 441, and in Rizzi, *Lo sguardo del potere*, p. 66.

'the first champion of the "political" army as we intend and practise it (bearer and defender of *one* idea, and therefore not party biased)'.[78] Today we know that, in the internal equilibrium of the Fascist power system, the full unfolding of this drive to politicise the armed forces was checked by the logic of compromise between the party and the military hierarchies, leaving the traditional military with a fairly wide leeway for self-management as both a corps and a career.[79]

But the war obeyed a yet more stringent logic, which put paid to any compromise between velleity and opportunism, and showed how vain it was to attempt to 'mobilise' the masses after having gone to such pains to 'demobilise' them.[80] In his speech to the party directorate on 17 April 1943, Mussolini himself had to acknowledge that the ideal of the political army – for which he held up the SS as a model – was still a long way from being achieved.[81] In an earlier speech to the same audience, on 3 January of the same year, Mussolini had declared that 'the Armed Forces can never be political enough, never Fascist enough … Because this is a war of religion, of ideas.' The question as to 'whether twenty years of Fascist rule have changed things only on the surface, leaving them much the same below', was for Mussolini purely rhetorical. The answer was 'that the Italian people will hold firm and astound the world'.[82] But it was precisely the Fascist 'new man' who did not appear on the battlefields, however much the trial of war had been taken as the elective testing-ground for him to manifest himself.[83] An RSI soldier was to number this very 'absence of the *homus novus*' among the 'three squalors, one greater than the others', that he saw as weighing on his death.[84] As early as the beginning of the war, a major in the Royal Army had

---

78 The passage, taken from the preface to a book on the *arditi*, is quoted by Rochat, *Gli arditi della grande guerra*, p. 79.

79 See G. Rochat, 'L'esercito e il fascismo', in G. Quazza, ed., *Fascismo e società italiana*, Turin: Einaudi, 1973, pp. 89–123.

80 I use these expressions in the sense that G. Germani gives them in *Autoritarismo, fascismo e classi sociali*, Bologna: Il Mulino, 1975. The notice, posted in the public offices during the war, 'Here one does not discuss high politics and high strategy, here one works', offers shameless proof of this failure. Compare Moltke's last letter to his wife, where the maxims proclaimed by the people's court that tried the 2 July 1944 conspirators are paraphrased: 'Whoever discusses questions of high politics with persons who in no respect whatsoever have the competence and particularly with those who do not in any way belong to the Party are preparing high treason …Whoever dares express opinions on questions to be decided by the Führer is preparing high treason' (*LRE*, p. 414).

81 'War', the Duce prophesied on that occasion, 'will be won by the army that becomes a political army more quickly than its opponents' (Deakin, *The Brutal Friendship*, p. 320).

82 Cited in ibid., p. 132.

83 For a keen but unsuccessful search for the new Fascist man, see R. De Felice, *Intervista sul fascismo*, ed. M. A. Ledeen, Bari: Laterza, 1975.

84 'Spiritual testament' addressed to his wife on 16 April 1944 by Mario Moretti, a

written to his son that Fascism 'had failed to create a new youth, and with this terrible crime Fascism has foreclosed its outlet towards the future'.[85]

These different attitudes to being at war, briefly outlined above, fostered germs of *reducismo* (diehard veteran's spirit) partly akin to the experience of the First World War,[86] as it has been studied, and indeed partly peculiar to the Italians of the Second World War. In general, it has been rightly observed that trench warfare 'seems to have left a more salient psychological mark than earlier or more recent experiences of combat', and that consequently 'the Second World War generated less sense of political mission in its former soldiers than the First'.[87]

The Italian war had this peculiarity: in the Resistance (and, in its way, in the RSI as well) vent was given to some of the tensions we might call *proto-reducistiche* that had built up during the conflict. They were condensed in formulae like, 'When we return, we'll put things in order', generated by the illusion of being able to transfer into civilian and normal life the exceptional and totalising character of the wartime experience, whose traumatic aspects one believed one had the right to redress.[88] Obviously, the shirkers (*imboscati*) were the first and immediate targets of this resentment. They were despised as those who 'complain about the radiator, about the inconvenient timetables of the theatres'; they were hated as 'scum' who deserved to be sent 'into the desert and then see what they have to say', as 'armchair heroes who make high-sounding utterances in the cafés and write *vincere* to you on every scrap of paper they can find'; like those who 'are here in town laughing and living it up ... while the women forget their most sacred duties in the arms of profiteers'.[89]

The desire to take revenge on all such people is equally apparent: 'but let's hope to find these malingerers one day and settle accounts with them!'; 'but

---

twenty-eight-year-old Neapolitan, former combatant in 1940–43, who died the following June (*LRSI*, p. 78).

85 Letter of 8 December 1940, in Rizzi, *Lo sguardo del potere*, p. 133.

86 I am referring above all to P. Fussell, *The Great War and Modern Memory*, New York: Oxford University Press, 1975; E. J. Leed, *No Man's Land: Combat and Identity in World War I*, New York: Cambridge University Press, 1979; A. Prost, *Les anciens combattants dans la société française 1914–1939*, Paris: Presses de la fondation nationale des sciences politiques, 1977. For the Italian experience see, in a predominantly political key, G. Sabbatucci, *I combattenti nel primo dopoguerra*, Bari: Laterza, 1974.

87 R. O. Paxton's review of Prost's book, in *Journal of Social History* XIV: I (Fall 1980), pp. 157, 160.

88 This theme is widely covered by Leed, again as regards the First World War, in the last chapter of *No Man's Land*, 'The Veteran Between Front and Home', and particularly in the section 'The Economy of Sacrifice and its Collapse'.

89 This is a series of examples treated by Ceva, *Cinque anni*, p. 98 (it is Captain Gabardini, mentioned above); Rizzi, *Lo sguardo del potere*, pp. 131, 149; diary of paratrooper Pallotta during leave (quoted in M. Di Giovanni's degree thesis).

the day will also come when I'll be able to get my own back'; 'but God will keep our memory in shape'; 'sooner or later you'll be found out'; 'we'll make a clean sweep of the defeatists (*mormoratori* – 'murmurers'); and that whole rabble of individuals who are now looking contemptuously at the army will have to pay or think differently after the Victory'.[90] These utterances already reveal the variety of possible directions the combatants' reactions might take.

Certainly the most absurd anger was that of the staunch Fascists, for it was an anger against themselves and their own myths. If a woman could write to her husband in Russia, 'It's nonsense for them to write that this was a war for all – for all the poor yes, but not for the rich who are the ones making millions out of the war',[91] the only way a Fascist could vent his feelings against 'i signori della doppia camicia' ('the double-shirted signori'), against the '"let's-arm-ourselves-and-off-you-go" gang', was by swathing himself again in his language: 'It is better to die in war than live uselessly … We are Italians and Fascists only when we have smelled the scent of the trench, the whistle of the machine-gun.'[92]

Paradoxically, the Fascists at the front had to take issue with other Fascists, the ones who had stayed at home – thus anticipating one of the themes of the contradictory polemic of the Republican Fascist Party against the Fascist National Party. Carlo Scorza himself, soon to become the last secretary of the PNF, was to say to Fidia Gambetti, who was departing for Russia in the summer of 1942: 'Make sure you come back; then we'll settle up with everyone, even the Duce, if necessary.'[93] At a certain point Edgardo Preti, lieutenant-general of the militia in the Italian Army in Russia (ARMIR) Command, began to speak of 'counter-revolution when the war's over' and pronounced grim threats against 'those signori in Rome'.[94] Berto Ricci, an intellectual of the so-called Fascist left, expressed a similar point of view: 'For the time being let's get on with winning the war … We'll sort out the English in our ranks later.'[95]

It is not surprising that the officer who, from the end of 1942, edited the paratroopers' newspaper *Folgore*, where many diehard positions appear, later found himself in the Social Republic.[96] We should add, however, that even in the Social Republic the diehard component had, as such, limited room for political

---

90 Letters quoted in Rizzi, *Lo sguardo del potere*, pp. 150, 130, 132; diary quoted in the previous note.

91 Letter of 9 July 1942, quoted in Rizzi, *Lo sguardo del potere*, p. 105.

92 Corporal's letter to a woman of Poggio Rusco (Mantua), 15 June 1942, quoted in Rizzi, *Lo sguardo del potere*, p. 130).

93 This is what G. Mayda recounts in 'Morto Scorza, l'ultimo ras del fascismo', in *La Stampa*, 27 December 1988, according to the testimony of Gambetti himself.

94 Tarchi (G. Tolloy), *Con l'armata italiana in Russia*, p. 163.

95 Undated letter from Tripoli, quoted in A. Asor Rosa, 'La cultura', in *Storia d'Italia*, Turin: Einaudi, 1975, vol. IV, p. 187.

96 See M. Di Giovani's degree thesis.

action, as witness the failed 'conspiracy' promoted by the 'party of the "*medaglie d'oro*".[97]

Many other former combatants wanted to 'sort things out', in a deeper and more global sense – that is, by participating in the Resistance. When the hardship of wartime experience fused with repudiation of the military hierarchies and the values they embodied (or should have embodied), the way was paved for this, whatever paths individuals might have taken.[98] To this day, a survivor of deportation still writes resentfully: 'I've read a lot about the events of those few days on the western front, but I've never read anything about the shitty idiocies the officers committed and which I witnessed.'[99] A soldier's letter says: 'I never expected to be treated so badly or that the officers would be such a crew.'[100] With candid malice, another soldier recounts from the Marmarica desert: 'Here I can see officers who were so cocky in Italy, and yet in only a few, in only a very few days they've bowed their heads and their morale and no longer seem to be even privates.'[101]

In the next section we shall see how the repudiation of the Royal Army accounts for much about the attitudes and behaviour of the partisans. Here I only wish to recall the lieutenant described by Primo Levi, where this rejection was kept problematically bottled up, finding, as yet, no outward expression:

---

97 For the 'Congiura detta dei "tre B"' ('The So-Called Conspiracy of the "Three Bs"'), namely Francesco Maria Barracu, mutilated in one eye, and undersecretary for the presidency of the Council, Carlo Borsani, blinded in war and president of the 'Associazione combattenti nella RSI', and the great disabled Fulvio Balisti, see Bocca, *La Repubblica di Mussolini*, p. 148. Bocca also recalls the brusque way in which, at the Verona congress, Alessandro Pavolini greeted the proposals of a trade-unionist, Lequio di Milano, to include agriculture among the activities to be socialised, by way of reparation for the promises of land that had been made but not kept to the peasants who were First World War veterans (ibid., p. 94).

98 Rochat justly writes that at least part of the memoirs about the campaign in Russia highlight values, such as *esprit de corps*, that were 'only partially alternative to the traditional ones … which however … acquire a significance as a criticism and rejection of the structure and tradition of the army and potentially of the political structures which are at the origin of so much suffering and grief'. And he adds that 'Nikolaevka and all the fighting during the retreat are, in a certain sense, partisan battles because they were faced by those who were convinced that they wanted to do it' (Rochat, *Memorialistica e storiografia*, pp. 472–3).

99 Testimony by Gaudenzio Peroni, from Novara, born in 1919, street vendor, condemned in 1942 for desertion, in Bravo and Jalla, *La vita offesa*, p. 76, where similar expressions appear about officers on the Greek–Albanian front.

100 Report by the Mantua provincial censorship commission, 13 July 1942, in Rizzi, *Lo sguardo del potere*, p. 73.

101 Letter by Igino Carbone, peasant (5th year Elementary school certificate), 15 August 1942 (later killed in Tunisia), in Revelli, *L'ultimo fronte*, p. 18.

One could see that he wore the uniform with revulsion ... He talked about Fascism and the war with reticence and a sinister gaiety that I had no trouble interpreting. It was the ironic gaiety of a whole generation of Italians, intelligent and honest enough to reject Fascism, too sceptical to oppose it actively, too young to passively accept the tragedy that was taking shape and to despair of the future; a generation to which I myself would have belonged if the providential Racial Laws had not intervened to bring me to a precocious maturity and guide me in my choice.[102]

On 2 April a 'captain of the Alpini' revealed the existence of *reducismo* 'andato a bene' ('for a good cause'); or, if one prefers, of '*reducista* anti-Fascism',[103] sending this letter to a clandestine paper:

The survivors bear with them a legacy and mission received on the field from their comrades: to ensure that justice is done and to strike at those responsible for the disaster that is pounding our country. We shall be up in the front line for the vindication of liberty and for a better social order ... I am with the Italy of Vittorio Veneto which goes back to the traditions of our Risorgimento.[104]

Hard on the heels of this, and aggressively, came a young man's broadsheet:

Above all we respect those who are fighting, both in the ranks of the revolutionary forces and in the ranks of the armed forces. Fighting, mind you, not hiding themselves away in headquarters or the censor's office or else sporting coffee-room anti-Fascism and meanwhile enjoying the many girls available, going off to the pictures or the races.[105]

As if in distant countermelody to this, in the same period Giaime Pintor was reflecting on his own 'anti-militarism ... which took shape in a privileged military atmosphere.'[106]

To discredit the heir to the throne, Prince Umberto, who 'is staying afloat ... in that distant Italy', Nuto Revelli called him an 'imboscato', or draft-dodger ('we'll have to shoot him'); and in another page of his diary Revelli gave an exemplary outline of the *itinerarium mentis militaris in Resistentiam* (itinerary of the

---

102 P. Levi, *Il sistema periodico*, Turin: Einaudi, 1975, p. 66 (published in English as *The Periodic Table*).

103 The expression is used by G. Fogar, 'Le brigate Osoppo-Friuli', in Istituto di storia medievale e moderna dell'Università di Trieste, *Fascismo-guerra-Resistenza. Lotte politiche e sociali nel Friuli-Venezia Giulia 1918–1945*, Trieste: Libreria Internazionale Italo Svevo, 1969, p. 292.

104 *Ricostruzione*, April 1943.

105 Bollettino *Popolo e Libertà*, July 1943.

106 Pintor, *Doppio diario*, p. 112.

Resistance military mind) – an itinerary following which a regular officer like himself, who had believed in the military virtues, had come to reconvert, integrate and sublimate them into partisan life.[107] The 'poetry of military life', which in August 1942 an officer of the occupying troops in Greece had recognised as something that could not possibly be felt by 'thirty or thirty-one-year-old men, veterans of two wars, some of whom had been away from their homes, some for two years, some for three', was, we can infer, found again among the partisans in command of whom that officer was to die.[108] We can see proto-*reducismo* taking an anti-Fascist turn in many other testimonies. Witness this passage: 'Once again the war has surprised our good faith, playing upon young men's instinctive patriotism – this war! the culmination of the twenty-year-old crime ... each one of us has a friend who has died far off, in the ranks of a prostitute army.'[109]

A few months earlier, a university students' underground paper had spoken about young men 'exploited until only yesterday on the battlefields in a senseless war'.[110] This link between proto-*reducismo* and anti-Fascism is endorsed by many biographies, and emerges too from other passages in this book.[111] In a vain attempt to save himself, a youth who failed to report for service in the Social Republic, about to be shot in Florence in March 1944, invokes his past as an honest combatant: they shouldn't do it because I've always done my duty, I've always fought, 'and I've never been punished'.[112]

To those who had fought in the 1940–43 war, the old-guard anti-Fascists generally showed an attitude in which obvious pragmatism prevailed (the important

---

107 Revelli, *La guerra dei poveri*, pp. 186–7 (24 March 1944) and pp. 166–7 (27 January 1944). During the days of 8 September Revelli had performed a symbolic stripping gesture: 'It was almost morning when I got home. I took off my uniform: never again will I wear it!' (p. 1370).

108 Letter of August 1942 by Gino Prinetti Castelletti, member of an ancient Milanese family, who had been a student at the Turin artillery and engineers school. A Garibaldino, he was to be killed in Valsesia in 1944 (Ceva, *Cinque anni*, pp. 24–6).

109 'Trovarsi smarriti', article signed 'Un giovane', in *Avanguardia. Giornale della gioventù socialista*, June 1944.

110 ' Impegno', leading article of the first number of *La Nostra Lotta* (Rome), organ of 'Unione studenti italiani (unitari)', 26 March 1944.

111 Here I shall recall two cases. The first is that of second lieutenant Domenico Mezzadra, 'constructed', with the name 'Americano', as Garibaldino commander of the Pavese Oltrepò ('Relazione dell'ispettore Giorgio sulla 3ª divisione Aliotta', 6 March 1945, in *Le Brigate Garibaldi*, vol. III, pp. 441–3). The second is that of Candido Pinazza, knifegrinder from of a peasant family, gunner, who on 12 August 1943 wrote from Greece: 'I'll continue to preserve myself always with my honour, offering all that is necessary, because I want to return to my native country with my head held high.' Having joined the Greek partisans after 8 September, he was killed on 5 May 1944. (A. Ventura, 'La società rurale veneta dal fascismo alla Resistenza', in *Società rurale*, pp. 59–60).

112 Testimony about Guido Targetti by Chaplain Lieutenant Angelo Beccherle, in Bilenchi, *Cronache degli anni neri*, p. 59.

thing is that they join us); it also included respect for the sufferings they had endured; recognition (at times with a fair share of opportunistic rhetoric),[113] however it had been deployed; satisfaction at noting so great a capacity to set things right, so much 'profound moral rebellion which had matured particularly in the course of the war'.[114] There was less of an urge to get to the heart of the complexity and contradictions in the itineraries of so many individual lives. Some expressed the fear that scepticism would take hold of the ex-combatants, 'save the minority who had chosen the Resistance and the (slimmer) one that had chosen the Social Republic'.[115]

As if to reassure the mass of ex-servicemen who began to flock down into the South, Adolfo Omodeo, trying to make good use of what he had written about the 1915–18 combatants, said: 'The rejection that has accompanied the military venture from the beginning does not mean failure to recognise the positive value of the rich human experience gained on the battlefields ... Thus the energies lavished by the combatants do not seem vain to the men who are now setting about restoring Italian society.'[116]

The anti-Fascist leaders were, in fact, mainly concerned with the problems of the imminent post-war period, when the great mass of survivors who had not been filtered through the Resistance, nor foundered into the Social Republic, might represent a huge political problem that would have to be handled differently from the way it had been handled after 1918. The line taken towards the soldiers enrolled in the Royal Army, which during the war had been chiefly a matter of principle, an invitation, with little hope of immediate success, not to leave the bodies and souls of soldiers to the Fascist generals,[117] became, at the

---

113 See for example *Il Popolo*, Rome edition, 31 December 1943, where it is asserted that the most 'serious and combative', the 'most assiduous' anti-Nazis are the officers and soldiers who have fought alongside the Germans.

114 *Orientamenti programmatici*, edited by Lombard regional federation of the Italian Liberal Party, p. 12 (the author of the pamphlet is Paolo Sereni).

115 Inverni (V. Foa), *I partiti*, p. 82. In the constituent assembly Foa was to propose, in vain, an inquiry into those responsible for the disaster of the war, in order to prevent them from the indecency of presenting themselves as representatives and avengers of the fighting (Foa's own testimony to the author).

116 Words probably spoken in Naples and quoted by *Risorgimento Liberale*, northern edition, March 1944, in an article entitled 'Parole ai combattenti'. In Omodeo's speech broadcast on Naples radio on 22 December 1943, the words quoted by the Liberal paper do not figure; but the inspiration of the speech is identical. Omodeo said: 'No one will outrage your grief, the sufferings you have borne, the blood you have spilled'; and added: 'It is not we, O friends, who have betrayed Italy, even if with our hearts we were on the side of those who defended, beyond the frontiers, the traditions of human civilisation' (A. Omodeo, *Libertà e storia. Scritti e discorsi politici*, Turin: Einaudi, 1960, pp. 134–8).

117 This, for example, is the concept contained in the *Note sul 'lavoro militare'*, drawn up by the Centro Estero Socialista (Socialist Foreign Center) of Zurich in spring 1942

end of the war, a thorny question that had to be solved if the reconstruction of democracy was well and truly to get under way.

3. The repudiation of the royal army

The corollary of the *resistenti*'s ethico–political condemnation of the Fascist war was their bitter and contemptuous dissociation from what had been its instrument, the Royal Army, both as a military institution and ruling class, and as a style of life. Testimonies of this repudiation, which seemed obvious to many *resistenti*, abound. The most drastic and unequivocal are those that speak baldly of the Royal Army as of a 'dissolved' army. This, literally, is how it is put by a document – which is nevertheless very 'military' in form, insofar as it forbids political activity in the nascent partisan formations – written at the end of December 1943 for the Committee of National Liberation of Northern Italy.[1] And it was likewise to be expressed again by the 'internal regulation of the Corpo volontari della libertà' of 18 April 1945.[2] Ugo La Malfa trenchantly wrote: 'Badoglio's great army succumbed and died in Italy on 8 September 1943.'[3] At the end of March 1944 a circular of the Justice and Liberty political commissar for the 2nd sector asked that 'it be made quite clear to the partisans that they are soldiers of a new and revolutionary army, the National Liberation Army, which does not identify with, nor even succeed, as heir and continuer of the old Royal Army, which has failed so miserably'.[4]

In November 1944, and then towards the end of the war, two authoritative Communist leaders, careful as ever, though at times with evident effort, to toe the political line that their party had indicated for relations with the institutions, also spoke of the 'dissolved royal army'.[5] If the epithet *disciolto* (dissolved)

(see Landuyt, *Un tentativo di rinnovamento*, p. 95). See also a Communist circular of winter 1942–43, which delineated the 'type of discourse to give in the meetings held during flying visits when addressing soldiers and officers'. The document, conserved in ACS, is quoted by Ragionieri in the cyclostyled text of the talk given in Milan in 1968. In the printed version of the talk the quotation is omitted (see Ragionieri, 'Il partito comunista', in Valiani, Bianchi and Ragionieri, *Azionisti, cattolici e comunisti nella Resistenza*).

1 'Proposta di una delibera del CLNAI per la costituzione di una commissione responsabile delle operazioni militari in Lombardia' (*Atti CVL*, Appendice i/D, p. 525). See, in general, G. Rochat's survey, 'La crisi delle forze armate italiane nel 1943–45', in *Rivista di storia contemporanea* VII (1978), pp. 398–404.

2 *Atti CVL*, p. 491.

3 'Per la rinascita dell'Italia', pamphlet published in December 1943.

4 See Bianco, *Guerra partigiana*, p. 63.

5 See the letters of the Command of the group of Garibaldi divisions of the Valsesia, Ossola, Cusio, Verbano to the Command of the 1st division, 24 November 1944 (IG, *BG*, 07078). The commander of the group was Eraldo Gastone (Ciro); and, again signed

registers a reality that can by now, one hopes, be taken for granted, *fallito* (failed), or similar epithets, which were also recurrent, express a political and moral verdict that was taken to be equally incontestable. A Verona CLN leaflet reads: 'Our army has come to a tragic end, but an array of Patriots still holds high Italian valour.'[6]

A few fundamental points account for the condemnation of the Royal Army. To this day, in a survivor's memory, these can be said to come under the heading of betrayal: 'There was no longer any doubt. We had been ignobly betrayed [by the High Commands] and handed over to the Germans.'[7]

The attitudes towards the high-ranking officers had been severe and unsparing, and not just in the days immediately following the collapse. Dante Livio Bianco tells of an Alpini lieutenant turned partisan leader who, in Cuneo, 'proposed to kill without hesitation the colonel commanding the regiment, and possibly those superior officers who had wanted to throw in their lot with him', and remarked: 'Events would then show that what might at the time have appeared brusque ruthlessness was actually proof of wise foresight.'[8]

In a bitter attack on the regular officers, *Il Segno*, a Roman young people's Catholic paper, already noted for a certain freedom of spirit, spoke of a 'caste' which 'was the direct parallel of the party hierarchs'.[9] Even the 1 October edition of *Risorgimento Liberale*, though crediting the army, 'badly armed and badly run', with the wish to 'fight against its real enemy, against the Nazi oppressor', recognised that it had been 'deceived, disoriented, made to disarm, dispersed'. As we shall presently see, a smaller clandestine group like the Italian Labour Party (present almost exclusively in Romagna and Milan) was induced to reject the war against the Germans for fear that it might once again fall under the hegemony of the Royal Army. Its paper, *La Voce del Popolo*, reads: 'We don't want our young men to be enrolled in the monarchic army, which they joyously abandoned on 9 September, and to be compelled to fight under incompetent – as well as dishonest – generals and by mainly cowardly and spineless officers.'[10]

The book published clandestinely by this movement is shot through with

by Ciro and Cino, the 'Observations and proposals ... concerning the project of the communist delegation of the CLNAI for the transformation of the partisan units into regular formations of the Italian army', 21 January 1945 (*Le Brigate Garibaldi*, vol. III, p. 265).

6 Undated, entitled 'Guerra invisibile', in IVSR, *Archivio*, section I, envelope 49, *CLN, Stampa non periodica*.

7 Testimony relating to Trieste by Major Stefano Mascioli from La Spezia, in *L'Unità*, 4 September 1983.

8 Bianco, *Guerra partigiana*, pp. 5–6.

9 Article entitled 'Risanamento. L'Esercito', signed Filatete, 1 March 1944.

10 Article entitled 'Realismo', 15 October 1943. The newspaper under that date was actually still published by the Union of Italian Workers, which was unifying with the movement named People and Freedom to produce the Italian Labour Party.

a withering indictment of the high-ranking officers of the ARMIR.[11] The 'military' and 'autonomous' formations, who appeared to the Justice and Liberty and Garibaldi ones as a more or less direct continuation of the Royal Army, often paid dearly for this hostility, whatever the line pursued by the political parties that the *giellisti* (members of GL) and Garibaldini followed. 'May all our comrades rest assured that there are no Badogliani in our midst', the joint Osoppo-Garibaldi Command reassured its men in the brief period of its existence.[12] The 'committee for the Faenza zone' was enjoined to overcome the repugnance that the partisans felt at fighting alongside Badoglio's officers.[13] But another Communist document lets slips the word *purtroppo* (unfortunately) when having to explain the reasons inducing one to avail oneself also of high-ranking officers from the army.[14] A symptomatic episode is recounted by Vittorio Cerri, second lieutenant of the Green Flames (Fiamme Verdi), who, on 1 May 1945, immediately after the Liberation, was surrounded by a group of Garibaldini from the Pavese Oltrepò bent on tearing off his stripes, plumes, Alpine cap and eagles, who partly succeeded in doing so; as they moved off, the Garibaldini 'made jeering remarks about the army'.[15]

'Because of the prejudice against the officers in [Effective Permanent Service] I found myself, as everyone knows, in a moral condition of dire humiliation' – this was how, on 27 August 1944, Colonel Roncioni, who had become commander of the *patria* battalion of the 4th Osoppo Friuli brigade, complained about a formation in which, it should be recalled, Catholic influence and anti-Communist (and anti-Slav) polemic were rife even at those moments when formal agreements were reached with the Garibaldi brigades. Speaking of the armed forces being put together again in the South, the colonel added polemically: 'An army which is said to be destroyed and no longer existent, despite the fact that it is continuing to fight with the allies, as we are repeatedly informed by the radio.'[16]

It was in its behaviour that the Royal Army appeared to the *resistenti* as something remote, squalid and immoral. In his diary Guido Quazza wrote: 'one is cleansed from the detritus of the army'.[17] The profound difference of the

---

11 Tarchi (G. Tolloy), *Con l'armata italiana in Russia*.

12 Letter by the Command of the Ippolito Nievo brigade to the unified Garibaldi-Osoppo Command, 14 September 1944 (*Le Brigate Garibaldi*, vol. II, p. 332).

13 Letter with no sender's name, undated, in IG, BG, *Emilia-Romagna*, G.IV.3.2.

14 Letter of the Bologna federation to Grisaldi, commissar of the Stella Ross-Leone, 11 September 1944 (ibid., G.IV.2.8).

15 Report by Vittorio Cerri, 1 May 1945 (INSMLI, *CVL*,envelope 90, folder 13).

16 Letter sent by Roncioni to the Udine CLN, the Veneto regional military Command, and the Commands of the 1st, 2nd, 3rd and 5th Osoppo Friuli brigades (IVSR, *Archivio*, section 1, envelope 51, *Divisione Osoppo Friuli*).

17 Quazza, *Un diario partigiana*, p. 136.

partisan bands was declared with pride. This too is a fact that became imprinted on people's memories, according to formulae like 'there was draft as in the Italian army', 'the commander was always the first into action', 'before an action, we all discussed it together'; 'there were neither those who commanded nor those who simply obeyed'.[18]

Distrust was mutual. When the Gappist Giovanni Pesce reported to an HQ that was to supply him with arms, he was asked: 'Are you an officer? What rank are you?' Furious, Pesce managed to restrain himself from voicing this reflection: 'So, everything that's happened in Italy and the world, the 8 September breakup, the partisan recovery, had not the slightest effect on that man's way of conceiving existence in terms of fixed and immutable hierarchies.'[19]

Ferdinando Mautino speaks of officers who conserved 'a gangrened putri-fied mentality of supremacy and privilege', regarding a group of them who were 'far more intent on finding a bolt-hole than a place of combat', and who would soon move off 'in search of a less uncomfortable patriotic job'.[20] In a Garabaldi brigade document of autumn 1944, the 'social disparity and consequently the disparity of treatment between officers and troops' was stoutly denounced as 'one of the reasons that have caused the collapse of the Royal Army'. In contrast with this, 'in our formations we have got off on a footing of absolute democracy, and it is on that basis that we intend to remain'; and therefore 'the establish-ment of an officers' mess' is incomprehensible. 'The Garibaldino officer shares his bread, pallet and fire with the private.'[21]

When, in homage to unification, the political commissars became war com-missars, Francesco Moranino stressed that they had to share mess-tins, pallets, scabs and lice with their men.[22] In a party document, Vincenzo Moscatelli candidly reiterated the verdict on the Royal Army, describing it as a 'bourgeois army'.[23] Giovanni Battista Lazagna was convinced that the only useful job that

18 Testimony by Ermenigildo Mazzini, worker of Cassolnovo (Lomellina), who fought in Albania after various attempts to evade military service, and then chief of the Pizio Greta band of the Valsesia Garibaldi division (see A. Ballone, 'Una sezione, un paese: appunti per una storia del militante comunista 1921–1981', in *Rivista di storia contemporanea*, vol. X, 1981, p. 439).

19 Pesce, *Senza tregua*, p. 243.

20 Mautino, *Guerra di popolo*, pp. 38–9.

21 The Lombardy delegation of the Command of the Garibaldi brigades to the Command of the 3rd Lombardia Aliotta (Oltrepò pavese), 26 October 1944 (IG, BG, 0338).

22 *Bollettino periodico del commissario politico* of the 12th Garibaldi division, column entitled 'I commissari di guerra' (no. 1, undated, but late March 1945, quoted in Dellavalle, *Operai*, pp. 276–7).

23 Report to the secretary of the Milan federation of the PCI, 15 September 1944 (IG, BG, 06320).

could be found for the officers after the war was to send them for ten years to clear up the rubble.[24]

Even at their stormiest, relations between comrades were very different from the tantrums that occurred in the *naja* (regular army), warned Moscatelli;[25] and, again in the Ossola zone, fear was expressed that the return home of many officers interned in Switzerland, with a view to the final dissolution of the army, was accompanied by a style which was by now intolerable.[26] In one of the first Giustizia e Libertà (GL) bands in the village of Paralup in the Cuneo area, rejection of everything that smacked of the Royal Army was such that a partisan refused to don a grey-green greatcoat in the rain. On this score Dante Livio Bianco, who recounts the episode, recalls what Carlo Rosselli had written in his *Giornale di un miliziano*: that, as they trooped through the streets of Barcelona, they did their level best not to march in step.[27]

'I made a rather demagogic little speech,' Emanuele Artom, political commissar of a GL division, wrote in his diary: 'The soldiers of Badoglio's bands would do well to come here and see how you are living: those who are on their best behaviour with the officers and live as they used to in the old army, where a soldier worked and got a lira a day and the officer commanded and got fifty.'[28]

The trust placed in some cases, immediately after the Armistice, in military formations that were, or were supposed to be, to a greater or lesser extent organic, and which had repaired to the mountains – traces of which can be found even in the wary *L'Italia libera*[29] – and the shortly ensuing disillusion contributed to increasing contempt for the army and its leaders and the distrust of the 'military' bands on the part of the 'political' ones. In a 'Report on the military situation in the Biella area' (November 1943), the condition of the 'soldiers who had taken refuge in the mountains' (about 700 men at the end of October) is described as disastrous because of the inertia, the political and organisational incapacity, the lack of surveillance, the nonexistent or contradictory commands. Thus, when the final, total breakup occurred at the beginning of November, only on new Garibaldini bases was it possible to start the work of reconstruction. And, as

24 Lazagna, *Ponte rotto*, p. 147.

25 'Extract' from a letter by the political commissar of the unified Command of the Ossola and Valsesia divisions to the commissar of the 81st Volante Loss brigade, Santino, 26 August 1944 (*Le Brigate Garibaldi*, vol. II, pp. 267–71).

26 Letter by the Ossola zone Command to the subordinate Commands, 24 February 1945 (ibid., vol. III, pp. 412–15).

27 See Bianco, *Guerra partigiana*, pp. 21–2. For this episode see C. Rosselli, *Oggi in Spagna, domani in Italia*, Turin: Einaudi, 1967, p. 29.

28 Artom, *Diari*, p. 172 (under the date 18 February 1944).

29 Rome edition, article entitled 'Franche parole ai soldati italiani', 25 September 1943. For similar illusions existing in northern Italy, see M. Giovana, *La Resistenza in Piemonte. Storia del CLN regionale*, Milan: Feltrinelli, 1962, p. 41, which quotes a broadsheet issued on 20 October by the Piedmont CLN.

the Communist author of the report was keen to point out, this was done in the teeth of the sabotage work of the 'Military Committee', which, in cahoots with the industrialists, 'spread the rumour that the Communists wanted to use the soldiers for their own ends'.[30] Another report, on the Belluno area, speaks of the disbanded soldiers of the Royal Army, passive and fence-sitting, organising themselves into squads, leaving one no option but to organise other, Garibaldi ones;[31] while a former combatant in Spain, who became the commander of the 8th Garibaldi brigade in Romagna, spoke ironically of the generals' and colonels' pretentious claim to create a regular army in the Apennines immediately after 8 September.[32] Such episodes are but a few of the many that Resistance historiography has generally placed in its 'first phase', the one called in very approximate terms 'military', and soon to be superseded by the more mature phase that saw the birth and flowering of the bands connected in various ways with the political parties.

I shall be dealing with the process of politicisation and its links with militarisation in the next chapter. What needs be stressed here is that the 8 September collapse marked a fracture that could not easily be made good in the history of the Italian military institutions and, still less so, in the country's perception of them. The radical stances taken by the *resistenti* are simply the clearest manifestations of this fracture. Those stances even upset the role of father figure that had been entrusted above all to the reserve officers and had constituted the most human face of the Italian military hierarchy. That role had proved capable of tempering the bureaucratic dimension that makes the modern mass army officer 'a special category of official in contrast to the knight, condottiere, tribal chief or Homeric hero'.[33] (Traces of such figures – apart from the Homeric hero – were, for that matter, to be found in the partisan leaders themselves.)

By its very nature, the presence in the partisan formations of Royal Army officers who had enrolled in them contributed to this process. In the first few weeks the political forces had mainly sought superior officers, to whom command duties could be entrusted. Behind this search lay the complex political question

---

30 *Le Brigate Garibaldi*, vol. I, pp. 144–6. In A. Poma and G. Perona, *La Resistenza nel Biellese*, Parma: Guanda, 1972. The document, quoted on pp. 65–6, is attributed to Francesco Scotti, 'perhaps also to Gian Carlo Pajetta'.

31 'Relazione sulle condizioni dell'organizzazione di Belluno, fino al dicembre 1943' (*Le Brigate Garibaldi*, vol. I, pp. 230–41).

32 'Pietro Mauri' (Ilario Tabarri), the author of this 'General report on military activity in the Romagna' up to 15 May 1944, recalls having vainly appealed to the guerrilla movements, to 'the experience of China, of Spain and of all the other European countries' (ibid., pp. 407–21).

33 See M. Weber, 'Parliament and Government in Germany', in *Political Writings*, Cambridge: Cambridge University Press, 1994, p. 146 (original edition: *Parlament und Regierung im neugeordneten Deutschland. Zur politischen Kritik des Beamtentums und Parteiwesens*, Munich-Leipzig: Duneken & Humblot, 1918).

of the relationship with Badoglio's government; and, insofar as it directly bore on the problems of the nascent partisan organisation, it was based on a residual overrating of the technical abilities of the military men, regarded as 'experts' whom one could under no circumstances do without. Even in intensely anti-militarist circles, like those of the first Cuneo GL bands, some such prospect had been fostered.[34] As Bianco recalls, the failure of these searches consolidated the anti-militarist spirit.[35] Drawing no general conclusions, but unequivocally, Ermanno Gorrieri (the Christian Democrat commander) was later to write in his book about the Resistance in the Apennines that 'the regular officers, with a few laudable exceptions, stayed at the margins of or even outside the Resistance.'[36]

A case in point is the affair of General Raffaello Operti, who was nominated to be military commander of Piedmont. Already in October an authoritative Communist leader, in dubbing (with a reservation in favour of the Action Party representative) the members of the military Command of the Piedmontese CLN as fence-sitters, gas-bags and vainglorious stuffed shirts, had summed up his view of things by describing those gentlemen as capable only of thinking of the Royal Army.[37] Before Operti's candidacy, the PCI member responsible for military work in Piedmont levelled extremely harsh criticisms at the general;[38] and the PCI delegation in the committee recalled that Operti had 'been part of the corps commands in the occupied countries, whose actions can only be judged by organisms appointed or to be appointed by the victim peoples of occupation.'[39]

The Communist representatives had evidently wanted to bring up a question that put the committee in a spot; but they had touched on the sore point of war criminals, which was one of those questions on which the ruling class was soon to close ranks. Not only was there to be no handing over of Italian war criminals to the Yugoslavs, the Greeks, the Albanians, the Russians, the Ethiopians, but no extradition of war criminals would be included in the programmes declared by the Resistance. The exchange of obedience for impunity between the generals who signed the surrender and the Allies, institutional continuity, the wish to safeguard the all-absolving myth of the 'goodness of the Italians', Italy's new

34 See a testimony along these lines in Giovana, *Storia di una formazione partigiana*, pp. 34–5.

35 Bianco, *Guerra partigiana*, p. 23.

36 See Gorrieri, *La Repubblica di Montefiorino*, p. 103.

37 Report by Giovanni, 10 October 1943 (*Le Brigate Garibaldi*, vol. I, pp. 104–6).

38 Sandrelli's letter to the political commissars, 11 November 1943, where the reader is referred to what was published in *Il Grido di Spartaco*, undated, 9, article entitled 'Guerra popolare', and to *Il Garibaldino piedmontese* (*Le Brigate Garibaldi*, vol. I, pp. 127–30). For the 'caso Operti' ('the Operti case') see Spriano, *Storia del Partito comunista italiano*, vol. V, *La Resistenza. Togliatti e il partito nuovo*, Turin: Einaudi, 1975, pp. 197–9, and De Luna, *Storia del Partito d'Azione*, pp. 107–8.

39 'Dichiarazione della Delegazione del Partito comunista di Torino nel CLN', November 1943 (IG, *Archivio PCI*).

international position in the incipient Cold War – all of these factors would be opposed to it; nor would contempt at the incriminated General Mario Roatta's flight from a Roman hospital on 7 March 1945 be enough to reverse this trend.[40] Not even in the climate of November 1943 was the preliminary objection by the Turin Communists, interpreters of a sentiment that went beyond their party interests and contained some of the deepest reasons for rejecting the Royal Army and the war, successful. The directive declared so often by the PCI even then – that everything was to be subordinated to the war of liberation – rebounded against the PCI itself, not least because of the stance taken by the Action Party, which took Operti's part, pleading greater military as well as financial needs (Operti was the depository of the 4th Army 'treasury').[41]

But pride in being even technically more competent than the regular officers was to become a strong point of many partisan commanders. We find it proudly expressed by the Command of the Tollot (Veneto) Garibaldi brigade, which urges its men to give the Fascist enemy 'the certainty that he is up against forces organised possibly with greater know-how and technical skill than their own, which number in their ranks wiseacres of their so-called General Staffs of the notorious former Fascist war schools'.[42] The moral superiority that could offset even technical deficiencies was the main point stressed by the GL formations' Lombardy commands, who rejected the commander of the Oroboca division's request to be replaced by a person of greater military competence: 'Twenty years of bad government and Fascist corruption have taught us that only when disinterest, abnegation and self-sacrifice govern one's decision to serve one's country, is the nation served as it should be, by people who also know how to make up for their lack of specific technical specialist skills.'[43]

The downright inefficiency of the Royal Army came under fire, too. Care should be taken, wrote the Garibaldi command of Valsesia, Ossola, Cusio and Verbano, on 24 November 1944, to ensure that 'circulars do not remain dead letters in HQ files as happened in the disbanded Royal Army'.[44] Snide quips

---

40 In the article entitled "'Imperialismo" di vasalli', which he was to publish in *L'Unità*, 12 September 1945, Togliatti denounced the sabotage by the reactionary classes, who had prevented 'the trial of all our war criminals being seriously begun and not of just one of them, Roatta, who was in any case allowed to escape' (in P. Togliatti, *Opere scelte*, ed. G. Santomassimo, Rome: Riuniti, 1974, p. 394). On the failure to punish Italian prisoners-of-war see the BBC November 1989 broadcast, which provoked a clumsy reaction by the Italian embassy in London.

41 'Dichiarazione del Partito d'Azione di Torino', 9 November 1943 (IG, *Archivio PCI*).

42 Report on the meeting of the Tollot brigade Command, 27 March 1945 (INSMLI, CVL, envelope 35, folder i).

43 Letter by the regional Command to the commander and political commissar of the Alpi Orobie zone Command, 17 March 1945 (ibid., envelope 93, folder 5).

44 See the letters of the Command of the group of Garibaldi divisions of the

were made about the arrival of a general sent to 'take command of our boat, which is not, when all is said, to be sniffed at … and which, if this happens, will certainly become something very chic'.[45]

The fact is that relations with the regular officers, but also with those reserve officers who sought their identity in that rank, always remained somewhat tense (Barbato-Pompeo Colajanni – the most popular Garibaldi commander in the Cuneo area, had been a permanent regular officer, but did not act in this guise in the Resistance). Those relations are a particularly fitting terrain for identifying how the broad political lines of the parties and the average conscience of the *resistenti* intertwined. For the parties, the problem had to be seen in terms of what attitude should be taken towards the old institutions being reconstructed in the South, as well as the general view of the war of liberation in Italy, or indeed the world war as a whole. For the *resistenti*, the officers, their uniforms, their language, their behaviour took on a symbolic significance that went beyond the merits or demerits of individuals. Some of the officers who came into contact with the bands seemed, indeed, to be going out of their way to make themselves disliked, or at least ridiculous. On 21 April 1944, Colonel Silvio Marenco, head of SIMAR, an organisation operating in the Siena territory, which took its name from the first letters of his first and surname, declared: 'We are making the recruits born in 1924–25 who are reporting to us take the oath of allegiance to King and Country as before; in other words, we are recreating our army here'.[46] Likewise, Rita, the regular officer who had become commander of the Pasubio division, a formation of uncertain identity, created by the singular figure of Giuseppe Marozin, awarded decorations for military valour (among others, to Marozin himself), 'availing myself of the faculty granted in Russia to the commander of the regiment, for exceptional cases, by His Excellency Marshal Messe'.[47] In the report on the activity of another small Tuscan formation, where after sundry adversities a number of officers were dispatched to take command, Lieutenant Colonel Antonio Malinotti, in an engagement, 'gave orders with a pistol in his hand standing behind a big tree together with his son. The colonel's orders were completely wrong (as the entire formation can testify)'; then,

---

Valsesia, Ossola, Cusio, Verbano to the Command of the 1st division, 24 November 1944 (IG, *BG*, 07078).

45 The Lombardy Command of the GL formations to the Command of the Valtellina Alpine division, 28 January 1945. On 22 February the Lombardy Command would write, 'as for the General, for the time being we have suspended his coming, which I think will probably prove useless' (INSMLI, *CVL*, envelope 93, folder 5).

46 See R. Manno, 'Le bande SIMAR dal settembre 1943 al giugno 1944: aspetti della lotta partigiana nell'Italia Centrale', in *Il Movimento di liberazione in Italia* 101 (October–December 1970), pp. 68–110, and 102 (January–March 1971), pp. 45–81.

47 'Relazione sull'attività svolta dalla divisione', sent on 13 December 1944 to the 'central' CLN in Milan (IG, *BG*, 09487).

finding himself before a German action, 'the colonel, almost with tears in his eyes, insisted on abandoning arms and commending his soul to God since all of them would die'; finally, another three officers arrived: 'giving military orders, filing us up in squads; reluctantly we obeyed. The officers immediately understood that the partisans weren't soldiers, a captain spoke up saying he and his companions demanded the formal "Lei" address, that he would brook no argument, that the affairs of superiors were no concern of ours.'[48]

Certainly, in the reactions towards the army and the officers, different time-frames must again be distinguished. In the first weeks and months, what was involved was an immediate consequence of the moral crisis of the army and of disillusion in the residual hopes reposed in it. In a central phase, individual officers would be received into the more or less politicised formations, while the autonomous ones, generally led by military men, would provide structures which, despite a sometimes flaunted continuity with the Royal Army, would actually acquire a high degree of self-legitimisation. Lastly, in the final phase, when 'militarisation' sought institutionally guaranteed expression, the officers, as such, were once more to play at least a formal role, above all in the unified commands. For example, the zone Command for the province of Modena would consist of General Marco Guidelli – Max – and nine other members, eight of whom were officers, whose style would impress itself upon, if not the men's conduct, at least the documents they drafted.[49]

Typical of the first phase is the order sent on 9 November 1943 by a regular officer, who described himself as 'military commander of the Biella CLN', 'a tutte le baite' ('to all the huts'), ordering the consignment of all weapons, which he would redistribute according to new criteria, and declaring anyone who failed to obey a 'dissident' and 'rebel', to be prosecuted as such: 'It has finally been made unequivocally clear', the order explained, 'that there is no such figure as a political commander or a political officer or a civil commander. There is just the one commander and he is to be obeyed.'[50]

---

48 'Relazione del residuo della formazione Magni Magnino passati poi alla Buscaglia', dated Castelfiorentino, 28 August 1944. Lieutenant Colonel Malanotti is accused of incompetence and abandonment of his post, also in the 'Relazione sulla formazione di "Bustinchini" fatta dal commissario politico Nello Gilardetti' (the two reports are in ISRT, *Fondo Salvadori – PCI Castelfiorentino*, insert 59).

49 See the 'Relazioni sulle operazioni che hanno portato alla liberazione della provincia e della città di Modena', edited by the Command and signed Max, undated, but shortly after the liberation (copy in IG, *BG, Emilia-Romagna*, G. IV. 3–1). A panorama of the officers present in the zone and city Commands of Emilia-Romagna is in L. Bergonzini, *La lotta armata*, Bari: De Donato, 1975 (vol. I of *L'Emilia Romagna nella guerra di liberazione*, edited by the local delegation), pp. 214–15.

50 A copy of the ordinance, signed 'Il comandante Gorizia' (Lieutenant Graglia) is in IG, *Archivio PCI*. It is published from another copy in Poma and Perona, *La Resistenza nel Biellese*, pp. 431–2. On the activities of this lieutenant see pp. 63–7.

Positions of this kind could only rekindle convictions like that expressed in a document kept in the archives of the Garibaldi brigade general headquarters: 'It will be a long time before the Italian officers are able to redeem their reputation for incompetence and indifference to the *patria*, or even treason, which they earned for themselves in the most critical days of the Badoglio period'.[51] More brusquely, a partisan said to Pietro Chiodi, 'The regular officers who aren't partisans are traitors and one day we'll shoot them'.[52]

On the other hand, still in the early days, the officers who joined the Garibaldi formations, particularly in the areas under strong pressure from the Slavs, received requests that the Communist directives would duly not only exclude but partly overturn into prohibitions. Thus, on 27 September Mario Lizzeri, a leader who was later to perform highly responsible functions in Friuli, reported, with a mixture of indignation and resentment, that the officers, windbags and pedants, wanted to be called patriots, refused to make the closed-fist salute, and wished to do away with the name 'political commissar'.[53] Witness, by contrast, the firm tone with which a similar problem was dealt with in a Piedmontese Garibaldini document of 10 October 1944, which tells the story of a captain who 'has done his level best to persuade us to give up our positions and become exclusively soldiers [*militari*]. How can we get him to understand that we are soldiers in the true sense of the word and not as he would have it, for interests decidedly against the Italian people?'

The document goes on to say that the captain 'will help us the day after the war is over ... we are very sorry if we do not receive help, [but] like the inhabitants of Warsaw we know where our duty lies and shall do it whatever the cost, since we are sure of being able to give [*sic*] alongside the entire people'.[54]

In fact, the largest formations – the Garibaldi and GL – came to develop remarkably flexible attitudes to the officers, out of both political expediency and faith in the new solidarity that the partisan struggle was capable of fathering and developing, recreating within its own ranks plainer hierarchies of value. Witness what Vanni [Giovanni Padoan], political commissar of the Natisone Garibaldi division, wrote on this score in his memoirs. The ranks held in the Royal Army, he explains, 'did not count; on the contrary, at times they could be a hindrance. There were cases of former officers who rose again from the ranks to became fine partisan commanders loved and respected by their men.' Not so, Vanni polemically goes on to say, in the Osoppo formations (which were

---

51   Undated, but not long after 8 September 1943 (IG, *BG*, 005488).

52   Chiodi, *Banditi*, p. 28 (26 June 1944).

53   'Relazione su reparti di patrioti italiani della zona di Subit, Porzus e Foran (Udine)' (*Le Brigate Garibaldi*, vol. I, pp. 98–9).

54   'I compagni responsibili' to the 'cari compagni' of the 3rd Piedmont division (ibid., vol. II, pp. 424–8).

prevalently national–Catholic).[55] It is interesting to read this testimony by Vanni, who was an experienced Communist leader, parallel with that of Carlino, the chief of the General Staff of the same division, who was in fact one of those officers, mentioned by Vanni, who had re-qualified themselves (Carlino – the Ferdinando Mautino whom we have already encountered several times – had been an officer with the occupying troops in Croatia, and had ended up with the Natisone division in January 1944, after fighting with the Croat and Slovene partisans). Carlino thus writes that every officer, 'royal or republican', 'was asked to abandon positions acquired in very different settings and for a very different combination of reasons; each was obliged to assume the maximum responsibility that his intellectual, moral and military capacities, and the requirements of the struggle, demanded of him'.[56]

The internal rehabilitation described by Vanni and Carlino is altogether different from the sudden arrival of the officers, 'relics of the militarist face of Fascism' – as a GL document put it – with their ambition of taking command of formations that had come into being and developed autonomously.[57]

Significant differences have been noted here between the Action Party–GL formations and the Communist Party–Garibaldi formations (in both cases, it must always be remembered, the political and military organisms never fully coincide), independently of their different attitudes to the institutional problem and the Badoglio government. In the GL formations there was no preconceived social distrust of the officers, but often a high degree of moral distrust, albeit tempered by willingness to recognise a certain role, in the best cases, for the professionalism of their technical military know-how. Some GL documents, particularly high-level ones, display a tone of military aristocracy, coupled pedagogically with the democratic aims of the movement. A case in point is a Piedmont Command circular whose form is very much in the tradition of the army, while its content exhorts the men to break away from it. The purpose of the circular is formulated as follows: 'Collaboration with the other divisions of partisan troops'. *Reparti* (divisions) and *truppe* (troops) are words utterly at odds with the plainer partisan language, as is *soldati*, which nevertheless recurs also in the diary of the GL intellectual Emanuele Artom. But the circular then expresses the concept that our struggle is 'essentially political', even if the GLs are not 'the expression of a party', and reminds its readers that 'we do not want to recreate the essentially static, bureaucratic situations of the old army, in which the

---

55 See G. Padoan (Vanni), *Abbiamo lottato insieme. Partigiani italiani e sloveni al confine orientale*, Udine: Del Bianco, 1965, p. 122.

56 Mautino, *Guerra di popolo*, p. 39.

57 Circular of the Command of the GL formations, written 9 May 1944, when, in concomitance with the predicted Allied offensive, the arrival of Anglo-American and Badoglian officers was thought to be imminent (*Formazioni GL*, p. 89).

high Commands were the sole depositories of the Word'.[58] Also valuable is Beppe Fenoglio's description of a partisan who has 'the face of a GL': in an English uniform, 'with the air half of an intellectual and half of a regular officer'.[59]

In the Garibaldi brigades, by contrast, superimposed on a high degree of social distrust – though often more for reasons of party discipline than out of deep conviction – there was the line that rallied anyone showing a genuine wish to fight, and therefore, indeed often with particular emphasis, the army officers as well. Initially the appeals, when they were not highly stereotyped repetitions of those preceding 8 September, are less confident; but they then draw strength from the very development achieved by the formations. In this case, too, we would do better to refer not to the general PCI directives, which are sufficiently well-known and where the appeal to a policy of unity after the Salerno 'turning-point' went so far as to attempt to attach the 'military' and 'autonomous' formations as well to the CLN,[60] but to intermediate or low-level documents. 'We have said', reads a Turin Communist document of 10 October 1943, 'that the partisan formations organised and controlled by us are formations of the National Guard emanating from the people and that they recognise no authority other than the CLN. This does not mean that we deny the officers faithful to the old army and the monarchy' the right to keep their opinions and to fight, even in formations that 'appeal to and regard themselves as units of the Royal Army and obey Badoglio'.[61] Around about the same time, a violent attack against cowardly officers, but a hand held out to honest ones, appears in a Garibaldi General Command document.[62] And if some formations balked at this, they were told the error of their ways. Thus the Casotti brigade, which had not wanted as commander a certain captain Bellinzona, alias Saetta, 'with the excuse that he hasn't served with partisans long enough or something of the kind', was told in answer that he was an officer 'of unquestionable merit because a captain at the age of twenty-six', and that 'his position as regular officer who since 8 September has not reported for service is to his credit'. Thus, the reprimand concluded, 'this is an error, comrade, because we are after the necessary political creed, but we also

---

58 *Formazioni GL*, pp. 106–8. See Foa's invitation to practise 'assiduous vigilance' to prevent 'the influence of the old military caste', which had been eliminated, with effort, from reflowering (Inverni, *I partiti*, p. 21).

59 B. Fenoglio, 'Golia', in *Un giorno di fuoco e altri racconti*, Milan: Garzanti, 1963, p. 568.

60 See for example the article entitled 'Il Fronte Nazionale unitario ed i suoi compiti di lotta', in *L'Unità*, northern edition, 25 May 1944. The article says that 'after the formation of the national democratic war government, there is no longer any reason to maintain a division which is wholly damaging to the anti-German movement and not to establish political collaboration in common organs'.

61 'Informazioni per l'ufficio di organizzazione', signed by Alfredo (IG, *Archivio PCI*).

62 See the undated document, IG, *BG*, 005488.

want people keen to fight against the common enemy'; and besides, we must 'give the Voghera lot some joy and not rub them up the wrong way'.[63] The fear that, by means of the CLN ('the Voghera lot'), the officers would make a bid for positions they didn't deserve is expressed with great frankness in this other document:

> If we get the CLN to intervene now, before having the Command under our belts, they might send along their usual majors (they always have them tucked away some-where or other and you know very well what they're worth and what orientation they have) and be ousted, and so let control slip away from us, after working so hard to keep those forces on their feet.[64]

Even in documents containing self-criticism for disrespectful behaviour towards the officers, it was said that the latter did not manage to get themselves taken too seriously, particularly when they flocked in during the euphoria of the summer of 1944. The SAP divisional Command of Turin writes (though it should be borne in mind that the SAPs were support formations for urban guer-rilla warfare, certainly the type least suited to Royal Army officers):

> Possibly we can criticise ourselves for not having known how to behave with the officers, expecting from youngsters, with a petit-bourgeois mentality, what one could expect from already well-proven comrades. Perhaps we are not diplomatic enough and incapable of that tact and delicacy needed when dealing with daddy's boys, who are easily upset by rough proletarian forms ... Our belief is that the offic-ers, unless they are very intelligent elements or comrades of proven faith, can be used as technicians, without command functions.[65]

Greater faith, and also greater tact, was expressed, instead, by a 'scheme for the organisation of a Garibaldi assault brigade Command', issued a few months earlier by the general Command, which considered the possibility of giving posi-tions of command to 'the officers who maintain a proud and firm anti-German and anti-Fascist stance'.[66]

---

63 Letter by Giorgio, undated, to a 'caro compagno' (INSMLI, *CVL*, envelope 93, folder 4).

64 For the same reason, the document went on to say, there is no need to ask the CLN, bureaucratically, for 'the promotion of those detachments to Garibaldi brigades. When it is already established we can present the CLN as something that exists and that gives its unconditional support to the Committee itself': the military Committee of Piedmont to the Command of the 4th Cuneo brigade, 18 March 1944 (*Le Brigate Garibaldi*, vol. I, pp. 310–16).

65 'Rapporto sul lavoro SAP', 30 October 1944 (IG, *BG*, 06051).

66 The document bears two dates, 15 and 20 May: the second is also that of the

Still more brusquely, and almost upending the terms of the question – in order, possibly, to prevent the worst from occurring – on the eve of the Insurrection, the regional triumvirate for Emilia-Romagna would declare: 'There is no doubt that the officers who take command are to be *apolitical*: they will be officers and no more. Even if the majority will probably belong to no party, supporters of parties cannot and must not be excluded – that would be the limit!'[67]

In the appeals made to the officers who had joined the Social Republic, or even those who merely lay low without committing themselves, their soldier's status is stressed in a clearly instrumental way. Thus, shortly after the Salerno turning-point, the north Italian edition of *L'Unità* also invoked the duty to obey the orders of 'superiors';[68] while, more emphatically, a poster of the 7th Garibaldi division (Valle d'Aosta), addressed to 'officers, non-commissioned officers, Alpini, our Brothers!', made a direct appeal to the wartime experience of 1940–43:

> We are former officers, former soldiers of the old Royal Army, who have however done our duty on all the fronts and now want to redeem the honour of an Italy which is derided, humiliated because of a regime of swaggerers, of thieving fathers- and sons-in-law … so you can't fire at your former colleagues and fellow-combatants of the old battles bitterly fought together and lost only because they were poorly armed and poorly led by incompetent Fascist officers.

It is no accident that a document of this tenor, which constitutes a sort of *summa* of 'continuismo' between the 1940–43 combatants and those of 1943–45, contemptuously rejects the description of the partisans as 'rebels', 'bandits', 'outlaws', let alone, obviously, 'cowards'.[69] A fairly late document of the military Command of the Ossola area offers a clear summary of the main lines of the attitude that had been taking shape towards the officers, who, given the imminent end of the war, were flocking in in ever greater numbers. The spirit of the document is that one should not disappoint the officers, that one should give them a good welcome, but that it was necessary to take care not to create misunderstandings, and to bring it home to them how different the atmosphere of the partisan army was from that of the Royal Army – no *naja* (military service), a political but not a party mentality; no ranks save those recognised by the

---

circular that transmits the 'schema' of the dependent organisms (INSMLI, *Brigate Garibaldi*, envelope 1, folder 4).

67 The triumvirate of the Communist federation of Modena, 23 March 1945 (ISRR, *Archivio del triumvirato insurrezionale Emilia-Romagna*).

68 Appeal to 'Ufficiali italiani!', 25 May 1944.

69 Appeal to 'Ufficiali, Sottufficiali, Alpini, Fratelli nostri!', undated (IG, *BG*, 05631).

patriots; the use of the officers, mainly – even after the period of re-education provided for – only as military advisers.[70]

Just one corps, the Alpini, were well thought of in the Resistance. Nevertheless, even the Alpini myth was to be critically scrutinised, both to see how much personalities like Nuto Revelli retrospectively contributed to the creation of that myth (Revelli's work, moreover, has become part of a literary tradition that no other Italian military corps can boast), and to identify the dissent or at least doubt that already existed at the time of the Resistance. Hitler himself could be called to testify in favour of the Alpini: at his Klessheim meeting with Mussolini on 23 April 1944, he classed them as being 'among our worst enemies'.[71] Certainly, if the spirit of the Bersaglieri – to name another of the traditional and, in their way, popular corps of the Italian army – is compared with that of the Alpini, it appears clear why the latter, and not the former, became assimilated into a sort of Resistance ethos, most widespread in the GL formations, many of which took the name 'divisione alpina Giustizia e Libertà'. In his book on the Russian campaign, Giusto Tolloy says: 'Bersaglierismo in fact had its beginnings in Garibaldinismo in a purely formal sense, and the red fez is still there to recall its origins' – so it is hardly surprising that it is found alongside Fascist squadrismo, 'which itself adopted its half-brother's fez, dyed black'. Against this brusque verdict – which took no account of the date of birth of the Bersaglieri (1836), but distinguished affinities underlined by Fascism itself – Tolloy affirmed that 'in no Italian corps was there a greater democratic spirit and convinced discipline' than in the Alpini, even if that corps had in its turn been polluted by Fascism.[72] This seems to be borne out by the Alpini of the Pusteria division, who carried out a scorched-earth policy in the Balkans.[73] And an Alpino from the Greek front had spoken of 'old scarponi [as the Alpini were nicknamed] moulded in a Mussolinian atmosphere, and we have no fear of death'.[74] These words seem to bear the imprint of a spirit much akin to that of the bersagliere who wrote from Dalmatia to a fellow-soldier: 'The bersaglieri are the true soldiers, they are the symbol of vitality, they perpetuate the race of

---

70 Circular of 24 February 1945 'to all formations dependent operative sectors', concerning 'officials who flock to the formations'. The document is signed by the political commissar Livio and by the military commander Colonel Delle Torri (Le Brigate Garibaldi, vol. III, pp. 412–15)

71 See Deakin, The Brutal Friendship, p. 679. For 'l'alpinità' partigiana see M. Giovana, 'Tradizioni e stereotipi militari nella guerra partigiana italiana', in Notiziario dell'Istituto storico della Resistenza in Cuneo e provincia 29: 1 (September 1986), pp. 27–87 (esp. p. 69–87).

72 See Tarchi (G. Tolloy), Con l'armata italiana in Russia, pp. 72, 186.

73 See Collotti, L'occupazione nazista, p. 543.

74 Letter by Nicola Di Febo di Pescasseroli, who died in Bari of wounds received on the Greek front (in Ceva, Cinque anni, p. 28).

those created [by God] to dare'.[75] Against the *bersagliere* with his hundred feathers and the Alpino with just one, the partisan, in one of his songs, would affirm the value of those who were up in the mountains fighting without possessing a single feather.

The fact is that the Social Republic too managed to organise its own Alpine division, the Monterosa, which arrived in Italy in August 1944. As in the case of the other three divisions put together in Germany, for many enlisting was simply a means of getting back to Italy and then deserting.[76] The keenest remained, giving sorry proof of themselves in the armed forces of Salò. Here is the testimony of a report by the Conegliano CLN: 'We have managed to unmask the wicked activity of the Alpini in our area led by a well-known war criminal, Attilio Pillon.'[77] The memory of the execution of three GL partisans at Casteldelfino provoked this comment from Mario Giovana: 'In this way even our illusions about the Alpini were waning.'[78] In his diary Pietro Chiodi records that a partisan who had been taken prisoner related how he had been 'beaten and tortured by the SS and the Alpini ... The latter amused themselves by sticking their plumes up his nostrils. An officer kept repeating amid the quips of his men: while you're here, your wife is having fun with others.'[79]

Fascist sources tell the same story. Unpopular with and insulted by the population, who call them 'traitors', 'men who've sold themselves', 'down-and-outs', the Monterosa Alpini 'are often compelled to use an iron hand'; they react to provocation 'immediately and energetically ... shooting numerous elements', and intend that at the end of the war they'll be the ones to sort out the Italians who 'need to be purged'.[80]

Detached and slightly embarrassed, Dante Livio Bianco placed the word 'Alpini' in quotation marks when referring to those of the Monterosa left in the valley, even if 'they don't appear to be too numerous or bellicose'.[81] But Revelli can't hold back this cry of anguish: 'It seemed impossible to me that my Russian Alpini were wearing German uniforms. I saw them come out huddled together

---

75 Letter of 10 July 1942 (Rizzi, *Lo sguardo del potere*, p. 97).

76 'You say that the Alpini haven't yet arrived, but I have to tell you that they have all managed to flee'. Letter sent from Vigliano d'Asti ('Esami della corrispondenza censurata al 30 giugno 1944', in ACS, *SPD, CR, RSI*, envelope 9, folder 3).

77 Information sent to various CLNs and Commands of the CVL, 23 March 1945 (INSMLI, *CLNAI*, envelope 7, folder 2, subfolder 11).

78 See Giovana, *Storia di una formazione partigiana*, p. 278.

79 Chiodi, *Banditi*, p. 56 (25 August 1944).

80 See Pansa, *L'esercito di Salò*, pp. 192–3: GNR report of 19 August and 19 October 1944, relating to the zone of Sestrini Levante (the first was written just twenty days after the division's return to Italy).

81 Letter to Nuto and Dado, Pradleves, 31 October 1944 (see Revelli, *La guerra dei poveri*, pp. 467–8).

like a flock of sheep. I tried to make out at least one of my comrades among them, but they were all alike'.[82]

The link, which was also its limit, between the Alpini of the ARMIR and the 'alpino' spirit of some of the Resistance, can be gleaned from what Giorgio Rochat says about the Russian campaign. The compact and united attitude of the Alpini, which he sees as a 'furious hope to save themselves in the teeth of those who had driven them out there, the German master and the proud enemy',[83] Rochat considers 'far more defensive than offensive, aimed at the group's survival on the socio-cultural plane more than on the military one'. In other words, it was an instrument 'to defend a collective identity', where 'the weakening of "national" values gave way to closer and more limited "municipalistic", values, like, indeed, *esprit de corps*'.[84]

In connection with the problem of local partisan recruitment, Revelli observed: 'It's the nucleus of *montanari*, the Alpini partisans, that keeps the brigade in one piece'; and, comparing his memory of the Don line and the experience of the Alpine huts of Paralup, he pointed out: 'The discipline, the hierarchy, at Belogore as at Paralup, was not a matter of form, but of substance. The Alpini respected the corporal, the NCO, the officer whom they esteemed. Ranks counted for nothing ... Our soldiers were waging war in grey-green uniforms, but underneath, on their skin, they wore bourgeois stuff, from home, made of warm wool'.[85]

Here, we are among the GL units of the Cuneo area. But in other *resistenti*, for example among the Garibaldini of the Isontino, Alpine solidarity could appear, instead, in the guise of old-style paternalism. The commanders of the Osoppo formations – national Catholics, but with a vein of *azionismo* as well[86] – struck the political commissar of the Natisone division as being 'distant from their men and when they approached them they did so in the paternalistic spirit of the Alpini officers'.[87] For that matter, still less politicised autonomous formations of the Osoppo brigade and plainly 'military' ones, like the divisions commanded by Major 'Mauri' (Enrico Martini), had also dubbed themselves *alpine*. In the first section of one of their 'Regulations', the Brescian Green Flames, disliked both by

---

82 Those involved were the Alpini of the Tridentina division – the case is therefore different from that of the Monterosa – captured at the Brenner pass and concentrated, in Italian SS uniforms, in a barracks in Cuneo. See ibid., p. 154, beneath the date 30 November 1943.

83 Tarchi (G. Tolloy), *Con l'armata italiana in Russia*, p. 187.

84 Rochat, *Memorialistica e storiografia*, p. 481.

85 Annotations beneath the dates 23 August and 14 February 1944 (Revelli, *La guerra dei poveri*, pp. 322, 172–3).

86 Fogar has drawn attention to this component of the Osoppo formations in *Le brigate Osoppo-Friuli*, pp. 269–360.

87 See Padoan (Vanni), *Abbiamo lottato insieme*, p. 190.

the Garibaldini and the GL, wrote, with gestures drawn from patriotic rhetoric: 'The Green Flames are continuing the glorious tradition of the Italian Alpine battalions, which have never known defeat.'[88]

As already with the Arditi, the Alpini were compared with the *paracadutisti* (the paratroopers), the army's latest speciality.[89] We have already seen how, after 25 July, with the collapse of the National-Fascist motivations for fighting the war, a powerful *esprit de corps* had sought to take their place. After 8 September this identity – expressed in the formula, 'We are above all *paracadutisti*'[90] – found itself with a still heavier and more contradictory task. On the one hand, it meant that the paratroopers became one of the most solid divisions of the CIL (Italian Liberation Corps); on the other hand, by insisting on a high degree of continuity between the two wars (1940–43 and 1943–45), and consequently refusing to accept any serious criticism of the recent past, it rendered impossible any genuine moral participation in the new experience. The case of the *paracadutisti* thus lays bare how a merely combative ethic was incapable of carrying the weight of such profound historical upheavals. The Fascist-type conduct of the *paracadutisti* in the Kingdom of the South, which made them resemble their fellow-soldiers of the Social Republic, was rooted in the fact that the 'wide horizon of myths, symbolic references and values which had found expression and exaltation in Fascism, precipitating into the world war even in the identity of the corps born from it, did not appear to be called into question.'[91]

It is easy, therefore, to understand not only the denunciations and protests from the democratic side,[92] but also the distrust that made General Umberto Utili advise against dropping *paracadutisti* behind the lines,[93] and finally the fact that after the war the *paracadutisti* of the North and South cancelled the Gothic line, converging into a single association. Frustration and the incapacity to overcome it characterise these soldiers. Paradigmatic of this is the episode which sees the *paracadutisti* triumphantly entering a liberated village in the Marche: joy at this rediscovered unison with the spirit of the people is immediately wrecked by their seeing those applauding them with clenched fists.[94] This gave birth to

---

88 See the 'Regolamento', undated, in sixteen paragraphs, conserved in INSMLI, *CVL*, envelope 90, folder 12.

89 For a comparison between the Alpini and the *arditi*, see Rochat, *Gli arditi della grande guerra*, pp. 72–3.

90 See *Folgore. Foglio da campo del paracadutista italiano*, 15 October 1943 (cited in Di Giovanni, degree thesis).

91 See Di Giovanni, degree thesis.

92 One of the most authoritative is the one that Togliatti was to make in his report to the 5th Congress of the PCI (Togliatti, *Opere*, vol. V, p. 192).

93 See Di Giovanni's degree thesis, which also records the fears that in the transfer from Sardinia to Naples the *paracadutisti* would divert the ship towards the territory of the RSI.

94 This episode is recounted by Gaetano, regular NCO, in his answer to a

defeatist velleities which, *excusatio non petita*, induced someone to write in the corps newspaper: 'There's no getting rid of the so-called squadristic spirit'.[95] On the opposite side, the army put together by the Social Republic in turn found itself in a tricky relationship with the tradition of the Italian army. If the armed forces of the Social Republic seemed to have broken drastically with those of the Royal Army, this formal fracture with the institutional authorities of the state was not matched by a corresponding fracture in the institution of the army as such. Moreover, continuity with the war alongside the German ally – indeed, continuity with 'all the wars', as the Fascists were forever fond of putting it – provided a legitimising framework for the army, and also to a great extent the RSI as such. It was inevitable that a high degree of continuity should derive from the two wars even in the armed forces which had fought them, and which had to continue fighting them. Badoglio might well be dubbed the 'felon marshal'; but could all the marshals, all the generals, all the high-ranking officers of the army, be dubbed felons? Could the whole structure be considered irremediably corrupt?

The dilemma that the Social Republic encountered when it attempted to furnish itself with a military organism was, if truth be told, but one aspect of the more general contradiction with which the Social Republic and the republican Fascist Party had to grapple as regards the Kingdom of Italy and the Fascist National Party, i.e. the twenty-year-old Fascist–monarchic regime. It is well-known that, in the case of the armed forces, this contradiction was shown in the different ideas as to how they should be organised that were held, on the one hand, by Marshal Rodolfo Graziani, who had become minister of defence, and on the other, by the old *squadrista* ringleader Renato Ricci, now chief of the militia, and Alessandro Pavolini, secretary of the Republican Fascist Party (PFR).[96] The communiqué issued on 27 September 1943, after the first meeting of the renascent Fascist government, reads as follows: 'The land, sea and air forces will be respectively incorporated into the militia, navy and air force of the republican Fascist state. Recruitment will be by conscription and by voluntary choice.'[97]

In line with their programme of creating a 'new', political and Fascist army, Renato Ricci and Alessandro Pavolini were in favour of voluntary enlistment; whereas Rodolfo Graziani, an old regular officer, was for conscription and recruitment in the internment camps in Germany (the Germans wanted

---

questionnaire given to him by M. Di Giovanni (see the latter's degree thesis).

95 'Saluto al Gruppo Folgore', in *Folgore*, 15 November 1944 (cited in the degree thesis of M. Di Giovanni).

96 See the chapter entitled 'The Battle for the Republican Army', in Deakin, *The Brutal Friendship*; Bocca, *La Repubblica di Mussolini*, chapter entitled 'Il riarmo'; Pansa, *L'esercito di Salò*; Setta, *Renato Ricci*, pp. 251–58.

97 See Deakin, *The Brutal Friendship*, p. 575.

conscription but, to be on the safe side, training in Germany). Deakin is right when he says that the result of the internecine struggle for control of the armed forces was that the RSI found itself again with 'a series of private armies and police forces owing but tenuous allegiance to any central authority'.[98] This state of affairs made it hardly likely that there would be the recovery, so frequently boasted of by the Fascists, from the collapse suffered by the armed forces on 8 September; but it opened up new possibilities for those who somehow or other managed to pick themselves up. On the one hand, there was a small minority of diehards, easily swallowed up by the more violent aspects of the Italian military tradition. On the other hand, there was a certain quantity of conscripts, again wearing grey-green uniforms, with the *gladius* rather than stars, who instead reproduced the most depressing features of the old army. The censors recorded disbandments, desertions, 'oaths taken passively', 'humanitarian- or religious-based defeatism', and above all impatience with, or even hatred of, barrack-room life and military service.[99] Very probably, the choice of the title *Naja repubblichina* – a small newspaper published by the Cuneo GL, and addressed to the soldiers of the Monterosa and Littorio divisions[100] – was prompted by an accurate intuition of this reality. 'Getting their pay and fence-sitting' are the distinguishing features of the officers of the RSI army, according to a report by the Cremona Republican National Guard of 4 October 1944;[101] and many other Fascist sources do not skimp on unsparing descriptions of the low morale and scant or even nonexistent fighting spirit of the new Republican army. 'We're sick of being soldiers', one soldier writes, in the hope that the censors of his letter will get a clear 'concept of us'.[102]

Already, at the end of 1943, a report from the Modena area speaks of recruits born between 1923 and 1925 who had presented themselves 'solely for fear of something worse befalling them', and who lacked 'the spirit of sacrifice, love of their country, youthful enthusiasm for anything military; in short, they bore with them the whole wretched bourgeois mentality which lately has completely disoriented almost the entire Italian population'.[103]

On the threshold of summer 1944, a German document describes the

98 Ibid., p. 602.

99 'Esame della correspondenza censurata al 30 giugno 1944'. 'È un'altra volta come prima', 'It's again like before', says one of the censored letters (ACS, *SPD, CR, RSI*, envelope 9, folder 3).

100 See Bianco, *Guerra partigiana*, pp. 120–1.

101 See Pansa, *L'esercito di Salò*, p. 139. Pansa's book has a wealth of documents similar in tenor to this.

102 See Rizzi, *Lo sguardo del potere*, p. 153.

103 Report by Captain Gino Greco, commander of the Sassuolo infantry training battalion, to the provincial chief and the military Command of the province of Modena, 18 December 1943 (see Gorrieri, *La Repubblica di Montefiorino*, p. 56).

situation in the Biella area as follows: 'The Italian commands of the different units place themselves behind the German commands and take no initiatives of their own ... The Italian commands are not a hundred percent committed to the struggle, the troops are not committed at all. One can't rule out the possibility that many will go over to the enemy.'[104]

The German Colonel Jandl made this general observation: 'The men who must form the new army, and particularly the higher-ranking officers, may be inferior in number; but otherwise they will always be the same. The September 8th revolution has not brought about a spiritual change.'[105] Similar views are found in the Anglo-American documents.[106] Even an Italian SS division, 'all southerners', who have donned that uniform 'in order to get back from Germany', are mocked in a GL document for 'not being employed except to look after the horses'.[107] And, as had already happened in the Royal Army, the choral war-song, an 'element of spiritual invigoration', was given the task of reviving the troops' spirits, forgetting once again the distance separating a spontaneous song (including the Fascist ones) and a song ordered from above, between 'the manly youth who with Roman determination will fight' and 'I'm a poor deserter', sung by the Alpini in Russia.[108] Towards the Royal Army and their symbols, the volunteer Fascist soldiers, or at least the more highly motivated of them, showed a hostility and contempt that vied with those of the *resistenti* – proving again how similar reactions found different outlets. Witness the letter of a soldier who, in the Balkans, had gone over to serve directly under the Germans:

> I've suffered a lot but have already forgotten. What I haven't forgotten, though, are those sons of bitches, the Italian officers who abandoned us in the mountains of the Balkans, naked, without a piece of bread, and I who went the rounds of the Muslims' houses asking for a piece of bread or *polenta* to appease my hunger, naked and unshod, without clothes in the depth of winter sleeping in the woods.[109]

---

104 'Rapporto sulla situazione di Biella e dintorni', signed by 'Zollrat', 15 June 1944 (IG, *BG*, 06139).

105 Quoted in Deakin, *The Brutal Friendship*, p. 599.

106 See for example the *Report on conditions in enemy occupied Italy*, n. 37, of the Italian Theatre, HQ, PWB, Secret, 7 February 1945 (ISRT, *Archivio Medici Tornaquinci*, envelope 3, 6, n. 1).

107 'Relazione fatta da Nardi per conto del Partito d'Azione, dalla zona Lecco-Brianza', 14 April 1945 (INSMLI, *CVL*, envelope 93, folder 5).

108 See the circular by General Mischi, head of the General Staff, quoted in Pansa, *L'esercito di Salò*, p. 140. For songs in the Italian military tradition, see M. Isnenghi, *Le guerre degli Italiani. Parole, immagini, ricordi 1848–1945*, Milan: Mondadori, 1989, pp. 71–113.

109 'Esame della corrispondenza censurata al 30 giugno 1944' (ACS, *SPD*, *CR*, *RSI*, envelope 9, folder 3).

In another letter, as was sometimes the case between 1940 and 1943 as well, when comparisons were made with the German army the latter came out best in every way, and not only in terms of military power. A soldier training in Germany writes:

> And then in the German army the officers have rights and duties like all the soldiers, they wear the clothes that the soldiers wear … When, seeing this, I think back, as I say, to our officers, it makes me want to laugh, they really seem like so many shop-window mannequins. They're capable of elegance, robbery and abuses of power of every kind. No distinction is made even for meals, even the generals eat the meals prepared for the troops in equal doses. The only difference is that these command and the others obey. With this system, what would seem very rigid discipline automatically becomes the most natural thing in the world; when a soldier is treated as a soldier in the true sense of the word, and not as a slave and wretch as we were treated, everything becomes pleasant and bearable.[110]

The Fascists who made their choice in Italy express themselves no less radically: 'Ranks no longer exist … The defeat has abolished them. We're all equal! Let them just try coming and busting our balls!'[111] Stars of rank become an 'abhorred symbol', which is torn off, but – remember the contradiction pointed out above – a lieutenant says: 'I've nothing to be ashamed of for wearing my stars, if anyone so much as tries I'll kill him.'[112] 'But what are they doing here?' the volunteers would say of the re-draftees. And their faithful interpreter recalls: 'There was a disconsolate atmosphere, of people doing things without conviction, reluctantly resigned to having to do them, and which the mess officer's clowning certainly did nothing to dissipate … We didn't mix with them.'[113] A Fascist newspaper of 29 February 1944 speaks of young men who signed up 'with enthusiasm and faith and who now say that they are discouraged'. There was even a drop in the morale of the 'volontari della morte' ('volunteers of death'), contaminated by the many badogliani with whom they were incorporated.[114] 'They seem like the royal army', a partisan chief said of a group of deserters who went over to the ranks of the Resistance.[115] Yet this 'seem like the royal army'

---

110 Ibid. The director of SIM, C. Amè (Guerra segreta in Italia, 1940–1943, Rome: Casini 1954, quoted in Rizzi, Lo sguardo del potere, p. 64), has spoken of the impression that the 'different … form of mutual spiritual relations between officers and troops' made on the Italian troops in North Africa.
111 Mazzantini, A cercar la bella morte, p. 41.
112 The episode is recounted in ibid., p. 170.
113 Ibid., pp. 143–4.
114 See Rizzi, Lo sguardo del potere, p. 91, and 'Esame della corrispondenza censurata al 30 giugno 1944' (ACS, SPD, CR, RSI, envelope 9, folder 3).
115 M. Bernardo, Il momento buono. Il movimento garibaldino bellunese nella lotta

would also be the salvation of the RSI officers when the tribunals appointed to judge them after the Liberation felt, as has been written, a 'sense of guilt' towards them.[116]

This sort of low-level continuity – as we might call it – this sort of drawn-out, dragging 8 September, is found, too, in an opposite political and international context, in the army that the Kingdom of the South was endeavouring to put back on its feet. The inefficiency, the mediocre fighting spirit, the lack of motivation, the widespread draft-dodging (the 'we're not going' sentiment), the desertions, the scant influx of volunteers, are well-known phenomena.[117] They need to be recalled here as confirmation of the fact that the moral disenchantment with the Royal Army was as widespread a phenomenon in the South as in the North, though obviously it manifested itself in very different forms. Nor, in the case of the South, can this phenomenon be said to have been reabsorbed by the process of bureaucratic reconstruction that the old military institutions somehow succeeded in setting in motion. On the contrary, this very restructuring, in the small part that was successful as in the large part in which it suffered setbacks, reveals (with due exceptions) how historically mistaken it is to speak of the moral unity that was created between the combatants – the partisans of the North and the regular soldiers of the South.

Privileged testimonies are provided by the partisans fighting in the territories gradually liberated by the slow advance of the Allies or by those (the most notable being possibly that of the Modena Garibaldi division commanded by Armando),[118] who, for various reasons, crossed the lines and found themselves once more before a military machine by now utterly alien to their way of thinking. News circulating in the North about the 'difficult encounter between partisans and liberation troops', and the whole state of affairs in the South, hardly boded well.[119] The real, new Italian army is the partisan one, wrote the

---

di liberazione del Veneto, Rome: Ideologie, 1969, p. 91.

116 Neppi Modona, *Giustizia penale*, p. 75.

117 See particularly M. Occhipinti, *Una donna di Ragusa*, preceded by E. Forcella, *Un altro dopoguerra*, Milan: Feltrinelli, 1976, and the above-mentioned collection of essays, edited by N. Gallerano, *L'altro dopoguerra*. See also Rizzi, *Lo sguardo del potere*, p. 84.

118 See Gorrieri, *La Repubblica di Montefiorino*, Chapter I, 'Il passaggio di Armando [Mario Ricci] oltre il fronte', and Chapter LIII, 'L'esodo in massa oltre il fronte'. On 5 June 1944 the PCI leadership for occupied Italy had sent all the federal committees orders against changing sides (*Le Brigate Garibaldi*, vol. II, pp. 15–19).

119 See Bernardo, *Il momento buono*, pp. 125–6. The circular with the pessimistic news about the South, to which the author alludes, is probably that of 20 December 1944, conserved in IG, BG, 09505. See also the 'Relazione militare' (Military Report) to the 'ufficiale di collegamento' (liaison officer) of the CUMER, Toetti (Bruno Gombi), regarding the situation of partisans in liberated Tuscany, undated, but winter 1944–45 (IG, BG, Emilia-Romagna, G.IV.3.2).

newspaper of the 1st GL Alpine division, not the one formed from the relics of the 'regular' army which 'is on the other side of the front doing lord knows what'.[120] 'Insurmountable distrust of an organism which is considered without a doubt an instrument of the monarchy' is attributed to 'several partisan commanders' at a meeting of the Florentine executive committee of the Action Party;[121] while the black picture painted, in some 'Appunti' ('Notes') by the Presidency of the Council, of the situation at the Cesano training centre in Rome is completed by noting the tendency of the former partisans, along with other left-wingers, 'not to recognise the authority of the officers of the army'.[122]

On 17 February 1945, speaking on Radio Roma, the Liberal Aldobrando Medici Tornaquinci, under-secretary for occupied Italy, might well hail the 'day of the partisan and of the soldier' in the name of the 'fusion between the regular and volunteer elements of the armed forces', blithely invoking precedents from the Risorgimento;[123] but the denunciation that had been made on 27 July 1944 at a PCI leadership meeting comes closer to the truth.[124]

The former partisans were not alone in showing intolerance towards the officers. A Military Information Service report on the irregular divisions reads that 'all in all resentment, hatred and contempt are often to be observed towards the officer category, who are regarded as responsible for the material ill-being of the troops'. The officers were accused of enjoying innumerable privileges even now that their ineptitude had brought about the collapse. Accordingly, morale was low in the officers and NCOs, 'depressed' by the evident lack of esteem that they sensed in the lower ranks and among civilians, as well as by the difficulty of living conditions and the scant manifestation of patriotism.[125]

---

120 'Il nostro esercito', article by 'quelli della montagna' ('those of the mountains'), republished in *L'Italia Libera*, northern edition, 6 February 1945.

121 Report by Tristan Codignola: minutes of the 15 June 1945 session, in ISRT, *Carte Carlo Campolmi*, envelope 2.

122 Anonymous 'Appunti' ('Notes') of 9 March 1945, in ACS, *Carte Casati*, folder S.

123 The text of the radio conversation is in ISRT, *Archivio Medici Tornaquinci*, envelope 10.2, n. 2. But in a report of 27 February 1945 the same under-secretary would complain that in Romagna enlistment was being impeded, and that it had not yet been possible to obtain parity of treatment between the families of regular soldiers and those of the partisans fighting alongside them (ibid., envelope 3.3, n. 1).

124 Minutes in IG, *Archivio PCI*, 'Direzione'. See G. Conti, *L'esercito italiano sulla linea gotica fra alleati e partigiani*, and G. Boatti, 'Partigiani voluntari nel Regio Esercito: l'esperienza del gruppo di combattimento Cremona', in G. Rochat, E. Santarelli and P. Sorcinelli, eds, *Linea gotica 1944. Eserciti, popolazioni, partigiani*, Milan: Franco Angeli, 1986, pp. 143–60. See also, in general, G. Conti, 'Aspetti della riorganizzazione delle forze armate nel regno del Sud (September 1943–June 1944)', in *Storia contemporanea* VI (1975), pp. 85–120, and L. Rizzi, 'L'esercito italiano nella guerra di liberazione: appunti e ipotesi per la ricerca', in *Italia contemporanea* 135 (April–June 1979), pp. 53–81.

125 'Sintesi delle relazioni deli uffici militari censura di guerra del mese di settembre 1944', in Aga-Rossi, *La situazione politica ed economica*, pp. 128–36.

'I curse all Italian officers, let's hope all these Italian officers spill blood, let's hope that things go badly for them too', says a soldier's letter. And in a carabiniere's letter:

> I loathe myself for wearing this kind of dress ... Again I remember how I was abandoned on 8 September 1943 by a coward of a captain and by a lurid carabiniere marshal who let me fall into the clutches of the Germans. Now they expect to be respected by us; seeing officers makes me want to spit in their faces. Among us here in Florence are carabinieri and foul NCOs who've sworn the oath to the republic, and are now treated almost better than us.

Significant here is the overlapping of emotions and motivations, and the nagging memory of 8 September. In another letter, this generates derision for the generals who 'have betrayed the country, handing it over to the Germans without fighting'. Or again: 'Then someone will pay with his infamy to us, the world has changed, the time of Mussolini is over, those *signori*, the officers, will have to work and earn their bread with their own sweat.'[126] In many of these letters, there is a telling comparison with the organisation and spirit of the Allied armies, also made by the partisans when the Anglo-American missions begin to arrive, and wholly favourable to the Allies. It is just the good-for-nothing officers who would prevent the Allies from doing all the good they might. This extract from a letter is typical: 'Now we're more barefoot and naked, so we make a sorry sight walking through the street, but all this comes from the Italian commands who would like to send us all to a concentration camp because the Americans wanted to clothe us but they replied that they didn't need clothing, while we're the ones who have to suffer.'

Less rancorously, another letter speaks of the English as 'human folk, very different from what they wanted us to believe in Mussolini's times'.[127] A Military Censorship Office statistic, eloquent not least in its obvious approximation, gives the figure for those favourable towards the national government as 65.69 percent, while for those favourable towards the Allies the figure rises to 88.66, and patriotism must make do with 55.19.[128] Mirroring such judgments are those given by authoritative Allied officers, which pitilessly reveal the contradictions of the Italian government's debating over the question of the war effort against Germany. A prime example is Major General Browning's severe sermon, addressed on 15 January 1945 to the war minister, the Liberal Alessandro Casati, because he had not yet cleared refugees out of the Cesano barracks allocated for training the Italian Liberation Corps combat groups: 'Italy is expecting much of

---

126 Ibid.

127 Ibid.

128 See Rizzi, *Lo sguardo del potere*, p. 83. For the impact of the culture and organisation of the Allied armies, see in particular N. Gallerano's essay in *L'altro guerra*.

her Combat Groups. You must give them the facilities to obtain the best possible reinforcements. Failure to do this is a definite hindrance to, even sabotage of, the war effort.'[129]

Certainly, the Allies themselves could be accused – at the centre as on the periphery[130] – of sabotage, or at least of discouraging the Italian war effort; and the reasons for and contradictions of this attitude have been widely investigated.[131] But one act of sabotage does not exclude the other, while both contributed to throwing into disarray the improvised new Italian soldiers. Small wonder, then, that some of them came to see in the rigid correctness of the allied Commands the only point of less unstable reference. A couple of months earlier, General Browning, who supervised the training of the Combat Groups, had written: 'The rank and file are of first-rate quality; give me two years with British officers and NCOs ... and we'd have an army as good as any in Europe.'[132] Almost in anticipated counterpoint with the British general, a clandestine paper of the North (commenting on an episode that had occurred in the South) had written, with a touch of white man's arrogance sustained by wounded national pride: 'So the English have ended up incorporating our anti-Badoglian volunteers with their officers, as they do with the Indians and the natives of Kenya.'[133] True, the testimonies of the grim legacies of the collapse refer above all to the divisions not deployed on the front (the majority), while generally, but not always,[134] those on the fighting line are described as being more cohesive. But it is also true

---

129 ACS, *Carte Casati*, folder U.

130 On the ill will demonstrated by the Allies in Rome immediately after the liberation of the city, see the 'Notizie varie sulla Capitale', sent by Orlando, General Commander of the Carabinieri, to Bonomi, prime minister and minister of the interior, 10 August 1944 (quoted in Aga-Rossi, *La situazione politica ed economica*, pp. 109–11). On the obstructionism practised by a local military governor, see the minutes of the 28 January 1945 session of the Empoli CLN (ISRT, *Archivi comunali*, envelope 2, folder I, S., folder 3, *CLN Empoli*).

131 See in particular Kogan, *Italy and the Allies*; P. Secchia and F. Frassati, *La Resistenza e gli Alleati*, Milan: Feltrinelli, 1962; D. Ellwood, *Italy 1943–1945*, Leicester: Leicester University Press, 1985.

132 'Weekly Bulletin' of the Allied control commission, 26 November 1944 (cited in Kogan, *Italy and the Allies*, p. 73).

133 *La Voce del Popolo*, 24 February 1944, article entitled 'Fuori dall'equivoco'. The newspaper referred to the activities of the Gruppi combattenti Italia, for which see C. Pavone, 'Combattenti Italia: un fallito tentativo di costituzione di un corpo di volontari nell'Italia meridionale', in *Il Movimento di liberazione in Italia* 34–35 (1955), pp. 80–119. On the repercussions that the episode had in the Actionist circles of the North, who tended to overestimate its republican significance, see *L'Italia libera*, Lombard edition, articles entitled 'La situazione', 20 November 1943, and 'Il congresso' (of Bari), 18 February 1944.

134 See, for example, the letter by Second Lieutenant Sforzino Sforza (Carlo's son) to Minister Casati, where the Corpo italiano di liberazione (Italian Liberation Corps), and particularly its officers, cut a very poor figure (ACS, *Carte Casati*, folder A).

that views like those expressed by General Browning refer to a more general picture including the entire armed forces of the South, which never managed to regain legitimacy in the eyes of the country. Their identity as an instrument against the anti-German war remained always uncertain even for the government itself. Apolitical patriotism, vaguely and rhetorically proclaimed, could provide no solid cement to so unliveable an endeavour as 'traditional military enterprise'.[135] An example of the rhetoric of the time is given by Under-Secretary Medici Tornaquinci's invectives against the 'wretched sophistries' of those who want to know 'whether the officer who will command them will be monarchic or republican'.[136] An example of rhetoric shot through with diehard nostalgia can be found again in the position taken by the 'Associazione nazionale combattenti della guerra di liberazione' deployed in the regular divisions of the armed forces: one of their representatives wanted retrospectively to sew military stars (*stellette*) on the shabby tunics of the partisans, who were in fact defined as 'italiani con le stellette'.[137] There is, however, some extenuation here in the fact that, at the PCI national council of 7 April 1945, Togliatti had deprecated 'volunteers who do not want to wear stars'.[138]

The 'staggering fact of the meagre number of those who have answered the call-up', as the CLN of Teramo put it,[139] or the young men's repugnance 'for a war whose cause they do not know' (according to the view of General Pietro Pinna, high commissioner for Sardinia),[140] are borne out by General Utili's complaints about the silence over the Liberation Corps and the failure to support it.[141] General Angelo Cerica would declare to the Tuscan CLN: 'This army, which feels itself to be held in contempt and forgotten by the country, can in no way accept the sacrifice, and will do all that it can to do as little as possible.'[142] The failed influx of recruits, moreover, fanned the exhausted war veterans' feeling that it was 'always the same ones who had to risk their lives'.[143]

---

135 These are Rizzi's words, from *Lo sguardo del potere*, p. 81.

136 'Il partito liberale e i doveri dell'ora', conversation broadcast on Radio Roma, 22 January 1945 (ISRT, *Archivio Medici Tornaquinci*, envelope 10, 2, n. 1).

137 Information taken from Agostino Bistarelli's degree thesis on Italian Second World War veterans (University of Pisa). The 1982 article referred to is by G. Gerosa Brichetto, 'Come nacque la nostra associazione'.

138 Togliatti, *Opere*, vol. V. p. 137.

139 AS Teramo, *CLN provinciale*, envelope I, folder 4/C: minutes of the session of 23 October 1944, which register, among other things, the fear that the recalled servicemen had of being used in the Far East.

140 Letter to the Presidency of the Council, 29 January 1945 (ACS, *Carte Casati*, folder S).

141 Letter to Casati of 30 July 1944 (ibid., folder A).

142 Minutes of the session of the CTLN of 11 January 1945 (ISRT, *Carte Francesco Berti*, envelope I, folder I).

143 Words of a memorandum of 20 April 1944 of the Ufficio operazioni dello Stato

South of the Garigliano, and then of the Gothic line, the Italians were in fact living in the profound conviction that, 'for them, the war had really ended with the arrival of the Allies, and that what followed was a painful and mostly incomprehensible epilogue in which they felt they had no part'.[144] Out of this grew an atmosphere of widespread depression and impatience with the authority of a state that had made itself so little trusted or believed. In those conditions it was 'often dangerous – often loathsome'[145] to perform the service of keeping the peace. But above all it was an atmosphere that helps us better understand, on the one hand, the Fascist traces whose presence is indicated by many documents among both the troops at the front and those in the supply lines, as well as the draft-dodgers, and on the other hand the explicit manifestations of left-wing tendencies revealed by the same documents relating to similar situations. Thus in Sassari, on 20 February 1945, several hundred re-draftees, hostile to the war, marched down Via Roma shouting 'Duce! Duce!'; and on the very next day, another 200 abandoned the camps 'with a red cloth around their heads'.[146] The peacekeeping authorities were happy to bracket the Fascists and Reds together as 'anti-monarchic'; but, quite apart from their slovenliness and archaic cunning, in the demonstrations against the calls to arms these opposite persuasions did at times overlap and become mixed, in a widely politically naive confusion. Well and truly Fascist, on the other hand, were those armed divisions who, like the Fiesole *paracadutisti*, went through the city singing Fascist battle songs or, like the Alpini in Fiesole, attacked the Communists.[147]

Such contrasts and confusions indicate the contradictory attitude of the parties of the left, and particularly the Communists, to the reconstruction of the armed forces in the South. On the one hand, the policy of national unity, which aimed at waging war against the Germans, required that every effort be concentrated on making the army efficient, and thereby overcoming the Allies' mistrust. On the other hand, an opposite kind of mistrust of the Italian military class and awareness of the mood of the population made it difficult to proceed coherently and efficiently towards that goal. The equation of partisans of the North and soldiers of the South was, moreover, often made by the northern

---

Maggiore (Operations Office of the General Staff), quoted in Rizzi, *Lo sguardo del potere*, p. 219.

144 H. S. Hughes, *United States and Italy*, Cambridge: Harvard University Press, 1953, p. 128.

145 Letter to the author (2 July 1945) by reserve Second Lieutenant Antonio Niccolaj, stationed at the time in Sicily.

146 Anonymous 'Appunti' ('Notes'), dated 8 March 1945, in ACS, *Carte Casati*, folder S.

147 The first episode was reported by the Fiesole CLN to the CTLN, 29 June 1945; the second was denounced to the CTLN on 7 February 1945 by the Florentine federation of the PCI (ISRT, *CTLN*, envelope II, folder 5).

underground press, with different nuances – with more conviction by that of the right,[148] but proposing the gradual diminution of 'distinctions' by that of the left. As long as hope remained that volunteers' divisions might spring up in the South independent of the old army, this was the card that had been played, in the full knowledge of how that tallied with the mood rife among the *resistenti*. Thus *L'Italia Libera* hailed the 'Gruppi combattenti Italia', on the very day that saw their definitive failure, as 'the first nucleus of the Italian popular army … without any relationship with the royal authorities' – a position which did not, however, prevent them from associating the partisans with the soldiers who had fought at Monte Lungo from 8 to 16 December in the first, hapless, attempt to bring Italian regular troops back into the line.[149]

As early as 19 September, *L'Unità* had written: 'And in the regions that have already been liberated we need to set up, we need to impose the setting up of Garibaldi volunteer formations to participate under the Italian flag in the anti-German war.'[150] A couple of months later, a local Communist party petition, more or less deliberately forcing the facts, claimed that 'The Guardia Nazionale and formations from the former army are already operating alongside the Anglo-Americans.'[151] *L'Unità* saluted 'with faith and enthusiasm' *the first Italian divisions fighting on the southern front*.[152] A faith that scarcely tallied with the facts was placed in voluntary enrolment as a means of transforming the army from within, creating a more credible symbiosis with the partisans of the North. The orator who at the assembly of the 'youth committee for the war of liberation', held at Rome in the Teatro Quirino, argued that the young were not joining up 'because first they want a republican army',[153] gave an explanation which was to some extent true in politicised city circles, but which over-simplified the infertile terrain on which calls to arms were falling. Here, too, a good example is a case from Rome where, in a demonstration at the university, weariness and

---

148 See, for example, in *Il Risorgimento liberale*, Piedmont edition, June–July 1944, the article entitled 'Il partito liberale italiano ai fratelli dell'Italia occupata'. The same newspaper published the 'Radiomessagio di Messe ai Patrioti', giving it a prominent position.

149 Article entitled 'Il volontari della libertà, Roman edition, 30 October 1943, in italics, in the 20 January 1944 number of the Rome edition. See the *Italia Libera* articles, 'La situazione' and 'Il congresso di Bari', cited in note 133.

150 Article entitled 'La nostra guerra per l'indipendenza e la libertà', Rome edition, 19 September 1943.

151 'Dichiarazione programmatica da sottoporsi ai membri del CLN di Biella', 20 November 1943 (IG, *Archivio PCI*).

152 Title of an article that appeared in the Rome edition, 15 December 1943. See also 'L'eroismo dei soldati italiani sul fronte meridionale', in ibid., 30 December 1943.

153 See the undated account written for use by the PLI and conserved in ISRT, *Archivio Medici Tornaquinci*, envelope 5, I, 4, n. 9. The episode can be ascribed to the weeks straddling 1944 and 1945.

scepticism seek refuge in resentment of a nationalist feather. On the one hand, the young men contesting the parties' appeal claimed that they would not join up 'because too long a period of suffering must give us the right to be left in peace'. On the other hand, they cited the persisting armistice regime, the imprisonment that so many Italian soldiers were still suffering in Allied hands, and lastly the memory of the 'mutilated victory', the myth of which had been an intrinsic part of Fascist ideology. These young men argued that there was 'no reason to fight for those who at the end of the last war, at whose side we fought, did not recognise our efforts to achieve victory'.[154] Similarly inspired, a Liberal Reggio Calabria newspaper had published these reflections by a student: 'The university students have been forced to take up arms for the defence of a cause they do not even know ... The students ask today for many things to be set in order before they are made to fight'.[155]

Apart from desertions that occurred even among the volunteers,[156] voluntary enlistment still proved incapable of solving the problem of re-conquering moral and political unity between the country and the armed forces (it might have done so if it had been taken as the fulcrum of the new army – but this was a proposal that no one seriously supported).[157] Besides, there was doubt and wavering even among the forces of the left, particularly over whether preference should be given to group volunteering, the aim of which was to form politically homogeneous divisions, or to individual volunteering, which meant the scattering of volunteers in the ranks of the Royal Army. On this score, a confidential Communist document written shortly after the liberation of Rome, recalling the posters that appeared for enrolment 'in the various Red Army, Matteotti, and Pilo Albertelli brigades', concluded: 'While accepting the volunteers' applications, our party considered it opportune to aim at forming a more or less regular army, and was the only one, I believe, to refuse to form independent brigades'.[158]

Palmiro Togliatti's article, 'Per un forte e disciplinato esercito italiano' ('For a strong and disciplined Italian army'), which appeared shortly after the formation

---

154 Undated anonymous note, in ISRT, *Archivio Medici Tornaquinci*, envelope 5, I, 4, n. 20.

155 Article entitled 'Perché? Per chi?', in *L'Idea* 13, (January?) 1944.

156 On 28 March 1945 the Command of the 22nd Cremona infantry regiment wrote to the Tuscan CLN that, although the Tuscan volunteers behaved well, among them there were cases of desertion and abandonment of units; and the CLN examined the question at the session held the very next day (ISRT, *CTLN*, envelope II, folder 5; and *Carte Francesco Berti*, envelope I, folder I, minutes for 29 March 1945).

157 As proof of this, see the fruitless sally by General Arnaldo Azzi, 'La guerra e l'esercito', in *L'Italia Libera*, Rome, 24 December 1944.

158 Giovanni (former commander of the Pisacane and Gramsci central GAPs) to 'Caro G.', undated (IG, *Archivio PCI*). On this point, as on the entire line taken by the PCI towards the reconstitution of the armed forces, see Paolo Miggiano's laureate thesis, discussed at the university of Rome with Professor Gastone Manacorda.

of the Salerno government and aimed at making the most of the turning-point in military terms as well, lucidly outlined the PCI's fundamental thinking in this regard, but already highlighted its contradictions. These were interwoven with the recurrent demands that the military hierarchies be purged, and the proposal to insert partisans into the regular army. The objective difficulty that the Communist (and not only Communist) position had succeeded in gaining the recognition of both friends and adversaries without arousing misunderstandings or distrust was unwittingly and comically expressed in a few 'notes' sent by the carabinieri General HQ to Minister Alessandro Casati on 15 March 1945: 'Various soldiers frequent left-wing elements in their off-duty hours. It does not appear, however, that defeatist propaganda is practised among the divisions.'[159]

In the Communist press of the North, due recognition of the achievement of the 'national democratic government', with the presence of Italian regular divisions on the Gothic line, is coupled with insistent repetition that 'the decisive event' will have to be insurrection;[160] and even when a mannered tableau was given of the renovated army, as by Bülow (Arrigo Boldrini) in a broadcast on Radio Ottava Armata (Radio 8th Army), pains were taken to underpin it by emphasising 'the influx of thousands of volunteers, many of whom are former partisans',[161] or by speaking, as L'Unità did on 22 April 1945, of 'Italian regular divisions, reinforced by the Garibaldino spirit brought to it by the patriot volunteers'.[162]

We now have to see how the rejection of the Royal Army and its lifestyle, which had been one of the departure points for the Resistance in its aversion to the Fascist war, had to reckon with the growth and 'militarisation' of the bands, which interwove in diverse ways with their politicisation.

---

159 ACS, *Carte Casati*, folder S. It should be borne in mind that, almost a year earlier Orlando, the general commander of the carabinieri, had warned that the formation of the new government should abandon all prejudices against the parties, provided the cohesion and discipline of the units was guaranteed (circular of 25 May 1944, quoted in Di Giovanni, degree thesis).

160 See leading article entitled 'L'insurrezione nazionale per la salvaguardia e l'avvenire d'Italia', in *L' Unità*, northern edition, 8 October 1944.

161 The text of the radio message, from Cesenatico, 16 March 1945, is in ISRR, catalogue 2. XC, c. I.

162 Leading article, northern edition, entitled 'L' offensiva generale su tutto il fronte patriottico è iniziata'.

CHAPTER 3

Paths to a New Institutionalisation

1. MILITARISATION AND ITS LIMITS

The partisan bands, born of an initial reaction against institutions, or at least as an attempt to fill the void left by their eclipse, evolved rapidly and originally, becoming, in Weberian terms, no longer a simple 'community' or 'association' but a 'social group' governed by a 'set of regulations' in which conduct is orientated '(on average and approximately)' 'towards determinable maxims' that are 'in some way obligatory or exemplary'.[1] Experience itself seemed to call for new and adequate rules. 'There's a wish for everything to be set in order, for everything to be legalised', wrote Roberto Battaglia, commenting on the desire he saw among the men of the Lunense division to 'regain also the written expression of their thoughts, the documents to which they were accustomed: laws or sentences or orders'.[2] This re-emergent desire to establish normative standards may be interpreted in two ways, according to the frame of reference one adopts. The first reading is based on the premise that every movement born in society denies its origin and betrays its true nature when it takes even the most approximate institutional or juridical path. This reading is reductive because, while indicating a real risk, it ignores the opposite risk that those very initial driving forces will be dispersed and rapidly ebb away. To use organisation as a means of countering this process takes firmness of conviction and tenacity of intention that do not necessarily conflict with the fundamental values at stake. It is as if, at a certain point, one were to realise that putting one's life at risk is not enough to guarantee the pursuit of one's heart's desires. Only analysis can help us understand who, in this recurrent dialectic, the palm goes to – the most desirable victory being one that somehow manages to synthesise the two principles. While this reductive reading errs on the side of excessive generosity, the other, by contrast, belongs to that type of realism which transforms the viewpoint of established power into a criterion of value. According to this second reading, the

---

1 See M. Weber, *Economy and Society*, Berkeley: University of California Press, 1978, vol. I, p. 31 (original edition: *Wirtschaft und Gesellschaft*, Tübingen: J. C. B. Mohr, 1922).

2 Battaglia, *Un uomo*, pp. 196–7. See also p. 237: 'Nati come fuorilegge, tendevamo per istinto a ritornare nella legge' ('Born as outlaws instinctively we tended to re-enter the law').

irregular must look to legitimising itself with the regular, otherwise it becomes 'purely criminal because it loses the positive interconnectedness with some available regularity'.[3] All the European Resistance movements were, in fact, beset with the problem of whether there really did exist a pre-constituted 'regularity' 'somewhere' to appeal to: the different ways they answered this question might indeed serve as a criterion for distinguishing between the Resistance movements of the various countries, from Denmark to Yugoslavia. In Italy the most authentic resistance impulse lay in not feeling the need for any 'other legitimising parties'. This 'extremely hard alternative', which aimed at the 'imposition of a new regularity relying solely on its own strengths',[4] had to reckon with the slow re-emergence in the distant South of a government which was, furthermore, the only one recognised by the Allies. The only aspect of this question that we shall examine here, which culminated in the delegation of powers to the CLNAI by the Rome government,[5] is the process illustrated by the historiography of the Resistance as the militarisation and politicisation of the partisan bands. These two forms of institutionalisation, born as they were on the field from within the movement, would, however, eventually come to perform the work of mediation between the spontaneity of the movement itself and the 'regular' institutional order that was destined to re-emerge. Here a further distinction needs to be made. While the 'autonomous' formations believed that they could limit themselves to the first aspect, militarisation, and indeed saw it as a guarantee against the risks they regarded as implicit in the second, the formations that were in fact 'political' – and above all the Garibaldi and Justice and Liberty brigades – tended consciously to interweave one aspect with the other, though making every effort to keep them distinct.

During the Spanish Civil War, in an interview given to an English journalist, the Italian anarchist Camillo Berneri had said: 'Militarisation is certainly a good thing. But one needs to distinguish between military formalism, which is not just ridiculous but also dangerous, and self-discipline, even rigorously exercised, as it exists in the Durruti Column'.[6] Berneri's distinction, after the arduous experience of the first anarchic formations nourished by equal measures of

---

3 Schmitt, *Theory of the Partisan*, p. 65, paraphrase of R. Schroers, *Der Partisan. Ein Beitrag zur politischen Antropologie*, Cologne: Kiepenheuer & Witsch, 1961, and p. 73. For these authors, who are unable to include human liberty among the factors of history, the figure of the partisan without a 'powerful third party' is theoretically unthinkable, as distinct from that of the criminal.

4 The existence of this alternative is acknowledged, with the words quoted in the text, also by Schroers, for whom, however, the problem still remains, for the irregular, that of 'legitimising oneself with the regular' (see preceding note).

5 The protocol was signed by Pajetta and Bonomi on 26 December 1944, at the conclusion of Parri's mission to the South (see Catalano, *Storia del CLNAI*, pp. 341–3).

6 See *Guerra di classe*, 30 March 1937, cited in M. Oliviari, 'L' azione politica di Camillo Berneri nella guerra civile spagnola', in *Critica storica* XIX (1982), p. 225.

enthusiasm and disorder, was as simple to formulate as it was difficult to practise. The autonomous formations, only very few of whom had turned against the
Royal Army, generally tended to position themselves on the basis of the more
traditional 'formalism'. Nevertheless, the peculiarity of a situation unanticipated
by the regulations in which they too found themselves immersed, gave rise to
effects like those described by Beppe Fenoglio, with regard to Mauri's 'Blues', in
a page whose realism is slightly tinged with irony:

> In everything that concerned establishment, distribution and command structures,
> it was almost excessively evident that they *ranked* with the Royal Army, whereas the
> Garibaldini did their bitter best to distance themselves radically from it. The fact
> was that the Badogliani commanders, elegant, *gentlemanlike*, vaguely anachronistic,
> considered guerrilla warfare nothing other than the continuation of the anti-
> German war for which the disastrous hate of 8 September had not permitted detailed
> planning, but which was to all intents and purposes planned and declared. The offic-
> ers were, in large part, authentic army officers and this *flattered* the men, the other
> ranks. As little space as possible was given to natural hierarchies and that little with
> a *supercilious* grin … All this the troops were happy with, flattered and reassured.[7]

Dante Livio Bianco's testimony relating to the 'military' band of Boves is
similar: 'The uniform was identical to the Royal Army's, with *stellette* [stars],
insignias and badges of the traditional rank.'[8] Tallying with this picture is the
'supreme superior condescension' with which Mauri greeted the Garibaldini's
overtures to him.[9] But the security that the regular – career or reserve – officers managed in some cases to give to the 'truppa' can at times be identified in
the documents as felt even among the more politicised.[10] Midway between military tradition and the new spirit of the times were certain instructions issued
by another important group of autonomous formations, the Osoppo. Superiors
were to be addressed as 'comandante' – not as 'signor tenente' and the like, but
neither simply by their battle name. Fine, call your superiors by their first names
('si dia pure il tu'), they add, but remember that 'patriots are allowed no right to
criticise among themselves the actions of their commanders': complaints were
to go through hierarchical channels. However, even in the Osoppo there were
those, including don Moretti, who opposed the use of Royal Army stars and

---

7 Fenoglio, *Il partigiano Johnny*, p. 116. The 'Blues' were Enrico Martini's politically
autonomous band.

8 Bianco, *Guerra partigiana*, p. 21.

9 Letter by the Command of the 14th Capriolo division 'ai compagni responsabili', 23
January 1945 (*Le Brigate Garibaldi*, vol. III, p. 274). The bad relations between Mauri and
the Garibaldini are widely documented.

10 See for example the case of the cobbler Carnera, a courageous and courteous
Garibaldino from Spain, to whom the 'soldati', after an initially warm welcome, seem to
prefer 'bourgeois' ('borghesi') second lieutenants (Artom, *Diari*, pp. 85–97).

ranks.[11] The Green Flames of the Brescia area were at that time using expressions such as 'gregari, ufficiali, truppa'; but 'if they recognise the necessity of hierarchical differences, they are all united in brotherhood by the equality of free men'.[12] In another major autonomous formation, the DeVitis (Piedmont), the anti-militarist spirit gained ground widely.[13]

An exemplary case of the transition from pure militarisation to its fusion with politicisation is provided by Nuto Revelli. This passage is nourished by the high concept Revelli had of military life:

> I know almost all my men. I talk to them a lot, I never tire of listening to them. I'm interested to know why they came up into the mountains and where they were before and what job they had. This is the life I dreamed about in Modena, before I became an officer: this is what I thought military life was like.

Earlier Revelli had written: 'I was uncertain, I didn't want to bow to the fact: I didn't want to admit that the "politicians" are better than the "military".'[14] Piedmontese and mountain-dweller's seriousness favoured an encounter that appears to be embodied, not without some resistance from the officers in the band, in the partisan chief Marcellin, who belonged first to an autonomous, then to a GL band, a sergeant-major and skiing instructor, in whom Ada Gobetti traced 'the happy fusion, the just balance' between social and military qualities.[15]

Equally important for our present purposes are the tensions that military requirements created among the partisans. These tensions lay in the conflict between equality felt as a value founded on the choice of liberty and the common acceptance of risk,[16] and that contorted equality that, in time of war, cohabits with hierarchical order, becoming a function of it.[17] While the first kind of equality permits, and actually strengthens, the preservation of individuality, the second mortifies it.[18] This seems to me an indispensable key to understanding resistance to, and the contradictions regarding, militarisation – and not just in terms of the intractability, the indiscipline, and the scant understanding of higher political and military needs. The same irritability at the revival of a 'bloody and

11 Agenda no. 1, signed Bolla, 9 October 1944 (IZDG, envelope 272b, folder III/I); Fogar, *Le brigate Osoppo-Friuli*, p. 301.

12 'Atto di fede' ('Act of faith'), undated, in INSMLI, *CVL*, envelope 90, folder 12.

13 See Quazza, *Un diario partigiano*.

14 Revelli, *La guerra dei poveri*, pp. 189, 169 (29 March and 7 February 1944).

15 Gobetti, *Diario partigiano*, pp. 152–3.

16 Dante Livio Bianco has written that the keen egalitarianism of the initial stages, though destined to change, 'represented, in its way, that need for renewal and breaking from the past, which was the soul of the partisan' (*Guerra partigiana*, p. 23).

17 See, on this theme, Leed's remarks in *No Man's Land*, especially on pp. 26–7.

18 The partisan 'refuses to be drowned in the uniform level of a single mentality or discipline'. Battaglia, *Un uomo*, p. 216.

oppressive'[19] military service acquires a deeper significance than that springing from the mere rejection of the misdeeds of the Royal Army. In the mouths of the partisans, someone observed, the word *naja* (military service) could be 'the unconsidered expression of elements damaging to the formation', but it could also express a just rebellion against 'anti-democratic forms'.[20] In other words, one had to protect the new behavioural habits that had caused three sailors who joined a Garibaldi band to hesitate to call the commanders by their first names, and to be amazed that the chiefs were criticised at the meetings.[21]

Agostino Piol, vice-commander of a Garibaldi brigade, who had 'lost all his loved ones in the struggle for liberation', protested against the attempt to impose discipline on the unit, against the introduction of ranks, against the political commissars 'sitting there at their desks'; all this struck Piol as being a return to the *naja*. The divisional Command firmly but affectionately reprimanded Piol, reminding him that in the *naja* 'only a bestial system of direction reigned, not the fraternity that exists among us'. Unconvinced, Piol went his own way with some hundred men; and news then came that he had been gravely wounded, 'and by now may no longer be alive'.[22] The tragic fate of this Garibaldino, convinced as he was that, at the end of the war, 'they'll put us in a concentration camp', is a good indication of the tension I hinted at above. With a crudity that makes him miss the full complexity of the situation, Vincenzo Moscatelli (Cino) dealt with the same problem as follows:

> Everything that is a healthy mark of a military education in our formations is vaguely dubbed by that lot as *naja*, while personal habits, disorder, improvisation, lice, scabies and hanging about for hours or whole days on end, either lying or sitting by the fire in a state of utter mental inertia, in short what is characteristic of the *banda*, of the gypsy-like camp, is passed off as 'true partisan life'.

In reproaching these men, his own men, for their scant political conscience, Moscatelli remarked that if they were questioned about the reasons for their choice, they would reply: 'To drive out the Germans and Fascists. That's all. No more than that.' As for the future, all they can think about is 'a fine parade through the city', and above all home. 'At most', Cino added, 'they talk of liberty, of

---

19 Bianco, *Guerra partigiana*, p. 35. On p. 144 he would speak of 'months and months of a new-style *naja* but still "naja"'.

20 Letter by Michele, political commissar of the 1st Gramsci division, to the commissar of the 6th Nello brigade, *Atti*, 22 November 1944 (*Le Brigate Garibaldi*, vol. II, p. 621).

21 See Lazagna, *Ponte rotto*, p. 70.

22 See the letter by Piol of the Command of the 3rd Piedmont division, 12 September, and the one by the 'compagni responsabili' of the same division to 'cari compagni', 10 October 1944 (*Le Brigate Garibaldi*, vol. II, pp. 325–7, 424).

finally being able to express "our opinion", of a few people to sort out'.[23] Actually, this was no mean achievement; and in underrating it, Moscatelli revealed the tendency of many Communist chiefs to conceive of the growth of the bands in terms of the two exclusive routes of militarisation and indoctrination along party lines – with the consequent disparagement of that profound *humus* which gave birth not least to the capacity to bear lice and scabies. Besides, the political commissar of one of Moscatelli's divisions himself appeared horrified at a brigade commissar's order of the day proposing 'the military system of a genuine army' as a model, and prescribing the salute formerly used in the Royal Army.[24]

There were also curious cases of contamination between the 'old-style military imprint', 'which is to be applied a hundred percent', and new partisan ways, seen almost as a sublimation of military virtues. (This we have already noted in the case of Revelli, but it did not always occur with the same humanity.) Thus a circular on the subject of 'discipline' even prescribes an hour a day of 'closed order instruction', and in the same breath orders that 'the detachment commanders live together with the men serving under them', because, as a subsequent document repeats, 'you don't get to know the partisans by idling about at the café or strolling around town with girls'.[25]

Criticism of militarisation could be accompanied by that bureaucratisation and a combatant's intolerance of politicians. Both of these criticisms were present within the Communist organisation. This must have been the state of mind of those who reproached the Garibaldi commands for contenting themselves with 'sending directives and asking for reports'.[26] Accusations of bureaucratisation were exchanged between the Commands of various levels. One of these wrote resentfully:

> This Command would like to know what specific aspects of organisation you are reproaching us for. We have always made it a rule to prevent the bureaucratisation of the Commands in order to keep as close as possible to the men and urge them continually along the path of action. When it has not been possible we have not hesitated to leave them the circulars for using machine-guns.[27]

---

23 Moscatelli's letter to Walter, 31 October 1944 (IG, *BG, Emilia-Romagna*, 06754).

24 Report by Michele, commissar of the 1st Gramsci division, October 1944 (?) (ibid., 06746).

25 The style of these documents of the Command of the 11th Torino brigade reveals the author – 'È mio intendimento', 'Insisto' – as being a regular officer (*Le Brigate Garibaldi*, vol. II, p. 19 and n. 2, under the dates 7 and 10 June 1944).

26 See the resentful letter sent on 15 February 1945 by the delegation for Lombardy to 'compagno Italo' (ibid., vol. III, p. 364). For the 'valanga burocratica' ('bureaucratic avalanche') which at a certain moment descended on the Command of the Lunense division, see Battaglia, *Un uomo*, pp. 193ff. For the 'sea of duplicated and typewritten papers' that reached the formations, see also Mila, *Bilancio della guerra partigiana*, p. 417.

27 Unaddressed letter by the Command of the 40th Matteotti brigade (1st Lombardy division) of 14 August 1944 (IG, *BG*, 0592).

For some time *L'Unità* had warned against the re-establishment of anti-quated and reactionary hierarchies, claiming the superiority of working-class leaders over fence-sitting 'competenti' ('experts') and 'technicians'.[28] Even the Christian Democrat commander Claudio writes, with regard to the Republic of Montefiorino (the free zone established in the Modenese Apennines from 18 June to 31 July 1944), that there was no need for 'officers transplanted at the last moment in the place of the natural leaders of the units', but of leaders experienced in the partisan struggle and who acted as an expression of the Resistance[29]

In fact, the selection of the leaders reveals a characteristic feature of partisan ways, which would have to reckon with the growth of the formations and, in the final phase, with their unification. What Guido Quazza has called a 'microcosm of direct democracy'[30] required the election and, if necessary, the dismissal of chiefs; but it became increasingly difficult to follow this practice, apart from the already arduous problem of introducing 'technical' leaders from the Royal Army. On several occasions Bianco speaks of appointing commanders from below.[31] In the statute of the '1st Mazzini brigade' (Valle d'Aosta) things appear more fully worked out:

The military commanders and vice-commanders of the brigade and group are assigned and designated by the Command of the 7th GL division, which will appoint elements internal and external to the brigade according to military capacity and aptitude, moral gifts and qualities, influence over the men, and length of service in partisan life. The vote of confidence by the men, required only in exceptional cases, and decided only at the discretion of the brigade political commissar, may constitute for the Command of the 7th GL division an expression of opinion and not a determining element.

On the other hand:

The squad and nucleus commanders are elected by the men and appointed by the GL 7th divisional command, which will make appointments after consulting the brigade commander and political commissar. The brigade and group political commissars are elected by the men and appointed by the GL 7th division Command, and those elected can be dismissed only in 'exceptional cases'.[32]

---

28 Rome edition, 30 December 1943, article entitled 'Organizzare la Guerra partigiana'. On 'La formazione dei nuovi quadri' ('The training of new leaders'), see the record of occurrences clearly delineated by Poma and Perona, *La Resistenza nel Biellese*, pp. 207–12.

29 See Gorrieri, *La Repubblica di Montefiorino*, p. 390.

30 Quazza, *Resistenza e storia d'Italia*, pp. 241–52.

31 For example, on p. 51 of *Guerra partigiana*.

32 The statute, of September 1944, is in *Le formazioni GL*, p. 171.

Another Actionist saw the indiscipline among the Garibaldini, again from the Valle d'Aosta, as the fruit of having concentrated exclusively on the partisans' rights and 'the principle of the elective nature of their chiefs'.[33] Indicating just how confused things had become in the Rosselli GL brigade deployed on the French side of the Alps, Nuto Revelli himself noted: 'In one band they've reached the point of holding a referendum among the men to choose the commander!'[34]

The 'responsabile militari' ('person responsible for military affairs' – note the formula used in the place of 'commander') of a Garibaldi detachment was elected 'by secret vote'; but the higher command, to whom the report was addressed, put a question-mark in the margin by way of comment.[35] It was Lazagna's boast that in his formation the chiefs were elected, and that their power, 'except in case of emergency', was subject to the approval of the whole formation, even in the matter of dismissal.[36] This question is raised in a highly polemical letter in which the commander is accused of refusing to submit himself to the judgment of his men:

Hadn't we made it clear in the discussion that the commanders are such only if they have the unanimous approval of their Garibaldini? In this struggle ... it is the *gregari* [privates] (which in any case remains an ugly military term) who elect commanders and not those who impose themselves by virtue of the stripes they received from a regime whose last representatives we are now fighting.[37]

As I suggested in the last chapter, being a Royal Army officer could even count against one. In order to be elected commander of the Arno division, Aligi Barducci first had to overcome the distrust aroused by the fact that he had been a second lieutenant of the Arditi.[38] An officer's past could become a point in

---

33 Medical second lieutenant Dario Diena, 'Relazione sulla situazione e sugli avvenimenti partigiani nella Valle d'Aosta come li ho visti io alla fine di agosto al 28 ottobre 1944' (INSMLI, *CLNAI*, envelope 4, folder I, subfolder I).

34 Revelli, *La guerra dei poveri*, p. 392 (25 January 1945).

35 'Rapporto del distaccamento Calcagno' of the Cascione division, 24 February 1944 (IG, *BG*, 09941).

36 Lazagna, *Ponte rotto*, p. 31.

37 Open letter by Filippo, commander of the Nanetti division, to Olivi, commander of the Piave brigade, 29 August 1944 (*Le Brigate Garibaldi*, vol. II, p. 285). In the minutes of the discussion to which the letter refers there are the following words: 'The ranks that the men bore in the old army are not valid in the partisan formations ... here ranks and responsibilities are given according to the abilities and partisan determination' (ibid., p. 287).

38 See G. and E. Varlecchi, *Potente*, p. 83; the report conserved in ISRT, *CVL*, Comando militare toscano, envelope 5, folder 7; the 'Relazione sull'attività clandestine e operativa svolta dei patrioti toscani nel periodo 8 settembre 1943–7 settembre 1944', compiled by Major Achille Mazzi: here one reads that 'the chiefs were elected by the *gregari* (passive yes-men) – a secret and tacit pact linked them' (ibid.).

his favour only after all the other necessary qualities were recognised; but even where this criterion was applied, one saw former captains being placed under former lieutenants.[39] A 'regime of progressive democracy' is how a Garibaldi document describes a situation in which the chiefs spring not from ties of wealth, family genealogy or the authoritarian designation of restricted political circles, but from the free choice of those concerned based on the value of the actions of individuals; this happens when positions of command are well and truly positions of responsibility, guidance, sacrifice:[40] – a principle aimed at combating the regressive tendency that had surfaced here and there that 'length of service had to create merit'.[41]

Possibly the most interesting criticism of rank-and-file appointments, in view of what motivated it, is the one, inevitable enough in itself, made by General Raffaele Cadorna after being parachuted into the North to take command of the CVL:

> Two characteristics strike one immediately: the political nature of most of the formations; the election of the chiefs by grassroots consensus rather than designation from above and their close political control. These characteristics, which are clearly incompatible with the requirements of a national army in a democratic nation and regime, have their raison d'être in this wretched phase of civil war.[42]

Comparison of this document with the one quoted above appealing to 'progressive democracy' helps throw light on the two profoundly different meanings that could be given to the word 'democracy' as applied to the fighting men. The latter could be seen merely as the age-old arm of a will, albeit democratic, that had been formed elsewhere; or else as bearers in their own right of values, practices, and democratic ends. General Cadorna must at least be credited with having realised, albeit reluctantly, how difficult it was to apply the first of these two models to a civil war.

A danger in some respects more subtle than that feared by Cadorna lay in the possibility of the partisan chief slipping into the role of the charismatic leader, insofar as he was recognised as having proved himself to possess a 'quality ... considered extraordinary'.[43] The same could happen among the partisans as what Jean-Jacques Langendorf imagined for his hero von Lignitz, who during

---

39 See Giovana, *Storia di una formazione partigiana*, p. 76.

40 Agenda item no. 1 of the Command of the Lombardy Garibaldi division, 8 October 1944 (IG, *BG*, 01186).

41 'Relazione sulla situazione della brigata Calvi Cadore dai primi di ottobre al suo scioglimento', dated Milan, 24 November 1944 (ibid., 012).

42 Memorandum of 4 September 1944 (INSMLI, *CLNAI*, envelope 10, folder I, sub-folder I).

43 Weber, *Economy and Society*, vol. I, p. 241.

the battle of Jena came across a squad of scattered hussars: 'Without hesitating, he took command of them. None of them asked himself what right that civilian had to give them orders. His natural authority commanded their respect.'[44]

The 'irrational' character of this kind of power – in the sense that 'it has no system of formal rules'[45] – was somehow rationalised in the Resistance by appointments through election from below. The charisma gained on the field became the de facto premise guiding the group's choice. This is why the partisans were so often reluctant to be deprived of their 'natural' chiefs, in whom they saw a natural synthesis of charismatic and democratic power; the partisans saw that their natural leaders recognized hard facts and had respect for standards that they themselves had adopted. A British officer penetratingly described partisan discipline as 'based on the personal relationship which exists between the leader, who is elected, and the man who selected him to be his officer. This makes their discipline a curiously personal thing.'[46]

A woman partisan was convinced that, 'while the bureaucratic assignment of commanders may be all right for a regular army it might mean the downfall of a partisan formation whose cohesion is due above all to the prestige enjoyed by the leader'. Therefore, she continued, the men would regard the substitution of the commander Montagna 'as an impairment or an act of high-handedness and this would lead to the break-up of the group'.[47] The 'bond that best keeps a band together is political conviction or trust in its leader', wrote the chief of an autonomous formation who was not insensitive to political considerations;[48] and a political commander saw trust in and human harmony with the chief that one chose for oneself as a channel of that very same politicisation.[49] At times the leader's glamour provoked excesses. A Communist in the province of Brescia who had addressed a brigade commander (who came, what is more, from the Green Flame autonomous units) with expressions like 'you, only you are the commander', 'your brigade', 'the brigade is entrusted to you' and the like, was reprimanded as follows: 'In our party all the best comrades are valued but in such a way as to avoid the adulation that marks the parties we are fighting against ... The brigade does not belong to a person, a commander

44 J.-J. Langendorf, *Elogio funebre del generale August-Wilhelm von Lignitz*, Milan: Adelphi, 1980, p. 60.

45 Weber, *Economy and Society*, vol. I, p. 240.

46 Report by Major Healy of the 8th Army on the partisans of the Ravenna area, 23 January 1945 (in Casali, *Il movimento di liberazione a Ravenna*, vol. II, p. 332)

47 Report on the 13 Martiri di Lovere (Bergamasco) brigade, 2 August 1944 (IG, BG, 1055).

48 Quazza, *Un diario partigiano*, p. 191 (16 July 1944).

49 See Battaglia, *Un uomo*, pp. 189–90. In the Lunense division, of which Battaglia was commissar, free election of the chiefs was practised (ibid., p. 130). For the fascination of the chief, see the testimony of Tersilla Fenoglio Oppedisano, who associates it with *esprit de corps* (Bruzzone and Farina, *La Resistenza taciuta*, p. 154).

may even be transferred. The brigade is entrusted to the Command and not to one man.'[50]

It was worse still when the commander, however valorous, abandoned himself to the arbitrary exercise of his power in an 'utterly bourgeois' way insofar as he cuffed his comrades and even threatened them with a pistol. He made the actions seem like banditry, got the young men to blacken their faces, put on fake beards and moustaches, and got bed linen and silverware included in the spoils.[51]

It has been pointed out that, in partisan fiction, the commanders often play the lion's role.[52] This is probably a consequence of the chief's glamour, as well as of the adoption of an easier literary model. The truth is that, though in some cases there was a tendency to make the Command a collegial organ, militarisation led to this collegial character being reduced in practical terms to very little. Commenting on the Communist proposal 'for the transformation of the partisan units into regular formations of the Italian army', Cino (Vincenzo Moscatelli) and Ciro (Eraldo Gastone) advanced a number of modifications which, while reiterating the supremacy in operative decisions of the commander and commissar, tried to leave space in all other matters to some form of collegiality, with a view to 'avoiding the tendency of some commanders towards centralisation', especially if they were regular officers.[53]

In a later chapter we shall see how the exercise of justice constituted one of the channels leading to a more or less definite institutional order. Likewise in the field of discipline and its visible signs. For example, the first partisans did not wear uniforms, refusing to regard themselves as the possible shreds of those of the Royal Army. Hatred of the uniform was a part not only of what I have called the repudiation of the Royal Army, but of a more radical feeling of repulsion for militarism.[54] Gian Carlo Pajetta recounts that he had always imagined

---

50 Letter of the delegation for Lombardy to the Brescia federation of the PCI, 18 September 1944 (*Le Brigate Garibaldi*, vol. II, p. 353).

51 Andrea's report to 'cari compagni' (Parmense), 14 March 1944 (IG, *BG, Emilia-Romagna*, G.IV.2.2).

52 See Falaschi, *La Resistenza armata*, p. 79, which paraphrases and disagrees with a judgment expressed by Alberto Asor Rosa (*Scrittori e popolo*, Rome: Samonà e Savelli, 1965, p. 250), according to which it would seem to be a question of a 'transference of the intellectual who in this way recognises himself as having the right to command'.

53 Cino and Ciro's 'Osservazioni e proposte', 21 January 1945, are published in *Le Brigate Garibaldi*, vol. III, pp. 259–69 (the words quoted are on p. 265). The proposal of the Communist delegation of the CLNAI, 8 January 1945, ibid., pp. 206–8. See also the observations of General Cadorna, who obviously repeats the hierarchic principle, in Secchia and Frassati, *La Resistenza e gli Alleati*, pp. 292–3. It had been the General Command of the CVL that had requested, since 17 August 1944, the integration of the Corps 'as such' in the 'new national army' (*Atti CVL*, pp. 158–60).

54 For the proto-antipathy of young workers towards the uniform (as cadets), see

a 'popular army' in workers' overalls.[55] Then, little by little, dress with at least some common features begins to become a distinctive sign of group identities. An imaginative and whimsical liking for individual variants persists, revealing a deep repugnance for 'the uniform'.[56] Even the armed corps of the RSI often wore somewhat motley uniforms; but in their case the model was that of the 'non-regulation uniform', an extravagance conceded to the confused desire, which they in turn had, to appear irregulars. It is no accident that the most distinctive corps on this score – the *paracadutisti*, the Decima Mas, the Muti – flaunted, even in the name of elegance, these deviations from complete uniformity.

In its 'internal regulations' issued after unification – as late as 18 April 1945 – the general Command of the CVL would content itself with prescribing that, without prejudice to the use of the partisan badge and/or armband, 'if possible one should aim at having uniformity in the equipment. The essential items of the uniform are: windbreaker and long skier's trousers'.[57] A Garibaldi chief noted: 'It's strange to observe how the uniform would raise us in the esteem as much of the civilian population as of the enemy';[58] in fact it was not that strange, but it is interesting that a Garibaldino should have considered it so.

Uniforms meant that recognisable ranks were adopted. On this score the general Command of the CVL issued meticulous instructions, taking care among other things to point out, after initially taking a different line, that 'there are no ranks in the CVL, but only command assignments';[59] and this had for example been the practice of the Lunense division[60] and the Italia Libera band of the Val Maira.[61] Cino and Ciro, though aiming at a firm military organisation of their formations, had urged: 'Symbols of rank will have to be simple and not too conspicuous.'[62] The Biella zone Command was to complain that 'the badges

---

the suggestions offered by Passerini, *Torino operaia*, p. 156.

55 But those whom he met dressed like that turned out to be soldiers of the 4th Army fleeing from France. G. C. Pajetta, *Il ragazzo rosso va alla Guerra*, Milan: Mondadori, 1986, p. 12.

56 'Usually there were enough uniforms for a hundred carnivals', writes Fenoglio in his description of 'the wildest parade in modern history', that of the partisans entering Alba (B. Fenoglio, *I ventitré giorni della città di Alba*, Turin: Einaudi, 1975, pp. 8–9).

57 *Atti CVL*, p. 493. For the badge and armband, see the orders of 20 August and 1 September 1944 (ibid., pp. 164–5, 177–8).

58 Lazagna, *Ponte rotto*, p. 240. For the adoption of uniforms, see Dellavalle, *Operai*, p. 187.

59 See the regulation in *Atti CVL*, p. 490. For the preceding orders of 21 July, see Dellavalle, pp. 122–3.

60 See Battaglia, *Un uomo*, p. 127.

61 See Giovana, *Storia di una formazione partigiana*, p. 76.

62 See Cino and Ciro's 'Osservazioni e proposte', in *Le Brigate Garibaldi*, vol. III, p. 268.

of duties indicated seem to us to be real badges of rank'.[63] In short, if one really couldn't do without them, let there be ranks, but with discretion. A discretion which, at a distance of years, Pajetta no longer felt the need to respect when he wrote: 'We established the forms and the colour of the ranks, even if the Garibaldini continued to sing: "There's no lieutenant nor captain", echoing the infancy of the Red Army'.[64]

In almost all the expressions issued to outline the most suitable discipline for the partisans, there is the dialectic between the necessity that it be firm and incontrovertible and the need felt equally strongly that it be based on self-conviction. Even the infelicitous formula used in a Garibaldi document – 'prompt, unconditional, absolute obedience' – is ennobled by the motivation sustaining it – 'because my chiefs have been freely accepted by me' – and by the duty given to each combatant to check that his chief did not degenerate.[65] It is a document which, much as it recommends 'getting the men used to discipline towards hierarchies', feels the need to specify: 'We certainly don't want bourgeois barrack-room discipline, but nor do we want anarchy'.[66] The advice that Antonio Prearo, the commander of the GL column of the Val Pellice, gave to his partisans included that of 'being disciplined not in the sense and style of the old *naja* but disciplined in spirit ... Remember that our discipline is the discipline of the volunteer: it may turn a blind eye to trifles but is inflexible in the things that are essential for us'.[67] General joint discussions, 'where the bond of close dependence on and disciplined obedience to hierarchical bonds disappears for a few moments' are recommended by a Garibaldi political commissar.[68]

The insistence on reserving discipline only for the great occasions was extremely widespread: 'However, while discipline leaves a lot to be desired in moments of truce and calm, when there is alarm or the need to come out for actions, the response is unanimous and at such times discipline is felt'.[69] A highly mannered reconciliation between discipline as *habitus* and discipline as

---

63 See the letter, regarding unification, of the Biellese zone Command to the Piedmont regional military Command, 4 April 1945 (ibid., pp. 581–2).

64 Pajetta, *Il ragazzo rosso va alla guerra*, p. 50.

65 So runs the commitment ('impegno') to be assumed by anyone enlisting in the 7th Piedmont division (IG, *Archivio PCI*).

66 Letter of the Piedmont military committee to the Command of the 4th Cuneo brigade, 18 March 1944 (*Le Brigate Garibaldi*, vol. I, p. 311).

67 The circular is published in *Formazioni GL*, pp. 100–1. Prearo, who was a captain, failed in his command action, and was to be substituted by young GL politicised lieutenants. My thanks to Giorgio Rochat for this information.

68 Michele, of the 1st Gramsci division (Ossola-Valsesia), to *Atti*, 14 November 1944 (IG, *BG*, 06914).

69 Letter to 'Cri' (Giuseppe Alberganti), who was in charge of the insurrectional triumvirate of Emilia-Romagna, to the General Command, 14 July 1944 (*Le Brigate Garibaldi*, vol. II, p. 125).

mere military necessity is proposed in a letter by Cino and Ciro: 'Iron discipline in combat or on duty, free-and-easy behaviour off duty, contempt for the sterility of formal discipline'.[70]

Indicative here is a certain diehard distrust of the partisan police:[71] these police, for whom the need was felt at a certain point, might not appear 'that distant from the all-too-well-remembered royal carabinieri'.[72] But championing 'Garibaldi humanism' against 'the traditional Teutonic automaton'[73] produced a variety of attitudes that cannot be defined that easily in terms of discipline, whatever adjective might accompany it.

What proved to be a particularly sticky issue was the 'soldo' (soldier's pay) paid to the partisans, the object of widespread distrust, despite acknowledgments of its opportuneness as a channel for financing the bands.[74] Neither salaries for the officers nor pay for the men, insisted Dante Livio Bianco with regard to the Cuneo GL.[75] On 9 November 1943 the Communist representative of the Turin CLN declared:

> We regard the projected increase of pay of thirty lire to the soldiers and relative salaries to the officers as politically mistaken. This is a people's war fought on a volunteer basis and animated by a lofty patriotic spirit. If it must be introduced, the *soldo* should not exceed five lire, that is, the small change necessary for small personal expenses.[76]

But a year later a Garibaldi chief, Achille, who had reported that his men refused to accept differentiated pay according to rank, first of all received compliments on his style as an 'old partisan, the jealous guardian of the fraternal egalitarianism of the bands', and immediately after a lesson against

> 'flat' high-quality egalitarianism, to define it from a class point of view, utterly petit-bourgeois ... In any case, the history of the edification of socialism in the USSR itself

---

70 Cino and Ciro's letter to the CVL General Command, 9 December 1944 (IG, *BG*, 07324).

71 See Dellavalle, *Operai*, p. 183.

72 'On the other hand', it is added, 'it is hard to keep an army together' without a military police force: 'Relazione del commissario politico del Comando piemontese delle formazioni Giustizia e Libertà', 31 December 1944, written by Giorgio Agosti (*Formazioni GL*, p. 283).

73 See the 'Bollettino n. 33', 8 August 1944, of the 52nd Clerici (Comasco) brigade, quoted in *Le Brigate Garibaldi*, vol. II, p. 171. In another document this brigade appears under the name 'Fronte popolare'.

74 See, for example, Quazza, *Un diario partigiana*, pp. 177, 178, 183, 197, where the words 'paga', 'gratifica', and 'indennizzo' ('pay', 'allowance', and 'indemnity') are used.

75 Bianco, *Guerra partigiana*, p. 103.

76 'Dichiarazione', conserved in IG, *Archivio PCI*.

teaches us that salary differentiations are necessary and that to stimulate emulation it is necessary to apply the principle that distinguishes this phase from that of Communism, 'from each according to ability, to each according to his work'.[77]

The issue involved is well summed up by the GAP commander Elio Cicchetti:

One day Ambro arrived and brought us a thousand lire. He said that the Command had decided to let us have that small sum every month, a kind of salary, to enable us to meet our most elementary needs. All in all the measure in itself was right, but there and then it seemed to me distasteful and even offensive. I was repelled by the idea of being paid to be a partisan; I hadn't seen a lira for at least six months and all the same had always managed to get by, without needing to turn to the laws of the market to survive. I didn't want to accept that money. The question acquired a symbolic significance for me. It was certainly exaggerated to take it that way, but pride prevented me from seeing the thing in a practical light.[78]

In other documents there is a rejection of any economic differentiation whatsoever between commanders and simple partisans. 'Giving different pay to officers, NCOs and soldiers', Pajetta wrote, 'would be doing things more army style; the way we want it, egalitarianism means doing things more partisan style, which suits us fine.' The Green Flames, who in fact wanted 'to do things army style', established a monthly allowance of 1,000 lire for the commander and vice-commander, and 500 lire 'per la truppa'.[79] Inadmissible, on the other hand, in the view of the Biella zone Command, were 'the awarding of command allowances and the differences in family allowances'.[80] The allowance granted to dependents was already regarded as a different and acceptable practice.[81] The same could probably be said of the one-off gratuities, like that decreed by the Action Party, for Christmas 1944, of 1,000 lire for each GL partisan.[82] The weekly

77 Letter by the Command of the 1st Gramsci (Ossola-Valsesia) to Achille, 21 October 1944. The Command offered a compromise: in order to improve the rations, to put the money refused by the partisans into a kitty (IG, BG, 06647).

78 E. Cicchetti, Il campo giusto, Milan: La Pietra, 1973, p. 179.

79 See Pajetta, Il ragazzo rosso va alla guerra, p. 128 (Pajetta was referring to the formation commanded by Arrigo Boldrini, which was by now incorporated in the Allied army); a circular of the Command of Tito Speri division of 9 August 1944, in ISRBS, Q IV, 2. My thanks to Gabriella Solaro for having drawn my attention to this document.

80 See the above-mentioned document, (IG, BG, Emilia-Romagna, G.IV.2.2). For egalitarianism of this kind, see also Artom, Diari, p. 92 (28 November 1943).

81 For example, the Valsesia military zone organised (18 April 1945) an 'ufficio assistenza' which established a 'table of checks, indemnities and pensions' (IG, BG, 08594).

82 See the folder entitled 'Formazioni GL. Circolari e direttive' of the Lombardy Regional Command (INSMLI, CVL, envelope 93, folder 5).

awards decided on in November 1944 by the government junta of the free zone of Alto Montferrato provided for differences only between unmarried men, married men, and married men with children.[83] But a cash reward for a successful action could give rise to the comment: 'come si trattasse di mercenari' ('as if we were mercenaries').[84] In the same spirit, the 'financial recompenses for acts of sabotage' were considered by Roberto Battaglia a sign of the intemperance of the highly courageous Diavolo Nero (Black Devil), before he and his band were called to order by the Communist Party.[85]

Indeed, what was to be avoided at all costs was the figure of the mercenary: the partisan had to remain a volunteer out of pure ethical and political choice. Understandable therefore was the disdain with which a Garibaldi document reacted against manoeuvres, attributed to Major Gufo ('Owl' – Tito Cavalleri), to get the Garibaldini detachments of the Valle d'Intelvi under his command by offering them higher pay: 'cornering soldiers by means of money (120 lire a day coming from the dollar exchange, rather than the Garibaldine 5 lire) is no longer practised in any civilised army in the world'.[86] A document characteristic of partisan (and sub-Alpino) moralism complains: 'The Turin CLN money began to pour in, contributing to making the environment less healthy.'[87] And this is negatively confirmed by the fact that, among even the most scrupulous orders issued gradually by the CVL general headquarters, there are none relating to the 'soldo' – uncertainty and shame, probably, rather than an oversight.

The process of militarisation interwove with the local character of the bands. To those drives towards centralisation, inherent in this process as in that of politicisation, local recruitment acted as a counterweight. Particularly close bonds of solidarity grew between the men, even when it did not previously exist, underpinned by the use of dialect, and a greater propensity to fight in defence of what was, obviously one's own land. The small local *patria* was felt to be threatened in a more immediate way than the large *patria*, Italy, and the motivations necessary to inspire men to take up arms could not always be transferred onto the plane of the great ideals of political and human redemption.

83 Respectively 200, 350 and 500 lire (A. Bravo, *La Repubblica partigiana dell'Alto Monferrato*, Turin: Giappichelli, 1964, p. 134).

84 See the document cited above (IG, *BG, Emilia-Romagna*, G.IV.2.2).

85 See Battaglia, *Un uomo*, p. 173.

86 Letter by Neri, vice-commander of the group of Lombard divisions, to Major Cavalleri, 22 September 1944. The major had the reputation of having at his disposal a great deal of money coming from America (*Le Brigate Garibaldi*, vol. II, pp. 362–4). For an analogous denunciation of certain breakaway groups, see the report by Moro, of the 4th Piedmont division, to the General Command of the Garibaldi brigades, which is also dated 22 September 1944 (IG, *BG*, 04940).

87 Report by Belloni on 'L'azione partigiana in Valle di Susa (5 mesi di attività)', 8 February 1944 (ibid., 004861).

Roberto Battaglia speaks of 'regional interests that had weakened the guerrilla movement' in Umbria; but for the Apuan and Garfagnana zone, he recognises the importance both of regional recruitment, which meant that almost every family had a young man among the partisans, and the wide and complementary presence of those whom he calls 'partigiani contadini' ('peasant partisans'), who did not abandon their work in the fields.[88]

'Le quattro giornate di Napoli' (The four days of Naples'), remembered in the whole story of the Resistance as the glorious and spontaneous episode of auroral promise, have a truly exemplary significance from the point of view of the struggle *pro aris et focis* (for the altars and the hearths). A stone placed in the park of Capodimonte reads: 'Died fighting for the defence of the hearth. 29 September 1943'.[89] It was the first time in history that the 'lazzari' found themselves on the right side. They therefore deserved to be recalled in the appeal that Benedetto Croce prepared, in the name of the 'National Liberation Front', for the call-up of volunteers of the 'Gruppi combattenti Italia': 'Men, women, children of Naples have demonstrated, despite the few weapons they have managed to procure for themselves, that heart and that pugnacious spirit and that spontaneous heroism which in the past shone in famous defences of our city against foreigners'.[90] Palmiro Togliatti, too, speaking to the Neapolitan partisan leaders, would first recall the Jacobins of 1799, but then add that in the 'people's struggle against an invading army … whatever explanation one might wish to give to it, one is however compelled to recognise the dawn of an instinctive manifestation of national force and patriotic spirit'.[91] Nor was this just a Neapolitan phenomenon. *Pai nestris fogolârs* (For our Hearths) is, for example, the title of a periodical of the Friulian Osoppo brigade.[92] The Resistance does, indeed, have this dichotomy running subtly through it: on the one hand, the solidity guaranteed by moral and material rootedness *in loco*; on the other hand, the risk, which could stem from it, of there being a shrinking of the ideal and political horizon. The leading national Resistance movements gave the first characteristic its due, but were at the same time concerned about the second. In a report 'on the feats of arms from 13 to 17 March 1944' in the Monregalese valleys, Major Mauri wrote:

As regards recruitment, I prefer that, for the time being, it be done directly under the charge of the group leaders, who thus have the opportunity to choose their men: as a general rule I aim also to form the groups with elements from the same village

---

88 Battaglia, *Un uomo*, esp. pp. 171–2, 140.

89 The memorial stone notes Salvatore Palumbo, Ciro Palumbo, Egidio Bramante, Angelo Ciorcari, Gaetano Rescigno.

90 The poster, affixed in Naples on 10 October 1944, is Appendix V of B. Croce, *Quando l'Italia era tagliata in due. Estratto di un diario*, Bari: Laterza, 1948, pp. 154–6.

91 Report given on 11 April 1944, in Togliatti, *Opere*, vol. V, p. 6.

92 See Fogar, *Le brigate Osoppo-Friuli*, p. 283.

or from a specific area, so as to avoid the enrolment of untrustworthy or suspicious individuals.[93]

One of Nuto Revelli's annotations almost gives the lie to this: after a harsh rounding up, out of twenty-four men who abandoned the formation, nine were from the same village.[94] And what should also be noted is the greater security that fellow-villagers, and dialect, offered against infiltration by spies. Ada Gobetti tells of a man 'small, very, very dark, a southerner, as you can hear from his accent', who for these reasons alone was suspected in Susa of being a spy.[95] According to Fenoglio, the mere fact of speaking Italian was already a bad sign.[96] Of a group that formed in the mountains around Modena between Communists, Action Party members and Catholics from Sassuolo, Ermanno Gorrieri writes: 'I think one can say that the Sassuolesi, who constituted a fair share of the partisans active in the mountains, at least in the initial phase, felt greater solidarity with their fellow villagers than with the party.'[97] Still with regard to the Modenese Appennines, behind 'the old idea of creating a robust and determined local formation', launched again in autumn 1944, were 'apolitical' and anti-Communist aims.[98] But even the Command of the '13 Martyrs' Garibaldi Brigade of Lovere not only adopted the criterion of 'pochi ma buoni' ('few but good'), but made the 'buoni' coincide with local lads, and dubbed the city folk with the pejorative militarist term 'vaselina'. For this attitude the formations were sternly rebuked,[99] just as a La Spezia Giustizia e Libertà formation was taunted with the epithet of 'patrioti casalinghi' ('stay-at-home patriots').[100] Another Garibaldi document, respectable by contrast, describes the mountain dwellers of the Oltrepò around Pavia as 'excellent elements, but difficult to drag into operations outside their village; while they fight like lions near the walls of their houses, the moment they have to move away from the area many of them abandon the formation'.[101] This attitude, another report explains,

---

93 Quoted in Revelli, *La guerra dei poveri*, p. 455.

94 Ibid., p. 234 (2 May 1944).

95 Gobetti, *Diario partigiano*, p. 148 (January 1944).

96 Fenoglio, *Il partigiano Johnny*, p. 338.

97 Gorrieri, *La Repubblica di Montefiorino*, p. 66.

98 See the 'Relazione di Alpino Righi', cited in ibid., pp. 517–18.

99 See the 'Relazione n. 3 (Macchi)', 15 July 1944 (IG, BG, 010547: see the passages in this report quoted in *Le Brigate Garibaldi*, vol. II, p. 178). Attention is drawn to strong antagonism between the local (Bergamasco) partisans and those who had come from the city in another 'Rapporto sul Distaccamento 13 Martiri' (summer 1944?) (IG, BG, 010566).

100 See the 'Relazione del "Comando Federale bis" di La Spezia del PCI sulla "situazione militare e politica della IV zona operativa"', 28 March 1945 (*Le Brigate Garibaldi*, vol. III, p. 542).

101 'Rapporto informativo e osservazioni' of Medici, inspector for the Pavese

meant that, as soon as the Anglo-Americans arrived, these units disbanded and each member returned home.[102] A group commanded by a certain captain Raul – well-armed, and composed for the most part of Communist sympathisers, almost all fellow villagers who carried home with them spoils they had captured – not having wanted to move in time, is said to have been attacked and decimated.[103]

The Valtellina only to Valtellinese partisans, as their commander Retico seemed to want? But that way – ran the answer – 'you are treading on Fascist ground. There is no worse policy, no worse action than to divide one Italian from another, whether he be a Sicilian, a native of Veneto, a Piedmontese or a Tuscan'.[104] A Garibaldi detachment from Boves was criticised because 'it smacks rather too much of the local situation insofar as the majority are from the village and before general interests come local ones: this could be prejudicial'.[105]

Alongside these criticisms inspired by strong national pedantry, there appear others that are more immediately connected with contingent situations. The local partisans – it is claimed – revealed themselves to be particularly sensitive to the risk of reprisals against the hearths that sweetened their existence. This gave rise to *attesismo* (waiting on events) and, with the formation of free zones, an excess of defensive attitudes.[106] On those occasions the local elements could 'fuel the general euphoria',[107] then be ruinously involved in dispersal and gradual ebbing away. In that way they offered the enemy the opportunity to concentrate forces each time on a single point, allowing them to 'arrange their attacks in grades, using first one formation, then another' and 'to be always

Oltrepò, to the PCI federal committee of Pavia, 10 August 1944 (ibid., p. 238).

102 'Relazione sulla situazione delle Brigate Garibaldi dell Oltrepò Pavese', 3 September 1944, by Piero, political commissar of 73rd Crespi brigade, to the delegation for Lombardy. The commissar adds, in view of a necessary displacement, that the locals had to be disarmed in favour of those coming from the plain (ibid., vol. II, pp. 303–7).

103 'Relazione sull'attività svolta dalla Brigata Caiani', Florence, 16 August 1944 (ISRT, envelope 231, *Brigata Garibaldi Caiani*).

104 Letter by Fabio, military person in charge of the insurrectional triumvirate of Lombardy, to Retico, 23 February 1945 (*Le Brigate Garibaldi*, vol. III, p. 407). See also Domenico's 'Relazione sulla mia ispezione in Valtellina' to the 'Delegazione Comando', 4 August 1944 (IG, BG, 0540), and the letter by the delegation for Lombardy to the Command of the 1st and 2nd division group as well as the group of the 1st Lombardia-Valtellina division, 17 October 1944 (*Le Brigate Garibaldi*, vol. II, pp. 444–5).

105 'Relazione sul lavoro svolto', signed Giasone, 18 August 1944 (IG, BG, 04383).

106 See, for example, the letter by Pietro, commander of the 8th Romagna brigade to Franz, liaison officer of the CUMER, 31 July 1944; the 'relazione militare-politica' of the Command of the 6th Liguria zone to the Regional Command, 7 October 1944; the anonymous report on partisan movement ('movimento partigiano') in Friuli, 24 October–1 November 1944 (*Le Brigate Garibaldi*, vol. II, pp. 180–4, 412–14, 562–6).

107 The expression is used in Dellavalle, *Operai*, p. 151, relating to the Biella valleys in summer 1944.

stronger than us'.[108] Finally, we should not forget those homeless villagers, the southerners blocked in the North. Among them there seemed to be the reappearance of the tendency to group themselves according to their areas of origin, as in the Royal Army.[109] Revelli recalls the case of forty disbanded Sicilians from the 4th Army who on no account wanted to be separated from a *carabiniere* who was their fellow villager, and in whom they had recognised a leader's authority: when the *carabiniere* was killed, the Sicilians dispersed.[110] With the Sardinians of the Natisone division and the Triestine brigade at a certain moment there was the idea of creating a Sardinian battalion.[111] We do not know what came of that proposal, most likely nothing, just as we are unable to say whether similar episodes occurred elsewhere.

It is revealing however to compare this with the different behaviour of the Sicilian soldiers who were on the island at the time of the Allied landing and, still more, with the view of the landing given them by a *paracadutista* officer who believed in the Fascist war: 'It was a grave psychological error, too ingenuous not to have been deliberate, to send the inhabitants to defend their own land. When a soldier is close to home he is unlikely to make a good combatant.'[112]

At times, the local character of the bands led to mimicking the only lively and popular rite in Italian military tradition, the festival of the young recruits. In June 1944, in the province of Biella, the new partisans

> even took the country bus up to the assembly points, celebrating the occasion with the same enthusiasm with which the date of conscription was celebrated in the villages. From the plain and from the city of Vercelli as well a large group of youths reached Postua by bicycle accompanied by their wives and girlfriends.[113]

The problem of the growing number of bands, of which the local character is but one aspect, reached a turning-point with the beginning of the influx of the youths who had wanted to dodge the drafts improvidently issued by the Fascist

---

108 See the letter by the Piedmont delegation to 'dear comrades' (of the General Command?), 19 April 1944, and the one by the Lombard delegation to the Command of the 1st and 2nd division group, 24 October 1944. The latter takes its cue from the failure to support another unity that was heavily attacked (*Le Brigate Garibaldi*, vol. I, pp. 355–8; INSMLI, *Le Brigate Garibaldi*, envelope 2, folder, I, S folder I).

109 Antonio Gramsci's analogous reflections on prisoners are well known (*Lettere del carcere*, Turin: Einaudi 1965, pp. 72–3, letter to his sister-in-law Tania, 11 April 1927).

110 Revelli, *La guerra dei poveri*, pp. 144–5, 152–3.

111 The proposal was made by Virgilio, chief of the General Staff of Natisone, to the Command of the 9th Yugoslav Corps (IZDG, envelope 223, folder II/4b).

112 Ugo Bodon, draft officer of the Nembo, reply to a questionnaire given to him by M. Di Giovanni (see Di Giovanni, degree thesis).

113 This is how Dellavalle, *Operai*, pp. 146–7, paraphrases the oral testimonies that he collected.

government (the so-called Graziani bands), and the various German call-ups. These new partisans gave rise to problems of cohabitation with the older ones, who already tended to swathe the memory of the initial phase, the dawn of the movement, in jealous nostalgia. 'Things, Nuto, aren't what they used to be! Everything's changed! There were few of us, then, in the fine times of Palanfré! How wonderful the evenings were, all of us gathered together singing our songs, joking, laughing':[114] that's how Nini of the GL Rosselli brigade, by now deployed on the French side of the Alpine front, recalled beginnings which were not actually that distant.

The veterans suspected that they had before them people who regarded being a partisan as a mere refuge. A GL commissar inveighed 'against that way of considering the partisan formations as a sort of charity organisation, aimed at welcoming, protecting and assisting draft dodgers and deserters, so as to prevent their meeting a worse end, imprisonment in Germany or dispatch to the battlefields'.[115]

Still more unsparing was a Garibaldi commissar concerning Colonel Libero Descalzi, 'squadrista, persecutor of the people of Stradella, volunteer in Spain etc.', who had formed a brigade near Varzi 'composed essentially of daddy's boys whose fathers financed Descalzi to make sure that he saved their sons. No combative spirit animated those dodgers, who had come into the mountains to play the dandy and save their skins'.[116] 'Butter and jam' partisans or 'evacuee partisans' were the names given to those who poured into the mountains in summer 1944, convinced of being able to tranquilly await 'the good moment'.[117] These stances reflect the problem of the evolution from mere self-defence to the exercise of even aggressive violence, which, furthermore, required different and greater armaments. The fact is that at a certain point the influx of men exceeded the availability of weapons, as well as the means of subsistence. The presence in the mountains of so many unarmed men could only be a cause for concern. 'When the fighting starts I'm going to disappear. I'm not going to stay here and get myself killed',[118] said an unarmed partisan, expressing a point of view that was widespread among those who did not intend to risk their lives in a challenge that was too unevenly matched.

In this matter there were two schools of thought among the leaders. The first, in the name of political and human responsibility, claimed that it was not

---

114 Revelli, *La guerra dei poveri*, p. 376 (29 December 1944).

115 This is point five of a circular by the commissary of the 2nd sector, 26 March 1944 (in Bianco, *Guerra partigiana*, p. 64; then in *Formazioni GL*, p. 79).

116 Report by a political commissar of the 3rd Aliotta Lombardy division, 31 December 1944 (IG, *BG*, 01728).

117 See Bernardo, *Il momento buono*, p. 57, and the report of Vice-Commander Neri of the Lombardy group to the Command delegation, 9 November 1944 (IG, *BG*, 01237).

118 Testimony by Angelo Repetto, in Bravo and Jalla, eds, *La vita offesa*, p. 85.

possible to turn anyone away. A Garibaldi document reads: 'To find excuses and
fail to do everything possible to solve the inevitable difficulties stemming from
such an influx of men indicates poor political work with little understanding.'[119]
And in another one: 'We have deemed it opportune, despite the fact that they are
unarmed, not to reject them, so as to remove them from the enemy's clutches.'[120]
On 18 October 1944, the provincial military command of Vicenza issued a circular ordering the suspension of new enrolments for lack of weapons and because
'it is all too easy to present oneself at 11.55 [i.e. the eleventh hour] and enjoy
the same recognition as those who presented themselves at zero hour'. But the
general command of the Garibaldi brigades severely criticised this attitude of the
veterans, and reminded them that weapons can be won and that the only condition to be put to anyone asking to enlist is that he be 'fired by a firm will to fight'.[121]
These Garibaldi directives undoubtedly contained an attempt to re-launch the
volunteer spirit on that terrain of combat whose arguments were invoked by
those who balked before the influx of so many unarmed men. But there was
wavering even among the Communist and Garibaldi leadership, initially above
all for practical reasons, and then in a second phase above all because of the
resistance of the now consolidated formations, animated by a growing *esprit de
corps*, to being diluted by too many newcomers. A report from Emilia at the end
of 1943 observed: 'It does not seem to us advisable to send them into the mountains without weapons and with the near certainty of not being able to supply
them. We will in short make every effort to find the best solution for them: the
important thing is that they don't fall back into the clutches of the Germans.'[122]
Similar perplexities existed in the GL formations, where the concern was for the
'disturbance' that might be caused by the continuous influx of men, and there
was the warning not 'to be fanatical about the number'; but alongside this, it was
recommended to leave the doors open 'to the workers who are on strike and to
avoid their being deported to Germany'.[123] In another GL document satisfaction

119 Circular by the Command of the 2nd Piedmont division to the brigade
Commands, 13 June 1944 (IG, *BG*, 04648).

120 Riccardo, inspector of the 3rd Aliotta Lombardy division, to the delegation for
Lombardy, 14 November 1944 (ibid., 01621).

121 Letter to the 'Delegazione Comando per il Veneto', 9 November 1944 (*Le
Brigate Garibaldi*, vol. II, p. 556). Analogous concepts are expressed in other Garibaldini
documents.

122 'Rapporto al Centro del Partito' by Banfi (Vincenzo Marini), 16 December 1943
(IG, *Archivio PCI*). Analogous concepts in Cri's report to 'cari compagni' from Bologna,
late December 1943 (ibid.). Again, on 17 February 1945 Ciro, the Ossola commander, in a
report sent to Switzerland, was to speak of the impossibility of enlisting everyone owing
to the lack of armaments (IG, *BG*, 07942).

123 'Notiziario e direttive' of commander 'D' of the Piedmont GL formations to the
military commanders of the formations and for the information of the political commissars of the work zones, 30 June 1944 (ISRP, envelope 29, folder B).

is expressed that 'the number of regular officers has always been deliberately kept low through a process of rigorous selection', contrary to what was happening in the Garibaldi brigades, which take 'whoever presents himself'[124] – though we have seen that this was not always true.

The problem went beyond the political differences between the formations. The Communist Bernardo was not tender towards indiscriminate recruitment, on which, using an identical argument to that of the GL document quoted above, he laid much of the blame for the disastrous outcome of the September 1944 roundup on the Grappa.[125] 'In the band or in the district', was the bald invitation of a poster put up in the Canavese region by GL and Matteotti formations, addressed to young re-draftees; and the area command remarked: 'This poster has appeared at a moment when we are having difficulty keeping within reasonable limits the influx of recruits who are arriving from everywhere, in order not to increase excessively the load of dangerous unarmed men in this period. The way it is expressed seems inopportune.'[126]

Since February 1944 the military Command for Northern Italy had been urging that 'the temptation be resisted to swell the ranks in the bands by indiscriminately taking in disbanded men who take to the mountains. Let those who after a fit period of moral and material preparation prove their worth as combatants be accepted.'[127] In this prose, in which Parri's hand is recognisable, the meaning of 'non combattente', of 'disarmata', tends to assume a morally negative connotation. This tallies with the spirit of the bands, who not only feared the presence of the unarmed men during the recruitment sessions, but came to regard the sessions themselves as an instrument of selection, a sort of God's judgment which served to sort the wheat from the tares.

> It is necessary to proceed with an energetic and inexorable purging in grand style of all those unreliable elements who have entered the brigades only to seek refuge or to eat or steal. In other words, we need to free ourselves of all the dead weights, of all the rotten, cowardly elements, who are only ready to take advantage of the situation.

---

124 'Relazione del commissario politico del Comando piemontese delle formazioni GL' (the author is Giorgio Agosti), 31 December 1944 (ISRP, envelope 29, folder C; published in *Formazioni GL*, pp. 267–86).

125 Bernardo, *Il momento buono*, p. 100.

126 The manifesto is signed '5ª Brigata G. Mazzini (formazioni GL) – Divisioni d'assalto Davito Giorgio (formazioni Matteotti)'; the criticism is found in a report, 23 March 1945, by the Biellese zone Command (IG, *BG*, 05373).

127 Par. 7, 'Leggerezza e mobilità', of the 'Direttive per la lotta armata', in *Atti CVL*, Appendix I, document P (p. 550).

– so runs a report about a recruiting session in Emilia.[128] And Nuto Revelli, after a severe roundup in Valle Stura, observes: 'The selection is starting. The sick, the flat-footed, the accidental partisans will go. Our attitude is sympathetic: we are almost inviting them to leave the formation.'[129] At the other end of the Alpine arc, the Garibaldi-Osoppo division felt the need for similar reasons to rid itself of 'much dead weight'.[130] Writing about the winter of 1944–45, the ever rigorous Ferdinando Mautino says:

> Some individuals of no moral substance, who flocked into the partisan ranks when it looked as if there was going to be an easy and imminent triumph, who have now fallen into the hands of the Nazi-Fascists or are just plain terrified of the latter's temporary excessive power, had turned into the vilest of spies ... The purged formations are stronger from the point of view of these dangers as well.[131]

'Pochi ma buoni' ('Few but good') is the moral which Emanuele Artom drew from the roundups in late 1943; whereas in Tito Speri's Green Flames division this moral is tempered by frequent enjoinders not to send men away, both because they might talk, and because, as the commander Romolo Ragnoli writes, 'not everyone is born a lion, but lions can be made'.[132] 'Buoni', for Artom, means morally, even more than materially, fit for combat (he himself had a paralysed leg), while 'pochi' had two meanings – one military, the other political – which did not always coincide.

The problem that emerges in these documents brings us back to the basic reasons for deciding to resist, above all when it was provoked by new circumstances that could not be avoided. The difference lay in the fact that those of the 'innovatori' and 'primi adottanti' who had weathered the test had created out of

128 Letter by Gracco, commissar of the 12th brigade, to the 'delegato ispettore delle brigate Garibaldi Nord Emilia', 2 August 1944 (*Le Brigate Garibaldi*, vol. II, p. 188).

129 Revelli, *La guerra dei poveri*, p. 324. On that occasion the number of men descended from over 400 to 250. See also ibid., pp. 453–4, 234–5, where, finding himself before 'a list of little cowards and sick evacuees', prepared by the quartermaster after another roundup, Revelli remarks: 'Many sick: no cowards'.

130 'Relazione sui fatti d'arme di Faedis-Attimis-Nimis del 27 settembre 1944' of the Command of the division, 15 October 1944 (IZDG, envelope 272b, folder I/A). See Bernardo, *Il momento buono*, p. 57: 'I grandi rastrellamenti liberarono i reparti di questa zavorra e costituirono il banco di prova per chi veramente intendeva combattere per la liberazione del paese' ('The great roundups freed the units of this dead wood and constituted a test for those who really intended to fight for the liberation of the country)'.

131 Mautino, *Guerra di popolo*, pp. 149, 168.

132 Artom, *Diari*, pp. 149–50 (2 January 1944); letter by C. (Ragnoli) to 'carissimo C.I.', 22 August 1944, in ISRBS, Q IV, 2. My thanks to Gabriella Solaro for drawing my attention to this document.

nothing a complex armed organisation which the 'first' partisans and 'the late-comers' found themselves mixed together as a consequence of their choices.[133] The voluntary nature of the resistance was constantly reiterated by the 'innova-tori' and 'primi adottanti' above all by the very fact of persevering, and then by intransigent affirmations of principle: 'Recruitment into our ranks is absolutely and strictly voluntary. We believe that any other criteria would only weaken our formations', is how a Garibaldi document that can be considered exemplary puts it.[134] But there was no lack either of incitements to full mobilisation. '25 May call-up of volunteers of liberty' was how *L'Unità* entitled one of its articles;[135] and however ambiguous or even distasteful the word 'leva' ('call-up' or 'conscrip-tion') might have sounded (though possibly it contained a distant memory of the 'leva in massa' of the great revolution and of the Commune), it did not go beyond a moral and political appeal. The same may be said of this appeal for all the forces to mobilise in the light of the enemy retreat: 'Each person, be they man or woman, must be ready to carry a stone on the road, to fell a tree, a tel-ephone pole, to contribute, in short, by every possible and imaginable means to interrupting or blocking the road.'[136]

Nevertheless, there were tendencies to transform these appeals into coercive measures, or at least there was the intention to do so. The controversial, inde-pendent-spirited and 'extremist' commander Libero [Riccardo Fedel] responded to the Fascist enlistment proclamation for men born between 1922 to 1925 by issuing his own proclamation, threatening those who did not enrol with the partisans instead with penalties still harsher than the Fascist ones; and he was severely reprimanded.[137] A similar initiative was taken by the Garibaldini of the Valsassina and the Valvarrone on 24 May (a date obviously not casually chosen)

---

133 As has already been recalled, these expressions are used, with sociologi-cal rigidity, in the research directed by Ardigò, *L'insorgenza partigiana*. See, in particular, S. Porcu's contribution, *Il processo di diffusione territoriale. Un' analisi morfologico-strutturale e socio-demografica*, pp. 68ff, which adopts the scheme proposed by E. M. Rogers, *Diffusions of Innovations*, New York: Free Press, 1962.

134 Letter by the Command of the 1st Gramsci (Ossola-Verbano) to the 'Centro informazioni e polizia', 26 February 1945 (IG, BG, 08025). See also the letter by the group Command, same zone, to the Command of the 2nd division, 30 January 1945 (ibid., 08060).

135 Northern edition, 25 May 1944.

136 Circular of the 'Comando Gruppo brigate A. Garemi' (Veneto) to 'all the depen-dent Commands', November 1944. The General Command of the Garibaldi brigades appreciated this text to the extent that it proposed it as a model in one of its circulars to all the delegations of 9 November 1944 (*Le Brigate Garibaldi*, vol. II, pp. 553–6).

137 See the 'Rapporto generale' by Pietro Mauri, commander of the 8th Romagna brigade, on military activity in Romagna up to 15 May 1944 (ibid., vol. I, pp. 407–21). Regarding the episode, see Flamigni and Marzocchi, *Resistenza in Romagna*, p. 169; see also, p. 706, n. 20.

1944,[138] while in the area of Chiavenna all the men who had matriculated from 1910 to 1926 were mobilised.[139] The Belluno division enjoined the able-bodied men to enlist at the commissions set up for the purpose, and the women to do likewise as dispatch riders and auxiliaries.[140] The results of initiatives of this kind were scant or insignificant (the Belluno command had, moreover, been so inept as to organise this general mobilisation for a time following the arrival of the Allies, with the aim of continuing the struggle alongside them). But these 'coercive and restrictive systems'[141] indicated not so much a brutish 'militaristic' evolution as a certain blurring of the voluntary character of the struggle and a reversion to 'regular' and institutionalised combative models which, by compelling men to practise violence, made it morally less problematic.

It is telling that a note about the unification plans, probably written by an Actionist, reads:

Army of National Liberation [Esercito di Liberazione Nazionale – the formula used also by Mauri] no longer CVL. ELN is a no less political or progressive denomination. It better expresses the imperative character of our military organism which, answerable to the CLN, draws from the latter, which is a government, the necessary, and also present, authority to order requisitions of means and materials, to compel men to perform specific tasks, to establish conscription, to proceed to mobilisation. None of this would be possible if the corps continued to be exclusively voluntary. Furthermore, the ELN is tomorrow's army in the making, which will absorb the one that they are laboriously scraping together in liberated Italy. Also, the concept of liberty in the name CVL is more limited than that of liberation, which means political liberty within and independence of our country from the foreign foe.[142]

---

138 See the letter by the Command of the 55th Rosselli brigade to the brigade group Command, 24 August 1944 (IG, BG, 0646); 24 May is significant as the anniversary of Italy entering the First World War on the Entente side.

139 See the communications by the Command of the 1st division to the Command of the Lombardy divisions' group and to the 90/A brigade Command, 7 September and 5 October 1944 (ibid., 0671 and 0724).

140 Bernardo, Il momento buono, pp. 209–10.

141 These words appear in a report by Costa, commissar of the 8th Asti division, to the delegation for Piedmont. These systems, the commissar warned, 'could provoke ill feeling in the populations, and some regrettable accidents have been provoked' (Le Brigate Garibaldi, vol. III, p. 520).

142 The note, probably dating from January 1945, is conserved in INSMLI, CLNAI, envelope 10, folder I, Subfolder 2. In summer and fall 1944, Mauri's formations used the name 'Esercito italiano di liberazione nazionale' (see the documents conserved in INSMLI, CVL, envelope 26, folder I, Subfolder 6, and envelope 27: Diario di Mauri, 7 October 1944). The Green Flames defined themselves as 'Armata italiana dell'Interno', possibly taking their cue from the French (ibid., envelope 90, folder 13b, relating to August 1944).

It was not just a question of names. But the name, or better to say names, that the movement gave to its protagonists and organisation are indicative of the stages of militarisation. In the first few weeks after 8 September, various names had appeared. The one that circulated most widely was 'guardia nazionale', linked to the residual illusions of some form of collaboration with the remains of the Royal Army. In the days immediately preceding 8 September, the National Guard had been put forward, by the Communists, precisely in this key. A workers' delegation had said to the prefect of Milan: 'The authorities must favour the formation of an armed National Guard, organised by officers of the Army, composed of the popular masses, to flank our Army in order to put an end to the Nazi-Fascist danger'.[143] After the Armistice this path was attempted again in some cities, even if in Milan Ferruccio Parri appeared sceptical about 'lawyers marching with muskets on their backs to Porta Ticinese'.[144] The Communists stuck to this line for some time, probably because the name must have sounded reassuring to bourgeois ears. They launched appeals and spoke of the Guard as if it already definitely existed. *L'Unità* assured its readers that 'the young men of the whole of Italy are flocking into the ranks of the National Guard created for the defence of peace in a wave of enthusiasm', and that the Guard and army units that had reorganised in the mountains 'are repelling the barbarians'.[145] The 1 October 'general directives reserved for comrades alone' include that of 'reinforcing the National Guard in the factories and in the districts, with ever more intense mobilisation'.[146] But a letter of 7 October written by Mauro Scoccimarro from Rome to Milan already warned: 'Bear in mind that here the name hasn't caught on: none of the parties have liked it because it is too old: it recalls 1848. To my mind, there has been no political sympathy for it, because the old, well-remembered Guardia Nazionale often had an anti-popular function'.[147]

---

143 'I rappresentanti delle Commissioni interne ricevuti dal Prefetto', in *La Fabbrica*, September 1943 (quoted in Spriano, *Storia del Partito comunista italiano*, vol. V, p. 14).

144 See the *Intervista sulla guerra partigiana* given to L. La Malfa Calogero and M. V. de Filippis, p. 22. For Turin, and in general, see Giovanni's 'rapporto' from 5 to 15 September 1943, in P. Secchia, *Il PCI e la guerra di liberazione 1943–1945. Ricordi, documenti inediti e testimonianze*, Milan: Feltrinelli, 1973, p. 117 and note. For Florence, the report by A. Pieri, of the Arno Garibaldi division, in ISRT, *CVL*, Comando militare toscano, envelope 5, folder 7, p. 2. See also G. Grassi, *Nota storica*, prefacing *Atti CLNAI*, p. 10.

145 Northern edition, 29 September 1943. On 31 October the newspaper was to publish an article entitled 'A Lecco e nel Friuli la Guardia Nazionale infligge duri scacchi agli aggressori nazi'. See also the 7 and 25 November 1943 issues.

146 *Bollettino del Partito*, 1 October 1943.

147 IG, *Archivio PCI*. 'Form the National Guard? It was no longer the times of the Risorgimento, we had said to each other', is what Pajetta writes today, *Il ragazzo rosso va alla guerra*, p. 7.

A 'report from Liguria' of 4 December was a sort of 'extremist' counter-melody to the Roman leader: 'Actually, rather than speak of "national guard" formations mixed with Badoglian-nationalistic-Gascon cadets, it might be more appropriate to speak of formations that are highly agile, but primarily fired by the spirit of the party, manoeuvrable as the nucleus of a genuinely proletarian army.'[148]

The CLNA itself came to realise that the dissolution of the army had put paid to any project for a National Guard – a name that would be used by the Fascists with their GNR (Guardia Nazionale Repubblicana).[149] Moreover, significant hendiadyses had appeared – 'join the National Guard, reach the formations of the Partisans'[150] – as well as less innocuous variants, like 'Guardia Nazionale del Popolo' and 'Guardia Nazionale Popolare'.[151] The latter then reappeared in various forms to denote more or less permanent organisms to put alongside the active partisan units. The Friuli Garibaldi division would provide 'norms for the establishment and functioning of the Guardia del Popolo', which 'will have to rise in all the inhabited centres' with men from sixteen to fifty-five;[152] the name 'Guardia del Popolo' was even given to the police of the free zone of Carnia;[153] in some Tuscan *comuni* there would be talk of a 'Guardia Civica' to flank the partisans.[154] The SAP were partly to answer these needs.

The name *partigiani*, instantly popular though it was, thus encountered some difficulty in being assimilated at a high level. Officially it never was assimilated, preference being given to that extremely noble, but somewhat cold name 'voluntari della libertà', which had already vanished from current usage,[155] but

---

148 IG, *Archivio PCI*.

149 See the 'Breve monografia sul movimento partigiano in Italia', contained in the first number of a bulletin edited by the press office of the CLNAI (ISRT, *Carte Francesco Berti*, envelope II, folder 3).

150 Manifesto of the Modena CLN, 14 November 1943, quoted in Gorrieri, *La Repubblica di Montefiorino*, p. 85.

151 See *L'Unità*, Roman edition, 3 November 1943, article entitled 'Il primo e l'ultimo 28 ottobre del facismo repubblicano', and *Il Combattente*, 7 December 1943, article entitled 'La Guardia Nazionale Popolare e la Guerra di liberazione nazionale'.

152 See the minutes of the session of the Carnia (free zone) CLN of 7 August 1944, in IRSFVG, Fondo Magrini, envelope CLV, folder III.

153 *Istituzioni di un corpo di polizia nella zona liberata. Relazione approvata da CLN zona liberata nella seduta del 30 settembre – 1 ottobre 1944*, quoted in M. Leganani, 'Politica e amministrazione nelle repubbliche partigiane', *Quaderni del Movimento di liberazione in Italia*, Milan, undated, vol. 2, p. 46.

154 Letter of the delegation of the Command of the Garibaldi brigades for Tuscany to the Command of the Arno division (quoted in G. and E. Varlecchi, *Potente*, pp. 207–8).

155 See for example *Avanti!*, Roman edition, 30 December 1943, article entitled 'Per le bande dei volontari della libertà', where the word 'partigiani' and the distastefully sounding expression 'milizia popolare e volontaria' are also used.

which was adopted in the internal statute of 9 January 1944 of the military Junta appointed by the Central Liberation Committee.[156] A Communist document re-launched it in the form of 'attivisti della libertà' ('activists of liberty').[157] In the word *partigiano* there was a remote meaning of defending one's own land, dating back to the war of independence that the Spaniards had waged against Napoleon; but there was also something red – 'a reference to Lenin roused the partisans'– which exalted its aggressive and irregular component, and aroused distrust among the right-minded and orthodox.

'All the representatives have rejected the name "partigiano" for the fighting forces; they must be called "esercito" or "armata", etc.', states a Communist report from Turin.[158] Albeit late in the day, *Il Popolo*, the Christian Democrat paper, took a clear contrary stance. Addressing the young men fighting 'bare-breasted and bare-headed', it wrote: 'You won't return as "partisans", because even on the "partisan" mountains and scrublands you will never have been them, but will on the contrary have fought in order not to be them.'[159]

In Florence, the Action Party, too, showed some perplexity, and proposed the replacement of 'partigiano' with 'patriota'.[160] The word 'patriot' certainly rang more sweetly in the ears of all those who identified chiefly with the patriotic war (but the word was not to have too stirring a future since, in the official post-Liberation honour ceremonies, the term 'patriota' was to be placed on a rung lower down the ladder than 'partigiano combattente'). Dante Livio Bianco attributed the political success of the GL spirit to the fact that the word 'partisan' had undermined both 'patriot' and 'rebel' – the latter, in his curious view, not exceeding 'the limits of a phenomenon which was of interest only to the crime squad'.[161] A Vicenza document seems, for that matter, to bear him out, when it speaks of 'our folk who say with moving faith "not rebels: partisans" and who consecrate this word, born elsewhere, which in principle we were surprised to pronounce, but which has been dear to us since we heard women on the roads of our hills greeting our armed youths with "God bless our partisans!"'.[162]

---

156 *Atti CVL*, Appendix I, document L, p. 539; *Avanti!*, Rome edition, 12 January 1944; *L'Italia Libera*, Rome edition, 19 January 1944; *L'Unità*, Rome edition, 30 January 1944; *La Punta*, 2 February 1944.

157 Letter by Ciro, commander of the group of Valsesia, Ossola, Cusio, Verbano, and Costanzo divisions, delegate of the Command in Switzerland, 29 January 1945 (*Le Brigate Garibaldi*, vol. III, p. 304).

158 Report signed Giovanni, 10 October 1943 (IG, *Archivio PCI*).

159 *Il Popolo*, northern edition, 25 September 1944, 'Saluto ai giovani studenti'.

160 'Relazione sull'attività del CLN dal 1 dicembre 1943 al 15 febbraio 1944', written by the Communist member (IG, *BG*, Toscana).

161 Bianco, *Guerra partigiana*, p. 46.

162 *Fratelli d'Italia. Organo del Comitato veneto di liberazione, 'edizione per Vicenza'*, 30 July 1944, article entitled 'I partigiani del popolo'.

Risorgimento Liberale wrote, with apparent detachment: 'All right, let's accept this term, which has nothing offensive about it: the cause those partisans are defending is Italy.'[163] In fact, the term 'ribelle' ('rebel') was never abandoned. It sounded distasteful to those who, in a rather legalistic fashion, feared it might imply a recognition of the Social Republic. But the root both of the aversion it aroused and of the way in which it was proudly adopted by those who recognised themselves in it, lay precisely in its ancient and profound semantic content. In this case too there are many variants: from the words of the partisan song *Fischia il vento* (The Wind Whistles), 'every *contrada* is the rebel's *patria*', to the current phrase 'ribelli della montagna' ('rebels of the mountains'),[164] to Teresio Olivelli's 'ribelle per amore'.

Still more defiant were expressions such as 'fuori legge' ('outlaw')[165] and 'bandito'.[166] The latter, while deriving literally from 'bande' ('bands') and/or 'messo a bande' ('banned'), and while rebutting the 'Achtung! Banditen!' of the German road signs, contained the problem of the distinction between bandits and highwaymen, which I will come back to. 'Guerriero' ('warrior') is, by contrast, a word that was rarely adopted: destined in recent times to enjoy renewed fortune, the term must then have appeared a trifle *recherché* and archaic,[167] even if the word 'guerriglia' enjoyed wider circulation.[168] A similar discussion could be devoted not just to the names the partisans were called by, but to the way in which the units into which they formed were designated. 'Banda' is undoubtedly the original and most spontaneous name, used in the first few months even by the Military Command for Northern Italy. Giancarlo Pajetta has written: 'The *giellisti* of Cuneo, fine and courageous … called their formations "bande", to make it clear that platoons, companies, battalions, regiments and brigades

---

163 Rome edition, 15 March 1944, article entitled 'Italia che nasce e Italia che muore'.

164 See for example Gorrieri, *La Repubblica di Montefiorino*, p. 296.

165 This was the title of a newspaper 'a cura della 7a Brigata GL "P. Stefanoni", Divisione patrioti Valtoce, Raggruppamento "Di Dio"'.

166 Giancarlo Puecher was commemorated, for example, by calling him 'Bandito Puecher!' (see G. Bianchi, *Giancarlo Puecher, a vent'anni, per la libertà*, Milan: Mondadori, 1965, p. 134).

167 In fact it is the name given to a 'giornale delle Brigate Mazzini', while the 'Formazioni Mameli' chose the more bizarre one, *Il Guerrigliatore* (see *Saggio bibliografico*, nn. 4114–15 and 4100–02).

168 For example, on 7 December 1943 *L'Unità*, Rome edition, published an article entitled 'Guerriglia', which describes the characteristics of the 'guerra partigiana' in a very traditional, one might say scholastic, manner. 'Guerra partigiana' is spoken of in the 'rapparto di Ermete' (Agostino Novella) from Rome, 26 March 1944 (see G. Amendola and F. Frassati, eds, 'Documenti inediti sulle posizioni del PCI e del PSIUP dall'ottobre 1943 all'aprile 1944', in *Critica marxista* 2 [1965], pp. 131–9). In both cases the sources are Roman.

would no longer exist. We, on the other hand, said "brigades", and dreamed of soon being able to call them "divisions".[169]

Indeed, the GL formations too ended up organising themselves into divisions, even if their Command re-divided them only into squads, detachments and brigades.[170] The autonomous formations certainly had no semantic taboos about adopting names of the organic units of the army. Thus, when the 'technical consultant' of the CMRP (Comando Militare Regionale Piemontese) advised against several Garibaldi brigades being grouped together into the 1st Piedmont division, which had for that matter already been created, it is hard to know how much of this was a 'technical' move and how much it may be put down to political caution.[171] 'Brigade' too was successful, in the wake of the Spanish international brigades. Towards the end of 1943 the PCI leadership was speaking of detachments, battalions and brigades;[172] and 'Garibaldi assault detachments and brigades' was to be the definitively adopted name (where that word 'assault' recalled, with questionable opportuneness, the 'reparti d'assalto' ('assault units') of the First World War – the *arditi*).

'Platoon' or 'company' do not appear for the smaller units, and still more understandably 'regiment' was avoided, since it smacked too much of barracks (the mythical 'fifth regiment' of the Spanish Civil War was not enough to rehabilitate it).

Recourse to traditional terminology was made necessary not only by the growth of the formations and the consequent need to group them into higher-level units, but also by the political wish to acquire, as far as possible, the physiognomy of an army – paying the price of an attenuation of the original egalitarianism. There were those who insisted on carrying things too far. From the Ossola-Valsesia came the proposal to create in that free zone and in Lombardy as many as four 'corpi d'armata della liberazione' ('liberation corps') and to transform the Lombard regional Command into a Command of the 'assault army of Liberation'. The CVL General Command dryly expressed its dissent.[173] A 'corpo d'armata Centro Emilia' appears in other documents; but when Pajetta had an 'enormous headline' printed in the *Combattente* – 'Partisan corps gives chase to the Germans' – Longo became irritated and explained that 'the most important thing was to get oneself taken seriously'.[174]

---

169 Pajetta, *Il ragazzo rosso va alla guerra*, p. 27.

170 'Circolare interna n. 3' of 26 September 1944 (*Formazioni GL*, p. 162).

171 This opinion was sent on 10 June 1944 to the regional CLN and to the Command of the 1st division itself (IG, BG, 04653).

172 Letter 'ai compagni delle formazioni partigiani', 23 November 1943 (*Le Brigate Garibaldi*, vol. I, p. 136).

173 See the minutes of a meeting of 14 March 1945, amply summarised in ibid., vol. III, p. 489, note 2, and *Atti CVL*, pp. 469–70 (6 April 1945).

174 See 'ordine del giorno n. 4' ('agenda item no. 4') of 10 July 1944 (*Le Brigate*

For its part, the CVL General Command devoted considerable care to the subject and eventually, following unification, sanctioned the ascending scale of squad–detachment–battalion–brigade–division.[175]

One should not, however, assume that the construction of an increasingly complex hierarchical pyramid meant a corresponding effective and regular organisation. Neither the Garibaldi nor GL General Command were equipped with General Staffs or operational offices that drew up battle plans, issued the consequent orders, and so on. The unity ensured by these General Commands was above all politically orientated, and broadly speaking organisational. Likewise with the General Command of the CVL (Corpo Volontari della Libertà), and with more reason.[176] Even when the final phase of unification was reached, the General Command and the single peripheral Commands responded essentially to political perspectives and equilibria. The more unadulterated current of the partisan formations, which were territorially and politically differentiated, was in reality to unite more into a sort of federal form than into the rigid framework of a hierarchical machinery. Even the partial fusions that occurred locally were often more fictitious than real. Such was the case, for example, with the amalgamation into the Piave division of the Battisti and Perotti formations. And, again in the Ossola zone, when it was decided to create a single Command for the free territory of the 'republic', and the commander of the Matteotti formations was put in charge of it, nobody objected, because 'we were all convinced that anyway no one would obey a single command'.[177]

2. RELATIONS WITH THE PARTIES

Military-style organisation, which, as we have seen, in many respects remained more a programme than a reality, would not have been enough to keep so variegated a partisan army, and one so jealous of its autonomy, united. With a realism verging on excess one partisan chief has written: 'The absolute lack of higher control would have allowed us with a certain ease to reign over the territories that were subsequently occupied with a despotism and an irresponsibility that might, besides, have justified the urgent military needs.'[1]

Garibaldi, vol. II, pp. 115–16, and relative bibliographical cross-references). Pajetta, Il ragazzo rosso va alla guerra, pp. 83–4, presents this as one of its journalistic discoveries.

175 See the circular of 3 April 1945, which issues the CLNAI decision of 29 March (Atti CVL, p. 461).

176 'We had organised the semblance of a General Staff; but the only thing that really counted remained the collaboration between Parri and Longo' (Pajetta, Il ragazzo rosso va alla guerra, p. 62).

177 See N. Chiovini, 'I giorni della liberazione di Cannobio', in Novara. Notiziario economico 2 (1987), p. 7; and Pajetta, Il ragazzo rosso va alla guerra, p. 76.

1 Lazagna, Ponte rotto, p. 31.

A partisan chief with a certain degree of charisma might, that is, have found himself tempted down the slope of some form of *rassimo* (petty despotism).[2] The ties established with the parties acted as a counterweight to this tendency, as they did, for that matter, to local pressures. These ties made the individual formations more internally homogeneous, differentiating them from others of a different persuasion, but at the same time they were a unifying factor: they not only transmitted the CLN policy of unity to the rank-and-file, but fostered the conviction that it was political commitment as such that established the essential bond between the partisans. Undoubtedly one of the presuppositions of the way the parties took root in post-war Italian society was their having been present in the Resistance – a factor which to this day gives legitimacy to the 'constitutional arc' of the parties of the Italian Republic. Some clarification is necessary, however. Above all, we need to recognise that there was some degree of fortuitousness in the 'politicisation' of a certain number of formations. This was clearly seen by Anna Bravo, when, writing of the Alto Montferrato, she said that, since the partisans were, so to speak, a politically amorphous material, those who first managed to help them, stimulate them, and give them advice with a wider experience, were able to orientate them towards their own political positions. The need to organise set in motion political conquest.[3] It was thus that the military organism itself became a 'natural channel for the current of political ideas'.[4] Financing, access to Allied airdrops, assistance of various kinds, CLN recognition, as well, naturally, as the prestige that they had succeeded in gaining, were the instruments of which the parties availed themselves to lead the bands into their respective orbits. Some GL formations, an Action Party document complained, had regressed into apoliticism because they were convinced that this was the way to obtain greater funding and airdropped supplies. For the same reasons, it added, these formations could end up gravitating towards the Garibaldi or Matteotti brigades.[5] The diary of the Rosselli brigade tells us that, while freedom of individual political orientation held good, 'given that the

2 This sort of phenomena is indicated in the report by Grossi (Francesco Scotti), who was in charge of military matters in the Piedmont insurrectional triumvirate, on his visit to the free zone of southern Monferrato and of the Langhe from 19 to 25 October 1944 (*Le Brigate Garibaldi*, vol. II, p. 494).

3 Bravo, *La Repubblica partigiana dell'Alto Monferrato*, p. 39. In the preceding pages the author had also highlighted the initial distrust towards the Garibaldini-Communists.

4 Battaglia, *Un uomo*, p. 185.

5 See the 'Osservazioni sulla situazione militare del Partito d'azione nell'Alto Novarese', signed T. Moro for the Novara federation, sent to the Military Command of the party for the Lombrady, 24 March 1945 (*Formazioni GL*, pp. 347–9). The technique of absorption practised by the Green Flames of the province of Brescia in order that 'the party to which the formation possibly belonged came to lose all influence' is described, by another *azionista*, in the 'Relazione sopra il distaccamento Barnaba', 19 January 1943 (INSMLI, CVL, envelope 93, folder 5).

brigade must however rely on one of the parties at the CLNs, it is logical and right for the 'Carlo Rosselli' brigade to rely on the representative of the Action Party'.[6] The 'non-political nature' of the autonomous bands came in for a severe upbraiding from the General Command of the CVL, which reminded Mauri that 'the struggle being conducted against the Germans and Fascists is absolutely political and must be conducted raising the political conscience of the various formations to the highest degree'.[7] Non-politicalness was generally denounced by the politicians as false non-politicalness.[8] And indeed it did lend itself well to use by the Christian Democrats and Liberals, who did not have many bands of their own, to exert their influence over the autonomous bands. A Garibaldi document gives a colourful and angry description of this process:

> The Christian Democrats are hard at work on the 'autonome'. They're sending them military chaplains, bigwigs from the curia, trusted and pretty sharp elements. They're well received and don't miss the chance to 'advise' and perhaps pretend in God's name to participate at the zone Command meetings. We are being as tactful as we can not to provoke them; but it's clear that sooner or later we won't be able to tolerate positions and insinuations against us.[9]

On the other hand, some formations became 'of a political leaning only because of the political profession of one or two of the men in charge of them'.[10] Other formations, or at least some of their members, may be said to have gone looking for 'politics', without ever fully encountering it.[11]

The Communist Party and Action Party, those most engaged in the armed struggle, inevitably dedicated particular attention to relations with 'their' formations. Some of the problems arising from this will be discussed in the chapter

---

6 Quoted in Revelli, *La guerra dei poveri*, p. 483.

7 Letter to the CMRP of 18 August 1944 (*Atti CVL*, p. 163).

8 For example, in September 1944 Brandani (Mario Mammuccari), Communist representative of the military command of the city of Turin, wrote these words about the 'New Movement of National Redemption' ('Nuovo Movimento di Redenzione nazionale'): 'The apolitical character of the movement is suspect. No movement is apolitical. Even soldiers, if they are not mercenaries or adventurers, think politically' (G. Vaccarino, C. Gobetti and R. Gobbi, *L'insurrezione di Torino*, Parma: Guanda, 1968, p. 78).

9 Letters by 'compagni responsabili' of the 3rd Piedmont division to 'cari compagni', 10 October 1944 (*Le Brigate Garibaldi*, vol. II, p. 427). Battaglia mentions formations that were 'military', but which in fact had relations with Democrazia Cristiana in *Un uomo*, p. 126.

10 Report by the Command of the Nanetti division, Pesce, 31 May 1945 (*Le Brigate Garibaldi*, vol. III, p. 720).

11 Such was the case with the De Vitis division (on which see Quazza, *Un diario partigiano*, esp. pp. 190, 199, 202, 205, 238), and what was subsequently said about the influence that the Turin strikes of March 1944 had on the commander Giulio Nicoletta.

of this book dealing with the class war. Let me just recall here that, in the PCI documents, complaints about what was considered scant politicisation are accompanied by a commitment to politicisation–militarisation along the party line, as a means of reabsorbing the manifestations of spontaneous leftism or, as commissar Davide writes, of 'a more or less anarchic tendency, however much they profess Communist sympathies'.[12] 'How far are the GL formations following today and how far will they follow tomorrow the line of the Action Party?' was the question that Giorgio Agosti, political commissar of the GL Piedmontese Command, asked himself on 31 December 1944.[13] He gave a very full answer; and what needs highlighting is the point where he observes that, while the first bands were well and truly *azionisti*, of their own free choice, by now the GLs, following, as it were, an inverse path to the one traced above, were a small army that was more military than political. It would be wrong to think that they were fast becoming like the *autonomi*, but 'it would be a mistake to confound the GL *esprit de corps* with adhesion to the programme of the party and fidelity to its directives'.

Militarisation and politicisation did not, therefore, always keep in step with each other; on the contrary, again according to the author of this report, it was a harder business politicising the partisan today than it had been yesterday. Today the partisan, especially since the start of the 'pianurizzazione' (that is, descent into the plains) which had brought him out of the Alpine valleys,[14] was acquiring too much of 'a soldier of fortune's mentality', assuming an '"ardito's temperament"' and beginning to nurture a "passion for the *bel colpo* [the coup]" ... There is more of a squadrista's spirit than one might think'.

The two main parties were, moreover, the first to be of one mind in repeating that politicisation under their aegis did not mean adhesion to the parties themselves. A document drawn up by Duccio Galimberti in April 1944 is quite explicit on this count, where it still claims continuity with the column commanded by Carlo Rosselli in Aragon; likewise a Piedmontese regional command document of the following July, in which the distinction between political awareness and party membership is said to be 'not a dialectical game', that is to say, not a game of side-taking.[15] The recognition of freedom of opinion, even within

---

12 See the letter by Davide, commissar of the Modena division, to the regional Garibaldi delegation, 29 May 1944, quoted in Gorrieri, *La Repubblica di Montefiorino* p. 280. See also the accusations of sectarianism, due to the lack of 'un serio lavoro politico', addressed to the bands of the valleys of Lanzo and the province of Genoa by inspector Gr. (Francesco Scotti) in May 1944 (*Le Brigate Garibaldi*, vol. I, p. 385).

13 See the above-mentioned report in *Formazioni GL*, pp. 267–86. On the report between the Action Party and GL formations, see De Luna, *Storia del Partito d'Azione*, pp. 295–302.

14 On 'pianurizzazione', see Battaglia, *Storia della Resistenza*, pp. 455–60.

15 See them in *Formazioni GL*, pp. 84–5, 118–20. See also a letter of 13 October 1944

the politically defined formations, is one of the ways in which this relationship with the parties was manifested. Giovana gives an account of the GL formations he studied that is in line with the documents just quoted.[16] As for the Garibaldi brigades, it is enough to quote this declaration of principle: 'In the political field the patriot can express and support any opinion and doctrine and must conversely respect those of others, even if they should conflict with his.'[17] This full individualistic guaranteeism, the affirmation of whose principle is recurrent, did not always combine easily with another widespread directive: that the only political line that it was legitimate to practise was the CLN's unitary one. There was the risk, on the one hand, that this programmatic humanism would lower the political tone of the formations, and on the other hand that it might encourage the branding as anti-unitary of those who did not share the interpretation given to the unit by the political tendency prevailing in one or other formation. Thus one might reach the paradox that one did indeed have the right to be non-political, but 'on the understanding that this was meant in the sense of espousing the CLN line, and no other one'.[18] Relations between the parties could be regulated with a formalism hardly in line with circumstances. This is what the Dronero CLN did when it decreed that, in the Maira valley occupied by the GL and Garibaldi brigades, party newspapers could be distributed only 'subject to authorisation' by the CLN itself, and that the parties had to abstain from public demonstrations where not all of them were represented, 'except for the private meetings of each single party'.[19] A vast range of situations lie between these more or less solemn declarations, and the reality of the collective climate, characterised by a greater or lesser degree of political intensity, that was being created in the bands. Here, a central figure was that of the political commissar. Invented by Trotsky to control the Tsarist officers whom the newborn Red Army could not do without, the political commissars had accompanied the fortunes of the Communist and democratic formations (one need only think of Spain). In the Italian Resistance the commissars, whom not all the parties accepted easily,[20] were called upon to play a role that complicated and greatly altered their

---

by the GL delegation of the Lombard Regional Command to Colonel Bassi (Bergamasco) (INSMLI, *CVL*, envelope 93, folder 5). Again, on the eve of the Liberation the newsletter of the 10th GL Alpini division, 'lungo il Tanaro', would feel the need to repeat that the GL were not Action Party formations, though they recognised themselves as being tied to them (article entitled 'Chiarificazione', April 1945).

16 See Giovana, *Storia di una formazione partigiana*, pp. 61–2, 103–4, 291–3.

17 'Proposta di riordinamento', undated, no author (Parma zone) (IG, *BG*, Emilia-Romagna, G.IV.3.2).

18 See Bernardo, *Il momento buono*, p. 144. See also point 7 of the 'Vademecum del volontario della libertà', edited by the CUMER commissariat, 25 August 1944 (*Le Brigate Garibaldi*, vol. II, p. 263).

19 Minutes of the meeting of 6 July 1944 (IG, *BG*, 04348).

20 See on this point L. Longo, *Un popolo alla macchia*, Rome: Riuniti, 1964, p. 119.

image and function. The basic justification for their existence was expressed in these words: 'In the Garibaldi brigades there cannot be combatants who do not know what they are fighting for';[21] or, in these other words, written by way of a comment on the difficulties raised by the autonomous units in accepting the commissars: 'This tendency for ... the soldiers to fight and ask no questions, to fight and stay clear of politics, is a militaristic reactionary tendency that must be combated.'[22] Major Mauri actually refused to have commissars in his units: in his view, all that was needed, not least to understand the meaning of liberty, democracy and social justice, were arms, body and soul (*cuore e braccio*), and the Italian flag, the *tricolore*.[23]

Albeit after uncertainties and equivocations (even among the Communist and Action Party leaders),[24] the political commissar came to be recognised as being equal in rank to a commander: 'solidly responsible' and 'equal in law' is what they were called in a document of the Garibaldi leadership; 'equal in rank, in all the orders' is how a document of the Action Party leadership put it.[25] Transformed, with their power reduced so as to make them acceptable to everyone, at the act of unification,[26] the parity of rank of the 'war commissars'

21 Letter to the Cremona SAP Command, 13 November 1944 (INSMLI, *Brigate Garibaldi*, envelope 2, folder I, subfolder 2).

22 Letter by Oreste (Giordano Pratolongo), responsible for military matters in the Piedmont insurrectional triumvirate, to 'cari compagni', 11 September 1944 (*Le Brigate Garibaldi*, vol. II, pp. 322–3). Oreste adds that 'the GL Command is in full agreement with the garibaldino Command'.

23 See E. Martini Mauri, *Partigiani penne nere*, Milan: Mondadori, 1968.

24 In a letter of 13 December 1943, Amendola wrote that the identification between commander and commissar seemed 'dangerous' (Amendola, Letter a Milano, p. 236). For the *azionisti*'s doubts about the very opportuneness of the commissar, see, as regards Galimberti, Parri's testimony (*Intervista sulla guerra partigiana* given to L. La Malfa Cologero and M. V. de Filippis, pp. 23–4), and what Bianco wrote, moving on the basis of the certain political character of the military GL chiefs (Bianco, *Guerra partigiana*, p. 90). See also Giovana, *Storia di una formazione partigiana*, pp. 194ff. A fine portrait of a GL commissar is given by N. Bobbio, 'Il commissario Mila', in *La Stampa*, 5 February 1989.

25 See 'Schema di organizzazione of the Command di una brigata d'assalto Garibaldi', circulated 20 May 1944 by the General Command (ISRT, *CVL, Comando militare toscano*, envelope 5, folder 7, *Delegazione toscano delle Brigate Garibaldi*); and the 'Relazione sullo schema di decreto per l'unificazione delle formazioni partigiane nel CVL' of the Alta Italia executive of the Action Party, 9 January 1945 (INSMLI, *CLNAI*, envelope 10, folder I, subfolder 2).

26 Fearing that unification would lead to the complete disappearance of commissars, some Garibaldi formations had started to appoint commissars as commanders; see the report by Albero (Alberto Cavallotti), inspector at the 3rd Aliotta division, to the Lombardy insurrectional triumvirate, 24 February 1945, and the letter by the Lombardy delegation to the above division, 27 February 1945 (*Le Brigate Garibaldi*, vol. III, pp. 417, 419–20).

with commanders was reiterated by CVL headquarters.[27] As channels of communication, the commissars obviously mirrored the points of view of the
parties they came from; but they also came to figure as representatives of the
CLN's unitary policy. They are clearly defined as such by Roberto Battaglia.[28]
In the Di Dio formations, for example, this function was interpreted extensively almost as a prohibition to talk politics.[29] The Communists in turn would
increasingly insist on this CLN and unitary–patriotic nature of the commissar, though always pointing out that this was precisely the line of their own
party.[30] If we compare the 'guide del commissario' ('commissar's guides') and
the instructions for the 'ora politica' ('political hour') with some original texts
drawn up at Communist headquarters, we can see how the primitive political
and class emphasis was diluted into that of the CLN.[31] Mario Bernardo ruefully
recalls: 'The content of the political hour which had constituted the critical and
constructive force of the first formations had gradually been debased, being
transformed itself into lectures by commanders and commissars.'[32] Nevertheless,
clear traces of party spirit remain, as in the report recommending that a good
political commissar must 'give a clear explanation of the social constitution of
the Soviet regime, [and] should be capable of giving some lessons on Leninism
and if possible in political economics'.[33] More soberly, but still stepping beyond
CLN bounds, the instructions sent to the 188th Ferruccio Ghinaglia (Cremona)
SAP brigade included a request to talk about progressive democracy;[34] while
'Andrea Lima' (Mario Lizzero), commissar of the Friuli Garibaldi division,
urged his colleagues to explain 'the principles of progressive democracy
that will guide Italy after the invader and the traitors have been driven

---

27 See the 'Decisione' of the CLNAI of 29 March 1945 (*Atti CVL*, p. 463). There
was to be no difference in the command badges ('distintivi di commando'); see the
'Regolamento interno del CVL', 18 April 1945, already cited (ibid., pp. 490–2).

28 See Battaglia, *Un uomo*, p. 129.

29 See R. A. Webster, *The Cross and the Fasces*, Stanford: Stanford University Press,
1960, pp. 166, 210.

30 Among the many documents along these lines, see the letters sent by the delegation for Lombardy 15 November 1944 to the Command of the 1st and 2nd division group,
and 2 November 1944 to the Command of the '13 Martiri di Lovere' brigade (INSMLI,
CVL, envelope 93, folder 4).

31 See M. Legnani, 'Documenti della guerra partigiana: le 'Guide del commissario',
in *Il Movimento di liberazione in Italia* XVII: 81 (1965), pp. 61–74. Comparison with the
party texts, conserved in ISRP, was suggested to me by Gianni Perona, to whom I give
my thanks. See G. Perona , 'Le forze della resistenza e l'insurrezione', in *L'insurrezione in
Piemonte*, Milan: Franco Angeli, 1987, pp. 311–43, esp. pp. 335–46.

32 Bernardo, *Il momento buono*, pp. 63–4.

33 'Relazione sulla visita fatta da me il 14–15 agosto [1944] alla formazione 13
Martiri' (Bergamasco), signed Lesia (?) (IG, *BG*, 010560).

34 INSMLI, *CVL*, envelope 93, folder 4 (November 1944).

out'.[35] It should come as no surprise, then, if the Communists themselves reprimanded the commissars who 'confuse the life of the party with the political line of the Fronte Nazionale',[36] and if in some cases the commisars were substituted for their blatant sectarianism.[37] At the opposite extreme of sectarianism, or simply of faith in one's deep convictions, the figure of the commissar was diluted to the point at which he faded into a sort of lay chaplain or 'social assistant', just as the chaplain could in his turn blur into a commissar. In the Osoppo brigades, Fogar writes, there were 'lay commissars in the complete and official sense of the term, and priests' – that is to say, chaplains who devoted themselves not only to religious but also to ideological–political assistance, above all in an anti-Communist and anti-Slav sense.[38] In this case, given the nature of the Osoppo brigades, we have an example of the paradox by which the Italian partisan bands were perhaps the only military formations in which political commissars and chaplains lived side by side,[39] where the stress falls on the side of the chaplain. Elsewhere it is the commissar who intrinsically recalls the chaplain. A Piedmontese partisan has written: 'They called them chaplains; they were rather like an equivalent of Catholic chaplains. But they were marvellous figures, always!' The adversative conjunction 'but' is in this context all the more significant insofar as the traditional opposition between culture and lack of culture characterising the relationship between the chaplains and the soldiers is turned on its head: 'I knew how to use the subjunctive, they didn't. I knew how to use it in Latin, they didn't. Not only that, but they got accents on words wrong.'[40] At other times the commissars' resemblance to the chaplains

---

35 It is curious that this proposal was made in a report to the provincial CLN of Udine, 31 January 1945, which advocated unification with the Osoppo (*Le Brigate Garibaldi*, vol. II, p. 319). For the tasks entrusted to commissars in the brief period of the 'Comando Coordinamento GOF' (Garibaldi – Osoppo Friuli), see order of the day no. 7 of 2 November 1944 (IZDG., envelope 272b, folder I/B).

36 'Relazione sulla mia ispezione in Valtellina', signed Domenico, 4 August 1944 (IG, *BG*, 0540).

37 Such was the case with Remo, transferred to a post other than that of commissar of the 51st Capettini brigade. See 'Relazione dell'ispezione alla 3a divisione Lombardia Aliotta', 12 October 1944, signed Giorgio (IG, *BG*, 01492). For Remo's intemperance in his articles in *Il Garibaldino*, see the document cited in *Le Brigate Garibaldi*, vol. II, pp. 529–30, n. 9.

38 See Fogar, *Le brigate Osoppo-Friuli*, pp. 330–41, which gives a balanced reconstruction of the activities performed in the Osoppo formations by the commissars or, as they preferred to call them in that environment, political delegates. During the brief period of Garibaldi–Osoppo unification, the Christian Democrats had been concerned that the positions of command did not all remain in Communist hands.

39 See Webster, *La Croce e i Fasci*, p. 228.

40 Tersilla Fenoglio Oppedisano's testimony, in Bruzzone and Farina, eds, *La Resistenza taciuta*, pp. 153–4. The commissars referred to by Fenoglio 'had studied in jail'.

is mentioned in a quite different sense. In Giorgio Agosti's long report about the GL brigades, which I have already recalled, it is argued that often the commissar, rather than politicising the commander, militarised himself: 'Thus at a certain point in his talk sten guns and explosive pencils recur more often than the ideals behind the partisan war.' An anonymous hand scribbles in the margin: 'This is what happened to many military chaplains in the army.'[41] Moreover, this frustrated the 'anti-Bonapartist' function, which some wanted to attribute to the commissars in their relations with the commanders, 'in the sense of guaranteeing themselves against the possibility of excessive autonomy and safeguarding themselves against presumed bids for independence ... even if there's no sign of there being any Napoleon capable of undermining the authority of the governing body'. The alarmed author of this is a general writing to another general: in fact he concludes by stating that the commissars are necessary in the party formations, but not in those autonomous ones commanded by military men – an opinion shared by General Cadorna, the addressee of this message, according to whom commissars, whom he likens to the officers responsible for propaganda and to the chaplains, are admissible only in the formations without officers.[42] Less paradoxical, in its ingenuousness, is the fact that an officer who declared that he had been sent by CVL headquarters, 'after having made comments about the weakness of the Bonomi government', asked the members of the Veneto Regional Command how they would view the rise of General Cadorna to head of government after the Liberation. (The people consulted obviously said that they were against the idea.)[43]

There was also the risk of the commissar assuming the guise of a factotum, through being too caught up in the duties of administrator, supply assistant, and storekeeper.[44] A commissar might devote himself to assistance functions (in some formations the commissars seem to have been mainly medical students);[45]

---

41 See the text of Giorgio Agosti's account *Formazioni GL*.

42 See the 'Memoria per generale Valenti' (Cadorna) by General Trabucchi, 28 February 1945 (INSMLI, *CLNAI*, envelope 10, folder I, subfolder 2) and R. Cadorna, *La riscossa, Dal 25 luglio alla Liberazione*, Milan–Rome: Rizzoli 1948.

43 'Informazioni sul movimento partigiano nel Veneto', February 1945, anonymous (*Le Brigate Garibaldi*, vol. III, p. 423).

44 See the complaints against this evolution expressed in a letter by Michele, political commissar of the 1st Gramsci (Ossola-Valsesia) division, to Marco, commissar of the 82nd Osella brigade, 16 November 1944 (ibid., vol. II, pp. 598–9), as well as the report on the 'visita alla 47a brigata Garibaldi' (Parmense), 29–30 December 1944. Signed Pini (?) (IG, *BG, Emilia-Romagna*, G. IV.2.6). See also the pamphlet 'Funzioni del comandante e del commissario politico', edited by the Command of the 8th Asti division (IG, *BG*, 05816).

45 See the report by Ferrarini (Enzo Costa) on the inspection at the forces of the Parma Apennines, July 1944, in which it is added that 'only two commissars are proletarian and old comrades' ('solo due due commissari sono proletari e vecchi compagni') (*Le Brigate Garibaldi* vol. II, p. 121).

and it is no accident that this feature became most marked in the unified commands that saw Communist and Christian Democrats working alongside each other.[46] Some Communist commissars limited their political initiative for fear of being criticised by Christian Democrats.[47] An authoritative Communist leader gave this rather unsparing picture of the commissars of one formation: 'The commissars have greatly lowered the function and characteristics of the commissariat. Idlers, no courage, chatterboxes, or else sloggers, but not in their activity; full of life, but not in military terms; *gerarchi* at times but not commissars.'[48]

When Boldrini, by now deployed with his formation in the British 8th Army in Rome, wanted to reassure General Berardi, chief of the General Staff, he described the commissars as 'head cooks', 'head quartermasters', 'those responsible for daily shopping'. Pajetta, who recounts the episode, ironically commenting on the general's simple-mindedness, does not, however, bear in mind that there was some truth in this parody given by Boldrini, and that it was very much in the general's interest to give it credence.[49]

Certainly, one needs to have a better idea of who the commissars were. Evidently not all of them were of the excellent quality described above by Tersilla Fenoglio or the lamentable quality described by Andreis. Faith, enthusiasm, honesty and 'giudizio' ('good judgment'), as one document states, could make up for lack of political expertise;[50] but that does not mean that they always succeeded in doing so.

The specific character of the single formations exalted the principle of the 'free choice of unit by the aspiring volunteer',[51] but often made transferring from one unit to another a tricky business. A military man like Mauri had lost no time in solving this problem: in his formations anyone who passed from one unit or one command to another without the commander's written permission was

---

46 This occurred, for example, in the Modena division in the period of unified Command: see the 'relazione sull'attività del commissariato' (undated, but attached to a report to the CUMER dated 2 January 1945), quoted in ibid., vol. III, p. 187, note 2.

47 This reticence is observed in the report on an inspection of the Ateo Garemi brigade group (Vicentino), 20 February 1945 (ibid., p. 381): perhaps the brigade's name suggested particular prudence.

48 Report by Andreis on the inspection of the 6th Langhe division, 12 October 1944. As a remedy, Andreis had organised a school for commissars (ibid., vol. II, pp. 434–5).

49 Pajetta, *Il ragazzo rosso va alla guerra*, pp. 127–8.

50 See order of the day no. 3 of 5 January 1945 of the 9th Cuneo division (IG, BG, 04490).

51 This is what Cino and Ciro wrote in their 'Osservazioni e proposte' for the Communist project for 'the transformation of the partisan units into regular formations of the Italian army' ('la trasformazione delle unità partigiane in formazioni regolari dell'esercito italiano', 21 January 1945 (*Le Brigate Garibaldi*, vol. II, p. 264).

considered a deserter, and as such could be shot.[52] On 14 November the CVL General Command, which certainly could not brook such a crude way of going about things, issued a circular, as peremptory as it was unrealistic, against the 'buying up of combatants from other units'. The Command recalled that all units were open to all parties, but that all therefore followed the policy of the CLN alone. Only with the authorisation of one's own commands (or, if appropriate, of the higher ones) could a partisan, from that moment on, switch formation; but no penalties were envisaged for transgressors.[53]

Only a few days earlier, the Lombard delegation of the Garibaldi brigades had decreed that transfer could be ordered neither by the military commands nor by the parties, 'unless a reinforcement of the formations results from it', but the safeguarding of the individual's freedom of choice was accompanied by that of the group's solidarity: the decision for transfer was to be 'taken by all the men of the formation'.[54] A commander asked twenty or so men who presented themselves to bring him authorisation by the Command they came from.[55] But in that same period the soliciting of men between formations was denounced in the Cuneo area.[56]

In fact, worthy unitary intentions were not sufficient to resolve all the conflicts that could arise between the free choices of single partisans and the reinforcement of the military and political character, and *esprit de corps*, of the individual formations. At times this reinforcement generated clashes and abuses of power on both sides. In both the Garibaldi and GL documents, the denunciation of acts of incorrectness by others is always accompanied by the reaffirmation of the wish to collaborate.[57] Emulation, not competition and bullying between the bands, was the appeal launched by the Cuneo zone command on 3 February 1945,[58] which sums up the repeated declarations of good-will on this score.

Tensions between formations, which reached the point of attempts at mutual disarmament,[59] also beset the Matteotti brigades and the various autonomous

---

52 See the edict of 24 July 1944, attached to the letter of 8 October to Lieutenant Colonel Vanni quoted later, (INSMLI, CVL, envelope 27, folder 2, subfolder I.)

53 See *Atti CVL*, pp. 235–7.

54 The delegation to 'comandante Gufo', 1 November 1944 (INSMLI, *Brigate Garibaldi*, envelope 2, folder I., subfolder I).

55 Report by Pierino, commander of the 46th brigade, to Piedmont delegation, 11 March 1945 (IG, *BG*, 05051).

56 Circular of the (unified) zone Command to all the dependent formations, 3 February 1945 (ibid., 04504).

57 See for example the letter by Andrea, political commissar of the group of Liguria brigades, to the General Command, 3 August 1944, and the circulars of the Piedmontese and Ligurian GL Commands of 8 July and 25 August 1944 (respectively in *Le Brigate Garibaldi*, vol. II, pp. 192–4, and *Formazioni GL*, pp. 106–8, 147–8).

58 IG, *BG*, 04504.

59 For example, Sciabola (Lionello Santi), the GL representative, who was

groups such as the Osoppo brigades, the Green Flames and Mauri's divisions. Here facts and suspicions mingle in a way that is hard to unravel, and coexist with flattery addressed by various commands to individuals or entire units. An example of this can be found in the letters that the Command of the Valle di Susa divisions addressed to the commander of the De Vitis autonomous division, showering him and his men with praise and offering him a paternalistic 'recognition'.[60]

Indeed, in the Garibaldi formation there arose a certain tendency to regard every fine and valorous partisan as a natural Garibaldino. The Communists sought in this way to reap the fruits of their choice for their formations of such a widely and universally resonant name which, at the beginning, had been used sometimes without any particular political or organisational reference in mind.[61] Condemning the behaviour of those who had forcefully compelled several units of the Monviso GL brigade to go over to the Garibaldi, the General Command actually developed the concept that Garibaldini are all those who 'offer themselves as an example and model for all combatants', wherever they may be serving. These 'garibaldini d'onore' were to be awarded the red scarf with *tricolore* stitching.[62] For their part, during the occupation of Alba, the autonomous units of Mauri, who were defined as the expression of the Italians 'who would like to empty the partisan movement of all popular and democratic content',[63] represented a sore temptation for the Garibaldini, who were more poorly armed, shod and fed.[64] In his turn, Nando, chief of one of Mauri's bands, went over to the GL brigades simply because they were better armed and, 'if they could have greater supplies', he said, he 'would go over to the Garibaldini, because war is waged with arms, not politics'.[65] The process of politicisation which gives

---

parachuted with an allied mission protested (late October 1944) against attempts to disarm him by the Garibaldini of the Biella area (INSMLI, *CLNAI*, envelope 6, folder 3, subfolder 9), who, according to one of their documents, felt denigrated (report by inspector Gigi, 15 December 1944, in *Le Brigate Garibaldi*, vol. III, p. 79). For the significance of this whole affair, see the section entitled 'I rapporti tra garibaldini, giellisti e missioni alleate', in Poma and Perona, *La Resistenza nel Biellese*, pp. 220–4.

60 The letter, of 31 December 1944, is in *Le Brigate Garibaldini*, vol. III, p. 165.

61 See in this regard a reference, rather too emphatic, in Gorrieri, *La Repubblica di Montefiorino*, p. 72.

62 Letter to the delegation for Piedmont, 9 November 1944 (INSMLI, *Brigate Garibaldi*, envelope I, folder 4, partly published in *Le Brigate Garibaldi*, vol. II, p. 607, n. 2). See also, in ibid., the same General Command's' letter to the Piedmont delegation, 17 November 1944, pp. 604–7.

63 Letter of 17 November 1944, in *Le Brigate Garibaldi*, vol. II, p. 607.

64 See the report, signed Antonio, on the 'ritirata [retreat] della 2a divisione Garibaldi Liguria "F. Cascione" in Piedmonte', late October 1944 (IG, *BG*, 010247).

65 See the report by Nestore, political commissar of the 8th Asti division, to the

pride of place to the CLN did not always correspond to the reality of the presence of politics in the bands. The CLN tended to present itself as the civilian government presents itself to the armed forces. The Piedmontese regional CLN reminded the formations of the 'necessary bond of subordination and discipline ... for everything relating to political and administrative activity'.[66] The Ligurian CLN called on the Command of the 1st Liguria (Garibaldi) division to adhere to the principle that 'political authority lies exclusively with the CLN'.[67] A clear-cut distinction between civilian power and military power is also made in a Garibaldi document.[68] Dante Livio Bianco, for whom the CLN was the 'true and authentic national government of invaded Italy', attributed the distrust of the 'gentlemen of the committee' to the 'usual "trincerismo"' ("diehard trench mentality"), an all too familiar phenomenon of the 'small-mindedness' of the 'military formations'.[69] On one occasion Major Mauri acknowledged that he, and his Blues, were under the orders of the CLN; but 'so deep-seated was his "trenchman's"' spirit as to induce him then to write: 'In twenty months' warfare waged over two-thirds of the Cuneo territory, there was never a sign of there being a provincial CLN in Cuneo. But it doesn't bother me in the least that I don't have to know it even today'.[70] But distrust of the CLN cannot be put down merely to a priori aversion to politics on the part of the 'pure' military men,[71] which was also present at times in the political formations, such as the GL.[72] Even the CVL (Voluntary Liberty Corps) command proclaimed the autonomy of the military organisms in deciding who should be appointed to the commands.[73] Nor would it be correct to attribute certain manifestations of hostility

---

delegation for Piedmont, 18 February 1945 (*Le Brigate Garibaldi*, vol. III, p. 374). For Nando (Ferdinando Pagliassotto), see *Formazioni GL*, p. 408.

66 Circular of 8 November 1944, in 'Bullettino' n. 2, p. 35.

67 Minutes of 11 January 1945, in P. Rugafiori, ed., *Resistenza e ricostruzione in Liguria. Verbali del CLN ligure, 1944/1946*, Milan: Feltrinelli, 1981, p. 190.

68 Letter by the delegation for Piedmont to the Command of the group of Langhe divisions, 9 April 1945 (Le Brigate Garibaldi vol. III, p. 590). On this point, see in general Pajetta, *Il ragazzo rosso va alla guerra*, p. 47.

69 See Bianco, *Guerra partigiana*, pp. 63–5.

70 Letter by the General CVL Command to the CMRP, 18 August 1944 (*Atti CVL*, pp. 162–4) and Martini Mauri, *Partigiani penne nere*, p. 229.

71 A minor, but very clear example is given by Colonel Marenco's SIMAR band in Tuscany, *Partigiani penne nere*, p. 229.

72 Cerri (Norberto Duzioni), one of the organisers of the GL in the province of Bergamo, abandoned them when he realised that, instead of working for the *patria*, he was working for the Action Party. See his letter of resignation, 15 September 1944, in *Formazioni GL*, pp. 158–60. For the anti-partyism of Tuscan band chief tied to the GLs, see the minutes of the executive committee of the Florence Action Party, 7 April 1945 (ISRT, *Carte Carlo Campolmi*, envelope 2).

73 See the letter to the Regional Command for Lombardy, 16 August 1944 (*Atti CVL*, pp. 151–2).

to the CLN only to the fear that they were dominated by Communists.[74] The 'stuttering CLNs' could be seen as being infected by the 'highly dangerous gangrene' of *attesismo* (waiting on events).[75] Before an invitation to call a truce in the guerrilla war, 'the conviction, which had been deep-rooted for some time, grew all the stronger that in the CLNs there lurked the spectre of betrayal'.[76] One CLN, though composed almost solely of Communists, could be defined as 'partisans of pious works'.[77] 'The bias of our Garibaldini against these committees' was considered 'widespread and deep-rooted'.[78] 'The bands' hatred of the Modena and Bologna Committees reached the point of threats'.[79] Even a Communist chief was unaware of the very existence of the Ravenna provincial CLN.[80] Words with a Tocquevillian emphasis appeared in a Garibaldi document. The CLN, 'created for liberty, was performing the function merely of making slavery more accommodating'.[81] Bandied back and forth increasingly were accusations of incompetence in directing the struggle, of falling short in the work of assisting the partisans, of improper and incompetent interference in things military, of totally irrational behaviour.[82] Distrust might go so far as to advise that

---

74 This seems to have been the case with a Parma province formation that distanced itself from the CLN (also accused of inefficiency). See the report by 'Dario' (Luigi Marchini) titled 'al compagno federale e al compagno commissario', 7 June 1944 (*Le Brigate Garibaldi*, vol. II, p. 21). See also the report of the Nanetti division Command to the General Command, 10 August 1944 (ibid., pp. 245–7).

75 See Mautino, *Guerra di popolo*, pp. 34–5. For similar views of the CLNs of the provinces of Mantua and Biella, see the report to the Lombardy delegation by the Command of the group of lower Po Sap brigades, 8 January 1945, and the letter to the Biella federation, 27 November 1943 (*Le Brigate Garibaldi*, vol. II, p. 212, and vol. I, p. 141).

76 See Bernardo, *Il momento buono*, p. 109.

77 This is the CLN of Cassolnovo in Lomellina. See Ballone, *Una sezione, un paese*, p. 445.

78 See the letter by Michele, commissar of the 1st Gramsci division, to the commissar of the 124th Pisio Greta brigade, 1 April 1945 (*Le Brigate Garibaldi*, vol. III, p. 555).

79 'Situazione delle bande nella zona preappenninica a est e a ovest della via Emilia', signed Emilio, undated (November 1944?) (INSMLI, *Brigate Garibaldi* envelope I, folder 4).

80 Asdrubale's letter to Matteo, in Casali, *Il movimento di liberazione a Ravenna*, vol. II, pp. 283–4.

81 Letter by the Command of the group of northern brigades of the Friuli Garibaldi division to the Carnia CLN, 18 March 1945, after the end of the free zone (IRSFVG, *Fondo Magrini*, envelope CLV, folder I).

82 See Celso Ghini's report 'sul movimento della zone di confine umbro-marchigiano', 16 August 1944 (*Le Brigate Garibaldi*, vol. I, p. 256); the protest of the commander of the 2nd Cascione division to the Cuneo, Imperia and Mondovì CLNs, 6 December 1944 (ibid., vol. III, p. 33); the letter by the Lombardy delegation to the Regional Command, 18 May 1945, inspector Giorgio's report on the 3rd Aliotta division, 6 March 1945 (ibid., pp. 247–8, 443); the report by the PCI 'Comitato federale bis' of La

'no plan, no method, no tactic for action is to be communicated to any political organ'.[83]

In some cases the local CLNs were more highly thought of than the provincial ones, insofar as they relieved the partisans of civilian duties,[84] duties which, however, the partisans themselves sometimes claimed, using their power directly to settle disputes and right wrongs. This is what Ciro and Cino did when they severely warned the Sub-Alpine Railway and Navigation Company of Lake Maggiore against reporting unauthorised absentee workers to the Fascist authorities.[85]

In recalling all this, my intention is not to reopen the debate on the nature and real substance of the CLN, at the various levels, nor on the consequent intermingling, in the exercise of power, between the committees, the military formations and, in the free zones, the variously constituted popular governing juntas.[86] I simply want to emphasise that the problem of the presence of politics in the Resistance goes beyond simple adhesion to the single parties and/or their coalition expressed by the CLN. This kind of politicisation and its limits was put to the test in the unification of the various formations. I do not mean the initial efforts,[87] nor the unification, which remained mainly formal, that occurred from 19 to 20 June 1944 with the creation of the CVL General Command, but that, which was intended to be substantial, decided by the CLNAI (National Liberation Committee for North Italy) on 29 March 1945.[88] Initially the Communists had resisted this prospect. On 9 November 1943, in Turin, they had declared it 'unviable' and 'an error'.[89] If in this case it was a question of avoiding the controversial General Operti being appointed commander, a letter the following month from

---

Spezia on the 'situazione militare e politica della 4ª zona operative', 28 March 1945 (ibid., pp. 543-4).

83 This is what the Command of the group of Lombardy divisions wrote to the Command of the Nanetti battalion, 24 December 1944 (IG, *BG*, 01326). For a Nanetti detachment of the Certosa-Rho zone, see ibid., 011055 (5 September 1944).

84 See battaglia, *Un uomo*, pp. 134, 197-8. The criticism is addressed to the Apuania CLN.

85 'This is a warning: just words. If you don't change your attitude you will learn very quickly what our habitual style is: facts', 12 October 1944 (*Le Brigate Garibaldi*, vol. II, pp. 437-8).

86 Regarding the free zones see Legnani, *Politica e amministrazione nelle repubbliche partigiane*. For the general problem, dealt with in all histories of the Resistance, here I shall just mention G. Quazza, L. Valiani and E. Volterra, *Il governo dei CLN*, Turin: Giappichelli, 1966, and Quazza, *Resistenza e storia d'Italia*, Chapter VII, entitled 'I CLN direzione giacobina'.

87 See Bianco, *Guerra partigiana*, pp. 26, 42.

88 See *Atti CVL*, pp. 41-2, 459-65; *Atti CLNAI*, pp. 136-7. The decision to create the CVL had been taken by the central CLN on 9 January 1944 (*Atti CVL*, p. 538).

89 'Dichiarazione del rappresentante del PCI nel CLN' (IG, *Archivio PCI*).

the Milan to the Rome party headquarters expressed the broad conviction that the appointment of 'un responsabile', a 'dirigente', a 'capo', could not fail to have an anti-Communist significance: therefore, it is stressed, 'we demand parity within the political committees and within the military committees', but nothing else.[90] In expectation of a popular national army being created by a 'government of national liberation', the Communists insisted on the absolute parity of the parties in the committees and the denial of any 'operational directional function' to the committees themselves.[91] The growth of the Garibaldi brigades and the Salerno 'turning-point' led to a change in this position. In the 'Instructions for all comrades and for all the party formations', drawn up by Togliatti in Naples on 6 June 1944, the demand appeared for 'a single armed organisation, with a single military command, which should be entrusted to the most energetic and determined anti-Fascists and to the most militarily capable'.[92] Two days before this, the northern edition of L'Unità had published an article titled, 'The immediate formation of a single command for the whole partisan movement is necessary', in support of a proposal formally presented by the party in March, where 'essentially' coordination, orientation and aid duties were envisaged for the 'unified central Command' as well.[93]

The unfolding of events that led to General Cadorna's appointment as Commander, with Luigi Longo and Ferruccio Parri as vice-commanders – Longo representing the Garibaldi, Parri the GL brigades – is well enough known. But it is worth recalling that, in the Action Party too, which then became a convinced champion of unification,[94] initially some perplexity was expressed out of fear that the partisan struggle would be emptied of its political significance.[95] When, on 9 January 1945, the party's North Italy executive drew up the 'Report on the outline for a decree for the unification of the partisan formations in the Corpo volontari della libertà [Volunteer Corps for Freedom]', it maintained:

---

90 Letter of 10 December 1943 (IG, *Archivio PCI*).

91 See the 'Promemoria della delegazione del PCI presso il CLN per l'Alta Italia', late December 1943 (in *Atti CVL*, pp. 526-33). On the entire controversy over this question, above all with Parri, who had been dragged along until March 1944, see ibid., documents in Appendix I.

92 Minutes in IG, *Archivio PCI*, 'Direzione. Verbali della Delegazione PCI per l'Italia Meridionale'. It is published under the title 'Istruzione per l'insurrezione di tutto il popolo', in Togliatti, *Opere*, vol. V., pp. 41-2.

93 See *Atti CVL*, pp. 576–9.

94 The inclusion of the partisans in the army and in the public safety forces was a request that the Action Party pressingly made to the recently formed Bonomi government. See the article entitled 'Guerra, Governo e Popolo', which appeared in *L'Italia Libera*, northern edition, 19 June 1944.

95 See Catalano, *Storia del CLNAI*, p. 165, which refers the reader to a June 1944 issue of *Il Partigiano alpino*.

Unification cannot be 'military–apolitical'; relations between CLN and CVL cannot be those that regularly come into play between government and army, precisely because *this is a war of political deliverance* and the freedom fighters are fighting as much against the foreign invader as the interior and still more contemptible Fascist reaction. This can never be forgotten, especially by those who longed for a CVL of pure military men; if it were to lose its anti-Fascist, anti-imperialist, anti-reactionary and therefore democratic, liberating, popular and progressive line of political orientation and justification, the CVL would be incapable of fighting and would be devoid of justification and purpose ... All the commands are quite as much political organs as they are military ones.

In its proposal the Action Party was to present an international argument: the Greek experience could easily have been avoided if the partisans had presented themselves to the Allies as a united bloc. France and Yugoslavia were in fact showing the advantages of fusion and incorporation into the regular army.[96] As their documents repeat,[97] the Communists' fundamental objective was the transformation of the partisans into a regular army and their incorporation with the one being reconstituted in the South, even if this meant paying the price of an operation of a watered-down political value. The Action Party, by contrast, saw unification as the creation of an anything but blind military arm of that new organ of government, transcending the parties, which was how the party, or at least part of it, was fond of viewing the CLNs – as instruments of 'democratic revolution'.[98] The two parties most deeply engaged in the armed struggle were those that tried to tackle the question of unification and its political signifi-

---

96 'Relazione sullo schema di decreto per l'unificazione delle formazioni partigiane nel CVL', written by the party's Alta Italia executive on 9 January 1945 (INSMLI, *CLNAI*, envelope 10, folder I, s, folder 2). The concepts expressed in the report are amply illustrated in a pamphlet, *L'Unificazione*, published 15 March 1945 by the 'Edizioni del Comando delle formazioni partigiane Giustizia e Libertà'. As regards France, the Corsican partisans who were appointed officers in the army – 'gli Hoche e i Marceau della Resistenza' – must have come to a thousand, while about 60,000 elements of the FFI (Forces Françaises de l'Intérieur) were included in General Jean Lattre de Tassigny's army deployed on the Rhine (see Michel, *La guerra dell'ombra*, pp. 313, 333).

97 See, as an example of all, the project presented by Longo, 8 January 1945, to the CLNAI, which is in fact entitled 'Per la trasformazione delle unità partigiane in formazioni regolari dell'esercito italiano' (*Le Brigate Garibaldi*, vol. III, pp. 206–8), as well as Togliatti's speech at the Brancaccio theatre in Rome, 9 July 1944, his declarations to the party's national council, 7 April 1945 (Togliatti, *Opere*, vol. V, pp. 69, 117), and his letter to the insurrectional triumvirate of Emilia-Romagna, 2 March 1945 (*Le Brigate Garibaldi*, vol. III, pp. 430–1).

98 See in particular the proposal presented to the CLNAI, 31 December 1944, conserved in INSMLI, *Carte Damiani*, and amply summarised in Catalano, *Storia del CLNAI*, pp. 352–3.

cance, whereas the Christian Democrats and Liberals presented no proposals. The Liberals and Christian Democrats, and General Cadorna with them, on the one hand seemed concerned at the prospect that unification might bring with it;[99] on the other hand, they were ready to take advantage of the benefits that the initiative of others might bring them, sensing that the prize catch was flapping in their hands. The position of the Italian Socialist Party of Proletarian Unity (PSIUP) was isolated: it appeared unenthusiastic – even though it eventually fell into line – about placing under the command of reactionary generals an army, like the partisan army, whose purpose was to remain 'the efficient force for the conquest and defence of democratic liberties'.[100] The PSIUP raised another objection: it demanded that those concerned, namely the partisans, be consulted. Documents widely attest that the latter were somewhat suspicious about what was, as Leo Valiani has subsequently written, not a super- but inter-party unification being imposed from above.[101] Scepticism was widespread about the true results of an operation by now aimed more at measuring out forces among the parties with a view to the post-Liberation period than at creating an effective fighting instrument. In his report of 31 December 1944, Giorgio Agosti was already prophesying that, given the different formations' political leanings and their extremely powerful *esprit de corps*, it would be a 'unity of appearances': that was the only way he himself was prepared to accept it.[102] A young Garibaldino of the Piacenza zone, though favouring unification, was convinced that 'many things will go back to being as they were'.[103] The difficulty of finding enough party representatives, as well as officers, to fill all the posts in the jumbled unified commands was an accepted fact. Gorrieri made fun of General Marco Guidelli who, at the suggestion of the Communists, was put in charge of the Modena Command zone: up in the mountains this high-ranking officer's letters-cum-proclamations were 'greeted with utter indifference'.[104]

---

99 A note sent by the Liberals to Under-Secretary Medici Tornaquinci during his mission to the North (or possibly written by the under-secretary himself) contains these words: 'Communisti promotori della unificazione per evitare lo scioglimento delle bande' ('Communists promoters of unification in order to avoid the dissolution of the bands') (ISRT, *Archivio Medici Tornaquinci*, envelope 4, 5, n. I). For Cadorna's fears, see Catalano, *Storia del CLNAI*, pp. 356–8.

100 See his stances in the CLNAI meetings of 28 January and 5 February 1945 (ibid., pp. 355–6).

101 See L. Valiani, 'Gli azionisti' in Valiani, Bianchi and Ragionieri, *Azionisti, cattolici e comunisti nella Resistenza*, p. 98.

102 *Formazioni GL*, p. 278.

103 Alberto's letter to Pierino, 24 February 1945 (IG, *BG, Emilia-Romagna*, G. IV. 2.11).

104 See Gorrieri, *La Repubblica di Montefiorino*, p. 638. On the difficulties the Matteotti brigades had in finding the necessary men, see a letter sent to Citterio, 10 April 1945, by Gianni (Ridella), vice-commander of the GL formations in the unified zone

Indeed, the impression one gets skimming through the Resistance documents of the last two or three months before the Liberation is that, while the documents of the preceding months hint at a richer reality, which they do not succeed in fully expressing, things now are the other way round. The later documents mainly testify to the setting in motion of an organisation aimed at spreading a vast and uniform network of commands, appointments, and so on, carefully and punctiliously measured out, in such a way as to pre-establish *faits accomplis*, if not in reality at least on paper. This could even lead to increased quarrelling between the formations: involved though they were in the process of unification, they dragged behind them old resentments, born at times of their experience in the single commands they had formerly fought under.[105] The bands, therefore, almost closed ranks in order to prevent new and unexpected ones, which might modify power relations, from springing up at the last minute.[106] Moreover, these relations in the unitary organisms agreed over the table did not always tally with the reality that had established itself on the field. This was a source of concern for the Garibaldi general command in a directive adopted by the Piedmont delegation, which urged 'doing way with the great disproportion currently existing between the influence and prestige enjoyed among the partisans and the population by the Garibaldi formations ... and the actual forces deployed ... For all this, a special effort must be made by all to create new brigades.'[107]

The Commands' and the parties' mental reservations and the partisans' moral and emotional reservations do in fact punctuate the process of unification. An interesting indication of this is the persistence, in several Garibaldi documents, of the leave-taking formula *saluti garibaldini* (Garibadinian greetings). 'We can use it with each other, can't we?' wrote Fabio, who was responsible for military affairs in the insurrectional triumvirate for Lombardy, to Ciro and Cino on 13 April; and on 15 April Ciro replied: 'best Garibaldini wishes (despite everything)'. Again, on the same day, Ciro 'in the name of Cino too', returned with 'Italo' (Luigi Longo) 'the most cordial Garibaldini wishes (seeing that you still use this adjective which is so dear to us ... I'm taking advantage of the fact;

Command of the Pavese Oltrepò, and by Albero, sector commissar (INSMLI, *CVL*, envelope 93, folder 5).

105 For the poor relations with the Action Party and 'a certain major Mauri'), see the 'Relazione dell'ispettore B. sulla Iª divisione Piemonte', 25 May 1944; and, for relations with another group of *autonomi*, the 'Relazione del Comando unico di zona brigate Garibaldi e Fiamme Verdi di Reggio Emilia alla Delegazione del CUMER', 5 January 1945 (*Le Brigate Garibaldi*, vol. I, pp. 430-2, and vol. III, pp. 201-4).

106 See for example the report by Riccardo, inspector in the Pavese Oltrepò, to the 'military delegation ', 26 March 1945 (ibid., vol. III, pp. 536-7, n. 6).

107 'Highly confidential' document sent by the Piedmont delegation to 'compagni responsabili di P', undated, but later than June 1944 (INSMLI, *Brigate Garibaldi*, envelope 2, folder 4, s. file I).

and on 20 April Italo in turn insisted: '*Saluti Garibaldini*, mark you, because this isn't an official letter and no one can cancel Garibaldi from life and history (I'm not exaggerating).'[108] It was in this spirit that the Piedmont delegation (and it was certainly not the only one to do so) asked that 'detailed news about the ex-Garibaldi formations' continue to be sent. This contact needed to be kept up to 'keep the bond between you from weakening.'[109] 'Rife discontent' was reported among the Garibaldini of the Pavese Oltrepò;[110] while until 25 January those of the 6th Langhe Salis division had declared their names and emblems to be inalienable, and had warned: 'Some men, even among the politically more mature, have expressly declared to us that, the day they have to abandon their Stella Tricolore, they would sooner go home.'[111]

In the Cuneo GL divisions, preference was shown for stopping unification at the level of the zone and squad commands. On this score the *Notiziario* (Newsletter) of the 2nd Alpine division appealed to the 'libertarian' and 'rebellious' spirit of the bands, and the solidarity born in them during twenty months of common struggle. In no mean terms, this paper denounced as 'undemocratic' the 'general approval' for a unification which smacked of the orders from above that used to come from Rome and now came from 'the *impastatori* [pasta-makers] of the partisan movement'.[112] Even a GL pamphlet, while supporting unification as a necessary thing to aim for, dotted its 'i's many times and warned against the danger that unification might favour last-minute 'absentees' and 'renouncers' exemplified by the colonels, among others.[113] There were those who were prepared to recognise the political opportuneness of unification as the premise for transformation into a regular army, and those who made no disguise of their scepticism as to the fact that it would induce the Allies to go back on their intentions to disarm and disband. Others preannounced a reluctant 'obbedisco' ('I obey'): 'As for the cautious form with which our Garibaldini are familiar, we have to tell you that their political education and military understanding is such as to give them no difficulty in accepting possible evolution towards centrality.'[114] The core of the problem was summed up by a partisan chief as follows: 'The partisans felt themselves to be combatants in an army of civilians.'[115]

108 *Le Brigate Garibaldi*, vol. III, p. 619, and IG, *BG*, 08564, 08584, 08585, 08604.

109 ISRP, *II* and *IV Divisione Garibaldi Piemonte. Carteggio con organi militari superiori*, C. 7 a.

110 Report by Giorgio, 20 March 1945 (*Le Brigate Garibaldi*, vol. III, p. 509).

111 Letter to 'compagni responsabili' (IG, *BG*, 056617).

112 See the article entitled 'L'Unificazione', April 1945, quoted in Giovana, *Storia di una formazione partigiana*, p. 346, and the balanced judgments that the author expresses on the question (pp. 343–7).

113 'L'Unificazione', 15 March 1945.

114 Report by the 'Comando della 2ª divisione Garibaldi Gardoncini Battista' (Piedmont), 4 March 1945, signed by Commander Maggi (IG, *BG*, 04848).

115 Bernardo, *Il momento buono*, p. 162, where the author writes that 'le stellette

The Resistance press played a prominent role in the relationship between the parties and this 'army of civilians'. It was not just 'a combat unit ... an army rather than an instrument to spread an idea'.[116] The aim of the press was to form new cadres and to perform a pedagogic function both for the partisans and for the mass of the population. Who should write, for what end, and for whom, was a frequent subject of discussion. Pietro Secchia took the Rome edition of *L'Unità* to task for having 'become more a directional organ of the leaders than an organ for directing and organising the masses ... more a bulletin and magazine than a combat newspaper'.[117] The objective of 'activating the masses of the civilian population' is indicated as being essential in other Communist documents too.[118] Conversely, workers' criticisms appeared denouncing *L'Unità* for 'addressing the population a lot, but the workers little and comrades hardly at all',[119] while in a partisan formation, the Belluno division, the main criterion was that the press should serve 'as a means of educating and orientating party-members because, it was claimed, propaganda among the anonymous crowd should be conducted by individuals, with their example and their words. The best kind of propaganda against the enemy was in military actions'.[120] The Turin leaders discussed the limits of editorial intervention. Some believed that corrections could only be made to syntax, while for others this was not enough: 'Those who are writing are novices, they shouldn't be over-sensitive ... you learn to write by writing'.[121] The objective was to have 'simple and immediate pieces which mirror the daily activities of our units' and which were 'the voice of the detachments', besides being 'the guides for the commissars'.[122]

---

ricordavano il triste periodo dell'esercito' ('the stars recalled the sad period of the royal army').

116 Michel, *Les courants*, pp. 794–5.

117 Letter of December 1943 (IG, *Archivio PCI*). For Secchia's criticisms of the Rome edition of *L'Unità*, see also his previous letter of 19 December, which partly includes the Milan edition as well (Longo, *I centri dirigenti del PCI*, pp. 127–31).

118 Circular of the Lombardy delegation, 29 September 1944 (INSMLI, *CVL*, envelope 93, folder 4, subfolder a). See Bernardo, *Il momento buono*, p. 143, regarding the Nanetti division.

119 'Rapporto da Torino', 6 October 1943, by Giovanni, where the view expressed about *Il Grido di Spartaco* is wholly positive (IG, *Archivio PCI*).

120 Bernardo, *Il momento buono*, p. 144.

121 Exchange of letters between Rossi and Alfredo, 9 and 13 November 1943 (IG, *Archivio PCI*).

122 Letter by the Command of the 1st Gramsci division to that of the 118th Servadei brigade, 6 February 1945, and by the delegation for Lombardy to the Command of the Valsesia, Ossola, Cusio, Verbano group, undated (IG, *BG*, 07870, and INSMLI, *CVL*, envelope 93, folder 4, subfolder a).

It doesn't matter if the leaflets and articles are written in incorrect Italian; what is important is the concept and substance. This collaboration will, besides, habituate our comrades to thinking and to expressing their ideas, and will therefore help them to become skilled elements for tomorrow's struggle.[123]

The Lombard edition of the (GL) *Partigiano Alpino* published, for partisan use, an appendix to Alfredo Panzini's *Dizionario moderno*, while the newspaper of Mauri's divisions, *Il Risorgimento* brought out, a 'vocabolario del patriota' ('patriot's dictionary').[124] There are fairly frequent complaints about the poor distribution of the press, which seemed to make its production almost a waste of effort.[125] True, each copy was generally read by several people; but there were also those who 'as soon as they had read the paper destroyed it out of fear'.[126] Congestion occurred, as in Genoa; attempts at capillary distribution were attempted, with a personal accompanying letter.[127] Collective reading appeared to be a method aimed at strengthening the press's pedagogic functions. The party official responsible was advised to be the first to read and comment on 'the article out loud; that way those who are interested in the subject draw near and listen and little by little the others in turn draw near; that's how propaganda works'.[128] Less ingenuous than this is another invitation to read and comment, which starts with the statement that 'the press is not read by the partisans. Like most of the Italian people they don't read newspapers: they're not in the habit of doing so. We need to overcome this resistance little by little, get them interested, ask their opinions about the articles, comment on them, etc. If *we* don't begin this job it will never be done.'[129]

---

123 Minutes of the meeting of the 'Comitato esecutivo del PCI presso la divisione Garibaldi Nanetti', held 17 April 1945, which was sent to the political brigade and battalion committees (INSMLI, *CVL*, envelope 34, folder 3, subfolder 2).

124 See Falaschi, *La Resistenza armata*, pp. 14, 11.

125 See the letters by 'compagni responsibili della delegazione per il Piemonte' to those of the Valle di Susa brigades, 12 July 1944; by Neri, vice-commander of the Lombardy group to the 'Delegazione Intendenza 52ª brigata', 7 November 1944; of the Lombard Command of the GLs to the 'Servizio Stampa' ('Press Service') of the Action Party, 23 December 1944 (*Le Brigate Garibaldi*, vol. II, pp. 116–20; IG, *BG*, 01231; INSMLI, *CVL*, envelope 93, folder 5, subfolder a).

126 Letters by the Command of the 1st Gramsci division to the Command of the Ossola, Valsesia, Cusio, Verbano group, 7 December 1944. The most enterprising readers were advised as to the possibility of 'posting up at least two copies in every village' (IG, *BG*, 07288).

127 'Appunti sull'organizzazione di Genova', undated, but late November 1943, quoted in Gibelli and Ilardi, *Lotte operaie: Genova*, p. 119; circular letter of the Command of the Carnia brigade, dated 25 March 1945 (IRSFVG, Fondo Magrini, envelope CLV, folder I).

128 Minutes of the meeting between commissars and party officials of the 3rd Lombardy division (Oltrepò pavese), 20 October 1944 (IG, *BG*, 01519).

129 Letter to Franz, a brigade vice-commissar of the Command of the 1st Gramsci

The mural newspaper, which was widely used by the Garibaldi formations, was the most immediate channel for the apprentice to express himself.
Incitements to do so smacked of Soviet didacticism: 'It's an extremely effective
instrument of criticism and self-criticism. It's very popular in the Soviet Union,
as it was in Spain'.[130] But there was also the sincere faith 'that every Garibaldino
has something to say, that he knows how to say it, that he is capable of writing
it ... even when the writer doesn't have a perfect grasp of spelling'. The person
expressing this conviction also showed a great respect for the writer: one needed
'to correct without ever changing the form', and possibly discuss the substance.[131]
The mural newspapers needed to deal with concrete things, even the simplest
things: from how the mess kitchen was working to the organisation of guard
duties; to enable readers to question the quality of the commanders and commissars; to stimulate emulation of the partisans; to frame the great political
problems – even if in some formulations suggested to them, the answer was, as
in school essay questions, already implicit.[132] Thus, the mural newspapers, and
for that matter all the minor partisan press, often swung between public soul-
seeking, didactic purposes, and the instrument of direct democracy – between
the expression of the way one was and the way one ought to be. It was difficult
to find the meeting-point between the desire to impart and the desire to acquire
knowledge. Referring to a cycle of lessons on the French Revolution, commissar
Michele wrote: 'I've been informed that there was a crowd of attenders at the first
two lessons, but mass desertion for the third. The way the theme was treated and
the theme itself more than ever justify this desertion. I've had this course suspended immediately'.[133] The 'combattente bibliotecario' ('librarian combatant') is
a figure envisaged in several organisational schemes;[134] and after the temporary

---

division, 11 December 1944 (ibid., 07341).

130 Instructions 'a tutti i commissari politici' by the Cuneo brigade commissar,
undated (ibid., 04291). Some newspapers displayed the front page of their daily editions
on walls around the city, as mural newspapers (*giornale murale*).

131 Circular to the commissars of the Command of the 3rd Piedmont division, 4
August 1944, on the subject of mural newspapers (*Le Brigate Garibaldi*, vol. II, pp. 198–201).

132 See the circular cited in the previous note; the letter of the Piedmontese delegation to the Command of the detachment of the lower Valle di Susa, undated, but spring
(or summer) 1944 (IG, *BG*, 004897); and a further circular of the Command of the
Piedmont division, 14 September (ibid., 005003). As one of the many examples of mural
newspapers, see the one mentioned in Lazagna, *Ponte rotto*, p. 156.

133 Report to the Command of the Valsesia, Ossola, Cusio, Verbano group, 11
January 1945 (IG, *BG*, 07612). But the French Revolution is a relatively widespread
subject: for example, as regards the difference between bourgeois revolution and proletarian revolution, see the plans of the lessons held at the 1st Garibaldi Osoppo division, in
IZDG, envelope 272b, folder I/A.

134 'Istruzioni per i compagni commissari politici' of the Parma federal secretariat
of the PCI, 18 December 1943 (IG, *BG*, *Emilia-Romagna*, G.IV.2.2). The request for books

conquest of the enemy garrisons, one commander wrote, 'the partisan with a typewriter on his back was a typical sight'.[135]

The books circulating among the partisans ranged from the history of the country to that of the working-class movement, from novels preferably with a social background to works of economics, to the canonical *Storia del PC (b)* (*History of the Communist Party*). Fascist propaganda books captured from the enemy were also read and discussed.[136]

The further they were from the top, the more the press and collateral activities succeeded, to a more or less widespread degree, in not being just channels for transmission of the political line but also the expression of the ideas, feelings and contradictory ideas of the party members. Indicative of this are the differences between the party newspapers and those of the bands. The great flowering of the underground press made it an instrument of aggregation of men and ideas, not only within the parties – and favoured the widening and enrichment of the political meaning of the entire Resistance process.[137]

---

for the formations appears in many documents.

135 Bernardo, *Il momento buono*, p. 255.

136 Ibid.

137 Laura Conti's catalogue (*Saggio bibliografico*), frequently cited, registers (and it is incomplete) 2,357 newspaper titles and 2,623 pamphlets and leaflets. Some partial information can be given regarding their circulation. In Romagna the Communist newspapers would seem to have sold between 1,500 and 3,000 copies (Flamigni and Marzocchi, *Resistenza in Romagna*, p. 191, in which four newspaper titles are recorded). According to the person in charge of the cultural section of the 50th Nedo brigade, the newspaper *Baita* had a circulation of 4,000 copies (report of 25 September 1944, in IG, BG, 05187). For *Stella Alpina*, Moscatelli, in a letter to Moro (the diplomat Mario Lanza, who was in Switzerland at the time), speaks in terms of 10,000 copies (IG, BG, 07850). The Florence edition of *Il Popolo* would seem to have had a circulation of 9,000 copies (Webster, *The Fasces and the Cross*, p. 170). Attention was drawn to the aggregative function of the press, for party ends, from 26 December 1943 by Sandrelli (?), the person in charge of military work for Piedmont, writing to the party leadership (*Le Brigate Garibaldi*, vol. I, pp. 183–8).

CHAPTER 4

The Patriotic War

1. REGAINING NATIONAL IDENTITY

Who had been defeated in the Fascist war fought between 1940 and 1943? Only Fascism? Or the Italian state with which Fascism had identified itself? Or even Italy herself, as an historically defined national entity?

For the Fascists the defeat of Fascism and the defeat of Italy were one and the same thing: it was this not least that gave rise to their stubborn refusal to face facts, their continuing to desperately play the losing card. Some Roman youths who immediately after 8 September had presented themselves to the Germans in order to continue fighting alongside them were reminded by the officer that 'Italy no longer exists; there is no longer a government, an army', and he asked: 'Do you want to become German soldiers?'[1]

The anti-Fascists obviously distinguished Fascism from Italy; but the more thoughtful of them realised that merely changing sides was not enough to put to flight all the shadows that had gathered around the nation's identity. Taken in its most elementary sense, the war against Germany, declared by the Royal Army of the South on 13 October 1943, might seem nothing other than the continuance of the preceding war, on the right and, what is more, the winning side; and undoubtedly to a certain number of combatants in the partisan formations, and not only in the 'autonomous' ones, it seemed just this. But we have seen how not even to those called to fight in the army of the South did this motivation appear sufficient.

To give legitimacy to the new war, it seemed that the anti-Fascists needed to take the full blame for the defeat suffered first at the hands of the Anglo-Americans and the Soviets, and then of the Germans; and that it was at the same time indispensable to uncouple the difficult business of recovery from any connection with the Italian nationalist tradition, which had been exacerbated by Fascism. This was an extremely arduous task, and the attitudes taken towards it help define the positions manifested at the time among the Italians.

The most radical and at the same time fecund attitude was the one which took for granted the *finis Italiae* as an autonomous state. This position is expressed with particular lucidity in a memorandum by Giorgio Diena and Vittorio Foa, according to whom 'the responsibility for creating the new state of affairs that

---

1 Mazzantini, *A cercar la bella morte*, pp. 23–4.

may save Italy falls completely on those anti-Fascist forces which, in the absence of any authority, must themselves become the authority with autonomous initiative. Only on this condition will Italy, today a passive battlefield, cease to be a simple geographical expression.'[2]

In the same spirit Ugo La Malfa wrote: 'Between 28 October 1922 and 8 September 1943 Italy, as a great national state inherited from the Risorgimento, was destroyed.'[3]

Strongly Mazzinian in inspiration, both in its denunciation and in the desire to redeem things, the *Bollettino Popolo Libertà* stated that 'there is no longer a *patria* for the Italian people. It is right that things be so', otherwise Mussolini and Victor Emmanuel III, beating the old patriotic drum, would gull the people once again. Yet 'to rise again into a nation' was 'the duty we set ourselves to seek together to accomplish'.[4]

It has been justly observed that, in the Italian Resistance, the 'idea of the *patria* [is] less elementary, less physical than was the case outside Italy'.[5] This was due precisely to the difficulty in reconstituting a univocal concept of the *patria*, capable of giving a human face back to the nation'.[6] Above all in the first few weeks, outbursts of individual pride, aimed at safeguarding one's own personal identity, fuse with the reaffirmation of national identity. At other times in history as well the sense of individual and collective unhappiness had been seen, in Enlightenment terms, as the generator of patriotism.[7]

A demonstration of dignity in defeat was given by the old general called on to command the volunteer corps, which was one of the very first things the Americans attempted to establish in the *Mezzogiorno*, independently of the Badoglio government:

I said and repeated that I would only ever fight and serve under the Italian flag (I am not Graziani!). That I was aware that they were victors and I one of the vanquished

---

2 This memorandum was written in Val Pellice, 17 September 1943, for internal use by the Action Party. My thanks to Foa for having given me a copy.

3 U. L Malfa, *Per la rinascita dell'Italia*, edited by the Action Party, 1943, p. 4.

4 'Orientamenti gennaio 1944', in *Bollettino* n. 7, pp. 8–9.

5 Enzo Enriques Agnoletti in the preface to *LRI*, p. 13.

6 This paraphrases an expression by G. L. Mosse, *Masses and Man: Nationalist and Fascist Perceptions of Reality*, New York: Howard Fertig, 1980. Mosse writes of 'humanistic nationalism', p. 18.

7 This observation was made by Franco Venturi at a seminar on the birth of the nation held in 1986 at the 'Scuola normale superiore di Pisa'. Venturi gave the examples of Italy, Poland and Greece, and recalled that the nexus between unhappiness and patriotism had first appeared in Pasquale Paoli's Corsica: 'We are an unhappy people ...'. For a fuller development of this theme, see F. Venturi, *Settecento riformatore*, vol. V, *L'Italia dei lumi (1764–1790)*, vol. I, Turin: Einaudi, 1987, Chapter I, 'Patria e libertà: la rivoluzione di Corsica'.

insofar I was not personally responsible for [the victory]. I said this to distinguish myself from all the fervent supporters of the victor, beyond a certain limit. The general was a bit surprised, then he commended me.[8]

Another anti-Fascist had difficulty getting an English general to understand that he was not 'dealing with adventurers'. The general was amazed that 'men of value could devote their lives, and risk those of persons dear to them, for a cause which involved as a logical consequence the defeat of their own country in war'; and the anti-Fascist, giving his explanation to the general, was grieved 'to lay bare his sorrows and those of his people'.[9]

A testimony of the difficult situation faced in Yugoslavia by the soldiers who, having succeeded in avoiding being captured by the Germans, joined the partisans, reads: 'But for us Italians one reason for national pride still held: we needed to redeem our name from the shame inflicted on it by the anti-men who spoke our language'.[10] A sailor who had toured the world was to recall that for a long time, 'Wherever we went, nobody could stand us. Oh: "Italian? 'eaven forbid!" Nobody could stand us because of this 'ere fact of the dictatorship that this 'ere Fascist party 'ad. And it was then we began to understand: "Why is it no one can stand us?" No one could stomach the sight of us'[11]

After 8 September it was true that 'no one could stand' the Italians because they were 'branded as treacherous by old and new allies alike', and because 'one way or another, we had fought against everybody'. In the hierarchy of the concentration camps, the Italians found that they were superior only to the Jews. 'Mamma mia, to see the look of hate in people's eyes', a woman imprisoned at Ravensbrück recalls.[12]

But consciousness of the abyss could turn into that of an unexpected rediscovery. Pietro Chiodi was struck by the revelation that had enlightened him as early as 27 July 1943:

---

8 This is what Giuseppe Pavone says in his diary about the 23 September 1943 meeting at Paestum with General Donovan, head of the OSS (Pavone, *I gruppi combattenti Italia*, p. 85). See the letter that the general sent on 12 October to Benedetto Croce, inspirer of the Groups: the general was insistent about 'not accepting a dependence that had even the slightest semblance of inferiority or of less moral, military and political consideration' (ibid., p. 93).

9 Anonymous 'Romagnolo', *1943–45*, p. 47 (conversation with General Neame).

10 These words occur in the E. Sequi's Preface, datelined Belgrade, 10 July 1964, to A. Bressan and L. Giuricin, *Fratelli nel sangue. Contributi per una storia della partecipazione degli italiani alla guerra popolare di liberazione della Jugoslavia*, Rijeka: Edit, 1964, p. 5.

11 The Communist Cafiero Canali's testimony, in Portelli, *Biografia di una città*, p. 239.

12 See Bravo and Jalla, *La vita offesa*, p. 185 (the authors' comment) and p. 187 (testimonies by Natalino Pia, artisan, survivor from the Russian campaign, and of Giuseppa Doleati Soardi, Turinese factory worker, partisan dispatch rider).

I had never realised that the Liceo was so shining and full of light. I feel that it is a small part of my *patria*. That part in which I am called on to do my duty towards her. It is the first time that I have realised I have a *patria* as something that is my own, entrusted, in part, to me as well, to my intelligence, to my courage, to my spirit of sacrifice.[13]

On 9 September Emanuele Artom noted in his diary: 'Half of Italy is German, half is English and there's no longer an Italian Italy'; and then on 16 December, with a combination of shame and clarity of conviction, he wrote that to his parents he spoke only of the practical reasons for his decision to be a partisan,

and I kept quiet about those ideals: I don't quite know why, but I'm ashamed to talk about them. Perhaps so many years of patriotic and political rhetoric inhibit one from speaking of these subjects with fresh and spontaneous simplicity. Yet here too great progress is being made. The mysticism of the last century, both the cause and effect of the Romantic and Mazzinian concept of nations that have a mission to accomplish, has by now had its day.[14]

Natalia Ginzburg has effectively evoked the stupor and emotion that many anti-Fascists, or simply non-Fascists, of her generation had on rediscovering their sense of a *patria* to defend:

The streets and squares of the city, which had once been the theatre of our adolescent's boredom and the object of our haughty contempt, became the places that it was necessary to defend. The words 'patria' and 'Italia', which had nauseated us between the school walls because they had always been accompanied by 'fascista', because they were swollen with emptiness, suddenly appeared to us unqualified by adjectives and so transformed that we seemed to be hearing and thinking about them for the first time. All of a sudden they rang true to our ears. We were there to defend the *patria* and the *patria* was those streets and those squares, our loved ones and our childhood, and all the people passing by. So simple and obvious a truth seemed strange to us because we had grown up with the conviction that we didn't have a *patria* and that we had been born at a point swollen with emptiness. And what seemed still stranger was the fact that, for love of all those unknown people who were passing by, and for love of a future unknown to us but whose solidity and splendour we could make out in the distance, between privation and devastation, each of us was ready to lose him- or herself and his or her life.[15]

---

13 Chiodi, *Banditi*, p. 14.
14 Artom, *Diari*, pp. 76, 124–5.
15 N. Ginsburg to G. Falaschi, ed., *La letteratura partigiana*, pp. 8–9.

Mixed with all this, perhaps, was the more or less conscious desire to free oneself of the recurrent oscillation between self-denigration, which had also acquired the guise of a defence from the stereotypes imposed by the regime,[16] and self-pity, fed by the myth of the 'goodness of the Italians', which others stubbornly refused to recognise. 'Since the formation of the first groups of so-called "rebels", we have seen the name "Italy" pronounced with a certain sense of admiration, no longer with contempt', a Garibaldi commissar was to write.[17]

The 'Preliminary Report on the Activity of the Partisans of the Province of Arezzo' states that the birth of the patriot formations 'had, through a psychological process that was quite comprehensible in a Fascist climate, initially to overcome the reluctance to believe that finally something essentially "Italian" was taking shape, authentic in the true sense of the word.'[18]

In another document a Tuscan partisan recalls that, when his band liberated a village, 'our greatest satisfaction was to speak in Italian to people who were expecting to hear other, guttural sounds. The liberated Italians understood then that even if there was a defeated Italy there was however a victorious Italy as well. And the victorious Italy was us.'[19]

It is this kind of profound expectation that allowed even the regular troops of the Italian Liberation Corps to be in many cases gratified by the warm welcome they received from the populations of the liberated territories.[20]

'Italia, Italia, cosa importa se si muore' ('Italy, Italy, what does it matter if one dies'), sang a wounded partisan in an SS prison, using the words of a national-Fascist song, re-utilised also by the partisans; and the same partisan, hearing the Italian SS men singing 'Italian songs to German rhythms', remarked, almost as if to explain these reversals, 'They've poisoned them.'[21] The fact that Italians were fighting against Italians and that both were invoking Italy in fact made the reacquisition of a sure sense of the *patria* more difficult, but also more tormenting.

'The spring of patriotism against the German on home soil has been released', recounted a Garibaldi partisan educated by the nuns, who was sensitive to the nationalist myths of Fascism, but after 8 September had felt the

16 See Passerini's observations, *Torino operaia*, p. 82.

17 *La popolazione deve essere con noi*, document written by Eros, general commissar of the joint Garibaldi and Fiamme Verdi Command for Reggio Emilia, 26 January 1945 (*Le Brigate Garibaldi*, vol. III, pp. 89–91).

18 Undated report by the 23rd Pio Borri Garibaldi brigade (ISRT, *Carte Francesco Berti*, envelope I, folder 7).

19 Undated short report by the Bianconcini formation (ISRT, *Carte Carlo Campolmi*, envelope I, folder c, subfolder *Monte Foggiola*).

20 See for example a combatant's letter quoted in the 'syntheses of the reports' of the military offices, war censorship, of September 1944, conserved in ACS and quoted in Aga-Rossi, *La situazione politica ed economica*, p. 129.

21 See Chiodi, *Banditi*, pp. 53, 42 (August 23 and 18, 1944). In the national-Fascist song, instead of 'Italia', 'Dalmazia' or 'Frontiera' were sung; in the partisan song, 'Valsesia'.

'fascination of the rebel linked to the Italian Risorgimento in anti-Austrian terms'. And she added: 'At that moment I jettisoned not the *patria*, not what Mussolini had taught me: I jettisoned Mussolini'.[22] A Bolognese butcher tells this tale of a carabinieri marshal: 'the marshal first served the Fascist state, then as an Italian he recognised the value of the "resistance", for which he gave his life'. In 1937 the marshal had arrested the butcher's brother, who was then sentenced to four years by the Special Tribunal.[23]

In explaining his decision to join the Resistance to his family, a police chief's son wrote: 'For a long time I'd been seeking the truth in myself ... it would have been a poor show if I, who have always professed the religion of the *patria*, backed out at the moment of action. Here what is involved is not heroic spirit, it's the human spirit which is on its feet and every man with it'.[24]

Revelations, discoveries, reworkings of ancient cultural undercurrents, continuities going under a different name, interweave in this attempt to reconstitute an idea and a sense of the *patria*. It is hardly surprising, therefore, if in those who unambiguously and painfully had committed themselves in this enterprise – the declaration of war against Germany by the Royal Army of the South – aroused, beyond strictly politico-diplomatic evaluations, a sense of extraneousness, if not irritation or even anger. Ada Gobetti wrote in her diary:

> The news has left me cold. It makes no difference to us. Perhaps it will have a certain importance for those who were awaiting orders from Badoglio (who have, however, calmly gone home by now): not certainly for our mountain folk from here, nor for the Turin workers. It's we who are fighting the war, our war – and the official benedictions of a debased authority that no one believes in any more mean little to us.[25]

---

22 Tersilla Fenoglio Oppedisano's testimony, in Bruzzone and Farina, *La Resistenza taciuta*, pp. 146–7.

23 Testimony given by Roberto Marocchi and Mariano Fenudi, whom I thank for having communicated it to me. The butcher writes: 'So, on 8 September 1943, when the roads were crowded with frightened people, I was at work preparing meat for the "Italiani", as the Marshal had said! On 8 September 1943, I was working, as a Communist, as a Partisan.'

24 Letter by Maurizio Giglio, who was shot in the Ardeatine Caves (March 1944). Wounded in Greece, he had decided to leave the commission for the armistice with France, in Turin, which had seemed to him 'a kind of shirker's hideout'. Having made contact with the OSS, he had enlisted in the RSI auxiliary police in order to supply information. He was discovered by the Koch band. Today he is celebrated as a real hero of the police of the Italian Republic, which confirms the fact that the confusion of languages regarding the concept of the *patria* has not yet ceased, and has indeed been revived by the 'continuità dello Stato'. See A. Baldinotti, 'Il diverso silenzio di Maurizio Giglio', in *Polizia moderna* XXXVII: 8–9 (August–September 1985), pp. 38–42.

25 Gobetti, *Diario partigiano*, p. 39.

The same position was expressed by the Action Party's Rome newspaper:

> If the king and Badoglio formally declare war on Germany now ... it's a gesture that
> fools nobody and adds nothing to the present state of affairs. The real war against
> Germany has been declared by the Italian people since 9 September ... And it's war
> declared not against Germany, but against Nazism, which is so much more inhuman
> and reactionary than Fascism.[26]

Avanti! in its turn stated that the war against Nazism and Fascism was being
waged by the people, and the king and Badoglio had nothing to do with it.[27]
More brusquely, the newspaper of the Communist Movement of Italy defined
the declaration of war as 'another instance of royal buffoonery'.[28] In its poster
launched for the occasion, the Communist Party stated that unity, which was
indispensable for war, required trust in one's leaders, but 'this trust can't be
given to men who, co-responsible for Fascism and the Fascist war, have deceived
and betrayed the Italian people'.[29] In a longer and more closely argued article,
L'Unità went back to the authoritative pages of the *Storia del PC* to establish the
distinction between just war and unjust war, naturally bracketing that against
Nazi Germany in the former category, 'of immense, unprecedented significance',
but for that very reason denying that it could be directed by the Badoglio government: 'How can this government which has feared the people conduct a
people's war?'[30] Even *La Democrazia del Lavoro*, the newspaper published by
the bloodless party of that name, which on 20 March had called the war against
the Germans a war 'of redemption', on 23 March 1944 warned that, to avoid the
war being fought only as a selfish Italian affair, it must not be conducted by men
compromised by Fascism.

The high party ranks were to change their tune after the Salerno 'turning-
point' and the creation of governments of national unity whose declared aim
was indeed to give priority to the war. Nevertheless, it is highly significant that in
the *resistenti*'s conscience the war against the Germans/Nazis needed no external legitimisation appealing to criteria of legality embodied in the institutions of

---

26 Article entitled 'Guerra regia e guerra di popolo', in *L'Italia Libera*, Rome edition,
17 October 1943.

27 See, among others, the leading articles 'Combattere' and 'Nostra guerra', 11 and
25 October 1943.

28 Article entitled 'Proletari in guardia!', in *Bandiera Rossa*, 15 October 1943.

29 The manifesto was published in *L'Unità*, Rome edition, 18 October, and in *Voce
Operaia*, 22 October 1943. It can now be read in *Il comunismo italiano nella seconda
guerra mondiale*, pp. 217–19.

30 Article entitled 'Guerra giusta e necessaria', in *L'Unità*, Rome edition, 18 October
1943. See also ibid., 1 December 1943, the article entitled 'Necessità di un governo', which
repeats that, under Badoglio's leadership, the war against Germany cannot be fought.

the old state. On the contrary, it was these very institutions that had to legitimise themselves by conducting the war with moral scruples. Only one newspaper of declared monarchic inspiration could write that the war had to be fought under the orders of the legitimate head of state, namely the king.[31] Most *resistenti* must also have found needlessly contorted Benedetto Croce's thesis that the laceration suffered by the soul of the Italians between one war waged by Fascism, 'legal in appearance but odious', and another, which was 'dear to the heart of every true Italian' and 'tenaciously pursued the spirit of the Risorgimento', had been finally healed: in fact the second war had, according to Croce, become legal 'because it is carried out on the same priniple as that marked by the sole government legally existing now in Italy'. (The scant clarity of this argumentation may also be ascribed to the fact that Croce was inviting men to enlist for a war that had not been declared, in a volunteer corps that was not recognised by the royal government.)[32] Among the *resistenti*, even those who sought the help of legality like this saw it only as 'legal clothing' provided after the event to the 'popular declaration of war' that had already occurred.[33] Only to the Italian partisan formations in the Balkans did the declaration of war bring, within certain limits, tangible and immediate benefit, because it gave them greater legitimacy in the eyes of their former enemies. The Command of the 2nd corps of the People's Liberation Army of Yugoslavia (Montenegro) issued a communication in which, even going beyond the way things actually stood, it stated: 'With the declaration of war against Germany and the recognition of Italy – by the Anglo-Soviet-American coalition – as an ally in war, its international position has changed.'[34]

Rejection of the king, the generals and the discredited government of the South as guides, or even simply as fully fledged comrades in the war against the Germans, could even reach the point of questioning the very opportuneness of that war. By this I do not mean certain strictly class attitudes, to which we will have to return, but to a form of abstract moralist–revolutionary intransigence,

---

31 See *Italia nuova. Giornale del Centro della democrazia italiana*, Rome, 1 March 1944, leading article entitled 'Dopo il discorso di Churchill'. The reference is to his 22 February speech to the House of Commons, in which the premier had repeated his support of the king and Badoglio: 'When you have to hold a hot coffee-pot, it is better not to break the handle off until you are sure you will get another equally convenient and serviceable, or, at any rate, until there is a dish-cloth handy!' (quoted in Degli Spinosa, *Il Regno del Sud*, p. 284).

32 See the *Manifesto*, signed by the National Liberation Front and written by Croce, put up in Naples on 10 October 1943, calling for volunteers for the Gruppi Combattenti Italia (Appendix V to Croce, *Quando l'Italia era tagliata in due*, p. 155).

33 See *Il Combattente*, actually a somewhat atypical organ of the 'Garibaldi assault detachments of Tuscany', 3–4, undated, but between January and March, 1944.

34 For the proclamation, signed by Major General Peko Dupcevic, see Bressan and Giuricin, *Fratelli nel sangue*, p. 400.

which was nonetheless able to identify several genuinely problematic questions. The clearest formulations of this sort of populist, aristocratic and self-punitive fence-sitting are found in the press of the small Partito Italiano del Lavoro. A people still widely polluted by servile behaviour was not – it was claimed – worthy of participating in a war that free peoples were waging. To avoid being confused with the turncoat reactionaries, the only viable path remaining was to abstain from fighting the new war that the latter were now sponsoring, following the 'umpteenth betrayal' by that 'despicable dwarf', the king.[35] A declaration inspired along these lines states:

> The reasons for which the Italian revolutionaries have been fighting against the Germans since 1 September 1939 and those for which the monarchic clique has been fighting since 13 October 1943 are too different to reconcile. The former are fighting for liberty against tyranny; the latter for the winners against the losers. The former are fighting for the people; the latter against the people.[36]

From this it was deduced that 'Italy's war against Germany is immoral and politically absurd'.[37] Within this moralising pessimism, which underrated the northern population's capacity to react and fight, immediate objectives were nevertheless posed that did not widely differ, save in the stress laid on the defensive spirit, from that envisaged by those who strongly advocated war against Germany and the Fascists: armed defence of people, houses and cities, assistance to the persecuted and their families, refusal to collaborate in public services and public offices. Almost a year later another newspaper of the same group was to write: 'It's wrong to think that the mere fact that we speak of defensive struggle means that we're lukewarm in the struggle itself: what we're doing is exactly the same as what the partisan or Gappist is doing.'[38] But this group was a unique case in Resistance circles in knowing how to give a positive connotation to what would then be the southern 'non si parte', ('we aren't going'): 'If Badoglio doesn't manage to scrape together those divisions – which will however unfortunately happen – to offer as cannon fodder to the English, that would give the Allies the impression of a real popular will which no speech or congress will succeed in giving.'[39]

---

35 These expressions are contained in the commentary that *La Voce del Popolo*, 15 October 1943, dedicated to the declaration of war on Germany, which, the newspaper wrote, had caused 'a sort of dismay'.

36 Ibid., 15 October 1943, article in the series *Fuori dall'equivoco*, later collected in a booklet.

37 Ibid., 1 November 1943, article entitled 'Il nostro "fare"', and 20 February 1944, 'Fuori dall'equivoco'.

38 'Conoscerci', in *La Voce dei giovani*, Milan: Sesto Giovanni, chiefly edited by Delfino Insolera.

39 'Fuori dall'equivoco', in *La Voce del Popolo*, 20 February 1944. The allusion is to

Emerging from these positions was a problem that, to varying degrees of intensity, as hope or fear, ran through the Resistance: that of the link between war and revolution, to which we shall need to return. For *La Voce del Popolo* the answer was drastic: 'The possibility of coupling the war with social revolution is lost for the Italian people: by stubbornly insisting on pursuing it we'll end up doing neither the one nor the other'.[40]

Emphasis on the nation could lead to the two foreign armies occupying Italy being mechanically equated with each other. This formula, which led to the anti-Fascist character of the war being placed in parenthesis, was appealed to instrumentally, in some cases, even by voices above all suspicion, such as Radio London which, through its commentator Candidus, broadcast the appeal to accelerate, fighting alongside the Allies, the liberation of Italy from the 'two foreign armies'.[41] Some strictly observant Mazzinians equated the Germans who had 'brought Fascism to Italy' with the Allies who 'are bringing the monarchy back to Rome ... and it's not enough simply to serve, one must also applaud in order to serve the interests of the foreign government that is protecting the adversary'.[42] At times there are traces of this argument, stripped of its Mazzinian emphasis, in the Action Party press, which uses it in anti-monarchic and anti-Badoglian terms.[43]

In the Republican Party press the equation of the two foreign armies led to populist – or rather *prequalunquistico* – words like those that appeared in Rome on the monument to the early nineteenth-century Roman dialect poet Giuseppe Gioacchino Belli: 'Clear off, the lot of you. Leave us to weep alone!' This appeared to *La Voce Repubblicana* as 'an exclamation vibrating with all the dejected anguish of the drama of our nation ... in these words there's the light of a new conscience. This withdrawing into ourselves, this probing our hearts embittered by grief is what it means. *Andatevene tutti!*'[44]

In deeply considered and heartfelt terms, the student newspaper *La nostra lotta* declared on the one hand that 'the struggle for liberation and independence will make us independent of the allies as well', and on the other showed as strong a contempt for the monarchic regime of the South as repulsion for the Social Republic. In fact, between these two poles 'which are opposites only

---

the congress of the CLNs held in Bari, 28 and 29 January 1944.

40 'Fuori dall'equivoco. Variazoni', ibid., 20 April 1944.

41 Candidus was John Joseph Marus, born in London of Friulian parents, tried in Italy by the Special Tribunal for the Defence of the State (see Piccialuti Caprioli, *Radio Londra 1940–45*, pp. xv, 16).

42 Article entitled 'Dignità', in *L'Italia Repubblicana*, organ of the Partito Repubblicano del Lavoro, Rome, 1 November 1943.

43 Article entitled 'Scopi di guerra e di pace', 7 May 1944 (Lombardy edition).

44 *La Voce Repubblicana*, 4 June 1944.

geographically ... a large number of the Italian people are again sinking wretch-edly into an attitude of passivity and fatalism'.[45]

One of the minor Roman newspapers spoke ironically (we are still in 1943) about the fact that Radio Munich and Radio London both broadcast Garibaldi's hymn, 'Va fuori d'Italia, va fuori stranier!', while the Italians stood by watching the two foreign armies confronting each other, both courageously, on their terri-tory.[46] More cautiously and realistically, a Christian Democrat newspaper invited its readers not to delude themselves, but recalled too that the Anglo-Americans would never treat us as the Germans were treating us, and that linked to the victory of the former was the future of democracy in Italy.[47] *La Democrazia del Lavoro* drew a parallel with the wicked neutralism that had broken out against the other war,[48] while at the other extreme, *La Voce del Popolo* spoke of the 'two current stumps of capitalism in Italy', each protected by a foreign army, so that one had to fight 'against every occupation'.[49] Even the most circumspect equation of the two foreign armies could give grist to the mill of monarchy. 'Friends? Enemies? Allies?', a clandestine paper of that persuasion asked itself. And answered: 'From natural tendency, confirmed by experience, the foreigner who in any guise whatsoever sets foot on the soil of others wants somehow or other to assert himself as master.' Only the legitimate sovereign – this was the moral – could place himself above the two foreign armies contending for Italy.[50]

On the other front, some Fascists too tried at the eleventh hour to re-play the card of 'stretching our arms again above the foreign bayonets'.[51] There are

---

45 The subtitle of the newspaper is 'Organo degli studenti italiani' and in its first number, datelined Rome, 26 March 1944, it announced that it had been founded by the Unione Studenti Italiani, as a transformation of the agitation committee that had come into being the previous December. The constitutive document is signed by PdA, PCI, PSIUP, PRI, Communist and Christian-Socialist Catholics. The extracts quoted are in two articles of the first number: 'Volontà di democrazia' and 'Impegno'.

46 Articles entitled 'Tra i fuochi' and 'Gli assenti', in *La Rinascita. Organo dell'Unione italiana per il rinnovamento sociale*, bitterly and confusedly critical towards the old ruling class as a whole (1, undated: number 2 is dated 10 December 1943).

47 Article entitled 'Italia e Antitalia: gli eroe di Monte Canino', in *Il Popolo*, Rome edition, 23 January 1944.

48 Letter published under the title 'Neutralisti, no', in *La Democrazia del Lavoro*.

49 *Il Partigiano*, Rome, 23 January 1944, which prints a speech made on 2 January by the political commissar of a 'Comando superiore partigiano', of which it claims to be the organ; a speech said independently of both the Royal Army and by the CLN. See on this Comando superiore, E. Piscitelli, *Storia della Resistenza romana*, Bari: Laterza, 1965, p. 141.

50 See the first number cyclostyled in Rome, 15–23 January 1944, of *L'Alleanza italiana. Settimanale del Centro politico italiano. Dio-Autorità*, which invokes, alongside the king, the heart of Jesus and the name of the Virgin Mary.

51 Leading article entitled 'L'assente', which appeared in *La Stampa*, 20 February 1945, signed by the editor, Concetto Pettinato. Regarding the episode and the entire

countless traces of these final transformist dartings, and indeed they bespeak the appeal to create new forms of solidarity against the foreign armies, which-ever they might be. For example, an officer of the Decima Mas, one of the Fascist formations that tried to exploit this most, on presenting himself to the striking workers of the Borletti company in Milan on 16 April, said to them: 'The situation has reached the end of the road and … we mustn't scrap but find a way of coming to terms to ensure that neither the Germans nor the English take advantage.' The workers did not prove, on that occasion, to be well enough vaccinated, since they agreed to send a delegation to the provincial head, who gave it short shrift.[52]

Indicative of these Fascist velleities, if only indirectly, are the invitations made to the partisans on several occasions to open their eyes about the fate that the Allies had in store for them. 'Ecco la gratitudine dell'Inghilterra!' ('There's England's gratitude for you!') was the caption on a poster representing Churchill giving a partisan a kick.[53] An apocryphal number of L'Unità reproduced an appeal by Ercole (Palmiro Togliatti), substituting Germans with the English: 'A prime and indispensable condition for this successful outcome is the struggle against the English invader, exploiter of peoples.'[54]

The upshot of equating the two foreign armies, however it was suggested and whatever the motivation, was that it gave force to 'attesismo' (waiting on events). Thus there was the confirmation that blurring the anti-Fascist character of the new war inhibited the reconquest of national identity. 'There are no liberators, only men who liberate themselves!' a leaflet proclaimed,[55] underlining the commitment to defeat the selfishness, apathy and sloth that were weighing

position of Pettinato, who was in the habit of making such statements, which eventually cost him his job (but never did a dismissal so benefit the person dismissed), see Pansa, L'esercito di Salò, pp. 687–8. The northern Italian edition of L'Unità, commented, 'not for nothing is La Stampa owned by Fiat, one of those monopolistic trusts which have financed Fascism and which have been profiteers of Fascism, and are the main culprits for the Fascist policy that has led our country to catastrophe' (lead article entitled 'I piani criminali del nazifascismo devono essere e saranno sventati col ferro e col fuoco dell'insurrezione nazionale').

52 See Informazioni da Milano, 22 April 1945, which is unsparing in its criticisms of the gullibility of the workers (Le Brigate Garibaldi, vol. III, p. 673). L'Unità, cited in the previous note, had written, 'The bandits of the "Mas", with their chief, the rogue Prince Julio Borghese, will meet the same fate as their "comrades".'

53 Fondo RSI, no. 340. See also nos 538, 603, 612, 703.

54 A note penned on the copy of this issue, dated 'agosto 1944', in the possession of the Istituto Gramsci in Rome, reads: 'Here is a number of L'Unità falsified by Chief Pantono of Alessandria on the orders of the Fascist federation. We have already taken care to reply with a leaflet'.

55 Text proposed by the 'Comando militare settore Magenta' to the Comando piazza of Milan, 1 March 1945 (IG, BG, 0435).

on the Italians both as individuals and as a people. 'Our historic curse, oppor-tunism', wrote an Action Party broadsheet.[56]

National identity could thus only be re-established by shaking off the age-old destiny that had made of Italy only the stage of great historical dramas enacted by the protagonists of other peoples. It thus became natural to go in search of episodes that lent themselves to offering a less depressing vision of the history of the *patria*. Commonplaces, rhetoric, recycling of memories and cultural stereotypes, autonomous reflection on one's past as a people – all circu-late in Resistance circles, and above all stress the Risorgimento, whose wars had been the most Italian and anti-German of all. The Resistance drew strength and at the same time ambiguity from the Risorgimento, as witness the much abused expression 'Secondo Risorgimento'.[57] More or less all the political and ideologi-cal positions of the Resistance movement, and indeed of the Fascists too, chose their special bit of the Risorgimento to refer to.[58]

The two largest movements – the Garibaldi brigades militarily, the Action Party politically – gave themselves names that evoked the Risorgimento veins which, in the struggle for hegemony in the new state, had succumbed to the liberal-moderate-monarchic solution. Implicit in these names is the programme of again calling into question the post-Risorgimento orders – not just the Fascist one, but the Liberal one as well. On the other hand, the Risorgimento, with the force of its hagiographic and homologising stereotypes, made a fitting ideological screen for both the left-wing and moderate versions of the policy of unity. *Il Risorgimento Liberale* explicitly stressed as much on one occasion.[59]

The great powers at war with Fascist Italy had themselves been the first to set the liberating version of the Risorgimento against the one entangled in Fascist nationalism-imperialism: not only the English, for whom numerous tes-timonies could be cited (Radio London, for example, had a soft spot for the expression 'Secondo Risorgimento', and throughout the war commemorated

---

56 'Responsabilità', leading article of *L'Italia Libera*, Rome edition, 11 November 1943.

57 See C. Pavone, 'Le idee della Resistenza: antifascisti e fascisti davanti alla tradizione del Risorgimento', in *Passato e Presente* 7 (January–February 1959), pp. 850–918.

58 See the opinion expressed soon after the war by a distinguished Risorgimentist: 'The constituent parts of the world of the Risorgimento – and someone who has been reared to revere it cannot write this without anguish – have been decomposing and each element is going all alone to seek its historical origins'. W. Maturi, 'Gli studi di storia moderna e contemporanea', in C. Antoni and R. Mattioni, eds, *Cinquant'anni di vita intel-lettuale italiana*, vol. I, Naples: Edizioni scientifiche italiane, 1950, p. 247.

59 See the leading article 'Per la solidarietà fra i partiti', northern edition, October 1944. Compare, in the January issue of the same year, the placing side by side of the names of Cavour, Settembini and Mazzini, of Garibaldi and Matteotti.

the anniversary of Garibaldi's death),[60] but even the Greek dictator Metaxas. The latter, in a radio broadcast on 22 November 1940, shortly after the Italian invasion, said: 'Greece forgets neither Santarosa, nor Fratti, nor Garibaldi, nor the many other Italians who shed their blood for her, for the liberty and independence of Italy in the last century.'[61] Nor had the Fascists dared to call their war the 'fifth war of independence', despite the objectives set for it: 'Nice, Savoy, fateful Corsica, Malta bulwark of Romanità', as one of their songs listed them.

From the Kingdom of the South the voice of Victor Emmanuel III at once hastened to remind the Italians what 'the inhuman enemy of our race and our civilisation' was;[62] and, still in the South, an 'Appeal to the King' to resign, written by an intellectual of some prestige, concluded with the enjoinder to Italy to resume 'the tradition of its Mazzinian and Garibaldinian risorgimento, and the mission that Fascism, in a dominion of ignorance and brutality, had dis-owned and divided'.[63]

The memory of the Risorgimento sustained the spirits of the military intern-ees in the German camps. Already at the Brenner Pass there rose from one of their troop-trains the chorus of Verdi's *Va' pensiero* or *Oh Signor che dal tetto natio*.[64] And, to the request that they join the RSI, 'the choice [was] between the Italian Italy of the Risorgimento, of the old war, human and honest, and the Germanised Italy, of the Fascist myth, inhuman and dishonest because, though unreal and unrealisable, it was preached as being real and true'.[65] After 8 September, it might seem that the miracle of 1848 was reviving, when 'Alle irruente orde straniere/studenti e popolani/per improvisa concordia terribili/ il petto inerme opponendo/auspicarono col sangue/il riscatto d'Italia' ('Against the violent foreign hordes/students and common folk,/grown terrible from sudden concord,/presenting their unarmed breasts,/hoped with their blood/for

---

60 See Piccialuti Caprioli, *Radio Londra 1940-45*, pp. 116, 199, 358, 601. 'The Remaking of Italy' was dedicated 'to the glorious memory of Fortunato Picchi who died Palm Sunday 1941, a martyr of the new Risorgimento'.

61 The text of Metaxas's speech is published in the appendix to M. Cervi, *Storia della guerra di Grecia*, Milan: SugarCo, 1965, pp. 467–8.

62 Speech from Radio Bari of 24 September 1943 (see Degli Espinosa, *Il Regno del Sud*, pp. 80–1).

63 The appeal, dated 6–10 November 1943, is published by Francesco Flora as an appendix to his book *Stampa dell'era fascista*, Rome: Mondadori, 1945, pp. 115–45.

64 Carocci, *Il campo degli ufficiali*, p. 46.

65 G. Zaggia, *Filo spinato*, Venice: Rialto 1945, p. 64 (cited in Rochat, *Memorialistica e storiografia sull'internamento*, p. 37). For an analogous appeal to the ancient memories of the *patria* (or, in this case, *patrie*) see the title of a clandestine French newspaper, *L Bannière, Bulletin des amis de la vieille France et sympathisants de la résistance*, the first number of which was printed on 1 May 1942.

the redemption of Italy').[66] The following words appear in a newspaper of an 'extremist' group, the Roman Communist Movement of Italy, on the anniversary of the October Revolution: 'It is not under the sign of the monarchy and with the army of the monarchy that Italian unity was formed and is defended, but with the heroic deeds of the Risorgimento which has created the nation's fibre and makes it inviolable!'[67]

Unity 'as in the epoch of the Risorgimento' was a desire expressed on one occasion by Pietro Nenni, with some reservation however on the part of his party, sensitive as the latter was to the risk that the Resistance would turn out disappointingly, as the Risorgimento had.[68] This concern was extremely strong in the Republican Party, which was always ready to denounce the 'absurd concordance' between 1859, 1860, 1866 and 1915.[69] Nor did the 'vague patriotic vocabulary' used against the 'enemy of the Piave' appeal to an intransigent GL member who considered it 'a step backwards', to which however 'it was necessary ... to adapt', while another GL member was convinced that it was a mistake to confuse the Risorgimento with the present struggle.[70]

In the Catholic world too there were residues of anti-Risorgimento intolerance, early expressed by the preacher who in the church of Sant'Agostino in Rome, in May 1943, had remarked ironically: 'There's never an end to our famous Risorgimento: we started from Eritrea, then Libya and then the world war; to obtain a scrap of land in the sun we went messing around in Abyssinia, then we went knocking our heads in Spain, then ended up in Russia. Where, where on earth will we end up this time!'[71]

But favourite among the Catholics are the suggestions of neo-Guelphism. The new Risorgimento must be finally conducted not against the Catholics but with the Catholics, so that 'the *patria* and the true God are circumfused

66 Memorial tablet placed by the *comune* of Padua in 1885 on the wall of the University in front of Caffè Pedrocchi.

67 *Bandiera Rossa*, 7 November 1943.

68 Nenni's words figure in the text – prepared, but not approved – of the message that the central CLN was to send to the Bari congress (*Documenti inediti sulle posizioni del PCI e del PSIUP*, p. 106). The perplexities of the PSIUP are expressed in a document, dated 1 May 1944, on the Salerno 'turning-point' and the 'problems of the unity of action and anti-Fascist unity' (*Avanti!*, Rome edition, 6 May 1944).

69 See the declaration, 'Il Partito repubblicano italiano ai partiti politici del congresso di Bari', published in *La Voce Repubblicana*, 30 January 1944.

70 See Giovana, *Storia di una formazione partigiana*, pp. 214–16, and Battaglia, *Un uomo*, p. 181. When he became a Communist, Battaglia was to collect several of his essays under the title *Risorgimento e Resistenza*, Rome: Riuniti, 1964 (the first essay is entitled 'Primo e secondo Risorgimento').

71 'I am convinced', concluded that preacher who didn't mince his words, 'that the leaders of the government are either imbeciles or are acting in bad faith' (quoted in A. Riccardi, *Roma 'città sacra'?*, Milan: Vita e Pensiero, 1979, p. 191).

with the light of a single love'.[72] Piero Malvestiti founded the Guelph Action Movement, which was then merged with the Christian Democrat party; and free rein was given to appeals regarding the 'providential mission' assigned by God to the Italy of Girolamo Savanarola, Francesco Ferrucci and Matilde of Canossa.[73] More wayward still, Il Risveglio, the Christian Democrat weekly of the South, refigured the history of Rome, claiming Christ, as a Roman, lumped together with St Francis of Assisi and St Catherine of Siena, the Madonna del Grappa and the Carroccio, St Nicholas of Bari, and proclaiming that the Alps were placed by God as the sacred boundary of Italy.[74] Unfortunately the Action Party and the Group for the Defence of Women were no better when, in some of their Genoese leaflets, they tried to claim Balilla as their own.[75] In Piedmont, the Babel of Risorgimento languages led to the assumption of the name 'Nuovo Risorgimento Italiano' by a movement formed from the remnants of the 4th Army and inspired by General Operti. After provoking tense discussions within the Piedmontese cities' military command, this movement, through the intransigence of the Communists and the regional CLN directives, ended up being identified as an enemy to fight 'on a par with the Nazi-Fascists'.[76]

Naturally the Fascists too, though hindered by their German comrades, descended onto Risorgimento ground. They placed Mazzini's effigy on their stamps, invoked Mameli and his national anthem,[77] pitted a truly patriotic

---

72 These words were spoken by lawyer Gino Fratti, Modenese member of Catholic Action, referred to in Gorrieri, La Repubblica di Montefiorino, pp. 254–5. See, in the same spirit, the newspaper Unità e Libertà, published 28 September 1944 in free Domodossola.

73 See the poster Agli italiani di libertà, with which the Guelph Action movement invited all Catholics to join Democrazia Cristiana (INSMLI, CLNAI, envelope 8, folder 9); the article 'Il risorgimento morale degli Italiani', signed by 'Il Guelfo', in Il Popolo, Rome edition, 28 November 1943; the poster put up in Florence, immediately after the liberation of the city, by the Tuscan regional committee of the DC (ISRT). Matilde di Canossa was the name of a detachment of Green Flames of the Reggio Emilia area (another one bore the title of don Albertario). See G. Franzini, Storia della Resistenza reggiana, Reggio Emilia: ANPI 1966, p. 515.

74 See Il Risveglio of Bari, 26 December 1943, article entitled 'Saluto ai valorosi' ('Greetings to the courageous', those troops fighting alongside the Allies).

75 'Genovesi! Le ossa dei vostri grandi, di Balilla, di Mameli, di Mazzini ...'; 'Donne genovesi! ... Che non ci sia un nuovo Balilla che dica: che l'inse? ...' (Saggio bibliografico, nn. 2196, 3049).

76 See the minutes of the meeting of the Command held in the second half of August and in September 1944 (in Vaccarino, Gobetti and Gobbi, L'insurrezione di Torino, pp. 66, 75–6, 78, 95). See also the regional CLN's notification to the CMRP (INSMLI, CLNAI, envelope 6, folder 3, s, folder 16) and the Diffida (Warning) published in the March–May 1944 issue of La Riscossa italiana. Organo piemontese del Fronte di liberazione nazionale. See also Secchia and Frassati, Storia della Resistenza, pp. 879–80.

77 An example of propaganda postcards with this motif is kept at the ISRT.

Garibaldi of their own against the one besmirched by the 'bandits',[78] and proclaimed that 'the RSI is the heir of the Roman Republic' of 1849.[79] One university student volunteer loftily invoked the Risorgimento virtues (which numbered among other things virility too), and reproached his wife for not wishing to read *Le confessioni di un italiano*, which would have enabled her to 'penetrate deeply into my soul'.[80] The Fascists for their part made no excuse about claiming for themselves the glories of the history of Italy: they too invoked St Francis and St Catherine, Francesco Ferrucci and Marcus Furius Camillus; they named one of their battalions Pontida (possibly more out of ignorance than impudence) and, naturally, brought Balilla over to their side.[81]

This vying for even the distant past was not, however, an exclusively Italian phenomenon. In France Vercingetorix and the victorious defence of Gergovia against the Romans in 52 BC were subject to it. When Vichy organised a ceremony in which all the French regions had to bring a handful of their earth to Gergovia there were outcries of profanation, because Vercingetorix 'is the hero of the Resistance.[82]

Irritated, the anti-Fascists replied sarcastically to what seemed to them unwarranted appropriations. 'Why don't the Fascists quote these words of Mazzini's?' asked an Action Party youth paper, after quoting some of the Genoese's thoughts inspired by the theme of liberty.[83] From the microphones of Radio London, Umberto Calosso noted that '*Giovanezza* [Youth], the hymn of the old men of the Fascist hierarchy was increasingly being replaced by other

78 See the article entitled 'Garibaldi e le brigate Garibaldi', in *Valanga repubblicana*, Fascist newspaper of Modena, 15 December 1944 (quoted in Gorrieri, *La Repubblica di Montefiorino*, pp. 210–11).

79 These words appear on a poster conserved at the 'Museo del primo e del secondo Risorgimento' in Bologna. On the theme of the defence of Rome in the name of the Republic of 1849, see the three posters published by Piscitelli, *I bandi*, pp. 183–4. Appeals to the Risorgimento are widely present in the posters, single issues and booklets conserved in *Fondo RSI*. Figuring in them are, among others, the Cairoli brothers (n. 447) and Princess Trivulzio Belgioioso (n. 70), but the prevailing figures are Garibaldi and Mazzini.

80 Letter of 5 March 1944 by Mario Moretti, who fell in Rome on 6 June (*LRSI*, pp. 76–7). I have already mentioned this paratrooper's 'spiritual testament'.

81 See, in *Fondo RSI*, nos. 12, 481, 740, 1093, 192, 389. For the Pontida battalion, see Dellavalle, *Operai*, pp. 146, 143. For Balilla, see the title *Che l'inse?* of a Genoa newspaper, the first number, of 6 February 1944, issued as a 'settimanale giovanile' ('youth weekly'), explained that that appeal had been made only in the name of patriotism, not in that of anti-Germanism.

82 See 'Gergovie', 93, August 1942, which draws attention to the loss of Alsace and Lorraine, as well as 'our beautiful Indochina, watered with the most generous of French blood'); and *Libérer e Fédérer*, 1 September 1942, article entitled 'La Manifestation de la Légion Gervovie est un insulte à la mémoire de Vercingétorix'.

83 See *Giovani*, Rome, 1 March 1944.

hymns, including those of Garibaldi and Mameli.[84] Disdainful and concerned, *La Riscossa italiana* wrote that the Fascists were profaning Mazzini, Garibaldi, and the Roman Republic, and mentioned the free Comuni and Archbishop Ariberto into the bargain.[85]

When we look at the counter-evidence of the names of the clandestine newspapers and formations, and the *noms de guerre*, the impression that the neo-Risorgimento spirit was spreading assumes more modest proportions. General titles prevail in the newspapers, pivoting on words like 'libertà', 'liberazione', 'lotta' ('struggle'), 'battaglia', 'rinascita' ('rebirth'), 'riscossa' ('recovery'), 'combattente', 'volontario' and the like, often associated with geographical, or else political and ideological names.[86] On the other hand, not many newspaper names appeal to the Risorgimento: *La Giovane Italia* of the Youth Front of Tuscany, the *Fratelli d'Italia* of the Veneto CLN, *L'Italia e il secondo Risorgimento*, and only a few others, even if we consider titles inspired by patriotism of a general kind, such as a *Stella garibaldina* of the Piedmontese Garibaldi brigades (flanked, to be on the safe side, by a *Stella partigiana*), *Il Tricolore* of the Pavese Oltrepò operative sector, and *Patria* of the Lazio Christian Democrats. In acquiring, at a medium level, a firm ideological commitment, as expressed in the names of the newspapers, the Risorgimento clearly had less space, as a motivation for war against the Germans and Fascists, than that given to it in the more solemn and official writings and speeches or in the schools, where those writings and speeches turned up again. By contrast, the great Revolution figures considerably more, indeed massively, in the titles of the French underground press, where there frequently appear 'La Révolution française', 'Valmy', 'Père Duchesne' (which indicates 1942 as its '151e Année: ô drapeau de Wagram! ô pays de Voltaire!'), 'La Marseillaise' and the 'Ça ira', the '14 Juillet' and the 'Quatre-vingt-treize'. One of the newspapers with the latter title is specified as being 'journal of the descendants of the French Revolution'.[87] 'To re-make France', it states 'we must repeat 1792 and Valmy'; or even '1794–1944. The youth of France greet the 150th anniversary of the death of the young fighter for Liberty: Saint-Just'.[88]

---

84 See 'Lo specchio' ('The Mirror'), comment broadcast 28 November 1943 (in Piccialuti Caprioli, *Radio Londra 1940–45*, p. 219).

85 Leading article entitled 'Saldezza del fronte antifascista', January–February 1944. The battle of Legnano is also evoked, in Verdinian fashion.

86 I have in mind the 4,647 periodical titles that appeared in the *Saggio bibliografico*, mentioned earlier.

87 I have in mind the 1,106 titles registered in the *Catalogue des périodiques clandestins*.

88 See *La Pensée française. Organe des intellectuels du Front National du Nord et du Pas-de-Calais*, July–August 1944, leading article entitled 'Intellectuels! Au combat, avec toutes vos armes', and *L'Avant-Garde. Organe central des jeunesses communistes*, 15 July 1944.

Pétain, the victor at Verdun, is compared to Dumouriez, the victor at Valmy: both of them traitors.[89] Bloch recalled that in May 1940 the *Marseillaise* had still signified 'the cult of the *patrie* and the execration of tyrannies'.[90] But the *Marseillaise* was a popular song, while the Risorgimento had become a bombastic and scholastic concept. Besides, there are explicit Jacobin echoes in Italy too: in a speech given in Naples on 3 September 1944, Nenni called the partisans 'sans culottes of the French revolution', and both *Avanti!* and *L'Unità*, at least in the first few months, invoked a government of public health.[91]

The Risorgimento appeared more insistently perhaps in the names of the partisan formations, above all in Veneto, but never on a large scale.[92] Here, when the formation was not designated by a number alone, geographical names prevailed as well as the names of those who had died fighting in the Resistance itself – as if to underline the local roots of many formations and the preponderant bond that they felt with their own immediate past. Names indicating the political and ideological patrimony to which the formations appealed were, in turn, more numerous than the purely Risorgimental ones. There was an intermediate group of broadly patriotic inspiration – Italia, Italia Libera (the most widespread of this type), Fratelli d'Italia, Patria, Italiano, Dante, and the like.

Significant too was the dose of Risorgimento-inspired names in the different formations. Of the seven detachments making up the 2nd Garibaldi (Biella) assault brigade, three had plainly Risorgimento names, in the democratic vein – Bixio, Mameli, Fratelli Bandiera; one, Pisacane, a heretical, already tendentially Socialist, Risorgimento name; one, Piave, a name from the 'fourth war of independence'; and finally, two that were political names inspired by unity between the parties of the left – Matteotti and Gramsci.[93] But the most recur-

---

89 Leading article, 'Les Paysans de la France et le 14 juillet', in *Le Paysan Patriote. Organe des Comités paysans du Midi et du Sud-Ouest*, 14 July 1943, where Laval is the tyrant born of the modern 18th Brumaire.

90 Bloch, *La strana disfatta* p. 138.

91 P. Nenni, *Che cosa vuole il Partito socialista*, Rome: Casa Editrice Avanti!, 1944, p. 11. See *Avanti!*, Rome edition, 30 December 1943 (leading article 'Né opportunismo né oltrantismo'), and *L'Unità*, northern edition, 31 October 1943 (article entitled 'Giusta guerra di popolo').

92 Luigi Longo noted that in Veneto 32 formations out of 112 associated themselves with the Risorgimento (*Un popolo alla macchia*, pp. 466–9). The list of cases that follows is based essentially on the index of organisms (registered as amounting to 1,059, widely diverse in terms both of consistency and of persistence), which furnishes the *Guida agli archivi della Resistenza*, edited by the archive-library committee of the Istituto Nazionale per la Storia del Movimento di Liberazione in Italia, Rome: Pubblicazioni degli Archivi di Stato, 1983. Also used are the analogous indexes of the three volumes of *Brigate Garibaldi*, and of the *Formazioni GL*.

93 See the 'Rapporto del mese di gennaio 1944' (IG, *BG*, 05076). And see Dellavalle, *Operai*, p. 115.

rent Risorgimento names circulating in the Garibaldi formations appear to be Mazzini (at least five times), Pisacane, Bixio, Fratelli Bandiera (three times each), Cattaneo, Nievo, Nullo, Mameli (twice), and then Anita Garibaldi, Mazzini and Garibaldi, Manin, Cairoli, Calvi, Pellico, Menotti, and also a Camicia Rossa (Red Shirt) between the Risorgimento and the workers' movement.[94] Still rarer, perhaps surprisingly, seem to be the Risorgimento names adopted by the GL formations, even if we take into account that there were fewer of these than the Garibaldi brigades: Cattaneo and Mazzini (twice each, as if to symbolise the dual, traditional inspiration of Italian political radicalism) and, here too, Nullo. Cattaneo figured among the minor politicised formations like the Socialist Matteotti ones, while we should recall there were also some Mazzini brigades inspired by the Republican Party.

Appearing among the Lombard Liberal organisation were the Fratelli Bandiera and Goffredo Mameli, alongside San Giusto and San Fermo.[95] The Osoppo in their turn recalled Mameli, and the Green Flames drew inspiration from Tito Speri. Among the formations of not clearly definable political leanings, again there were Mazzini, Cairoli, Mameli, the Fratelli Bandiera, as well as Silvio Pellico, Luciano Manara, Santorre di Santarosa, Cinque Giornate, Dieci Giornate, Curtatone and Montanara.

A survivor of one of the Yugoslavia formations gives a desecrating explanation of what motivated the decision to take the name Garibaldi: Mazzini was too republican, Matteotti too political, while 'Garibaldi, let's face it, is all right for everybody and was all right for us too, and so we became the "Divisione partigiana Italia Garibaldi".[96]

If we descend from the names of the formations and newspapers to the *noms de guerre* chosen by, or given to, the partisans, things become trickier. Mixed with political, ideological and autobiographical motivations was a vast range of attitudes to that partial mutation of one's identity that a change of name involved.[97] At times, 'subtle reasons' preceded the choice of a name; and it is

---

94 In this case, as in those that follow, the figures are only indicative, based on the indexes recorded above, which are obviously incomplete with respect to reality, but also at times provide a distorting image, as for example when they register formations generated by each other as distinct.

95 Declaration, made after the Liberation, by the regional federation of the PLI (INSMLI, envelope 90, folder 15).

96 Testimony by avvocato Umberto Zaccone (in various authors, *Aspetti religiosi della Resistenza*, Atti del Convegno nazionale, Turin, 18–19 April 1970, Turin 1972, pp. 155–62). One needs to bear in mind the probable desire of the witness, who was a Catholic, to differentiate himself from the Communist Garibaldini.

97 On the *noms de guerre* adopted by the partisans, see F. Castelli, 'Miti e simboli dell'immaginario partigiano: i nomi di battaglia', in ISR Asti, *Contadini e partigiani*, *Atti del Convegno storico, Nizza Monferrato, 14–16 dicembre 1984*, Alessandria: Edizioni dell'Orso, 1986, pp. 285–309. On the loss of identity due to the adoption of a false name,

not right to call them 'Arcadia'.[98] The panorama is vast, a veritable pattern book of popular fantasy and culture, in which patriotic remembrance seems to play only the most modest part. We find classical and mythological names (Ajax, Euclid), names from noble literature (Carducci, Alighieri),[99] the most learned names (Bede), names from popular literature of various tongues (D'Artagnan, Gordon, Radiosa Aurora), English names (Bill, Tom) and Russian ones (Boris, Ivan); barbarians' names (Attila, Alimiro) and exotic names (Alì, Ataman), names of sports champions (Bartali, Nuvolari and the thoroughbred Nearco), cocky and violent names (Ardito, Uragano, Mitra – meaning machine-gun), defiant names (Boia – hangman; Caino – Cain), the names of animals (which were among those most often adopted: from *tordo* – thrush – to *bufalo*) and of plants (*bambù* and *grano* – wheat), names deriving from physical (Baffetti) and psychophysical features (Bestione), place names that take their cue from a Royal Army tradition, great military commanders (Scipio, Napoleon). In such varied company, the Risorgimento makes a very scanty showing.[100]

Evidently there was not much inclination among individual *resistenti* to recognise themselves, even ironically, in the heroes of the Risorgimento. We do find a Piedmontese Garibaldini named Garibaldi, and a Veneto who calls himself, with generous unitary sentiment, Cavour, but there is no way of telling how much of a bearing physical resemblance had in cases like these. A couple of Nullos and a Nievo are recorded (in Veneto), a Cecilia deriving from La Cecilia,[101] and precious little else. When forty-five Garibaldini of the Natisone division asked to enrol in the Italian Communist Party, they were asked to choose a name for

---

see the testimony of Pietro Secchia, who used a great number of false names in his life, in G. Pesce, *Quando cessarono gli spari*, Milan: Feltrinelli, 1977, p. 203. Nelia Benissone has observed that concealing one's name for reasons of safety at times resulted in one's well and truly forgetting it. Bruzzone and Farina, eds, *La Resistenza taciuta*, p. 47. It would certainly be interesting to compare Italians' *noms de guerre* and their real names. See E. De Felice, *Nomi e cultura. Riflessi della cultura italiana dell'Ottocento e del Novecento nei nomi personali*, Pomezia-Venezia: Sarin-Marsilio, 1987. According to the author, about a quarter of the 1,200 forms examined 'have an ideological stamp'. But while the Resistance, the First World War and Fascism occur very frequently, 'no explicit and direct onomastic reflex exists for the Second World War, the War of Liberation and the Resistance' (p. 29).

98 Battaglia, *Un uomo*, p. 58 (see also pp. 153, 230–1); Meneghello, *I piccoli maestri*, p. 280.

99 A Garibaldino band included both Dante and Ceka (Chiodi, *Banditi*, p. 110: 18 gennaio 1945).

100 It is evident that, still less than for the names of the formations, in this field it is impossible to make a rigorous quantification. What is said on this score, both here and elsewhere, in the present text is based on my personal research and on fuller indexes of the names present in texts devoted to the Resistance.

101 Anna Cinanni was given this name by her brother Paolo, a Calabrese, in homage to Giovanni La Cecilia, 'because, if I'm not mistaken, there was a revolutionary of our Risorgimento who bore this name' (Bruzzone and Farina, *La Resistenza taciuta*, p. 100).

themselves: nine chose their own names; four, Slav names; three, Anglo-Saxon names; six drew inspiration from romantic war fiction; one from the novels of Salgari (Yanez); three opted for national-patriotic and almost irredentist names (Adriatico, Roma, Pisino); and one even recognised himself in Balilla.[102]

The detached, solemn, scholastic figure that the leading personalities of the Risorgimento had did not favour their adoption as partisan *noms de guerre*. The fortune enjoyed, in contrast, by the adjective *garibaldino*, 'impetuous', must be attributed not only to the choice made by the PCI, but also to the fact that this name allowed one, without going so far as to identify with the great men of the history of the *patria*, to recognise oneself in the only phenomenon of voluntary and democratic combativeness that the Risorgimento and the post-Risorgimento had known.

The Great War of 1915–18 was an intermediary between the Risorgimento and certain motivations of the new anti-German war. This was the result not only of the version of it taught at school as the 'fourth war of independence', but also of the vaguer and more complex sense of a sort of posthumous means by which democratic interventionism, vilified and suffocated by Fascism to the advantage of Mussolinian interventionism, got its own back. Ferruccio Parri was the symbol of this path, sometimes punctuated by self-criticism.[103] It is above all in the Action Party that suggestions of this kind circulated. A poster addressed to the people of Cuneo began: 'The Action Party, heir of the parties which in 1914 wanted war against the Germans, not for a limited ideal of nationalism, but solely in the name of liberty and greater Justice.'[104]

In Venezia Giulia the Action Party also appealed to Oberdan,[105] which was,

---

102 The other names are hard to classify: 'Elenco dei compagni che intendono iscriversi al PCI' ('List of comrades who intend to enrol in the PCI') (IRSFVG, *Fondo Rapuzzi*, envelope I, folder IV *Gruppo Intendenza* 1944). A Balilla appears also in the Modena division, which, after the reconstitution of the Command whereby the Communists became the minority in favour of the Christian Democrats (12 December 1944), had as its Chief of Staff a 'Barba Elettrica' ('Electric Beard'), which had been the nickname of the Fascist general Annibale Bergonzoli, commander in the Spanish Civil War of the Littorio Division. See order of the day no. I of the new Command, 19 December 1944, and Command's report to the CUMER and the commander of the British mission, Wilcockson, 24 January 1945 (*Le Brigate Garibaldi*, vol. III, pp. 113–14, 281).

103 It has been rightly recalled that 'anti-Fascism had to be created through the self-criticism of democratic interventionism' (A. Lyttleton, 'Storia di un'antologia fra vecchie e nuove storiografie', in *Il Mulino* XXXIII [1984], p. 200). And the comment on the anthology *Il fascismo*, edited by Costanzo Casucci, which firmly vindicates the fundamental value of democratic interventionism.

104 INSMLI, *CLNAI*, envelope 8, folder 12 (undated).

105 See the typescript 'Per il 61° anniversario del martirio di Guglielmo Oberdan: 20 dicembre 1882–20 dicembre 1943' (registered in *Saggio bibliografico*, n. 2213; see also n. 2214).

furthermore, the name given to a Garibaldi battalion and chosen also as a *nom de guerre*; while in Verona it was the CLN that began one of its leaflets as follows: 'On 24 May 1915 Italy sided with the United Nations to defeat the Prussian idea of world supremacy, which means bullying. 24 May 1944 finds Italy again at the side of the United Nations, engaged, for the second time in thirty years, in a terrible war to disinfect German skulls of a still more oppressive conception.'[106]

Among the accusations that it levelled at the king, *La Voce Repubblicana*, organ of a party that was not part of the CLN, included that of having shilly-shallied in 1914–15, out of love for the reactionary sovereigns of the Triple Alliance.[107] Numerous testimonies of this kind can be found in the names of some formations (Battisti, Piave), or also in explicit appeals by well-qualified people like Luigi (Gigino) Battisti, son of Cesare, who on 19 February 1945, in a letter from Lugano to the minister of war, the Liberal Casati, asked to be enrolled in the Combat Groups, 'recalling the motives of the Risorgimento and of the democratic interventionism of 1915'.[108] Here too one could overdo things. The 'Partito della Democrazia del lavoro' invoked the Italy of the Risorgimento and of Vittorio Veneto and, in the same breath, also included that of the 'Libyan enterprise'.[109]

The Socialist and Communist parties, though not dissociating themselves from these appeals to the First World War, indeed contributing importantly to them, displayed some uncertainty and wavering on this score. On the one hand, the two parties were keen to shake off the reputation of being anti-patriots who had spat on the officers' medals; but on the other hand they were not prepared to publicly disclaim their consolidated verdicts on the great imperialistic world war. A southern edition of *Avanti!* emphatically recalled 'the victory of democratic Italy over Prussian militarism', and for the entire world expressed the wish for 'the second inevitable victory for the definitive elimination of every kind of militarism'.[110] It is an article in which the renewed theme of the anti-militarist, and therefore final, war coexists with the re-proposal of one of Fascism's most pitifully ridiculous propagandist formulae: 'inevitable victory'. The Milan edition of the same paper published, again on the anniversary of the 4 November 1918 armistice, this half-title:

> *Flowers for the dead*. Our invitation to place flowers on the monuments of the war dead has been taken up everywhere generously. In some places, as for example Milan, the militia has attempted to oppose it. In the homage to the dead of the 1915–18 war it has seen an offensive [*sic*] against Nazi and Fascist vices.[111]

---

106 IVSR, *Archivio*, section I, envelope 49, CLN, *Stampa non periodica*.
107 Article entitled 'Un profilo del re decaduto', 4 June 1944.
108 ACS, *Carte Casati*, folder H.
109 Editorial of *Azione democratica*, 31 January 1944.
110 'Radiomessaggio per il 4 novembre 1943', in *Avanti!*, Bari, October 1943.
111 *Avanti!*, Milan edition, 8 November 1943.

Still in the Socialist sphere, in Rome the official party organ attempted a fuller and at once more traditional argument: 'The spiritual confusion of today's Italy stems essentially from the drama of two generations: that of the world war of 1914, and that of the present war.' The paper then goes on to define as 'subsidiary and secondary' the motives espoused in 1915 for entering the war, such as 'hatred of Germans, Latin solidarity, Bissoloti's democratic war or Corrdoni's revolutionary one, or else Trento and Trieste'.[112]

The Communists had attempted to mediate between patriotic war and revolutionary war by adopting the name Garibaldi, but they generally remained reserved and prudent about the 1915–18 war, even if there were cases of patriotic ingenuity such as that found in a Garibaldi poster in the province of Bergamo: 'Hitler today wants to follow the same fate as the Hapsburgs. Whoever lays a hand on Italy dies.'[113]

Particularly revealing is the Communist Party's criticism of an article about the 4 November 1918 armistice that appeared in *Liberazione*, the Perugia CLN newspaper – though edited, to all effects, by the Communists. What was wrong in that article was the statement that 'the '14–18 war was a war of national liberation. We cannot accept this point of view. Certain references may be made to the '14–18 war but must avoid that way of thinking.'[114]

The fact that the writer of this letter replaced ''15–18' with ''14–18' is itself indicative of his non-patriotically Italo-centric viewpoint. Moreover – and this is worth noting in order to highlight the contradictions of censor and censored alike – he also criticised another article in the same newspaper, of 7 November, that had seemed to him to smack a good deal more of a Communist organ than of any kind of national front.

Appeals to the 1915–18 war certainly offered an alibi to the 'anti-Fascism of the Fascists'.[115] At times languages become almost grotesquely mixed up in them, as in the case of an Alpino who had fought in the 1915–18 war. That First World War veteran told the Social Republic general who shook his hand before the coffin of his son killed by Slav partisans that he was proud that his son had given his life '"for the *patria* and for the king". No one dared contradict him.'[116]

But, besides their ideological content, the appeals to 1915–18 presumably found an echo because they referred to an event that was close in time but not so close as to prevent memory from having the chance to transfigure

---

112 *Avanti!*, Rome edition, 12 January 1944, 'Messaggio di capodanno ai giovani'.

113 Late 1943 poster, entitled *Il terrore nazista non piega l'Italia. Come i tedeschi possono aiutare i patrioti* (IG, Archivio PCI).

114 'G.' to 'Caro C.', 6 February 1944 (in ibid.).

115 For the use of this expression see Quazza, *Resistenza e storia d'Italia*, Chapter III, 'Il Fronte resistenziale'.

116 The episode is recounted in G. Manni's unpublished diary, cited earlier, Ch. 1: 3, note 101.

it, parenthesising its horrors. The First World War was an event that had been recounted to the younger men by their fathers as a fundamental, formative experience, punctuated by exceptional gestures, which struck their imaginations. 'The action which has the flavour of the hoax played on the Bulgarians [sic]', runs a report about an attack on a Fascist barracks.[117]

The memory of the First World War, like that of the Risorgimento, in any case led to the rediscovery both of one's traditional allies and of one's traditional enemy.

2. THE TRADITIONAL ALLIES

One of the instructions which, after Italy's entry into the war, the British issued as propaganda for our country was to avoid all 'sentimental references to Anglo-Italian "traditional friendship"'.[1] From June 1940 to September 1943, many things had certainly changed, and in fact after 8 September the Italian rulers let no chance slip to appeal to the 'traditional allies'.[2] But British distrust of pro-Italian sentiment had not weakened much, even though declarations by Labour MPs in favour of the Italian people were forthcoming. These openings were greeted with satisfaction by the Resistance press, which nevertheless did not fail to recall, albeit discreetly, Churchill's pro-Mussolinian lapses.[3]

British hostility to and lack of esteem for the Italians had been fuelled by

---

117 Anonymous report relating to the Valsassina (IG, *BG*, 0941).

1 *Directive on British propaganda for Italy*, 20 September 1940 (see Piccialuti, *Radio Londra 1940–45*, Appendix I, I, p. cxiii). The directives of 20 April 1940, when the British government still hoped to keep Mussolini from declaring war, insisted on two points: to foment anti-German sentiments by recalling that 'European civilisation and traditions are based on the Roman Empire and the Christian Church'; to reassure the Fascists: 'We have the greatest admiration for the achievements in Italy of Fascism' (ibid., p. xxx).

2 See, for example, the replies sent by Badoglio to Churchill and Roosevelt's message of 11 September 1943, and the proclamations of 15 September 1943 and 11 February 1944 (See Badoglio, *L'Italia nella seconda guerra mondiale*, p. 126; Degli Espinosa, *Il Regno del Sud*, pp. 53–8, 273).

3 *L'Italia Libera*, Rome edition, 17 October 1943, and *La Riscossa italiana*, 20 October, gave prominence to the words pronounced by MPs Greenwood and Thomas to the House of Commons in the debate held on 21 and 22 September. See Churchill, *The Second World War: Closing the Ring*, Chapter 3, and Degli Espinosa, *Il Regno del Sud*, pp. 63–79). *L'Italia Libera* expressed its hope in an accord between the two peoples in 'questa guerra di liberazione europea' (articles entitled 'Da popolo a popolo' and 'Iniziativa degli italiani'). On 7 May 1944 *L'Italia Libera*, Lombardy edition, republished an article that had appeared in the *New Statesman and Nation* that was critical of Churchill's attitude and line regarding Italy. *Il Risorgimento Liberale* reminded the British prime minister that, if he had been deceived about Mussolini, why did he not realise that the Italians too could be deceived? (*Nel 1928 ...* northern edition, November–December 1944).

three years of war. Scepticism ran high about the capacity of such a devastated people to recover.

The impression that Churchill had drawn from the first armistice approaches made in Lisbon by the diplomat D'Ayeta had been that, fundamentally, it was a 'plea that we should save Italy from the Germans as well as from herself, and do it as quickly as possible'.[4] At the beginning of the war, Churchill had also said to his private secretary, Sir John Colville, that the Italians 'know how to excel in countless fields ... And yet they have insisted on doing the only thing that they have never managed to do very well, fight.'[5] More unsparingly, the British foreign minister, Eden, in a note sent on 14 January 1943 to US Secretary of State Cordell Hull, had declared that, rather than the prospect of Italy as an ally, he preferred that of a collapsed Italy, which the Germans would be compelled to occupy, thereby diverting immense forces from other fronts.[6] A leaflet air-dropped in the North by Allied, presumably British, aircraft in November 1943, crudely warned: 'You cannot expect only us to fight for you and for your liberty, while Italian men stand to one side, or even fight against us alongside the Germans ...Those who stay inactive at home do not deserve a place alongside the victor.'[7]

In a broadcast of 8 October 1943, which seemed to prefigure the directive to consider the Italians a 'logical but volatile people', Candidus, the most caustic of the commentators in Radio London's Italian broadcasts, and the one who seemed to have been assigned the task of telling the Italians the bitter truth, stated things yet more baldly:

> Let no one think that the Allies landed in Italy from love of the Italians; they landed from strategic necessity ... The liberation of the peninsula is not, and could not be, the final aim of the Allies; it is a means of defeating Germany; but fortune would have it that what is only a means for the Allies coincides with what is an end for the Italians; who therefore – if they have the slightest consciousness of their present and future interests and a minimum of political awareness – must not simply wish that their liberation will come quickly, but must contribute to hastening it by their own efforts.[8]

---

4 Communication to Roosevelt, 5 August 1943, in Churchill, *The Second World War*, vol. V, book I, p. 90.

5 Interview given by Colville to R. Cianfanelli, *Corriere della Sera*, 8 June 1980: 'Per vedere le rovine d'Italia non dovremo arrivare a Pompei' (cited in Casucci, *Il fascismo*, p. 14, note).

6 See Toscano, *Dal 25 luglio all'8 settembre*, pp. 14–17.

7 The leaflet is conserved in the 'Museo del primo e del second Risorgimento', in Bologna.

8 The text of the broadcasts, entitled *La strada difficile e aspra*, is published in *Parla Candidus. Discorsi dal 13 aprile 1941 al 3 dicembre 1944*, Milan: Mondadori, 1945,

Certainly, in the twenty months of German occupation the Allies were not unforthcoming in their appeals and tributes to the fighting spirit and valour of the Italians, even if in anti-Fascist and Resistance circles they often appeared to be too parsimonious.[9] At some moments these appeals were clearly instrumental in character; at others they expressed genuine wonder at the unsuspected gifts demonstrated by the Italians. But it was the very manifestation of this wonder that confirmed the widespread presence of the limited view of their combative virtues that the Italians sensed in the Allies, as they had already sensed it in the Germans (and in any case, in their heart of hearts many Italians considered that judgment to be not altogether unfounded). In a broadcast about the March 1944 strikes, Candidus said: 'Admiration is all the greater for the fact that – let's face it – opinion was widespread abroad that the Italians would never have done such a thing … The idea that they lack not so much physical courage as military virtue and even the will to fight, is an old story.'

But, shifting emphasis, Candidus went on to say that by refusing 'to fight for what is not felt as being essential and inalienable to the national community', the Italians had shown that they 'had outgrown the vanity of militaristic glory' and demonstrated that they were 'perhaps the most civil and wise people on the earth'; so much so that now, when 'their very historical personality is in jeopardy', the Italians have demonstrated, once again, that they possess 'courage' and 'virility'.[10]

Words like those, in the 25 May 1944 issue of *L'Unità*, should not therefore sound rhetorical: 'A profound sense of emulation is stirring our national pride'[11] – emulation regarding both the Allied armies and the Resistance movements of the other European countries. The Resistance leaders made a tenacious effort to shake off the narrow role of 'obscure fifth column auxiliaries', in which, as Parri put it on one occasion, the Allies wanted, at least initially, to confine

---

pp. 180–1, and in *Piccialuti Caprioli, Radio Londra 1940–45*, pp. 209–11. The directive for propaganda towards Italy is in a memorandum relating to the period from 31 January to 31 May 1944 (see ibid., vol. I, p. cxxiii).

9 See, for example, a letter of … to 'Carissimo' (Damiani?), in Switzerland, of 8 December 1943, asking him to ask Radio London for 'more Italian' ('più italiana') propaganda, and to give more appreciation to anti-Fascism (INSMLI, *Carte Damiani*, envelope I, folder I); the stance taken by the CLNAI on 16 June 1944, recalled by Catalano, *Storia del CLNAI*, pp. 206–7; the protest by the organ of the Mazzini Society, 'Nazioni Uniti', against the fact that the American press was giving far more coverage to the French and Yugoslav Resistance than to its Italian counterpart (article entitled 'L'organizzazione dei partigiani', 1 July 1944, quoted in L. Valentini's laureate thesis).

10 The text of the broadcasts is published in *Parla Candidus*, pp. 261–3, and in Piccialuti Caprioli, *Radio Londra 1940–45*, pp. 235–7.

11 Northern edition, article entitled 'L' offensiva alleata e il popolo italiano'.

the unexpected capacity for fighting back demonstrated by the Italians.[12] One of the most well-known and significant documents attesting to this attitude of the Allies is the letter that John McCaffery, the British representative in Switzerland, sent to Parri on 16 August 1944. The letter began by recalling that 25 July had been made possible only by the Allied victories, and then went on to say:

> A long time ago I said that the greatest military contribution you could bring to the Allied cause was continuous, widespread sabotage, on a vast scale. You wanted bands. I supported this desire of yours, because I recognised its moral value for Italy. The bands have worked well. We know that. But you've wanted to form armies. Who asked you to do so? Not us. You've done it for political reasons, and to be precise, to reintegrate Italy. No one will blame you for this idea. But don't blame our generals if they work, at least essentially, with military criteria.

Shortly before this, the Englishman had come out with this scoffing exclamation: 'But, for heaven's sake, you don't mean now to direct military operations instead of Eisenhower or Alexander!' The letter concludes with a warning: 'One last word of advice. You have friends. Don't actually try to lose them.'[13]

The Allied point of view, expressed by McCaffery with realistic baldness, generated a mixture of sentiments and resentments among the *resistenti* that combined in varying ways with the image, often vague and filtered in any case through their respective political sympathies, that they had of the British and Americans. The most deeply felt positions were held by those who could not forget that they belonged to a defeated and guilty country (their most burning sense of guilt was towards the French and Yugoslavians);[14] the most distrustful were those who could not get it out of their heads that the British and American armies were still always the instruments of two capitalist and imperialist powers. The Milanese Communist leaders were taken to task

---

12 Parri's words are in Maurizio (F. Parri), 'Il Movimento di liberazione e gli Alleati', in *Il Movimento di liberazione in Italia*, 1949, I, p. 8; republished in Parri, *Scritti 1915–1975*, pp. 512–28. According to Salvemini, Churchill, for the Italians, admitted only 'sabotatori e vuotacessi' ('saboteurs and john-cleaners'). Postcard to the author, 1955.

13 McCaffery's letter is published in Secchia and Frassati, *La Resistenza e gli Alleati*, pp. 99–100.

14 'I'll never forget shouting 'Viva Nizza italiana!' Revelli said to himself when he heard a Frenchman mockingly say, 'Italian partisans, why do you no longer shout *viva il duce*?', and noted: 'Here in the Nice area the French haven't forgotten June 1940' (Revelli, *La guerra dei poveri*, pp. 328 and 357, 30 August and 25 October 1944). A girl who was hostile to the Garibaldini because they were friends of the Slavs was reminded by a political commissar that, for everything that had been done against that people 'in the name of the Italian people, we had to pay the consequences, even if they were unjust' (Vanni [G. Padoan], *Abbiamo lottato insieme*, p. 197).

by their Roman colleagues for having expressed this concept all too clearly in *L'Unità*.[15]

A Tuscan Action Party newspaper summed up well the difficulties distinguishing relations with the Allies: 'For some time now we have been saying that what has happened in Italy in the last few years has happened against the will of the people. Now, we can be totally convinced of this, without however succeeding in convincing others, if at the present moment we fail to play our part in the victory of the Allies.'[16]

The use of the Allies as an alibi for everything of democratic worth that one was failing to do in Italy – a tendency in which a considerable part of left-wing historiography was to indulge – is rejected outright in this other Action Party document: 'It's we who are to blame, not the English or anyone else, if we haven't been capable of getting rid of the king and the reactionary forces.'[17]

As the Resistance came to be recognised by the Allies – for whom, it should be noted, recognition was the best way of controlling it – there were increasing manifestations of intolerance of their presence and of the way they provided their help, which, nevertheless, the Allies knew they could not do without.

As Henri Michel has written, towards the Allies the entire European Resistance 'manifests both gratitude and unease, a faith that weathers the worst trials and a desire for self-determination, that is to say for revolt'[18] – all the more so in the case of the Italian Resistance, which had to reckon with an 'enemy ally'. The attitude circulating in many Garibaldi formations typifies this: they felt their being discriminated against in the air-drops as a lack of recognition and legitimisation, not least with respect to the formations that were their competitors. Regarding a request for heavy arms, a Garibaldi command wrote:

And this is also intended to show the men once and for all that the manoeuvring of enemy propaganda and of other formations is quite unjustified. Up to now we have fought it strenuously with words, but the Garibaldini demand tangible proof that the Allies, the Higher Commands, are interested in their needs and that they demonstrate their recognition of their efforts in concrete action. This therefore becomes not just a material but a moral necessity, which would give an elevation

15 Letter of 13 December 1943, in Longo, *I centri dirigenti del PCI*, p. 256. The criticism related to an article entitled 'Perché è necessario che prenda il potere il Comitato di liberazione nazionale', which appeared 7 November in the northern edition of *L'Unità*.

16 Article entitled 'Al popolo italiano, agli amici, ai nemici', in *La Libertà*, 27 October 1943.

17 Undated document of the Action Party of the North, commenting on the Salerno turning-point (mutilated, in INSMLI, *CLNAI*, envelope 8, folder 12). Probably it concerned the 'plan for a political declaration to submit for approval by the Central Executive in Rome'.

18 Michel, 'Gli Alleati e la Resistenza in Europa', p. 62.

of tone to their enthusiasm and galvanise their fighting spirit, appealing against disheartenment.[19]

So one could not do without the Allies, but one needed to maintain autonomy and dignity in one's dealings with them, differentiating oneself, in this respect as well, from the way the Fascists were behaving towards the Germans. As early as October 1943, *La Riscossa italiana*, the Piedmonetese newspaper of the National Liberation Front wrote:

> In siding with the English, the Americans and the Russians, we shall take care in our dealings with them not to fall into that spirit of humiliation and servility with which Mussolini had put himself in the retinue of Hitler ... We shall be and we shall fight at the side of the United Nations with the dignity of a people who, having regained dominion over themselves, is fighting for a common ideal that transcends particular differences, and wishes, with the active contribution it will give to this struggle, to redeem the shame of Fascism.[20]

In May 1944, the Command of the GL formations ordered that the formations themselves were never to be placed under foreign officers nor (the juxtaposition is significant) under the command of 'relics of the militaristic expression of Fascism': only 'technical directives' could be accepted from foreigners.[21] An 'indomitable spirit of independence towards the foreigner, even if he is an ally' is insisted on by the commander of the 4th zone (Piedmont),[22] while a Garibaldi report from Reggio Emilia complains about the head of an American mission who was in the habit of throwing his weight about.[23] The insurrectional Veneto (Communist) triumvirate stated plainly that the partisan formations depended 'directly upon the CLNAI and the CVL Command, and

---

19 Report by the Command of the 8th Asti division to the delegation for Piedmont, 14 November 1944 (*Le Brigate Garibaldi*, vol. II, p. 576).

20 Leading article entitled 'Riscossa', in *La Riscossa italiana*, 20 October 1943.

21 'Norms of a general character for the forthcoming events', sent to the commanders of the formations 3 May 1944 (ISRP, envelope 29, folder b). On the refusal by the Val Varaita to submit to the orders of Captain Patt, chief of the American mission, see Giovana, *Storia di una formazione partigiana*, p. 266.

22 Letter to the Piedmont regional military Command, 13 February 1945, in which advice is asked about how one should behave towards another captain, Chape, suspected of being an agent of British espionage (IG, *BG, Piemonte*, document 3). The fears displayed by this captain that the workers and the population would provoke disorder during the transition phase are mentioned in a letter that 'the comrades' sent Pietro and Barbato of the 1st Piedmont Garibaldi division on the eve of the Liberation (IG, *BG*, 04426).

23 Letter of the inspector of the CUMER delegation for North Emilia to 'dear comrades', 13 December 1944 (*Le Brigate Garibaldi*, vol. III, pp. 74–6).

that from these organisms, with which the Allied Command and the Rome government are in contact, they receive orders, instructions, directives ... We must defend our national dignity, so badly mistreated by certain Allied orders and certain Allied commanders. We must do this tactfully, but with dignity' – all the more so because all too often the Allied Commands seemed to do nothing other than re-propose Christian Democrat and Liberal positions already encountered elsewhere.[24] Major Tucker, head of the British mission, mooted the idea of dropping British paratroopers in Friuli, but withdrew the proposal, which was supported by the Osoppo formations, when the Natisone Garibaldi division command asked the paratroopers to operate under them.[25] The eastern border was an arduous test-case for the affirmation of a sense of national dignity which differed from the old and arrogant anti-Slav nationalism; this accounts for the different ways in which the Garibaldini and Osovani behaved towards the British proposal. But the commitment not to let oneself be deprived of authority by the Allied Commands, especially in the guise of the parachuted missions, is to be found in more or less all the partisan formations, whatever their political persuasion. It appears particularly acute, a veritable point of honour, when the Allied missions 'rubbed into us the crimes weighing on our country'.[26]

Manifestations of disappointment and irony at the slowness of the Allied advance in Italy were fairly widespread. Among the Communists and Garibaldini, these sometimes took the form of denunciations of the bad faith of the Allies, which was generated by 'clear political motives', as claimed in a meeting of Milanese Communist workers.[27] The Allies' slow progress is made particularly clear by comparison with the overwhelming Soviet advances. Before the grandiose spectacle of the Allied armies north of Bologna, one GAP member was to remark: 'At the sight of so much power, it was hard to understand why we had had to wait so long for that day!'[28] Justifying his modifications to an article due to be published in Stella Alpina, Vincenzo Moscatelli wrote to the author: 'It is neither my fault nor yours if the Russians are moving so quickly ... I've put the Allies in as well, because, after all, even if they're not doing much we can't ignore

---

24 The Veneto insurrectional triumvirate to the PCI representative in the regional CLN, 19 March 1945 (ibid., p. 501).

25 This is what Vanni (G. Padoan) relates in Abbiamo lottato insieme, pp. 149–51.

26 This is what is said in the protest against the increasing interference and arrogance of the British Cherokee mission that the Biella zone Command sent on 7 April 1945 to the Piedmont delegation of the Command of the Garibaldi brigades and on 8 April to the CMRP (Le Brigate Garibaldi, vol. III, pp. 586–8). Regarding the Cherokee mission, see Poma and Perona, La Resistenza nel Biellese, pp. 386–9.

27 'Estratto di un rapporto da Milano', 15 December 1944, in Secchia, Il PCI e la guerra di liberazione, p. 709.

28 See Cicchetti, Il campo giusto, p. 260.

them, least of all in a patriots' paper ... in short ... have it out with Barbisun'[29] – Barbisun being the nickname given to Stalin by northern Italians.

A Lazio Communist claimed that 'the Anglo-Americans don't want to wage the war in Italy', and drew an apparently paradoxical conclusion from this: 'We therefore have plenty of time and, if we work well without wasting it, we'll be able to develop our political movement and the partisans' war so that the liberation of Italy will be the work of the Italians themselves.'[30] Other Garibaldi documents accused the Allied missions of counselling 'attesismo', and reveal the difficulties encountered by the partisan chiefs in stilling the apprehensions aroused by the disarmament to which the partisans were subjected in the zones as the latter were liberated ('they say ... they'll never let themselves be disarmed even if this means opposing the English, and if the worst comes to the worst they will disarm themselves, bolting home and hiding their weapons').[31]

This intolerance towards the Allies, which became more acute and widespread after events in Greece and British General Harold Alexander's proclamation,[32] drove parties and commands alike to try and damp things down. The 'same old expression – what are these Anglo-Americans doing?' was stigmatised by political commissar Michele as a mask for *attesismo*.[33] Likewise, against 'the word "betrayal"', with reference to the Allies, which 'recurs insistently, we have decided to react energetically'.[34]

If the events in Greece induced some partisans to say: 'So that's how it is, now we're being shot at by the Nazi-Fascists and tomorrow we'll be on the

29 Moscatelli to Livio (Paolo Scarpone), commissar of the Ossola zone single Command, 12 February 1945 (IG, *BG*, 07901).

30 March 1944 report by V.B., who had worked close to the front (IG, *Archivio PCI*).

31 See the undated (late 1944?) report on the 'military solution' in Carnia (IG, *BG*, 09332).

32 On 13 November 1944 the English General Harold Alexander, commander-in-chief in Italy, issued a proclamation in which, declaring the conclusion of the summer campaign, he invited the partisans to 'cease operations organised on a large scale'. This proclamation has been the centre of much controversy, for a recent re-examination of the question, see E. Aga-Rossi, 'La politica anglo-americana verso la Resistenza italiana', in *L'Italia nella seconda guerra mondiale e nella Resistenza*, pp. 150–4. The proclamation had a depressing effect, but its provisions were only partly carried out, not least because of the ambiguously interpretable circular, written by Luigi Longo, that was issued on 2 December by the CVL General Command. The proclamation and the circular are published in Secchia and Frassati, *La Resistenza a gli Alleati*, pp. 151–9.

33 Undated report (October 1944?) by the 1st Gramsci (Ossola-Valsesia) Garibaldi division (IG, *BG*, 06746).

34 'Rapporto informativo dall'Emilia (da parte del PCI, novembre 1944)'. In the Communist federation of Modena there was a justifiably intense concern to avoid a situation of the kind that had occurred in Warsaw (*Le Brigate Garibaldi*, vol. II, pp. 666–71).

receiving end of the English cannon-blasts, machine-gun volleys and air-raids', it was explained to them that this kind of language 'was not very different from that used by the Fascists'.[35]

A Garibaldi newsletter is criticised as follows: 'We must never speak ironically in our newspapers about the efforts being made to defeat the Nazi-Fascists. If we wish to ridicule someone, it should always be our enemies and certainly not ... General Eisenhower's hernia.'[36]

Some Modena partisans who had complained about the 'customary respects paid to the representatives of the Allied armies' received a reprimand that recalls McCaffery's: 'It is the Allied Command that is leading and directing the war in Italy against the Nazi-Fascists.'[37]

Likewise, there was the enjoinder always to give the Allied troops a friendly welcome. It is worth mentioning the motivation for this obvious directive that was given to persuade the Milanese militants who seemed to question it. The Allies, it is recalled

> have spilled their own blood and not just ours to liberate us from Fascism. The distrust that they may nourish for us is justified: we should not forget that guilt weighs on the Italian people too. It will be for us [note the different meaning that this second *us (noi)* acquires], the people's vanguard, to show the Allies that we have made a clean break with Fascism and taken a new road.[38]

If these were the warnings coming from the Communists, committed as they were to keeping their members' class spirit in one piece, as well as the policy of unity firmly championed as an international prospect,[39] more predictable still were those coming from elsewhere. *Il Risorgimento Liberale* cautioned against

---

35 'Rapporto informativo n. 4' of the Command of the group of Padana (Po valley), SAP brigades inferior to the delegation for Lombardy of the General Garibaldi Command, 15 December 1944 (ibid., vol. III, pp. 80–2).

36 The commissariat of the group of Valle di Susa divisions, 17 December 1944, to the Command of the 17th brigade regarding the newspaper *Il Partigiano* (ibid., p. 103).

37 Cecco 'ai compagni Livio e Cyrano', 20 December 1944 (ibid., pp. 118–20).

38 'Information from Milan' on a meeting of the 4th sector, 14 April 1945 (ibid., p. 622). Compare the clumsiness of the poster put up on 9 October 1944 by the new mayor of Forlì, Franco Agosto, for the liberation of the city: 'We salute the Allies, who made a decisive contribution in blood to the victory', quoted in Flamigni and Marzocchi, *Resistenza in Romagna*, p. 316. The two authors record also the chilly welcome that the Allied troops were given in Forlì (ibid., p. 246).

39 The reactionaries were trusting in the break-up of the coalition, but would be disappointed – this was the line taken by the party and made known in a 'circular' of 1 January 1945 by the Command of the group of Milan city and province SAP brigades (*Le Brigate Garibaldi*, vol. III, pp. 180–3).

inopportune criticisms of the slowness of the Allies: other peoples 'more deserving than us' were destined to wait still longer.[40]

The Allied missions at times seemed to be held responsible for the bad news that they brought from liberated Italy. 'Why are things not going well in liberated Italy?', the Liguria mission was asked. The answer, as typical as the question, was above all that it was often the Italian rulers who did not even reach the threshold of action conceded by the Allies. Then came the admission:

> We've made mistakes, but down there the liberation movement was all but nonexistent, and if there were Fascists in the administrations and the industries we couldn't substitute them because we had no one else. Here things are completely different. You can act, provided you avoid disorder in the administrations and the industries and in every branch of life and keep out of trouble.[41]

Quite apart from the difference between the respective political lines which were unknown or little known to them, the partisans grasped the differences between the British and the Americans with whom they were in direct contact, wholly to the advantage of the Americans, whose greater generosity was also attested by the news filtering through from liberated Italy.[42] This preference for the Americans, identified *tout court* with the prospect of something new, provoked the astonished and slightly resentful remark of a Garibaldino: 'Contrary to all expectations, a good number of the population of the valley were awaiting not so much the "liberation" as the Americans.'[43]

But others had no such perplexities: 'The Americans are very democratic and have a different view of the way Italy should be sorted out from the British. Both today and tomorrow, we'll have to lean on the former greatly.'[44] Or again: 'They say the Americans intend to help us more than the British, and when they let their folks know what they've found here they'll send us all sorts of good things.'[45] An American officer parachuted down to a Matteotti formation in the

---

40 Article entitled 'Parole agli impazienti', Rome edition, 5 January 1944.

41 See 22 February 1945 reports on the 'colloquio con la missione alleata per la Liguria' and on the 'incontro fra i delegati del CLN per la Liguria e la missione alleata della 6a zona' (*Le Brigate Garibaldi*, vol. III, pp. 389–91 and p. 392, n. 2).

42 This, for example, is the opinion expressed by the Communist Alfredo in his 'Impressioni generali riportate durante la mia permanenza nella zone liberata (24 January–14 March 1944)', ibid., vol. I, pp. 308–10.

43 Testimony of a partisan recorded in Bernardo, *Il momento buono*, p. 171.

44 The Command of the 6th Liguria zone to the person responsible for military matters of Linguaria insurrectional triumvirate, 21 January 1945 concerning contacts that had been had with the mission in Liguria (*Le Brigate Garibaldi*, vol. III, pp. 270–1).

45 'Responsible comrades' to 'dear comrades', val di Lanzo, 7 August 1944, 'segreto'. The subjects of the verb 'dicono' ('they say') are three Italians, two of whom are Communists, who had enlisted in the American army and parachuted into the zone (ibid., vol. II, p. 214).

province of Alessandria is said to have stated that 'the American Command takes a hostile view of the agreements between the British Command and the Italian conservatives', and that 'the Americans intend to create a banking trust and a commission that is to come to Italy to make loans at 0.50 percent interest'.[46]

Earlier, the Third International had already regarded the Americans more favourably than the British. A Communist veteran who had met Gramsci and Togliatti recounted: 'I am present at the meeting between a major in the British army and the American airman I'm accompanying. A cold, stiff cordiality, consisting only of words: the cordiality of a conservative with a follower of the third estate.'[47] Another old Communist militant stressed that 'the English fought against the Nazi-Fascists only because this corresponded to their imperialistic interests and not because they were anti-Fascist like us'.[48]

Probably the younger and less politicised generations were influenced by the many forms in which the 'American myth' had spread so widely, as well as the influences of Fascist propaganda that had furiously attacked 'il popolo dei cinque pasti' ('the five-meals-a-day people'). In any case, among the Communists attempts emerged to make political use of the differences encountered between the two Anglo-Saxon allies. The Modena Communist federation issued this directive:

> We shall need to pay great attention to the disagreements between the Americans and the British, since we must avoid creating tension with the British. With the latter we must benefit from the better disposition of the Americans, in order to induce them to modify their attitude, while we must make it clear to the Americans that our behaviour towards the English has to be correct, because they are one of the allies.[49]

In fact the Communist-inspired bands' attitudes to the British could range from prudent erasures of wall graffiti that were 'blatantly pro-Soviet ... exterior manifestations that could both be an impediment to normal relations and create difficulties in aid supplies',[50] to sending, with typically excessive zeal, birthday greetings to King George VI.[51] In the case of Britain and the United States, too, it had to be borne in mind that the people were not to be confused with the

---

46 See the *Informazioni da Torino*, undated (IG, BG, 04031).

47 Anonymous report, undated, on the zone of Montefiorino (IG, *BG, Emilia-Romagana*, G.IV.3.3).

48 See Vanni (G. Padoan), *Abbiamo lottato insieme*, p. 140.

49 The Communist federation of Modena to the party committee for the mountains, 8 January 1945 (ISRR, *Archivio del triumvirato insurrezionale Emilia-Romagna*).

50 'Rapporto di un partigiano', undated, on the battle of Montefiorino, which began 30 July 1944 (IG, *BG*, 02255-57).

51 This is what the Nanetti Garibaldi division did. See the Command's 'communications' to De Luca, inspector of the Triveneta delegation (*Le Brigate Garibaldi*, vol. III, p. 61).

governments, or rather, with the reactionaries who had sway over the governments: 'We must always distinguish between the popular masses of the Allied countries and a certain inevitable resistance, which can and must be overcome, on the part of the reactionary cliques that try to exercise their sway over the governments and General Staffs.'[52]

Clearly the reactions towards the British and Americans, with whom not only the combatants but the great mass of the population were coming into contact, did not all stem from opinions and preferences regarding the great political issues. The impact between Italian society and the customs, behaviour, and culture of the British and, above all, American troops – a prologue to the process of Americanisation that developed in the post-war period – was particularly visible in Rome and the South, where the Allied occupation lasted longer and was largely conducted by an army that was still belligerent, and therefore a generator of particularly acute tensions.[53]

Here, the *resistenti*'s experience of things was particular. The British and American prisoners who, having escaped from the concentration camps, joined the partisan bands, often constituted an original channel for re-establishing genuine ties with the 'traditional allies'. Involved in this were the rural populations who, often risking their lives and possessions, gave the prisoners refuge and assistance. In fact, some of the former prisoners were thinking of seeking refuge in Switzerland.[54] Others, though of working-class background, made no effort to disguise their suspicion of anything smacking of Communism.[55] But there were also those – like Tony, a British regular officer who was one of the protagonists of the guerrilla war in Garfagnana and the Apuan Alps – who genuinely chose to fight in the Resistance.[56] In some cases the parachuted missions too

52 Mutilated letter to 'caro Osvaldo', 21 October 1944, Ossola zone (IG, BG, 06645).

53 See the proceedings of the conference *L'altro dopoguerra*, esp. part II, *La gente e la guerra*, ed. Paolo Sorcinelli, of the proceedings of the conference *Linea gotica 1944*. A lively description of the impressions aroused in 'G.I. Joe dell'armata americana e Tommy Smith della 8a armata brittanica' by an Italy so different from what they had imagined it to be like was given by G. Spini, 'Alleati e Resistenza', in *Fascismo e Resistenza (1936–1948). Lezioni e testimonianze*, Milan: Feltrinelli, 1962, pp. 565–76.

54 This is the reason why Bianco, for example, does not have an enthusiastic memory of the Anglo-American ex-prisoners who joined the GL formations: little fighting spirit, and moreover they preferred Switzerland, in fact. By contrast, Bianco had an excellent opinion of the behaviour of the French, who were evidently more highly motivated (Bianco, *Guerra partigiana*, p. 124).

55 See, for example, the testimony of private Edwin Hogg, protected by sharecroppers in the Prato area, in R. Absalom, 'Ex prigionieri alleati e assistenza popolare nella zona della linea gotica 1943–44', in Rochat, Santarelli e Sorcinelli, *Linea gotica 1944*, p. 471, note 28.

56 See what Battaglia writes, *Un uomo*, esp. pp. 76–8. There is a relatively large number of memoirs and reminiscences about Allied prisoners who, in various ways,

were a vehicle of mutual esteem and understanding, all the stronger for the fact that both parties were risking their lives. Bernardo recalls the case of a British mission which 'won the indisputable affection of the partisans by stating, unlike other missions, that they would remain on the spot as long as even one partisan was left alive there'. Of another mission, consisting of Americans, Bernardo writes that 'confidentially ... they let us know that the orders they had received, and agreed on with the Rome government, were not the most flattering and that difficult times lay ahead for the partisans'.[57]

Perhaps the most burning issue in relations with the Allies was the aerial bombings of the cities, which indiscriminately hit the entire population (even if it is excessive to suppose, with Alessandro Portelli, that they aimed at 'wiping out civilian society').[58] In some of the Resistance documents containing protests against the bombings, these are attributed unambiguously to the British, no mention being made of the Americans (in the memoirs, by contrast, the Americans actually have the edge on the British on this score).[59]

'Today the masses see the aerial bombing as the cruellest thing that Britain can do against them. All are of the opinion that it is no longer necessary to bomb the factories, because in consequence they would be the predestined victims, and then, why destroy all that is the patrimony of labour?' This is how a Turin Communist document puts it.[60] The British came to be deemed capable of deliberately bombing the partisans too, and not just the Garibaldini, but even the 'azzuri' (the non-Communist Blues).[61]

Whatever weight the massive and indiscriminate bombings of Turin, Milan, Naples, and finally Rome may be regarded as having had in the collapse of the Fascist regime and Italy's surrender, after 25 July, and above all after 8 September, the scenario and people's expectations had changed too greatly for the air-raids over the cities not to produce a new and disturbing reaction.

---

joined the Resistance forces. Here I shall simply record S. Hood, *Pebbles from My Skull*, London: Hutchinson, 1963; see also P. Ginsborg, *A History of Contemporary Italy: Society and Politics 1943–1988*, Harmondsworth: Penguin, 1990, pp. 2–3.

57 See Bernardo, *Il momento buono*, pp. 115, 177–8.

58 To be exact, Portelli refers to the city of Terni, where the bombardments actually did compel the population to engage in an almost total exodus. See the essay 'Assolutamente niente. L'esperienza degli sfollati a Terni', in the proceedings of the above-mentioned conference, *L'altro dopoguerra*, pp. 135–44.

59 See one of the few accurate enquiries on the subject: C. Rosati, 'La memoria dei bombardamenti. Pistoia 1943–1944', in Rochat, Santarelli and Sorcinelli, *Linea gotica 1944*, pp. 409–32.

60 'Rapporto sulla situazione nelle fabbriche', signed Giovanni, December 1943 (IG, *Archivio PCI*). The document is quoted, with the title 'Aeronautica d'Italia', in Dellavalle, *Operai*, p. 222.

61 See what Fenoglio writes, *Il partigiano Johnny*, p. 216 (English translation by Stuart Hood, *Johnny the Partisan*, London: Quartet Books, 1994).

The above-mentioned Turin Communist document reads: 'What was justified before the Armistice is today denounced by everyone and creates in their minds exasperation and hatred, a possible prey for Nazi propaganda.'[62]

And indeed, German and Fascist propaganda did not let the occasion slip, and it was necessary to set about finding a way of combating it.[63] The tone is often one of defensiveness and retort. The Salò authorities are accused of giving the air alarms deliberately late, so as not to hamper war production and 'so that the Germans don't lose time'.[64] Even the destruction of Montecassino by the Allies was blamed on the Germans.[65] Some drew attention to the launching of the V1 and V2 on London.[66] Particularly bitter was the reaction to the occasional Fascist accusation that the bombings had been requested by the anti-Fascists, and particularly the Communists.[67]

The most widely accepted argument was that, in the final analysis, the Fascists were responsible for the bombings, that they had wanted the war and had ruthlessly waged it. A recent Turin document reads: 'I knew the British because

62 For the attribution to the Fascists of responsibility for the bombing raids preceding 25 July, see Gallerano, Gli italiani in guerra, pp. 308–16.

63 A vast assortment of posters, postcards and pamphlets stigmatising the Allied bombings is contained in Fondo RSI. Italia cattolica demanded the excommunication of the bombers, in support of the thesis of the Venetian Fascist newspaper Fronte Unico, and in controversy with the bishop of Cremona, who claimed that the excommunication of non-believers was out of the question. Catholicus, Parole chiare di un cattolico 15 January 1955 (quoted in C. Scagliola, L'Italia cattolica, 'Un foglio al servizio della RSI', in Poggio, La Repubblica sociale italiana, p. 159). The bishop of Padua, monsignor Agostini, explicitly invoked 'divine punishment on the enemy bombers'. See Canfora, La sentenza, p. 79.

64 See, for example, in the northern edition of L'Unità , the articles entitled 'Lo sciopero generale a Torino contro gli industriali profittatori', 25 November 1943 and 10 July 1944, '500 workers assassinated by the Nazis (at the Dalmine plant), as a consequence in fact of their failure to sound the alarm'; a leaflet distributed by the CLN of Forlì after the 19 May 1944 air-raid ('those responsible are the Fascists'), quoted in Flamigni and Marzocchi, Resistenza in Romagna, p. 192; the article entitled 'Umanità nazifascista', in La voce della realtà. Giornale murale per la populazione a cura della XIX brigata d'assalto Garibaldi Eusebio Giambone (Piedmont), 13 August 1944 ('after all', this article explained, 'if the Fascists hadn't helped the Germans things wouldn't have come to this pass'). One Fascist reply was that it had been the Gaps who had cut the wires of the alarm system (report from Cremona by Luciano, 1 and 11 July 1944, in IG, BG, 011211).

65 See in the Catholic Il Segno and the monarchic L'Italia nuova the articles entitled 'Le opere e i giorni del nazifascismo' and 'Dopo 14 secoli', both 1 March 1944.

66 See the mural newspaper La voce della realtà, quoted above.

67 See, for example, the undated poster Al popolo di Vicenza of the local CLN on the air raids of 14 May and 18 November (IVSR, Archivio, section 1, envelope 49, CLN, Stampa non periodica). A specific accusation against the Communists is contained in a poster that was put up on the orders of Grazioli, the provincial chief of Turin, 18 April 1944 (Vaccarino, Gobetti and Gobbi, L'insurrezione di Torino, p. 209).

they were dropping bombs on us, but I had realised that it had been Fascist Italy that had asked for these bombs'.[68] Togliatti's argument was no different;[69] and a Marche Communist paper explained: 'The main culprits for so many monstrous crimes are always the Nazi beasts who bring and attract death and destruction wherever they pass'.[70]

The argument was extended, a fortiori, to the considerably more destructive bombings of the German cities, though little mention was made of them. On the one occasion that it does mention these bombings, *Il Popolo* justifies them on the principle that 'Germany will fall victim to that weapon that it has so rashly used to attack defenceless peoples'.[71]

Stances at various levels were, however, taken against the indiscriminate aerial warfare conducted by the Allies. 'But why have these English come to vex *us*, when they could quite easily go and bomb the Duce at Gargnano?', demanded a woman in an air-raid shelter in Brescia.[72] Vent is given to an elementary desire for reprisal in a censored letter: 'I know this sounds malicious, but, I swear, I'd be cruelly gleeful to hear news of the destruction of some American cities and I'm only sorry it isn't possible'.[73] A 'wave of contempt' was reported in Bologna for the bombing that came shortly after 8 September, claiming 4,000 victims and 'ably exploited by the Germans and Fascists'.[74] 'Terrorist bombings' was the

---

68 See Nelia Benissone Costa's testimony in Bruzzone and Farina, *La Resistenza taciuta*, p. 58. Benissone Costa relates how she refused a reward of 20,000 lire offered to her after the Liberation for having accompanied some British escapees from a concentration camp into Switzerland. The aerial bombings of Turin had in fact been carried out above all by the RAF.

69 See his article entitled 'Condizioni di armistizio', in *Rinascita*, July 1944, quoted in Canfara, *La sentenza*, p. 269.

70 'Bombardamenti', in *Aurora*, 2 December 1943 (quoted in G. Bertolo, 'Le Marche', in *Operai e contadini*, p. 301).

71 'Qui gladio ferit gladio perit', article that appeared in the Rome edition, 23 January 1944. See what Thomas Mann declared in April 1942 from an American radio station after a British air raid on Lubeck: 'I think of Coventry, and I have no objections to the theory according to which we shall all pay' (quoted in Canfora, *La sentenza*, p. 38).

72 And she added (8 December 1943): 'We hate the Germans because it was they who liberated the Duce'. Her husband, a functionary in the prefecture, was as a result dismissed from his job (ACS, *SPD, CR, RSI*, envelope 24, folder 170, *Pozzetti Giordano*). See the parody that the Neapolitans had made of the popular song *Oi Marì*: 'Se sente 'na sirena / Nu brivide m'afferra / Ciurcillo ha fatta a guerra / Pe' tante infamità. / Putisse ave' ragione / Ma nuie che ce trasimme? / A Roma sta a sfaccimma / Iatela a bumbardà!' 'One hears a siren / A chill seizes me / Churchill makes war / With so much infamy / Maybe he is right / But what does it have to do with us? / The scum is in Rome / Bomb over there!'

73 Letter sent from Como: 'Esame della corrispondenza censurata al 30 giugno 1944' (ACS, *SPD, CR, RSI*, envelope 9, folder 3).

74 'Fu necessario un manifestino' ('A leaflet was necessary'), explains Cri. in a report to 'cari compagni', late December 1943 (IG, *Archivio PCI*).

bald definition given to those of the Terni steelworks.[75] *Fratelli d'Italia*, organ of the Veneto CLN, ruled out the idea that the Allied actions could be considered terrorist 'in the strict sense of the word', but expressed concern that 'raids like those on Treviso and Padua wreak immense damage on the Italians, very little on the Germans, and cost a considerable amount for the Anglo-Saxons', who are clearly motivated 'by cynicism, or poor training or selfish prudence'. The main culprit, however, still remains Fascism.[76] The CLNAI itself protested against the 'morally and politically disastrous effect of the bombings carried out on urban centres of Italian cities, the military utility of which does not appear to be sufficiently well demonstrated'.[77] *La Democrazia del Lavoro* prudently remarked that some of the sufferings and destruction wrought by the Allies seemed to the Italian population 'neither necessary nor just'.[78] Since before 8 September, *L'Italia Libera* had written that it was 'an extremely sad psychological error' to believe that Italy's recovery would be accelerated by the bombings: 'A people fleeing amid the smoking ruins of a destroyed city is momentarily lost for the cause of the revolution.'[79]

By contrast, *Voce Operaia*, the newspaper of the Catholic Communists, took satisfaction in pointing out that, of all the belligerent nations, the USSR was the only one that had not bombed enemy cities.[80] The censor's remark about several letters from Reggio Emilia seems to bear this out when it complains about Allied machine-gunning of cyclists and peasants: 'All this has cooled the Anglophiles greatly. But there's little to hope for, because the upshot has been

---

75 Article entitled 'Problemi operai. L'acciaieria', in *L'Unità*, organo umbro del PC, 10 January 1944 (ACS, *SPD, CR, RSI*, envelope 9, folder 3).

76 Article entitled 'I bombardamenti aerei', in *Fratelli d'Italia*, 5 May 1944. On 7 April 1944 Treviso had suffered a massive air raid, which the newspaper described as a 'catastrofe'. The article said that 'both Badoglio and the Allies have been repeatedly informed' of the scant military results of the destruction caused.

77 See the document 'Da parte del Comitato di Liberazione per l'Alta Italia', 3 April 1944 (INSMLI, *CLNAI*, envelope 3, folder 3), brought to the notice of the Allies through the Lugano delegation (see Catalano, *Storia del CLNAI*, p. 152). The document gives the example of Padua. For analogous reactions in Genoa see A. Gibelli, *Genova operaia nella Resistenza*, Genoa: Istituto storico della Resistenza, 1968, pp. 162–3.

78 Article entitled 'Parole agli Alleati', 20 March 1944.

79 Article entitled 'Bombardamenti', August 1943. On the complaints by the members of the French Resistance against the Allied bombing see Michel, 'Gli Alleati e la Resistenza in Europa', p. 88. The fault of Vichy, certainly, wrote *Provence Libre. Organe régional des Mouvements unis de la régionale des Mouvements unis de la résistance française*, 'mais les fautes des uns ne sauraient excuser les fautes des autres', 'the faults of one does not excuse the faults of the others' (Les bombardements Anglo-Américains, 1 June 1944).

80 *Voce Operaia*, 19 November 1943, article entitled 'I cannoni del Cremlino tuonano'.

that Russophilia has grown vertiginously. We've really come to a sorry pass.'[81]

There is a clear distance between the attitudes towards the Allies examined so far, and the military, political and diplomatic relations between the states. Those who set store by the latter tended to confuse national dignity with the international position of the country, and ended up setting objectives for the Italy that had gone over to the victor's side that were excessive, to say the least. The Resistance was not always free from attitudes of this kind, which reveal considerable uncertainty as to what the post-war world order would be and the status that Italy would have in it.[82] Positions appeared that were inspired by a tardy and faint-hearted nationalism, but which nonetheless found (and were later to find) confirmation among a fair proportion of average public opinion, with the emergence of issues relating to borders, particularly the eastern ones, and to the dismantling of the Italian armed forces, the colonies, and the terms of the Armistice (and later of the peace treaty). In these positions, what was a drama of the collective conscience became the request, oscillating between superficiality, effrontery and servility, to cash in the reward for changing sides, as if Italy were able to repeat the operation that had led Restoration France to sit at the Congress of Vienna alongside the victorious powers.[83] Togliatti, a minister in the Salerno government, wrote a letter to the Premier Badoglio recommending realism and dignity, and urging him to establish relations with the Allies in the grand style, though without pursuing the myth of promotion to the status of allies, and avoiding 'querulous complaints'.[84] A more or less analogous note is

---

81 'Esame della corrispondenza censurata al 30 giugno 1944' (ACS, *SPD, CR, RSI*, envelope 9, folder 3).

82 It is enough to cite this testimony, which is if anything too drastic, by Altiero Spinelli, about the scant echo of the federalist manifesto of Ventotene: 'We had in no way foreseen that, after the end of the war, Europeans would no longer be their own masters in their quest for their future, but that, having ceased to be the centre of the world, they would be heavily conditioned by extra-European powers', Spinelli, *Io Ulisse*, pp. 311–12.

83 *L'Osservatore Romano* of 10 November 1943 reported that, on 7 November, de Gaulle, inaugurating the consultative assembly of Algiers, had complained that France had not been invited to the Moscow conference (held from 19 to 30 October 1943), and had contrasted this with what had instead occurred at the Congress of Vienna, where the new French rulers, wrote *L'Osservatore*, 'were regarded as interpreters of that part of the nation which had no responsibility for the policy of the fallen regime'. A pamphlet, 'Breve storia di cinque mesi' (which declares itself as Actionist-inspired, though independent of the party), maintained (quoting pp. 95–6 of the Vatican paper) that this 'is the situation of today's Italy, which could, *eadem ratione*, aspire to be considered an equal': provided, mind you, that it was not the king who would be sending his representatives to the peace talks.

84 Letter of 18 May 1945, marked as 'secret', and with Togliatti's marginal note 'parlatone con Badoglio' ('talk about it to Badoglio') (IG, *Archivio PCI*, 'Direzione Verbali della Delegazione PCI per l'Italia Meridionale'). Togliatti took an identical public position in the already-mentioned article 'Condizioni di armistizio' in *Rinascita* of July 1944 (quoted

struck in *Avanti!*: 'Let us not delude ourselves that we will win the hearts of the victors by obeying their every order, and that we will then save our country by wresting a few wretched concessions in the diplomatic discussions at the green tables of the conferences.'[85]

The *resistenti* could generously repeat that peoples are not responsible for the sins of their governments.[86] But peoples and governments were one thing, and states another; and if the Italian state had signed an armistice inspired by the anti-Fascist principle of unconditional surrender, this was the point of departure that had to be free of any kind of reservation (like Foa and Diena's memorandum, quoted at the beginning of this chapter). Participation in the war of liberation therefore had to be utterly alien to the 'shameful cynicism with which Mussolini demanded ten thousand dead' to wield at the peace table.[87] By contrast, according to the Roman monarchic newspaper *Italia nuova*, co-belligerence 'nullifies, by abrogating them de facto and by law, all the clauses of the armistice regarding any form of disarmament'.[88]

The first public declaration of foreign policy made by the government of national unity set up in Salerno condemned the 'invasions [the word 'aggressioni' was avoided] that had occurred in France, Greece, Yugoslavia, Russia and Albania – the last of which we wish to see independent as soon as possible'; and the wish was declared 'to adopt a policy of friendly cooperation to repair the ravages of the war and to conduct careful and rigorous investigations to identify Fascist misdeeds and acts of violence and to adopt the most severe penalties for the culprits'.[89] This is the least that could be asked in public declarations. But it is possible that the non-participation of France and Greece at the armistice negotiations with Italy fed some absurd hope in what remained of Italian diplomacy,

---

in Canfora, *La sentenza*, p. 269). In the party's national council of 7 April 1945, he would repeat that 'we could not expect that Italy would be treated as a country to be put on the same plane as the great Allied democratic countries'. Togliatti, *Opere*, vol. V, p. 115.

85 'Rivoluzione dall'alto?', Rome edition, 20 May 1944.

86 See the text of the agreement of the upper Val Maira, stipulated on 30 May 1944 between D. L. Bianco and M. Juvenal (Giovana, *Storia di una formazione partigiana*, pp. 120–2).

87 Togliatti's words in his speech at the Brancaccio theatre in Rome, 9 July 1944 (Togliatti, *Opere*, vol. V, p. 60).

88 The rumoured consignment of a third of the fleet to the USSR was considered an insult which, fortunately, London and Washington seemed to intend to spare us (leading article entitled 'Cobelligeranza', 20 March 1944).

89 The declaration of the Council of Ministers of 23 May 1944 is published among the *Fonti dell'Archivio centrale dello Stato relative al Governo di Salerno (febbraio-giugno 1944)*, in A. Placanica, ed., *1944. Salerno capitale: istituzioni e società*, Naples: Edizioni scientifiche, 1986, pp. 683–4. See the enthusiastic comment by *L'Unità*, Rome edition, 28 May 1944, article entitled 'Il governo all'opera. Energica azione contro la quinta colonna fascista. Una dichiarazione programmatica di politica estera'.

nostalgic for the old mythical card of the 'determining weight' of Italy in the contest between the powers.[90]

The declaration just quoted made no mention of the borders and colonies. The government, represented by Carlo Sforza, made its first semi-official declaration about these on 20 August 1944: independence for Ethiopia and Albania, the Dodecanese islands to Greece, the old colonies (Eritrea, Libya, Somalia) to be entrusted to an international organisation or to be left in the possession of Italy.[91] Sforza was the minister without portfolio in the government presided over by Ivanoe Bonomi, a revenant who believed that the problem could be placed once again in the context of the debates at the beginning of the century. In fact, in Bonomi's preface to an old and well-known book of his, he underlined his claim that it might be in Socialism's interest to support colonial expansion.[92]

Behind this preoccupation with the organisation of the international scene lay different convictions and intentions. It might have been a mere tactical ploy and a message sent to the other colonial countries. The memory of the old League of Nations mandates might have had something to do with it.[93] Finally, there might have been a genuine desire to give the problem of the colonial peoples an international breathing space. But this breathing space was choked in several Liberal, Christian Democrat and Action Party writings by appeals to prejudicial formulae such as 'porta aperta' ('open door'), free access to raw materials, and outlets for emigration.[94]

---

90 On the exclusion of France and Greece, and their protests, see Toscano, *Dal 25 luglio all'8 Settembre*, pp. 55–7.

91 See Kogan, *Italy and the Allies*, p. 168. As regards the Dodecanese, Sforza had done no more than recognise that Greece had a 'moral right' to it and express his hope in 'friendly negotiations' between the two countries. By contrast, Lussu and Nenni's positions were unequivocally in favour of Greece. See Sturzo, *L'Italia di domani*, pp. 5–6; E. Lussu, 'La ricostruzione dello Stato', June 1943 (*Quaderni dell'Italia Libera*, I), p. 15; P. Nenni, *Che cosa vuole il partito socialista*, speech given in Naples, 3 September 1944, p. 15.

92 See Bonomi's introduction, datelined 'Roma, giugno 1944', to the reissue of *Le vie nuove del socialismo*, which dated from 1907, entitled 'Travaglio di dottrine e di metodi in mezzo secolo di movimento socialista' (partly reproduced as an appendix to L. Cortesi, *Ivanoe Bonomi e la socialdemocrazia italiana*, Salerno: Libreria internazionale editrice 1971, from which I quote p. 131). On 20 March 1944, *La Democrazia del Lavoro*, the clandestine newspaper closest to Bonomi, had written that Italy, 'within the parameters established by the same allies after the other world war, will participate with her capacity for work in the colonising activities that will begin with the peace'. Article entitled 'Parole agli Alleati'.

93 It is well known that this was the solution then adopted for Somalia.

94 For the Action Party, see the *Progetto di piano di lavoro* of the Alta Italia executive committee, edited by the regional secretariat for Emilia and Romagna (copy in ISRT); regarding this document, of which a later edition of December 1944 is attributed to Altiero Spinelli and conserved in INSMLI, *Carte Damiani* (envelope I, folder 7, where,

The long and the short of it was that no clear-cut anti-colonialist stance was taken that sought in unilateral renunciation the only argument that could give it credibility.[95] This is probably one of the cases where the distance is greatest between the diplomatic preoccupations of the governments and, to at least some extent, the parties, cowed by the old Fascist accusations of 'rinunciatari' ('renouncers'), and the conscience of the *resistenti*. The latter, even when they did not openly proclaim anti-colonialist principles, certainly did not regard Italy's preservation of its colonies as one of the motivations for their choices. On the contrary, there is good reason to believe that most Italians, at heart, could not have cared less about the colonies, which represented, at the very most, as Parri put it, a 'question of *amour propre*'.[96]

Writing about the PCI, Ernesto Ragionieri has said: 'Nationalism, definitely a dead letter rejected in terms of dealings with the European peoples, still conserved a certain vitality when it came to colonial peoples', so that opinions about the fate of the Italian colonies were 'divided'.[97] To this frank confession it needs to be added that, in the middle ranks of the older Communist militants, anticolonialism was too deeply ingrained to be easily placed in parenthesis. The

---

however, a still later manuscript note reads 'Valiani'), see E. Rotelli, *L'avvento della regione in Italia*, Milan: Giuffrè 1967, pp. 106–8; *L'Italia Libera*, northern edition, 8 January 1945; R. Lombardi, *Il partito d'azione: cos'è e cosa vuole*, December 1943 (reprinted in May 1945). For the Italian Liberal Party: the *Orientamenti programmatici della federazione regionale lombarda*, written by Paolo Sereni. For Christian Democracy: 'Idee ricostruttive della Democrazia cristiana', in Andrea Damilano, ed., *Atti e documenti della Democrazia cristiana 1943–67*, Rome: Cinque Lune, 1968, p. 8. Sturzo had expressed the view that the pre-Fascist colonies should not be treated in the same manner as Ethiopia, and then he too looked to a general European solution of the 'problema africano' (Sturzo, *L'Italia di domani*, pp. 6–7). Among the Socialists, Nenni too used the formula 'libero accesso alle materie prime' ('free access to raw materials'). Speech in Naples, 3 September 1944. For the permanent presence of these themes among the Actionists even during the phase of the peace treaty discussion, see Tristano Codignola and Enzo Enriques Agnoletti's letter, 14 August 1946, in ISRT, *Carte Enzo Enriques Agnoloetti*.

95 Compare, for example, the request formulated by the anarchist Camillo Berneri, when the Confederación Nacional del Trabajo entered the Spanish Republican government, to give Morocco its independence immediately, without allowing itself to be held back by the colonialistic fears of France and Great Britain (article entitled 'Che fare', in *Guerre di classe*, 24 October 1936, quoted in Olivari, *L'azione politica di Camillo Berneri*, p. 224).

96 Declaration to the *New York Times*, 24 January 1946 (see Kogan, *Italy and the Allies*, p. 167). One should, however, bear in mind that, as Kogan himself points out, Parri, as prime minister, had defended the North African possessions, appealing to Italy's need for an open port to the Mediterranean.

97 See Ragionieri, *Il partito comunista*, p. 410. Ragionieri refers to the debates that followed, in the various party petitions, at the conference of the insurrectional triumvirates held in occupied Italy from 5 to 7 November 1944.

leaders, on the other hand, felt themselves bound to prudence until the USSR made its position in the matter clear (it is well known that at a certain point there was talk of a Soviet request for a mandate to govern Libya).[98] Worthy of mention, therefore, are both the clear stand taken by *Italia all'Armi!*, the newspaper printed by the PCI in Switzerland for the Italian internees, and a discussion between the leaders and workers of the Milan party membership. The Italo-Swiss paper vindicates the USSR's anti-colonialist birthright, and adds:

> Besides being a danger for peace and their aggressive tendencies, Pan-Europeanism, all pan-theories [*sic*] and racism, falsify the history of humanity by establishing fallacious proportions and perspectives of historical evolution and even falsifying the facts. It is precisely for this reason that the study of the history of the colonial countries in relation to the history of the whole of humanity has been organised on a vast scale in the USSR.[99]

The second example, recorded in a report from Milan, is the intervention of a comrade, presumably a *quadro* (senior party member), who, 'in the matter of the abandonment of the colonies', recalls: 'Socialists have always been for the autonomy of peoples. The colonial peoples have always been exploited by the capitalistic countries, with the excuse of bringing them civilisation. We need to liberate them and offer them solidarity, but we must offer solidarity above all to the USSR in its thrust for socialist construction.'

A correspondent from *Il Centro* was more clear-cut on this score, and more realistic too. He explained: 'If we declare the liberty of the peoples of our colonies we'll put England in difficulty: if instead we insist on conserving them, England will appear as a liberator.'[100]

Against the 'empty nationalist affirmation of the inviolability of borders', *L'Italia Libera* resolutely declared that it was a matter of safeguarding 'national

---

98 In an article, 'Il problema delle colonie', published in *L'Unità*, 14 September 1945, Togliatti was to put an end to a series of contradictory statements by inviting his readers 'not to weave in the shadows intrigues against the Soviet Union'. Togliatti, *Opere scelte*, pp. 397–9.

99 Article entitled 'La storia dei popoli coloniali ed oppressi, elaborati dagli scienziati sovietici', in *Italia alle Armi!* , 5 April 1945.

100 'Informazioni da Milano: riunione del settore E. I e del sottosettore E. I', December 1944 (IG, *Archivio PCI*). The document is published with the date 15 December, which is however that of the report from which part of the 'informazioni' is taken, in Secchia, *Il PCI e la guerra di liberazione*, pp. 707–9. Secchia omits the passage relating to England. The 'informazioni' are published, without any omissions, in *Le Brigate Garibaldi*, vol. III, pp. 169–80. On the end of Italian colonialism, see A. Del Boca, *Gli Italiani in Africa orientale*, vol. IV, *Nostalgia delle colonie*, Bari: Laterza, 1984. The first chapter is wisely entitled 'Una battaglia inutile'.

integrity' rather than 'territorial integrity'.[101] The aim of this affirmation was to sound the alert against German manoeuvres for the annexation of the Alto Adige, Trentino, Venezia Giulia and Istria. All the more reason why the principle should hold with respect to the Anglo-American, French and Yugoslav victors. Despite the difficulties it had to face on the eastern border, the 'patriotic war' of the Resistance was not a war over borders. In fact, implicit in the reconquest of national identity was the principle of respect for the wishes of all peoples, who must no longer be 'traded in the gaming house of diplomacy'.[102]

But what does appear, in some far-sighted writings, is a deeper concern, though one held in check by enthusiasm for the alliance between the great powers that was bringing Nazi-Fascism to its knees: namely, the concern that Europe and tomorrow's world would be governed by a directorate of victors. It was the old theme, dear to Carlo Rosselli, of the international autonomy of anti-Fascism, which was here singing a noble and anxious swansong.

Since June 1943 Emilio Lussu had considered it 'highly unlikely that the Anglo-American occupation could allow free political action'; and, providing one of the few instances of a realistic prediction of the post-war order, had added: 'The influence that the great nations will exercise over continental Europe will in itself be immense in every field: it is up to us not to contribute to making it excessive.' The Italians, in fact, would have only a 'second-class freedom, overseen and measured out'.[103] *L'Italia Libera*, repelled by a vision of the future so much at odds with the Resistance spirit, came to criticise as 'rhetorical and vague' the formulae of the Atlantic Charter, and openly denounced the risk of a new Holy Alliance being born, 'without the seriousness and concreteness that yet animated that alliance initially'.[104] A stand was taken against either direct or indirect expansionism, called *direzione politica dei popoli*, by a Christian Socialist newspaper, which sharply criticised 'the game-playing of the old, myopic and selfish diplomacy'.[105]

Avanti! reminded its readers that in 1918 the victors had not essentially interfered in the internal politics of the defeated countries. But this time, it added, when everyone had become used to seeing ideology incarnated in a state, things would be different, 'even though they're still talking in terms of

---

101 *Integrità nazionale*, Rome edition, 4 October 1943.

102 This is how the New York Italian anarchist newspaper expressed itself, with a clarity that was hard to find in Italy. 'Questioni non territoriali', in *L'Adunata dei refrattari*, 29 July 1944 (quoted in Laura Valentini's degree thesis, where another article, dated 3 February 1945, and entitled 'Confini scellerati' is also mentioned).

103 Lussu, *La ricostruzione dello Stato*, pp. 2, 9–10.

104 Article entitled 'Scopi di guerra e di pace', 7 May 1944 (edizione della Lombardia).

105 Article entitled 'Politica e Religione. Superamento', in *L'Azione dei lavoratori*, 10 February 1944.

the self-determination of peoples'.[106] The Socialists did in fact oscillate between claiming a classist and, for some of them, revolutionary autonomy and opting for the USSR. *Avanti!* wrote:

> If Italy gets bogged down in conformism, it will be an Anglo-American colony whose lot it will be to grow old on the crumbs of the decomposing capitalistic economy. If it aligns itself with the revolutionary countries, marching at the head of which is the Soviet Union, it will regain its joy in living in the creative effort of a new civilisation.[107]

The Communists had little doubt as to how things stood. Maintaining the alliance between the three 'great powers', even after the end of the war, represented for them an objective that they had stressed many times, and one that might be thwarted only by the forces of reaction.

3. THE REDISCOVERED ENEMY

Appeals to the Risorgimento, to the First World War, to traditional allies, converged in the figure of the German as enemy and invader, an invader who this time had not been stopped on the Piave but had got as far as Naples. From arrogant ally, the German became once again the 'real enemy',[1] far more 'real' than the Frenchman, the Englishman, the American, or the Russian had ever been. The negative epithets to attribute to the German enemy, elaborated by a long tradition, could lead to the German being made into an 'absolute enemy', disqualified 'in moral as in other terms' and thus transformed into an 'inhuman monster'.[2] Justifying their struggle by appealing to the great values that went beyond 'the political', the *resistenti* tended on the one hand to see their enemies as actually incarnating absolutely negative values; while on the other hand, in the values they professed, insofar as they were universal, they had the antidote

---

106 *Rivoluzione dall'alto?*, Rome edition, 20 May 1944. It is well-known that the most candid recognition of this novelty came from Stalin. See M. Djilas, *Conversations with Stalin*, Harmondsworth: Penguin, 1967. 'This war', said Stalin in April 1945, 'is not as in the past; whoever occupies a territory also imposes on it his own social system. Everyone imposes his own social system, as far as his army has power to do so; it cannot be otherwise.'

107 *Appello di Capodanno ai giovani*, Rome edition, 12 January 1944.

1 This is how, on 20 November 1943, *L'Azione* defined him in the already cited article 'Non c'è tradimento', appealing to the authority of Cesare Balbo and Pietro Colletta.

2 See Schmitt, *The Concept of the Political*, pp. 36, 37, 110, and *Theory of the Partisan*, p. 78. For a criticism of this point of view, which sees the 'political' as being the sole guarantee against the inhuman, see Chapter 3.1, above.

2

52 A CIVIL WAR

against this degeneration. It was, in reality, the enemy's ruthlessness that went well beyond 'the political', but that ruthlessness needed to be combated without being imitated.

The risk inherent in using old stereotypes against the Germans were denounced in a GL document that spoke ironically of expressions like 'barbarous invader', 'age-old enemy', 'hated German', 'sacred soil of the *patria*': these formulae, dear to 'a few more or less conscious latecomers or a few nostalgic traditionalists', merely demonstrated the 'inadequacy of stale patriotic models'.[3]

In effect, these and similar expressions often appear in the Resistance press, in unison with the widespread opinion that German barbarity was capable of every kind of excess. As early as 10 September 1943, Emanuele Artom noted in his diary: 'The Germans entered Turin yesterday and the wildest rumours are going around; that they're cutting off people's hands to take their wrist watches, et cetera.'[4]

It seems clear here that the memory of 1914–18, when in Belgium it was sworn that the Germans had cut off children's hands and when Giovanni Preziosi, who later became one of the most fanatically racist and Germanophile Fascists, spoke of the 'German octopus which stretches its tentacles and applies its suckers everywhere'.[5] The appeal to eternal German barbarity had already appeared in the period of non-belligerence,[6] and is present in the entire European Resistance.[7] In Italy, Fascist propaganda had rechristened the Germans ('tedeschi') as 'Germanici' (not Germani, so as to avoid classical reminiscences), but during the Resistance the word 'tedeschi' became dominant again, flanked by

---

3 See *L'Unificazione*, 'Edizioni del Comando delle formazioni partigiani Giustizia e Libertà, 3', 15 March 1945, p. 4. The words 'sacro suolo della Patria' ('sacred soil of the Patria'), 'l'Italia, madre comune di tutti noi', 'secolare nemico' and 'barbarie teutonica' were also used by Togliatti (in his *Appello agli italiani* of 1 April 1944 and in his speech to the Brancaccio theatre in Rome, 9 July 1944: Togliatti, *Opere*, vol. V, pp. 39, 59). 'Nemico millenario' ('Millenary enemy') appears in *Italia nuova*, the right-wing Roman clandestine newspaper, 24 January 1944.

4 Artom, *Diari*, p. 76.

5 This and other passages from *La Germania alla conquista dell'Italia*, published in 1916, are maliciously quoted in an anonymous note about Preziosi conserved in ACS, SPD, CR, RSI, envelope 24, folder 166.

6 On 14 May 1940 a Milanese informer expressed the view that the German threat to shoot ten prisoners for every paratrooper killed behind the lines 'lent itself to a revival of Barbarossa's acts of barbarity, the story of the hostages of Crema'. Quoted in M. Rigotti Colin, 'Il soldato e l'eroe nella letteratura scolastica dell'Italia liberale', in *Rivista di storia contemporanea*, XIV, 1985, p. 342, which then refers the reader to Cesare Balbo's *Storia d'Italia*.

7 'L'éternelle barbarie' is the title of an article that *Avenir. Journal provisoirement clandestin destiné aux jeunes de France*, printed in Paris, published after a German reprisal.

the still more fearsome word 'teutoni'. According to the Christian Democrats of *Il Popolo*, 'the truth of the matter is that the Germans have remained exactly as Caesar's and Tacitus's Romans had found them to be'.[8]

This recurrent theme appeals to history, and may come to refer to the race: 'The descendants of the Teutons, whom not even twenty centuries of history have tamed and refined out of their savage, primitive nature';[9] or again: 'people of Genoa, barbarous Teutonic power is falling apart'.[10]

More elaborately, a Veneto newspaper writes: 'German people, you are powerful: you crave world supremacy: you are also capable of appearing civil and kind, or shall I say courteous, but beneath the skin you are savage! For you civilisation remains a myth, and every effort you make to achieve it ends in a bestial snarl!'[11]

If here the enjoinder is not to let oneself be deceived by the good manners that the Germans are at times capable of displaying, elsewhere the discourse touches on 'the Nazi enigma, the sinister phenomenon of a learned people, turned beasts'.[12] The most elementary form of this enigma lay in the fact that the Germans, whose technical civilisation was beyond question, were devoid of a more profound human civilisation. A Friuli Communist paper says:

> It's undeniable that in Germany the inventive spirit is highly developed, that she occupies one of the foremost places in industry and the sciences; but that she has the delusion of being designated by God to dominate the whole world is ridiculous and rash. Let her keep her precious culture when this has to be paid for with blood. Let her also keep her inventions and her astounding inventions, when to make use of them it is necessary to pay in terms of the grimmest slavery … We want one thing only: Liberty … Better naked and free than snugly padded and slaves.[13]

In this text there appear echoes of the ancient chants of revolt, like that of the Lyonese *canuts*, and reminiscences of the propaganda of 1915–18 against Kaiser Wilhelm's Germany: 'The modern Huns, free of moral scruples and other technical imperfections, advance with the aid of science … The Germans don't

---

8 'Atrocità e rapine tedesche', in *Il Popolo*, Rome edition, 23 October 1943.

9 This is what is said in the cyclostyled broadsheet *San Giusto! Organo democratico per la lotta di liberazione*, August 1944.

10 Undated Ligurian leaflet of the Action Party (*Saggio bibliografico*, n. 2195).

11 *Sui monti*, broadsheet of the Verona CLN, 1 July 1944.

12 These words belong to C. Antoni, 'Il nazismo, fenomeno culturale', in *Nuova Europa* I: 2 (17 December 1944), p. 9. Antoni wrote: 'One is left terrified before the bewildering weakness of that 'spirit which Germans of other times had so assiduously cultivated'.

13 Article entitled 'La civiltà', in *L'Aratro e il Martello. Organo del Partito comunista del Friuli occidentale*, 15 October 1944.

understand that one can possess a hundred universities, a thousand laboratories, innumerable perfect factories, the most thriving commerce and still be barbarians. In 1915, shortly after Italy's entry into the war, that is how the *Rivista di patologia nervosa e mentale* ('The Review of Nervous and Mental Pathology') was speaking about the Germans.[14] A Resistance document was to set 'the most ferocious obscurantism, the scientific kind' against 'the most open enlightenment: that which draws its origins from ineluctable historical premises'.[15]

The formula 'Teutonic automaton' well sums up the loathing of the ancient barbarian and the dehumanised technician, enemies of 'Garibaldino humanism'.[16] This sensation aroused by the Germans is described by Ada Gobetti in a page of her diary that recounts how a group of women who had come to bring food and messages to their imprisoned spouses were dispersed with rifle butts: 'While they were performing the brutal act, their faces didn't even express brutality: impassive, soulless; and in their brutal deeds there was no fury, nor cruelty, but something frighteningly mechanical'.[17]

More traditional appear the appeals to the women not to fraternise with the invaders: 'Girls of Italy! Not a look, not a smile for the German occupiers. Women of Romagna! You who more than anyone hear the Prussian's insult, you who feel yourselves dishonoured by the bestial German'.[18]

By contrast, there is a biblical tone in this appeal by the Belluno Garibaldi division: 'Prune the fruit-trees, so that they bear no fruit for the invaders!'[19]

The German soldier had often aroused admiration and shyness in the shabby, uncertain Italian soldier.[20] 'They fascinated us', an RSI Fascist was to write of the Germans.[21] The *resistenti*, by contrast, felt satisfaction at having lib-

---

14 E. Lugaro, 'Pazzia d'imperatore o aberrazione nazionale?', in no. 7 (July 1915), pp. 23, 29 of the extract. Lugaro was professor of psychiatry at the University of Turin. During the Second World War Churchill often called the Germans 'Huns'.

15 'Bollettino n. 33', 8 August 1944, of the Command of the 52nd Clerici (Lombardia) brigade, named 'Fronte Popolare' in another document (IG, *BG*, 0565).

16 The expression is in 'Bollettino n. 33', cited in the preceding note. See *Le Brigate Garibaldi*, vol. II, p. 171, n. 3.

17 See Gobetti, *Diario partigiano*, p. 147 (June 1944).

18 This is how two leaflets begin: one of the Bologna 'Gruppi di difesa della donna' ('Groups for the Defence of Women'), the other of the Forlì PCI (*Saggio bibliografico*, nn. 3138 and 1890).

19 'Manifesto alla popolazione', 10 February 1945, in Bernardo, *Il momento buono*, p. 216.

20 See Collotti, *L'alleanza italo-tedesca*, p. 33.

21 Mazzantini, *A cercar la bella morte*, p. 165. A soldier training in Germany admired the 'fighting spirit' and the 'will to victory' that animated the German people but not, alas, the Italian people. Last page of Nicola Tufano's diary, 21 September 1944 (*LRSI*, p. 165).

erated themselves from any sense of inferiority. Typical of this is the pleasure they feel at seeing that also the Germans flee: this is the exhilarating essence that Revelli draws from the tale of the first day of a roundup in Valle Stura. For that matter, he had already seen them in Russia fleeing 'like hares'.[22] From some SS men who had turned tail, Chiodi captured a document with the words: 'The bandits are cowards who flee the moment they hear the word "German"'; on it he affixed the stamp of the 103rd G. Nanetti brigade and mailed it to the Turin SS Command.[23] 'Eccoli i conquistatori del mondo!' ('So these are the conquerors of the world!'), thought an anti-Fascist on seeing two Germans escaping through a train window following an air-raid alarm.[24] 'They too were scared of dying', says a partisan about the Germans engaged in a roundup.[25] Seeing the Germans escaping and being afraid of death was the confirmation that they were men like the rest of us. This was the discovery made, with a sense of liberation, by one of Sartre's characters.[26] The Germans, who were in the habit of underestimating their adversaries, were moreover the first to arouse these reactions in those capable of standing up to them.[27] And when the partisans had the cheek to break the rules of the game, the Germans grew more arrogant, and the partisans more gleeful at getting their own back.[28] The prestige of the German warlords nevertheless remained such that at times the partisans actually seemed to be awaiting from them some acknowledgment of their own military qualities. This

----

22 Revelli, *La guerra dei poveri*, pp. 202–7. In Russia Tolloy had noted the satisfaction felt by many Italians in seeing that the Germans too stole (Tarchi, *Con l'armata italiana in Russia*, p. 40).

23 Chiodi, *Banditi*, p. 126 (23 March 1945). Leonardo Cocito had recounted to Chiodi: 'We arrested two Germans who, trembling all over, showed us Communist documents'. In Innsbruck, during his imprisonment, Chiodi had noted: 'I felt joy seeing so many Germans running like madmen' (ibid., pp. 25, 81, 20 June and 23 September 1944).

24 Anonymous, 'Romagnolo', 1943–45, p. 342.

25 Claudio Locci's testimony in Portelli, *Biografia di una città*, p. 282.

26 Mathieu in *La mort dans l'âme* (English title *Iron in the Soul*). In the French underground press the Germans are often called 'Seigneurs': '14 Français fusillés pours un Officier Nazi envoyé "ad patre" [*sic*]. Il appartenait il est vrai à la caste des Seigneurs' (L'Unité de la Sarthe. Organe régional du Parti communiste français: half-title of the September 1941 number).

27 Hillgruber speaks of the 'continuity in error' encountered in the Germans. He himself, however, when dealing with the Norwegian resistance to the invasion in April 1940, described it not only as 'unexpected' but also as 'stubbornness'. A. Hillgruber, *Hitlers Strategie. Politik und Kriegführung 1940–1941*, Munich: Bernard & Graefe, 1965, and *Der Zweite Weltkrieg 1939–1945*, Stuttgart–Berlin: Kohlhammer, 1982.

28 See the German consul Moellhausen's testimony: the partisans' presence was 'anomalous … an affair that regarded Wolff and the SS' (Bocca, *La Repubblica di Mussolini*, pp. 104–5). Wolff was commander of the SS in Italy.

is what was written about the Garibaldi commander Rocca, who negotiated an exchange of hostages with the Germans: 'He was received and treated with the greatest respect and paid the honours due to a military chief, a recognition of our valour.'[29] Another Garibaldi commander recalled with satisfaction that some German divisions preferred to surrender (a rare event) to the partisans rather than to the Americans.[30]

Beppe Fenoglio has a sure intuition of these contradictory sentiments when he describes the impression aroused in the people of a village by the sight of a German captured by partisans: 'They kept silent, beginning to explain to themselves the mystery of 8 September, when a dozen of these men had subdued a barracks with entire regiments of ours in them.' This prisoner is admired, particularly by the women, for his patently racial attributes: tall, blond, extremely strong, golden-skinned. And one partisan says to another: 'God, Ivan, doesn't it seem quite something to you that one of Hitler's men, from the army that brought France and Poland and half the world to its knees, is there washing plates for us poor down-at-heel Italian partisans?' In the end the prisoner will be killed by a little partisan, just so that the latter can free himself of his angry sense of inferiority – while a similar sense of liberation had been produced in other partisans by seeing how the Germans' arrogance was mixed with opportunism towards those who at that moment had the upper hand.[31] Thus there are partisans who gleefully recall how many German prisoners were glad to be packed off to Switzerland in their underpants.[32]

But the more the Germans shrunk to human size, even to the lowest scale, the more they aroused the problem of their capacity for redemption. Here it is hard to distinguish the conditioning effect of the victors' perspectives as to what lay in store for Germany. To what degree did one's pragmatic or purely ideological stances affect the attitudes aimed at instilling one's values even into the enemy?

The conviction was widespread among the *resistenti* that Germany should be punished more severely than Italy because its crimes were greater and its insistence in pursuing them more stubborn. A Communist worker says this, for example: 'It is natural that the greatest weight of the defeat of the Fascists will press most heavily on the Fascist peoples. Germany will suffer the greatest

29 Article entitled 'Cambio d'ostaggi', in *Voce nostra*, organ of the 9th Garibaldi division A. Imerito (Piedmont), 18 March 1945.

30 Lazagna, *Ponte rotto*, p. 283.

31 Fenoglio, *Golia*, pp. 250–4. See what padre Gemelli wrote about the treatment of prisoners in the 1915–18 war: 'When they take a prisoner, our soldiers look at him as a child looks at a toy he's never seen before, and soon they become friends with a cigarette or a piece of bread' (Gemelli, *Il nostro soldato*, p. 66).

32 N. Chiovini and A. Mignemi, 'Il 44 sulle sponde del Lago Maggiore', in *Novara. Notiziario economic* 2 (1987), p. 47.

weight. It is natural that Germany will be dismembered even if this goes against the Marxist principle of nationalisation.'[33]

Interlaced with this kind of attitude was the widespread conviction that one of the aims of the struggle was to sweeten, by comparison, the treatment reserved for Italy. This expectation of greater severity for Germany was at times expressed in crudely self-gratifying formulae. For example, the Democratic Labour newspaper *Azione democratica* recognised that, among the German troops, there were 'many decent Germans who are in the very same condition that so many decent Italians were in before 25 July. But today all of them – with their acquiescence and their herd-spirit (which is much stronger than in the Italians) – are behaving and have to be considered as Nazis. And treated as such.'[34]

But there was a strong desire that Germany too would manage to throw off the yoke before the final catastrophe, above all because this would bring the war to a swift conclusion, then because many felt that the distinction between people and regime, invoked for the Italians, could not be denied a priori to the Germans, and lastly out of a genuine repugnance to admitting that there was such a thing as an irremediably infected and damned people. This repugnance could even take the form of the aberrant paradox that appears in *La Voce del Popolo*, the newspaper of the Italian Labour Party. As a corollary of the way the Yalta Conference had been criticised for its incapacity to ensure a real recovery for Germany, the paper wrote that if the German people really could not be re-taught the meaning of liberty, it would constitute a danger by its very existence and 'the United Nations would be duty-bound to exterminate it, in the same way that the Germans have tried to do with the Jews – naturally without their senseless acts of cruelty, but also without any senseless pietism.'[35] Another smaller, extreme left-wing formation, the 'Movimento comunista d'Italia', expressed the more humane wish that the German people would know how to liberate themselves from Nazism, and warned: 'Let it be clear that we are fighting against Nazism and not against the Germans and that we are not prepared to play the game of a new anti-German nationalism.'[36]

A typical kind of argument is to be found in *La Riscossa Italiana*, the Piedmontese CLN broadsheet:

> The Italian people do not intend to pour on the German people that stream of hate and that river of insults which Fascism, in the anger generated by its moral and material inferiority, habitually directed against the peoples of the united nations:

---

33 'Relazione da Milano', on a meeting of the 4th sector, 14 April 1945 (*Le Brigate Garibaldi*, vol. III, p. 621).

34 Article entitled 'Libere Opinioni', 31 January 1944.

35 Article entitled 'La Conference di Crimea', in *La Voce del Popolo*, 15 March 1945.

36 *Bandiera Rossa*, 5 October 1943, 'La funzione dell'URSS nel conflitto mondiale', and 22 October 1943, 'Anche Benedetto Croce per la Repubblica?'

Anglo-Saxons and Russians. We know the exceptional contribution which at other times Germany too has been capable of giving to the cause of civilisation, but its people must today cure themselves [a metaphor widely used about the Germans] of the turbid and fearsome ideologies which, in the name of militarism, pan-Germanism, and racism, have perverted it, making it the blind instrument of f erocious oppression.[37]

The Germany of Goethe, Schiller and Kant was also appealed to by *Il Risorgimento Liberale*,[38] which was not alone in invoking the great spirits of German civilisation, and the glorious episodes of German history. Thus a Communist poster printed in the province of Bergamo at the end of 1943 urged the German people to 'rediscover itself and those forces that saved it under Frederick the Great, that made it rise up against Napoleon, that have always fought against the Hohenzollerns, the Kruppses, the Trendelenburgs, the Bosches and partners, those forces that have always wanted a Germany that is truly united, free, independent, loved and respected by all the peoples of the earth'.

The same poster recalled that in 1918 Germany had been rescued from total ruin by a revolution which had unfortunately been betrayed – whence Nazism.[39] Among the last words of Leone Ginzburg, a prisoner of the Germans, are those 'about the need after the war to become missionaries of civilisation in Germany'.[40]

The difficulty in making a clear-cut distinction between Nazis and Germans, resisting the idea that the former were but the expression of the deep essence of the latter, is revealed by the fact that some posters and appeals are directed against the 'Nazi Germans', and others simply against the Germans. The different treatment often given to prisoners who were soldiers of the Wehrmacht on the one hand and the SS and other explicitly Nazi corps on the other was a concrete way in which the distinction between people and regime sought to gain ground. In a zone where instructions were that all German prisoners were to be treated indiscriminately according to the laws of war, a squad handed seven prisoners over to the Allies. But two, when questioned, confirmed that they were Nazis and war volunteers. On hearing this declaration the partisans immediately executed the two enemies, thereby retrieving two automatic pistols.[41]

---

37 Leading article entitled 'Riscossa', in *La Riscossa Italiana*, 20 October 1943.

38 Leading article entitled 'Il Partito liberale italiano ai fratelli dell'Italia occupata', July 1944 (Piedmont edition).

39 The title of the poster was 'L' Armata Rossa spezza ogni resistenza: la Germania è sconfitta' ('The Red Army breaks all resistance: Germany is defeated'). IG, *Archivio PCI*.

40 Letter written by Manlio Rossi-Doria to Leone's sister, Marussa, and published by Parri with the title 'Ricordo di Leone Ginzburg', in *L'Astrolabio*, 14 March 1977, pp. 22–5.

41 See the order given on 21 September 1944 by the Command of the 28th Mario

Opinions differed about the possibility that the German generals might attempt a coup like the successful one conducted on 25 July by their Italian colleagues, but mostly tended to be sceptical.[42] For example, not long before the attempt on Hitler's life of 20 July 1944, the Liberal paper *Risorgimento Liberale* wrote:

> The generals feel that their destiny is united with that of the Nazis, despite all the repugnance that the best of them may feel, despite all their feelings of repentance. Together, Hitlerian chiefs and generals will be called before the judgment of the world: one might just as well, therefore, think the chiefs of the German general staffs, carry on fighting to the end.[43]

This prediction was essentially correct and was founded on the belief that in the psychology of the German people there existed 'the suicide point', which was in fact close at hand.[44]

These opinions appeared to be called into question again by the episode of 20 July 1944. The Communist reactions include both a typical and a specific case in point. In their public stances the Communists, just like the other parties, could only approve the coup, albeit failed. Evidence of this is clear, above all initially. A Garibaldi proclamation gives this assurance: 'The German people too are stirring against Hitler and the Nazi scoundrels. The German generals … wanted to show the world and above all their people that the Nazi war is definitively lost. With the attempt, the soldiers and the German people are in open rebellion.'[45]

A headline on the front page of *L'Unità* reads: 'After the blows dealt by the Red Army and the Allied Armies, pressed by all the peoples fighting for their liberty, the internal German front is collapsing.'[46] On 7 August the tone is naturally more muted: 'The colonel's bomb was not the desperate gesture of a

---

Gordini brigade (ISRR, 2, LXXIII, i., 23), and the report on the 'attività svolta dalla compagnia effettiva al distaccamento della bassa romagna', ('activity engaged in by the company in withdrawing from the lower region of Romagna'), undated (ISRR, 2, CVI, d. 7).

42 On the repercussions of 25 July on the Germans and on the scant chance of analogous events occurring in Germany, see Collotti, *L'amministrazione tedesca*, pp. 44–7.

43 *Risorgimento Liberale*, Rome, 15 March 1944, article entitled 'Perché perderanno'.

44 Ibid., 15 April 1944, 'Il punto del suicidio'. It seems one should connect to this observation the fact that, of the thirty-one letters of Germans included in *LRE*, only one, written by the Communist Cato Bontjes Van Beek, contains an explicit and impassioned profession of love for Germany (p. 379). In the others there are no expressions such as 'long live Germany' or 'long live free Germany'.

45 Proclamation by the Command of the 40th Garibaldi Matteotti (Lombardia) brigade, 22 July 1944 (IG, BG, 0515).

46 *L'Unità*, northern edition, 25 July 1944.

small clique, but the expression of revolt that is rife in the German army.'[47] The Communist paper establishes a link, clearly dear to its heart, between a possible internal change in Germany and the invitation to surrender formulated by 'as many as seventeen of the thirty generals taken prisoner this summer on the eastern front'.[48] An explanation of events expressed in doctrinaire terms, rare in the public declarations of the Resistance, is given instead by a Garibaldi political commissar: 'As the Italian capitalistic bourgeoisie, with the occupation of Sicily, and thus the appearance of certain defeat, resolved to liquidate Fascism, since the Fascist government or committee of capitalist bourgeois interests no longer responded to their interests, so in Germany Hitler and Nazism no longer respond to national and capitalistic bourgeois interests.'

We, the commissar concluded, using our method and our philosophy, 'which is that of historical and dialectical materialism', must prove capable of interpreting 'all events and consequently of drawing our directives and marching orders towards our boundless social goals'.[49]

That the two peoples' fates, common in the tragedy that had led them to hate one another, should be common too in their recovery, is the animating spirit of a Communist-inspired article or manifesto, written in the Bergamo zone at the end of 1943: 'Only through the common struggle against Nazism and Fascism can the Italian and German peoples save their nations and once again become brothers.'[50] The extreme expression of this wish is that the two peoples would find fraternity in socialism, for which Germany was regarded as being fully ripe.[51]

L'Italia Libera wrote: 'The heavy bombings have then made tens of millions of people homeless, creating a proletarianisation still more frightening than that produced in its time by inflation.'[52] More realistically, Togliatti was to express concern about the absence of the German working class 'in the front for the struggle for liberation'.[53] A reminder of the sufferings and 'innocent blood' of 'our Catholic brothers of the other invaded lands' and 'the German Catholics themselves, oppressed by Hitlerian persecution' and by 'pagan and

---

47 *L'Unità*, August 1944, leading article entitled 'L' Armata Rossa alle porte della Germania'.

48 Ibid. The allusion refers in particular to Marshal von Paulus, the defeated commander-in-chief at Stalingrad.

49 This is what Ario wrote, in the name of the Command of the 40th Garibaldi-Matteotii brigade, 'ai compagni della Brigata', 21 July 1944 (IG, *BG*, 0512).

50 At the foot of the typescript, conserved in IG, *Archivio PCI*, is this note: 'Di L. Da tradurre in tedesco e stampare, Può andare?' ('By L. To translate into German and print? Is it OK?').

51 See, for example, in *Avanti!*, Rome edition, 30 December 1944, the article entitled 'Il discorso di Smuts e il federalismo europeo'.

52 'La situazione interna tedesca', Lombardy edition, 9 June 1944.

53 Speech to the PCI national council, 7 April 1945 (Togliatti, *Opere*, vol. V, p. 132).

THE PATRIOTIC WAR 261

racist' Nazism, is contained in an issue of the Catholic-Communist paper *Voce Operaia*.[54]

The way in which the soldiers of the Social Republic – a unit stationed in Turin – reacted to the assassination attempt on Hitler is described cautiously, but transparently enough, in a Fascist report:

> The soldiers are astonished at what has happened in Germany. They claim that now the Germans won't be able to proclaim themselves paladins of national integrity since what happened in Italy on 25 July was about to happen in their nation as well … They also add that the fact of having actually wanted to make an attempt on the very life of the Head of State demonstrates that in Germany hostility to the Führer, though not represented by wide strata of the population, is characterised by a more intense hatred. (In Italy on 25 July this had not happened to Mussolini.) As regards the 'failure' of the attempt, the soldiers fear a certain indifference, which cannot be due to ill-concealed disappointment. Their way of seeing and judging things has vaster horizons: all the present heads of the warring nations, they say, should be outlawed and eliminated from the political scene (and not only the political one …) insofar as they are all responsible, to a greater or lesser extent, for this terrible and inhuman conflict, which, degenerating into vendettas and reprisals, is increasing still further death and grief in the families.[55]

The stances taken towards the German people, also present in other European Resistance movements,[56] had to reckon with the reality of the repression exercised by the Germans as occupiers, and with the hatred aroused by their uniforms and the way they wore them, for the symbols of their power, for the sound of their incomprehensible language, for their whole way of being and behaving in Italy and among other men.

The Resistance therefore found itself facing – as had already happened in the war, but now more starkly – the problem of how vehemently one should hate the enemy. For some there was no problem, just an uncontrollable impulse; and it is understandable why testimonies in this regard are mainly offered by death-camp survivors: 'There was such hate in me, I think it was hate that made me

---

54 'Per l'indipendenza nazionale, per la società nuova, guerra alla germania nazista!', in *Voce Operaia*, 22 October 1943.

55 'Relazione P. del mese luglio 1944. XXII' of the Distretto di Torino, Ufficio assistenza e propaganda (ACS, *SPD, CR, RSI*, envelope folder 165, Tombari Alberto).

56 See for example, for France, the presentation, September–October 1940, of *La Révolution française. Bulletin pour un mouvement national révolutionnnaire français*: 'It is not to our advantage to fall into a vengeful and sterile Germanophobia'; for Holland, the letter with which a Communist sentenced to death enjoins his son: 'do not grow up blindly hating the German people'. Gau Postma to his wife Nel, 24 July 1944, in *LRE*, p. 694.

survive'; 'And all this time there was a great hatred, an enormous, terrible hatred of the Germans'.[57] Those who were prepared to grant that not all Germans were the same called the worst of them 'German Germans'.[58] When on 18 April 1945 Ada Gobetti met up with a German armed to the teeth and scared out of his wits, she noted: 'Despite my inveterate sympathy for the defeated, I just couldn't feel pity for him.'[59]

Revelli has illustrated the difference he sensed between hating the enemy, which he explained somehow in terms of a 'natural' relationship, and fighting him with cold professionalism. The difference, that is, between the 'individually motivated warrior', as the *resistente* prided himself on being, and the bureaucratic soldier of 'rational' modern armies.[60] When, on the other side of the Alpine front, he met up with the first American units, Revelli noted:

> I get the impression that the Americans can't get around to hating the Germans. In the German they see the soldier, not the beast. You'd think they were ignorant of the concentration camps, the reprisals, the destruction that they're encountering as they advance. Theirs is a regular war, waged with a superiority of equipment, armaments, which are formidable. Their country is far away, out of harm's way, and not being carpet-bombed. At times it almost seems as if they don't know what they're fighting for. Perhaps they're unable to grasp the reasons for the terror and misery surrounding them.[61]

The Americans thus found it hard to understand how such a high degree of rationality and ferocity coexisted in the German army. And, by recalling the carpet-bombing, of which the German cities were victims, Revelli is suggesting, unwittingly perhaps, a link between the two 'rational' armies, precisely on the plane of ruthlessness. There was in turn an awareness of the risks involved in hatred. From Radio Bari, 'Astolfo' had urged that children be taught to

---

57 Testimonies by Giovanni Aliberti, a Turin doctor and member of GL, and Augusto Cognasso, a Turin student and Actionist, in Bravo and Jalla, *La vita offesa*, pp. 262, 378.

58 Testimonies by Natalina Bianca Giai (Pasqualina), from Susa, in ibid., p. 166. On the 'hostile and contemptuous' attitudes, save for 'rare exceptions', of the German population towards the Italian military internees, see Rochat, *Memorialistica e storiografia sull'internamento*, pp. 46, 65.

59 Gobetti, *Diario partigiano*, p. 348.

60 On this definition see Weber, *Economia e società*, vol. I, p. 221.

61 Revelli, *La guerra dei poveri*, pp. 387–8, under the date 16 January 1945. See General Patton, who, on the eve of the Normandy landings, explained to his collaborators that the problem of Fascism and Democracy 'was no more important than the electoral battles periodically fought by Republicans and Democrats in the United States' (quoted in Michel, *The Shadow War*, p. 8).

hate the Germans; and one of the minor Roman papers replied to him: 'Yes, we are fighting the Germans and holding them up as enemies even to children; but why instil hatred into those young hearts?'[62] Though not without its share of apocalyptic tones and reminiscence of Churchillian 'tears and blood', an Action Party pamphlet warned: 'The war of liberation is not inextinguishable hatred of the German people, but of the diabolical power which today it incarnates.'[63]

It is precisely the elements of the civil and ideological war, which gave birth to the ruthlessness of the struggle, that acted as a counterweight to the all-absorbing aversion to the German, as such. When at Carigno, on 7 September 1944, Pietro Mancuso, 'born in Palermo on 14 July 1920, chemist, resident in Milan', was made by the Germans to mount the scaffold, he shouted: 'Long live Italy and long live a free Germany!' The officer asked him: 'Long live a free Germany?' – 'Yes, long live a free Germany...' was the reply.[64] Before being shot by the Germans, the French partisan Boris Vildé wrote: 'My death must not provide sustenance for hatred of Germany.' One of 'very few' such cases, Henri Michel noted.[65] In the letters written by Italian *resistenti* awaiting execution, explicit expressions of this kind are equally rare and should be distinguished from enjoinders to forgiveness with a more universal meaning. Equally rare, however, are incitements to hate the German people. When, during the struggle, Ada Gobetti, who, as we have seen, could not bring herself to feel sympathy for the vanquished Germans, had entered a trattoria where some German soldiers were having a moment's break, she had described them as

> good-looking blond, cheerful lads. Stripped of their uniforms, of the hated symbols, in what way were they any different from our lads? I thought that if one of them had been in the place of young Davide [a dead partisan, whose corpse she had seen shortly before] I would have felt the same feeling of rebellion and the same pain.

She then recalled an old woman from Meana, with a son on the African front, who prayed 'for him and for all of them. For all of them. For the *others* too.' Again, Ada Gobetti seemed to discern with anxiety, and relief, human sentiments – albeit fleeing – in the German automatons. Thus, she recorded these words uttered by a German who was participating in the burning of a village: 'Cursed war! I have children too. And I've been fighting in this war for four years. But I hate this kind of thing. It's those from HQ who order them. They're

---

62 Article entitled 'Odio', in *L'Italiano. Organo del Partito d'unione*, 26 February 1944.

63 *La guerra di liberazione*, December 1943, p. 4.

64 'Promemoria dei fatti del 7 settembre 1944', written by the doctor, the prefectorial commissar and the parish priest the day after the execution, in Chiodi, *Banditi*, p. 153.

65 Michel, *The Shadow War*, p. 247.

bad, bad.' But a little later, 'on his face the cold, impassive, lifeless mask had descended again'.[66]

Indeed, only rarely did the Germans open up, and when they did only rarely was this taken as being other than the 'effeminate gracefulness of the occupiers'. So it is worth recalling the curious romantic tone with which the provincial police of Belluno addressed the partisans to persuade them to 'stop their restless roaming and re-enter the orbit of ordinary life'.[67]

Between *pietà l'è morta* (pity the dead), which is to be taken not only as a tragic statement of fact but as an imperative for intransigence, and recognising in the German enemy a human object of pity, there is thus a vast range of feelings and behaviour. Often the choices resulting from them are hard, for fear of the consequences they might have on other men. A report of the 3rd Garibaldi brigade fighting in the area between Piombino and Pisa states that the shooting of three German prisoners was demanded by some partisans, 'particularly the foreigners' (in the band there were Russians, Ukrainians, Mongols, and two Americans; and the fact that it was the 'foreigners' who were the most severe is stressed with evident satisfaction); but,

> having ascertained that the two Germans are Austrian and the other can prove his anti-Nazi sentiments, we have decided not to grant the request. We are explaining things in order to clarify the thinking behind our decision: the partisans are judges not murderers. They do not use the vile methods of the enemy. The decision is approved by a large majority.[68]

But another Tuscan report tells of a partisan patrol that captured two Germans 'who on being disarmed were released because of their insistence on joining the partisans, thereby demonstrating that they were anti-Nazi in sympathy; instead, as soon as they'd been freed they told the German command about the incident'.[69] It was, then, a real problem to ensure that one ran no risks from having too excessive a humanitarian spirit.

The invitation to go over to the just side while there was still time became particularly dramatic in this context. Witness the emphasis with which a minor

---

66 Gobetti, *Diario partigiano*, pp. 116 (late March 1944) and 182 (7 August 1944).

67 Appeal by the German Command (December 1944), in ISBR, 1943–1945. *Occupazione e Resistenza in provincia di Belluno. I documenti*, Belluno 1988, p. 115. The expression about the *garbo femmineo* ('effeminate grace') that the Germans displayed in Venice (reminiscent of *Death in Venice*?) is in an appeal by the 'Comitato d'azione', undated (typescript in IVSR, *Stampa antifascista*).

68 The report, dated 16 June (but in fact July) 1944, is signed by the commissar and the political vice-commissar (IG, *BG*, 011699).

69 'Relazione sulla formazione Busticchini fatta dal commissario politico Nello Ghilardetti' (ISRT, *Fondo Salvadori – PCI Castelfiorentino*, insert 59).

Roman newspaper of that part of the left which did not identify itself with the CLN, addressed an essay as 'A Word to a German Soldier'). He was threatened with terrible reprisals, which could only be avoided by going over outright to the side of the workers and the revolution. At the same time, it is boasted that no attempt is being made to instil hatred for the German as such, but the German soldier is warned that, if he does not get a move on, something worse than defeat will befall him – namely, 'being excluded for ever from the category of civil beings. And I will no longer be able to save you.'[70]

Desertion was therefore the main highway offered to the Germans as proof of their desire for salvation, the only one that could concretely act as a counterweight to the hatred they incurred. These enjoinders to desert not only express the obvious desire to weaken the enemy (and here hope far outdistanced reality), but appear to be motivated by confidence that the deserter, like the prisoner, could be won over to one's own side. This confidence is unknown in 'normal' warfare, where prisoners are, indeed, protected by international conventions against forced enlistment into the ranks of those who have captured them. By contrast, the civil war nature of the struggle, extended to the Germans as well insofar as they were Nazis, made for a different kind of attitude aimed at breaching one of the cardinal points of German military ethics, whereby it would have seemed inconceivable that German honour, in those circumstances, could be saved only by desertion and going over to the enemy.[71]

This complex attitude to the Germans appears in many documents. Emblematic is the case, be it real or invented, mentioned in a Communist report: 'In a large Turin factory, while the workers were raising funds in favour of the partisans, they were surprised by German soldiers. Four German soldiers gave ten lire each to the fundraisers.'[72]

Expectations that a crack would appear in the German army were greater in the weeks immediately following 8 September, when the hope was cherished that the mess Italy was in might have repercussions on the German monolith.[73] Such hopes grew slimmer in the difficult central months of the struggle, though appeals to desertion never ceased, nor appeals to make the most of whatever

---

70 *Il Partigiano*, 9 February 1944, which contains, alongside the title, 'When it comes to liberty, one mustn't wait, one must take: Blanqui'.

71 The German translator of *Se questo è un uomo*, Heinz Riedt, fought in Veneto with the GL formations. After the war 'his political past was held against him', even if 'nobody ever told him in so many words' (Levi, *The Drowned and the Saved*, London: Abacus, 1989), p. 140.

72 'Informazioni dal Piemonte', referring to September 1943. The episode is also recounted in another report of the same month, sent by Giovanni (IG, *Archivio PCI*).

73 See Zangrandi, *1943*, p. 20. After 25 July in Rome word spread that Hitler had committed suicide. See the telegram to the *questori* by Senise, the head of the police force, 28 July 1943, quoted in various authors, *L'Italia dei quarantacinque giorni*, p. 195.

desertions occurred. They were to flourish again when it was clear that things were heading for the final breakup and the Germans themselves on various occasions appeared less determined.[74] Thus, the September 1943 issue of *Informazioni da Piemonte*, mentioned earlier, states:

> In Turin and the region the German soldiers are hostile to the SS and are tired of and demoralised by the war. Many of them have looked for civilian clothes in order to desert. Especially in the factories, the German soldiers are trying to chum up with the workers ... While taking care about what might be provocative in this, we must set about exploiting this state of affairs.

The Rome edition of *Avanti!* assured its readers that German deserters were going over to the partisans,[75] while the fact that two prisoners were a bricklayer and a farmhand who decided to fight with the partisans was stressed, by way of guarantee, in a Garibaldi document.[76] Gorrieri recalls that in the Republic of Montefiorino there were German deserters in a battalion formed by men of various nationalities.[77] On 28 May 1944 the Rome edition of *L'Unità* announced that in the Magliano zone (where the German army was in retreat) '120 German soldiers are going over to the partisans'. Generally, announcements of this sort that appear in the underground press are inflated; more sober and accurate are the facts given by the documents of the formations. The creation, or attempted creation, of units formed exclusively by German deserters should be regarded as borderline cases. A Communist document from Friuli notes:

> A German battalion is being formed with Austrians and Germans who have been in our Garibaldi formations for some time and have proved to be reliable elements. Once it has formed and got its bearings, the battalion will be sent into Austrian territory to act and to start a partisan movement. A small propaganda section will stay behind in the division's zone to work on German soldiers.[78]

---

74 Reports of this kind are contained, for example, in a 'highly confidential and secret' communication, signed Simon, 13 November 1944, of the inspectorate for the 1st Ligurian zone to the Command of the 2nd Garibaldi Division 'Felice Cascione' (INSMLI, *Brigate Garibaldi*, envelope 3, folder 4, subfolder 2); in a report, 20 January 1945, by a prisoner, Giglioli, who had escaped from the Germans during a roundup in the province of Piacenza (IG, *BG, Emilia-Romagna*, G.IV.2.6); in a report for Switzerland, signed Ciro, 17 February 1945, by the Comando Garibaldino della Valsesia, Ossola, Cusio, Verbano (IG, *Archivio PCI*).

75 Article entitled 'La lotta partigiana in Piemonte', 12 January 1944.

76 Report by Andrea to 'dear comrades', 14 March 1944, Parma area (IG, *BG, Emilia-Romagna*, G.IV.2.2).

77 Gorrieri, *La Repubblica di Montefiorino*, p. 352.

78 'Relazione su un'ispezione in Friuli dal 24 ottobre all'11 novembre 1944', undated (*Le Brigate Garibaldi*, vol. II, p. 565). On 24 November of the same year an order of the

Recurrent mention is made of the Austrians as being the most ready to desert, and in any case, save some contrary indications,[79] the most human among the enemy. This came to be writ large in people's memories. Many years later, Silvio Rivoir, who was imprisoned in the 'Carceri Nuove' of Turin along with Emanuele Artom, recounted how his comrade and a German sentry 'spoke about the important things in life, of the moral and human motives that must inspire us; Artom quoted classical authors to give force to his argument and the other understood and was seen to be deeply upset'.[80] Though requested to do so, a GL commander of the Grappa zone took his time over enlisting the five Austrians present among six prisoners in his hands. Recaptured during a roundup, and denounced by the sixth, a 'Prussian', the five were hanged, and the commander was seized by remorse for having distrusted them.[81] On 23 November 1943, the Rome edition of Risorgimento Liberale had believed that it could announce that 'the Austrian units stationed in the vicinity of Rome have been disarmed. For some time now German soldiers of different ranks, and Austrians in particular, have been buying civilian clothing at any price so as to be able to flee at the opportune moment.'

The February 1944, 'Directives for the armed struggle' of the military Command for Northern Italy recommended directing propaganda for the German troops, which 'has already been successfully tried out here and there', above all at the Austrians, Czechs, Poles, and so on.[82] 'The German army is dis-integrating' ran the title of an article in Italia Libera reporting the desertion above all of Bohemians, for instance of two hundred of them above Arona.[83] Some hundred Volksdeutschen (ethnic German) deserters are mentioned in a Garibaldi report from the Bibbona area in Tuscany.[84] These last examples already bring us onto different ground: the urging of those who had, it was generously assumed, been press-ganged into the oppressor's army to have done with it.[85] As

---

day of the Slovene liberation army announced its decision to create an Austrian battalion (see Etnasi, La Resistenza in Europa, I, p. 45.

79 See Chiodi, Banditi, p. 181.

80 See Artom, Diari, p. 181.

81 Manuscript of the unpublished diary of G. Manni.

82 See paragraph 18 of the 'Direttive', in Atti CVL, Appendix I, document P, p. 558.

83 Northern edition, 22 July 1944. On the Czechs see P. De Lazzari, La resistenza cecoslovacca (1938–1945), Rome: Napoleone, 1977.

84 See the 'Relazione', undated but post-Liberation, of the 7th detachment, 1st section, of the 3rd Garibaldi brigade (IG, Archivio PCI).

85 'Incorporés de force' is the name given to Alsations, Lorrainers and Luxembourgers enlisted in the German armed forces. See A. Wahl, 'L'incorporé de force d'Alsace-Moselle, analyse de récits de guerre', and G. Trausch, 'Le long combat des enrolés de force luxembougeois', in Centre de Recherche Histoire et Civilisation de l'Université de Metz, La mémoire de la seconde guerre mondiale, Metz: Centre de recherche Histoire et civilisation de l'Université de Metz, 1984, pp. 227–42, 181–99.

for the Germans as such, it is worth recalling the existence in Carnia of a battalion called 'Fries Deutschland'[86] and of the newspaper *Germania Libera*,[87] as well as a 'German Committee for National Liberation' whose existence in Milan was reported at the eleventh hour by the Information Service.[88]

---

86 See the mention made of it in the description in the *Fondo ANPI* at the IRSFVG (*Guida agli archivi della Resistenza*, p. 542).

87 See *Saggio bibliografico*, n. 4539. See also, in the same text, the numerous appeals, bilingual or in German, registered in the index of the categories, under the entry *Wehrmacht e SS*. Compare with the titles of the newspapers in German that figure in the already cited *Catalogue des périodiques clandestins: Deutsche Freiheit, Freies Deutschland, Volk und Vaterland*, and others.

88 See Deakin, *The Brutal Friendship*, p. 720. On German deserters, labelled in the death camps with a red star, and the unsatisfactory state of the studies regarding them, see G. Schreiber, 'La linea gotica nella strategia tedesca: obiettivi politici e compiti militari', in Rochat, Santarelli and Sorcinelli, *Linea gotica 1944*, pp. 25–67. On the repression practised by the German war tribunals, 'which passed more than fifty thousand death sentences on their own soldiers: a figure a hundred times higher than any other army in the Second World War (except the Red Army)', see L. Klinkhammer, 'Le strategie tedesche di occupazione e la populazione civile', in M. Legnani and F. Vendramini, eds, *Guerra, guerra di liberazione, guerra civile*, Introduction by G. Quazza, Milan: Franco Angeli, 1990, p. 115. These are the proceedings of the Belluno conference of 27–29 October 1988.

CHAPTER 5

The Civil War

1. A CONTROVERSIAL DEFINITION

The interpretation of the struggle between the Resistance and the Italian Social Republic as a civil war has, until very recently at least, met with hostility and reticence on the part of the anti-Fascists – so much so that the expression has come to be used almost exclusively by the defeated Fascists, who have provocatively waved it in the face of the victors.[1] The anti-Fascists' diffidence has consequently grown, fed by the fear that talk of civil war leads to the two warring sides being confused with each other and put on a par under a common condemnation or absolution.[2] In fact, never so much as in civil war, which Concetto Marchesi

---

1 On all counts see G. Pisanò, *Storia della guerra civile*, Milan: FPE, 1965–66, and G. Almirante, *Autobiografia di un 'fucilatore'*, Milan: Edizioni del Borghese, 1973. For a summary of fascist positions on this score, see M. Isnenghi, 'La guerra civile nella pubblicistica di destra', in *Rivista di storia contemporanea* XVIII: 1 (1989), pp. 104–15 (including, on p. 105, a reconstruction of the trajectory followed by Pisanò in his writings on the subject). See also P. Corsini and P. P. Poggio, 'La guerra civile nei notiziari della GNR e nella propaganda della RSI', in Legnani and Vendramini, eds, *Guerra, guerra di liberazione, guerra civile*, pp. 245–98 (on pp. 231–44 they republish the aforementioned report by Isnenghi).

2 See, among others, the intervention by Gian Carlo Pajetta at the Brescia conference on the Italian Social Republic, in Poggio, *La Repubblica sociale italiana*, pp. 431–4; E. Sarzi Amadé, 'Delazione e rappresaglia come strumenti della "guerra incivile"', in Legnani and Vendramini, *Guerra, guerra di liberazione, guerra civile*, pp. 323–53; M. Palla, 'Guerra civile o collaborazionismo?', in ibid., pp. 83–98 (another version appeared with the title 'Italia 1943–1945: guerra civile o collaborazionismo?', in *Passato e Presente* 19 [January–April 1989], pp. 165–71). Sarzi Amadé further expressed his positions in a piece entitled 'Guerra civile o Resistenza?' in *L'Unità* of 4 November 1988 (the response by the author of this present work appeared in the 9 November edition). These authors all polemicised against the positions expressed by Pavone in 'La guerra civile' in Poggio, *La Repubblica sociale italiana*, pp. 395–415, and in his 'Le tre guerre: patriottica, civile e di classe', in Legnani and Vendramini, *Guerra, guerra di liberazione, guerra civile*, pp. 25–36 (a paper delivered at the 1988 Belluno conference, now published in *Rivista di storia contemporanea* XVIII, 1989, pp. 209–18. For a first balance-sheet of this still ongoing discussion, see C. Bermani, 'Guerra di liberazione e guerra civile', in *L'Impegno* X: 1 (April 1990), pp. 10–16 (on pp. 7–9, the interventions of various readers are reproduced).

called 'the most ferocious and sincere of all wars',[3] are the differences between the belligerents so clear-cut and irreducible, and hatreds so profound. 'We're the ones they hated most of all', an old *resistente* put it recently.[4]

To say that the Resistance is also civil war does not mean that we have to seek out protagonists who experienced it exclusively in these terms. On the contrary, it means doing our best to understand how the three aspects of the struggle – patriotic, civil, and class – analytically distinguishable, often coexisted in the same individuals or groups.

Immediately after the Liberation, as during the struggle itself (and this we shall see in the pages that follow), the taboo against the notion of a civil war had been less strong. In his report given on 6 August 1945 at the first CLN congress of the province of Milan, Emilio Sereni had spoken repeatedly of the 'two years of civil war' (Sereni wanted to show that another civil war would lead the country to destruction).[5] In 1947 Carlo Galante Garrone had no qualms about stating that 'a bloody civil war had been fought'.[6] Leo Valiani had denounced 'the way people's souls turn ferocious' as being 'the innermost and at the same time most profound danger that any civil war (and the struggle against the Fascists was just this) brings with it.'[7] Luigi Meneghello has also used the expression.[8] Aligi Sassu painted the picture *La guerra civile 1944*.[9] And in a series of lectures in the 1960s Francesco Scotti claimed that the Resistance had been 'also a civil war against Fascism and for the creation of a completely new, socially more advanced state'; [10] and Paolo Spriano also uses the expression 'guerra civile' intermingled with 'guerra di liberazione', even if he does not place it at the centre of his treatise.[11]

But in the volume of Palmiro Togliatti's *Opere* covering the years 1944–55,

---

3 These words appear in the January 1946 essay *Storia e poesia* (quoted in Canfora, *La sentenza*, p. 13).

4 See Corrado Stajano's interview of Carlo Dionisotti, in *Corriere della Sera*, 3 January 1989.

5 See 'Democrazia al lavoro. Una guida per lo sviluppo dei CLN sulla via della ricostruzione', stenograph-report of the interventions at the First Congress of the Milan provincial CLN, 6 August 1945.

6 C. Galante Garrone, 'Guerra di liberazione (dalle galere)', in *Il Ponte* III (1947), p. 1054.

7 L. Valiani, *Tutte le strade conducono a Roma*, Florence: La Nuova Italia, 1947, p. 172.

8 Meneghello, *I piccoli maestri* (a 1964 book). The term 'Civil War' also appears frequently in *Bau-sète*, Milan: Rizzoli, 1988.

9 The canvas is conserved at Rome's Galleria Nazionale d'Arte Moderna, listing number 4710

10 F. Scotti, 'La nascita delle formazioni', in *La Resistenza in Lombardia*, Milan: Labor, 1965, p. 64.

11 Spriano, *Storia del Partito comunista italiano*, V, p. 340.

the words 'guerra civile' never once appear, so great was the Communist leader's desire to give his party national status. This need tallied with the widespread tendency to conceal the elementary fact that 'the Fascists too, despite everything, were Italians'.[12] 'Italiani' does not refer only to an ethnic fact. Both sides intended to reintegrate 'the paradigm of the modern state as sovereign political unity', since both felt themselves to be representatives of the whole of Italy.[13] The first way of exorcising what is regressive and frightening in the breakdown of the unity of the national state lies in denying shared nationality to those who bring about that breakdown. The Fascists had always called their adversaries 'anti-nazionale';[14] and the latter had always retorted by expelling them – at least those of the RSI – from the history of Italy, if not from humanity itself. Franco Calamandrei rightly defined as 'esorcistica' ('exorcistic') the formula 'uomini o no' ('men or not-men'), which was the title Elio Vittorini gave to his bad novel about the Resistance.[15] And it is no accident that Giorgio Bocca, one of the few non-Fascist writers who have unreservedly spoken in terms of a civil war, was reviewed under the title 'Anche Salò è storia nostra'.[16] Assertions like Ermanno Gorrieri's 'there was no civil war' are in fact the mechanical corollary of others, like 'Republican Fascism found no correspondence in the popular conscience'.[17] The fundamental truth of this statement does not eliminate the problem of the Fascists who, though not very numerous and largely unheeded, chose to fight alongside the Germans. The description of the Fascists as lackeys of the foreigner was not enough to cancel their being described as Italians, nor does it authorise us to evade the task of reflecting on the ties, not new but extremely close here, between external war and internal war. Nor can one overlook those Italians, far more numerous than the militant Fascists, who actually accepted the RSI government, paying it various forms of obedience, though with a greater or lesser degree of mental reservation.

In line with the fundamental continuity of the state between Fascism and the Republic, and particularly with the failure of the purges, is a bland, reassuring vision of the Resistance, where all trace of civil war has been scrubbed out. The anti-Fascist unity embodied in the system of the CLNs, which is still the

---

12 Words from Emilio Sereni's intervention, reproduced in Quazza, Valiani and Volterra, *Il governo dei CLN*, p. 195.

13 For a definition of the modern state as overspill from the wars of religion, see Fioravanti, *Stato (Diritto intermedio)*, part 3.

14 In the preamble to the 1926 PNF statutes, entitled 'Faith', one could read that 'new Italians' were those born in the struggle 'between the Nation and the anti-nation' (See Missori, *Gerarchie e statuti del PNF*, p. 355).

15 According to Ottavio Cecchi's preface to Calamandrei, *La vita indivisibile*, p. 16

16 'Even Salò is part of our history.' This is the title of N. Tranfaglia's review of Bocca's *La Repubblica di Mussolini* in the 20 February 1977 edition of *La Repubblica*.

17 Gorrieri, *La Repubblica di Montefiorino*, p. 762.

legitimising source of the Italian Republic and of what has been called its 'arco costituzionale', is thus reinterpreted as mere anti-German unity, almost as if the Republic was founded on opposition to Germany and not to Fascism.

The truth is that inherent in civil war itself is something that feeds the tendency to bury the memory of it. In order to exorcise the civil war, the French have coined the expression 'guerres franco-françaises', thereby bracketing together all the fractures which, in armed or unarmed combat, have divided their people, at least since the great revolution.[18] Even in Yugoslavia, at least at the official and political level, it is denied that the Resistance was a civil war.[19] And yet it is hard not to recognise the struggle without quarter between Tito's partisans, the Chetnicks of General Mihajlović, Ante Pavelic's Ustaše, the anti-Tito Slovenian Belagardists, and the other Fascist bands that infested the country between 1941 and 1945, as being a civil war. Indeed, Yugoslavia is the only European country in which the Resistance took the form of a successful social and political revolution. This Yugoslav paradox can be explained with reflections that may hold good for Italy, too. The members of a people who place themselves at the service of a foreign oppressor are considered guilty of so radical a betrayal as to extinguish their membership of that people. By behaving as they do, they annihilate within themselves the very fact that makes their treachery immense and unforgivable. The religious concept of the renegade might be a useful way of explaining this process, which deprives those who have placed themselves against the community of their people of ideal and moral – more so even than political – nationality. 'Renegade' was the name given to a partisan shot by his comrades as a spy.[20] 'Renegades scattered on the mountains' is how a Fascist militant consul referred to the partisans.[21] To destroy an internal enemy of this sort, the use of violence appears all the more legitimate the more that enemy is ranked with the external one. Against an external enemy, far more than against an internal one, a millenary tradition justifies violence which 'may do away with limits and restrictions on the exercise of power', and which for this very reason wishes to be rapidly forgotten.[22] What is more, the renegade may repent and return to his original community, may convert and counter-convert, as in the numerous shifts from Social Republic to Resistance and vice versa. The

---

18 See the special edition – No. 5 (January–March 1985) – of *Vingtième Siècle*, and within this, on pp. 55–79, H. Rousso's essay, 'Vichy, le grand fossé'.

19 October 1985 conversation with Milica Kacin Wohinz of the Institute for the History of the Workers' Movement of Slovenia.

20 G. Pesce, *Soldati senza uniforme (Diario di un gappista)*, Rome: Cultura Sociale, 1950, p. 15.

21 Mazzantini, *A cercar la bella morte*, pp. 203–04 (see also pp. 67, 207).

22 Schnur, *Rivoluzione e guerra civile*, p. 138. See also Hannah Arendt's observations in *Sulla rivoluzione*, Milan: Edizioni di Comunità, 1983, pp. 4–5 (original edition *On Revolution*, New York: Viking, 1963).

abandoned party made the following words its maxim: 'There is no greater traitor than the sincere convert.'[23] False conversion could be tolerated, just as it is in religious wars – but not heresy.[24]

The link between civil war and revolution in turn should be numbered among the factors that contributed to the rejection of the notion that a civil war was fought in Italy between 1943 and 1945. But this undeniable link can be viewed in two ways. On the one hand, revolution may be seen in positive and eschatological terms, making civil war appear by comparison, in one's evaluation of it, synonymous only with disorder and horror.[25] Conversely, civil war appears as the almost inevitable outlet of revolution, in such a way as to carry in its wake the positive or negative connotations given to revolution.[26] And since no one has ever claimed that the Italian Resistance was a revolution, its link with civil war has remained in memory only as a danger that was avoided. It has always been the Communists' boast that they managed to save Italy from the 'Greek prospect', by preventing the Resistance movement from developing into a devastating post-liberation civil war. The Action Party invoked democratic liberty, but gave that formula a powerfully innovative meaning compared to the current use of the word 'revolution' and the spectres it calls up (as we have already noted, the 'actionist' tradition has always been the least reluctant to speak in terms of civil war).[27] In effect, only a victorious revolution has the force to have no fears about inscribing the sufferings caused by civil war into its history. Even a defeated revolution can claim to have been the protagonist of a civil war when it does not intend to hide its revolutionary character. Marx's *The Civil War in France* is proof of this.

The prevalence of the formula 'war, or movement, of national liberation' rather than 'civil war' thus conceals that part of reality that sees Italians fighting Italians. The Spaniards conceal things in like fashion when they define the war against the French as a war of independence, ignoring the fact that there were also the Iberian proponents of Enlightenment ideals, the *afrancesados*.

Concealment makes the formula 'war of national liberation' so tranquilising that its use has withstood the great semantic reinforcement in the post-war

---

23 See C. Berneri, *L'ebreo antisemita*, Preface by A. Cavaglion, Rome: Carucci, 1984, p. 84 (original version *Le Juif antisémite*, Paris: Editions Vita, 1935).

24 On renegades, see L. Scaraffia, 'Il rinnegato', in *Prometeo*, June 1986, pp. 38–47.

25 On this, see P. P. Portinaro's Introduction to Schnur, *Rivoluzione e guerra civile*, p. 8 and passim, as well as Schnur's own text, p. 129 and *passim*.

26 On this connection, with particular regard to 1789 and 1917, see J. W. Borejsza, 'La guerre civile dans l'Europe contemporaine', in *Vingtième Siècle* 5 (January–March 1985), pp. 143–4.

27 For Action Party members' propensity to speak of civil war, see V. D'Alberto, 'Tra Resistenza e guerra civile. Nota su GL', in *Protagonisti* IX: 32 (July–September 1988), pp. 5–9, and the testimonies quoted therein.

period, in which the formula has come to denote the anti-colonialist and anti-imperialist movements of the Third World, all of which have had their bitter share of civil war.[28] As we shall see, the identification of the main enemy – the German or the Fascist – is a problem running throughout the Resistance. An astute American investigator of things Italian has written: 'Within a very short time ... the average citizen of Northern Italy came to hate the Neo-Fascists even more than the Nazis.'[29]

This surcharge of hate is a phenomenon that needs investigating, not least for the fact that it finds a mirror-image among the Fascists, who in their turn were busy attributing the entire responsibility for the beginning and exacerbation of the civil war to the anti-Fascists, and particularly the Communists. Mutual accusations of having set the fratricidal struggle in motion were and remain numerous. Which does not mean that we should forget those who, while feeling the civil war as a tragedy that generated massacres and grief, also felt it as an event to undertake with pride, in the name of the choice they had made and the conscious acceptance of all the consequences it involved. From this point of view, the current deprecation can be reversed: it was in fact in the very tension innate in its 'civil' character that the negative elements typical of war as such found a way of vindicating themselves. Franco Venturi once said that civil wars are the only ones worth fighting.

2. THE REAPPEARANCE OF THE FASCISTS

There is no point in lingering over the dispute as to whether it was the Fascists or the anti-Fascists, and the Communists in particular, who fired the first shot. Giorgio Bocca's remarks on this point are correct but not exhaustive: 'It

---

28 Sergio Cotta has maintained that the formulation 'war of national liberation' is more comprehensive than, and thus preferable to, 'civil war', 'war of independence', 'ideological war', and so on. See his *Lineamenti di storia della Resistenza italiana*, as well as this author's reply (*Rassegna del Lazio* XII [1965], pp. 111–15), and that of E. Passerin d'Entrèves, 'Un recente saggio sui problemi di storia della Resistenza', in *Il Movimento di liberazione in Italia* 78 (April–June 1965), pp. 92–100. Vittore Branca has in turn written: 'Not, then, so much a "civil war" as a war of "national liberation" from the foreigner and his servants.' In short, a second Risorgimento, moreover comparable to the first Risorgimento in that then also there had been 'reactionary Italians', allied to the Austrians. See V. Branca, 'La città dell'Arno nella Resistenza e nella liberazione', in *Nuova Antologia*, CXIX: 2152 (October–December 1984), p. 98. See also, by the same author, 'Liberazione nazionale o guerra civile? (lettera a Carlo Francovich)', in *Il Mulino* 135 (January 1964), pp. 40–2.

29 Hughes, *United States and Italy*, p. 128. Non-Italian students have obviously felt less unease about facing up to the reality of a civil war. See M. Clark, *Modern Italy, 1971–1982*, London–New York: Longman, 1984, pp. 299, 316, where he speaks of 'civil war and popular vendetta' (I thank Angelo Gaudio for bringing this to my attention).

is obvious that the anti-Fascists should make a move before the Fascists: it is up to them to prove by fighting that there are Italians who are ready to fight, ready to pay for the return ticket to democracy. The best thing for Neo-Fascism, obviously, is inner calm, proof against consensus or popular resignation.'[1]

Certainly that would be the best thing, but it would leave unsatisfied some of the basic motivations that led to the rebirth of Fascism and which drove it, from within its own ranks, onto the terrain of civil war.

First of all, one had to dispel the sense of frustration rife among the Fascists from 25 July[2] and exacerbated by the inglorious collapse of the regime. The prediction of the old turncoat police chief, Carmine Senise, proved all too true: 'as for the party, I reassured the Duke [Acquarone] that all that was needed was a dissolution with no worry whatsoever about a possible resistance by the Fascists.'[3]

In his *Storia della guerra civile*, in answer to the inevitable question – Why did the Fascists fail to act? – Giorgio Pisanò first gives this pat answer: the best Fascists were at the front; then follows it up with another, more convincing one: they took the declarations of loyalty to the alliance with Germany seriously; and finally resorts to an argument that echoes RSI propaganda: the beginning of Fascist reorganisation was cut short by the murder of the former party secretary Ettore Muti, perpetrated for that very purpose. But Pisanò too is obliged fundamentally to recognise that the Fascist Party was involved in a general crisis afflicting the Italian people as a whole.[4]

This crisis had been experienced by the Fascists in various ways. Those who had not been content simply to step down could be stimulated by the collapse to radically review their past and the entire system of Fascism, along the path that led Fascists, not for reasons of opportunism, to become anti-Fascists. Those in whom this process was not at work had shifted psychologically for themselves, suffering without understanding. After 8 September, some at least could not let slip the occasion, offered by the Germans, to show (themselves above all) that they were still alive. And the simplest answer to the question 'How could the collapse have happened?' was to blame it all on traitors, with whom the time had now come to settle accounts.

Revenge is mentioned in the first radio appeals launched from Germany by Alessandro Pavolini and Vittorio Mussolini immediately after 8 September

---

1 See Bocca, *La Repubblica di Mussolini*, p. 97.

2 See Deakin, *Brutal Friendship*, Chapter: 'The "Last Wave" of the Fascist Party', and L. Balestrieri, *Stampa e opinione pubblica a Genova tra il 1939 e il 1943*, Genoa: Istituto storico della Resistenza in Liguria, 1965, pp. 66–7.

3 See Senise, *Quand'ero capo della polizia*, p. 193 (this episode is dated 19 July 1943).

4 See Pisanò, *Storia della guerra civile*, pp. 4–36. For evidence of this at a local level – 'on 26 July the PNF showed not a single sign of life' – see M. Calandri, 'Qualche considerazione sulla RSI nel Cuneese', in Poggio, ed., *La Repubblica sociale italiana*, p. 191.

1943, when the Duce was still a prisoner on the Gran Sasso, and was reckoned by many to be physically dead as well. Exemplary punishment of the 'vile traitors' was pre-announced by Mussolini in the speech recorded for the radio immediately after his arrival in Germany.[5]

Even if we wish to give some credence to the hypothesis that Mussolini was not enthusiastic about having been liberated by the Germans,[6] once he had received this gift he had no choice but to go along with things and play his hand again. The circle of traitors to be punished went well beyond the members of the Grand Council, who were later to be dealt with at the Verona trial. It extended to all those who during the twenty years of Fascism had mutilated the Fascist victory, just as that other victory, which it had been Fascism's historic task to reintegrate, had been mutilated.

A Fascist paper wrote about the anti-Fascist declaration of faith made on 17 August 1943 by several medical professors at the University of Modena: 'These men are morally unworthy to teach not because they professed anti-Fascism after 25 July, but because, by accepting like sheep the discipline of a party which in their heart of hearts they deprecated, they are unworthy today to teach young people that dignity which they lacked and which is the essential basis of any severe academic discipline.[7]

The very youngest and the old guard could find themselves close to each other in their desire for revenge, the former bringing to it the energy of a generation conflict, the latter clinging to the myth of the 'return to origins', when the enemy, then too, had been other Italians unworthy of the name. When punishing the party hierarchs (gerarchi) proved to be 'a fake Terror',[8] the area of those to be punished widened still further, until it potentially embraced the entire Italian people in whose very name, however, revenge was being invoked.

The contradictions of the two elements that had been the hallmark of much of the history of Fascism – elitist tendencies and demagogic populism – were thus revealed particularly clearly in the Social Republic. Ardengo Soffici, an intellectual who had had his day, could still delude himself that one could keep together, in the name of faith in the figure of the Duce, contempt for the people and optimism about the final outcome. He wrote: 'It will turn out that Mussolini had not deceived himself so much as to deem a people of time-servers worthy of an empire.'[9] But a twenty-two-year-old Fascist grants no respite: 'Mussolini's mistake is that of having overrated his people, [a people who] do not want to

---

5 See Bocca, *La Repubblica di Mussolini*, pp. 14, 25.

6 See Zangrandi, *1943*, p. 243.

7 The author of this article, published in the *Gazzetta dell'Emilia* of 22 October 1943, was Enrico Cacciari, who in other pieces displayed his thirst for revenge (quoted in Gorrieri, *La Repubblica di Montefiorino*, esp. p. 48).

8 An expression used by Bocca, *La Repubblica di Mussolini*, pp. 124–7.

9 A. Soffici, *Risaliremo l'abisso*, in the *Corriere della Sera* of 1 November 1943.

suffer in order to become great, powerful, rich.'[10] Another complains about the 'tardy reawakening' of the people, and adds:

> There are too many Italians who are sleeping, there are too many traitors who are exulting, there are too many pacifists who want the ruin of Italy at all costs so as to enjoy the fat booty stolen from the Fallen on all the fronts, from the workers who have always worked and suffered. But the hour of judgment and reckoning will come.[11]

'Mussolini has been betrayed by everyone! It is the fault of the cowards who have betrayed [him]!', said a Fascist on a Roman tram after an air-raid alarm.[12] With a vulgarity made almost pathetic by the equivocal pass to which he had come, a *squadrista* and member of the Black Brigades from Fiume exulted thus: 'Life is beautiful and is worth living only when there is spirituality, when one rises above the grey mass of the majority: it is the few who dominate the many, it is the few who make History, the many have to endure it! I prefer to be on the side of those who impose it on the others!'[13]

A Blackshirt from an M battalion wrote that the Duce 'once again against the will of a people that believes itself to be Italian (and is not) has succeeded in warding off chaos, with a mere handful of men ... Even against the will of the people we shall fight alongside our German ally who has shown himself to be the true friend of the Italian people.'[14]

Mussolini was the first to feel that he was the victim of an act of betrayal. 'He is full of rancour against the Italians, by whom he feels he has been betrayed', recounted Leandro Arpinati, the former *gerarca* who had been out of favour for some time, after a meeting with the Duce.[15] In those months Mussolini recalled a memorial stone that Carlo Dossi had dedicated to former prime minister Crispi:

> Francesco Crispi / great in spirit dreamed that Italy / would be great / and sought to arouse in the Italians / awareness of their worth. / But the crowd replied / that it

---

10 Diary of Ottaviano Rocchi, shot by partisans in Parma province in November 1944 (*LRSI*, p. 24).

11 Letter of 17 November 1944 by Azelio Facini, who met his death on the Umbrian front two days later (*LRSI*, p. 177).

12 See Calamandrei, *La vita indivisibile*, p. 142 (7 March 1944).

13 Letter to the mother of Umberto Scaramelli, written on 28 October 1944 (*LRSI*, p. 168).

14 'Esame della corrispondenza censurata al 30 giugno 1944' (ACS, SPD, CR, RSI, envelope 9, folder 3).

15 'Anonimo romagnolo', *1943–45*, p. 79. For the invective hurled against traitors in the Milan Lyric Theatre speech of 16 December 1944, see Deakin, *Brutal Friendship*, p. 742.

wished to be small and cowardly/ and among the many eager pigmies / more gigantic appears the figure of Crispi.

'This epigraph', remarked the Duce 'necessarily takes us back to present times.'[16] Fundamental to positions of this kind is the idea that it was not Fascism that ruined Italy, which was unworthy of it. Julius Evola would write:

> It wasn't Fascism that acted negatively on the Italian people, on the Italian 'race', but vice versa: it was this people, this 'race' that acted negatively on Fascism, that is to say on the Fascist attempt, insofar as it showed itself incapable of providing a sufficient number of men who were equal to certain noble demands and certain symbols, elements healthy and capable of promoting the development of the positive potentialities that could be contained in the system.[17]

Even Hitler, for that matter, in the last months manifested an ingratitude towards the German people that they can scarcely be said to have deserved. His 'ill humour' drove him 'to speak more and more frequently and angrily to the effect that if Germans were not ready to follow him to victory they must perish'.[18] In a conversation with Albert Speer, Hitler was still more vindictive and apocalyptic: the German people had shown themselves to be too weak and the future belonged 'exclusively to the stronger eastern people. What was left after the battle was only inferior beings; the good ones have been killed.' In line with this, in the same days, the Führer ordered the destruction of vital German structures.[19]

A disturbing aspect of the path which led to republican Fascism, felt not only as a continuer of the war but as the driving force of vengeance, is given by those who, though lukewarm Fascists before 25 July, discovered the flame of militancy in themselves after 8 September. In certain respects these itineraries are more interesting than those pursued by front-ranking figures who, having wholly or half changed sides after 25 July, changed yet again after 8 September. The most illustrious case of the latter is unquestionably Giovanni Gentile; but equally exemplary is Renato Ricci.[20] There were, instead, humble folk who

---

16 Quoted from the papers of the Duce's private secretariat in Mazzatosta, in *Educazione e scuola nella Repubblica Sociale Italiana*, p. 91.

17 J. Evola, *Il fascismo. Saggio di un'analisi critica dal punto di vista della Destra*, Rome: Volpe, 1964, p. 98 (quoted in P. Rauti and R. Sermonti, *Storia del fascismo*, vol. I, *Le interpretazioni e le origini*, Rome: Centro editoriale nazionale, 1976, p. 46).

18 K. Hildebrand, *The Third Reich*, New York: Routledge, 1984, p. 71 (original edition *Das Dritte Reich*, Munich: Oldenbourg, 1979).

19 The order – *Nero-Befehl* – is from 19 March 1945. See Hillgruber, *Storia della seconda guerra mondiale*, p. 176. See also, by the same author, *La strategia militare di Hitler*, p. 611.

20 For a detailed reconstruction of the Gentile affair see Canfora, *La sentenza*,

committed themselves specifically to the Social Republic – like the elementary school teacher Franco Rubbio Nosso, who participated in the Fascist occupation of the Quirinale after the Via Rasella attack,[21] or the pharmacist Oreste Millone, who had become commissar of the republican *fascio* and was shot by partisans, but previously 'had never distinguished himself in special manifestations of Fascist faith, though he proudly described himself as a *squadrista*.'[22] Franco Calamandrei notes in his diary that, 'During the German occupation of Florence, N., kind-hearted, cordial N., to all appearances the mildest of men, was killed by the GAPs together with his father as a systematic denouncer of Jews to the SS.'[23] This path was pursued also by some fairly important personalities, like Professor Goffredo Coppola, like the former nationalist Giotto Dainelli, who on 25 July did not follow his old chief Luigi Federzoni and then became *podestà* of Florence and Giovanni Gentile's successor as president of the Accademia d'Italia,[24] or like the director of Pirelli, Count Franco Grottanelli, who ended up in the RSI because, he said, 'I can't stand betrayal.'[25] These are not the only cases on record.[26] Beppe Fenoglio sums them up in the figure of Lieutenant X, brother of the partisan Kyra, who 'had not been particularly enthusiastic during the whole of the war ... But after 8 September the elder one changed, he was ablaze, he erupted, he was among the first and most determined and bloodthirsty Fascists.'[27]

Even in a distant and isolated universe like that of Italian POWs in Allied hands, there were similar reactions to those recorded above. One need only mention the testimony of General Umberto Cappuzzo, a prisoner in India at the time: 'There were those very extreme Fascists who claimed to have always been anti-Fascist; and those who had been 'only a soldier' and for moral reasons suddenly felt closer to the defeated regime.'[28]

It should come as no surprise, then, if immediately after 8 September the

---

pp. 54–64; on Ricci, see Setta, *Renato Ricci*, p. 247

21 Testimony of Matteo Mareddu, communicated to me by Elvira Gencarelli.

22 Giovana, *Storia di una formazione partigiana*, p. 70.

23 Calamandrei, *La vita indivisibile*, p. 213 (19 August 1945).

24 See Francovich, *La Resistenza a Firenze*, p. 136.

25 See Bocca, *La Repubblica di Mussolini*, p. 81.

26 Ibid., pp. 26–7, 78–9; Gorrieri, *La Repubblica di Montefiorino*, pp. 48–9; on the Teramo *fascio*, where some 150 of the 482 PFR members had not been signed up to the PNF, see L. Ponziani, 'Teramo 1943–1944. Condizioni di vita e mentalità', in Gallerano, ed., *L'altro dopoguerra*, p. 160.

27 Fenoglio, *Il partigiano Johnny*, p. 124.

28 'The younger ones' – Cappuzzo adds – '(I was twenty-one) reacted better'. See *La Repubblica* of 7 September 1983. For an analogous situation in the USSR's prison camps, see F. Gambetti, '"L'Alba", giornale dei prigionieri italiani in URSS', in Istituto storico della Resistenza in Cuneo e provincia, *Gli italiani sul fronte russo*, p. 344. On fascist memories of the prison camps, see Isnenghi, *La guerra civile nella pubblicistica di destra*.

Fascists reappeared here and there spontaneously, without awaiting the resurrection of Mussolini and the establishment of the RSI government. Some, as we have seen, went directly over to serving the Germans, in Italy and the Balkans.[29] Some federations of the republican Fascist party were formed before the arrival of the provincial chief (*capo della provincia*),[30] the figure in which the RSI, in an attempt to supersede the old dualism, wished to bring together the prefect and the federal secretary (the *capi delle province* were summoned to Milan by Minister of the Interior Guido Buffarini Guidi only on 25 November 1943).[31]

It has by now been brought to light how the German leaders were in two minds as to the advisability of giving life to a neo-Fascist government, its seeming to many of them more rational, for the better conduct of military operations and a more intense exploitation of the economic resources in the Po Valley, to have a regime of direct occupation.[32] It was Hitler who, judging the disastrous political effect that the reduction of the 'senior partner' of the Axis to a conquered land would have, above all on his minor satellites, gave the go-ahead to the creation of the Social Republic, though naturally taking the due precautions. The Führer, who in the past had had some difficulty justifying his excessive faith in Fascist Italy to high-ranking German officials, once said to Ambassador Rudolf von Rahn: 'On no account be taken in by the Italian heart.'[33]

The Fascists, for their part, have always attempted to legitimise their republic as a providential shock-absorber placed between the Italian people and their enraged German comrades. Only somewhat paradoxically, Victor Emmanuel III himself was to adopt this thesis, which facilitated the reconciliation between monarchic Fascists and republican Fascists. The RSI government, the king once said in his Egyptian exile, 'prevented the establishment of an extremely harsh, ruthless German government in Northern Italy.'[34]

The fact of the matter is that the RSI would not have lasted a single day without German support. All the same, this obvious reflection does not make it

---

29 See also the case of two blackshirt battalions near Rome, recorded in Zangrandi, *1943*, p. 145. 'Abandoned and ignored by the *Madre Patria*' – namely, by the Social Republic – these soldiers remained at the Germans' side in the Balkans ('Esame della corrispondenza censurata al 30 giugno 1944', in ACS, SPD, CR, RSI, envelope 9, folder 3).

30 See M. Legnani, 'Potere, società ed economia nel territorio della RSI', in Poggio, ed., *La Repubblica sociale italiana*, p. 12.

31 Ibid., p. 11.

32 See, among other authors dealing with this topic, Schreiber, *La linea gotica nella strategia tedesca*, pp. 25–6. See also Klinkhammer, 'Le strategie tedesche di occupazione'.

33 An instruction to Rahn, in ACS, SPD, CR, RSI and quoted in Bocca, *La Repubblica di Mussolini*, p. 151. On Hitler's clear disappointment with Mussolini's new Italy, see J. Petersen, *L'organizzazione della propaganda tedesca in Italia*, a talk given at the aforementioned 'L'Italia in guerra 1940–43' conference, page 81, note 18.

34 See P. Puntoni, *Parla Vittorio Emanuele III*, Milan: Palazzi, 1958, pp. 352–3.

a useless exercise to seek the intrinsically Fascist motivations that led to the birth of the Social Republic and thrust it along the path of civil war in a more intense way than that of mere collaborationism.

We have seen how the need to show that one was still alive manifested itself above all as a desire for vengeance. We now have to add that, in the first few weeks, genuine desires for pacification were also revealed, desires which are not to be confused with the opportunistic ones of the last months of the war, let alone the clumsy attempts to divide adversaries made above all on the Socialists.[35] Several incidents can be cited as occurring in Tuscany and Emilia-Romagna, the two regions where the memory of the *biennio rosso* and the Fascist action squads were most powerful and where the civil war was to be particularly bitter. Many years later a Communist from Montelupo Fiorentino recalled: 'The first Fascists to reappear on the scene initially proved to be submissive and to have sized up the new situation; in fact they vainly tried to make an approach to some anti-Fascists to seek their collaboration; then, as time went by, when with German support the RSI was founded, they reverted to their old methods.'[36]

Sergio Flamigni and Luciano Marzocchi have written of the initial tendency to conciliation and moderation displayed by the province of Forlì, and have recalled the case of a Fascist who pulled out, saying: 'I've given blows, I've taken blows, we're even and I don't care anymore.'[37] In Umbria, in the first few weeks the militia was 'quiet and subdued'.[38] In Alessandria and Asti the Fascists attempted talks with the CLN and the anti-Fascist representatives, and a Communist chief who had agreed to a meeting with them and with the *carabinieri* was dismissed from the federal committee.[39]

Some of this behaviour on the part of the Fascists assumes the tone of a generational appeal against the old men who had ruined Italy: the king and Badoglio headed the list, but they were not the only ones. In this regard, they would survive the failure of the bids for conciliation of the first few weeks, and rather than seeking pacification they would aim at shifting the clash between the generations, thus attempting to revive another of the Fascist myths. A leaflet distributed by the Aldo Resega Black Brigade in Milan was to set the young

---

35 See on this Bocca, *La Repubblica di Mussolini*, pp. 306–8, on the 'Bonfantini affair', and also Canfora, *La sentenza*, esp. pp. 183–4, 193, 196, where these initiatives are credited with exaggerated significance.

36 *La resistenza al fascismo a Montelupo nel 1943–1944*, the October 1966 written testimony of Giuseppe Romano (ISRT, *Raccolta di biografie*).

37 See Flamigni e Marzocchi, *Resistenza in Romagna*, pp. 115–16.

38 It was 'propaganda at all cost' and the 'printed press bands' that changed the climate. See Battaglia, *Un uomo*, pp. 36, 30–1.

39 See the 'Rapporto di Giovanni' of 22 September 1943 (IG, *Archivio PCI*) and that by Alfredo (Arturo Colombi) on 'the political–organisational situation' from 10 October of that year (Secchia, *Il PCI e la guerra di liberazione*, pp. 123–6).

against the 'old, oft-foundered wrecks of the past', who (and here even Pavolini and Farinacci figure) 'are diabolically attempting to submerge the purest Italic youth'. Lest there should be any misunderstanding, the following were held up to this *giovinezza* as models: Ettore Muti, Gino Pallotta, Niccolò Giani and Berto Ricci. This particular case, quite clearly, was a call to battle; and in fact in the leaflet there was the invocation: 'Borsani, the youth of the trenches is with you!'[40] Smacking less of battlefield memories (but we are already in October 1944) is the appeal that the Modena paper *Valanga repubblicana* addressed to 'noi giovani' ('we young men') who 'tomorrow, come what may, shall have to impose our will on the country. Old men and old systems continue to dominate more or less everywhere: and it is from this old ruling garbage that we must make a clean break so as to present ourselves as free and rejuvenated for the post-war fray'.[41]

Other appeals to the young could slip into a patriotic and leftish populism different both from the cloying and manipulative declarations in favour of 'socialisation' promoted by the RSI, and Fascist 'sinistrismo', which was interpreted above all in terms of the cudgel and of violence. A leaflet addressed to the 'giovani' of the province of Forlì began like this:

> Don't let yourselves be seduced by the vain erudition and inane theories of those who out of personal interest and because all they know of life is books and libraries, forget that the real life of the people who suffer is something else ... Give your faithful and firm support to the cause of the Poor against the Rich ... Garibaldi is watching you from the heaven of heroes and is exhorting you to save the *patria*. *Patria* or death.[42]

Similar positions expressed in a more refined way, with Mazzini in place of Garibaldi, appear in a neo-Fascist rag, *Patria*, published, it seems, under the editorship of a philosophy teacher at the Liceo of Fano with a programme to 'build bridges between people's minds and not dig abysses'.[43]

A far cry also from the intrigues in high places appear clumsy advances such as that attempted at Castelfiorentino immediately after 8 September, when some

---

40 See Pansa, *L' esercito di Salò*, pp. 72–3, which cites a GNR report of 2 August 1944. Blinded during the war, Borsani had been awarded the Medaglia d'Oro, and was president of the Associazione Nazionale Mutilati e Invalidi. He is now remembered on account of the 'conspiracy of the three Bs' (see Bocca, *La repubblica di Mussolini*, p. 148.).

41 The paper was directed by a young officer, Rino Lavini, who was relieved of his post after three issues, one of which was seized as soon as it hit the newsstands (see Gorrieri, *La Repubblica di Montefiorino*, p. 201).

42 Quoted in Flamigni and Marzocchi, *Resistenza in Romagna*, p. 278.

43 See M. Isnenghi, 'Verso una stampa post-fascista. Episodi di giornalismo marchigiano (1943–44)', in Rochat, Santarelli and Sorcinelli, eds, *Linea gotica 1944*, pp. 568–9.

Fascists requested the 'approval' of the local Communists, on condition 'that they informed them of their every movement and of all the orders that were imparted to them by the federation'. The author of the report is careful to point out, 'our refusal was always disdainful', even if he has to recognise that, with the arrival in Florence of lieutenant colonel Bartali with fifty militiamen, and his having requested 'collaboration with our men (for the good of the people: sic!)', there was some 'sidestepping' ('scantonamento') in the neighbouring villages, though this was short-lived: 'From then our illegal activity recommenced.'[44] 'Serenades' to Communists and Socialists is the name Gorrieri gives to those that appeared in October 1943 in the *Gazetta dell'Emilia*;[45] and, in the moderate underground press, there were those who did not fail to sound the alarm about this, or pretended to do so, with a tacit but clear anti-Communist polemic.[46]

The moves towards reconciliation of the first few weeks produced some agreement in certain places. At Sant'Arcangelo di Romagna a document of mutual commitment not to attack one another was signed in September by the Fascists and the Rimini CLN (the five Communists who participated in the initiative were duly expelled from the party); and a similar attempt occurred at Forlì.[47] In Ancona immediately after 8 September Fascists and anti-Fascists signed a pact for the maintenance of order, while in Venice various anti-Fascist representatives (excluding the Actionists) replied to the appeal addressed to them by the *federale* (the provincial party secretary), Montesi 'with a pure heart, transcending party egoism and passions', and participated in a meeting of reconciliation. Other meetings and other appeals are recorded elsewhere.[48] Even Concetto Marchesi, who subsequently, at the inauguration of the academic year at Padua, would address a message to the students which has become a classic of Resistance literature, but of which the ambiguities and multiple readings have recently been highlighted, needed to be taken to task by the Communist Party before disentangling himself from polluting relations with the Fascist education minister, Carlo Alberto Biggini.[49]

Some of the documents recorded above mention the moment at which attempts at reconciliation cease and there prevail, inexorably by now, drives

---

44 'Relazione della sezione comunista di Castelfiorentino alla federazione comunista fiorentina', 15 August 1944 (ISRT, *Fondo Salvadori – PCI Castelfiorentino*, insert 59).

45 See Gorrieri, *La Repubblica di Montefiorino*, pp. 212–13. The Modena newspaper, under the dubious leadership of Vittore Querel, would continue to harp on about this theme in subsequent months.

46 See 'I due fascismi', an article in the 5 January 1944 Rome edition of *Risorgimento Liberale*, which terms the left fascists' manoeuvre as 'very subtle Machiavellianism'.

47 See Flamigni e Marzocchi, *Resistenza in Romagna*, pp. 117–18.

48 See Bocca, *La Repubblica di Mussolini*, pp. 17, 75–7.

49 See Canfora, *La sentenza*, above all Chapter 4, 'Lo Stato del lavoro nella parola del rettore'.

towards civil war. We shall have occasion to return to the anti-Fascist responses to 'the tremulous attempts at reconciliation', as the central CLN called them.[50] As for the Fascists, on 15 October Fernando Mezzasoma, the minister of popular culture, decreed: 'The newspapers are to desist from publishing appeals for the reconciliation of souls, for the concord of spirits, for the fraternity of Italians. After forty-five days of poisoning of public opinion, scandal-mongering, preaching hate and man-hunting, certain pietistic manifestations represent an indication of pusillanimity and half-heartedness.'[51]

Sincere though it might have been in some Fascists, the desire to hold out against foreign bayonets was thus doomed to give way to the deeper urge to wreak vengeance on the anti-Fascist Italians in the shadow of those very bayonets. With the establishment of the Social Republic, the need that its restricted and motley group of leaders must not lose face nor incur the suspicion of their German ally, who had become yet more demanding and arrogant in his new guise of occupier, led towards this outcome.

'But what is this Fascism which has dissolved like snow in the sun?' Hitler asked Mussolini at their first encounter after 8 September.[52] It seems that Field-Marshal Wilhelm Keitel said that 'the only Italian army that will not be able to betray us is an army that doesn't exist'.[53] From this point of view, the civil war was a further pledge given to Nazi Germany, which recognised its value all too well. The best way to bind the collaborationists was to 'load them with feelings of guilt, to make them bleed, to compromise them as much as possible'.[54]

Even that small hold that the RSI managed to have on that part of the population who had been left frightened by the institutional void created after 8 September drove it, paradoxically, towards civil war. This was not a case of 'returning to origins'. On the contrary, it was a case of establishing the maximum continuity with the twenty-year-old regime that had had as a source of essential legitimation the very re-establishment and maintenance of order. 'I needed order', wrote an auxiliary in the women's service,[55] speaking for many. 'Finally we shall have a government!' shouted a man in Venice on hearing the news of Mussolini's rescue.[56]

---

50 See the 'Diffida' carried in the 31 December 1943 Rome edition of *Il Popolo*.

51 See Amicucci, *I seicento giorni*, p. 122. On 31 May 1944 Mezzasoma re-established pre-emptive censorship: see De Luna, 'Giornali e giornalisti nella RSI', in Poggio, ed., *La Repubblica sociale italiana*, p. 116.

52 According to F. Anfuso, *Da palazzo Venezia al lago di Garda*, Bologna: Cappelli, 1957, p. 326.

53 Amicucci, *I seicento giorni*, p. 69.

54 Levi, *I sommersi e i salvati*, p. 30.

55 E. Curti, 'Impressioni', in *Donne in grigioverde*, 18 February 1945, cited in M. Fraddosio, 'Donne nell' esercito di Salò', in *Memoria* 4 (June 1982), p. 60.

56 See Calamandrei, *La vita indivisibile*, p. 112

The Fascists, who had always kept the action of creating disorder as their special preserve, were at the same time convinced that what the mass of men longed for, more than anything else, was order. They could not therefore fail to be driven to ruthlessly repress the rebels who were giving them trouble. Disorder as an instrument of order, a fundamental feature of Fascism, would come to achieve, on this road, paroxysmal results. The Social Republic would in fact be riddled with a multiplicity of police forces, armed corps, militias, bands picked up here and there in search of adventure or booty, who acted without any coordination and often in competition with each other. With bureaucratic caution, Giovanni Tebaldi, the *questore* of Bologna reported to the chief of police:

> Despite the awareness and the rapid, effective intervention by the provincial authorities responsible, we must still note here and there arbitrary police actions, at times of considerable gravity, on the part of members of the Militia and of some provincial *gerarca*. Naturally, when the personal, or in any case unconfessable, motive for these actions comes to light, regular denunciations are made.[57]

Revealing the real state of affairs, one Fascist wrote:

> The Armed Corps, by which I mean the Guardia, the Police, the Italian SS and the various battalions, 'Nembo', 'San Marco', 'Barbarigo', 'Roma o Morte', 'Muti' et cetera, are creating real bewilderment in the minds of the masses with their multiplicity and their enlistment methods. It's like being in an old-style market with each of the various Jewish hawkers trying to corner the buyer by lauding his goods to the skies.[58]

Of the two indissoluble faces of modern totalitarianism – the rigid hierarchical order imposed on the whole of society and the chaos created by the

---

57 'Relazione sulla situazione politica e sullo spirito pubblico nella provincia di Bologna (quindicinale)', 31 December 1943, which begins: 'The political situation in this province remains delicate' (ACS, Direzione Generale di PS Divisione Affari Generali e Riservati: I take the quote from the photocopy at the INSMLI. My thanks to Gabriella Solaro for having made me aware of this as well as the document mentioned on note 60, below page 286). On 20 March 1944 the same *questore* issued a report condemning the Bologna PFR federation led by Franz Pagliani, a 'moderate' Fascist at the centre of murky dealings with 'millionaires' (see Legnani, *Potere, società ed economia*, p. 14). On pp. 13–15 he cites other police reports of analogous situations, or else 'an almost idyllic portrayal' of reality. A letter ultimately falling into the censor's hands spoke of 'opportunists and sharks, thieves and vultures' who had infiltrated the party ('Esame della corrispondenza censurata al 30 giugno 1944', in ACS, SPD, CR, RSI, envelope 9, folder 3). A convinced Fascist who joined the MSI after the war, he was unwilling to join the PFR on account of the 'arrivistes' and 'profiteers' who flooded into that party (testimony of Mario Sassi, in Portelli, *Biografia di una città*, p. 263).

58 Memoir of Dr Edmondo Leppo, n.d. but September 1944, in ACS, SPD, CR, RSI, envelope 24, folder 165.

fragmentation of juridically unregulated powers (Neumann's Behemoth) – the RSI thus primarily displayed the latter.[59] Instead of consensus, albeit forced, one had at best to content oneself with a discipline born of low spirits.[60]

It was the congress of Verona, inaugurated on 14 November 1943, that marked the decisive turning-point towards civil war, based on the convergence between the young and the old *squadristi*, who immediately thereafter perpetrated the Ferrara massacre as a reprisal for the killing of the *federale* (provincial party secretary) Igino Ghisellini; and the party secretary Pavolini, who used the occasion to try to lead Fascist chaos back into the hive of the single and, at least theoretically, united and intransigent party.[61] From that moment on, RSI documents and political journalism are full of references, explicit or implicit, to civil or fratricidal war.[62] The political or ideological character of this war made it obvious that it would be compared to the one that the German comrades were continuing to wage against the monstrous coalition of the demo-pluto-Judaic-Masonic-Bolshevik powers. As we have noted with regard to 1919–22, 'in Fascism's mythology of struggle and war, war and civil war make an indissoluble pact'.[63] Commenting on the Ferrara massacres, Farinacci wrote in *Regime fascista*: 'The watchword was: an eye for an eye, a tooth for a tooth … It was thought that perhaps we wouldn't have the force and courage to react. Now the facts have spoken'.[64]

The creation of the Black Brigades, announced by Pavolini on 26 July 1944, a year after 25 July, on the basis of a decree by Mussolini of the previous 30 June, constituted the culminating point of Fascist commitment in the civil war. The

---

59 At the Brescia conference, Mario Isnenghi spoke of the 'refeudalisation' of the state, while Luciano Violante illustrated the splintering of criminal law, in which state bodies tended to exert jurisdiction over their own constituent parts (M. Isnenghi, 'Autora: presentazioni dell'ultimo fascismo nella riflessione e nella propaganda'; L. Violante, 'L'administrazione della giustizia', in Poggio, ed., *La Repubblica sociale italiana*, pp. 99–111, 289–94).

60 'The mood of the population is, undoubtedly, depressed, but it remains obedient to discipline', the head of the Padua province assured the Interior Ministry in his 26 January 1944 monthly report: the workers and intellectuals were highlighted as the most hostile elements, while the proportion of young men called to arms who actually showed up for duty was judged to be one-quarter (ACS, Direzione Generale di PS, Divisione Affari Generali e Riservati; photocopy at the INSMLI).

61 See Deakin, *Brutal Friendship*, pp. 613–21.

62 For the central – if not always explicit – role of the civil war in GNR reports, see Corsini and Poggio, *La guerra civile nei notiziari*. See also P. Ambrosio, ed., *All' attenzione del duce. I notiziari della GNR della provincia di Vercelli*, Borgosesia: Istituto per la Storia della Resistenza in Provincia di Vercelli, 1980, and M. Calandri, ed., *Fascismo 1943–1945. I notiziari della GNR da Cuneo a Mussolini*, Cuneo: L' Arciere, 1979.

63 See J. Petersen, 'Il problema della violenza nel fascismo italiano', in *Storia contemporanea* XIII (1982), p. 990.

64 See the article 'Dalle parole ai fatti', in the 17 October 1943 issue (quoted in Bocca, *La Repubblica di Mussolini*, p. 99).

initiative stemmed not least from the failure of the republican National Guard as backbone of the internal military machinery, and of the creaking, in the summer of the partisan offensive, of the entire RSI structure. The most determined Fascists had somehow or other understood that they would have to manage the final reckoning directly. This too, for that matter, could be considered a return to origins. The 1921 statute of the National Fascist Party (PNF) had in fact established that 'all Fascists belong to the combat squads'; and on 24 April 1923 the Grand Council had ordered that 'all Party members be officially registered in the militia'.[65] Pavolini's announcement was: 'All members of the republican Fascist party aged between eighteen and sixty constitute the auxiliary corps of the Black Shirts.'

The instructions that followed, which were again Pavolini's, reiterated and specified the meaning of this total militarisation of the party, which was also a further attempt to reabsorb the neo-action-squad 'federal police', who, springing up in the weeks immediately following 8 September, were 'in many cases survivors of the government's attempted dissolution of them'.[66] Thus the party secretary wrote: 'As of this moment all Fascists are to consider themselves in a state of emergency for the struggle against the activity of the rebels and for the defence of their own families'; consequently, the house of every Fascist is to be transformed into 'a small fortress where it is not possible to be surprised in one's sleep'.[67] Shortly before, on 27 June, writing to Mussolini, Pavolini had stressed, against Graziani's 'apolitical' velleities, the need to place oneself on a 'terrain which is that of armed politicians against armed politicians'.[68] Now, in his radio broadcast of 25 July, Pavolini publicly developed this concept, remarking: 'It is not enough to profess oneself to be for Italy when there is also an Italy of Badoglio and Palmiro Togliatti.' The divisions returning from Germany 'bear on their bayonets a political idea. Nor could it be otherwise at such a time as this, during this war which Mussolini defines as a religious war.'

In the same speech, flaunting unscrupulousness and gall, which served to cover up a sense of frustration and almost of envy (sentiments not new to the Fascists, above all in their attitude to the Communists), Pavolini said that the Italians

> do not fear combat ... They don't, however, like being shut up in barracks, organised, regimentalised ... The partisan movement is successful because the combatant in the partisan ranks has the impression of being a free man. He is proud of what

---

65 See Missori, *Gerarchie e statuti del PNF*, pp. 338, 352.
66 See Legnani, *Potere, società ed economia*, pp. 11–15.
67 Document held in ACS, SPD, CR, RSI, cited in Bocca, *La Repubblica di Mussolini*, p. 271.
68 Paraphrased in Deakin, *Brutal Friendship*, p. 700.

he is doing because he acts independently and develops the action according to his personality. It is therefore necessary to create an anti-partisan movement on the same bases and with the same characteristics.[69]

No doubt the party secretary had in mind the experience that had already been tried out by the 'franchi tiratori' (snipers) or Gruppi d'Azione Giovanile (GAG) who had been organised in Florence in opposition to the Gruppi di Azione Patriottica (GAP), and with a view to a sniping campaign that was to be conducted after the arrival of the Allies.[70] In a letter to Mussolini of 18 June Pavolini had written that, in the disintegration of the civil and military authorities that was taking place in Tuscany, only the Fascists were holding out.[71] A practical translation of the concepts expressed by Pavolini can be found in a plan devised by Mussolini himself the following 16 August: 'The partisans captured during and after the fighting are immediately shot. The disbanded who are captured with weapons are shot in conformity with the well-known ministerial ordinance'; the unarmed were to be sent to Germany; those who present themselves, 'to work or to military service'.[72]

In fact, the party secretary's directives were obeyed only to a limited extent. The Black Brigades only rarely entered the city gates; nor did they manage adequately to take the place of the garrisons of the fast-dissolving republican National Guard.[73] In Trieste, in July 1944, out of 8,500 party members only 500 formed part of the Black Brigades.[74]

The sporadic Fascist sniping in Florence and Turin, where provincial party secretary, *federale* Giuseppe Solaro seems to have been planning it for some time,[75] should be considered the last, albeit faint-hearted Fascist contribution

---

69 'Il partito in armi', in the *Corriere della Sera* of 26 July 1944. The 30 June decree 'Duce della Repubblica Sociale Italiana' stated (article 1): 'The political structure of the Party is transformed into a military-type body, including the creation of the Auxiliary Corps of the Blackshirt Action Squads.

70 Pisanò, *Storia della guerra civile*, pp. 739–40, and Francovich, *La Resistenza a Firenze*, pp. 283–5. The GAGs are discussed in a 15 June 1944 report from the Inspector Paolo ('Cari compagni', *Le Brigate Garibaldi*, vol. II, p. 34).

71 Cited in Deakin, *Brutal Friendship*, p. 692.

72 ACS, SPD, CR, RSI (quoted in Bocca, *La Repubblica di Mussolini*, p. 268).

73 Bocca, *La Repubblica di Mussolini*, pp. 266–9, and Legnani, *Potere, società ed economia*, p. 24.

74 As Francesco reported in a 13 December 1944 meeting of the PCI leadership in Rome, laying great stress on the blow to the Blackshirts in their first sortie in the Canavese region (IG, *Archivio PCI*, 'Direzione. Verbali 1944'). Francesco was probably referring to the clashes in August, during which Alessandro Pavolini himself was wounded at Cuorgnè (see Bocca, *La Repubblica di Mussolini*, pp. 268–70).

75 See the documents in Section V of Vaccarino, Gobetti and Gobbi, *L'insurrezione di Torino*, pp. 213ff; Gobetti, *Diario partigiano*, p. 370; the letter sent to Moscatelli by

to the civil war. Their chances of doing any harm were overrated by the Resistance organisms. The Communist Party 'Direttive per l'insurrezione n.9' of 15 September 1944 warned against a 'particularly dangerous occult resistance' and against the fifth column.[76] On 1 April 1945 the 'Direttive operative per il piano E.27' of the Biella zone command mentioned foreseeable Fascist guerrilla warfare for the period following liberation.[77]

Only a very minor and abortive contribution to the civil war was given by the extremely rare Fascist attempts to conduct actions south of the Gothic line.[78] These are not to be confused with the sporadic and vague manifestations of nostalgia or sympathy for Fascism that occurred in liberated Italy, and that were far more the fruit of local situations than of Pavolini's directives. Still pursuing the mirage of mirroring the anti-Fascists, Pavolini had in fact decreed that the Fascists left in situ or deliberately sent behind the lines should stir up a 'clandestine Fascism, similar in its manifestations to the activity of the clandestine parties of our adversaries or at any rate of our opponents generally in the provinces controlled by us'.[79]

The result of these directives can be seen not so much in the facts as in the propaganda of the RSI.[80] What should be stressed, rather, is that as a rule both the Royal Army and the Fascist government, evidently in agreement with their respective allies, avoided deploying their regular units against one another on the front.[81] This confirms the fact that the civil war was not fought between the Kingdom of the South and the Italian Social Republic. It was a war fought between Fascists and anti-Fascists, on the only territory where

---

Moro, an Italian diplomat in Switzerland, on 10 February 1945 (IG, *BG*, 07887). Pisanò, *Storia della guerra civile*, p. 780, gives the blatantly exaggerated figure of 2,000 snipers in Turin.

76 *Le Brigate Garibaldi*, vol. II, pp. 332–5

77 IG, *BG*, 05417.

78 Some post-Liberation Tuscan CLN reports make reference to Fascist operations, for example those of 27 September and 14 December 1944 (ISRT, *Carte Francesco Berti*, envelope 1, folder 1). For the Fascists' activities to the south of the Gothic Line, see G. Conti, 'La RSI e l'attività del fascismo clandestino nell'Italia liberata dal settembre 1943 all'aprile 1945', in *Storia contemporanea* X (1979), pp. 941–1018.

79 Directives to federation commissars 11 June 1944, held in the ACS and quoted by Conti, 'La RSI e l'attività del fascismo clandestino', p. 976

80 See, for example, in the Fondo RSI: No. 1141, 'Rifrapa racconta' (10 November 1944); No. 1145, 'Lettere censurate' (9 December 1944) and No. 1197, 'Il fascismo nell'Italia invasa ha impugnato le armi' (1945).

81 However, Professor Seton-Watson (whom I thank for his testimony) recalls how, as a liaison officer placed with a CIL division, he saw a confrontation with a GNR unit. Similarly, Richard Lamb (whom I also thank) told me that there are documents in the Public Record Office reporting on clashes between the Friuli Gruppo di Combattimento and RSI forces.

they were present politically and militarily, in a contest that was nonetheless acquiring a significance that involved the entire Italian people – just as *squadrismo*, a central and northern phenomenon, had left its mark on the fate of the whole nation.

Graziani's regular troops also participated in the civil war, particularly the four divisions organised in Germany. In a poster Tito Agosti, commander of the Littorio division, gave warning of reprisals in the event of partisan attacks on Italian or German soldiers; in another poster Agosti gave news of a reprisal that had been carried out (four partisans shot). Again, by means of a poster a military command announced the execution of three partisans in reprisal.[82] 'The round-ups are being conducted by the traitors who have re-entered the country from Germany', Chiodi wrote in his diary.[83] In Garfagnana, when the Monterosa and Italia divisions arrived, things took a turn for the worse compared with the period in which the front had been held by the Germans: requisitions, thefts, reprisals to stem desertions.[84] In one of his writings many years later, Ferruccio Parri, engaged as ever in transfusing anti-Fascist tension into the national significance of the war of liberation, saw the arrival of Graziani's divisions from Germany as marking the moment when the struggle took on the 'character of a real civil war', and added vehemently: 'We could even go so far as to say that if the Germans had had more means at their disposal, or had not been forced into a tight corner by the way the war was going, more numerous and well-organised Graziani divisions could have created difficult problems.'[85]

The desertions that decimated these divisions only accentuated their Fascist character. Those who remained – and, up to the very last weeks, they were more numerous than the *resistenti* had bargained for – were in some cases the most cowardly, but in many other cases the most highly motivated and diehard. In Monterosa, according to a Garibaldino report, the Fascists were about 40 percent of the troops, and all the officers.[86] In short, in the

---

82 Fondo RSI, Nos. 292, 293, 309

83 Chiodi, *Banditi*, p. 32 (8 August 1944).

84 See E. Ronconi, 'Note sui rapporti fra il clero toscano, la Repubblica sociale italiana e le autorità d'occupazione tedesche', in Comitato regionale toscano per le celebrazioni del trentennale della resistenza e della liberazione, *Il clero toscano nella Resistenza, Atti del convegno di Lucca, 4–6 aprile 1975*, Florence: La Nuova Europa, 1975, p. 138. Ronconi based his work above all on parish priests' reports.

85 See F. Parri, 'La mancata Resistenza nel Sud', in *L'Astrolabio* XI: 1 (January 1973), p. 55. In *Il movimento di liberazione e gli alleati*, Parri had written: 'The dire influence of Graziani's army helped aggravate the horrors of the civil war' (Parri, *Scritti 1915–1975*, p. 523).

86 See the 'Relazione di ufficiale (ex partigiano) rientrato dall'internamento in Germania con la divisione Monterosa', sent to the Piedmont delegation by the Command of the 6th Langhe Division on 27 August 1944 (*Le Brigate Garibaldi*, vol. II, p. 276). On desertions, see the – far from precise – figures collected by Pansa for all four divisions:

controversy between 'national' army and 'political' army, force of circumstance proved Pavolini right.

It was not easy for the RSI Fascists to recognise the very existence of the partisan movement. After many years a Fascist described the first partisan prisoners with whom he came into contact as being very different from 'a kind of opposite version of ourselves'.[87] The Fascists in fact found it hard to understand how one could not be heroic, according to the image they had of heroism, yet nevertheless not banal. Apart from their propagandist aim, the use of expressions like 'bandits' or, worse still, 'hired assassins in the pay of the enemy' manifest their strong unease at an unexpected phenomenon, which they sought to exorcise by attributing its birth and development to external agents. This idea was reinforced by the tendency to refuse, at first, to make a careful distinction between partisans and escaped prisoners, above all if they were Slavs.[88] Communists and Jews – both linked, in the haunted Fascist imagination, to dark and powerful international organisations – lent themselves well to being indicated as those most directly responsible for a banditry directed by others.[89] The expression 'comunisti badogliani', used above all in the first months to describe the partisans (this was the name given to the Via Rasella assailants in Rome), while aiming on the one hand at compromising and disqualifying both by juxtaposing them, on the other hand presented itself as the internal version of the monstrous capitalistic–Bolshevik coalition against which Fascism and Nazism were fighting.

At the heart of the Fascist attitude lay deep-rooted incredulity in the very capacity of the anti-Fascists to fight. The memory of the all-too-easy Action Squad victories of 1920–22, when Fascist violence was organised while Socialist violence was not,[90] the long-enjoyed security of institutional protection, and contempt for the adversary (it is typical for the Fascists to call their enemies 'bastards', i.e. racially impure) left the Fascists unprepared to face a real civil war fought by both sides. It was one thing for them to vent their desire for revenge by reviving the punitive expeditions, and quite another to face other organised, armed Italians. Perhaps the altogether particular hatred that the Fascists

---

between 10 and 15 percent according to Graziani, 25 percent according to the Germans (thus around 16,000 out of 65,000). Pansa, *L' esercito di Salò*, pp. 207–8.

87 Mazzantini, *A cercar la bella morte*, p. 124.

88 A testimony that Ugo Tucci (who I thank) gave me regarding Umbria devoted some attention to this point.

89 See the example given by Bocca ('La Resistenza incomprensibile', in *La Repubblica di Mussolini*), where on p. 103 he cites a report from the Turin *questore* speaking of the CLN as led by 'Jewish communist types and elements in the pay of the enemy'.

90 See, on this observation, A. Lyttelton, 'Fascismo e violenza: conflitto sociale e azione politica in Italia nel primo dopoguerra', in *Storia contemporanea* XIII (1982), p. 979.

later reserved for the figure of Parri derived precisely from their incapacity to understand how such a fragile-looking man, discreet and no worshipper of violence, had managed in the end to be stronger than themselves. Allowing for the obvious differences, we might all the same suggest an analogy with Churchill's remark about Hitler's incapacity to understand what unshakable strength of will lay hidden, despite everything, in that frail gentleman with the umbrella, Arthur Neville Chamberlain.[91]

Thus, the reality of the partisan Vendée, as Mussolini called it,[92] was gradually brought home to high- and low-ranking Fascists alike, to extremists like Giorgio Almirante and moderates like Giorgio Pini. In June 1944 Graziani, in a memorandum to Mussolini, was compelled to acknowledge: 'Only the flat lands of the Po Valley were under effective Republican control. All the rest was virtually in the hands of the rebels.'[93]

Once they were forced to take stock of the real state of affairs, eliminating the rebels could not but be an essential objective. Above all, it would have been intolerable if even this task was dealt with by the Germans alone. 'You see? To do in the subversives there's no need of the Germans, we're enough!' said a Fascist to a comrade before the bodies of partisans displayed in Piazzale Loreto in August 1944.[94]

The Fascists had always been afflicted by fear of not being taken seriously by their allies. Even in Spain the Francoists had sung:

Guadalajara no es Abisinia
Los españoles, aunque rojos, son valientes
Menos camiones y mas c ...[95]

[Guadalajara is no Abyssinia
The Spaniards, even the Reds, are valiant
They have fewer trucks and more b[alls]

Now the Fascists had at all costs to show that, even if they were unable to fight seriously against an external enemy, they could at least, by the very fact of

---

91 See W. Churchill, *The Second World War*, vol. I: *The Gathering Storm*, New York: Houghton Mifflin, 1948, p. 495.

92 See Bocca, *La Repubblica di Mussolini*, p. 256 and Pansa, *L' esercito di Salò*, p. 155. Already in a letter to Hitler of 1 November 1943, Mussolini had spoken of the Apennine armed bands, albeit adding that there was no need to worry about this (quoted in Deakin, *Brutal Friendship*, p. 594).

93 Cited in Deakin, *Brutal Friendship*, p. 704.

94 Testimony of the partisan Lara, in 'Anonimo romagnolo', *1943–45*, p. 375.

95 See G. R. Zitarosa, 'Parentesi ventennale', in *Aspetti letterari. Lucania d'oggi* XIII: 4–6 (December 1953), p. 100.

being Fascists, crush the internal one. Taking seriously the distinction between the armed forces of the state and the party militias, Giovanni Tarabini, Modena regent of the republican *fascio*, theorised this unrealistic distinction of tasks: 'While the state will see to the war against the enemies at the front, the Fascists will see to fighting against the anti-Italian elements at home.'[96]

'I was captured only because I'm a Fascist. For no other reason', wrote forty-year-old Andrea Perusini, secretary of the Ronchi *fascio*, shot by the partisans of the Natisone Garibaldi division, in his last letter; and he was appreciated by them for his dignified behaviour in the face of death.[97] Umberto Scaramelli, the black *brigatista* from Fiumi, a veteran of the March on Rome, showed clear awareness of how hard the struggle was, and of how it had burnt bridges for both sides: 'If by some wretched chance our adversaries should win the day, they certainly won't have any pity on us; we must therefore be manly in character, continue fighting for the Idea, and if necessary die for it; at least that way our adversaries will have to respect us and recognise us as men worthy of the name!'[98]

Another Fascist accepts the consequences of defeat in the civil war, though still following the logic of revenge, which appears in him to be intrinsic to the cult of life. He declares: 'I've been sentenced to death by the partisans, by whom I've been taken prisoner. They've won and are therefore right to take their revenge on those fighting them ... I was wrong. I bet on the losing horse and now I'm paying for it. Let me say however that not for one moment do I repent my error', which was due to his choosing the path 'of honour and of life'.[99] A nineteen-year-old *paracadutista* appears more arrogant, calling 'the patriots' (his quotes) 'illusi' ('dupes' or 'dreamers'), but also 'wretched renegades' and 'cowards' and, assuring his parents that 'the *paracadutista*'s cudgel is hard, you know!', identifies himself with the *squadristi* of the mythicised old guard.[100]

Characteristic of the civil war are direct, personalised relations between combatants on opposing sides, from whom there pours forth not only rage and ferocity, but also a vast range of reactions and attitudes – from defiant bravado to the hurling of abuse, from pity to bewilderment, to a curious readiness to 'talk to each other'. Nuto Revelli tells of a telephone conversation that he had consisting of insults, while in the mountains, with a Cuneo *gerarca* (Fascist party

96 See the article 'Squadra di polizia federale' in *La Gazzetta dell'Emilia*, 22 November 1943. According to Tarabini every Fascist had to join the militias (cited in Gorrieri, *La Repubblica di Montefiorino*, p. 49).

97 *LRSI*, p. 110; and see Padoan (Vanni), *Abbiamo lottato insieme*, pp. 52–3.

98 *LRSI*, p. 168, letter to mother of Umberto Scaramelli, 28 October 1944.

99 Letter of 29 April to the mother of Paolo Comelli of Udine, born 1907, shot in Valsassina on 30 April 1945 (*LRSI*, p. 231).

100 Letters of 30 November 1944 and another undated from Sergio Mannucci, of Florence, fallen fighting the partisans on 21 November 1944 (*LRSI*, p. 172).

official).[101] An exchange of songs during combat well highlights some of these factors peculiar to civil war:

> At a certain moment the devilish shooting fell silent, and the low, calm voice of the vice-commander of the Bufalo battalion for the first time enjoined the enemy to surrender, to which the Fascists replied with volleys of machine-gun fire and with the usual cawing of the dying crows: *Battaglioni del Duce, battaglioni* ... The fighting continued like this, with greater or lesser intensity, for many hours. The enemy no longer sang, instead it was our valorous garibaldini who, heedless of the danger that had come very close to many of them, were singing: *Cosa importa se ci chiaman banditi* ... *Ma il popolo conosce i suoi figli* ... ['What does it matter if they call us bandits? ... But the people knows its sons'][102]

A man from the province of Bologna wrote to his wife in another key:

> I also don't think that the 'patrioti' will harm you, knowing my conduct as an Italian who for six years has been fighting in grey-green. If they should ask about me, tell them that I'll go to the front and that when the war's over, if we are the victors, will come back calm and content to my small village; if they are the victors, I won't go into hiding, but will give myself up to their courts, sure of receiving a serene verdict, in an Italy sanctified by so many sacrifices.[103]

A very young paratrooper addressed his parents as follows: 'I myself would like to go and see the partisans to have a drink with them and tell them that we must join forces to drive out first of all the real invaders, who are the English, Americans and company, then the Germans if they should refuse to go.'[104]

A case of genuine bewilderment, to be solved only by the intervention of the officers, is recounted by Franco Calamandrei, after a shoot-out in Rome in front of the barracks in Viale Giulio Cesare:

> A Fascist comes along the sidewalk firing a machine-gun. Then he turns around, enters [the tavern where Calamandrei has taken refuge], he's young, distraught, in a black leather jacket: and says to the women who are looking at him in terror and contempt – 'If you knew how I too am feeling! I've had it! That we have to do this kind of thing between Italians!' – and bursts into tears, throws down his weapon,

---

101 Revelli, *La guerra dei poveri*, p. 200 (17 April 1944).

102 'Relazione sull'attacco al presidio di Fara', by the Command of the 81st Brigade Volante Loss, 21 March 1945 (IG, *BG*, 08315).

103 Letter of 3 September 1944 from Myrio Montanari, born 1917, shot in early May 1945 (*LRSI*, pp. 160–61).

104 Letter from Mario Amprimo, born in Trieste in 1926, shot by the partisans in March 1945.

sinks to the ground and sits there in a half faint. Moved, the women gather around him, shake him, and cry as well.[105]

It would be wrong to think that the RSI survived exclusively, inasmuch as it survived, on its commitment to the civil war. The militant Fascists were a slim minority, far more isolated than the Resistance minority, which was much larger. The Fascists conducted their civil war on the wide strata of the population who found in the Republic their own peculiar modus vivendi. For Fascism, which, under the cloak of gaudy forced politicisation, had covered a far more penetrating and widespread depoliticisation of the Italians, it was now impossible to re-politicise, to their own advantage, great masses of the population in a situation of dire emergency – a situation which had increased the profound and widespread weariness produced by the war. Probably Mussolini – with what conviction, who can say? – tried to play once again the old double card of violence and normalisation, of the stick and the carrot, to use one of his last felicitous journalistic quips.[106] In reality, the RSI leant not only on the violence of the old and new *squadristi*, and certainly more so than on the demagogy culminating in 'socialisation', but also on the 'stuffy and oppressive atmosphere' breathed in the territory under its control. Roberto Battaglia had already drawn attention to this atmosphere in likening it, with an idea that was to be taken up again only recently, with that of the Kingdom of the South.[107]

The process of normalisation practised by the RSI should not be seen as a true re-establishment of order founded on a sufficient degree of certainty and law, but as an acquiescence obtained, within certain limits, to the commands of an authority that had suddenly stepped in with the purpose somehow or other of filling the void that had been created after 8 September.

Those who had experienced those days as a source of liberating exultation were upset and almost incredulous before what seemed a rapid and unjustifiable return to normality. Shortly after 8 September, Ada Gobetti noted in her diary: 'Outside, in the streets, on the tram, external life appeared squalidly normal. Incredulous bewilderment, enraged rebellion, was now giving way, in most people, to the indomitable resigned weariness of the Italian people.'[108] To cope

---

105 Calamandrei, *La vita indivisibile*, p. 137 (2 March 1944).

106 'Il tempo del bastone e della carota' ('The time for the stick and for the carrot') was the subtitle Mussolini gave to the anonymously published series of articles appearing in the *Corriere della Sera* in nineteen non-consecutive instalments from 24 June to 18 July 1944, under the title 'Storia di un anno'. In the last piece, the author revealed his true identity. See B. Mussolini, *Opera omnia*, edited by E. and D. Susmel, Florence: La Fenice, 1951–64, XXXIV (1961), pp. 301–444.

107 See Battaglia, *Storia della Resistenza*, p. 138, and Gallerano. ed., *L'altro dopoguerra*.

108 Gobetti, *Diario partigiano*, p. 25. This sense of becoming estranged from normal life, continuing in its ordinary rhythms, was described with particular intensity by those who were deported to extermination camps. 'The tracks that honeymooning couples'

with this problem, *L'Unità* drastically stated that 'between the occupiers and the occupied there is no possibility whatsoever of normalisation'.[109] But even the Jews were partly deceived by this spurious normalisation, thereby inscribing in the painful part of their memory the passivity with which they awaited the catastrophe.[110] And, to contaminate things further, even in those who actually accepted some form of normalisation, antipathy for the armed units that supported it remained and grew, fanned by the conviction that those units were formed by volunteers.[111]

Military disobedience, which was directed at the highest of the positions at stake, was not accompanied by equally extensive civil disobedience, though there were the appeals by the committees, the partisan commands and the parties, even to the point of inviting the population to boycott German goods and to abstain from public spectacles, and even of threats.

On the eve of the liberation of the city, the Florence CLN, which was the first to put itself forward explicitly as an organ of government, sent the vice-*podestà* a warning against the reporting, ordered by the Germans, of motorised vehicles and other materials: 'We therefore kindly ask you and your collaborators to refrain from such a practice ... We also think it opportune to inform you that, should you decide differently from our desires, you will be shot without further warning.'[112] The partisan commands were no less resolute. Commissar

trains glided along were no less smooth under our weight, and by day, in the countryside, people would stand to watch as our train passed'. R. Antelme, *La specie umana*, Turin: Einaudi, 1954, p. 31 (original edition: *L'espèce humaine*, Paris: Gallimard, 1947), cited in A. Rossi-Doria, 'Memoria e storia dei Lager nazisti. A proposito di "La vita offesa"', in *Movimento operaio e socialista* X (1987), p. 94. We could also cite the final scene of the Losey film *Monsieur Klein*, where the Jews are taken away while all around them the everyday activity of a market continues.

109 'Organizzare la guerra partigiana', *L'Unità* Rome edition, 30 December 1943.

110 See, for example, how it is recorded in Artom, *Diari*, p. 72. See also the audio-visual collection on the deportations from the Rome Ghetto of 16 October 1943, produced by the Istituto Romano per la Storia d'Italia dal Fascismo alla Resistenza, the Comunità Israelitica di Roma and the Comune's Prima Circoscrizione, which can be consulted at the Archivio Storico Audiovisivo del Movimento Operaio in Rome. An echo of the absurd trust in the Fascists can be found in M. Michaelis, *La persecuzione degli ebrei*, in Poggio, ed., *La Repubblica sociale italiana*, pp. 367–85. In Paralup, the area where the first GL bands were being formed in the Cuneese region, the partisans, particularly those who were themselves Jewish, called in vain on the Jewish families there seeking refuge before the predictable fascist raid, which, indeed, led to their capture (testimony to the author from Mario Giovana, whom I thank).

111 'The population is a little hostile to us, because it is said that we are all volunteers', wrote one airman ('Esame della corrispondenza censurata al 30 giugno 1944', in ACS, SPD, CR, RSI, envelope 9, folder 3).

112 The 26 July letter is published as an appendix in Francovich, *La Resistenza a Firenze*, pp. 296–7.

Cino [Vincenzo Moscatelli] and commander Ciro [Eraldo Gastone] warned a firm that had declared its intention to denounce unauthorised absentees from work to the Germans that they were laying themselves open 'to very bitter and overdue attention by the force of partisan law. This is a warning: only words. If you do not correct your attitude you will very soon learn what our style is: facts.'[113] The Communist press is full of warnings to those who collaborated in whatever form: policemen, hall porters, functionaries, actors.[114] Luciano Bolis has recorded that 'luckily, the greatest understanding reigned between conspirators and doctors (when it wasn't spontaneous, threatening letters made sure that it was equally active and effective!)'.[115]

But it was above all the activity of the CLNAI (the CLN for Northern Italy), which in the last few months of the war, after the written authority received on 31 January 1944 by the central committee and the following 26 December by the Rome government, should justify its recognition as the 'third government' or, if one prefers, the shadow government,[116] that was 'bent on making the actions of the Social Republic appear in an illegal light'.[117] Particularly notable, in terms of civil disobedience, was the exhortation not to pay taxes, which had already appeared in the 8 November 1943 issue of *Avanti!*. On 14 September 1944 the CLNAI decreed the suspension of the existing fiscal legislation,[118] and

---

113 'Lettera inviata dal Comando del raggruppamento alla Società subalpina di imprese ferroviarie di navigazione del lago Maggiore, 12 ottobre 1944' (*Le Brigate Garibaldi*, vol. II, pp. 437–8). See also the 11 June 1944 warning given by the Piacenza province divisions' command to the director of the local prisons (ibid., p. 31). In the summer of 1944 this author personally warned the director of the Castelfranco Emilia prison that if he was handed over to the Germans to be deported to Germany or to the Fascist firing-squad – which had recently decimated the political prisoners – then his friends would really make him pay for it.

114 See, for example, in the Rome edition of *L'Unità*: 'Dopo l'ultimo movimento dei questori. Avvertimento!' (17 November 1943); 'Gesto nazionale di alcuni attori' (7 December 1943); 'Il coprifuoco a Roma. Avvertimento alla polizia' (30 December 1943); 'Stiano in guardia i poliziotti ("la Giustizia popolare sarà senza pietà")' (6 January 1944); 'I portieri debbono aiutare i patrioti' (6 January 1944); 'Ultimo avvertimento alla polizia' (12 February 1944). Togliatti gave a stark warning on Radio Milano Libertà (Radio Mosca) on 30 December 1943 (Togliatti, *Opere*, vol. IV: 2, p. 514). 'Lettere ai funzionari di polizia' and paragraph 6 of the PCI leadership circular to all federations of 1 January 1944 (*Le Brigate Garibaldi*, vol. I, p. 212).

115 Bolis, *Il mio granello di sabbia*, p. 75

116 The RSI interior minister Paolo Zerbino himself spoke of the CLNAI's functioning in its latter phase as a 'shadow government', in a statement made to Giorgio Bocca (see Bocca, *La Repubblica di Mussolini*, p. 319). For the 'third government' formulation, see Pavone, *Tre governi*.

117 See G. Grassi, 'Introduzione' to the *Atti* CLNAI, p. 21, which refers to some efforts made in this manner.

118 *Atti* CLNAI, pp. 172–7.

the Ligurian CLN warned the citizens against paying taxes and the collectors' offices against forced payment orders, on pain of answering for them after the Liberation.[119] On 3 February 1945 the military command of the Piave zone issued a similar warning, and the Belluno partisans saw to it, as far as was in their power, that it was respected.[120]

On 15 March 1944 the CLNAI warned against subscribing to the 'prestito città di Milano' ('city of Milan loan') launched by Piero Parini, *podestà* and subsequently head of the province, who was fond of flirting with self-rule in Milan and *Risorgimento Liberale* urged the people of Milan not to subscribe to a loan that 'does not possess the qualifications and authorisations provided for by Italian laws'. But in a fortnight a billion lire were raised and the loan, after being annulled by the municipal council by decree of the CLN, was to all effects recognised as valid in 1946 by the city administration that won the election.[121] This Fascist success was all the more significant for the fact that it appeared to go against the trend of 'tesaurizzazione' ('accumulation' or 'hoarding'), which back in June 1943 had caused the 'scant success' of the issue of multi-year treasury bonds, compelling the government 'to rely increasingly on the pressure of bank-bills'.[122]

Only analytic research will be able to give an adequate indication of the outcome of the injunctions to fiscal disobedience. But Massimo Legnani's findings do seem to give us some idea:

> About 14 percent of the payments made by the RSI were covered by tax revenue, a percentage about 6 points lower than the margin assured by the fiscal revenue of 1940–43. Considering the general conditions in which the administrative machinery was operating, the difference between the two percentages appears undoubtedly significant, but not so much as to become a vertical fall.[123]

Sometimes it was the practical needs of small town councils that made it difficult to put fiscal boycotting into practice. This is revealed by the 31 October 1944 request by the 'CLN, Ufficio collegiale di Valsusa' to the CVL Command of the Alta Valle to put up a poster urging payment, given that, in the absence of tax collections, they were proving unable to provide essential services.[124]

---

119 Proceedings of 1 December 1944 (*Resistenza e ricostruzione in Liguria*, p. 160).

120 See Bernardo, *Il momento buono*, pp. 268, 158.

121 For the position taken by the CLN, see *CLNAI*, pp. 121–2. On the loan affair as a whole, see L. Ganapini, 'Lotte operaie: Milano', in *Operai e contadini*, pp. 175–80, 189–92, and then the section 'Un miliardo per la Repubblica ambrosiana', in Ganapini, *Una città, la guerra*, Milan: Franco Angeli, 1988, pp. 116–20.

122 See P. Baffi, *Studi sulla moneta*, Milan: Giuffrè, 1965, p. 232.

123 Legnani, *Potere, società ed economia*, p. 20.

124 INSMLI, *CLNAI*, envelope 6, folder 3, subfolder 3.

In fact, appeals not to pay taxes, and other similar appeals, do not always appear to carry complete conviction. The president of the CLNAI himself, the independent Alfredo Pizzoni, implicitly acknowledged this when he reminded the parties that 'as a rule what is decided at the CLNAI level serves for a well circumscribed interval of time'.[125]

The government of the South, for its part, was to take measures for 'legislative order in the liberated territories' without taking account of what the CLNAI was decreeing.[126] When a delegation of the prime minister's legislative office subsequently arrived in Milan after the Liberation, it was to write in its report: 'We feel no desire at all that the measures of the CLNAI or the various liberation committees be recognised as having legislative value.' The delegation thus toed the line of 'throwing in the sponge' over the clearly widespread practice of ignoring the CLNAI's injunctions of non-collaboration and civil disobedience.[127]

The double-crossing and opportunism, the absences and presences, the doing and not doing characterising the activity of the public administration which went over to the service of the RSI, often corresponded to the more or less widespread expectations of an exhausted population that needed to use certain essential services, and for which the dividing lines between acquiescence to de facto established authorities, fence-sitting and passive resistance were not well defined, thus making for a toing-and-froing from one territory to another. The 'resigned fatalism' that Mussolini himself could not help drawing to Hitler's attention on 3 October 1943 – though he considered it as coexisting with the opposite pole of a 'volontà di ripresa' ('determination to recover') – the oscillation of the large majority between scepticism and pessimism, which the Duce

---

125 See his letter 'Ai compagni del CLNAI', 8 August 1944 (*Atti CLNAI*, p. 155).

126 I am referring to the *luogotenenziale* (king's lieutenant's) legislative decree of 5 October 1944, No. 249. In the report presented to the commission charged with preparing its text, no reference is made to the CLNAI's position. The report is in ACS, Presidenza del Consiglio dei ministri 1948–1950, envelope 37, folder 1.1.26/13504, subfolder o. Its author, Arturo Carlo Jemolo, communicated its main substance in a 'note' in *Le fonti di diritto vigenti in Italia. Profili giuridici della tragedia italiana*, which can be found in the *Atti della Reale Accademia Peloritana* V (1944), pp. 127–50; see also, F. Margiotta Broglio, ed., in *Nuova Antologia* CXX: 2153 (January–March 1985), pp. 12–30.

127 The report of the commission, comprising Jemolo, the lawyer Antonio Galamini and a civil servant, dated 26 July 1945, is in ACS, Presidenza del Consiglio dei Ministri: 1948–1950, envelope 37, folder 1.1.26/13504, subfolder 9. For the affair as a whole, see Pavone, *Tre governi*, pp. 450–2. The Versailles National Assembly of 1871 took more drastic measures to confront the decrees emanating from the Paris Commune. It went so far as to deny the validity of registrations of marital status, but to avoid the inevitable bother arising from this, it was forced to accept marriages and the registration of one's natural children being written up *ex novo* on the initiative of the parties concerned, or, failing this, upon the request of the state attorney (see Jemolo, *Le fonti di diritto vigenti in Italia*, p. 26).

would again mention to Hitler at the Klessheim meeting of 22 April 1944,[128] the 'grey zone of the indifferent and the resigned' undulating between 'il popolo sano' and the 'rebels',[129] are like their counterpart, in Fascist guise, of the *attesismo* insistently denounced by both the Communists and the Actionists. The latter were all too aware how the moderate anti-Fascist parties had their eyes on the weary and uncertain mass whose numerical weight would count when it came to elections.

A strongly partisan and GL province like Cuneo would later give most of its votes to the monarchy and Democrazia Cristiana. The provincial head, who complained about not managing to get himself taken seriously 'because the population felt that the established authorities had less force than the rebels', traced this picture with pessimistic perspicacity:

> Here at present they are not very Fascist and do not seem to have been very much so in the past, but they were very great lovers of public order and legality; they are extremely attached to their possessions and almost all are small proprietors, workers, individualists, monarchists, or at least were so at one time – people who would like to have everything and give nothing.[130]

There was a great deal of Fascist propaganda against 'sceptics, fence-sitters, Anglophiles', as a poster of 20 April called them.[131] Another poster quoted these words of Eleonora Duse: 'He who despairs betrays'.[132] A propaganda postcard read: 'Sfiducia [here meaning "disheartenment"]. Away with that S', which was represented in the form of a serpent.[133] A leaflet of 5 October considered 'the Italians' attitude of equivalent detachment from the English and the Germans a way of not doing their duty towards the *patria*'.[134] Republican Fascism missed the fact that, though it makes sense to play a waiting game vis-à-vis a winning cause whose fruits one is waiting to gather, contributing as little as possible to it, it makes no sense to do so when it comes to a losing cause. In the latter case, fence-sitting can mean no more than waiting, without taking any risks, for by now inevitable, definitive defeat.

Between the small amount of possible ordinary administration swathed in vague Fascist phraseology and act upon act of increasingly barbaric violence, no

---

128 See Deakin, *Brutal Friendship*, p. 364.

129 See the SID (Defence Information Services) report of 29 February 1944, cited in Rizzi, *Lo sguardo del potere*, p. 87.

130 'Relazione al ministro dell'Interno del capo della provincia (prefetto) Quarantotto', 7 January 1944, cited in Revelli, *La guerra dei poveri*, pp. 437–8.

131 *Fondo RSI*, No. 889.

132 Ibid., No. 283.

133 Ibid., No. 485.

134 Ibid., No. 1039.

middle way lay open to the RSI. A twenty-one-year-old auxiliary, sentenced to death by the partisans of the Valle d'Aosta, expressed this contrast in the bitterest terms, blaming his fate on the uselessness of a war fought for those who preferred not to lift a finger: 'It's terrible to think that tomorrow I'll no longer exist; I'm still unable to convince myself. I don't ask to be avenged, there's no point; but I'd like my death to serve as an example to all those who call themselves Fascists and who sacrifice nothing for our Cause except words.'[135]

3. THE ANTI-FASCISTS' ATTITUDE TO THE CIVIL WAR

Anti-Fascist and Resistance circles sometimes refused, but more often than not agreed to recognise, implicitly or explicitly, what was taking place as a civil war, though with various inflections. These range from reticence to deprecation, from the rejection of all responsibility for the Fascists to the firm acceptance of the phrase as describing an incontrovertible fact.

The monarchist 'Centro della Democrazia italiana' adopted an extreme position. As late as April 1944 it accused the CLN of not having grasped the fact that, after the great event of 25 July, 'liberation', after 8 September as well, could only have 'the value and meaning of liberation from the foreigner', as well as the restoration of 'the reign of law' violated first in 1919–22 and then in 1922–43. The monarchist newspaper *L'Italiano* did not hesitate to use the formula 'war of national liberation' and, while going so far as to speak of 'war of religion', did so in the extremely literal sense of identifying the right side with the Catholic Church. The 'Centro' declared that it had been born to give voice to the increasingly large number of people who disapproved of the CLN and of whom, certainly, and above all in Rome, there were more than a few.[1] This was not an isolated position, as regards either the present, the past (the *biennio rosso* being bracketed with Fascism), or a near future, above all in Rome and the South. It amounted to the partisans being saddled with responsibility for the civil war even by those who were not Fascists. Another minor Roman underground paper had already done as much, albeit in the guise of an impartial condemnation of both parties. The parties, it says, 'under the influence of extremist positions', have 'unleashed the civil war', and it is difficult to distinguish right from wrong in it.[2] Victor Emmanuel III had come cleaner when, in his speech on Radio Bari of 24 September 1943, he had denounced those who 'either by betraying the oath they had given, or by forgetting the repeated assurances of loyalty given

135 Letter from Franca Barbier di Vercelli, 24 July 1944 (*LRSI*, p. 135).
1 See the editorial of *Italia Nuova* of 4 April 1944, 'Chiarimenti'; the 24 January 1944 issue; and the 1 March 1944 issue's article, 'Le premesse fondamentali della ricostruzione'.
2 See the article, 'Monarchia e sinistra', in *L'Italiano*, Rome, 15 March 1944. On 15 December 1943 the paper had taken a position against the 'so-called revolution'.

to me personally, foment civil war by inciting the Italians to fight against their brothers'.[3]

A few months later, what was happening in the North would be recognised in no uncertain terms as being a civil war by the general commanding the *carabinieri*, while explicitly denying a similar contraposition between the Kingdom of the South and the Social Republic.[4]

In its famous order of the day of 16 October 1943 (asking that it be given 'all the constitutional powers of the state'), the central CLN laid the entire blame for the civil war on the Fascists, maintaining all the while some uncertainty as to the effective outcome of the initiative that the latter had taken. In fact it spoke of 'Mussolini's last-minute attempt to raise, beneath the mask of a self-styled republican state, the horrors of civil war'.[5] The Modena CLN, to cite a peripheral example of some months later, resolutely declared:

> It is not [the patriots], it is not we who are responsible for the civil war. It is the Fascists who have wanted to unleash it in the crazy, criminal and desperate attempt to avoid the end that they deserve. And they are so vile as often to send to fight against the patriots young men who are our kindred spirits, blood of our blood. They are so impotent that they have to seek help from the Germans.[6]

Equally clear-cut was the position taken by *Risorgimento Liberale*: 'Mussolini is to blame for the blood being spilled today in the streets and jails of Italy, even the blood of his extreme and wretched supporters. It is he who has stimulated his followers, compelled his enemies, urged his allies to be violent. It is he who has unleashed the civil war.'[7]

Notable, in these two texts inspired by the 'moderate' parties, is its being taken for granted that the Fascists are worse than the Germans.

Views of the civil war appear to oscillate in the Christian Democrat press. On 23 October 1943 *Il Popolo* recognised its existence and laid all the blame on the Fascists; on 23 January 1944 it went back on this. On 12 December it had declared that the Italian front was the internal one.[8] The Christian

---

3 Cited in Degli Espinosa, *Il Regno del Sud*, p. 81.

4 'Relazione mensile riservatissima, dal luglio al novembre 1944, del generale Taddeo Orlando al presidente del Consiglio e ministro dell'Interno Bonomi' (in the ACS, cited in Aga-Rossi, *La situazione politica ed economica*, pp. 102–27).

5 The order of the day was widely reproduced in the Resistance press. See its text in Bonomi, *Diario*, pp. 123–4.

6 Leaflet of 2 April 1944, written by the Modena CLN's chair, the Christian Democrat Alessandro Coppi (see Gorrieri, *La Repubblica di Montefiorino*, p. 175).

7 See the article, 'Sangue', in its 5 May 1944 Rome edition.

8 See its Rome edition's articles 'Gli artefici della guerra civile', 'Italia e Antitalia: gli eroi di Monte Canino', and 'Il nostro fronte'.

Democrat view of things would be influenced by fear that the 'civil war' would swing in favour of the left and degenerate into revolution. Indicative of this is a document sent to Alcide De Gasperi by the Christian Democrats of Turin on 15 January 1945.[9] After giving a picture of the Garibaldi (and also Matteotti) partisan movement which anticipates many of the themes of 18 April, it said that unfortunately Democrazia Cristiana and the Liberal Party had not managed to impose the idea of 'keeping the rebels' movement on purely patriotic and military ground under a single command, which should also have been military in character'; Actionists and Communists had clashed because above all the latter aimed to make the partisan formations into 'an instrument of oppression for tomorrow, more so than a means of anti-German and anti-Fascist struggle for today'. Without too much thought to coherence, the authors of the document strongly underlined that 90 percent of the population were extremely hostile to the Germans, but even more so to the Fascists. Moreover, at roughly the same time, in one of its propaganda booklets the Ministry of Occupied Italy, run by the Communist Mauro Scoccimarro, published the famous words of the song *Fischia il Vento* (The Wind Whistles) with one variant, 'a conquistare la *bella* primavera' (rather than *rossa*), and another which had the partisan waving the Italian flag.[10]

Even in the left-wing press there were defensive, reticent or oscillating attitudes. On 7 February 1944 *Avanti!* wrote that Mussolini, 'before disappearing, wanted to build the premises of the new civil war'.[11] But more incisive lines of argument appeared, too. Above all the Fascists were reminded that their responsibility for the explosion of civil war was not just today's: they had been busy unleashing fratricidal war against the Italian workers for twenty years now.[12] There was also pride in taking up a challenge. Commemorating Mario Fioretti, a youth killed by the Fascists – baldly defined as a 'subversive', a very rare form of description for the Resistance press – *Avanti!* wrote that 'the murder of our comrade is to be regarded as being among the first signs of civil war'. And it added immediately:

---

9 The document is republished in part, without any indication of its source (probably the De Gasperi archive) in Bianchi, *I cattolici*, pp. 268–71.

10 See the pamphlet *CLNAI – Comando del CVL. Guerra di liberazione. Esperienze e figure del CVL*, Rome 1945.

11 See the Rome edition's articles 'Risposta al Primo Ministro inglese' and 'Che cosa vogliono gli operai'.

12 Such was the response of the Astigiano Gruppi di difesa della donna to the appeal for peace that the *podestà* had made for Easter 1945. They add that it was 'all too easy' to invoke concord now that the time to settle accounts was approaching (cited in Bravo, *La Repubblica partigiana dell'Alto Monferrato*, p. 230).

This war that Fascism has insisted on unleashing as the last act of the tragedy into which it has thrown the country will be waged by us without quarter. Only from this war, from what by now are its decisive discriminations and its bloodbath, will social justice and liberty for the Italian people and all Europe be able to rise as inviolable conquests.[13]

More soberly, *L'Italia Libera* wrote: 'So Fascism wants civil war? All right, then. And let it be the CLN that will wage it until Fascism is exterminated.'[14] In another 'actionist' article the undertaking was made with greater pride: 'We know that we have to achieve our idea in the fire of a war which is also civil war.'[15]

For the Action Party the civil war was an aspect, or an initial phase, of democratic revolution. Dante Livio Bianco spoke of 'true civil war, and ideological and political war if ever there was one' in a context in which democratic revolution was discussed.[16] Vittorio Foa wrote that 'the people's war has to be the first act of the people's revolution.'[17] Closer still is the tie established in a small GL newspaper: 'The opportunity to assert the rights and claims of the people and the workers is given us today now that the people and the workers are armed and can defend themselves, or never again … And this armed struggle has a name: Revolution!'[18]

From its opening lines a GL pamphlet vehemently emphasised that the Second World War was a war of religion: 'Fractions of Italians, Chinese, French and Russians are fighting today on both sides … We partisans feel the anti-Hitlerian German to be our brother and the Italian Fascist our deadly enemy.'[19]

Another, internal Action Party document recognised the civil war 'between opposing religions' as inevitable.[20] If anything, it was on tactical grounds that the need was felt to draw distinctions. Giorgio Agosti wrote: 'The tactic of "the worse it is the better it is", which consists of involving even the lukewarm and indifferent with the partisan cause and rousing the atmosphere of civil war in

13 *Avanti!*, Rome edition, 30 December 1943, article 'La figura del Caduto'.

14 Northern edition, 22 July 1944, editorial 'La tragedia'.

15 Editorial 'La rivoluzione italiana', in *L'Italia Libera*, Lombardy edition, 22 May 1944.

16 Bianco, *Guerra partigiana*, p. 20.

17 Inverni (V. Foa), *I partiti*, p. 73

18 '*Guerra di rivoluzione*', editorial of *Giustizia e Libertà. Notiziario dei patrioti delle Alpi Cozie*, September 1944 (cited in Giovana, *Storia di una formazione partigiana*, p. 199).

19 *Introduzione alla vita politica (per gli italiani cresciuti sotto il fascismo)*, Edizioni del Comando delle formazioni partigiane Giustizia e Libertà, p. 2. The author was Massimo Mila.

20 Circular of 31 October 1943, cited in Valiani, *Il partito d'azione*, p. 77.

the most indolent zones, is useful when insurrection is imminent, but becomes dangerous when one is forced onto the defensive.'[21]

Talk of civil war in any case took the refusal of continuity with the Royal Army to its extreme consequences: this refusal indeed already contained within itself the descent into civil war, in the strong sense of the term.[22]

The Communists regarded the civil war as an incontrovertible fact; but, while not shrinking from calling it by its name on many occasions, they did not insist on the use of the expression. This attitude may be ascribed to the Communists' prevailing commitment to making some class needs converge with the national and unitary character of the struggle for liberation, and to incorporating in this design the specifically anti-Fascist objective that was, by contrast, the core of the democratic revolution championed by the Actionists. In the course of events, however, it was the requirements of the struggle itself that often influenced the ideological pattern. On 19 September 1943 *L'Unità* wrote: 'The struggle against the Germans is inseparable from the struggle against Fascism. Nazi Germany and Fascism are locked in a mortal embrace: one cannot strike one without the other.'[23]

And immediately after this, on 29 September, the same paper explained: 'We mustn't forget that interwoven with the struggle against the Germans is a civil struggle that is already taking place.' Fascism is dead, 'but national life has certainly not been purged of Fascism. And some Fascists are taking advantage of the presence of the Germans to give vent to their base instincts of rancour, hatred and vengeance ... The struggle against the Germans and the struggle against the Fascists are one and the same thing.'[24]

A few days later *L'Unità* again clearly indicated the three tasks facing the Italian people: 'War against the Nazi aggressor; civil war against the Fascists, their allies; political struggle against the reactionary forces that lie across its path in the attempt to display all its energies and capacity for action and for fighting.'[25] The party's theoretical review authoritatively endorsed this point of view, writing: 'It is the time for battle, the time for the partisans' war, the time for civil war, the time for war actively fought against the Germans and against the Fascists.'[26] As for personal experience, a concentration camp survivor has

---

21 'Relazione del commissario politico del Comando piemontese delle formazioni Giustizia e Libertà', 31 December 1944 (*Formazioni GL*, p. 273).

22 See Giovana, *Storia di una formazione partigiana*, p. 256.

23 Rome edition, editorial 'La politica di Badoglio'.

24 'Per l'unità del popolo italiano nella lotta contro il nazismo e il fascismo', a long, notable article in the Rome edition, which, in a bitter polemic against Badoglio, reflected the Rome leadership group's understanding of the left turn that had followed 8 September 1943.

25 Rome edition, 5 October 1943, article 'Governo di Partiti'.

26 'Due svolte. La nostra organizzazione di fronte ai compiti nuovi', in *La nostra lotta* 1 (October 1943), p. 19.

recounted how, spurred to make the initial choice by his hatred of the Germans, he had then 'transferred the image of the German onto Fascism'.[27]

The operational instructions for fighting the Fascists often implied, above all when drafted by Actionists, Communists and Socialists, or under their influence, the enjoinder to go beyond the notion of the Fascist as a contemptible and dangerous but circumscribed residue. Paragraph 2 ('Azione prima di tutto' – 'Action before all else') of the 'Direttive per la lotta armata' ('Directives for the Armed Struggle'), issued in Milan in February 1944 by the military Command for Northern Italy, states:

> Let not only spies, *agents provocateurs* and traitors be our objective in the civil struggle, even if they are the main target. Let us aim at the petty local tyrants, the swine who are terrorising the populations, the political and military hierarchies in general, and particularly those whose disappearance could be most damaging and demoralising for the enemy. Let us deal with the offices and institutions of the Fascist party. Let us attack wherever possible the units, detachments and barracks of the militia.[28]

No less drastic, more than a year later, were the PCI 'Direttive n.16' for the insurrection, written by Luigi Longo and issued on April 1945:

> In the cities the GAP and SAP units must attack and unsparingly destroy as many Fascist *gerarchi* as they can get to; all those agents and collaborators and Nazi-Fascists who continue to betray the *patria* (*questori*, commissars, high state and municipal officials, industrialists and technical managers of production subservient to the Germans); all the Nazi-Fascists and 'republicans' who remain deaf to the *patria*'s injunction to surrender or perish.[29]

If we descend from these lofty declarations of principle and maxims to a more close-range view of things, this picture is not belied, but becomes more complex – at times more homogeneous, at times more blurred and differentiated. Here, too, the dividing lines between attitudes and sentiments do not always coincide completely with those that distinguish the top ranks of the parties.

A sentiment that was certainly widespread, and which stoked the loathing that was immediately manifested for the republican Fascists, lies in the way the latter assumed the character of dismal but brazen revenants. True, the forty-five

---

27 Testimony of Lidia Beccaria Rolfi, a primary-school teacher, in Bravo and Jalla, *La vita offesa*, p. 82.

28 *Atti CVL*, Appendix 1, p. 546.

29 The 'Direttive' were published in *La Nostra Lotta* III: 7 (10 April 1945), pp. 31–3. Secchia republished them in *Il PCI e la guerra di liberazione*, pp. 1010–11, but omitting the passage here cited, which can instead be found in Longo, *Sulla via dell'insurrezione nazionale*, p. 344, or on pp. 591–2 of *Le Brigate Garibaldi*, vol. III.

days of Badoglio's rule had been days of false liberty, of military dictatorship, of turbid compromises. But the headlong collapse of so much of Fascism's specific machinery and symbols had been such as to strike people's souls as an event from which there could be no turning back. Popular conscience had, to a large degree, galloped along this road, well beyond the intentions, fears and manoeuvres of the king and Badoglio. Now the resuscitated Fascists seemed, against nature, to be making time flow backwards. They had only just risen from the tomb, and there they were immediately giving orders. The vindictive attitudes they were flaunting (the conciliatory intentions recorded above were not so visible), the way they roamed about the cities in black shirts and motley uniforms, theatrically re-hoisting the symbols of the regime and restoring the Fascist names of streets and squares, the recapturing in Rome of Palazzo Venezia and the headquarters in Piazza Colonna, miming punitive expeditions and warlike assaults against nonexistent enemies – these were all spectacles that shook, frightened and saddened even those who had not completely clarified their ideas on whether they should join the Resistance. In Piazza Colonna, Franco Calamandrei's sharp eye came to rest on the 'people stopping in the square to watch, with a mixture of curiosity, fear, commiseration and mockery, and an expression of mutual understanding'.[30] Not so different from this is a Fascist's memory of things: 'The passers-by on the pavements raised their eyes, slightly astonished at seeing something so unexpected; they sought us with incredulous faces, but we were already some way away.'[31] The fact that the Fascists could once again play the bully like this because they were protected by the Germans deprived that resurrection of any glimmer of even the most obscure heroism.

Certainly, as I have already noted, the Fascists in this way re-qualified themselves in their own eyes and recharged themselves against their enemies. But the anti-Fascists recharged themselves too, many of them beginning to repent having been too temperate after 25 July, having confused their personal feeling of liberation with a reality that was in fact a good deal more irksome and difficult. In a climate that was 'more tuned to joy than revenge', an error had been committed out of too much generosity and failure of foresight: 'We mocked them, insulted them, and that was all.'[32] The Germans had been feared, not the Fascists. During the forty-five days, as Ferruccio Parri, who had always been vigilant of German moves, testified many years later, 'the Fascist revival was not taken as certain; it might have been probable, but I have to say that it was not viewed as being imminent'.[33]

---

30 See Calamandrei, *La vita indivisibile*, p. 113.
31 Mazzantini, *A cercar la bella morte*, p. 29.
32 Testimonies of Edovillo Caccia, in Dellavalle, *Operai*, p. 58, and of Alberto Todros, a Jew, in Bravo and Jalla, *La vita offesa*, p. 78.
33 See the *Intervista sulla guerra partigiana* he gave to L. La Malfa Calogero and M. V. de Filippis.

The error was not to be repeated, however. 'Don't delude yourselves with the memory of the forty-five days. This time you won't get off so lightly', wrote *L'Unità* on 4 June 1944.[34] And in the instructions circulated on the eve of the insurrection, the PCI leadership declared: 'We can't have a second 25 July.'[35] Running through the whole Resistance is this constant concern. *Il Combattente* wrote explicitly that on 25 July the Italian people had been too temperate.[36]

An article relating to Captain Mazzuoli, defined as 'one of Matteotti's murderers', reads: 'Not eliminated when he should have been, this scoundrel, like so many of his fellows, was able, after 8 September, to join the SS and commit other murders.'[37] In Rome, at a meeting of the Socialists in charge of the Appio-Tuscolano-Prenestino military sector, Giuseppe Lopresti, an extraordinarily noble-hearted and fine-spirited young man, said: 'The Fascists have returned because on 25 July Fascist blood was not spilled.'[38] The GL partisans who sang *La Badoglieide*, with the words 'ma il fascismo restava il padron' ('but Fascism remained the boss') expressed regret at not having acted at the right time. A curious piece of counter-evidence is furnished by an article in *Il Popolo* which, wishing to deny the existence of the civil war, argues: 'If that's how things were, why didn't it break out on 25 July?'[39] But it was precisely because it didn't break out on 25 July that it broke out on 8 September.

> We're telling you once and for all: we don't want to see your pre-25th July faces anymore. We don't want to see them anymore because *you are all responsible for the catastrophe that has engulfed us*; we don't want to see your faces anymore because you still have the old mentality, because you have the old methods, because, lastly, as long as you stay in the seat where you've placed yourselves again, no one will be able to believe in the possibility of renewal, in the new marching impulse, in the new idiom that you're preaching. We want new people, and by new people we mean: morally healthy and limitlessly honest.[40]

---

34 Northern edition, article 'L'ultimo quarto d'ora'.

35 'La Direzione del PCI per l'Italia occupata ai triumvirati insurrezionali e ai comitati federali', 24 April 1945, morning (*Le Brigate Garibaldi*, vol. III, p. 683).

36 Article 'Chi sono i ribelli! Chi sono i patrioti!' (n.d. but between January and March 1944, No. 3).

37 See 'Ricordi di un allievo ufficiale' (Luigi Bocci), in Bilenchi, *Cronache degli anni neri*, p. 38.

38 From the author's own recollections (Lopresti was later shot at the Fosse Ardeatine).

39 Rome edition, 23 January 1944, article 'Italia e Antitalia: gli eroi di Monte Canino'.

40 A passage from the Fascist paper *Emmerossa* (an unusual title), 'news-sheet of the youth militia', republished with some satisfaction in the Rome *L'Italia Libera* of 20 January 1944, in the article 'Riesumazioni'.

These are the words of young men who still believed in Fascism and its capacity to regenerate itself. But the sight of the old faces of the regime triggered in them reactions to some extent akin to those of the anti-Fascists.

On the other hand, the new-style Fascists had no better effect on them:

> [T]hey looked athletic, extremely efficient, infinitely more so than similar units of the late Royal Army, very modern, *Germanlike*, all with smiles of exploding faith, with a lousy visual effect, openly, deliberately fratricidal. But the acme was contained in the photograph of Ettore Muti's legionaries, who carried ultramodern weapons in the old fancy-dress of the March on Rome, tommy guns slung over black ski-tops, with the tin badge of the skull. But, on examination, unbalanced units, made up of old men and children, veterans, raw recruits and mascots.[41]

In the first few weeks an Action Party pamphlet had shown that it under-estimated the perilousness of the reappearing Fascists: 'No, poor, black-shirted Fascists, you won't manage to destroy Italy!'[42] Certainly, the Fascists were no longer capable of destroying Italy any further; but they were capable of inflicting cruelties upon it and of involving the anti-Fascists in a bloody final reckoning. 'They are using terror to defer the moment of reckoning as long as possible', wrote Eusebio Giambone in his last letter.[43]

The civil war between Fascists and anti-Fascists can in fact be seen as the recapitulation and final enactment, under the cloak of the German occupation, of a conflict that began in 1919–22. A similar interpretation has been advanced for the struggle between Vichy and the French Resistance, interpreted as a summing-up of the fractures that had marked the history of modern France: 'Sous le regard de l'occupant, se règle un formidable arrière de comptes.'[44]

In Italy the phenomenon had a special impact, because the conquest and management of power by the Fascists had been wholly autochthonous. This is precisely why the republican Fascists, coming as they did at the end of the cycle of Fascism's fortunes, had nothing new to offer, nothing to hope for; they themselves appeared desperate and became the object of a more intense hatred. By contrast, in the *resistenti* the reckoning, which looked back to the past, was capable of being charged with hopes and projects for the future.

---

41 Fenoglio, *Il partigiano Johnny*, p. 9.

42 'Che cos'è il Comitato di liberazione nazionale', *Quaderni dell'Italia Libera*, 1 October 1943, No. 3, p. 6. In the preceding pages we read 'Let us be clear: the black-shirted Fascists today leave the Italian people rather indifferent: a few lowly personal vendettas or raving displays of revenge do not change the overall situation.'

43 LRI, p. 106.

44 'Under the gaze of the occupant, there will be great reckoning.' Rousso, *Vichy*; J.-P. Azéma, 'Une guerre de deux cents ans?' – an essay from which (p. 148) the citation in the text is taken, in *Vingtième Siècle* 5 (January–March 1985), pp. 147–53.

I have already mentioned the retrieval of the memory of the *biennio rosso*, which was conducted by some of the older *resistenti*, and which seduced the younger ones. Two Communist leaflets addressed to the people of Florence proudly recalled the defence of the San Frediano district against the *squadristi*.[45] Flamigni and Marzocchi have spoken of town councils in Romagna that proudly cherish the memory of not having let the Fascist squads through, citing for example San Leonardo di Forlì, which was to became a centre of the Resistance and a firm seat of CLNs, partisan commands and PCI organisms.[46] To this day, in their reminiscences the elderly Turin workers interviewed as part of an oral history research project compare 1919–21, the period of the *biennio rosso* and of *squadrismo*, with 1943–45. As the interviewer observes, this is no mere repression of the Fascist *ventennio*, but 'has the merit of being an interpretation of history, a way of speaking about recovery from defeat'.[47]

It is true that the definition of 1919–22 as a civil war is disputable, even if it was used, both then and later, by Socialists, Communists and Fascists alike. In his report to the 7th Congress of the International in August 1935, Togliatti spoke of the 'most barbarous civil war' that took place in Italy after the war.[48] And in 1943, in his speech to the directorate of the Partito Nazionale Fascista (PNF) on 17 April, Mussolini said that the highly 'unpopular' war of 1915–18 'was the first result of the first episode of the civil war that ended in 1922'.[49] Jens Petersen has remarked how, 'in Fascism's mythology of wars and struggle, war and civil war make an indissoluble pact with each other', and how in 1919–22 there had been a 'unilateral distribution of the causes for violence';[50] and Adrian Lyttelton has made the point that Fascist violence was organised, whereas socialist violence was not.[51]

In 1943–45 revenge was indeed taken against this iniquitous distribution of violence, which was made to pay for the sense of frustration experienced in the uneven fight against the action squads:

> Ste quattro facce gialle color del sego
> portavano la morte e il me ne frego
> anche noi ce ne saressimo fregati
> se il governo com alor ce avesse armati

---

45 Held in the ISRT, Raccolta volantini, PCI Firenze (clandestini 1943–1944).

46 See Flamigni and Marzocchi, *Resistenza in Romagna*, p. 35.

47 See Passerini, *Torino operaia*, p. 76.

48 Togliatti, *Opere*, vol. III, book 2, p. 758.

49 Cited in Deakin, *Brutal Friendship*, p. 319, which adds the comment: 'Mussolini might have added that the second part of the civil war began, for similar reasons, in 1943.'

50 See Petersen, 'Il problema della violenza', p. 990.

51 See Lyttelton, 'Fascismo e violenza', p. 978.

[These four yellow faces the colour of tallow
bringing death and the motto 'I don't give a damn'
we too would have been screwed
if the government had armed us like then]

Sung in 1922 in Rome and Viterbo to the tune of 'La Leggenda del Piave', probably by the Arditi del Popolo, this song was then rediscovered by the partisans.[52] For their part, the Fascists who cultivated the myth of the return to origins dreamed of it as an opportunity not to repeat the errors committed in 1922 out of stupid indulgence. One of them, terrorised in the days of the insurrection by the stories he had heard about the 'Sarzana massacre' and the 'Empoli massacre', on seeing what remained of a Black Brigade, remarked: 'The last 18 BLs who left twenty-three years before.'[53]

The *resistenti* made the necessary distinctions between Fascists, offering them in the weeks immediately following 8 September a still possible choice to save themselves. That is to say, if exceptional events produced in the Fascists the temptation to damn themselves once and for all, the same events also offered the chance of redemption 'to the gentlemen who feel blood coming to their cheeks at the very memory of having been Fascists': these, wrote *L'Unità*, would certainly not allow themselves to be gulled by the resuscitated Mussolini and Farinacci.[54] A Modenese leaflet said: 'We offer a hand to all Fascists who have repented, and bullets for the *gerarchi* who persist along the path of betrayal.'[55]

The *resistenti* also distinguished between those who by now were fighting under the flags of the RSI. This was chiefly due to the obvious intention to divide and scatter the enemy, to the point of imposing the drastic final dilemma 'surrender or perish'. It was also due to genuine understanding for those who had answered Graziani's call-ups reluctantly or performed other acts of forced submission. And lastly it was due to the tendency already mentioned, a typical feature of civil war, to consider a more or less large proportion of those deployed on the opposite side as being recoverable on the field (which is an altogether different problem from the recovery of the defeated by the victors after the event).

This problem was faced squarely in two Communist documents. The 'Direttive di carattere generale riservate ai soli compagni' ('General directives reserved for comrades only') warned:

---

52 Portelli, *Biografia di una città*, p. 161. In the testimony given by Agramante Androsciani a direct link is made between the Arditi del popolo and the partisans (p. 163).

53 Mazzantini, *A cercar la bella morte*, p. 250. The 'BL', the first-mass-produced truck from Fiat, was often used in fascist parades and spectacles.

54 See the short piece 'Buffonate' in the Rome edition of 19 September 1943.

55 Article without byline or date in *Evviva i partigiani!*, No. 1 (see *Saggio bibliografico*, n. 4875).

Our policy towards the Fascists, including *squadristi*, must prove capable and must tend to dissolve those forces. We must tell them squarely that our future attitude towards them will depend on the position that they take at this moment. We need to bring home to them that the moment of their rehabilitation has come, and it will happen only insofar as they show themselves to be good Italians in the struggle against the Germans and against the Fascists who have sold themselves to the Germans.[56]

The 'Direttive', with evident reference to the attempted agreements recorded above,[57] hastened to add: 'This attitude of ours towards the Fascists must not lead us to make pacification pacts, whether they be made by single comrades or still less in the name of our party'; and not only because free credit should not be given to those who 'have always been our declared enemies', but to put a stop to a 'demagogic propaganda which has the cheek to demonstrate to the people the possibility of an accord with the Communists'. In other words, the crux lay in the dilemma posed by an appeal published in *L'Unità* on 5 October: *Fascists! This is the crucial point*: either save yourselves together with the dignity of Italians, or perish branded as traitors!'[58]

On 21 October the 'Direttive di lavoro' returned to the question of 'what line should be taken with the Fascists and the capitalists', making many distinctions between them.[59] Relations with the RSI, which had shown its colours, could only be combative. The 'anti-German Fascists' were not forbidden to fight the Germans if they really wished to; but this did not mean one should forget that the object of the struggle was the destruction of Fascism. The category 'anti-German Fascists' appears very rarely indeed, in such bald terms, in the Resistance press and documents. It does however raise, one might say preter-intentionally, a real problem that was deliberately passed over at the time by the immediate needs of the struggle, by subsequent political opportunism, and still more by the general need to feel purified. Namely: was it enough to become anti-German to cease being Fascist? As we have seen, the Communist document's answer seems to be 'no'; and certainly, no 'antitedesco' continued to describe himself as 'Fascist'. But if we take 'Fascist' in its strong sense, the perspective immediately became less linear; and the suspicion with which the merely military and patriotic 'autonomous' formations were viewed appears attributable not just to

---

56 Published in the 'Bollettino di partito', of 1 October 1943.

57 See also, in *L'Unità*'s Rome edition of 26 October 1943, the article 'Aberrazioni fasciste', which laments that some anti-Fascists, 'whether out of fear or foolishness, have swallowed the bait'.

58 Rome edition, article, 'Fascisti, attenzione!'

59 IG, *Archivio PCI*. The document is partly quoted, without any indication as to its date, in Flamigni and Marzocchi, *Resistenza in Romagna*, p. 135. On the part of the 'Direttive' concerning the PCI attitude to the capitalists, see the next chapter.

political sectarianism, but also to the perception of a difference in substance and to an unresolved tangle of the national conscience in wrestling with the problem of its responsibility for Fascism and the war.

The distinction between *gerarchi* and *gregari*, the high-ranking Fascist officials and the rank-and-file, offered a first possible way out. The Communist 'Direttive' of 21 October unreservedly criticised an article that had appeared in the southern edition of *L'Unità* on 12 October, according to which, 'if the representatives of the regime up to 25 July ... want to redeem themselves and become our brothers again', only one way is open to them: the struggle. Too easy! protested the 'Direttive': 'They have done too much harm to Italy and to our people for their present participation in the struggle against the Germans to absolve them completely. They, and above all the most senior of them, will always have to answer to the people for their misdeeds.'

By contrast, the 'ex-Fascists from the ranks, duped and deluded' must certainly be helped to take 'the road to redemption'.

The Fascists who did not seize the last opportunity offered by the catastrophe that they themselves had brought about, and who persisted instead in the wrong choice, appeared then as the symbolic essence of the twenty-year-old offence suffered by the Italian people. Facing them in a final showdown meant getting rid of something that went beyond their capacity to do harm (which was itself considerable) and then surviving as an organised political force (which was practically non-existent).

Probably, it is precisely during the civil war that the word 'Fascist' acquired, with particular intensity, a meaning that went beyond the concrete and specific historical experience of Fascism, eventually coming to denote a kind of human being with negative connotations from every public and private point of view. A Garibaldino's description of a Fascist is typical of this:

> Spy and agent provocateur, delinquent and pimp. He has punctually supplied information to the Tizzano carabinieri and was constantly on the lookout for information about our activities. He captured and disarmed Truk (Allegri), handing him over to the police. He has abused women with violence and death threats. A bestial, dangerous, hated man. He martyred his wife.[60]

A moderate paper is no less damning, with the possible difference that it stresses not so much the absolute wickedness of the man as his inconsistency on a plane that goes beyond mere ferocity: '*Repubblichino* in name and unchanged in substance, more bestial than before, more incompetent and incoherent,

---

60 To the partisans who took his wife, he essentially said, 'Do what you like with her'. See the 'Relazione del commissario politico Remo al Comando di brigata', regarding the Giordano Cavestro division, of 23 May 1944 (IG, *BG*, *Emilia-Romagna*, G.IV.2.2).

nonexistent save in acts of ferocious repression: a mob of violent and unhinged wretches, the object of scorn and the most exacerbated execration.'[61]

The persistent use of *fascista* as an epithet that was insulting, global, and expressive of all the ignominy that could reside in a human being may be regarded as the extreme consequence of this expansion, to which the RSI gave a decisive contribution, of the semantic content of the word beyond historically verifiable limits.

Resistance journalism, by and large, offered confirmation of the recapitulatory character acquired by the struggle against the Social Republic – and not just because it devoted thorough attention to the RSI as such, if only to denounce its subjection to the Germans, its repressive ferocity, and its demagogic manoeuvres culminating in *socializzazione*, but because it took its cue from the present experience to formulate differentiated long-term judgments on Fascism *tout court* – above all its origins, its 'nature', and the catastrophe it had brought about in the war. It is not one of the purposes of this study to analyse the intrinsic value of these judgments and their relationship both with the studies conducted during the Fascist *ventennio* and with subsequent historiographical studies. It will suffice here to give a few examples of the need that was felt to give historical and social, we might say 'objective', weight to Fascism – not least to give better support to the dislike of the republican Fascists, who found themselves being regarded as at once nonexistent and all too real. On 5 October 1943, *L'Unità* wrote:

> The re-creation of a pseudo-Fascist government does not mean the resurrection of Fascism: that is well and truly dead in the souls of the Italians. This government is nothing more than a branch of the Berlin Nazi government. It is both a grotesque and a tragic fact. It is the last act truly worthy of Fascism, the one that sums up all its acts of baseness and its crimes: betrayal of the *patria*.[62]

There could be different lines of argument. It was difficult to disentangle the search for the sub-base that had generated and sustained Fascism from the intrinsic inconsistency of the soul of Fascism itself. Fascism, a liberal pamphlet says, had been the 'improvisation of an unreasoning and uneducated faction which was supported by the self-interested complicity of classes who should have been in command of the country and accepted with indifference by the masses'.[63]

---

61 'Il Partito liberale italiano ai fratelli dell'Italia oppressa', in *Risorgimento Liberale*, Piedmont edition, July 1944.

62 Rome edition, article, 'Astuzie di ladroni'.

63 'Primi chiarimenti', a pamphlet of the Movimento Liberale Italiano, dated 1 May 1943, p. 1.

This was the 'aristocratic' version of Fascist inconsistency. A variant lay in attributing to Nazism a more solid historical and cultural structure. *La Riscossa italiana*, the 'Piedmontese organ of the National Liberation Front', wrote:

> It is well known that while Fascism sprung up fortuitously after the end of the war in 1918, with scant and vague Crispist and nationalist derivations, and with no coherent or constant ideas save that of hanging on to power at all costs ... Nazism, on the contrary, is linked to a vast, organic movement of ideas which for about a century has had a foothold in Germany under the auspices of Prussian militarism, pragmatism and racism.

It began with Fichte, the paper explains, continued with Treitschke, and then went from bad to worse.[64]

Inquiring into the fundamental nature of Fascism was, however, a means of warning against the tendency to identify it wholesale with the discredited republican Fascists in a sort of levelling and general absolution that let all the other Fascists off lightly. This line of argument took a wide variety of directions. A GL newspaper warned against forgetting those who 'pull the strings of these clumsy puppets whose heads are crudely carved in wood, and which have for so long been got up in the most disgusting and gaudily ridiculous variety-show uniforms'. The paper listed the puppet-masters as follows: 'the inhuman capitalism of the great industrialists and landowners, of the gigantic firms, unbridled militarism and high finance', backed by a king who had betrayed the Constitution.[65] This sort of *summa* of the convictions of the left, ranging from a section of the Action Party to the Communists, was given a clear Third Internationalist slant in a Garibaldi brigade document:

> Many ingenuous people still marvel at the fact that a theory like Nazi-Fascism, which is inconsistent from the ideal point of view and shameful from the civil point of view, has been able to turn the world upside-down. They forget or do not know that Nazi-Fascism is simply an aspect of polyhedric capitalist imperialism; it is a death-throe of great capital seen as a political force of world hegemony.[66]

---

64 *La Riscossa italiana* 1: 3 (December 1943), article 'I precedenti dell'ordine internazionale di Hitler'.

65 *Giustizia e Libertà. Notiziario dei patrioti delle Alpi Cozie*, June 1944, No. 4, article 'I nostri nemici' (cited in Giovana, *Storia di una formazione partigiana*, pp. 101–2).

66 As we read in the piece signed 'Cap. G. Neri', in the *Bollettino* No. 35 of the Command of the 52nd Garibaldi Brigade (Upper Lombardy), 13 August 1944 (IG, *BG*, 0589).

Even the Christian Democrat paper *Il Popolo* wrote: 'Behind the handy screen of Fascism, for twenty years the capitalist classes have imposed themselves on the state, dominated its politics, paid its men, inspired its ideas'.[67]

In the moderate Resistance press too, the capitalistic and landowning classes were frequently accused of collusion. But when very general, fulsome, at times rhetorical statements gave way to rather more pertinent arguments, the ideological and political differences reappeared. A case in point is the contrast between the lecture entitled 'Il Fascismo' from the *Breve corso per commissari* (Short course for commissars), given on 15 September 1944 by the 1st Garibaldi Osoppo divisional command, in the brief period from 27 July when the Garibaldini and Osovani achieved uneasy unification, and a discussion topic – 'political theme: the disunion first of the Italian, then of the German people permitted the advent of Nazi-Fascism' – developed on 1 November by the Friuli Osoppo division, which had again become autonomous.[68] The first text states that reaction, having repelled the revolutionary forces, sought a way 'of eliminating the class struggle once and for all', and found it

> in the nascent Fascist party which, run by a man with no precise political line, driven by his ambition to the conquest of power by any means, reunited in its ranks the most reactionary elements of the bourgeoisie and all the elements living on the margins of society, who were prepared to sell themselves simply to avoid having to work.

By contrast, the second text, which was mainly Catholic in inspiration, attributes the advent of Fascism not so much to the defeat suffered by the working class as to the very fact that there had been the outbreak of a struggle that had created 'unbridgeable abysses between the various classes, in other words the disunion of the Italian people'. In these words it is not difficult to glean retaliation against the vaunted unitarianism of the Communists. The document appears to have absorbed many of the views that Fascism had given to the post-First World War crisis: disorder, degenerate parliamentarianism, extremism, 'disillusion at the concrete results of the war'. The lack of 'quick and efficient' legislation, capable of ensuring a 'more equal distribution of wealth', had thus left the field free to 'extempore and charlatan demagogues'. Only when everything was already compromised did the parties, 'reduced to a scanty group of shadows, understand the mistake they had made, and they went off to ponder things on the Aventino, from which they were duly sent packing scornfully and derisively by the dictator and his thugs. A pathetic, wretched spectacle!'

---

67 Rome edition, 20 February 1944, article 'Demagogia repubblicana: la socializzazione'.

68 IZDG, envelope 272b, folder 1/A and B.

It is remarkable that, in a scenario so full of conventional elements, there should have been this final outburst of youthful moralism and opposition between generations, which more closely resembled Communist-inspired polemics than the defence of the Aventino still to be found in the 'New Year's Message to the Young' that appeared in *Avanti!*. Recognisable in that appeal is the soundness of the 'cruellest criticisms' on the 'plane of news and tactics', but it is solemnly stated that 'in spirit and in its historical achievement [the Aventino] was a memorable event'.[69]

Circulating in the Resistance press are a collection of opinions about the nature of Fascism that are not well amalgamated – not even in the Communist writings, which could have used a more rigid ideological frame of reference. Reflections, attempted inquiries, and the challenging of facts converge here – together with expressions of moral repulsion, either lengthily argued or the most rapid generalisations; judgments about the social and economic forces that had fathered and sustained the regime; denunciations of the responsibility of individuals, classes, social groups or the entire national community; and finally a desire to go beyond, while not prematurely burying, a past that was truly so arduous a task to put behind one. In an Action Party pamphlet a visible attempt is made to keep all these threads together. It talks in terms of 'institutional crystallisation' and 'social reaction', of 'mentality, in the deep sense given to this word by political speculation', of a 'psychological aspect' by which Fascism is 'a combination of distrust and fear which corresponds to the letter with the defence of very precise interests'.[70]

This widening of the significance to be given to the struggle against Fascism meant involving firstly the entire Italian ruling class, which was getting itself together again in the South, and then the whole of the nation's past, at least from the time of unification. The repression of the concept of civil war was certainly rooted in this subterranean awareness of its implicit potentiality to embrace Fascism in the widest sense of the word, to the point of overstepping it. 'No further proof is needed of the political failure of the ruling classes', wrote the Rome edition of *L'Unità* during the phase of stiffening anti-Badoglio sentiment following 8 September:

It is nonsense to say that the struggle against the Germans is not simultaneously a struggle to the end against Fascism. But the struggle against Fascism implies the mobilisation of large masses of the population, and Badoglio shrinks from this in horror [because] at the basis of the Badoglio government are those same plutocratic and imperialist groups which were formerly the soul of Fascism.[71]

---

69 Rome edition, 13 January 1944.

70 'Che cos' è il Comitato di liberazione nazionale'.

71 Editorial 'La politica di Badoglio', 19 September 1943. See also, in the same issue, 'Il vergognoso fallimento del governo Badoglio'.

More radically, *Avanti!* bore this half-title: 'The King's appeals from Palermo [*sic*] are echoed by Mussolini's speeches from Vienna: the dialogues of the dead!'[72] And *L' Azione*, organ of the Christian Socialists: 'The Italian people do not want to fight either for one (the monarchic government) nor the other (Mussolini's government).'[73] In an article entitled 'Il congresso di Bari', *L'Italia Libera* was to speak of 'two phantom governments' flapping this way and that against the backdrop of the Italian tragedy.[74]

The attitudes taken towards the purges are an excellent index of the different meanings given to Republican Fascism and to that of the *ventennio*[75] (just as in Restoration France they were compelled to distinguish between the followers of Napoleon during the 'normal' period and those of the hundred days).[76] The fact that the proposals were generally more drastic in the North than the South, or than in Rome, should be seen as being closely linked with the radicalising experience of the civil war.

For their part, the republican Fascists obviously polemicised against the purges set under way in the Kingdom of the South. But they do not seem to have taken advantage of that stimulus for self-criticism that they had claimed they wished to conduct; on the contrary, they were unable to hide a certain embarrassment. They declared the need for retaliation, played the victim, consoled themselves – Mussolini most of all – with repeated charges of conspiracy; in short, they revealed their fear of alarming their comrades by harping on too much about so burning an issue. The Duce himself was keen to put his seal on this question: 'None of this naturally can frighten us Fascists. We have committed ourselves to a struggle in which what is at stake is life itself.'[77]

The two sides engaged in the civil war also vied for the past of the nation, and above all the Risorgimento. In the last chapter attention was drawn to the anti-German use of the Risorgimento and the different evaluations given to it by the Resistance. Here we might add that there was nothing new in the different

---

72 Rome edition, 26 September 1943. In the same issue we read, 'With the tomfoolery of the Fascist restoration and the harlequinades of the monarchy's *volte-face*, the saddest twenty years of the *patria*'s history is now complete' (in the article 'Benito Pulcinella').

73 'Un popolo e due governi', in *L' Azione*, 20 October 1943.

74 Rome edition, 20 February 1944.

75 On the purges see Pavone, *La continuità dello Stato*, pp. 228–67, and M. Flores, 'L' epurazione', in *L'Italia dalla liberazione alla repubblica*, Milan: Feltrinelli, 1977, pp. 413–67. Also see L. Mercuri, *L' epurazione in Italia, 1943–1948*, Cuneo: L' Arciere, 1988.

76 See B. Constant, *Mémoires sur les Cent Jours en forme de lettres*, Chez Béchet aîné, vol. II, Paris, 1822. 'De l'hypothèse de la légitimité de Bonaparte jusqu'en 1814, et de son illégitimité en 1815', pp. 102–5.

77 Gabrielli, *La stampa di Salò*, pp. 163–74. The comment by Mussolini is taken from Note 46 of Radio Repubblicana, 'I puri e gli epurati', 31 July 1944.

interpretations of the formative process of national unity being used as instruments of political struggle. But, precisely because of the civil war, 1943–45 saw the final breakdown of the unity of the Risorgimento tradition as an instrument of 'nationalisation of the masses', independently of the fact that the RSI's appropriation of Mazzini and Garibaldi was largely illegitimate. The RSI could not but take to its extreme consequences the vision of a Risorgimento that aimed essentially at creating a strong, united nation-state, with the odd splash of populism perhaps, but in any case not undermined by liberal-democratic fancies and poisons. It was the most crudely Savoyard interpretation that the RSI inevitably made its own, even though it was compelled to expel the Savoy royal family. It was at the same time the interpretation that many of the groups of young Resistance intellectuals (and not just the Actionists) had learned to criticise and scorn in the pages that Luigi Salvatorelli had published on the eve of the regime's collapse.[78]

The objective of the Risorgimento dispute was the appropriation of the essence of that movement, whereby those who joined with the opposite side were rejected with the word 'anti-Italian'. There was nothing new about this phenomenon either. It has always been denied that the Risorgimento was a civil war, even in episodes like the Expedition of the Thousand, which saw only Italians fighting against Italians. This process is analogous to that described in regard to the 'war of national liberation', which led to the annihilation of the very nationality of compatriots fighting on opposite sides. The success of the appeals to the Risorgimento made between 1943 and 1945 probably lies also in their capacity to place the internal enemy on the same plane as the external one, in line with the reassuring vision of the founding process of the unitary state.

At times the recapitulatory thrust of the 'day of reckoning' that occurred between 1943 and 1945 transcended the very opposition between Fascism and anti-Fascism and its links with the Risorgimento. Fractures emerged, together with resentments, ancient desires for vengeance, more far-reaching and deeply rooted conflicting conceptions of the Italian man and the Italian nation. In a pamphlet written in December 1943, Riccardo Lombardi claimed that '1922 is simply a repetition, befitting the changed times, of 1898', just as Luigi Salvatorelli in 1919 had linked the crisis of the end of the century, the radiant May of 1915, and the Fascist reaction.[79] But comparisons and questionings could go well beyond this. There were imprecations against 'our historic curse, opportunism'.[80] There

---

78 I am referring to the slender volume *Pensiero e azione del Risorgimento*, published in the Saggi Einaudi collection in 1943.

79 Lombardi, *Il Partito d'azione. Cos' è e cosa vuole*, p. 8; L. Salvatorelli, *Sovversivismo conservatore*, in *Il Tempo*, 24 September 1919, and then in Salvatorelli, *Nazionalfascismo*, Turin: Piero Gobetti Editore, 1923, pp. 34–8.

80 'Responsabilità', in *L'Italia Libera*, Rome edition, 11 November 1943, reproduced 'from the Turin organ of the Partito d'Azione'.

was the wish to liberate oneself from the diagnosis of Fascism as a 'revelation' or as the 'autobiography of the nation'.[81]

4. THE MAIN ENEMY: THE FASCISTS OR THE GERMANS?

Once the figure of the Fascist enemy had been redefined, alongside that of the German enemy, the unifying category 'nazifascista' was not always enough to keep the two parties together, even though the category was viscerally understood by the majority of *resistenti*, and not invalidated by the fact that the Fascist was the servant of the German – not an occasional servant, but a servant morally and politically in accord with his master.

Let us take another look at a page from Beppe Fenoglio, whose initial title, we should remember, for *The Twenty-Three Days of the City of Alba* had been *Tales of the Civil War*.[1] Note this dialogue between two partisans:

Sandor says: 'I've got it in for the Germans, of course I have, for lots of reasons. But that doesn't compare with how I've got it in for the Fascists. As I see it they're the cause of everything'.

Ivan says: 'True ... but what kind of people are we Italians? We're in a war in which you can hurt everyone, you must hurt everyone, and we only do it among each other. What is this? Cowardice, idiotic goodness, justice maybe? I don't know. I only know that if we catch a German, rather than kill him we end up keeping him like one of our own. If the Fascists over there nab an Englishman or an American they'll certainly rough him up a bit, but they don't kill him. But if instead we nab each other, you've had it, and if we try to explain that we're brothers they laugh in our faces'.[2]

In this dialogue the claim, ideally so clear-cut and so often repeated, that the German is being fought only insofar as he is a Nazi and the Italian only insofar as he is a Fascist,[3] is unable to contain and control all the emotions and doubts that the civil war arouses in relation to the war against the foreigner. What is more, in Beppe Fenoglio's words there emerges one of the most perturbing aspects of the civil war.

---

81 Giustino Fortunato is the source of the first, well-known definition. The second appeared in an article by Piero Gobetti in the *Rivoluzione Liberale* of 23 November 1922, then again featured in P. Gobetti, *La Rivoluzione Liberale*, Turin: Einaudi, 1947, p. 185.

1 Falaschi, *La Resistenza armata*, p. 183.

2 Fenoglio, *Golia*, pp. 255–6 (the discussion is about the appropriate treatment of a German prisoner).

3 See, as a very clear example, an untitled article appearing in the Roman *Italia Libera* of 30 October 1943, where the cause being fought for is defined as 'universal', as against a Nazi-Fascism 'that denies and tyrannises humanity'.

The civil war was generally described by both sides as 'fratricide', so as to fan its horror and to lay a more infamous condemnation at the feet of the enemy, who was held up as the only culprit. There were families whose different members had chosen to fight on opposite sides.⁴ But the fratricide metaphor sprang most forcefully from fraternity as a category extended to the entire nation. Giancarlo Puecher, shot by the Fascists, forgave them because 'they know not what they do and do not know that brothers killing each other will never produce concord'.⁵ 'I'm not going to fight against my brother' – this was the reason a prisoner in Germany gave for refusing to join the ranks of the RSI.⁶ A southerner cut off in the North did not join the Fascists because he did not want to fight against his brothers; he did, however, join the partisans because, evidently, the Fascists appeared to him to have fallen from the rank of brothers.⁷ A soldier conscripted by the RSI did not intend 'to defend an idea that doesn't concern me ... kill a brother for no reason ... stain my hands and my soul with our [own] blood'.⁸ Fascist leaflets distributed in the South denounced the call-up to fight the brothers of the North.⁹

In the page from Fenoglio quoted above, fratricide appears as a fact that aggravates the struggle and which, in place of mutual pity, generates mutual scorn. Umberto Saba raised this theme of fratricide almost to the status of an interpretive canon for the whole of Italian history:

The Italians are not parricides; they are fratricides. Romulus and Remus, Ferruccio and Maramaldo, Mussolini and the socialists, Badoglio and Graziani ... 'We shall fight,' the latter had printed in one of his posters, 'brothers against brothers' (a great favourite, not determined by circumstances, it was a cry from the heart and a cry from one who – having got things straight in his mind – finally gave vent to his feelings). The Italians are the only people (I believe) who have at the basis of their history (or their legend) an act of fratricide.¹⁰

4 At the Brescia conference on the RSI I have already referred to several times – Poggio, *La Repubblica sociale italiana*, pp. 440–1 – Mario Venanzi recalled the case of two brothers, one partisan, the other in the Decima Mas; however, remarkably, this episode was used in defence of the view opposing the use of the term 'civil war'. At the same event a statement from Aldo Gamba, *Cenni sui servizi militari e politici di spionaggio e di informazione* (pp. 275–87), spoke of a partisan who was the nephew of Valerio Borghese. See also the case of a prisoner of the Allies, who remained a Fascist, whose brother, a partisan – 'he over there ... and I here' – was shot by the Fascists, 'thus by my own side'. G. Tumiati, *Prigionieri nel Texas*, Milan: Mursia, 1985, pp. 150–2.

5 *LRE*, p. 489.

6 Testimony of Pierino Vero, a carpenter, in Bravo and Jalla, *La vita offesa*, p. 124.

7 Testimony of Rocco Giovinazzo, a barber, in ibid., p. 80.

8 In a letter to his parents, from Montebelluna ('Esame della corrispondenza censurata al 30 giugno 1944', in ACS, SPD, CR, RSI, envelope 9, folder 3).

9 See Conti, *La RSI e l'attività del fascismo clandestino*, p. 950.

10 U. Saba, *Scorciatoie e raccontini*, Milan: Mondadori, 1946, pp. 13–14.

Saba forgot Cain and Abel, Eteocles and Polynices, Wagner's Fasolt and Fafner, and whoever else was to make Hannah Arendt write that the whole of human history 'is born from fratricide, any political organisation ... has its origin in murder'.[11] But Saba intended to provide a profound motivation for Italians' incapacity, even at the height of the fratricidal struggle, to perform a true revolution, which is inevitably parricidal.

In fact, if we skim the most direct and spontaneous Resistance documents, hatred of the Fascists seems to prevail over that against the Germans. This may naturally depend on the way Fascist repression was viewed: for example, in December 1944 (when Graziani's divisions had already arrived) the Piedmontese command of the GL formations considered it far more severe than German repression.[12] In the same period the group command of the Valsesia, Ossola, Cusio and Verbana Garibaldi divisions reported that 'the Germans opposed the conducting of roundups which the Fascists would like to conduct' – naturally, they were careful to add, without there being the least compromise between the patriots' formations and those of the German Commands.[13] At the same time, it might depend on the ordinary behaviour of the Germans and the Fascists: in that same period, Ada Gobetti saw the former as 'unbelievably stolid and indifferent (at times one would even say blind, deaf and dumb)' and the latter as 'far more curious and wide-awake'.[14] But there also emerges an intrinsic and profound loathing of those who, though Italian, had led Italy to ruin. A young man on his way to enlist in the *Stella Rossa* was asked by the commissar: 'What do you have in mind?' 'To kill Fascists.' 'Enough,' said commissar Ferdi, 'to go on with, more than enough.'[15] In Cernobbio, during the days of the Liberation, the population raised no protest against Germans being sent to Switzerland, but wanted to lynch the Fascists of the Republican National Guard (GNR) on the spot.[16] Many preferred to go with the Germans rather than the Fascists.[17] At a distance of a few years, an Actionist would state that 'the German was fought almost solely because he was the last incarnation of Fascism, his ally and accomplice'.[18]

While the Actionist did not unduly object to the tendency to see the Fascist as the main enemy, the Communist leaders often felt the need to curb

---

11 Arendt, *Sulla rivoluzione*, p. 13.

12 'Relazione del Commissario politico del Comando piemontese delle formazioni GL', 31 December 1944 (Formazioni GL, p. 268).

13 Letter sent on 31 December 1944 to the Lombard delegation of the General Command of the Garibaldi Brigades (IG, *BG*, 07501).

14 Gobetti, *Diario partigiano*, dated 11 December 1944, p. 251 (see also p. 260). The observation relates to the Baulard garrison in the Val di Susa.

15 B. Fenoglio, 'Il padrone paga male', in *Un giorno di fuoco e altri racconti*, p. 126.

16 Chiovini and Mignemi, *Il 44 sulle sponde del Lago Maggiore*, p. 9.

17 Testimony of the Istrian Francesco Del Caro, in Bravo and Jalla, *La vita offesa*, p. 84.

18 E. Enriques Agnoletti, 'Prefazione', in *LRI*, p. 14.

it, concerned as they were that it might lead to the national character of the struggle being blurred. The Communists, moreover, were more closely identified with the thinking of the coalition between the great powers, which had been adopted as an essential element of the new party strategy. They warned that the struggle against the Germans ought always to be considered the main one.

'There always remains', says a Garibaldi document of winter 1944, 'the conviction in the GAPs that those most responsible are the Fascists and that the Germans will be dealt with later. But we are doing our utmost to combat this way of thinking and reckon to have concrete results soon.'[19] From the Marche, the following June, it was reported that 'the actions have been directed principally against the Fascists but there have also been those against the Germans, though to an insufficient extent'.[20] And in Lombardy again:

> It is not right to maintain that our struggle should be conducted only against the Fascists. By doing so, we would play the German enemy's game ... Therefore, the struggle against the Germans should be the principal struggle that we must conduct in order to liberate the soil of our country for good. Act then indiscriminately against Germans and against Fascists as common enemies.[21]

This was the Solomonic and not altogether coherent conclusion.

With a view to the insurrection, a Ravenna Communist document says, a new 'line' must be adopted, responsive to a *revolutionary* need. The 'most feared enemy', the one most hated by the people, was no longer the Fascist but the German, and so the latter was the 'enemy who needs to be struck at' with a 'continuous, ruthless fight to the death ... in order bring the masses ever closer to our action'.[22]

Behind the greater inclination to fight the Fascists 'impregnated with ferocity and defeat',[23] there might well have been, in some cases, the greater fear inspired by the German warlords; but there was also the hatred aroused by the Fascists themselves, whose subaltern position to the Germans seemed to generate, almost by way of compensation, a touch more violence.

---

19 'Rapporto del Comitato sportivo', Reggio Emilia, n.d. but February or March 1944 (IG, *BG, Emilia-Romagna*, G.IV.2.7).

20 From the Divisional Command delegation for the Marche to the Garibaldi Assault Brigades Central Command, 27 June 1944 (IG, *BG*, 01229-97).

21 Lombard delegation of the Garibaldi Brigades General Command to the Command of the 54th Valcamonica Brigade, 17 September 1944 (INSMLI, *Brigate Garibaldi*, envelope 2, folder 1, subfolder 1).

22 See the 'Circolare n. 13', containing the 'directives for action' of the Ravenna provincial military committee of 3 July 1944 (cited in Casali, *Il movimento di liberazione a Ravenna*, vol. I, pp. 71-2).

23 Meneghello, *Bau-sète*, p. 25.

'I was able to ascertain', reads another Garibaldi document, 'that while the Germans reserve the fighting for themselves, they leave the dirty work, such as that of hangman and jailer, to the *repubblichini*.'[24] While the Germans, recounts a prisoner who managed to give them the slip, succeed in 'exploiting down to the finest detail the errors committed by the partisans towards the local populations ... they leave the Fascists in charge of the reprisals and acts of violence against civilians and partisans'.[25] In a Ligurian band it was ruled out, incorrectly of course, that 'the Germans got involved in such operations', namely the reprisals.[26]

When in Florence, in December 1943, there was the reprisal against the killing of Colonel Gino Gobbi, the Germans refused to hand over five officers they were holding.[27] In this particular case it might have been a question of formalistic respect being paid to different competences; but the impression aroused was nevertheless always an increase in the odiousness of the Fascists, even when the Germans handed over to them for execution prisoners whom they had previously tortured.[28]

In a discussion between Veneto Garibaldini the opinion clearly emerged that what was done to shorten the war – the destruction of vehicles, for example – would undoubtedly count with the Allies and the decisions they would take about the future of Italy 'more perhaps than the number of Fascists eliminated, although morally, for the whole partisan movement, the elimination of the Fascist lackeys is the most powerful tonic sustaining us'.[29]

Ferdinando Mautino (Carlino, head of the Natisone Garibaldi division General Staff, mentioned earlier) argued this irrepressible priority given to hating the Fascists with a reflection that seemed to reverse the trend: that it wasn't so much the Germans who were sustaining the Fascists but vice versa. 'The work of local traitors, without which no foreign force would have been able to manage, was indispensable.' If, Mautino explained, the Germans were able to organise themselves rapidly, it was because they had 'found at their feet cowardly and irresponsible officials and public functionaries, greedy and corrupt

---

24 See the report by 'Oreste', the military organiser of the Piedmont insurrectionary triumvirate, 'Sulla situazione della brigata e distaccamento Garibaldi dislocati nelle Prealpi verbanesi (Gruppo Zeda)', 24 June 1944 (*Le Brigate Garibaldi*, vol. II, p. 64).

25 Giglioli's report of 20 January 1945 (IG, *BG*, Emilia-Romagna, G.IV.2.6: see *Le Brigate Garibaldi*, vol. III, p. 288, n. 4).

26 'Rapporto del commissario politico', 27 March 1944 (IG, *BG*, 09965).

27 See the testimony of G.B.A., 'Fucilazione alle Cascine', in Bilenchi, *Cronache degli anni neri*, p. 71.

28 Such was the case of Walter Magri, shot by the Fascists at Poggio Renatico on 27 March 1945 (*LRI*, p. 125).

29 'Relazione della riunione del Comando brigata Tollot a Coledi', 27 March 1945 (INSMLI, *CVL*, envelope 35, folder 1, subfolder 3).

industrialists and speculators, and the ignoble thugs of the Fascist hierarchy'.[30]

Recognition is given to the Germans in contrast to the Fascists even by a member of the insurrectional triumvirate for Emilia-Romagna. This Communist leader took the Modena GAP brigade command to task for having sent letters, for an exchange of prisoners, not only to the German command but to the prefect and to the Black Brigade command. He points out that

> The German Command is waging the war more or less within the international rules. We can denounce its acts of brutality, but essentially we can deal with it as belligerent to belligerent, but not the Fascists! They are traitors in the service of the foreigner and it is precisely by writing to the Germans that we must brand with fire this shameful fact of sold flesh.[31]

Whenever possible, the Germans were the first to speculate on the distinction they saw being made between themselves and the Fascists. A German officer said of the partisans: 'They attack us because they want to take our weapons in order to fight the Fascists.'[32] The Germans had general orders from above to avoid if possible entering 'into direct contact with the Italian population, but to use the Italian authorities as executive organs'.[33] And they even flattered themselves with the belief that the Italians would appreciate 'their objectivity, to which they were hitherto unaccustomed'.[34] The Germans thereby turned to their advantage, with how much intentional perfidy it is hard to say, the role of mediation with the population that the protagonists of the Social Republic (and its retrospective apologists) have attributed to it. On the field several German attempts were made to divert the force and anger of the partisans against the Fascists.

In the Marche, before the failed attempt to get the Macerata brigade to hand over their arms pacifically, the SS offered (again unsuccessfully) 'to leave them

---

30 Mautino, *Guerra di popolo*, p. 47.

31 Cecco 'to comrades Livio and Cyrano', 20 December 1944 (*Le Brigate Garibaldi*, vol. III, p. 119).

32 See the unusual encounter between a German official and the GAP commander Cicchetti in an Emilian peasant's house, recounted in Cicchetti, *Il campo giusto*, p. 209.

33 See the 'Direttive per la collaborazione fra il plenipotenziario del Grande Reich [Rahn] e il generale plenipotenziario della Wehrmacht in Italia', Toussaint, n.d. (in Collotti, *L'amministrazione tedesca*, pp. 276–9).

34 As the Milan military commander, Colonel Seeberg, adjudged the action he had taken in the city's factories to quell the tensions being fomented, as he put it, by the foolishness of the Italian authorities (18 January 1944 report, cited in Collotti, *L'amministrazione tedesca*, pp. 197–8). The Japanese ambassador was also impressed by the Germans' efficiency and discipline, as against the egoism, arrogance and tyranny 'as it was before' of the Fascists (see his report to the Mikado, n.d., in Ragionieri, *Italia giudicata*, p. 804).

in peace, provided they undertook not to fight the German occupying troops, so [gave them] ... free rein to do in the ... Fascist ... allies'.[35] In the Pavese Oltrepò, too, the Germans showed themselves willing at certain moments to come to an agreement, 'promising the patriots that they would leave them ample freedom in their struggle against the Fascists'.[36] In the zone of Imperia a German commander 'made pacification proposals, namely that they were not to attack the Germans and they for their part would take no measures against Italians who dissented from the Fascist regime. In the presence of the Italian SS he added: that the Italian dissidents could do what they wanted against the Fascists, that they washed their hands of them etc.'[37]

It was by now spring 1945, and the document I have just quoted also recalls symmetrical attempts to reach an accord on the part of the republican National Guard, the San Marco division, and the provincial head of Savona. The truth is that, out of the corner of their eye, the Fascists had always kept close watch over the Germans for fear of being ditched. 'Throughout the zone complicity between the partisans and Germans is in the normal run of things', a bitter and frightened Fascist had written with regard to the Valtellina.[38] The Germans, however, knew all too well that they had the whip-hand. The Val Pellice commander did not mince his words with the GL partisans who, earning the contempt of the Garibaldino Barbato, had sought to speculate on the disagreements between Fascists and Germans: 'Coming to terms with us you avoid the Fascists, but coming to terms with the Fascists you don't avoid us.'[39]

It has always been a good tactic to divide one's adversaries, in peace as in war. The *resistenti* also tried it out, but came up against two very powerful obstacles. The first lay in the almost fatally fanciful character that the action assumed, as soon as it went beyond the mere recognition of the Germans' low regard for the frustrated Fascists. 'Open disavowal of Fascism by the Germans' was the optimistic moral that *L'Italia Libera* believed it could draw from the way the Milan strike of December 1943 had gone.[40] The 'shrewd line' to pursue, suggested

35 'Relazione dell'ispettore Dario sulla situazione nelle Marche, nella Toscana e nell'Emilia', June 1944 (*Le Brigate Garibaldi*, vol. II, p. 58). See also the analogous case in the inspector Paolo's report, 'Cari compagni', of 15 June 1944 (ibid., pp. 33–5).

36 'Relazione sulla situazione delle Brigate d'Assalto Garibaldi dell'Oltrepò Pavese', signed by the commissar Piero, 3 September 1944. Piero comments that 'this is a symptom of their weakness' and an attempt to buy time while awaiting reinforcements (*Le Brigate Garibaldi*, vol. II, p. 304). Indeed, this was during the period of the partisans' great summer offensive.

37 PCI report 'Sulla situazione militare e politica dal 19 ottobre al 4 novembre', n.d. (INSMLI, *CLNAI*, envelope 8, folder 2, subfolder 9).

38 See the note to the letter of Aminta Pruneri, class of 1891 (*LRSI*, pp. 148–9).

39 See Artom, *Diari*, pp. 165, 167 (dated 10 and 13 February 1944).

40 The subtitle of the article, 'Lo sciopero a Milano', covered the whole first page of the 20 December 1943 Lombard edition of *L'Italia Libera*.

by a document submitted to the Tuscan CLN, of avoiding compelling 'Germans and Fascists to bolster, for reasons of defence, their ill-matched solidarity', was easier to preach than to practice.[41]

The other and more substantial obstacle lay in the fact that the only viable form that these divisive attempts could take was to stipulate separate agreements with one enemy or the other. Here, a dual reality has to be registered. The political directorates and the central partisan commands always issued the firmest prohibitions about resorting to this kind of thing. Witness the military command for Northern Italy's 'Direttive per la lotta armata' of February 1944 and the CLNAI's 'Appello agli italiani' of 3 December 1944.[42] There may at times have been some sign of a certain gratification in seeing the arrogant adversaries compelled to come to terms. Thus *Avanti!* informed its readers with satisfaction that, in many places in Piedmont, 'the small Nazi garrisons are negotiating with the partisans, who have the control of that zone in their hands'.[43] And *L'Unità* wrote: 'Kesselring would like to come to terms', terms that naturally are not considered.[44] The gratification was completely justified, seeing that Mussolini found himself compelled to complain to Ambassador Rudolf von Rahn that 'in many places the German military local authorities have come to modus vivendi terms with the partisans; forming true and proper agreements ... which has increased the power and prestige of the partisans'.[45] This power and prestige seemed still greater for the very fact that the advances were rejected. *L'Unità* writes proudly: 'After having sought to obtain from our commands a sort of "neutrality" at least towards the German troops, the German Command was compelled to give battle.'[46]

At the basis of this firm stance on the part of the leaders, there was not only political and moral intransigence but 'Gobettian seriousness', as Dante Livio Bianco put it[47] – the conviction that agreements with the Germans ultimately put the partisans in an invariably inferior position. In fact, even with the good faith of the local Germans or Fascists, it only took an order from above for them to feel obliged to violate the agreements that had been reached, and they did

---

41 See the *Informazioni per il CLN* 2 (18 January 1944) (ISRT, *Carte Francesco Berti*, envelope 1, folder 3, subfolder *Informazioni*).

42 See *Atti CVL*, p. 559, and *Atti CLNAI*, pp. 206–8.

43 'La lotta partigiana in Piemonte', *Avanti!* Rome edition, 12 January 1944.

44 'Un Corpo d'Armata sulle retrovie della linea gotica', *L'Unità* northern edition, 7 August 1944.

45 See Deakin, *Storia della Repubblica di Salò*, Turin: Einaudi, 1963, p. 714. A secret circular of the RSI Regional Military Command, 11 September 1944, archived in the IVSR speaks of contacts between the Pasubio Division partisans and the Italian and German police, without 'resulting in clarification'.

46 'Una spina nel fianco', *L'Unità* northern edition, 7 September 1944 (on the liberated zones of the Emilian Appennines).

47 Bianco, *Guerra partigiana*, p. 99

just this. By contrast, a partisan could find himself plummeting into the crisis of conscience that beset comrade Ferrarini (Enzo Costa): Did you have to keep the word you had given to the Germans?[48]

At the local level, however, alongside firmly intransigent stances ('our intentions, in keeping with the principles of our struggle, are contrary to any form of compromise', declared one Garibaldi command with reference to some German advances),[49] several cases of agreements both with the Germans and with the Fascists need recording. Weariness, disheartenment, irresponsibility, fear, difficulty in relations with the populations who feared reprisals, scant political awareness, rivalry between bands of different political persuasions – these and other similar motivations can be traced from one case to another, apart obviously from the cases of deliberate betrayal, in the agreements struck or even just attempted. The very possibility of this behaviour would have been absent outside the framework of civil war waged in the form of a partisan war. In fact it is the high degree of autonomy that the individual partisan formations possessed that allowed them to size up contingent situations with a freedom unknown to regular armies. Those who stipulated these agreements were generally convinced that what was involved was a purely local necessity that left the fundamental principles of the struggle intact.

Indeed, if civil and ideological war is tendentially war without quarter, it also contains a greater readiness for encounters and transactions. Simplistic tactical calculation and an inclination to 'talk' to the enemy could thus converge in encouraging contacts that were not mere invitations to desert. The fact that it was a game between three players, or rather that one of the two parties presented itself in dual form – Germans (Nazis) and Italians (Fascists) – heavily influenced the interweaving, which reappeared at this level, between national affinity (and hostility) and politico-ideological affinity (and hostility).

Documentary traces of these contacts have remained above all in the denials, condemnations and injunctions not to make them by the political and military leaders of the Resistance – and, with particular vigour, by the Communists and Actionists. Used at times as an argument in these appeals was the failure of the 'deceptive armistices (like those in Rome and Milan last September)'.[50] At other

---

48 The episode is recounted in the 'Relazione di Marelli sul lavoro svolto fra i volontari della libertà in montagna' (Piacentino), 26 December 1944. Marelli argued that they would not keep their word (it was a matter of freeing an imprisoned German lieutenant in exchange for Ferrarini) (*Le Brigate Garibaldi*, vol. III, pp. 142–3).

49 Communication from the Ugo Muccini Garibaldi Brigade (La Spezia) to the local CLN leadership, 12 November 1944 (ISRT, *Carte Enzo Enriques Agnoletti*).

50 Such was the reasoning of *La Riscossa italiana* (organ of the Piedmont CLN) of January–February 1944, in its editorial 'Saldezza del fronte antifascista', where it praised the freedom-fighters who had 'almost unanimously' proved able to foil the enemy's manoeuvres.

times a unitary organ like the military Command for Northern Italy, which denounced several cases that had occurred especially in Piedmont, was distrustful about taking part in the manoeuvres of the Badoglians, who, as the Fascists boasted, were collaborating with them and the Germans 'to combat extremist bands and common criminals'.[51] Here too the Communists tended to turn to account the formation in Salerno of the government of national unity, which 'perhaps ... may be able to have some sway over these gentlemen and persuade them to change course: the course piloted, in fact, by former army officers, of compromises with the enemy'.[52] On 27 September, on the eve of the autumn crisis, the Lombard regional command issued a circular which again identified any compromise, such as agreements for the delimitation of neutral zones, as treason: the only contacts allowed were those for the exchange of prisoners.[53] On 27 November 1944 the Veneto regional command denounced the fact that mountain units had consented to work for the Todt organisation in the hope of avoiding the roundups: 'Whoever comes to an agreement betrays the cause and must and will be treated as a traitor.'[54]

There were also mutual denunciations between the formations, and generally it was the Garibaldi who most insistently accused the others, and not only the 'autonomous' or 'Badoglian' formations. For example, the scene at the mouth of the Val Pellice was bitterly denounced: 'Guards beyond the Santa Margherita bridge; on the other side there are partisans under the influence of the Action Party. Both sentries can see each other and protect the entrance in their respective zones of influence in utter peace.'[55] The Novara Socialists come in for the severest accusation for having, with the support of the Catholics, appeared to have negotiated with the Fascists, swallowing this line of reasoning: 'Since we're all against the foreigner ... stop firing at the Fascists and Germans from 6 January, and wait for the foreigners to clear off when the war's over.'[56] Tendencies

---

51 See paragraph 20, 'Direttive politiche' of the 'Direttive per la lotta armata', Milan, February 1944. According to the document, 'there is a national pact ... and anti-communism must not become the cover for the struggle against it' (*Atti CVL*, p. 560).

52 The Piedmont delegation letter 'Cari compagni', of 19 April 1944, referring in particular to an episode taking place in Val Sangone (*Le Brigate Garibaldi*, vol. I, pp. 355–9).

53 'Circolare del Comando regionale lombardo alle formazioni dipendenti', 27 September 1944 (INSMLI, CVL, envelope 90, folder 1).

54 The circular is kept in IZDG, envelope 272b, folder 1/C.

55 The Cuneo No. 4 Brigade's political commissar P.'s letter 'Cari compagni', 28 February 1944. The matter was reported with disdain by the Command of the Brigade to the Piedmont CLN's Military Committee on 15 March (IG, *BG*, 04211).

56 'Dal colloquio con un compagno del Comitato federale di Novara', 30 December 1944. Also in December, a report on the organisational and political situation in the province signed by 'Valbruna' (Vittorio Flecchia) for the attention of the PCI secretariat, held that 'the Socialists, at first "radical" to the point of wanting to exclude the bourgeois

on the part of the GL and Matteotti formations to come to terms with the enemy were denounced by the Piedmontese Garibaldini in August 1944.[57] Another compromise with the Germans, proposed by the 13th zone command and the GL but disdainfully rejected by the Garibaldini, is the subject of a document of the Oltrepò in the province of Pavia.[58]

The Garibaldini-Communists' particular insistence in making these denunciations may be explained on the one hand by the feeling they had that they were bearing the greatest weight in the struggle, and on the other by the fear that the agreements were being made behind their backs, in order to isolate them politically and militarily. This can be gleaned in some of the documents quoted above, where real facts are mixed with suspicion and sectarianism. The aim behind the intransigence demanded of everyone, therefore, was also to guarantee oneself against unpleasant surprises that might be contemplated by the other partners in the coalition (allowing for the due proportions and differences, it was a guarantee analogous to that implicit in the formula 'unconditional surrender'). Naturally, the Communist leaders felt committed to taking an equally vigilant line towards their formations, when it was reported that they were going astray.

'The energetic action of our men prevented the negotiations from having a completely positive outcome', said a Garibaldi document about the Canavese area, where it was again claimed that the Germans were being driven to seek compromise by the strength of the formations.[59] From Valcamonica a command reported that it had rejected the German advances ('give us weapons and we'll accompany you to Switzerland'); while, again in the province of Bergamo, at the end of August 1944, there were reports of negotiations opened, out of ingenuousness, by the 13 Martiri di Lovere formation.[60] A case in Valtellina was deprecated, and the opportunity was taken to repeat that anyone who set about

---

currents from the CLN, have now become nothing less than capitulationist faced with the Fascists'; as a consequence of these changing positions, 'it has thus far not been possible to implement the pact for unity in action' ('Rapporto sulla situazione politica organizzativa', IG, *Archivio PCI*).

57 'Relazione sull'attività militare', sent on 26 August 1944 to the Regional Command of the Command of the 4th Piedmont Division (*Le Brigate Garibaldi*, vol. II, pp. 272–3).

58 Report from the inspector Riccardo (Alfredo Mordini) of the 3rd Lombard Division 'Aliotta', 25 November 1944. On 28 November he would inform the General Command's military delegation that the GL had made an agreement on its own, and thus the Garibaldians had been forced to bear the German assault alone (IG, *BG* 01652 and 01654).

59 'Situazione militare della zona sotto il controllo del Comitato militare di ...', n.d., around mid-April 1944 (IG, *BG* 03974).

60 Command of the 54th Valcamonica Brigade to the Command delegation, 'Notiziario-Bergamo', n.d. (IG, *BG* 010564 and 010734).

doing this kind of thing was a traitor.[61] The tragic results that bargaining of this kind could lead to were pointed out.[62] Also denounced was 'the naivety of thinking one is negotiating with the enemy to 'screw' him ... Even if the accords have not been accepted, whoever has negotiated has made a mistake and the mistake must be highlighted, discussed with those concerned, brought home to them, and they must perform severe public self-criticism, if the encounter occurred in good faith.'[63]

A request for authorisation, in exceptional cases, to engage in 'negotiations limited to the time necessary for overcoming extreme temporary difficulties' was firmly and disdainfully rejected. One could negotiate, it was repeated, only for the exchange of prisoners.[64] If this rule was breached the punishments were exemplary: on 15 September the group Command of the Lombard divisions communicated 'to the dependent Commands' that Carlo, *intendente* (quartermaster) of the 1st battalion of the 40th brigade, had been sentenced to death 'for having negotiated and bargained with the German invader'.[65]

The Nazi-Fascists 'vainly try to get in contact with the formations, arguing, promising etc. until someone swallows the bait': this was what the Lombard regional Command reported to the general Command of the *volontari della libertà* in January 1945, citing the case of the GL Orobica division, which had emerged drastically reduced and whose commander had been committed for trial by a partisan court. With the same rigour as the Garibaldini, the GL authorities had immediately taken measures to proceed against the commander, Marcello, describing him as a traitor.[66] The political commissar of the same division became rattled over the fact that he had had a

61 The 'Delegation for Lombardy' to the 1st and 2nd Divisions Group Command, 24 September 1944 (INSMLI, *CVL*, envelope 93, folder 4, subfolder a).

62 For example, the cases of Nevio in the Valle di Gressoney and of Gastone (86th Brigade) in Valtellina. See the 'Relazione sulla Valle di Gressoney. Rapporto del commissario della Valle, Negri' of 11 November 1944; the 'Breve relazione riassuntiva per i compagni della Delegazione per la Lombardia', signed by Maiocchi, 2 December 1944; the communication from the Lombard Divisions Group Command to the Command delegation, 4 December 1944 (IG, *BG*, 05694: see *Le Brigate Garibaldi*, vol. II, p. 585, note 3, and vol. III, pp. 13–17; IG, *BG*, 01287); as well as the very harsh reprimand, calling for revenge, from the delegation to Group Command (INSMLI, *CVL*, folder 4, subfolder a).

63 'The comrades responsible' to the Vice-Commander Pietro and the 'Comrades responsible for the 2nd Piedmont Division', 16 December 1944 (*Le Brigate Garibaldi*, vol. III, p. 101).

64 See the 'Comunicato del Comando della 3a divisione Piemonte', 2 October 1944 (*Le Brigate Garibaldi*, vol. III, p. 393).

65 IG, *BG*, 01152.

66 Report dated 1 March 1945 and letter from the Lombard Command of the GL formations to the Command of the GL Division Orobica, 15 December 1944 (INSMLI, *CVL*, envelope 93, folder 5, subfolder a).

conversation with an SS captain and asked whether he should resign. (He was told he should not.)[67]

One could continue to cite cases of this kind – which also involved, often with particular intensity, the autonomous formations. For example, between August and September 1944 the ill-starred Fiamme Verdi (Green Flames) of the province of Brescia struck various pacts with the Germans, who left them a free hand to deal with the Fascists.[68] The fact that formations inspired by essentially patriotic ideals bargained not only with the Fascists but also, and possibly even more, with the foreign invader, with the express purpose of being better able to fight their fellow countrymen on the other side, confirms the complex web of motivations which, for all their differences, sustained all the *resistenti*.

A Garibaldi Command of the Ossola province warned against contacts with the units of Graziani's army, of the Decima Mas and the like, who were trying in this way to 'differentiate themselves from the real Fascists', in the name of a second-hand nationalism that would lead them to fight against the English and Americans today and the Germans tomorrow. One of our men, this warning goes on to say, is giving himself free rein in these colloquies to compromising remarks, like the commander who 'for instance, let out this howler: that he too hated the English and Americans'.[69]

Obviously, when offers of this kind were made by the Fascists in spring 1945 they appeared particularly suspect – not any longer because they hid traps for the partisans, but by virtue of their obvious and tardy opportunism.[70] Greater alarm, by contrast, was aroused by episodes of fraternisation – albeit sporadic

---

67 Regional GL Command for Lombardy to the Commissar Mario, 11 April 1945 (INSMLI, *CVL*, envelope 93, folder 5, subfolder a).

68 The suspicion that the Fiamme Verdi were prone to deals and bargaining with the enemy is illustrated by the 'Relazione riservata del rappresentante delle formazioni GL nel Comando militare regionale lombardo sulla situazione politico-militare delle formazioni Fiamme Verdi e del generale Fiore', 18 March 1945 (INSMLI, old classification, Comando militare regionale lombardo, Delegazione Brigate GL, Corrispondenza). Similar reports appear in various Garibaldian documents: for example, a report from the inspector Remo to the Lombard Regional Command, the CLNAI and the Lombard delegation of 10 March 1944 (INSMLI, *CVL*, envelope 90, folder 4). For the arguments over the Fiamme Verdi and General Fiore, see the letter from the Bergamo zone-commander 'Bassi' (Mario Buttaro) to the Lombard Regional Command, n.d. but January 1945 (IG, *BG*, 010605). The formation's commander, Captain Gianni, soon repented, asking to be readmitted into the movement (see letter from 'Bassi' to the Lombard Regional Command, 20 March 1945, IG, *Archivio PCI*).

69 'Circolare a tutti i commissari politici di brigata sui colloqui con i Comandi nemici', from the Command of the 1st Gramsci Division, 20 October 1944 (*Le Brigate Garibaldi*, vol. II, pp. 457–9).

70 See, for example, the 'Circolare n. 19 sulle relazioni col nemico', from the Piave Zone Command, 20 March 1945 (ibid., vol. III, p. 511).

– again with a nationalistic emphasis, like that reported at Venaria Reale, where Garibaldini and Fascists dined together in a restaurant 'extolling the liberation of Italy from the Germans, the English and the Americans'.[71]

Of a different feather were the contacts made with the civilian authorities of the Social Republic with a view, as we saw earlier, to asserting somehow the authority of the 'third government' over them as well. Locally established power relations were in many cases more effective than the solemn appeals of the CLN bigwigs. This gave rise to curious and sometimes ambiguous coexisting powers. The partisans of the Pinan Cicero Garibaldi division ordered the various *podestà* to put up posters decreeing that Fascist spies be executed.[72] In Postua, in the province of Biella, the prefectorial commissar placed himself under the partisan command that had been set up in the town.[73] In the free zones of the province of Belluno, in the spring of 1944, 'many prefectorial commissars and local authorities, who were to become collaborators of the movement, were invited by the partisans to stay in their posts for reasons of convenience';[74] and it was certainly convenient for both parties. Thus some *podestà* came to act more as shock absorbers between the population, on the one hand, and the Germans and the Fascist government, on the other, than as representatives and time-honoured right hands of the latter.[75]

A report on the province of Macerata says: 'Often, spontaneously and at their own expense, the local Fascists indemnify individuals' or comrades' families who have been the victims of thieving or devastation committed by bullies from other zones brought into those zones to conduct funerals or reprisals after the killing of some Fascist or spy'.[76]

The partisan Rosanna Rolando has told the story of how, having to get a supply of bombs out of the Turin tobacco factory for the GAPs, she went to

---

71 'Informazioni da Torino', 13 December 1944, from the Piedmont insurrectionary triumvirate official Alfredo, who had sufficient scruple to say that this news was still yet not confirmed (ibid., p. 68). An apparently analogous case of GL members – or supposed GL members – fraternising with fascists was mentioned, and denounced, in a 3 April 1945 document sent from the Lombard Divisions Group Command to the delegation and insurrectionary triumvirate for Lombardy (ibid., pp. 574–8). The tendency not to trouble the Germans without having first been attacked was mentioned in a document of the Military Command of the Valli di Lanzo, 30 January 1944 (IG, BG, 04205).

72 See Lazagna, *Ponte rotto*, pp. 94, 167; on p. 172 there is a fine description of the population's many efforts assisting the partisans.

73 See Dellavalle, *Operai*, p. 119. On the coexistence of RSI and CLN authorities in peripheral areas, see pp. 210–11.

74 Bernardo, *Il momento buono*, p. 50.

75 See the observation made on this score in Chiovini and Mignemi, *Il 44 sulle sponde del Lago Maggiore*, p. 9.

76 'Relazione sull'attività partigiana nella zona di Macerata', n.d. but late March 1944, probably written by the Communist federation (*Le Brigate Garibaldi*, vol. I, p. 343).

the director and said to him: 'I am the CLN chief. If you think fit, have me
arrested immediately. Now or never, because they'll do you in', and the director,
though 'dumbfounded' and 'all in a sweat', obeyed.[77] In the Cansiglio forest the
Garibaldini approached the forestry militia (one of those corps which had for
some time now been Fascist only in name and because of the black shirts its
members wore), who 'terrorised, accepted a pact of mutual respect. The militia
were to do their job by supplying the partisans with all the armaments and
information they might need'.[78]

In Albano, at the request of the pontifical villa of Castel Gandolfo, the CLN
created a commission that included the *podestà* and dean.[79] There was also
the borderline case of the negotiations for coexistence of a sort in the Monte
Cetona zone, conducted by the military-style SIMAR autonomous formation
with Giuseppe Chiurco, provincial head of Siena and historian of the Fascist
revolution. The ambiguity of such behaviour, however, also cost the RSI dearly,
since, by getting mixed up in this double-dealing, its local authorities, from
the *podestà* to the *fascio* secretaries and the *carabinieri*, disintegrated and went
into hiding.[80]

There is also documentary evidence of agreements for the formation of local
government organisms, which were very limited in number, even on the part of
formations a good deal more important and better informed than the SIMAR,
led by the modest and muddleheaded Colonel Silvio Marenco. This occurred in
the Lanzo valleys, where the Garibaldini established contact with the prefectorial commissars to set up new municipal administrations.[81] It occurred in the
Biella area too.[82] In Dronero it was the prefectorial commissar who attempted
to create a civil guard enlisting partisans into it as well; and the CLN seems
somehow to have got in on the negotiations: the Socialists and Actionists above
all, but also the Garibaldini, to judge by the warning addressed to them too.[83]
This civic guard ploy was a recurrent attempt to bridle the most intransigent

77 Bruzzone and Farina, *La Resistenza taciuta*, p. 23.

78 Bernardo, *Il momento buono*, p. 38.

79 See the 'Relazione riguardante la zona dei Castelli Romani dal 22 gennaio 1944,
data dello sbarco in Nettunia, al 15 febbraio 1944', n.d., unsigned (*Le Brigate Garibaldi*,
vol. 1, pp. 261–2).

80 See Manno, *Le bande SIMAR*, pp 47–50.

81 See the letter sent from the Command of the 2nd Piedmont Division to the Valli
di Lanzo CLN, 22 July 1944 (*Le Brigate Garibaldi*, vol. II, pp. 155–7).

82 See 'Relazione dell'ispettore Gigi sulla ispezione al Comando del raggruppamento divisioni biellesi', 15 December 1944 (ibid, vol. III, p. 78).

83 See the sharp denunciation in the 'Relazione sul lavoro svolto in Valle Maria',
unsigned, 30 July 1944 (ibid., vol. II, pp. 172–4) and the warning sent to the Garibaldini of
Dronero and the surrounding area by the commander, Steve, and the political commissar, Copeco, of the 104th Carlo Fissore Brigade, 15 January 1945 ('Ai garibaldini di Dronero
e dintorni', ibid., vol. III, p. 238).

Resistance demands, and was a terrain for privileged encounters between the moderates of both sides. The Communists and Actionists were frequently compelled to take up baldly contrary positions.

In evaluating episodes of this kind it is always a good idea to bear in mind dates and circumstances. What Mario Lizzero, one of the ablest and most influential Communist leaders, wrote on 27 September 1943 was clearly a bitter pill to swallow from the point of view of the Resistance. Concerned as he was about relations with the population, Lizzero saw a possible interlocutor in the 'non-reactionary authorities', with whom he urged the 'maintenance and increase of good relations', listing the following examples: 'parish priests, *carabinieri*, village worthies'.[84] In the Montefiorino zone, after the roundup of July–August 1944, the democratic administrations that had been created in the period of the partisan republic stayed in their posts, accepting a modus vivendi with the RSI. Certain town councils (*comuni*) thus had 'sindaci popolari' ('people's mayors') and 'commissari prefettizi di comodo' ('compromise prefectorial commissars') at one and the same time, so that the municipal archives still contain traces of correspondence with both the mountain CLN and the authorities of the RSI. Ermanno Gorrieri remarks: 'On both sides, a sense of responsibility had prevailed with regard to the excessively rigid political organisation of things, thereby preventing the consequences of the civil war from weighing yet more heavily on the populations.'[85] It should be added that this process occurred at the time that control of guerrilla warfare in the Modenese mountains passed temporarily from the Communist to the Christian partisans, commanded by none other than Gorrieri.

In a town like Carrara, located at one of the confines of the Gothic Line, agreements with both the Fascist and the German authorities created a situation that was on the one hand grotesque, and on the other highly dangerous for those partisan formations that refused to accept this kind of compromise:

Further to incidents and consequent contacts with republican and German authorities, the activity of the CLN of Carrara is by now public knowledge; the president is known; various commissions, including the food commission, function in collaboration with the state bodies; but German negotiations with the Julia partisan formation to obtain free passage across the Cisa, have been 'conducted irresponsibly', and several spies who were sent among the formations [which had not accepted the agreements], have facilitated and possibly caused a massive roundup'.[86]

---

84 Report from Andrea 'Dal Comando battaglione partigiani Friuli' (ibid., vol. I, pp. 95–7).

85 See Gorrieri, *La Repubblica di Montefiorino*, pp. 545–9; see also p. 561, n. 22. The words 'civil war' (p. 547) are, in Gorrieri, an obvious slip of the pen, given that he denies the legitimacy of such an expression (see p. 222, n. 17).

86 See the 'Promemoria per il CLN della Liguria d'incarico del presidente del CLN

On several occasions, agreeing to dialogue with the Fascist authorities could offer an opportunity to make provocatively unacceptable requests to them. The Communist delegate sent by the CLN (along with a Christian Democrat) to the provincial head and the *podestà* of Modena, who undertook to save the installations if the partisans refrained from attacking the retreating Germans, declared that on the contrary the struggle needed stepping up, and demanded both the immediate resignation of the two functionaries and that they make a public anti-German declaration.[87]

The final transitional phase would obviously be that in which contacts with the enemy intensified, taking on a different, increasingly differentiated meaning according to whether they were with the Germans or the Fascists. In the case of the former, once they had surrendered, all that remained to be done was to hand them over to the Allies as prisoners of war. With the latter, the question was a good deal more complex because it predetermined, at least in part, the future of the Italians who had chosen to fight for the wrong side. The watchword 'surrender or perish' did not rule out discussing the terms of surrender; but there was always the risk of slipping towards a negotiated and rather too tranquil handover of powers. Witness this motion presented on 27 June 1944 to the Tuscan CLN by the Action and the Communist parties:

> The CTLN, having come to its knowledge that in many municipalities of the province the CLN have accepted the passage of public powers on the part the Fascist authorities and are acting in tacit accord with the occupying troops, wishes to remind them that the task of the CLNs is to lead the people in the struggle against Nazism for the liberation of Italy, and disavows such actions, inviting the CLNs of the province to return to their duties, resuming at once and immediately the direction of the struggle against Nazi-Fascism.

---

di Apuania', 28 December 1944. On 7 January 1945, the Apuania CLN president, Christian Democrat Enzo, drafted a 'Relazione di massima sul movimento patriottico nella provincia di Apuania, per il CLNAI', which contained a section entitled 'The truce with the Germans'. The truce entailed the mutual recognition of 'zones of influence': the partisans could even circulate in the German zone, 'if disarmed and not in uniform'; the Germans could enter the free zone 'only in small platoons, out of urgent necessity and, if possible, with prior notice' (INSMLI, *CLNAI*, envelope 7, folder 3). See also 'Relazione sulla insurrezione armata e conseguente liberazione delle città di Massa e Carrara', sent from the local PCI federation to the party leadership in Rome on 24 April 1945, which speaks of the 'farce' of the German platoons and partisans passing through the city without troubling one another (*Le Brigate Garibaldi*, vol. III, pp. 687–92).

87 See the 'Rapporto d'informazioni' from the Modena PCI federation, October 1944. The CLN did not accept this demand, but all the same posed very tough conditions of its own (ISRR, *Archivio triumvirato insurrezionale Emilia-Romagna*).

The motion was not passed, and the CTLN limited itself to recalling a less drastic one, which had been passed the previous 24 May, when the Christian Democrats had polemicised against the 'political infantilism', 'ideological prejudices' and 'romantic sentimentalities' that appeared to them discernible in the intransigent positions.[88] Things were to change in April 1945 with the general collapse, but the Communists' insistence on insurrection, which they were prepared to start alone if need be, should nonetheless be attributed to the firm commitment to avoid not only another 25 July at the topmost level, but also a creeping series of widespread events of the same nature.[89] Even if 'insurrection' was scarier than 'liberation',[90] when the showdown came this sort of prudence was shelved in favour of a formula championed from the beginning of the movement,[91] implicit in which was the anti-Fascist, and not just anti-German, character of the victory, and which could be imprinted in the collective memory as summing up the entire event. It is symptomatic that the ex-partisan workers questioned in a recent research inquiry tend to call the whole Resistance an 'insurrection'.[92]

---

88 ISRT, *Carte Francesco Berti*, envelope 1, folder 1, Verbali del CTLN, 19, 23, 24, 26 and 27 June meetings. On this whole affair, see Francovich, *La Resistenza a Firenze*, pp. 233–6, according to which all negotiation was broken off on 26 June.

89 See the 'Direttive n. 9' of 15 September 1944, probably drawn up by Secchia, and the 'Direttive n. 16', drafted by Longo, of 10 April 1945 (*Le Brigate Garibaldi*, vol. II, pp 332–5; vol. III, pp. 591–5). Secchia, republishing some lines from the 'Direttive n. 16', comments: 'It is remarkable that serious historians have not brought out the full importance and proper value of these directives, which, in settling the matter once and for all, and ordering all Communists to act, if necessary, even by themselves – with full respect for the unity of all democratic forces and in the name of the CLN – were decisive for the success and ultimate triumph of the national insurrection' (*Il PCI e la guerra di liberazione*, p. 101).

90 'It will perhaps also be better to speak of the liberation of Milan and not of an insurrection, a word that, for some, can make this concept seem more suspect and even forbidding', wrote Citterio on 13 February, in the name of the GL Lombard Command, to Ludovico of the 'GL Provincial Command 734' (INSMLI, *CVL*, envelope 93, folder 5, subfolder a).

91 The title 'Prepariamo l'insurrezione nazionale inseparabile dalla liberazione dai tedeschi e dai fascisti' ('Let us prepare the national insurrection, indivisible from liberation from the Germans and the Fascists') stretched across the whole front page of *L'Unità*'s northern edition of 25 November 1943, while the editorial of the 5 December issue was entitled 'Dalla guerriglia partigiana all'insurrezione nazionale' ('From partisan guerrilla-struggle to the national insurrection'). Similar titles appeared in the 10 January and 21 June 1944 issues. The CLN had called for insurrection with its 20 September 1944 appeal (*Atti CVL*, pp. 176–7). On the uncertainties of the CLN itself with regard to drawing up a general plan for insurrection, see G. Grassi, 'Nota storica', *Atti CLNAI*, pp. 36–7.

92 See Passerini, *Torino operaia*, p. 11.

5. THE CATHOLICS AND THE CIVIL WAR

The civil war presented the Catholic Church and its various components with more arduous problems than those connected with the patriotic war. The latter could always be seen as falling within the traditional framework of conflicts between states, even between Catholic states, before which the Church, from long experience, knew how to conduct itself. Already the ideological character that the 1940–43 war had acquired – that of both a Fascist war and an anti-Bolshevik war – had created for the Catholic Church, as an institution and in relation to individual consciences, the particular problems that have been mentioned earlier. After 8 September the only problem that seemed to have been definitively solved was the identification of the victor. But even here, the mere question of what attitude it should take towards the strictly national aspect of the war became difficult for the Church – and not so much because of the change of sides, which in fact allowed the Church to feel easily in unison with the anti-German sentiments of a large part of the Italian population (as in fact occurred in the South), but because there came to the fore, as we shall presently see, the problem of obedience owed to the occupying foreign authorities as guardians of order.

It was the civil war, however, that created a particularly difficult situation. It revealed the line of 'tranquil loyalism' to the government followed during Badoglio's forty-five days as being no longer viable.[1] It complicated the process of what has been called 'the succession'.[2] It made dramatic what for most Italian Catholics had never constituted a serious problem of conscience, namely being both Catholic and Fascist. At a still higher level, it revealed the conflict between observing the fifth commandment and killing in time of war, now that it was necessary to kill other Italians. While in normal wars each of us, when he returns home, can be absolved for having done his duty, the civil war opened up a problematic field that it was not easy for the ecclesiastical authorities to occupy with clear and unambiguous directives.

In any case, several distinctions need to be made from the start – distinctions that are not limited to that between the higher and lower clergy, incontestable though that distinction is. This distinction has been emphasised by left-wing historiography, starting with Roberto Battaglia's *Storia della Resistenza* (which is naturally wholly in favour of the lower clergy), but is already present in the contemporary sources[3] and then in the memoirs,[4] as well as in the way

---

1 Bianchi's definition, in *I cattolici*, p. 176

2 On this point, see G. Poggi's deft essay, 'La Chiesa nella political italiana dal 1945 al 1950', in S. J. Woolf, ed., *Italia 1943–1950. La ricostruzione*, Bari: Laterza, 1974, pp. 255–82, and E. Rotelli, V. Onida, M. Reineri and F. Margiotta Broglio, *La successione*, Rome: Edizioni Lavoro, 1980.

3 See, for example, 'Timori in sagristia', in *Avanti!*, northern edition, 10 January 1944.

4 See, for example, Bianco, *Guerra partigiana*, p. 36.

things actually were. On the other hand, it has been minimised or even denied in Catholic-inspired historiography and journalism. The fact is that an exceptional situation like the civil war, inserted in a great international ideological war, brought to light the multiplicity of planes on which the Church moved, all of them real enough but all resistant to any *reductio ad unum* – be it the appeal to a providential game between parties in which each would perform his office, or a bishop condemning partisan violence, or the tendency to highlight a rather too lucid and 'objective' ecclesiastical strategy capable of controlling and transporting to the glory of the institution the multiple threads of the often contradictory experiences lived by Catholics.[5]

The contradictions throng around one fundamental one: to remain *super partes* and at the same time to take sides. This is not simply a question of opposition between being religious and being political, for both elements were to be found at both poles of the dichotomy. The political (and military) choice of the Resistance, in a situation which called into question automatic institutional forms of legitimisation, was inevitably supported by profound, deep-rooted motivations for a Catholic who wanted to choose his allegiances as a Catholic, according to his religious convictions. On the other hand, Catholic piety was embodied in an institution, which as such operated politically.

The hardest distinction to mediate was thus that between religion as an institution – administrated, though not exclusively, by the leaders of the hierarchy – and religion as a question of conscience. Both levels contained the duality of being *super partes* and of taking sides. At the first level, this duality generated diplomatic prudence, broken at times by compromise with, or opposition to, the Nazi-Fascist authorities. At the second level, emphasis was laid on the religious piety shared by friends and enemies, victors and vanquished, and active engagement alongside one's friends against the enemy, out of a religious inspiration to rebel against oppression and injustice. 'Thou source of free life, give us the force to rebel' is written next to an image of Christ.[6] 'Pastoral activity', to which Catholic historiography has often appealed, though failing to devote as much attention to the sheep as to the shepherds, does not appear to be sufficient as a mediating category. In fact, pastoral activity took the form of diplomatic caution, provoking the reactions of those who 'had by now made a clear choice of sides'.[7]

---

5 A trap not totally avoided even by such excellent essays as those of G. Miccoli ('Problemi di ricerca sull'atteggiamento della Chiesa durante la Resistenza con particolare riferimento alla situazione del confine orientale', in *Società rurale*, pp. 241–62) and of S. Lanaro ('Società civile, 'mondo cattolico' e Democrazia Cristiana nel Veneto tra fascismo e postfascismo', in Isnenghi and Lanaro. eds, *La Democrazia cristiana*, pp. 3–71).

6 A card kept in IVSR, folder Stampa antifascista.

7 The words of F. Malgeri, 'La Chiesa di fronte alla RSI', in Poggio, ed., *La Repubblica sociale italiana*, pp. 313–33, at the end of a passage (p. 321) in which he dwells on pastoral activities.

Nor is the distinction exhaustive between a plane on which the Church performs a 'Benedictine' function of preserving society from chaos, and a plane where it orientates the masses over which it exercises its influence in a pro-Resistance direction.[8]

The function of the shepherd who must never abandon his sheep could lead the Church – and this was no novelty, either – to paying the price of submission to, or collaboration with, established power, whatever that power might be. From an ethico-political point of view, it is legitimate to speak in such cases of opportunism, but from a pastoral–institutional point of view one has to recognise the coherence of those priests who considered it more important to tend the souls of others than to tend their dignity as citizens or, if one prefers, to think too deeply about the reasons for a choice made by so many people as men and citizens. This attitude seems to me to be exemplified by a chaplain of the Pusteria Alpine division who, on being captured by the Germans in Grenoble, refused to follow the deported officers because they had refused to collaborate and were defined by him as 'rebels': 'I didn't want to go to Poland, my ministry didn't permit me to starve to death among barbed wire, thus cutting short work that was so useful for the soldiers.' When, subsequently captured by the Allies, he was taken to England, this priest 'immediately became an enthusiastic collaborator of the victors.'[9] An opposite example is don Olindo Pezzin. Chaplain of the 13th sector of the Frontier Guard, stationed at Malles Venosta, where the South Tyrolese handed fugitive soldiers over to the Germans but wanted to hide the priest even though he was dressed as an Italian officer, don Pezzin gave himself up to the occupiers as a prisoner in order to remain close to the men who had been entrusted to him.[10]

In reality the Church, in the multiplicity of forms it took on RSI territory, found itself facing the same problems of the relationship between political and legal morality with which all the Italian inhabitants of those regions had to reckon. It seems to me at least as useful to try to understand certain features of the complex and not always coherent behaviour of this sizable portion of the Italian Catholic world as to conduct research into 'the Catholics of the Resistance'.

Consider above all the classic problem of the obedience that should be withheld, in principle, from a government deemed illegitimate, but accorded in

---

8 See E. Brunetta, *Correnti politiche e classi sociali alle origini della Resistenza nel Veneto*, Vicenza: Neri Pozza, 1974, p. 65, quoted in Tramontin, *Contadini e movimento partigiano*, p. 289.

9 These last words were used by Rochat, *Memorialistica e storiografia sull'internamento*, p. 49 and n. 98, to describe the attitude of the chaplain, referring back to the memoirs of P. Bettotti, *Noi della Pusteria. Diario di guerra*, Trento: Tipografia AOR, 1951.

10 As don Pezzin recounted to the author.

practice to the same government insofar as it was acting as guardian of common interests, and above all of public order. As one descends from diplomatic formulations, and first and foremost those of the highest Vatican authorities, to how individual priests and individual Catholics accounted for their conduct, it becomes increasingly hard to face this problem simply by remaining irenically and cautiously equidistant. And so prudence and diplomatic ability, and the age-old claim of being non-political, slip in the direction of ambiguity.

In October 1943, Monsignor Evasio Colli, bishop of Parma and director general of Catholic Action, published in *L'Avvenire d'Italia* – in reply to a libellous statement that had appeared, as a *ballon d'essai*, in the Fascist newspapers – a declaration that 'this association has never made mention of the state, nor of Fascism, nor of the Republic in any written document. Catholic Action must not engage, has not engaged, does not engage and will never engage in politics. If it were to do so it would betray its mission.'[11]

The Secretariat of State's general directives would maintain 'an attitude of superior impartiality before the armed conflict', avoid 'manifestations that might appear either as purely political proclamations or as statements of preference towards one of the belligerent forces'.[12] But when asked for advice by the vicar cardinal of Rome, Marchetti-Selvaggiani, as to how he should behave in response to Fascist pressure to collaborate in dissuading the young from draft-dodging, the assistant secretary of state, Monsignor Giovanni Battista Montini [the future Pope Paul VI], replied with words whose meaning slid from diplomatic prudence to what was to all effects acquiescence. Montini said that one should 'confine oneself to recommending calm and obedience to the public authorities. To give other advice would mean entering what is still an open question.'[13]

On 15 October 1943 Monsignor Ambrogio Marchioni, secretary of the nunciature in Italy, had a meeting with General Rodolfo Graziani. To the marshal's request that he take the part of, or at least express sympathy for, the cause of the Social Republic, the monsignor replied by insisting again on the neutrality of the Church and 'still more of the Vatican', which did not permit any 'political intervention in favour of one of the belligerents or in favour of one part of the citizens against another of the same nation'. The duty of priests, rather, was to 'instil calm, tranquility, order, so as to ensure that ill-advised actions do not produce serious reprisals against so many innocent people or the entire population'.[14]

The authoritative prelate incidentally let slip a few words – the Church 'does

---

11 See A. Fappani and F. Molinari, *Chiesa e Repubblica di Salò*, Turin: Marietti, 1981, pp. 7–8. The two priests commented 'The sharp reply was not without effect.'

12 Telegram from the secretary of state's office to monsignor Cicognani, 31 May 1944, cited in Malgeri, *La Chiesa di fronte alla RSI*, p. 320.

13 Cited in Malgeri, *La Chiesa di fronte alla RSI*, p. 318.

14 The report of the colloquium is cited in Miccoli, *Problemi di ricerca*, p. 248; and in Malgeri, *La Chiesa di fronte alla RSI*, p. 320.

not and cannot remain neutral between good and evil' – which, while sounding, on the one hand, like a necessary if vague appeal to the highest principles, on the other hand did not help orientate individual believers in a situation that compelled them, if necessary, to risk 'calm', 'tranquility' and 'order' in choosing between positions which also needed to be defined in relation to the problem of 'good' and 'evil'.

The polyvalence of the appeals issued, above all by the bishops, with their various tones and emphases, stemmed very largely from the fact that they gave no precise indication as to who were to be the recipients of the condemnations and warnings. It was a repeat performance of 'deprecating the deeds' without 'denouncing the culprits', which had characterised the attitude of ecclesiastical teaching regarding Fascism and the war.[15] The intransigent Fascists were the first to resent this ambiguity; the anti-Fascists were offended by it; most people were bewildered or, conversely, felt authorised to set their consciences at rest, without any undue traumas, delegating the government once again to the hierarchy. The root problem – namely that of the legitimacy of the political command exercised by the actually existing authorities – was evaded.[16] Thus it might happen that declarations by manifestly pro-Fascist papers such as *L'Italia Cattolica* turned out to be very similar to stances taken by the highest ecclesiastical authorities. In that Venetian magazine the following words are quoted from St Paul's *Epistle to the Romans*: 'Let every soul be subject to authority. Whoever resists authority, resists God's design and merits eternal damnation. Therefore, according to your duty pay the tributes, enlist and fight. In these things too the authorities are instruments which God uses.'[17]

There is clear assonance here not only with the bishop of Mantua, who urged respect for the authorities and for the German troops, only to find his admonition immediately re-launched by an RSI poster,[18] but also with many of the vague appeals to respect for unnamed authorities. Even in one of the most well-known episcopal documents, the *Lettera degli arcivescovi e vescovi della regione piemontese al clero e al popolo nella Pasqua 1944* ('Letter of the archbishops and bishops of the region of Piedmont to the clergy and the people at Easter 1944'), the effort seems to be to reconcile 'obvious considerations of prudence with constant concern about not letting oneself be dragged into performing actions that were in any sense compromising and binding', maintaining for that end 'on the

---

15 See G. Dossetti, 'Introduzione' in L. Gherardi, *Le querce di Monte Sole*, Bologna: Il Mulino, 1986, p. xxxvi.

16 F. Traniello has drawn attention to this question in 'Il mondo cattolico nella guerra e nella Resistenza', in *L'Italia nella seconda guerra mondiale e nella Resistenza*, pp. 325–69.

17 See the May 1944 instalment (cited in Scagliola, *L'Italia Cattolica*, p. 158).

18 The poster (n.d., printed in Treviso) begins by invoking Francis of Assisi, patron saint of Italy (Fondo RSI, n. 739).

principal point ... an able and eloquent silence' – where, however, 'ability' was such as to be to the detriment of eloquence, if the latter was taken to mean the vehicle of an emphatic strength of conviction.[19] And ability revealed itself as ambiguity when the bishops condemned the 'bloody guerrilla warfare of armed bands' (the Fascists in no way regarded themselves as bands involved in guerrilla warfare) and 'any form of reprisal and violence from whichever side it may come and whatever justification it may flaunt'. On the fundamental point of the RSI's legitimacy, the Piedmontese bishops took cover behind St Thomas: 'The use of power will be God's if it is exercised according to the precepts and norms of divine justice; instead it will not be God's if he who holds it uses it to commit injustice', and behind Leo XIII: 'In all things in which the law of nature or the will of God is violated, commanding is as iniquitous as obeying.'[20]

Of an altogether different feather was the moral tension that had inspired the letter of the Dutch bishops of 25 July 1941, which was immediately circulated in France as well.[21] In contrast to so many instances of caution, greater clarity must be recognised in the pragmatic argumentation of Monsignor Giuseppe Angrisani, bishop of Casale Monferrato:

> We find ourselves before an established government, which has in its hands the force to make its laws observed and will not allow itself to be ignored or ridden roughshod over. Even if one does not wish to invoke higher principles, it is well to say that prudence at least suggests that we avoid the greater evil by adapting to the lesser. This rule of common sense, even though it may seem prompted by mere personal advantage, will be of value in illuminating us about the practical way to resolve many intricate situations.[22]

When all was over Monsignor Angrisani wrote: 'The bishop, like all the other bishops of this wretched northern Italy, torn between brothers and bloodied by fratricidal massacres, had not the slightest intention of taking one or the other side.'

This bishop is, moreover, an example of how in the very person of a prelate simple practical prudence and genuine religious ardour could coexist. In fact,

---

19 The pastoral letter was published in pamphlet form by the Opera Diocesana per la Stampa Cattolica. It is quoted and discussed at length in Rovero, *Il clero piemontese nella Resistenza*, pp. 41–75 (the words cited in the text are from p. 47).

20 Ibid.

21 See the 18 October 1941 issue of *Veritas*, a daily newspaper for the clergy, and the December 1941–January 1942 edition of *Témoignage chrétien*. *Veritas* also referred to the previous decision of 26 June, by which the Dutch episcopate forbade sacraments being given to 'those Catholics known to have given notable assistance to the National-Socialist movement'.

22 'Relazione sulla stampa cattolica', in ACS, SPD, CR, RSI, quoted without reference to its date in Malgeri, *La Chiesa di fronte alla RSI*, p. 318.

344 A CIVIL WAR

on 14 November 1944 Monsignor Angrisani asked to be shot in the place of 150 hostages from Ozzano.[23]

Another exemplary case of the question of obedience or disobedience to the existing authorities is that of don Aldo Moretti, awarded the *medaglia d'oro* in North Africa, when still convinced that it was not an 'unjust war', and one of the organisers of the Friuli Osoppo partisan formations. The semi-formal annexation to Germany of the province of Udine led to the existence of a particularly close intertwining of the patriotic and anti-Fascist aspects of the struggle. Don Moretti recognised the illegitimacy of the government installed by the Nazis (it was illegitimate enough in Germany, its standing in Italy can only be imagined), but at the same time recognised the occupier's 'right to govern within the bounds of what regards public order'. He then sought to save himself from contradiction by clinging to the argument that annexation to the Reich of the territories of the Pre-Alps and the Adriatic coast was not altogether perfect: if it were so, 'in theory, it might make it difficult in all honesty entirely to legitimise the armed resistance and to equate it with that provided for by Holy Scripture'. The declaration of war on Germany by the 'Italian state that had constitutional continuity' had then, don Moretti goes on to say, remedied the situation.[24] Don Moretti did nonetheless get the local branch of the Christian Democrats to reject the orders prepared by the CLNAI against Fascist traitors and collaborationists.[25] These contradictions reoccurred in don Moretti's direct superior, the bishop of Udine, but weighted the opposite way, in the name of public order on the one hand, and on the other – and this is the thorniest point – of respect for human life. Monsignor Giuseppe Nogara, whom Bianchi defines as an 'uomo possibilista', published, in the *Rivista diocesana udinese*, one of his declarations of 12 December 1943, in which he recommended obedience to the legitimate ordinances of authority – because in matters relating to the maintenance of order even a de facto government has to be obeyed. The following January the bishop, who had previously even offered himself to the Germans so long as 'you leave my children in peace', invoked 'respect for life', without naming anyone in particular who had violated it; and then in March and April, with the other bishops of the Adriatic coast, he condemned the occupier's abuses of power, but

---

23 See Rovero, *Il clero piemontese nella Resistenza*, pp. 63, 62. Angrisani's words reported in the text are taken from his brochure *La croce sul Monferrato durante la bufera*, Casale Monferrato: Tipografia Casalese, 1946, p. 18.

24 Don Moretti espoused these ideas in the *Cenacolo di studi sociali*. See Bianchi, *I cattolici*, pp. 182–3, no date indicated. Bianchi comments: 'Thus also the Catholics who had not asked for or wanted the prosecution of the war had to accept the war among Italians; so, too, because they were convinced that legality was on their side.' The biographical notes on Moretti (pp. 179–80) recall the 'decisive meeting' with Giorgio La Pira.

25 See Fogar, *Le brigate Osoppo-Friuli*, pp. 296–301, which also features an even-handed judgment on don Moretti's 'justificationism through theology and doctrine'.

also the acts of violence and excesses of those opposing him.[26] On 30 November 1944 the same prelate addressed a letter to his parish priests enjoining them to exhort the partisans to present themselves and to hand their weapons over to the Germans, on the guarantee that they would not be deported. A Garibaldi source has no hesitation in defining this policy as treason, since in a phase of the most violent roundups, such as that taking place, it induced surrender. The Germans, for their part, had made sure that they distributed safe-conduct passes to those parish priests who presented themselves. Even the commanders of the Osoppo brigade repudiated the bishop's letter, alleging – 'hypocritically', comments the Garibaldi document – that it had been extorted from him. The Christian Democrats managed to get the bishop to withdraw the controversial document.[27]

There are, besides, many cases of priests urging the partisans to present themselves – in the Chiavenna zone, for example, or in Piedmont, where the priests appealed to family reasons.[28] Ada Gobetti recounts the case of a youth who presented himself, induced by a 'foolish priest', was hanged by the Germans, and died crying 'Viva i partigiani!'[29]

The notification of 5 December 1943 after the Fascist reprisal for the killing of Colonel Gino Gobbi, and the homily subsequently pronounced for Christmas that year by Cardinal Elia Dalla Costa, Archbishop of Florence, are among the documents that best lend themselves to several of the present reflections. Both were widely circulated, being published by L'Avvenire d'Italia on 7 and 28 December, and then the homily in a pamphlet entitled 'The paths of peace'.[30] The cardinal deprecated 'the struggle between sons of the same land', deprecated 'the acts of oppression, the impositions, the acts of violence, the excesses', warned that 'rash actions produce reactions that often go beyond the provocation'. The speaker's most astute and subtle words, and the most equivocal for his listeners, were those in which he reminded them that 'every act of violence, every blow, every illegal use of arms is criminal, because no one can take the law into his own hands, unless it be to apply the well-known principle: each law permits

---

26 See Bianchi, I cattolici, pp. 192–4.

27 Fogar, Le brigate Osoppo-Friuli, pp. 328–30. For the Garibaldian reaction, see the letter from Marco, 'A cari compagni', 3 December 1944 (IG, BG, 09453).

28 See the letter from the Lombard Divisions Group Command to the delegation for Lombardy, various commands and the CLNs of Chiavenna and Sondrio, 1 December 1944, as well as that of the Piedmont insurrectionary triumvirate official Alfredo to the PCI leadership for occupied Italy, 12 December 1944 (Le Brigate Garibaldi, vol. III, pp. 12, 68).

29 See Gobetti, Diario partigiano, p. 186, under the date 9 August 1944.

30 Florence: Libreria fiorentina. Ronconi carried out a diligent analysis of the documents produced by the cardinal Dalla Costa, already traced in outline in cardinal Schuster's prior texts. See Note sui rapporti fra il clero toscano, la Repubblica sociale italiana e le autorità d'occupazione tedesche, pp. 133–4.

violence to be rejected with violence'. Was this, then, a go-ahead, for those of a mind to take it as such, even for armed resistance against violence exercised by an illegal authority? In fact, Dalla Costa went on to assume almost the guise of counsellor to the prince. The cardinal asked 'those holding public office or exercising public functions' to respect first and foremost the law prohibiting violence, and to show an example of equanimity 'in their own interest' and 'because nothing increases the influence of he who is in command than the use of means that are in keeping with perfect justice'.

It was *Voce Operaia*, the Roman newspaper of the Communist Catholics, which – jealous guardian of a dual orthodoxy – was most directly affected, and missed no opportunity to make the most of the clergy's contribution to the Resistance, that assumed the task of giving an answer, respectful in form but firm in substance.[31] The cardinal was reminded that he could, if he wished, choose not to speak out, but there was no way in which he could steer a middle course; and then the paper went so far as to vindicate, in principle, the liberty to judge even the actions of legitimate authorities. If – the open letter argued – it is still lawful for a Catholic to discuss case by case whether one need obey the legitimate authority or what the nation and people feel to be the true authority (always to exclude the latter would mean excising Catholics from any historical movement), here this problem did not even arise, because it was clear that the Nazi-Fascists were *also* an illegal authority.

At times indiscriminate condemnations pronounced by the clergy acquired greater intensity when the victims of abuses of power and acts of violence were priests. In such cases there seems to emerge a sort of request for special, institutionally guaranteed treatment for those exercising the sacerdotal function. The bishop of Padua, Carlo Agostini, promoter of Fascist-style patriotic manifestations, protested in a letter to the provincial chief when some priests were arrested, claiming that they were 'holy persons', sanctioned by the laws and conventions in force both in Italy and in the 'Great Germanic Reich'.[32] The bishop of Reggio Emilia, Eduardo Brettoni – who on 21 December 1943, in a telegram to the GNR Command, had deprecated as 'private violence ... the brutal crime that had destroyed the life of the *primo seniore* Fagiani', killed by partisans – protested, with a message published in the 'Bulletin' of his diocese, against the execution of don Pasquino Borghi for having given refuge to partisans and allied prisoners. Eight other people had been shot with the priest; but the bishop, without so much as a word about them, wrote that 30 January 1944 'will be sadly

---

31 'Lettera aperta a S.E. il Cardinale Dalla Costa Arcivescovo di Firenze', *Voce Operaia*, 5 January 1944. Enzo Enriques Agnoletti replied to the 5 December notification with a letter of his own (see Francovich, *La Resistenza a Firenze*, pp. 104–5), against which Vittore Branca polemicised – in the cardinal's defence – as late as 1984. See the aforementioned 'La città dell'Arno', in *Nuova Antologia*.

32 See Briguglio, *Clero e contadini*, pp. 324–5.

remembered in the annals of this Diocese ... for the execution ... of one of our priests'. The bishop passed no comment on the charges and the sentence ('they are the tasks reserved for the dispassionate judgment of history'); but warned that if, as was rumoured, 'grave acts of violence in the form of insults and blows' were 'used ... [the culprits] have incurred excommunication ... in accordance with canon 2343, paragraph 4, of the code of canon law'.[33]

Hand in hand with this tendency to practise a sort of separatism was the other, predominant one that saw the force of the clergy springing from the fact that they lived among the people and, in the case of active warfare, among the combatants. From this point of view, military chaplains of the RSI and partisan chaplains were driven at times by similar motivations. On the one hand, there was the Vatican, which managed to get Germany to concentrate all prisoners who were priests at Dachau, though this meant separating them from those they were meant to be assisting; on the other hand, there was the reaction of a deported priest, don Roberto Angeli, who regretted this measure: 'If our priest-hood was not for others, what value did it have? That sterile sacred selfishness could only devalue us morally both in our own eyes and in those of others.'[34]

In a declaration by Giovanni Sismondo, bishop of Pontremoli, the double standard is particularly evident. Writing about himself, the bishop, who was awarded the Resistance's silver medal for military valour, wrote of himself: 'Our approach was always impartial ... We always tried to maintain relations with all the Commands of the various warring parties.' From the military commands the bishop then descends to the men: 'Hide the outcasts; betray not him that wan-dereth' (Isaiah, 16.3) and 'Feed the hungry, give drink to the thirsty, clothe the naked, house the pilgrims (Mark, 25, 33).'[35] These words were pronounced after the event (in 1946), when the Christian Democrat hierarchy and leadership were beginning to distance themselves from the Resistance, following a process that

33 See the texts quoted in Gorrieri, *La Repubblica di Montefiorino*, pp. 177–8, which also recalls the violent reply from the local Fascist daily *Diana repubblicana*, with its article 'Difesa del crimine'. The canon cited by the bishop reads 'Qui violentas manus in personam ... aliorum clericorum vel utriusque sexus religiosorum iniecerit, subi-aceat ipso facto excommunicationi Ordinario proprio reservatae', 'Whoever would lay a violent hand on the person of ... and other members of the clergy or religious persons of both sexes, should by default be subject to excommunication of the kind specific to his own order.' On the shooting of don Borghi and of the eight patriots, see Bergonzini, *La lotta armata*, p. 70.

34 R. Angeli, *Vangelo nei Lager*, Florence: La Nuova Italia, 1975, quoted in Tramontin, *Il clero italiano e la Resistenza*, p. 35. Don Olindo Pezzin (p. 697, n. 10), after having been separated first from his soldiers and then from his official accompaniment, saw the motives for his own choice frustrated.

35 Quoted in Bianchi, *I cattolici*, pp. 187–8. Monsignor Sismondo did not cease celebrating Mass 'for our king Vittorio Emanuele' (See also Tramontin, *Il clero italiano e la Resistenza*, p. 29).

in the years of the Cold War would lead the Catholics almost to mute their participation in it.[36] This attitude, like the opposite one of vindicating the Catholic contribution, shifts a contradiction onto the plane of journalism and historiographic reconstruction.

The habit of negotiating on an equal footing with the powers that be from one institution to another was so deep-rooted that contacts with the German and Fascist authorities must in another respect have appeared obvious to the ecclesiastical authorities. But here too the existence of the RSI posed knotty problems. The Germans, as occupiers, could in fact be recognised as having an authority with which it was legitimate to have contacts in a 'climate of formal and bureaucratic mutual respect'.[37] This was the line taken by Northern Italy's most representative cardinal archbishop, Idelfonso Schuster, who in May 1944 not only accepted the visit of General Wening, commander of the German forces in Northern Italy, but sent one of his prelates, Monsignor Giuseppe Bicchierai, on a return visit. By contrast, in the same month Schuster agreed to receive the *podestà* and two *vice-podestà*, but did not return the visit.[38] Less careful, or simply more spontaneous, the bishops of Modena, Boccoleri, and of Carpi, Dalla Zuanna, paid an official visit to the head of the province, with the easily predictable result that on 30 March 1944 *La Gazzetta dell'Emilia* published an exultant communication which concluded by recalling how victory was 'the sole guarantee of salvation also for religion, the indispensable spiritual nourishment for our profoundly patriotic and Catholic people'.[39]

Oscillating conduct and coded messages are borne out by the judgments, contrasting in time and place, found expressed in the reports of the Fascist authorities. Thus early reassurance arrived from Grosseto that 'the clergy has given no cause for comment, supporting the authorities in the campaign of internal resistance'.[40] But after a few months the censor of the correspondence pointed out that 'the clergy is very sharply rebuked for its hostile demeanour to the republican state, and for the favour it has shown towards the partisans which feeds the spirit of rebellion'.[41]

---

36 See on this the observations made by Reineri, *Per uno studio comparato*, p. 270.

37 Ronconi, *Note sui rapporti fra il clero toscano, la Repubblica sociale italiana e le autorità d' occupazione tedesche*, p. 143.

38 Malgeri, *La Chiesa di fronte alla RSI*, p. 321, n. 32.

39 Gorrieri, *La Repubblica di Montefiorino*, p. 230.

40 'Relazione sulla situazione politica ed economica della provincia di Grosseto', sent by the *questore* Vincenzo Mancuso to the chief of police, 31 December 1943. I thank Gabriella Solaro for having made me aware of this document, kept in ACS, Direzione Generale di Pubblica Sicurezza, Divisione Affari Generali e Riservati; there is also a photocopy in the INSMLI.

41 'Esame della corrispondenza censurata al 30 giugno 1944' (ACS, SPD, CR, RSI, envelope 9, folder 3).

For a strongly partisan zone, Mario Giovana's detailed and balanced description of the conduct of the lower clergy of the valleys around Cuneo comes closer to reality: 'reserve that was flaunted but lacking in hostile acts', 'assistance conceded with caution and moderation', 'inactive sympathy', rare cases of 'active collaboration with the partisans, leading to the death of some parish priests'.[42]

One point was particularly dear to the heart of the RSI, and interwove with another that attracted less attention on the part of the ecclesiastical hierarchies: the Holy See's recognition of the Republic and respect for the Lateran Pacts.[43] Recognition – for which, for that matter, risky official applications do not appear to have been made – was never granted, despite pressure to do so.[44] On 27 September 1943 a note by the secretary of state, Cardinal Luigi Maglione, explained that the Holy See

> does not as a rule recognise de jure governments that are set up in wartime, because of the war, when there is already a legal government. If the new Mussolini government has de facto power in one part of Italy, one could at the most – bearing this fact in mind – have some not official but confidential and I should say private contacts with it, because there might be questions to solve at the practical level.[45]

Sometimes the fact that the highest ecclesiastical authorities avoided appointing new bishops to the sees that fell vacant during the twenty months of RSI government, so as not to have to ask for the assent of that government, was offered as proof of their firm determination not to recognise the Fascist Republic.[46] In fact this behaviour touches on the second question mentioned above: the request that the Lateran Pacts be respected by a government that one did not, however, wish to recognise. Nothing would have prevented the Holy See from seeking the assent of the government of the South, which had certainly not renounced its potential jurisdiction over the entire national territory. But such a patent gesture would have been at odds with the cautious line that had been chosen, and might have led to RSI reprisals precisely in the concordatory sphere which the Holy See had most at heart (the threats to establish a national church,

---

42 Giovana, *Storia di una formazione partigiana*, pp. 307–11 (also see p. 211).

43 See on this A. Cicchitti-Suriani, '"La Repubblica sociale italiana" ed il Concordato del 1929', in *Nuova Antologia* LXXXVI: 1810 (October 1951), pp. 118–27.

44 See Malgeri, *La Chiesa di fronte alla RSI*, p. 314. On the hard-won recognition of the RSI on the part of the Axis's residual satellites, see F. W. Deakin, 'Prolusione', in Poggio, ed., *La Repubblica sociale italiana*, pp. 5–6. Generalissimo Franco, Deakin adds, refused to recognise the RSI in 'humiliating' fashion. The *Caudillo* was, at that time, more than ever alert to the behaviour of the Vatican (Malgeri, p. 309).

45 See Reineri, *Per uno studio comparato*, p. 271, n. 16.

46 See, for example, the intervention of L. M. De Bernardis at the Brescia conference on the RSI (Poggio, *La Repubblica sociale italiana*, p. 439).

bandied about by Roberto Farinacci, 'Crociata italica' and Lando Ferretti[47] were all too clearly senseless). In abstract terms, even a clear anti-concordatory, and even persecutory, act on the part of the Fascists might not have been altogether unwelcome for the Church, insofar as it could then have turned this to its own honour and advantage. All the same, prudence and experience taught that it was better for certain privileges, such as those assured by the Concordat, not to be undermined by anyone, not even by an illegitimate authority, since it was easy to mar but difficult to mend them, and the public spectacle of their violation was in itself scandalous. Indicative of this is the episode of the extra-territorial convent of San Paolo, which Pietro Koch's band of Fascists overran, capturing the numerous people who had sought refuge there.[48] The Fascist press posed a dilemma that had its share of logic: either the Vatican recognised the RSI and renewed the Lateran Pacts with the republic, or else it did not recognise it and 'the matter therefore becomes Badoglio's affair'. The reaction of *Il Popolo*, organ of the Christian Democrats, was extremely violent, but conducted on extremely slippery ground:

> Is it necessary to recall that ... the obligations of the Italian state are automatically assumed by the occupying authorities, the only real and integral authority responsible for the San Paolo incident? Does it need recalling that if even the international juridical personality of the republican government is highly problematic or non-existent, that government nonetheless has as its head a physical person who is the very same person who signed the Lateran Pacts?[49]

Another Christian Democrat newspaper of the capital, *Il Segno*, went to great pains to refute the thesis by which the appeal to the Lateran Pacts had no value if the Social Republic was not recognised.[50] An irreverent comment, however,

---

47 On this, see S. Tramontin, *Il clero e la RSI*, in ibid., p. 338. See also Gorrieri, *La Repubblica di Montefiorino*, pp. 228–9.

48 On this episode, see Piscitelli, *Storia della Resistenza romana*, pp. 278–9, and Malgeri, *La Chiesa di fronte alla RSI*, pp. 316–17.

49 'La criminosa aggressione di San Paolo', *Il Popolo* Rome edition, 20 February 1944, headed 'I patti del Laterano violati da Mussolini e da Hitler' ('The Lateran Pacts violated by Mussolini and Hitler'), and subtitled 'La ferma protesta della S. Sede contro il vile oltraggio al diritto delle genti e all'opera caritativa della Chiesa' ('The Holy See's resolute protest against the base offence against people's rights and the Church's charitable works'). See the sharp polemic on a point of law – the extraterritoriality guaranteed by the solemn treaty – in the article 'Violata immunità del monastero di S. Paolo', *La Civiltà Cattolica* LXXXV (4 March 1944) – XXII, Vol. I, §2249, pp. 323–7.

50 'Le opere e i giorni del nazifascismo', signed 'Ardito', 1 March 1944. In the *Regime fascista* of 20 February 1944, Farinacci had written: 'If, then, they do not want to respect our Republic, why do we have to uphold and respect the pacts tying us to the Holy See? In short, will we have to take shelter in the strong and pure fortress of a national

came from a minor paper, expressing what was very likely the view of many *resistenti*, but paradoxically deeming it best not to voice it publicly: 'Both of them are right', the Church and the Fascist regime both in bad faith since 1929.[51]

In many Fascists genuine stupor can be detected both at the ingratitude that the clergy and Catholics in general were showing them, and at the *fin de non-recevoir* with which they now greeted the request that for so many years had not fallen on deaf ears: We have the same enemies, why aren't you with us? After recalling the 'debt of recognition' that Fascism deserved from the Church a note from the *Corrispondenza Repubblicana*, inspired by Mussolini himself, stated: 'The reasons for which the clergy should be at our side have already been mentioned: because we are fighting against all its age-old and relentless enemies.'[52] Lower down the hierarchic ladder, the secretary of the *fascio* for Firenzuola expressed the same concepts: how can the priests not side with those who are fighting 'against masonic sectarianism, against Bolshevism, against atheism and against anarchy?'[53]

We might think that the small minority of ecclesiastics who came out openly in favour of the RSI did so precisely because they were receptive to appeals of this kind.[54] Responsive to them certainly was that *medico condotto* (district doctor) from Fabbrico (Reggio Emilia) who expressed the wish for a 'perfect fusion between religious and military forces. Only then will Italian conciliation between the state and the Church be a true, profound and absolute reality.'[55] Also responsive to them appears to have been the canny republican army colonel, a member of the Republican Fascist Party (PFR), who kept only a photograph of the pope in his office in Udine.[56] Highly responsive, naturally, was the group headed by don Tullio Calcagno and the Cremonese 'Crociata italica' ('Italic Crusade'),[57] as well as the more moderate group that gathered around

---

Catholicism, in order to defend our religion?' These words formed part of a long list of the attacks Farinacci had made on the behaviour of the Church that appeared in the June 1944 northern edition of *Risorgimento Liberale*.

51 See 'La violazione del Collegio di San Paolo', *La Voce del Popolo*, 15 March 1944.

52 'Stato e Chiesa', in *Corrispondenza repubblicana* 63 (14 July 1944), reproduced in Mussolini, *Opera omnia*, XXXII, *Dalla liberazione di Mussolini all'epilogo. La Repubblica Sociale Italiana*, 1960, pp. 380–1

53 Letter of 12 November 1943 to cardinal Dalla Costa (?) (there is a copy in the ISRT), quoted in Tramontin, *Il clero italiano e la Resistenza*, p. 46, n. 70.

54 This is also Tramontin's opinion: *Il clero e la RSI*, Section 2.

55 Letter to don Tullio Calcagno from Dr Francesco Davolio Marani, 25 May 1944 (*LRSI*, p. 50).

56 See the report from the High Command chief Mischi, which somewhat absolves Colonel G.Z., who had been accused of administrative improprieties (ACS, SPD, CR, RSI, envelope 24, folder 169).

57 On this, we can refer back to A. Dordoni, *'Crociata italica'. Fascismo e religione nella Repubblica di Salò (gennaio 1944–aprile 1945)*, Milan: SugarCo, 1976.

the Venetian review *Italia Cattolica*, issued directly by the Ministry of Popular Culture.[58]

It would have been wishful thinking for the Fascists to imagine that don Tullio Calcagno or the head chaplain of the Black Brigades, don Eusebio Zappaterreni, a Franciscan survivor of the Russian campaign, could, with their scanty and discredited followers, mobilise the uncertain, let alone constitute a powerful counterweight to the far larger minority of priests who openly sided with the *resistenti*, to the extent that some even became chaplains to Garibaldi partisan formations.[59] In the Verona Charter it had been repeated that 'the Religion of the Republic is the Roman Catholic Apostolic one' (words which figured as the half-title of *Italia Cattolica*, mentioned earlier). But by and large the Fascist authorities appeared somewhat prudent, if not resigned, aware as they were of the impossibility of opening another highly risky front. Mussolini might well say to Padre Eusebio, on 26 September 1944, that 'when the priests see the black shirts they ring the church bells to warn the red shirts';[60] but he could do nothing to prohibit those bells from being rung. In the twilight of the Social Republic, his well-chosen definition of himself as 'Catholic and anti-Christian', which had inspired him so fruitfully on so many occasions, was doomed to be irremediably frustrated.[61]

The odd tough and testy stance by the Fascists did not change matters. Farinacci's paper, polemicising against the director of Catholic Action, Monsignor Evasio Colli's declaration of disengagement, mentioned earlier, wrote that 'at a tragic hour like this one cannot, in albeit deliberately equivocal prose, urge the young towards absenteeism, desertion, anarchy'.[62] Reproaches for blindness and ingratitude were coupled with denunciations of the clergy's absenteeist and fence-sitting attitudes, which were frequent in the reports of the peripheral RSI authorities.[63] Some particularly suspicious Fascists even went so far as to see don Calcagno himself as 'the Church's hand in our ranks, and

---

58 On this review, under the direction of Giovanni Vettori, which appeared between December 1943 and February 1945, see Scagliola, *L'Italia cattolica*. The 20 February 1944 Rome edition of *Il Popolo* commented in a brief section of its 'Osservatorio' column that *L'Italia cattolica* had 'a different tone from that of *Civiltà italica*, though with the same desire to adhere to republican Fascism as a means of professing religious faith' – words marked by irony more than bitterness.

59 On the chaplains of the partisan formations, see the sample offered by Tramontin in *Il clero italiano e la Resistenza*, p. 43, n. 38. See also Miccoli, *Problemi di ricerca*, p. 253, and Tramontin, *Contadini e movimento partigiano*, p. 291, n. 63.

60 Fappani and Molinari, *Chiesa e Repubblica di Salò*, p. 42.

61 Mussolini made this self-definition, based on his theory of the 'Catholic-paganisation of Christianity', on 8 August 1938, in conjunction with the publication of the Racial Laws (See G. Ciano, *1937–38. Diario*, Bologna: Cappelli, 1948, p. 217).

62 Cited in Gorrieri, *La Repubblica di Montefiorino*, pp. 226–7 (30 October 1943).

63 See the cases cited by Malgeri, *La Chiesa di fronte alla RSI*, p. 319 and n. 28.

one of her pilasters in our formation. You never know, think the old Vatican foxes'.[64]

Again, Farinacci, not altogether wrongly, considered the formula that the military RSI chaplains had to 'mutter' in place of the oath 'eel-like and Pharisaic': 'I declare that I am aware of the obligations inherent in the service of spiritual assistance with the military forces of the Italian Social Republic and am fully conscious of the regulations governing the position of military chaplains. I declare furthermore that I undertake to perform all my chaplain's duties properly with all diligence and zeal'.[65]

In fact, even if they attached different weight to it, the figure of the RSI military chaplain constituted a mutual pledge given on the institutional plane by the Fascist state and the Church. The former (at odds, it seems, with German thinking)[66] respected the Concordat and obtained indirect backing. The latter demonstrated that the Concordat was in any case in force. In fact, in addition to those who had volunteered (generally survivors from the 1940–43 campaigns), some bishops took the initiative of sending chaplains to the military formations of the RSI, including the black brigades, both 'to try and do a bit of good even among wolves', and to 'establish useful relations with the parade-ground commanders in order to be able to make use of them later at an opportune moment'.[67] The chaplains, wrote *Italia Cattolica*, 'continue to do what they have always done';[68] but some put excessive zeal into it, like those who wore the badges of the SS above the cross.[69]

The authorisation for religious assistance to the partisans, granted by Pope Pius XII in October 1944 at Schuster's request,[70] and the presence, in various forms, of chaplains in the Resistance formations also answered both a religious need and a need for politico-ideological presence, aimed at combating the influence of doctrines that were dangerous for the Church.[71] An

---

64 Report to the *Duce* of 6 August 1944 by the naval lieutenant Ernesto Vercesi, who had witnessed the liberation of Rome and then slipped back into the RSI (ACS, cited in Malgeri, *La Chiesa di fronte alla RSI*, p. 318, n. 23).

65 'L' equivoco continua', *Il Regime fascista*, 11 April 1944, and the circular from monsignor Casonato, fulfilling the role of a castrensial vicar for the RSI. Both cited in Tramontin, *Il clero e la RSI*, pp. 344–6.

66 Tramontin, *Il clero e la RSI*, p. 344.

67 Tramontin, *Il clero italiano e la Resistenza*, p. 36. The first words cited are those of Tramontin himself: those that follow are taken from the responses the bishop of Padua made to the Consistorial Congregation's circular of 10 April 1944, requesting news on what was happening to the diocese under the German occupation.

68 'Patriottismo dei nostri sacerdoti', 31 March 1944, cited in Scagliola, *L'Italia cattolica*, p. 160.

69 See Chiodi, *Banditi*, p. 42 (18 August 1944).

70 See Malgeri, *La Chiesa di fronte alla RSI*, p. 321.

71 Malgeri, *La Chiesa di fronte alla RSI*, p. 322, which, however, seems to

identical web of motivations was at work in the bands who accepted or even requested chaplains: genuine respect for religious conscience, and demonstration of the fact that the clergy were on your side, both against the Fascists, and, perhaps still more important for the Communists, as part of the policy of unity with the Christian Democrats. On one occasion Vincenzo Moscatelli ('Cino') said: 'From tomorrow you'll have two chaplains because I don't want there to be no Mass on Sundays, and in case you should die you won't die like dogs!'[72]

The borderline case of the RSI military chaplain raises the question of the role as stand-ins for the institutions that the clergy had played so extensively under German occupation and the RSI. This role, to which Federico Chabod has already drawn attention,[73] reveals the clergy's great capacity for filling, to a considerable degree, the void which neither the RSI nor 'the government of the CLNs' was capable of filling completely, thereby incorporating acts of human and religious assistance into their diplomatic caution and political ambitions. Their role as substitutes was immense and all too evident in the city of Rome, where it fed the myth of *defensor urbis*;[74] but it spread extensively and in the most various forms throughout the whole of the occupied territory. In August 1944 the Northern edition of *Il Popolo* could write emphatically that 'while [Italy's] governing class has betrayed its duty', the clergy 'has remained all but intact against the misdeeds and acts of baseness into which many compatriots have fallen'.[75] Still earlier, *Il Popolo* again, in its Roman edition, had indicated the parish priests as being the only active authority in the villages located in the zones of the front.[76] In the Lower Po valley, the IOUs that substituted for coins were accepted only if they bore the parish priest's stamp.[77] The dean of Malo imposed a ceiling price on black-market prices.[78] A parish priest was appealed to as mediator in disputes that broke out within the ranks of a Garibaldi formation.[79] And many more examples could be cited, both in this minute sphere and in that of relations with the Fascist and German authorities in negotiations for the exchange of prisoners.

---

underestimate the political content of this last motivation.

72 Tramontin, *Il clero italiano e la Resistenza*, p. 20.

73 Chabod, *L'Italia contemporanea*, pp. 125–6.

74 On this point, we can refer back to the aforementioned work of Andrea Riccardi, *Roma 'città sacra'?*, Chapter 6, 'La Chiesa e la guerra a Roma'.

75 'Il Clero', *Il Popolo*, 20 August 1944.

76 'Retrovie', *Il Popolo*, 20 February 1944.

77 F. Camon, *La vita eterna*, Milan: Garzanti, 1972, pp. 151–80 (cited in Lanaro, *Società civile*, p. 25).

78 Testimony taken from Lanaro, *Società civile*.

79 Such an initiative was taken on 14 July 1944 with the appeal to the 'parish priest' of Roncaglia (Valtellina) by the Command of the 40th Garibaldian Brigade Matteotti (*Le Brigate Garibaldi*, vol. II, pp. 123–4).

The main ambition behind this type of presence and activity was to transform the work of triangular mediation between the population, the Fascist and
German authorities, and the partisans and CLNs into genuine political mediation at the highest level. Against this prospect the CLNAI took a stand on 19
January 1945 'in the most energetic way' with a painstaking document that left
its trace through then being published only in *Avanti!*, *L'Unità* and the Genoese
paper *L' Attivista*.[80] When the final surrender came, the ecclesiastical authorities'
tendencies to present themselves as intermediaries would emerge particularly
clearly: from the parish priests of the province of Belluno to Cardinal Schuster,
prelate of the Ambrosian Church. The latter, who had already offered his services as mediator between 'the supreme Italian and German authorities' and the
'dissident government' of the Ossola area, felt, according to Gianfranco Bianchi's
interpretation of him, that it was 'an evangelical duty to avoid general insurrection', and was fond of appearing as a protagonist and indeed almost primate
of the northern Church, which irritated the supreme authorities of the Roman
Church.[81] If on the one hand the ecclesiastical hierarchies together cultivated to
the end the ideal of an Italy reduced wholly to the state of an open city under
their protection,[82] the CLNs, for their part, could not, in the delicate phase of
transition, abdicate in favour of the ecclesiastical authorities. The CLNs had
given their personal word to the Allies that they would safeguard public order,
and generally they succeeded in doing this so well as to induce a British officer
in Turin to exclaim: 'You pulled off a revolution and it's all so calm, so orderly. I
feel I'm in England.'[83]

The insurrection and the disturbance of public peace were, according to the
ecclesiastical view, dangerously close to that disturbance of people's minds that
Church teaching has always numbered among its duties to avoid. An undisturbed 'public peace' ('ordine pubblico') does in effect offer fewer opportunities
for people's consciences to be ruffled, and makes it easier to govern them. The
war fought on national soil had instead created a particularly treacherous terrain
when it came to safeguarding traditional morality and customs, of which the
Church felt itself to be the guarantor. The category of 'public peace' thus broad-
ened until it came to include moral order. A research study of the diocese of

---

80 See the text of the motion in *Atti CLNAI*, p. 240. On the prior discussions, see
Catalano, *Storia del CLNAI*, pp. 316–20.

81 See Tramontin, *Contadini e movimento partigiano*, pp. 310–11; Bianchi, *I cattolici*, pp. 271ff, p. 215; Traniello, *Il mondo cattolico italiano*, pp. 353–8; and Malgeri, *La
Chiesa di fronte alla RSI*, pp. 330–3.

82 See, for example, the response from the Florence diocese to the already mentioned Consistorial Congregation circular. The archbishop had done everything possible
to push events in this direction, and been somewhat successful (See Tramontin, *Il clero
italiano e la Resistenza*, p. 40, n. 12).

83 See Gobetti, *Diario partigiano*, p. 283.

Fano[84] has shown how the parish priests were concerned about the novelties that the war had brought with it, above all in the sphere of sexual morality. From this point of view, it was principally the German and the Allied troops – made up of foreign, even coloured, and mainly non-Catholic people – who were bracketed together in the condemnation. This deprecation was of a different kind from that regarding the 'calamity of the civil war ... originating from high quarters, supported and stoked in every way possible by the two sides', where if anything what was highlighted were the 'increasingly ferocious, implacable and bloody'[85] features of the conflict. All warfare was in any case classed as exceptional. And if it is true that in the religiosity of the Italians 'the quotidian revealed the sacred',[86] the appearance of the exception might indeed reveal the sacred more clearly, but it could also put it in jeopardy.

Among the functions involved in the stand-in role for the institutions exercised by the clergy, the one that has left the clearest traces, in the vast social consensus won by the Catholic ruling class after the war, is that of assistance, which also falls into the no-man's-land between institutions, religious devotion and political projects. Assistance was a field in which the Church moved with a time-honoured confidence that was destined in the post-war period to achieve new triumphs under the protection of Christian Democrat power. During Badoglio's forty-five days the new possibilities being offered by the situation had already been glimpsed. On 12 August Monsignor Ferdinando Baldelli, leader of Opera Nazionale Assistenza Religiosa e Morale agli Operai (ONARMO), had urged Cardinal Maurilio Fossati, archbishop of Turin, to step up the activity of the chaplains in workplaces; otherwise, he wrote, 'tomorrow we won't be able to give the sense of the continuity of our work, above and beyond all party rivalries'.[87] And again ONARMO, pursuing the logic of *super partes*, laid down this policy in a circular of 5 October 1943: 'No collaboration with political parties of any tendency.'[88]

In the period of the civil war and the German occupation, the work of assistance covered a vast field. It ranged from the organisation of Catholic succour to fugitive anti-Fascists (OSCAR), which operated from Milan in the college

---

84 A. C. Federici, 'Il passaggio del fronte (giugno-agosto 1944) attraverso le relazioni dei parroci della diocesi di Fano', in Rochat, Santarelli e Sorcinelli, *Linea gotica 1944*, pp. 335–80.

85 Words that don Damiani, a parish priest in the Brescia mountains, sympathetic to the RSI, wrote in his diary, where he also defined the partisan phenomenon as 'the most poisonous mushroom of the War' (Fappani and Molinari, *Chiesa e Repubblica di Salò*, p. 137).

86 See M. Cassin, 'Quelques facteurs historiques et sociaux de la diffusion du protestantisme en Italie méridionale', *Archives de sociologie des religions*, July–December 1956, 2, pp. 55–72.

87 Quoted in Reineri, *Per uno studio comparato*, p. 268.

88 Ibid.

of San Carlo from 12 September 1943,[89] to assistance given to escaped Allied prisoners,[90] to refuge in monasteries and convents, of which even prominent lay anti-Fascists like Pietro Nenni availed themselves. This resuscitated right of asylum was bitterly contested by the Fascists (as in the San Paolo episode in Rome). They even went so far as to have false orders by the Congregazione dei Riti published in the press, prohibiting priests from taking strangers into their houses.[91] By contrast, Il Popolo lost no time in approvingly noting the judgment expressed by one of those who were assisted by the clergy: 'For the next fifty years at least anti-clericalism will be impossible in Italy.'[92]

So unanimous and luminous an image of this work of assistance and recovery has been transmitted as to make us almost forget the shadows clouding it at times. A case in point is the great roundup conducted by the SS in the Rome ghetto on 16 October 1943, when, alongside the many fine pages written by the clergy, monasteries and convents were other, far from noble ones, like the demand that children be baptised as a condition for granting them asylum.[93]

In L'Osservatore Romano an article entitled 'Christian Charity' appeared, written by the priest Sergio Pignedoli (whom we have already encountered as the author of the letter 'To you, student and soldier', which vindicated the evangelical duty of offering charity to everyone: 'In a Roman Catholic priest's house anyone can go [even if he is opposed to his ideas] and find there a bed and a loaf of bread.'[94]

Clearly, this attitude is very different in kind from prudent diplomatic equidistance between the warring parties. Nevertheless, it was precisely the most deeply pondered and acutely felt positions that gave rise to the contradiction between a religious sense that made no distinction between friends and enemies and a religious sense that presented itself by contrast as the basis of a radical choice of sides. The beautiful simplicity with which a priest led out to be shot by the Fascists wrote that his fate was simply the consequence of his having

---

89 The organisation was led by the priests Andrea Ghetti, Aurelio Giussani, Giovanni Barbareschi and Natale Motta (see Enrico Mattei's report to the Christian-Democratic National Congress, Rome, 24 April 1946; the duplicate copy of the text is in INSMLI, old classification, CLNAI, envelope 8, folder 9). See G. Barbareschi, ed., Memoria di sacerdoti 'ribelli per amore', Milan: Grafiche Boniardi, 1986, p. 44.

90 See, for example, Absalom, Ex prigionieri alleati, pp. 453–73.

91 See 'La criminosa aggressione di San Paolo', Il Popolo Rome edition, 20 February 1944.

92 'Miracoli di carità e banda Calcagno', Il Popolo, Rome edition, 20 February 1944.

93 See the testimonies recorded in the Istituto Romano per la Storia d'Italia dal Fascismo alla Resistenza, the Comunità israelitica di Roma and the Comune's Prima Circoscrizione, which can be consulted at the Archivio Storico Audiovisivo del Movimento Operaio in Rome.

94 'Carità cristiana', L'Osservatore Romano, 30 December 1943.

done his job as a priest[95] left the fundamental question unanswered. Just as the continuity between religiousness, patriotism and anti-Fascism, suggested by the author of the following words, was by no means obvious: 'The clergy ... far from standing by like inert spectators of the nation's tragedy, have taken to the trenches of heroism with charity as its weapon.'[96]

Likewise, a parish priest of the diocese of Saluzzo, recounting that he hid partisans who risked being killed, made this comment: 'This in the name of evangelical charity which is the cause of true patriotism.'[97] Giuseppe Rovero himself, who quotes these words, nevertheless points out the full problem inherent in the fact that 'the charitable and welfare activity of the priest takes on a patriotic significance, without losing any of its religious significance ... We can simply say that these are exceptional circumstances.'[98]

The parish priest of Cadola, monsignor Viezzer, who was arrested twice, wrote in his diary: 'A priest could not help seeing the human and patriotic side of what was happening.' And the report by the parish priest of Valle di Seren del Grappa to the bishop of Belluno says, almost defensively, regarding the partisan couriers who had used the canon's house as an address: 'And I couldn't avoid it.'[99] At a higher level, Monsignor Giovanni Cazzani, bishop of Cremona, had answered don Calcagno more confidently and realistically: 'The Italian clergy cannot be against the majority of the Italian people, who are against Fascism.'[100]

It was not only the Italian clergy and Catholics who faced the problem of the relationship between religion and patriotism. 'Patriotism is a Christian virtue', wrote a Belgian priest before being shot.[101] But if the letters written by Italians sentenced to death are compared with those of another Catholic country, such as Belgium, the Italian ones reveal a religious sense which, while being in line with patriotism, is experienced principally, at the final hour, as faith in individual salvation, as the hope of finding one's loved ones in heaven, as forgiveness often accorded to one's slayer. In the Belgians, by contrast, there appear the themes of an ideologised Catholic culture conforming to the tradition of that country. One is dying for the Church, to restore Belgium to Christ, for the advent of Christian

---

95 'Il povero Don Aldo Mei' ('Poor Don Aldo Mei'), as he signed, had, among other things, sheltered a young Jew, 'whose soul he wish[ed] to save' (*LRI*, pp. 142–5).

96 See L. Zuliani's Introduction, 'Eroismo e carità del clero nel secondo Risorgimento: testimonianze e documentazioni', Rome 1946 (cited in Tramontin, *Il clero italiano e la Resistenza*, p. 39).

97 See Rovero, *Il clero piemontese nella Resistenza*, p. 55.

98 Ibid., p. 66.

99 See Tramontin, *Contadini e movimento partigiano*, pp. 284, 298.

100 Report by don Calcagno on a colloquy of 25 January 1944, sent to Mussolini by Farinacci, including comments damaging to the bishop (kept in ACS, SPD, CR, RSI, quoted in Bocca, *La Repubblica di Mussolini*, p. 230).

101 Letter by the parish priest Joseph Peeters, shot on 31 August 1943, addressed to 'my dear Vicars, my dear Congregation' (*LRE*, pp. 92–3).

society, even for Christ the King – which was the motto of Rexism (Belgian Fascism), whose head, Léon Degrelle, had become an active collaborationist.[102]

Difficult indeed, then, were the problems inherent in the passage from Christian solidarity to the bloody struggle against people who spoke the same language, belonged to the same national community, and by and large professed the same religion. On 23 September 1943 a meeting was held in Como for 'cases of conscience'; and a priest, don Onorio Cairoli, drew up a declaration that reads like a court sentence (with a justification and verdict):

> With all the attenuating circumstances of a political muddle around which informative facts are scarce, and with the psychological justifications put forward from opposite points of view in support of conflicting convictions, admitting the considerations which discounted the good faith of others, there is but one, objectively certain solution: to oppose the Germans, an unjust foreign occupier, and their collaborators, within the limits dictated by the commandments.[103]

A Veneto priest, 'questioned by the Germans as to whether he had offered lodging to the British, replied that he hadn't, justifying his mental reservation by distinguishing between board and bed for a few nights and real accommodation'.[104]

In Rome, in the church of San Marcello al Corso, the prior, Clemente Francesconi, celebrated a mass offered for the soul of Ettore Muti. An indignant letter then appeared in *L'Unità*, attributed to 'a young member of Catholic Action', which granted that a priest could not refuse to celebrate that service, but added that he should have taken care to keep it within the sphere of a purely private event. Instead the mass had acquired a political significance of which Catholics would be the first 'to demand tomorrow that prior CF justify himself for his cowardly formalistic, anti-Christian and Pharisaic conformism'.[105]

The question of funeral rites, in which the right of priests to celebrate them was never contested by anyone, is the thorniest question relating to the issue of convergence or divergence between religious and political spheres. The patriarch of Venice, Cardinal Adeodato Giovanni Piazza, agreed to solemn obsequies

---

102 'I lived to restore Belgium to Christ': letter from the priest Emmanuel de Neckere to his father, 31 October 1942; another priest, Jules Gengler, in a letter to his parents of 9 November 1942, promised to shout out 'Long live Christ the King!' when he faced the firing squad (*LRE*, pp. 87, 81). The letter cited in the previous note concludes with the words, 'Long live God and the Holy Virgin, Long live the Catholic Church, Long live Belgium and Long live Comblain au Pont [his parish]'.

103 Cited in Tramontin, *Il clero italiano e la Resistenza*, p. 41, n. 23.

104 P. Polesana, *Eroismo e martirio di Anno distrutta dal fuoco*, Feltre, 1947 (paraphrased by Tramontin, *Il clero italiano e la Resistenza*, p. 39, n. 5).

105 See 'Lettera di un cattolico', *L'Unità*, Rome edition, 5 October 1943.

being celebrated in San Marco for the thirty soldiers of the GNR killed in the explosion caused by the GAPs at Ca' Giustiniani – and then celebrated, in San Moisè, the funeral of thirteen anti-Fascists shot in reprisal.[106] In some cases the parish priests risked their lives to bury partisans who had been killed.[107]

L'Unità reported with satisfaction the news that Cardinal Schuster had, in Milan Cathedral, openly prohibited confessors from giving absolution to informers working for the Germans.[108] *Voce Operaia*, organ of the Catholic Communists, devoted an enthusiastic commentary to the episode, with an opening in the spirit of Manzoni and Gioberti and a finale in that of Togliatti: 'Ancient and immortal Catholic faith, linked to all the fortunes of our people, today you reaffirm yourself as the indestructible binding force of popular unity!'[109] But when, little more than a couple of months later, Schuster made some anti-Communist declarations and participated in the funeral of Aldo Resega – the *federale* (provincial party secretary) of Milan killed by the GAPs – the same *Voce Operaia* attacked him bitterly, accusing him of not having attended the funerals of the eight hostages shot in reprisal, and adding with rage and anguish: 'We won't lose our faith because of this. Which doesn't, clearly, absolve those who are doing everything in their power to make us lose it.'[110]

A priest refused to bless the flags of a Garibaldi formation, provoking 'a murmur of disapproval'. The commissar then addressed the following sermon to the cleric:

> Your behaviour makes you unworthy to serve the God you claim to believe in. Do not forget that He drove out of the temple the false priests, who had him crucified for this. Remember that He too died to redeem the oppressed, as we today are fighting to redeem our country. Certainly God, who can see it, disapproves of your action.[111]

Monsignor Giacomo Bortignon, bishop of Feltre and Belluno, climbed the scaffold to administer holy oil and kissed four hanged partisans. The bishop of Padua, monsignor Carlo Agostini, at the station of Chiesanuova, opened the railway trucks full of soldiers being deported to Germany. But both prelates participated in the episcopal conference in the Veneto of 20 April 1944, which pronounced itself in favour of the separation between politics – the sphere into which the war was conducted – and the Church, which was 'outside and above' it, and whose resolution, though regarded as one of the clearest and

---

106 See Tramontin, *Il clero italiano e la Resistenza*, p. 28.

107 See Rovero, *Il clero piemontese nella Resistenza*, p. 57.

108 See 'Per I fascisti che si confessano', *L'Unità*, Rome edition, 28 October 1943.

109 'Esempio', *Voce Operaia*, 26 October 1943.

110 'Pastorali politiche', *Voce Operaia*, 15 January 1944.

111 Padoan (Vanni), *Abbiamo lottato insieme*, pp. 173–4. As he handed the flag to the standard-bearer, Vanni said that it was blessed with the tears of mothers.

most enlightened documents of the northern Italian episcopate, reminded its 'subjects' about the duty of 'disciplined obedience' and those governing about the imperative of 'justice' and the 'common good'. Monsignor Agostini then, justifying himself before the *questore* for having circulated the document in his diocese, took the opportunity to declare his 'sentiments of patriotism and sympathy towards the Germans, having also given public proof of it'.[112]

It is no easy thing to find an organic framework for positions inspired by such contradictory impulses and the proclamation of one's duty to disobey the laws of the Social Republic made by so prominent a Christian Democrat politician as Paolo Emilio Taviani.[113] The exhortation by Teresio Olivelli, who died at Mauthausen, to become 'rebels for love' is interpreted by his biographer as a choice made precisely by virtue of his Christian spirituality.[114] The same need to come down clearly on one side or the other was felt by Alfredo Di Dio, the Catholic partisan leader of the Val d'Ossola, who, replying to his mother, who was exhorting him to hide, said that he regarded those who were neither partisans nor Fascists as 'mediocre'.[115]

Still more significant is the itinerary of Giuseppe Dossetti. In the summer of 1942, at the inter-regional conference of the Catholic graduates of Emilia-Romagna, Dossetti had maintained that Christian morality considers rebellion against tyranny legitimate. Immediately after 8 September he was recommending that one keep clear of the fratricidal struggle and direct one's energies at offering fraternal assistance to the persecuted and suffering. Dossetti was then to become president of the provincial CLN.[116] Gorrieri clearly saw where Catholic engagement in the Resistance would lead politically. The Catholics, he wrote, had grown convinced that their organised presence in the armed struggle would constitute a qualification for participating in the construction of the new democratic state soon after the Liberation.[117]

The contradictions of the Catholics were mirrored almost identically in the contradictions and uncertainties of the 'lay' *resistenti* they found before them. When the *laici* found themselves again alongside the Catholics, they showed incredulity, positive surprise, suspicion, at times almost contempt, together with

---

112 Malgeri, *La Chiesa di fronte alla RSI*, pp. 329, 325–7; Briguglio, *Clero e contadini*, pp. 323–4.

113 See the article 'Serriamo le fila: la lotta per la liberazione è incominciata', signed 'Pittaluga', *La voce d'Italia*, organ of the Ligurian CLN, 21 November 1943 (cited in Bianchi, *I cattolici* p. 277).

114 Caracciolo, *Teresio Olivelli*

115 Bianchi, *I cattolici*, p. 275.

116 See Bianchi, *I cattolici*, p. 178, and Gorrieri, *La Repubblica di Montefiorino*, pp. 80–1.

117 As Gorrieri wrote (*La Repubblica di Montefiorino*, p. 282) with regard to the Modena youth group he headed.

manifestations of a unitary spirit, at times instrumental, at times sincere. Sincere certainly was the wish to avoid the rebirth of anti-clericalism, though this attitude does not simply bespeak a civil ideal of tolerance, but also inadequate attention to the great problems of theory and morality, sacrificed to the political need for agreement between Catholics and the representative role assumed for them by the Christian Democrat party. If on the one hand this party constituted the visible proof of the Catholics' commitment, on the other hand it might instead have aroused suspicion exactly by virtue of its being a bridge between religion and politics, over which it was hard to tell what might cross in future. 'We started hearing talk of Christian Democrat units', writes a pungent Veneto Action Party–inspired author in his memoirs: 'Late in the day but sure enough, they too arrived. The participation of priests and of some church folk in the first phases of the Resistance had been admirable; but now one might almost have thought that this organisational intervention, coming rather late in the day, was an opportunist, competitive move.'[118]

Many *laici* also hoped that the Catholics, and the clergy in particular, would take sides – without, however, altogether giving up hoping for a clergy that was somehow, in humanitarian terms and without political pretensions, above the struggle. The humanitarianism of the clergy could then be seen with satisfaction both insofar as it constituted the humus in which the Resistance sunk its roots, and in its being a counterweight to a politicisation that was welcome, but not unreservedly so. At the same time it could be criticised as being a brake on the struggle. A Communist report says: 'A good many clergy, with the pretext of humanitarianism, are seeking to reach a compromise with the enemy, saving him from just punishment, and the masses, not being politicised, will be easily influenced.'[119]

In the *laici* there was, in short, a contradiction that mirrored the contradiction we have encountered among the Catholics: a desire for the Church to take the right side, but also a fear, which generally remained hidden, that they would overstep the mark.

6. THE EUROPEAN CIVIL WAR

Many of the aspects of the civil war seem, as it were, to have been sublimated in the conviction that a great European civil war was taking place. This concept is almost as controversial as that of a civil war applied only to Italy. The controversy becomes richer in significance when the entire 'thirty years war' that took place in Europe between 1914 and 1945 is regarded as being a 'civil'

118 Meneghello, *I piccoli maestri*, p. 291.
119 'Informazioni da Milano', 14 April 1945 (*Le Brigate Garibaldi*, vol. III, p. 621).

war.[1] This interpretation of the war as civil, ideological and religious, while not denying the geopolitical reasons for the conflict, does not consider that they tell the whole story.[2] It is clear in fact that, if one sets off from the view that 'the real dominant tendency' of the Second World War, 'for all the ideological embellishments', was that of 'a contest between the great powers for a distribution or the preservation of their international positions, that is to say, a problem of strategic and economic spheres of interest', one cannot but conclude that the groups who had taken it 'for a sort of "international civil war"' were mistaken.[3] On the other hand, if the European civil war is seen, as it has been, as a question regarding only Bolshevism and National Socialism, one ends up with a reductive and distorted vision, leading to the aberrant conclusion that all the Nazi horrors, including the extermination of the Jews, were an 'excessive response' to the violence practised by the Bolshevik revolution and the Soviet regime.[4] As we have already seen, there is undeniably a link between revolution, civil war and war between nations, but in a far more complex sense than the link theorised in these terms by Ernst Nolte. As Hannah Arendt wrote, 'a world war appears as the consequence of a revolution, a sort of civil war unleashed over the whole of the Earth's surface: it is in fact as such that much public opinion – and not without reason – regarded the Second World War'.[5]

Indeed, the discourse needs to be extended in three directions. Above all, the very technique of the war inaugurated by the Germans 'against the defensive euphoria of the French' – parachute drops behind the enemy lines, action by 'fifth columns', often formed by local Nazis in civilian dress, innumerable ways of terrorising the civilian populations – was something that 'smacks more

---

1 G. Barraclough, *An Introduction to Contemporary History*, London: Penguin, 1967, p. 30. The English historian argues that 'for most European historians' the 'great civil war' in Europe had begun in 1905. On the '1914–45 Thirty Years' War', I refer back to the intervention I made at the Brescia conference mentioned above (for its proceedings, see *L'Italia in guerra 1940–43*, Brescia: Fondazione Luigi Micheletti, 1992).

2 Benedetto Croce, in an autobiographical note referring to 29 August 1941, spoke of a war of religion. See B. Croce, *Etica e politica*, Bari: Laterza, 1981, p. 373. Mussolini spoke of this theme in a speech to the Italian divisions stationed in Germany. The *Corriere della Sera* of 25 July 1944 even gave the title 'war of religion' to one of the sections of the report on his speech. On the contemporary interlinking of civil war and war of religion, see R. Koselleck, *Futuro passato. Per una semantica dei tempi storici*, Genoa: Marietti, 1986 (original edition: *Vergangene Zukunft. Zur Semantik geschichtlicher Zeiten*, Frankfurt am Main: Suhrkamp, 1979). On the religious aspects of the Spanish Civil War, see G. Ranzato, 'Dies irae. La persecuzione religiosa nella zona repubblicana durante la guerra civile spagnola (1936–1939)', *Movimento operaio e socialista*, XI (1988), pp. 195–220.

3 Hillgruber, *Storia della seconda guerra mondiale*, pp. 131–2.

4 This being the well-known thesis of Ernst Nolte's *Der Europäische Bürgerkrieg. Nationalsozialismus und Bolschewismus*, Berlin: Propylaen, 1987.

5 Arendt, *Sulla rivoluzione*, p. 10.

of a civil war or a coup d'état than the traditional employment of the various weapons in combat.[6] This technique of war and resistance against the invader and his accomplices had, moreover, the effect of stripping spying activity against the occupying regime of the despicable features traditionally associated with it: no longer hired spies, but informers who were freely contributing to the cause of recovery.[7]

Secondly, the very fact that the peoples of Europe were fighting each other for the second time in twenty years was widely felt as a fratricide which crudely highlighted the fracture that had taken place between the normal development of civilisation and the lack of an adequate *jus publicum Europaeum* for the reality of the new century, and capable of coping with nationalistic degeneration in its different guises.[8] The federalist projects that flowered during the Resistance stemmed not least from this state of affairs.

Finally, the civil and ideological war crossed the borders of the various countries and was a war of coalition, like that fought by the great Allies. There was in fact an extremely close interweaving between the war between the nations that became civil war and the civil war that became a war between nations; and the features of the one reverberated against the other. Alongside the figure of the German enemy there was the common figure of the Fascist-collaborationist enemy who drew together the different European Resistance movements, in other respects so various and heterogeneous. Collaborationism was born from within the invaded countries themselves and gave a glimpse of a possible Europe that was truly and wholly Nazi-Fascist, body and soul. 'The unforgivable crime of Vichy is not having simply deferred to the enemy force but to quickly give it its full collaboration.'[9]

The desire to collaborate did more than boost the German request for collaboration. In Hitler at least, the will for dominion overwhelmed the convenience

---

6 As one Italian observer, O. Blatto, remarked in 'Strategia classica e tecnica rivoluzionaria', *Nuova Antologia* of 1 June 1940 (LXXV, 1637), pp. 216–20. See also the lucid prediction of these events by a German author, according to which it was necessary to encourage the 'disaggregation of the organs of state and of government authority, and the destruction of any state order' (L. Schuttel, *Fall schrintruppen und Luftinfanterie*, 1940, cited in W. Hahlweg, *Guerrilla. Krieg ohne Fronten*, Stuttgart: Kohlhammer, 1968).

7 It would have been difficult to devote a volume such as that entitled *Spie per la libertà* (Spies for Freedom) by Franco Fucci, Milan: Mursia, 1983, to any other type of war: indeed, it deals with the secret services of the Italian Resistance. A hint of the importance, in this field, of the *réseaux* formed by 'dilettanti', appears in Michel, *Les courants*, p. 305.

8 According to Schnur (*Rivoluzione e guerra civile*, esp. p. 59) the first world civil war took place in 1791–92, this marking a lasting rupture of the *jus publicum europaeum*. See also the Introduction to this volume, edited by P. P. Portinaro, pp. 35–6.

9 Conference staged by A. Philip in London in 1943 (cited in Michel, *Les courants*, p. 187).

of making widespread use of collaboration that was not merely manual labour to use and discard. It was above all the more esoteric component of Nazism, the SS, that became the bearer of a National Socialist European ideology, on the basis of which it seemed possible to give the war, particularly from 1942 onwards, the character of a crusade open in one way or another to all healthy and Aryan Europeans, and not the exclusive preserve of the German people and their Führer.[10]

The Italian *resistenti*, who were all too familiar with the part the Fascists had played in their country in dragging the European peoples into that terrible showdown, gained strength and faith from feeling that they were involved in an event whose dimensions were so vast and whose significance so profound as to sweep away, or at least attenuate, the distrust which, as Italians, they knew they had to overcome. A French partisan wrote of an Italian partisan to whom he had spoken about 10 June 1940: 'There was too much sadness in his voice for me to doubt his sincerity, and then four years under the Vichy regime helped me understand what I could not admit in May 1940.'[11]

In 1942 *Nazioni Unite*, the organ of the Mazzini Society, entitled one of its articles 'Cronache della guerra civile europea' ('Chronicles of the European Civil War').[12] A Tuscan Action Party newspaper stated that civil war had been going on in Europe for years.[13] In its opening paragraph, a GL pamphlet, written by Massimo Mila, forcefully stressed that the Second World War was a European war of religion and explained: 'Fractions of Italians, Chinese, Frenchmen and Russians are today fighting on one side or the other ... Today we partisans feel the anti-Hitlerian German to be our brother, and the Italian Fascist our deadly enemy.'

Similar concepts were expressed by Adolfo Omodeo and Carlo Dionisotti, the latter of whom defined the whole period that began with the First World War as a 'European revolution'.[14] It is no accident that these quotations bear the 'actionist' stamp: the 'democratic revolution', in which the Action Party synthesised its programme, was in effect conceivable only in the context of a European revolution, even if this involved civil war. *L'Italia Libera* published two articles side by side: 'La rivoluzione italiana' and 'La rivoluzione europea':

---

10 See Hillgruber, *Storia della seconda guerra mondiale*, pp. 131–2, 144–7.

11 *Provence Libre. Organe régional des Mouvements unis de la résistance française*, 1 June 1944.

12 The article was published in its May 1942 issue (11), and is quoted in Laura Valentini's laureate thesis from the University of Pisa, cited above.

13 'Guerra civile per la libertà', *La Libertà*, 27 October 1943.

14 *Introduzione alla vita politica (per gli italiani cresciuti sotto il fascismo)*, Edizioni del Comando delle formazioni partigiane Giustizia e Libertà, p. 2; A. Omodero, *La confederazione europea*, a pamphlet published in Naples in late 1943 (later reproduced in A. Omodero, *Libertà e storia*, pp. 66–7); Dionisotti (C. Botti), *Giovanni Gentile*, p. 90.

Jugoslavia'.[15] And as early as September 1943 it had written: 'European solidarity has been re-established. The Italians have by now taken their place among the peoples who are fighting for liberty', alongside the French, the Greeks and the Yugoslavs, whom the soldiers had silently learned to admire.[16]

The aspiration to create a European federation was the natural outlet for this attitude.[17] At the Action Party Conference of 5–6 September 1943, Leone Ginzburg had explicitly argued in favour of 'participation in the anti-Nazi war as essential in allowing the Action Party to pursue its Risorgimento and Europeanist mission'.[18] This was the only path considered practicable, even if it meant paying a very high price, if one was to avoid the abyss of that *finis Europa* that had instead appeared inexorable to many of the major intellectuals who had come of age before 1914, from Benedetto Croce to Thomas Mann. And it was also the generous final card that could be played by the old claim, dear to Carlo Rosselli, of the international autonomy of anti-Fascism or, as one reads at times in *Avanti!*, of a socialism that did not want to get itself crushed between the two blocs that were taking shape among the victors.[19]

The internationalist tradition of the workers' movement also tended to view the European civil war approvingly, and spurred the Italian partisans 'to feel tied to the partisans of the whole world': that is how a Garibaldi commander replied to the officer of a British mission who wished to convince him that the Greek partisans were 'just rebels'.[20] The Communist cadres, however (more so than in the Garibaldi and workers' rank-and-file), trod more cautiously, governed as they were by Stalin's policy, which was unitary on the international as it was on the internal plane. To harp on too much about a European civil war might in fact clash with the cause of the great coalition, by evoking that 'transformation of the imperialist war into a civil war' which had been definitively proscribed after 21 June 1941. In this sense the case of Greece exemplifies the confusion of political meanings, projected into the future as well, that the 'civil war' acquired both internationally and internally, and at the level of both ideological involvement and, emotionally, of sympathies and fears. Two very differently inspired documents bear this out. The first is the hotly contested approval of the contradictory motion hailing the Greek patriots that was passed by the CLNAI on 6 January

---

15 *L'Italia Libera*, Lombard edition, 22 May 1944.

16 *Gli Italiani e la solidarietà europea*, *L'Italia Libera*, Rome edition, 25 September 1943.

17 Salvemini had the scruple to note that a European federalism proclaimed by Italians could seem like a cop-out designed to 'escape punishment'. See his letter to Ernesto Rossi of 29 November 1944 (Salvemini, *Lettere dall'America*, pp. 44–5).

18 Testimony of Manlio Rossi-Doria, taken from Valiani, *Gli azionisti*, p. 67.

19 The article 'Ammistrazione o Rivoluzione' in *Avanti!*, Rome edition, 16 March 1944, speaks of a 'great European revolution'.

20 See Bernardo, *Il momento buono*, p. 126.

1945, and contested by the liberals at the following session on 12 January.[21] The second is the declaration made at a party meeting by a Communist worker from Milan: 'The Greek question is looked on favourably by some comrades, because by rising up [against the British-supported government] the Greek people would seem to have shown their maturity. The liberation of Greece is a result of the Russian advance.'[22]

The exemplary value assumed in the eyes of the Italian partisans by those of other countries was forcefully affirmed especially by Actionists, Communists and Socialists. A Garibaldi document lists French, Estonians, Latvians, Lithuanians, Czechoslovaks, Hungarians, Romanians, Bulgarians, Yugoslavians and Greeks;[23] but generally it was the French, the Yugoslavians and also the Russians who were held up as examples. The Yugoslavians exerted a particular fascination on the Communist and working-class rank-and-file, not least because they seemed in their struggle to unify three wars – patriotic, civil and class. A Roman 'extremist' newspaper underlined that the Yugoslavian partisan war was a 'people's war not just against enemies from without, but also and above all against the enemy from within'.[24] But the myth too of Paris, mother of all revolutions, was bandied about at the moment of the liberation of the French capital, alongside that other myth of revolutionary fraternity between the two peoples.[25]

At work in the Resistance was the memory of the Spanish Civil War, seen as the great rehearsal for the European conflict precisely in the 'civil' and ideological sphere. 'It started in Spain' was how *L'Italia Libera* entitled one of its evocative articles,[26] to show, as it were, that Carlo Rosselli's famous prophecy from Radio Barcelona – 'Today in Spain, tomorrow in Italy' – had been fulfilled; and the

---

21 See the motion's text, 'The CLNAI, while confirming its full solidarity with the United Nations in the struggle for democracy, and the conscious discipline of the formations of the volunteers for freedom, makes the most enthusiastic salute to the Greek patriots fighting against the domestic forces of reaction in order to establish the rule of freedom in their country' (*Atti CLNAI*, pp. 222–3, 227–8).

22 See 'Estratto da un rapporto da Milano', 15 December 1944, in Secchia, *Il PCI e la guerra di liberazione*, pp. 708–9.

23 See the 'Rapporto informativo n. 2' from the Group Command of the Lower Po SAP to the responsible official of the Lombard delegation, Fabio, 27 October 1944 (*Le Brigate Garibaldi*, vol. II, p. 497).

24 *Il Partigiano*, 23 January 1944.

25 'Il saluto del popolo italiano a Parigi liberata', *L'Unità*, Northern edition, 1 September 1944. For an overall view of the 'expected but missing' (Foa, *La crisi*, p. 18) contacts and accords with neighbouring Resistance forces, the paper that Ferruccio Parri and Franco Venturi gave at the II Congresso internazionale di storia della Resistenza held in Milan in March 1961 remains of enduring importance. See 'La Resistenza italiana e gli Alleati', in INSMLI, *La Resistenza europea e gli Alleati*, pp. 237–80.

26 *L'Italia Libera*, Northern edition, 22 July 1944.

GL paper recalled that the tradition of the movement's struggle was born precisely in Spain.[27] *L'Unità* in its turn celebrated the beginning of the heroic and luckless struggle of the Spanish people, giving the version of it canonised in the Third International.[28] On the other hand, this interpretive conformism – yoked to the probable concern that it was inopportune, particularly as far as relations with the Catholics were concerned, to labour the point too much – resulted in Spain's being given less space in the Italian Communist press and the PCI's other Resistance documents than one might have expected. The newspaper *Democrazia Internazionale* drew attention to this, lamenting the fact that the glorious name 'Fronte Popolare' was being kept hidden for tactical reasons.[29] But the prestige enjoyed by the veterans from Spain, some of whom arrived via the French Resistance, was great – from Luigi Longo to those partisans – but here we are among those incorporated in the 9th Yugoslav Corps – who sang:

> Noi siamo giovani garibaldini
> della Spagna i reduci noi siam
> combattiamo contro i fascisti assassin
> contro chi angoscia l'intera umanità.[30]

> [We are young Garibaldini
> we are the veterans of Spain
> we fight the fascist assassins
> who torment all of humanity.]

The memory of the 'enormous political contribution by the party in Spain among the first "volunteers" to make them into soldiers of a cause' had been immediately invoked by a Piedmontese Communist leader in support of his conviction that 'the partisan formations in Italy today have a function exceeding that of sniper in the strict sense of the word'.[31] But the Spanish model could seem so noble that emulating it seemed an object beyond one's reach. Speaking of Umberto, a veteran from Spain, the Garibaldini 'ask[ed] themselves' whether 'in any of our formations there is an Italian with the same qualities'. The comment of a party representative, torn between nostalgia for Communist solidarity and duty towards CLN unity, is crude and ungenerous: 'Don't come to me with the

---

27 'Ai Partigiani', editorial of *Lungo il Tanaro*, April 1945.

28 'Otto anni fa ed oggi', *L'Unità*, Northern edition, 7 August 1944.

29 See the article 'El Frente Popular', *Democrazia Internazionale*, No. 3, n.d. *Il Saggio bibliografico* 4219 attributes this publication to the Bordigist Partito Comunista Internazionalista, but this is unconvincing.

30 The text of the song appears in IZDG, envelope 272a, folder II/B.

31 See the report from the responsible official for military work in Piedmont, Sandrelli, to the PCI leadership, 26 December 1943 (*Le Brigate Garibaldi*, vol. I, pp. 183–8).

example of the Spanish International Brigade, because here things are very different. There they were men united by a faith, here they are men united only by contingent circumstances but who then have particular interests that are very different from each other.'[32]

Parallel with this were vivid hopes and longings that the Axis defeat would bring with it the fall of Franco's regime. *L'Italia Libera* warned that the European revolution that was taking place should not bypass Spain.[33] *Avanti!* assured its readers that 'the progressivist and revolutionary forces of the whole world would make sure that they did not allow' the saving of Franco, whose destiny remained 'linked with that of Mussolini and Hitler.'[34]

The Fascists too cultivated the memory of the exploits of their legionaries in Spain.[35] If they did not make too much of this point, however much it lent itself to use in their approach with Catholics and the contemplation of the new European order, this is probably because things were made awkward for them by the ingratitude shown by the Generalissimo, over which it was prudent to draw a veil of silence.

In any case, if the Fascists had read the Spanish press of those months they would have noted how the Franco regime was progressively and clearly distancing itself from the losing powers, albeit amid reticence and ambiguities cloaked in exaltation of the Church, of Pius XII and of the 'crusade against communism' (the headline under which news from the Russian front was generally collected). On 30 July 1943 the Barcelona edition of *La Vanguardia Española* called the 'constututional situation ' created by Mussolini's defenestration 'simple and legalistic'; and on 9 September, in an article entitled 'A momentous step' , wrote that in any case Italy had the 'inmense good luck ' to house 'in its heart ' Vatican City. Mussolini's liberation, which on 15 September was defined as an 'heroic undertaking ', on 18 September was considered a fatal signal of civil war. The main thing for which Mussolini was reproached in the respectful obituary dedicated to him on 1 May 1945 would be – and who can doubt the

---

32 See the report from the responsible PCI official and vice-commissar, Italo, to the Command of the 3rd Lombardy Division Aliotta (in Oltrepò), 10 November 1944 (IG, BG, 01600).

33 'La Spagna e l'Europa', *L'Italia Libera*, Lombard edition, 10 April 1944. See also (in its Northern edition, 6 February 1945) 'Problemi della democrazia europea. Per la rinascita della Spagna'.

34 'Che vuole?', *Avanti!*, Rome edition, 30 December 1943, on an amnesty given by Franco, and 'Inquietudine spagnola', 12 January 1944, which, however, began from the correct understanding that neutrality had strengthened Franco. In autumn 1944, Spanish exiles, above all Communists, attempted in vain to establish a guerrilla base in the Val d'Aran in the Pyrenees, riding the wave of the liberation of France (see E. Pons Prades, *Guerrillas españolas 1936–1960*, Barcelona: Planeta, 1977).

35 See, for example, the propaganda flyer 'Volontari in terra di Spagna' (Fondo RSI, No. 966).

journalist's sincerity? – that of having committed the 'colossal error' of entering the war.

The theme of the defence of Europe was widely present in Fascist propaganda – or, rather, Europe's defence against external enemies and from internal enemies, who were in many respects still more insidious. In the old polemic which in June 1927 Telesio Interlandi (one of whose articles at that time had borne the title 'Anti-europei perché fascisti') had set against Francesco Coppola's argument in favour of the union of the European West against 'Asiatic subversivism',[36] the RSI adopted the latter position, now in the form of submission of the peoples of the European continent to the New Order imposed by Germany on the Western powers. Even the fond hopes of Fascist internationalism[37] had had to give way to the patent fact of German predominance; and all the more so in the light of the maladroit attempts that the part of Italian diplomacy headed by Under-Secretary Giuseppe Bastianini had made to create around Italy and in the name of Europe a constellation of smaller states with a view to disengaging from Germany.[38] It was, moreover, the very process of subjection that led to an accentuation of this kind of SS-type Europeanism and the hatred it generated among Europeans: 'Hitler saved Europe, and for this reason Rexists had the effrontery to shout: Heil Hitler', Léon Degrelle had said in a speech that he gave in Liège on 5 January 1941.[39] A French poster calling for enlistment in the SS proclaimed: 'With your European comrades you will conquer under the banner of the SS!'[40]

This attitude, mentioned earlier, had been reinforced after the attack on the USSR, when Hitler himself, in a proclamation to the German people on 22 June 1941, had described himself as the 'conscious representative of European culture and civilisation'.[41] Now, in Italy, immediately after 8 September, a poster of the Livorno *Kommandantur* also urged that the words 'Long live the new Europe under the leadership of Adolf Hitler!' be shouted.[42] An SS proclamation in the province of Forlì denounced as outlaws those who wanted 'the annihilation of every cultural value of the West, of religion, and consequently of the spiritual patrimony of every upright person'.[43] Of all people, it was Mussolini who seemed the

---

36 On this argument and its development, see G. Carocci, *La politica estera dell'Italia fascista (1925–1928)*, Bari: Laterza, 1969, pp. 197–9. Interlandi directed his polemic against a corrupt Paris and the degenerate Weimar regime, whereas Coppola instead envisaged a great and strong European bourgeoisie.

37 See M. A. Ledeen, *Universal Fascism: The Theory and Practice of the Fascist International 1928–1936*, New York: Howard Fertig, 1972.

38 On these efforts, see Deakin, *Brutal Friendship*.

39 Quoted in the laureate thesis of M. Di Giovanni.

40 See Etnasi, *La Resistenza in Europa*, vol. I, p. 182.

41 See E. Collotti, *La seconda guerra mondiale*, Turin: Loescher, 1973, p. 128.

42 ISRT, Raccolta volantini.

43 'Ultimo monito ai sabotatori', 16 September 1944, cited in Flamigni and Marzocchi, *Resistenza in Romagna*, p. 239

most uncertain on this score. When he was a prisoner of the king and Badoglio's and was taken to Ponza, it appears that he said to Admiral Franco Maugeri that it was nonsense to consider Russia a peril for European civilisation.[44] As head of the RSI he had the weekly *Avanguardia Europea*, edited by Felice Bellotti, closed down.[45] Some Nazi-Fascist propaganda posters and other news-sheets appear, therefore, more eloquent than the Duce's customary wavering or the vague European-toned propositions of the Verona manifesto.[46] A leaflet assured its readers that the 'victory of European arms' was 'sure and imminent'.[47] A poster was entitled 'The European Crusade', and bore in its background the flags of the SS and of several European nations. Other posters proclaimed: 'The New Europe: Enough with the tyranny of money'; 'Germany defends Europe'; 'Read and think it over: Europe rushes forward'; 'Italian SS Legione. Awaits the youth for the benefit of Italy and Europe'; 'Europe will resist the new barbarians'.[48] An airman wrote to his brother Benito: 'I'm glad I've enlisted in the SS and I can't wait to be able to offer my tangible contribution to the cause of the New Europe, the only hope that Europe can have for life and well-being tomorrow'.[49]

'Long live fascism! Long live Europe!' were the last words written to his mother by a Fascist shot as a spy by the British in Santa Maria Capua Vetere on 30 April 1944.[50] In comparison to this, a medical officer appeared kind-hearted and bewildered when, thinking of the Holy Roman Empire, he wrote to the 'Very Reverend Don Tullio Calcagno': 'Many years ago, at school, I learned that European civilisation consists essentially of three elements: "Romanism, Christianism and Germanism"'.[51]

The Europeanism inspired by the SS's murky esotericism was one of the channels through which RSI Fascism assimilated the trappings of Nazism in a particularly marked fashion, bequeathing them to the post-war neo-Fascists.[52]

---

44 See F. Maugeri, *Mussolini mi ha detto*, Rome: Tip. Agricoltori, 1944, p. 23.

45 See Bocca, *La Repubblica di Mussolini*, p. 217.

46 See Deakin, *Brutal Friendship*, p. 668

47 ISRT, Raccolta volantini.

48 Fondo RSI, Nos. 330, 385, 547, 669, 672, 991.

49 Letter from Arrigo Gasparini Casari, from Modena, class of 1922, 11 January 1944 (*LRSI*, p. 30).

50 The eighteen-year-old Roman Franco Aschieri (*LRSI*, p. 102).

51 Francesco Davolio Marani, a medical officer from Fabbrico (Reggio Emilia), 25 May 1944 (*LRSI*, p. 50).

52 On SS esotericism, see A. Del Boca and M. Giovana, *I 'figli del sole'. Mezzo secolo di nazifascismo nel mondo*, Milan: Feltrinelli, 1965; F. Jesi, *Cultura di destra*, Milan: Garzanti, 1979. On the neo-Fascists' inheritance from the RSI, in contrast with other European collaborationist movements, see E. Collotti, 'La Repubblica Sociale Italiana', *Ulisse*, XXX, Vol. XIII (October 1976), folder LXXXII, esp. pp. 101–2. On the twilight of French SS who fled in 1944, retreating to Sigmaringen Castle, see H. Rousso, *Un château en Allemagne*, Paris: Ramsay, 1980. See also M. Revelli, 'Panorama editoriale

Earlier I suggested how the events in Greece offered a glimpse of the possibility of the meaning of 'civil war' slipping from a war between anti-Fascists and Fascists to a war that might explode *after* the defeat of the Fascists. An article in *Risorgimento Liberale*, the Liberal newspaper, in its ambiguity, straddles these two possible meanings. Fascist propaganda, it says, 'could have created the premises for a civil war': the unity of the CLN had averted the danger, because the parties proved to be 'conscious that a civil war would only lead to final irreparable disaster and to reactions as predictable as they would be iniquitous.'[53]

For the right, brandishing the 'Greek prospect' was a way of curbing the fearsome developments, charged with international significance, that were coming to light in Greece. For the left, it was useful to suggest, albeit discreetly, the bogeyman of similar developments elsewhere in order to obtain the greatest possible shift of the unitary faction over to their side, in return for the guarantee that events would take a different turn in Italy. This second attitude emerged clearly at a meeting held in the Langhe in February 1945 between the British captain O'Regan (Chape), Mauri, commander of the autonomous brigades, and Andreis (Italo Nicoletti), a Garibaldi inspector. O'Regan, in agreement with Mauri, had proposed the unification of the formations under his command. Andreis replied that, if one wished to avoid offending Italian national sentiment, unity could only be achieved in the ambit of the CLN and the Piedmontese regional military command, which was under the authority of the committee, and added that what had occurred in Greece was impossible in Italy, 'since we have a government which is recognised both by the Allies and by the partisans; and any decision taken by this government would be carried out by us'. There were not, then, the conditions in Italy for a post-Liberation civil war; but, Andreis warned, with the attempts at dispersal that were being made, with the attempts being conducted 'outside the CLN and the Italian government, conditions for civil war were being concretely created.'[54]

It was precisely the radical nature of the struggle, both Italian and European, that might drive people to brandish the prospect of a civil war in the immediate future, if the present one failed to have all the effects hoped for. This threat was

---

e temi culturali nella destra militante', in 'Nuova destra e cultura reazionaria negli anni ottanto', *Notiziario dell'Istituto storico della Resistenza in Cuneo e provincia* 23 (June 1983), pp. 49–74.

53 'Per la solidarietà tra i Partiti', *Risorgimento Liberale*, Northern edition, October 1944.

54 See Andreis's report, 'Sulla riunione tenuta a Cortemilia col rappresentante della missione inglese', 6 February 1945. On 1 February, the Garibaldian commander Nanni expressed similar ideas following a 27 January meeting. In a postscript for his comrades, Andreis added: 'For our part, while doing everything to strengthen unity, we vigorously struck down any anti-democratic or anti-Italian initiatives by reactionaries if necessary' (*Le Brigate Garibaldi*, vol. III, pp. 332–5 and n. 8).

explicitly formulated in the unlikely context of the 'Outline for the manifesto of the Committee for the defence of teachers and intellectuals'. Here, the government of the South was warned about jeopardising its future by taking decisions without consulting the entire Italian people: only by working without falling into this error would those governing in the South 'be able to avoid incurring responsibility for a civil war that would be no less inevitable for having to be deferred for a few years'.[55]

In the speech he gave at the Brancaccio theatre in Rome on 31 December 1944, Pietro Nenni did not hesitate to state the equation: 'political centre bloc' equals 'civil war'.[56] This was certainly a case of verbal intemperance. But that intemperance contributed to fostering alarm for the future. Just back from his mission to the North, Aldobrando Medici Tornaquinci, under-secretary at the Ministry for Occupied Italy, voiced this alarm to the Liberal national committee, which met in Rome from 1 to 4 March 1945: 'There are some parties (which yet form part of the CLN), that are demonstrating in the most blatant way that their war propaganda does have the liberation of the North as its aim, but also, or possibly above all, the formation of armed groups, or ideally, of an army which is the army of a particular party.'

The situation, Medici Tornaquinci explained, 'is not marked by the red of the CLN, but there is the risk that it will be dominated by a darker red'.[57] It is this red, darker and more dazzling, feared by some, hoped for by others, that now takes us on to examine the third aspect of the struggle that was being waged in Italy at that time: the class war.

---

55 *Attività clandestina dell'Associazione professori e assistenti universitari (APAU) e del Comitato di liberazione nazionale di professori e assistenti universitari (CLNPAU) in Milano negli anni 1944-1945*, published by the Comitato Direttivo Provvisorio dell'Associazione Professori e Assistenti Universitari, Milan, July 1945, pp. 17–18. The 'Outline' was datelined 23 May 1944, Milan.

56 *Il partito socialista e la crisi ministeriale (novembre 1944)*, Rome: Società Editrice Avanti!, Biblioteca 'I documenti del partito', 2, p. 30.

57 ISRT, *Archivio Medici Tornaquinci*, envelope 5, 2, 3.

CHAPTER 6

The Class War

1. CLASS, NATION, ANTI-FASCISM

In April 1916, James Connolly, on the eve of the desperate attempted insurrection against the English that would lead him to the gallows, wrote:

> We are out for Ireland for the Irish. But who are the Irish? Not the rack-renting, slum-owning landlord, not the sweating, profit-grinding capitalist; not the sleek and oily lawyer; not the prostitute pressman – the hired liars of the enemy. Not these are the Irish upon whom the future depends. Not these, but the Irish working class, the only secure foundation upon which a free nation can be reared.[1]

The identification, here, of the nation's enemy with the class enemy is peremptory but not new. One of the most radical of the seventeenth-century English 'Levellers', Gerrard Winstanley, had identified the rich with the Norman invaders.[2] To this way of seeing things employers and capitalists are, as such, enemies and foreigners. From the Fascist point of view, by contrast, capitalists are enemies only if they are foreigners (or Jews), in continuity with the nationalistic tradition that exalted national labour and declared that it wished to defend it against foreign exploitation.[3]

Illustrating his socialisation plans to ambassador Rudolf von Rahn, Mussolini presented them as a punitive measure against the industrialists who were pro-British and guilty of the 8 September act of treachery. Hitler concurred, in the name of inflicting a just punishment on entrepreneurs who sabotaged war production.[4] Socialisation thus became a form of political punishment.

---

1 The article 'The Irish Flag' was published in *Workers' Republic* of 8 April 1916, and republished in P. Mac Aonghusa and L. Ó Régáin, *The Best of Connolly*, Cork: Mercier Press, 1967, pp. 195–7 (I thank Paul Ginsborg for giving me this information).

2 See Christopher Hill, 'Gerrard Winstanley: 17th Century Communist', lecture at Kingston University, 24 January 1996.

3 See *Autoritarismo*, p. 246; and the arguments of M. Barrès in *Scènes et doctrines du nationalisme* (Paris: Plon-Nourrit, 1925, vol. I, p. 105) with regard to the defence of the worker against the foreigner, cited by Marco Diani, 'Metamorphosis of Nationalism: Durkheim, Barrès and the Dreyfus Affair', *Jerusalem Journal of International Relations* 13: 4 (1991) pp. 71–94 (my thanks to Manco Diani for making me aware of this).

4 Collotti, *L' amministrazione tedesca*, p. 159 (the episode took place in February 1944).

During the Resistance, and not only in Italy, the coincidence between the two enemies – enemies of the *patria* and class enemies – was called into question by the inevitably interclass policy of national unity pursued by the major parties of the left. It is possible, though, to detect, above all in the Communist leaders, an effort not to allow all class opposition to drown in the waters of national unity. The proletariat thus found itself with an extra burden of national responsibility, which was taken to coincide with 'its economic interests that cannot be defended, nor its demands obtained if the Nation perishes'. This position was a sort of updated exegesis of the Marxist motto: 'The proletariat have no country'. This motto, it was explained, 'does not mean that the proletariat should not feel the need to conquer the country for themselves', a country that they do not have, another text emphasises, because the bourgeoisie steal it from them.[5] At the same time, oscillating in various ways according to time and place, distinctions between capitalists were reintroduced, culminating in that between collaborationists and good patriots. The 'struggle for national independence' therefore joined hands again with the class struggle against the homegrown *alta borghesia* regarded as the slave and ally of foreign imperialism.[6]

An upended version of the same problem can be found in some Action Party documents: recognition of the elements of social confrontation present in the struggle, and at the same time the affirmation that this is not the whole story. Riccardo Bauer wrote: 'It is the battle not between two economic classes – even if such a polarisation coincides – but rather between two conceptions of life, between two political religions, namely: the conception of life as creative liberty and that of life as subordination and hierarchic order'.[7]

In reality two class motivations are identifiable in the behaviour of many *resistenti*, above all if they were of working-class or even peasant origin; and these motivations often coexist with patriotic and anti-Fascist ones in the strict political sense. For workers who were to a greater or less extent politicised, the ideal enemy, the clearest and most representative enemy-figure would have been that of a *padrone* who was also a Fascist and a brazen servant of the Germans,

---

5 Letter from the Turin SAP Division Command to the Command of the 1st Sector, 25 January 1945 (IG, *BG*, 06106); letter from the PCI central commission for agitation and propaganda to the Lazio committee, which had requested advice on what reply to give to a request for clarification made on 12 December 1943 by Carla, Nistro and Leone, as regards the concept of *patria*. (*Documenti inediti sulle posizioni del PCI e del PSIUP*, pp. 125–31); 'La Patria', Voce Operaia, 28 January 1944.

6 'La classe operaia e la questione nazionale', *L'Unità*, Rome edition, 3 November 1943.

7 'Circolare riservata ai comitati locali', 31 October 1943, published with the title 'La politica del Partito d'Azione nei primi mesi della lotta armata', in *Formazioni GL*, pp. 48–53: p. 49.

and as such no longer a real Italian (according to the process of annihilation of the national identity of turncoats already emphasised when speaking of the civil war). The condemned men who were shot crying 'viva il comunismo, viva l'Italia, viva la libertà' or 'viva l'Italia, viva Stalin, viva il comunismo!'[8] synthesised in this final message of theirs the multiple reasons for their choice. A leaflet addressed to the Bolognese rice-workers, and therefore expressive of an attitude mediated by exhortative and programmatic ends, starts with an attack on 'our *padroni* [who] have repeatedly demonstrated that they have no desire to grant us any of our vital demands'; and, in a typical crescendo of concentric circles, concludes with 'viva la nostra libertà! Morte ai tedeschi e ai traditori fascisti!' ('Long live our freedom! Death to the traitorous German fascists!').[9] Blunter is this slogan proposed for the workers of Massa Lombarda: 'Fuori i tedeschi e 10 lire come minima di paga oraria!' ('Out with the Germans and 10 lire an hour as the minimum wage!')[10] 'Pour la défait de Hitler. Pour l'augmentation de nos salaires' ('For the defeat of Hitler. For higher wages') was the appeal that appeared in a clearly Communist-inspired French newspaper.[11] In a 'Letter to the peasants from a city worker' the contextual occurrence of the three objectives of the struggle is voiced in accents – we are in Romagna, remember – that echo an old Mazzinian social vision, which in its time was also committed to convincing people of the complete congruity between the interests of the working classes and the interests of the *patria*:

What does it matter, *fratello*, that the oppressor of our *patria* is called Nazi or Fascist and ours called landowner rather than industrialist? They're all much the same, they all oppress us ... Get it into your head that so long as there is a Fascist lording it in the cities and so long as there's a German trampling on our soil there can be neither peace, no liberty, nor freedom for you. Remember that if the emancipation of peoples can only be the work of the peoples themselves, the emancipation of Italy from all oppressors can only be the work of us ourselves; therefore you too O *fratello contadino*, must do your bit, must cooperate with all your strength for the expulsion

8 'Relazione attacco al ... Val d'Ossola dal 12 al 24 giugno 1944' (IG, BG, 08648); Gorrieri, *La Repubblica di Montefiorino*, p. 451. The condemned man could also take solace in religion.

9 N.d., unsigned, in MRB, Raccolta Adversi. The leaflet was printed on the eve of the rice-workers' 12 June 1944 strike (see L. Arbizzani, 'Manifesti, opuscoli, fogli volanti', in L. Bergonzini, *La Resistenza a Bologna. Testimonianze e documenti*, Istituto per la storia di Bologna, vol. IV, Bologna, 1975, p. 187). See also the first issue (n.d.) of *La Mondariso. Organo delle mondine bolognesi*.

10 *La Lotta*, 30 June 1944, cited in Casali, *Il movimento di liberazione a Ravenna*, vol. I, p. 61.

11 *Le Réveil des métallos. Organe de défense des métallos de la région rouennaise*, 1 September 1941.

of the Nazi-Fascist oppressors of our country and for our liberty and for the triumph of the working class.[12]

A Turinese *resistente* and Communist militant, when they wanted to give her the [Bulgarian] 'diploma Alexander', said: 'I don't want foreigners' stuff; I'd take it if it came from Italians.'[13]

One of the first problems, then, lies in the coexistence of these distinct motivations in the same individuals or, conversely, their being split between different individuals. First of all, there was the fact that not all employers, industrial or agrarian, were collaborationists, nor were they all Fascists, or at any rate still Fascists. And, mirroring this, there was also the fact that, if we set aside the different collective stance towards Fascism, not all workers were, strictly speaking, *resistenti*; which means that the oft-used hendiadys that the Resistance was essentially the work of the partisans and workers, needs examining, as does the relationship between these two main protagonists of the Resistance movement.

In fact in the consciousness of the *resistenti* there were distinctions and preferences that led to the three enemy-figures being isolated or combined in various ways. Thus, the insistence on casting the *padroni* in a hostile light contributed to that different way of viewing the Germans, not as a pure incarnation of the Devil, which I have already mentioned.

A February 1944 leaflet, distributed in Cittadella in the province of Padua, after enjoining its readers to hide wheat and to feed British prisoners and German deserters, concluded: 'Don't hate the Germans. Let us hate the Italian exploiters, the false prophets, the traitors. Let us hate the *arristograzie* [*sic*, misspelling], let us draw up a blacklist.'[14] A case of class consciousness sublimated in politico-ideological consciousness may be encountered in that 'organizzatore del lavoro militare' ('organiser of military work') in the province of Novara who asked 'how it was possible to shoot at a German who, for all one knew, was a Communist.'[15]

The clandestine *L'Unità* always bore the subheading 'Proletari di tutti i paesi unitevi!' ('Workers of the world unite!'). On 30 April 1945 this had already disappeared from the Milan edition. The Rome edition of the clandestine *Avanti!* placed that motto next to the other one in its half-title: 'The first duty of the proletariat is to achieve democracy: Marx-Engels.' In the period of armed struggle, the internationalist appeal, dear to the workers' hearts, represented a kind

---

12 The letter, which appeared in the Imola *La Comune* of April 1944, was cited in M. Legnani, 'Aspetti economici delle campagne settentrionali e motivi di politica agraria nei programmi dei partiti antifascisti (1942–45)', in *Il Movimento di liberazione in Italia* 78 (January–March 1965), pp. 21–2.

13 Testimony of Rosanna Rolando, later forgotten by the Republic and the Communist Party itself, Bruzzone and Farina, eds, *La Resistenza taciuta*, pp. 30–1.

14 Cited in Briguglio, *Clero e contadini*, p. 337.

15 See Pajetta, *Il ragazzo rosso va alla guerra*, p. 42.

of ideal pole, a natural but remote premise, to offset the policy of national unity, but only in rare cases was it made explicit and argued autonomously, rather than as part of the exaltation of the international role of the Soviet Union. One such case can be found, for example, in an 'ora politica' ('political hour') held at the 1st Garibaldi-Osoppo division (in the brief period when the formations fighting on the eastern border were unified), when it was explained that 'the concept of class goes beyond that of the nation, since individuals belonging to different nations belong to the same class', and are driven to fight against each other by the ruling classes: only the creation of a single state, therefore, will prevent 'the frequent repetition of fratricidal wars'.[16]

In July 1943 a French Trotskyist newspaper had spoken out against Gaullist and Stalinist propaganda that talked of 'dirty Krauts' and 'despicable macaronis.'[17] I mention this only to point out how the traditional formulae identifying class consciousness and internationalism were compelled to contend with a reality characterised not so much by the opposition as 'the contiguity of consciences between the struggle between classes and the struggle between nations',[18] and where 'partisan internationalism', mentioned in the previous chapter, took priority over proletarian internationalism.

In the case of Italy the presence of autochthonous Fascism made the picture yet more complex and gave a particularly strong sense to the objective of 'achieving democracy'. If the day of reckoning was to be truly decisive, it had to go beyond the dismal epigones of Salò and strike at the very roots of Fascism, which indeed everyone was proclaiming that they wanted to sever. Intransigence in the struggle against the Fascists, who were doomed to defeat, was thus coming to be like the mark of this wish to go beyond Fascism itself. A pamphlet dedicated 'to the glory of the national hero Dante Di Nanni, a twenty-year-old Garibaldino who fell fighting in Turin on 18 May 1944', says that in Di Nanni instinctive repugnance for Fascism, generated by his coming from a working-class family, had been transformed into the realisation that 'one needed to dismantle and destroy the whole social system that had generated and perpetrated this oppression' and the conviction that the Italian Communist Party (PCI) was 'the revolutionary party, the only party capable of defending the interests of the working class'. After 8 September, Di Nanni had dreamed of seeing 'the armed proletariat at the head of all true patriots.'[19]

---

16 Text of the 'political hour' on 'social classes' held by the 1st Osoppo Brigade Command, Le classi sociali, in IZDG, envelope 272b, file. I/A.

17 'Si tu veux la paix, main tendui aux ouvriers Allemands et Italiens', La Vérité, 30 July 1943 (editorial).

18 The expression is from V. Foa, La Gerusalemme rimandata. Domande di oggi agli inglesi del primo Novecento, Turin: Rosenberg e Sellier, 1985, p. 201.

19 See La giovane vita di Dante Di Nanni raccontata da un suo compagno di lotta, undated, without page numbers.

The coincidence between armed proletariat and true patriot had moreover to be constantly verified, even in the area influenced by the PCI. This we shall see more clearly presently. But mention can be made even now of one of the first Forlì mountain bands, where the class spirit did not so much evolve in a patriotic direction as violently generate manifestations of social hate, thereby giving rise to a particularly strong link between class war and civil war and leaving the patriotic war in the background. The behaviour of this band has been described as follows in a Communist-inspired book:

> The principal objectives are *carabinieri*, Fascists and spies, while the Germans are, with rare exceptions, left in peace. This activity was accompanied by requisitions, carried out against the major landowners of the area, medium and small owners ... There were many reasons for this conduct: the persistence of a new form of fence-sitting characterised by the renunciation of opposition to the main enemy and the manifestation of a class impulse which saw the solution to 'foodstuff' problems in provisioning to the detriment of farmers. The first partisan units mainly consisted of farmhands and workers in general. For the persecution and acts of oppression they had suffered these were prone to regard as 'enemies' that category of farmers who had been Fascist and had taken advantage of the favourable conditions to subject them to the injustices of Fascism. The excesses that had occurred created tensions that prevented the formation of collaborative relations with important strata of the rural population. There was a resurgence of the old maximalism which bedimmed the national vision of the Resistance.

The commander of this band, Libero, was a captain (Riccardo Fedel), a veteran from Yugoslavia, where he was said to have fought with the partisans. He was blamed for having obtained 'the consensus of his command and the sympathy of many partisans precisely by supporting the mistaken tendencies just described'. A Garibaldi document came down very severely against Libero, and even considered his physical liquidation, if only to bring the formation back to its senses. Demoted to chief of staff, Libero was to desert during the great roundup of April 1944, and after the Liberation his name would figure on the lists of the OVRA (Opera Vigilanza Repressione Anti-fascista). Thus, what was alarming in the social revolt of 'farmhands and workers in general' could be laid at the door of a traitor.[20]

The memory of 1920–21 in its turn re-soldered the link between class war

---

20 See Flamigni and Marzocchi, *Resistenza in Romagna*, pp. 137, 165–6, 178. The quote is from p. 165, while on p. 172 one of the accusations against Libero's partisans is that of having established a 'Dipartimento del Corniolo' in the image of the Cisalpine Republic. The document to which it refers is a 'Rapporto generale' by the Commander of the 8th Romagna Brigade, Pietro Mauri, on military activity in Romagna up to 15 May 1944 (*Le Brigate Garibaldi*, vol. I, pp. 411–21).

and civil war. ''21-type individual … '21-type lad, that's it', is how a worker from
the Galileo plant describes a smart youth after recalling the role that the presence of 'folk who'd done '21, who'd done '22', elderly people who 'venian per
tradizione di famiglia' ('who come out of family tradition'),[21] had had in creating a class consciousness in the factory. It was a memory that culminated in the
verdict against 'reformists also called traitors'[22] and in the judgment on the 1921
split,[23] which was very similar to the one passed by a French Trotskyist paper:
'The workers of Milan, Turin and Rome have not forgotten the lesson of 1921.
This time, they will not relinquish the weapons that the traitors of social democracy made them turn in to Mussolini'.[24]

The identification of the Fascist regime with the regime of the *padroni*
encouraged the belief that the moment had come for a showdown on the social
plane as well. Conversely, and highly favourable to the identification of the
working class and Communism, there was the stark dilemma that had been
posed for more than twenty years by Fascist propaganda: either Fascism or
Communism.

'In many countries there is no evidence of other political leanings. The division seems to be clear-cut: either Communists or Fascists. The situation only
needs to pick up a bit for us to be masters of the situation.' While this schematic
optimism of the Ancona Communist leaders is neither justified nor can it be
applied across the board, it does indicate a widespread conviction. The Ancona
Communists complete the picture by introducing the connection between the
Fascists and the German connection: 'The local Fascists, especially those from
the hinterland, are giving no trouble, on the contrary they are doing their utmost
to show their goodwill towards the anti-Fascists: we know, however, that this is
due to the fact that the invaders haven't yet arrived in these zones.'[25]

'The enemy is the Nazi German', declared *Avanti!*, and only the working
classes, it added to square the circle, can wage a struggle that is not only a 'war
against the foreigner who is trampling on the soil of the *patria*, but it also and
above all a war against the scourge of our century, inside and outside Italy, against
Fascism'.[26] And in another appeal it urged: 'National insurrection against the

---

21 Interview with Angelo Raffaelli, born in 1902, a Communist, in G. Contini,
Memoria e storia. Le Officine Galileo nel racconto degli operai, dei tecnici, dei manager,
Milan: Franco Angeli, 1985, pp. 359, 351–5.

22 Remo Righetti, in Portelli, *Biografia di una città*, p. 146.

23 On this, see the calmly worded yet sharp exposition of the issue, stressing the full
value of the Livorno split, in the 26 October 1943 *L'Unità* Rome edition's commentary on
the pact for unity in action with the Socialists.

24 *La Vérité*, 30 July 1943.

25 'La Federazione di Ancona alla Direzione centrale del Partito: relazione politica',
n.d., but early December 1943 (*Le Brigate Garibaldi*, vol. I, pp. 147–8).

26 See 'La nostra guerra', *Avanti!*, Rome edition, 26 September 1943.

Nazi invader; national insurrection against the remains of Fascism ... national insurrection against the accomplices of Fascism.'[27]

Several Action Party–GL documents also ended up affirming the privileged coincidence between working class and nation: 'Every strata of the population can be activated ... never forgetting, obviously, that the working class is the avant-garde class, the politically national class par excellence.'[28]

In the pages that follow I shall try, within the scenario outlined above, to highlight some elements which, at various levels and in various situations, may be said to come under the category of 'class war', in the broadest sense of the term, appearing isolated one moment and at the next, interwoven in various ways with purely anti-Fascist or patriotic impulses and motivations. I shall avoid reopening the discussion, which was useful in its time in calling a halt to Resistance oleography but which had become a dead letter, as to whether the *Resistenza rossa* could have prevailed over the *Resistenza tricolore* if it had not been curbed by the Communist party's unitary policy.

In PCI policy and, partly, in that of the PSIUP – and this is the first point to which it is worth drawing attention – there were several themes which, in their repetitiveness as in their oscillations and contradictions, fostered what can well claim to be 'class' attitudes and expectations. This phenomenon has often been called *doppia anima* (dual soul), ambiguity – winking. What needs emphasising, rather, is that there was a 'dual soul' among the leadership and a 'dual soul' among the rank and file, and that the latter was partly induced by the former and came to coincide with it, and partly had a physiognomy of its own, which the leadership generally called incomprehension, tardiness, deviation. The efforts to which the leaders went to suppress these attitudes constitute one of the few sources available for approaching the attitudes themselves.

What needs considering above all, as I have already suggested, is the use of adjectives which in the Communist press (and not only there) more often than not accompanied the nouns *capitale* and *capitalisti*, when they were indicated as enemies: '"*grande" capitale*', '*capitalisti "collaborazionisti"*', and the like. In both cases, but above all in the second (in the first case the reference was more 'objective' and 'scientific', coming to coincide with the categories of monopolistic and financial capital), so much hostility was levelled at the adjective that it inevitably redounded on the noun. Above all the workers to whom the message was addressed could easily take that hostility as being directed at the noun. If anything, there was the question as to whether being 'grandi' necessarily coincided, in the case of the capitalists, with being collaborationists. Of the French Communists' attitude it has been written that '[T]rusts, even when they are

---

28 See 'Norme nell'attuale situazione politico-militare', probably produced by the Command of C Division, 25 December 1944 (*Formazioni GL*, p. 259).

appointed, appear to belong more of the category of traitors (or foreigners) to the Fatherland than to the class of exploiters and capitalists.'[29]

This reflection is equally applicable to the Italian Communists. But it can be added that several hendiadys used by the Communist press seem to suggest a coincidence between *grandi* and *collaborazionisti* which is the expression at once of theoretical expectation, didactic purpose and political desire. What is almost a telling lapse appears in these words from the top demanding clarity: '*Today we must regard the industrialists as accomplices of the Germans and Fascists*, because they are exploiting the situation created by the latter to make the workers' conditions worse and worse.'[30]

More pragmatically, but with equal optimism, an Action Party document, championing nationalisation or at any rate the placing of the monopolistic or almost monopolistic companies under public control, explained, 'These measures will be immensely facilitated by the fact that the Italian financial-industrial oligarchy has not only benefited greatly from Fascism, but has also collaborated with the German occupying authorities and with the neo-Fascists.'[31]

There were, in reality, many oscillations, linked not least to the way the situation was evolving. A comment in *L'Unità* on the November-December 1943 strikes attempted to provide an explanation, in terms that might be called traditional, of the social forces on which the RSI could not help leaning. 'Financial capital and reactionary groups that are lackeys of the Nazis and Fascists today constitute a bloc opposing the liberation of the country', and the author hastens to add: 'Unfortunately this bloc is being supported also by some high-ranking prelates of the Catholic Church, as witness the pastoral releases by the Fascist press, significant among which are those of the cardinals of Milan and Florence.'[32] 'Whatever the attitudes of the chameleons of big industry and high finance', *L'Unità* had written on 31 October 1943, 'in concrete terms Hitlerian Fascists and plutocrats are getting together to ring the neck of the working class.'[33]

In the days immediately following 8 September, by contrast, numerous distinctions had been made in defining the behaviour of the capitalists. The title of an article in *L'Unità* had contrasted the 'representatives of big capital who

29 M. Agulhon, 'Les communistes et la libération de la France' (paper to the 'Colloque international "La libération de la France"', 28–31 October 1974), cited in Quazza, *Resistenza e storia d'Italia*, p. 188.

30 Letter of 10 November 1943 from the 'Secretariat of the Communist Party' to the Turin organisation, which criticises the inadequate link that No. 8 of *Il Grido di Spartaco* drew between economic demands and the struggle against the Germans and fascists. The letter was written by Longo (Secchia, *Il PCI e la guerra di liberazione*, p. 177).

31 *Progetto di piano di lavoro del Partito d'azione*, INSMLI, *Carte Damiani* (envelope I, folder 7).

32 'La via giusta', *L'Unità*, Northern edition, 24 December 1943.

33 'Giù la maschera agli affamatori del popolo', *L'Unità*, Northern edition, 31 October 1943.

sided with the invader', with the 'vast majority of honest industrialists who with increasing determination are steering in the direction of the struggle against the Germans'.[34] A few months later, this opening of credit would be almost reproved by another newspaper, according to which there were capitalists and industrialists about who 'have already tired of their patriotic poses of the first few days', have taken to collaborating with the occupier and 'would rather the patriots didn't disturb them in their dealings with the enemy'.[35]

Particularly severe was a stand taken by *L'Unità*, still at the beginning of 1944:

> The great monopolist industrialists will increase their collaborationist zeal to support the German plans for prolonging the war which enables them, by starving out the working class, to secure for themselves the most handsome profits and to facilitate for the Nazis the availability of cannon and labour fodder: the recent strikes have completely exposed the anti-worker and anti-national spirit of these great industrialists.[36]

Togliatti himself, speaking at the Brancaccio theatre in Rome of 9 July 1944, starkly contrasted the armed workers with 'the groups of the plutocracy who have proved to be anti-national, ever ready to betray the country if it means serving their pockets'.[37]

Often, and particularly from the Communists, there were denunciations naming traitor capitalists, which inevitably acquired particular significance. The 29 September 1943 issue of *L'Unità*, mentioned already, denounced the henchmen of the Volpi, Pirelli, Donegani and Boccardo works, who did business with the Germans in the name of their masters, who sought to keep a low profile. The Fiat directors – towards whom, in actual fact, attitudes vary – were said to be 'openly backing Nazi-Fascist action' and Professor Vittorio Valletta was said to be 'one of these shady figures, for all his efforts to appear as a friend of the workers, a man sensitive to national interests'.[38] The Roman industrialists Peroni

---

34 *L'Unità*, Northern edition, 29 September 1943.

35 'Via dalle file del CLN I capitalisti – i traditori' ('Kick the capitalists-traitors out of the CLN') *Il Combattente*, 1 January 1944. Again, this combination of the two terms might have more than one interpretation: did it mean expelling all of the capitalists as well as all of the traitors, or only those capitalists who were also traitors? Or, perhaps, that capitalists could not but be traitors?

36 'Non c'è tempo da perdere', editorial of *L'Unità*, Northern edition, 10 January 1944.

37 Togliatti, *Opere*, vol. V, p. 76. See the article in *L'Unità*, Northern edition, 20 February 1944, 'I grandi capitalisti vendono le nostre macchine ai tedeschi'.

38 See 'Informazioni da Torino' by Alfredo, official responsible for the Piedmont insurrectionary triumvirate, of 13 December 1944, *Le Brigate Garibaldi*, vol. III, p. 67) and

and Manzolini come in for severe denunciations in the column entitled 'La voce dei lavoratori' ('The workers' voice').[39] On 29 December 1943 Alberto Damiani, representative of the CLNAI in Lugano, was sent an 'urgent note' to be broadcast by the BBC and Radio New York. 'The resistance of the industrialists, particularly the small and medium ones, has been notable, while other big industrialists have immediately placed themselves zealously at the service of the Germans'; there then follow the names of the 'most shameless and active', including Franco Marinotti of the Snia Viscosa plant and Senator Piero Puricelli.[40]

The denunciations, whether they were generic or explicitly named names, could be transformed into genuine warnings, again the more effective the more individualised they were. This too was a form of struggle that had been tried out in France, where appeals of this sort had been made 'Aux Patrons':

> A list is prepared for the bosses who, in collusion with Laval, lend themselves to the systematic exploitation of their factory workers. From this moment on their names are written down. These scaffolds prepared for Laval and his clique will be usable again for the bosses.[41]

'We shall remember it at the day of reckoning!' – this is how 'the Piedmontese organ of the National Liberation Front' concluded a *Monito agli industriali* (Warning to the Industrialists) – and particularly the major ones, 'with Fiat top of the list' – who were denounced for having assumed a demeanour which 'is a far cry from what one should have expected from them'.[42] 'In tomorrow's Italy there will be no place for anyone who has not given his all to the struggle. The *signori industriali* would do well to remember this' is how a severe article condemning the directors of San Giorgio of Sestri Ponente concludes.[43] The Communists managed to get a fairly sizable part of their viewpoints into the stances taken by the various CLNs. Thus the 'decree' of the Lombard CLN of November 1944 warned the industrialists against carrying out lockouts, since they represented 'an attempt to suffocate the liberation movement with starvation and deportations, striking at its most efficient and combative sectors'.[44]

'Scioperi e dimostrazioni di popolo in tutta l'Italia occupata', *L'Unità*, Northern edition, 10 December 1944.

39 *L'Unità*, Rome edition, 23 March 1944.

40 *Atti CLNAI*, p. 111.

41 *93. Organe des héritiers de la Révolution française*, July 1942, p. 3, which even invokes 'the ancient land of Gaul'. The first issue of the paper, published in St Étienne in May 1942, bore these words by Joseph Barthélemy as an epigraph: 'Liberty is still spelled in French letters.'

42 *La Riscossa italiana*, June 1944.

43 'Sestri Ponente – Dalla San Giorgio', *L'Unità*, Ligurian edition, 5 September 1944.

44 INSMLI, *CLNAI*, envelope 8, folder 2, subfolder 10.

Similar stances were taken by the Savona CLN, which ordered the industrialists to pay their employees three months' advance wages by 15 December, on pain of being denounced to the 'police commission or the Military Tribunal'.[45] Bitterly, and using populist tones, the Asti CLN addressed the industrialists who were obeying the RSI rather than the Committee itself: with the enormous profits they had accumulated the industrialists were buying farmhouses and precious objects ('we have a long list of these purchases') rather than using them for the benefit of their workers. Only a choice of this kind 'will help make the people view with less aversion your position which has until now been one of absolute privilege'.[46] The Piedmontese CLN defied Signor Primera, 'president of the Milan textile fibers industrial committee' and 'all the textile firms of the region of Piedmont' to commit those 'out-and-out war crimes' consisting of drawing up lists of materials to place at the disposal of the Fascists and Germans.[47]

As for the CLNAI, among the many documents on this count, which were not always issued without internal resistance, we need only recall the 'Appello agli industriali' urging them to refuse to collaborate with the Nazi-Fascists, to grant the workers' requests and pay them for the days of the strike (3 March 1944). This appeal should be read alongside the warning that had been formulated back in November 1943: 'Let the industrialists remember that their conduct is being carefully followed and will be examined closely and the right punishment will be dealt to those of them who reduce their workers to poverty'.[48] When the CLNAI created its economic commission it passed a motion maximalistically forbidding the commission itself and its individual members to have 'in any circumstances contacts even of a personal or informative character with individuals who were formerly political or economic representatives of the Fascist regime'.[49]

The *industriali* – a word that, in the CLN documents, generally appears in the place of *capitalisti* (*padroni* is totally absent) – thus appeared as a social group to keep a special eye on. This was an undoubted success not only for the Communists, but for the whole left wing of the anti-Fascist front. To the workers' ears all this could not fail to sound as an incentive or confirmation

---

45 Ibid.

46 The document is published, undated, as an appendix to Bravo, *La Repubblica partigiana dell'Alto Monferrato*, p. 234.

47 The text of the warning is in ISRT, *Archivio Medici Tornaquinci*, envelope 4, IV, 1, No. 7. The CLN recalled its own decree No. 11 of 4 February 1944.

48 *Atti CLNAI*, pp. 121, 107–8. On the PCI's insistent work to involve the CLNAI in the March 1944 strike by means of the aforementioned appeal, see Ganapini, *Lotte operaie: Milano*, p. 182 (and also the elaboration of this essay in *Una città, la guerra*).

49 INSMLI, *CLNAI*, envelope 5, file 2. On the economic commission, see the record of the 5 February 1945 CLNAI meeting in *Atti CLNAI*, pp. 243–7.

of their class sense. But the industrialists were also asked to do their patriotic duty; and, apart from the distinction between big and small industrialists, this invitation could become so broad and general as to call into question their very class assumptions, which were indeed screened and protected by the patriotic ones, but also watered down. The Communist leaders realised as much – above all the northern ones, who, whether from their specific education or from fear of losing contact precisely with the most class-conscious part of the working class, sought to remedy matters. Above all in the first months, when the party line was still being run in, there are numerous interventions along these lines. Criticising the editors of *La Fabbrica*, the newspaper of the Milanese federation, Pietro Secchia warned that 'the struggle against the Germans and the Fascists … must not allow us to forget the actual living conditions of the workers and the class struggle', and considered it 'somewhat exaggerated' to devote 'an entire page out of two to appeal to the industrialists cordially and imploringly to give benefits to the workers who are fighting etc. etc.'.

Even in the matter of saving the factories, which was to become part of Resistance hagiography, Secchia recommended caution: one couldn't 'give the impression that today the workers are fighting essentially to save the factories and the industrial patrimony'. And from this political warning, Secchia rose to a sentiment of genuine moral indignation, denouncing that fact that this

> is tantamount to saying that the workers are willing to give their blood, their lives to saving the factories and that the industrialists for their part at least will provide the dough, help their families etc. Don't you feel how undignified this language is, whatever the intention of the writer, and how much it smacks of the reformist and the mercenary?[50]

The Actionist Vittorio Foa obeyed the dictates of a similarly noble inspiration when he proposed that the Piedmont CLN reject the *obolus* (or pittance) of 50,000 lire periodically sent by Professor Valletta and instead impose a war tax of a considerably higher sum on Fiat.[51]

---

50 October 1943 letter, in Secchia, *Il PCI e la guerra di liberazione*, pp. 173–5. In a subsequent letter of 10 November, Secchia recognised the improvements made in No. 4 of *La Fabbrica*, but again criticised an appeal devoted more to inciting the 'patriotism of the industrialists' than the 'workers' spirit of struggle', and considering the title of the article 'Gli operai non temono la fama' ('The workers are not afraid of hunger') to be 'absolutely wretched'. (pp. 177–8).

51 The proposal fell, having been backed by the Communists alone (testimony of Vittorio Foa to the author, September 1986). According to the ISTAT index, 50,000 lire in 1944 corresponded to 3,850,000 as of 1990.

Addressing the industrialists, the Turin paper *Grido di Spartaco* (The Cry of Spartacus) had written: 'Those, at this decisive moment, who fail to offer this solidarity, can hope for no remission of their misdeeds and their sins, and will be excluded for ever from the national community and a severe blow will be dealt to their lives and possessions.' Which brought Luigi Longo's pungent comment: 'The language is rather more ecclesiastical than communistic; the punishment is projected rather more into the future and then it is by no means clear how and by whom they will be punished, etc.'[52]

Around about the same time the party direction was warning:

The mellifluous and submissive attitude taken by the party towards the industrialists and capitalists in general is not right ... Never forget that the present struggle in no way suppresses class conflicts and that we must always defend our actual interests as the exploited against the exploiters. We must not prostrate ourselves at the feet of the capitalists simply because some of them profess to be anti-Fascist (and who knows how sincere they are!) or aid the struggle against the Germans. This aid must not be considered an act of generosity but as a binding duty for all those who possess it.[53]

Parallel with these interventions were those aimed at giving back to the party a clear and predominant working-class physiognomy, after the all too open-handed admissions made in the Badoglian period: 'It would be a grave error to forget that the good proletarian composition of the governing organisms is a guarantee of the just political line.'[54] From Venice came the complaint that there were no workers in the federal committee; from Pistoia, that the presence of the workers 'in leading positions is almost non-existent' and that far too many street cells have been organised'.[55] The steering committee of the federation of Trieste reported, almost by way of confirmation, that it had obtained good results by passing from an organisation based exclusively on street cells

---

52 Letter to the Turin organisation, 10 November 1943, in Secchia, *Il PCI e la guerra di liberazione*, p. 176.

53 'Direttive per l'atteggiamento da prendersi nei confronti dei fascisti e dei capitalisti', 21 September 1943 (*Le Brigate Garibaldi*, vol. II, p. 109). Gibelli and Ilardi have a rather reductive interpretation of this document, insofar as they believe it speaks to the PCI's foreignness to the shop floor, as expressed in their *Lotte operaie: Genova*, pp. 120–1.

54 'Due svolte. La nostra organizzazione di fronte ai compiti nuovi', in *La nostra lotta*, 1 October 1943, p. 17. On the 'reproletarianisation' of the PCI in the period after 8 September, see Ganapini, *Lotte operaie: Milano*, pp. 154–5. On the social composition of the PCI during the Resistance, see Spriano, *Storia del Partito comunista italiano*, vol. 5, Chapter 4, 'I quadri decidono di tutto'.

55 'Rapporto del Federale di Venezia', signed 'Spino', 4 February 1945 (IG, *Archivio PCI*); Brunetti's report, 'La situazione politico-militare nella città di Pistoia e le sue province', 10 February 1944 (*Le Brigate Garibaldi*, vol. I, p. 260).

to a factory-based one.[56] 'Workers who think like workers always understand each other'[57] is the moral implicit in these organisational measures, which seem to dig up an old bone of contention between Amadeo Bordiga's *Bordighisti* and Antonio Gramsci's *Ordinovisti*.

The head office of *L'Unità* in Milan criticised the Rome edition for not giving 'the impression that it was a workers' paper', nor even the paper of that party 'which wants to be at the forefront of the war of National Liberation'.[58]

The Communist position oscillated throughout the lifespan of the Resistance. Pietro Secchia himself, at the 5–7 November 1944 conference of the insurrectional triumvirates, complained that it was a 'grave weakness' that the social basis of the party was 'still almost exclusively working-class'.[59] A provincial edition of *L'Unità*, printed in an area with a dense working-class population, wrote confidently: 'Take no notice of those who say you must give up the class struggle' and declared the congruence between 'proletarian unity' and the 'union of the people in the struggle for national liberation'.[60] At a party meeting, 'Albero' (Alberto Cavallotti), a neophyte intellectual sent from Milan to the 1st Lombardia Aliotta division in the Pavese Oltrepò, 'explains the reason for the suppression of the class struggle and its transmutation into an insurrectional struggle'.[61] The contradiction may go back to that between the demand for a monopoly (or near-monopoly) of working-class representation, in the traditional sense, and the use of the force thereby acquired within the policy of broad national unity.

In the last months above all, declarations were to abound aimed at turning to account the inclusion of honest capitalists in the patriotic front, it being, besides, those very capitalists, honest or dishonest, who would cross over, with increasing resolution, into the CLN camp.

---

56 Letter 'Cari compagni', n.d. but February 1944 (IG, *Archivio PCI*).

57 'Perché i comunisti lottano per l'unità della classe operaia', *L'Unità*, Northern edition, 8 October 1944 (in the section 'Domande e risposte').

58 According to a 26 November 1943 letter with which Secchia communicated (and expressed his agreement with) Longo's viewpoint; and another letter, also by Secchia, of 19 November (Longo, *I Centri dirigenti del PCI*, pp. 157, 130).

59 See his 'Rapporto d'organizzazione', *La nostra lotta* II, 19–20 (25 November 1944), pp. 21–2.

60 'Perché dobbianto essere marxisti?', *L'Unità*, Ligurian edition, 23 November 1944 (in the section 'Domande e risposte').

61 'Riunione del PCI tenuta ad assemblea', 1 April 1945 (*Le Brigate Garibaldi*, vol. III, p. 560).

2. WORKERS AND WORKERS' REPRESENTATION

The events that had led, during Badoglio's forty-five days of rule, to the birth of the internal commissions are well known.[1] The different attitudes to them that the Communist Party and the Action Party had adopted have also been pointed out – differences implying a different vision of the relationship between economics and politics. The Communists had stressed the general political value of the commissions in the 'struggle for the salvation of the country and for a better future for the workers'.[2] The Actionists, on the other hand, had stated the need to make the commissions the expression of a 'fundamental need' which linked back to the past but was capable of going beyond 'the fundamental organ of the democratisation of the factories ... in perfect parity with the *ceti padronali* [master classes]... for the control of the running and economic administration of the company with a view to workers' profit-sharing' – that is to say, all this capable too of 'transcending ... the economic aspect of the life of the company'.[3]

The Social Republic and the German occupying regime inherited the Badoglian commissions. The Germans showed an inclination to keep them alive, guaranteeing them for the Fascists as well, provided, needless to say, that the commissions collaborated in ensuring productive efficiency.[4] But initially there was some wavering among the anti-Fascist left as well. In Turin, at the very beginning, the Communist leader Remo Scappini had maintained that the internal commissions had 'to be supported and turned to account, taking special advantage of the anti-Fascist and anti-German position of many industrialists and in order to conduct a vast propaganda job'. But only a few days later Scappini's position, in line with party directives, had changed radically.[5]

---

1 See N. Gallerano, L. Ganapini, M. Legnani, eds, *L'Italia dei quarantacingue giorni*, Chapter 4, 'Gl: scioperi contro la guerra e la questione sindacale'; and 'L'accordo sulle commissioni interne (2 semptembre 1943)', in V. Foa, *Sindacati e lotte operaie*, Turin: Loescher, 1975, pp. 43–6.

2 'Salutiamo nelle Commissioni Interne una vittoria della iniziativa e della decisione degli operai italiani', *L'Unità*, Northern edition, 7 September 1943. See also the previous issues of 4 and 22 August.

3 'Volontà ed azione operaia', *L'Italia Libera*, 21 August 1943, see also the 5 August issue.

4 For the case of Genoa, see Gibelli, *Genova operaia*, p. 61. For the position taken against the Badoglian commissions by the Milan 'Fascio' squadrists, see Ganapini, *Lotte operaie: Milano*, p. 161.

5 The first quote is taken from C. Dellavalle, *Lotte operaie: Torino*, in *Operai e contadini*, p. 203. Dellavalle refers to the 'Considerazioni sulla situazione generale del Piemonte con particolare riferimento a Torino, 30 settembre 1943', held in IG, *Archivio PCI* and reproduced in Secchia, *Il PCI e la guerra di liberazione*, pp. 119–23 – though the version of the text published in Secchia's volume does not include the words cited by Dellavalle. The second quote is taken from 'Rapporto da Torino', 6 October 1943, also cited in Dellavalle, *Lotte operaie: Torino*, p. 203.

Thus another Communist report, this time from Bergamo, complained that, while the commissions were created 'with great difficulty' in the Badoglio period (at Dalmine solely through the work of the Action Party), 'after 8 September the comrades on the commissions did not resign; they thus got themselves into a blind alley: compromised in the eyes of the management, the Fascists, the Germans, and the workers. They were forced to choose: either leave the internal commissions or leave the Party.'[6]

Again, on 7 November 1944, a document signed 'Trade Union committee of the province of Varese' appeared in L'Unità, under the title 'Basta con le commissioni interni!' This document stated that the Fascists had not abolished Badoglio's commissions, mainly because they couldn't do so 'without openly antagonising the masses', and in the second place to obtain hostages in the persons of the best workers. But by now, the document concluded, the workers had understood that 'the internal commissions are a farce'.

When, moreover, it was the Fascists themselves who wanted to set up internal commissions, the anti-Fascist front, and not just the Communists,[7] spoke out against this measure, considering it, together with the socialisation decree that followed it, the last demagogic swindle of Fascism. It is a known fact that the Fascist commissions were essentially a failure.[8] Even where the commissions had been set up, as in the Biella area, 'they had been liquidated by the Fascists themselves' because, as even a Fascist paper wrote, 'they did not respect the factory environment' and had been elected by only a few voters, most of whom were 'not Fascists'.[9] The scant turnout at the elections and the remarks abusive of Fascism and extolling liberty and Communism that abounded on the few ballot papers that were completed, are proof of this failure. In the province of Como abstentions and blank ballot papers reached 100 percent.[10] Soon after this, news arrived from Lecco of the successful boycotting of the election, though there had been some cases of incomprehension and two expulsions had proved necessary.[11] In one Vicenza plant, out of little more than a thousand voters more than nine hundred ballot papers bore 'protests against the industriali affamatori (starver

6 'Rapporto sul lavoro di partito in Bergamo', 29 December 1943 (Le Brigate Garibaldi, I, pp. 191–2). Even harsher reproaches had been made in a previous report of 16 December (IG, Archivio PCI).

7 For instance, 'I rappresentanti socialisti e cattolici del comitato sindacale torinese' ('The Socialist and Catholic representatives of the Turin union-committee') called for non-participation in the internal-commission elections (the document, presumably from November 1943, can be found in IG, Archivio PCI).

8 See, among the many analyses drawing such a conclusion, Gibelli and Ilardi, Lotte operaie: Genova, pp. 137–43; and Ganapini, Lotte operaie: Milano, pp. 153–9.

9 Dellavalle, Operai, p. 22. The newspaper quoted is Il Lavoro biellese, 22 March 1944.

10 Nino's 'Relazione', regarding Como province, November 1943 (IG, Archivio PCI).

11 According to a 19 December 1943 report (IG, Archivio PCI).

industrialists) – against the Germans – long live Stalin – death to the Fascists, etc.'[12] At the Ducati works in Bologna there had been a 50 percent abstention and 25 percent blank ballot papers, while written on 'the majority of the rest' there had been: 'Cut it out, scoundrels, clear out *venduti* (i.e. you who've sold yourselves), enough with hunger, long live Stalin'; and the reprisals had at once begun: dismissals and dispatches to the evacuated factories in the provinces.[13]

After the March 1944 strikes, Ernesto Marchiandi, the labour commissar of the RSI, ordered that company bosses were no longer to negotiate with the workers' representative bodies, but only with the Fascist trade unions, which were ignored by the workers even more than the commissions were. Despite the opposition of Hans Leyers, the German general responsible for controlling Italian industry, Marchiandi does not seem to have revoked his order.[14]

Augusto Spinelli, the RSI Minister of Labour (the new ministry had been set up on 19 January 1945), admitted, in a letter to Mussolini, that the elections at Fiat had been a fiasco; only 30 to 40 percent of the clerical staff and 10 percent of the workers had voted; half the ballot papers had been left blank, while the other half contained votes and various things written on them.[15] Even if the figures reported by the minister exceed those recorded on the notes that Under-Secretary Medici Tornaquinci took during his mission to the North – 0.16 percent[16] – and to those given by *L'Unità* – only forty-six voters[17] – the fact remains that the blow dealt to the Fascists was unmistakable.

'The masses refuse to receive anything from us', wrote Anselmo Vaccari, head of the Fascist Federation of Employees with disconsolate realism, and added: 'The workers affirm that there will be no socialisation, or if there is, it will continue to reinforce the capitalist classes and to keep labour in a state of subjection … The workers … regard us, wrongly mind you, as the thugs of capital.'[18]

But the situation described above did not prevent some of the Fascist committees, poorly elected though they were, and moreover often with a larger white-collar than blue-collar representation, from managing to make their presence felt. This is not, as workers' historiography would ideologically have it, a

---

12 'Rapporto trimestrale agosto-ottobre 1943' (IG, *Archivio PCI*).

13 Cri., 'Cari compagni', late December 1943 (IG, *Archivio PCI*).

14 See Collotti, *L'amministrazione tedesca*, p. 202.

15 Letter of 1 March 1945, cited in Deakin, *Brutal Friendship*, p. 748.

16 According to the liberal under-secretary, the anomalous votes were given by 'Greta Garbo, and such like'. As for abstention, according to an explanation of workers' behaviour widespread in subsequent years, this was so high on account of the fact that 'two Communist workers stood very close to the ballot boxes in order to watch the voters' (ISRT, *Archivio Medici Tornaquinci*, envelope 4, IV, 2, No. 4, Socializzazione).

17 'La coscienza proletaria rigetta le truffe della "socializzazione" fascista', *L'Unità*, Northern edition, 9 April 1945.

18 Report of 20 June 1944 in Deakin, *Storia della Repubblica di Salò*, pp. 664–5.

case of the 'workers' using the Fascist trade union'.[19] Such a vision of things, whether democratic or Communist, while laying so much emphasis on the working class as to make it into a metaphysical entity which regally chooses what it finds most agreeable in the Fascist arsenal, actually offers an extremely reductive picture of that class, its complexity, its contradictions, and the difficulties it encountered, in that situation, in keeping the three figures of the adversary that it found before it united.

Above all, at least in several cases, there was the memory of the Communist Party's past enjoinders to avail oneself of the legal instruments of the Fascist regime. The Milan federal committee felt the need to warn: 'Today we are no longer in the period of the exploitation of Fascist legality, today we are in a period of extra-legal struggle, of open struggle, of armed struggle.'[20] And several times L'Unità reiterated: 'No internal commissions under an occupying regime.'[21]

A realistic low-down of the situation and of the difficulties in giving it an unambiguous definition may be found in a December 1943 report from Turin sent by 'Alfredo' (Arturo Colombi) to the PCI leadership:

So far we have not managed to prevent the committees from being elected. Even if it is true that in the elections previously promoted by the Fascist republicans 80 percent of the voters abstained and the other 10 percent scribbled insults, in the end a list of avant-garde individuals managed to get elected … The workers set great store by their delegations and don't understand the danger of them; on the other hand, when tens and tens of thousands of workers are in motion one can no longer direct them anonymously and we have therefore given orders to our comrades not to be too concerned about putting in individuals who see more or less eye to eye with us, but individuals who have energy and who carry out our directives, and know how to talk to workers, know how to spur them to resist and who will resist even when the struggle gets more violent.[22]

If Colombi's percentages are exact, it follows that the 10 percent of workers who cast valid votes comprised both the more or less convinced Fascists and those who voted for the 'elementi d'avangardia'.

There is a very pragmatic explanation of this tendency towards entrismo (that is, working from within) in another Communist report from Turin of the same period. According to this report not only socialist elements 'or those claiming to be such' accede to the Fascist manoeuvres, but also some comrades,

19 This being the title of a section of Dellavalle's essay 'Lotte Operaie: Torino', p. 15. A comparable concept can be found in G. De Luna, Lotte operaie e Resistenza, in 'Rivista di storia contemporanea', 1974, pp. 517–18

20 Letter to the Breda leadership committee, November 27, 1943 (IG, Archivio PCI).

21 The title of an article in the 12 February 1944, Rome edition.

22 Le Brigate Garibaldi, vol. I, p. 164.

'citing the pressure of the mass, who if it means obtaining provisions are not over-particular, want this participation in order to have individuals of proven honesty and energy in the said commissions'.[23] By contrast, a more doctrinaire and generalising line of argument was followed in another report, again from Turin:

> We still know that in the bourgeois regime the work of the internal commissions is constantly impeded by the dominant class, especially the Fascists; therefore in my view it would be opportune to boycott them. It is not with a small wage raise that the proletariat will solve the problem of the high cost of living; the vampires, the speculators, the blood-suckers are all ready to annul everything that the workers will have obtained. It is the system that we have to demolish.

The author of the report recalled that 'the Fascist unions were created to serve the bourgeoisie', and concluded by swinging back and forth between commissions *tout court* and Fascist commissions:

> We shall agree to be part of the commissions only when we have the opportunity to be of use to the proletariat, when we have expelled the German oppressor and Fascism, in the pay of the bourgeoisie, when we are able by means of our organisations to make a clean sweep of the present regime, then, yes; therefore the duty of true Communists at the present hour is one only, to get rid of this putrescence.[24]

Indeed, 'some illusions' about the Fascist commissions were reported from Emilia.[25] And a report about Varese denounced the federal committee for being badly orientated regarding the commissions;[26] from Brescia warning comes that 'it is extremely hard to persuade the internal commissions to desist from their activity', that some 'particularly compromised' comrades have had to be expelled and that, alongside the fear of reprisals, there is the hope that it is possible 'to do something advantageous for the workers even in the present circumstances'.[27] At the De Micheli works in Milan, only at the end of 1944, on the initiative of a group of women, did it prove possible to get the Fascist commission dissolved.[28] A Socialist justified his presence on a Lombard factory commission by saying that he intended to keep an eye on the commission itself; but the

---

23 IG, *Archivio PCI*.

24 'Rapporto sulla situazione delle fabbriche', section 'Le commissioni interne tedesco-repubblicane', 23 December 1943, signed 'Rosa' (IG, *Archivio PCI*).

25 'Rapporto al Centro del Partito', signed 'Banfi', 16 December 1943 (IG, *Archivio PCI*).

26 Anonymous report, late 1943 (IG, *Archivio PCI*).

27 Undated (December 1943?) anonymous report (IG, *Archivio PCI*).

28 'Informazioni da Milano', 15 December 1944 (IG, *Archivio PCI*).

mere fact of being part of it created difficulty for the PSIUP's entry into the local CLN.[29]

A significant case, worth dwelling on by virtue of the analytic documentation of it that survives, is Padua, where as late as the eve of the Liberation the workers could be seen to be having difficulty extricating themselves from the Fascist factory organisms. At a meeting of Communist leaders the representatives of the Rizzato workshops (120 workers, three Communists, eight sympathisers), faced with the management's initiative, following the intervention of the Fascist unions, of creating shop commissions, reported, 'we too think that the commission may be able to do something for the workers'. The Breda representative (250 workers, five Communists, thirty sympathisers) tells how, as it was originally composed, at the third attempt the commission had been elected by a hair's breadth:

> When it was set up there were five comrades, including the spokesman. We sabotaged this commission and, seeing that they prevented us from resigning, we started not to work by playing the overseers, which provoked the resentment of management. In March [1944] we went on strike like all the other workers ... Now they've set up a new commission, this time a truly Fascist one.

The representative of the Veneta works (300 workers, three Communists, thirteen sympathisers) related: 'When the Fascist commission was set up again I found myself in it, but the only time I showed up was the first time and that was to hand in my resignation. On that occasion the comrades who were already there approached me so as to get me tied up with the Party.'

The representative of SAER trolley-bus lines (250 workers, seven Communists, thirty-five sympathisers) tells how, at the end of 1944, 'for firewood (through the usual Fascist commission) something was obtained, but only to the advantage of single individuals'. The new commission that the management wanted to re-establish was to be sabotaged. At Stanga, where there were more Communists (600 workers, twenty-five Communists, 150 sympathisers), the situations appears to have been rather different. In late November 1944 the Fascists, by means of threats, urged people to vote. At the third attempt, one of the shop stewards reports, 'some of the workers voted not only for the individuals they trusted but for the known Fascists, with the intention of sabotaging them ... It is clear that on any question relating to the workers only the clandestine workers' or flying commission is consulted.'

Another shop steward from the same workshop, and the most authoritative

29 As referred to by a PCI report of 14 April 1945, concerning Arcioni (IG, *Archivio PCI*). On the Communists' reproaches against the Socialists for having collaborated with the internal commissions for banking staff in Sesto San Giovanni and Varese, see Salvati, *Il Psiup Alta Italia*, p. 87.

one to boot, who wound up the meeting, added that there were plans for a propaganda campaign to get the Fascist commission to resign, and warned: 'Anyone
who continues to be part of it will be regarded and judged as a traitor to the
working class', the significant thing here being the by no means isolated appearance of this specific figure: the betrayer.[30]

This reference to clandestine commissions brings us on to the workers'
organisms that sprang up in the factories in opposition to the Fascist ones. The
downward slide to the Fascist commissions – said one of the speakers at the
Padua meeting mentioned just now – was due to the scant understanding of
the duties of the agitation commissions. And from Verona it was pointed out
that the inadequacy of Communist organisation – 'the mass has proved to be
more advanced than our comrades believed' – had driven the workers to turn
to the Fascist commission, which 'has made promises'.[31] Since September 1943
L'Unità had announced the birth of the clandestine workers' commissions as
something that had already come about.[32] Shortly after, the *Bollettino di partito*
(Party Bulletin) had urged its readers to 'study on their work sites the possibility
of both illegal and semi-legal commissions functioning'.[33] And the 'Directives
for trade union work' issued by the PCI leadership the following November contained the appeal to form 'secret factory trade union commissions' in the place
of the Fascist commissions.[34] *L'Italia Libera* as well urged the 'new organisms of
workers created during the anti-Germanic resistance' to lose no time in choosing
responsible elected chiefs, and to recognise neither the Badoglian nor the Fascist
commissions.[35] Subsequently the agitation committees appeared, at differentiated times and in various cities, where they were active to varying degrees.[36]

---

30 Record of the 'Riunione dei rappresentanti di Partito' ('Meeting of Party representatives'), in a Padua workshop, 18 March 1945 (IG, *Archivio PCI*; reproduced in part in
Le Brigate Garibaldi, vol. III, pp. 490–4). For a severe denunciation of those who offered
themselves up for the game played by the 'union bureaucrats in the pay of the Germans',
see 'Commissioni interne e comitati segreti di fabbrica', *Il Lavoratore. Giornale di politica
proletaria*, 1 November 1943 (see above for details of the group in charge of this paper).

31 'Ispezione alla Federazione di Verona', 27 January 1945 (IG, *Archivio PCI*).

32 'La classe operaia riorganizza i suoi quadri per la lotta contro l'oppressore. Lo
scioglimento dell'unione dei sindacati e delle Commissioni interne. La costituzione di un
Comitato operaio clandestino', *L'Unità*, Northern edition, 29 September.

33 'Direttive di carattere generale riservate ai soli compagni', *Bollettino di partito*, 1
October 1943.

34 The 'Direttive' was a document of significant importance, and was reproduced
in R. Luraghi, *Il movimento operaio torinese durante la Resistenza*, Turin: Einaudi, 1958,
pp. 311–15. However, Luraghi attributes it to the Turin organisation of the PCI (see
Dellavalle, *Operai*, p. 90).

35 'Attualità dell'azione operaia', *L'Italia Libera*, Rome edition, 30 October 1943.

36 On Turin, see Luraghi, *Il movimento operaio torinese*, chapter 'Dallo sciopero
di marzo ai comitati d'agitazione'. As regards Venice, in a 4 February 1945 report signed

After the March 1944 strike, the utilisation of the committees, as organs autonomous from the parties, was seen as indicating the Communist Party's readiness
'to abandon itself trustingly to the spontaneous initiatives of the masses' ('but
one should be under no illusions', added the Action Party leader, Vittorio Foa).[37]

What role did the memory of the post–First World War councils play in
the workers' creation or taking up of the enjoinders to establish factory organisms? Immediately after the November 1943 strikes this report was issued from
Turin: 'I have said what I think about a certain superficiality on the part of some
comrades who think that they can already set up their own stable organisms
(internal commissions and even company unions) in the factories and that these
organisms can be directed by us.' This is impossible, says the Communist leader
who wrote the document, above all for reasons of clandestinity, and also because
these organisations would inevitably end up 'collaborating with the German
military authorities for the good order of war production'.[38] For the Communist
Party it would have made no sense to go back to the council phase; and then,
paradoxical as the prediction might appear of the councils inevitably slipping
into collaboration, it did pinpoint a real problem, to which we shall shortly need
to return.

The demand for councils had appeared in 1942 in a newspaper whose title
and subtitle were themselves very much a remembrance: 'L'Ardito del Popolo:
Organ of the Workers, Peasants and Soldiers'.[39] The 'Milanese Libertarian
Communist Federation' appealed to the provincial CLN, informing them that
they had participated 'with other revolutionary movements in the creation of
a movement for the establishment of factory councils, taking up the Turinese
idea of the last post-war period', and that they had consequently formed the
'council brigades', which asked to be able to operate 'in agreement with those of
the CLN'. The *bordighisti* of the international Communist Party also vindicated
the councils as an organ of revolution; and in December 1944 their newspaper,
Rivoluzione, reported the establishment of a league of revolutionary councils.[40]

'Spino', we read that there were committees 'in a number of factories, but they have not
carried out any activity for some time' ('Rapporto del Federale', IG, *Archivio PCI*).

37 Inverni (V. Foa), *I partiti*, p. 50.

38 'Rapporto sulla lotta nelle fabbriche torinesi', signed 'Giovanni', n.d. (IG, *Archivio
PCI*).

39 The paper had no issue number, but was dated 4 May 1942. It featured expressions of both the old Socialism – 'divided we are a rabble, together we are powerful' – and
the old Bolshevism: indeed, Bolshevism had substituted 'the heroic conception of life' for
the 'utilitarian' one and 'true, practical idealism' for 'philosophical materialism'.

40 Undated letter. The reply approved the idea of collaborating in accordance 'with
the orders of the CLN' (INSMLI, *CLNAI*, envelope 6, folder 2, subfolder 4). In December
1944 appeared the first issue of *Comunista libertario. Giornale della Federazione comunista libertaria italiana*, which claimed the adherence of those disappointed with the
'supposedly revolutionary parties'. As regards the Bordigists, see 'Sui consigli operai',

The marginality of these groups and the minority position of the Socialists headed by Lelio Basso, who were also in favour of the councils, bear out the view recently expressed by one of the most sensitive among the leading figures most actively involved in those events to the question of the councils. Vittorio Foa has in fact ruled out the idea that the Resistance in fact saw the re-emergence of 'the revolutionary line of the factory councils', which were, in his view, irreparably defeated in the years immediately following the First World War. The councils of the Resistance period were – and not just in Italy – 'instruments of class collaboration and of the democratisation of the social system'.[41] Balder still is the view expressed by another Action Party leader, Leo Valiani, according to whom only 'in historiography or political journalism could the libertarian character of the post–First World War workers' councils be re-exhumed (I myself did so, in articles and pamphlets published in exile and then in the Resistance), but there was no way of reviving them then'.[42]

The autonomistic council–spirit animating one wing of the Action Party centred not so much on the councils as on the CLNs, attributing to these inter-party organs the role of bearers of democratic petitions that would indeed transcend party forms of political action. Foa wrote at the time, in one of his pamphlets, that 'coherently' the Action Party 'had become an advocate of the factory councils ... The autonomy of the factory councils and the broadening of the working-class basis of the revolution are two aspects of the same reality.'[43]

It is in one of Franco Momigliano's writings that we find what is probably the concentrated essence of Action Party philosophy regarding the councils. Co-existing in those pages are political vision and a technical-productionist vision, the opposition between the *sindacato* (union), which represents legality, and the *consiglio* (council), which represents democratic and non-class-based revolution, a desire for conciliation between state planning and company autonomy, criticism of the councils of 1919–20 for having been based only on Turinese experience, and appeals as a precedent to the German and Austrian laws of 1919

Prometeo, April 1945. See also the articles 'L'unità nei consigli' and 'Idee sui consigli. Classe e partito' in *Rivoluzione*, No. 2 (February 1945).

41 Foa, *La Gerusalemme rimandata*, p. 269. For Basso's position, see *Bandiera Rossa. Organo del Partito proletario rivoluzionario*, whose 9 June 1944 final issue published a set of 'Theses'; see also Salvati, *Il Psiup Alta Italia*, p. 65.

42 Valiani, *Il partito d'azione*, p. 135. Among the pamphlets he wrote during the Resistance, as described in the text, see *Antonio Gramsci. Le origini del movimento rivoluzionario e antifascista del proletariato italiano* (signed 'Federico', one of the 'Quaderni dell'Italia Libera' published by the Milan Province Federation of the Action Party). For a more general view, see, De Luna, *Storia del Partito d'Azione*, Chapter 4, 'La questione operaia: le tesi consiliari fra liberalismo e pianificazione'.

43 Inverni (V. Foa), *I partiti*, pp. 62, 71.

(the latter being models which must have meant precious little to the Italian working-class consciousness).[44]

Prominent space was given to the 'company council' in the Action Party's 'Progetto di piano di lavoro' ('Project for a Labour Plan');[45] while *L'Italia Libera*, in demanding the 'military expropriation of the great Fascist and collaborationist capitalists', also demanded that the companies be entrusted to councils composed of both blue- and white-collar workers.[46] The Tuscan CLN, at the proposal of the Action Party, decided that the companies that were to be sequestered be administered by councils 'consisting of workers' and office employees' delegates … representing the various political currents existing therein'.[47]

The institutionalised presence in the council of the various political currents referred to in this document already takes us some way away from the *consiglio* in the strict sense of the word to company CLNs and their relations with the workers' councils or commissions. Again, on the eve of the insurrection, at a meeting with the factory CLNs, a Lombard Communist representative complained that not all his comrades were capable of distinguishing between party work, CLN work, and the work of the agitation committee.[48] Mirrored in this difficulty is, on the one hand, the tricky business of keeping together the various motivations and objectives of the struggle, and on the other hand the fact that it was mainly left-wingers, and generally Communists, who were present in the various types of organisms. Thus at the Breda works in Padua – to name but one of many cases – both the agitation committee and the CLN consisted only of 'comrades and sympathisers'.[49]

Luigi Longo, in an article published in *Nostra lotta* (Our Struggle), clearly distinguished between agitation committees (organs of class unity in the factory) and company CLNs (organs of national unity).[50] Longo had evidently felt it

---

44 See Uberti (F. Momigliano), 'Le commissioni di fabbrica. Lineamenti politici', *Quaderni del Partito d'Azione*, December 1943, No. 6).

45 INSMLI, *Carte Damiani*, envelope 1, folder 7.

46 Piedmont edition, June 1944 (declaration following the formation of the first Bonomi government).

47 Record of the 4 July 1944 meeting (ISRT, *Carte Francesco Berti*, envelope 1, folder 1).

48 See 'Informazioni da Milano', April 14, 1945 (*Le Brigate Garibaldi*, vol. III, p. 620).

49 Record of the 'Riunione dei rappresentanti di Partito' ('Meeting of Party representatives'), in a Padua workshop, 18 March 1945 (IG, *Archivio PCI*; reproduced in part in *Le Brigate Garibaldi*, III, pp. 490–4).

50 'Comitati di agitazione e Comitati di liberazione nazionale d'officina', *La nostra lotta*, vol. II, 12 July 1944, pp. 10–13 (later reproduced under the title 'Gli organi di combattimento degli operai nelle fabbriche', in Longo, *Sulla via dell'insurrezione nazionale*, pp. 196–203). The same ideas were developed in the article 'Comitati di agitazione e CLN di fabbrica', *L'Unità*, Northern edition, 10 July 1944. At the bottom of the *La nostra lotta*

necessary to give an authoritative interpretation to that passage in the note sent out to the regional and provincial CLNs by the CLNAI on 2 June (when the final showdown was reckoned to be imminent) – which, while making explicit mention, at the request of the Communists themselves, of the 'factory commissions of the workers, office staff and technicians', tended however to place them under the aegis of the system of the CLNs, one possible embodiment of which was indicated in 'both factory and village' commissions.[51] The 'fear that the working class would be diminished by the existence of the liberation and works commissions', which had been clearly manifested, was deemed by Longo to be a sign of 'distrust in the working class' and in its capacity to fulfil its national function – a distrust which 'remains such even when it is cloaked in extremist and classist expressions to which an opportunist practice corresponds'. Longo probably had it in for positions like those expressed by Lelio Basso, according to which the distinction between the two types of commissions was being annulled in favour of the agitation committees, defined as 'classist organs that guide the masses not only in the war of liberation but also in the struggle against capitalism'.[52]

The fact of the matter was that things were rather more complicated, both from Longo's point of view or from Basso's. In the Genoese factories a far from linear relationship was created between the agitation committees and the company CLNs – as well as between the latter, which somehow had been vitalised by the situation in the factory, and the regional CLN. A Genoese Communist Party document of December 1944, in agreement with the Socialists, undertook to show the other parties of the regional CLN – and especially the Liberals, who had declared themselves to be a non-class party – that the committee 'cannot and must not defend the interests of all, that is to say, put the workers on the same plane as the capitalists'.[53]

If the CLNs had followed this line to the letter, they would have been legitimised to issue orders even in the matter of strikes. But on this point it was precisely the PCI that proved recalcitrant. In the Tuscan CLN, all the other parties accused the Communists of having encroached upon a province of the committee itself by issuing a strike order for the streetcar service. The Communist representative did not hit back by claiming that exclusive competence lay with his party and the workers' organisms, but endeavoured to lead the strike back

---

article, the editors announced that there would be a wider take on the subject in the next edition, but this did not in fact appear in any of the following issues.

51 See *Atti CLNAI*, pp. 129–30.

52 Undated circular 'Ai segretari provinciali della Lombardia', in Salvati, *Il Psiup Alta Italia*, p. 68. Salvati notes, however, that the PSIUP was not present at the agitation committees' conference of 21 January 1944 (p. 80).

53 See Gibelli, *Genova operaia*, pp. 167–74, 237–48 (the document cited here is on p. 242).

onto the general direction adopted by the committee. A laborious compromise was reached, which included the principle that the suspension of public services lay within the competence of the CLN.[54]

In Gallarate, but only on the eve of the Liberation, the PCI was also taken to task by the CLN, and the Communist representative made the following declaration: 'Our party will do everything to ensure that strikes occur wherever possible and at any moment, so that all the movements are involved in the liberation movement and are therefore useful for it, for which I assume full responsibility. In the event of a general movement arranged by the CLNAI, it would be disciplined.'[55]

It was a knotty question. The answer given to the Varese provincial CLN on 23 July 1945 by the CLN for Lombardy retrospectively indicates as much: 'As regards an employer's representative being admitted into the provincial CLNs, this is excluded by the very principles of this organism, which is an expression of the force of the resistance.'[56]

3. POLITICAL STRUGGLES AND ECONOMIC STRUGGLES

If from the great political options and ideological options we proceed to take a closer look at their presence in the factory, or at any rate among the workers, we run up against further difficulties and problems. I have already pointed out how the highest aspirations – driving out the Germans and Fascists – could rub uneasy shoulders with immediate demands – a rise in wages. It would certainly be reductive to see this dichotomy in terms of the classic one between economic and trade union struggle on the one hand and political struggle on the other. The urgent need to do something about particularly harsh working and living conditions and the grandiosity of the political objectives, which could furthermore be pursued only by military means, on the one hand made the struggle cruder, and on the other hand swathed it in the conviction, or rather, the intuition that only the re-establishment of a minimum of democratic conditions for everyone (employers included) would guarantee the full exercise of the workers' very identity, from the smaller to the larger demands. This is why it is reductive to see the workers' struggles during the Resistance merely in 'national' or 'labour' terms, both of which are, for opposite reasons, hagiographic.

One of the foremost leaders of the PCI, Pietro Secchia, wrote in a letter from Milan to his Roman comrades: 'Even if the working class is facing far more important tasks, nevertheless day after day the workers have to face and struggle

---

54 Records of the CTLN meetings of 27–28 July 1944 (ISRT, *Carte Francesco Berti*, envelope 1, folder 1).

55 'Informazioni da Milano', 18 April 1945 (*Le Brigate Garibaldi*, vol. III, p. 650).

56 The letter, signed 'G. Morpurgo Tagliabue', is in the AS Varese, *CLN*, envelope 10.

with these problems of daily life … We have to make sure that we link the immediate demands of the working class to the more general and political ones of the
struggle against the Germans and Fascists.'[1]

At the middle-ranking level, the Genoese Communist leaders warned that 'it
would be a gross error to set the struggle for essential, immediate, vital demands
against the insurrectional struggle' and denounced the 'rash and superficial
extremism' of those who proclaimed: 'Enough with economic agitations; there's
nothing more we can do on the economic score, we must strike once and for all:
either the strike of insurrection or nothing!'[2]

More passionately a leaflet urged:

Workers of Romagna! In putting forward your demands you cannot help protesting about all the sorrows of our country … The workers and their families are cold,
hungry, they have no wood, they have no shoes, they have the lowest possible wages,
their *padroni* are in cahoots with the enemies of the country, looming over them are
the dangers of bombings, pillaging, deportation to *Germany*. Must they keep quiet?
… Must they continue to tolerate the bloodthirsty prostitution of the *padroni* and of
the Fascist scum?[3]

An attempt was made to get around the problem of the relationship between
the general situation and immediate demands by stressing the political character that those demands easily acquired. Thus the PCI leadership asked the
Turin federal committee to see whether there were 'other demands which were
partially political in character' that 'can be united with the economic ones', the
examples given being the watchword: 'Don't negotiate with the Germans and
refuse the Fascist intermediaries' and the demand for the abolition of the curfew
and the removal of the Germans from the factories and the city.[4]

The coupling of economic claims and political demands – at times argued
in depth, at times stated more schematically – was in the tradition of left-wing
anti-Fascism. Shortly before the turning-point marked by the Resistance, in the
Communist newspaper *L'Azione*, the first number of which appeared in the
Biella area on 1 November 1942, said 'the watchwords of the struggle against
Fascism find … their just mediation in grasping a situation that the working
class was living every day in the factory'.[5] A manifesto preceding 25 July, signed
by 'a group of young men', began by denouncing the repudiation 'of all the dead

---

1 Letter of 26 November 1943, in Longo, *I Centri dirigenti del PCI*, pp. 156–7.

2 Circular on 'The struggle against cold, hunger and Nazi-Fascist terror', 30
November 1944, cited in Gibelli, *Genova operaia*, p. 261.

3 The leaflet, n.d., signed 'Comitato d'azione romagnolo', was published twice
over in Casali, *Il movimento di liberazione a Ravenna*, vol. I, pp. 16, 57; in the second case
it is erroneously ascribed to the March 1943 strikes.

4 Letter of 13 November 1943 (IG, *Archivio PCI*).

5 Dellavalle, *Operai*, p. 42.

and disabled of the 1914–18 war', went on to exalt the Russians, 'intensely loyal to their country and their government', and concluded by demanding the 'abolition of ration cards (an antechamber to indemnity)'.[6] But whereas before 8 September the most current watchword was peace, from that day on it became armed struggle. Those who continued to demand 'bread, peace and liberty' received this answer: 'Bread and liberty, fine. But why peace? You should be saying: we want the war of liberation'.[7]

This line was not taken only by the Communists. *Avanti!* also followed it, though at times giving the impression of bringing it back under the old dualist umbrella of a maximum programme and a minimum programme. Announcing the revival of the glorious 'Tribuna dei ferrovieri' ('Railroad workers' tribune'), the paper charted the programme of the re-established National Group of Socialist railroad workers, the first point being the struggle for national liberation; then, listed among the 'class vindications' are: 'regularisation of the position of casual labourers, revision of wage scales, adoption of the eight-hour working day, etc.'.[8]

The Catholic paper *Conquiste sindacali*, printed in Rome, devoted a great deal of space to 'interessi di categoria', but made no specific reference to the political and military struggle that was taking place.[9] In the stances taken by the Action Party over the economic struggles, which it sometimes prided itself on having triggered, the connection with the greater struggle in progress is there;[10] and on one occasion Gian Carlo Pajetta was compelled to acknowledge that, in commenting on the strikes, the Action Party paper had been quicker off the mark than *Il Grido di Spartaco*.[11] If anything, it might be said that alongside its great historic affirmations – for example that the first thing Fascism did was to cut wages[12] – the Action Party press, even on labour issues, displayed

---

6 'Basta con la guerra, vogliamo la pace', cited in Flamigni and Marzocchi, *Resistenza in Romagna*, pp. 269–70.

7 'Direttive per l'agitazione economica in corso', Milan, 13 December 1943, with criticisms of a leaflet put out in Turin (IG, *Archivio PCI*).

8 *Avanti!*, Rome edition, 30 December 1943.

9 See the first issue, 9 April 1944, with the subtitle 'Christian voice of Italian labour' and the claim that the paper 'is associated with the tradition of *Il Domani Sociale*, organ of the Confederazione italiana dei lavoratori'.

10 See, for example, the letter from 'Nada' (Franco Venturi) of 22 December 1944, 'Carissimi', concerning the strike 'over economic issues' sparked in Galbiate and 'across the whole vast sphere of small and medium-sized businesses, where wages are particularly low and where we have sunk strong roots' (INSMLI, *CLNAI*, envelope 8, folder 12, sub folder 4).

11 'Note sugli scioperi di Torino', *Il Grido di Spartaco*, 6 December 1943, written by 'Luca' (Giancarlo Pajetta) (IG, *Archivio PCI*).

12 'Lotta di massa contro la riduzione dei salari', *L'Italia Libera*, Northern edition, 8 January 1945.

the greater capacity for analytic planning that characterised that party. Thus the pamphlet entitled 'Occupation of the factories and direct running of the companies' raises the question of how to ensure the smooth running of the occupied factories in a phase of transition 'from capitalistic management to direct workers' management'. It recalls that 'too often in capitalist-run industries the wages system is fixed to ensure the minimum administrative difficulty', and declares the need for 'new systems of retribution and planning, which must necessarily be more elastic and more in tune with the performance of each individual factory'.[13]

Making demands relating to labour relations and factory life in general implied the need to identify an interlocutor. Here the facts themselves revived the problem of the convergence, or separation, between *padrone*, Fascist and German. The latter two figures were explicit enemies; and we have seen how contacts and negotiations with them, on the political and military plane, were considered as amounting to treason. The *padrone*, by contrast, was an ambiguous figure. It is not surprising therefore that, generally speaking, the Communist directives dug their heels in, indicating the employer as the interlocutor in the factory. An intervention by the Milan federal committee is particularly clear on this point: it recommends against refusing contacts with the industrialists 'for fear of being contaminated and compromised', because by so refusing 'we do not show strength; on the contrary, we show that we are weak, that we are afraid, in other words, that we are not sure of ourselves'.[14] A year earlier, at the time of the strikes, *L'Unità* had made its position clear: 'We must exclude in the most determined way every Fascist (and even more so German) representative; we must negotiate directly with the *padrone*.'[15]

Several of the objectives of the struggle declared by the same issue of the Communist paper were such however that even the best-intentioned employers could not have fulfilled them alone: for example the 'doubling of basic foodstuffs', the 'distribution of clothing and fuel', 'housing for the casualties and adequate means of transport at reduced prices', but above all the 'liberation of workers who had been arrested for having defended the interests of the working class' and, still more, the 'return to the normality of civilian life, with the lifting of the curfew and the withdrawal of the Germans from the plants'. Indeed, that same issue of *L'Unità* indicated the Fascists, the Germans, and the 'great profiteer industrialists in their service' as the adversaries against whom the strike was directed.

Two days later *L'Unità* was denouncing 'the underhand maneuvers of the industrialists', who first pretend to give way on certain points, then say 'We can't

---

13 *Voci d'Officina*, supplement No. 2.

14 Letter 'Cari compagni', 19 September 1944 (IZDG, envelope 272b, folder V/1).

15 'Avanti fino alla vittoria!', editorial of *L'Unità*, Northern edition, 16 December 1943.

do anything about it. Go to the Germans'.[16] The Breda workers, stated a report written at the time, had refused to take up an enjoinder of this sort.[17]

During those very days a 'Letter from the Directorate to the Organization of Turin' was sent to explain why the Germans were not to be negotiated with:

It is not only a question of principle. It is evident that if we were fighting for demands that depend on the Germans, it will be difficult, if the struggle has to be concluded, not to negotiate with the Germans. But, in this particular case – the letter hastens to explain – the Germans don't come into it. It is a question of a labour contract involving only the workers and the employers: the intervention of the Germans can only have an intimidating character and for this reason we must reject it. For the same reason we must reject any intervention by the Fascists: neither one or other of them have anything to do with workers' affairs; if they intervene, they intervene only to give a strong hand to the employers, which is why we want to deal directly with the employers, as equals.[18]

This letter readopted and, one might say, gave order to the arguments used on 13 December to criticise the Turin Communists for their contradictory behaviour during the strike: in a first leaflet they had not indicated the Germans as enemies of the country; in a second leaflet they had, but had then gone to negotiate with them.[19] A note about this from Turin had in fact presented the situation with remarkable realism:

It is not that members of the illegal internal commissions negotiating with them [the Germans] are inspired to collaborate, but it is the constant pressure from the mass that wants its action to achieve concrete results at all costs. This was how some 'comrades' negotiated with the enemies of the proletariat, not for want of political conscience, but dragged into doing so by the desire not to come short of the trust that the mass placed in them … We must recognise that the action, in terms of every union relationship, was in itself dignified, since while it negotiated economic questions with the real *padroni* of the country, it refused to have any contact with the Fascists.[20]

Many tales have been told of the German interventions in the factories, various in number and diverse in outcome, especially when, in the major cities

16 *L'Unità*, 'second extraordinary' Northern edition, 18 December 1943.
17 'Rapporto sugli scioperi', Milan, 13 December 1943 (IG, *Archivio PCI*).
18 Letter of 16 December 1943 (*Le Brigate Garibaldi*, vol. I, p. 168).
19 IG, *Archivio PCI*. See also 'Note informative sull'agitazione degli operai torinesi', 27 November 1943, signed 'Alfio' (IG, *Archivio PCI*) and, on these, *Le Brigate Garibaldi*, vol. I, p. 168, n. 1. Collotti notes the nuances of Milanese workers' attitude towards the Germans in his *L'amministrazione tedesca*, p. 195.
20 'Dalle fabbriche', n.d., signed 'L'attesista' (IG, *Archivio PCI*).

like Milan and Turin, they were guided by the able General Zimmerman. Here we can recall the case of a small city, Piacenza, where in the Arsenale plant 1,900 workers out of 2,500 had participated in electing the Fascist internal commission, but many had written on their ballot papers: 'Long live freedom, long live Italy, long live the Soviet Army, long live Stalin, long live communism'. On 2 December 1943, during the strike that some members of the commission had tried to sabotage, the Germans arrived 'who having learned from the workers that the stoppage was not due to anti-German sentiments, but to the very low wages, promised that they would immediately see to getting their wages increased! And, absurdly, the applause of a group of women workers crowned the Nazi promise. What this lot are interested in is war production.'

The writer of the report, however, did not reproach the workers but the party comrades who were 'obtuse and sectarian' and 'claim that the workers are pig-headed, people who think only of their sordid interests, indifferent to our struggle – hence this step and these heresies'.[21]

The web of situations and desires outlined so far is particularly evident in the strikes, which were extensive, frequent and incisive in the Italian Resistance. Under the occupying regime and an internal regime which in its history and most profound aspiration prohibited strikes, (a legislative decree of 21 June 1944 introduced the death penalty for organisers of strikes and lock-outs), the strikes exalted their very character as affirmations of collective identity, instruments of liberation, discovery (or rediscovery) of direct action – all elements whose moral value, as we have already suggested, is in no way at odds with their being instruments for satisfying immediate needs which even in those conditions the strike could assume. This does not mean that we should not seek the differences and conflicts manifested in the declared aims given to the strikes and among the strikers themselves, beyond declarations of principle like: 'the struggle for the defence of the daily bread of the workers is an aspect of the struggle to drive the invader off Italian soil, for the total destruction of every form of Nazism and Fascism'.[22]

The impossibility of there being the joyful and festive aspect found in strikes that occur in quite different circumstances made the Resistance strike experience a particularly harsh one, accentuating the dramatic nature of the options

---

21 'Rapporto sull'Arsenale di Piacenza', attached to the 'Rapporto al Centro del Partito' by 'Banfi', northern Emilia, 16 December 1943 (IG, *Archivio PCI*). This latter report (republished, without the attached piece, in Secchia, *Il PCI e la guerra di liberazione*, pp. 230–3), gives a very negative take on the Party's situation in Piacenza.

22 'The hopeless manoeuvres of the traitor Mussolini. The meaning of the increase in wages and taxes', *L'Unità*, Rome edition, 1 December 1943. In reality, as is clear from this article itself, it was not an increase in taxation but rather of the minimum level from which private property was taxable.

and consequences involved, including the roundup of laborers and deportations to Germany.[23]

The interweavings, overlappings, differences in emphasis over workers' rights or the political objectives, and the latter's downward slide towards insurrectional, military action traverse the whole Resistance period and, by and large, but not mechanically, follow the evolution of the general politico-military situation. The immediate demands were not just wage-demands, though obviously these figured prominently; they tended to spill over from factory life to life as such, thereby accentuating, by this route as well, the existential and political significance of the agitation. An increase in foodstuffs, the distribution of winter clothing, shoes, and coal, the heating of the units with window-panes shattered by the bombings, the setting up of canteens, an increase in the gas and electricity supply, figure among the requests of this nature.

A powerful egalitarian impulse is often present. For example: a minimum guaranteed wage; specific pay claims for women, young people, and labourers; equal advances on wages for everybody, labourers, women and young people included; still further improvement in conditions for the sick, the laid-off and 'those unable to work for reasons beyond their control';[24] 'granting the same treatment as that given to workers in the protected industries';[25] the extension of war indemnity to all workers; the setting up of canteens in every plant, etc.[26]

Other demands are expressly political, such as a guarantee against the continuous persecutions, arrests and deportations,[27] the liberation of hostages and

23 See Deakin, *Brutal Friendship*, pp. 675; Legnani, *Potere, società ed economia*, pp. 16–17. Among the people deported from Piedmont to Germany, some 36 percent of survivors were workers and engineers, 15 percent peasants, 10 percent artisans and apprentices, and 9 percent small shop owners and traders – see Bravo and Jalla, eds, *La vita offesa*, p. 55. See also p. 120, where one survivor says that the working-class presence was more like 90 percent.

24 'Gli operai militanti in lotta per gli anticipi', *L'Unità*, Northern edition, 7 September 1944.

25 'Le nostre rivendicazioni', *L'Edilizia*, Turin, 22 December 1944. Dellavalle ('Lotte operaie. Torino', pp. 238–41) notes that the Germans often turned a blind eye to the presence in the protected industries of workers from the age-groups that had been called to arms, whom management claimed to be indispensable.

26 See, on this, Dellavalle's 'Lotte operaie: Torino', p. 224; Ganapini, 'Lotte operaie: Milano', p. 173; De Luna, *Lotte operaie e Resistenza, passim*. The 'Adorno contract' decreed on 29 March 1945 provided for almost full wage-equality between men and women: clearly an attempt to make use of Resistance conditions to make a mark on the situation after Liberation (Dellavalle, *Operai*, pp. 268–71).

27 As we often read in *L'Unità*. Four hundred people were deported from Turin after the March 1944 strikes, according to Fascist sources; 132 of them came from Fiat alone, according to the research of Ernesto Bolognesi (himself a deported worker): see ANED, *Gli scioperi del marzo 1944*, pp. 38, 65–8. According to another estimate, after the March 1944 strikes, the proportion of workers, anti-Fascists and partisans in Piedmont

prisoners, an end to the reprisals. But the fundamental political nature lay in the very fact of striking. The passage from one plane to another is clearly traced in a document of the Trieste Communists, which urges the organisation of economic/wage strikes, and adds:

> In this case economic action will be transformed into political action, since we'll find ourselves up against the Germans and Fascists, who will oppose it. We therefore need to see how the internal struggle in the factory can be made to develop into a street struggle. It is through this development of the struggle that the premises will be created for the political development (political strikes) and thence insurrectional development (insurrectional strikes).[28]

In this document, which belongs to the initial phase of the Resistance and to a zone that was feeling the pressure of the dynamism of the Yugoslavian partisan movement, the passages from one phase to the other are anticipated as being rapid and almost contemporaneous. But in the same period, while the Rome edition of L'Unità was hailing the strike that had occurred in Turin, the Roman leaders were asking their Milanese counterparts whether, in an occupying regime, the watchword 'political and insurrectional strike' was 'possible and realisable';[29] and as in subsequent appeals for a strike in the capital, this one would be called 'peaceful', 'protest', and 'demonstrative'.[30] In March 1945 experience would teach that, without renouncing the final outcome, 'a general strike, like for that matter an insurrection, does not materialise overnight, pre-prepared and ready', and that therefore 'it would be ... a grave error for the individual factories of our province to defer the claims relating to everyday problems in order to present them all in one block at the moment of the general strike'.[31]

Again at the end of March 1945, a meeting held by the Garibaldini at the Triplex plant in Milan was criticised for having urged the workers 'not to resume work as long as there are Germans in Milan'; and in mid-April in the two Lombard cities of Busto Arsizio and Gallarate, workers who had come out on a strike that they considered 'the final blow', 'do not want to work again until

---

who were arrested amounted to over 60 percent: see Bravo and Jalla, La vita offesa, p. 55.

28 Letter from the 'Comitato della Federazione comunista di Trieste' to the Commander of the Trieste Battalion (which was, among other things, invited to adopt the name 'Garibaldi Trieste'), late December 1943 (Le Brigate Garibaldi, vol. I, p. 180).

29 See 'Lo sciopero in regime di occupazione', L'Unità, Rome edition, 15 December 1943, and the letter from Rome to Milan of 13 December (in Longo, I Centri dirigenti del PCI, p. 258).

30 L'Unità, Rome edition, 13 and 20 April 1944.

31 Record of the 'Riunione dei rappresentanti di Partito' ('Meeting of Party representatives), in a Padua workshop, 18 March 1945 (IG, Archivio PCI; reproduced in part in Le Brigate Garibaldi, vol. III, pp. 490–4).

the liberation', and branded the Communists leaders who were urging them to return to work as traitors.[32]

The watershed represented by the March 1944 strikes brings several questions to light.[33] 'With the abandonment of the initial hypotheses of an insurrection' (linked to the vainly hoped-for effects of the Anzio landing) and the definition of the platform as *politico-rivendicativo*,[34] differences appear in comments hot from the event that mirror the diverse ways in which the strike had been experienced and interpreted.

'A wrong interpretation ... of some of our watchwords, like for example, "let us get ready for the national insurrection"', the Communist paper recognises, had led to the illusion that an insurrection was about to break out; but 'insurrection is no joking matter', even if the workers 'understand that there can be no real solution to the impossible conditions of today's life without having done with Nazi-Fascism'.[35] In these words there is once again the clear Communist attempt to square the various aspects of the struggle.

As for the Actionists, alongside their obvious recognition of the value of the strike,[36] what we can call an optimistically idealistic comment appears, at odds with the moralistically pessimistic position that they had expressed only a few weeks earlier. An Action Party trade union document had said: 'The workers are still too uninformed about problems of a general nature; they are too concerned with solving their particular problems; they are still too closely tied to trade union life to be able to see national life with a certain breadth of vision.'[37]

One might almost say that here the 'autonomy' of the working class is interpreted as obtuseness. By contrast, here is Leo Valiani's comment about the strikes: 'The workers have asked for nothing because they don't intend to ask their enemies for anything, because they don't want to negotiate with their adversaries. No partial and particular demands that could be the subject of negotiations ... It is the very problem of the Italian revolution that they have posed.'[38]

---

32 'Informazioni da Milano', 14 and 18 April 1945 (*Le Brigate Garibaldi*, vol. III, pp. 621, 648–50)

33 See, on this, *Operai e contadini*.

34 The situation is summarised thusly by C. Dellavalle, in ANED, *Gli scioperi del marzo 1944*, p. 30.

35 'Lotte parziali ed insurrezione nazionale', *L'Unità*, Northern edition, 20 March 1944.

36 'Sciopero politico' ('Political strike' was the headline of the 7 March 1944 Lombard edition of *L'Italia Libera*).

37 'Rapporto sulla situazione operaia a Torino', written by the Action Party's trade-union committee, presumably dating from January 1944 (kept in the archive of Giorgio Agosti and cited in De Luna, *Lotte operaie e Resistenza*, p. 522).

38 *Voci d'Officina*, No. 2, March 1944 (cited in De Luna, *Lotte operaie e Resistenza*, p. 526).

There seems to be less certainty in the opinions expressed by the workers' rank and file. Perplexities of this sort emerge: 'Who have we been fighting for? For the British, for the capitalists? By failing to obtain satisfaction for our economic demands, haven't we lost the strike?': which was precisely a criticism made by the *bordighisti* as well.[39]

The complexity and morality of the workers' attitude can be gleaned particularly well in the nuances of a testimony made forty years later by a worker deported to Mauthausen: 'With that general strike, on the pretext, for that matter legitimate, of improving wages and the rations of general foodstuffs, the workers openly manifested their impatience with Fascism, their reaction to the war and to the Nazi reprisals.'[40]

In counterpoint to this we might recall some comments by the anti-Fascist right-wing, which oscillated between openly declared, duty-bound, satisfaction and embarrassment. Addressing the workers, *La Democrazia del Lavoro*, the Roman paper of the Democratic Labour party (the *demolaboristi*), wrote: 'By virtue of our example, the strike, as an instrument of economic revenge and class struggle transcends this and becomes a means of political struggle, a creator of national liberation.'[41] For the monarchist paper *Italia Nuova*, 'political' was too strong a word, as the Fascist press wrote too: the strike was only 'national, patriotic'.[42] *Il Risorgimento Liberale* saw the strike as a manifestation of interclass national solidarity, which it polemically set against the 'strike-mongering collusion between Communism and plutocracy', of which Alessandro Pavolini, following an old Fascist pattern, had spoken in one of his reports to the party directorate.[43]

And indeed in relations between industrialists and workers one encounters attitudes of solidarity that certainly fit into the vaster framework of national solidarity, but also appear on occasions as the recognition of inalienable cohabitation in the bosom of the company. From the employers' point of view, this cohabitation entailed physically safeguarding the factory as a whole, machines and men alike. One thus encounters, in the industrialists too, taken as a whole, a plurality and overlapping of policies. This attitude can be seen above all as testifying to ambiguity; but within it genuinely paternalistic attitudes were to be found (protection, one might say, even in the presence of scant and dwindling deference), or, if one prefers, of accepting the challenge, or invitation, to collaborate

---

39 De Luna, *Lotte operaie e Resistenza*, p. 527. As regards the Bordigists, see the article 'In margine agli scioperi. Un esperimento e il suo bilancio', *Prometeo*, 1 April 1944.

40 Testimony of Marco Gatti, in ANED, *Gli scioperi del marzo 1944*, p. 54.

41 'Saluto agli operai dell'Italia occupata', *La Democrazia del Lavoro*, 20 March 1944.

42 'Non è l'ultimo', *Italia Nuova*, 20 March 1944.

43 'Scioperi e Resistenza', *Risorgimento Liberale*, Rome edition, 15 March 1944. The Northern edition of March 1944 published article 'Il successo dello sciopero politico', which described the strike's 'unexpected' success.

in the liberation struggle.[44] Even a Communist report of the first weeks, while giving pride of place to utility rather than solidarity, gave this assurance: 'The industrialists, in general, are well-disposed towards the workers; the Germans are taking everything away from them and in the end blowing up their plants ... so that the industrialists are thinking of using the workers to defend them etc. That's why [Fiat owner] Agnelli seems to be prepared to give lots of money to the CLN.'[45]

In its direct relations with the workers, Fiat showed both severity and ambiguity, as when, during the March 1944 strike, it first declared a lockout, then interpreted it as a holiday and paid the workers for their days off work.[46] A comparison could be made between the industrialist class and the Catholic Church as an institution. The industrialists too, frightened though they were, but ultimately sure of the continuity of their function, could allow themselves to remain above the warring parties, biding their time until they found themselves on the winner's side. Meanwhile, they knew how to accumulate points for good service with the Resistance and maintain, all the while, good relations, particularly business relations, with the powers that be, and above all those who held the real power – the Germans. Again hot from the event, a leading industrialist like Enrico Falck, treasurer of the Christian Democrat party for northern Italy, described the situation of the industrial manager under the Germans as 'extremely difficult': 'On the one hand it was important to ensure that one had the indispensable commodities, on the other hand one needed to manifest apparent good will to avoid the measures that were threatened at every corner to dismantle plants and send machinery and labour to Germany'.

Falck also spoke of the 'united front assumed by workers and reciprocally by the managers' and recalled the organisation of the 'company conferences of San Vincenzo'.[47]

A Fascist *gerarca* sent to Turin on a tour of inspection reported that, against the threat of the equipment being transferred to Germany, 'the agitation was fomented by the Fiat management whose prestige is ever increasing as they are at the head of the only organisation in Turin capable of feeding a large number of people'.[48]

In short, in the industrialists too, especially the major ones, as in the Church, there was the ambition to perform a stand-in role for the institutions. The

44 For an analysis of such an attitude among the medium and small industrialists in the Biellese, see Dellavalle, *Operai*, pp. 54–6, 68–72, 166.

45 'Rapporto da Torino', signed 'Giovanni', 6 October 1943 (IG, *Archivio PCI*).

46 See ANED, *Gli scioperi del marzo 1944*, p. 37.

47 See E. Falck, 'Fabbriche in Lombardia', in *Anche l'Italia ha vinto* 16 (December 1945), pp. 259–63.

48 Report from the head of the Party's political secretariat, June 1944 (cited in Deakin, *Brutal Friendship*, p. 702).

intransigent Fascists got irritated, just as they did with the ecclesiastical hierarchs, at what seemed to them to be unjustifiable privileges granted to shifty and
ungrateful potentates. Giuseppe Solaro, the provincial party secretary for Turin,
wrote angrily: 'The lower class rebel is imprisoned or shot; Ingegnere De Rossi,
who supplied him with arms, is not. The sons and protégés of capitalism don't
go into the army nor into the *Servizio del lavoro* and are provided with untouch-
able exemptions; the workers on the contrary bear the brunt of the transport
problems, the bombings, the food difficulties.'[49]

Understandably, Resistance austerity branded the behaviour of a good many
industrialists as playing a double game. Vittorio Foa wrote: 'Certain sectors of
big business [note, here too, that limiting formula 'certain'] are running with
the hares and hunting with the hounds, ... they serve the Germans, doing very
good business, subsidise the Fascists, prepare the white guards, keep in permanent touch with Messe and Badoglio, and give ludicrously small donations to the
liberation movement.'[50]

Foa's view, which fell on deaf ears, was that these donations should be
rejected and replaced by a war tax deliberated by the CLN.[51]

At the end of 1943, the Rome edition of *Avanti!* also expressed the view that
the industrialists were giving dough only for the purpose of dividing and isolating the proletarian elements, and of tying the bands to a wait-and-see attitude
(*attesismo*).[52] The fact was that 'as the Allies advance, the industrialists are
getting jittery and reaching for their wallets; and it's no bad idea to take advantage of this.'[53]

The Milan PCI federal committee, in the letter of 19 September 1944 mentioned earlier, in which it advised against being afraid of getting one's hands dirty
by negotiating with the industrialists, placed at the top of the list the need to
accept aid from the industrialists 'in money, provisions, technical instruments,
vehicles, arms, etc., in full awareness, however, that the industrialists were acting
like this for their own future advantage.[54]

---

49 Bocca, *La Repubblica di Mussolini*, p. 187. Bocca gave his tenth chapter the title
'Il partito dell'industria' ('The party of industry').

50 Inverni (V. Foa), *I partiti*, p. 22.

51 The author in dialogue with Foa, September 1986. See Note 51 of Chapter 6.1.

52 'Per le bande dei volontari della libertà', *Avanti!*, Rome edition, 30 December
1943.

53 Gobetti, *Diario partigiano*, p. 199 (entry for 20 September 1944).

54 Letter 'Cari compagni', 19 September 1944 (IZDG, envelope 272b, folder V/1).
In AS Genova, CLN, packet 2, folder 7, there are many documents on the aid given by
various firms to the CLN. A list of Pirelli's contributions to the Resistance – the conspicuous financial support appears, here, alongside the fact that 'a son of Doctor Alberto
(Giovanni) was a partisan in Valtellina' – appears in a 2 May 1945 memorandum 'For
the attention of His Excellency Aldobrando Medici Tornaquinci (ISRT, *Archivio Medici
Tornaquinci*, envelope 11, 1, n. 16).

At times, and particularly in the Garibaldi bands, there was the gleeful relish at shaking loose the purse-strings of the frightened capitalists: 'The answer to your question regarding Donegani is to knock very hard. That fellow is a scoundrel and a millionaire, so the thing to do is to press for a much higher figure than the one you originally had in mind; to save his skin when the time comes, he'll certainly be obliging now.'[55]

'Blackmail', 'extortion' are the terms used by the partisan Tersilla Fenoglio Oppedisano in recalling her exploits in obtaining money from the industrialists ('they were scared silly! ... and I was scared silly too!'). The crudeness of these words – tempered, as far as she personally was concerned, in her other 'unarmed extortions' – conveys not so much an idea of the authors as of the targets of these operations, people with whom, one had become convinced, no other language was possible.[56] But the *borghesi* who financed the PCI because they were blackmailed and frightened were contemptuously compared by one of the small Roman underground papers which elsewhere I have called *pre-qualunquista*, to those who financed Fascism.[57]

In relations between employers and workers the most subtle piece of blackmailing attempted by the former towards the latter, when they were defending their jobs and struggling for survival, may be summarised as follows. The industrialists would say: in order not to dismiss anyone, we have to keep the factories working; to keep them working we have to accept the orders that are offered us; the only people who are offering substantial orders today are the Germans. Which leaves us with two options: either we dismiss employees or we work for the Germans. But, if we choose the second, don't come telling us that we're collaborationists: if we were, we would at least be so to the extent that you are workers.[58]

It was no easy thing for the workers to get around this attempt at making national solidarity slip into company complicity. The workers could have replied: 'That's your affair.' This amounted to saying that, for the industrialists, it was 'objectively' impossible not to be collaborationists, for which they would in any case be called to account. What actually were pitched against each other, in a dispute of this sort, were the perspectives that the two social classes had on the power relations that would emerge between them at the end of the war. Clearly, if one of the two parties had enjoyed absolute superiority, it could have accused

---

55 Francesco to Amos, 16 April 1945 (Upper Lombardy) (*Le Brigate Garibaldi*, vol. III, pp. 636–7).

56 Bruzzone and Farina, eds, *La Resistenza taciuta*, pp. 147–8.

57 See 'Paura', *L'Italiano*, 15 March 1944.

58 An explicit, provocative argument of this nature was made by the Liberal and Christian-Democrat representatives at a meeting of the Ligurian regional CLN of 6 December 1944, when the layoffs at San Giorgio were discussed (see *Resistenza e ricostruzione in Liguria*, pp. 162–6).

the other of collaborationism, if it saw fit, with no fear of reprisals. But neither party could rest serene in the prospect of its own absolute predominance, whatever its respective hopes and fears.

And in fact there were different and far less straightforward situations. The appeals against dismissals and against working for the Germans were constant and parallel, but could also intersect, producing distinctions and nuances of various kinds. Above all war production could be isolated as an object of the refusal,[59] even if it was not that easy to define the boundaries dividing it from peace. One could attempt to separate the fact of working from drawing a salary, by asking the industrialists to use the war profits they had already accumulated to pay the workers even in the absence of orders placed by the Germans. Thus *L'Unità* could at one and the same time report 'agitations at Breda against the dismissals' and denounce 'the fabulous war profits' of those companies,[60] or write baldly: 'The Italians workers must not be reduced to poverty and starve to death. There are millions and millions of war profits, of autarkic profits which can feed the workers even if they don't work, or work little.'[61]

In a discussion with their employers some Turin workers are said to have asked the Lancia managers for 'the necessary wage to cope with the cost of living, and don't oblige us to produce it; that way the Nazi *padroni* will have precious little to take away from Italy to fuel this war of imperialism and famine. Remember, traitors of the Italian people are to be shot.'[62]

Dismissals were rejected also because they put at the Germans' disposal a mass of human beings to enlist in the Todt organisation or deport to Germany. Appeals of this kind were numerous and resolute: the industrialists who do not go over directly to serving the Germans, wrote *L'Unità*, 'are going about dismissing their workers, thereby preparing on the market so much good human flesh for Todt's and Sauckel's slave-drivers'.[63] The agitation committee of a Milanese factory warned management against letting the German Command have a list of the people they had dismissed, and enjoined them to make a public

---

59 See, for example, the editorial 'Sciopero generale' in *L'Unità*, Northern edition, 25 January 1944.

60 These being the titles of two articles published in the 25 November 1943 Northern edition of *L'Unità*.

61 'La classe operaia non deve pagare le spese della guerra imperialista', *L'Unità*, Northern edition, 12 October 1943.

62 'Rapporto sulla situazione nelle fabbriche', signed 'Giovanni', December 1943 (IG, *Archivio PCI*).

63 'Spezzare la coalizione dei negrieri e degli affamatori', *L'Unità*, Northern edition, 7 November 1943. The Todt Organisation was in charge of the work that needed to be carried out for the German armed forces. Kurt Sauckel was plenipotentiary for sourcing manpower. See, similar to the sense of the piece in the Milan edition, the 10 November Rome edition's article 'La disoccupazione e i piani nazisti'.

recantation with a notice to be posted for at least a fortnight.[64] In the Genoese factories it was believed that if the Germans shifted responsibility for the deportations onto the industrialists, then they must have had some reason for doing so.[65] In Modena it was the Fascist authorities who 'made every effort to carry out Ernst Sauckel's programme'.[66] 'Directives for the struggle against deportations' were issued by the General Command of the Garibaldi brigades on 27 June 1944.[67]

If the dismissals made the men idle, beyond a certain limit they made the machines idle too, and therefore also subject to transference to Germany. Slogans like 'Not a man nor a machine for the Nazi slave-traders and plunderers'[68] were intended as an alert against the dual threat arising from the German concern about not managing to use the considerable productive possibilities of Italian industry *in loco*.[69] On the other hand, sabotage ('work but sabotage'), which hit Germans and employers alike, if taken all the way, conflicted with the objective of saving installations: a Garibaldi formation reminded a GL formation of this after a sabotage operation carried out by the latter.[70] However, sabotage could create risks for the occupiers analogous to those produced by the idleness of the factories. Hence, appeals like 'Act! Sabotage! Destroy! Prevent the Germans from taking possession. What they take away from us we'll feel the lack of, and it will be used against us. It's more necessary than ever to act immediately! Burn everything!' met with criticisms from above and perplexity from below. This would be seen when the partisans, showing that they had taken the appeal literally, burned down three factories which, like for that matter all the others in the zone, were working for the Germans.[71] Total sabotage could be admissible only as an *extrema ratio* when faced with deportation to Germany: 'Rather than that,

64 See INSMLI, *CLNAI*, envelope 8, folder 2, sub folder 10 (12 February 1945).

65 See 'Rapporto di un organizzatore comunista sulle agitazioni operaie di fine ottobre [1944] contro le deportazioni', cited in Gibelli, *Genova operaia*, p. 336.

66 See Gorrieri, *La Repubblica di Montefiorino*, chapter 'Operazione 'mano d'opera' per la Germania', p. 321.

67 *Le Brigate Garibaldi*, vol. II, pp. 72–4. The directives were published in *La nostra lotta*, 2, 11, 10 July 1944, pp. 7–9.

68 See, for example, the 21 June 1944 Northern edition of L'Unità, and similar appeals made in the 10, 15 and 25 July and 7 August issues.

69 On this, see Collotti, *L'amministrazione tedesca*, pp. 162–3, 190.

70 See the letter from Valle di Susa Group Divisional Command to the Command of the Lera Brigade of the GL 5th Alpine Division, 30 December 1944 (*Le Brigate Garibaldi*, vol. III, pp. 159–60).

71 The appeal to Biella workers – drawn up by local Communists, who signed it in the name of the CLN (the same appeal calling on them to refuse participation in the elections for the Fascist internal commissions) – was criticised by the PCI leadership on account of its weak links with shop floor reality (see, on this episode, Dellavalle, *Operai*, pp. 90–2).

wreck the machines and make them unusable' said an appeal by *L'Unità*.[72] On the other hand, it was insinuated even by Fascist propaganda that closure of the factories was playing the industrialists' game.[73]

The most level-headed words written about this messy question, which was both political and moral, appeared in the Action Party press. The pamphlet *La guerra di liberazione* of December 1943, stated with analytic clarity that it was proving difficult to achieve what was emphasised by the Communist appeals:

> The industrialist who accepts orders from the Germans is betraying his country. If the consequence of his refusal to serve them is the total unemployment of the workers, or worse still the firm's passing under enemy control, he can agree to produce for the latter, but he shall make the execution of the contract vain by means of the most energetic and determined obstructionism.

A few days later *Italia Libera* was compelled to recognise that, with the continuance of the occupation, 'it was difficult to avoid a minimum of collaboration'. The workers, the Action Party paper went on to say, by striking and sabotaging, redeem the sin of working in factories producing goods for the Germans. But when it came to the employers, 'there has been one sole example of an industrialist shutting up shop, paying his employers a few months' salary and taking to helping the partisans; but one example is not enough to save the mass'. As for the industrialists who were indeed making tidy sums out of the German orders, the article concluded, referring to future power relations (and also the good functioning of the economic laws), 'their industries – if essential – will be saved, but not them, nor the fortunes they have accumulated with the greed of the speculator and dishonesty to the *patria*'.[74]

An atypical solution, but one which signals a pressing problem for the free zones, was practised for some time by the 50th Garibaldi brigade commanded by Francesco Moranino. How was one to prevent the free zone that had come into being in the Biella area from dying without selling the Germans the cloth produced with raw materials supplied by the Germans themselves? In October 1944, Moranino proposed that in exchange for the supplies received they sell the Germans the finished product, but not more than a fifth. Despite the severe reprimand of the higher Commands, for whom there could be no exceptions to the rule about not dealing with the enemy, the agreement worked for

72 'Operai in guardia! Gli industriali vi vendono ai tedeschi. Non un operaio né una macchina in Germania!', *L'Unità*, Northern edition, 25 January 1944.

73 See, for example, the leaflet distributed among the workers of Forlì on the occasion of the March 1944 strikes (cited in Flamigni and Marzocchi, *Resistenza in Romagna*, p. 289).

74 'L'ultima piaga: il collaborazionismo', *L'Italia Libera*, Lombardy edition, 18 February 1944.

a couple of months until it was swept away by the roundups at the beginning of 1945.[75]

In the occupied zones south of what was to be the Gothic line, there is the striking case of Galileo, the Florentine firm, where almost all the workers (around 80 percent) refused to follow the machinery which, as agreed between the Germans and management, was mostly being sent to the North. Again on 25 July 1945 the Tuscan CLN had to intervene to make sure that these workers, and those who chose to behave in a like manner, were treated at least as well as the workers returning from the North, 'in view not least of [the Committee's] responsibility, since in the period of clandestinity it always urged the workers to refuse to go to the North'.[76]

How much of a backward turn things would take in a matter of two years is proven by the fact that the minister of Labour, the old Socialist Ludovico D'Aragona, was compelled by the third legislative commission of the Constituent Assembly to withdraw the measure for re-employing workers who had dodged work during the German occupation: Christian Democrats, Liberals and Monarchists had opposed it, and the left-wing parties had taken the matter no further, showing that they were sensitive to what would befall those who had been employed in their place, who would probably risk dismissal.[77]

The imprint given by the great political forces to class relations, as outlined above, was also the result of their mediating role regarding initiatives arising from those relations. Some of the moods of the rank and file can actually be seen through the top-level documents, when they report the rents showing in the declared political warp. Particularly in the first few months, the Communist leaders lamented at times the disproportion between the organisational deficiencies of the party and the influence it exerted among the masses.[78] At other times they reached 'the truly sad recognition that the proletarian avant-garde is marching at the tail of the masses.[79] Or else they took cold comfort from observing that 'the working class is more advanced than the Party', with the other observation that it 'recognises our Party as its Party'.[80] There existed a vast

75 See Dellavalle, *Operai*, pp. 229–33.

76 ISRT, *CVL*, envelope 205, folder Officine Galileo, and *Carte Francesco Berti*, envelope 1, folder 1, Verbali del CTLN; Contini, *Memoria e storia*, p. 309.

77 Archivio della Camera dei Deputati, Atti Assemblea Costituente, 3a commissione per l'esame dei disegni di legge, 24–25 January 1947. The record of the meeting is republished in R. Romboli and C. Fiumanò, *Il contributo della Costituente alla legislazione ordinaria*, Bologna: Il Mulino, 1980, pp. 532–6.

78 See, for example, Sandrelli's 2 November 1943 report from Turin ('Al Centro', IG, *Archivio PCI*).

79 See the 'Lettera agli attivisti del Partito' and 'Rapporto sulla situazione nelle fabbriche', both from Turin, December 1943 (IG, *Archivio PCI*).

80 'Rapporto sul lavoro di Partito in Bergamo', not signed, 29 December 1943 (*Le Brigate Garibaldi*, vol. I, p. 191).

area of the working class that contaminated the party's slogans and watchwords, sometimes concealing the contradictions within them, at other times highlighting them.

Of the hope that with the fall of Fascism capitalism too would be swept away only a scholarly, doom-laden and Third Internationalist version existed, explicit formulations of which can also be found in the PSIUP and clear traces in the Action Party. Giorgio Diena, for example, was of the opinion that capitalism had transformed itself 'from the instrument of production' 'into an obstacle to and brake on the forces of production.'[81] Another version of this hope was experienced through the pat identification of the Fascist with the employer and hope in a new world of Socialism and Communism. (The distinction between the two terms, while clear-cut on the party and pragmatic plane, blurred to the point of dissolving on the plane of ideological principles.) At the same time, the tactical caution of the Communist Party could intersect with the workers' demands for immediate and 'reformist' improvements. If for the Party mediation lay in Togliatti's elaborate policy of progressive democracy, for at least part of the rank and file workers mediation or, if one prefers, the overcoming of contradictions, rested heavily, as will presently become clearer, on the myth of the USSR and hope in the arrival of Barbisun or Baffone (Stalin), however one wished to call him. Myth and expectations in turn often coexisted with the demand for the re-establishment of the elementary conditions of democracy, inside and outside the factory. At work here was the historical memory of the fact that the *padrone*'s authoritarianism in the factory, reinforced during the 1915-18 war, had offered Fascism a model.[82]

Explicit manifestations of unadulterated class hatred made their way into the close-weft fabric of anti-Fascist national unity, not only on the part of the workers, but also, if less patently and leaving few traces – on that of the employers. In Turin Cavaliere Viberti alternated between paternalistic tones ('you're like sons...') and tongue-lashing the workers for having clapped 'every time a Fascist *gerarca* showed up' with scoffing and provocative declarations: 'Whatever turn the war takes, under whatever sky or flag, remember that I will always be better than you.'[83] A Paduan woman landowner protested to Farinacci and the local *capo di provincia* because 'our managers ... favour ... that class ... which most ferociously hates Fascism and which already counseled, and organised dispersal, rebelliousness ... those ferocious *rurali*, with no country and no honour ...

---

81 G. Diena, 'La rivoluzione minimalista', *Quaderni dell'Italia Libera*, April 1945, 16, p. 17.

82 See, on this, V. Foa, 'Introduzione' in P. Grifone, *Il capitale finanziario in Italia*, Einaudi, Turin 1971.

83 See 'Sunto di quanto avvenuto in questo ultimo periodo che va dal 19 novembre al 24 novembre alla Viberti', unsigned, and 'Rapporto sulla situazione nelle fabbriche', signed 'Rosa', 23 December 1943 (IG, *Archivio PCI*).

they only hate, hate, hate us'[84] – and it is worth noting here that the reassuring word *rurali*, used so much by the Fascists, is turned on its head by the blind fury of this landowner into a blanket term for her class enemies. An Emilian landowner felt himself to be under attack from the 'Gruppi armati proletari' ('Proletarian armed groups') and the 'Squadre di azione proletarie' ('Proletarian action squads') (preferring to shake the initials GAP and SAP out into their full forms).[85]

The arrogance of the landowners, or at least of some of them, comes across as being greater than that of the industrialists: in this respect, the Fascism of the RSI had well and truly returned to its origins. This time too, the industrialists found themselves caught up in a wider game and a wider perspective.

From the opposite side, testimonies of class hatred abound. 'There are insistent rumours that if the strike isn't settled by the 16th, responsibility will be laid chiefly on them (the *padroni*) and that four or five of them will be shot. (A good thing too)' – so runs a report from the Breda works in December 1943.[86]

An able and ambiguous figure like Professor Valletta is the object of fiery denunciations. *Voce Operaio*, the Catholic Communist paper, wrote: 'This shady slave of the Germans contemptuously dismisses workers, threatening them with the Nazi firing squad.'[87] On 26 November 1944 the provincial agitation committee of Turin denounced the entire Fiat management to the CLN for collaborationism, defining Valletta as a 'traditore della patria'. At the suggestion of the Action Party representative (Mario Andreis) the denunciation was transmitted to the *comitato per l'epurazione* (purging committee), whence began a long and complicated process which would peter out at the beginning of 1946. A further denunciation, to the agitation committee of the fourth sector, still during the period of clandestinity, gave the initiative a more clearly classist imprint: 'The workers of Fiat have not forgotten and ... will not forget the abuses of power and outrages and the exploitation suffered at the hands of this management and its cops'.[88]

'There's the dictatorship of the *padrone*. Because that was Fascist property', is what is said of the Terni company. And it is recalled that 'to get the work done' an engineer from the same firm 'was prepared to get himself killed ... And he went around with a riding whip, saying 'Forza! Forza!' ('Come on! Come on!').

---

84 See Briguglio, *Clero e contadini*, p. 340.

85 Unpublished diary of G. Manni

86 Quoted in A. Scalpelli, 'Quinta Sezione: Sciopero!', in *La Resistenza racconta*, Milan: Il calendario del popolo, n.d.

87 See the article on the Turin strike in *Voce Operaia*, 16 December 1943.

88 See Colombi's 13 December 1944 'Informazione da Torino' (*Le Brigate Garibaldi*, vol. III, p. 70) and R. Gobbi, 'Note sulla commissione d'epurazione del CLN regionale piemontese e sul caso Valletta', in *Il Movimento di liberazione in Italia*, October–December 1967, No. 89, pp. 57–73.

The partisan movement deemed C's excessive zeal to be culpable, and he was sentenced to death'.[89]

The case of this engineer prompts one to discuss the physiognomy of the Fascist as seen by the factory. In the Fascist there was a fusion of the figure of the *padrone* and that of the superior: a manager of the Galileo works makes this plain, in explaining adherence to Communism as 'rebellion against the *padrone* as superior, and their being superior in that they are part of the class of *padroni*'.[90] But the employer was often absent; while the arrogant boss and the slave-driving overseer were visible daily. From this point of view, the re-born Fascists of the Social Republic appeared as the epitome of the Fascist *qua* class enemy. When the black-shirted Fascists showed their faces at the factory 'they were greeted with hisses and told to beat it; which did not happen in the case of the Germans' – this is what is written about the Milan strikes of December 1943:[91]

> The *padrone* had no need to be present because there were the Fascists. The Fascists hit people. They were among the workers, among the workers themselves … there were people who'd been put there in the factory because there they had to report what it was doing. In the factory the Fascist workers … in short they were isolated because they were a small minority, they were factious … they were the least able of many, … they were the least intelligent, they weren't great kicks at work.

This is the factory Fascist as he had remained fixed in the memory of the Galileo workers.[92] The *gerarchia* in the factory, a Terni worker recalls, 'was a *gerarchia* of charge hands, it wasn't a technical *gerarchia*'.[93] To have liberated oneself from the bullying of the corporals and overseers – 'the liberation struggle was necessary to eliminate this affront to the workers represented by the searches et cetera'[94] – was to remain in the workers' memory as one of the most tangible signs of the change that came about with the Liberation.

Hatred of the henchman-Fascist could be so intense as to blur that of the *padrone*-Fascist. Another Galileo worker says of his father, a horse-broker and veteran of the Scandicci barricades: 'He didn't realise that behind these Fascists

89 Testimonies of Dante Bartolini and Comunardo Tobia, in Portelli, *Biografia di una città*, pp. 209, 286.

90 Interview with the Engineer Brini, in Contini, *Memoria e storia*, p. 209.

91 'Insegnamenti ed esame critico', a PCI document cited in Ganapini, *Lotte operaie: Milano*, p. 168.

92 See the testimonies of Corrado Polli, Berto Guarducci and Ugo Cellini, collected in Contini, *Memoria e storia*, pp. 95, 159, 294.

93 Testimony of Emilio Ferri (Portelli, *Biografia di una città*, p. 92).

94 Testimony of Raffaele Chiavacci, PCI member, laid off from the Officine Galileo in 1954 (Contini, *Memoria e storia*, p. 328; see also p. 342).

there was the *padrone*, he hated those littl'uns, but wasn't keen on the idea of striking the big'uns. Eh, anarchoide...' and then expressed in eloquent and effective words the pride of the generation that had become Communist: 'Such a personal hatred: and little by little it turned into organisation.'[95] This is, as it were, the other, more sanguine face of the proletarian virtue of sacrifice which leads in its turn to organisation.[96]

The 'organisation' itself, by dealing a blow to the general and symbolic aspect of Fascism, appeared to be moved both by hatred of individuals and by collective conscience. The Genoa trade union committee's request that the regional CLN for Palazzo Patrone, seat of the PFR (*Partito fascista repubblicano*), in Piazza Corridoni in the city centre, be allocated to the *Camera del Lavoro* seems significant: 'Because it would be symptomatic of and a source of obvious satisfaction for the working masses to use premises that housed their uniformed (*sic*) oppressors as the seat of the class organisms'.[97]

The meaning that the workers attributed to the word *fascista* can be seen particularly clearly in the criteria used for weeding out Fascists in the factory, suggested, and when possible applied, by the rank and file. The first manifestation of this phenomenon had been during the forty-five days of Badoglio's rule,[98] when, however, essentially magnanimous attitudes to the Fascists in general, already recorded, had prevailed in the factory too.

'Since 25 July I ain't taken off me 'at to anyone', recounts a Galileo worker who had previously been persecuted by the regime, 'I've saluted and that's all, I've kept them at a distance like the plague': at the most the '*fascisti fascisti*' had been jostled a bit, spat in the face once or twice, escorted to the gate: 'What 'appened outside I dunno'.[99] Later, even this magnanimity in the factory came to be regretted. For example, the director of the Turin firm, Aeronautica Italia, would be defined as a swine who was mistakenly spared after 25 July.[100]

Reasons are frequently given, during and after the Resistance, for expulsions from the factory: 'because disliked by the working class' (thus, for example, in Genoa);[101] or 'scorners of the working class, bloodhounds and persecutors of the workers'. These expressions, in a peripheral zone like the Garfagnana, appear

---

95 Testimony of Corrado Polli (Contini, *Memoria e storia*, pp. 101–3).

96 'Sacrifice and organisation: ... proletarian virtues' – so commented *L'Unità*, Rome edition, 15 March 1944, with reference to the strikes in Northern and Central Italy.

97 Faced with this request (made on 3 April 1945), on 8 September the CLN decided not to answer (AS Genova, *CLN*, packet 2, folder 7). See *Resistenza e ricostruzione in Liguria*, p. 234.

98 See De Luna, *Lotte operaie e Resistenza*, pp. 508, 511.

99 From the aforementioned testimony of Angelo Raffaelli (Contini, *Memoria e storia*, pp. 346, 351).

100 'Rapporto sulla situazione nelle fabbriche' by Giovanni, December 1943 (IG, *Archivio PCI*).

101 See Gibelli, *Genova operaia*, p. 47.

among the reasons of 'moral unworthiness' that are kept distinct from 'political reasons'.[102]

This is how the *stato di accusa* (committal for trial) against an industrialist from Abbiategrasso was worded: 'A jackal grown rich to the order of many hundreds of millions during twenty years of fascism, when a workers' committee asked for assistance for the needy and the patriots, with a handsome gesture, offered 5,000 lire to divide among 105 employees. He is held up to the contempt of the workers'.[103]

The comment on a series of interviews with workers from the Piombino steelworks read:

> Fiercely negative judgments were expressed about the director of the plant and his managers, but also a certain respect. The injustice of their initiative seems implicit in the role they occupy, and not in themselves as persons. Implicit in their judgments there seems to be the view that after all each was playing his own game, to the end; this 'extenuating circumstance' is not conceded to the [internal] guards. They are simply defined as 'ruffians', or 'errand boys'.[104]

Togliatti was to sharply condemn this radical aspect of workers' morality, when it shifted from mere henchmen to technicians. Speaking at the congress of the provincial federation of Turin, the leader complained that 'some twelve hundred technical experts have been removed, and not under the accusation of atrocities and collaborationism, but simply because they are disliked by the mass. This is a grave error; here political motives go by the board and the old trade union rivalries between technicians and workers come into play'.[105]

With these words Togliatti put his finger on a real problem, but his reading of the worker's attitude is reductive. The workers' distrust of the factory managers, indicated several times during the Resistance, did not tally with the party line, but was rooted in a strong sense of social differentiation, which was not eliminated by the general reduction of hunger. At times this reduction was invoked as the unifying element,[106] in the hope of seeing in a contingent fact the

102 'Istruzioni del PCI di Fornaci di Barga ai suoi delegati nel CLN locale e nella commissione di epurazione interna' (quoted in the laureate thesis of Giovanna Nannini, Università di Pisa, 1976, on the Resistance in Garfagnana).

103 See 'Informazioni da Milano', 22 April 1945 (*Le Brigate Garibaldi*, vol. III, p. 671).

104 Laureate thesis of Katia Sonetti, Università di Pisa, 1980, on post-war reconstruction in Piombino.

105 Quoted from *La Nuova Stampa* of 3 November 1945, in Quazza, *Resistenza e storia d'Italia*, p. 387. Quazza noted that the phrase does not appear in the version printed in Togliatti's *Discorsi di Torino* (pp. 38–62).

106 This argument was used to overcome the diffidence that Paduan workers showed towards engineering staff. See the record of the 'Riunione dei rappresentanti di Partito' ('Meeting of Party representatives'), in a Padua workshop, 18 March 1945 (IG,

final realisation of the long looked forward to proletarianisation of the *ceti medi* (middle classes). These contradictory attitudes were not to be found only among the Communists. On one occasion the trade union committee of the Action Party, a party, that is, deeply engaged on the middle class front, distributed this outraged leaflet: 'Mirafiori employees! Your behaviour during the lock-out was scandalous!'[107]

For their part, the CLNs, when they hadn't preferred to equivocate, as the Ligurian one did, had chiefly concerned themselves with preparing criteria and norms for purging the company executives.[108] The economic commission of the CLNAI deemed that those norms had to be interpreted with extreme prudence,[109] concerned as they were that the executives, who were not guaranteed 'a minimum of personal physical safety' would abandon their posts, thereby throwing production into chaos.[110] The resolve to deal a blow to the industrialists who had financed Fascism from the beginning and were now doing roaring trade with the Germans appeared clear and linear.[111] But to individualise, that is to say transform into subjective responsibility, the historic responsibilities of the industrialist class for the role they had had in bringing about Fascism and then keeping it in power was an objective that the failure of the purge would reveal to be, at least in those conditions, unattainable.[112] Presumably, the workers sensed that the achievement of so grandiose an enterprise could only be entrusted to the overall force of the class and its political and trade union representative bodies. But meanwhile the workers did not want to continue to see the most odious faces in the factory.

The powerful sense of workers' dignity underlying these attitudes is manifested in a variegated range of positions and incitements. Some workers who had gone to a Fascist scoundrel about certain problems of theirs received the following reproof: 'Let the feckless reflect well and think of the future if they want to enter the free unions with heads held high alongside their comrades.'[113] A worker

---

Archivio PCI; reproduced in part in *Le Brigate Garibaldi*, vol. III, pp. 490–4).

107 INSMLI, *CLNAI*, envelope 8, folder 12, sub folder 4 (without date, presumably from March 1944).

108 See the meeting records published in the volume edited by P. Rugafiori (*Resistenza e ricostruzione in Liguria*): they demonstrate frequent but far-from-conclusive discussions on this theme, referring back to the decisions of other bodies.

109 See 'Delibera sulle commissioni di epurazione', 26 October 1944, in *Atti CLNAI*, pp. 199–200.

110 See the 16 October 1944 remarks by the president of the commission, Cesare Merzagora, cited in Ganapini, *Una città, la guerra*, p. 178.

111 A principle enunciated, for example, in the Lombardy edition of *L'Italia Libera*, 9 June 1944, in the article 'L'epurazione dell'industria'.

112 Something of this idea appears in Foa's 'Introduzione' in Grifone, *Il capitale finanziario in Italia*, p. xvi.

113 'Un po' più di dignità', in *Lavoranti chimici*, Turin, 23 December 1944.

got the Fascists to give him money and then handed it on to a Communist to distribute; but the latter refused to do so because 'accepting meant receiving alms', as well as 'lending oneself to a demagogic manoeuvre by the fascists'.[114] Another worker, who was offered the chance of being re-employed at Fiat as a white-collar worker told his interviewer many years later: 'But I hadn't fought in the Resistance to become a clerk at Fiat.'[115]

Shortly after the Liberation, a reconstruction committee set up in Sesto Fiorentino would give this reply to a reprimand from the prefect: 'But it should be borne in mind that there exist other laws over and above those that the state issues: the laws of conscience, violated by the industrialists'; and in the Tuscan CLN the Christian Democrat representative would record that very often 'when people who had been expelled turned up for work again with a certificate from the local Committee, they were thrown out'.[116]

As I have already underlined more than once, anti-institutional animosity and a desire for better institutions, traverse much Resistance conduct, and remained as one of the Resistance's most tenacious legacies but also one of the hardest to administer. Among the workers they set in motion both egalitarian and solidaristic drives. 'Solidarity, a moral thing, the sharpened tool of struggle', is the title that the Catholic Communists in Rome gave to one of their articles, urging their readers, after so much *arrivismo personale* (personal self-seeking) 'to identify their lot with the lot of everybody'.[117] These appeals for universal brotherhood acquired particular connotations when they appeared as incitement to workers' solidarity. An appeal by the railroad workers agitation committee to condemn failure to participate in the current struggle punctually recalls the sad memory of blacklegging: 'The old system of the past struggle, where even blacklegs always ended up receiving the same benefits wrested by the strikers, is over for good.'[118]

Solidarity appeared to be intrinsic to a work ethic, which had in no way been submerged by the exceptional circumstances of those months, about which it makes no sense to talk in terms of workers' absenteeism.[119] If anything, the sheer fatigue of labour served, yet again, as a reagent against Fascist heroics.

---

114 The story of the episode is told in an anonymous report on the November 1943 strikes in Turin, entitled 'Cause e sviluppi dell'agitazione' (IG, *Archivio PCI*).

115 Interview with Emilio Guglielmino in *A voi cari compagni*, edited by S. Tatò, Bari: De Donato, 1981, p. 27

116 ISRT, *CTLN* envelope II, folder 9 (17 September 1945); record of the 2 March 1946 meeting, featuring a discussion of a strike taking place in one Castelnuovo dei Sabbioni factory in protest against the readmittance of an engineer who had already previously been purged (ISRT, *Carte Francesco Berti*, envelope 1, folder 1).

117 *Voce Operaia*, 16 December 1943.

118 'Noi ferrovieri', *L'Unità*, Northern edition, 10 March 1944.

119 See the use of this expression in *Operai e contadini*.

Speaking about his early development, the Gappist Elio Cicchetti recalls the effect it had on him seeing these words of Mussolini's daubed on the walls: 'We are against the easy life!': 'To earn my living I'd started working even before I finished elementary school: frankly I didn't like that motto one little bit.' On another page Cicchetti again writes of a Communist worker, arrested under the regime, who had been a kind of master to him, and whom he met up with again after 8 September: 'In the factory they had taught me that work is a serious business, to be done with precision, participation and dignity; only in this way can one firmly claim a decent living wage.'[120]

'I couldn't be faulted at work' is one of the recurrent expressions in a collection of testimonies of women's political participation. Or again: 'I always worked. I was capable of doing anything.'[121] The old Galileo worker, a manager recalls, 'even when he was athirst for Communism was still proud of being part of Galileo.'[122]

The passage from the work ethic – 'we were those Communists who liked to do our duty first and then claim our rights', declares another Galileo worker[123] – to company pride could be a short one. And there could even be a borderline case like that of the Mirafiori works committee which asked for 'the honour of giving the name Fiat to an assault brigade, undertaking to maintain it with men and equipment'.[124] A woman worker from the same plant was to declare many years later: 'I feel myself to be a real worker because I'm from Terni and my mum's dad worked in the factory; they always made me see the factory as a place where there's satisfaction.'[125]

Numerous other testimonies of this kind could be accumulated, and projected onto the ethics of reconstruction, which might in turn be a useful way of understanding many aspects of the ethics of the Resistance. It seems, however, that much can be learned by setting an at once rigid and radiant formulation of the ethics of future socialist labour alongside the doubts of those who were at that time feeling the sting of forced labour. *Il Nostro Avvenire*, 'spokesman of the Italians of the Litorale who adhered to the movement for the new Yugoslavia'

---

120 Cicchetti, *Il campo giusto*, pp. 17, 34.

121 See the preface to B. Guidetti Serra, *Compagne*, Turin: Einaudi 1977, pp. XV; and V. De Grazia and L. Passerini, 'Alle origini della cultura di massa. Cultura popolare e fascismo in Italia', in *La Ricerca Folclorica*, April 1983, 7, p. 24.

122 Interview, cited above, with the Engineer Brini, in Contini, *Memoria e storia*, p. 200.

123 Interview with Ugo Cellini, born 1911, in Contini, *Memoria e storia*, p. 296.

124 IG, *Archivio PCI*. Out of 14,000 workers at Mirafiori, seventy were Communists, in addition to those who entered the partisan bands, according to the 'Rapporto sulla situazione dell'organizzazione di Torino e provincia', 25 December 1943, signed 'Bianchi' (IG, *Archivio PCI*).

125 Testimony of Lucia Vernaccioni, in issue zero of *Orsa Minore*, summer 1981 (quoted in Portelli, *Biografia di una città*, p. 76).

denounced the erroneous opinion rife among the workers according to which 'We'll work less, everybody will receive the same pay, there won't be the hated "capi" in the units and the works, there'll be no discipline, each person will be able to do as he pleases without fear of comments, fines, punishments or dismissals.'

By contrast, 'later, under the guidance of leaders who have come from the common people [not the daddy's boys but the best] perhaps the most severe too, because the more competent they are the more demanding they are ... we shall have to work more intensely', each person will be paid according to his ability, and it is ridiculous to think of 'an age of plenty in which by then work will be done by others ... In God's name, who are the others?'[126]

A textile worker deported to various concentration camps considered it an intolerable humiliation – 'to be humiliated on that score too!' – to see Polish civilians take only a quarter of an hour over a job that would have required a whole day for the convicts.[127] Primo Levi speaks for cases of this kind, of the dignity – 'a rough-and-ready ascesis' – that could be found even in the forced labour at Auschwitz. But he specifies:

> I frequently noticed in some of my companions (sometimes even in myself) a curious phenomenon: the ambition of 'a job well done' is so deeply rooted as to compel one to 'do well' even enemy jobs, harmful to your people and your side, so that a conscious effort is necessary to do them 'badly'. The sabotage of Nazi work, besides being dangerous, also meant overcoming atavistic inner resistances.

Levi's conclusion is that 'love for a job well done is a deeply ambiguous virtue'.[128] It is this basic 'ambiguity' that the following warning seeks to exorcise: 'If there are comrades who work punctually and work well for the war production, these comrades are not Communists.'[129]

This problem seems to have been solved in the period of reconstruction, when the will to survive combined with faith in the advent of socialism and 'political ideology absorbed ... the previous labour cultures'.[130] At that time there was the widespread conviction that by now one was working for oneself, by virtue of the force gained through the Resistance movement by the working class and its party: 'There was this conviction that by now [the factory] had become theirs. It was marvellous, there was a truly moving harmony ... Work

---

126 Typewritten copy, signed 'F.S.', in IZDG, envelope 534, folder III/B.

127 Testimony of Cornelio Giuseppe De Taddeo (Bravo and Jalla, *La vita offesa*, p. 232). Of course, there also exist reports of work done badly on purpose (pp. 216–17, 256).

128 Primo Levi, *The Drowned and the Saved*, p. 98.

129 'Vita di Partito' in *L'Unità*, Northern edition, 21 June 1944.

130 Contini, *Memoria e storia*, p. 9.

was in full swing, and even if there are always black sheep, isn't that so? It was his work-mate who said to the other, "Eh, see that you work because things ain't as before!"[131]

Some workers even offered free overtime hours for the reconstruction of the factories; while a group of company CLNs declared on the one hand that 'only in work lies the reconstruction of the Patria that has been torn to pieces by Fascism', and on the other hand asked in the same breath for the dismissal of all the Fascists who had adhered to the Social Republic and 'for 75 percent of workers' representation in the running and management of the companies to be devolved to the workers and 25 percent to the owners'.[132] For a worker from La Spezia it went without saying that, since the aim of the Resistance was to bring down Fascism, the destruction of capitalism would follow on from that:

> We had a socialist prefect and a communist *questore*, we had the power centres in our hands, things being like this, it was logical to think: well, comrades, let's get down to the job of reconstruction because now it's we who are in the power. Given our situation, we thought that Socialism was here, when we had our meetings in the evening, we spoke about how to build a socialist society, about communism, about nothing else.[133]

That it was not just desirable but impossible for reconstruction to come about if it was not 'on completely new bases', socialist ones, was argued in a rather scholarly fashion by the Socialist press as well.[134] In the period of recon-

---

131 Testimony of Arnaldo Menichetti, in Portelli, *Biografia di una città*, p. 300 and of Alfredo Mazzoni, born 1905, in Contini, *Memoria e storia*, p. 311.

132 'Festa del lavoro all'Ilva', in the Naples *La Voce* of 18 May 1945, signalled that the workers had contributed in various ways to the reconstruction of Bagnoli, above all by means of offering their labour out-of-hours. A similar tale with regard to Alfa Romeo workers in Pomigliano d'Arco was published in *Il Risorgimento* of 12 August 1945, in the article 'Com' è risorta un'industria' (I thank Gloria Chianese for having given me this information). However, this zeal was not always appreciated, even among workers who felt reconstruction to be their duty: see the testimony of Pietro Cornaglia, concerning Breda in Marghera, in *A voi cari compagni*, p. 97. For the other episode referred to in the text, see 'Dichiarazione comune fatta dai CLN aziendali riuniti il 1a giugno 1945 presso la sede del gruppo comunista di Busto Arsizio' (AS Varese, CLN, envelope 10).

133 Paolino Ranieri, cited in the laureate thesis of Chiara Federici, Università di Pisa, 1976, on post-war rebuilding in La Spezia.

134 See, for example, 'Dichiarazione', a statement approved by the national council of the PSIUP held in Naples from 2 to 5 September 1944, with the participation of representatives of the occupied regions (*Il Partito socialista e la trasformazione politica e sociale del paese*, no date or location). In the first issue of *L'Avanti!* printed in Bari, it said that if the workers had to pay for reconstruction, this reconstruction could not but be socialist in character ('Caos e ordine socialista', in the October 1943 edition).

struction, the hope in a tomorrow that is already almost today, was to give birth to a 'grande tensione ideale' ('great ideological tension') which for several years was to outlive the 'illusion of revolution'.[135]

This climate in the period immediately following the Resistance cannot be explained if we fail to identify the expectations created among the workers during the Resistance, when, though failing to settle into a coherent programmatic picture within or without the mediation of the parties, those expectations give us a glimpse of 'a rationality that does not deny desire':[136]

> We were fighting to change the world, and I think I fully did my duty to attempt to change things. It seems to me that, to an extent, there have been changes ... But we wanted to destroy private property, we wanted work to be everyone's possession, everyone's right. We aspired to a society with no exploited nor exploiters, and it seems to me that we're still a very long way off this. Certainly, in fighting we wanted a different future. First of all we fought to drive the Germans out of our country and the Fascists who were their servants ... then we fought to create a democratic Italy, but a new Italy ...[137]

– where that 'but' (*ma*) contains the disillusion underlying these words.

A worker from the Reggio Emilia area, a long-standing anti-Fascist but not a partisan, the son of a socialist worker who would have liked him to join the PSI and not the PCI, has recounted:

> At that time we were always talking about the development of a socialist society whose model was the Soviet Union. We were convinced that we'd achieve it soon, that we'd construct the new man: committed, hard-working, capable of constructing a world with neither exploited nor exploiters; and this discussion was nourished by the fact that 'inside yourself the deep conviction had been created that the movement demanded a total commitment and you couldn't refuse it, otherwise it was a sort of betrayal'.[138]

In the PCI leaders themselves there was the longing for Communism, and bald manifestations of hatred for the rival class that was not fully dissolved in the politics of national and democratic unity, however sincerely it might be affirmed.

---

135 Testimony of Ida Rovelli, from Milan, a PCI member since 1940, in *A voi cari compagni*, p. 71.

136 An expression used by Portelli with reference to the years 1919–22, in his *Biografia di una città*, p. 146.

137 Testimony of Fioravante Zannarini, from Bologna, a Communist from 1921, in *A voi cari compagni*, p. 68, and that of Nelia Benissone Costa, a working woman, a Communist from 1938, in Bruzzone and Farina, eds, *La Resistenza taciuta*, p. 57.

138 Testimony of Silvano Consolini, in *A voi cari compagni*, p. 79.

L'Unità therefore gave a reductive interpretation of reality when it affirmed: 'The political line is only known to the leaders of our basic organisations, but it is not sufficiently assimilated by the great mass of party members.'[139] It was not, in fact, just a question of getting to know the party line at more or less the opportune moment, but of even the middle-ranking leaders experiencing a situation according to their own fundamental inspirations. Riccardo, inspector in the Pavese Oltrepò, an old party official, an emigrant, and a combatant in Spain, as severe with himself as he was demanding with others, solid and loyal, wrote in a letter: 'We're democratic, but we don't forget that we have a blacksmith's hammer under our jackets.'[140]

Stefano, an inspector operating in Lazio, didn't mince his words in denouncing the traces of extremism that he encountered; but at Paliano, in order to activate comrades, he said: 'The policy of the Party is nothing other than that of the revolver in one's hand.'[141] The political commissar Due, speaking to the Communists of the Ravenna (Liguria) detachment, who were 'indignant' at American and British behaviour towards the USSR, assured them that, once the objective of the defeat of the Germans and Fascists had been achieved, 'other more arduous ones await us', that the 'war of liberation' is also a war 'for the destruction of capitalism' and that the government will have to be 'the expression of the working and peasant class itself'.[142]

'We are living in a full revolutionary climate', an old militant who had known Gramsci and Togliatti felt he could write of the Republic of Montefiorino;[143] that the 'Italian people are well and truly decided to fight to the end for the proletarian cause' is the assurance given in a message sent to commander Bülow in Ravenna.[144] The shape of things just after the war was charged with great revolutionary potentiality: witness some Milanese workers who, 'though accepting the line of the party', distrust the British ('look at Greece and Belgium') and 'think that a civil war is indispensable to achieve our goal'.[145] There was the conviction that Europe was inevitably heading towards Communism[146] and that 'socialism

---

139 'Politica e azione', in the Northern edition of 25 July 1944, part of the 'Vita di Partito' series.

140 Letter 'Cari compagni', January 1945 (IG, *BG*, 01755).

141 Report 'Caratteristiche generali della zona', March 1944 (IG, *Archivio PCI*).

142 Commissar's report on the meetings held on 31 October and 1 and 3 November 1944 (IG, *BG*, 010286).

143 IG, *BG, Emilia-Romagna*, G.IV.3.3.

144 'Annibale' to 'Buloff [*sic*] and Falco', 5 December 1944, in Casali, *Il movimento di liberazione a Ravenna*, vol. II, p. 246.

145 'Estratto da un rapporto da Milano', 15 December 1944, in Secchia, *Il PCI e la guerra di liberazione*, p. 708.

146 'Relazione sull'attività di V. in O.', Liguria, April 1944 (?), where the 'lively discussions' on this point dated back to the forty-five days under Badoglio before the armistice (IG, *BG*, 09977).

is in the hearts and minds of everybody', the only remaining obstacles to demolish being Nazi-Fascism and Prussian militarism.[147]

In their biography of Potente (Aligi Barducci), commander of the Arno Garibaldi division, Emirene and Gino Varlecchi wrote, hot from the event, that, 'Sure, he was fighting against the Nazi-Fascist enemy, but in his blazing red shirt he was considered, and rightly so, the combatant of a "greater war", that of all the oppressed against the oppressors, of poverty against wealth, of injustice against injustice.'[148]

Potente himself, in a short piece that he wrote in March-April 1944, had expressed the conviction that the battle of the Resistance and of national unity was simply a 'tactical battle' on the road to revolution, which he defined as the 'subversion of the existing order of values and interests'. Timpanaro's comment on this is appropriate when he says that, while one should not go so far as to describe declarations of this kind as 'heretical', they nonetheless expressed a profoundly Communist aspiration.[149] A similar aspiration can be found in the testimonies of workers who recount that they had been attracted by Communism insofar as it was a new type of society.[150]

The intrinsic and altogether natural fusion between the Resistance impulse and the proletarian cause that could occur in the minds of the Communists is candidly revealed by the words addressed by Gina (Pasqualina Rossi Battistini), a leader of working-class origin, to a young Turinese Jewish intellectual: 'And yet a lad like you should become Communist; you're too intelligent not to be one and you've given too much proof of idealism by coming to fight without anyone obliging you to.'[151] The same position was expressed in another way by those who died before the firing squad shouting 'Viva il comunismo!' or, since they were Communists, refusing the last rites.[152]

Demands for greater clarification and explanation about the party's programme, which bespoke an eye turned powerfully towards the future – 'we eagerly discuss what will happen tomorrow'[153] – generally met with little success. The replies restated the party line caption-style and/or referred inquirers to the supreme principles of Marxism-Leninism, the ultimate guarantee. But ordinary

147 'Avanti la gioventù socialista!', editorial of *Avanguardia. Giornale della gioventù socialista*, June 1944.

148 See G. and E. Varlecchi, *Potente*, p. 87.

149 G. and E. Varlecchi, *Potente*, pp. 35, 193–5.

150 As can be deduced from many of the interviews cited in this volume.

151 Artom, *Diari*, p. 98 (2 December 1943).

152 'Notizie varie del 27 gennaio 1945', by the Command of the 8th Asti Division, which speaks of the shooting of Tom (IG, *BG*, 05845); the last letter of Eusebio Giambone (*LRI*, p. 106); *Il Combattente*, 3–4, January–February 1944, on the shooting of Gino Bozzi.

153 'It is more difficult to make it understood that this tomorrow is not in contradiction with the Party's policy today', continued Osvaldo Negarville's report from Turin, 12 January 1944, cited in Dellavalle, *Lotte operaie: Torino*, p. 230.

party members demanded to know more about these as well.[154] As prominent a leader as Mauro Scoccimarro wrote from Rome:

> We've been asked by some comrades to draw up a party programme, that is an up-to-date programme. For the time being we'll start publishing articles about reconstruction in *L'Unità*, but a genuine programme might even be inopportune at this moment. Our fundamental programme now is war against the Germans and the destruction of Fascism and we wouldn't like to formulate programmes of economic and social reforms that might upset the unity of the national front.[155]

A party leader answered Potente's piece, mentioned above, as follows: 'We mustn't forget the political line of our party today. It's useless talking about what the party will have to do tomorrow.'[156]

The Garibaldi paper *Tre Vedette* had written: 'I want to fight against the fascist traitors today and tomorrow I'll fight against their capitalist friends to obtain equality and liberty'. Then comes this reprimand:

> Today the communists are fighting the Nazi-fascists and tomorrow they'll fight for Italy to be reconstructed, sparing the Italian People further sufferings. The communists ... are not fighting today [the word 'oggi' is added in pencil] for the proletarian revolution but for the liberation of the Nation. Tomorrow's problems are to be decided by the Communist Party tomorrow, that is when the country, liberated from the Nazi-Fascists, is able to freely express its will.[157]

'Some valorous comrades' from the province of Faenza, who 'pride themselves on being an integrally Communist detachment' and 'are proud to wear a red handkerchief around their necks with the emblems of the proletarian revolution', had asked 'for the Party to explain what the programme of action will be tomorrow', maintaining 'that such an explanation is supremely useful

---

154 See, for example, the article 'Collaborazione dei lettori' in *L'Unità*, Northern edition, 7 September 1944, on the responses to a questionnaire distributed by the Party's Milan federation. See also the series of articles 'Per la formazione ideologica dei quadri' ('For the ideological development of the Party's cadre') in the Rome edition. On the Marxist texts with the greatest circulation during the Resistance, see Ragionieri, *Il partito comunista*, pp. 400–1.

155 Scoccimarro to the Milan comrades, 20 December 1943, in Longo, *I centri dirigenti del PCI*, p. 267.

156 See M.A. and S. Timpanaro's introduction to G. and E. Varlecchi, *Potente*, p. 37 (see also p. 195).

157 See the letter from the Commissariat of the Val di Susa Divisions Group to the Command of the 17th Brigade, 17 December 1944 (*Le Brigate Garibaldi*, vol. III, pp. 102–4).

for the purpose of winning over the working masses to the struggle'. The reply to this was that the objective was certainly the creation of a socialist society: 'that [objective] remains clear to the eyes of the avant-garde of the proletariat', who yet have difficulty understanding the intermediate objectives, the only ones however which 'interest the vast mass of workers whose minds are still closed to our ideology'. From this sort of incommunicability between initiated and uninitiated springs the moral of the discourse: 'How can one pretend from a party such as ours a clear-cut definition of the tactic to be pursued some time in the future?'[158]

A local (Asti) issue of *L'Unità*, and as such closer, presumably, to the mood of the rank and file, published one of the few explicit and simple expositions of the aims of Communism, including the non-denominational state, liberty for all religions, education for everyone and not only 'for the sons of the *signori*, even if they are of poor intellect', parity between men and women: 'No parasite must pretend any longer, as has always happened and is still happening today, that others work for him. The scandalous bourgeois system of kicking the workers around and the monstrous fascist pretension that forces the workers to work and keep quiet must be cancelled from the face of the earth.'[159]

Intolerance of the unitary policy and doubts as to its real efficacy, fear that it would end up being a work of Sisyphus for those who were sinking all their energies in it, are further indications of an attitude that did not always succeed in sinking all its ideals and all its hopes in the line of a party, in which it nevertheless rested its faith. The numerous top-level documents which signal these positions of uncertainty did so in order to repress them; but they also had to grant, as 'Vineis' (Pietro Secchia) did, in answering the complaints of the Veneto insurrectional triumvirate, that 'you're right not to let anyone tread on your feet and you mustn't let them be trodden on';[160] or else they must take care not to interpret the unitary policy too literally, as the 'responsible comrades' do in the case of the occupation of Alba: 'We must show a broad unitary spirit, but we mustn't sacrifice all our positions just to achieve it … We mustn't pass from a rigid position to the widest concessions;'[161] or again, they feel obliged to remark that 'among the comrades there's a misunderstanding of the political line of the

---

158 Unsigned letter, no date, 'Al Comitato della zona di Faenza' (IG, BG, Emilia-Romagna, G.IV.3.2).

159 'Linee programmatiche generali del Partito Comunista', in the 15 October 1944 edition. The paper also featured a letter from 'a woman comrade' on the tasks of education 'in a democratic or COMMUNIST system'.

160 Letter of 2 April 1945, in Secchia, *Il PCI e la guerra di liberazione*, pp. 1012–13.

161 Letter of 24 October 1944, to the Command of the 6th Langhe Division. The authors recommend an attentive reading of the article 'Responsabilità', published in *La nostra lotta*, vol. II: 17, 13 October 1944, pp. 14–15 (*Le Brigate Garibaldi*, vol. II, pp. 480–2).

party. Many are upset and afraid that the Party will end up following a political line that is closer to the interests of others.'[162]

News from Belgium and, above all, from Greece, spread disquiet, prompting the leaders to remind their members that 'the alliance on the international front is no idyll, just as it is no idyll on the national front'.[163]

The uncertainties and resistance with which the Salerno 'turning-point' was greeted may be interpreted from the same perspective. They are also linked to generation differences. An ex-partisan, Anna Cinanni, has recalled that 'the Salerno turning-point was like a betrayal, but, I would say, more so for comrades of a certain age than for the younger ones.'[164] Emilio Sereni expressed a similar opinion. A prisoner in the Turin jails at the time, he wasn't the least bit surprised by the turning-point: 'All the same I don't deny that that initiative did however leave other comrades perplexed, especially those who'd been in prison for years and had inevitably been somewhat detached from the general policy of the party.'[165]

Within the Communist Party, relations between generations, to which we must necessarily return, took a particular form, above all differentiating the older members. Those who had managed to keep apace with the evolution of the party were programmatically, but not always emotionally, well-disposed towards the young men coming from the Fascist drafts. The others showed the distrust that had developed in the isolation in which they had lived, when the mediating influence of their families had had no way of operating.[166] This mixture of trust and suspicion gave rise to a complex web of positions. At the November 1944 conference of insurrectional triumvirates, when membership had risen from the 6,000 of September 1943 to 70,000, almost exclusively workers, the 'real professional revolutionaries according to Lenin's conception' had on average been party members for twenty-three years, in prison or political exile for eight years and were not more than forty-five years old.[167] They were both suspicious of their contemporaries who had not fully adapted, and full of hope in, but also of reticence and caution towards, the young ones.

'Those who are keen to do everything are the young ones, and this is good,

162 'Verbale riunione COM-ORGA', Milan, 5 December 1944 (INSMLI, *CLNAI*, envelope 8, folder 2, subfolder 12).

163 Ibid.

164 Testimony of Anna Cinanni, in Bruzzone and Farina, eds, *La Resistenza taciuta*, p. 106.

165 Piergiovanni Permoli, ed., *Lezioni sull'antifascismo*, Bari: Laterza, 1962, p. 285.

166 Many good examples of this mediating influence appear in Guidetti Serra, *Compagne*.

167 'Serrare le file e vincere ogni difficoltà per la vittoria dell'insurrezione nazionale', an article filling almost the whole of the 25 November 1944 Northern edition of *L'Unità*.

but somehow or other the older party members are put aside too rigidly as if they could no longer do anything good.'[168] If in this report from Piedmont the veterans appear benevolent towards the younger ones, hoping only that they won't overdo things, from the other zones they come in for very severe criticism. 'Some old party members have held back the actions of the younger ones, even threatening to denounce them if they went ahead' – that is how things stood in Mantua.[169] And from Cremona reports came of strong resistance to truly engaging in military work, while having to recognise in those who behaved like this the attenuating circumstance of age, habits and 'family responsibilities'.[170]

This reluctance to engage above all in military action is generally classed, in Communist language, as opportunism and, in this case, *attesismo*. At other times, by contrast, but this is not necessarily a contradiction, the older members were accused of sectarianism. A drastic denunciation came from the eastern border, where many things were said to be going well and others badly,

> but above all there's the obstacle of the 'old comrades' who with their 25 years of party membership haven't a frigging clue (sorry) about the far-reaching policy that we're practising today. Sectarianism, superiority, the clenched fist salute, the red star, integral policy, distrust and criticism of everything, especially of individuals from the past regime or ex-*carabinieri* or fascists who have moved into line only today. It's a terrible effort working with them. We'd do better to dig a 1,000-meter hole and chuck them all in it, since if they haven't understood today they'll never understand.[171]

Sometimes extremism and prudence were reported as coexisting in the same person. Thus, in the 'vecchi compagni' of Aosta a 'sectarian spirit' and reticence 'about going ahead with our work' seem to dwell together.[172] Among so many contradictory accusations and counter-accusations, a document from the province of Biella grasps a crucial point, independently of ancient class and/or anti-Fascist purity: 'In the detachments we have marvellous young anti-Fascists. These are ex-Fascists whose moral revolt against Fascism is of great political interest.'[173]

---

168 'Rapporto del compagno Do. sull'organizzazione della quale ha assunto la direzione' (IG, *Archivio PCI*).

169 'Rapporto d'attività del mese di maggio', sent on 10 June 1944 from the Lombardy Delegation to the General Command (*Le Brigate Garibaldi*, vol. II, p. 23).

170 'Storia dell'organizzazione sportivo-militare del Partito Comunista della provincia di Cremona', compiled by the Command of the SAP Brigade F. Ghinaglia, dated 1 November 1944 (IG, *BG*, 011242). Varese and Como provided a similar story.

171 'Relazione del compagno Bruno al Centro regionale del PCI sulla situazione in Benecija', 13 September 1944 (*Le Brigate Garibaldi*, vol. II, pp. 327–30).

172 'Appunti sull'organizzazione di ...', 8 December 1943 (IG, *Archivio PCI*).

173 'These young people', the document proceeds, 'love the Communists and want

It would, however, be reductive to equate the veterans with those who kicked against the party line and the young as its enthusiastic followers; and it would also mean relegating to a parenthetical position the difference between sectarianism and extremism. Sectarianism is an attitude that exalts the sense of belonging to the party to the point of impairing the party line itself: it stresses, completely in its own favour, its differences from the other parties, particularly the Socialists and Christian Democrats. The latter, said a Communist worker from the Milanese firm, Pracchi, 'are never around, and what's more when they do show up it's to be able to say that the Christian Democrats and Socialists have participated in the victory too, but without fighting ... But if then, besides not participating in the struggle, they put a spanner in the works, I'm not prepared to have our way blocked.'[174]

Reprimands against behaviour of this kind, found in both the political and military organisms, were numerous, covered all the geographical zones, and appealed to the demands of the policy of national unity. At times there were more fully articulated judgments, as when it was reported that 'the socialists are influencing more workers, office employees etc. than might at first sight be thought' by those who let themselves be misled by their scant organisational presence;[175] and as when it was said the Christian Democrat workers who sympathised with the Communists were to be considered 'the vanguard of their party' and not elements to capture.[176] Explicit appeals are made to those 'whose only thought is to occupy towns and cities with partisans, GAPs and SAPs belonging to the party'.[177] Sectarianism could even assume the conformist guise of pushing things too far in unitary terms; and criticism of this attitude was useful not least in reassuring the less enthusiastic about that line. Thus at times there was the reminder that 'nobody is saying we must lose sight, even slightly, of the aims that must fit our action'.[178] At other times one's own caution was viewed with self-irony, as in the remark that one must think twice about writing certain articles, otherwise 'the friends of the CLN ... raise a hue and cry against our sectarianism!?!!?!'[179]

Extremism, on the other hand, went more deeply into the question and

---

to become Communists' – 'Rapporto di Giordano sul lavoro militare nel Biellese', 19 January 1944 (IG, *BG*, 05081).

174 'Informazioni da Milano', 15 December 1944 (IG, *Archivio PCI*; it appears in part in Secchia, *Il PCI e la guerra di liberazione*, see p. 709).

175 Salvati, *Il Psiup Alta Italia*, p. 78: 'The material on trade-unions in the [Basso] archive confirms how far behind the Party was organisationally'.

176 See the 'Circolare al comitato cittadino e al comitato provinciale', a letter to the city and provincial committees of the P. (Padua?) federation of the PCI – undated, but from after the Salerno Turn (IG, *Archivio PCI*).

177 'Informazioni dall'Emilia', 4 October 1944 (IG, *BG, Emilia-Romagna*, G.IV.2.8.)

178 'Relazione della riunione del Comando Brigata Tollot del giorno 27 marzo 1945', in Bernardo, *Il momento buono*, p. 228.

179 Letter to the 4th Piedmont Division (IG, *BG*, 04998).

offered different contents and quick results, making the greatness of the objective coincide with the immediate possibility of achieving it. It was not so much a question of childish impatience as of the intensity of the demand.

What was actually happening was that an intricate game of relations between sectarianism and extremism was being played out, giving life to various forms of 'leftism'. There was a *sinistrismo* that led to *attesismo* in the name of the purity of the class struggle, which had to be preserved against the struggle between Fascism and anti-Fascism and the war between the states. As a French Trotskyist newspaper wrote, 'against the servants of Roosevelt and Hitler, the Italian Revilution continues'; or, as an Italian *bordighista* paper stated, 'the proletariat responds to the three stock masks of the class enemy (democracy, Fascism, Sovietism)', by transforming the war into revolution.[180]

A variant of this attitude was summed up as follows in a Communist document criticising it: 'Waiting for the struggle between Fascism and anti-Fascism to run its course until the contestants are exhausted. In order then to take up the struggle for proletarian claims.'[181]

In fact, in the history of Italian socialism and the working class there was nothing new about the working class, or whoever presumed to speak in its name, stepping aside like this, not only from the war but, initially at least, from the conflict between Fascism and anti-Fascism as well. One need only think of the refusal either to adhere or sabotage, and many of the first uncertain reactions to the March on Rome. It would be incorrect therefore to blame all the *attesismo di sinistra* (left-wing waiting game) on *bordighismo* or Trotskyism. During the Resistance, however, such attitudes could only take the form of a stoppered dogmatism. Even Concetto Marchesi was tempted by it when, while still Rector of Padua University, he showed some reticence and incredulity towards the anti-Fascist and anti-German struggle.[182]

There was also a *sinistrism* that took the form of red hyper-belligerence. This is how a Communist document sums up the opposition between the two stances: 'opportunism on the one hand and militant sectarianism on the other.'[183] The former is criticised for its ideological deviationism, a residue of a past to be put behind one once and for all; the latter, to which we must necessarily return, is criticised above all because of the practical damage that might be done by political miseducation and the crude enthusiasm of the younger generations who above all embraced it. Neither the former nor the latter form of deviationism

---

180 Title of the editorial of *La Vérité* of 15 September 1943; 'Sulla guerra', *Prometeo*, 1 March 1945.

181 'Circolare del PCI sui CLN', 29 October 1943, from the Rome federation of the PCI (*Documenti inediti sulle posizioni del PCI e del PSIUP*, p. 103).

182 Canfora, *La sentenza*, p. 72.

183 Report from Giacomo, Modena, to the Emilia-Romagna insurrectionary triumvirate, 27 March 1945 (IG, *Archivio PCI*).

need necessarily be viewed as alternative political lines to that of the PCI. On the contrary, they reveal attitudes, moods, and expectations – rife among the militants and, in general, the workers' rank and file.[184] Pietro Secchia would not have written his infelicitous letter 'Il sinistrismo maschera del Gestapo' ('*Leftism* mask of the Gestapo') if his target had only been the small dissident groups outside the party[185] rather than a wider internal 'danger of dissidence'.[186] On the contrary, it may well be that a leader with a certain reputation for being a *sinistro*[187] should have been the very person expected, in accordance with Third Internationalist custom, to launch so severe and crude an attack. On the other hand, as was pointed out at the time, 'for the Communist Party dissidence constitutes not only an excellent tactical cover but also an excellent index or thermometer of the radicalism of the masses; from the point of view of the official Communists, if Trotskyism didn't exist it would have to be invented'.[188]

The Communists randomly bracketed under the label *trockista* – that text goes on to say – left-wing opposition of whatever type it may be: *trockista* had in fact become the most demonising epithet of all.

Actually, the term *livornismo* would have been more in key with the tradition of Italian Communism.[189] The *bordighisti* (Internationalist Communist Party) should be considered *livornisti*: their presence in the party was however altogether marginal, even if several alarming traces of them were reported. In Turin it was considered disgraceful that 'there is not the aversion on the part of the comrades to the worm-eaten sectors of Prometeo and Stella Rossa that there ought to be'.[190] One of the first things Togliatti wanted to know as soon

---

184 For example, a 9 March 1944 report by Remo Scappini to his local federal committee speaks of the Genova PCI 'resembling an old maximalist formation' (Gibelli and Ilardi, *Lotte operaie: Genova*, p. 115).

185 For a quick overview of these groups, see A. Peregalli, 'L'altra Resistenza. La dissidenza di sinistra durante la RSI', in *Studi bresciani. Quaderni della Fondazione Micheletti*, 1986, 1, pp. 31–7.

186 This being the expression used by Spriano, *Storia del Partito comunista italiano*, vol. V, p. 125.

187 As seen from Rome, 'The Northern comrades, starting with Longo and Secchia, were not, by any chance, still developing the "leftist" tendencies of not long before?' (Pajetta, *Il ragazzo rosso va alla guerra*, p. 105).

188 Inverni (V. Foa), *I partiti*, p. 79. See also how Ragionieri wrote of sectarianism as 'a safety-valve of that never-tamed class spirit whose needs could never be satisfied by means of the national-unity policy' (*Il partito comunista*, p. 396).

189 A term advanced in the literature by L. Cortesi: see in particular 'Storia del PCI e miseria del riformismo', in *Belfagor*, XXXII, 2, 31 March 1977, esp. from p. 204, and 'Pietro Secchia da Livorno alla Resistenza', *Belfagor*, XLI, 6, 30 November 1986, esp. pp. 436–7.

190 'Commento al rapporto organizzativo', signed 'Alfredo', 25 December 1943 (IG, *Archivio PCI*); and Luraghi, *Il movimento operaio torinese*, pp. 43–4.

as he landed in Naples, regarded Amadeo Bordiga; and to justify his entry into the second Bonomi government before the party leadership, Togliatti explained that 'a different solution would have brought about, even within the party, the danger of reinforcing left-wing currents through the excessive development of one aspect of the party's character to the detriment of others'.[191]

The *bordighisti*, according to whom the USSR was a capitalist state, reduced the immense tragedy that was convulsing the peoples of the whole world to a dogmatic formula, and in that formula they were appeased: 'Between two imperialisms that are fighting each other in our country, there is no advantage in the proletariat's choosing one way or another.'[192] The genuine Trotsykists were around as well. And here too comrades or those presumed to be so 'are not loath to have contacts and attend meetings and discuss things with such tools of Fascist policy' whereas the 'little group of Trotskyist riff-raff should have their skulls bashed in'.[193]

The Trotskyists' total condemnation of Stalin and Stalinism – 'Of course! They're Stalinist cadres!', wrote a French Trotskyist about the collaborationist Vlasov[194] – and their opinion of the USSR, as a socialist state maybe, but a degenerate one, could only stoke the Communist leaders' hate, also given the international network that the Trotskyists, unlike the *bordighisti*, had at their disposal. Individuals with Trotskyist sympathies were reported among the Garibaldini of the Valsesia and the Ossola brigades. Two of the four Trotskyists, in good faith, who arrived in a band were said to have been rehabilitated and the other two, in bad faith, had been 'treated as they deserved', and hadn't shown their faces again. Naturally, in evaluating these reports we need to bear in mind the extreme suspiciousness of those who made them and the fears shown towards, for example, 'one of those eternal grumblers who at the moment is very much under the influence of the Trotskyists'.[195] There is the curious case, governed, it would seem, by the law of 'an eye for an eye', of the Turinese Socialist leader, a foreman, who, when accused by the Communists of having sabotaged a strike, replied that he had been afraid of playing the Trotskyists' game.[196]

---

191 See the record of the 16–18 December 1944 meetings (IG, *Archivio PCI*, 'Direzione. Verbali riunioni 1944').

192 These words appear in Secchia's article 'Il sinistrismo maschera della Gestapo', p. 17.

193 See the leadership's instructions 'to all party-activists' who reached Turin on 4 November 1943 (*Le Brigate Garibaldi*, vol. I, p. 122).

194 'De Staline à Vlassov', *La Vérité*, 20 July 1943.

195 See the letter from the Lombardy Delegation to the Command of the 1st Valsesia Division, 9 August 1944 (*Le Brigate Garibaldi*, vol. II, p. 231); the letter from M. N. of the 1st Division to the Secretariat of the Milan Federal Committee of the PCI (IG, BG, 06199); and the letter from M. 'on behalf of the Secretariat of the Federal Committee', 10 August ('Caro Michele', IG, BG, 08729).

196 See Giovanni's report of 2 December 1943 (IG, *Archivio PCI*).

Trotskyists and *bordighisti* were 'historic' embodiments of dissidence, and drew prestige from this quality, but a heavy legacy of hatred and bloodshed as well. The *anarchici* and *libertari*, who had re-appeared in the zones that had been their traditional hunting-grounds, like the Carrara area, where they established their own partisan bands and entered the CLNs,[197] fell more into the category of historic diversity than of dissidence. But anarchic diversity, though it had been tragically shattered in the Spanish war, belonged in Italy to what was by now distant history and did not prevent a Communist partisan from recalling Errico Malatesta as 'a marvellous, truly exceptional man, whom I don't know why the party has isolated'.[198]

Rather more interesting, by virtue of their novelty, were the groups that were formed in those months. Though coming under the influence above all of the Trotskyists, they were in fact adjacent to the PCI, reabsorbable by and to a great extent reabsorbed into it. The absence of anti-Sovietism and, indeed, the frequent exaltation of the USSR and of Stalin favoured this process. This undoubtedly was 'a spitting image Stalinist policy';[199] but this observation could equally well apply to many of the Communist rank-and-file. The appeal of these groups, in the eyes of their critics, was the '*diciannovista*' (1919) jargon that is such a favourite with the radicalised but politically immature masses: for example, the watch-word 'peace against capital, against the *patria*', etc.[200] A PCI leader wrote of Stella Rossa (an integral Communist party) – a Turin group, but present elsewhere as well, as far as Padua[201] – that it was inspired by the criterion of 'class against class' and that 'the workers rather like its classicism [*sic*]'.[202] What they probably liked was the presence in the group of a seventy-year-old – who was given the name of Kurtimes – 'who says he was with Lenin in Switzerland' and of a fiery Russian student who went under the name of Arnault.[203] An important role in getting re-absorption of the group under way was played by the 'Lettera aperta ai

197 See 'Relazione sulla insurrezione armata e conseguente liberazione della città di Massa e Carrara', sent from the local federation to the PCI leadership in Rome on 24 April 1945 (*Le Brigate Garibaldi*, vol. III, pp. 687–92). A vigorous call to armed struggle was published in *Azione libertaria* of 15 September 1944, such that the masses would not be 'shapeless and docile' upon the arrival of the Allies.

198 See the testimony of Nelia Benissone Costa, in Bruzzone and Farina, eds, *La Resistenza taciuta*, p. 34.

199 Peregalli, *L'altra Resistenza*, p. 33.

200 This judgment on *Stella Rossa* was made in Osvaldo Negarville's report of 12 January 1944, cited in Dellavalle, *Lotte operaie: Torino*, p. 230.

201 'Riunione dei rappresentanti di Partito' ('Meeting of Party representatives'), in a Padua workshop, 18 March 1945 (IG, *Archivio PCI*; reproduced in part in *Le Brigate Garibaldi*, vol. III, pp. 490–4).

202 Report by Colombi on *Stella Rossa*, No. 20, August 1944 (cited in Ragionieri, *Il partito comunista*, p. 395).

203 Report by Giovanni, 8 December 1943 (IG, *Archivio PCI*).

compagni di Stella Rossa' ('Open letter to the comrades of Stella Rossa'), which appeared in the 10 September 1944 issue of *Il Grido di Spartaco*. The letter was utterly weighted in a 'Bolshevik' and anti-centrist direction (though obviously condemning opportunism from the opposite side); it rejected accusations of Machiavellianism and stressed the principle that outside the Communist Party, *nulla salus* (nothing is healthy).[204]

Only partly analogous to the case of Stella Rossa was that of the group that congregated, in the Milan area, around the Venegoni brothers and the newspaper *Il Lavoratore* (The Worker). This group, as Luigi Longo wrote in Rome, 'is oriented in an extremist, but not anti-party, direction', and consequently Longo exempted it from classification under the mask of the Gestapo.[205] The group exerted an influence that reached as far as Moscatelli's Garibaldi formations.[206] In it, as in similar groups, there was the conviction that Fascism had been well and truly, in the literal sense, the last card of the bourgeoisie; but, if that was so, the radical class revolt found support in the objectivity of the course of history. It followed that 'the Italian bourgeoisie, guilty of so many misdeeds, of causing so much grief and so much ruin ... must perish together with the monarchy and Fascism'.[207]

This optimistic extremism did not, however, come in for any less vigorous reproach than the pessimistic variety. When a Garibaldi paper of the Pavese Oltrepò wrote that on 25 July the bourgeoisie had ably shaken off Fascism, it was tartly rebuked with the reminder that it had been the working class, especially with the March strikes, who had brought about the fall of the regime and there was thus no cause to fear that the fruits of the operation would fall into the hands of the class enemies.[208]

Optimistic, to be sure, was the 'Movimento comunista d'Italia', which was widespread in Rome and Lazio, and which published the newspaper *Bandiera Rossa*. Confident in the revolutionary character of the situation, convinced that 'Fascism has worked for us' because 'the period of collaborationism and reformism finished with the establishment of the dictatorship', sure that September 10th

---

204 A shadow was cast over the absorption of *Stella Rossa* into the PCI by the mysterious death of one of the group's leaders, Temistocle Vaccarella, in Milan in May 1944 (see, among others, Anonimo Romagnolo, *1943–45*, pp. 328–35). On *Stella Rossa*, see Luraghi, *Il movimento operaio torinese*, pp. 202ff and 241ff.

205 Letter of 6 December 1943 in Longo, *I centri dirigenti del PCI*, p. 172.

206 See the criticisms made by the commissar of the 1st Gramsci Division, Michele, in a letter to the commissar of the 118th Servadei Brigade, Aldo Tuto, of 3 March 1945, and Moscatelli's severe reprimand of Fagno on 6 March (*Le Brigate Garibaldi*, vol. III, p. 434 and n. 2).

207 'Il congresso di Bari', *Il Lavoratore*, 3 March 1944 (cited in Peregalli, *L'altra Resistenza*, p. 34). On the Venegoni group, see Ganapini, *Una città, la guerra*, p. 67.

208 The article 'Borghesia e fascismo' was criticised in a letter 'From the Party's inspector' 'To the 3rd Division comrades', 8 November 1944 (IG, BG, 01589).

had seen the lowering forever of the *tricolore* (the Italian flag), full of admiration for Balcania, where they did not content themselves with a 'melancholy
we'll settle accounts later', extolling the decisive role of the USSR in preventing a
compromise peace between Hitler and the Anglo-Americans, but ready at the
same time to remind the USSR of its 'obligation to defend the world proletariat
at the peace table'[209] – in its positions the 'Movimento' appears as an elementary mixture of ideas and sentiments that were rife in a vaster area than that to
which it explicitly adhered, and which invested the Communist rank-and-file
itself. The influence of *Bandiera Rossa*, 'among certain comrades of ours' is in
fact reported by Communist sources.[210] For the 'Movimento' the PCI was an
organisation distinct from it but not different, 'because the cause is but one,
the goal but one', and if one sincerely believes in it, it will be encountered in
the Revolution.[211] In the meantime, however, the 'Movimento' put this common
sense question to its elder brothers: how 'can one pretend at one and the same
time to enjoy the trust of the adversary who has to be put to sleep and that of the
masses who have to be awakened?'[212] Precisely by virtue of its popular character,
the 'Movimento comunista d'Italia', which liked to define itself as 'subversive'
and showed sympathy for the anarchists,[213] did not have wait-and-see (*attesis-
tiche*) leanings. On the contrary, 186 of its members had been killed (52 at the
Ardeatine Caves on 24 March 1944) and 137 arrested and deported;[214] and had
fought not only in Rome but also in the province of Lazio.[215]

The closeness of these movements to the PCI did not prevent their being
close to the PSIUP as well – to several of its generic, maximalistic formulae,

209 See the *Bandiera Rossa* articles 'Orizzonte rivoluzionario' (22 October 1943);
'Perché collaborare?' and 'Chiarificazione' (5 October 1943); 'L'ora presente e noi' (29
October 1943); 'L'URSS e le realizzazioni comuniste' (7 November 1943); and 'La funzione
dell'URSS nel conflitto mondiale' (5 December 1943).

210 See 'Riassunto di un intervento del compagno Giulio nel federale di Roma',
27 November 1943 (*Archivio PCI*).

211 See 'Equivoco da chiarire?', *Bandiera Rossa*, 22 October 1943, responding to
an article with a similar title (but without the question-mark) in *L'Unità* of 10 October.
L'Unità's reply, 'Punto e basta', on 26 October, was haughty rather than violent in tone.

212 'La via maestra', *Bandiera Rossa*, 7 November 1943.

213 See the *Bandiera Rossa* article 'Noi sovversivi!', 22 October 1943, and 'Necessità
e base di un accordo', 5 January 1944, which dealt with the need to work with the anarchists, who had first awoken 'the clouded minds of the Italian proletariat'.

214 See S. Corvisieri, *Bandiera rossa nella Resistenza romana*, Rome: Samonà e
Savelli, 1968, p. 8. On p. 67 he also reports that the MCd'I had 2,098 recognised combatants in Rome (as against the PCI's 2,336).

215 The MCd'I was militarily active in Zagarolo, Palestrina, Olevano, and Anagni:
see the PCI reports 'Caratteristiche generali della zona' and 'Relazione politica 5a zona
Prenestina', March 1944 (IG, *Archivio PCI*). On the guerrilla struggle in the Prenestini
mountain area, see V. Tedesco, *Il contributo di Roma e della provincia nella lotta di liberazione*, Cassino-Roma: Amministrazione provinciale di Roma, n.d., pp. 320–4 and 482–8.

which when it came to predicting the consubstantial collapse of Fascism and capitalism were no fewer than those of the dissident left-wing groups,[216] and above all to the positions that found their most explicit exponent in Lelio Basso.[217] In this case there was not so much closeness between militants arising from instinctive sympathy, as an aspiration on the part of the PSIUP's left wing to 'polarise the dissenting forces of the mass parties'.[218] And it turned out that some of these forces came to see the PSIUP as being a less risky habitat than that offered by the PCI.

4. STRUGGLE IN SOCIETY AND THE STRUGGLE FOR SURVIVAL

During the Resistance the class struggle stepped out of the factories and the ideological moulds most closely connected with them, above all along two roads. The first of these was that of the struggle for the physical survival of strata of the population far more extensive than those of the workers as such; and in this struggle a particularly important role was played by women.[1] It seemed almost like a situation in which 'the market was reborn as the arena of class war'.[2] The second road joined up with the path of armed struggle, in the cities and the mountains. The Communist formula, 'the struggle against cold, hunger and Nazi-Fascist terror' attempted, once again, to keep social, patriotic and military objectives together.[3] In the social as in the military sphere, the struggle could

---

216 *Avanti!* of 22 August 1943, which gives news of the foundation of the PSIUP: 'Capitalism … is rapidly marching towards its own ruin, in Italy in particular as well as everywhere else'.

217 After the fusion of the MUP (Movimento di unità proletaria) with the PSI and the subsequent formation of the PSIUP (6 August 1943), in October Basso left the Party, founding the Fronte proletario rivoluzionario in Milan. Its paper was called *Bandiera Rossa*. On this whole series of events, see Salvati, *Il Psiup Alta Italia*, pp. 61–88. See also the documents on the CLN by the left wing of the PSIUP from September to October 1943, reproduced in *Documenti inediti sulle posizioni del PCI e del PSIUP*, pp. 93–8.

218 This is how Salvati, *Il Psiup Alto Italia*, p. 63, summarises the stance of Basso and the group of which he was leader.

1 See the appeals aimed at women in the 'Stampa non periodica' section of 'Gruppi di difesa della donna', in *Saggio bibliografico*, nos. 3023–145. Compare this to 'Esame della corrispondenza censurata al 30 giugno 1944', in ACS, SPD, CR, RSI, envelope 9, folder 3.

2 E. P. Thompson writes in his 'Moral Economy of the English Crowd in the Eighteenth Century', *Past and Present* 50 (1971), pp. 76–136 that the 'market-place was as much an arena of class war as the factory and mine became in the industrial revolution' (p. 120).

3 See, for all this, 'I Comitati di Liberazione Nazionale nella lotta contro il freddo, la fame e il terrore fascista', *La nostra lotta*, III/1 (1 January 1945), pp. 2–5. The Northern edition of *L'Unità* published, within some of its issues (for example, those of 10 and 30 January 1945), a *Bollettino della lotta del popolo italiano contro il freddo, la fame e il terrore*.

escape the political picture of national unity in the name of which it was solicited. Traces of social and/or partisan *sinistrismo* can therefore be identified that do not always coincide with the openly political *sinistrismo* internal or external to the parties, though often tending to merge with them; and on the other hand, in the struggle for mere subsistence the most general principles of human solidarity and assistance could be invoked that went beyond the class struggle in even the broadest sense of the term. In both cases the hasty observation of an American woman journalist that, faced with cold and hunger, it was not possible to be political was belied.[4] That journalist did not take account of how ragged and mobile in that situation the boundaries were between being political and being other things, whatever the intentions and declarations of the protagonists. The Catholic Communists of Rome, while urging that 'parish committees' be set up 'to organise a mass mobilisation – marches, protest demonstrations, parades of women asking for bread and work', were eager to emphasise that this was not 'political work, but simply work of Christian charity'.[5] In Milan Christian charity could take the form of civic solidarity. In this register, *Avanti!* reminded the industrialists that national solidarity must also mean social solidarity;[6] while 'una compagna', sending a letter to *L'Unità* on 25 December 1944, in which she tells how she has succeeded, regarding the problems of electricity and wood, in setting up a committee 'di casamento' ('a tenants' committee'), fuses the traditional Milanese civic sense with the political pride of someone who has been able to arouse a democratic initiative from below.

'Occupation by the homeless of empty premises, apartment buildings, hotels, schools, barracks currently occupied by the Germans and the Fascist organisations!' declared an early appeal in *L'Unità*.[7] 'All casualties must have a house!' was the title of an article published still earlier by the Rome edition of the same paper, which urged the population to go ahead and install themselves in the empty houses.[8]

It was a short step from these appeals to positions like the one that the intellectual Franco Calamandrei irritatedly registered ('Infantilismo!'): 'Tonino [most likely an intellectual too] says that the party will have to urge its comrades to sack the houses of the well-to-do, to guide them and support them in this. I tell him that his is the position of "Bandiera Rossa".[9]

In a famished city behind the front, as Rome was – I am still referring to the Communist press – incitements in which the patriotic and anti-Fascist spirit

---

4 Ellwood, *Italy 1943–1945*, p.113, which cites an article from the 11 September 1944, *New York Times* by Ann McCormick.

5 'Tutti uniti per la difesa del nostro pane', *La Voce operaia*, 16 December 1943.

6 'Battaglie sindacali', in the 8 November 1943 edition.

7 Northern edition, 25 November 1943.

8 See the 29 September 1943 edition.

9 Calamandrei, *La vita indivisibile*, p. 145 (9 March 1944).

mingle with elementary claims and denunciations are particularly recurrent: 'The right to live without having to work for the oppressor'; 'Let us make sure that the Nazi plan to starve out Rome fails'; 'The German creates famine! Famine creates the black market! The black market is black hunger for the workers' population!' 'Nurses at the end of their tether. What are the waiters waiting for to get organised? Claims of the Garbage Service'; 'Evacuees demand human treatment. Casualties of Portonaccio evicted by the Fascists and plundered by the Germans. Atrocities against the disabled'; 'Inhuman life of the FF.SS [State Railways] goods guards. The Railway Administration must come to the aid of the famished porters. An agitation to get bus 210 back into operation. The problem of eggs' – and so on and so forth.[10] The fact that in Rome the PCI took root, immediately after the Liberation, in the hazardous as well as the industrious classes certainly has a premise in appeals of this kind, too.[11]

But this was not a phenomenon limited to a restricted Roman sphere. In northern Italy too there were manifestations that recall an old tendency towards social rebellion – and bring to light again what has been called the 'symbolic tie between bread and liberty, rooted in popular culture from time immemorial'.[12] The political forces of the left would have liked to make use of these ferments providing that they didn't slip their grip. Indicative of this were the answers given, at a meeting of the Piedmont regional military command, to the question, put by the Allies, about possible popular uprisings at the moment of the transfer of powers. The GL representative 'has expressed scepticism as to the maturity of our people and has again raised the question of the police, the need for technical experts et cetera'. The representative of the Garibaldi brigades stressed that, 'where in certain quarters popular strata were driven by hunger to rash actions, only the partisan police would be capable of calming them in a friendly way without recourse to force. Which is what no technician could do.' 'But what if naturally, after such an intervention, the agitation were to continue?', demanded the general who represented the *autonomi*. The Garibaldino's reply was as dogmatic as a manual: 'In this case we would surely be dealing with *Lumpenproletariat*, with elements led and instigated by Fascists and troublemakers. And … our partisan police would use arms with the greatest energy.'[13]

---

10 *L'Unità*, Rome edition, 24 November, 7 and 24 December 1943, 30 March and 18 May 1944.

11 T. Lombardo, 'Il mercato nero a Roma', in Gallerano, ed., *L'altro dopoguerra*, pp. 181–90, and F. Anania, 'Linee di ricerca sui partiti di massa a Roma dopo la liberazione', in M. I. Macioti, ed., *Oralità e vissuto: l'uso delle storie di vita nelle science sociali*, Naples: Liguori, 1986, pp. 150–9. Anania makes reference to Edoardo D'Onofri's review, 'Le borgate di Roma e il romanzo di Pasolini' (on Pasolini's novel *Una vita violenta*), published in the second 1960 issue of *Rinascita*.

12 Bravo and Jalla, *La vita offesa*, p. 40.

13 IG, *Archivio PCI*.

This reply anticipates the Communist attitude which often, in the immediate post-war period, really did risk throwing into the arms of an unduly feared right-wing sedition the revolts of unemployed, evacuees, ex-servicemen, housewives – in short, all those irregulars that the party was unable to control and who did not fit easily into its ideological picture. Palmiro Togliatti was to express irritation at those who, in the Mezzogiorno, meant by the word 'popolo' only the wretched and the 'sfardati' ('the ragged').[14]

A SAP document says: 'Our greatest concern is to avoid reaching the point of excesses being committed owing to hunger, excesses that the reactionaries can take advantage of to obstruct the establishment of the popular democratic government on the grounds of the immaturity of the masses.'

Yet the situation was such that in the very same document, alongside the denunciation of *sinistrismo* as the 'main danger ... which defeated but not completely eliminated Fascism might exploit', the 'preparatory actions' listed include the following: 'Raiding of town council treasuries, custom-houses, registry offices, and destruction of all the files relating to taxes, stockpiles, rallies, agrarian censuses and anything that might be useful for control of production and for possible withdrawals. The fruit of the taxes, the proceeds from duties, et cetera can be withdrawn.'[15]

At about exactly the same time *L'Unità* published the following appeal: 'The workers have asked for bread and coal. The enemy has replied by starving and arresting them. There is only one answer: to raid the provisions and fuel depots.'[16] The reports of the republican National Guard 'are dense with news of sackings of and raids on the stockpile granaries and on goods trains, grocers' shops, bakeries.'[17] The correspondence censored by the RSI confirms the malaise, the discomfort, the anger at a situation that raised the prospect of 'black-market trade that is the ruin of us poor workers. Even the Germanic Authorities are incapable of purging these irresponsible rascals; they will pay for it at the end or after the war, but meanwhile we're the ones to suffer and class hatred is growing.'[18]

Social revolt could leave even a young Action Party intellectual greatly perplexed. Emanuel Artom wrote in his diary: 'Many lads interpret communism as a system of anarchy, disobedience and looting. The day before yesterday one was declaring that there are no longer any officers and soldiers, while another was

14 P. Togliatti, 'Il PCI e l'autonomia', in *Cronache meridionali*, IV, 7–8, July–August 1957, p. 428.

15 'Istruzioni del Comando della divisione SAP Torino alle brigate SAP della provincia', 10 November 1944 (*Le Brigate Garibaldi*, vol. II, pp. 557–61).

16 Special edition in leaflet form, 25 November 1944 (for the Milan strikes).

17 De Luna, *Lotte operaie e Resistenza*, p. 512.

18 Letter from Pordenone, transcribed in the 'Esame della corrispondenza censurata al 30 giugno 1944' (ACS, SPD, CR, RSI , envelope 9, folder 3).

intending to appropriate one of Agnelli's villas for himself ... I try to calm them down in the name of the Fronte Nazionale.'[19]

The fact is that, outside the factory, old drives towards social revolt emerged, while inside the factory they were incorporated in the class spirit. As was often the case, some Communist leaders lost no time in spotting this slide. Secchia wrote: 'Revolt of the weak against the strong? ... That's a language and a formula that has nothing in common with our doctrine.'[20]

What was really at work was the drive to identify the Nazi-Fascists not so much with the rigorous but circumscribed category of owners of the instruments of production, as with that, full of ancient echoes, of the rich and strong, whom one finally felt able to oppose on an equal footing. The 'insurrectional plan' of a Garibaldi brigade reads: 'The numerous rich are totally behind the Nazi-Fascists and are tough. The poor are totally behind the patriots and they too are tough.'[21]

In the Belluno area, the Garibaldini of the Nanetti brigade got a hearing above all 'among the poor folk', to whom they spoke 'of a world and a future society that would put an end once and for all to all the acts of oppression, injustices and privileges of the ruling classes, that is say all those evils which for centuries have afflicted the populations of our country'.[22] On 9 April 1945 the provincial agitation committee of Asti addressed a manifesto full of pathos to the hungry: 'In your unity lies your force, learn to know the force of your hunger and your wretchedness ... The good words of your *padroni* today will certainly be of no use to you tomorrow to season your food.'[23]

A young man of twenty-three enrolled in the Communist Party because 'he has always wished to be part of a class of men who defend the interests of the oppressed against the tyrants'. Another, of nineteen, 'is a poor labourer, he has understood the injustice of this infamous world and wants too to be among the defenders of human rights. He is mild, good, just, he has a big heart, an unshakable faith: he's a Communist!' Or again: 'Although they are serving in an autonomous formation they almost all declare themselves Communists ... For them Communism signifies social justice and radical, intransigent anti-Fascism.

---

19 Artom, *Diari*, p. 85 (under the date 23 November 1943). Artom placed his hopes in the arrival of a veteran officer of the International Brigades in Spain; but he was then forced to recognise that not even Carnera – the *nom de guerre* of the officer concerned – would be able to get the men to obey him (p. 97).

20 Vineis (Pietro Secchia) to the Valli di Lanzo military committee, 21 December 1943 (*Le Brigate Garibaldi*, vol. I, p. 177).

21 This was the plan of the '4th Zone Ruggeri Brigade' with regard to Polvareto and Solarolo in Cremona province, from 26 March 1945 (IG, *Archivio PCI*).

22 Bernardo, *Il momento buono*, pp. 71, 57.

23 See Bravo, *La Repubblica partigiana dell'Alto Monferrato*, pp. 232–3.

One of them believes in Communism as the first Christians believed in the life eternal.'[24]

In many of these declarations there is a full-bodied and almost religious sense of social antagonism. The rich acquire a meaning that goes beyond their identification with the enemies of the country, as they are seen by a tradition present in an underground French newspaper where these words of Robespierre's are quoted: 'Abuses are the work and the domain of the rich, they are the scourge of the people, the people's interest, their particularly interest'.[25] The Communist attempt to classify behaviour smacking of social revolt in terms of the pauperisation brought about by the Fascist war, which has afflicted 'peasants, artisans, intellectuals, office workers, professional people' – that is, all the allies, real or presumed, of the working class – appears doctrinaire.[26]

The intellectuals' dislike of the rich resembles, rather, certain of Malraux's characters, who directed it not 'so much against the possessors as against the stupid principles they spout to defend their possessions', and who did not hate 'the happiness of the rich, but their good opinion of themselves'.[27] It was unlikely that an intellectual or professional person, however impoverished or desperate, would set about burning the municipal archives; if anything, it would have made him 'happy like a boy finally burning his school-books'.[28] By contrast, the partisan bands, which had many peasants in their ranks, could do so in an altogether different spirit.[29]

'Town Hall: burn the papers relating to the innumerable Fascist acts of harassment (contribution of wheat, cattle etc.), but respect the registry office ones which are necessary for the normal life of the population', a Garibaldi command urges.[30] A patrol occupying the town of Fosdinovo in the Lunigiana area reported

---

24 The first two quotes are from a report by Falco, 'I nuovi e vecchi compagni. Mie impressioni', of the Nino Franchi detachment of the 58th Garibaldi Brigade, 5 November 1944 (INSMLI, *CLNAI*, envelope 8, folder 2, subfolder 12); the third from Chiodi, *Banditi*, p. 33 (12 August 1944).

25 *Le Père Duchesne*, September 1942. Robespierre's words were attributed to his speech on universal suffrage given to the National Assembly on 22 October 1789. However, they do not appear on the pages dedicated to this speech (pp. 130–3) in Œuvres de Maximilien Robespierre, VI, *Discours*, I, *1789–90*, ed. by M. Bouloiseau, G. Lefebvre and A. Soboul, Paris: PUF, 1950.

26 *L'Unità*, Northern edition, 10 January 1945: 'A 24 anni dalla fondazione del PCI. Il PC forza essenziale della Rinascita'.

27 A. Malraux, *The Conquerors*, Chicago: University of Chicago Press, 1992, pp. 85, 109, on Garine and Hong (original version: *Les conquérants*, Paris: B. Grasset, 1928).

28 Battaglia, *Un uomo*, p. 37. The destruction of the municipal archives is not to be confused with what happened to the Fascist archives immediately after 25 July 1943 on account of the popular ferment (on this, see Missori, *Gerarchie e statuti del PNF*, p. 89).

29 As Battaglia himself notes in his *Storia della Resistenza*, p. 240

30 See 'Note sull'azione svolta a Nizza Monferrato il 10 luglio 1944', composed by

that it had executed three Fascists, and that in the town hall not only pennants and other 'black stuff' were destroyed but 'the tax registers on cattle, the draft lists, the food checks and other bumf were torn up.'[31] In a village in the Romagna Appenines a *carabinieri* barracks was occupied and 'having carried off the weapons and smashed the telephone installation the lurid mass of paper is set fire to.'[32] The town council offices of Sorico, 'which in the twenty years of Fascism have become the centre for the irradiation of every act of harassment for the local country folk', is the target of raids by a partisan band: 'a general clean-out was made of the draft lists, cattle stockpile distribution lists, wheat production lists, various documents, various stamps, a typewriter, shoes.'[33] In the town hall of Frassinoro (Modena), 'the partisans burned the archive and the material of the *fascio*. They then distributed the stockpile wheat to the population.'[34] In 1876 the (anarchist) band of the Matese (near Benevento) would have done no differently in terms of the destruction of instruments and symbols of power, and acts redressing wrongs done to the population.

A Bolognese leaflet urged the distribution of wheat 'to individual families ... to all the categories of citizens, excluding no one'.[35] The salvaging of wheat from the Nazi raids – distribution of the stockpiles to the masses was considered the premise of these raids – represented above all the counterpart of the food contributions that the partisans asked for from the peasants and that, as we have seen, gave rise to manifestations of solidarity but difficulties in relations as well. In the second place, salvaging became the central motive of what was called 'the battle for wheat': with a degree of linguistic reserve on the part of the CLNAI, which felt it fit to add the adjective *vera* ('this is the *true* battle for wheat');[36] or without any such inhibitions engendered by the use Fascism had made of that formula, in other documents, as in the following leaflet: 'The Ferrarese peasants have won

---

the Command of the Asti Brigade, 11 July 1944 (IG, *BG*, 05772). The Ligurian edition of *L'Unità* repeatedly published news in this spirit.

31 Report by the Ugo Muccini Brigade, n.d. (IG, *Archivio PCI*).

32 Report on the 'Gruppo Salvatore', written by Salvatore Auria, n.d. but late 1943 (IG, *Archivio PCI*).

33 *Bollettino* No. 49, 28 August 1944, by the Command of the 52nd Fronte Proletario Brigade (IG, *BG*, 0652).

34 See Gorrieri, *La Repubblica di Montefiorino*, p. 119. Similar behaviour was reported in Teramano, Montieri in Tuscany and in the Belluno region: see Ponziani *Teramo 1943–1944*, pp. 157–70; 'Scontri di partigiani', a list of actions by the Spartaco Lavagnini detachment (IG, *BG*, 011670); and Tramontin, *Contadini e movimento partigiano*, p. 296, on the array of parish reports and diaries.

35 Leaflet 'Il grano a tutti i cittadini', seemingly from July 1944, signed 'Il Comitato di unità sindacale' (republished in in Arbizzani, *Manifesti, opuscoli, fogli volanti*, p. 245).

36 Appeal of 10 June 1944 to farmers and peasants (see Catalano, *Storia del CLNAI*, p. 189). The Fascist regime had initiated a 'battle for wheat' to make the country self-sufficient and not require imports.

the wheat battle.'[37] For that matter, in France too filching wheat from the Krauts and from Vichy is called 'la bataille du blé'.[38]

An ambiguous relationship existed between behaviour that bespoke social revolt and that denoting political sectarianism – not least because at times it was the party documents themselves that, as we have seen, called for social extremity, while trying duly to lead it back onto the straight and narrow of the official line.[39] At times social subversion found in sectarianism an elective channel of expression, and at other times it was, on the contrary, repressed by it; at still others it appeared to be compromised by it, in the sense that political sectarianism dried up the source of popular sympathy that only subversion could feed off. The political commissar Federici [Virginio Barbieri] was criticised for having set his men along the road 'towards a certain extremism both in word and action', which necessarily went hand in hand with 'a certain rigidity in dealing with the population'.[40] 'Sectarian and extremist conferences which have somewhat frightened the population' and had prompted the parish priest to escape were reported in the area of Zavattarello.[41] Anti-Catholic and anti-religious demonstrations, which 'place the Catholics on the same level as the enemies', were particularly scandalous forms of these attitudes. The first of the two documents mentioned above attributed this phenomenon to the isolation and narrowness in which the party had been compelled to live for twenty years, but also to the 'residue of the 1919 and 1920 mentality' – that is to say, to a longer wave than that of the life of the party.[42] The Modenese Christian Democrats were suspected of, and had to deny, circulating *Il Contadino*, one of those apocryphal Communist rags whose paternity was generally attributed to the Fascists or the Germans:[43]

---

37 Undated leaflet, signed by the Ferrara PCI federation (ISRR, A. VIII, f. 1). See also the chapter 'La battaglia del grano' in Flamigni and Marzocchi, *Resistenza in Romagna*, and L. Arbizzani, *Azione operaia, contadina, di massa*, Bari: De Donato, 1976, Chapter 1.1.

38 See 'Le Paysan Patriote. Organe des Comités paysans du Midi et du Sud-Ouest', editorial of the 30 August 1943 *Notre pain quotidien*.

39 Like, for example, the Modena and province edition of *L'Unità*, in its 4 November 1944 special edition, which, reporting on the destruction of conscription and taxation records in Soliera, attributed this action to 'the hatred against the Nazi-Fascist oppressor'.

40 See Dario's 22 May 1944 report on the Capelli formation (in the Apennines near Parma). Federici was a longstanding militant, who, arrested in around 1934, had to defend himself from the charge of having asked for a pardon, which he now claimed to have been merely an act of clemency (*Le Brigate Garibaldi*, vol. I, pp. 428–9).

41 The inspector attached to the Aliotta division, Albero, to the insurrectionary triumvirate for Lombardy, 24 February 1945 (*Le Brigate Garibaldi*, vol. III, p. 416).

42 See 'Rapporto', given by 'Sala Walter' to the Modena PCI federation, 6 October 1944 (IG, *Archivio PCI*).

43 These falsifications did, however, make it rather easier to issue 'a serious warning to all those ragbag so-called "left" groups, whose political irresponsibility ... serves Hitlerite propaganda and ultimately assumes the objective role of provocation':

the paper illustrated 'that ideological complex which Fascism has always attributed to Communism in matters of religion, the family, etc.'[44] The sectarianism
of the political commissar Davide – again in the province of Modena – combined with the presence of 'a politically backward mass, animated only by the
class instinct', is blamed for the loss of the populations' sympathy as well as the
total hostility of the clergy suffered by the Modena division, which had in fact
passed under Christian Democrat control. It is a sign of a curious inversion of
evaluative criteria that the Christian Democrat commander Claudio attributed
Davide's initial successes not to the 'class instinct' but to the 'vague anarchico-
rebellious instincts of the young mountain-dwellers'.[45]

Beneath the wrapping of national unity, Christian Democrat anti-
Communism began to build its foundations in these Resistance stances, which
aimed at vying with the Communists for hegemony over the popular masses,
including the workers, to whom a leaflet circulated in Tuscany offered 'the figure
and the idea of the worker of Nazareth' as a model.[46] The 'determined stance
against any kind of dictatorial extremism', the enjoinder not to fall 'into another
dictatorship', the explicit labelling of the Communists as 'red Fascists', to the
extent that all the red paper in Domodossola was requisitioned to prevent the
town council from printing its bulletin on it – these, and other similar ones (apart
from the excessive zeal of the confiscation of paper ordered by commander Di
Dio) were the recurrent formulae of the Christian Democrat press, directed
against both PCI policy and social subversion.[47] The Christian Democrat press

---

see the box 'Manifestini provocatori', *L'Unità*, Rome edition, 15 March 1944.

44 See the letters from 'the Communist leaders of the Modena formations' to the
Modena PCI federation, 2 December 1944, and that of 15 December from the insurrectionary triumvirate to the federation (*Le Brigate Garibaldi*, vol. III, pp. 20, 91). As an
example of the over-the-top Fascist falsifications, we might cite the leaflet distributed
in the name of the Florence PCI, which expressed the desire to 'destroy the family and
traditional culture and exterminate intellectuals, idealists and priests' (see 'L'ultima arma
dei fascisti' in *L'Unità*, Tuscany edition, 12 July 1944). The fact that the Fascists did print
leaflets and attribute them to anti-fascists is clear from the report by the minister of
labour, Spinelli, to Mussolini on 1 March 1945: in this case, it was a matter of propaganda
in favour of socialisation (see Deakin, *Brutal Friendship*, p. 748–9).

45 See the letter from the insurrectionary triumvirate to the federation of 15
December 1944, cited in the previous note, as well as that from the Modena federal
committee to the triumvirate, from 4 January 1945 (*Le Brigate Garibaldi*, vol. III,
pp. 194–201). On the fate of the Modena division, later returning to PCI control, see
Gorrieri, *La Repubblica di Montefiorino* (the comments on Davide appear on p. 283).

46 'Appello all'operaio', leaflet held in the ISRT, Raccolta volantini, DC Firenze
(clandestini 1943–1944).

47 See, among the many possible examples, *Libertà. Organo del movimento democratico cristiano*, 15 April 1944 (quoted in Bianchi, *I cattolici*, p. 264); 'Attenzione' in
Il Popolo, Northern edition, 20 August 1944; the 'Strictly personal report' from Ossola
to the DC central military committee (held in the De Gasperi archive and quoted in

was forever engaged in warning the workers against false masters and corrupting doctrines, and at the same time in defending its good name from those who considered it to be dedicated to extremism. An 'Address to the workers' published in *Il Popolo* concludes with the invitation not to read 'our words' hastily: 'Read them this evening in the peace of your poor house, while your wife frugally mends your jacket again and your children rest their heads on the table, overcome by sleep.'[48]

The fight for physical survival did bring the population together, but at the same time risked fomenting the hostility against the peasants typical of the famished cities. Resentment against peasants who 'are selling everything on the black market and raking in the money' is indicated by the reports on the censored correspondence.[49] If the memoirs of an Emilian landowner are to be credited, there were, on the other hand, peasants who said: 'From the point of view of food let's enjoy these last days of war.'[50]

The Fascists were the first to attempt 'more than ever to extol the workers at the expense of the peasants (see the fight against the black market etc.)',[51] and were eager to describe the peasants as 'selfish, starvers and black-marketeers',[52] thereby provoking, from a peasants' defence committee, the condemnation of 'Fascist scheming aimed not only at dividing the workers and peasants, but at setting them against each other.'[53] In retaliation against such scheming, the organ of the National Liberation Front of Piedmont wrote: 'Not the peasants, but the Germans and Fascists are the cause of the present economic hardship of the workers.'[54]

But the perfidy of the Fascists was not always necessary. As can be seen from many of the incitements to them to behave differently, the workers, both

---

Bianchi, *I cattolici*, p. 247); and Terracini's 30 September 1944 complaints to the CLNAI, protesting the squadrism of the kidnappings carried out by the Val Toce division commanded by Di Dio (see Catalano, *Storia del CLNAI*, pp. 276–7). One example of this type of argument appears in the leaflet 'Lavoratore, tu devi ragionari', held in the Archivio Osoppo in Udine.

48 *Il Popolo*, Northern edition, 25 November 1944.

49 See 'Esame della corrispondenza censurata al 30 giugno 1944' (ACS, SPD, CR, RSI, envelope 9, folder 3). The words cited appear in a letter from Milan.

50 Manuscript of G.M.'s memoirs,

51 As Alfredo wrote to the PCI leadership in December 1943 (*Le Brigate Garibaldi*, vol. I, p. 163). See also his (unsigned) 'Rapporto sugli scioperi di Torino' from late November 1943, which appears in the same volume.

52 See Flamigni and Marzocchi, *Resistenza in Romagna*, pp. 148–9.

53 See the order of the day passed at Scurzolengo (Asti) on 22 July 1944 (IG, BG, 05481). On the Fascist efforts to set workers and peasants against one another, see Legnani, *Aspetti*, p. 21; Ganapini, *Lotte operaie: Milano*, pp. 152, 177–8; and G. Bertolo, 'Introduzione a Le campagne e il movimento di resistenza', in *Operai e contadini*, p. 267.

54 'Gli scioperi torinesi e il loro significato', *La Riscossa italiana*, December 1943.

as a class and as city-dwellers, often, of their own initiative, showed hostility towards the peasants or at any rate indifference to their problems. In the emergency situation, the complex web of ancient peasant culture and factory culture running through the history of the workers' movement was, as it were, stripped of its flesh and taken back to the two extreme poles of invincible distrust among the oppressed, and solidarity. While the former prevailed in the country areas where the partisans were active, in the cities the latter often emerged. A Perugian Communist document complains:

> Most of our militants and the leadership itself still appear to have difficulty grasping the problems [of the peasants]. In some cases we have had to fight against the tendencies shown in some strata of the population against the peasants (connected with the present food supply problems and the dominion of the black market) and echoed among some party militants.[55]

'Sectarianism' and 'incapacity' regarding the peasants were reported from Terni as well.[56] Widespread hostility 'towards this important category of exploited workers of the land' was denounced in the province of Forlì, where *panzane* (tall stories/yarns) of this kind circulate: 'The peasants are selfish. The peasants are conservative and reactionary. The peasants have not the slightest importance in the revolutionary process for the progress of the human race.'[57] In the provinces of Cremona and Mantua there was widespread 'distrust of the peasant masses, their being branded as having become bourgeois and loafers'; and in particular in Mantua, with a singular loss of historical memory, the causes of *attesismo* were sought in the 'absolute prevalence of peasant masses who are slower and more hidebound than the workers'.[58] Still more offensive, in intention, is the opinion given of the Bassa Milanese where, it was said, twenty years of Fascism had 'practically *meridionilizzato* [southernised] the agricultural worker.'[59] By contrast, the Gappist Cicchetti was respectful of the difference of the peasants, to whom it was difficult to speak in the language of the workers.[60]

---

55 Report from the commissar of the Perugia federation, Comparozzi, 'Sulla situazione politica nella nostra provincia', 27 January 1944 (IG, *Archivio PCI*).

56 See 'Relazione sulla situazione politica e militare della nostra provincia', Terni, 1 February 1944 (IG, *Archivio PCI*).

57 See the letter from the 'federal political secretariat' of the Forlì PCI to 'the committees in the countryside, to all our responsible officials', undated but concerning the 25–29 March 1944 strike (cited in Flamigni and Marzocchi, *Resistenza in Romagna*, pp. 290–1).

58 See 'Relazione del lavoro militare di Cremona provincia e Mantova', 3 November 1944, signed 'Mario' (IG, *BG*, 011248) and 'Relazione su Mantova', undated but late 1943, in *Le Brigate Garibaldi*, vol. I, p. 195.

59 Report of 10 November 1943, quoted in Ragionieri, *Il partito comunista*, p. 342.

60 See Cicchetti, *Il campo giusto*, p. 46.

The presence in the factories of workers who had not yet altogether severed their peasant roots could produce further incomprehension and distrust. In Turin the commuters, who had fewer food difficulties than those living in the cities, were considered to be taking too much time in becoming proletarianised.[61] In Varese the failure of the November 1943 strikes was attributed to the 'half peasant' workers who 'do not lack the essentials'.[62] In Bergamo it was deemed that the presence of a 'working-class workforce coming from the country and living in the country', though creating 'favourable objective conditions' for mutual understanding, in fact does not succeed in eliminating 'the prejudices of the mass of urban workers: the peasants sell themselves at a low price and eat white bread; they are the servants of the *padroni*'.[63]

These were the consequences of a political culture that, though proclaiming the unity of workers and peasants, was incapable of grasping 'the element of mutual enrichment which rural diversity introduces into the relationship with the worker's movement [and which] takes unity for uniformity'.[64] Appearing indiscriminately in the documents are the expressions 'workers who live in the country' and 'peasants who work in factories'; and these workers from the country often appear to be most in danger of dismissal.[65]

This 'war between the poor' might help explain the subsequent success of Christian Democracy in the country areas,[66] despite the great post-war peasant struggles. A 'Galileo' worker has recently recalled the decline suffered by the company, 'where there was a less mature working class ... because a huge number of workers from the country areas had been admitted during the period of the war'.[67]

Among the instances of solidarity that helped counterbalance this phenomenon was that created between the evacuees from the towns and the country-dwellers.[68] In these cases the counterbalance was only partial because,

61 Anonymous note of 17 November 1943 (IG, *Archivio PCI*).

62 See 'Rapporto del caposettore', undated. Another report, from 27 September 1944, signed 'Tommaso', comments that 'the greater part of the workers – including our own comrades – are tied to the countryside and thus do not feel a compelling need for wage increases and thus taking action over such demands'.

63 See 'Rapporto sul lavoro di Partito in Bergamo', unsigned, 29 December 1943 (*Le Brigate Garibaldi*, vol I, p. 192).

64 As Portelli puts it in *Biografia di una città*, p. 68.

65 'We Communists ... must absolutely oppose these manoeuvres' – see the record of a 'Riunione dei rappresentanti di Partito' ('Meeting of Party representatives'), in a Padua workshop, 18 March 1945 (IG, *Archivio PCI*; reproduced in part in *Le Brigate Garibaldi*, vol. III, pp. 490–4).

66 The expression, and the subsequent consideration on it, appear in Ballone, *Una sezione, un paese*, p. 441.

67 Testimony of Renato Castaldi, in Contini, *Memoria e storia*, p. 119.

68 See on this Bertolo, 'Introduzione a Le campagne e il movimento di resistenza',

for those compelled to remain in the towns, the evacuees were likened to the better-fed and less bombed country folk. A borderline case was Terni, with the 'exodus of an entire city' destroyed by the bombings and the 'reduction to the state of nature' of its inhabitants who had fled into the country areas.[69] City-dwellers' distrust found an incentive in the tendency of the agricultural areas to withdraw into themselves, fomenting a sort of provincial autarky with a reversion to different forms of bartering. These autarkies, which were sometimes encouraged by the partisan commands, would in their turn have after-effects in the immediate post-war period.[70]

One would nevertheless be mistaken to think that the hostility to and distrust of the peasants present in some sectors of the working class means that in the country areas during the Resistance there were not, as various studies have highlighted, autonomous forms of class struggle, in some cases linked to the presence of partisan bands and to the individuals of peasant origin serving in them. Certainly, the linear development from the struggle against the stockpiles to that against the landowners and the Germans – a rural version of the superimposition of the three figures of the enemy: the *padrone*, the Fascist, the German – did not follow the model sketched by *L'Unità* in an article in which, in typical Communist style, objectives and desires are described as a reality that is already coming about:

---

pp. 271, 300–03; Ardigò, ed., *Società civile e insorgenza partigiana*, p. 21; Portelli, *Biografia di una città*, p. 266.

69 Portelli, 'Assolutamente niente', pp. 135–44.

70 Among the Resistance's proceedings in this sense, we can include the Valle Maira CLN's ban on exporting essential goods (15 July) as well as that made by the popular junta of Castiglione Falletto (7 September 1944) (IG, *BG*, 04534 and 05502); the 'wine blockade' imposed on the Valsesia-Ossola-Cusio-Verbano region by the political commissar of the Creola Battalion of the 1st Garibaldi Division (see the letter from the Command of the Silvio Loss Brigade, 24 November 1944, IG, *BG*, 07083); and the instruction that 'Nothing can leave the area in which it is produced', justified with the argument that city-dwellers would be better disposed to rise up if they were going hungry ('Direttiva di massima e particolari sul servizio di intendenza e sul rifornimento alle formazioni di montagna', from the political commissar of the 3rd operations zone of the Friulian plain, Ario – *Le Brigate Garibaldi*, vol II, pp. 640–44). In terms of the aftermath of Liberation, we can note the firm position taken by the Arezzo CLN, backed by the prefect (a discharged *Bersaglieri* colonel, nominated by the AMG) against exports of food-goods from the province, on 23 October and 7 November 1944; a contemporary debate on sending two butchers beyond the borders of the province to procure meat (ISRT, envelope 7, folder 1, Verbali del CLN di Arezzo); the 22 May 1945 order by the Command of the Pisacane Brigade forbidding people exporting timber out of Belluno province (Bernardo, *Il momento buono*, document 24). On the issue as a whole, and in particular on its local manifestations in the final months of the RSI, as the central government declined, see Legnani, *Aspetti*, p. 46.

The struggle of the urban masses, guided and spurred by the working class is also making its contribution to the very conditions of this struggle which, having begun as a defence against the Fascist agents of the stockpiles and against the Fascist plunderers of human flesh, is now transformed into an attack against all the self-styled Fascist authorities of the country areas.[71]

The time taken for Communism to penetrate the country areas was indeed insistently denounced in party documents from Emilia, the Marche, Veneto and Lombardy.[72] This raises the question of how much the PCI's rootedness in agricultural areas like that of Emilia was due to Resistance mobilisation and how much to its capacity to gather the socialist legacy, both maximalist and reformist, along multiple roads. The imperfect and tardy encounter between the Resistance and the peasant world, made still more so by the RSI call-up, is a more general phenomenon.[73] It has been justly written that 'Partisan action to fight Fascism in the country areas had the laborious task of finding a politico-social meaning and of reconciling a series of conflicting interests, as well as procuring the aid and provisions indispensable for military activity in the plain and for the sustenance of all the combatants.'[74]

The difficulties are signalled by the uncertain nature of the concrete political proposals addressed to the country areas:[75] to the 'silent proletarians of the fields', as the Communist press put it at times, or to the 'soul of the dear and hard-working people of the fields', to use an expression dear to the Christian Democrats.[76]

71 'Sulla via dell'insurrezione si rafforza l'unità fra il popolo delle cino e il popolo delle campagne' in the (duplicated) July 1944 'abridged edition published by the Mantua Communist Federation'. See the (printed) Northern edition of 10 July.

72 See, for example, Banfi's 'Rapporto al Centro del Partito', from Emilia, of 16 December 1943 (IG, Archivio PCI, cited in Ragionieri, Il partito comunista, p. 343; Ragionieri writes, on p. 373, that matters later improved, which is certainly true, at least in the case of Emilia); Dario's report on the Marches, n.d. but late spring 1944 (?) (IG, Archivio PCI); 'Rapporto del membro del triumvirato insurrezionale del Veneto, Oreste, sulla Federazione di Venezia', 7 March 1945 (Le Brigate Garibaldi, vol III, p. 452), and a document sent by the Veneto insurrectionary triumvirate on 10 March 'A tutti I comitati federali' (IG, Archivio PCI); and the 14 April 1945 and the 4 March meetings in the eastern sector of Milan (IG, Archivio PCI). See also the self-critical article 'Lotte parziali e insurrezione nazionali', which appeared in the 23 March 1944 Northern edition of L'Unità (cited in Bertolo, 'Introduzione a Le campagne e il movimento di resistenza' pp. 271–2).

73 See Bertolo, 'Introduzione a Le campagne e il movimento di resistenza', esp. p. 259, and Ventura, La società rurale veneta, esp. pp. 66–7.

74 Poma and Perona, La Resistenza nel Biellese, p. 186.

75 Legnani brought attention to this in Aspetti and Politica e amministrazione nelle repubbliche partigiane.

76 Bertolo, 'Introduzione a Le campagne e il movimento di resistenza', p. 261; and the document quoted in Legnani, Aspetti, p. 41.

But it was the Action Party press that treated the agrarian problems most thoroughly and competently.[77]

The demands regarding farmhands' wages and agrarian agreements found support in the memory of 1919–21, which was nevertheless revived in the landowners as well.[78] The *consigli di cascina* (farm councils), born on the wave of the Resistance, were to be violently opposed by the landowners.[79] Above all, though, it is the manifestations of perilous solidarity with and assistance given to fleeing soldiers, Jews, partisans, Allied prisoners, deserters and draft-dodgers that give a particular tone to the Resistance as it was experienced in the country areas. In this sense, the Resistance becomes once again a broader category than that of class struggle.

5. CLASS STRUGGLE AND ARMED STRUGGLE

> There is ... in the Garibaldini the tendency to consider themselves the leaders of the whole political and trade union movement. Comrades and non comrades have to be taught that the partisans have the duty to support the workers' struggles, but that these struggles are promoted and directed by the appropriate organisms: the Party organisation and the Agitation Committee. The workers need solidarity, not supervision.[1]

> Turin was liberated by the SAPs and the workers. When the partisans arrived, Turin was already free ... But Turin practically was liberated by them, the workers.[2]

---

77 On all this, see M. Rossi-Doria, *Prospettive della agricoltura italiana* (Rome: Partito d'azione, 1945, published as No. 1 of the 'Quaderni agrari'). On this point, see 'La questione agraria: dall'efficientismo tecnocratico al meridionalismo rivoluzionario', Chapter 7 of De Luna, *Storia del Partito d'Azione*, pp. 238–68.

78 See, for example *Terra e lavoro. Organo del comitato provinciale dei contadini* (Romagna), 1 November 1944 (quoted in Casali, *Il movimento di liberazione a Ravenna*, p. 62). According to *La Lotta*, organ of the Bologna PCI federation, in its 11 March 1945 editorial 'Seminare', the landowners hoped that the Allies would arrive soon, and even that a new squadrism would arise to defend them against the 'accursed' revived Federterra agricultural labourers' union.

79 See, on this, G. Crainz, 'I braccianti padani', in G. Chianese, G. Crainz, M. Da Vela and G. Gribaudi, *Italia 1945–1950. Conflitti e trasformazioni sociali*, Milan: Franco Angeli, 1985, pp. 173–326; *Il '48. Le lotte dei lavoratori cremonesi della terra negli anni 1946–1953*, Cremona: Lega di cultura di Piadena, 1976.

1 'Il responsabile del triumvirato insurrezionale del Piemonte, Alfredo, alla Direzione del PCI per l'Italia occupata' (*Le Brigate Garibaldi*, vol. III, p. 69).

2 Testimonies of Nelia Benissone Costa and Teresa Cirio (Bruzzone and Farina, eds, *La Resistenza taciuta*, pp. 55, 89). For a factual verification of this, see Vaccarino, Gobetti and Gobbi, *L'insurrezione di Torino*, pp. 248, 261. Teresa Cirio lamented that 'in the [version of events told in] schools the solely military aspect has come through too strongly' (p. 86).

Our combatants have to view the agitations of the working class with sympathy, in that they too are directed at the same goal of liberation. *The strikes must therefore have the active support of our formations.*[3]

The partisan struggle is welded with that of the workers and peasants to drive out the Germans and exterminate the Fascists.[4]

I will respond with obedience to an order of the Party. But don't count on my commitment at the zone command. I remain a Garibaldino in the mountains.[5]

We [Garibaldini] have taken good care not to take the place of the workers' commission.[6]

Three declarations of workers' and party pride, one contemporary, the others consolidated in memory; an incitement of the unitary military organ; a Communist appeal that takes the customary form of a statement tallying more with ideology than with the facts; a brusque preference for the war in the mountains; an insistence on respect for reciprocal autonomy. These quotations show how complex the relationship between the factory struggle (in town) and the armed struggle (in the mountains) was, with viscous effects in the post-war period too. It has in fact been remarked that while the 'country partisans', of the mountains, felt misunderstood and betrayed, the 'partigiani di città' would prove to be better inserted in both the factory and the parties.[7] Pietro Secchia has told of answers, which were mostly just common sense, given to Yugoslav representatives critical of the fact that the workers had not been urged to go over in mass to the partisan formations.[8] The impossibility of following the Yugoslav example (for that matter, the Slovene Urban recognised that Italian originality lay precisely in the combination of mass struggle and armed struggle),[9] and alongside this the need to avoid fighting two parallel wars,[10] in other words, to get around a situation

3 'Direttive per la lotta armata', February 1944, by the Military Command for Upper Italy (*Atti CVL*, p. 560). Parri's hand in composing these directives is clear from the text.

4 *Il Combattente* (Tuscany), February–March 1944.

5 Letter from Milo, Commander of the Nanetti Division, to the Zone Command Commissar De Luca (Giuseppe Landi), 20 March 1945 (*Le Brigate Garibaldi*, vol. III, p. 513). On this episode, see Bernardo, *Il momento buono*, pp. 154–5.

6 'Relazione del Comando della 3a divisione Piemonte alla Delegazione per il Piemonte', send to the Piedmont Delegation and the Military Commands, 15 September 1944 (*Le Brigate Garibaldi*, vol. II, p. 340).

7 L. Lanzardo, 'Fonti orali e storia della classe operaia: indagini sulla coscienza di classe alla Fiat', *Rivista di storia contemporanea*, X, 1981, pp. 255–81.

8 In a conversation between Secchia and the present author.

9 See the 23 March 1944 cited in Ragionieri, *Il partito comunista*, p. 355.

10 'Up to February [prior to the support given to the March 1944 strikes] the war that we were waging was almost a parallel one', Giulio Nicoletta recently recalled. He was Commander of the autonomous S. Devitis Division (see ANED, *Gli scioperi del marzo 1944*, p. 56).

in which, as was noted at the time, 'the union sector is going its own way, with scant ties with the military movement',[11] created problems for which there was no pat solution. The difficult connection between the struggle in the factory and the armed struggle that was created at the time is well expressed in the verses of Dante Bartolini, a proletarian poet from Terni, about an imaginary episode:

> La fabbrica d'armi di Terni
> andammo migliaia di operai
> fu rotto il cancello
> spalancato
> prendemmo le armi
> una parte
> poi si partì per la montagna.[12]

> [To the arms factory of Terni
> Thousands of workers we went
> The gate was broken
> Flung open
> Some of the arms
> We made off with
> Then off to the mountains we went.]

In a quite different situation, with the Red Army beating at the gates, a clear proclamation was made: 'Our insurrection, our revolution is above all an affair regarding us workers. We know why we're fighting. We know why we're dying. Not only for the liberty of the Patria, but also for our social liberation.'[13]

The Communists had to deal not merely with the organisational problem of how to distribute the *quadri* (leaders) and the more expert militants between the factories and the mountains. It might even happen that 'comrades' initiatives in all the mass organisational fields created in the eyes of the party supporters the impression that everything and everyone was gravitating around the

---

11 According to Inverni (V. Foa) *I partiti*, p. 22. For critical remarks on the disjuncture between strikes and military activity, also see the report by Sandrelli – the official responsible for military work in Piedmont – to the PCI leadership, 26 December 1943 (*Le Brigate Garibaldi*, vol. I, pp. 183–8) and the article 'Dallo sciopero generale all'insurrezione nazionale' in *Il Combattente* (Tuscany) 17 April 1944. See also *Operai*.

12 Portelli, *Biografia di una città*, pp. 261–2. According to Portelli, Bartolini 'gave life to a metaphor'.

13 Proclamation of the Czech National Council, 4–5 May 1945, cited in Etnasi, *La Resistenza in Europa*, vol. I, p. 139.

partisan movement'[14] – an overstatement that redounded more to the glory of the partisan movement than of the party.

Oscillating and conflicting worries can be recorded in the Communist Party. At times one seems to be confronting reluctance to enter the armed bands: How many Communists, and especially *quadri* enlisted in the fighting formations?, *L'Unità* was early to ask itself;[15] and a report from Biella related that in order to induce the 'exhausted comrades' to enter the formations 'we had to resort to the question of discipline'.[16] At times, instead, fear is expressed that military commitment would overwhelm every other activity (as for example in the province of Vicenza),[17] causing, as we have seen, a sort of jealousy in those detailed for political work.[18]

The 'Direttive di lavoro' ('Work directives') of 21 October stated that no fewer than 15 percent of the party members were to join the ranks of the partisans.[19] Evident in the first phase in fact is the 'politically and militarily urgent and necessary' commitment to send workers and Communists into the bands, which had often formed spontaneously.[20] In this context 'Workers and Communists' are not synonymous but constitute a hendiadys that expresses both faith in the objectivity of class and faith in the subjectivity of politics. In a document from the centre, slightly earlier than the one just quoted, the assertion that the best forces of the party were to join the formations of partisans and snipers is in fact followed by another: 'The Communists must not leave for the front on their own; they must know how to mobilise the most energetic and combative of the workers, above all of the younger ones.'[21]

---

14 Report by Secondo Saracco on the Valle Sessera, 19 March 1945 (quoted in Dellavalle, *Operai*, p. 232).

15 Northern edition, 25 November 1943: article 'Tutto per il fronte' in the section 'Vita di Partito'. A similar concern appeared in the same section of the Rome edition, 20 December 1943, under the title 'Azione partigiana'.

16 Undated, unsigned report (late 1943?) (IG, *Archivio PCI*).

17 See 'Rapporto trimestrale agosto-ottobre' (August-October 1943) (IG, *Archivio PCI*).

18 See, for example, 'Nota informativa sull'agitazione degli operai torinesi', signed Alfio, 27 November 1943, which explains: 'The ranks of the leadership have been impoverished, with the best comrades sent away from Turin and the rest given military tasks' (IG, *Archivio PCI*).

19 *Le Brigate Garibaldi*, vol. I, p. 110

20 On the implementation of this directive, see Lazagna, *Ponte rotto*, p. 22. See the letter from Alfredo to Sandrelli, the official responsible for military work in Piedmont, 10 November 1943. The following day, Sandrelli wrote to the political commissars that the bands 'had to be continuously reinforced with those among our ranks with adequate preparation' (*Le Brigate Garibaldi*, vol. I, pp. 125-9).

21 See the circular 'A tutti gli attivisti del Partito', which reached Turin on 4 November 1943 (IG, *Archivio PCI*).

A crucial point was armed support of strikes, requested for example by the Milanese Communist organisation in the light of their experience of the strike of mid-December 1943.[22] Again in Milan, during the March 1944 strikes, the workers had high hopes of armed intervention but these hopes were dashed because of the number of Gappists who were arrested.[23] In Turin as well the interventions were limited.[24] This armed backing of the strikes, which failed to be forthcoming or was limited, were a sort of equivalent of the scant commitment of the city's organisms to the mountain war so often bemoaned by the partisans.

The March 1944 strikes, however, marked a turning-point in the relationship between struggle in the factory and armed struggle, in the sense that the Communists would set greater store by the latter.[25] Essentially, it was a question of re-stipulating the 15 percent norm mentioned above. From Modena 'in very few weeks dozens of comrades including a great many *quadri* and three members of the federal committee itself, were invited into the mountains'.[26] The Ligurian CLN, anticipating inevitable dismissals, proposed that the industrialists pay several months' advance wages and that the dismissed workers join the partisans, a prospect made impracticable by the German deportation of 16 June 1944. On the other hand, the San Giorgio workers appeared to have little desire to abandon the factory.[27]

Many documents indicate the problematic nature of the triumphalist hendiadys 'with strikes and guerrilla warfare towards the decisive battle'.[28] At a meeting of the secretariat of the 2nd Milan sector, held on 15 December 1944, voices opting for internal strikes in which 'the worker doesn't abandon his machine' vie with voices demanding that 'the mass be given in short the trust of the street'.[29]

Indeed, as the final showdown approached, military presence in the factories become more frequent, leading to stances that were reproved as being extremist. On 3 March 1945 at Borletti, Garibaldini of the 170th brigade not only

---

22 See Ganapini, *Lotte operaie: Milano*, p. 170, and the documents cited therein.

23 Ganapini, *Lotte operaie: Milano*, pp. 183–5.

24 See Dellavalle, *Lotte operaie: Torino*, p. 250.

25 See Ganapini, *Lotte operaie: Milano*, pp. 187–8; Dellavalle, *Lotte operaie: Torino*, p. 250; De Luna, *Lotte operaie e Resistenza*, p. 528.

26 See the letter from 'Cri', official responsible for the insurrectionary triumvirate for Emilia-Romagna, to the General Command, 14 July 1944 (*Le Brigate Garibaldi*, vol. II, p. 125). For Milan, see the unsigned May 1944 report simply entitled 'Relazione' (IG, BG, 011011).

27 Gibelli, *Genova operaia*, pp. 211–12, 229–37. See *Resistenza e ricostruzione in Liguria*, pp. 112–37 (from 3 October to 3 November 1944).

28 This being the title covering the whole front page of *L'Unità*, Northern edition, 9 April 1945.

29 'Informazioni da Milano', 15 December 1944 (IG, *Archivio PCI*).

held an assembly, not only made those present give one another the clenched fist salute but 'one Garibaldino forced some hesitant individuals to do it at gunpoint. Finally, they sent a greeting to Stalin and the USSR, and not to the Allies'.[30] In Legnano on 24 March the Garibaldini 'to stir the *attesiste* [fence-sitting] masses' threw bombs in one plant.[31] On 9 April at the Pavan works, fear of a repetition of this action, which occurred in a Milan factory, prompted the Gruppi della Difesa della Donna (Groups for the Defence of Women) to organise a stoppage of a few hours, though it had no 'male backing'.[32] In Milan it was recorded with satisfaction that 'the masses are electrified because [they feel] the presence of the Garibaldini'.[33] In Turin the April 18th strike, which had armed protection, would then be considered 'pre-insurrectional' – and legitimately so.[34]

The GAPs (Gruppi d'azione patriottica) and the SAPs (Squadre d'azione patriottica) were assigned the specific task of conducting the armed struggle in the cities. The former were the more carefully picked,[35] better trained and committed to isolated actions, though having also the ambitious task of 'organising and directing the great masses of the workers of the plants towards insurrectional combat'.[36] We shall return later to several particular features assumed by urban violence as practised by the GAPS, which never consisted of more than a few dozen people living in total clandestinity. This helps explain why in some cases a clear preference was manifested to take to the mountains rather than join the GAPs.[37] The composition of the GAPS remained essentially Communist, even if intakes from other parties or of unaffiliated people were not excluded[38] – (in Turin two alleged Liberal Gappists were shot).[39]

---

30 'Informazioni da Milano', 14 April 1945 (*Le Brigate Garibaldi*, vol. III, p. 620).

31 'Informazioni da Milano', 22 April 1945 (*Le Brigate Garibaldi*, vol. III, p. 668).

32 'Informazioni da Milano', 22 April 1945 (*Le Brigate Garibaldi*, vol. III, p. 669).

33 'Informazioni da Milano', 22 April 1945 (*Le Brigate Garibaldi*, vol. III, p. 674). See also Informazioni da Milano', 14 April 1945 (*Le Brigate Garibaldi*, vol. III, p. 620).

34 See Vaccarino, Gobetti and Gobbi, *L'insurrezione di Torino*, p. 192.

35 According to a biography of GAP cadre in Emilia-Romagna, dated 28 December 1944, we find that Pietro was a mechanic who had joined the PCI in 1928 and spent three years in prison; Luigi was a bricklayer who emigrated to Paris in 1927, joined the PCI in 1929, was wounded at Guadalajara, went to the USSR, was arrested in France and Belgium and then held at Ventotene; Jacopo was a former medical officer who had joined the PNF in 1932 (though not assuming any rank) and then the PCI in 1941 (IG, BG, Emilia-Romagna, G.IV.2.10).

36 'Relazione' (IG, BG, 011011).

37 See, for example, an anonymous report on Valsesia-Valdossola, 4 March 1944 (IG, BG, 08631).

38 See 'Circolare n. 19', 19 July 1944, from the Command of the 28th Garibaldi Brigade GAP Mario Gordini (Romagna) (IG, BG, 02209–12).

39 See the record of the meeting of the Piazza di Torino Command, between late March and early April 1945, and the SAP document giving a quite different explanation of the episode (Vaccarino, Gobetti and Gobbi, *L'insurrezione di Torino*, pp. 143–5).

The SAPs were organisms recruited from a wider spectrum and for largely defensive purposes. Moreover, the different ways in which their nature and function were interpreted present some interesting features. Though less marked than with the GAPS, there was a Communist presence in the SAPs, at least as regards their intentions, even if it had to be solicited by the leaders: 'Most of the elements belonging to the SAPs joined the squads out of party discipline and not out of a voluntary wish to fight'.[40] Again in Turin, this definition which might be called canonical is given: 'The SAPS are patriotic mass organisations organised by the PC; they are not PC organisations but supported and organised by it and they depend on the CLN, by whom they are recognised'.[41]

But a 'mobilisation order' issued by the federation of the Ravenna PCI in October 1944, when the Allies were at the gates, baldly stated that the SAPS were an 'armed organisation of workers and peasants' and that it was necessary to 'sapizzare' the whole party.[42] The SAP as a vehicle of alliance between workers and peasants is also mentioned by a Piedmontese document,[43] while, again in Turin, the fusion that had occurred between the Communist and Socialist SAPs was hailed as 'the material and spiritual reinforcement of the proletarian united front'.[44]

Indeed, in the province of Ravenna, out of more than seven thousand (very poorly armed) members, the great majority were Communists; but there were also 138 Republicans (one of whom declined the post of commander), 19 Actionists and 15 Christian Socialists.[45] And an Emilian document says: 'There are no longer any SAPs organised from elements from other parties, except for a few in the *bassa* (lowland), in the same old places',[46] which could include Ravenna itself. But rather than mentioning inevitably imprecise figures, it should be noted that in many areas the SAPs came to assume the reductive

---

40 'Rapporto sul lavoro militare', by the Turin SAP Command, 1 September 1944 (IG, *BG*, 06048).

41 As explained on 16 December 1944 by the 'comrades responsible' to Vice-Commander Pietro and the 'comrades responsible for the 2nd Piedmont Division', who had shown themselves not to be 'clear' on this. On 15 January 1945 the Command of the Turin SAP Division reproached the Command of the 4th Zone Brigade for having made the SAP, 'a true and proper Party organisation' (*Le Brigate Garibaldi*, vol. III, pp. 98–102, 234–7).

42 Casali, *Il movimento di liberazione a Ravenna*, vol. I, pp. 104–5.

43 See the letter from the Command of the Piedmont SAP Division to the Command of the Gardoncini Battista Brigade (undated – January 1945?) (IG, *BG*, 06045).

44 See the order of the day of the 2nd Sector SAP Military Command, 30 March 1945 (in Vaccarino, Gobetti and Gobbi, *L'insurrezione di Torino*, p. 164).

45 These figures appear in Casali, *Il movimento di liberazione a Ravenna*, vol. II, p. 253. 'Christian Socialists' here is probably meant to mean Christian Democrats.

46 'Informazioni dall'Emilia', November 1944 (*Le Brigate Garibaldi*, vol. II, p. 668).

role of organising, often only on paper,[47] all those who intended in one way or another to be in on the scene, with a view to the epilogue. This accounts for the distinction between defence units mentioned in a Turin document, according to which the Communists in the SAPs were only a minority, 'while the rest are either sympathisers or vague patriots', and the commander more often than not an ex-army officer. This document also testifies to the peculiar kind of relationship that the SAPs succeeded in establishing with the industrialists: not only to get money out of them, but also to get taken on as 'surveillance staff, firefighters, guards'[48] – a collaboration which was compromising for the SAPs and risky, initially, for the industrialists.

The interweaving between the various forms of *sinistrismo* and the generational differences, to which I have already drawn attention, produced widely divergent ways of viewing the armed struggle too. It is the older comrades who, throughout the twenty-month span of the struggle, and more or less in all the zones, were reported to be 'for the most part faint-hearted', prey to a 'mood of passive resistance and negative *attesismo*'. These are 'old comrades coming from the Livorno split' [January 1921 split of the PSI into the PCI], men 'who refuse to join the bands', or who 'are scared stiff of employing the young', who are 'sectarian, fearful', and whose *attesismo* is 'il punto nero' ('the real blot').[49] Speaking of an encounter with an old *bordighista* in Acqui, shortly after 8 September 1943, Giovanni Pesce recounted: '*I* want to act. *He* ladles out a fine lesson on the red army'.[50]

The older men also felt the tradition of the party of *quadri*, according to which it was indispensable 'to form the organisation, to educate the *quadri*, then act'.[51] Instead,

---

47 'Rapporto del membro del triumvirato insurrezionale del Veneto, Oreste, sulla federazione di Venezia', 7 March 1945, spoke of 350 SAP members who were 'largely paper members, in that they lack weaponry', while the other parties gave 'inflated figures' (stir them up in order to control them!). In the same report, the Venetian GAP were termed 'almost nonexistent' (*Le Brigate* Garibaldi, vol. III, pp. 449–53).

48 Rapporto sul lavoro militare', by the Turin SAP Command, 1 September 1944 (IG, *BG*, 06048).

49 See 'Rapporto sul lavoro di Partito in Bergamo', 29 December 1943 (*Le Brigate Garibaldi*, vol. I, p. 193); 'Relazione sulla situazione politica della nostra provincia', Perugia, 27 January 1944 (IG, *Archivio PCI*); 'L' organizzazione di Terni e il lavoro militare', 8 February 1944 (*Le Brigate Garibaldi*, vol. I, pp. 255–6); the report by the Yugoslav Urban, 23 March 1944 (cited in Ragionieri, *Il partito comunista*, p. 355); 'Informazione da Udine', December 1944 (*Le Brigate Garibaldi*, vol. III, pp. 166–9); 'Rapporto sulla federazione di Venezia', 7 March 1945, by Oreste, a member of the Veneto insurrectionary triumvirate (*Le Brigate Garibaldi*, vol. III, pp. 449–53).

50 Pesce, *Senza tregua*, p. 23.

51 Such was the gist of the critique Pietro (Antonio Roasio) levelled against G. (Giuseppe Gaddi) in an undated note (but possible to attribute to December 1943) on the

Attraverso valli e monti
eroici avanzano i partigiani
per scacciare l'invasore
all'istante e non domani.

[Through the valleys and the mountains
the partisans advance heroic
to drive out the invader
instantly, not tomorrow.][52]

An outraged Communist reports the presence in the CLN of Cremona, one of the most *attesista* of the provinces, together with Mantua, and both in the great tradition of the labourers' struggle,[53] of 'a phenomenon contrary to what usually occurs in these committees. The representative of *Italia Libera* is for action, while our representative is a fire-fighter, because he says we're not yet ready for the offensive.'[54]

A few months later another Cremonese Communist leader recounted that he had spurred his men to act 'not only from the military point of view but also from the political point of view; in fact our party is revolutionary because it conceives action as being a means of winning and of keeping oneself healthy'.[55] And this, furthermore, paved the way for combative activism, which, as we shall see, in its turn came in for criticism.

No particular reasons are given for the many instances of reluctance to engage fully in the armed struggle. Here and there one comes across attitudes resembling those of vague *attesismo* – 'things will run their course in any case without our participation'[56] – or mirroring those of the *attesisti* of the right, who were awaiting the arrival of the Anglo-Americans; while those of the left put their trust in the victories of the Red Army.[57] In the organisation of the

---

Belluno federation (*Le Brigate Garibaldi*, vol. I, p. 202).

52 An adaptation, made by the Natisone Division, of the Soviet song *Les Partisans* (see Padoan [Vanni], *Abbiamo lottato insieme*, p. 178)

53 See the Party report of 20 June 1944 (cited in *Le Brigate Garibaldi*, vol. II, p. 30, note 2); the news report from the Command of the Lower Po Division to the Lombardy Delegation, 5 October 1944 (*Le Brigate Garibaldi*, vol. II, pp. 401–3); and 'Rapporto informativo n. 2' to the Lombardy Delegation from the Lower Po SAP Brigade Group Command, 27 October 1944 (*Le Brigate Garibaldi*, vol. II, pp. 496–502). In this last document, the wait-and-see attitude is attributed to the role of the fear of reprisals in alienating peasants.

54 Handwritten document from December 1943 (IG, *Archivio PCI*).

55 Report by Luciano, 11 July 1944, 'Il lavoro sportivo provinciale' (IG, *BG*, 011211).

56 See the circular by the PCI federation of 'P.' (Padua?), undated but after the Salerno Turn (IG, *Archivio PCI*).

57 See, for example, Dellavalle, *Operai*, p. 263 (concerning February 1945).

Milan party, 'incomprehension' and 'underestimation' of the job being done by the military were reported and some comrades even thought that 'going into the mountains is something of a punishment'.[58]

The risk also appeared that relations with the partisan commanders were being compromised by 'party comrades' behaving like 'the most tenacious saboteurs of the actions of the Garibaldini', with the reverse effect that, 'to the extent that military activity continues to be conducted independently of mass agitation, the factors expounded above will come to affect and diminish the fighting spirit of the Garibaldini'.[59] Parallel with this, another document states that the military comrades 'must support the demonstrations of the masses, and not impose them with methods that upset their feelings ... and vice versa, naturally'.[60]

The important thing was to repeat that the reactionary classes 'fear the armed populace more than the Germans and Fascists' – that is how *L'Unità* put it, and it seemed almost to be echoing the polemic against 'better Hitler in Paris than the Popular Front in power'.[61] Vittorio Foa attributed to the *attesisti* conservatives the capacity to understand, in fact, that 'a complete engagement of the masses, and one coming at the present time, even if it be for the purpose of the anti-German war ... would liberate new energies, the developments of which would be hard to foresee, but without doubt contrary to the present interests of order and property'.[62]

Along similar lines, *Bandiera Rossa*, the newspaper of the 'Movimento Comunista d'Italia' answered those who were saying our best comrades are dying and at our expense the bourgeoisie is giving itself an anti-Fascist facelift, that the calculation of the bourgeoisie 'seems right but isn't!', because the bourgeoisie cannot halt our destiny and will pay dearly for every dead comrade.[63] Some PCI documents express concern that the bleeding to death of the 'healthy Communist forces' was viewed with approval in order to 'reduce them and wear them out' and render them 'innocuous' for the 'opportune moment'.[64]

Traces of what was earlier called 'red hyper-belligerence', with mixed shades

---

58 See the report 'Il lavoro militare in Piemonte, Liguria e Lombardia', 7 May 1944, and 'Rapporto di attività del mese di maggio', sent from the Lombardy Delegation to the General Command, 10 June 1944 (IG, *Archivio PCI*; and *Le Brigate Garibaldi*, vol. II, pp. 23–7).

59 See the report from the Commander of the Milan SAP Brigade Group, Franco, 'Il lavoro militare al 30 novembre 1944'. The sharp critique concerns events in the Valle dell'Olona (*Le Brigate Garibaldi*, vol. II, p. 675).

60 'Informazioni da Milano', 22 April 1945 (*Le Brigate Garibaldi*, vol. II, p. 668).

61 See 'Attesismo: un'insidia da sventare' in the 31 October 1943 Northern edition.

62 Inverni (V. Foa), *I partiti*, p. 24.

63 'Azione', *Bandiera Rossa*, 5 January 1944.

64 'Relazione del comandante della brigata d'assalto ligure', 20 April 1944, on the Benedicta massacre (IG, *BG*, 09981).

of satisfaction and concern, occur in many documents, revealing the discrepancy between scant political training and great military audacity.

A report relating to the province of Cuneo reads: 'There is this characteristic often encountered in the formations: the difficulty of coupling the technical fighting capacity of the partisan war with the political quality of the Command.'[65] And in one report about the Alto Monferrato: 'Very active Garibaldi forces are continually performing marvellous actions, but leave much to be desired when it comes to their political organisation and orientation, their Anglophobia and their *sinistrismo*. We're hard at work getting them into step.'[66] Often 'lack of political know-how' meant no more than a vaguely classist radicalism out of tune with the party line, yet not meriting the precise political definition 'sinistrismo'.

The Communist *quadri* often found themselves facing this dilemma: what was to be feared most? What today would be called grass-roots ingenuity or poor indoctrination? A May 1944 report reads: 'Judging by divers elements who show off their doctrinaire knowledge in theory while being fence-sitters in practice we have to conclude that they are preferable to those comrades who don't know the principles of Marxism and who have never read Lenin, but who are active in practice.'[67]

In line with this, before the 'low political level of the basic comrades and of some *quadri* too', one can only 'hope that the military factor will influence the political one'.[68] Or also, commenting on a renovation of political commissars that was conducted, drawing from the new recruits: 'If the younger ones were untrained they were also free of sectarian and extremist tendencies encountered in the men with greater experience of partisan life.'[69]

The PCI made every effort to keep the 'great family of the Proletarian Avant-garde' under control.[70] But this was made difficult both by the formal denial of the political and class character of the brigades themselves, and by the need to appeal to the fighting spirit of the young. This spirit, as we shall see immediately, found in the very colour red the symbol of its

65 'Rapporto sul sopraluogo alla 6ᵃ zona bis del 14–15 febbraio 1945' (IG, *BG*, 04508).

66 'Rapporto di informazione. Piemonte', dated 22 February 1945, Turin (IG, *BG*, 04082).

67 Cited in Ragionieri, *Il partito comunista*, p. 398

68 See the report by Tommaso on the political and organisational situation in Varese, 27 September 1944 (IG, *BG*, 010834).

69 As Carlo, Commissar of the 50th Brigade, put it at the meeting of the Biella and Valsesia region Garibaldi Brigades commanders held in Callabiana in November 1944 (see Dellavalle, *Operai*, p. 196).

70 The Garibaldi Brigades were defined thusly in a report by Giorgio (Oltrepò Pavese) to the Lombardy Delegation, 1 September 1944 (*Le Brigate Garibaldi*, vol. II, p. 302).

identity and a safeguard against being reabsorbed into the merely military and patriotic war.

It has been written of the French Communists that 'politically they put national fronts etc. into their programs', but 'militarily they organise their own troops who don't fuse with the others even if they cooperate with them' and even if they remain essentially faithful to the unitary policy.[71] In Italy this problem was to be at least formally solved with the unification of the formations sanctioned in the last months of the struggle; but the whole span of the twenty months is shot through with incitements to reinforce the party presence in the Garibaldi formations. In the 'Directives for the constitution and functioning of the party nucleus within the partisan formations', issued on 1 March 1944, there is the enjoinder to 'do your job with tact and ability', avoiding useless outward manifestations of discord and friction with non-Communists. Should the commander and commissar, who in any case maintain their functions, be party members – the instructions go on to say – they, together with the person in charge of the nucleus, are to 'form a triangle', jointly answerable to the party for the progress of the unit. The commander and the commissar, again if they are party members, may be denounced to the superior authorities who shall take opportune measures, including dismissal; but in cases of urgency, the party members in charge may act also on their own initiative.[72] It was the dwindling of the historic figure of the political commissar, who after unification was to be called 'commissario di guerra' ('war commissar'), which led to the emergence of the 'responsabile del nucleo di partito' ('person in charge of the party nucleus').

The tact and ability, the 'necessary watchfulness' (as one command interprets it),[73] required by the instructions could become so blurred as to render the life of the party in the formations almost clandestine,[74] or 'rigorously secret and illegal', as one command recommends, out of excessive zeal and conspiratorial viscosity, but also from the need to camouflage themselves in the presence of the Allied missions.[75] The political commissar of the Natisone division candidly

---

71 See Michel, *Gli Alleati e la Resistenza in Europa*, pp. 40–1.

72 *Le Brigate Garibaldi*, vol. I, pp. 292–3. The constitution of the 'Party triangle' was recommended by the Piedmont delegation to the 'comrades responsible' for the lower Val di Susa detachments, in a 26 April 1944 communiqué (p. 363).

73 See the report from the 8th Asti Division, 14 January 1945 (cited in *Le Brigate Garibaldi*, vol. III, p. 239ff).

74 As was lamented at a meeting between Party organisers and commissars of the 3rd Lombardia Aliotta Division (Oltrepò Pavese) on 20 October 1944 (record in IG, *BG*, 01519).

75 See the directive sent from the 'Group Command for the 40th, 52nd and 55th Brigades' to the Commander and the Commissar of the 40th Brigade, 22 August 1944 (IG, *BG*, 0638). At a meeting of 'the Executive Committee of the PCI with the Command of the N. Nanetti Garibaldi Division', on 15 April 1945, there was talk of the need not to alarm 'outside elements' within the ranks (the record of the meeting is in IG, *Archivio*

wrote in his memoirs: 'From the start I made it a point of honour to succeed in winning over to Communism all the partisans and above all the commanders and commissars of various ranks';[76] and the commander of the Nanetti division would recall the 'responsabile di partito' as being

> something of the coordinator and controller of the combined action of the commander and the commissar together. Often he performed an excellent demo-cratically inspired action, at other times, if he was one of those elements who were not too well-fitted for the task, he created divergence and discord among the parti-sans, above all for the fact of being, at least partly, imposed from above.[77]

In this scenario, the militia of the Garibaldi brigades was seen as an instru-ment of recruitment and preparation of the '*quadri* for the immediate future'.[78] From the partisans, in fact, '*quadri* and popular chiefs must spring who will facilitate things for us immensely in tomorrow's work of ordering the nation on new bases'.[79]

For this end, it was indispensable to overcome reticence about opening the party's doors to the Garibaldini, replacing a party candidature with a partisan one (infiltrating oneself also among the GL partisans), judging the aspirants only 'as Garibaldini because they're young and we can't ask more of them'.[80] The party nucleus of the 8th Asti division was to reproach the commanders for having done too little to introduce into 'the family of the party' its many sympa-thisers; and the delegation of the brigades for Veneto levelled a similar rebuke at the 'Party comrades' of the Nanetti division.[81] In a long article commenting

---

PCI). A circular from Orel, 'responsible Party organiser attached to the division' had only recently (10 April) made reference, without mincing his words, to the Allied missions (*Le Brigate Garibaldi*, vol. III, pp. 601–2).

76 Padoan (Vanni), *Abbiamo lottato insieme*, p. 42.

77 Bernardo, *Il momento buono*, p. 47.

78 As described in a missive from 'Lucio Nino' to the Genoa Delegation (IG, *BG*, 09939).

79 From the aforementioned letter by Sandrelli: *Le Brigate Garibaldi*, vol. I, pp. 125–9.

80 See the letter to the Command of the 1st Piedmont Division, 30 September 1944, signed 'comrades' (*Le Brigate Garibaldi*, vol. II, pp. 379–80); the record of the 3 March 1945 Party meeting with the 3rd Lombardia Aliotta Division (*Le Brigate Garibaldi*, vol. III, pp. 435–6); a report from Albero, of that same division, to the insurrection-ary triumvirate for Lombardy, 9 March 1945 (IG, *BG*, 01880); the record of a later Party meeting in the Aliotta Division, 21 March 1945 (IG, *BG*, 01933). See also the position taken by the Political Commissar of the Arno Division, Giobbe (Danilo Dolfi), repro-duced in M. A. and S. Timpanaro's 'Introduzione', in G. and E. Varlecchi, *Potente*, p. 34.

81 See the letters from the Cell to the commands of the Division and of the 45th,

on the conference of the insurrectional triumvirates held at the beginning of November 1944, *L'Unità* calculated the partisan Communists as being at least fifteen thousand, and sympathisers some tens of thousands, 'on whom our party can count as much as it can on our comrades'. Contemporaneous with this satisfaction there was however the firm enjoinder to 'rid the formations of a party character'.[82]

It is easy to see how hard it was to get the other parties to agree on this last point, and not only because of the composition of the General Command (Luigi Longo and Pietro Secchia) and the numerical ratio between Garibaldini and Communists, but because the latter generally held the positions of command, exclusively or almost so.[83] Dante Livio Bianco recalls: 'Then (and, for that matter, subsequently), more than *garibaldini*, they were generally called Communists'.[84] Here Bianco is referring particularly to the Valle Varaita and January 1944; and in fact a few months later a Garibaldi document relating to the same area complained that an Action Party article had spoken of 'Communist bands', but then had to recognise that, for their part, the Garibaldini 'considered the other Badogliani ... in the pejorative sense',[85] an accusation that the *giellisti* (members of GL) certainly did not deserve.

The Communist Party's denials about its close connection with the Garibaldi brigades were therefore not very credible. But this does not make them any less interesting for the language they use and the reality they reveal, both when they turn outward, and, still more so, when they assume the guise of appeals and rebukes addressed to the brigades themselves. The language is defensive and often considers the label 'Communist' given to the brigades an unjust accusation, a speculation, a calumny on the part of their adversaries, an attempt to

98th and 100th Brigades, 15 January 1945 (*Le Brigate Garibaldi*, vol. III, pp. 238–9); and the letter of 10 March 1945 from the Veneto Delegation (ISBR, *Carte Landi*).

82 'Serrare le file', Northern edition, 25 November 1944.

83 In the Biella region, out of around 1,850 Garibaldini in the 5th and 12th Divisions, 600 were Communists and 'all the commissars and almost all the commanders (if not all) are members of our Party'; moreover, 'almost all of the intellectuals in the two Divisions' were Communists ('Relazione del lavoro di Partito', signed 'Bibi', 3 December 1944: IG, *BG*, 05299). Other reports soon afterwards gave even higher figures, and also added to these the – significant in themselves – figures for members of the Fronte della gioventù (*Le Brigate Garibaldi*, vol. III, pp. 77–9 and notes). See Dellavalle, *Operai*, pp. 77, 200. The Ligurian Garibaldi Division commanded by a Catholic (Bisagno), to take another example, had a 'significant' proportion of Communists, including the vice-commander, the commissar, the vice-commissar, and the head of the High Command, while the intendant was a priest: 'Note particolari, 1 agosto 1944' (IG, *BG*, 010075).

84 Bianco, *Guerra partigiana*, p. 42.

85 See the report from Pietro, Commissar of the 1st Division, to the Piedmont Delegation, 23 June 1944 (*Le Brigate Garibaldi*, vol. II, pp. 61–4).

depreciate and belittle the formations, to deprive them of the sympathy they enjoy among the populations.[86] But to whom did one of these documents assign the task of removing every last bit of party varnish from the Garibaldi brigades? To the party nucleus of the brigades.[87] And if they were then taken literally, there was the outraged protest that at a meeting to set up the Ligurian unified command, the Socialist and Actionist representatives 'went so far as to question whether the Garibaldi brigades are truly representative of us, because in them there are elements of every political tendency; but in concrete terms they have been unable to produce any specific facts.'[88]

General Headquarters was compelled to lament that 'a just but exaggerated concern to explode 'the myth that the Garibaldi brigades are Communist' had meant that 'hardly any of our large units bears the name of Antonio Gramsci'.[89] In fact, not many Garibaldi formations bear the name of Antonio Gramsci: eleven, according to the copious 'Index of Organisms' of the three volumes of documents of the *Brigate Garibaldi nella Resistenza*; seven according to that of the *Guida archivi della Resistenza*. But no more numerous in those indexes are the other great names of the workers' and Socialist-Communist' tradition. 'Carlo Marx' is coupled with Benedetto Croce in designating two detachments of the 40th Matteotti Garibaldi brigade, operating in Upper Lombardy alongside a Rosselli brigade and a Proletarian Front, which would duly assume the name of the fallen Luigi Clerici (note in this case the perfect equilibrium of the names). Matteotti (the name most frequently used for their formations by the PSIUP and in some cases also by Giustizia e Libertà); Buozzi, Fratelli Rosselli (who obviously figure in the GL formations as well) in effect appear as names with a unitary intent. Only in a few rare cases are the names explicitly Communist: Togliatti, Tito, Stalin (chosen, furthermore, by a group of Cossack deserters

---

86 See, for example, the letter from the 'comrades responsible' for the Piedmont Delegation to their equivalents in the Val di Susa, 12 July 1944 (*Le Brigate Garibaldi*, vol. III, pp. 116–20); the letter from the Command of the 3rd Piedmont Division (the person who penned this must have been an old member, since they wrote 'Partito Comunista d'Italia' rather than 'Partito Comunista Italiano') to the Command of the Giustizia e Libertà formations, Susa Alpine battalions (IG, *BG*, 004944); 'Camicia rossa', an article in *La voce della realtà. Giornale murale per la popolazione a cura della 19a brigata d'assalto Garibaldi Eusebio Giambone*, 13 August 1944 (IG, *BG*, 04741); and the letter from the Lombardy Delegation to the Command of the 3rd Aliotta Division, 10 November 1944, which issues a reprimand for the paper *Il Garibaldino*, speaking as if it were an organ of the PCI (INSMLI, *Brigate Garibaldi*, envelope 1, folder 1, subfolder 2).

87 *Le Brigate Garibaldi*, vol. III, pp. 116–20.

88 'Relazione del responsabile militare del Triumvirato insurrezionale della Liguria, Gi', 5 July 1944 (*Le Brigate Garibaldi*, vol. II, pp. 97–8).

89 Note to the Command Delegations, 4 December 1944 (INSMLI, *Brigate Garibaldi*, envelope 1, folder 4).

who showed up at the Natisone division),[90] Serrati, Gastone, Sozzi, Spartaco Lavagnini. Some clearly ideological presences are marked by Spartaco, Stella Rossa,[91] and Volante Rossa, by a proletarian brigade formed in September 1943 with Slovene support.[92] Edging the border of Risorgimento names (which, as has been duly noted, figure widely in the Garibaldi bands too), are names such as Camicia Rossa and Pisacane; these words uttered by the latter are recalled in the half-title of a Socialist paper: 'Socialism or slavery: there is no other alternative for our society'.[93] The names of the war-dead variously combined with geographical names are by far the most frequent in the Garibaldi bands.

Compared with the names of the formations, the mastheads of the Garibaldi local papers seem to present a greater number of proletarian and Communist stances.[94] Some could have sounded so only to those who had been politically educated along Leninist lines: thus 'La Scintilla' ('The Spark') and 'Nuova Scintilla' (and in France too 'L'Étincelle' appears several times). Other are more explicit: 'Il Compagno', 'Fazzoletto Rosso' ('Red Scarf'), 'La vigilia operaia' ('Workers' Vigil'), 'Gioventù proletaria' ('Workers' Youth'), 'Il Proletario', 'Savona proletaria', 'Rivoluzione proletaria', 'Bandiera Rossa'. Others still hark back to an ancient working-class and popular tradition: thus for example 'La Barricata', 'La Fabbrica' ('The Factory'), 'La Forgia' ('The Forge'), 'Il Martello' ('The Hammer'), 'La Squilla' ('The Blast'), 'L'Aratro e il Martello' ('The Plow and Hammer'), 'L'Aurora' ('Dawn'), 'Il Lavoro' ('Labour'), 'La Solidarietà'. 'La Comune' also appears, just as in France there was 'La Commune' (the title – 'La Commune de Paris' – chosen likewise by the *Journale des marraines de la compaignie des franc-tireurs et partisans*, to replace 'Jean Jaurès', which preceded it).

Extremely rare, by contrast, were the *noms-de-guerre* adopted by (or assigned to) the Garibaldini which had a proletarian and/or Communist ring. It would seem that the tradition of naming one's children after great figures of the working-class movement was not renewed when one had to choose it for

90 According to the Division daily report (IZDG, envelope 272a, folder 1/A.C.7).

91 A Stella Rossa Brigade operating in Piacentino was commanded by a communist ('who behaved very badly, and added to that was a Montenegrin, obtuse and rigid as steel'). It published the paper *L'Umanità nuova*, termed 'indecent' – such was the judgment passed in the report 'Comando della 6ª zona ligure al responsabile militare del triumvirato insurrezionale della Liguria, Giovanni', 2 November 1944, which guaranteed that the paper would change its name to *Guerriglia* (*Le Brigate Garibaldi*, vol. II, pp. 527–30, rich in commentary on the regional press). The Montenegrin was probably unaware (and the writer of the letter probably did know) that *Umanità Nova* was an anarchist title.

92 See Mautino, *Guerra di popolo*, p. 36, and Fogar, *Le brigate Osoppo-Friuli*, p. 278.

93 *Avanguardia. Giornale della gioventù socialista*, June 1944.

94 Here, we are essentially referring to the oft-cited *Saggio bibliografico*.

oneself.[95] Only sporadic Matteotti's and Spartaco's and, should we wish to stress Russian echoes, the odd Ivan, and little else, are on record.

'Il rosso' is, on the contrary, widespread in the symbolism of the scarves, shirts, stars, hammers and sickles, clenched fist salutes and in the songs. Even the RSI recruits seem to have marched off singing *L'Internazionale* and *Bandiera Rossa*.[96] This abundance of red is attested to above all by the frequency with which the Communist directives repressed it throughout the twenty-month span of the struggle. If in some cases satisfaction is expressed that red has been replaced by the *tricolore*,[97] very often the insistence on reiterating requests, even 'in modo duro' ('sternly'),[98] that this be done reveals refractoriness about meeting those requests. 'Let's get the red stars removed immediately', reads a document relating to the Valtellina; and in one about the Parma area: 'No badge apart from the fine tricolored cockade is to be allowed. Likewise for songs, which must not be party-songs, but only national in character.'[99]

A report on Umbria, shortly after the liberation of that region, bitterly recorded that the movement had 'a rowdy character based on verbal extremism, closed fists and *Bandiera Rossa*'.[100] In Valle d'Aosta the Garibaldini, solely 'for love of unity', agreed to wear the *tricolore* armband and the 'red and black shield, the colour of the valley'.[101] On the eve of the liberation of Ravenna, the commander Bülow urged his men not only to adopt the *tricolore* and the military salute but 'not to sing the *Internazionale* nor other political songs. Learn *Il Piave* and the Garibaldi hymns'[102]

---

95 On this tradition, see De Felice, *Nomi e cultura*, pp. 37–9, where he recalls how the 'habit of conveying social protest and the hope for a new, different life by means of one's children's names' was signalled in Ernesto Ragionieri, *Dall'Unità a oggi*, vol. IV, Book 3, *La Storia d'Italia*, Turin: Einaudi, 1976, p. 2076.

96 See the GNR reports cited in Pansa, *L' esercito di Salò*, pp. 33, 54–5, 76–7; and Bocca, *La Repubblica di Mussolini*, p. 152.

97 See the report 'Il Sopraluogo in Valle di Lanzo', 24 February 1944, signed Garelli (*Le Brigate Garibaldi*, vol. I, pp. 268–71).

98 See Dario's report 'Cari compagni' (n.d., but late Spring 1944) reporting upon the sectarianism of the brigades in Tuscany (IG, *Archivio PCI*). See also the eponymous report from the inspector Paolo, 15 June 1944 (*Le Brigate Garibaldi*, vol. II, p. 34).

99 See the report of the Command of the 40th Matteotti Brigade to the Milan PCI federation, 10 July 1944 (*Le Brigate Garibaldi*, vol. II, pp. 113–14; and the letter from the Commissar Gracco addressed to the 'delegate-inspector of the North Emilia Garibaldi Brigades), 2 August 1944 (*Le Brigate Garibaldi*, vol. II, pp. 188–9).

100 'Relazione sul movimento partigiano della zona di confine umbro-marchigiana', by Celso Ghini, 16 August 1944 (IG, *Archivio PCI*).

101 Report by the Command of the 7th Garibaldi Division, 1 September 1944 (IG, BG, 05640).

102 See the instructions issued on 7 September 1944 (Casali, *Il movimento di liberazione a Ravenna*, vol. II, pp. 269–70). See also the circular from the Ravenna Provincial SAP Command, 8 September 1944, which conclude with the appeal 'Unity! Unity!

Reports came from the Langhe of 'red scarves, red stars, hammers and sickles, chants, clenched fist salutes, talk about revolution and against priests'.[103] From the province of Como, by now on the eve of Liberation, that is to say when the formal unification of the formations had occurred, scarves and red stars and clenched fists were still being denounced as marks of sectarianism and 'lack of capacity'; and, around about the same time, the delegation for Lombardy warned the group command of the Valsesia, Ossola, Cusio, and Verbano divisions against 'indulging in closed fists and red flags, symbols among your men of limited education ... The good Communists will be the first to understand that it is not in the interest of their party to make divisive gestures and manifestations'.[104]

A month after the Liberation (but we are on the eastern border) a report by Nilo (Francesco Pesce), commander of the Nanetti division, was still denouncing sectarian manifestations by comrades, starting with the customary red scarf.[105]

Probably the most vivid description of the sporting of red has been left by 'Vanni' (Giovanni Padoan), political commissar of the Natisone division:

The red scarf they wore around their necks was enormous, it wasn't a scarf, but a shawl that descended from the neck down to the waist and beyond. On their beret they had a red star whose points extended from one rim to another and gave the unpleasant impression that a squid was enveloping the head of the person wearing it. But not only the beret, the whole uniform was literally strewn with red flags. They were everywhere, applied with extreme lavishness: on their breasts, on their jackets, on their sleeves and even on their trousers. Machine-guns and rifles were full of stars of every dimension, some of them tastefully engraved.[106]

Unity!'; and also the letter from the Commander of GAP Sector No. 3 (Russi) to the squad-leaders, 16 September (Casali, *Il movimento di liberazione a Ravenna*, vol. I, p. 76, and vol. II, p. 317). In the same area, on 18 February 1944 Asdrubale wrote to Matteo on the issue of propaganda, commenting that 'any text is fine, as long as it's revolutionary', this propaganda being distributed among young people, soldiers and women (*Il movimento di liberazione a Ravenna*, vol. II, p. 283).

103 'Relazione sulla 6ª divisione', by the inspector Andreis, 12 October 1944 (*Le Brigate Garibaldi*, vol. II, p. 435).

104 See 'Relazione del responsabile militare del Triumvirato insurrezionale della Lombardia, Fabio, sulla situazione delle forze patriottiche di origine garibaldina', 16 April 1945 (*Le Brigate Garibaldi*, vol. III, pp. 626–36).

105 'Relazione personale sulla situazione generale politico-militare della zona della divisione Garibaldi Nino Nanetti', Rome, 31 May 1945 (*Le Brigate Garibaldi*, vol. III, pp. 718–22).

106 Padoan (Vanni), *Abbiamo lottato insieme*, p. 119. The description refers to the GAP battalion commanded by 'Giacca' (Mario Toffanin) which, on 7 February 1945, massacred the Osoppo Brigade Commander 'Bolla' (Francesco di Gregori), the political commissar, the Action Party's 'Enea' (Gastone Valente) and seventeen partisans at the Porzûs *malghe*. On the killing, see the letter from 'Libero' (Italo Romanelli) addressed

In Perugia too 'the great and uncontrolled display of red flags' at the moment of the Allied entry into the city was attributed to sectarianism and backwardness; and in Terni an identical phenomenon was bracketed among 'petit bourgeois excesses'.[107] An Emilian commissar, describing the worst part of a formation, states: 'It is, however, the keenest squad when it comes to displaying red stars and other badges.'[108]

In another document the need to proclaim red is coupled with the need to 'avoid swearing at all costs'.[109] This makes the opinion expressed by a party envoy about the parading of red in the Republic of Montefiorino all the more thoughtful and respectful. After recalling that nearly all of the young men belonging to the Modena division 'have joined our party and strongly insist on calling themselves Communists', the author of the report writes:

> Hundreds of these youths are wearing the red shirt with the hammer and sickle and those who don't have it fervently wish to wear it; these youths are among those most fired with the fighting spirit and the spirit of sacrifice with a marked class spirit as well. Both Davide [the commissar] and Armando [the commander] insist (rightly) that if one were to take their red shirt away from these youths, with it one would be taking away the fighting spirit with which they are animated.

The party envoy therefore did no more than have the hammer and sickle replaced with the *tricolore* cockade and in any case suggested a shift in the meaning to be attributed to the red shirt, which, he points out, 'has had its importance in the formation of the units of our country'.[110]

It didn't escape the author of this report, nor partisan leaders like Davide and Armando, that there was a risk that insistent Communist pedantry aimed at obtaining not only the application but the interiorisation of the party's unitary

---

to the 'Segreteria del Partito d'azione per l'Alta Italia', February 1945 (*Formazioni GL*, pp. 317–22 and their respective notes).

107 'Relazione del compagno Silvio sugli avvenimenti dalla fine di maggio ad oggi nelle province di Terni e Perugia', 25 June 1944 (IG, *Archivio PCI*, published in the 23 June 1964 *Rinascita*.

108 'Relazione del commissario politico Remo al comandante di brigata', on the Giordano Cavestro detachment, undated but from 23 May 1944 (IG, BG, Emilia-Romagna, G.IV.2.2).

109 See the instructions from the political commissar of the 2nd Piedmont Division to all the other political commissars, 'A tutti i commissari politici', n.d. (IG, BG, 04667).

110 Letter from the official responsible for the insurrectionary triumvirate for Emilia-Romagna, Cri., to the General Command, 14 July 1944 (*Le Brigate Garibaldi*, vol. II, p. 126). We should also add that this same Cri. lamented the commanders' failure to salute one another. On the refusal of the Christian-Democrat partisans in Montefiorino to adopt the red star and the clenched-fist salute, see Gorrieri, *La Repubblica di Montefiorino*, pp. 379–80.

line would wither the very roots of participation in the struggle. This was not just an Italian problem. Djilas, who, heading a delegation of Yugoslav partisans, presented himself at the Kremlin with a red star on his beret, came in for a contemptuous cold dowsing from Stalin: 'What are you doing with red stars on your beret? Form isn't important, what's important are concrete conquests, and you ... want red stars. What use do you think red stars are?' Djilas' reply had been respectful but firm: 'It is impossible to abolish the red stars because they have already become a tradition and have come to mean something to our fighters.'[111]

Fear of deviationism and *sinistrimo* led to attitudes that actually preceded specific party choices being taken for possible political lines. Indeed often the reddest, the most zealous in declaring themselves Communists were not even members of the party. One gets closer to the truth by transferring into a very different situation Edward P. Thompson's critical remarks to Keith Thomas, who had resorted to the explanatory categories of 'inadequacies of popular education' and of 'popular religious ignorance':

> Possibly so: but is it also a glimpse into that process of translating doctrine into a more meaningful, an altogether more relevant [red!] symbolism – of accepting from the church [the Party!] only so much doctrine as can be assimilated to the life experience of the poor... 'Ignorance' is far too blunt an analytic tool, for ignorance may indicate evasion, or translation, irony in the face of the church's homilies, or very often, active intellectual resistance to its doctrines.[112]

The symbolism of red served to affirm one's individual and group identity before those who used other symbols, like the light blue scarf and the green scarf. Red – and a cross-current Umbrian document complains about the opportunism of those leaders who don't like it[113] – signified that the struggle taking place was seen as being a radical innovation, while the colours of the Badogliani and of the *autonomi*, green and light blue, indicated a desire for mere restoration. When the Piave brigade was incorporated, against its wishes, into the Nanetti Garibaldi division, the commissar Ugo accused the commander Olivi of wishing to make his men wear 'instead of the red scarf, which was the symbol of Garibaldi, of his heroism and his sacrifice, the light blue scarf, which was the symbol of a reigning house upon whose legality the people have not yet been

---

111 Milovan Djilas, *Conversations with Stalin*, London: Penguin, 1967, p. 61.

112 E. P. Thompson, 'Anthropology and the Discipline of Historical Context', in *Midland History*, vol. 1, p. 3 (1972). K. Thomas (*Religion and the Decline of Magic*, London: Penguin, 1971) had applied his interpretative criteria to the fact that an old man 'who had attended sermons his whole life' thought of God as 'a kindly old man', Christ as a 'docile young man' and his soul as a 'great bone in his body'.

113 See 'Relazione di C. sulla prima visita alle formazioni partigiane della zona di Foligno', 3 February 1944 (*Le Brigate Garibaldi*, vol. I, pp. 251–5).

able to pronounce'. Here, the cautious wording of the formula far from attenuating, reinforces the rebuff.[114]

In the Modenese Appenines the Communist representatives saw themselves compelled to denounce the fact that while, according to them, the Garibaldini did not wear party badges and sang only patriotic songs, the same could not be said of the Christian Democrats, who had the letters *DC* and a cross embroidered on their *tricolore* scarf.[115]

One measure at which the Garibaldini particularly balked at was the adoption of the military salute. True, the appeals to adopt it make use of expressions such as 'regular army of free Italy', 'salute formerly in use in the ex-royal army', which are in tune with what I have called 'the repudiation of the royal army',[116] but it is also true that this was not always the case. In fact, anodyne formulae appear like the 'traditional salute of the Italian army': thus an enjoinder made in northern Lombardy commits the gaffe of implicitly comparing the salute with the clenched fist and the Fascist salute: 'No outstretched arm, neither with hand open nor with fist clenched'.[117] And it is still truer that the military salute was a symbol that was very hard to stomach, smacking of the idea of a discipline which one of the above-quoted documents actually, and approvingly, called 'iron'. Likewise, in another document great satisfaction is expressed at having 'succeeded in applying the military salute, in imposing ranks'.[118] And the misunderstandings, exchanges of words and convergences with the GL brigades that could occur on this count make singular reading. When a group of *giellisti* from the Pavese Oltrepò turned up at a Garibaldi headquarters asking to be incorporated into the brigade, their reason for doing so was that 'in the *Giustizia e Libertà* column there is still an old-style militaristic spirit involving the military salute, the *signorsì* (yes, sir), and differential treatment in the mess'.[119]

---

114 'Lettera aperta ai Garibaldini della Brigata Piave', 29 August 1944; first appendix to the letter from the Nanetti Division Command to the Command of the Mazzini and Tollot Brigades, 29 August 1944 (*Le Brigate Garibaldi*, vol. II, pp. 283–4).

115 See the letter from the PCI representatives in the Modena Division to the CLN for the province and mountain-region, the CUMER and the representatives of the Christian Democrats, Action Party and Socialists, 22 February 1945 (*Le Brigate Garibaldi*, pp. 379–80); and Gorrieri, *La Repubblica di Montefiorino*, pp. 379–80, which underlines the Christian Democrats' pride in wearing their own symbols.

116 See the order of the day of the Central Emilia corps, no. 4, 10 July 1944 (*Le Brigate Garibaldi*, vol. II, pp. 115–16); and the circular from the 3rd Piedmont Division Commander, Massimo, 'A tutti i Comandi di brigata e di distaccamento', 4 September 1944 (IG, *BG*, 004990).

117 'Bollettino n. 43', 22 August 1944, from the Command of the 52nd Luigi Clerici Brigade (IG, *BG*, 0625)

118 See 'Relazione politica generale' by the political commissar Lamberti, of the 47th Brigade, 27 October 1944 (IG, *BG*, Emilia-Romagna, G.IV.3.4).

119 See 'Rapporto informativo e osservazioni per il Comitato federale', for the Pavia

An Actionist from the Modena area complained about seeing 'too much red and very little *tricolore*', though he acknowledged that 'the work and speeches of the political commissar and the commander are *Fronte nazionale* in character and content'.[120] Among both the Garibaldini and the *giellisti* the not very successful idea was born of adopting factory overalls as a uniform. More soberly in a Garibaldi document – 'provisionally we recommend overalls, no matter what colour they are'[121] – more emphatically in a page written by a prestigious GL leader: 'The overall, the finest and most meaningful uniform, for volunteers fighting a revolutionary war (remember Carlo Rosselli's vibrant words in Spain: only the anonymous genius of revolution could invent this extraordinary but at the same time natural uniform: the overall. The war of the workers' will be waged in the uniform of work)'.[122]

The memory of Spain also influenced the Communist leaders, but in the reverse direction, for their rigid stance over the salute and other aspects of military discipline was undoubtedly influenced by the memory of how hard and bloody it had been settling accounts with the libertarian character of the anarchist militias. And possibly there was the memory too of the error committed in 1921 of not backing the 'Arditi del popolo', opposing them with the formation of party squads. This tendency was manifested initially in Romagna and again in summer 1944 in Piedmont.[123]

The ambiguity of the red shirt was utilised, oscillating between a sort of philological homage to the hero of the two worlds and a proletarian updating of it. This dual meaning of red is evident in a letter of Moscatelli's: 'Let the Garibaldini consider it as they like; for our part we are proud to wear the red scarf, and to fittingly wear this symbol of our great Hero and of the purest patriotic expression of the Italian Risorgimento'.[124]

Federal Committee, by the inspector Medici, 10 August 1944. 'For now', it continues 'we made the fine gesture of sending back the first ones who came to us, though with the proviso that if this incident should be repeated, the same approach should not be taken again, as men must have full freedom of choice' (*Le Brigate Garibaldi*, vol. III, p. 237).

120 See the letter from Libero Villa to the Modena representative of the Partito d'azione (no date – June 1944?), cited in Gorrieri, *La Repubblica di Montefiorino*, p. 375. A similar GL attitude was cited in the case of the 43rd Garibaldi Brigade, adding that 'the peasants are in large measure influenced by the Garibaldini'. See the letter from the political commissar of the Liguria group to the General Command, 3 August 1944 (*Le Brigate Garibaldi*, vol. II, p. 193).

121 See circular no. 14 of the 'Comando Raggruppamento Brigate Garibaldi di Milano e provincia', 13 February 1945: interesting as an urban-focused document, and for its late timing (IG, *BG*, 011084).

122 Bianco, *Guerra partigiana*, p. 96.

123 Flamigni and Marzocchi, *Resistenza in Romagna*, p. 29, and a letter from the commissariat of the Piedmont Delegation to the Commissar of the 2nd Piedmont Division, Paolo (Antonio Giolitti), 18 June 1944 (*Le Brigate Garibaldi*, vol. II, pp. 37–8).

124 Letter to Moro, in Switzerland, 30 January 1945, in which, together with Ciro,

With still greater transparency the commissar of the 2nd Cascione division operating in Liguria had written: 'For the time being, the red of our shirts and of our flags has a Garibaldi, not Communist, tone.' 'But where are these flags in the divisions?', had been the irritated retort of Simon, the commander of the 1st zone of Liguria; and as for that 'for the time being', he had warned: 'This phrase seems intended to still the impatience and fears of certain sectarian Communists and to calm them with the promise that the shape of things today will change tomorrow. What are the non-Communist Garibaldini to think of this? That the present shape of things is nothing but deception.'[125]

In another document, also aimed probably at 'calming' the impetuous, it is the *tricolore* star that is explicitly identified with the Garibaldi star.[126] The General Command of the brigades itself undertook to demonstrate that 'the red scarf, with its fine tricolored points, is the symbol and badge of the Garibaldino and not of Communism or Socialism'.[127] At the Bracco pass:

> the red flag has been replaced by a fine *tricolore* which in the place of the Savoy shield bears the red star ... The men of the formation wear large red stars on their breasts, and on their berets; an order abolishing them would be extremely ill-advised. The obstacle has been overcome by proposing, and the proposal has been accepted by the Command, to attach to the beret a *tricolore* cockade to which the red star will be attached ... There is also the proposal to wear a red scarf around one's neck, but we hope to obtain a *tricolore* scarf with a small red star at the corners.[128]

The search for stratagems stimulated imagination: the adoption of the *tricolore* star, offset by the 'Garibaldi red scarf and toggle with a medallion of Garibaldi';[129] the affixing of a tricolore armband to the red shirt;[130] the tricolore against a red background, like the one which was consigned by the provincial CLN to the Nanetti division, 'but soon the flag was forgotten by the partisans as a useless object'.[131] As for the salute, a form of compromise was the introduction

Moscatelli laments the discrimination to which the Garibaldini forced to cross the border were subject. Cited in *Le Brigate Garibaldi*, vol. III, pp. 308–9, note 6.

125 See the critical letter from Simon to the commissariat of the 2nd Liguria Cascione Division, 23 November 1944 (ibid., vol. II, p. 628).

126 See the circular from the Command of the 3rd Piedmont Division, 2 October 1944 (ibid., vol. II, pp. 393–4).

127 See the letter to the Delegation for North Emilia, 9 November 1944 (INSMLI, *Brigate Garibaldi*, envelope 1, folder 4).

128 'Rapporto informativo e osservazioni', from the inspector for Oltrepò, Medici, to the Federal Committee, 10 August 1944 (*Le Brigate Garibaldi*, vol. II, p. 237).

129 See the report of Renzi and Schiavi on the 47th Brigade (Emilia), 2 August 1944 (IG, *BG*, 03433).

130 See the letter from the Lombardy Delegation to the Command of the 3rd Aliotta Division, no date (INSMLI, *Brigate Garibaldi*, envelope 2, folder 1, subfolder 1).

131 Bernardo, *Il momento buono*, p. 35.

of the military one 'if at the moment they make it they have their service cap, and the clenched fist salute if they don't' – which was the utmost case of innovation in continuity, given that in the Royal Army of the regime the bare-headed salute had been the Fascist one.[132]

It is hard to say what the symbol of red was reckoned to contain, beyond a vague aspiration for radicalism, an assertion of identity and (though this be may be found only in the older partisans and in the most acculturated) the desire that the 'temporary defeat of the proletariat in 1919' be redeemed.[133] When the partisans, managed, as they did in the free zones, to exercise power, the important decisions were taken along the general lines of national and unitary action,[134] whether or not they were convinced that this was the only manner, in those circumstances, of paving the way for the revolution or, as was said at a party meeting, of 'preparing the men and the ground for the accomplishment of our social and economic plan'.[135] Moreover, more radical measures and proposals were not lacking. In the Fucino area it was the Communist party itself, in the person of a leader of the stature of 'Palmieri' (Giorgio Amendola), who urged his reticent Avezzano comrades to give pride of place to the watchword 'Torlonia must be seized' and, what's more, arrested, with the proviso, however, that this 'in no way means a socialist, but a democratic, revolution'.[136] But while Amendola dogmatically based his assertion on the fact that Torlonia was a case of fusion between a semi-feudal structure and monopolistic capital, a circular issued by General Headquarters recalled that the Garibaldi brigades 'do not carry out expropriations against anyone who is not pro-Nazi'.[137] Thus the political commissar Renato, who 'wanted to socialise the oil companies of the zone, dispossessing the capitalists', was said to be valorous, but incompetent.[138]

In the Pavese Oltrepò Actionists and Christian Democrats were alarmed at the fact that 'wherever the brigades stayed for some time there was a rapid re-flowering of democratic institutions, a series of anti-capitalistic measures,

132 See the letter from Andrea (Mario Lizzero) 'per il Comando delle Tre Venezie' to 'Direttivo comunità di …' and to the Command of the Friuli Battalion, 9 October 1943. Andrea explains that 'the essential thing is never to speak of being revolutionaries, but to be so in reality, without saying so' (IZDG, envelope 534, folder III/1).

133 Words contained in a questionnaire of February 1945 prepared by the commissar of the F. Ghinaglia (Cremona) SAP brigades, seeking some insight as to the cause of this defeat (IG, *Archivio PCI*).

134 I defer to the already vast literature on the free zones, in particular Legnani, *Politica e amministrazione nelle repubbliche partigiane*.

135 IG, *BG*, 01519

136 See 'Verbale seduta Segreteria (26 novembre 1943)' (IG, *Archivio PCI*).

137 This Spring 1945 circular can be found in INSMLI, *Brigate Garibaldi*, envelope 1, folder 4.

138 See Marelli's report 'Sul lavoro svolto fra i volontari della libertà in montagna (21–25 dicembre)', 1944 (Piacentino) (*Le Brigate Garibaldi*, vol. III, p. 141).

[which] while uniting the multitude of poor peasants and artisans to us made the rest of the country hostile to us'.[139]

In this document satisfaction is mitigated by concern. In others there is only concern: for example about the 'socialisation of the rural funds' which was to occur in the zone of the Mingo division.[140] The controversial Romagnolo partisan Libero, whom we have already encountered, promoted 'agrarian reform and sharing out 75 percent of the harvest', with the corollary that the owners' part of the Fascists' holdings should be used to assist the partisans.[141] One command urged the taxing of the well-to-do, above all the Fascists and war profiteers; some councils formed in liberated areas abolished the 'purely and typically Fascist taxes'.[142] And so on.

There was a risk of the more incisive and summary social measures smacking of brigandage. This, above all, was the interpretation that the anti-Fascist front as a whole tended to give it. A Turin document reads: 'In the Committee [the CLN] there is the wish to define every determined act that harms the industrialists as brigandage.'[143]

That the adoption of red symbols did not signify a precise acceptance of a political program, but adhesion rather to what the word Communism triggered in the imagination, seems to be borne out by those documents containing expressions like 'apolitical but sympathising with the social conception of the Party', or 'sympathy for the social conception of our Party';[144] by those which speak of a 'spontaneous pro-Communist sentiment in the young', which was taken by Liberals and Actionists as the 'fruit of a preordained work of propaganda';[145] and finally by those which justify the fact of having formed party nuclei, 'because there weren't any comrades', with elements who 'feel themselves to be communists and who are among the best Garibaldi in terms of courage, discipline and intelligence'.[146] This force of attraction exerted by Communism, understood as an

---

139 See the report by Piero, political commissar of the 3rd Aliotta Division, to the General Command, 27 December 1944 (ibid., pp. 144–9).

140 See a note referring to the 'most serious matters' that the inspector Dario had noted with regard to the formations of the Alessandrino area, April 1945 (ibid., p. 617, n. 1).

141 See Flamigni e Marzocchi, Resistenza in Romagna, p. 172.

142 'Il Comando della 11a divisione Cuneo al Comando della polizia divisionale', 14 January 1945, and 'Il Comando della 6ª zona ligure al Comando militare regionale e al CLN della Liguria', 24 November 1944 (Le Brigate Garibaldi, vol. III, p. 230, and vol. II, pp. 637–9).

143 From an anonymous document of 23 December 1943 (IG, Archivio PCI).

144 See the two reports by Andrea 'from the partisan command of the Friuli battalion', both from 27 September 1943 (Le Brigate Garibaldi, vol. I, pp. 95–9).

145 According to the intendent's report 'on the military events subsequent to the date of 27 March 1944', n.d., referring to the Benedicta killings (IG, BG, 09955).

146 See the letter from the inspector stationed with the 3rd Division, Albero (Oltrepò

at once radical and vague mutation, is well described by Moscatelli in a letter in which he remarks on the vast gap between the quantity and quality of the party members and the inclination of the others to call themselves all Communists. The latter, if they could,

> would have the hammer and sickle stamped even on their buttocks. Barbison [Stalin] is a God Almighty. Woe betide anyone who says anything against Russia and above all against the Red Army. They all salute with their fists [but] (almost all of them) have the holy medallion around their necks, the holy image in their wallets. [He, Cino, doesn't salute with his fist] while I am saluted like that even by priests, by *carabinieri*, by the whole population indiscriminately.[147]

Here, there was, certainly, opportunism, at least in the priests and the *carabinieri*. But Moscatelli's conclusion, that it is easier to pick good military leaders than party ones, confirms the existence of red belligerence, where both noun and adjective were real, independently of any ties with the Communist Party, which was nonetheless felt to be the party of revolution. Many years later a Communist partisan from Terni was keen to explain that 'there were precious few of us whose direction was Communist idealism', but added:

> I mean, at that moment maybe we'd started heading towards anarchism, complete liberty, because after the oppression there had been in these parts, the poverty, misery, malnutrition, everything, folk no longer bothered to distinguish political leanings. It was almost all a common idea. The only aim was to take up arms and pursue a sacrosanct struggle, as we defined it in those times.[148]

Some partisans were convinced that 'the march on Genoa [was] the definitive taking possession of the city as a proletarian revolutionary movement'.[149] Others let slip remarks such as: 'Damn it, now of all times when we have weapons and ammunition the war is about to finish!' and were deemed to be 'clearly politically immature', but of great fighting spirit.[150] From the factories

---

Pavese), to the insurrectionary triumvirate for Lombardy, 24 February 1945 (*Le Brigate Garibaldi*, vol. III, p. 416).

147 Report 'Alla Segreteria federazione milanese del PCI', 15 September 1944 (IG, BG, 06320). Moscatelli gives the following figures: seven had been signed up to the Party prior to 25 July, nine recruited during the '45 days', and '66 promoted to Party ranks at the meeting in tribute to the Red Army': a total of 82 among around 1,000 men.

148 Testimony of Guglielmo Vannozzi, in Portelli, *Biografia di una città*, pp. 264–5.

149 'Alcuni rilievi sull'organizzazione della 3a divisione' (Liguria), n.d. (IG, BG, 010473).

150 See the letter from the Command of the divisions in the Valsesia, Ossola, Cusio, and Verbano areas (Cino and Ciro) to the Delegation for Lombardy, 12 February 1945 (IG, BG, 07907).

came the response of one who, at an assembly held a few days before the insurrection, said: 'And it is precisely because the Allies are at the gates that I tell you
to get a move on, because we haven't much time.'[151]

These were, so to speak, elementary confessions of the longed-for bond
between war and revolution, clearly stated by an 'extremist' newspaper – 'modern
war is always revolution'[152] – and supported by the observation: 'so there are a
lot of these Garibaldini, then …'.[153] Regret and nostalgia for the heroic times
were to appear in these words written many years later: 'The end of the war also
meant the end of the authority of the military formations, which represented the
revolutionary drive of the movement', and the partisans 'practically entered the
museum of all veterans. Like the Garibaldini of the Argonne, the Alpini of the
Grappa, and the infantrymen of the Piave.'[154]

6. The myth of the USSR

'We could hear a roaring … it was the voice of Stalin, that cannon there', recounts
a Garibaldino partisan, Meo Bigatti, deported to the Flossenbürg concentration
camp.[1] On 3 February 1945 the PCI official in charge of mass labour in Milan
wrote a long, highly critical report on the situation in the factories: scant organisation, insufficient activity, conspiratorial slipshoddery, an *attesista* (wait and
see) attitude, distrust of Socialists and Christian Democrats. But 'right the way
along the line morale is high because of the Red Army advance. Everyone hopes
… that it isn't a question of months but of days and then *el Barbisun* [Stalin] is
coming to liberate us.'[2]

In these two very different situations, a similar concentration of hopes is displayed in the USSR, the Red Army, and Stalin – symbols of an ideologically and
emotionally sanctioned liberation, which carries more weight than the fact in
itself of being liberated even from a concentration camp. 'It was the Americans',
wrote an Actionist held in a lager, 'and some were disappointed because they

---

151 Testimony of Nelia Benissone Costa on the assembly held at the Turin
Microtecnica plant (Bruzzone and Farina, *La Resistenza taciuta*, p. 55).

152 Thus commented *Il Partigiano*, published by Rome's Comando Superiore
Partigiano (headed by Carlo Andreoni, after his departure from the PSIUP) in the article
'Vecchi stomaci', 9 February 1944, which also states, 'We are not prepared to set any ques-
tion aside …').

153 Thus commented *Carnia Libera*, 1 March 1945, in the article 'Noi Garibaldini',
which estimates the Garibaldi formations as accounting for 73 percent of all partisan
forces.

154 Bernardo, *Il momento buono*, pp. 167, 196.

1 Bravo and Jalla, *La vita offesa*, p. 296.

2 INSMLI, *CLNAI*, envelope 6, folder 2, subfolder 6.

were expecting the Russians, and they turned their backs on them and walked off.[3] The arrival in Trieste and eastern Veneto of the 'armies of Stalin and Tito' was the hope expressed by the SAP command in Milan.[4] In other documents the desire to see the arrival of the Red Army is expressed in what is a sometimes not very circumstantiated but always sure form.[5]

Given the difficulty of providing anything more precise than a generic desire for a radical change, and given the parsimonious indications about the future offered by the party, the myth of the USSR and of Stalin proved particularly fitted for filling the void. *L' Azione Libertaria*, a clandestine paper close to the Communists, realised as much, but in its very title showed the distance it wished to keep. It wrote that in Italy we know what we don't want and we give what we want the name of Communism and Socialism. But, not knowing really what these ought to be, 'we turn to Russia and the PC, hoping and trusting that through our spirit of revolt they will bring about Communism: as if someone could do for a people what he can do himself. Only he himself ...'[6]

The war had made the role of the USSR essential, by virtue of its having been the coadjutant that it had appeared to be to some young people whose anti-Fascism had ripened under the regime.[7] From this point of view, the contradictions of PCI policy (its dual soul, its turning a blind eye), which have been extensively analysed at the political and ideological level, turn out to be deeply rooted in the consciousness of the militants and of a vast area influenced by them. This was not 'a justification of one's personal passivity',[8] but an objective compulsion, springing from the history of the last twenty-five years and revived by the experience of what was happening at the time.

The watchword of the years immediately following the Revolution, when among the duties of Communist parties pride of place was given to the 'defence

---

3 Testimony of Bruno Vasari, an Action Party member from Trieste born in 1911 (Bravo and Jalla, *La vita offesa*, p. 300).

4 See the 'circular' from the Command of the SAP Brigades group for Milan and its province, 1 January 1945. The same conceptions appeared in the subsequent 'Circular No. 12' of this same Command, from 30 January (*Le Brigate Garibaldi*, vol. III, pp. 181, 311–12).

5 See, for example, the letter from the political commissar of the Friuli division, Andrea Lima, to the Udine CLN, 31 January 1945 (ibid., pp. 312–19).

6 From the article 'Del comunismo', 15 September 1944, which begins 'Each country makes *its own* revolution'.

7 Their illusions in the American people quickly having collapsed, Aligi Barducci and his friends convinced themselves that 'only the Russian people, which had made its own revolution, could help the Italian people to do likewise'; thus did M.A. and S. Timparano sketch out the development of a group of young people born under fascism (G. and E. Varlecchi, *Potente*, p. 75, n. 1).

8 This reductive interpretation, tied into the polemic against *attentismo*, appears in Ragionieri, *Il partito comunista*, p. 402.

of the USSR,[9] was reversed. Now it was the USSR that helped, guided, showed the way. The party's unitary line, which deferred the revolution *sine die*, accepted it in the meantime insofar as it felt guaranteed by the country of the Revolution and, on behalf of that country, by 'Barbisun-Baffone' ('Stalin'), whose force would, come what may, safeguard Italy from relapsing into a new Fascism and from the seductions of reformism. Those who hoped for an autonomously Italian revolution (the writers of the small newspaper quoted above, the Actionists of the 'democratic revolution', the small group of the PIL, mentioned in the preceding chapters, and some other heretics) were unable to unravel this maze of uncertainties that was deeply implanted in the masses. Indeed, the international situation that was clearly taking shape and that seemed to leave no space for the breaking of that identification between revolution and the expansion of the Soviet sphere of influence, of which the arrival of the Red Army was the symbol even before it became its effective cause, also helped to reinforce this maze – that is, it fed both the hopes and fears that it aroused. This is borne out by the fact that the dissolution of the Comintern – so significant on the plane of international relations and ideology[10] – had no appreciable effect on the force exercised by the myth of the USSR during the Resistance, in Italy and elsewhere.

The PCI could not but foster this myth. But the enthusiasm with which it was fostered could not always be contained within the limits most in tune with the party line. At times the intransigence of Communist principles and the Communist faith, and the need to galvanise the privileged recipients of the message, conflicted with the intention to present the party's position reassuringly to a vaster public. For example, the celebration of 7 November, a canonical, fundamental date, left an extremely reduced margin of tactical elasticity. If we read the Rome edition of *L'Unità* for 1943 together with the northern edition, and the manifesto launched for the occasion, we find the following statements: the ultimate cause of the Soviet victories lies in the October revolution; the essential merit of the victory goes to the USSR, which 'has saved the world from the barbarities of Nazism and Fascism', stamped its democratic character on the war, and 'proved capable of linking the nations allied to it to this progressive character'; the army of Marx, Lenin and Stalin is invincible; the Soviet proletariat is 'the force of humanity' and 'the victorious vanguard in the struggle for the liberty of Europe'; Stalin is 'the genius expressed by the working class in the decisive moment for the fate of humanity'; among his merits is his implacable

---

9 A paraphrased version of this old argument was used in the aforementioned 'open letter' to the dissidents of Stella Rossa, writing that it was necessary to alleviate 'the burden that has weighed down on the Red Army for over three years'. The dissidents had, moreover, spoken in their paper of the 'tortured flesh of the Russian people' (see Dellavalle, *Lotte operaie: Torino*, p. 208).

10 On the repercussions of the dissolution of the Comintern, decreed on 15 May 1943, for PCI cadre, see Ragionieri, *Il partito comunista*, pp. 310–18.

struggle against 'social-democratism' (that is, the pretence of social-democratic feelings): the USSR is the '*patria* of all workers'; the USSR 'certainly will oppose any measure that aims to suffocate the liberty and progress of the Italian popular forces'.[11]

Particularly recurrent is the attribution to the USSR of the essential merit of victory. The Soviet offensive thus finds no more than 'a useful complement in the offensive of the Anglo-American armies in France and Italy'; and, if the Red Army is 'glorious', the Anglo-American armies are only 'powerful'.[12]

In this scenario, the victories of the USSR, and its very existence, acquire a pedagogic value. With a language in which rhetorical gesture does not succeed in stifling sincerity of inspiration, a 'mural newspaper for the population' writes of Stalingrad: 'After the French Revolution a Russian Revolution has arisen in Europe teaching the world once again that the invader can be repelled however strong he may be, if one truly entrusts the destinies of the *patria* to the poor, the humble, the proletariat, the workers'.[13] A local (Alessandria) edition of *L'Unità* wrote with an emphasis that was no less sincere: 'Since 7 November 1917, on the vast Soviet territory, the flag of universal brotherhood has been waving. With the victorious Russian Revolution the oppressed peoples exult and begin once again to hope!'[14] When the Soviet armies entered eastern Prussia, the Ligurian edition of *L'Unità* commented: 'On the lands consecrated by the most glorious traditions of Prussian militarism and aristocracy, the armoured columns of the army of workers are advancing victoriously, led by young generals, by marshals who are sons of the people, sons of workers and peasants'.[15]

---

11 See the Rome edition of *L'Unità*, 3 November 1943, whose whole front page was covered with the title 'On the 26th anniversary of the Russian Revolution, the people of the whole world see the dawn of the victory of freedom and of national independence'; see various titles and subtitles of the northern edition of 7 November 1943, and the article 'Perché è necessario che prenda il potere il CLN' ('Why it is necessary for the CLN to take power') which sought to dispel 'leftist' qualms; and the 7 November poster in which the USSR, following an old formulation, was defined as the 'fatherland of all workers', in P. Secchia and F. Frassati, *Storia della Resistenza*, Rome: Riuniti, Rome 1965, vol. I, p. 300. At the same time, *L'Unità* referred to 'the victory of the Soviet Union and of its allies'; and the article 'Con l'URSS per la vittoria e per la libertà!' ('With the USSR, for victory and freedom!') concluded with the statement that 'the Soviet Union is guiding the United Nations to victory, the liberation of peoples' (northern edition, 29 September 1943).

12 See the article 'La schiacciante vittoria dell'Esercito Rosso (oltre la Vistola)' in the Emilia-Romagna edition of *L'Unità*, 30 July 1944, and the 3 July 1944 letter from the Lombardy Delegation of the General Command of the Garibaldi Brigades to the formations of Como province, n.d. (INSMLI, *Brigate Garibaldi*, envelope 2, folder 1, subfolder 1).

13 'Ottobre rosso', in *La voce della realtà*, published by the 19th Eusebio Giambone Brigade, 13 August 1944 (IG, BG, 04741).

14 Editorial 'Saluto al popolo sovietico', 1 March 1945.

15 'L'Unione Sovietica combatte in Germania', 7 November 1944.

On the occasion of previous Soviet victories, *L'Unità* had exhorted its readers to consider them as 'examples to study and understand, as the highways to follow', not least as regards 'the rapid and ruthless purging of traitors and the fifth column [and] the consequent impossibility of the Germans finding in the USSR a Quisling, a Laval, a Farinacci, a Mussolini'.[16]

The lesson provided by the USSR was at once moral, political and doctrinal. Illustrating the democratic regime that 'must provide the spinal column of our formations', a Garibaldi command wrote: 'It is precisely this which is the secret of the marvellous results obtained in Russia and wherever our comrades have been able to act and organise'.[17] On the occasion of 7 November 1944, *L'Unità* repeated that the victories of the USSR were the victories of the 'superior form of democracy', the 'proletarian Soviet' form; and, extending the notion for Italian use, added that in the Soviet Union democracy 'is open to the initiative and active participation of the broadest popular masses'.[18]

Soviet democracy is often held up as the key for interpreting the progressive democracy championed for Italy by the party;[19] and in some cases specific references are made to the Constitution of 1936.[20] The lessons devoted to the 'realisation of Sovietism' in a 'short course for commissars' organised by the 1st Garibaldi-Osoppo divisional command in fall 1944 appear scholastically doctrinaire – though this was the eastern border. It was explained that in the USSR 'the law of surplus value has been overthrown'.[21]

All these suggestions became part of common parlance – or, if one prefers, of the faith of Communists who were signed up party members, but also of those who were not signed up. A Florentine worker recounts:

> Frankly I have never lost my faith: only once have I wept, I swear by my son, when I came out of 'Galileo' and saw in *La Nazione* that word was going around that the

---

16 'L' Armata proletaria ha sfondato lo schieramento tedesco sul Nipro e a Melitopol', Northern edition, 31 October 1943.

17 Letter from the Command of the 1st Zone, signed 'Curto', to the inspector Simon, 8 July 1944 (IG, *BG*, 010046).

18 Article in the series 'Domande e risposte', in the northern edition of 7 November 1944.

19 Thus, for example, Pietro addressed himself to his 'dear comrades' in the Cuneo area on 14 December 1944, exhorting them to read the articles which *La nostra lotta* was publishing on the USSR and on progressive democracy (IG, *BG*, 04467). On the connection between Togliatti's conception of progressive democracy and the Soviet experience of state-building, see F. Sbarberi, *I comunisti italiani e lo Stato 1929–1945*, Milan: Feltrinelli, 1980, especially the fifth chapter.

20 See the article 'La Costituzione sovietica' in *L'Unità* (Asti), 15 November 1944, *La Costituzione sovietica*, and the 4th Piedmont Division Command's request for the text of the Constitution, on 25 February 1945 (*Le Brigate Garibaldi*, vol. III, p. 419).

21 The text of these lectures is held at IZDG, envelope 272b, folder 1/A.

Russian war was over and done with: all that remained to be done was grab them and give them you know what ... at that moment I wept, but then picked up straight way, and [since then] I have always hoped.[22]

The victories of the Red Army demonstrated in fact how well founded this faith was. And it is no accident that the anniversary of the creation of the Red Army was solemnly celebrated in the Garibaldi formations.[23]

Another Galileo worker so strongly identified the vision of the Soviet Union with the war of liberation in his memory ('this new society in which there was no longer man's exploitation of man, right? This brotherhood, this no more fear of dismissal') as to make the mistake of saying that he had joined the PCI in 1945, 'when there were the Germans', when in fact in that year they had already left Florence. (This is no oversight but an indirect manifestation of regret at not having joined the party at the heroic and unifying moment.)[24] The same worker attributes to Radio Moscow the highly popular signature tune of Radio London 'You could hear, "Tum, tum, tum Moscow speaking, it's Moscow speaking. Workers of the world unite." It was Togliatti speaking then.'[25] As a snub to Fascist-era dating, a presumably very raw Communist recruit dated his report: '5 maggio 1944–XXVII'.[26] Enthusiasm for the Red Army advance could be such as to drag *Il Grido di Spartaco* into gaffes such as that of calling it 'il rullo compressore' ('the steam-roller'), which was what the tsarist army had customarily been called: criticism from the party secretariat was swift and severe.[27]

---

22 From the aforementioned testimony of Angelo Raffaelli (Contini, *Memoria e storia*, p. 352).

23 On 24 February 1944 the Commissariat of the General Command circulated 'outline political report for political commissars, on the events of the week, no. 3' with the theme of 'The 26th anniversary of the Red Army and the military situation (INSMLI, *Brigate Garibaldi*, envelope 1, folder 4). On 27 February, Rino communicated from the Valli di Lanzo to his 'dear comrades': 'Today we have marked the 26th anniversary of the Red Army amidst an openly patriotic and revolutionary atmosphere' (*Le Brigate Garibaldi*, vol. I, p. 273).

24 Testimony of Corrado Polli, born 1921, adding: 'Russia was, for us, a mirage'. A manager of the factory, the engineer Francesco Brini, commented 'They claimed already to have become Russians' (Contini, *Memoria e storia*, pp. 90–2, 214).

25 Ibid., p. 82.

26 See the report on the Picelli detachment, written by 'Facio' for the Command of the North Emilia Brigade (IG, *BG, Emilia-Romagna*, G.IV.2.2).

27 Thus was signed Luigi Longo's 10 November 1943 letter to the Turin leadership, held at IG, *Archivio PCI* and published in Secchia, *Il PCI e la guerra di liberazione*, pp. 176–7, with the passage cited in the text omitted. However, the error made by a 'candidate' intellectual, in speaking of the 'nationalism' of Stalin, was instead considered 'possible to overcome, with the right clarification' (anonymous document, presumably from late November 1943, with regard to the Marche: IG, *Archivio PCI*).

A Terni partisan song, an adaptation from the French of the famous civil war song 'A l'appel du grand Lénine s'avançent les partisans', succeeds in concentrating the three motifs of the patriotic war, the civil war and the class war, projecting them onto the Soviet myth which is unambiguously identified with Communism. The enemies are identified as the 'Fascist puppets' and the 'German destroyer'. The appeal is addressed to all Italians, before whom the partisans present themselves as 'the partisans for your liberty' (a clear reference to the Fascist hymn 'Giovinezza': 'in Fascism lies the salvation of our liberty'). A particular appeal is, moreover, addressed to the workers and peasants; there is a reference to Filippo Turati's hymn to the workers ('Su fratelli su compagni'): but the *padroni* are never named. Instead the red flag of Communism flutters and, above all, 'all'appello di Stalin siamo i primi partisan' ('we're the first partisans at Stalin's roll-call').[28]

This text can be compared with two rather colder reports by party leaders, again in the province of Terni. In the first of these there is the complaint that recruitment has been done 'not too well', and this explanation is given: 'The prevailing mentality is to enlist all those who are for Russia and against Fascism, but in practice these individuals do not give good results.' The second report complains about the scant political and class conscience, and the cause of this is seen as lying in the lack 'in the *mezzogiorno* [sic] of a well-informed and capable organisation of our party, whose function and prestige here is perceived more than anything through revelations of the ['exceptional' has been crossed out] economic, strategic possibilities of Russia.'[29]

These two party functionaries were guilty not only of a shaky sense of geography but of scant generosity towards their new, enthusiastic and combative comrades, who were practically all, as they themselves wrote, of proletarian and popular extraction. But they also signal the risk that the discourse would slip from 'Russia is winning because she is right' to 'Russia is right because she is winning'. Associating the USSR with a great, ideal loftiness in order to find the strength to level criticisms at it was an antidote – not in fact widely used – to this risk. A Communist who 'declares himself to be an anarchist and who seems to be in the Party because without organisation you can't do anything' expressed his contempt for 'the Soviet ambassadors in London, because they have been

---

28 The song's text appears in Portelli, *Biografia di una città*, p. 263 (see also p. 314: 'Thus we went to fight, thus we lived Stalin'): 'Brothers, comrades, villages and cities / We're the partisans of your liberties / Workers and peasants, in struggle we'll unite / On Stalin's call we are first to the fight / Workers and peasants destroy the invader / The Fascist stooges and the German destroyer / Now's the time for battle, Italians arise / See now, Communists, the red flag flies'.

29 'Relazione sulla situazione politica e militare della nostra provincia', Terni, 1 February 1944; 'Relazione militare', n.d., but early 1944, Alv. (Alviano?) (IG, *Archivio PCI e BG*, 012373).

wining and dining while thousands of men are dying on the Russian front'.[30] The pro-Sovietism of the Movimento Comunista d'Italia, mentioned earlier, may be taken as being in some measure similarly inspired – forever astonished, as it is, that the PCI fell short of the standard set by the Soviet model, and fond of recalling the words of the *Manifesto*: 'Communists disdain to hide their principles and aims.'[31]

Stalin – and testimonies on this score abound – was the symbol that summed up the Soviet myth. He was able to enjoy all the advantages of the charismatic leader without, given his physical distance from the scene, having to endure the drawbacks. In seeking to understand how a figure who emerged as the head of a bureaucratic machinery managed to focus onto his person so much utopian longing, we might get a glimpse from these words of an elderly anarchist who in his turn had gone over to the Italian Communist Party: 'Pietro Gori was the ideal, Stalin the reality.'[32] In other words, the figure of Stalin represented the idea made flesh, taking on its burdens and sullying his hands, and, in order to preserve them, reducing the supreme principles to didactic formulae or, as one intellectual puts it, to 'rarefied logic' breathed 'with a sense of repose'.[33]

People died crying 'Viva la libertà! Viva Stalin!' or simply 'Viva Stalin'.[34] And the fascination of the figure of Stalin could extend also to those who were not Communist. A partisan who enlisted in the Cremona Gruppo di Combattimento of the CIL has recounted: 'In the battle that we were fighting, in which we were taking a heap of blows from the Germans, and were about to flee, the officer had yelled "Avanti, Savoia!" three times and no one budged. A

---

30 See Fredo's report from the Varese, November 1943 (IG, *Archivio PCI*).

31 'Dichiarazioni sulle direttive politiche del MCI', in *Bandiera Rossa*, 28 December 1943.

32 K. Sonetti, 'La présence du mythe dans un fragment de conscience ouvrière: Pietro Gori et Staline parmi les ouvriers de l'entreprise Ilva à Portoferraio', in Institut d'Histoire du Temps Présent, *IV Colloque international d'Histoire orale, Aix-en-Provence, 24–26 septembre 1982*, Université d'Aix-en-Provence, n.d., pp. 428–34. My thanks to Sonetti for making me aware of this.

33 Calamandrei, *La vita indivisibile*, p. 161, under the date of 27 March 1944. This was four days after the Via Rasella attack, of which Calamandrei was one of the protagonists.

34 One man to shout 'viva la libertà' at the firing squad was Luigi Clerici, whose name was then adopted by the Fronte Proletario brigade (see the *Bollettino* No. 45 of the brigade command, 24 August 1944, in IG, BG, 0626). For the partisans who fell shouting the name of Stalin, see again the report signed by Sandro, 28 January 1944, on the Fratelli Bandiera detachment active in the Biellese, where another partisan – evidently moustachioed – had the *nom de guerre* 'Whiskers', so as not to confuse the sacred with the profane; and 'Rapporto della compagna Milena sull'attività della formazione partigiana Ugo Stanzioni', Modena, 8 April 1944 (IG, BG, 05087 e 03001; another part of this latter document is quoted in *Le Brigate Garibaldi*, vol. I, p. 342).

comrade – a republican – stood up and said "Avanti Stalin!" The whole company moved.'[35]

The USSR was presented as the one who reaches out a 'fraternal' hand to us (in effect, the USSR tried to benefit from its indirect involvement in the occupation regime in Italy) and as 'the first paladin and most effective guarantor of the loyal application' to Italy of the resolutions of the Moscow conference.[36] On the thorny question of the fate of the Italian prisoners in Russia, Togliatti personally undertook to ensure that they 'are living well today. The overwhelming majority of them breathe an atmosphere of condemnation of Fascism and are anxiously awaiting the moment when they will be able to be free to take up arms for the liberation of the *patria*.'[37]

The granting of autonomous seats to the Ukraine and Byelorussia in the United Nations, which was being created at the time, was presented as a great conquest of principle, due to the coherent application of the doctrine of Lenin and Stalin to the different nationalities; and the compromising prediction was made that from now on all the Soviet republics would be able to 'establish their own diplomatic relations with foreign states and levy their own national army, which will however be part of the Red Army'.[38]

This article makes explicit and reassuring mention of the Baltic, Karelo-Finnish and Moldavian republics, which were about to be liberated by the Red Army; just as it insists on the 'independence, liberty, integrity guaranteed by the USSR to Romania'.[39] This was actually a difficult line of reasoning, aimed among other things at nipping in the bud any hint of 'extremism' which, taking the open and worldwide nature of the Union of the Soviet Socialist Republics literally (the possibility of acceding to or withdrawing from the Union was provided for by the 1936 Constitution, as it had already been by those of 1918 and 1924), might plead the case for a pure and simple entry into the Union of those peoples who were gradually being liberated from the Nazis and from the *padroni*. This was an utterly unrealistic hypothesis, but one that must somehow have been circulating if Riccardo Lombardi accused the PCI of seeing European unity only as

---

35 Ferruccio Mauri's testimony in Portelli, *Biografia di una città*, p. 314.

36 'Ripresa delle relazioni diplomatiche con l'URSS' in *L'Unità*, Rome edition, 23 March 1944, and 'La conferenza di Mosca' in the northern edition, 7 November 1943.

37 Interview with Libero, *L'Unità*, Rome edition, 18 May 1945.

38 See 'La recente riforma della costituzione sovietica. Il riconoscimento della più completa autonomia nazionale ai popoli dell'URSS' in *L'Unità*, Rome edition, 12 February 1944. So, too, did *L'Italia libera* speak of the 'great reform, daring in conception and prompt in implementation' ('La riforma costituzionale dell'Unione Sovietica', Lombard edition, 12 February 1944). Even the royalist *Italia nuova* praised the reform, mocking the Fascist interpretation according to which it was a mere ruse ('Le riforme costituzionali in Russia', 4 April 1944).

39 See the commentary in the northern edition of *L'Unità*, 10 April 1944, on Molotov's statements as Soviet troops entered into Romania.

'an expansion of the borders of the USSR',[40] and if in retort to the South African Prime Minister Jan Smuts, who had presented entry into the Commonwealth as the sole path of salvation for the countries of the European West, *Avanti!* wrote that if that were the case it would be better to join the Soviet Union, which is 'another "Common Wealth" which for years has been offering all countries the opportunity to enter and participate, with parity of rights and duties'.[41]

Equally unfeasible was the not entirely new hypothesis, echoed in *Azione Libertaria*, of creating the Federation of Soviet Socialist Republics of the Balkans.[42] It is well-known how vigorously Stalin condemned the project of this kind put forward by Dimitrov and Tito.

Predictions about the novelties that, through enlightened Soviet initiative, were to characterise the post-war international order, should be linked to the hope that the victorious outcome of the severe trial of war, and the loyalty to the regime that the people had demonstrated by isolating cases of collaboration-ism, would inaugurate a process of democratisation in the USSR. Those who cultivated the myth of the USSR as a foreshadowing of the future did not feel the least need to nurture such hopes. But those who would sincerely have liked to see a more ductile and realistic, politically useful and morally acceptable 'myth', did in fact put some losing cards on this very prospect. The PSIUP executive did just this in a declaration of 1 May 1944;[43] Franco Venturi argued likewise in one of the most acute and carefully pondered attempts at interpreting Soviet Russia to appear during the Resistance;[44] and this too is how Eugenio Colorni already thought during his internment in the prison of Ventotene.[45] It was, furthermore, a hope that was internationally widespread in vast socialist circles that were not prejudicially anti-Soviet.[46]

---

40 See the pamphlet *Il partito d'azione: cos' è e cosa vuole* (The Action Party: What It Is and What It Wants), December 1943, p. 12.

41 'Il discorso di Smuts e il federalismo europeo', in the Rome edition of 30 December 1943.

42 Editorial 'Considerazioni sulla guerra', 15 September 1944. See, on the precedents of this idea, V. C. Fišera, 'Communisme et intégration supranationale. "La Fédération Balkanique" (1924–32)', in *Revue d'histoire moderne et contemporaine* XXXIV (July–September 1987), pp. 497–508.

43 'L'Esecutivo del partito definisce la posizione dei socialisti di fronte al nuovo Governo Badoglio ed ai problemi della unità d'azione e della unità antifascista', *Avanti!*, Rome edition, 6 May 1944. The text has been reproduced in S. Neri Serneri, *Il partito socialista nella Resistenza*, Nistri-Lischi, Pisa 1988, pp. 142–50.

44 See the pamphlet printed under the pseudonym 'Leo Aldi', 'Socialismo di oggi e di domani', (*Quaderni dell'Italia Libera*, December 1943, p. 17).

45 See the testimony of Spinelli, *Io, Ulisse*, pp. 316–17. Spinelli adds that he and Ernesto Rossi did not share in Colorni's optimism.

46 On the long ascendancy of this type of hope (the Two-and-a-Half International, Guild Socialism, etc.), ripening again during the war, see G. D. H. Cole's *History of*

As far as the Soviet Union itself was concerned, Djilas subsequently wrote:

> As I look back, I can say that the conviction spread spontaneously in the USSR that now, after a war that had demonstrated the devotion of the Soviet people to their homeland and to the basic achievements of the revolution, there would be no further reason for the political restrictions and for the ideological monopolies held by little groups of leaders, and especially by a single leader.[47]

And note Konstantin Simonov's description in 1958 of the enormous emotion aroused by the speech made by Stalin on the radio shortly after the start of the German invasion. When one of the listeners, a war casualty, heard Stalin address the people using the words 'Brothers and sisters! My friends!', he asked himself: 'Was it possible that only a tragedy like war could revive those words and that sentiment? ... But what Stalin's speech had left in the souls of everybody was primarily the feverish hope for a change.'[48]

It is hard to know whether aspirations of this kind were rife among the Russian partisans fighting in Italy, as Michel has suggested that they were in some way present in the partisans fighting in the occupied territories of Russia.[49] It is equally hard to understand, if we go back beyond the apologias made after the event, how much the Russian partisans fighting in Italy contributed to feeding the myth of the USSR. Testimonies conflict. The Christian Democrat Ermanno Gorrieri extols their valorous and disciplined behaviour in the Republic of Montefiorino, criticising, if anything, the sycophancy of the Communist press towards them.[50] In the Communist documentary sources, along with the many and obvious positive recognitions, expressions of 'unitary' concern appear, kindled by the fact that the Soviets did not intend to remove the hammer and sickle from their caps. But behaviour of this kind could aid the myth, and in any case it showed that *sinistrismo* was not just a 'mask of the Gestapo'. Concerns

---

Socialist Thought, vol. IV, *Communism and Social Democracy 1914–1931*, and Vol. 5, *Socialism and Fascism*.

47 Djilas, *Conversations with Stalin*, p. 40.

48 See Ehrenburg's testimony cited in Valiani, *Il partito d'azione*, p. 129. At the 12th International Congress of Historical Sciences held at Vienna in 1965, I asked the Soviet scholars present whether, among the peoples of the USSR, such expectations had really arisen. The response was that only a bourgeois in hock to imperialism could foster the idea that the Soviets had fought for something other than the Soviet system, as it then existed. So they said in public; but then, in private, their delegation leader, Evgeny Boltin, apologised for their having been so aggressive.

49 Michel, *Gli Alleati e la Resistenza in Europa*, pp. 75–7.

50 Gorrieri, *La Repubblica di Montefiorino*, p. 373. 'The Russians and Slovenes', an anonymous and dateless 'report by a partisan' on the Apennines near Modena commented, 'upheld the necessity of an iron discipline and were rather predisposed to neglecting the educational aspect' (IG, *BG*, 02255).

about social extremism appear, because the Soviets 'are plundering villas and houses of *signori* only because they are such even if they aren't Fascists, and of small land-owners'. But this too could, in some cases, feed the myth. Finally, there arose what might be called perplexities concerning public morality (*buon costume*), because the Soviets got drunk and made 'unbridled use' of food, creating problems above all with the peasants.[51] Iron discipline and lack of restraint were qualities that seemed to coexist in the Russians and Yugoslavians, arousing both admiration and fear. Again, the Soviets' wish to go it alone was not appreciated,[52] while problems were created by the difficulty in distinguishing escaping prisoners from deserting collaborationists, Cossacks and 'Mongols'.[53]

That the name *mongoli* was attributed to all, or almost all, Soviet collaborationists, excluding Cossacks, with whom one came into contact indicates how marked was the tendency to saddle that distant and terrifying Asian people with an undeniable fact that might cast a shadow on the myth of Soviet Russia.[54] And it could so happen that Germans and Fascists 'pretended to be Mongols so as to do what they liked without shame. One Mongol had a southern Italian accent.'[55]

---

51 See 'Rapporto generale sull'attività militare in Romagna (dall'8 settembre 1943 al 15 maggio 1944)', and a 12 March 1944 proposal to constitute 'Garibaldi Brigades of Romagna', where, out of a total of 218 men, there were eighteen Soviets – including a company commander – two German deserters, six Czechs (presumably also Wehrmacht deserters), fourteen Slovenes, two Poles and five Englishmen (IG, *BG, Emilia-Romagna*, G.IV.I.4 and G.IV.2.7).

52 See the documents cited in the previous note, and the 9 March 1945 letter with which the commander and commissar of the divisions-group for Valsesia, Ossola, Cusio and Verbano – Cino and Ciro – explained to the 'Russian Georgian Garibaldians of the 10th Rocco Brigade' that, though understanding their intentions, they did not consent to their request to be organised in a single unit: would fraternisation with their Italian comrades not suffer from such a move, and how would the Georgians be able to extricate themselves in the event of a raid, for want of any knowledge of the Italian language? Not without a certain wryness, Cino and Ciro recalled that the greater part of the Georgians who had wanted to set up their own unit in Val d'Ossola had, in fact, crossed over into Switzerland (*Le Brigate Garibaldi*, vol. III, pp. 453–4).

53 See 'rapport di un partigiano', IG, *BG*, 02255, and the 22 November 1944 communication from commissar Franco of the Pisacane battalion of the Natisone division to the Command of the 4th BBO battalion (Briški Beneški Odred), to the effect that he had been authorised by the Soviet mission among the 9th Corps to try to secure the desertion of the Cossacks occupying Carnia desert (IZDG, envelope 221, folder III/3).

54 A Communist leader who was for some days a prisoner of the 'Mongols' during the January 1945 raid in the Piacenza region described it thusly: 'All the troops were Russians – and add to that the fact that they were workers, intellectuals, peasants – who justified their subservience to the Germans by invoking the fact that they had been continually beaten up in prison, and not given anything to eat' (Report by Giglioli, 20 January, in IG, *BG, Emilia-Romagna*, G.IV.2.6).

55 Lazagna, *Ponte rotto*, pp. 205–6.

CHAPTER 7

Violence

1. The Problem of Violence in the Context of War

Common to the three aspects of the Resistance distinguished in the preceding chapters – the three wars – is the exercise of violence. Resistance violence lends itself, therefore, to a synthetic discourse that, though it will be impossible to avoid returning to some of the themes that have already come to light, nevertheless gives us the opportunity to get them into clearer focus. Bloody violence lies at the centre of this discourse; but around the problems that it poses can be grouped several of the arguments that have come to be part of the historiographical tradition of the Resistance.

I shall not attempt a quantitative, and inaccurate, reconstruction of the acts of violence committed by the two warring parties. If we remember that in the Second World War around 50 million human lives in all were lost, the number of Italians killed between September 1943 and April 1945 is relatively small: 44,720 partisans who fell fighting and 9,980 killed in reprisals, to whom should be added 21,168 partisans and 412 civilians mutilated and disabled.[1] The total toll after the Armistice was 187,522 fallen (120,060 of whom were civilians) and 210,149 missing (122,668 of whom were civilians). Between 10 June 1940 and 8 September 1943 the Italian armed forces had had 92,767 fallen (to whom 25,499 civilians should be added), while the missing had been 106,228. Altogether, then, Italian losses in the Second World War (dead and missing, soldiers and civilians, men and women) came to 444,523. Other countries had far bloodier experiences: in the Soviet Union, 20 million dead, 7 million of whom were civilians (altogether, 10 percent of the population); Yugoslavia, 1,690,000; Poland, 6 million (22 percent of the population – the highest percentage in the world, due to the almost total elimination of 3.5 million Jews). Germany suffered about 5 million human losses, Japan 1.8 million.[2] The enormity of the violence unleashed in the

---

1 Official figures of the Italian Prime Minister's Office (Presidenza del Consiglio dei ministri) reported in Battaglia, *Storia della Resistenza*, p. 561, notes. Battaglia adds that, according to ANPI figures, some 32,000 partisans died abroad, and that the number of Fascists and Germans who fell in the anti-partisan struggle is impossible to define.

2 Figures from the Istituto Centrale di Statistica, *Morti e dispersi per cause belliche negli anni 1940–45*, Rome 1957, Table 1.1 and M. L. Salvadori, *Storia dell'età contemporanea dalla restaurazione all'eurocomunismo*, Turin: Loescher, 1976, pp. 924–5. I thank Giorgio Rochat for having made me aware of an error in the original edition of this book.

First World War[3] might therefore seem to have revisited Italy, during the Second World War and the German occupation, in a relatively modest measure.

The question, however, cannot be circumscribed in quantitative terms, not only because the number of victims is in any case high and the reaction it arouses instantly transcends the materiality of a mere numerical count, but because in doing so one would run the risk of sidestepping the fundamental historical and moral problems posed by the killing of other men and women, and by the recognition or denial of its lawfulness. Today, with so much violence going on in the world, the dichotomy is clearly recognisable – in Italy, particularly, after terrorism – between the total and meta-historical rejection of violence, especially bloody violence, and reference instead to the historical situation as founder, or denier, of the lawfulness of killing, or indeed the duty to kill, other men. The historian, and the contemporary historian most acutely, feels that espousal of the first position means stepping beyond the bounds of the discourse which, given his profession, he is called upon to conduct, and consequently reducing all wars, all revolutions, all massacres, all executions to the same level: in a word, to consider everything 'la stessa pappa' ('the same pap') (as a central European friend of mine, Irene Nunberg, a Jew, one of the few members of her family to survive extermination, has put it). On the other hand, the second position leaves one deeply troubled by virtue of the authorisation it grants the 'philosophers of history', whose perilousness, when they speak in the name of the powers that be, our century's events have amply demonstrated. And yet the historian cannot duck the task of placing in the flux of time and contextualising in the situation in which he sees them occurring the manifestations of violence that he encounters in the course of his research. In doing so he should not forget that there exists a problem of life and death that it is not his task to resolve. All the historian can do is illustrate the forms in which this problem has manifested itself through the centuries, as Ariès's and Vovelle's by now classic works[4] have shown that it is possible to attempt to do.

The following pages have the far more modest aim of offering a contribution to the correct evaluation of the kind of violence that the resistenti and Fascists practised – on the one hand bringing it back into that framework of the Second World War that was common to everybody, Fascists and anti-Fascists, Italians and Germans alike, and on the other hand holding fast to the fundamental distinctions between the parties involved. The enemy himself, a partisan has written, 'had taught us all there was to know about death', but remained a disciplined man, 'sheltered from doubt', and discharged his acts of inhumanity upon us.[5] For this reason, too, quantitative facts, the importance of which should

---

3 As Hannah Arendt put it in her *On Revolution*, New York: Viking Press, 1963.

4 Philippe Ariès, *The Hour of Our Death*, New York: Knopf, 1981; Michelle Vovelle, *La mort et l'Occident de 1300 à nos jours*, Paris: Gallimard, 1983.

5 Battaglia, *Un uomo*, p. 157.

obviously not be denied, have not been given pride of place. As Thompson has written,

> the symbolic importance of violence – both the violence of the state and the law and the violence of protest – may have no direct correlation with its quantity ... Neither terror nor counter-terror can exhaust their significance in the light of a heavily quantitative examination, because the quantities must be seen within a global context, and this includes a symbolic context which attributes different values to different forms of violence.[6]

The great difference in symbolic value that the violence exercised by the men of the Resistance has compared with that practised by the regularly constituted armies and police corps stems from the breakdown of the state monopoly of violence. The citizens, hitherto more or less direct and conscious instruments and beneficiaries of state violence, became managers of violence in their own right. The moral problems springing from the immeasurable violence practised by tens of millions of men during the entire war were thus laid at the feet in a particular way, which demands more clear-cut answers of a few tens of thousands of partisans, who practised violence of their own free choice.

2. Resistance violence and fascist violence

The violence that flared up in Italy after 8 September 1943 came after a long period of practising and witnessing wartime violence, dating from 1940. But we have to go further back, to the Ethiopian war and the Spanish war and, for that matter, to the whole climate, of which Fascism and Nazism were both product and cause, that had shifted people's attitudes – and not just in a few fanatics – to the violence present in the world from the recognition of a fact to the affirmation of a value. In 1914 the explosion of violence had managed to appear as the breakdown of a world that was too bland, too monotonous, too enfeebled.[1] (Allowing for the obvious difference in scale, post-1968 violence, following a long period of unprecedented prosperity, would again have some of these characteristics.) In 1914 it had also managed to appear as the sudden unveiling of the intrinsically violent nature of the state.[2] In the Italy of 1940, and as a final proof in the Italy

---

6 E. P. Thompson, 'Folklore, Anthropology and Social History', *Indian Historical Review* III (1978), p. 2.

1 See chapter 2.1.

2 'The individual citizen can with horror convince himself in this war of what would occasionally cross his mind in peace-time – that the state has forbidden to the individual the practice of wrong-doing, not because it desires to abolish it, but because it wants to monopolise it, like salt and tobacco. A belligerent state permits itself every such

of 1943, the exercise of violence seemed rather to be the outflow of what had been building up for a long time. This made the violence on the one hand more obvious, and on the other more ruthless; but at the same time it paved the way for the passage to a reconsideration of the limits of resorting to violence and the possibility of using it in a contingent way in order to render it impossible in the future. Violence as seduction and violence as harsh necessity thus clash openly, though coexisting at times in the same people.

In a country like France, which, until the advent of war, had had no experience of Fascism in power, still in the 1930s the discovery of 'paradoxes, ambiguities conflicts, still unresolved' had led to violence being set against 'the sweet dreams of our professors'; but, Sartre goes on to say, 'it was a wretched violence ... which risked leading us to Fascism'. And again: 'It was the war which shattered the worn structures of our thought: war, occupation, Resistance, and the years which followed'.[3]

In Italy the dilemma appeared in an ostensibly simpler light: anti-Fascist violence against Fascist violence. The historicist foundation – in its idealist or Marxist version – of nearly all anti-Fascist political thought favoured this simplification. Moreover, we have seen how, faced with what Carlo Rosselli called the 'war that returns', the attitude of the anti-Fascists had been neither easy nor univocal. The German occupation and the birth of the Social Republic made the contrast between the two kinds of violence once again clear; but the global situation, created by the war, still involved all those who, on opposite fronts, were experiencing it.

Giaime Pintor, who did not live long enough to see things mutate into the Resistance, had traced this image of the war as 'place of the demoniacal':[4]

And everywhere the war has spread a facile cruelty, an unthinking, dull cruelty which is the worst secretion of man. The horrible sense of the gratuitous, of the unnecessary murder. Once the constraints have been removed, killing becomes a habit and punishing has become a routine exercise. The horrible weakness of man has emerged, the weakness of the man who can command.[5]

Pride in the Resistance must not make us hastily conclude that only the Fascists of the RSI were heirs of this attitude to killing other men. They were certainly the heirs in a growing and prevalent way, because this kind of behaviour was in tune with the basic nature of their culture; but traces are to be found

misdeed, every such act of violence, as would disgrace the individual.' Sigmund Freud, 'Thoughts for the Times on War and Death' (1915), in *On Creativity and the Unconscious*, New York: Harper, 1958.

3 Sartre, *The Search for a Method*, New York: Knopf, 1963, pp. 19–20.

4 On this, see the comments and quotes used in Langendorf, *Elogio funebre*, esp. p. 50.

5 Pintor, *Doppio diario*, pp. 120–1.

among the *resistenti* as well. In *The Drowned and the Saved*, Primo Levi wrote that the oppressor and the victim 'are in the same trap, but it is the oppressor, and he alone, who has prepared it and activated it'.[6] Levi devotes a chapter of his book to the 'grey zone', which, in the strict sense, he sees as being that of collaboration (*protekcja*) as the indispensable ring in the mechanism of the extermination camps; but, as he himself suggests, that phrase also indicates the border zone between the territory of good and the territory of evil, which vie with one another for it. The higher the rate of collective violence taking place, the more likely it is that conduct in some way common to the two great opposing territories will spring from that grey zone.

While the current practice and the constant spectacle of killing could lead to the sad habituation of which Pintor speaks, it could also prompt one to question oneself about the sense of staying alive, thus taking the problem of life and death back into the realm of one's personal experience with particular immediacy. 'It did not seem to me to be very natural that I should stay alive among so many dead companions', wrote a partisan on the eve of being shot by a firing squad.[7] 'Are you ashamed to be alive in the place of another?', was the kind of question that was asked in a death camp.[8] Parallel with this, the death that you unjustly underwent could be accepted as a destiny that you shared with so large a number of your fellow men.

Many *resistenti* felt this sentiment before the risk of death and the certainty of being condemned. 'I think today that the whole of humanity is suffering, that I'll be neither the first nor the last to die in this war', wrote a young man before attempting to escape from a training camp in Germany.[9] General Perotti, on the eve of execution in April 1944 with the other members of the Piedmontese regional military command, wrote to his wife: 'I consider myself one of the war dead, because war has been ours. And in war death is a risk everyone runs ... so many are dying every day and most of them, innocently; I at least have fought'.[10]

And an Italian participating in the French Resistance: 'There's nothing extraordinary about my death, no one should be surprised and no one should grieve; so many are dying on the front and in the air-raids that it is not at all strange that I, a soldier, should fall as well'.[11]

---

6 Levi, *I sommersi e i salvati*, p. 14.

7 Letter to the mother of the twenty-one-year-old Valerio Bassavano, an electrical mechanic from Genoa, shot on 19 May 1944 (*LRE*, p. 523).

8 See the chapter 'La vergogna', in Levi, *I sommersi e i salvati*.

9 Letter to the relatives of Sergio Papi, a state employee from Milan, of twenty-three years of age. Captured by the SS, on 18 October 1944, Papi was condemned to death by the Littorio Division tribunal, presided over by the general Tito Agosti, who later hanged himself in Rome's Forte Boccea (*LRI*, pp. 159–60).

10 *LRI*, pp. 174–5.

11 Letter to the relatives of Spartaco Fontanot, shot on 21 February 1944 (*LRE*, p. 337).

Identical sentiments were present in those of other countries awaiting execution. A French intellectual: 'I consider that at this moment thousands of soldiers of all countries are dying every day, dragged into the great wind that is sweeping me away too.'[12] A Belgian engineer: 'Hundreds of thousands of soldiers have died in this war: I am one of them.'[13] A Yugoslavian woman worker: 'Today when millions of men are going innocently to their deaths, I too find myself among them. This is what destiny has wanted and I do not grieve the fact.'[14] A Soviet Communist: 'Millions of men are perishing: are we any better than them?'[15]

This playing down of one's own violent death does not stem only from the desire to assuage the grief of those who remain, and is at the same time a far cry from mystical identification with death. It should be linked rather with the attitude assumed before the exercise of violence as an unavoidable consequence of a choice made in the name of political and civil ideals, an integral part of which consists in calling into question violence as an instrument and a value. There was not only a reappearance of the utopia of the 'last war', which was fought as a war to end all wars and sustained the morale of the great mobilised imperial armies, saddling the enemy with full responsibility for the first shot. It was also a question of living, as indeed a Piedmontese woman partisan has said, 'the first time in history in which one is rebelling against war and the promoters of war', even if today the Communist comrades of this partisan, extollers of combative voluntarism, are loath to acknowledge (the testimony dates from the early 1970s) that 'deep down' there was 'that aspect of the rejection of war' ('nobody says these things to the Party, nobody says them at school').[16] The words of another woman protagonist, whose husband was a prisoner, are along the same lines: 'And so that hatred, that antipathy to war, bullying, violence reawakens ... Then came 8 September and ... and I joined the partisans.'[17]

It is certainly no accident that these last two quotations come from women. But at the other end of the scale a similar distancing from the arms ethic can be detected in a vice-brigadiere of the *carabinieri*, turned Garibaldi partisan, who, on the eve of execution, wrote to a priest asking him to urge

---

12 Letter to the parents of Daniel Decourdemanche, shot on 30 May 1942 (*LRE*, p. 293).

13 Letter to the mother of Richard Altenhoff, shot on 30 March 1944 (*LRE*, p. 101).

14 Letter to a female friend of Alexandra Ljubic, shot by the Ustaše on 9 November 1942 (*LRE*, p. 582).

15 Letter to the family of Ivan Charitonovic Kozlov, 27 December 1942 – adding 'Such a shame! I have a mad desire to live!' – shot at the end of December 1942 (*LRE*, p. 787).

16 Testimony of Tersilla Fenoglio Oppedisano (Bruzzone and Farina, *La Resistenza taciuta*, p. 151).

17 Testimony of Margherita Bergesio Coccalotto (Bravo and Jalla, *La vita offesa*, p. 81).

his wife 'to do all she can not to try to make their children into soldiers or militarists'.[18]

The general problem raised by declarations and behaviour of this kind may be expressed by quoting Primo Levi: 'Is there such a thing as useful violence?' Levi replies: 'Unfortunately, yes', and adds that in it suffering is a 'by-product, something extra'.[19] We shall come back to this 'something extra' and the discriminating value of the attitude towards it. Meanwhile, the 'utility' of violence must be traced back to the just cause in the name of which it is exercised. In those circumstances, what does it mean to say that one must not *propter vitam vivendi perdere causam* (destroy the reason for living in order to stay alive)? The radical answer that violence is itself a *vivendi perdere causam* was utterly extraneous to the historical situation; but it is indicative that in 1946 Andrea Caffi, a lucid and committed intellectual who had experienced all the great upheavals of our century, from the Russian Revolution to the Resistance as lived on French soil, came to the conclusion that 'organised violence' is always negative, in any war, 'even against Hitler or ... Stalin'.[20] Echoing in these words is the trauma of Hiroshima and the onset of the Cold War; but they also bespeak disappointment in the results obtained by the exercise, during the Second World War, of so much 'just' violence.

The fact is that the *vivendi causa* of those human beings who underwent Fascist and Nazi aggression was also that of not tolerating the intolerability of that aggression.[21] It would have been paradoxical if *propter vitam* of the aggressor, the victim of aggression gave up sustaining his own *vivendi causam*, which led him in the first place to put his own life in danger. The 'truth' of the *resistenti* aimed therefore at giving an affirmative answer to the question put by Thomas Mann in 1918: 'Can truth be an argument, when life is at stake?'[22] Answering 'yes' meant committing oneself to finding, within a truth that does not make violence into a value, sufficient justification for a practice that seemed to belie it. I should like to venture a comparison with an experience that is in so many ways distant. The Maccabees who were fighting against the Seleucids were asked:

> Was it necessary to fight on the Sabbath against an adversary who didn't respect the rules of the game? The problem had arisen at once, at the beginning of the revolt; experience led them to conclude, 'if we all do as our brothers have done and do not

---

18 Remo Sottili, shot in Munich on 29 August 1944 (*LRI*, p. 209).

19 Levi, *I sommersi e i salvati*, p. 83.

20 A. Caffi, 'Critica della violenza', an essay written for the journal *Politics* in 1946, included in an eponymous volume edited by N. Chiaromonte, Milan: Bompiani, 1966, pp. 77–104 (the words cited appear on p. 77).

21 To use Todorov's expression in *La tolleranza e l'intollerabile*, pp. 87–108.

22 T. Mann, *Ironie und Radicalismus*, cited by L. Ceppa, 'I fratelli Mann. Una biografia in parallelo', in *Rivista di storia contemporanea* XIII (1984), p. 115.

fight rather against the Gentiles to defend our lives and our institutions, very soon they will have wiped us off the face of the earth'.[23]

Concluding the chapter in his memoirs on 'The Tragedy of Munich', Churchill wrote: 'The Sermon on the Mount is the last word in Christian ethics. Everyone respects the Quakers. Still, it is not on these terms that Ministers assume their responsibilities of guiding States.'[24]

During the Resistance the problem of the fifth commandment was raised as a preliminary issue by several anti-Fascist Catholics. 'The *cristiano-sociale* [*sic*, Christian Democrat] has raised the question of conscience: Is it legitimate to kill?' says a Communist report from Turin.[25] As we recalled earlier, a professor at the seminary of Como, don Onorio Cairoli, claimed that it was right 'to oppose the Germans and their collaborators, within the limits dictated by the natural commandments and by the decalogue'.[26] In a Communist document, a Garibaldino, Catholic commander's hesitation about attacking the enemy and laying ambushes for him is attributed not just to 'exaggerated military honesty', but 'perhaps ... to religious prejudice'.[27]

Replying to a reader who had asked *Il Popolo* what canonical measures he would incur if he used 'Fascist methods of persuasion on the Fascist don Calcagno', the Christian Democrat writer replied that it was sacrilege to cause 'real offence' to a cleric who had not been reduced to lay status or banned *in perpetuo* from wearing the cassock (measures that were never adopted against the founder of 'Crociata italica'), and added, in poor taste:

It seems to us though that, more so still than canonical reasons, moral considerations and respect for legality, a necessary premise for a constructive anti-Fascism should dissuade us from the Matteottisation of don Calcagno or anyone for that matter. When the time comes, the law will deal with Farinacci and his lot as well.[28]

23 Vidal-Naquet, *Il buon uso del tradimento*, p. 69.

24 Churchill, *The Gathering Storm*, New York: Bantam, 1961, p. 286.

25 Report by Giovanni, 'from verbal information received from Giuseppe' (*Le Brigate Garibaldi*, vol. I, p. 105).

26 See above, Chapter 5.5 and compare the words that a Dutch Catholic, Johannes A. J. Verleun, condemned to death by the Germans and shot on 7 January 1944, recalled his father having told him: 'God wills that it should not happen, but should the Germans stamp their hefty feet on our Fatherland, then a cordial Act of Contrition, boy, and do not hesitate' (*LRE*, p. 689).

27 'Alcuni rilievi sulla organizzazione della 3a divisione', Liguria, November–December 1944 (?), signed 'Luigi' (IG, *BG*, 010477).

28 *Il Popolo*, Rome edition, 20 February 1944.

Not that recourse to violence, in exceptional circumstances, was extraneous to Catholic thought: one need only think of its justifications of tyrannicide.
Closer to home, though the sides here are inverted, in 1921 Alcide De Gasperi
had criticised 'those who intend to condemn every Fascist action under the
vague condemnation of violence'. Violence, De Gasperi had recalled, is sometimes legitimate: the violent one might appear to be Renzo (in Manzoni's novel
I Promessi Sposi) resisting an abuse of power, while the real violent one was don
Abbondio.[29] The fact is, however, that the Catholics did not always find it easy
to separate the problem of violence, considered in principle, from the questions, discussed chiefly in Chapter 5 of this book, of order and legality. This
slippage was favoured on the one hand by the extensive interpretation of the
principle, to which we shall return, that it is permissible to kill only for legitimate defence,[30] and on the other hand by the fact that, when the Christian
Democrats (like, for that matter, the Liberals) spoke about today's violence their
thoughts ran to the violence of a possible and perilous tomorrow: revolutionary
violence, against the existing social order, proletarian violence. *La Libertà* took
a stand 'against all political violence'.[31] *Conquiste sindacali* appealed to the doctrine of Christ – revolutionary, yes, but not violent.[32] More problematically, the
Christian Socialists wrote that 'a clean sweep is always necessary, to kill is almost
always useless' for those who do not want to give the class struggle 'a metaphysical significance, a mystical essence in order to make it into a bloodthirsty
God of hate'.[33]

The problem of the connection between violence and legality was not,
however, the invention of some scrupulous and fearful Catholic consciences.
By long tradition, both Christian and lay, what made it legitimate to kill, sus-
pending the authority of the fifth commandment, was primarily, if not quite
exclusively, the cover of legality – in other words, the recognition of the state
monopoly of violence. Now, the theme of the institutional void and the all-
determining choice, which has been central to our argument so far, finds its
critical point precisely in the exercise of violence – that is to say, of the legitimisation of exercising the *jus vitae ac necis* (right of life and death) without any
secure institutional cover. The preference of many Catholics for purely military

---

29 See the article 'Il fascismo nella campagna elettorale', in *Il nuovo Trentino*,
7 April 1921 (cited in R. De Felice, *Le interpretazioni del fascismo*, Bari: Laterza, 1969,
p. 143).

30 See, for example, don Giuseppe Menegon's reprimand of the band-leader
Masaccio, in Ventura, *La società rurale veneta*, p. 69, n. 115.

31 This paper, 'organ of the democratic Christian movement', 15 April 1944, is cited
in Bianchi, *I cattolici*, p. 264.

32 'Cristo e il lavoro', an article from 9 April 1944.

33 'Perché Cristiano-Sociali', in *L'Azione dei lavoratori*, 'Roman organ of the
Christian-Social Movement', 25 January 1944.

partisan activity can be interpreted, in this regard, as a quest for the traditional guarantee of a non-guilty use of arms.[34] The authorisation given to the military was, in short, more reassuring than the choice of the political; and it was an authority introjected by the conscience of each single individual and endorsed by the age-old authorisation given by the Church to the secular arm of Christian principles. This could give rise to the paradox that the more one harboured religious doubts and scruples, the more readily one had recourse to this authority, either by taking up arms oneself or saddling others with the more unpleasant aspects that went with doing so. In the Modena partisan division the Christian Democrats wanted order and regular and inflexible tribunals, but preferred the firing squads to be composed of Communists.[35] A lay conscience like Primo Levi has baldly laid bare the contradictions, and not the consolations, generated by this kind of behaviour:

> I demand justice – he writes of himself – but I am not able, personally, to trade punches or 'return the blow' … I prefer to delegate punishments, revenges and retaliations to the laws of my country … It is indeed because of this that my career as a Partisan was so brief, painful, stupid and tragic: I had taken on a role that was not mine.[36]

If the partisan was no longer protected by the moral anonymity guaranteed a priori to the regular soldier at the moment in which he kills an equally anonymous soldier, the enemy also emerged from anonymity. Both as a German and, still more, as a Fascist, the enemy came to acquire a concrete and far more individualised physiognomy: the enemy ceased to be 'only a collective identity'.[37] The emotional and moral attitude towards him thus became in its turn more personal and all-absorbing. Even in regular wars, for that matter, as we have already seen, the combatants find themselves compelled to live one of these two alternative experiences: that of being an atom of an indistinct mass shooting in cold blood at the faceless enemy, preserving oneself from blind hatred but with the risk of slipping into indifference and cynicism; or else of shooting in hate, but running the risk of being dragged towards rage and ferocity against individual enemies. The *arditi*, for example, set off action 'with an explosion of barbaric joy' and, when they returned, 'each boasted about how he had laid in

---

34 Note the contrast between the positions expressed, within the Osoppo formations, between the 'military men' don Ascanio De Luca and don Attilio Ghiglione (a former Alpinists' chaplain) and the 'politician' don Moretti (Fogar, *Le brigate Osoppo-Friuli*, pp. 289–90).

35 See the letter from the Modena PCI federation to the Party committee for the mountain areas, 8 January 1945 (*Le Brigate Garibaldi*, vol. III, p. 200).

36 Levi, *I sommersi e i salvati*, pp. 109–11.

37 Fussell, *La grande guerra*, p. 97.

with his knife'; and in March 1943 *Gerarchia*, Mussolini's magazine, read: 'War can't be fought without hating the enemy'.[38]

A letter to his fiancé written on 28 April 1917 by Fernando Schiavetti, who was to become a severe critic of the 'the Fascist aesthetic of violence', reveals clearly how difficult it was to strike a balance between the two positions:

I am very aware that I don't harbour blind hatred of the Austrians [in a letter written six days earlier he had spoken of a 'personal resentment which was completely absent in me before'] and that I am capable of understanding that in war we die, they die and no one is a murderer: but I have no pity for them, none whatsoever. The other day we hit one and I was good enough to exclaim: I'm sorry for his mother but I'd hit him another time.[39]

Just before being shot by the Germans, a Soviet partisan wrote: 'Can you imagine with what courage, with what fury and with what boundless pleasure I would destroy these loathsome reptiles? Yet only two years ago I was afraid of killing a chicken!'[40] And Roberto Battaglia would ask himself: 'But how can you be so happy because you have killed other men?'[41]

In the partisan war, ideological and civil, the knot that Fernando Schiavetti was attempting to unravel in the 'regular' war of 1915–18 became still more tangled. In a page of her diary, Ada Gobetti described the concern that she felt at how her son Paolo might react to the execution of a suspect that had been ordered by a partisan chief: 'While Paolo was recounting it, I was observing his face with a certain anxiety, afraid that I would find there satisfaction or indifference. Instead he said, with restrained shame – 'It rather upset me' – and I heaved a sigh of relief. It may be necessary to kill, but heaven forbid that one should find it simple and natural.'[42]

---

38 M. Carli, *Arditismo*, Rome-Milan: Augustea, 1929, pp. 26–7, and A. Gatti, *Caporetto. Dal diario di guerra inedito*, ed. A. Monticone, Bologna: Il Mulino, 1964, p. 230, cited in Rochat, *Gli arditi della grande guerra*, pp. 35, 49. Marinetti told the Arditi, in an October 1918 speech: 'All right is on your side when you slit an Austrian's throat' (appendix to F. Cordova, *Arditi e legionari dannunziani*, Padua: Marsilio, 1969, p. 207). See, finally, the title of an article by M. Risolo in *Gerarchia* XXII: 3 (March 1943), pp. 103–5.

39 Cited in N. Tranfaglia, 'Tra Mazzini e Marx. Fernando Schiavetti dall'interventismo repubblicano all'esperienza socialista', in *Rivista di storia contemporanea* XIII (1984), p. 223, n. 6. Tranfaglia adds as an appendix the article 'Repubblica e fascismo (commento alla lettera di Benito Mussolini)', published by Schiavetti in the *Iniziative* of 20 November 1920 (see p. 235).

40 From the aforementioned letter by Ivan Charitonovic Kozlov, 27 December 1942 (*LRE*, p. 787).

41 Battaglia, *Un uomo*, p. 83

42 Gobetti, *Diario partigiano*, p. 100 (13 March 1944).

On the one hand it is precisely the not very 'technological' character of the partisan war that tended to make the enemy more visible; on the other hand there was the active, indeed growing, 'totalitarian character of modern warfare, which made no distinction between soldiers and civilians, that – contrary to all expectations – recreated the conditions of band warfare.'[43]

Nobility of ethical commitment and the risk of totalisation coexisted, therefore, in the partisan war waged against the enemy – Fascism and Nazism – which had all the prerequisites for being described as the total enemy. I have already drawn attention to the inhuman character that the enemy acquired when viewed in the light of extermination and inhumanity that, in this manner, he tended to reverberate on those who, precisely because he was like that, opposed him.[44] And I have also recalled that one cannot free oneself from this tangle by invoking a rigorous autonomy of the political, in whose sphere the war ought to be circumscribed, in order to prevent 'the logic of value and non-value from unfurling its full, devastating consequences'.[45]

During the Resistance, the Catholic Communists came singularly close to this Schmittian position when, though following Saint Thomas's teaching in vigorously practising the concept of a just war, thereby judging the partisan war as well in terms of value, they also saw politics and the war, which is its armed right hand, as being indispensable and neutral instruments that morality, without compromising itself, 'employs just as they are'. The revealed law that man needs insofar as he is tainted with original sin regards the person, not the techniques that he or she uses – not therefore the medicine, not the chemistry, not that 'technique of killing' which is war, a mere mechanism to which it would be absurd to apply the Law, in this case the fifth commandment. The fullest exposition of this line of reasoning led Felice Balbo to write that when in the 'construction of techniques' it is necessary

> to be violent to men as persons even to the point, at times, of killing some of them; in such cases one is not going against the charity which religiously unites men, but

---

43 *La Democrazia del Lavoro*, 10 February 1944. I wanted, here, to quote a moderate publication, which used an old-fashioned expression – bands at war – and appealed to Risorgimento-era (and, as such, reassuring) examples, such as Mazzini and Pisacane.

44 Two texts by Carole Beebe Tarantelli have confronted this terrible question in lucid fashion: 'Io, vedova delle BR vi dico', and a conversation with Doris Lessing on her novel *The Good Terrorist* (both appearing in *La Repubblica*, 1 February and 25 May 1986). To understand the different ways in which one can deal with these questions, compare these texts to Guido Almansi's fatuous review of Lessing's novel, 'Attentatrice offresi' (also in *La Repubblica* – 20 November 1985).

45 Schmitt, *Theory of the Partisan*, referring back to *Concept of the Political*. Schmitt succeeded in producing eloquent pages on the inhuman invention of the absolute enemy, which he attributes to Leninism, without citing Nazism.

frees it from facile and lazy good intention. In this way the claim that killing a man can be an act of charity will not seem paradoxical.[46]

Positions springing from such different cultural contexts thus seem to converge, leaving aside Balbo's tortuous and, indeed, paradoxical reasoning, towards a conception of wartime violence which, to get itself out of a fix, takes refuge in an apparent and 'technical' asepticity. But the dropping of the bomb on Hiroshima would not be aseptic, just as Ernst Jünger had not been aseptic when he had written: 'We are soldiers and the rifle is the instrument that distinguishes us. Killing is our trade, and it is our boast and duty to do this job well and carefully, in a workmanlike fashion.'[47] It has to be recognised that on this path there seems to be no trace of sure, clear, definitive antidotes, given once and for all, to the risk of attributing a totalising value to violence against the enemy, if one tends to see him as absolute. Indeed the distinctions schematically appealed to above simplify, to the point almost of indecipherability, situations which on the one hand cannot but send one to the realm of ends – values – present in whoever practises violent action, and on the other hand arouse emotions and feed on symbols in which ends and means necessarily interweave. In an essay about Fascist violence, paraphrasing a passage from Natalie Zemon Davis, Adrian Lyttleton observes that, historically, what counts is 'the meaning and direction of violence', then warns that one should not interpret violent people only as crazy or frustrated, but rather 'in terms of the aims of their actions and in terms of the behavioural roles and models permitted by their culture'.[48]

There is some affinity between the *resistenti* and those souls full of contempt and violence, who have been credited only with the capacity to listen to the word of Jesus;[49] or with those whom Saint-Just taught that 'the war for freedom must be conducted with fury';[50] or, again, with those who recognise themselves in the maxim that 'people do not become revolutionaries out of science, but out of indignation'.[51] To a Catholic the contradiction might appear to be irenically appeased: only by virtue of the Resistance, one of them has written,

---

46 See 'Guerra di liberazione e di Giustizia', *Voce Operaia*, 26 October 1943, and above all 'Politica e morale', in the 15 January 1944 edition. For the application of these same conceptions to the violence implicit in the class struggle, see the article 'Il cattolico di fronte al problema della violenza', in the 9 November 1943 issue. Lastly, see F. Balbo, *L'uomo senza miti*, Rome: Einaudi, 1945, p. 80.

47 E. Jünger, *Feuer und Blut*, Magdeburg: Stahlhelm Verlag, 1925, p. 18.

48 Lyttelton, *Fascismo e violenza*, pp. 982–3, discussing N. Zemon Davis, *Society and Culture in Early Modern France*, Stanford: Stanford University Press, 1975, p. 186.

49 Referring to positions repeatedly expressed by Gianni Baget-Bozzo and other similar Catholics.

50 Letter to General Jourdan, 17 June 1794. These words are used as an epigraph by J. J. Langendorf in his *Elogio funebre*.

51 M. Merleau-Ponty, *Humanisme et Terreur*, Paris: Gallimard, 1947, p. 48.

have the Catholics (extremely timid at first) finally overcome the instinctive horror of arms: they have learned to fight – no longer unarmed – illegality and injustice; to do battle without hating; to love the unjust adversary, though killing him in order to re-establish law and justice, to the point of having 'succeeded, even while dealing out death, in remaining charitable'.[52]

In the letters written by those awaiting execution attitudes are more various and hard-won. The enemies may be the 'cursed enemy'; they may be the 'blood-thirsty human beasts', on whom, however, it is asked that one's blood should not rebound; they may be dubbed with many other equally crude and relentless expressions. But there may also be the enjoinder not to curse or bear hatred towards anyone, consigning the enemy to future popular justice, and to divine justice.[53] What may certainly have a bearing in these cases, which are more frequent in the letters of condemned Italians than in those of other countries, is the wish to make one's peace in extremis with the precept of the Gospel. But a Garibaldi brigade that had entitled its broadsheet *Vendetta* was taken to task as follows: 'The title *Vendetta* is badly chosen and gives no indication of what it is intended to mean. If by vendetta one means the struggle that we are waging against our enemies to liberate Italy, it strikes us as more appropriate to speak of *Giustizia* and not of *Vendetta*.'[54]

An apologue about the difficulty of getting final ends and the practice of violent means to coincide is recounted by Italo Calvino about himself and his younger brother. The elder brother was talking about Lenin and Gorki: 'he was capable of explaining what democracy and Communism are, he knew stories of revolutions, poems against tyrants; things which were useful to know too, but which there was time to learn later, when the war was over'; the younger brother, instead, spoke about 'the calibres of pistols and automatic weapons'.[55] Calvino himself explained how the practice of violence, as an unavoidable means in those circumstances, involved, in some of its deep echoes, the risk of being confused with the enemy, from whom only an appeal to ends, which had acquired objective value in the course of history, could save one:

That burden of evil which weighs on men of Righteousness, that burden which weighs on us all, and which gives vent to itself in shooting, in the killing of enemies, is the same as that which makes the Fascists shoot, and which leads them to kill with the same hope of purification, of redemption. But then there's history. There's the

---

52 E. Franceschini, 'Il mio no al fascismo', in *Vita e Pensiero* LVIII (1975), p. 831.

53 *LRI*, pp. 58, 240, 61, 74, 94, 191.

54 Letter from the commissariat of the Valle di Susa divisions group to the Command of the 17th Brigade, 17 December 1944 (*Le Brigate Garibaldi*, vol. III, p. 102).

55 I. Calvino, 'La stessa cosa del sangue', in his *Ultimo viene il corvo*, pp. 84–5. On the autobiographical character of this account, see Falaschi, *La Resistenza armata*, p. 123.

fact that we, in history, are on the side of redemption, while they are on the other side. Nothing must be lost by us, not a gesture, not a shot, must be lost, though identical to theirs – do you see what I mean? – everything will serve if not to liberate us, to liberate our children … This is the meaning of the struggle; the true, total, meaning, beyond the various official meanings.[56]

Grief for a common existential predicament and the desire to discover an objective fact that might guarantee one's difference fuse marvellously in this page. In another short story – it has been observed – the fact that of three German prisoners flung into a well one manages to save himself, fulfils 'a desire of Calvino the man'.[57]

The rift between thinking, saying and doing, the bridging of which should be identified as an essential factor in the decision to resist, reappeared at times in the very performance of the acts of violence which that decision gave rise to – almost as if the totalising commitment hesitated before the profundity of the prospects that were opening up, thus recreating from its bosom a new fracture. Franco Calamandrei tells of a priest who heard the confession of a Gappist in flight after an attack, got him to hand over his revolver and exhorted him to renounce violence.[58] The 'Anonimo romagnolo' described the crisis of conscience suffered by a young man who immediately after 8 September kills a German taken by surprise in an *osteria*.[59] A Garibaldini paper wrote edifyingly of a partisan who shoots at a Fascist marshal, and is then overwhelmed by anxiety and returns to his combat post only when he has prayed during the night 'as when he was a child, with his mother', because 'praying has done me good'.[60] Untroubled by doubts, in contrast, was the reply of another Garibaldino whose comrade Pietro Chiodi asked this question: "'Bill, if you woke up with two machine-gun barrels in front of your belly what would you do?" Shrugging his shoulders he replied: "I'd spit in his face".'[61]

This reply ignores all the mediations and the artifices of the science and art of war. Among these artifices is an age-old one that could to a large extent be transferred to the partisan war and which, in being transferred, brings with it and amplifies the moral snare of war seen as a game. What I have in mind are ambushes, which St Augustine had authorised, though condemning

56 Calvino, *Il sentiero dei nidi di ragno*, p. 147.
57 Falaschi, *La Resistenza armata*, p. 136, with regard to the piece 'Uno dei tre è ancora vivo' (in *Ultimo viene il corvo*, pp. 140–8).
58 Calamandrei, *La vita indivisibile*, p. 138 (under the date 3 March 1944).
59 'Anonimo romagnolo', 1943–45, pp. 91–2.
60 See the account 'La Croce di Sant'Uberto', in *Il Partigiano*, directed by the commissar Bini (Giovanni Serbandini), August 1944 (quoted in Falaschi, *La Resistenza armata*, pp. 20–1).
61 Chiodi, *Banditi*, p. 107.

'intemperate violence, profanation of temples, sacking, butchering or fires', as well as 'vendettas, atrocities and reprisals'.[62]

Chiodi tells of partisans and peasants whose 'faces are radiant' because of a successful ambush of Fascists.[63] Battaglia recalls that 'every ambush on the road was greeted with an inhuman hilarity'.[64] On this score there is a significant page in which Marc Bloch describes the Germans' undisturbed entry into Rennes:

> I was badly tempted ... to lie in wait for that damned column at the corner of some spinney of Breton countryside, which is so admirably suited by nature for the mounting of ambushes, even if we had nothing to fight with but the sparse equipment of an engineer detachment. Once we had produced enough confusion in the enemy ranks, it would have been easy enough for us to melt into the 'wild', and then repeat the same performance farther on. I am quite certain that three-quarters of the men would have jumped at the chance of playing a game like that. But, alas, the regulations had never envisaged such a possibility.[65]

Even in active *resistenti* the departure of partisan warfare from the 'regulations' generated the vague scruple that ambushing was still always a kind of warfare that to some extent involved betrayal. Ermanno Gorrieri considered night-time ambushes against the German vehicles along the Apennine road a 'harsh necessity', and boasted that his Italia brigade 'will distinguish itself more in open combat than in this kind of attack'.[66]

But the backslidings that brought the partisans close to resembling their Fascist enemy were manifest most alarmingly in the practice of excessive violence – that excess which the veterans of all wars generally prefer not to speak about.[67] Here, it is not enough to say that the cruel and sadistic can be found in every field and that there were incomparably more of them among the Fascists. We should look, rather, at the basic cultural structures sustaining the two warring parties, and ask why one party was better fitted than the other to select the cruel and sadistic and to bring out the darkest impulses of the human soul in the form of politically significant behaviour. For this fundamental reason, Communist

---

62 See R. H. Bainton's *Christian Attitudes Towards War and Peace* (Nashville: Abingdon, 1960), cited in G. Sofri, 'Riflessioni sull' educazione alla pace', in *Rivista di storia contemporanea* XIII (1984), p. 516.

63 Chiodi, *Banditi*, p. 119 (8 March 1945).

64 Battaglia, *Un uomo*, p. 156.

65 Bloch, *La strana disfatta*, p. 64.

66 Gorrieri, *La Repubblica di Montefiorino*, p. 87.

67 'Old soldiers have two types of memory: that which is allowed and that which is not allowed. They are not allowed to remember the extent to which they took pleasure from killing and torture' (Doris Lessing, in conversation with Carole Beebe Tarantelli, cited above).

Catholics are indulging in what is only a dialectical artifice when they deny the dignity of political status to the 'technique of killing' used for an unjust end, thereby deducing that when Mussolini and Italo Balbo had Giacomo Matteotti and don Minzoni murdered, 'they did not act as politicians, since their so-called policy was not a technique of human progress, but was the wicked regressive machinery, an agglomeration of gestures which had the deceptive appearance of Politics.'[68]

In a civil and 'irregular' war, politics and culture, the ends and the 'techniques' used to achieve them, interweave particularly closely in both fields, and the two different warps have some common threads running through them. At various levels of profundity and assimilation there were several kindred cultural substructures that could not be snapped overnight simply by taking opposite sides of the barricades, just as the viscosity of the language could not be eliminated.[69]

Traces of this affinity have been identified in the songs and the literature of the Resistance.[70] In Chapter 4 of this book some features that sprang from the matrix of Risorgimento culture were highlighted. Here we can give the example of the appeals to blood as a symbol of purification. A modern Italian version of this stereotype was clearly formulated in the words that Giovanni Gentile wrote to Adolfo Omodeo as early as 15 July 1915: 'I have faith above all in the great moral forces that will develop purified by this great bloodbath, for all humanity!'[71]

In 1945 one of two *resistenti* awaiting execution wrote that 'it is with blood

---

68 'Cantonate giovanili', *Voce Operaia*, 27 February 1944, replying to the criticisms that the paper of the young Christian Democrats, *La Punta*, levelled against the article 'Politica e morale'.

69 Falaschi considered this phenomenon 'rhetorical dross that hung on in partisans' language': a reductive reading, though serving the purpose of adding emphasis to the claim that the 'Resistance also represented a turning-point in the Italian language' (Falaschi, *La Resistenza armata*, pp. 19, 10).

70 Leydi, discussing the 'fascist derivation' of some partisan songs, wrote – forcing matters somewhat – that it was not a question, as Pasolini claimed, of imported material coming from former officials of the Royal Army, but rather the fact that 'there was now a generically Fascist spirit within any politically committed song' (R. Leydi, 'Introduzione' to *Canti della Resistenza italiana*, collected and annotated by T. Romano and G. Solza, Milan: Collana del Gallo Grande, 1960, pp. 72–3). Moreover, Falaschi himself – *La Resistenza armata*, pp. 73–4 – has observed that the changes to *La ragazza se ne va con Diavolo* introduced by Marcello Venturi in the 1965 reprint (the first edition was from 1946) served precisely to bring into focus the troubling question of kinship.

71 G. Gentile and A. Omodeo, *Carteggio*, ed. S. Giannantoni, Florence: Sansoni, 1974, p. 167. Remember, here, the contrary position of Croce, according to which war was a merely practical matter that should not interrupt the conversations between erudite types on the opposing sides. There was thus something of a division of the two greatest idealist philosophers into different camps: but the real war was not fully reducible to either of their two positions.

that the country in which one was born, has lived and has fought becomes great', while the other asked that the hem of the bloodstained shirt of Duccio Galimberti which he was conserving be bathed in his own blood. True, they were two officers in permanent active service, though the second was a member of the Action Party, to which in fact he bequeathed the bloodstained relic.[72] But even a Garibaldian song went like this:

> Rosso sangue il color della bandiera
> Siam d'Italia l'armata forte e fiera
> Sulle strade dal nemico assediate
> Lasciammo talvolta le carne straziate.[73]

> [Blood-red is the colour of the flag
> We are the strong, proud army of Italy
> On the enemy-besieged roads
> At times we leave our flesh in shreds.]

This is a very different symbolic vision of blood and bodily suffering from the 'rational' one imbuing statements such as 'a greater contribution of blood would be met by greater Allied recognition'.[74] Comparison should be made rather with documents such as the letter that a Fascist wrote to his wife on 29 August XIX (1941): 'What does it matter if men's flesh is in shreds, when the satisfaction of having done one's duty is stronger?';[75] or like the 'spiritual testament' of Aldo Resega, *federale* of Milan and *ardito* of the First World War, where there is, furthermore, a specific element of Fascist culture too – the appeal to the '"sacral" function of the shedding of blood' as more authentic than democratic legitimisation.[76] Resega's 'testament' in a poster that the Fascists put up after he was killed by a GAP, contains these words: 'The tragedy of Italy will perhaps be worth my blood. I am fighting with the impetus of my faith. Let it gush forth without parallel, without reprisals and without vendetta. Only in this way will it be dearer and more fecund for my *patria*.'[77]

---

72 Ugo Machieraldo, from Vercelli, shot by the Germans in Ivrea on 2 February 1945, and Pedro Ferreira, from Genoa, shot by the Fascists in Turin on 23 January 1945. See the letters to the wife of the former and Action Party comrades of the latter (*LRI*, pp. 123, 83).

73 However, in the Risorgimento-era song inspired by the flag given to the departing soldier by his weeping loved one, red was 'all the fire of my love'.

74 Bernardo, *Il momento buono*, p. 126.

75 Letter from Vito Severgnini, born 1904, later an RSI combatant, shot on 30 April 1945 (*LRSI*, p. 6).

76 On the persistence of this theme, see Revelli, *Panorama editoriale e temi culturali*.

77 *LRSI*, p. 48. On Resega's 'moderate' role, see Ganapini, *Una città, la guerra*, pp. 109–11.

A Fascist captured during the days of the insurrection saw the shedding of his own blood as a pledge of pacification among Italians: 'With the shedding of blood by us few, reasons for party hatred are done away with, for the future too. Thus everything will come about in that peace with justice for which all of us have fought, albeit with different ideas and opposite concepts.'[78]

It is on this very terrain which is so difficult to explore that the *resistenti* and Fascists diverge over the point of the innocence professed by those who shed their own blood. In the letters of *resistenti* awaiting execution declarations of innocence are frequent, even allowing for the fact that some may have been dictated by the desire not to compromise the recipients and their imprisoned companions-in-arms. Let us also isolate those cases in which the profession of innocence was intended to exclude personal participation in the spilling of blood: 'I have never killed nor had anyone killed ... my hands are free of blood, thefts and robberies.'[79] The fact remains that there were still many condemned men who, while firmly declaring their ideals and asking those left behind them to be proud of their deaths, affirmed their innocence with equal intensity. One of them wrote that he was 'dying innocent and like a partisan'.[80] This, then, is not an innocence that we could call 'technical' with respect to the event that led them to their death, nor even only a strong denial of legitimacy to those who had decided on that death. It is rather the vindication of a moral innocence which was not only identified with the very reasons for the choice they had made, but which gave the shedding of one's own blood the value attributed to the sacrifice of an innocent victim. In this context, the ambiguous metaphor used by a man about to die, 'it seems that I'm going to a wedding',[81] acquires the meaning of an offering up of one's own innocence.

In the Fascists too the culture of death did not exclude the figure of the innocent victim. But between the crucifix and the lictorian fasces, as Georges Bataille had seen in 1938, the symbol that the Fascists found most congenial was the latter, including as it did the executioner's axe.[82] When in Terni in 1936 a monument had been unveiled to those who had died in accidents at the Acciao

---

78 Letter by the Milanese Lorenzo Malingher, an officer in permanent active service and a combatant in Spain, to his wife, 29 April 1945, written when his ultimate execution was still in the balance (*LRSI*, p. 233).

79 Letter by the Turin engineer Lorenzo Viale, shot by the Fascists in Turin on 11 February 1945, to his loved ones (*LRI*, p. 239).

80 Letter by the Turin teacher Renzo Scognamiglio, GL, to his mother. Shot by Folgore parachutists at Rivarolo Canava on 22 March 1945 (*LRI*, p. 206).

81 Letter from Rovigo mechanic Amerigo Duò to his Action Party comrades. Shot by the Fascists in Turin on 23 January 1945 (*LRI*, p. 75).

82 See the Bataille quotes and associated comments by C. Ginzburg in his 'Mitologia germanica e nazismo. Su un vecchio libro di Georges Dumézil', in *Quaderni storici* 57 (December 1984), pp. 857–82; and his *Miti, emblemi, spie*, Turin: Einaudi, 1986, pp. 210–38 (see, in particular, p. 230).

steelworks, the newspaper of the local *fascio* had written: 'Not "victims", but virilely and Fascistically "caduti" ["fallen in battle"].'[83]

Fascism is well known for its abundant use of appeals to virility and of sexual metaphors, as for its intimacy with the metaphors and symbols of war.[84] Equally well known is how *arditismo* had been the cultural terrain for this symbolism: 'Youth ... which casts its smile at death, limpid as a virgin's kiss. The war in which we are going towards death as towards love.'[85]

Both before and after 8 September, the Second World War paratroopers, of the Social Republic as of the Kingdom of the South, nourished themselves with the same food. In spring 1943 one of them wrote to his commander: 'One day, speaking to the company, you said that we *paracadutisti* must make war as we make love. You exhorted us to make love a lot because we would be making a lot of war.' Likewise, a member of the Italian Liberation Corps (CIL): 'And we went into battle to joke with death as we had joked with girls.'[86]

Still in 1986, the RSI volunteer Carlo Mazzantini writes: 'The inebriation of that violation gave greater strength to our voices', and recalls the effect that the Fascist songs had on women 'with incredulous eyes' and men who 'shuffled off uncertainly'. A few pages later, to make things clear, Mazzantini says: 'We were exalted by that sense of violation, the impression of penetrating a hostile body which our songs made tremble'. And, to remove any residual doubts, he concludes: 'These songs were our whole culture.'[87]

Death dealt to others by attacking them is part of Fascist culture: both one's own death and the deaths of those fighting alongside one are an integrating element of this mysticism of death, which even drove the Fascists to exaggerate the numbers of their own dead.[88] In the *resistenti*, by contrast, as we shall see better presently, the possibility of being killed appears above all as a pledge given to one's conscience before the right one recognises in it to kill;[89] and in partisan

---

83 Portelli, *Biografia di una città*, p. 212.

84 Fussell, *La grande guerra*, pp. 345ff, draws our attention to the words 'assault', 'impact', 'push', and 'penetration'.

85 Editors' presentation, with the title 'Vita!' in *L'Avanguardia fascista*, 'Paper of the Bologna vanguard', 7 May 1921; P. Giudici, *Reparti d'assalto*, Milan: Alpes, 1928, p. 23, cited in Rochat, *Gli arditi della grande guerra*, p. 15.

86 Letters published in the paper *Folgore*, the second one on 15 January 1945 (cited in M. Di Giovanni, laureate thesis).

87 Mazzantini, *A cercar la bella morte*, pp. 52, 97.

88 For example, A. Tamaro, *Due anni di storia 1943–1945*, 3 vols, Rome: Tosi, 1948–50, vol. III, 1950, p. 49, supplies figures on the number of Fascists fallen in the battle over Rome in early June 1944 that it is difficult to consider anything other than excessive: according to his claims, out of 980 Folgore parachutists, 'only thirty were still alive' after four days.

89 I recall the lucidity with which this argument was developed by Giuseppe Lopresti, later shot at the Fosse Ardeatine.

bulletins the number of enemy killed increases, often excessively, but never that of one's own dead.

Carlo Mazzantini puts the following words into the mouth of one of his comrades engaged in roundups and executions:

> To die for the *patria*, for the idea! ... No, it's a pretext! Even at the front you kill ... To die is nothing: it doesn't exist. No one manages to imagine his own death. The point is to kill! To cross that border! Now, that's an act of your will. Because there you live, in another's death, your own. It's there that you show you possess something you feel is worth more than life: than yours and that of others.[90]

There are many variants on the theme of death in contemporary Fascist documents, even if, at the end of the day, they are pretty monotonous. A few examples will suffice, beginning with what might well be taken as a prototype: the paratrooper – later in the RSI – who describes the sensation he felt at his first jump: 'The kind of joy you feel when you are "side by side with death".'[91] These words faithfully followed those of a *paracadutisti*'s song inspired in its turn by D'Annunzio's 'Canzone del Quarnaro':

> C'è a chi piace far l'amore
> c'è a chi piace far danaro
> a noi piace far la Guerra
> con la morte paro a paro.[92]

> [There are those who like making love
> There are those who like making money
> We like to make war
> Face to face with death.]

In a poster that appeared in Rome, death figured both as the enemy and as a cause for pride: 'To arms. Youths of Rome, liberate Italy from death, from the enemies who are liberating you from life. The Battalion of Death.'[93] A young man

---

90 Mazzantini, *A cercar la bella morte*, p. 136. 'I went for the sake of experience ... to know what I would have to endure ... to make myself a man', said another Fascist, volunteer in a firing squad (p. 93).

91 Letter from Primo Pata, 17 November 1942, to his mother. He would later fall on the Nettuno front, on 16 February 1944 (*LRSI*, p. 7).

92 I take this information from the laureate thesis of M. Di Giovanni, cited above, in which he speaks of the first jump as symbolic of a challenge to death, itself victorious even before the fight has begun. Not for nothing did a chaplain of the Tarquinia college say to the parachutist cadets: 'You are already heroes!'

93 Undated poster in Piscitelli, *I bandi*, p. 191.

training in Germany wrote to his mother: 'Now I'll no longer be able to go by the name "Volontario della Morte!" Now I'll no longer be able to wear the black flames of the Arditi! ... I'll have to resign myself instead to being a Bersagliere.'[94] A Dannunzian friar, who had been a chaplain in the wars of 1915–18, of Spain, and of 1940–43, and who was subsequently shot by the partisans, says: 'I love sister death like a creature who takes me to my God and Father. I await sister death living in the grace of God and working in the vineyard of the Lord. I desire sister death as the Saints yearned for her and I prepare my heart for the coming of the Bridegroom.'[95]

In the letter of a nineteen-year-old this kind of attitude is accentuated by a paroxysmal nihilism that lacks, however, the tragic sense given by the levelling of everything with nothing:

> The whole world, with the weight of its rottenness, is about to come crashing down on us. Let us stiffen ourselves! Let us dehumanise ourselves! Let us forget sentiments, everything regarding ourselves ... Let everything, everything perish! Men, things, cities of yesterday and today. Let the whole of a past and the whole of a present die. Let the only idea that remains great be for victory and in victory. Let us lose everything! Friends, relations, joys. Let us remain naked! Let only our soul remain! But may the enemy clambering over our dead bodies feel on himself the condemnation of the blood crushing him, the invincible breath of a Faith that has moved mountains and overwhelmed skies and oceans.[96]

In another letter a woman auxiliary sees things in terms of a duel with death: 'I shall be able to look death in the face, flee it, amuse myself with it; it must be fun playing hide-and-seek. As you can see, the blackshirted volunteers don't fear death and take everything philosophically. That's how we live ... looking death in the face with a smile on our lips.'[97]

This tone, passing as it does from one's own death to that of the enemy in a kind of exalted coming and going, aroused the greatest indignation in the other camp. 'Enough with thirteen-year-old brigands who kill for fun!', reads a poster addressed by the GL Women's Movement to the 'women of Piedmont'.[98]

---

94 Letter from the Sicilian Oscar Lo Surdo to his mother, '17.VI.XXII' (17 June 1944, as rendered in the Fascist calendar starting from the 1922 March on Rome). Enlisted in the Italia Division, he fell at Pontremoli on 23 April 1945 (*LRSI*, p. 127).

95 'Spiritual testament' of Crisostomo Ceragioli, a.k.a. 'friar Wolf', shot near Montepulciano on 24 May 1944 (*LRSI*, p. 117).

96 Siena's Fernando Mugnaini, in a letter to his mother of 9 August 1944. He fell on 18 April 1945 in Mirandola, fighting against partisans. In the letter he wrote: 'Now for the first, and perhaps for the last time, I at least feel that I am a somebody' (*LRSI*, p. 140).

97 Letter by Sara Corsellini, 14 March 1945, quoted in Fraddosio, *Donne nell'esercito di Salò*, p. 73.

98 INSMLI, *CLNAI*, envelope 8, folder 12 (March 1944?).

The Fascists sang:

> A noi la morte non ci fa paura
> ci si fidanza e si fa l'amor.

> [We do not fear death
> We embrace it and make love to it.]

and

> Le donne non ci vogliono più bene
> perché portiamo la camicia nera.

> [The women no longer love us
> Because we wear the black shirt.]

The second song concludes concentrating all of Fascist virility in the encounter with 'la Signora Morte', while flesh-and-blood women are left to the malingerers, sissies, incapable of conquering them with violence.[99] Compared with certain songs of the Rumanian Iron Guard, models of paroxysmal mysticism of blood and death ('Legionnaires are born to die', 'death is a gladsome wedding for us'),[100] there is something Catholicly materialistic about these Fascist songs, and the cocky tone fails to conceal the consternation pervading them.

Two extreme poles can thus be identified in the Fascist expressions. Fitting to the first are Georg Simmel's words, born in a quite different context, about the 'aesthetic form of the destructive impulse, which seems to be part of the existences of all pariahs to the extent to which deep down they are not completely slaves'.[101] The second pole is one of arrogant defiance, as displayed by Enrico Vezzalini, chief of the province of Novara, who before being executed wrote that he disavowed nothing and that he would like to 'die shouting: for Italy and for Fascism, Viva la Morte!'[102] – a baldly Fascist retort to the 'death to the kingdom of death' in Filippo Turatti's hymn of the workers. The approach of the final disaster enveloped the traditional elements of the Fascist culture of violence in a lugubrious and desperate atmosphere, which far from excluding ferocity could actually stimulate it. The 'moderate' Fascist Zerbino, minister of

---

99 See the article 'Fiaccola di vita', which took up this theme, quoted in Gorrieri, *La Repubblica di Montefiorino*, p. 306.

100 Laqueur, *On Terrorism*, p. 73.

101 Simmel, *La moda*, p. 41.

102 A letter to his wife on 23 September 1945 (*LRSI*, p. 301). Vezzalini had a Garibaldian grandfather, and his father was a volunteer in the First World War.

the interior, was being no more than consolatory when, on 23 April 1945, he telephoned Francesco Saverio Grazioli, high commissioner for Piedmont, to say: 'Bella agonia finisce.'[103] A university student appears to be more sincere when he confesses: 'I am young and I have reached a point at which life and the beauty it is purported to have repels me, and that is a crime.'[104]

Mazzantini summed up the sense of his experience like this, and not just because he was writing a posteriori: 'And there was no afterward to that business.' Mazzantini also puts these words into the mouth of one of his comrades: 'We are burnt out ... Once this war is over we'll be of no use to anyone, we must disappear'; and recalls how Ernst von Salomon's I proscritti (Die Geächteten, 1930) was a book that had an initiatory value for the Fascists of the Social Republic.[105]

This culture of death is a far cry from the sense that Piero Gobetti gave to the words 'volontari della morte' ('volunteers of death') when, as his wife Ada wrote after the killing of Sandro Dalmastro, he spoke of his generation 'who face destiny as it is in its tragic aridity, with no need to embellish it, to clothe it in heroic auras: all the more heroes in that they do not want to be so, do not even know that they are.'[106]

'Pietà l'è morta' ('Pity the dead') is an invention of Nuto Revelli, and owes much of its popularity to the forlorn and at the same time proud connotation that it carries. But the same words engraved on the machine-guns of the Decima Mas[107] change meaning, becoming the motto of one of the most ferocious Fascist units which reckoned to flee the desperation of the exiled by flaunting gestures of aristocratic elegance borrowed from its leader, Prince Junio Valerio Borghese. When the Garibaldini of Chiodi sang 'Siamo figli di nessuno / siamo carne da plotone' ('We are foundlings / we are platoon fodder'), there was nothing grim about this, but a case rather of knocking on wood or even, as Chiodi himself interprets it, of being tongue-in-cheek about oneself, in reply to Radio London which spoke of 'cavaliers of liberty'.[108] In some songs there also emerges the ancient tradition of making misery and sorrow reasons not for desperation but for revolt. The same song mentioned earlier, which speaks of the red blood of the flag and of rent flesh, also has the archaic and far from Fascist words: 'We

---

103 The phone call was intercepted by the information office of the regional military command of the CVL: reported in Vaccarino, Gobetti and Gobbi, L'insurrezione di Torino, p. 215.

104 Twenty-four-year-old Dante Corti in a letter to his mother, dated 2 April XXII (1944). A Lombard, later killed by partisans, he tried to finish his letter on a positive note – 'one consolation is left to me' – invoking the fatherland and Fascism (LRSI, p. 91).

105 Mazzantini, A cercar la bella morte, pp. 168, 172. Life is defined as 'something great and trivial' on p. 95.

106 Gobetti, Diario partigiano, p. 125 (6 April 1944).

107 Chiodi, Banditi, pp. 137–8 (17 April 1945).

108 Ibid., p. 108 (12 January 1945).

live on privation and affliction'. In another song death is defined as 'cruel'. In the letters of those awaiting execution it can be called a 'sad and at the same time fine moment', a 'majestic step';[109] one might marvel at the ease and resolution with which one faces it;[110] one might point to its harshness: 'I die murdered', 'shot dead', 'they are killing me', 'don't make a fuss about the body or anything else. Where they fling me they fling me.'[111] More frequently, compassion is asked for one's mortal remains: a Sienese brigadier of the *carabinieri* speaks almost like Dante's Manfredi: 'My corpse lies this side of the river.'[112] Elements of the culture of death appear almost exclusively in the Christian and Catholic transfiguration of the certainty of eternal life.

In the letters of condemned Italians, religious invocations, which were very frequent and far more numerous than in those of other countries, centre in fact on the life to come and on the heaven that awaits oneself and one's loved ones. Out of 112 Italian letters, only forty do not contain religious appeals, and of these only a few contain explicit affirmations of laicity. With regard to European letters, Thomas Mann pointed out the shades of meaning that appear in appeals to divinity, and added that 'it is singular to note that those who do not speak of God find higher, more spiritual and more poetic expressions for the idea of survival'.[113]

In the Fascists the lack of a future not only heightened their obsession with death, but made the figure of the enemy particularly monstrous in their eyes, contributing to his being transformed, far more than occurred among the partisans, into the 'absolute enemy'. The enemy was no longer an obstacle to remove along the way, but became something whose annihilation absorbed the entire project of violent action. Even in this, its final incarnation, Fascist violence bore within itself the ambiguity that had always been its hallmark. On the one hand it was flaunted as the right of the strong over the weak, depicted as a coward and racially inferior, a *bastardo*, and was practised with 'the proud cynicism which affirms the incurable mediocrity of a crowd to be dominated with a stick to the greater glory of few supermen'.[114] On the other hand that violence precluded the gratification inherent in beating a strong enemy: and it may well be that most of

109 Letter from an unknown man to his father, and from the priest Aldo Mei to his parents (*LRI*, pp. 35, 143).

110 Letter from captain Franco Balbis to his father, and from the worker Quinto Bevilacqua to his parents (*LRI*, pp. 41, 48).

111 Letters from the student Achille Barilatti to his fiancée; from the trader Arturo Cappettini to his mother; from the student Bruno Frittaion to his fiancée; and from the accountant Fabrizio Vassalli to his parents, adding 'When you can, put a notice in the papers. Viva l'Italia!' (*LRI*, pp. 44, 63, 92, 236).

112 Letter from Vittorio Tassi to his wife (*LRI*, p. 218).

113 T. Mann, in the Preface to *LRE*, p. xii.

114 As it was described, with rather overwrought stress, in 'Né a destra né a sinistra', *Risorgimento Liberale*, Rome edition, 15 April 1944.

the cruelty of Fascist violence was generated not least by the sombre attempt to fill this hiatus. It should be added that, as was suggested in Chapter 5, the Fascists of the RSI, whatever their aspirations to return to their origins, were unable, through the exercise of violence, to recreate that 'paradox', which is so well illustrated by Lyttleton when he speaks of the 'ability to tie antisocial sentiments to the defence of the existing social order'.[115] Even if their cultural roots remained the same, their fruits, in a context that did not allow any prospect of real success, could not but manifest themselves as pure violence. The Fascist thug had no space left to cultivate in himself the man of order whom he had borne in his breast from his origins and which he was used to embodying in the form of bullying and oppression. Moreover, the weakness of the RSI, its splintering into unmanageable bands and, of course, the birth of the partisans, made another of the historical characteristics of Fascist violence less solid: that of acting under the de facto and legal cover of established authority.

This contradictory aspect was grasped by Concetto Marchesi in an 'open letter' which, because of its somewhat contorted argumentation, has lent itself to various interpretations.[116] Its basic meaning, however, appears clear. Addressing the Fascists, Marchesi writes: 'The adversary [the Gappist] is assailing you with revolver shots in the streets. Honour compels you to seek to punish the culprits, or to do the same yourselves, to act as judges or as enemies: not both together.'

These words denounce RSI Fascism's brazen summation of the two ways in which Fascism had, from its origins, exercised violence: the illegal and the legal way. You Fascists, says Marchesi, do not respond to violence as risk like men of honour, that is as equals, but with the customary cowardice of illegal violence protected by 'justice', that is to say, the established power of your republic.

The Fascists shot partisans who gave themselves up after promising them that their lives would be spared, a practice that ties in with their oft-expressed desire to have a free hand against rebels.[117] They flaunted their joy at having killed three other outlaws with the weapon they had taken off the first partisan to be killed.[118] They simulated executions to terrorise the prisoners[119] (though it

---

115 Lyttelton, *Fascismo e violenza*, p. 983.

116 Canfora, *La sentenza*, pp. 150–4, and as an appendix (pp. 315–18), the text by Marchesi, in the form of an 'open letter' to Gentile, appearing in the Lugano Socialist daily *Libera Stampa* on 24 February 1944. Spriano's interpretation of this in his *Storia del Partito comunista italiano*, vol. V, p. 209, seems rather reductive, defining it as a 'paean to the GAP militant'.

117 See, among many others, Chiodi, *Banditi*, p. 101 (17 December 1944) and the letter from an officer of the 12th GNR legion, based in Moncalieri, reported in the 'Esame della corrispondenza censurata al 30 giugno 1944' (ACS, *SPD, CR, RSI*, envelope 9, folder 3).

118 'See, now, I am satisfied, and even if I must die, I die contented': letter from a *carabiniere* from Aidussina (Gorizia) in the service of the RSI (ibid.).

119 Unpublished diary of G. Mauni, c. 39 (August 1944) and the testimony of Elsa Oliva (Bruzzone and Farina, *La Resistenza taciuta*, p. 134).

needs recalling that simulations of this sort occurred at times at the hands of the partisans as well).[120] They took pleasure in the sufferings they inflicted.[121] They urged the SS to treat those whom they tortured ferociously.[122] A Fascist himself told his parents of the horror he felt at seeing his comrades laughing over the corpse of a nineteen-year-old boy they had shot.[123] A monumental, and unintentional, documentation of the torture inflicted by the Fascists on those who fell into their hands[124] was left by the Supreme Court of Cassation when, after the war, in its zeal to exclude the particular savagery which, according to the infelicitous formula used by the law, made the Togliatti amnesty inapplicable, it constructed a painstaking survey of torturing practices.[125]

The RSI introduced the practice of public executions and of leaving the bodies of the hanged and shot in the place of execution for a long time. 'Afterwards they will display me to the public hung by a piece of cord', wrote a condemned man.[126] This was, as it were, a revival in the key of brutal contemporaneity of the 'splendour of the executions' of which Foucault has spoken in relation to the *ancien régime*. Indeed, some of the features that Foucault analyses are matched by the display of the corpses of the condemned which was to have it symbolic reversal in Piazzale Loreto. Foucault writes:

> On the part of the law that imposes it, the execution must be clamorous, it must be observed by everyone, rather as its triumph. The very excess of the violence exercised is one of the elements of its glory ... Hence, without doubt, those tortures that go on after death: corpses burned, ashes thrown to the wind, bodies dragged on trellises, and exhibited on the roadsides.[127]

---

120 Testimony given to the author by Nuto Revelli.

121 'I also learned how to pretend to faint, giving me a few moments of peace, because these sirs no longer enjoyed striking me when they saw that I was not suffering' (Bolis, *Il mio granello di sabbia*, p. 21), where this ferocity is counterposed to the guards, who 'it must be said, looked after me well' (p. 27).

122 Such was the behaviour of a chaplain 'a sorry sell-out figure', in the Carceri Nuove in Turin: 'Relazione del garibaldino Oscar sulla prigionia del commissario politico Emanuele [Artom], 15 aprile 1944', quoted in an appendix to Artom's *Diari*, p. 180.

123 Letter from the Tagliamento militiaman Francesco D'Ambrosio, 27 April 1944 (not using 'XXII'), who was in turn shot by partisans on 12 March 1945 (*LRSI*, pp. 146–7).

124 See, for example, the letter of protest addressed to Mussolini by the patriarch of Venice, Cardinal Adeodato Piazza, of 24 January 1945 (cited in Malgeri, *La Chiesa di fronte alla RSI*, p. 329, n. 73).

125 See Pavone, *La continuità dello Stato*, p. 252.

126 Letter from Umberto Ricci to his parents and friends, 23 August 1944 (*LRI*, p. 193). See M. Mafai, *Pane nero. Donne e vita quotidiana nella Seconda guerra mondiale*, Milan: Mondadori, 1987, pp. 226–52, which describes some cases of corpses being exhibited.

127 M. Foucault, *Surveiller et punir*, Paris: Gallimard, 1975, p. 38.

In another key, Thompson speaks of the public executions as a theatre aimed at generating the 'terror of the example'; and, comparing the sophisticated resources available, for this purpose, to the contemporary state and those of the eighteenth-century state, adds that the latter had to resort 'to forms of increasing the terror against transgressors' by insulting the corpses in ways that 'deliberately struck at popular taboos'.[128] The republican Fascist state found itself compelled by its weakness to regress to these ancient forms of ostentation of their capacity to punish.

'Any cyclist or pedestrian caught circulating in the territory in the possession of firearms without the authorisation of the competent authorities will be shot on the spot', ran a proclamation by Armando Rocchi, head of the province of Perugia.[129] The words 'sul posto' ('on the spot') indicated both the immediacy and the visibility of the punishment. As we shall see better presently, this formula and this practice were to become widely used and would be adopted by the partisans too when they wanted to demonstrate that they knew how to punish those among them who stepped seriously out of line. Thus the 'provisions in the case of occupations of villages and towns issued by a command' establish: 'the death penalty will be inflicted by means of shooting in the back on all Garibaldini caught in the act and guilty of private violence, theft, vandalism. The execution is to take place in public in the same place where the offence is committed'.[130] Or again: 'The corpse of the executed man has been left with a card on his breast bearing the following words: "Executed by the partisans because unworthy of belonging to their ranks. Reason: rape and robbery"'.[131]

The Fascists, though holders of so much vaunted power, had a paroxysmal fear of not being taken seriously, and this fear drove them to imitate and outdo the Germans in the practice of reprisals. The *podestà* and political secretary of Saluzzo insisted on the Germans shooting six hostages, and the secretary said that he wanted the town to have a 'Christmas of blood'.[132] 'All the soldiers stationed in Florence were to be made to see with our own eyes that one was not joking', recounts one of them who was forced to witness the

128 E. P. Thompson, 'Folklore, Anthropology and Social History', in *The Indian Historical Review* III (1978), p. 2.

129 INSMLI, *Manifesti e volantini*. See the account of the public display of the barefooted corpses of partisans, 'heaped on the pavement' in Turin's Via Cibrario, as described by Angiolina Fenoglietto (Guidetti Serra, *Compagne*, vol. I, p. 16).

130 Instructions from the Command of the Vittorio Veneto brigades group, 1 April 1945 (*Le Brigate Garibaldi*, vol. III, p. 565). See also the communication from the Command of the 1st Gramsci division to the Command of the Valsesia, Ossola, Cusio, and Verbano group, 29 November 1944 (IG, *BG*, 07163).

131 Letter from the Command of the 6th Bixio brigade (Liguria) to the detachment commands, 7 October 1944 (*Le Brigate Garibaldi*, vol. II, p. 415).

132 Testimony of the canonical Francesco Raspino, who was present at the executions, in Rovero, *Il clero piemontese nella Resistenza*, pp. 73–5.

shooting of five draft-dodgers.[133] 'This will be your end', said the Fascists to a captured partisan, pointing to his comrades who were hanging from the gallows.[134] And we have already recalled Farinacci's comment on the Ferrara massacres.

When presently we come to examine the theme of reprisals, we shall return to the real significance of the exemplary effect of these bloody spectacles. What needs registering here are the disturbing effects they had on the minds of those who were compelled to witness or even collaborate in them. In the Florence episode recalled above, the conscripts who had been pressed into the firing squad and had fired at the victims, if only minimally, so that it had become necessary for the orderly officer to use his revolver,

> sometimes regarded themselves as voluntary perpetrators of that massacre, sometimes as victims of the officers' high-handedness. They yelled, wept and often woke up suddenly in the night crying 'no, no' or repeating the same cries as the executed. They would appeal to their mothers, say that they did not want to die, let out yells of terror and invocations of help.[135]

A prisoner aware that his end was nigh said to one of his comrades: 'Hanging leaves an ugly memory for those who remain.'[136] The specific and, intentionally, infamous horror of hanging lies in the fact that rifles and machine-guns are weapons, while the gallows is not. Hanging cannot therefore even simulate the final act of a combat engagement. It is telling that the hanging of two of the leading and most detested local *gerarchi* in Turin, immediately after the Liberation, had to be authorised by the governing regional council 'notwithstanding the provisions in force'.[137]

Hanging, moreover, lay utterly outside that personal relationship that a weapon creates in combatants. This relationship was felt particularly intensely by the Fascists, being part of their culture, but it can also be found in the partisans:

> Ma la mitragliatrice non la lascio
> Gridò ferito il legionario al passo
> Grondava sangue al conteso sasso
> Il costato che a Cristo somigliò

---

133 Bocci, *Ricordi di un allievo ufficiale*, p. 47.

134 Testimony of Diego Verardo, in Bravo and Jalla, *La vita offesa*, p. 112.

135 Bocci, *Ricordi di un allievo ufficiale*, pp. 48–51.

136 Chiodi, *Banditi*, p. 57 (25 August 1944). These are the words of Leonardo Cocito, later hanged.

137 Legislative decree no. 5, 29 April 1945. The two men hanged from the trees were the *federale* Giuseppe Solaro and Giovanni Cabras (Vaccarino, Gobetti and Gobbi, *L'insurrezione di Torino*, pp. 318–19).

Ma la mitragliatrice non la lascio
E l'arma bella a un tratto lo lasciò.

[The machine-gun I will not abandon
Cried the wounded legionnaire at the pass
As his blood poured on the contested stone
The machine-gun I will not abandon
but the beautiful weapon he did leave behind.]

– ran a verse of the legionary's song.[138]

After 8 September this value attributed to one's weapon became still more exclusive in the Fascists:

We had witnessed the collapse of an army, we had seen weapons rejected, dispersed, become useless overnight, faint-hearted, worthless. They had acquired a mythical value in our imaginations … The more patent the unreality of that war became, and little by little the more confused the aims, the motivations of that life, the more we clung to our weapons as the only thing in which we could recognise ourselves … It became a kind of fetishism.[139]

In the partisans a wider and less clear-cut range of attitudes can be observed, running from shame and trembling at handling an instrument of death for the first time, to attractions of an ambiguous kind: from satisfaction at finally being able to fight as equals, to pride at having done so thanks to the weapons captured from the enemy. The many controversies about the Allied airdrops and the distribution of weapons raining down from the sky may be explained in these terms as well.

A Garibaldini commander distributed the much longed-for submachine Stens to his men, and noted in his diary: 'I don't know quite how to put it, but in their eyes I can see a light that I shall never forget again.'[140] And Ada Gobetti: 'They were a bit riled at the order to hand over their weapons to me (the almost amorous jealousy these boys have for the weapons is curious).'[141] The Gappist Franco Calamandrei, describing the attack on the Flora hotel in Rome, occupied by the Germans, recalled: 'Having torn off the paper in which my rifle was wrapped I put it on the window-sill there in front of me. It was again a pleasant, reassuring sensation placing that metallic solidity on the solid surface of the marble.'[142]

---

138 Referring to the Uarieu Pass in Ethiopia.
139 Mazzantini, *A cercar la bella morte*, pp. 160–1.
140 Chiodi, *Banditi*, p. 36 (16 August 1944).
141 Gobetti, *Diario partigiano*, p. 196 (2 September 1944).
142 Calamandrei, *La vita indivisibile*, p. 124 (20 December 1943).

It was at the moment of the final surrender of weapons that these feelings were to prove particularly powerful, in the form of disappointment, but mixed with hope in those weapons that had, instead, been hidden. A Terni partisan recounts: 'That clause about surrendering weapons was immediately applied, but arrogantly. I remember how painful some partisans found it to part with their weapons'.[143] In Belluno, the scene of the disarmament is described in the following way:

> Disarmament at the barracks took place with great pomp, great eulogies and declarations of gratitude that were never to be forgotten. The partisan was laying down his machine-gun, his Sten, his rifle, and with his weapon he was prostrating his soul. For months his weapon had been his faithful daytime and nighttime companion, in her he had placed all his trust for twenty months. In that weapon which now he had to give up and in whose hands he already knew where it would end up, for twenty years he had seen the key to his freedom. The moral shock was very violent and found expression in forms of distrust of democracy, of disorientation and often of useless rebellion.[144]

Mirroring this love for one's weapons was the frequent manifestation of reluctance or even repugnance about using them. Here I do not mean those who had chosen not to participate, but those who had openly taken sides. This was particularly true with the women, for whom the age-old affirmation of difference seemed, in that emergency situation, to be summed up in the choice between shooting and not shooting. The problem is present even among the Fascist women auxiliaries, who were not allowed by regulations to use cosmetics, smoke or bear arms, for the use of which they were to train only for legitimate defence: a conjunction of prohibitions which nicely symbolises Fascism's contradictory attitude to the objective of militarising the 'exemplary wives and mothers'.[145]

A female auxiliary, shortly before being shot in Turin on 30 April 1945, wrote in her last letter, which still bore the Fascist-era date: 'I know that I have not shed blood: this comforts me in these last moments'.[146] But another, on the eve of the final catastrophe, had written to her mother: 'All I do is wash piles of plates, bed linen, sew, tidy the rooms we sleep in and deal with all the office work, telephone left, right and centre, decipher coded messages'; and had added

---

143 Testimony of the Communist Ambrogio Filipponi, in Portelli, *Biografia di una città*, pp. 287–8.

144 Bernardo, *Il momento buono*, p. 178.

145 On the women auxiliaries, see Fraddosio, *Donne nell' esercito di Salò*, and, by the same author, *La mobilitazione femminile: i Gruppi fascisti repubblicani femminili e il SAF*, in Poggio, ed., *La Repubblica sociale italiana*, pp. 257–74.

146 Letter from Laura Giolo to her family (*LRSI*, p. 241).

with satisfaction that 'the boys' called her 'their little sister' and the commander 'who is very nice and is pleased with us' had promised to take them in turns up to the front line. When, however, she puts on the camouflaged uniform, this woman feels like 'a real clown', though she does then pick up: 'I finally feel in my element.'[147]

A Red Cross nurse, after expressing the hope that 'those cursed rebels all croak', wrote:

> You know, when they go out on the roundups I always try to sneak in too. The other day I went with papa [who had asked to enlist in the SS] – I was so happy, you know. The soldiers are always saying I shouldn't because I bring bad luck (Red Cross nurses must stay at home) but I, you know ... when I can I go.[148]

The reactions of the anti-Fascist men and women to the appearance of the bush-jacketed Fascist women-soldiers ranged from vulgar jibes depicting the auxiliaries as ugly and unfitted for the kinds of combat that best suited their sex to the more thoughtful ones which started from the observation that they enlisted even though they were not obliged to do so, and concluded that 'the women of the Republic are demonstrating this today: that a certain female energy exists, only it hasn't been guided and directed.'[149]

Even the partisans were not so easily convinced that women could and indeed had to shoot. A very impassioned letter written by an imprisoned Communist ('and then I will take revenge because an idea is an idea') reads: 'There is no legitimate pretext for a lack of weapons; there are weapons for everyone, children, men and old men', but says nothing about women.[150]

> They had rather discarded me, insofar as we're women, the usual problem. So I escaped, reached the hillock where they were. I remember I was wearing a light blue sweater and they all shouted 'down' at me, because with a light blue sweater, in full daylight ... I didn't even know that there were any arms at my home. Then – in those days, the world was very different, and in the period I was with them, I saw

---

147 Letter from Imola sixteen-year-old Luciana Minardi, 17 March 1945, later shot (*LRSI*, pp. 197–8). Compare with the similar way in which a parachutist expressed himself: 'Marvellous, these cannonades, machine-gun fire etc. etc. Finally, I am in my element!' (Luciano Dal Soglio, 26 May 1944, *LRSI*, p. 119).

148 'Esame della corrispondenza censurata al 30 giugno 1944' (ACS, *SPD, CR, RSI*, envelope 9, folder 3).

149 See, on the first case, 'Surrogati' (understood as 'sexual surrogates'), an article in *La Fiamma*, 'organ of the Comitato di coordinamento femminile' (Genoa?), March 1945; on the second case, see 'Quelle in sahariana', *La Nuova Realtà*, 'organ of the Movimento femminile Giustizia e Libertà' (Piedmont), 27 February 1945.

150 Letter from the carpenter Violante Momesso to his mother. Shot by the Fascists in Venice on 28 July 1944 (*LRI*, p. 147).

how they cleaned them, I had my own little revolver which I didn't give to anyone … I tried it out, it worked well. There were wounded, dead, but whether I was the artificer, I can't say.[151]

In this account by a Terni woman partisan shooting at the enemy is seen, despite the distancing that comes at the end, a challenge won (including the pale blue sweater) not least over one's own comrades. The climate of partisan life – 'go, shoot and escape, right?' – is directly expressed by this other testimony:

The commander was very wary; he said that women were most useful at home. At first I was worried because I was afraid of not being up to it. In short, it seemed to me to be more a man's job than a woman's, but, finding myself having to and then seeing that there was no way out … Yes, I was proud … At first, I wasn't.[152]

'I should have been born a man' is how one woman sums up her regret at not having participated actively in the Resistance.[153]

A case in some respects extreme, but in others exemplary, is that of Elsa Oliva. A rebellious girl, she escaped from home at the age of fourteen. In Ortisei, during the war, she quarrelled with the inhabitants of Upper Adige to defend the good name of the Italian soldier. After 8 September in Bolzano she witnessed the first acts of violence against the Italians and 'from that moment I understood that all I could do was kill them, the Germans. The choice came immediately.' She was convinced that 'the liberation struggle was a complete non-experience, a complete invention'. She blew up with a bomb the automobile containing the fiancée of a friend of hers at whom, to obtain permission to enter the barracks, she had 'made eyes'.[154] When, in Maderno, she saw the 'mugs' of 'all those Fascists', she said to herself: 'There are not only the Germans to bump off, there are the Fascists too.' She made her way to the partisans of the Valtoce division, commanded by the anti-Communist Catholic, regular lieutenant Alfredo Di Dio – a curious choice, dictated no doubt by the fact that they were *autonomi*, a name that must have made them appear more in line with her expectations. But she was then compelled to recognise that, if it had not been for the reaction of her men, the *clero* (clergy) would have had her removed from the command of

---

151 Testimony of Gianna Angelini, in Portelli, *Biografia di una città*, p. 277. Battaglia speaks of a girl who asked to be allowed to shoot, in *Un uomo*, pp. 206–7.

152 Testimony of Anna Cherchi, from a peasant family, born in 1924 (Bravo and Jalla, *La vita offesa*, p. 85).

153 Testimony of Luigia Varusco, born in 1890, whose regrets included not having been able to ground her own identity in her own efforts (Passerini, *Torino operaia*, p. 55).

154 On the recourse to seduction in order to trick the Fascists and Germans, see Bruzzone and Farina, *La Resistenza taciuta*, and L. Mariani, *Quelle dell'idea. Storie di detenute politiche 1927–1948*, Bari: De Donato, 1982, p. 150.

the unit assigned to her. Indeed, if they had had their way, the Valtoce leaders would have made her only a dispatch-rider and nurse. But she 'wanted to shoot, take part in the engagements', and replied:

> I haven't come here to look for a sweetheart. I'm here to fight and I'll stay here only if you give me a gun and put me in the ranks of those who have to stand guard and fight in the actions. Added to that, I'll be a nurse. If it's all right by you I'll stay, if not I'll be off … In the first engagement I showed that I wasn't holding my gun just for show but to take aim and fire … I looked after my comrades but I didn't serve them … the men were often lazy.

Elsa Oliva's stance, writ larger no doubt in memory, is crowned by a series of episodes – and it is this coherence of hers that bears out the truth of this testimony. 'As commander' she was 'very severe' and had the men tied to poles. She respected the Muti brigade lieutenant who kept her prisoner for some time because he was courageous (just as the lieutenant respected her for the same reason). Without a moment's hesitation, together with other comrades, she executed a Fascist who had taken them prisoner and who, in the days of the Liberation, was sickeningly applauding the partisans, but said to him: 'Idiot, couldn't you stay hidden away in some hole?' The only thing that she didn't understand, because it was in fact hard to understand, was how this Fascist died crying 'Viva Stalin!': 'Did he think he'd save himself that way?' Finally, after the Liberation, she admitted: 'All of us had guns at home because we thought we'd still have to use them. With the liberation we hadn't seen what we had dreamed about so much in the mountains.'[155]

By contrast, there were women who refused to shoot and kill out of individual choice and conviction. Testimonies of this kind are numerous. Albina Caviglione Lusso tells of women partisans who took care of the wounded and brought arms and ammunition to the combatants: 'They never fired, though.' Tersilla Fenoglio declares: 'I never used arms; I would never have used them and I would never have fired, because I've always had a great fear of doing harm to my neighbour. I only performed defensive actions. It's absurd, but that's the way it was, perhaps because of the residual Catholicism that I had.'[156]

Even a Communist partisan in so fierce a Resistance movement as the Yugoslav one writes that the Ustasha are killing her 'because she is honest and has not killed anyone, has never harmed anyone, has helped her brothers and comrades with her thoughts only for them.'[157]

---

155 The testimony of Elsa Oliva appears in Bruzzone and Farina, *La Resistenza taciuta*, pp. 118–44. The quotes in the text appear on pp. 125, 126, 138, 130–31, 140.

156 Testimonies of Albina Caviglione Lusso and Tersilla Fenoglio Oppedisano, ibid., pp. 69, 155.

157 Letter from the *liceo* student Anka Knežčvic to her brother. She was shot in

These women were convinced that life was not in itself an absolute value ('it's better to die honestly than live unworthily', the Yugoslav writes) but refused to take the lives of others by their own hand. Though having made a clear choice of sides, they did not intend to sacrifice the claims of pity to the political and armed struggle. This model seems to be exemplified not only in women such as 'mamma Lucia' (Lucia Apicella), who at Cava dei Tirreni buried both German and Anglo-American soldiers,[158] but also mothers, like that of the partisan Nelia Benissone Costa, who, in idealistic solidarity with her daughter, devoted herself to honouring and burying the dead.[159] Another partisan, Teresa Cirio, speaks of women who 'when they learned that that there were dead people in town ... cut the hanged men down from the gallows, washed them, and laid them out. Others took red carnations to the cemetery. The graves of the partisans were always all adorned with flowers.'[160]

After the Liberation there would be mothers who would prevent those responsible for the killing of their sons from being executed: 'There's already one dead person, why do you want to kill another one ... who's a child [14 years old]? You mustn't take them; you people are guilty too.'[161]

Male perplexities, oscillations and contradictions before the women combatants are numerous, for all the encouragement and acknowledgment of the contribution of women in general to the Resistance cause. One command complained of the failure to form women's SAPs.[162] Rumours circulated of the presence of exclusively women's bands in the area of the Turchino pass in Liguria.[163] But, while accentuating the armed presence of individual volunteers, the prevailing tendency was to assign to women tasks that were technically more suitable in that they aroused less suspicion in the enemy, like those of dispatch-riders and informers, or else the more traditional, separate and subaltern ones, of nurse, cook, darner and the like. The general command of the CVL issued a report to all the formations, thereby setting it up as an example, announcing the establishment of a unit of women who 'iron, sew and darn', commanded by 'a Garibaldino who is also head-tailor'. 'These women', the report concludes, 'are

April 1944 (*LRE*, p. 590).

158 See G. Crainz, 'La 'legittimazione' della Resistenza. Dalla crisi del centrismo alla vigilia del '68', in *Problemi del socialism* 7 (January–April 1987), p. 76.

159 Bruzzone and Farina, *La Resistenza taciuta*, esp. p. 39.

160 Ibid., p. 88. See also the testimony of Teresa Bosco, in Guidetti Serra, *Compagne*, vol. I, p. 46.

161 Testimony of Carolina Griffanti, in Passerini, *Torino operaia*, p. 23. Note also the episode recounted by Nelia Benissone Costa: 'Upon Liberation, the partisans wanted to go and grab the woman who had made the denunciation, but the mother was opposed' (Bruzzone and Farina, *La Resistenza taciuta*, p. 53).

162 Letter from the Command of the Turin SAP division to the Command of the 1st Sector, 15 January 1945 (cited in *Le Brigate Garibaldi*, vol. III, p. 237, n. 2).

163 Testimony of Teresa Cirio (Bruzzone and Farina, *La Resistenza taciuta*, p. 83).

given a medical check-up weekly', this provision being indignantly condemned by the Piedmontese GL.[164] 'Putting clothes away, wrapping parcels ... treating the wounded, organising first-aid stations, nursery schools, et cetera' were the duties that the Communist Party indicated to the women's sections that were being created in the South, 'bearing in mind the southern mentality',[165] but clearly this mentality was equally widespread in the North as well.

What stands out here is a rare and explicit appeal to the combative pacifist tradition of women: 'You are the worthy daughters of those women who in 1915–18, to prevent the departure for the front of young men who were due to go off and get themselves killed by the Germans, lay down across the railroad tracks heedless of the danger to their lives. Your gestures are as admirable as those of your mothers.'[166]

Male reticence is particularly visible at the moment of the final parade, after the victory. In Milan – again it is Elsa Oliva who is telling the story – 'in the march-pasts, the dispatch-riders were made to wear nurses' arm-bands!':[167] and dispatch-riding was, as I have already said, a function recognised as being particularly suitable for women. When the partisans had entered Alba on 10 October 1944, thereby initiating the brief experience of the free zone, 'with the men', wrote Fenoglio,

> the women partisans paraded, in men's dress, and here some folk began to murmur: 'Ah, povera Italia!' ['Heaven help Italy!'] – because these girls had expressions and bearings that made the citizens start winking. On the eve of the descent the commanders, who had no illusions on this score, had given orders for the women partisans at all costs to stay up in the hills, but the latter had told them where to get off and had come rushing down into the town.[168]

---

164 *Atti CVL*, pp. 187–8. The detachment (of thirty-eight women) was set up alongside the 19th Garibaldi brigade 'Eusebio Giamone'. It was Vittorio Foa who told me of the GL's reaction to the uncouth suggestion of a gynaecological check-up. On the tension between women's traditional roles and their handling weapons, see L. Passerini, 'Ferite della memoria. Immaginario e ideologia in una storia recente', and B. Guidetti Serra, 'Donne, violenza, politica, armi: una esperienza giudiziaria', *Rivista di storia contemporanea* XVII (1988), pp. 173–245 (p. 231 features three testimonies of partisan women, one opposed to shooting a gun, one undecided and one in favour: the latter woman is Elsa Oliva); R. Anni, D. Lusiardi, G. Sciola and M. R. Zamboni, *I gesti e i sentimenti: le donne nella Resistenza bresciana*, Introduction by L. Passerini, Brescia: Tipografia Quiriniana, 1990.

165 Minutes of the 'Delegazione del PCI per l'Italia meridionale', 8 May 1944 (IG, Archivio PCI, 'Direzione. Verbali riunioni 1944').

166 Open letter from 'a political commissar' and 'a commander' to 'Our mothers, wives, sisters' in an undated special issue of *Noi donne* dedicated to the 'Volontarie della libertà'.

167 This testimony appears in Bruzzone and Farina, eds, *La Resistenza taciuta*, p. 141.

168 Fenoglio, *I ventitré giorni*, p. 9.

In the final parade in Turin the Garibaldi formations decreed that the women were not to participate in the march-pasts, to avoid unpleasant reactions, including the risk of their being called whores. Tersilla Fenoglio Oppedisano, who recounts the episode, recalls the disappointment and anger that she and her companions felt at seeing that in the autonomous formations the women paraded with the men as equals, but then adds that she recognises the justness of the ban.[169] Evidently 'Mauri' (Ilario Tabarri) and his men, who were bourgeoisly open-minded, felt free not to give a damn whether their women were called whores; not so with the Communists, both because their policy of alliance with the petit-bourgeois classes and the Catholics led them to cultivate their prejudices, and because several of the Garibaldi women at least were themselves sensitive to that risk.

In fact, at times the partisans themselves mirrored this tendency by calling Fascist women auxiliaries whores. On both sides, this was the most rapid way of avoiding the conflict between political and military commitment, regulated by new and uncertain codes, and sexual morality, regulated by ancient and solid codes.[170]

The protective attitude towards women and the limited function assigned to them are borne out in the name given to the unitary women's organisation sponsored above all by the Communists: 'Gruppi di difesa della donna per l'assistenza ai combattenti della libertà' ('Groups for the defence of women for the assistance of the freedom fighters'). On the one hand, women were seen here as beings to defend – on a par, it should be noted, with the peasants; on the other hand, the only active role they were assigned was that of assistance. Because of this, many women did not like the formula, Ada Gobetti included.[171] The Italian name followed the French one: 'marraines des francs-tireurs et partisans'. The still fresh memory of the grey Fascist invention *madrine di guerra* (godmothers of war) probably advised against using an identical formula. In France, however, the *madrine* declared themselves ready to fight, thereby vindicating their descent from the women of the great Revolution.[172]

---

169 Tersilla Fenoglio Oppedisano adds: 'Now I no longer make any judgments, but then I did' (Bruzzone and Farina, eds, *La Resistenza taciuta*, p. 160).

170 Considerations advanced by the student Emanuela Cortopassi in a seminar at the Modern and Contemporary History Department of Pisa University, in 1982.

171 See the testimony of Teresa Bosco, in Guidetti Serra, *Compagne*, vol. I, p. 43, and Gobetti, *Diario partigiano*, pp. 72–3. Nor did Gobetti like *Noi donne* as a title for the paper: 'But I accepted it, certainly, when they told me that it had already been the name of a women's paper in Spain, during the revolution' (ibid., p. 139, 9 June 1944).

172 See, for example, the paper *Quatre-Vingt-Treize*, published by the 'marraines du Détachement Victor Hugo'. The first issue, from 22 October 1943, contains this appeal: 'Do not forget, Hitlerites, that we are the descendants of the women of the French Revolution, those women who did not hesitate to throw themselves into the struggle together with the Revolutionaries.' The header of the second issue, 11 November 1943,

Perhaps the only people comparable to the women in their two-sided attitude to the armed struggle are those priests who chose to become chaplains with the partisan formations, and who therefore saw the contradictions of the Catholics at first hand.

In 1946 a periodical vindicating the clergy's contribution to the Resistance wrote: 'It's true: no priest took up arms, even if he was a chaplain of bands, because his pacific mission of love prevented him from using violent instruments of hate.'[173] When he went over from the Di Dio[174] to the Garibaldi formations, Don Sisto Bighiani, caressing his machine-gun, said to Moscatelli 'that he had prayed and was praying to the Lord never to be compelled to use it with his hands'.[175] By contrast, a chaplain to the Osoppo brigades, which took their inspiration from Don Aldo Moretti (a Resistance priest), fired and the next day said Mass, leaving a British major who witnessed the scene somewhat perplexed; and another priest had no qualms about shooting but did not want the political commissar in the band.[176]

Commitment for a good cause never completely cancelled the defensive character in Resistance violence. The decision to kill came later; it was a consequence of the fundamental decision to oppose the violence of the other side. Resistance violence could therefore be placed, broadly, in the category of legitimate defence, which involved the possibility of being killed oneself.[177]

Rousseau had written: 'Every man has the right to risk his life in order to preserve it ... He who wills the end wills the means also, and the means must involve some risks, and even some losses. He who wishes to preserve his life at others' expense should also, when it is necessary, be ready to give it up for their sake.'[178]

---

featured the image of a woman exhorting others to battle, sword in hand, in tune with the iconography of 1870. In the February 1944 header of another paper, *14 juillet. Organe des marraines de la compagnie des francs-tireurs et partisans Français 'Les Trois Glorieuses'*, there appeared on one side a man with a Phrygian cap, and on the other a proletarian in Third Internationalist style: each of the two men, who held a banner bearing the legend *14 juillet*, had a woman at their side, albeit of rather anodyne appearance.

173 'L' opera del clero e i partigiani', *Le Messager Valdôtain 1946*.

174 The Valtoce division had adopted the name of its commander, fallen in battle.

175 Tramontin, *Il clero italiano e la Resistenza*, p. 20 (with other examples and bibliographic references). On don Sisto and his relations with Moscatelli's Garibaldians, see *Le Brigate Garibaldi*, vol. III, p. 34.

176 See the contribution by G. Bianchi in *Aspetti religiosi della Resistenza*, pp. 73–4, quoted in Tramontin, *Il clero italiano e la Resistenza*, p. 20; Battaglia, *Un uomo*, p. 212 (see also p. 216).

177 Norberto Bobbio insisted on this point in a seminar held at Turin's Centro Gobetti on 28 April 1980.

178 Rousseau, *The Social Contract*, Book II, §5. See J. Goulet, 'Robespierre, la peine de mort et la Terreur', in *Annales historiques de la Révolution française* LXIII (1981), p. 219.

Many Resistance documents insist on the need to resort to violence. 'When we are compelled to kill one of our fellow men, one of our fellow countrymen, at times even an old friend, our hand does not tremble because we know we have had to act to defend ourselves, in that he wanted our death', says a GL newspaper – and adds immediately, almost as if it fears that a purely defensive vision might risk taking the colour out of the ultimate ends of the struggle: 'When, moreover, we remember again the sanctity of the cause for which our comrades are dying, we feel all the more that we are performing an act of true justice.'[179]

A Garibaldi unit's report expresses almost in the form of a fable this theme of defence that cannot help becoming offence: 'Two comrades were stopped by two militia-men of the Black Brigade, but on hearing their threat raised their pistols and shot them dead. In their enthusiasm at having captured them the Fascists had shouted: Partisan dogs, we'll kill you. And they were killed.'[180]

'Resentment at man-hunting' is indicated as one of the causes that led to the 'Four Days of Naples'.[181] Killing as a necessity helped to preserve one, at least as far as one's intentions were concerned, from taking pleasure in it, and from cruelty, that is from that *di più* (surplus) which was, by contrast, so greatly vaunted by the Fascists. 'We are not fighting to kill and exterminate', declared a Tuscan Garibaldino.[182] A Liberal newspaper wrote – and it is no easy business distinguishing the affirmation of how one should be from the statement of how things really are – that when one of the enemy dies there is no exultation, as there is with the sadistic Fascists: killing is always a grievous thing, even if today it is necessary.[183]

In Emanuele Artom's diary three subtly linked passages occur at a close distance from each other:

> The militiaman from Bagnolo who was a spy has been sentenced to death and then killed suddenly, without being aware of it until the last minute: this is the Soviet method, and if, at least in war, the death penalty is deemed necessary, this is the most human method: the anguish of the inevitable end is avoided, and never mind if the condemned man has no way of preparing himself and expressing his last wishes.

---

179 'Giustizia partigiana', *Il Partigiano alpino*, Piedmont edition, August 1944 (cited in Falaschi, *La Resistenza armata*, p. 23).

180 Report from the Montes organisation, December 1944, in Mautino, *Guerra di popolo*, p. 115. Note the episode recounted by Battaglia, *Un uomo*, p. 215, where a partisan killed two Germans who asked for his papers.

181 F. Caracciolo di Castagneto, '43–'44. *Diario di Napoli*, Florence: Vallecchi, 1964, p. 49 (29 September 1943 entry).

182 Testimony of the partisan Moretto (Guido Cavalcabò), in G. and E. Varlecchi, *Potente*, p. 232.

183 See the box 'Sangue' in *Risorgimento Liberale*, Rome edition, 5 May 1944.

Three days later Artom explained the reasons why he had not wanted to set a mousetrap and concluded: 'Last reason – last or first? – the desire to put this subtle examination of my conscience down in my diary'. Finally, Artom takes satisfaction in recalling a speech by his commander who, quoting D'Annunzio's motto 'I dare, I don't scheme', had recommended his men to 'dare as little as possible, in order to achieve the end, but not to make daring an end in itself'.[184]

The insistence on the defensive character of the struggle – in itself neither original nor significant, given that the aggressors too were in the habit of resorting to it brazenly – was therefore valuable for the *resistenti* above all as a moral guarantee, which was all the more necessary for the fact that the exercise of violence was the result of a personal choice. In many cases, direct and indirect, but always clear, manifestations of this conviction are identifiable; while in other cases the reasons for defence interwove in various ways, to the point of becoming almost invisible, with the active 'motivations' that sustained the struggle and that encountered the 'technical' reasons according to which the best defence is attack, above all in guerrilla warfare. Recalling our earlier examination of the *noms de guerres* with patriotic and class references, we can now underline that violent and truculent names appear only rarely, that they are best interpreted, as Fenoglio interpreted them, as 'formidable',[185] and that, when they do appear, they can often be taken as being ironical. For example, Fenoglio describes the crowd in Alba 'reading as one reads the numbers on the backs of cyclists' the *noms de guerre* that the partisans wore embroidered on their scarves, red and light blue alike, wrapped around their shoulders.[186] Names bearing the mark of real or feigned violence, self-attributed or attributed by others, include for example: 'Mitra' ('Machine-gun'), 'Mauser', 'Tritolo' ('TNT'), 'Bestione' ('Beast'), 'Boia' ('Hangman'), 'Caino' ('Cain'); and also the bad taste of 'Menefrego' ('I don't give a damn'), 'Ras', 'Ardito', 'Bastanaro'. For similar reasons, it is hard to say whether a partisan called Gandhi was a pacifist or a skinny lad with lightweight spectacles.

It has been repeated many times that the name 'Resistenza' is French in origin, and that in Italy it was taken up only after the event. This is true if one is referring to the canonised use of the formula 'movimento di liberazione'.[187] But if one looks at the press and at contemporary documents, one notices the

---

184 Artom, *Diari*, 8, 11 and 16 December 1943 (pp. 112, 115, 125).

185 Fenoglio, *I ventitré giorni*, p. 9: 'romantic, tremendous names, from Rolando to "Dynamite"'.

186 Ibid.

187 'Istituto nazionale per la storia del movimento di liberazione in Italia' ('National institute for the history of the liberation movement in Italy') was the name that Ferruccio Parri chose in 1949. The local institutes that sprang up in subsequent years, however, largely instead adopted names referring to 'the history of the Resistance' or similar.

frequent occurrence of the word, almost always with a small *r*, in the literal sense, implicitly and at times also explicitly 'defensive',[188] even if there is no lack of more solemn adoptions. It is telling that these should appear in a 'message from the CLNAI' to the CLN of emigrants to France,[189] that previously an Action Party newspaper had praised De Gaulle 'for strengthening French resistance against Nazi domination',[190] and that the expression 'movimento della resistenza' figures in the agreement of 7 December 1944 between the CLNAI delegation and Allied Command, which clearly had experience of French affairs.[191]

A leaflet dropped by British planes on the night of 22 October 1943 already reminded the 'Italians of the resistance' of the 'armed or passive resistance' taking place in the other occupied countries.[192] Passive resistance still fell short of even defensive violence, and the newspaper of young Roman Christian Democrats defended the latter, arguing that already during the Fascist *ventennio* it had been an authentic Italian masterpiece.[193] The newspapers of the more committed movements tended rather to use qualifying adjectives such as *attiva, organizzata*, or *armata*.[194] At times *L'Unità* speaks of resistance as simply a first step;[195] and the same concept recurs, for example, in an unsigned leaflet of November 1943 addressed to the young men of Arcugnano: 'Let us find ourselves again as soldiers even if in civilian dress and let us begin our battle of resistance at once, for the time being: let us not yield.'[196]

The principle of self-defence gave rise to complex developments. Mere individual self-defence was not feasible unless one lay low in isolation. Getting together in groups immediately posed the problem of the use of weapons. A Communist document severely criticises a *professore* who ordered his men to remain hidden in the village, the result being that they were all arrested in the taverns and houses. This episode demonstrates, the document concludes, that 'only with weapons in our hands and with a perfect military organisation can we save ourselves and at the same time inflict heavy blows on the enemy'.[197] Earlier,

188 According to 'Fuori dall'equivoco. Variazioni', in *La Voce del Popolo*, 15 March 1944.

189 The text was published in *L'Italia Libera*, Paris, 1 February 1945. Here, we read, 'We are particularly close to the people of France, which has been able to write the heroic pages of the Resistance, a name that has now become epic, European.'

190 'Al popolo italiano, agli amici, ai nemici', *La Libertà* (Tuscany), 27 October 1943.

191 The text of the agreement appears in Catalano, *Storia del CLNAI*, pp. 339–40.

192 An example of the leaflet is held at the MRB.

193 'Resistenza passiva', signed by 'the man in the street', *La Punta*, 28 February 1944.

194 See *L'Unità*, *L'Italia Libera* and *Voce Operaia*.

195 'Non c'è tempo da perdere' ('No time to lose'), northern edition, 10 January 1944.

196 IVSR, *Stampa antifascista*.

197 Letter from the Command of the 40th Matteotti brigade to the 'Delegazione Comando e al Comando regionale (unificato) lombardo', 20 July 1944 (IG, *BG*, 0507).

L'Unità had written: 'We mustn't let ourselves be butchered. We must arm and defend ourselves.'[198]

More calmly, but no less forcefully, a Garibaldi commander later wrote: 'It made no sense having abandoned civilian life to take ourselves off to live wretchedly in the mountains without starting that guerrilla warfare which would justify our daily privations and provide experience for future developments.'[199]

3. SELF-DISCIPLINE AND THE ORGANISATION OF VIOLENCE: THE PUNITIVE SYSTEM

The steady growth of the network of CLNs, culminating in the CLNAI and the coming to the fore as a military and unitary organism of the Corpo dei Volontari della Libertà (Corps of Volunteers for Liberty) headed by the General Command, may be regarded as signalling a growing political and institutional legitimisation of violence. It was not so much general and top-level legitimisation – relations with the monarchy, the government in Rome and the Allies – as the process of organisation springing from the very heart of the movement that saw the establishment of a series of guarantees against an indiscriminate and blind use of violence. It is this normalisation with the nascent state, to which attention has already been drawn, that distinguishes the immediate context within which single acts of violence took place.

Naturally a system of norms, however approximate, and organisation, born again in the name of liberty, recreated authority as well. The norms within which Resistance violence sought to discipline itself did not correspond to those that the enemy followed, or claimed to follow. The upshot of this was that the expression 'fuori legge' ('outlaw') mirrored the conflict between two different 'laws'. At the same time the *resistenti* tended, within certain limits, to revert to customary practices, such as the adoption of a uniform, which, according to even the most labile international law relating to war, should have guaranteed their status as combatants. One of the most noticeable differences between the 'political' bands (above all the Garibaldi and GL) and the 'autonomous' ones was that the latter were more inclined to adopt norms and styles belonging to military tradition. Indeed, in the conditions of complete autonomy in which he found himself operating, as prestigious a commander as Mauri (the major on permanent active service Enrico Martini) could give free rein to the militaristic concept that he had of his men as cavaliers and defenders of order. In his capacity as commander of the 1st Group of the Alpini divisions, Mauri thus reprimanded a lieutenant

---

198 Subtitle of the article 'La strage di Ferrara', Rome edition, 29 November 1943.
199 Bernardo, *Il momento buono*, p. 31.

colonel under him – and this in itself was quite a departure from the traditional hierarchy – for his behaviour towards the men in his charge:

> Permit me to say, signor Colonello, that I do not approve of your excessive goodness. In the war we are waging, and from knowledge of Italians, being good is a defect and we must not and cannot be so in the interest of our *patria* and of the Cause for which we are fighting. Every so often it is necessary to shoot men, if only to try out weapons.[1]

Not, of course, that this drastic and cynical policy was carried out to the letter; but the very fact of declaring it is a sign of the presence of a hyper-militaristic cultural structure, seen as the only alternative to the laxity which was in turn so much a part of the Italian military tradition.

The most pressing problem that had to be faced was that of distinguishing oneself from the robbers and plunderers who got busy on the wave of dissolution of the Royal Army and the pillaging of military stores that had followed it. The phenomena of the days immediately following the Armistice still lie this side of the distinction between robberies and plundering, on the one hand, and acts committed by the bands in order to sustain themselves, on the other. Little by little, the CLN, CVL and party organisations would, at least to some extent, take charge of this aspect of the struggle too. A late Action Party report which announced that 'the demarcation line' between partisan activity and banditry 'is often highly uncertain', said that the prestige of the Commands and of the CLNs greatly depended on the regularity of the financing they received.[2] But the first bands had had to fend for themselves.

Intent on distinguishing between criminality and politics wholly within the practice of killing, Nuto Revelli wrote in his diary with his customary frankness:

> The phenomenon of banditry is spreading. Disbanded ex-servicemen of the 4th Army and local delinquents, passing themselves off as partisans, are terrorising the population. All it takes to muddy the waters is an Alpino cap, a grey-green tunic. As we catch them we'll shoot them. If we want to ensure that the Germans and Fascists don't lump things together, cashing in on them so as to defame us, we must show no pardon.

---

1 Letter of 8 October 1944 to the lieutenant colonel Pier Alessandro Vanni, commander of the formations deployed across the Casotto, Mongia and Tanaro valleys (INSMLI, *CVL*, envelope 27, folder 2, subfolder 1); I thank Gabriella Solaro for making me aware of their existence.

2 Report from the political commissar of the Piedmont Command of the GL formations, Giorgio Agosti, 31 December 1944. Agosti refers to the 'numerous shootings of common criminals, in some cases also our partisans' (*Formazioni GL*, pp. 267–86).

Consequently, adds Revelli, the bandits 'are more scared of the partisans than they are of the *carabinieri*: the partisans shoot them ... To close the circle around these delinquents our squads are also operating in collaboration with the *carabinieri* of the valley' – i.e. with the *carabinieri* in the service of the RSI. But elsewhere Revelli also distinguished between rigour and inhumanity when, about the proceedings instituted against six false partisans, he wrote:

> 8 September has broken a false and confused world; it has thrown men's consciences in at the deep end. It's a painful business being hard with people like this. Mild sentences because they are not real bandits. These mountain folk who live in poverty, who do not want to and cannot come down from the mountains to look for a job, at times risk the firing squad because they interpret *ribellismo* [rebelliousness] in their own fashion.[3]

Revelli also recalls having vainly hunted the robbers of a group of Jews at Demonte in order to shoot them, but of having given a 'suspended' death sentence to some youths on their way to commit a robbery almost as an act of bravado, granting them the opportunity to rehabilitate themselves by fighting – which was what in fact happened.[4]

A Piedmontese band took the initiative of putting up posters asking for the collaboration of the population in repressing 'bandits outside the army'.[5] Phenomena of this kind were reported in many areas, from western Piedmont to the province of Biella and Friuli. In Friuli there was the execution of 'elements who, passing themselves off as partisans, were harassing the populations', while in the Apuan Alps 'three brothers [were shot], the first for having stolen and the other two for having tried to avenge his death'.[6] There are youths who 'say that they want to fight the enemy and not to be burglars in order to fatten up those of the Command', quite clearly a Command lacking in any prestige.[7] Others seem

---

3 Revelli, *La guerra dei poveri*, p. 144 (16 October 1943), p. 177 (29 February 1944), and p. 184 (15 March 1944). See the comments of the partisan Gin, from the Ligurian-Emilian Appenines: 'They want to make us live by stealing, so that tomorrow they might blackmail and slander us' (Lazagna, *Ponte rotto*, p. 155).

4 Conversation of the author with Nuto Revelli. Some Jews took refuge in Demonte, escaping the arrests of those who had been locked up in the Borgo San Dalmazzo camp after having come from Saint-Martin-Vésubie. On this affair, which speaks well of the Italian troops occupying southern France, see A. Cavaglion, *Nella notte straniera. Gli Ebrei di Saint-Martin-Vésubie. 8 settembre – 21 novembre 1943*, Cuneo: L'Arciere, 1991.

5 Artom, *Diari*, p. 93 (28 November 1943); see also p. 141 (28 December 1943).

6 Dellavalle, *Operai*, p. 84; Quazza, *Un diario partigiano*, pp. 154–6 (December 1943); Mautino, *Guerra di popolo*, p. 42; Battaglia, *Un uomo*, p. 130.

7 C.'s report 'on the first visit to the partisan formations in the Foligno zone', 3 February 1944 (*Le Brigate Garibaldi*, vol. I, p. 252).

to suggest that banditry descended from the art of fending for oneself, which was a cornerstone of the ethics of the Royal Army.[8] Still others distinguish between the requisitioning from civilians by means of coupons, 'recovery' – 'total or partial removal of foodstuffs and material belonging to the partisan movement, entrusted to civilians' – and 'confiscation' – 'compulsory removal of material and foodstuffs from organisations or persons who used them for purposes contrary to our ends'.[9] In other documents any expeditious appropriation of useful articles is vaguely defined as an 'act of recovery', possibly with an unintentional reminiscence of the aspiration to expropriate the expropriators.

One consequence of the tendential re-monopolising of violence in the hands of the 'third government' of the Resistance was that the formations that refused to recognise the authority of the CLNs and the CVLs – especially when the latter became formally unified – were to be looked on with distrust: lacking the official blessing of the new legitimacy, they would always seem to be on the point of falling into street banditry. The Command of a Garibaldi brigade reminded a commander who was stubbornly resisting the unification of the forces that those who remained outside would be treated as 'bandits' and 'saboteurs of liberty' and be given the death penalty.[10] Another Garibaldi formation warned that those who used ration coupons without supporting the CLN, but usurping its name, would have to answer before a people's tribunal, while if they did not even use the name, they would certainly be shot.[11] No less severe was the GL Lombard Command with its reminder that only membership of the CVL legitimates a formation, 'which otherwise would at present, and still more so after the Liberation, be considered altogether differently'; and which, to make things still clearer, added that uncontrolled initiatives led to damaging actions and useless losses, even 'when they do not degenerate into more or less open forms of banditry'.[12]

Naturally, this more or less unavoidable necessity lent itself to political vendetta – for example the denunciation, mentioned earlier, of 'sinistrimo as a mask of the Gestapo', and to acts of discrimination against those who saw 'irregularity' as being still an innate component of their decision to join the Resistance

8 'Informazioni per l'Ufficio di organizzazione', Turin, 10 October 1943 (Secchia, *Il PCI e la guerra di liberazione*, p. 122).

9 Circular from the 'Comando unificato Divisioni Valsesia Divisioni Ossola', 6 September 1944 (IG, *BG*, 06274).

10 Letter from the Command of the 40th Matteotti brigade (Valtellina) to Onit Nass, 14 July 1944 (ibid., 0490). On Onit Nass (Sandro Costantino), commander of the Gek group, see the letter from the Command of the 40th brigade to the vicar of Roncaglia, 14 July 1944 (*Le Brigate Garibaldi*, vol. II, pp. 123–4 and the relevant notes).

11 Letter from the Command of the Nanetti division to the Command of the Mazzini and Tollot brigades, 29 August 1944, and related attachments (ibid., pp. 283–9).

12 Circular of 12 February 1945, 'Inquadramento, disciplina, organizzazione' (INSMLI, *CVL*, envelope 93, folder 5, subfolder a).

and the increasingly rife ferments of social revolt. A typical case is Giuseppe Marozin, an intriguing popular ringleader from the Vicenza area. While no one questioned his courage and enterprise, orders were given that, if he was caught in the act, 'one should intervene with the maximum determination and with all the means at one's disposal.'[13]

The danger was also felt on the left that nuclei of future white guards were nesting in the irregular formations. Above all, and particularly in the last months, the Communists were on the lookout on this score; and the efforts made to defend the factories by means of the SAPs and other CLN-recognised formations aimed also at preventing a last-minute collapse, to their own disadvantage, of that unification of forces in the name of which so many of the class 'differences' most deeply felt by the militants had been sacrificed. On the other hand, the very presence of armed workers in the factories could tempt the owners to organise their own squads. When in Turin the DC became spokesman for such a request, the PCI's reaction was extremely severe. 'Any other organisms [that are not SAPs] directed and financed by the forces of reaction will be fought with every means': 'In fact, the Turin Communists had earlier warned: the industrialists, especially the management of the Fiat plant, would do well to remember that the workers will not tolerate management's private squads entering the factories, since they are considered real corps of white guards and are treated as such.'[14]

Similar warnings were given in Milan and elsewhere.[15] An extremely precocious denunciation of this kind had come from *L'Italia Libera*, the Action Party newspaper: 'Watch out for squads that the capitalists themselves are promoting

---

13 Letter from the regional military command in the Veneto to the Vicenza provincial command, 15 September 1944, held at the Istituto veneto per la storia della Resistenza. Bernardo passes very severe judgment on Marozin: *Il momento buono*, pp. 76–8. Nor was there any succour for Marozin in the *Enciclopedia dell'antifascismo e della Resistenza*, insofar as he is named in the piece devoted to the Pasubio division, written by Renato Sandri.

14 Minutes of the January 1945 and late September 1944 meetings of the Comando Piazza di Torino, in Vaccarino, Gobetti and Gobbi, *L'insurrezione di Torino*, pp. 116, 95. On the sense of alarm that arose among Turin's Communists, on this score, see the warning sent to SAP companies, 25 January 1945 (*Le Brigate Garibaldi*, vol. III, pp. 283–4) and the 15 June 1944 *Grido di Spartaco*'s denunciation of 'Il nuovo Risorgimento italiano, movimento antitotalitario d'ordine e di ricostruzione' as a 'White Guard Movement'.

15 See the 24 March 1945 circular from the 'Comando Raggruppamento Brigate SAP Milano e Provincia' (*Le Brigate Garibaldi*, vol. III, pp. 522–4). The birth of a 'White army' was referred to, with some apprehension, in the Bergamasco 'Notiziario militare' of December 1944 (IG, BG, 010599). On 26 February 1945, the 'Comando della Divisione Belluno' gave news, speaking in alarmed terms, of 'irregular units who are taking it upon themselves to act as a police corps after the end of hostilities', in a communication to all formations under its watch (Bernardo, *Il momento buono*, p. 247).

for their class interests, under the guise of the appeal to 'national solidarity' and 'sacrifices to bear in common' and under the promises of 'concessions on the social terrain'.[16]

Leaving aside for the time being developments that would lead us back into the theme of the class war, the organisation of violence as an instrument against its own degeneration had to reckon with the revolutionary tradition which did not always draw a clear dividing-line between rebels and bandits.[17] The severity towards robbers disguised as partisans sprang also from the need to be rid of this atavistic ambiguity, which threatened to reappear in the very bosom of the established partisan bands. The 1848 Garibaldini despised the regular army, but demanded discipline and severely punished pillagers.[18] In 1924–25 the young Communist Altiero Spinelli answered the complaint that the party was not minting false money or organising large-scale robberies by saying that, if one went about things in that way, one would transform oneself 'without even realising it, from revolutionaries into common criminals, participants, albeit irregularly, in the common exploitation practised by the bourgeoisie'.[19]

The Communist federation of Venice was to act along these lines when it enjoined the partisans operating in the zone between Mestre, San Donà and Portogruaro to stop getting well-to-do people to hand over money at gunpoint.[20] But it is certainly true that sometimes exceptional circumstances prompted criticisms against the positions expressed by Spinelli and by Giuseppe Dozza. A report from Bologna reads:

We are still encountering in the men who currently make up our GAPs a fundamental weakness which is the residue of a false sentimentalism, namely uncertainty about, nay aversion to, acts of expropriation. They are of the view that a Communist cannot act as a robber would act, and on this point all they see is the form while forgetting the substance.[21]

16 'Le squadre di fabbrica', *L'Italia Libera*, Lombardy edition, 18 February 1944.

17 On all these points, I refer back to Eric Hobsbawm's *Bandits*, New York: Delacorte Press, 1969, especially Chapter 7. See also P. Brunello, *Ribelli, questuanti e banditi. Proteste contadine in Veneto e in Friuli, 1814–1866*, Venice: Marsilio, 1981.

18 P. Del Negro, 'Garibaldi tra esercito regio e nazione armata: il problema del reclutamento', in F. Mazzonis, ed., *Garibaldi condottiero. Storia, teoria, prassi*, Milan: Franco Angeli, 1984, pp. 253–310.

19 Spinelli, *Io, Ulisse*, pp. 82–3. This response was praised by the organiser Giuseppe Dozza, because it was at odds with the kind of petty-bourgeois spirit that one might have suspected to lurk within the young Roman militant, given his social origin.

20 Letter addressed to 'caro Nagi', undated, INSMLI, *CLNAI*, envelope 8, folder 2, subfolder 4.

21 'Rapporto del triangolo dal settembre al dicembre 1943', Secchia, *Il PCI e la guerra di liberazione*, p. 131.

But a document from the Bergamo area denounces the excess of retrieval operations, stimulated by granting prizes and percentages: 'Either we work for the cause, in which case it's a patriotic and political action, or else we work for a prize or percentage, in which case it's banditry, even if it's hidden beneath a political veil.'[22] Requisitions, a GL Command decreed, were to be carried out 'in cases of urgent and absolute necessity', and in any case only at the expense of the most prosperous.[23]

The Communist and Actionist leadership were always well aware of the risk that the fragility of political education would degrade the partisans, turning them into 'adventurers with neither scruples nor restraint, undisciplined to the point of insubordination, strong, daring in action but out for their own ends and for no other purpose'.[24] This was a risk that was becoming particularly serious following the dispersal provoked by the roundups.[25]

There was thus not only the problem of an abstract normativeness, but of the discipline in which this was to be embodied as an instrument to distinguish the 'flower' from the 'dregs'. This distinction, which figures in Fenoglio's work as a hendiadys, could however become blurred since not everyone accepted GL's severe and diffident proposal, 'neither heroes nor bandits', and since at exceptional moments even the dregs could turn into flowers and possibly revert later into dregs.[26] It was no easy transformation, as witness the case of the murderer who, having joined the partisans, purportedly to redeem himself, when tried for desertion and rabble-rousing, saw his past recoil against him.[27]

---

22 'Compagni della Delegazione' to 'caro Pietro', 1 April 1945 (IG, *BG*, 010653).

23 Circular from the Lombard Regional Command of the GL formations, to Provincial Command 734, 28 November 1944 (INSMLI, *CVL*, envelope 93, folder 5, subfolder a). 'The watchword which is almost always respected is to take millions from the industrialist, but to pay the peasant for his hen': according to Giorgio Agosti, in his above-cited 31 December 1944 report (*Formazioni GL*, p. 275).

24 Words used in 'Considerazioni sul lavoro della montagna e GAP', concerning the Novara area, from late 1943 (IG, *Archivio PCI*).

25 Note, for example, the case of the Basso brothers, who ultimately handed themselves in to the Fascists, and the commander Leo Vigna, who surrendered during a roundup – leaving his men at liberty – and was then shot together with two of them, having confessed to 'violence against mountain-dwellers'. Dellavalle, *Operai*, p. 139. See also Giorgio Agosti's 31 December 1944 report (*Formazioni GL*, pp. 267–86) and the account of Gino Pieri, *Storia di partigiani*, quoted in Falaschi, *La Resistenza armata*, p. 52.

26 Fenoglio refers to the volunteers as 'flowers and dregs' in his *Il partigiano Johnny*, p. 154. Giovana uses the formulation 'Neither heroes nor bandits' in *Storia di una formazione partigiana*, p. 290. For the dregs who acted as flowers, but who the flowers could not vouch for, note the thieves of Rome's San Lorenzo district, who in 1921 gave brave and disciplined support to the Arditi del Popolo in the fight against the Fascists (see L. Piccioni, *San Lorenzo. Un quartiere romano durante il fascismo*, Rome: Storia e Letteratura, 1984, p. 31).

27 'Verbale del processo nei confronti del comandante di battaglione della

Acts of banditry committed by the partisans therefore met with the greatest severity, and the documentary sources attest to the sternest application of them, even if they are more reticent about recording actions that remained unpunished. Above all, there was the need to distinguish oneself, on this plane as well, from those Fascist formations which were the first to behave like bands of robbers. This was the reputation deservedly gained in Rome by the Bardi and Pollastrini band, who had their den in the headquarters of the 'federazione dei fasci dell'Urbe', in Palazzo Braschi, and who were eventually arrested by the Italian police.[28] Likewise, Chiodi brands as robbers a unit of the Italian SS 'who are stealing jewels, automobiles, money, giving part of the booty to their German masters'.[29]

For the partisans who behaved like robbers or highwaymen the punishment was almost always death. On the eastern border the chief of a Garibaldi band who imposed a tribute on the population, thus 'abusing the name of the partisans', was captured and shot 'after an interrogation'.[30] In the free zone of Montefiorino those guilty of carrying violent conduct too far were shot.[31] A Terni partisan who had burgled the stores of the Slavs was sentenced to death.[32] A partisan who stole 10,000 lire from an arrested Fascist was shot, while the Fascist was released under caution.[33] At a higher level, the Piedmont CLN issued an appeal against the acts of brigandage and the robberies that that were polluting the partisan movement,[34] while the tribunal of the Val Germanasca brigade of the 5th GL Alpine division expelled from all the patriotic formations a squad commander who 'tolerated his men's performing unspeakable actions against private and public bodies, thereby mystifying the just and sacrosanct work of his comrades in the brigade and of the other patriotic formations'.[35] In Val Seriana, the tribunal of the Gabriele Camozzi GL brigade sentenced to death six men

---

47a brigata, Juan', 19 October 1944, in *Le Brigate Garibaldi*, vol. II, pp. 453–5. Juan was shot.

28 Piscitelli, *Storia della Resistenza romana*, pp. 230–1, and Perrone Capano, *La Resistenza in Roma*, vol. I, chapter 6.

29 Chiodi, *Banditi*, pp. 21–2 (20 April 1944).

30 Mautino, *Guerra di popolo*, p. 62 (9 March 1944). See, in ibid., p. 86, the information on the Montes organisation, which had tried and executed partisans who had admitted their guilt in carrying out similar crimes (29 September 1944).

31 Gorrieri, *La Repubblica di Montefiorino*, pp. 383–4.

32 Portelli, *Biografia di una città*, p. 291.

33 Lazagna, *Ponte rotto*, p. 61.

34 Undated, printed poster, in INSMLI, *CLNAI*, envelope 6, folder 3, subfolder 17.

35 Note from the Command of the 4th Piedmont zone to all formations under its watch, 24 October 1944 (IG, *Archivio PCI*). On the justice enforced by partisans in the Valle Germanasca, see D. Gay Rochat, *La Resistenza nelle Valli Valdesi (1943–1944)*, Preface by L. Valiani, Claudiana, Turin: Claudiana, 1969, pp. 140–1.

'guilty of robbery, refusal to obey and mutiny'.[36] In the Nino Bixio brigade operating in Liguria, in the space of only a few days, two partisans were shot for
rape and robbery, one for theft, another for robbery, and one because he was 'a
robber, thief and spy'.[37]

Disciplining violence could therefore mean going the whole way in exercising it against those on one's own side who were making abusive use of it.
The very circumstances of the partisans left precious little alternative to extreme
punishment. A page in Emanuele Artom's diary, which begins by recalling the
singular request by the *carabinieri* in the service of the RSI to remove some partisan robbers from the bands so that they could arrest them, recalls also that
the commander and his men 'are afraid that if they hand them over to the *carabinieri* they will give away information about the camp and the bases. They
would prefer to eliminate them'; and immediately after this they repent not
having killed a general and two of his men who had been allowed to go free.
Artom, who had argued that one had to be generous, makes a comment that is
acute even if not altogether generally applicable: 'I've noticed that those who are
most inclined to favour the death sentences are always the ones who don't have
to issue them, but who just prattle'.[38] These words clearly reveal the personal
doubts of Artom, whose father had recalled 'the Talmudic saying that a court
that pronounces the death sentence even once in a century is to be considered
very severe', and who on another occasion proposed the death penalty for three
partisans who had stolen, but undertook to commute it 'into a few hours of
lookout duty and being deprived of cigarettes and money prizes for the whole of
the war'.[39]

In some cases, moral scruples (Guido Quazza's diary records arguments and
perplexities)[40] could be accompanied by fears for the future. A circular of the
Piedmontese regional military command, which stigmatised executions without
trial and recalled one's duty not to confound oneself with the Fascists, reprov-
ingly drew attention to an episode in which no one had wanted to take part in a
tribunal for fear of being called to account later for 'illegal judgment'.[41]

---

36 Communication from the 'Comando Divisione Orobica', 12 November 1944
(INSMLI, *CVL*, envelope 93, folder 5, subfolder a).

37 Note the reports from 1 to 8 October 1944 held in IG, *BG*, 010202, 010203,
010205, 010206 (the first among them was published in *Le Brigate Garibaldi*, vol. II,
p. 415).

38 Artom, *Diari*, pp. 174–5 (20 February 1944, when he was still with the
Garibaldians).

39 Ibid., p. 90 (27 November 1943) and p. 170 (18 February 1944).

40 Quazza, *Un diario partigiano*. In the autonomous De Vitis division, hanging
was also used to carry out capital sentences.

41 Circular addressed 'Ai Comandi dipendenti', 1 January 1945, which adds, 'Refusal
to take responsibility clashes with the very nature of the Command' (INSMLI, *CVL*,
envelope 23, folder 1, subfolder 8).

Experience often provided tragic confirmatory evidence of the need to take a hard line. Chiodi recounts that a partisan who was sentenced to death for thieving, but managed to avoid execution, went over to the Black Brigades and then took revenge by killing a former comrade whom he took by surprise while the latter was on his way home for Christmas.[42] In the trials instituted against partisans after the Liberation, it is telling that robberies would either be struck out, being defined as requisitions for war needs, or considered particularly infamous.[43]

Robberies and thefts were not the only occasion for the exercise of punitive violence within the formations. Deserters, instigators, those guilty of grave acts of insubordination could in their turn undergo the death penalty. There have been many case studies in this field, too. The partisan Tigre, who had shot at an envoy of the Tuscan CLN, piercing one of his arms, was immediately executed.[44] A squad leader who during an action wanted to withdraw a machine-gun pit was shot on the spot by his men.[45] One Command decreed: 'No kind of disbandment will be tolerated. I explicitly authorise the killing on the spot of *anyone* who flees.' And another, still more drastically: 'shirkers are to be shot'.[46] Major Mauri, an example of whose militaristic severity I have already given, ordered the shooting of anyone who absented himself with weapons for more than twenty-four hours, of anyone who went over to another unit without being authorised, of anyone who gave information to the enemy (to be shot 'without fail'), of anyone who abandoned his position during an action (he would be shot by his commander in person), of anyone who in an action refused to carry out an order ('to be shot immediately'), of anyone who spread discontent and disorder among the patriots ('shot at once'), of anyone who committed acts of sabotage ('shot without fail'), of anyone who did not hand over to his commander objects that had come into his possession ('shot'), of those who stole from their companions-in-arms, of anyone who falsified Command documents for their own advantage.[47]

Dante Livio Bianco writes of the death sentence inflicted 'with a perfectly serene conscience' on three partisans who were preparing to desert at

---

42 Chiodi, *Banditi*, p. 103 (29 December 1944).

43 See Neppi Modona, ed., *Giustizia penale*, p. 183.

44 See the records of the trial carried out by the Rosselli brigade No. 2, 17 July 1944 (ISRT, *Carte Ramat*, envelope 1, folder 2, subfolder 6).

45 See the 'brown report' on the Nazi-Fascist attack of 2 July 1944, by the 1st Garibaldi division, Ossola-Valsesia zone, 4 August 1944 (IG, *BG*, 06202).

46 Instructions from the Command of the 2nd Sector to the band and detachment commanders, 12 March 1944 (cited in Revelli, *La guerra dei poveri*, pp. 444–5); and the instructions from the head of the General Staff of the Garibaldi division 'Natisone', Carlino, 12 October 1944, on 'comrades unsuitable for military service', among them 'the several *carabinieri* who are asthmatic, have rickets or coughing fits' (ISRFVG, *Fondo Rapuzzi*, envelope 1, folder 1).

47 Decreed 24 July 1944.

the prospect of an imminent roundup.[48] The Triestina brigade set up a tribunal to judge deserters, and on 6 May 1944 reported two executions.[49] Another Command decided to be tough, 'not excluding execution', with some young men who presented themselves to the enemy, possibly with the intention of subsequently returning to the partisans 'so as to be in on the final reckoning as combatants'.[50]

These episodes are mentioned not in order to analyse the disciplinary and punitive system practised in the formations, which would merit separate treatment, but to add other facts in the attempt to reconstruct the atmosphere of violence in which the partisan war was necessarily immersed. The more responsible men did not fail to question themselves on the legitimacy of violent action when it was directed against those who, for their own part, had been infected by that atmosphere and had allowed themselves to be dominated by it.

A page written by the ever blunt and severe Ferdinando Mautino, which begins by recalling that 'discipline was not imposed, but requested', continues thus: 'And we have seen the men of entire formations demanding even the death penalty for comrades who had been found gravely wanting; and those very same men confirming the need for that law which was about to strike them so terribly'.[51] Lazagna tells of a partisan robber who accepted his execution as being just, and of protests, which appeared in the mural newspapers, against the sentence, deemed too mild, inflicted on a partisan who had stolen a sack of wheat; but an Allied mission too demanded the immediate execution of partisans who had made off with two parachutes.[52] That a partisan should pay more dearly than a civilian was powerfully stated in a December 1944 leaflet of the Vittorio Veneto brigade.[53]

At the heart of this wish to punish even to the point of inflicting the death penalty was unquestionably the need the Resistance movement felt for complete self-legitimisation. For this very reason the need was felt to embody the determination to punish in procedural forms which in some way guaranteed that those irreversible means tallied with the ends. On 16 July 1944 the CVL General Command issued directives for the 'constitution and functioning of war tribunals at the partisan units'.[54] The offences which were to lie

48 Bianco, *Guerra partigiana*, pp. 56–7.

49 Letter to the Command of the 9th Yugoslav Corps, 6 May 1944 (*Le Brigate Garibaldi*, vol. I, pp. 381–2).

50 'Relazione politica', political report from the commissar Ilia and vice-commissar Boris of the Liguria Bonfante division (ibid., vol. III, p. 157).

51 Mautino, *Guerra di popolo*, p. 70.

52 Lazagna, *Ponte rotto*, pp. 177, 182, and a report from the Biella zone Command to the Piedmont Delegation, 7 April 1945 (*Le Brigate Garibaldi*, vol. III, p. 586).

53 Quoted in Tramontin, *Contadini e movimento partigiano*, pp. 304–5.

54 *Atti CVL*, pp. 82–3.

within the competence of these tribunals were 'military ones or in any case those concerning military operations (banditry, espionage, outrages against the populations or against their political organisations)'. The sentences were declared unappealable and to be carried out immediately; and it was specified that 'in cases of *flagrante delicto*, desertion of one's post before the enemy or betrayal, the culprits could be shot without the formality of a trial', though the General Command could reserve the right to 'express its opinion in the matter'. Besides being an attempt to produce uniformity and discipline, these norms endorsed the practices already being followed in the various formations.[55] The norms did not establish the punishments nor specify the offences all that precisely – for example, desertion was not explicitly named. Writing towards the end of 1944, a Command gave this extremely realistic account of things:

> Our tribunals are in no way whatsoever obliged to decree the penalties according to the exact interpretation of the code in force. It is logical that in the absence of the technical elements (the presence of attorneys and judges in the formations is an exception) the judgments that are passed are founded exclusively on equity and common sense. The function of the solemn character given to our trials even when they do not carry the death sentence is above all educational.[56]

And a book of memoirs reads that, before managing to create tribunals, 'in the early days sentences were passed in a somewhat primitive way by all the formations'.[57]

The military penal code was in fact appealed to fairly often in the sentences of the partisan tribunals, a case in point being a Command of the Piacenza area, which did however take care to describe the Royal Army as 'ex'.[58] In legal jargon, these references can be said to have been more often than not material, not formal: that is to say, they paid lip-service to the content of some norms, but did not regard the norms themselves as being in force as such. And indeed, when traditional legality came back into its own after the Liberation, the *res*

---

55 On 11 August 1944, the 1st Alpine GL division issued instructions in the same spirit as those of the CVL Command, insisting on the need to prepare regular trials, the only exception being flagrant acts of banditry (Revelli, *La guerra dei poveri*, pp. 460–1). Note, too, the 'Norme per la constituzione e il funzionamento dei tribunali marziali presso le unità partigiane', probably by the Emilia GL Command (August 1944?) (*Formazioni GL*, pp. 137–8).

56 Letter from the Group Command for the Valsesia, Ossola, Cusio, and Verbano divisions, to the Command of the 1st Division, 10 December 1944 (IG, *BG*, 07332).

57 Lazagna, *Ponte rotto*, p. 170.

58 'Ordinanza del Comando della 13ª zona', 12 December 1944 (*Le Brigate Garibaldi*, vol. III, pp. 64–7).

judicata value of the sentences passed by the partisan military tribunals was not always recognised.[59]

On the other hand, appealing to the norms of the code could have the paradoxical effect of highlighting the makeshift character of the procedure that was followed.[60] And those who, like Major Mauri, in his proclamation mentioned earlier, explicitly referred to the fundamental norms 'of the war military penal code of the Italian Royal Army', as far as procedure was concerned took no steps at all towards setting up tribunals, but bestowed the power to punish directly on the division, brigade and detachment commanders.[61]

In partisan justice, therefore, the stress fell necessarily on substance rather than form. In Weberian terms, partisan justice can be broadly classed under the ideal type of the justice of the Muslim *kadi*.[62] In Mosso the real partisans arrested four false partisans who were extorting money from the population, led them into the square and asked the crowd what they wanted to do with them; and the crowd replied that they should be taken into the mountains and made to suffer starvation.[63] The almost total absence of legal experts in the bands accentuated this state of affairs and would subsequently be polemically remarked on by the partisans brought before the tribunals for not having greatly respected courtroom regulations: 'Signor giudice, that's true, only you were not there and so *I* had to do it.'[64] Which is not to say that there was a mere 'simulacrum of jurisdiction' resorted to only to 'set one's conscience at rest'.[65] The ritual of the trial channelled the desire for vengeance, stirred a sense of guilt in the accused, encouraged all the other members of the group to question themselves about what was just and what was unjust, and reaffirmed that even in the most exceptional situation there existed a general norm – in this case on the confines between morality,

---

59 See the sentence passed by the Special Assizes Court of Turin, 22 November 1951, quoted in Neppi Modona, *Giustizia penale*, pp. 179–81. On p. 64, it is noted that there do not exist full and trustworthy records of the sentences emanating from partisan tribunals.

60 An observation suggested to me by Gabriella Solaro.

61 Letter of 8 October 1944 to Vanni, (INSMLI, *CVL*, envelope 27, folder 2, subfolder 1)

62 Weber, *Economy and Society*, Berkeley: University of California Press, 1978, vol. I, p. 976. On the same question, seen in terms of the 'political nature' of a justice assumed to be impartial, see R. Canosa, 'Un dibattito tra M. Foucault ed alcuni militanti maoisti sulla giustizia popolare', in *Critica del diritto* 1: 1 (January–April 1974), pp. 33–56. My thanks to Gabriella Solaro for making me aware of this text.

63 Quazza, *Un diario partigiano*, p. 154 (13 December 1943).

64 Interview with Ildebrando Bilacchi, carried out by Luca Alessandrini on 3 March 1987, held at the IRSRER. See the testimony of Bruno Zenoni, in Portelli, *Biografia di una città*, p. 285.

65 Schnur, *Rivoluzione e guerra civile*, p. 319, on the revolutionary tribunals operating during civil wars.

politics and legality – to which everyone had to submit. Roberto Battaglia has put this very well: 'Precisely because we were fighting for a need for justice and that need was the true reality that had rallied us from far and wide around the same banner, in our law we instinctively aspired to a norm that was superior and not practical in character.'[66]

The tragic sense of administering justice was made more acute by the impossibility of inflicting sentences of imprisonment. The penalties inflicted with bodily violence thus leapt to the forefront: the utmost in violence, like execution, or partial but humiliating violence, as in the use of the stake. The partisan formations frequently resorted to this archaic form of punishment,[67] even in the very rare cases in which they were commanded by a woman.[68] A perverse continuity, almost by way of retaliation for the worst practices of the Royal Army, appears in this episode:

> A boy stole wheat from the band and sold it. Zama, his officer, got him to strip completely, except for his shoes and underpants, and had him tied to a stake for several hours in the snow at 1400 meters. He untied him when he became completely blue. He told how in Africa once he was tied to a stake for seventeen hours in the heat of the day, always turned towards the sun, with a small bowl of water under his eyes. We're arguing as to whether he did right or wrong.[69]

The sobriety of this comment of Artom's is a reminder that not everyone saw eye to eye about the stake as a form of punishment, widely used though it was. If the stake inflicted on two partisans who had dozed off during night guard duty was considered by the very men who had undergone it 'a more than just punishment because they could have come up from the Val de Susa and done the lot of us in',[70] in the Tollot Garibaldi brigade fighting in Veneto it was collectively decided to abolish the stake and all other forms of corporal punishment.[71] In another formation, 'after careful examination', a whole series of punishments were abolished 'as not in keeping with the spirit of the Garibaldi formations.

---

66 Battaglia, *Un uomo*, p. 240.

67 See, for example, the 24 October 1944 order of the day of the Command of the 3rd Aliotta Division (IG, *BG*, 01541); the draft statute of the Nanetti division, 2 December 1944 (ibid., 09448); Bianco, *Guerra partigiana*, pp. 53–4; Quazza, *Un diario partigiano*, pp. 189, 193; Revelli, *La guerra dei poveri*, p. 337; and Dellavalle, *Operai*, p. 121.

68 See the testimony of Elsa Oliva, in Bruzzone and Farina, eds, *La Resistenza taciuta*, p. 133.

69 Artom, *Diari*, p. 105 (4 December 1943).

70 Testimony of Raimondo Vazon, who comments 'Perhaps these were precisely the episodes in which one became aware that the adventure was over' (Bravo and Jalla, *La vita offesa*, p. 85).

71 'Resoconto di discussione sulle direttive militari e politiche del movimento', 27 March 1945 (INSMLI, *CVL*, envelope 35, Folder 1).

Above all it is stressed that the partial withholding of food rations is not moral. Let there be rather the application of simple and solemn disarmament, in front of the assembled unit, temporary or definitive.[72]

This is the spirit inspiring the directives that the General Command of the Garibaldi brigades came to issue in this regard: 'We are against this old barrack-room form of punishment. The "stake" almost always depresses, it does not re-educate, it is a punishment with negative effects.'

Instead, a whole series of other punishments are suggested, from publishing the reprimand in the mural newspapers to expulsion.[73] A cook who stole some salami and was then sent packing aroused general satisfaction.[74] In the Republic of Montefiorino the possibility of sending undesirables behind the line of the front was adopted as an alternative to the execution of the sentences.[75]

If what has been described so far is the treatment, containing a high dose of violence, given to false friends and to friends who stepped out of line, things were only apparently simpler when it came to the way enemies were treated. Obviously I am not referring here to combatants in open battle, who were treated in the same way as in regular warfare, even when the typical partisan tactic of the ambush and the surprise attack was resorted to. What I have in mind rather are several features in which the partisan war most clearly displays its specific character. A word or two is therefore in order about the treatment given to prisoners, Fascist deserters, and spies.

Behind all this treatment were the admonitions, warnings and condemnations that were levelled *en bloc* against the enemies. These solemn stances varied considerably, according to whether they were addressed to the Germans or the Fascists and, in the case of the latter, to army draftees or to volunteers of the Black Brigade, Muti, and so on. Orders issued by the CVL General Command and the CLNAI do not always tally with what was actually practised in single zones and by single formations. They were issued rather in the not always successful attempt to discipline widely divergent behaviour. In these documents, the Germans are, generally speaking, more bluntly named because all that could be asked of them was a pure and simple surrender, with the promise that they would be treated as prisoners-of-war and, in the final phase, handed over to the Allies.[76] As we have had occasion to see, it was not an unfamiliar phenomenon

---

72 Letter from the Command of the 1st Division to the Command of the 6th Nello Brigade (Ossola), 27 October 1944 (IG, *BG*, 06720).

73 Instructions of 4 December 1944 (INSMLI, *CVL*, envelope 20, folder 1). On expulsions from the bands, see Quazza, *Un diario partigiano*, pp. 194, 221.

74 Lazagna, *Ponte rotto*, p. 78.

75 Note the sentence passed by the military tribunal of the Modena division, 13 February 1945: the tribunal first sentenced the condemned man to death, then sent him out beyond the Allied lines (Gorrieri, *La Repubblica di Montefiorino*, p. 572).

76 As stipulated in the CLNAI decree on the surrender of Nazi-Fascist units, 19

for German troops to desert and go over 'with arms and baggage to the side of the patriots';[77] but the trust that could be placed in such conduct was minimal, and the arguments that had prompted it inevitably less mordant than in the case of the Fascists. In the case of the Germans, rather, doubts were expressed, explicitly or implicitly, against war criminals, of whom the absolute need to punish was particularly insisted upon by the Actionists and Communists. On 27 March 1944 the CLNAI itself, denouncing the atrocities committed against the Italian soldiers interned in Germany, warned that those responsible would be executed as war criminals.[78]

At times a distinction was made between the German army and the SS; at other times the Germans were bracketed with the Fascist volunteer forces rather than the 'regular' ones, almost as it were to disqualify their army more effectively, reduced as it was by now to 'a band of savages and predators'. In some cases even class appears as a discriminating factor, interwoven with a bias in favour of the Austrians. Thus the commander and commissar of a Pisacane brigade have no doubts about executing two 'chiefs', a captain and corporal 'of Germanic nationality'; but for four soldiers 'of Austrian nationality', who were elderly and all 'workers and peasants', they proposed further distinctions. And they were thus inclined to shoot a tailor 'with a petit bourgeois, arriviste and wait-and-see mentality' who, coming from the Alto Adige, voted for Germany in the 1939 plebiscite and 'can never be of any use to the people', whereas, in agreement with 'almost all the Garibaldini', they intended to be clement with a second soldier who 'is in a wretched physical condition and has clearly worked very hard', with the third, Trentino in origin, who had become 'a poor peasant of Austria', and with the fourth, a bricklayer who 'is our brother and the red partisans haven't killed Italian workers either'.[79]

Behind the appeals – promises and threats – made to the Fascists lay a dual purpose. Above all they aimed at fostering the breakup of the enemy forces, by alternating the awesomeness of the punishments provided for with the offer of a way out for those who surrendered or mended their ways.[80] The final manifesto,

---

April 1945 (*Atti CLNAI*, pp. 308–9).

77 This expression was used in the 27 March 1945 instructions issued by the General Command of the CVL regarding the dissolution of enemy forces (*Atti CVL*, pp. 448–9).

78 *Atti CLNAI*, pp. 123–4.

79 The quotes are taken from a CUMER poster directed to the population of Bologna, of 24 November 1944 (IG, *BG*, 02439), and a report by the commander and commissar of a detachment of the F. Tamberi battalion of the Pisacane Brigade, to the Command of the Nanetti Division (ISBR, envelope *Pisacane*). My thanks to Gabriella Solaro for making me aware of this document.

80 On 6 October 1944 the General Command of the CVL issued a five-day ultimatum, after which all those who remained in the service of the enemy would 'be considered guilty of high treason and, as such, [would] be liable to the death penalty' (*Atti CVL*, p. 206). But see also the 'fraternal invitation' made by the CLNAI on 6 August

Arrendersi o perire! (surrender or perish!), declared: 'May no one be able to say that, at death's door, he was not warned and not offered an extreme and ultimate path to salvation', and pointed out that, once disarmed, the soldiers of the RSI army would have to be allowed to go free, the Germans handed over to the Allies, and the Fascists of the Black Brigades, the Muti, etc. be 'kept in conditions in which they can do no harm'.[81] Again, on 22 April 1945 *L'Unità* published an appeal to the militiamen to desert and surrender their weapons as the only path to salvation: 'Make up your minds, tomorrow will be too late!'

The second purpose was to give a priori endorsement to the physical elimination of Fascists and collaborationists who 'have shown particular initiative and industry or in one way or another have acted in an executive capacity'. These were all condemned to death and their property confiscated; in the territories still occupied by the Nazi-Fascists *'the patriotic and armed formations* and *the partisans,* in the first place, are assigned the task of applying these orders, *without any formalities'.* Both in its Garibaldi brigade Command version, and in the subsequent CLNAI one, the decree blueprint from which these words are taken concludes with the invitation to the partisans to apply the orders without fail 'as from today' ('as from now').[82] Neither of the decrees, however, forgot the first of the purposes mentioned above: they made exception for those who, compelled to collaborate with the enemy, had redeemed themselves by doing him damage with acts of sabotage and by collaborating with the patriotic forces.

On 14 February 1944, in reply to the proclamation issued by Guido Buffarini Guidi, minister of the interior, the CLNAI had already laid down: 'All those who apply the proclamation of on-the-spot execution to *patrioti volontari della libertà* caught in the possession of arms will be deemed guilty of high treason against

---

1944, directed towards the officers and soldiers of divisions returning from Germany (*Atti CLNAI*, pp. 153–4), and the highly sympathetic appeal to young men in the RSI army who had not found 'the not always easy path to the mountains' even if 'from their faces' one could understand 'how much their uniform weigh[ed] down on them and their suffering on account of the disgrace of enslavement' (*Sui monti*, first issue, 12 July 1944, organ of the Verona CLN).

81 Thus concluded both versions of the proclamation – by the CVL and CLNAI – from 4 and 19 April 1945 respectively (*Atti CVL*, pp. 467–8, and *Atti CLNAI*, pp. 309–11). The slogan 'surrender or perish' was advanced by Longo in the report he gave to the enlarged meeting of the PCI leadership for occupied Italy, held in Milan on 11 and 12 March 1945. The report was published in *La nostra lotta* II: 5–6 (20 March 1945), pp. 5–20; and then in Longo, *Sulla via dell'insurrezione nazionale*, pp. 308–40.

82 See the decree *Contro i traditori della patria* (Against the traitors of the country) which the CLNAI, in assuming governing power in the occupied territories, intended to present to the government in Rome in June 1944, (*Atti CLNAI*, pp. 141–2). The text is similar to that proposed to the CLN by the Garibaldi Brigades, published in *L'Unità*, northern edition, supplement, 20 November 1943, then in *Fratelli d'Italia*, of the CLN in the Veneto, 15 January 1944 (See Canfora, *La sentenza*, pp. 195, 312–13).

the *patria* and as such condemned to death. The criminals whom the justice of the patriotic armed formations fails to reach will be inflexibly judged tomorrow by the people's tribunals.'[83]

In line with this, a GL newspaper wrote: 'Let the partisan war tribunals condemn as from now the definite culprits, even those in hiding. Their execution is deferred to the Liberation, but will need no other judgment (which will, on the contrary, be necessary for the uncertain cases).'[84]

Directives of this kind clearly had a spin-off on the way prisoners were to be treated, once their membership of a certain category that had been condemned to death *en bloc* had been ascertained. In the forces of the left the tendency was to interpret these texts extensively, at times by following the words used in them to the letter. As we saw in the previous chapter, this could lead to at least some of the class enemies being included among the recipients of the warning and condemnation. A couple of months after 8 September, *L'Unità* wrote: 'Those who, militarily or economically, actively or passively – functionaries, agents, soldiers – aid the enemy are to be outlawed from the nation and condemned to death.'[85] Pursuing this path of widening the field of those who were punishable, the Tuscan edition of the same paper warned tradesmen against speculating on the misery of the population.[86] When on 4 December 1944 the CLNAI issued a decree establishing a special war tax to be paid by 'all well-to-do persons and organisations', it stipulated that those who evaded were to be denounced 'as traitors of the national cause to the patriots' organs of justice which shall apply to them, by way of example, all those punitive sanctions which the organs themselves shall deem fit.'[87] The Communist leadership interpreted these words as follows:

> Naturally, it is not enough to send them [the industrialists] the extract of the CLN minutes: popular and partisan justice needs to proceed not only against the desperados of the black brigades, but also and principally against those old financiers and collaborators of Nazi-Fascism who by their refusal have made themselves definitively subject to the death penalty. This needs to be said and *published*, so that every patriot who has a weapon may know what to do if he meets them in the street.[88]

---

83 *Atti CLNAI*, p. 116. Buffarini Guidi was denounced as a war criminal on 27 September 1944, again by the CLNAI (ibid., p. 178).

84 'Giustizia partigiana', *Il Partigiano alpino*, August 1944.

85 'Giusta guerra di popolo', Northern edition, 31 October 1943.

86 'Chiare parole agli esercenti', 12 July 1944.

87 *Atti CLNAI*, pp. 209–10.

88 Instructions from the PCI leadership for occupied Italy to the insurrectionary triumvirates, 22 April 1945, in *Le Brigate Garibaldi*, vol. III, p. 664. The document also features the addresses of the Genoa SIAC, Bruzzo, San Giorgio, Eridania and Piaggio plants.

The 'Directives' for the insurrection issued by the PCI on 10 April 1945 give the following examples of traitors to be killed by the GAPs and SAPs: 'Questori, commissars, high-ranking state and municipal officials, industrialists and technical managers of production subject to the Germans'.[89]

In this context the denunciations and warnings addressed to people by name acquired a particular intensity: 'Prefect Mirabelli, your days are numbered!' wrote L'Unità on 7 August 1944, including in its denunciation two engineers employed by Ilva, one of whom was defined as 'diabolical'.[90] One CLN, the Ligurian regional one, for its part, cautioned the procuratore generale (attorney general) for not having taken any action against the Fascists responsible for the murder of patriots held in the prisons.[91] Even Radio London singled out individual Fascist personalities, reckoned to be war criminals, as targets.[92] And in the French underground press lists of collaborationists to be executed are frequent.[93]

Clearly, these initiatives and stances should also be interpreted as indicators of the ideas that were taking shape over the question of purging. Their immediate effect was to contribute to creating a climate of struggle in which at times the fearsome tones of certain appeals of the First International were heard once again. A message addressed to the Fascists of Monzuno (Bologna), guilty of not having kept faith with the pact stipulated for an exchange of prisoners and for having, in reprisal, attacked 'innocuous folk who were fighting only with their spades and hoes', reads:

> We warn you that our counter-measures will be *terrible and with no half measures.* Your destroyed possessions will illuminate with their flames the hour of the just punishment, your relatives killed regardless of sex or age will appease the just ire of those who, thanks to you, are weeping and dying today. Our reprisal will reach you wherever you may be, and no refuge, nor bodyguards, will avail to save you. Even at the ends of the earth we shall strike you.[94]

---

89 'Direttive n. 16', drawn up by Luigi Longo, published in *La nostra lotta* III: 7 (10 April 1945), pp. 31–8; later republished in Longo, *Sulla via dell'insurrezione nazionale*, pp. 344–50.

90 'Una canaglia', in the Northern edition. Filippo Mirabelli, already a national councillor of the Camera dei Fasci e delle Corporazioni, was head of Savona province from 25 October 1943 to 4 January 1945 (see M. Missori, *Governi, alte cariche dello Stato e prefetti del Regno d'Italia*, Rome: Bulzoni, 1978, p. 473).

91 Letter from the CLN to the public prosecutor, 19 January 1945 (INSMLI, old catalogue, *CLNAI* 8, folder 2, subfolder 10).

92 See Canfora, *La sentenza*, pp. 134–5.

93 For example 'Les traîtres', in *Le Patriote Martiguais. Organe du Front national de lutte pour la liberation de la France* (Organ of the French Resistance to Oppression), March 1944, and *Valmy*, June 1944: 'Frenchman, with a view to "the settlement of accounts", prepare the list of traitors and their friends'.

94 Command of the Stella Rossa brigade to the 'Republican Fascists of Monzuno',

Compare this with the challenge launched in 1873 'alla Borghesia' by neighbouring Rimini:

Be warned that in our hearts we have the idea of a vendetta which will be terrible and exemplary; the day will come in which you will know that we are again masters of our *piazze*. There will no longer be either grace or pity for the murderers of 1848 and 1871. We shall mow down your heads even if they are covered in white hair, and with the utmost calm. We shall have nothing but death to offer. Death for your mothers, for your fathers, for your relations, until your cursed race is completely destroyed. Goodbye shortly, lords of the bourgeoisie.[95]

The first general directives regarding the treatment of prisoners were issued by the CVL Command on 14 July 1944. These promised that 'the lives will be saved of those who give themselves up and solemnly undertake to do no further damage to the patriotic formations and the Allied armies', recommended that the promise of life 'must on all accounts be kept, and recalled that the prisoners were to be treated with humanity. Rapid exchanges are supported not least as a means of getting around the difficulty of setting up concentration camps.'[96]

The corollary of this last circumstance was the lack of prisons for the criminals, and it was recalled by protagonists as different from one another as the restless Communist Elsa Oliva and the solid Christian Democrat Ermanno Gorrieri as a decisive fact proving the impracticability of a middle way between killing the prisoners, if they were held guilty of crimes, and letting them free.[97] This line of argument was used to criticise the commander of the 3rd Garibaldi Liguria division, the Catholic Bisagno, who was 'reluctant about executions', when he should be convinced instead that the prisoners have immediately either to be sentenced by the tribunal and shot, or released.[98] 'Absolution or death' would be the conclusion reached even by the partisans of the Garibaldi division Pinan Cichero.[99]

In the final decree of 19 April 1945 regarding the surrender of the Nazi-Fascist formations, a distinction was made between simple soldiers in compulsory service, redrafted or conscripted, who, once they had been disarmed, were to be set free, and their officers and NCOs, who should instead be interned, on a par

---

June 1944 (*Le Brigate Garibaldi*, vol. II, p. 89).

95 Cited in C. Pavone, 'Aspetti della crisi della democrazia risorgimentale: mazziniani, garibaldini e internazionalisti nei primi anni dell'Unità', in *Il Cristallo* VI (1964), p. 78.

96 *Atti CVL*, p. 79.

97 See Bruzzone and Farina, *La Resistenza taciuta*, p. 133, and Gorrieri, *La Repubblica di Montefiorino*, pp. 569–70.

98 'Alcuni rilievi sulla organizzazione della 3a divisione', signed 'Luigi', November or December 1944 (IG, *BG*, 010477).

99 See Lazagna, *Ponte rotto*, pp. 59–60

with all the members of the Black Brigades, the Muti, the GNR, the Decima Mas, the police corps, the *paracadutisti*, and so on.[100]

In the twenty months of struggle, the treatment actually given to the prisoners was not only not completely in line with the directives just recorded, but revealed a remarkable variety of profound attitudes and motivations. 'The treatment that the partisan bands are to give captured Fascists ... has been discussed. There are those who are asking for the "Yugoslav" system to be introduced, but the majority are against this', Revelli noted very early on.[101] More closely argued doubts appear in another diary, concerning a prisoner who is nonetheless defined as 'a vile being':

> I am troubled by the idea that he might be killed. How pleased I am that *I* didn't capture him! Thinking of the possible end that awaited him, I would have let him escape. One can kill in battle, but not in cold blood. Perhaps it is no fault of his that he is who he is, because life is a terrible mystery: who destroys a mystery without having got to know it?

Before being shot, this prisoner, the diary page goes on to say, 'addressed a fellow villager, asking him to say good-bye to his wife for him, and the latter replied: "You must be crazy if you think I'm going to do a scoundrel like you a favour." This is what war turns men into; the ancients were right when they said that civil wars are far crueller than external ones.'[102]

A Garibaldino political commissar, acting in close contact with 'Yugoslav-type systems', has since written:

> I don't know whether all my comrades felt as I did, but every time someone was to be judged, I always asked myself how on earth I could judge another, who had given me the right, who had authorised me to sentence another to death, to take the life of a human being who had not done me any direct harm.

The answer the commissar gives himself 'after painful torment' – though he recognises how 'the profession of killing is a horrible profession' – appeals to the impelling value of experience: 'Very often we were too generous and this later cost the lives of many comrades, because after letting go individuals who with their tears had convinced us of their innocence, we were then attacked by Germans guided by these very same men.'[103]

'We had no other means of defending ourselves; there weren't any prisons, we couldn't hold him', a woman partisan recounts; and adds:

---

100 *Atti CLNAI*, pp. 308–9.
101 Revelli, *La guerra dei poveri*, p. 153 (29 November 1943).
102 Artom, *Diari*, pp. 131–2 (25 December 1943).
103 Padoan (Vanni), *Abbiamo lottato insieme*, pp. 67–8.

So it was a real problem putting together the firing squad. I remember that later I came across one of the lads from the squad, who was a very dear friend of mine. He was looking at his hands and saying to me: 'But Trottolina [Tersilla Fenoglio Oppedisano], would you still marry a man who has killed another one? I've fired with these hands, and I've killed a man!'

Trotollina's reply combines the criteria of obedience and justice: 'Take it easy, I'd marry him all the same, because you carried out an order which at this moment is highly moral.'[104] The difficulty of finding people to carry out the sentences was very widespread: 'The lads shuffled off as if to say: "But I haven't come into the mountains to do this sort of thing".'[105]

There was, then, a clash between appeals to force of circumstance and the goodness of the cause, but at the same time perplexity about the acts to be performed considered in themselves.[106] Other doubts appear about the methods of execution; but in matters of that sort methods and forms often redound back to the substance. Writing about roundups in Val d'Ossola, a partisan chief says: 'If I'd had my way, I'd have eliminated the prisoners, but that was impossible by now since it would have been extremely dangerous to shoot, thereby announcing our presence. Besides, none of us felt capable of killing with our bare hands some thirty prisoners like chicken, without causing wailing and moaning.'[107] Or again: 'Could you bring yourself to cut the throats of nine men with a knife?'[108]

Sometimes there was an intrinsic need not to let the most infamous crimes go unpunished. Chiodi recounts: 'They shot a sergeant who was generally thought by his companions to have made some partisan prisoners eat excrement.'[109] And Revelli:

Today one of our patrols met three German customs officers on the Lombard hills. They were the very same Germans of Isola, those who murdered Franceschi and the others last July. No pity. One of the Germans had a photograph of his children and

104 Testimony of Tersilla Fenoglio Oppedisano, in Bruzzone and Farina, *La Resistenza taciuta*, p. 158.

105 A. Clocchiatti, *Cammina frut*, Milan: Vangelista, 1972, p. 259.

106 Note, furthermore, the letter which a Garibaldian sent to the bishop of Belluno on 21 September 1945, speaking of the cracks in the 'granite certainties of an earlier time' (quoted in Tramontin, *Contadini e movimento partigiano*, p. 305).

107 Mario to the Lombard Delegation Command of the Garibaldi brigades, 26 July 1944 (IG, BG, 08688).

108 Such was Pesce's response to Di Nanni, who had reproached him for not having killed the captured *carabinieri*, who then rushed to sound the alarm (Pesce, *Senza tregua*, p. 119).

109 Chiodi, *Banditi*, p. 139 (17 April 1945).

was crying and trembling. The same old story: they understand everything, they become men again when they're lost.[110]

This theme of the German prisoners revealing themselves to be weak in the face of death appears widely in the partisan press and represents almost a counterpoint to the fear generated by the ruthless determination that the latter habitually displayed when it was they who did the killing. The face 'of that German who begged for pity in Piazza Cadorna showing me the picture of his children' remained impressed in a Gappist's memory.[111]

Another Gappist recounts: 'During the interrogation, as often happened in those circumstances, the two [German] prisoners declared that they were prepared to enter our ranks, simply to save their skins':[112] the two were executed. The newspaper of a brigade of *autonomi*, many of whom were Catholics, wrote:

> The German commander K ... he actually has a human heart and, like so many others, is bewailing the fate of his wife and daughters whom he hasn't heard from for some time. Do you remember that German K again ... the thirteen Italians he had shot at Borgo Ticino as a reprisal? Does he reckon that they didn't have wives, mothers, sisters, children who were bewailing their fate?[113]

A sergeant of the GNR was first acquitted for lack of proof from the accusation of having directed a roundup, then shot for high treason.[114]

By decreeing that the putting to death of captured men 'who truly proved to be prisoners of war' and of spies was to disregard any promise made to obtain their surrender, the military Command of the Ossola zone[115] contravened one of the norms mentioned above, but obeyed another which condemned war criminals to death, the execution being entrusted without more ado to the partisans. What actually happened was that the Fascists' resistance to the bitter end was stimulated once they became convinced that, come what may, they were doomed to be eliminated.[116] Some partisan Commands were so drastic as to leave no way

---

110 Revelli, *La guerra dei poveri*, p. 325 (25 August 1944).

111 Pesce, *Senza tregua*, p. 285.

112 Cicchetti, *Il campo giusto*, p. 145.

113 Note, here as in other cases, the invocation of mothers and sisters but not of fathers and brothers: 'Profili' in *Il fuori legge* (The Outlaw), organ of the 7th P. Stefanoni Brigade of the Valtoce division, Di Dio group, January 1945 (quoted in Falaschi, *La Resistenza armata*, p. 23).

114 Sentence issued by the extraordinary court martial of the Valle Stura Brigade of the 1st Alpine GL Division, 14 August 1944 (ISRP, envelope 35, folder c).

115 'Direttive operative', 13 February 1945, in *Le Brigate Garibaldi*, vol. III, p. 379, n. 4.

116 As referred to – though it was not the only case – by the Command of the 81st Volante Loss Brigade in its 'Relazione sull'attacco al presidio di Farà', 21 March 1945 (IG, BG, 08315).

out, as when they prescribed: 'Members of the republican armed forces who are captured are to be shot in the same place where they are captured as a warning and example. The same applies to members of the German armed forces.'[117] Similar conduct is represented in a more hesitant form with these words: 'From experience, the partisans were reluctant to take prisoners. A prisoner in partisan hands is always an encumbrance, besides being a danger.'[118]

As things turned out, if the instructions of the high-level unitary organs, the CLNAI and CVL, were not followed to the letter, nor were those, which were often notably different from each other, of the lower Commands and the single political organisms. One Command felt the need to repeat that if the 'outlaws' of the Muti, the Black Brigades, the Decima Mas, and so on, had to be executed, 'the prisoner must be treated with dignity', as prescribed by the norms, which were not always applied.[119] One Communist political commissar spoke ironically about the fact that

> the most pious bourgeois souls in the division were upset by the shooting of Fascist and Black Brigade elements, putting forward the excuse that it is pointless our adding other deaths to the millions of war dead, and saying that it is not against the Fascists or elements in the Black Brigades that one should be acting, but more realistically than the king, against the great capitalists whom we don't have in our hands.[120]

Pelle-di-biscia (Snake-skin), one of Calvino's characters, 'was saving men one moment, and killing them the next: he was changeable and ambiguous.'[121] 'The prisoners are going to pieces. We're releasing them, even if they'll rush back into the arms of the Germans!' This, Revelli recounts, was the line taken spontaneously during a roundup.[122]

There was no single attitude even about exchanges of prisoners. One protagonist, still offended by the fact that the formations were sometimes asked to capture prisoners in order to exchange them for arrested leaders, tells how a partisan

> did not consider it worth the trouble risking so much to exchange a prisoner for a leader whom nobody knew ... The fact that only high-ranking leaders were spared

117 'Disposizioni di carattere generale' of the 1st Garibaldi Division (Ossola-Valsesia), 26 August 1944 (ibid., 06239).

118 Bernardo, *Il momento buono*, p. 152.

119 Letter from the Command of the 8th Asti Division to the brigades for which it was responsible, 1 December 1944 (*Le Brigate Garibaldi*, vol. III, p. 7).

120 Report by Piero, of the 3rd Aliotta Division, to the General Command, 27 December 1944 (ibid., p. 146). 'Piero' was Orfeo Landini.

121 I. Calvino, 'Attesa della morte in un albergo', in his *Ultimo viene il corvo*, p. 93.

122 Revelli, *La guerra dei poveri*, p. 322 (22 August 1944).

by the enemy and that only they were granted the possibility of being exchanged, conflicted with the high sense of justice of the partisan, whose general and absolute principle was equality and the same right of all combatants to live.[123]

'Davide' (Osvaldo Poppi), the political commissar of the Modena division, once criticised the exchange, which he deemed inopportune, between a militia captain and the mother of a partisan.[124] Things are expressed more extensively, but in a similar spirit, in this letter written on the eve of the Liberation:

> We've never been able to do the slightest good outside the jails of Novara and Vercelli ... Negotiations of this sort were brought to a conclusion by Christian Democrats, Liberals and Socialists but, evidently, our comrades in the towns don't ... hit it off too well with the Nazi-Fascist Commands. On the other hand, since in Novara and Vercelli too they're screwing us over the exchanges because they're systematically packing the most valuable elements we request off to Bolzano, we've decided to waste no time and eliminate all the Nazi-Fascists who fall into our hands, except for those who give themselves up spontaneously. Just think, at the moment we still have, despite the notable bloodlettings that are being inflicted daily, some sixty prisoners, who eat and drink and keep a battalion of us busy. Sorry about the comrades who are inside, but, on the other hand, it isn't right either to save the worst at the expense of the best who are never liberated.[125]

The risks of magnanimity were pointed out with particular insistence. The released prisoners, it was said, not only should not be used for exchanges or to threaten reprisals, but they offered the enemy precious information, nor to be sure did they sweeten his behaviour.[126]

'The partisans have taken all the weapons off the Germans and Fascists, but have made the mistake of setting them free: they have simply assembled them on the road and got the townsfolk to keep an eye on them', the upshot being that when the German reinforcements arrived, many of these townsfolk were

---

123 Bernardo, *Il momento buono*, p. 153.

124 See Gorrieri, *La Repubblica di Montefiorino*, p. 384.

125 Ciro, commander of the divisions group for Valsesia, Ossola, Cusio and Verbano, to Fabio (Pietro Vergani), of the General Command, 23 April 1945 (*Le Brigate Garibaldi*, vol. III, p. 469, n. 2).

126 This was the flavour of the reprimand sent on 18 November 1944 by the Lombardy Delegation to the Command of the 53rd 13 Martiri di Lovere Brigade (in Bergamasco). The latter had offhandedly failed to grab 'the truncheon by the handle': the Germans, indeed, having secured the release of their imprisoned men in exchange for the promise not to carry out reprisals, did not keep their word (*Le Brigate Garibaldi*, vol. II, pp. 356–7).

captured in their turn.[127] 'When this happens they all declare themselves friends, but then, on being released, direct the roundups'.[128]

'If we look carefully at the question, we recognise that we've erred out of good-heartedness', says a report on the temporary occupation of the village of Bubbio in the Astigiano area, where the population would have liked the deaths of the secretary of the *fascio*, the *podestà* and the marshal of the *carabinieri*; but the partisans did not allow this, 'believing that a moral punishment was sufficient'. On the other hand, the officers and NCOs of the captured SS 'were gotten up in civilian dress and shot in a wood', while two German soldiers of the Red Cross 'are living with us like two friends; besides, a point in their favour is that one of them is of Austrian nationality'.[129]

'Moral punishment' recurs in another text, but this time, from both the ethical and practical point of view, in reverse form. Two former prisoners who had been roughed up led the Germans in the roundup; and the young Artom remarks:

> So now I understand the gravity of having killed some prisoners. Even at the time I had protested, but now I realise that it would have been better to remind him that the Germans kill partisans they capture, then point my revolver at him, reprieve him and keep him for an hour, explaining Hitler's certain defeat and the reason for our resistance. If he went back to the Fascists, never mind: one more or one less when there are so many makes no great difference, but there was some likelihood of his mending his ways, of his remaining our friend and doing us a good turn or two, or at least of his fighting against us more half-heartedly. The difference between the two systems would have been made clear, at least before the people and history.[130]

This page well sums up one of the horns of the difficult dilemma. The other horn is formulated with equal clarity, independently of its practical effects, in the following passage written by another hand many months later:

> It is also necessary not to let oneself be carried away by personal sympathies or by acts of exaggerated clemency; things which, though tolerated up to now, thanks to the experience acquired by the movement, can in no way be justified either in the

---

127 Testimony of Anna Cinanni (Bruzzone and Farina, *La Resistenza taciuta*, p. 102).

128 Barca's report on the 'inspection of 1 and 2 January' in the Val di Susa, 4 January 1944 (*Le Brigate Garibaldi*, vol. I, p. 216).

129 'Per il capo politico', 9 December 1943 (IG, *Archivio PCI*).

130 Artom, *Diari*, p. 145 (31 December 1943). On 20 December, faced with a case of ill-treatment, Artom asked 'What would Pisacane say?' Pisacane was the name of the Garibaldian formation in which Artom was active at the time.

case of the recruits or still less of the veterans ... The enemy shows us no clemency, so why should we show him any? Must we pardon those who are in cahoots with the enemy or who connive in his crimes?'[131]

Connected with this problem, but not always coinciding with it, was that of the ill-treatment and torture of prisoners. In the frequent severe reprimands of partisans who stained themselves with these crimes the chief argument was that one must not behave like the Nazi-Fascists. 'If he is guilty, shoot him! It is not possible to sink to the level of the Nazis', is how commissar 'Vanni' (Giovanni Padoan) reacted to one of the rare cases of torture.[132]

A GL newspaper replies to a hypothetical partisan who asks why the prisoners are being treated with so much clemency that this is happening in order not to put oneself on the inhuman plane of the enemies.[133] Revelli tells of a spy of the Muti brigade, 'a poor colourless, irresponsible wretch, who has been reduced to the level of the rabble by a school of bullying and cowardice. It will be hard to shoot him! A long interrogation, without harming a hair of his head, to make him understand that we are not like the "blacks"'. Revelli also tells of a thirteen-year-old, the mascot of the same Muti brigade: 'He's pathetic and infuriating. No one must touch him. What he deserves is a good hiding, but I ask them not to hurt a hair of his head. The most I've let them do is to shout "Balilla!" and "Camicia sporca!" ["dirty black shirt!"] behind him'. And then, of a woman spy: 'Don't hit her, don't touch her. We're not Fascists: no tortures, no vulgarity. We'll shoot her.'[134]

The Command of the Mario Gordini 28th GAP brigade operating in the Ravenna area recommended that German prisoners be treated 'according to the laws of war';[135] and a political commissar, who had learned through an Allied mission (a channel of information which made the news all the more galling) about tortures inflicted on a German prisoner, threatened the culprit with the death penalty, with the reminder that such acts 'we leave exclusively to the barbarity so often demonstrated towards our fellows by the persecutors of our people, holding it up as an example for popular indignation'.[136] More pragmatically, another Command explains: 'One should have no pity for the vile enemy,

131 'Il responsabile di zona' to the 'Comando della brigata Carrara' (Bergamasco), 23 March 1945 (IG, BG, 010642).

132 Padoan (Vanni), Abbiamo lottato insieme, p. 167.

133 Giustizia e Libertà. Notiziario dei patrioti delle Alpi Cozie, October 1944, article 'Ritorsioni' (quoted in Giovana, Storia di una formazione partigiana, p. 201).

134 Revelli, La guerra dei poveri, pp. 193, 196–7, 199 (12, 13, 14 and 16 April 1944).

135 Casali, Il movimento di liberazione a Ravenna, pp. 73–4.

136 Letter from Michele, political commissar of the 1st Gramsci Division (Ossola-Valsesia), to Picciolo, battalion vice-commander, 1 March 1945 (Le Brigate Garibaldi, vol. III, p. 428).

but one must make sure that the culprits, justly dealt with, do not inspire pity in public opinion.'[137]

The shortage of equipment and clothing could lead to the stripping of prisoners and the dead, a practice followed by the Fascists as well. On this score Commissar Vanni wrote: 'None of us has ever claimed that it was right to do such a thing, but to cite the Geneva convention about this is absurd.'[138] Commissar Giglioli was extremely harsh in his criticism of Garibaldini after a roundup in the Parma area:

> They have acted very badly against the prisoners, who during this period of imprisonment have accumulated a terrible hatred of the partisans, which will now have undoubtedly the gravest repercussions, for these prisoners are now in town and in town a sizable number of partisans have taken refuge. This accumulated hatred is not determined by political differences but by bad treatment, and this bad treatment was only determined by outrages committed against them, by the almost daily beatings and by the material privations that certain partisans imposed only because those men were prisoners. In fact, many of these prisoners did not occupy positions of responsibility and should not have been treated as such and instead unfortunately the most dangerous ones, either as a result of interventions or something else, were not ill-treated like all the others – which has created a very deep abyss between us and them. By this I don't want to defend these reptiles, but I'm keen to demonstrate that it was neither politic nor human to act in that way, and if there were responsibilities it would have been better to examine them and to take due action at the right time, not least to avoid the formations having to support hundreds of men who were an impediment, and this was demonstrated in the recent roundups that the formations have had to transport these people from one zone to another, subjecting them to harsh sacrifices and hunger, which is justifiable given the gravity of the situation, but if it was right to impose for elements responsible for misdeeds it could not be conceivable for simple prisoners many of whom had been in our hands for months without having committed serious offences.

Thus one would do well to bear in mind for the future that prisoners have to be treated as 'prisoners and if they are responsible they should be punished at once according to their responsibility, without hesitation and distinction; this will make it possible to instil the seriousness of our movement in the adversary, and will give him the chance to think more deeply before performing his actions against us'.[139]

---

137 Order of 18 September 1944, on the day of the Command of the 1st Piedmont Division (IG, *BG*, 04421).

138 Padoan (Vanni), *Abbiamo lottato insieme*, p. 240. On the Fascists, see Mazzantini, *A cercar la bella morte*, pp. 66, 99–100.

139 Report of 20 January 1945 (*Le Brigate Garibaldi*, vol. III, pp. 288–9, n. 4).

I have transcribed this long extract because in it are baldly displayed many of the points that I have been trying to highlight above. And in it there appears a tragic anticipation of the problem that not even the legal post-war purging would be able to solve: namely that of striking in high places and being clement lower down towards those who had not stained themselves with specific crimes. The rank someone held constituted the presumption of guilt, while those who did not take account of this criterion were reproached for their stolid benevolence.[140] The length of the period of detention, though indicated in Giglioli's report, raises another thorny question: how to treat the Fascists who were not captured in combat but arrested in the free zones. This is a problem well known to the rich body of literature on the partisan republics. It could appear particularly acute in the not very extensive territories that were liberated for periods of greater or less duration, and influence relations with the population. There were thus cases of posters put up to explain the reasons for an execution that had just taken place;[141] and for similar ends a French newspaper resorted to quotations from Montesquieu and Voltaire to recall that the executors of the sentence were as responsible as the judges who pronounced them.[142] There are also records of militiamen being set free because 'the local old folk had testified to their good conduct; this after a little sermon aimed, as usual, to point out the difference in behaviour between the patriots and the Fascists'.[143]

The recurrent invitations to desert, or indeed to desert en masse,[144] raised the question of what to do with the deserters: enlist them or send them away.[145]

---

140 On the first point, see the instructions from the PCI military official responsible for the Modena mountain area, from 10 to 25 May 1944, cited in Gorrieri, *La Repubblica di Montefiorino*, pp. 284–5 ('putting to death two enemy officers is always a political act: officers and sub-officers, apart from very few exceptional cases, must be rubbed out'). On the second point, remember that the forest militia in the Cansiglio, after giving the partisans some reinforcements, had asked to be disarmed, so as not to be too compromised in the eyes of the Germans; but the partisans were later reproached for having let a colonel and a captain go free (report from the Veneto detachment-command to the general command, 11 April 1944: *Le Brigate Garibaldi*, vol. I, pp. 349, 352, n. 8).

141 Letter from the Fregona CLN to the Command of the Vittorio Veneto brigades-group, 17 April 1945 (INSMLI, *CLNAI*, envelope 7, folder 2, subfolder 7).

142 'Aux magistrats de répression – Aux policiers trop soumis', in *Le Père Duchesne*, 'Year 151', September 1942.

143 Report from the Command of the 9th Liguria Brigade, 19 June 1944 (*Le Brigate Garibaldi*, vol. II, p. 43).

144 For example, a Verona CLN tract had called for 'a mass desertion, an armed desertion' (undated – IVSR, *Archivio*, I. envelope 49, CLN, Stampa non periodica).

145 On the extent of desertion, see the figures supplied by Pansa, *L'esercito di Salò*, p. 71. Up to the end of April 1944, there were between 25,000 and 26,000 deserters from the army, 'more than 10 percent of the total force and almost 17 percent of the levy from the classes called up before that date'. See also Deakin, *Brutal Friendship*, p. 664, on

Both solutions involved risks, intrinsic moreover to the possibility of 'conversion' which has already been said to be a distinguishing feature of civil war. The important thing was to verify the sincerity of the conversion, which could not, in principle, be denied even to prisoners. In fact, there were cases of their enrolling as well,[146] at times with the superficiality revealed by two militiamen of the Montefiorino zone who went around with a red star sewn onto their black shirts;[147] more often with the distrust aroused by the suspicion that at the moment of danger they could not be completely relied on,[148] and from the risk that spies might insinuate themselves into their ranks. Never however, Cino and Ciro wrote, would enlisted prisoners 'hold any rank in the formations'.[149] On the other hand, the difference between being captured, especially in the case of mass surrenders, and changing sides, was not always clear-cut, as the suspicious Fascist Commands themselves pointed out.[150] 'Appearing too humane' with the Alpini, says a document, 'had dire consequences during the last roundup'; consequently, before enrolling them it is necessary to 'subject them to a severe test' treating the 'waverers' as prisoners to assign to the auxiliary services.[151] This description is probably more realistic than the one which has the Alpini deserters 'embracing the Garibaldini as brothers' and large numbers of them asking to be enlisted.[152] The 4th Garibaldi Piedmont division set up an 'ethico-military training centre' for deserters, and a group of them complained of the too lengthy

---

German and Fascist worries, and the section 'Si disgrega la GNR' in Bocca, *La Repubblica di Mussolini*.

146 For example, after the assault on a barracks in San Vincenzo (Livorno), the prisoners – fifty-two Italian soldiers and twenty Mongols – were sworn in, and thus 'considered part of the formation' (report by Major Mario Chirici on the activity of the 3rd Brigade, 18 July 1944, in *Le Brigate Garibaldi*, vol. II, p. 148).

147 See Gorrieri, *La Repubblica di Montefiorino*, p. 350.

148 Mautino writes that the necessary purge among the prisoners brought into the Garibaldi-Osoppo division was pre-empted, in September 1944, by the fact that 'after three days of fighting, neither among partisan ranks nor among the mountains in that area was it possible to find a single one of these individuals' (Mautino, *Guerra di popolo*, p. 101). We can find more positive appraisals of at least some of the recruited prisoners – those who had not joined at the last minute – in Giovana, *Storia di una formazione partigiana*, pp. 139, 322–3.

149 Instructions sent to the Command of the 118th Servadei Brigade, 9 January 1945 (*Le Brigate Garibaldi*, vol. III, p. 222).

150 Note the 'serious incident' that took place in Saga (Cividale del Friuli), where on the night of 16 June 1944 a stronghold of around ninety well-armed men, almost all conscripts, disappeared without trace (Pansa, *L'esercito di Salò*, pp. 112–13).

151 Letter from the inspector Giorgio to Remo, the political commissar of the 51st Capettini Brigade (Oltrepò Pavese), September 1944 (*Le Brigate Garibaldi*, vol. II, p. 361).

152 Report from the commissar Remo on the history of the 3rd Aliotta Brigade, 31 December 1944 (IG, *BG*, 01728).

period of quarantine which prevented them from 'being free with their fists'.[153] Elsewhere deserters were transformed into workers, under the command of partisans.[154] Sometimes there was the fear that desertions by single individuals might provoke roundups, and that mass desertions might bring 'too close to our formations troops who were certainly better trained and more heavily armed'. In other words, there was the fear, as a dangerous by-product, of a shift in power relations (but it should be mentioned that in this case Mongolian troops were involved).[155]

The theme of spies has already been encountered several times in this book. All the formations had to be, and were, on the lookout for the presence of spies. Spies could be found everywhere: among prisoners, among deserters, among civilians, among the partisans themselves. The ambiguity of the figure of the spy was transformed into a halo of uncertainty as to their very existence. On the one hand this uncertainty was fed by frequent conspiratorial irresponsibility, and on the other hand it produced widespread and exaggerated suspiciousness and repressive harshness. In the Communist leaders the tragic experiences provoked by spies and the desire for vengeance against this particularly infamous incarnation of the figure of the traitor combined with excessive Third International training in revolutionary vigilance. If highly insidious spies had managed to hide themselves in the leadership of the Comintern and of the monolithic Communist Party, why on earth could the same thing not happen in the improvised Italian partisan bands? A PCI federation wrote that the suppression of spies was part of the 'concept of our Party', even if, for fear of reprisals, it was not part of that of National Liberation Front.[156] The CLN of Sassuolo, presumably under Communist hegemony, put up a poster which, giving the first names and surnames of spies 'responsible for having caused our people poverty, hunger, desperation and destruction' urged: 'Hand them over to our military tribunals. Eliminate them yourselves.'[157]

A Friuli document asserted that the elimination of spies was more important than acts of sabotage;[158] and an Emilian one announced still more drastically:

---

153 The deserters wrote a bombastic letter to the Command, held at IG, *BG*, 05065.

154 See Lazagna, *Ponte rotto*, p. 222.

155 'Bergamo Zone Operations Command' to the Lombard Regional Command, 10 April 1945 (*Le Brigate Garibaldi*, vol. III, p. 599, n. 1).

156 'Relazione politica', from the Ancona PCI federation to the Party leadership, undated but early December 1943 (*Le Brigate Garibaldi*, vol. I, p. 148).

157 Eleven people are listed: one is said to be 'with son', and two 'with family'. The – undated – poster is headed 'Popolo della zona di Sassuolo' (ISRM, Fondo Borsari, s.II.10, Miscellanea).

158 'Informazioni', undated, IZDG, envelope 272a, folder II/A.

When a spy is reported we must act with inflexibility, without sentimental weakness which could jeopardise the life of the unit. Even when in doubt we must eliminate the spy for the supreme reason of our safety. Those of us who are captured are shot and therefore we can do no differently with the active Fascist elements and those who aid them. Another vital consideration is that the execution of two or three traitors will bring terror among those who may be tempted to act as spies.[159]

Before the change in attitude of the population of a valley, from being favourable to being hostile to the partisans, a Garibaldi command became convinced that 'our only form of defence might be the elimination of spies and collaborators, in a word of the persons who are terrorising the population; this elimination will have to be ruthless'.[160] But in relations with the population the treatment given to spies or those presumed to be so could have the opposite results. Some Veneto parish priests' diaries testify to this,[161] while the report of an Emilian commissar describes an oscillation of opinions: 'As for the elimination of spies, some strata of the population had shown a certain disapproval more for sentimental reasons than anything else; after the roundup and the criminal conduct of spies against the villages and populations who had sympathised with the partisans' movement, these people have changed their minds'.[162]

The writer of this report would probably have put down to 'sentimental reasons' the behaviour of those three women from the Garfagnana who, finding a piece of paper with the names of three Fascist spies to be executed, went to tip off the threatened men.[163]

The following testimony from Umbria appeals explicitly to criteria of summary popular justice: 'Especially the spies, we've eliminated all of them. All of them. All the spies who we knew had spied, we looked for them even at the cost of spending entire nights walking'.[164]

A young intellectual subtly questioned himself about the action he was performing to identify a spy marked out for elimination. He feels 'like a fisherman tightening the net around an unwitting fish', and goes about gathering evidence 'without anger and without compassion, without any desire to lose him or to save him, only trying to get at the truth'. All the same, this is enough to burden

159 Instructions from the Command of the Modena detachment to the Stanzioni detachment, March 1944 (*Le Brigate Garibaldi*, vol. I, p. 341).

160 Letter from the Command of the Carlo Pisacane brigades-group to the Command of the Belluno division, 3 December 1944 (IG, *BG*, 09451).

161 See Tramontin, *Contadini e movimento partigiano*, pp. 301ff.

162 Report by Ilio, commissar of the 47th Brigade, to the Delegation for North Emilia, 3 August 1944 (*Le Brigate Garibaldi*, vol. II, p. 195).

163 'Esame della corrispondenza censurata al 30 giugno 1944' (ACS, SPD, CR, RSI, envelope 9, folder 3).

164 Testimony of Mario Filipponi, in Portelli, *Biografia di una città*, p. 284.

him with his share of 'responsibility for a human life and for the grief of the relatives who will remain'.[165]

The dilemma between absolutely necessary and excessive violence appears particularly dramatically in the treatment to be given to spies or those alleged to be so. We shall encounter this problem again shortly, when we discuss the activity of the GAPs, whose task it often was to eliminate spies. But first we need to turn our attention to another crucial aspect of the problematic question of violence: reprisals – though not without having first recalled, after so many examples of decisions to kill, the abolition of the death penalty decreed by the government of a partisan republic.[166]

4. REPRISALS AND COUNTER-REPRISALS

> For twenty-five centuries responsibility has been individual and has to be established by impartial judges. For twenty-five centuries punishment has no longer been conceived of as an act of vengeance, except in criminal associations. Well, that lot managed to do worse than the law of retaliation.

This is how a poster addressed to 'men and women of Padua' puts things in response to the reprisal killing of Flavio Buonasera and others.[1]

Ferruccio Parri wrote that 'clamorous events' like the Via Rasella attack in Rome, which was followed by the Ardeatine Caves reprisal, 'are born of a political vision, but embrace an unsolved and possibly insoluble problem of responsibility'.[2] It is the link between action, collective responsibility and individual responsibility which emerges in the reprisal and makes it, apart from the horror it arouses, a fact bristling with implications that are clear from its long and complex presence in history.

The distinction between the responsibility of the individual and the responsibility of the group of which he is a part was limpidly made by the Roman jurist Eneo Domizio Ulpian: 'Si quid universitati debetur, nec quod debet universitas singuli debent' ('If something is due from the community, it does not follow that the individuals owe what the community owes'). A medieval jurist, Godofredo da Trani, had applied this maxim, which was born in the sphere of civil law, to

---

165 Artom, *Diari*, p. 138 (28 December 1943).

166 See decree no. 5 of the CLN in the free zone, on the establishment and functioning of the people's tribunal, attachment no. 3 to the minutes of its 6–8 October 1944 session; F. Vuga, *La zona libera di Carnia e l'occupazione cosacca (luglio-ottobre 1944)*, Udine: Del Bianco, 1961, pp. 145–7).

1 The undated and unsigned poster is held in IVSR, Stampa antifascista.

2 Preface to Bianchi, *Giancarlo Puecher*, p. IX. Parri adds that 'the coils of this drama enveloped the last days of Giancarlo Puecher'.

the very theme of reprisals: 'Represaliis in singulos cives alicuius civitatis non dari ob sponsionem et debitum ipsius civitatis'[3] ('Reprisals against single citizens of a certain city must not be meted out because of the wager and debt of that same city').

In the medieval *Comuni*, the powerful identification between *civis* and *civitas* led, moreover, to the legitimisation of the right of reprisal as a relationship between individuals, disciplined by the community. A citizen who had been wronged by a foreigner was, in other words, recognised as having the right to exercise reprisal on a fellow citizen of the perpetrator of the wrong, though it was not legitimate to go so far as to resort to violence against persons. The *Comune* simply guaranteed the exercise of this right. It was the modern state that attributed to itself alone the right to carry out reprisals, gradually circumscribing, however, the possibilities and ways of exercising it.[4] Persons subjected to reprisal, wrote a late-nineteenth-century jurist, were to be 'treated gently'.[5]

War by its very nature has always constituted the most drastic denial of these civil principles. In war the bond linking *civis* to *civitas* is considered so obvious and absolute as to legitimise the citizen's right, for the *debitum* of *civitas*, to kill and be killed. Rousseau sought to get around this problem by claiming, in the very sphere of his classical ideal of the soldier-citizen, that war is not a relation 'between man and man, but between State and State ... Furthermore each State can have for enemies only other States, and not men; for between things disparate in nature there can be no real relation.'[6]

In fact the regulation and, within certain limits, the humanisation of war had led to the *cives*, who were also soldiers, being distinguished from everyone else, the result being that the extreme consequences of membership of the *civitas* was applied only to the former. But precisely for this reason the practice of reprisals – whether exercised against captured enemy combatants or, still more so, against civilians – was a harrowing, regressive fact. What, in fact, was questioned once again, on the most pressing of terrains, was that distinction between public and private, between the collective and the individual, which had relegated the doctrine of reprisals, seen as a 'sort of imperfect war',[7] into the sphere of international law, where the only subjects, active or passive, are states. It is no accident that reprisals against colonial peoples, whose members were not accorded the dignity of *civitas*, let alone that of citizenship, were found less

3 I take both quotes from M. Arduino, 'Rappresaglia (Diritto internazionale)', in *Digesto italiano* XX: 1 (1911–15), pp. 90–5.

4 G. S. Pene Vidari, 'Rappresaglia (Storia)', in *Enciclopedia del Diritto*.

5 'Rappresaglia', in *Nuova Enciclopedia Italiana*, directed by Gerolamo Boccardo, Turin: UTET, 1885.

6 Rousseau, *The Social Contract*, Book I, §4.

7 The expression is used by Arduino, 'Rappresaglia (Diritto internazionale)', p. 93.

shocking than the German reprisal against a French village, where some *francs-tireurs* had hidden in 1870.[8]

The historical memory of the connection between reprisal and the Germanic feud probably acted in the Nazis as an incentive to practise it and, in those who endured it, as proof of ineradicable Teutonic barbarity. It seems that the Germans exercised the first reprisal of the Second World War near Warsaw, on 26 December 1939, with the shooting of 107 Polish citizens.[9] In Italy the first episode seems to have been that of Rionero in Vulture, where the Germans killed sixteen civilians in reprisal against the killing of an Italian paratrooper who had gone over to their side.[10]

The Germans gave the word 'reprisal' an extremely wide meaning. They called the V1s and V2s launched against London in the last year of the war *Vergeltungswaffen* (reprisal weapons). Reprisal in fact was no longer an 'imperfect war', but the consummation of total war, which was seen as a gigantic reprisal against the forces of evil that wished to annihilate the Third Reich. Ernst Nolte would still be thinking along these lines when he interpreted the horrors of Nazism as an 'excessive response' to Bolshevism. The distinction between the collective and the individual was utterly extraneous to this vision of things: the great European civil war, consequently, was not lived as something different from the war between states, even if it was interwoven with it, but as a frightening reshuffling and polluting of relations and distinctions between the state and society.

It has to be added, however, that in a perverse form reprisals evoke one of the noblest principles of collective action, that of solidarity. Max Weber places the few lines he devotes to reprisals under the heading: 'The imputation of social action: representation and mutual responsibility'.[11] The distinction between representation, where the action of the representatives is imputed to those represented, who remain distinct from them, and solidarity, where 'certain kinds of action of *each* participant may be imputed to *all* others' inevitably takes reprisals into the sphere of solidarity, which is all the more present the more 'closed' the relations are (Weber actually cites war as an example), and the more the social relationship rests on 'various types of affectual, emotional or traditional bases'.[12] It is no accident that those, like Otto Brunner, who theorise the medieval constitutional model as 'authentically stable because founded on a rigorously organic–solidaristic perspective' assign a place of honour to the feud as 'a mechanism of

---

8 On this last episode, see ibid., p. 94.

9 *LRE*, p. 700.

10 See M. Di Giovanni, laureate thesis.

11 Weber, *Economy and Society*, vol. I, pp. 46–7.

12 This being Weber's definition of community, naturally making reference to Tönnies (ibid., p. 41).

defence and of protection of rights'.[13] Reprisal, by contrast, appears to our consciences as setting in dramatic collision the moral autonomy of the individual and his sense of belonging, in the sense of solidarity with the other members of the community of which he is a part. Individual conscience finds itself having to reckon with a network of relations which are indeed interpersonal but which somehow transcend it, so that it sees coming down on its head, contorted and brutal, the consequences of relations and principles in which it had put its trust and from which it had sought support. Perhaps the extensive use of the words 'martyrs' and 'martyrdom', even for those who were only 'victims' of the reprisals,[14] can be ascribed to the more or less consciously felt desire to bring under the category of testimony also those acts of violence and suffering endured (if we can speak in such terms) 'objectively'. So frightening is this objectivity that one writer who has sought to get to the heart of it has ended up, in the case of the Marzabotto massacre, going beyond the 'rational' concept of reprisal to speak of a 'caste' crime. At the root of this crime are metaphysical motivations of a kind that, strictly speaking, we ought to refer to in terms not of war crimes but of crimes 'occasioned by war'.[15]

If on the one hand reprisals drive terrorised individuals to seek individual safety, on the other hand they ultimately exalt that very sense of solidarity and co-responsibility that, by striking at its foundations, they had wished to undermine. Hence their essential failure. 'Humble and defenceless folk who tremble like a leaf, but react splendidly' were not accounted for in the plan for reprisals.[16]

---

13 As Otto Brunner's thought is paraphrased in Fioravanti, 'Stato (Diritto intermedio)', p. 24.

14 See, on this point, the observations made in A. Preti, 'Quale storia tra Marzabotto e Monte Sole?', *Rivista di storia contemporanea* XVII (1988), pp. 134–47, with regard to Gherardi, *Le querce di Monte Sole*. An analogous consideration could be made on the – debatable – use of the word 'holocaust' to designate the Nazi massacre of the Jews.

15 See Dossetti, 'Introduzione', in Gherardi, *Le querce di Monte Sole*, esp. pp. xvi–xvii. The fact that a narrow legal formalism can lead to the grotesque, in dealing with these questions, is demonstrated by the sentence Dossetti cites in support of the thesis that it was not a reprisal in the true sense: 'Even if one wanted, as an absurd hypothetical, to accept that only in the presence of the civilian population can one recognise a grave and immediate danger in the outcome of the operations being carried out, the possibility of keeping them alive would always have remained, and in no sense is it possible to identify a tie of necessity between this immense number of killings of women, the elderly, and children, and the success of the military action'. Dossetti, drafting a document by the Christian Democrat leaderships of Modena, Reggio Emilia and Parma, dated 25 February 1945, claimed 'In no way is it admissible, not even for reasons of defence, to kill in reprisal people who were surely not subjectively responsible'. This position was taken in opposition to the actions carried out by the SAP, many of which were adjudged 'neither legitimate, nor necessary, nor opportune' (quoted in Gorrieri, *La Repubblica di Montefiorino*, p. 538).

16 Dossetti, 'Introduzione', p. viii.

The passage from Weber cited above concludes by recalling that a reprisal may be seen as 'vengeance' or as an 'instrument of guarantee'. Germans and Fascists used it in both senses: the ruthlessness of the vengeance was intended to increase the effectiveness of the guarantee. In both cases the unequal value attributed to human life constituted an essential element. In Poland and Yugoslavia the ratio between the German soldiers killed and people shot in reprisals, belonging to the inferior race of Slavs, and what is more Communists, was of the order of 1-to-100.[17] In Italy, as for that matter in Western Europe as a whole, the ratio was lower (for the Via Rasella attack it was 1-to-10). But it could greatly increase in the case of indiscriminate massacres of entire villages, as at Marzabotto, and in France at Oradour-sur-Glane . 'The life of a German is worth that of fifty Italians', said a Nazi officer. The reply he got from a parish priest of the Belluno area is valid, whatever the proportion adopted: 'That is not true, an Italian is a man like yourselves, perhaps more human than you.'[18]

The RSI Fascists did everything possible to belie this greater humanity accredited to the Italians, when, starting with the Ferrara massacre, mentioned earlier, they embarked on the road of reprisals, vying with the Germans – in the wake, it must be said, of what the Royal Army had done in the Balkans and of what had been provided for by the war laws of 1938, referred to elsewhere. Reprisals against the relatives of deserters were decreed by the provisions of both the German and the Italian authorities.[19]

The stances taken by the *resistenti* to the Nazi-Fascist reprisals range from partisan counter-reprisals, through the positions of those who, while aware of the possibility of reprisals, did not intend to let themselves be discouraged from the struggle by this possibility, to a powerful urge, at the other extreme, to wait on events in the name of the need to spare human lives. Naturally, the focal point of disagreement did not lie in reprobation of the inhuman Nazi-Fascist vengeance, but in whether one agreed or denied that the 'instrument of guarantee' really worked in the enemy's favour. The point was that to bow before the reprisals might be considered an implicit recognition of the enemy's right to practise them. The enemy was indeed covered, in this barbarous practice too, by that patina of legality which the exercise of a state power, even the most ruthless, is always able to invoke – a legality, by contrast, not enjoyed by the bands of 'outlaws'.

In one of its documents of February 1944, the military Command for Northern Italy outlined how one was to behave in this sphere, claiming that 'causes for reprisals' should be 'avoided or limited whenever possible'. But it added that 'concern about reprisals must not constitute an insuperable impediment

---

17 See *LRE*, p. 700.
18 Quoted in Tramontin, *Contadini e movimento partigiano*, p. 297.
19 See Pansa, *L'esercito di Salò*, pp. 207–8.

to action and still less so be a mask for incapacity and unwillingness to act'. The document reiterated the condemnation of 'useless cruelties' and the need never to sink to the level of the enemy. It consequently sought to discipline counter-reprisals too, stipulating that 'if [the enemy's] cowardly ferocity demands reprisals only the chiefs have the right to order them'.[20]

From the very first weeks, the enjoinder not to fear reprisals is current in the Communist and Actionist documents and press. Their meaning can be summed up by borrowing these words from *France d'abord*: 'The Nazi terror is operative only for those who accept it.'[21] In the GL version: 'The force of the enemy exists because we fear it, not because it is real.'[22]

These drastic affirmations of principle were argued in various ways. Above all it was said that the reprisals bespoke not so much the force as the weakness of the enemy, against whom ultimately they could only rebound. 'Terror is nothing more than the cry of the savage who in his heart of hearts is weak and frightened', says the document just cited. The Gappist Giovanni Pesce wrote of the massacre perpetrated by the Fascists in Piazzale Loreto on 10 August 1944: 'The enemy realises that the weapon of terror is backfiring on him. We must insist.'[23] And on the occasion of attacks organised by him:

> Reprisals? – he replies to a Gappist who has broached the question with him – Yes, and more and more ferocious. That's why we must constantly keep our hands at [the enemy's] throat ... Not let ourselves be intimidated by the reprisals. It's the only way to keep our forces effective and to let the enemy know how useless his ferocity is.[24]

A Garibaldi Command repeated 'the necessity to attack the enemy and inflict losses on him without worrying about reprisals on the population, reprisals which ultimately always rebound on the enemy himself'.[25] In fact, if the Fascists were not attacked, a protagonist was to write, 'they scrupulously performed their canine duty ... on the presumption that they had no final reckoning to fear'.[26]

---

20 ' Direttive per la lotta armata', in *Atti CVL*, p. 547. Rochat, who published the document, deems that it was 'probably [drafted by] Parri, certainly by an Action Party member' (ibid., p. 11).

21 June 1944 (cited in Michel, *La guerra dell'ombra*, p. 266). See the article 'Le Maquis et la population', which holds that all French people had to accept the risks of war (*44. Organe des Forces françaises de l'intérieur et du Comité départemental de la libération nationale pour les Basses-Pyrénées*, 12 August 1944).

22 'Norme per gli ispettori', 25 December 1944, probably elaborated by GL Division C. (*Formazioni GL*, p. 258).

23 Pesce, *Senza tregua*, p. 206.

24 Ibid., pp. 211, 260.

25 Report by the Command of the 1st Piedmont Division to the Piedmont Delegation, 16 July 1944 (*Le Brigate Garibaldi*, vol. II, pp. 132–3).

26 Mautino, *Guerra di popolo*, p. 187.

'With action the weapon of terrorism is snapped'; 'Against the vile Nazis the audacious use of force is always the best weapon': these are notes struck over and over again by *L'Unità*,[27] widening out into still others: 'The sooner we chase the brown pest out of Italy, the fewer victims he will be able to slaughter, and the less ruin he will bring upon us.'[28]

And in fact the Fascists and Germans did not always carry out reprisals, whether from the impossibility of doing so or from calculation. The above quotations, and the many others like them, should therefore be seen not as mere voluntaristic exhortations. Reality, at least partly, bore them out. 'The decrees are not obeyed and the German authorities don't insist', wrote a parish priest from the Belluno area.[29] Curious confirmation is given by a German anti-aircraft Flakkorps unit that had gone over to the partisans of the Costrignano brigade without reprisals being visited on its families. It addressed its 'dear Italian comrades', urging them not to fear reprisals, given that the Germans were incapable of carrying them out.[30]

'The groups of partisans, the GAPs, disintegrate if they don't act'.[31] 'Down in the valley there was a military delegation which gradually died of exhaustion from having to wait so long for the day of struggle.'[32]

This theme, which here we find formulated at the beginning of the struggle as an incitement and at the end as a statement of fact, was another of the arguments used to overcome fear of reprisals. Ermanno Gorrieri, always so careful to steer as clear as he could of the crueller aspects of the struggle, drew from the experience of a band from Sassuolo, which had successfully conducted an attack on the GNR barracks of Pavullo, the moral that it was indeed successful actions that made formations grow.[33] The

---

27 The former words appeared as the title of an article in the Northern edition of 24 August 1944; the latter were the lesson drawn from the news that 'the women of Parma snatched thirty-seven young partisans away from the firing squad' (Northern edition, 25 May 1944).

28 Northern edition, 29 December 1943. See the Rome edition, 23 March 1944, and the article 'Per salvare Roma cacciare i tedeschi', where it is possible to find an implicit polemic against the growing myth of the Pope *qua* defender of the city. On 26 October 1943, the paper developed the idea that, seeing as the German reaction was going to happen in any case, it was worth forewarning of it ('Agire subito').

29 Tramontin, *Contadini e movimento partigiano*, p. 284.

30 Appeal of 26 October 1944 (ISRR, *Archivio del triumvirato insurrezionale dell'Emilia-Romagna*).

31 'Direttive di lavoro', by the PCI leadership, 27 September 1943 (?) (IG, *Archivio PCI*).

32 'Relazione sulla insurrezione armata e conseguente liberazione delle città di Massa e Carrara', sent from the federation committee to the PCI leadership in Rome, 24 April 1945 (*Le Brigate Garibaldi*, vol. III, p. 688).

33 See Gorrieri, *La Repubblica di Montefiorino*, p. 115

examples of Yugoslavia, of the USSR, and of France were often invoked on this score.[34]

The opinion was also expressed that the Nazi-Fascist reprisals fed popular hatred against those who practised them and thus, in this way too, fed the struggle. We shall shortly see that this was not always the case, but that sometimes it well and truly was. Above all among the partisans themselves: 'we turned nastier after that episode', recalls a partisan from the Terni area.[35]

In Valle Maira the German destruction of San Damiano and Cartignano (August 1944) provoked a bitter reaction in the population and fed the influx of recruits joining the bands.[36] 'The more the danger increases the more anti-German spirit increases', observed a Veneto parish priest as well.[37] Contempt was particularly strong when the Germans and Fascists failed to keep their word, following negotiations, that they would not carry out reprisals.[38] Fascist censorship drew attention, in the letters it examined, to the mixture of contempt for German reprisals and of fear of the actions of the partisans that provoked them.[39] The same view is expressed in the report by the GL political commissar Giorgio Agosti, which I have cited several times.[40] One could by no means be certain what direction popular reaction would take; on the contrary, there was a real fear that it would turn against the partisans, from awareness that the more hazardous actions might, as has been duly written, arouse 'both enthusiasm and reprobation'.[41] For example, a commissar expressed satisfaction at the

---

34 See, for example, the article 'Attesismo' in the 7 December 1943 *Il Combattente*, and the long lecture by Ilio Barontini to Giovanni Pesce when, after the first attack was brought to a successful conclusion, he was posed with the question of possible reprisals (Pesce, *Senza tregua*, p. 45). See also a circular from the Padua Communist federation (undated, but after the Salerno turn), on what would have become of the peoples of Europe had they all accepted enslavement on account of the threat of reprisals (IG, *Archivio PCI*).

35 Testimony of Mario Sabadini, on the shooting of a *carabiniere* who had fought together with the partisans, as a reprisal (Portelli, *Biografia di una città*, p. 283).

36 See Giovana, *Storia di una formazione partigiana*, p. 242.

37 Quoted in Tramontin, *Contadini e movimento partigiano*, p. 290.

38 See, on episodes of this type, the testimony of G. Nicoletta, commander of the autonomous De Vitis Division, concerning July 1944 (in ANED, *Gli scioperi del marzo 1944*, pp. 60–1); Quazza, *Un diario partigiano*, p. 176 (4 April 1944); and the stone on the Piazza di Boves, marking the killing of the priest Giuseppe Bernardi on 19 September 1943.

39 See 'Esame della corrispondenza censurata al 30 giugno 1944', which mentions this letter sent from Gabiano, Alessandria province: 'Too many massacres! In a village near here they shot fifty-seven villagers, all innocents, taken as hostages' (ACS, SPD, CR, RSI, envelope 9, folder 3).

40 See *Formazioni GL*, p. 273.

41 H. Michel, 'Le Maquis au-delà de la légende', in *Le Monde aujourd'hui*, 30–31 December 1984, p. xi.

fact that the Germans had not carried out reprisals – and to avoid them they had refrained from organising resistance in some villages – because they 'would have brought down on us the hatred and rancour of the population'.[42] German threats, says another Garibaldi document, 'have had repercussions on the morale of the population, which is not always up to understanding the situation'.[43] And still worse:

> Following such ruthless reprisal measures one can well imagine the consequences and repercussions on fighting spirit and the spirit of sympathy in the majority of peasant and mountain folk. From indirect news it appears that the mountain folk are chasing the partisans off, threatening (for the time being just threats) to denounce them to the Germans. The peasants have got it into their heads that these massacres happen because we are killing Germans and that it would be better not to kill them. Here in town as well that's the way people are seeing things.[44]

At times the population reproached the partisans for having put them in jeopardy and for not having then been able to defend them.[45] It is well-known that this was a central issue in the debate about the creation of the free zones. On the other hand, the lack of reprisals could sometimes induce the populations to look benevolently on the troops engaged in the roundups.[46]

But beyond predictions about repercussions that enemy reprisals might provoke in the local populations, repercussions which had however to be taken into the maximum account, the duty not to let oneself be intimidated was powerfully felt. All the human costs – the tragic destiny of the 'unknown heroes'[47] –

---

42 'Relazione sulla situazione delle brigate d'assalto Garibaldi dell'Oltrepò Pavese', 3 September 1944, signed 'Piero' (*Le Brigate Garibaldi*, II, p. 304).

43 Letter from the commissar Tino and the commander Nanni, of the 16th Perotti Brigade, to the Command of the 1st Piedmont division, 6 August 1944 (IG, *BG*, 04375).

44 Letter from the delegation of the Command of the Garibaldi Brigades for North Emilia, to the delegate of the province of Reggio Emilia, 27 July 1944 (*Le Brigate Garibaldi*, vol. II, p. 168).

45 See, for example, the report by the commissar of the 12th Brigade, Gracco, to the 'delegate-inspector of the North Emilia Garibaldi Brigades', 2 August 1944 (ibid., p. 187). See also Dellavalle, *Operai*, p. 111, and Quazza, *Un diario partigiano*, pp. 157–8, 164, 177. Today, superstitious partisans are reluctant to talk about their own absence during the massacre of the civilian population by the Nazi-Fascists in Guardistallo (Pisa). My thanks to Katia Sonetti for this information.

46 This case was reported – also being seen as a consequence of the bad behaviour of some partisans – in 'Relazione e ricognizione zona di operazione della Divisione Piave, Brigata C. Battisti', signed by the brigade commander, 14 November 1944 (IG, *BG*, 06963).

47 'Resistere con audacia, resistere attaccando', editorial in *Voce Operaia*, 15 January 1944.

were to be put on the enemy's account. This was the point which, in principle, it was urgent to insist on, even within the bosom of the Resistance itself,
which did not always accept it: those responsible for the reprisals were the Nazi-
Fascists who carried them out, not the partisans who performed the actions that
provoked them.

Eraldo Bassotto, leader of an autonomous band, declared to Benvenuto
Santus, a Communist from the Biella area, that he would consider him personally responsible for the reprisals that the Garibaldini's initiatives might provoke
not only against the civilian population but also against the men of his formation.[48] The vice-commander and political commissar of the 'Italia Libera'
brigade operating in the Grappa zone wrote in his memoirs: 'I didn't want ill-
advised killings to be performed in the zone under my control, which could
harm the population (with reprisals) and ourselves (with roundups).' To prevent
this, he even went so far as to stop the Garibaldi patrols from passing through
his territory.[49] After a German reaction that had atrociously befallen the population, it is a squad leader himself who declares: 'I do not want to be responsible
for so many murders.'[50]

The Via Rasella attack in Rome, with the ensuing massacre in the Ardeatine
Caves on 24 March 1944, is perhaps the episode that fed this kind of reflection most powerfully. The diary of one of the protagonists of the action, Franco
Calamandrei, records immediately after the explosion that 'some, above all the
women', commented unfavourably ('just when they were leaving …'); then, when
the reprisal had taken place, notes that 'public opinion is not too favourable
towards the action. They don't see its international political importance, which
may be worth the sacrifice.' Finally, Calamandrei speaks of the discussions about
it in the Rome PCI: intensify or hold fire? While initially the tendency seemed to
be in favour of intensification, the line in favour of holding fire then prevailed,
'but only provided that during the pause leaflets are circulated to the population
and the Germans, threatening a resumption of terrorism if evacuation has not
taken place by a certain date'.[51] The firmness of principles and the attention
given to the real state of affairs met in the conviction that an historian of the
European Resistance has expressed in the following words: 'Guerilla warfare is
less devastating than Verdun, the bombing of Coventry or Hiroshima'.[52]

---

48 See Dellavalle, *Operai*, p. 74.

49 Unpublished memoirs of G.M., c. 23.

50 'Rapporto della visita fatta dall'ufficiale di collegamento del CUMER alla 8ª
brigata Garibaldi' (Romagna), 2–7 August 1944. The author confided, 'however, this
form of opportunism will soon enough be wiped out' (IG, *BG*, 02226-29).

51 Calamandrei, *La vita indivisibile*, pp. 158–60 (under the dates 23, 25 and 26
March 1944). The leaflets were put out on 2 April (ibid., p. 163). On the (widely followed)
pause after the Fosse Ardeatine massacre, see Katz, *Morte a Roma*, pp. 183ff.

52 H. Michel, paper to the XII International Congress of Historical Sciences, 1965.

In the course of the struggle in Italy we find a noble expression of the firmness of principles in the words that Leonardo Cocito, kept in jail as a hostage, addressed to one of his cellmates: 'Whatever you do, don't abandon the struggle. Act without anxiety. If I am to come out of this, I'll come out, if I have to die let my fate be accomplished. But the important thing is *that you never give in!*'[53] A similar, though more abstract, dignity we find in the reply that Moscatelli sent to the German Command of Varallo Sesia, which had announced 'the execution of twenty-five hostages taken from among the civilian population, no distinction being made for sex and age, for every shot fired by the "rebels"'. Moscatelli replied that such conduct related to 'the justice of civil peoples, to which the names of those responsible, which are well-known to us, will be transmitted'.[54] Giovanni Pesce, after his reply, mentioned earlier, to the Gappist who was questioning him about the probability of enemy reprisals, added: 'We have all asked ourselves Azzini's questions, a thousand times, before the fallen, before the murdered, before the sacrificed innocents. They are a proof of honesty, of loyalty towards the hundreds and hundreds of comrades who are already dead, and towards those who are fighting with a weapon in their hands in every corner of Italy.'[55]

A Piedmontese woman partisan testified to the attention and concern for civilians: 'Certain actions had to be limited simply to prevent reprisals being carried out against the population. There was an enormous respect for the population.'[56] A GAP commander from the Ravenna area wrote that it would not have been difficult to kill Germans, but 'are we capable of facing [the enemy's] reprisal? No! So what should we do?' This attitude, he is quick to add, 'is neither fear nor cowardice, but prudence'.[57] But it is precisely 'the physical fear of getting killed' that is indicated in other documents as being a consequence of not having been sufficiently educated 'at the magnificent school of Bolshevism'.[58]

See 'I problemi della storia della Resistenza nei lavori del Colloquio di Vienna', in *Il Movimento di liberazione in Italia* 81 (October–December 1965), p. 40. Already in the nineteenth century, the Russian Romanenko held that terrorism 'cost infinitely fewer victims than a mass struggle' (Laqueur, *History of Terrorism*, p. 36).

53 Chiodi, *Banditi*, p. 139. Cocito was later hanged.

54 On 19 July 1944. See *Le Brigate Garibaldi*, vol. II, p. 149 and the documents cited in the notes therein.

55 Pesce, *Senza tregua*, p. 211.

56 Testimony of Tersilla Fenoglio Oppedisano, in Bruzzone and Farina, *La Resistenza taciuta*, p. 154.

57 Report by Mariano, 17 August 1944. This document clearly expresses the concerns raised by the peasants, not wanting 'to hear any more of having to hide wanted men, even if nothing had happened. Imagine, a little, them having to hide people in case of Germans' (Casali, *Il movimento di liberazione a Ravenna*, vol. II, pp. 298–9).

58 'Rapporto al Centro del Partito', by Banfi, from Emilia, 16 December 1943 (IG, *Archivio PCI*). See also the report from Mantua (undated, but from more or less the same

In order to avoid German reprisals, at a meeting chaired on 4 October 1943 by the commander Sante Danesin, a Garibaldi detachment of the Cecina zone decided to suspend all actions for forty-five days.[59] The Command of the 3rd Aliotta Pavese Oltrepò division decided on one occasion to 'defer offensive activities in order not to provoke roundups which, rumour has it, appear to be imminent'.[60] The commander of the Piedmont GL warned that 'action must not be confused with exhibitionism' and that one must not, by occupying 'positions *that cannot be held*', expose civilian populations 'to the harshest reprisals'.[61]

The acceptance of the human costs of the struggle generally went hand in hand with the commitment to reduce them to the minimum. It was on how this minimum was to be gauged, which was highly difficult to define, that differences were most marked. In fact it was not always easy to distinguish human concern about the shedding of blood[62] from political concerns about the intensification of the struggle. The distinction was particularly hard when Catholics who were also Christian Democrats were involved. In the diaries of parish priests from the Belluno area there is the recurrent motif of the need to avoid reprisals by limiting actions.[63] The vicar forane of central Garfagnana spoke of 'crude and useless reprisals'.[64] The parish priest of Cassolnovo in Lomellina spoke out against partisans who provoked reprisals.[65] The bishop of Casale Monferrato, mentioned earlier, also wrote that 'as a rule the partisans, having struck, fled. The population, who were absolutely innocent, remained and paid.'[66]

Here ethico-religious concerns are already shifting in the direction of a political stance. The shift is complete in this appeal by the Tuscan committee of the DC: 'Verbal effrontery, which would be a sorry repetition of the demagogic arrogance of dying Fascism, and rash and undisciplined actions would only provide a pretext for acts of enemy barbarity against the city and against the

---

time) which called attentism 'the firstborn son of the most genuine fears' (*Le Brigate Garibaldi*, vol. I, p. 195).

59 'Relazione generale sull'attività di guerriglia svolta dal Distaccamento F. Giaconi', written by Alessandro Favilli (ISRT, *Carte Carlo Campolmi*, envelope 1, folder 6, subfolder 1).

60 Report by the inspector Albero to the insurrectionary triumvirate for Lombardy, 24 February 1945 (*Le Brigate Garibaldi*, vol. III, p. 415).

61 'Notiziario e direttive', marked 'D' (Duccio Galimberti), 30 June 1944 (ISRP, envelope 29, folder b).

62 On this, see Ventura, *La società rurale veneta*, p. 69.

63 See Tramontin, *Contadini e movimento partigiano* (for example, p. 294, with regard to the parish priest of Seren del Grappa).

64 See Tramontin, *Il clero italiano e la Resistenza*, p. 22.

65 See Ballone, *Una sezione, un paese*, p. 440.

66 Angrisani, *La croce sul Monferrato durante la bufera*, p. 16 (quoted in Rovero, *Il clero piemontese nella Resistenza*, p. 50).

population and would be contrary to the useful and necessary war requirements themselves.[67]

The Christian Democrat president of the provincial CLN of Apuania complained that 'the carrying out of sporadic and inorganic attacks against individual Germans' had provoked 'a furious and ferocious reaction immensely superior to the actual damage done to the efficiency of the enemy'.[68] One of don Moretti's directives at the time the Osoppo brigade was created was to take account of the 'proportionality between the damage done to the enemy and the possible damage suffered by the populations in reprisals'.[69]

The Tuscan CLN of 24 June 1944 passed a motion affirming 'the duty to abstain from private vendettas and reprisals, save the right to react with violence to possible acts of Fascist violence', and on 30 June the Tuscan committee of the Christian Democrat party, in a manifesto addressed to its followers, paraphrased the text of this, dropping the adjective 'private'. At a subsequent meeting of the committee on 26 June the DC had, with the backing of the Liberals and Socialists, asked for the cancellation of this word from the motion; but the proposal had not gone through owing to the opposition of the Actionists and Communists.[70] In another Christian Democrat document, the aim of the struggle is indicated as being 'to make our contribution count at the peace table, namely by doing what the Allies expect of us, but always bearing in mind that for 'us, as Italians ... it is no less important to seek not to bring too much harm upon Italy through the Nazi reprisals'.[71] These words sound almost like an upended version, but stripped this time of cynicism, of the few thousand dead that, in June 1940, Mussolini wanted to make count at the peace table; and to send the Italians along the old road of reaping the maximum benefit from the sacrifices of others, while minimising one's own costs.

This, indeed, is the heart of the polemic about *attesismo*. In this polemic, in fact, the two principles of the value of life and the values that transcend life clash once again. This clash could neither be avoided nor remedied. Here there reappears the theme of expiation, which is to restore the Italians to the community of suffering peoples. Ferdinando Mautino calls it 'monstrous wrongheadedness'

---

67 Leaflet of 29 July 1944, in ISRT, Raccolta volantini, DC Firenze (clandestini 1943–44).

68 'Relazione di massima sul movimento patriottico nella provincia di Apuania', 7 January 1945, lamenting the local formations' weak obedience to the directives of the CLN (INSMLI, *CLNAI*, envelope 7, folder 3, subfolder c).

69 Tramontin, *Il clero italiano e la Resistenza*, p. 24.

70 ISRT, *Carte Francesco Berti*, envelope 1, folder 1, verbali del CTLN.

71 Circular from the executive secretariat of the Modena provincial committee, 1 March 1945, cited in Gorrieri, *La Repubblica di Montefiorino*, p. 357. Gorrieri notes that 'the concern to reduce the threat of reprisals against the population to a minimum constantly recurs throughout Christian-Democratic documents'.

not to make a move for fear of reprisals, 'as if we really imagined we could demonstrate that we were enemies of the Germans without facing their wrath, without undergoing the atrocities that all their enemies had undergone'.[72] *Fratelli d'Italia*, the newspaper of the Veneto CLN described as 'cowardly and tremulous souls' those who 'find it convenient to argue in favour of the need for a prudent and dishonourable inertia'.[73] A railway-workers' newspaper repeated: 'Either we act or we don't delude ourselves that others will act for us'.[74]

In the latter maxim, stated at that time and in that place, the word 'we' could acquire a dual meaning: 'we Italians' and 'we the working class'. It was this second meaning – rarely stated explicitly, in fact more often than not denied[75] – that stoked the suspicions and fears with which the fence-sitting attitudes of the conservative wing of the anti-Fascists were nourished. But both meanings contained a powerful wish for autonomous redemption, the desire to demonstrate that 'we are not a nation of cowards and loafers, nor do we have the souls of lackeys'.[76] And this not only had to serve to belie a view widely held by the Allies, but aimed also at countering Fascist claims about the cowardice of the Italian people and getting matters straight over the charges that the Fascists, rightly from their point of view, levelled at the folk who 'are sitting pretty getting by somehow in town', at those who are 'behind the blinds waiting on events'.[77]

Included in the condemnation of waiting on events (*attesismo*) were those who, though capable of offering active participation, preferred to take refuge in Switzerland. In her diary Ada Gobetti expressed disappointment in those who chose this path;[78] and Moscatelli was indignant at 'the foolish lamentations of

---

72 Mautino, *Guerra di popolo*, pp. 34–5.

73 A box in *Fratelli d'Italia*, 22 May 1944.

74 'Ieri, domani … e oggi', *Il Ferroviere* (Milan), February 1945.

75 *Voce Operaia* wrote: 'Only being present in the struggle, not leaving it to the old ruling class to lead it, can we arise above those old social relations that have led us to ruin' (editorial, 'Giornate decisive', 18 October 1943). For its part, *L'Unità* attacked attentism as the conscious sabotage of the popular insurrection, originating from those with an interest in giving credit to Nazi-Fascist talk of socialist and communist plots and of partisans 'coming down into the cities to liquidate the rich, and other nonsense of a similar type'. On this theme, see Chapter 6, above.

76 See the PCI's September 1943 appeal to the Italian people, in *Il comunismo italiano nella seconda guerra mondiale*, p. 216

77 See the article by Vittore Querel, director of the Modena *Gazzetta dell'Emilia*, in its 3 May 1944 edition (quoted in Gorrieri, *La Repubblica di Montefiorino*, p. 199), and the letter by seventeen-year-old Folgore parachutist Ferdinando Camuncoli (*LRSI*, p. 125). On GNR complaints of the attentism and cowardice of the Italian people, see G. Sciola, 'Avanzata alleata e popolazione civile nelle fonti della Repubblica sociale italiana', in Rochat, Santarelli and Sorcinelli, *Linea gotica 1944*, pp. 497–523.

78 See Gobetti, *Diario partigiano*, pp. 90–1. Here, I would like to pay homage to the memory of Delfino Insolera, who, when the other elements of the band in which he was initially involved crossed the border from Valtellina into Switzerland, instead went

irresponsible individuals who had crossed the border into Switzerland' after the fall of the Ossola Republic, contrasting them with everything that 'we have done, with our wretchedness, with our bare feet, with the few weapons at our disposal, with our dead, with our great determination to demonstrate that Italians know how to fight and die for liberty'.[79]

The dual outcome of the reprisals – of terrorising and thereby discouraging action, and of provoking reaction – must be linked to the fact that they also involved the 'territoriali', the 'true extremists of moderation', 'the naturally prudent', those who forwent the joy of fighting for justice and liberty, contenting themselves instead with enjoying the benefits that had been won by others.[80] An essential channel of this involvement was the taking of hostages, one of the many barbarous practices reintroduced by Nazi-Fascist warfare.

Already in the Franco-Prussian War of 1870, to prevent attacks on troop trains in occupied territory, the Prussians had forced distinguished French citizens to ride in them.[81] An international agreement entered into in Tokyo in 1934 had attempted to give a status also to hostages: when, 'in exceptional circumstances', a state deemed it indispensable to take hostages, 'they must not, under any circumstances, be subject to interrogation or corporal punishment'.[82] But as early as 12 September 1940 the German Command in France decreed: 'The hostages are locals whose lives guarantee the proper attitude of the population. Their fate is in the hands of their fellow villagers'.[83]

On 21 August 1941 General Schaumburg decreed that all French people arrested by the German or French authorities were to be considered hostages.[84] On 16 September of the same year, Field Marshal Keitel expounded the principle that Communists were whatever the case to be considered responsible for the attacks: 'It is only by this method, which has been used successfully in the history of the extension of the power of great nations, that one can re-establish order'.[85]

---

back to Milan, telling his sister Melina that he wanted to stay there where the battle for freedom was being fought.

79 Letter to a British officer ('Signor Rossi') in Switzerland, 1 December 1944 (IG, BG, 07194).

80 The words quoted are from Meneghello, *I piccoli maestri*, pp. 284–5; the rest is a paraphrase of the definition of 'free rider' in Hirschman, *Shifting Involvements*, p. 92.

81 G. Balladore Pallieri, 'La guerra', in P. Fedozzi and S. Romano, eds, *Trattato di diritto internazionale*, vol. III, Padua: Cedam, 1935, pp. 380ff. See, by the same author, *Diritto bellico*, Padua: Cedam, 1954, pp. 357–61.

82 Article III, 19 of the convention, cited in S. Klarsfeld, *Le livre des otages: la politique des otages menée par les autorités allemandes d'occupation en France de 1941 à 1943*, preface by M.-C. Vaillant-Couturier, Paris: Les Éditeurs français réunis, 1979, p. 19.

83 Ibid.

84 Ibid., p. 20. The decree was provoked by the killing of a German officer as a response to the shooting of two Communists.

85 Ibid., p. 23. The number of Communists to be shot for each German soldier

In the war that the Nazi-Fascists waged in Italy against the *resistenti*, all prisoners were considered hostages subject to reprisals, unless one preferred to use them for exchanges or to try to save one's skin on the final day. But not just this: not only the relatives of the *resistenti*, but all the civilian populations became potentially hostages in the hands of the occupiers. There was thus an expansion of the category of hostage that lent itself to aberrant inversions when it came to attributing responsibility. Thus in an article *L'Osservatore Romano* condemned both the capturing of hostages that involved civilians and the increasing number of attacks on *estranei* (outsiders, foreigners), and in its comment on the Ardeatine Caves called the partisans 'irresponsible' because they had provoked the killing by 'those responsible' of 'three hundred and twenty people sacrificed for the culprits who had fled arrest'.[86]

The journey from the First to the Second World War along the sorry highway of reprisals, counter-reprisals and hostages was long. In 1916 Maurice Barrès had called the Zeppelin raids on Paris 'horribles futilités', and had denied the usefulness of the reprisal bombing of Essen that had been requested.[87] In 1942 a French underground paper wrote that the unexpected generosity of the Germans who had not shot the 3,000 French prisoners, or thereabouts, captured at Bir Hacheim (outlaws, according to the Armistice), assured itself that if they had done so, 'The English will immediately shoot an equal number of Krauts'.[88] Another underground paper warned the rulers of Vichy who were having the relatives of those who were siding with the Algiers government arrested: 'But we still need charitably to remind these gentlemen that they also have a family, and it is still the case that we will be victorious'.[89]

In the Italian Resistance, numerous and authoritative stances were taken in favour of counter-reprisals, naturally against militant Fascists and German

killed was set between fifty and one hundred. To see the attention with which the Allies followed the question of hostages, see *The Axis System of Hostages*, London–New York: Inter-Allied Information Committee, United Nations Information Office, 1942. This document also speaks of the hostages taken by the Italians in Greece.

86 'Ostaggi', in the 7 January 1944 edition; a box in the 26 March 1944 edition entitled 'Un comunicato 'Stefani' sui fatti di via Rasella'. A box in *Voce Operaia*, 'Ancora sui GAP' reproached the Vatican's organ for having spoken of 'those sacrificed to vendetta and the reprisal for the vendetta' and of 'crime against crime'. Canfora, *La sentenza*, p. 158, aptly comments that, according to *L'Osservatore*, 'the attackers, the terrorists were, in reality, holding all the defenceless hostage'.

87 M. Barrès, *L'âme française et la guerre. Le suffrage des morts*, Paris: Émile-Paul Frères, 1919, pp. 281, 223–32, where the articles 'Le Crabe' and 'Les représailles? C'est le blocus resserré' are reproduced.

88 'Générosité ... ou intérêt bien compris', *93. Organe des héritiers de la Révolution française*, July 1942. This paper wrote 'Kollaborateurs' with a 'K'.

89 'L' épuration [i.e. the purge, termed an 'immense desire'] premier pas vers notre avenir', in *14 juillet. Organe de la résistance de la sous-région de Lyon*, 15 May 1944.

soldiers, not certainly against the local populations, however fence-sitting, absentee or opportunist they might have been. We have already recalled the February 1944 'Directives for the Armed Struggle' of the military Command for Northern Italy. In the instructions of 14 July of the same year, 'as part of their military activity', the CVL General Command explicitly provided for the capture, by the formations, of hostages 'to be sought among the German military and civilian authorities, and treasonous Fascist officers and functionaries'. The hostages – and Ferruccio Parri himself urged Tancredi Galimberti to take them ('We can't avoid it') – were to be treated as prisoners of war. Authorisation was given to proceed against them in reprisal for the shooting of civilians, prisoners and the wounded, and for the torturing and maltreatment of arrested patriots. It was also explained that, 'In no case may the measures consist of actions that are repugnant to the loyalty of those fighting valorously for the liberation of the *patria*.'[90] The Communist from the North, Francesco, was clearly referring to this directive when, on 13 December 1944, he communicated to party headquarters in Rome that the Command of the CVL had permitted the 'widespread use of partisan reprisals in response to Fascist and German atrocities'.[91]

From October 1943 *L'Italia Libera*, organ of the Action Party, had, on the other hand, declared: 'The Italian people must not fear reprisals. One reprisal leads to another, and the weapon of intimidation rebounds on those who use it.'[92] 'We shall respond to terror with terror' was Giovanni Pesce's reaction to the execution of Ateo Garemi in Turin.[93] Another Gappist has written, moreover, that the Fascist reprisals immediately gave birth to the partisans' desire for counter-reprisals, and that these – as we have already noted – were not always followed by a recrudescence of Nazi-Fascist actions, while in the local populations satisfaction at the performance of acts of justice prevailed over fear of their possible consequences.[94] For 'every young patriot killed ten Fascists die!' reads a leaflet announcing the slaughter of five young men on 22 March 1944.[95]

On 10 August, in view of the 'savage crimes' that the Nazi-Fascists were committing in Milan – torturing, shooting and abandoning the corpses in the squares – the Lombardy delegation of the Garibaldi brigade General Command issued this order to the formations under its jurisdiction:

---

90 *Atti CVL*, p. 80; letter from Parri to Galimberti, 11 August 1944 (*Formazioni GL*, p. 135).

91 'Direzione. Verbali riunioni 1944', IG, *Archivio PCI*.

92 Editorial in the 30 October 1943 Rome edition of *L'Italia Libera*.

93 Pesce, *Senza tregua*, p. 32. See. p. 237: 'We oppose the enemy's terror with our own terror'.

94 See Cicchetti, *Il campo giusto*.

95 The unsigned leaflet, 24 March, is held at ISRT, Raccolta volantini, PCI Firenze (clandestini 1943–1944).

1. Shoot the Nazi-Fascist prisoners at present in your possession (with the exception of those hostages for whom special exchange negotiations have already begun);

2. Such executions are to be communicated and popularised, indicating that they are carried out in reprisal for the Milan massacres;

3. If such massacres are repeated in Milan or in other cities, mass executions of Nazi-Fascist prisoners will have to be carried out immediately.[96]

On 27 September 1944 the CLN for Piedmont announced in one of its manifestos: 'We shall respond to persecutions with persecutions, to reprisals with reprisals. For every patriot killed five Nazi-Fascists will die; for every village set fire to fifty traitors will be shot.'[97]

At a meeting in late October 1944 the zone Command of the province of Belluno established, with the approval of the CLN representative, that one was to 'respond to terror with terror, completing the guerrilla actions with a rich dose of reprisals, aimed at making it clear that the movement was neither dead nor emasculated'.[98] The Vicenza CLN manifesto, referred to earlier, which rejected the accusation that some prisoners had requested the bombing of the city by radio, added that if the Fascists, under cover of that lie, were to kill the patriots in their hands, the GAPs would immediately execute 'those directly and indirectly responsible who are well-known to us'.[99] Towards the end of 1944 the Garibaldi delegation for Lombardy, faced with the fact that in Milan the Fascists, 'to avoid our reprisals', were rounding up and murdering 'our comrades' during the night and 'abandoning them along the roadside', decreed: 'No pity and no more crowding them into concentration camps.'[100]

These threats were not always followed up; but as the struggle grew more bitter, a voice like Elio Vittorini's resounded like a voice in the wilderness. Commemorating Eugenio Curiel, killed by Fascists in Milan on 24 February 1945, he wrote: 'He knew that taking vengeance and carrying out reprisals may be necessary for those who have nothing before them; it may be necessary for

---

96 *Le Brigate Garibaldi*, vol. II, p. 235; the notes mention the similar response by the Command of the 3rd Liguria Division, 25 August, to a Special Tribunal trial against 'thirty-one Italians', warning that for each shooting ordered by the tribunal, they would shoot 'two of the hostages we have in our hands ... (functionaries and agents of the Pubblica Sicurezza, GNR, officers and militiamen)'.

97 INSMLI, *CLNAI*, envelope 6, folder 3, subfolder 17. Already on 31 December 1943, this same CLN had announced: 'If the Germans continue to shoot imprisoned partisans, the same will go for the German prisoners' (ordinance no. 11, published in *La Riscossa italiana*, January–February 1944).

98 Bernardo, *Il momento buono*, p. 115.

99 Undated, available in IVSR, Archivio, S. 1, envelope 49, CLN, Stampa non periodica.

100 Letter to the inspector Riccardo, with the 3rd Aliotta Division (Oltrepò Pavese), 16 November 1944 (IG, *BG*, 0342).

the Fascists, but not for us who have much before us. We need something different: to fight for this *much*.[101]

In some very rare cases the intensification of the struggle could lead even the partisans to threaten to carry out reprisals on the families of Fascists.[102] At other times it was the partisan Commands themselves that avoided the reoccupation of villages that had for some time been under the Nazi-Fascists, in order to avoid 'reprisals by foolhardy individuals against those who had compromised themselves with the enemy'.[103] In cases like this, it was really more a question of vendetta than reprisal.

On 8 February 1945 the CLNAI sent its delegation in Switzerland, urging them to pass it on to the Rome government, a sorrowful appeal to ask for 'a ruthless action of exemplary reprisal' as the 'sole defence perceivable against inevitable future explosions of the impotent rage of the crumbling regime'. In this document the major political organ of the Resistance put the government on its guard against the 'deleterious influence' that 'the total lack observed so far of any gesture of active solidarity with the victims' had on the *combattenti della libertà*.[104]

In the absence of the Rome government, the partisans had to deal with the spiral of reprisal and counter-reprisal as well. A case in point is a document relating to the Cuneo area, which reads:

> In the war that the patriots of the partisan formations are waging enemy reprisals against the population are almost inevitable. It is up to us to intervene in the most suitable way in defence of the interests of the inhabitants threatened by the Nazi-Fascist reprisals. If the Nazi-Fascists burn down the houses of the peasants we shall have to burn down the houses of the Fascist chiefs, of the Fascists; if they kill the peaceful inhabitants of villages in reprisal we shall have to take to counter-reprisals against Fascists, Germans, and their families as well. Nazi-Fascist terror needs to be countered by patriotic terror.[105]

Exactly a year earlier, two German officers had been shot after being captured in the 27 December 1943 attack on Mondovì airport, conducted by almost

---

101 *L'Unità*, northern edition, 9 April 1945.

102 As stipulated by the disciplinary code of the 5th Piedmont Garibaldi Division (see Dellavalle, *Operai*, p. 182). See also *Le Brigate Garibaldi*, vol. III, pp. 152–3.

103 This happened in Varzi: see 'Relazione sull'Oltrepò pavese dell'ispettore Giorgio', 20 March 1945, in *Le Brigate Garibaldi*, vol. III, p. 510.

104 'Appello in favore dei detenuti politici'. On 30 January 1945, the Fascists in Milan had killed nine political prisoners (INSMLI, *CLNAI*, envelope 3, folder 2, subfolder 3/III).

105 As 'the comrades responsible' wrote to the political commissar of the 5th Zone (Cuneo area), Pietro, on 28 December 1944 (*Le Brigate Garibaldi*, vol. III, pp. 152–3).

all the Cuneo area formations under the command of two *bovesani* officers, i.e. regular officers.[106] In the autonomous division De Vitis, a Fascist lieutenant, was shot in reprisal for the killing of a partisan.[107] A long series of reprisals and counter-reprisals has been reconstructed for the Biella area.[108] A list of counter-reprisals that were carried out is contained in a letter of the Garibaldi Command delegation for Lombardy. These include thirty shootings (two against one) in response to the Piazzale Loreto massacre of 10 August 1944. If the Nazi-Fascists insisted, the document stressed, the proportion, in the counter-reprisals, would be raised to three against one.[109] A few days later, on 15 October, a poster, 'Al popolo di Milano! A tutti lombardi!', issued by the same delegation, gave news of this reprisal and added that the slaughter of civilians in the Pavia area had been answered with the shooting of eight prisoners, and the slaughter of fifteen patriots captured in the province of Varese with the shooting of forty-five Nazi-Fascists: 'The Garibaldini are waging war as soldiers of liberty, but they know how to be inexorable, and executioners!'[110] Against the shooting of two patriots in Varzi the Command of the 3rd Lombardia Aliotta division ordered that each of the brigades under it proceed to the killing of the same number of militia-men who were their prisoners.[111] In response to the shooting of five partisans captured and tortured by the Germans in a square of the village of Ivestria, the Baltera brigade shot twenty SS men kept as hostages.[112] On 8 October 1944 *L'Unità* reported the shooting of thirty-five prisoners in response to the murder of seven patriots.[113]

Particularly harsh was the reprisal for the killing of Duccio Galimberti, com-mander of the Piedmontese GL formations. On 12 December 1944 the regional

---

106 See Bianco, *Guerra partigiana*, p. 32.

107 See Quazza, *Un diario partigiano*, p. 217 (19 October 1944).

108 Dellavalle, *Operai*, pp. 123–4, 142, 144; Poma and Perona, *La Resistenza nel Biellese*, pp. 227–31, which recounts how a threatened counter-reprisal, for which authorisation was sought from the Allied Command (in August 1944) put a stop to mass reprisals for the whole of the rest of the year.

109 The letter, whose addressee is not indicated (but is probably the formations under their watch) is dated 12 October 1944 (INSMLI, *CVL*, envelope 93, folder 4, sub-folder 2).

110 Ibid., envelope 93, folder 4, subfolder a. On the role in carrying out these repri-sals attributed to the Valsesia, Ossola, Cusio and Verbano divisions-group (20 shootings), see the order sent from the Group Command to the 1st Division, 15 October 1944 (*Le Brigate Garibaldi*, vol. II, p. 442).

111 IG, *BG*, 01417 (15 September 1944).

112 Letter from Andrea, responsible for the organisational office of the Liguria Regional Command, to the Command itself, 6 October 1944 (*Le Brigate Garibaldi*, vol. II, p. 405).

113 'Contro il terrore, contro la fame, contro le deportazioni', northern edition, 8 October 1944.

military Command issued the following order 'to all the dependent formations': 'Shoot 50 bandits of the Black Brigades to avenge the death of commander Tancredi Galimberti.'[114]

When, between 28 and 29 April 1945, the Germans who were seeking to push their way through eastward massacred partisans and civilians in the zone of Santhià, in reprisal the partisans executed an equal number of Fascist prisoners in Vercelli.[115] In answer to another massacre of civilians carried out in extremis by German and Italian SS men, on 2 May 1945 at Avasinis, Garibaldini and Osoppo partisans shot all the members of the unit who did not manage to escape capture.[116]

This list, in which the victims are all enemy combatants and not civilian populations, is by no means complete. It should nevertheless be set alongside that of the reprisals and acts of violence which were avoided out of fear of partisan counter-reprisals. This list is far more difficult to compile, because what remains in terms of documentation is scant and unreliable, and the Fascist sources, which do not fail to denounce the *attesismo* of the population, are wary about levelling a similar and far graver accusation at their own armed forces (the same applies *a fortiori* for the Germans). Only one piece of evidence remains of Nazi-Fascist reprisals that were expected and did not come about. On one occasion the threat of a reprisal averted the shooting of some hostages.[117] A survivor from the death camps remembers a welcome ad hoc announcement of this by Radio London.[118]

5. Urban Guerrilla Warfare and the Gaps

A Fascist mailman was repeatedly warned that he could do the rounds of the town, but must do so without wearing the Fascist uniform. Having continued to wear it, he was killed by partisans, 'because it weren't just the *repubblichini*. The partisans did them there reprisals here too, understand?'[1]

The dividing-line between counter-reprisal, reprisal and autonomous initiatives was not in fact easily definable, even within a position that appeared, all things considered, as a response to the violence of others. 'To the arrogance of Nazism that presumes to reduce people to servitude with

---

114 ISRP, envelope 28, folder b.
115 See Poma and Perona, *La Resistenza nel Biellese*, pp. 422–7, and Dellavalle, *Operai*, p. 286.
116 See Mautino, *Guerra di popolo*, p. 195.
117 See Dellavalle, *Operai*, p. 161.
118 Testimony of Remo Scala (Bravo and Jalla, *La vita offesa*, p. 277).
1 Testimony of R. L., in Portelli, *Assolutamente niente*, p. 142.

violence and terror we must respond with violence and terror', declared the Communist Party's September 1943 appeal to the Italian people, cited earlier.[2]

The words *terrore* and *terrorismo* are used indiscriminately in the Resistance sources, uninhibitedly and without the echoes triggered today by the events that have occurred in Italy and internationally in the last two decades. The Resistance occurred in a situation that had seen the demise of the Romantic and anarchic tradition of the terrorist attack as an individual and exemplary act (propaganda of the deed) and which had simultaneously witnessed the outbreak of mass terror, to the point of genocide. In this context, Resistance *terrorismo* should not be confused with *terrore*, and appears as the extreme point of armed reaction to Nazi-Fascism, with motivations and implications as distant from those of the nineteenth-century assailants as from those of the terrorists of the 1970s and 80s. It is symptomatic that those who, like the Trotskyists – and, in Italy, also the *bordighisti* – regarded themselves as orthodox interpreters of the anti-anarchic Marxist tradition, took clear stances against any action that smacked of individualistic terrorism. The French Trotskyists, who were a good deal more authoritative than their Italian counterparts, published an article eloquently entitled 'Terrorism or mass organization?' . The answer was obviously all in favour of mass organised violence, not least because, if used against soldiers, 'the terrorist act widened the gap between French workers and German soldiers', and, if used against officers, the latter were easily replaceable, as for that matter were Laval and Déat. The *bordighisti* expressed similar concepts in an article that appeared in their newspaper, entitled 'Individual and class violence'.[3] Francesco Scotti , one of the first organisers of partisans and Gappists in Italy, has testified that some comrades 'maintained that it was not right to unleash individual terror which was contrary to Marxist-Leninist principles', and added: 'These and other objections had already had to be overcome in France in order to establish the Franc-Tireurs Partisans.'[4]

During the *ventennio* Italian anti-Fascism had also had to reckon with the problem of terrorism. The Communists had accused the activism of GL of reproducing the spectacular but sterile, or even harmful and counter-revolutionary, nineteenth-century and petit-bourgeois terrorism.[5] Riccardo Bauer and Ernesto Rossi had recognised a revolutionary character in their actions, but had firmly excluded the terroristic one, given the respect, which they imposed on themselves, 'for the elementary principles of humanity and

2 *Il comunismo italiano nella seconda guerra mondiale*, p. 216.
3 *La Vérité*, 25 September 1941; *Prometeo*, 1 February 1944.
4 Scotti, *La nascita delle formazioni*, p. 69.
5 See, for example, 'Il terrorismo individuale nella situazione italiana', *Lo Stato Operaio* VI (1932), pp. 326–31.

morality'.[6] Many years later, Ferruccio Parri recalled that in GL circles he was against terrorism because he thought that Fascism would collapse on its own – but that now he was no longer convinced that a violent action might not have speeded things up.[7] These swings of opinion merit attention. Pietro Secchia pointed out again that, if individual action was not sufficient, neither was mass action alone. He too had at one time urged action 'against things and persons'.[8]

In the practice of urban terrorism – of which the GAPs were the principal instrument – some of the thorniest political and ethical problems of the Resistance struggle come to light. The fact that the GAPs were very largely Communist in initiative and composition[9] makes the problem no easier; it only enriches it with a class and ideological component. Obviously, no mention was made of this component in the documents of the CVL General Command. But the Command preferred to speak of 'special action groups' 'to indicate in general terms formations like the GAPs, namely formations of special action groups of just a few men whose task it is to carry out terrorist actions against enemies and traitors, actions of sabotage against the enemy's communication channels and depots, etc.'[10]

A carefully argued account of the reasons why, in the last months of 1943, terrorism became 'feasible, even on a wide scale', was made by Leo Valiani, who vindicated the rightness of this choice not only for the Communists, but for 'all democratic parties', spoke admiringly of 'one of our [the Action Party's] terrorists', Pasqualino from Bergamo, and underlined that the attack on the *federale* (provincial party secretary) of Milan, Aldo Resega, and the exchange of shots at

6 See the pamphlet *Consigli sulla tattica*, in the GL archive, available at ISRT, S. IV, folder 2, subfolder I, insert 2, document 9. My thanks to Costanzo Casucci for making me aware of its existence.

7 Parri, in conversation with the author.

8 'GAP' in *Enciclopedia dell'antifascismo e della Resistenza*, Pietro Secchia, ed. Milan-Rome: Edizioni La Pietra, vol. II, 1971, pp. 475–9. Already in his article 'Perché dobbiamo agire subito' (*La nostra lotta*, November 1943, 3–4, pp. 20–1), Secchia had put together a clear *summa* of the Communists' positions. Luciano Canfora has noted that in the German edition of this text, from 1959, that the word 'persons' is replaced with 'institutions' (*La sentenza*, p. 158).

9 Secchia wrote that 'the PCI's GAP recruited exclusively Communists' and that the GAP were instituted upon the initiative of the General Command of the Garibaldi Brigade, towards the end of 1943 (see the encyclopaedia piece 'GAP', cited above). According to Ragionieri, the PCI had in fact already stipulated their creation with a circular in May 1943 (see Ragionieri, *Il partito comunista*, pp. 328–9).

10 Letter addressed to the Piedmont Regional Military Command, and for the information of the other Commands, 15 November 1944, to reassure them that the GAP should not mean 'formations of patriots of any particular political orientation' (*Atti CVL*, pp. 251–2). See also the subsequent confirmation letter, from 1 December (ibid., p. 264).

his funeral, 'galvanised the atmosphere of the Lombard metropolis'. According to Valiani, 'militant anti-Fascism decided to run this risk' – that is, the risk of reprisals and the effects of these on the population, and also

> the more hidden and at the same time profound risk that every civil war (and this was very much the case in the struggle against the Fascists) brings with it the danger of people's souls becoming ferocious, which after the victory could rebound, as a habit of 'taking the law into one's own hands', even against the democratic government itself that had come to power.[11]

A terrorism reminiscent of Vittorini's 'abstract furies'[12] appears in the article that *Avanti!* published as a comment on the Salerno 'turning-point', recalling that, from its order of the day of 9 February, the Socialist Party had pointed 'the way which was historically illuminated by the French precedents of the September and Maratian terror, when in order to eliminate the external enemy it was necessary first to eliminate the internal one, and of the Paris Commune'.[13]

In the passage referred to above, Leo Valiani took care to emphasise that 'terrorism, in the city, was not directed against all the enemy soldiers indiscriminately, but only against those who were assigned to duties of policing, repression, reprisal'. By and large this tallies with the truth, even if the distinction was not always easy to make. However, urban terrorism did not take truculent appeals like the following literally: 'The *repubblichini* Fascists are no longer men, they are ferocious animals from which one has to defend oneself. They must surrender unconditionally or be killed for legitimate defence. If you can do nothing else throw them down the stairs or out of the windows.'[14]

---

11 Valiani, *Tutte le strade*, pp. 169–72. Canfora has noted the author's subsequent (in truth, partial) self-censorship. In the 1983 reissue (Bologna: Il Mulino, pp. 128–30) 'militant anti-Fascism' becomes 'part of militant anti-Fascism', while the words 'all democratic parties' become 'and also other democratic parties'. See Canfora, *La sentenza*, pp. 155–7. On the Action Party's GAP, see the above-cited 'Relazione del commissario politico del Comando piemontese delle formazioni GL', 31 December 1944, which, in 'a substantially negative ... assessment' of the 'organisation of the urban squads', advanced a distinction between 'activists and terrorists' and other combatants (*Formazione GL*, pp. 284–5). See also the 30 January 1945 order from the Lombardy GL Command to 'Command 734', to proceed with the seizure of hostages who could be exchanged for Parri, himself captured by the Germans on 2 January 'with the promise of a major individual reward (even above 10,000 lire) if this coup can be pulled off' (ibid., p. 300).

12 See the preamble in Elio Vittorini, *Conversazione in Sicilia*, Milan: Bompiani, 1942.

13 'La bomba Ercoli', in the 5 April 1944 Rome edition. The 9 February order of the day, reacting to the conclusions of the Bari congress, appears in the 14 February issue.

14 The leaflet, datable to the third week of December 1944, is published in Arbizzani, *Manifesti, opuscoli, fogli volanti*, p. 454. Note the resemblance to Churchill's

What was involved rather were actions aimed *ad personam*; and this policy on the one hand excluded indiscriminate killings, and on the other made the Gappist into a combatant of a highly peculiar kind.

Dante Livio Bianco spoke of 'the elimination of particularly danger-ous and loathsome enemies (as in the case of Cumar, a boxer who had been the official torturer of the Fascist federation of Cuneo)'.[15] In Florence a GAP entered the home of the 'Fascist Nocentini Nello, spy, provocateur and right-hand man of Mario Carità', killed the bodyguard Pecchioli, 'a Fascist and ex-wrestler', and Nocentini's son, both 'Fascist SS men', but missed the main target.[16] *L'Unità* often published news with headlines such as 'Fascist Traitors Executed', 'Popular Justice Knows how to Shoot Traitors', and the like. In the French under-ground press announcements of this kind were highly frequent and detailed, and regarded the execution of spies, traitors, Gestapo agents, and particularly detested militiamen.[17]

There were recurrent exhortations not to commit errors in identifying the persons to be punished. In a hotbed like Trieste, the PCI federal committee enjoined:

> When you strike, strike in such a way as to demonstrate our objectivity, seriousness and sense of political justice; only thus will we have the solidarity and approval of the population of the area in which we are operating, only thus will we show that we are ... implacable, against the enemies of the people and of liberty, but at the same time upright and honest and above all revolutionary combatants, as Communists have always shown themselves to be and still do.

This document immediately listed first those to whom one should not abandon 'the tactic of the *foibe*':

> Fascists responsible for actions against the population, ex-leaders and holders of positions of responsibility in the Fascist regime who have shown themselves to be particularly reactionary; leaders and holders of positions of responsibil-ity of the present republican Fascism, of the government of Mussolini, who has sold himself, members of the republican militia and of the republican National

---

admonishment that, in the case of an enemy invasion, every English citizen should kill, if possible, one Hun, even if with a pitchfork.

15 Bianco, *Guerra partigiana*, p. 32.

16 See the report (unsigned and undated – the attack was on 7 April 1944), in *Le Brigate Garibaldi*, vol. I, pp. 348–9.

17 See, for example, *Quatre-Vingt-Treize. Organe des marraines des francs-tireurs et partisans. Détachement Victor Hugo*, January 1944, and *Vaincre*, whose 17 May 1944 'Supplément' is dedicated 'to the military communiqués of the partisans and *francs-tireurs* of Gascony and the Pyrenees'.

Guard; open, determined and active collaborators of the Germans, spies et cetera, et cetera.[18]

A meticulous list like this distances itself from the merely symbolic violence that strikes a human being, depersonalising him, only insofar as it sees incarnated in him something that transcends him. It is inspired rather by a violence that wishes to set an example only insofar as it strikes individuals deserving punishment, however broad – 'et cetera, et cetera' – the area of enemies punishable with this summary and radical procedure may be. The commander of the Cascione division is keen to offer this assurance: 'Up to now although we have taken action against a fair number of adversaries, we do not appear to have executed innocent people, and I do not deny that, given the situation, this too might just, by way of exception, occur, however much we try to do what is possible to avoid errors of that kind.'[19]

There appears to be not a shadow of doubt that 'patriotic terror' had deleterious effects on enemy morale. When in February 1944 the Germans organised an auxiliary police force in Bologna, the GAPs were initially ordered not to disturb them, in view of the fact that 'immature youngsters' had enrolled 'for the sole purpose of dodging the compulsory draft and not fighting the German war'. But when those policemen began to take part in anti-partisan repression, in five days the GAPs executed seventeen policemen, the result being that, out of 500, 150 seem to have deserted, while others actually went up into the mountains to join the partisans.[20] A great deal of fear was inspired, and at times it seemed that what was invoked by the Garibaldi brigade newspaper had come to pass: 'The third front must create for the Nazi-Fascists an atmosphere of hatred and terror; these criminals must no longer feel safe and sound anywhere; wherever they are they must feel hated and despised, wherever they are they must see enemies, wherever they are an armed hand striking them.'[21]

An RSI soldier about to go on leave to Milan received this letter from a relative: 'I advise you to come in civilian dress because the partisans are stopping trains and taking *carabinieri* and soldiers away with them, and they're knocking the black shirts off on the trains themselves.'[22]

---

18 Letter to the commander of the Trieste Battalion, December 1943 (*Le Brigate Garibaldi*, vol. I, p. 181).

19 Letter to Simon, commander of the 1st and 2nd zone Liguria divisions, 28 July 1944 (ibid., vol. II, p. 169).

20 See M. De Micheli, *70 GAP*, preface by Arturo Colombi, Rome: Edizioni di Cultura Sociale, 1954, pp. 145–7.

21 'Terzo fronte: guerra di popolo', Tuscany edition of *Il Combattente*, undated but between February and March 1944, issue 5.

22 'Esame della corrispondenza censurata al 30 giugno 1944' (ACS, SPD, CR, RSI, envelope 9, folder 3).

The dispatching of threatening letters *ad personam* to Fascist *gerarchi* and soldiers and to collaborationist bureaucrats was part of this policy aimed at terrorising the enemies. Threatening letters directed at Fascists by the Green Flames are reported by the censors – and one of them, from Bergamo, ends with these words: 'However things turn out, you shall not escape the punishment you have merited.'[23] The Florence CLN sent the *vice-podestà* Guido De Francisci, whom the Germans had enjoined to report vehicles and other material assigned for public services, the letter, mentioned earlier, that ended: 'Should you decide to go against our wishes, you will be shot without further notice.'[24]

I have mentioned the peculiar character that the urban violence of the GAPs acquired and (see Chapter 6), the not always easy relationship between partisan warfare in the mountains and guerrilla warfare in the city. Let me add now that it was not just a strategic problem which, in the final phase, took the form of making sure that a descent into town was not too premature.[25] And nor was this only an immediately political question. At the beginning of April 1945, for example, the Communists ordered the transfer into the mountains of about 1,500 Gappists and Sappists of the Carpi area, in order to regain control of the Modena division,[26] while the descent into town was feared by Edgardo Sogno, head of the Franchi organisation, because he saw in it 'baldly revolutionary intentions'.[27] Again, in terms of a short-term political project, Leo Valiani attributed the summons, which he supported, of sending the best *quadri* (leaders) from the mountains down to the town with the intention of using them in the negotiations with the Allies, not to feelings of contempt harboured by town-dwellers for the mountain bands. This in fact had been the accusation levelled at him by Mario Giovana, who, in an impassioned defence of the ethos of the partisans of the upper Piedmont valleys, had taken things beyond the strictly political terms of the controversy.[28] It was in fact precisely the overall figure of the mountain partisan that differentiated him not only from the *politico* who

---

23 Ibid.

24 Letter in appendix of Francovich, *La Resistenza a Firenze*, pp. 296-7.

25 For example, on 7 September 1944 the CUMER, expecting a German retreat (which did not then happen) prepared to descend on Modena and Bologna; instead, however, on 18 September the CVL General Command warned that mountain formations 'should absolutely not let themselves to be drawn into the cities' (see Gorrieri, *La Repubblica di Montefiorino*, pp. 459–60, which refers to 'Direttive operative per la battaglia della pianura padana', published in *Atti CVL*, pp. 194–6).

26 See Gorrieri, *La Repubblica di Montefiorino*, pp. 579–81.

27 See Catalano, *Storia del CLNAI*, p. 227, which refers back to E. Sogno, *Guerra senza bandiera. Cronache della Franchi nella Resistenza*, Milan: Rizzoli, 1950.

28 See the exchange of letters between Giovana and Valiani, published in *Il Movimento di liberazione in Italia* 89 (October–December 1967), pp. 125–9. Valiani told the version of events in the text above to Bianca Ceva, who related it to me in an 11 February 1968 meeting.

remained in town, but also from the urban fighter. Thus the Resistance too saw the re-emergence of the conflict between the ethic of the *alpino* and the ethic of the *ardito*, allowing for all the differences arising from the novelty of the times and the situation, and the obvious divergence between town and mountain. In fact, it is hard not to see in the name given to the 'brigate e distaccamenti d'assalto Garibaldi' ('Garibaldi assault brigades and detachments') some echo of the 'reparti d'assalto' (the *arditi*) of the First World War, filtered possibly by the albeit unorthodox memory of the 'Arditi del popolo'. The same could be said about the use of the word *fiamma* (flame), which had particularly compromising associations (the Fiamme Nere, and so on), as the title adopted by some newspapers and the name chosen by the *autonomi* of the Green Flames.[29]

'In order to act, dirty methods are necessary', wrote a SAP command. (The SAPs, seen in terms of a mass organisation, at times let themselves take their cue from Gappist practice.[30] But far from making these 'scoundrel's methods' a symbol or a myth, as the *arditi* had taken such pleasure in doing – and which were still best left to complete scoundrels – the Command added: 'This is how superficial and dishonest individuals went about things, troublemakers of our own and of other parties', causing numerous arrests.[31] Lest we overdo the comparison, it should be added that the 'golden slumber' of the *arditi* behind the lines, and the obsessively solitary and clandestine nature of the GAPs are two utterly contrasting situations.

At the suggestion of the Slovenians, the Natisone divisions decided to create units of *arditi*. But, as its commissar later wrote, 'it was a mistake, from both the operational and the political point of view': the non-*arditi* felt relegated to second-class combatants, while the *arditi* took to performing too many reckless

---

29 On the value of fire and flames as a political symbol, see Mosse, *L'uomo e le masse*, pp. 101–3. The *Saggio bibliografico* includes three papers whose title included the word *fiamma* (flame): one was specified as being a 'green flame' (*La voce delle Fiamme Verdi*, of the Sciatori Adamello), another as a flame 'of freedom' (the Garibaldians), and the third, without adjectives, as the 'organ of the Comitato di coordinamento femminile', presumably from Genoa (records 3419, 3528 and 4533). We can add a further *fiamma*, without adjectives and with no indications of provenance except the generic label 'CLN' (from Mantua).

30 Such was the reproach levelled against the Milan and provincial SAP by the document (no signature or date) 'I militanti di partito nelle SAP' (IG, *BG*, 011016). In Turin, 'SAP shock squads and manoeuvres brigades' were created, the former carrying out the same actions as did the GAP (Vaccarino, Gobetti and Gobbi, *L'insurrezione di Torino*, p. 177); the latter were reminded that they must not 'be some national guard from the last century, to be made fools of' (Turin SAP Divisional Command to all SAP brigades in the province, 10 November 1944, *Le Brigate Garibaldi*, vol. II, p. 560).

31 'Rapporto sul lavoro GAP' by the Turin SAP Divisional Command, 30 October 1944 (IG, *BG*, 06051).

acts. So those units were quickly dissolved.[32] The Alpino Revelli speaks of *colpisti* (strikers) in the same spirit: 'The most buccaneering *colpista*, if he is not sustained by conscientious courage, by a firm will, is worn down and collapses in combat. The "calm" courage of the *colpista* is not enough; what is needed is the courage that resists fatigue, exhaustion.'

Revelli draws a revealing comparison with an English paratrooper, Captain Flight, who, though finding himself with the opportunity to shoot at the Germans, did not do so: 'Perhaps the courage of these people runs out in the mechanical act of jumping, it all finishes there: a very striking courage, which we shouldn't set great store by, because it's like that of our *colpisti*.'[33] Dante Livio Bianco makes a clear-cut distinction between *soldati* and *colpisti*; he attributes greater 'fundamental' moral qualities to the former, and adds that the mountain band of the Cuneo area 'was, contrary to what many said, not at all a clandestine army.'[34] In the zone of the Piave Garibaldi brigade, its commander later recounted that 'the GAPs never showed any reason for existing and represented, if anything, a disturbance for the brigade, creating confusion and difficulties through their undisciplined and irresponsible actions.'[35]

These comments, and other similar ones that could be cited, call to mind a fine passage by Marc Bloch: 'It is a popular fallacy among officers that the man of hot temper, the adventurer or the hooligan, makes the best soldier. That is far from being the truth. I have always noticed that the brutal temperament is apt to break under the strain of prolonged danger.'[36]

It would be wrong, however, to put the Gappist on a par with the *ardito* and the *colpista*. To survive, the Gappists had to rely on an extremely difficult combination of qualities, and indeed there were very few of them, and not all managed to combine these qualities in an ideal fashion: coldness and determination of character, courage and physical dexterity, the most rigorous clandestinity, and solidity of political conviction which, given the need to interpret the struggle in the most severe, ruthless and relentless terms, was the only thing that could safeguard them from deviations and backslidings.

The commissar of the GAPs, says an instruction document,

> has to see to it that the altogether special life led by the Gappists does not corrupt their honesty and character. He must make it his business to see that every man who kills feels himself to be an executioner, and not a murderer; that he who does a

---

32 Padoan (Vanni), *Abbiamo lottato insieme*, pp. 60–1.

33 Revelli, *La guerra dei poveri*, p. 236 (4 May 1944) and p. 329 (2 September 1944).

34 Bianco, *Guerra partigiana*, pp. 95, 131 (on the political and human significance of the choice between the city and the mountains, see p. 28).

35 Bernardo, *Il momento buono*, p. 63.

36 Bloch, *Strange Defeat*, p. 104.

retrieval raid does so convinced of the justice of his action and not with the sense of feeling himself to be a thief.[37]

Another task that the commissar had, it was then recalled, was 'to keep the combatants' morale high, making clear to them the political aims of and ideals behind the actions, and to keep a check on their private lives, in order to avoid any form of degeneration'.[38] Absolute respect for the conspiratorial norms figures in another text, as both a physical and moral safeguard:

The habit that some GAPs have of going to the café every day to play cards, or enjoying themselves at the cinema or clubs, must cease. We must explain that we are soldiers, and thus mobilised in the fight against Fascists and Germans; explain to them how the Party demands that each of its members act as a member of the advance-guard in the fight against the Germans and Fascists, requires the maximum daily activity in seeking out objectives and in the struggle for national liberation; [the Party must] explain to them the danger that lies in frequenting public bars and restaurants, clubs, et cetera.

The author of this document firmly criticised those Gappists who had decided not to perform an action because a woman had shouted, 'Don't do it because they'll shoot my husband':

This must not happen again. We cannot look after the interests of a single person, one must always look to the general interest. Today there are thousands of men giving their lives every day for liberty, so we must show them our solidarity: we cannot be sentimentalists. We must strike the Fascists and the Germans and strike them hard, men and objects. Each of us must learn to hate the enemy ... We must give the enemy no respite: both day and night the GAPs must be the terror of the Nazi-Fascists.[39]

Incitements to strike with absolute intransigence appear in 'middle'- and 'low'-level sources, as they do in 'high'-level ones. An example of the former is the reprimand, made very early on, to a commissar because

several ringleaders have not been killed. Take note: no pity for the enemy. In town spies are more difficult to track down. These are doing us all the harm they can with the help of the SS. If they fall into your hands, why pardon or

37 Circular on the 'functions of the political commissar', from the Command of the 28th Mario Gordini GAP Brigade, 15 July 1944 (IG, BG, 02311–12).

38 Scotti, La nascita delle formazioni, p. 71.

39 Letter from the Milan GAP commander, Visone, to the detachment commanders and commissars, 17 July 1944 (Le Brigate Garibaldi, vol. II, p. 140).

spare them? Exterminate them without pity: and let that serve as a warning to all.[40]

These draconian commanders' orders on the field tend to disguise themselves not only as political appeals to fight relentlessly (as early as 10 September 1943 from Radio Milano Libertà, which is to say Radio Moscow, Togliatti had urged his listeners to 'destroy without pity traitors who place themselves at the service of the foreigner'),[41] but also as the directives, real or presumed, of the government of the South. Witness a document of 7 August 1944: 'Nicoletta must be made to see that both the Allies and our Rome government have given clear instructions in this regard, that is to kill as many of the enemy as possible, wherever and whenever they are found.'[42]

Another feature appears in the testimonies regarding the Gappists: the tense and obsessive sense of loneliness that hung over this combatant, who was generally compelled to live in absolute and often solitary clandestinity: 'An existence in which the sensation of being a hunted animal found respite only when it was overcome by the spur of action.'[43] A Torinese Gappist has written: 'The hardest thing to take was the complete isolation in which we were acting, an almost unbearable and at times pitiless isolation'; it had to be numbered among the reasons why 'even the best among the mountain partisans did not feel up to acting as Gappists in town.'[44] There are pages in the memoirs of a Bologna Gappist which well convey the atmosphere that was born when one had to spend days on end shut up in a tiny apartment: 'Another three days went by, three interminable days of solitude and hunger. We would spend them listless and inert, looking out of the windows, leafing through the few remaining books, hunting down lice and cursing fate.'[45]

The book by one of the most intrepid and cool-headed Gappists, Giovanni Pesce, mentioned earlier, is full of yet more tragic expressions: 'alone and hunted'; 'here I am back at home stretched out on the bed, my eyes fixed on the

40 Letter from Sandrelli, responsible for military work in Piedmont, 3 November 1943 (ibid., vol. I, pp. 116–17).

41 See his 'Appello agli italiani', in Togliatti, *Opere*, vol. IV, 2, pp. 479–83.

42 Letter from 'comrades' to the 'comrade responsible for Val di Susa', Valerio (*Le Brigate Garibaldi*, vol. II, p. 216). Just before, the comrades had written, 'The partisan did well to take the opportunity and kill the two Germans. If he had had to await the authorisation of the Command, the two Germans would have escaped.' Giulio Nicoletta was the commander of the autonomous De Vitis formation.

43 Mautino, *Guerra di popolo*, p. 55. For mountain partisans, however, liberation from the mindset of being hunted could come through defending a single location (see Giovana, *Storia di una formazione partigiana*, pp. 136–7).

44 Testimony of Irene Candera (Ines), in Vaccarino, Gobetti and Gobbi, *L'insurrezione di Torino*, pp. 48–9.

45 Cicchetti, *Il campo giusto*, esp. p. 169.

ceiling'; 'struggle against fear and solitude'; 'it's not the risk, it's the isolation that wears down the Gappist'; the Gappist 'no longer has a home, only addresses'; 'anguished waiting'; 'my own jailer'. The sublimation suggested to Pesce by a prestigious chief like Ilio Barontini is not enough to liberate him: 'When you're alone, the Party is you.' Pesce well understood those who 'rather than the terrible and draining isolated struggle prefer that of the mountain formations', and looked back nostalgically on Spain, where 'we faced the enemy in combat, face to face'.[46] The personalisation of the enemy, for example through tailing him prior to the action, endowed him with a 'private' face and demanded of the Gappist a firmer and more 'abstract' determination to eliminate him. When in Milan Pesce saw a new comrade coming towards him 'smiling and cordial', he immediately said to himself: 'no one smiles like that after the first actions', and sent him off to 'gain practical knowledge' with the partisans of the Pavese Oltrepò. As for Pesce himself, when a bomb exploded prematurely at Milan station, he found himself a prey to the 'absurd' doubt that the Gappist who had been assigned the action, previously reprimanded for being half-hearted in combat, might think he had been deliberately sent to his death.[47]

Being alone and shut up was, as it were, the symbol of a solitude born above all from the wearing effort to keep morality and inflexibility united in taking the lives of others. Franco Calamandrei, a Gappist with no past experience of anti-Fascist militancy, lucidly described in his diary the tension with which he lived his dual activity as assailant and intellectual. It was a distinction of planes which, though practised to safeguard one's own moral unity at its deepest level, was felt to be no less harrowing for that:

All day I've been dragging around with me a tiredness, a sense of heaviness, of nausea, and have had to struggle with myself not to fall back into the voids of conscience. Then it happens, at a certain point, that beyond disgust, when it is at its height, you find your strength, your faith, your will again ... I'm translating Diderot lazily: I'm finding this translation work more and more extraneous.

Elsewhere Calamandrei speaks of the 'voluptuousness of solitude', and again of detachment, lack of interest, indifference, tiredness – and exclaims: 'How much there still is to reclaim within myself!' When he remembers Giorgio Labò and the joy that his comrade had felt when he had been asked to write an article on Communism and architecture, Calamandrei notes: 'There was in him, in short, the more or less conscious anxiety to recover his terrain, to free himself from adventure, and the impossibility of actually being able to get away

---

46 Pesce, *Senza tregua*, pp. 8, 35, 36, 72, 99, 146, 147, 45, 35.
47 Ibid., pp. 166–7, 213.

in practice, and the vain effort to resign himself to this condition that he had inadvertently imposed on himself.'

Labò yearned 'to be sent out of Rome, into some band'; and faced with the death of his friend, Calamandrei needs to believe 'that death is always just, that the individual prepares it himself, day by day, that each of us dies only when he has to die.'

Making no comment, Calamandrei records the tale of a comrade who, having taken up position in Piazza di Spagna to prepare for the Via Rasella attack, on seeing the German column who were to be exterminated, first says to himself that he couldn't care less about the death of all those men, and then feels tears running down his cheeks. Calamandrei frees himself from the tragic sense of the situation with the successfully achieved action ('and I felt full of an elementary, childlike joy') and with the emotion he experienced at the immense misery of the refugees: 'Precisely because grief appears so out of proportion with the remedy, precisely for this reason we need to fight and fight so that an end is put to the disproportion.' Finally, Calamandrei appeals to political conscience as an antidote to the deviations that that type of fighting can lead to: 'I urge you to resume political life more actively in order to remedy a certain *sportismo* that is infecting us.'[48] In many Communist documents, 'sporting activity' meant military activity; and here possibly Calamandrei was keen to warn against the danger that might lurk in that conspiratorial formula.

A fine death and a gratuitous death were not in fact part of Resistance thinking, but of that of Fascism. Two Gappists wrote:

> Our Gappists are gifted with courage and they have been demonstrating it for the past ten months, but that doesn't mean that they feel themselves to be dedicated to certain death. A bullet through your head in a cornfield fighting against the enemy … That's not how we see things. We love life and put up with death with dignity and pride. Like [Giuseppe] Perotti and [Eusebio] Giambone.[49]

The GAP action that has aroused most discussion is, together with that of Via Rasella, the killing of the philosopher Giovanni Gentile, which occurred in Florence on 15 April 1944. The most considered comment to appear at the time,

---

48 Calamandrei, *La vita indivisibile*, pp. 156, 177, 171–3, 189–90, 144–5, 125, 132. Giorgio Labò was responsible for the Rome GAP's weaponry and bomb-making; he was captured by the Germans and shot on 7 March 1944 (*Enciclopedia dell'antifascismo e della Resistenza*, vol. III, Milan 1976).

49 Report to the CUMER from the Command of the 28th Mario Gordini GAP brigade (Ravenna), 29 August 1944 (Casali, *Il movimento di liberazione a Ravenna*, vol. II, p. 277); Pesce, *Senza tregua*, p. 90. In the former of the two documents, we read 'Our Gappista does not live amid a heroic, military environment like the mountain partisan, but rather is immersed among the masses, and feels their moods and influence.'

Carlo Dionisotti's, begins with the words: 'the violent end of Giovanni Gentile is only an episode in the crisis that Italy is going through'.[50] Another *resistente*, Enzo Enriques Agnoletti, who had originally expressed disapproval at the attack, has recently written that 'only the fame of the victim made him a special case'.[51]

These are opinions inspired by repugnance at giving preferential treatment to illustrious personages in the tragedy. But it is true that not only Gentile's fame, but also his being a great intellectual give his case a symbolic value that, on the one hand, particularly highlights the civil war context in which his killing took place, and on the other raises the question of the relationship between the responsibility of the man of culture and that of the politician. 'They are even killing philosophers', was Benedetto Croce's comment.[52] Necessary and useful, but marginal to this problem, appear the many investigations into the dynamics of the attack, into who its originators were, into when exactly the decision was taken to carry it out, into the possibility, claimed by some, of Fascists having been behind it.[53]

The essence of the problem was clearly formulated at the time by Antonio Banfi when, in an article devoted to the killing of the philosopher, he posed this question: 'He was a scholar, they say, a philosopher, a man of culture and a man who protected, defended culture and always celebrated the values of the spirit, and was this not a sufficient shield against his political errors?' The answer was a firm no, argued by denying whoever it might be in the 'inebriating and terrible struggle' that was in progress, a 'privilege of salvation', and all the more so in the case of someone who 'has made his intelligence and his knowledge into an instrument of deceit and perversion'.[54]

---

50 Botti (C. Dionisotti), *Giovanni Gentile*. Dionisotti's view was fully shared by the Action Party in the North (according to the testimony of Vittorio Foa).

51 E. Enriques Agnoletti, 'Ancora sul caso Gentile', in *L'Indice dei libri del mese* II: 10 (December 1985), p. 17. On the Florence Action Party's disapproval with regard to the attack, see Francovich, *La Resistenza a Firenze*, pp. 187–90, 295–6.

52 A comment made to his son-in-law, Raimondo Craveri (Craveri, *La campagna d'Italia*, p. 56).

53 From this point of view, the most detailed account is that of Luciano Canfora, *La sentenza*, cited above. It is a long and precise study of the 'instigators' who passed the 'sentence' against the philosopher; but his use of categories of little historiographical merit, the judicial terms 'sentence' and 'instigators', means the result of all this diligent scholarly effort is itself similar to an 'order of enquiry' (a hypothesis) in an evidence-based trial. Canfora replied to the observations I made on this point in 'Il mandante non fa storia', *L'Indice dei libri del mese*, III: 7 (July 1986) with a polemical vim not matched by the force of his argumentation, first in the Naples *Il Mattino*, then in 'Il punto non è questo', *Quaderni di storia* XII: 24 (July–December 1986), pp. 99–101.

54 'Storia di una vita: Giovanni Gentile', in *La nostra lotta* II: 9 (May 1944), pp. 14–16 (the words cited in the text are from p. 16). A briefer version of this article had already appeared in the 10 May 1944 northern edition of *L'Unità*, under the title

The problem was therefore that of the political responsibility of the intellectual, understood, in this case, as the basis of the legitimacy of the action aimed at killing him. In other words, the problem of the relationship between thought, word, and action. What needs identifying is the point at which the function of the word as an instrument of action prevails over its function of expressing and transmitting thought.[55] Any judgment on the link between Gentile's philosophy and Fascism is, from this point of view, marginal, even if it is natural that in those circumstances his famous speech about the cudgel being equal to the sermon as an instrument of thought was widely recalled, not least by Banfi.[56] But there is no doubt that the Gentile who supported the Social Republic and accepted important positions in it like that of president of the Accademia d'Italia, the Gentile who publicly thanked 'il condottiere della grande Germania', and who invoked 'yes, the cessation of the struggles, save that vital one against treasonous instigators, whether they have sold themselves or are in good faith, but inebriated with extermination', thereby faithfully repeating the words used by the Fascists, had stepped well beyond the threshold which, even with the flaring up of a civil war, ought to mark the zone of immunity accorded to a thinker.[57] In Gentile's case, however, his status as a philosopher conferred on him greater force as an active Fascist. It would have been odd if this circumstance had played in his favour.

When, in his speech to the Italians pronounced from the Campidoglio on 24 June 1943, Gentile had sought to champion a form of national unity in the form of Fascism, a newspaper of new generation anti-Fascists had commented in language which, though archaic, hit the nail on the head: 'He scorns us only because he is sufficiently able at leading innocents, namely the young and the masses further down the path of vice rather than that of virtue.'[58]

Now, in the course of the civil war, the frontier between 'vice' and 'virtue' was garrisoned, on both sides, with arms; and 'national unity' could only be proposed either wholly from one side or wholly from the other side of that frontier. Indeed, in order to achieve it on his side, Gentile demanded the elimination of those who sought it from the opposing side. If some credit is due to Gentile in those circumstances, it lies in his having taken sides without hesitation – though,

---

'Giovanni Gentile raggiunto dalla giustizia popolare'. On its attribution to Banfi, see Canfora, *La sentenza*, pp. 251–2, n. 14.

55 See, on this problematic, Todorov's considerations on Spinoza's *Tractatus theologico-politicus* ('La tolleranza e l'intollerabile', pp. 94ff).

56 An account of the identification between the cudgel and the sermon is at the heart of the piece 'Commemorazione di Giovanni Gentile', published in the 25 May 1944 issue of *Bandiera Rossa*, the Milan newspaper animated by Lelio Basso.

57 The plaudits for Hitler were expressed during the commemoration of Vico in front of the Accademia d'Italia on 19 March 1944; the attack against the partisans appeared in the article 'Ricostruire', *Corriere della Sera*, 28 December 1943 (see Canfora, *La sentenza*, pp. 172, 309–11).

58 *Bollettino Popolo e Libertà* 2 (July 1943).

as Dionisotti has pointed out clearly, with the ambiguity of the philosopher of history convinced that, whatever the situation may be, he has to be there at the centre of events. There is some truth, then, and, in the final part, ingenuous optimism, in this article in *L'Italia Libera*: 'This bloody death has somehow redeemed Giovanni Gentile, not certainly in comparison with the Italian intellectuals who have died fighting against Nazism, but in comparison with the Federzonis and Bottais who have abased themselves with some obliging protector, in the hope of avoiding the inevitable judgment that awaits them.'[59]

6. Insurrectional violence

The violence practised during the Insurrection and the phase immediately following it had a character of its own, when the direct 'settling of accounts' reached its acme, but at the same time headed towards its rapid conclusion, giving way to the process of punishment and purging that was to be conducted by the new institutional order. Coexisting in the climate of general euphoria of the last days of April 1945 were faith in and doubts about the near future, the fears of the Allies, the Rome government and the moderate parties that they might lose their hold on the situation, and on the other hand the urge to achieve, while time remained, as much as possible in the way of irreversible actions. On the one hand, in short, a determination to strike while the iron was hot, and on the other hand a ready commitment to cool the iron down. This is the background against which the explosion of violence that occurred in those crucial days has to be seen, when the exasperation accumulated in twenty months of civil war came out of hiding and was given vent in a way which, though legitimised by the victory, the victory itself might before long push down the slippery slope of mere and unseemly vendetta.

'Only justice which is *rapid and exemplary* will prevent an excessive number of massacres on the one hand and unmerited impunity on the other' – this is how the Piedmontese regional military Command had wisely sought in advance to steer the phase of transition in which excessive indulgence could only have added fuel to partisan radicalism.[1] The secretariat of the Action Party for Northern Italy had moved along the same lines early on, in urging the avoidance both of 'a bureaucratic and central purging process' like that promoted in Rome and a 'spontaneous movement of mob vendettas', which would simply have meant playing into the Allies' hands. There was in all this the awareness of how difficult it was to 'find a just middle way between inconclusive Jacobin

---

59 'La tragica fine di Giovanni Gentile', Rome edition, 20 May 1944.

1 See the preamble to the stipulations on justice, issued 28 September 1944 (Vaccarino, Gobetti and Gobbi, *L'insurrezione di Torino*, p. 98).

extremism and inertly waiting for a Constitution which in itself will be unable to solve anything if the way is not suitably paved by positive actions'.[2]

The news coming from the South was a spur to act swiftly if, as the PCI representative in the Piedmont regional military command had said at the beginning of the year, one wished to avoid repeating 'Rome's error as a result of which too many Fascists are still roaming the streets of the city undisturbed, and, what is worse, holding public offices and fomenting disorder of every kind'.[3]

Immediate problems of this order include the arguments and conflicts that occurred in the CLNs and in the CVL Commands about the role that the partisans ought to play in keeping the peace immediately after the overthrow of the Nazi-Fascist authorities. In the background there was the equally and perhaps still more important question of the inclusion of the partisans in the regular forces of the army and the police.

'Total and exclusive employment of military formations for purposes of warfare' was written in the agreement stipulated between the CLNAI and Under-Secretary Medici Tornaquinci on a mission to the North.[4] The distinction between military activity, police action and judicial proceedings was as clear on paper as it was difficult in practice in the days of the insurrection. Much as one wished to reduce the partisans to a pure military status, everyone knew full well that this was not how things stood: indeed, Edgardo Sogno, chief of the Franchi organisation, urged that the regular Italian Liberation Corps (CIL) troops should be the first to enter Milan, while the Communists were pressing the Garibaldini to liberate the city.[5]

On 20 April the CLNAI issued a 'regulation for the functioning of the commissions of justice' in order to 'offer the population a serious guarantee that justice will be done with serenity and promptness'. On 25 April, proclaiming the state of exception, it ordered the zone commands of the CVL to set up military war tribunals, and, the same day, issued a decree concerning its own jurisdictional powers.[6] This disciplining of the easily foreseeable violence during the phase of transition was fairly loosely woven, since much depended on those

---

2 Letter to the regional and provincial Party committees, undated but probably early 1945 (INSMLI, *CLNAI*, envelope 8, folder 12).

3 Vaccarino, Gobetti and Gobbi, *L'insurrezione di Torino*, minutes of the 24th session (December 1944–January 1945), p. 114.

4 ISRT, *Archivio Medici Tornaquinci*, envelope 4, IV, 1, no. 13 (29 March 1945).

5 See the note made by Sogno on 1 March 1945 in the San Vittore prison, which got through to the PLI delegation for upper Italy and, with its endorsement, the minister of war, Casati, in Rome (ACS, *Carte Casati*, folder H); and the letter from the General Command of the Garibaldi Brigades to the Command of the Valsesia, Ossola, Cusio, and Verbano divisions-group, 3 March 1945 (INSMLI, old cataloguing, envelope 148, folder 2).

6 See *Atti CLNAI*, pp. 316–21, 323–8.

who, when it came down to it, would act in concrete terms. This regulation, which repeated that 'every due regard should be shown' towards enemies who did not put up resistance, stressed that 'arms must be used against those who on the contrary put up resistance or are about to do so'.

In the proclamation of the state of exception it was explained, again by the CLNAI, that members of the Fascist armed corps were to be interned in concentration camps, while 'infringers are considered rebels punishable with death and will be shot on the spot'. At the same time death was reserved for saboteurs, looters, robbers, thieves: if caught in the act, these too were to be shot on the spot. Things, in short, were heading towards one of those moments in which, in order to feel that the nightmare of death was well and truly over, people, in exceptional cases, still had to die.

Some time before, in the Fortress Command of Turin, 'Brandani' (Mario Mammuccari), the Communist representative, had opposed a proposal by the Action Party, which duly withdrew it, to set up a police service with many 'technical' members, for the period immediately following the Liberation. The reasons Brandani gave for opposing this proposal deserve quoting for the general question that they raise:

> The police are a force and a political phenomenon, especially in the present phase of Italian life ... As for the excesses of the crowd, it is worth pointing out that the masses are the basic element of the insurrection. It would not do were active participation in this insurrection to be interpreted as excesses by the crowd. Naturally thefts and sackings have to be prevented, but this will be avoided with suitable appeals and with a garrison service at the stores and depots. The policing service during the insurrection must be performed by the citizen squads and the patriotic formations; from each of these the new police corps will spring. These squads and formations will be assigned the task of cleansing out the elements of the fifth column.[7]

At a later meeting of the Fortress Command, the Communist representative once again proposed the creation 'as from now' of a service of city police chosen from the GAPs and SAPs. According to the minutes of that meeting, the proposal was accepted.[8] At a 2 May assembly of the Piedmontese regional CLN, acting by now in the capacity of regional government council, Colonel Stevens, head of the Allied mission, accepted the principle of a police force

---

7 Minutes of the session of the second half of September 1944 (Vaccarino, Gobetti and Gobbi, *L'insurrezione di Torino*, p. 82). The establishment of citizens' and people's guards, primarily composed of partisans, was proposed in many documents relating to various different localities. The article 'I partigiani forza di ordine pubblico', published in the 20 October 1944 *L'Italia Libera*, expressed the Action Party's demand to this effect.

8 Session of late October/early November 1944 (Vaccarino, Gobetti and Gobbi, *L'insurrezione di Torino*, pp. 107–8).

entrusted to the partisans, 'apart from the *carabinieri* technicians', precisely in order to prevent 'all the partisans indiscriminately from regarding themselves as forces of order'. This high-ranking British officer was stressing an essential point. Essential too was the other point made at that meeting: the impossibility for the time being of stopping 'the present rhythm of the sentences being passed by the military tribunals' (as the prefect, the Socialist Pierluigi Passoni, said). On the same occasion, Colonel John Stevens made two provocative remarks that accurately pinpointed the state of affairs not only in Turin but elsewhere too: 'I should like to know in very simple words why we need the state of emergency here in Turin; whether we are afraid of the Germans or of the partisans ... It is curious that those of us present here, all civilians, apart from myself, should be defending military authority.'[9]

In fact, even this last point was not altogether indisputable. It was true that rapid and exceptional justice called for the work of the military tribunals; but those who wished to guarantee the pre-eminence of that political moment had at the same time to reaffirm the superiority of the CLNs to the regional Commands of the CVL (Corpo voluntari della libertà). And the PCI did just this, refusing to delegate to the Commands the maintenance of law and order, which was the exclusive task of the CLN.[10]

A realistic view of things during those days was also shown, in another way, by those officers of the Allied missions who 'confidentially urged the most rapid elimination of war criminals since, they said, once the Allied troops arrived a stop would be put to everything'.[11]

In many Italian sources it is, naturally, clearer that there should be the incitement to lose no time in taking the law into one's own hands. In response to General Mario Roatta's flight the Communist federation of Treviso made an appeal to the partisans to ensure that they secured 'all the peace-keeping and purging services in the country ... There is still too little attention and a kind-hearted and gullible spirit on the part of many partisans and certain anti-Fascists.'[12] More explicitly, Roberto Battaglia, former commander of the Lunense GL division and future historian of the Resistance, sent Renato Iacopini, the CLN-appointed *questore* of

9 Transcript, ibid., pp. 339–51.

10 See the letter from the PCI leadership for occupied Italy to the insurrectionary triumvirate for Liguria, and sent to all triumvirates for their information, 22 April 1945, (*Le Brigate Garibaldi*, vol. III, pp. 662–5).

11 Bernardo, *Il momento buono*, p. 165. Note this account of the moment of liberation of two extermination camp survivors: 'That day they began to get their just desserts; I say just desserts, others would say vendettas, and perhaps in some cases it was also a vendetta'; 'The Americans let us do it ... they saw us, and they let us torture them a bit, and then they took them away' (testimonies of Benito Puiatti and Eraldo Franza, in Bravo and Jalla, *La vita offesa*, pp. 306–7).

12 INSMLI, *CLNAI*, envelope 8, folder 2, subfolder 2.

La Spezia, the following advice from Rome: 'We must do the purging now, since after the Liberation we'll no longer be able to do it, because in war you shoot, but once the war's over you don't shoot anymore.'[13] In La Spezia too, the secretary of the PCI federation had, with a view to the insurrection, sent out an internal circular saying: 'Arrest all Fascists, remember that they will try to flee, and shoot those who try to flee.'[14]

Returning to Cuneo from France, Nuto Revelli saw the 'two-timers of the Littorio, yesterday's lions, now sheep', who, as prisoners, 'eat and drink' and 'are in seventh heaven', and flew off the handle: 'God forbid, I'm not saying we should disembowel all Fascists. But let's shoot because it's about time we did so.'[15] Pietro Chiodi's diary clearly sums up the behaviour that was rife at that time: 'Numerous prisoners are pouring in. On orders of the CMRP [Piedmont Regional Military Command] some categories are being tried and shot, while the majority are jailed for dispatch to Turin's Carcere Nuove.'[16] A confirmation of this attitude can be found, again in Piedmont, in the regional CLN Council minutes mentioned earlier:[17]

> *Presidente, liberale* [Franco Antonicelli]. Reports executions that have occurred at Pinerolo with highly summary verdicts. *CMRP* [Francesco (Fausto) Scotti, Communist, or Livio Bianco, Actionist]. Explains that five men were shot because circular 250 of the military command has been applied according to which the forces of the black brigades and the Decima Mas are war criminals and are to be eliminated, unless possible coercion be demonstrated. The complaints are therefore unfounded.

At the other end of the Alpine arc, in the Piave valley, the situation is described as follows: 'The ten thousand prisoners or thereabouts captured were consigned to the Allies a few days later. Only the Fascist prisoners were not consigned, though they were requested. The undersigned has assumed responsibility for the refusal.'[18]

When the shooting stopped, anger and violence could take other paths. Chiodi accompanied to Turin's Carcere Nuove the sister of a partisan who had

13 Iacopini's testimony, related in the degree thesis of Chiara Federici, cited above. The La Spezia *questura* counted seventeen summary executions of a political character in May, nineteen in June and five in July.

14 Quoted in ibid.

15 Revelli, *La guerra dei poveri*, p. 427 (27 April). On 28 April he repeated: 'The important thing, I tell myself, is that each man shoots as well as he can' (p. 430).

16 Chiodi, *Banditi*, p. 144 (28 April).

17 Vaccarino, Gobetti and Gobbi, (*L'insurrezione di Torino*, pp. 107–8).

18 'Relazione personale sulla situazione generale politico-militare della zona della divisione Garibaldi Nanetti', written by commander Francesco Pesce (Milo) in Rome, 31 May 1945 (*Le Brigate Garibaldi*, vol. III, p. 719).

been hanged in his cell, where both had been imprisoned, and found it occupied by six SS officers. Finding himself before the 'beast's face' of one of them, who had not stood to his feet, Chiodi, who remembers having given his word that he would not shoot, struck him 'savagely on the face with my pistol', while the hanged man's sister 'kicked in the face, knocking over' two who had gone down on their knees 'begging for pity'.[19] If the defeated proved to be cowards – Giuseppe Solaro, provincial head of Turin, 'before dying had said: Don't hurt me. I've always been a socialist'[20] – contempt could lead to ferocious treatment or, alternatively, transcend it. Before the anguish that he felt at the memory of his many dead comrades, Revelli said to himself: 'As long as I shoot, as long as I'm busy fighting, I manage to forget'; but when he came across a group of Fascists of the Littorio, who had become sprightly partisans at the eleventh hour, he gave up: 'It's hard to hit it off. Let them go to the devil!'[21]

At times there was repugnance, rooted in popular ethics, at reporting people to the authorities, whatever those authorities might be. A survivor from the German camps found a Fascist who had become a municipal guard, and, together with his comrades, gave him a thrashing: 'But we didn't go and turn him in. That had been enough to get it off our chests.'[22] Another partisan said to a spy who had him arrested and deported to Germany, and was now imprisoned in the Carcere Nuove: 'I won't denounce anyone, just make sure I never see you again as long as I live!'[23]

The feeling that reporting was akin to the very crime – denouncement to the enemy – that one was intent on punishing, could, on the other hand, be a further spur to summary justice: 'Then they took the one who had denounced him and shot him on the same spot.'[24]

Those, by contrast, who did the denouncing but to no effect could be driven to take things into their own hands. After the Liberation the partisan Rosanna Rolando handed over to a PCI inspector a report against the spy who had denounced her, 'but he lost it'. So she gave another one to two comrades, who said: 'Don't you worry, we won't lose the report.' The spy was arrested, 'given a people's trial' and shot.[25] 'One thing is sure', said another woman partisan, 'when the liberation came they took too little time to execute criminals.'[26] To make use of the time available, a commander insisted on regaining his

---

19 Chiodi, *Banditi*, pp. 149–50 (30 April).
20 Ibid., p. 152. Solaro was hanged from a tree on 30 April.
21 Revelli, *La guerra dei poveri*, pp. 431–2 (28 April).
22 Testimony of Biagio Benzi, in Bravo and Jalla, *La vita offesa*, p. 345.
23 Testimony of Raimondo Vazon, in ibid.
24 Testimony of Dachau survivor Elidio Miola, in ibid., p. 338.
25 Bruzzone and Farina, *La Resistenza taciuta*, pp. 28–30. Rolando and the two partisans were later sentenced to nine months' imprisonment.
26 Testimony of Elsa Oliva (ibid., p. 141).

'freedom of action ' in order to pass 'from theory to practice in making sure that the Fascists camouflaged as patriots get the justice that everyone is talking about'.[27]

Persistent and pent-up tension triggered tragic fates, like that of the partisan Mitraglia (Machine-gun):

> He loses his legs in combat. In Rome, immediately after the Liberation, he feels he has a leading role to play. At the meeting in front of the Coliseum about Roatta's escape, he harangues the crowd, incites them to storm the Quirinale. He goes back to his village, in the Valdarno. His life sinks gradually into indolence, demoralisation, loss of confidence. Until he beats to death an amnestied Fascist. He escapes. His wanderings. Milan. Attempt to cross the eastern border. An Allied patrol kills him.[28]

Disgust with the violence in which one had been immersed created, alongside the refusal to pardon, the inclination to pardon. A survivor from deportation to Germany has recently said: 'I have forgiven no one and still now forgive no one.'[29] But another concentration camp survivor has recalled:

> I, like others – I've spoken to others too – we were fairly tranquil, how can I put it? – a bit dim possibly, a bit shaken. But I believe that at least in me there was ... I don't want to use big words, but for me there was a sense of great pardon, in the sense ... we've squabbled but now it's over, good! And let bygones be bygones. I felt no need at all for vengeance.[30]

So pardon as virtue, pardon as guilt and political error, pardon as repugnance for 'beating them hollow' and as a desire to forget, interweave with the violence in those days of April and May 1945.[31] Formally, the matter was settled in Milan by the ordinance of the prefect, the Actionist Riccardo Lombardi, who

27 Letter to the CLN *questore* of La Spezia, May 1945, from the commander of the 4th operations zone, who invoked 'the moral imperative to defend law and freedom, which was principally conquered by us ourselves' (quoted in Chiara Federici, degree thesis).

28 Calamandrei, *La vita indivisibile*, p. 232.

29 Testimony of the partisan Renato Fracassi, a survivor of Mauthausen and Gusen I, in Bravo and Jalla, *La vita offesa*, p. 375.

30 Testimony of Attilio Armando, partisan, survivor of Flossenburg and Zwickau, ibid., pp. 345–6.

31 Renato Castaldi, a worker at Galileo in Florence, spoke of the many people for whom it was not important to ram home their triumph, once they believed that victory was theirs (Contini, *Memoria e storia*, p. 128). A popular poet from Terni later sang 'And dear comrade I want to tell you / It was a mistake to pardon those people' (Portelli, *Biografia di una città*, p. 300).

ordered 'the immediate suspension of arbitrary executions following summary proceedings by formations of volunteers and self-styled volunteers'.[32]

For many years the neo-Fascist press spoke of 300,000 people killed that April. The government waited until 1952 before giving the Chamber of Deputies, through the minister of the interior, Mario Scelba, the figure of 1,732 killed, supplied, it seems, by the General Headquarters of the *carabinieri*. Neither figure is very credible – one because it is excessive, the other because it falls short, despite its flaunted precision. It is almost impossible to work out rigorous data on this score: the very viscosity of the civil war makes such data difficult to trace. In their absence, here is Giorgio Bocca's estimate: 3,000 killed in Milan and between 12,000 and 15,000 in the whole of Northern Italy.[33]

The episode that symbolically sums up the violence during those days was the shooting of Mussolini and the hanging by the feet in Piazzale Loreto of his body, together with those of Clara Petacci and eighteen Fascist *gerarchi*.

The legality of the executions that occurred at Dongo stems from the complex institutional system that sustained the last phase of the Resistance, and then the insurrection. Without going too far back, on 12 April 1945 the CLNAI, ordering his capture, had denounced Mussolini and the members of the Fascist directorate as 'traitors to the country and war criminals';[34] and we have seen what consequences a declaration of this sort automatically involved. After the execution, the CLNAI fully endorsed it, deprecating only 'the explosion of popular hate which has on this single occasion gone so far as to produce excesses' – which was imputable, however, 'to the climate desired and created by Mussolini'.[35]

Italy, unlike France and England, had no regicides in its history as watersheds between opposing epochs. It had never fractured the monistic vision of power with the 'final decapitation of the king as symbol'.[36] Italy, the late comer even in this field had, in the very middle of the twentieth century, the execution of the Duce. Occurring in broad daylight, but without mob participation, along the road between Dongo and Giulino di Mezzegra, that execution of the charismatic leader fleeing 'disguised as a German'[37] was, immediately afterwards, made public in Piazzale Loreto. And in the most macabre manner, reviving the tradition of the dead body of the tyrant to be displayed to the people, and paying back Fascism, which had practised it in the self-same place, with the spectacle

---

32 The ordinance was published in *La Libertà*, Milan paper of the PLI, 1 May.

33 Bocca, *La Repubblica di Mussolini*, p. 339, featuring a brief examination of the various different estimates made. See also Isnenghi, *La guerra civile nella pubblicistica di destra*, pp. 104–6.

34 See *Atti CLNAI*, p. 295.

35 See the 29 April 1945 declaration, ibid., pp. 334–5.

36 These words appear in Foa, *La Gerusalemme rimandata*, p. 268.

37 This expression is used by G. Carocci in *Storia del fascismo*, Milan: Garzanti, 1972, p. 151

of the exhibition of the corpses. The symbolic value of this repayment, however, went very deep: the Duce's body, invulnerable to so many assassination attempts, was now hanging upended and lifeless.[38] And upended too was the Fascist symbology of the lictor's axe as an instrument of executions: the victim now was the Duce of Fascism himself, defeated and guilty. A sort of *lex talionis* was being put into practice, on the assumption that, in this case too, the 'forms of the execution referred to the nature of the crime'.[39] The killing of Clara Petacci, which had not been bargained for, was due to the fidelity, worthy of respect, that she showed to the person of Mussolini. But the exhibition of her corpse came to appear as a moralistic and public punishment for the tyrant's lasciviousness and a debunking of the myth, which had been cultivated so strenuously, of his virility.[40]

Piazzale Loreto lies, therefore, midway between 'posthumous lynching' and the 'splendour of the executions' which, with the 'spectacle of public punishment', engenders the fear that that spectacle might 'accustom the spectators to a ferocity from which one wished to divert them'.[41] Hence the emphasis on the exceptional character of the event to which the nature of a unique, unrepeatable last act of the tragedy, of 'an epilogue that had been amply prepared for in the years of war', was attributed by one and all.[42] Luigi Meneghello, who 'in his heart of hearts exulted' but feared that the 'upended puppet' might become 'our scapegoat', has subsequently written that 'naturally it was necessary to rid ourselves of Fascism in a way that was perceptible to the senses'.[43]

The huge crowd that immediately flocked to the scene reacted in ways in which the tragic and historic meaning of the situation seemed to get lost. 'An infantile people would have been the only way to describe those who clustered into Piazzale Loreto throughout the day to contemplate the illustrious corpses, recognisable by now only from the signs pinned to their clothes' – wrote one

---

38 On the symbolic significance of their being dangled upside-down in Piazzale Loreto, see Passerini, *Torino operaia*, p. 120 and n. 90, and her 'L'immagine di Mussolini: specchio dell'immaginario e promessa di identità', in *Rivista di storia contemporanea* XIV (1986), pp. 322–3.

39 Foucault, *Discipline and Punish*, p. 56. Fascist Party secretary Achille Starace suffered the blowback from his own lack of mercy: the man who had made the *gerarchi* jump through rings of fire was himself shot and hanged by his feet, dressed in sporting gear.

40 'We also have the Duce and Petacci here', said the widow of Leo Lanfranco – killed by Fascists – when a spy and his lover 'who had gone along with him' were shot in Turin (testimony of Rosanna Rolando, in Bruzzone and Farina, *La Resistenza taciuta*, p. 29).

41 'Technically, the Duce was not lynched, but just killed. The lynching part happened after, posthumously' (Meneghello, *Bau-sète*, p. 39). The other quotes are from Foucault, *Discipline and Punish*, p. 20.

42 Gallerano, *Gli italiani in guerra*, p. 321.

43 Meneghello, *Bau-sète*, pp. 38, 40.

eyewitness to whom the spectacle did not seem up to the standard of that revolutionary morality, that 'furor del popolo' which alone might justify it.[44] The
following comment is inspired by a still blunter intransigence:

> *Sic transit gloria mundi*: thus ends the glory constructed with violence and false-
> hood. They have paid, and this is right. But the scene is disgusting all the same:
> because the immense crowd now shoving their way forward towards those corpses
> is the same one that once trembled and lauded them when they were living men,
> at the height of their power and infamy. The crowd has remained servile as they
> were then. The Italian people has not liberated itself of its masters: it has crushed
> and killed them because they have been defeated by the Anglo-Americans. Now
> it presents the corpses to the victors, as Ptolemy offered the head of Pompey
> to Caesar.[45]

Another witness, a partisan mounting guard over some Fascist prisoners,
told one of them what he had seen in such terms that 'what emerged was the
picture of a festival, a sort of popular fête. All those folk going there, whole families leading their children by the hand.'[46] An upper-middle-class woman, on her
husband's arm, said: 'Well I never, what nice little legs Petacci had!'[47]

If the 'holiday atmosphere' could be fuelled in some measure by the plain
recognition of the irreversible end of a nightmare, so that the macabre and horrible character of the scene seemed to be placed in parenthesis, this very same
character was underlined instead by the fatuous way people conducted themselves and the comments they made. It was not, however, a spectacle that could
last long, and the Piazzale, to prove that the horror was well and truly over, had
to return quickly to being used for its original purpose – normal living. *L'Italia
Libera* put it discreetly:

> In the square sanctified, a year ago, by the blood of fifteen innocents – and we know
> that the blood of innocents cries out for vengeance in the sight of God – in the
> square there was a spectacle that satisfied every fantasy in search of the macabre …
> But let's empty our minds of that memory, just as the square was emptied, shortly
> after two o'clock, and became once again the city's busiest square, the square of trams
> going into the country, full of workers, trucks, bicycles.[48]

---

44 'Anonimo romagnolo', *1943–45*, p. 471.

45 Delfino Insolera to his brother Italo, 'late April 1945' (my thanks to Italo for
allowing me to quote this).

46 Mazzantini, *A cercar la bella morte*, p. 290.

47 My own recollection.

48 'L'animo di Milano torna a vibrare nel nuovo clima della libertà', signed 'gius.
gor', on the second page of the 30 April edition.

L'Unità's comment was more predictable: it exalted the 'historic importance of the fact that the greatest war criminals have been executed in Jacobin fashion, with an act of popular justice which is the inevitable corollary of the insurrection'. The exhibition of the corpses was written off by the Communist paper with a brief and contemptuous news item: 'The "carrion" of the duce of evildoers, surrounded by a good number of his acolytes, is lying in Piazzale Loreto, exposed to public derision'.[49]

The crowning comment came from *Avanti!*:

> Yesterday on a luminous sunny day a horrible spectacle took place. Necessary like so many horrible punishments … What 'legality' could have redressed the wrong committed, arbitrariness made law, violence erected into a normal part of life? No law, no legality that was not a 'legality' springing spontaneously from the very people who had suffered the affront. And the people have been compelled to execute their tyrant in order to liberate themselves from the nightmare of an irreparable offence … For the Italians there was no other way out … It was the only catharsis possible … Perhaps those who were all too willing to see Fascism only as a droll comedy will understand today what a tragedy it has really been for us, who have endured it, who have paid for it to the bitter end.[50]

---

49 'Giustizia è fatta', 30 April 1945 editorial.

50 Title across the whole front page, 30 April: 'The shooting of Mussolini and his accomplices is the necessary conclusion of a historical phase'. On the Piazzale Loreto events, see M. Isnenghi, 'Il corpo del duce', in S. Bertelli and C. Grottanelli, eds, *Gli occhi di Alessandro. Potere sovrano e sacralità del corpo da Alessandro Magno a Ceausescu*, Laboratorio di Storia, 2, Florence: Ponte alle Grazie, 1990, pp. 170–93, and M. Dondi, 'Piazzale Loreto 29 aprile: aspetti di una pubblica esposizione', in *Rivista di storia contemporanea* XIX (1990), pp. 219–48.

Politics and Future Expectations

1. POLITICS AND MORALITY

The *resistenti*'s relationship with politics did not end with their tie with the parties and their coalition in the CLNs.[1] The Resistance was in fact one of those moments in which politics figured as a tendentially all-engaging commitment – not in the sense that everything was seen, essentially, as being political, but in that many important needs aspired, in the eagerness to fulfil them, to take a political form and at the same time to go beyond politics in the name of the profound significance attributed to a future intensely desired. This attitude, which met with some resistance, bore with it many ambiguities; but, to use the language of current debate, it was the opposite both of the 'autonomy of politics' and of 'political exchange': in no way did political action occupy a separate sphere; nor did it figure only in the column of costs and sacrifices, but already in the credit column of benefits.[2] In the Resistance the relationship between politics, seen as a choice of ends and values and the means of practising them, and morality, was thus central, because the widening of the field open to moral judgment could not but involve politics first and foremost.

A partisan concentration camp survivor gratefully recalls a comrade because 'he was a man who without saying a word taught you the ABC of life. That was called political activity.'[3]

The technique and exercise of power were not therefore seen as the be-all and end-all of political action. Politics acquired once again a utopian function contemporaneously with its fundamental commitment to the here and now. It was precisely those who most aspired to concreteness to whom an only apparently backward passage from science to utopia seemed indispensable.[4] Reticence about instrumental politicisation, which even Ferruccio Parri had displayed

---

1 See Chapter 3.2.

2 For an example of this type of critique of the theory of political exchange, see Hirschman, *Shifting Involvements*, pp. 94–100.

3 Testimony of Raffaele Maruffi, mechanical engineer born in 1924 (Bravo and Jalla, *La vita offesa*, p. 195).

4 This image was used, with regard to the *impegno meridionalista* (i.e. post-war efforts to develop the socio-economic conditions of the South of Italy), by Rossi-Doria in his 1967 report *L'osso e la polpa dell'agricoltura meridionale*. See M. De Benedictis, 'Manlio Rossi-Doria', in *Belfagor* XLV (1990), pp. 284–5.

initially,[5] and the desire to give pride of place to the armed struggle in order to avoid being accused of indulging in party politics,[6] could both lead to a reductive vision of politics. But there existed, as both the basis and development of the initial decision to resist, a way of being political in which the deep convictions and inclinations of individuals and the contexts in which they operated found expression. A perfect example of this is the episode recounted in the form of a fable by Roberto Battaglia. It had to be decided whether to arrest a collaborationist industrialist, and if so whether to condemn him to death. On the first point the Communist was of the view that, as far as possible, the individual should be blackmailed and exploited for information, and only then arrested. The Christian Democrat agreed, but added that collaborationism was rife in Italy and that it would be unjust to make one person pay for everyone – and that, in any case, if arrested, the individual would have to be sent behind the lines to be given a regular trial by the Allied or Italian authorities. The Actionist considered that it would be a moral wrong exceeding other considerations to let an arms profiteer go free, and thus that one should proceed with his immediate arrest. When this occurred, the Communist claimed that the ransom offered by the family should be accepted, though without taking any account of it at the trial to which the industrialist had in any case to be subjected: that way he would simply have been made to give back 'at least in part, what he had stolen'. The Christian Democrat declared himself unqualified to speak, but asked the others to bear in mind the family conditions of the accused: 'There is already quite enough grief in Italy without adding to it with a ruthless act of repression.' The Actionist expressed the conviction that there was grave and clear proof justifying the death sentence, and objected to the Communist that 'the task of partisans is to see that justice is done; but in no way can one exploit the grief of an innocent family'. Battaglia's comment (and he should be identified with the Actionist) is that the views expressed on that occasion 'can throw more light on the nature of the Italian parties than any statement ... of their programmes'.[7]

These basic character studies did not necessarily coincide with formal adhesion to parties, given that in situations like that of the Resistance 'the very

---

5 See 'Intervista sulla guerra partigiana', an interview he gave to L. La Malfa Calogero and M.V. de Filippis, pp. 22–4. Note the statement that 'military formations are not the place for doing politics' in 'Proposte di una delibera del CLNAI per la costituzione di una commissione responsabile delle operazioni militari in Lombardia', late December 1943 (*Atti CVL*, Appendix 1, paragraph 5).

6 Though himself very political, the Garibaldian commissar Eros (Didimo Ferrari: see the fine pages devoted to him in Battaglia, *Un uomo*) wrote, together with the commander Monti, that 'doing politics merely means preparing the body, will and spirit for action' (report on 'operational activity', late October 1944 (?), IG, *BG, Emilia-Romagna*, G.IV).

7 Battaglia, *Un uomo*, pp. 186–9.

concept of adhesion to a party represents ... something infinitely more demanding but, at the same time, more elastic from the merely formal point of view than
any sort of regular "membership".[8]

Here the writer is mainly thinking about the Communist Party; but an
Actionist gives a similar description of the non-pedagogic but maieutic politicisation that occurred in the GL bands by means of few words and many actions,
in order to bring to light in the consciousness of each individual the 'ideals', the
'political motives', the 'historical reasons for the struggle' that were 'in the air'
and 'in the very reality surrounding the partisan'.[9] A sober description of how,
for that matter, politics gained ground in its own particular way in the Osoppo
brigades is given by Galliano Fogar, intent on squeezing all the positive juices
out of the much acclaimed apolitical character of those formations.[10]

There was a widespread conviction that politics constituted a duty. It was
as if, having turned away from the state that had failed, morality was seeking
a way of redefining its public dimension. A Garibaldi news-sheet announced
that a worker, a priest and a soldier had found that they all agreed that one had
a duty to participate in political life if one wished to avoid scourges such as
Nazi-Fascism repeating themselves.[11] There was some truth behind this instrumental unitary rhetoric. Addressing the 'Piedmontese workers of the land', an
Action Party leaflet urged them to concern themselves actively with politics: 'It
is time to convince ourselves that politics is a dirty business only when it is in the
hands of shady politico profiteers, as it was during the Fascist regime'.[12]

The partisans sought a way out of vulgar, trumpeting Fascist pan-politicism
not along the road that was to be the fortune of the 'Uomo Qualunque' movement, and would be successfully taken by the Christian Democrats as well, but
in vindicating the morality of politics and denouncing the fact that, beneath its
rhetoric, Fascism had prospered from the depoliticisation of the Italians.[13] In a
letter written to his friends before he was arrested, Giacomo Ulivi put his finger
on the fundamental contradiction that had, ultimately, marked the message
transmitted by Fascism: that politics is a dirty business and, at the same time, a
business reserved for specialists: 'We have copped out', wrote Ulivi, and here are

---

8 M.A. and S. Timpanaro, 'Introduzione' in G. and E. Varlecchi, *Potente*, p. 33.

9 Bianco, *Guerra partigiana*, pp. 62–3, on a document he drew up on 26 March
1944 in his role as a political commissar: later published in part in *Formazioni GL*,
pp. 78–80.

10 Fogar, *Le brigate Osoppo-Friuli*, p. 286

11 'Bollettino n. 43', by the Command of the 52nd Luigi Clerici Brigade, 22 August
1944 (IG, *BG*, 0625).

12 INSMLI, *CLNAI*, envelope 8, folder 12.

13 It would be interesting to compare this Resistance understanding with the
results of the historiography which, beginning with the studies of Alberto Aquarone, has
insisted on the gradual 'depoliticisation' of the Fascist Party.

the results, now that in political life we have been 'shunted aside by events. It's here that we're to blame.'[14] Equally unsparing about the Italians having placed their welfare in the charge of others is a Liberal pamphlet that concludes: 'They have given this sloth a new name: *gerarchia*.'[15]

'Accusa agli onesti' was the title of a leaflet of the Christian Democratic Movement of Modena; and the accusation was that 'serious, honest and able men' had kept away from politics 'on the basis of the old and anti-democratic mentality that the decent man, the serious person, ought not to interest himself in politics'. This stance was all the more remarkable for the fact that, coming from Catholics, the meanness of the 'selfish personal and family circle' was denounced: this was the only way to account for the fact – the essential point in the argument – that, in the absence of honest men, so many good-for-nothings had ended up among the partisans.[16] A Liberal newspaper traced the Italians' lack of interest in politics back 'to the years immediately preceding the advent of Fascism, which had in fact been engendered by that lack of interest. This was certainly historically false, if we consider the fervour of the *biennio rosso*, but, besides helping the Liberals to disassociate themselves from the responsibilities of the ruling class to which they intended to re-associate themselves, it was nevertheless a contribution to stances in favour of political engagement.[17] The Actionist Giorgio Diena wrote: not 'save us from the state!', but 'let us all be politicians!'[18] Clearly expressed, in some of these exhortations, is the anxiety to have done with selfishness and the invitation to ensure that it did not triumph at the very moment of deliverance.[19] On this score, even the fiery polemics against *attesismo* acquire a significance that goes beyond the mere incitement to fight. The aim now was to shake the Italians out of their atavistic inferiority, soaked in sloth. A medical student, a fine and active fellow, who declared that he had no political opinions, received this answer from Emanuele Artom: 'I wouldn't get that kind of answer from a young Russian or American of your age.'

In his impassioned apologia for political commitment, Artom draws a contrast between the workers who, 'driven by need, have concerned themselves in these years with political problems and have matured', and the 'foolish bourgeois

14 *LRI*, pp. 228–31 (the letter is from summer/autumn 1944; Ulivi was shot on 10 November of that year).

15 'Il principio (Orientamenti liberali)', edited by the Piedmont section of the PLI (supplement to issue 5 of *L'Opinione*, n.d).

16 The text is quoted in Gorrieri, *La Repubblica di Montefiorino*, pp. 390–1. See 'La Democrazia cristiana invita i giovani a lavorare per un'Italia migliore', editorial of the 25 September 1944 Northern edition of *Il Popolo*.

17 'Risveglio', *Risorgimento Liberale*, Rome edition, 15 March 1944.

18 Diena, *La rivoluzione minimalista*, p. 8.

19 As *Giustizia e Libertà. Notiziario dei patrioti delle Alpi Cozie*, April 1944, put it (quoted in Giovana, *Storia di una formazione partigiana*, p. 105).

youths … intellectually lazy and morally sceptical'.[20] But it was not just a question of economic drives. Fascism's depoliticising of people made words like the following particularly true: 'There is a sadness in the worker for whom the only medicine is political action'.[21] 'Comrade worker, listen!' was the title of an article in *Avanti!* which, in tones rather similar to those of Edmondo De Amicis, explained to the workers that it was not true that politics was a mug's game.[22] There were great expectations, also, in the parallel peasants' movements of the South,[23] for 'political answers' to the great questions emerging from Italian society.[24]

The risks that could arise from this view of politics – and it was a view of politics which at that moment was fast gaining strength – are clearly expressed in the retrospective testimonies of two leading figures: Fede and Roselli (as Carlo Levi rechristened them in his novel *L'Orologio*). Vittorio Foa has written, almost apologetically, that, immediately after the Liberation, 'many of us fell in love at that time with the technique of politics', which he sets alongside poetry and truth: 'and all of us fell for it together, poets (like Carlo Levi, Emilio Lussu, Guido Dorso and Ferruccio Parri) and *tecnici* alike'.[25] Altiero Spinelli speaks of many 'who without batting an eyelid took on the heavy commitment of anti-Fascists and partisans, and when all that was over, felt that it had been an ethical impulse of civil courage that had driven them along this path, but that they had no real political passion; and set their minds to other things, as peaceful citizens'.[26]

In Foa's words, there was nostalgia for the unity of politics, poetry and truth that was experienced in the blissful season of the Resistance, and together with this, though more secret, the aspiration not to renounce it.[27] In Spinelli's words, by contrast, there is the reminder of the harsh difference between politics and ethics: a harshness symbolised by that taste for command which in his clandestine and prison encounters had made him feel close to Pietro Secchia.[28]

---

20 Artom, *Diari*, p. 151 (26 January 1944).

21 The words of 'machine shop worker' Georges Navel in his *Travaux*, cited – though not agreeing with him – by Caffi, *Critica della violenza*, p. 93.

22 Rome edition, 12 January 1944.

23 See A. Rossi-Doria, *Il ministro e i contadini. Decreti Gullo e lotte nel Mezzogiorno (1944–1949)*, Rome: Bulzoni, 1983.

24 F. Traniello, 'Stato e partiti alle origini della Repubblica nel dibattito storiografico', in *Italia contemporanea* 135 (April–June 1979), pp. 3–15, esp. p. 5.

25 Foa, *Carlo Levi*, pp. 50–1.

26 Spinelli, *Io, Ulisse*, p. 117.

27 Note the sharpness with which Foa claimed that the parties had failed their first anti-Fascist duty: 'to tell the truth' (Inverni, *I partiti*, p. 17).

28 Spinelli, *Io, Ulisse*, p. 102. As he began to distance himself from the PCI, Spinelli remained moved by 'Secchia's immense rescue effort, which I could only manage to explain with the idea that he, at heart, wanted to save a friend, showing what was, for a Bolshevik, a reproachable weakness' (ibid., p. 247).

It was this all-embracing character, which politics tended to acquire in the Resistance experience, that revived within it the inevitable polarity between means and ends. This polarity rubbed shoulders uneasily with the aspiration to reunify oneself – 'an intimate accord of each of us with himself', Roberto Battaglia calls it[29] – that was at the root of the genuine decision to resist. The higher the stakes, and the greater the conviction that, 'at the present historical moment ... politics finds its true embodiment in ethics',[30] the more seriously one came to realise that 'political action often involves one in other activities of a very different nature – making strange alliances, dissimulating one's real objectives, betraying yesterday's friends – all of this, naturally, in the interest of the final 'end'.[31]

The conflict between the claims of 'verità' and those of 'tecnica' is evident in Anna Cinanni's account of her arrest. Interrogated, she denied everything: 'However, I did not want to renounce my ideal, renounce saying that I was indeed anti-Fascist. It was a question of principle for me; I could not, I did not want to renounce saying it.'[32]

What I have called the urge to reunify oneself was a way of reacting against the divorce between words and facts which, in Fascism, had been one of the things that 'most affronted human reason'.[33] In sociological language, Fascism had wanted both to 'mobilise' and 'demobilise' the population. Gino Germani, who has analysed this process, has shown how it leads to the apathy of the many and the fanaticism of the few – conformists in substance, fanatics in form.[34] The decision to resist aimed at overcoming this dichotomy, while that of the RSI militants exacerbated it in the vain hope of salvation. Even within the Catholic faith sincerely experienced, participation in the Resistance could come to mean a way out of a specific, individual contradiction within oneself: 'I received a religious upbringing in my family, but felt an abyss between the catechism and the lifeless and selfish actions that I and the others around me, even the members of my family, were performing.'[35]

29 Battaglia, *Un uomo*, p. 80. See also pp. 5, 6.

30 'Origini del movimento', *Bollettino Popolo e Libertà*, 1, pp. 2–3.

31 Hirschman, *Shifting Involvements*, p. 100, with reference not only to Machiavelli but also to Sartre's *Mains sales*. 'Sartre's epigones' have developed a true 'Manichean myth' around this play: 'to act implies sacrifice, in the superstitious sense of the term', forcing one to 'reduce to ashes that which one holds most dear'. E. Morin, 'La dialectique et l'action', in *Arguments*, April–May 1958, p. 13, quoted by L. Sciolla, 'Opposizione intellettuale e PCF: l'esperienza di "Arguments"', in *Rivista di storia contemporanea* X (1981), p. 132.

32 Bruzzone and Farina, *La Resistenza taciuta*, p. 110.

33 V. Foa, 'Le strutture economiche e la politica economica del regime fascista', in *Fascismo e antifascismo (1918–1948). Lezioni e testimonianze*, Milan: Feltrinelli, 1962, p. 281.

34 Germani, *Autoritarismo*, especially the concluding pages.

35 'Abbiamo intervistato un partigiano', in *Voce Operaia*, 19 November 1943.

'A state that obliges its subjects to become hypocrites works against its own interests':[36] it was precisely this that Fascism had done; and now a game which over the years had become more and more bare-faced and oppressive had to be unmasked. The Fascist ruling class had never felt sufficiently secure, and at the same time were too demagogic to parade, let alone practise, a dual morality.[37] They had thereby deprived themselves of the allure that the splendour of vices can exercise, without even managing to transform their hypocrisy into the homage paid to virtue.

Testimonies abound of this desire for coherence that was felt in the Resistance. A more difficult matter is to try to identify its contents, ambiguities and residues that had not been reabsorbed.

'Immediate coherence with their professed ideas is demanded of members, the only valid guarantee in times in which words have lost all value': this declaration, dictated by a minor group,[38] could well have been underwritten by a wide circle of resistenti. 'A New Set of Mores' is what Libérer et Fédérer, Silvio Trentin's newspaper, had called for on 5 January 1943 against political schemers. 'Gobettian sobriety', which was Dante Livio Bianco's constant point of reference, is another formula that synthesises this attitude, and that is echoed in Beppe Fenoglio's prophecy of an Italy that will be 'small but terribly serious'.[39] The formula would reoccur, with a show of irony that ill succeeds in concealing regret, in the words of another leading figure: 'It seemed to me ... that any hope I had had of making my private life somehow or other coincide with the public life of my country (which I had unfortunately believed to be the be-all and end-all of life) was dead.'[40]

2. PUBLIC AND PRIVATE

The commitment to reunifying conscience and to making action coherent with it therefore raised the question once more of the relationship between public and private. In recent years, which have been distinguished by the rediscovery of the value of 'the private', the Resistance, with the petering out of the wholly political accusations levelled at it from the left for having failed to transform itself into revolution, has been the target of the no less harsh criticism that it devoted scant attention to the private aspects of life, or indeed that it wholly sacrificed them.

---

36 Todorov, 'La tolleranza e l'intollerabile', p. 95, paraphrasing Spinoza.

37 'Only a ruling class which feels itself to be threatened is afraid to flaunt a double standard'. E.P. Thompson, Customs in Common, London: Merlin, p. 55.

38 'Dichiarazione costitutiva', by the Partito Italiano del Lavoro (pamphlet 'Partito italiano del lavoro – "Popolo e Libertà"', January 1944, p. 32).

39 See Bianco, Guerra partigiana, and Fenoglio, Il partigiano Johnny, p. 182.

40 Meneghello, Bau-sète, p. 69.

Speaking of his difficult relationship with his father Piero, Franco Calamandrei has given a thoughtful testimony on that dual border zone between the public and the private and between generations, which shaped the 'moral chiaroscuro that had hitherto remained on the sidelines' of the 'autobiography' of anti-Fascism. Calamandrei asks this question:

> Might it not be that also the separation between 'public' and 'private', if not the ousting of the 'private' by the 'public', which has become more accentuated in Italian life in these last few decades and has contributed to young people's estrangement from politics, had an embryo, at the origins of the present post-Fascist phase, in the relative obliteration of sentiments and persons in favour of ideologies, parties, classes, which, since those origins represent the memory of anti-Fascism, has oper- ated on objective laws, almost as one of the necessary conditions for re-founding politics rationally?[1]

For the majority of the combatants of the Fascist war the 'private' had been a refuge – memory, nostalgia, prefiguration of the return home – against being overwhelmed by a 'public' that they felt extraneous to them. In most *resistenti* the positions tended to be inverted, and the private, initially an instrument of salvation, became a risk of perdition. Analysing Giorgio Caproni's *I denti di Ada*, Giovanni Falaschi concluded that the private dimension of life was felt in the Resistance to be a snare. There is some truth in this observation, which Falaschi supports with a quotation from the Catholic Teresio Olivelli: 'rid yourself of the temptation of your affections';[2] but things do not end there. When Nazi-Fascist totalitarianism was over, there was a definite and active awareness that shut- ting oneself up in the isolation of one's private life had been one of the actual causes of totalitarianism, even if it did not have the critical clarity later given it by Hannah Arendt.[3] Hidden beneath a sometimes nobly rhetorical form was personal shame and respect for proportions: What! The world is ablaze and here am I thinking about my individual circumstances! Hidden too is a thread of subterranean regret at not having enjoyed one's private life more authentically when there was still time, interwoven with guilt at having possibly enjoyed it too much, until the terrible blow that had befallen the world. In *Una questione privata* Fenoglio chronologically traced the relationship between public and

---

1 F. Calamandrei, 'Piero Calamandrei mio padre', essay introducing P. Calamandrei, *Diario 1939–1945*, Florence: La Nuova Italia, 1982, pp. xii–xiii.

2 Falaschi, *La Resistenza armata*, pp. 163, 165. This concerned the story of a partisan who had to shoot a girl as a spy, but feared that he might previously have known her. But then he could tell from her teeth that this was not the case, and shot her without further hesitation.

3 See Arendt, *The Origins of Totalitarianism*, New York: Harcourt, Brace & Co., 1951, Part III.

private. 'The things of before – later, later!': where the 'things of before' are girls, who today 'are laughable. Disgusting and pathetic ... given the life we're leading and the job we're doing it takes nothing to go to pieces.'[4] It was hard to distinguish the 'private' from a normality that the emergency situation, fully accepted, made appear distant, extraneous and even inimical. At Villa Paganini, in Rome, Franco Calamandrei listens to 'the little girl saying to her governess "Miss, may I take off my coat?" What with everything that is happening or what you'd like to be happening, you feel on the other side of an abyss.'[5]

Public commitment, which has inscribed in it the dichotomy between life and death stripped to the bone, was loath to represent itself as a mere parenthesis; but was pervaded at the same time by nostalgia for the serenity of a normality that at times would come to be experienced as renunciation. 'When the war was over we got married', because 'then I couldn't, I didn't have time'; but then when this partisan got married and, at her husband's request, left political activity, 'this meant no longer being able to sleep! I grieved and suffered enormously.'[6] Another *resistente*, a Communist since 1940, said: 'I had the impression that with marriage everything would come to an end ... political commitment, personal freedom, the possibility of choosing.'[7] In women's testimonies the laceration between public and private appears particularly powerful and explicit; but it can also be experienced as obvious, to the extreme case of the partisan whose boyfriend was in the Black Brigades, 'but set great store by keeping personal affections and politics apart.'[8]

The years following the Liberation were to see the coexistence of regret for lost unity and remorse at not having managed to seize that exceptional opportunity to renew one's own individual life more completely.

It has been written about the crisis of the 1968 movement, but could equally well apply to that of the Resistance: 'When the movement flows again, the personal and the political always part ways again; the memory of unity rightly becomes again an obstacle to the suppression of the personal within the political, but at the same time, dangerously and ambiguously, again facilitates the suppression of the political within the separateness of the personal sphere.'[9]

But when the unity of the movement, never as great as it is made out to be, has led to the sacrifice of its two constituent parts, then one can say that

4 B. Fenoglio, *Una questione privata*, Milan: Garzanti, 1965, p. 28.

5 Calamandrei, *La vita indivisibile*, p. 119 (4 November 1943).

6 Testimony of Nelia Benissone Costa, in Bruzzone and Farina, *La Resistenza taciuta*, p. 60.

7 Testimony of Milan's Ida Rovelli in *A voi cari compagni*, p. 69.

8 Cicchetti, *Il campo giusto*, p. 220.

9 R. Sbardella, 'Movimento reale e critica della politica', in L. Vitale and C. Pavone, eds, *Contro l'autonomia della politica*, Turin: Rosenberg & Sellier, 1978, p. 64 ('Quaderni di Fabbrica e Stato', 6–7).

'militant ideology leaves the trenches of the individual life unmanned; and the territory that two centuries or so of the history of secular thought managed to remove from the theologians is on the point of falling into the hands of the necromancers'.[10]

One of the spheres in which public and private, collective and individual, interwove is that of the personal relations between the *resistenti*. Here things moved in two inverse but convergent directions: friendship evolved into political kinship and political kinship generated friendship. The trust between partisans, writes Battaglia, 'is a joy and a necessity': there was in fact the need for 'something that warmed determination with a sentiment'.[11] Ada Gobetti gave her diary this epigraph: 'It was precisely friendship – a bond of solidarity, founded not on blood relationship, or country, or intellectual tradition, but on the simple human relationship of feeling that you were two people together among many – that seemed to me to be the intimate significance, the hallmark of our battle.'[12]

Among the false foundations of friendship Ada Gobetti listed not class and party, but the *patria*. In her view, the urge to reconquer national identity was evidently not enough, after the degradations of National-Fascism, to recover Michelet's concept of one's country as 'the great friendship that contains all the others'. But many traces of the route traced by Michelet were present in the Resistance experience, by whatever name one might wish to call the final outlet:

> Our individual friendships are like the first steps of this great initiation, stations through which the soul passes, and gradually ascends to know and love each other on a higher, a better, a more disinterested plane that is called the fatherland.[13]

Ada Gobetti identifies friendship with solidarity. In fact, solidarity covered a wider, and in any case different, field than both friendship and politics, and revealed what it essentially was precisely when it sprung up between people who had neither personal nor political relations with one another. A girl who had been a partisan dispatch-rider, continuing all the while to go to school, later had this to say about what had motivated her: 'I don't know whether out of ideals or out of friendship. Perhaps for both reasons ... in this way I was taking part in what my comrades in the mountains were going through.' And another girl: 'What did I know of Communism and Fascism and things like that, at fifteen!

---

10 I. Calvino, 'La sfida al labirinto', in *Il Menabò di letteratura* 5 (1962), p. 95.

11 Battaglia, *Un uomo*, pp. 60–1.

12 Gobetti, *Diario partigiano*, p. 15.

13 J. Michelet, *Le peuple*, Brussels: Meline, Cans et Compagnie, 1846, pp. 205–6; with these words begins Chapter 1, 'L'amitié', of part III, 'De l'affranchissement par l'amour: La Patrie'.

I was a child! I went to take food to my partisan brothers. Who wouldn't have done it?'[14]

The meaning of friendship is extended in the 'Dichiarazione costitutiva' of the Italian Labour Party: 'Relations between party members will naturally be those among "friends" who love and respect one another, by virtue of the fact that their lives are inspired by the same ideal and that they have passed through the same sieve.' The rigour of this small group went so far as to sanction these relations between friends economically: all its members 'recognise the party's right to make use of their private assets, movable or immovable, at any given time, with the exception of articles of everyday use and the house they live in'.[15] A newspaper published by the group commented that with this 'direct and immediate testimony … we intend to anticipate, as far as is possible, the kind of society in which we believe'.[16]

The literature about the death camps and prisoner-of-war camps has shown how hard it was to reconcile solidarity with self-protection, when what was at stake was physical survival.[17] The *resistenti*, in general, were not put to such atrocious tests except when, subjected to torture, they had the lives of their comrades in their hands. Above all in the mountain bands friendship and solidarity became unaffected, cheerful fraternity. This was more a sincerely experienced fact than a carefully worked out programme.

The theoretical degrading that *fraternité* had suffered in the great revolutionary triad was not, in fact, redressed by the Resistance. If, because of its Proudhonian components, Silvio Trentin's *Libérer et Fédérer* had greatly insisted on the theme of solidarity, which was the version of fraternity assimilated by the workers' movement,[18] Proudhon does not seem to have been given prominent space in the Italian underground press. His name appears in what is at least an anomalous setting, *La Democrazia del Lavoro*, organ of the party of that name, consisting of old and grey, mainly southern, transformists.[19]

Solidarity as a category has been widely used to interpret the relations between the partisans and the population, especially the peasant population. The Allied prisoners who had escaped, above all at the beginning, were astonished

14 Testimonies of Maria Luisa Fasana Oggero and Natalina Bianco Giai (Bravo and Jalla, *La vita offesa*, p. 108).

15 *Partito italiano del lavoro* – 'Popolo e Libertà, January 1944.

16 'Conoscerci', *La Voce dei giovani*, 1 August 1944 (very likely written by Delfino Insolera).

17 On all this, see the chapter 'Conflitto, solidarietà, organizzazione', in Levi, *I sommersi e i salvati*.

18 See, on this development, A. Lay, 'Un' etica per la classe: dalla fraternità universale alla solidarietà operaia', in *Rivista di storia contemporanea* XVIII (1989), pp. 309–35.

19 The 20 March 1944 edition featured the subheading: 'We take liberty as our principle, equality as our means, fraternity as our end. Proudhon.'

and struck by the welcome they were given by the peasants.[20] An episode of extraordinary symbolic force was that of the Romagna peasant who washed the feet of an Allied soldier and was shot by the Fascists for the 'moral poverty and irresponsible servility' to which he had 'taken his sense of hospitality'.[21]

Friendship reduced the distance between public and private; but the ties established through it could sorely try the distinction, which is always a tension as well, between the two. Just as fraternity could slide towards terror and just as solidarity could represent itself in contorted guise in reprisals, so friendship proved inadequate to establish political relations single-handed. Saint-Just had written the noblest pages on friendship; but his attributing to it the character of a civic virtue had led him to the aberrant conclusion that 'he who declares that he does not believe in friendship should be outlawed' and 'if a man commits a crime, may his friends be outlawed'.[22] Those who saw religion as the foundation of human relations could declare the firm distinction between 'religious contact' – almost a sublimation of friendship – which 'occurs on a strictly personal plane, from soul to soul', and politics, 'which is created by mobilising masses and not individuals': political living is for everyone, political action only for a few.[23]

It is easy to see how in the Communist Catholics this distinction, which was in tune with their conception of politics as 'tecnica', favoured peaceful coexistence between Catholicism and Communism as well as an implicit appeal to the elitist doctrine of the Leninist party, in which professional revolutionaries must not let themselves be sidetracked by personal affections. 'I have no one, only my mother. First the Party and then my mother', the Communist Ettore Suatoni had said before the Special Tribunal.[24] Gian Carlo Pajetta later wrote: 'I often wondered, then, if there were cases when the "private" should be given pride of place over the "political". I've asked myself the same question at other times in

---

20 See Chapter 4.2, above. Note Hood's memoirs, *Pebbles from my Skull*.

21 Absalom, *Ex prigionieri alleati*, p. 462 and n. 43; Absalom draws his quotes from the article 'Fucilazione di un rinnegato' in *La Santa Milizia*, weekly of the Ravenna PFR *fascio*, of 8 January 1944; he adds that the Allied authorities later refused the shot man's father any compensation, because 'the help he provided was too little to justify any reimbursement'. However, his widow was paid the sum given for fallen 'helpers'.

22 Saint-Just, *Fragments sur les institutions républicaines*, §6, 2.

23 See the articles 'Contattismo e sedentarismo, malatti dei cattolici' and '"Contattismo" e contatto personale' in *Voce Operaia*, 16 December 1943 and 5 January 1944. The polemic was directed against the Catholic practice of operating politically by means of personal contacts (which would, in fact, be one of Christian Democracy's strong points). See also the articles 'Organizzazione rivoluzionaria' and 'Che fare, noi sacerdoti', in the issues of 4 October and 16 December 1943.

24 See Portelli, *Biografia di una città*, p. 231. See the letter from the Austrian Communist Franz Reingruber, who had been sentenced to death, to his mother: 'Yes, this [struggle] has completely absorbed me, but at the very bottom of my heart I loved you with all the intensity with which a son can love' (8 May 1943, in *LRE*, p. 49).

my life. The answer has always been the same: "Never".[25] But one of Fenoglio's characters, an aspiring partisan who became a fervent Garibaldino, replies to the political commissar of the Stella Rossa formation who in the exam that he puts him through includes the question, 'Would you prostitute your sister?', as follows: 'Not me ... I could never bring myself to use my sister like that, it wouldn't remotely occur to me.'[26]

In the Italian Resistance the split between the Communists themselves was partly healed, in the sense that not thinking 'only of oneself but of others too', seen as the essence of Communism,[27] was achieved not solely through one's dedication to the party. Many of the new adherents started by observing the 'shortcomings of the individual' and came to affirm the 'value of communistisation on morality and conscience'[28] – which was a way of expressing, in Communist fashion, what I have earlier called the process of self-reunification. But, in another respect, the divide grew wider. In order not to lose its grip on things, the party ethic, which found itself having to reckon with a far wider and more complex reality than the one it had known in clandestinity, tended to stress some of its more exclusive and severe features, which seemed furthermore to meet military needs extremely well.

This problem comes over particularly clearly in a document written by one of the protagonists (who later proudly vindicated his autonomy as a leader in the absence at that time of directives from Moscow and Togliatti).[29] Pietro Secchia, returning from a visit to the first Garibaldi formations of the Lanzo valleys, sent those comrades a long letter singing the praises of the priority of party organisation over individualism that degenerates into *faso tuto mi* (I do it all by myself). Secchia is unsparing in his criticism of the *famigliarismo* and 'friendly intimacy' 'characterising the whole life of this group, who, rather than soldiers, would

---

25 Pajetta, *Il ragazzo rosso va alla guerra*, p. 34.

26 Fenoglio, *Il padrone paga male*, p. 127.

27 Such was how Artom noted having heard one militant define communism: Artom, *Diari*, p. 102 (4 December 1943).

28 Albero, to the insurrectionary triumvirate for Lombardy, 9 March 1945 (IG, BG, 01880).

29 'At that time we had no "brakes" put on us, neither by events, nor by politicians, Party leaders standing over us [Longo and him] on account of their capacity and authority': a diary entry written in December 1954, *Pietro Secchia, 1945–1973*, ed. E. Collotti ('Annali dell'Istituto Giangiacomo Feltrinelli', XIX, 1978, p. 258). Such a situation of relative autonomy primarily concerned the early months of the Resistance. The Party's 'provisional organisational norms', drawn up by Togliatti in Naples on 27 June 1944, were also printed in the North just after Liberation, as No. 1 of *Le guide dell'organizzatore comunista*, Milan: Tip. Rosia, 1945 (my thanks to Giovanni Verni for supplying me with this information). These 'norms' held that 'every communist is a militant'; it is notable that Togliatti himself rendered the word 'party' with a lower-case 'p' (IG, *Archivio PCI*, 'Direzione. Verbali della Delegazione PCI per l'Italia meridionale').

seem to be composed of good friends who get together animated solely by the pleasure of being in each other's company'. 'Discipline', Secchia explained,

> does not exclude friendship. But it is friendship transformed into teamwork, shared aims, cohesion and union of will for the same end, a bond created in a particular atmosphere that stimulates emulation which brings out the best: so much so that the greatest friends, the true friends, are precisely the best. Because it is a friendship consisting of mutual and profound esteem, not that friendship of 'compaesani' which seems, rather, to be the kind that we have noted.

Two remarks made by Rino (Sandro Radice, one of the letter's addressees) come under particular fire from Secchia: 'My conscience refuses to do wrong to Colonel R., with whom I've always had friendly working relations.' Secchia explodes: 'Never, never let blasphemies like that one come out of the mouths of comrades like you ... The Party, the Party before everything and always.'[30]

Rino had also said: 'Give me your hand, otherwise I won't be able to sleep tonight, after your ruthless criticisms.' Secchia was intransigent:

> And what good do you imagine shaking hands will do? Is it meant to mean simply: friends as before? But scenes like this happen at the theatre, in the family or among friends. But we, beyond being friends, must feel ourselves to be, and to be above all, comrades. It's not with a friend that I want to be *reconciled*, it's with a comrade that I want to come to an *agreement* over this or that question. And when the comrade is a Party envoy, agreeing with this comrade means agreeing with the Party. This is the point. Afterwards, if you like let's drink a bottle and shake hands and ... embrace. But behind that handshake there is to be not the *reconciliation* of two friends, but the affirmation of a party line that we are undertaking to follow, because we're *convinced* it's right.[31]

When Stalin had begun his attack on Bukharin, 'He began by impatiently dismissing sentimental appeals to past friendship (Bukharin had read extracts from intimate letters exchanged): the Bolsheviks were not "a family circle" but a political party.'[32]

---

30 Secchia added 'I go to C ... to Colonel X and all his breed when the Party's interest demands it: that is the norm we live by'. In the margin Luca (Gian Carlo Pajetta) made a note: 'Could we be less *soldier-ish* in the old manner?'

31 The letter, sent from the 'commissar-general Vineis' to the Valle di Lanzo Military Committee, 21 December 1943, published in *Le Brigate Garibaldi*, vol. I, pp. 173–8. Note the article 'Lo spirito di partito', in *L'Unità*, Rome edition, 26 October 1943.

32 E. H. Carr, *A History of Soviet Russia, Foundations of a Planned Economy 1926–1929*, vol. II, London: Macmillan, 1971, p. 91. The passage refers to the Communist Party Central Committee meeting of 16–23 April 1929.

The Italian Communists had not always acted in perfect conformity with this line of conduct. Secchia himself, arriving at Civitavecchia jail after the turning-point of 1930, had pointed this out, availing himself of a judgment expressed by Dmitri Manuilski, who 'had reproached the Italian Communists for their tendency to be indulgent towards the defects of their comrades, and to conceive relations between each other as relations between friends rather than Bolsheviks, that is founded exclusively on loyalty to the Party. All this, however, now, after the turning-point, had to finish.'[33]

But when the very same Secchia – a man, in all other respects, of great humanity – re-encountered Spinelli, who was by that time out of the Party, at Ponza, he treated him with an affection that was reciprocated, because 'with weakness that was reprehensible for a Bolshevik he ultimately wished to save a friend.'[34] After the attempted assassination of Togliatti in 1948, it was again Secchia who said to Togliatti: 'Educate our comrades as friends.'[35] This is a sphere in which the figurative and metaphorical use of words such as friendship, solidarity, fraternity should make us think carefully before judging. It is not in fact easy to distinguish the various planes that intersect, and rarely appear in their pure state, from personal contradictions, cultural superimpositions or political opportunism. In an article about the relations between Togliatti and Longo (a man similar in temperament to Secchia), which *L'Unità* significantly entitled 'A relationship stronger than friendship', Nilde Jotti wrote: 'Togliatti said that if you are the leaders of a party you can't have "friends" among those who share the responsibility of running the party with you … This was a highly moral theory but also a very severe one, a sort of philosophy of solitude.'[36]

Here there is a curious contamination between the isolation of the man of power – classically, the tyrant – and the model of the full-time militant Bolshevik. So exclusive was this model that on the one hand it recreated, among those who succeeded in practising it to the full, 'an almost mystical sense of membership of the same family, of mutual devotion', which was particularly evident in underground and prison experience;[37] while on the other hand it seemed to constitute the only ideal of human perfection that one was able to propose, to the extent that those who still failed to meet it completely came to appear rather

---

33 Spinelli, *Io, Ulisse*, p. 193. Spinelli had been no less of this view in the Communist youth militia, where he was pestered by the 'problems of no significance' which the student comrades, unlike the workers, heaped on him; he termed the suicide of one of these students 'a petty-bourgeois act', the suicide having placed '"his own personal preoccupations above his duties as a Communist" … meeting an icy response from those present. "What are you, made of stone?" one of them said' (ibid., p. 76).

34 Ibid., p. 247.

35 See N. Ajello, *Intellettuali e Pci. 1944–1958*, Bari: Laterza, 1979, p. 187.

36 *L'Unità*, 17 October 1980, on the occasion of Longo's death.

37 See Spinelli, *Io, Ulisse*, pp. 159–60, with reference to Viterbo prison.

like catechumens. The relationship created in the Garibaldi brigades between the party nucleus and the partisans, referred to earlier, almost prefigured the difficult passage from the Bolshevik party to the 'new model party', as it were. Not everyone agreed in regarding the Garibaldi experience as a mass draft by the party. At a party meeting at the 3rd Lombardia division it was argued that 'the fact ... that the men claim they have the right to belong to the Party solely because they have been fighting as *patrioti* for months shows how much they still have to learn'.[38]

All this led to the formation of a sort of advance guard of the advance guard within the bosom of the same party. An eloquent expression of this is the directive sent to a political commissar, where the rhetoric of discipline smacks of Fascist language:

> While conserving what is good in the relationship of sympathy, friendship and particular affection, characteristics shared by the bands and which determine their orientation, we must however convince [the partisans] that today there is only one relationship that towers above everything: iron discipline, which is quick off the mark when it is felt and accepted with determination and enthusiasm. We must make the partisans feel that volunteerism is manifested in discipline more so than in combat.[39]

Giovanni Pesce was disconcerted by the easy-going nature of the Milanese Gappists, one of whom said to him: 'We're all friends. We live in the same block and the same quarter and we've known one another since we were kids.'[40]

As we have already noted, in the clandestinity of city warfare the sense of 'unpleasant isolation', which led to the severing of all human relations, reached an extreme level. The old leader Celso Ghini gave Pesce the sensation 'that the war is too harsh to allow its protagonists to concede anything to friendship'.[41]

The risks attributable to friendship presented themselves in two very

---

38 Transcript of 20 October 1944, in IG, *BG* 01519. Immediately after Liberation, such objections manifested themselves, and with their own specific tone, in the area around Gradisca, on the Yugoslav border. A document of the local 'Communist Committee' firmly argued that 'they must be considered Party members' and not sympathisers, generic anti-Fascists or members of the youth federation. With a characteristic leap into universal judgements, the document concluded: 'He is a member of the Party, he who is active and gives his whole self for the future development of humanity – independently of his political maturity' (document from the Osoppo archive, a copy of which Galliano Fogar gave to the IRSFVG).

39 'Estratto di una lettera del Comando unificato (Divisione Sesia – Divisione Ossola), ufficio del commissario politico', from the commissar of the Volante Loss Brigade, undated but from winter 1944–45 (IG, *BG*, 06560).

40 Pesce, *Senza tregua*, p. 166.

41 Ibid., p. 163.

different places. Above all in the mountain bands, which were composed of young and very young men, and in the chiefs who were the expression of the bands. Thus the *ispettore* 'Riccardo' (Alfredo Mordini), with twenty-three years of military life behind him, complained that they could not be granted that absolute trust which, in Italy and abroad, he was accustomed to having in his party comrades.[42] But there were also residual traces of Socialist and Communist culture dating back to the period prior to the 'bolshevisation' of the party; and, along the same lines as Secchia, *L'Unità* denounced these, criticising those old comrades who tended to 'take the Party for a little family or a group of friends'.[43] A few weeks earlier a party leader had complained that 'in some areas things were run along the lines of the patriarchal family; everyone knew everything, including the grandparents, the grandchildren and ... the mothers-in-law'.[44]

Yet it was this very continuity between being friends and being comrades that largely sustained the ethics of the rank-and-file: 'Those whom today we call comrades, [before Fascism] would have been called friends', said a worker from Terni; and an old militant, who had known prison and internment, was to complain many years later: 'The young are no longer brothers and friends as we were. It was enough for us to say: "He's a comrade" and "ciau".[45] Even strictly political watchwords like those following the 7th Congress of the International – 'in his report Georgi Dimitrov says that instead we need to work among all the young' – could be taken to mean that some space was set aside for human relations and that the internal barriers that had been erected, such as that against dancing with youths wearing the Fascist badge, had now collapsed.[46] It was the tissue that formed in a life shared together, as a mark of openness, that certainly counted more than quotations from Massimo D'Azeglio, Silvio Pellico, Cesare Cantù and Herbert Spencer, which were paraded by a Garibaldino newspaper.[47]

The corollary in the Communists to the severity of the party ethics, and

42 Letter from Riccardo to the Lombardy Delegation, n.d. (IG, *BG*, 01775).

43 'Rinnovarsi per progredire', in the 25 January 1944 northern edition. On top of this consideration, there was also the 'division between the recreational and political fields', much greater among the Communists than the Socialists, which has been discussed by Victoria De Grazia (De Grazia and Passerini, *Alle origini della cultura di massa*, p. 25).

44 'Rapporto al centro del Partito' by Banfi, Emilia, 16 December 1943 (IG, *Archivio PCI*).

45 Testimony of Arnaldo Lippi (Portelli, *Biografia di una città*, p. 26); testimony of Maria Francesca Accossato, widow of Sandrone, in Guidetti Serra, *Compagne*, vol. I, p. 31. On the lasting difficult relation between friendship and 'the cement of politics' among Communist trade union leaders after Liberation, see S. Tatò's interview of Emilio Guglielmino (*A voi cari compagni*, pp. 25–45). An analogy could be drawn between the Communist trade unionist among the workers and the Party militant among partisans.

46 Testimony of Teresa Cirio, in Bruzzone and Farina, *La Resistenza taciuta*, p. 74.

47 See *Unità e Libertà*, Domodossola, 28 September 1944.

the hegemonic pride inscribed in those ethics, was their severity towards themselves, their capacity to purge themselves 'so as not to give the bourgeoisie a pretext for denigrating us'.[48] A Communist was expected to refuse the plate of spaghetti offered him by a peasant, when it seemed like a privilege: 'Even if he was alone, even if the others would never have known.'[49] He had to be convinced that the terrible effort of transporting very heavy loads in the mud and rain was 'the necessary exercise to become revolutionaries'.[50] In every field, the Communists had to be the best.[51] This, among other things, was the only sure way of recognising each other.[52] 'Made of a special material', the Communists had to convince themselves that 'ours is the fault not only for what we ourselves fail to do, but also for what others fail to do'.[53]

There was a strong conviction that 'proletarian firmness, seriousness and morality'[54] could be fully achieved only in the party, which thus had the historic task of bearing witness in the name of all the workers, of all the oppressed.[55] Nothing in this picture lacked significance: 'In the life of the Party, in the work of the Party, it is a good rule never to consider anything as "unimportant", or worse still "without significance".'[56] Or again: 'If there are comrades who today are finding time to take it easy and enjoy themselves, they are not soldiers, they are not combatants.'[57] The idea that for the partisans, too, sloth is the father of all vices is repeated in many documents:[58]

---

48 'Informazioni da Milano', 15 December 1944 (Secchia, *Il PCI e la guerra di liberazione*, p. 708).

49 Testimony of Giovanni Serbandini, in G. Bocca, *Storia dell'Italia partigiana*, Bari: Laterza, 1966, p. 99.

50 Lazagna, *Ponte rotto*, p. 40.

51 Among the many firm statements to this effect, see the letter from the 'comrades responsible' for the Piedmont Delegation sent to those responsible for the Val di Susa brigades on 12 July 1944, and the 'Direttive organizzative e di lavoro', dated 28 January 1945, drawn up by the directorate of the Party Committee for the Friuli Division (*Le Brigate Garibaldi*, vol. II, pp. 116–20, and vol. III, pp. 299–302).

52 See IG, *BG*, 01519.

53 Such was Al's response to the comrades unwilling to accept his reproaches: transcript of the 'Riunione dei rappresentanti di Partito', the meeting of Party representatives from several Padua factories on 18 March 1945 (IG, *Archivio PCI*).

54 A circular addressed to 'all Party activists' arriving in Turin on 4 November 1943 lamented the lack of these qualities among 'inexpert, muddling and confusing … leaders and chiefs' who had emerged from the shadows after 26 July (ibid.).

55 Spinelli, *Io, Ulisse*, p. 101, which speaks of how the Communist Party had through twenty years been able to arouse an 'inexhaustible capacity for *martyrion*' in the 'humble classes' for the first time in the history of Italy.

56 'La Disciplina', in *L'Unità*, Rome edition, 7 December 1943.

57 'Passare all' offensiva' (in the regular 'Vita di Partito' section), *L'Unità*, Northern edition, 21 June 1944.

58 For example, the letter from the 'comrades responsible' to the political commissar

So a leader of the Belluno federation was balking at going into the formations as a commissar?: 'My decision was: to send G. into the mountains (precisely because he doesn't like the idea).'[59] Ludovico Geymonat, in proposing to Anna Cinanni that she be a dispatch-rider, said to her: 'We don't promise you anything. If they catch you, you'll get a bullet from them; if you betray us, you'll get a bullet from us. Is that clear?'[60]

Always deny everything, resist torture: this is

the only fitting conduct for a Communist militant who is conscious that he is fighting for a great and just cause; it is the only conduct that makes the Communist the worthy emulator of the greatest heroes of mankind; it is the only conduct that can instil fear and respect in the enemy and make him draw back from his criminal intentions.[61]

In short, the conviction is that virtue, always, pays.

Death was preferable to betrayal. A document dictating rules about conspiracy concludes: 'Whoever talks betrays and as a traitor must answer before tomorrow's tribunal. If need be, it's better to put an end to one's own existence like heroes than live like cowards.'[62]

An episode that occurred in Udine tragically sums up the conflict between ethico-political rigour and the bureaucratic spirit in which it could be applied. Thirty Communist partisans, sentenced to death, managed to spirit out of prison their request that 'their plea for grace and subsequent developments be seen to'. On 2 April 1945, Franco, on behalf of the federal committee, answered them with a long letter. The first part is shot through with genuine sympathy for the lot of the prisoners, but the conclusion is uncompromising:

Your fate is painful to us because we love you more than brothers ... Comrades, we understand that it's hard to die because all of us love life. We understand that it's easy to die as heroes on the battlefield but less easy under the refined moral torture to which the Nazi barbarian and his foul thugs are subjecting you. We understand all this, but ... tell the comrades not to ask for grace. You are patriots, you are soldiers. You can and you must demand treatment due to soldiers taken prisoner. But you must not ask for any grace.

---

of the 5th Zone in the Cuneo area, Pietro, 28 December 1944 (*Le Brigate Garibaldi*, vol. III, pp. 149–53).

59 As the inspector-general Pietro (Antonio Roasio) put it, towards the end of 1943, in a communication probably addressed to the PCI leadership (*Le Brigate Garibaldi*, vol. I, p. 202).

60 Bruzzone and Farina, *La Resistenza taciuta*, p. 99.

61 'Ancora sulla cospirazione', *L'Unità*, Rome edition, 1 December 1943.

62 Command of the Milan SAP Brigade to commands under its aegis, 1 January 1945 (*Le Brigate Garibaldi*, vol. III, p. 183).

A gloss jotted at the bottom of the page reads: 'On 9 April the thirty comrades were shot in the Udine jails.'[63]

The Communists and other anti-Fascists jailed during the *ventennio* can justly boast that they never signed the request for grace, even if this meant risking friction with their relatives. This, then, was the ultimate act of defiance by the condemned against the triumphant regime, a gesture that magnified the value of their testimony. But in the first days of April 1945 Nazi-Fascism was on its last legs, the Allies were about to arrive, the insurrection was at the gates. In such a situation, to apply a principle which in other circumstances had been of the highest value became a manifestation of abstract and indeed bureaucratic coherence, whatever the agony suffered by those who asked for it and those who agreed to submit to it.[64] 'An idea is an idea', one of the condemned had written from the Udinese prison; and 'if destiny and misfortune carried me off, I ask all of you for your pardon.'[65]

The developments of an intransigence that could make you a slave to your own virtue are not found only among the Communists. In November 1943, in France, Marc Bloch made a firm appeal to the Jacobin virtues against the tendency towards 'gigantic absolution for everyone': 'This limp inclination towards pardon undoubtedly expresses the most sincere side of an old tortuous soul. To be indignant and punish, one needs to believe a little in what our ancestors of '93 called, in their language devoid of false discretion, virtue.'[66]

Ernesto Rossi recounted that, when imprisoned at Ventotene, in his article 'Giacobinismo and liberalismo', he had expressed similar views to these of Bloch, he and Altiero Spinelli, who shared those views with him, were accused of neo-Fascism.[67]

A feature of Actionist intransigence distinguishing it from Communist intransigence lay in the fact that the former was compelled to manifest itself immediately in a recognisable way. Its novelty and its lack of a clear and unambiguous ideology made the Action Party visible above all through its behaviour and moral style. 'Unlike the other historic parties, which are evaluated on the basis of their traditional political line and their programmes which are known to all, the value of the Action Party lies only in what it actually

---

63 Ibid., pp. 569–71.

64 There are, moreover, testimonies of Communists who requested grace, in the letters of Resistance fighters across Europe condemned to death: see *LRE*, p. 347 (a Frenchman), p. 424 (a German), and pp. 515–17 (an Italian).

65 Letter from Luigi Ciol to his family, 14 March 1945 (*LRE*, p. 548).

66 'La vraie saison des juges', *Les Cahiers politiques*, November 1943. Bloch concluded with the statement that 'the renewed France will be an energetic, solid France'. Bloch was one of Secchia's favourite writers (from a conversation with the present author).

67 See 'Intervista con Ernesto Rossi', ed. L. Calogero La Malfa, in *Quaderni dell'Istituto romano per la storia d'Italia dal fascismo alla Resistenza* 1 (1969), p. 109.

does'[68] – so runs a declaration inspired by that pride in its novelty which circulated widely in the documents of the party. The party was presented as 'the only political formation of great importance which has arisen directly from the democratic crisis of the twentieth century which culminated in Fascism'.[69] To be admitted into the party, 'the ideals of the aspirant had to be accepted (and controlled)' – ideals, not ideology – together with his acceptance of the programme.[70] Precisely by way of contrast with the Communists, it was explained that 'We do not subordinate the programme of our party to a definite philosophical system compulsory for everyone', but, naturally, this does not mean that we don't have 'our ethical, political and economic principles: because otherwise we would not constitute a party'.[71]

In his pungent criticism of the 'sixteen-point programme' drawn up in Rome, Vittorio Foa came straight to the point: 'Ideological unity is a utopia, unless it is confused with the mythological unity of authoritarian parties ... The novelty of a party lies in its concrete political and organisational action; other than this it can be no more than an empty assertion'.[72]

But, at the same time, an Action Party newspaper wrote: 'Our belief is that the problem of the liberation of man has to be faced and resolved on all planes, that is to say for every aspect of his life, otherwise it is not solved at all'.[73] An exegesis of this principle, which seems to paraphrase Churchill's 'tears and blood', is found in a text that speaks in terms of the 'terrible and severe climate of sufferings, of social solidarity and unshakable determination' which distinguished the war of liberation and belied 'any presumed feebleness of the Italian character'. This climate 'is the destruction of affections, possessions and life's comforts, and the ruin of illustrious memories and the sharing of sacrifice and renunciations ... It separates people from their families. It wrenches men from their jobs ... It causes raids and reprisals, it exposes convicts and deportees to starvation'.[74]

To keep the tension at this pitch, the Actionists in their turn provided for political 'giornate', on the assumption that 'political work is educational work'.[75]

68 Letter from the Upper Italy Secretariat to the provincial and regional committees, n.d. but between late 1944 and early 1945 (INSMLI, *CLNAI*, envelope 8, folder 12).

69 Editorial 'Per un'Italia nuova' in youth paper *Giovani*, Rome, 27 May 1944.

70 'Circolare n. 2 riservata ai comitati regionali', written during Badoglio's '45 days' (ISRT, *Carte Enzo Enriques Agnoletti*, envelope 1, folder 2, subfolder Documenti che riguardano l'ideologia e la storia del PdA).

71 Pamphlet *Parole chiare ai comunisti*, signed by 'Eleandro', who described himself as a professor from a liberal-socialist background.

72 In Carocci, *La Resistenza italiana*, p. 187.

73 'Il Partito d'Azione è un partito socialista', in *La Libertà* (Tuscany), 27 October 1943.

74 *La guerra di liberazione*, pamphlet dated 1943, pp. 3–6.

75 'Norme per gli ispettori', 25 December 1944. All of these norms were imbued with

The powerful individualism and the equally powerful political passion in which that individualism was expected to find expression could not be easily reconciled with the unitary policy which was nevertheless pursued by the Actionists. At the end of 1942 Aldo Garosci had written from the United States: 'In the present phase I am in favour of the maximum sincerity, that is to say the minimum unity.'[76]

Even 'revolution in one go', which Vittorio Foa set against the two-stage revolution advocated by the Communists, arose from a need for sincerity and unity of conscience; and it is no accident that Foa attributed 'the difficulty experienced by the bloc of left-wing groups' to this.[77] The possible elitist consequences of such positions are clear. Leo Valiani was not mistaken in seeing the many losses suffered by the Action Party leaders as a surrogate for its lack of a mass base. This sprung not only from 'moralistic' subjective motivations – elsewhere Valiani has recalled the case of the *giellista* who, a latter-day Attilius Regolus, returned to Pietro Koch's jail[78] – but from a more intrinsic mode of being.[79] Here political ties and friendship, though distinct, formed a close-knit web, of which the correspondence between Giorgio Agosti and Dante Livio Bianco constitutes a monument.[80]

For the Catholic *resistenti*, whichever the formation they were fighting in, the relationship between politics and morality, between public and private, assumed peculiar characteristics. By Catholic I mean those for whom being so constituted an obvious fact, but implied also, in different grades and tones, a problem and a position – a distinction which does not necessarily correspond to the traditional one between practising and non-practising Catholics. Enjoinders to consider political commitment as a moral duty met with a wide variety of attitudes.

Above all there were Catholics who, convinced that they were in possession of a revealed truth that went to the heart of their being, felt less impelled, and in no way sensed the need to link the project of profound self-renewal to a historical contingency, however dramatic that contingency might be. Not that the sense, and the attraction, of self-reunification was unknown to them. But the Catholic faith had deposited in the depths of their souls a nucleus that did not need to be reunified with anything, because it was self-sufficient, absolute

a strong pedagogical spirit (published under the title 'La guerra in città', in *Formazioni GL*, pp. 257–63).

76 Letter to Umberto Calosso, sent from New York to London, 22 November 1943 (CSPG, *Fondo Calosso*, envelope 13).

77 Inverni (V. Foa), *I partiti*, p. 56.

78 See Bocca, *La Repubblica di Mussolini*, p. 198.

79 Valiani, *Azionisti*, pp. 80–1.

80 G. Agosti and L. Bianco, *Un' amicizia partigiana. Lettere 1943–1945*, introduced and edited by G. De Luna, Turin: Albert Meynier, 1990.

and eternal. To these Catholics the ultimate presuppositions of public and private, individual and collective, had to appear serenely distinct and serenely coexistent.

Other Catholics, of whom we have already seen some cases, sought instead in their very religiousness the profound motivations for their political commitment, which they saw as an instrument for affirming inalienable moral principles. This position generated torment and tension, all the more profound the harder it was to feel that the name 'religious' could confidently be given to the political actions performed by Catholics and, in particular, the clergy. In a lecture given at the Catholic University in Milan in January 1943, Giuseppe Dossetti had spoken of the active participation of the people as of a natural right.[81] To fight for the triumph of a right consequently became a duty.

Finally, there was a third Catholic attitude, which also made the religious factor the point of departure, but interpreted in a predominantly doctrinaire sense, as a model for a Christian society that was coming into being. These Catholics, in the name of coherence, were taking the dangerous paths of integralism, which is a Catholic version of totalitarianism.

There was no clear defining line between these different positions. Teresio Olivelli, for example, oscillated between the second and the third pole, not least perhaps from the lingering influence of his Fascist education.[82] One of the most upright Resistance groups, the Christian-Social Movement, started from the second position, but because of the simplistic manner with which it assumed it, ran the risk of ending up with the third. Christianity – say some of its writings – has made men equal before God and therefore before the law; but 'economic inequality' has made this great conquest meaningless: therefore the social problem and the moral one 'have to fuse in a happy synthesis'.[83] Or again, 'the forgoing of wealth preached by the Gospel constitutes an essential element for the solution of the social question [to be faced therefore] in the name of the ethic of justice and love of genuinely lived Christianity'.

All this afflatus, nourished by a Gospel that did not come to bear the sword, found its final outlet, moreover, in the apologia of the grey 'scuola sociale cristiana', presented as 'the application of the eternal and universal principles of the Gospel to the contingent needs of social life'.[84]

At the opposite pole, the Catholic Communists polemicised, with intellectual haughtiness, against the pretension of deducing politics from religion and

81 See Bianchi, *I cattolici*, p. 159.

82 On Olivelli's ambiguity, here, see Webster, *The Cross and the Fasces*, p. 210.

83 'Orizzonti economici e Principi' in *Rinascita*, 25 March 1944.

84 'Noi e i cattolici' in *L'Azione*, 10 November 1943, and 'Scuola sociale cristiana', in *Rinascita*, 25 March 1944. On the Social Christians, see A. Parisella, ed., *Gerardo Bruni e i cristiano sociali*, Rome: Edizioni del Lavoro, 1984.

from the ideals connected with it such as fraternity, justice and mutual love.[85] It is not remotely true, they maintained, that 'it is impossible to accept a political line without the philosophy that is behind it', otherwise the Catholics who call themselves democratic would have to accept the enlightenment and 'immanentist idealism'.[86] Lurking in the background of so much abundantly professed separatism lay a totalitarian integralism – a philosophy of history that saw in Communism (and precisely that of Stalin) the secular arm to which providence had assigned the task of realising the perfect Christian society.[87] Following such lines and such principles, truly the Christian God, the true God, will be, if we 'are worthy of our faith, the natural crowning, through supernatural grace, of the efforts of the atheist of good will'.[88]

In reply to these professions of faith came the warning that 'the unity of the Christian spirit' can never be broken.[89] And the *giornale di battaglia* of Christian Democrat youth' went on to explain: 'Catholicism, Christianity is by its very essence integralist, that is, it comprehends private and public life, projects its morality on all the problems of private and public life. In this sense we Christian Democrats or *Popolari* intend to define ourselves and to be integralist, with no oscillations and no discontinuity – in a word, coherent.'[90]

From this integralism the newspaper, paying little regard to coherence, drew a firm stance against the transfer of power: 'Only our organic conceptions of man, the family, society, the state places the most clear-cut limits on the action of those in power and the sphere within which mutual rights are to be exercised.'[91]

---

85 See, for example, 'Parole chiare al cattolico medio', in *Voce Operaia*, 15 January 1944.

86 'Parole chiare', *Voce Operaia*, 26 October 1943.

87 Note the several sharp observations in A. Del Noce, 'Genesi e significato della prima sinistra cattolica italiana postfascista', in *Storia contemporanea* II (1971), pp. 1035–124.

88 'Religione e comunismo', in *Voce Operaia*, 5 January 1944, in which Machiavelli, Galilei, Vico, the men of the Enlightenment, Kant, the romantics, the French revolutionaries, Hegel, and – albeit in different hues – Marx were termed 'angelic sinners'.

89 'Le fatiche totali di Voce Operaia', *Il Segno*, 18 May 1944. The utterly fundamentalist *Il Segno* – which held that 'the ultimate goal' of Christian Democracy should be the Catholicisation of the state – took a position towards that party which we would today call *collateralismo* (outside sponsorship by an organization that is not itself expressly political). See the editorial 'Posizioni', signed 'Signifer', from the first issue, 1 March 1944.

90 'A proposito di politica e morale', signed 'g', *La Punta*, 2 February 1944 (the first issue). The paper, whose motto was 'I cut and drive forth', was headed by Giulio Andreotti, Giorgio Tupini and Cesare Dall'Oglio (see Gorrieri, *La Repubblica di Montefiorino*, p. 134).

91 'Ai giovani', *La Punta* 2 February 1944 editorial, signed 'Grint'.

From their reading of some copies of *La Punta*, and from 'hasty readings of Giuseppe Toniolo', the Catholic partisans of the Modenese mountains attempted to 'invent an ideology of Christian Democracy'. At the party's first provincial congress (in October 1945), they affirmed the principle that the proposed reforms should not be seen 'as the limit that we put on the reforms requested by other currents', but should be deduced 'precisely from Christian doctrine'.[92]

Democrazia Cristiana adopted the first and third of the three positions outlined above – a feeble interest in politics specifically, the religious duty to participate, and integralism – some concessions being made to the second. This is one of the paths that led to that *realismo* on which they were subsequently to build so notable a part of their fortune. The Communists proved weak in their dealings with the Catholics in being so unaware of such complex facets of the latter's behaviour. The second position was naturally extraneous to Communist culture. Replying to a Christian Democrat protest against the lay funerals of partisans, 'Bülow' (Arrigo Boldrini) let slip that in the Garibaldi formations there were 'elements of various political tendencies and of *consequent* religious ideas'.[93] The Communists would have preferred it if all the Catholics had belonged to the first position: that way, at any rate, they could consider them a fact to acknowledge, and if possible govern, as such. The Communists were aware of the existence and strength of the third position, and knew they had to combat it, when it was not possible to reach any compromise with it. But here it was often the Catholics, and above all the clergy, who had no qualms about opening hostilities.

Sure of their hegemonic strength, but at the same time secretly wishing to be recognised as equals by so ancient and noble a potentate, the Communists often assumed an attitude of respectful and tactical forbearance towards the Catholics. Moscatelli wrote of one commander, 'our comrade since recently': 'He's still a bit weak on the religious side, but seems keen to overcome this. In any case it's almost a good thing that he should be like this; it will come in handier for our work among partisan believers.'[94]

Another document reads: 'In these countries there is also the question of the Church and comrades should not set themselves against it. Communists are not believers but they cannot go against Catholics who have twenty years of Fascism behind them. We must not go against the Church, although we know that Catholicism has always supported the bourgeoisie.'[95]

---

92 Gorrieri, *La Repubblica di Montefiorino*, pp. 542–3.

93 Letter to the Ravenna Christian Democracy, 15 March 1945 (my italics): *Le Brigate Garibaldi*, vol. III, p. 487.

94 Letter to Pippo, 6 July 1944 (IG, *BG* , 06162).

95 Transcript of a meeting of commissars and Party organisers attached to the 3rd Lombardy Division, 20 October 1944 (ibid., 01519).

Urging that the chaplain be given a good welcome, a political commissar wrote: 'Think of the USSR's change of policy over religion; they are excellent examples to follow.'[96]

Il Popolo might limit itself to being ironical about statements of this kind.[97] But other broadsides thundered much more loudly. One need only mention the *Estratto del catechismo sociale* published in Padua in 1944, under the editorship of the diocese's branch of Catholic Action, which enjoyed the freedom of the press granted it by the RSI. True to the best reactionary tradition, the pamphlet attacks, on every level, not only communism, but also socialism and liberalism.[98] As they had already done with regard to the war as such, the Catholic hierarchies seemed to be concerned that the current disorder was a source of immorality, in the most traditional sense of the word, and their concern was reinforced by the fear of a Communism which was a fomenter of dissolute customs. The patriarch of Venice, Cardinal Adeodato Piazza, extended this concern even to souls in purgatory. He wrote to Monsignor Nogara, bishop of Udine: 'It is to be hoped that the possible collapse does not also have damaging repercussions on people's souls, especially of those who have the greatest need in Purgatory (as it would indeed have if the Masses offered for souls were to be interrupted).'[99]

But it is from the same tissue of 'Christian and patriarchal solidarity', which favoured the indirect support given to the partisans by 'many parish priests of the so-called "peripheral" clergy ... a genuine governing class in Friulian agricultural society',[100] that the fear sprung that even the militia in the Osoppo brigades was a vehicle of immorality. Shortly after the Liberation a parish priest wrote:

---

96 Letter from Andrea Lima to the 'Communist directorate' and to the Command of the Friuli battalion, undated (IZDG, envelope 534, folder III/1). Curious evidence of what the Communists would have wished the Christian Democrats to have been like is given by the article 'Comunismo e democrazia cristiana', in the 5 September 1944 *L'Unità* (Liguria edition), which is presented as having been submitted by a group of Christian Democrats. The article is so made-to-measure as to give every impression of having been written by a Communist who is not ashamed to say that the greatest contribution to the liberation struggle came from the Communists and Christian Democracy.

97 See the short piece devoted to the freedom of religion which Stalin had guaranteed Italy on the basis of the third point of the Moscow Declaration (in the 14 November 1943 Rome edition).

98 The pamphlet, edited by the diocese's secretariat for social activism, was printed by the Antoniana printworks in Padua, its imprimatur dated 7 November 1944. See also the *Catechismo sul comunismo* (Catechism on communism) that the archbishop of Milan, Cardinal Schuster, had published in August 1943 and February 1944, and which Miccoli defines as 'rozzo centone' ('crude travesty') as well as an obviously political agenda, in *Problemi di ricerca*, p. 249.

99 Letter of February 1945, in ibid., p. 261.

100 Fogar, *Le brigate Osoppo-Friuli*, p. 292.

The partisans have returned home, who, to tell the truth, entered the *Osoppo* religiously and morally healthy and came out of it sick. Almost all of them belonged to Catholic Action and were also well educated, obedient, and church-going. Now ... *quam mutati!* The moment of liberty has come. And for so many youngsters liberty is continuing in the form of unbridled behaviour and merry-making ...[101]

And another priest, referring to the *osovani* (members of the Osoppo brigades) shows equal alarm about this liberty:

They've absorbed something that isn't right, something that can't be explained, that can't be understood. There's an evasion of every human and divine law, there's an unbridled tendency to abuse liberty against every precept of civilised living.[102]

'They go off and return ... different from when they left' complained the parish priest of Frassené in Cadore in his turn.[103] The arrival of 'that lot from Bologna, the damnation of our land' and particularly the infiltration of 'Emilian elements', again in the parish priest's view fomented a corruption in standards of conduct.[104] 'With the coming of the Gramsci', wrote the parish priest of Cergnai, 'the young are beginning to desert the church and abandon religious practices; immorality and acts of violence are constantly on the increase.'[105] And the parish priest of Chies d'Alpago: 'Even women are enlisting ... with consequences that are all too well known.'[106] A dean of Belluno cathedral, monsignor Palatini, even goes so far as to comment on the deportation of girls to Germany, as workers, writing in his diary: 'With what consequences for morality it is easy to imagine, all the more so since, with the due exceptions, in young women there is a noticeable slackening of morals and an appalling frivolity, the consequences of which are being felt.'[107] The retrospective reproaches of the Fascists as corrupters of

---

101 *Libro storico degli avvenimenti più notevoli avvenuti in questa Parrocchia di Rivalpo (Arta)*, dated 19 June 1945 (cited in Miccoli, *Problemi di ricerca*, p. 258).

102 *Libro storico della parrocchia di San Pietro al Natisone*, dated 30 December 1946 (cited in ibid., pp. 258–9).

103 Cited in Tramontin, *Contadini e movimento partigiano*, p. 308.

104 Reports by the parish priests of Longarone and San Gregorio nelle Alpi, cited in ibid., pp. 292, 300. On the migration of a large group of Bologna partisans to the Veneto, see E. Antonioni, 'La Resistenza veneta nel contributo dei garibaldini bolognesi', in *La Resistenza in Emilia-Romagna*, Bologna 1970, pp. 126–48, and L. Bergonzini, 'I bolognesi nel Veneto, nel Modenese e nelle Valli', in L. Bergonzini and L. Arbizzani, *La Resistenza a Bologna*, Bologna: Istituto per la storia di Bologna III (1970), pp. 169–265.

105 Tramontin, *Contadini e movimento partigiano*, p. 292.

106 Ibid., p. 291.

107 Ibid., p. 290.

youth made by another parish priest from the Belluno area sound a similar note to those used against the partisans.[108]

These Veneto priests, in their way, were paying homage to the pedagogic virtues of Resistance experience which redounded from the political and military into questions of ethics and conduct. The Resistance was, however, favourably recognised as possessing these virtues by two rather more enlightened churchmen, padre Luigi Rinaldini and don Giacomo Vender, for whom the rebel movement 'constitutes an educative environment' for the 'awareness it can give of the need to risk one's life for an idea, for liberty, justice, the life of one's country'.[109]

As the field open to judgments widened under the pressure of public events, the family came under fire as well. Witness the Fascist Roberto Farinacci, who did not hesitate to denounce the Italian family as 'incapable of being a school of civil, patriotic, and religious education'. The only future remedy would be to remove children from their families and gather them together in state boarding schools: 'And the parents? They'll just have to calmly recognise their incompetence and step down gratefully.'[110] The problem of the family was, however, faced only to a limited extent and, save only a few exceptions, warily, by the *resistenti*. The presence of the Catholics and, above all, the widespread wish not to irritate them in the name of a 'religious peace', the keys of which were left in the hands of the Catholics themselves, goes some, though not all of the way, towards explaining this reticence. The stances taken by the Christian Democrats on this score are well known. The last paragraph of *Idee ricostruttive della Democrazia cristiana* states that the democratic state 'will safeguard public morality, protect the integrity of the family and assist parents in their mission of educating the new generations in a Christian manner'.

In this context it was natural that the 'juridical efficacy of religious marriage' should be defended.[111] The evangelism of the Christian Socialists was no less intransigent and hide-bound on this point. 'When the moral unity' of the Italian people is at stake, wrote one of their newspapers, those who profess the theory of free love are 'free to keep it to themselves and good luck to them, but God forbid that it should affect the moral solidity of the Italian family with unhealthy ideas and scurrilous words'. Likewise, let those who are atheist 'go ahead and live their

---

108 See the sermon given by the Alpago parish priest on Sunday 6 May 1945 (ibid., p. 318).

109 See *Clero bresciano*, May 1944 (cited in Bianchi, *I cattolici*, p. 181).

110 'L' educazione nazionale problema del domani', *Il Regime fascista*, 19 August 1944, cited in Mazzatosta, *Educazione e scuola nella RSI*, p. 71. Japan's ambassador to the RSI was, nonetheless, critical of Italian women, 'especially those from the bourgeois and uppermost classes', because of their lack of dedication to caring for their families ('Rapporto al Mikado' in Ragionieri, *Italia giudicata*, p. 802).

111 *Idee ricostruttive della Democrazia cristiana*.

intimate drama: but God forbid that they should touch, or threaten the ethico-religious unity of our people'.[112] The Catholic Communists, then, transferred into Soviet socialism, as they imagined it to be, the full realisation of the Catholic ideal of the family, or at any rate the presence of the conditions for bringing it about.[113]

Even the most secular of the Resistance parties, the Action Party, trod very carefully on the question of marriage. One of its most elaborate programmatic documents proposed the 'restoration to the state of sovereignty in the matter of matrimonial legislation', but was careful to add: 'taking opportune measures to ensure that the religious wedding ceremony also is legally binding to all civil intents and purposes'[114] – that is to say, marriage regulated by the 1929 Concordat was to be saved. During Badoglio's forty-five days, *La Voce Repubblicana*, a newspaper which was to be on the margins of CLN policy, had written that 'regeneration' and the 're-consecration of the disrupted family, the *truly* essential nucleus of civil society' was necessary.[115]

'For the defence of the Italian family' was an article by Togliatti published in *L'Alba*, the newspaper printed in the USSR for the Italian prisoners. In it appears the argument that Fascism only chattered about defending the family, seeking all the while to take possession of it.[116] The reduction of divorce to a bourgeois luxury was not incompatible with an attitude which superimposed on ancient working-class traditions of scant attention paid to the ritual formalities of the union between the sexes the concern, once again, not to alarm the Catholics.[117]

Earlier we saw, in a stance taken by Secchia, how for relations between comrades the repudiation of the family model was the order of the day in the Communist Party, but how, at the same time, the metaphor of the party and/or the band as 'like a family' was widespread. Even at that time the 'ambiguity of the very concept of working-class cultural autonomy' appeared particularly difficult to resolve as far as social and moral conduct was concerned: 'Was it a question of being capable of thinking independently what the *borghesi* thought or else of thinking differently from the *borghesi* and even in opposition to them?'[118]

---

112 'Politica e religione. Superamento', editorial in *L'Azione dei lavoratori*, 10 February 1944.

113 'Liberazione della donna', in *Voce Operaia*, 4 December 1944, which expresses a singular faith in the Soviet and revolutionary value of introducing electrical appliances into the home.

114 *Progetto di piano di lavoro del Partito d'azione Alta Italia*, p. 12.

115 'Sì, imperialisti d'Italia!', undated, in the Badoglian paper.

116 Togliatti, *Opere*, vol. IV, 2, pp. 534–7.

117 In late 1946 Umberto Terracini, at a rally in Terni, would characterise divorce as a problem concerning the rich (see *L'Unità* of 3 December, quoted in Portelli, *Biografia di una città*, p. 359).

118 Foa, *La Gerusalemme rimandata*, p. 91.

Among the *resistenti* positions appear in which loyalty to the family and loyalty to the cause (whatever name one gave the latter) clashed frontally, and in conformity with classical tradition. 'At certain moments of life', wrote Moscatelli, in tune with Pajetta's positions, already mentioned, 'you cannot think of your family and your *patria* at the same time: either the one or the other. I have made my choice'. Moscatelli added that, although he had a sister who was arrested and ill-treated, 'in the exchange of prisoners I never give her name because the Garibaldini come first'.[119]

The few explicit stands in favour of changes affecting the very institution of the family are found almost exclusively in minor newspapers. One of these, which claimed to be written by 'well-informed *borghesi*', denounced the way in which the 'middle classes' lived 'the sense of the family, the real meaning of which – the cooperation of forces between blood-relations in the sphere of the affections and to a certain limited extent in the economic sphere – has been falsified, and is seen instead as an abstract entity dominating every member of the family from one generation to another'.[120]

Another newspaper, with a more powerful innovative drive, demands 'a profound revision of the intimate and private way of conceiving the family, religion, the *patria*, the condition of women in society and the education of one's children'.[121] Giorgio Labò, who was to die fighting in the Resistance, wrote in his diary: 'X has given me a strange definition of an enemy: "He who seeks and is able to kill my loved ones". It remains to be seen whether these "loved ones" count more than any ideal!'[122]

Involved here certainly, and particularly in *piccolo* and *medio borghese* circles, was real intolerance for the relations between the generations, to which we shall have to return. This intolerance had also been expressed by Fascism. But the war and the catastrophe into which the regime had plunged Italy now provided a kind of objective confirmation of it, laying bare the two faces of Fascism – conformism and false anti-conformism.

This is how we should read Resistance invective against the political apathy of Italian women, enclosed within the horizons of their family and now weeping their hearts out: 'Yet you raised no objection when your children in the schools were dressed up as *balillas*, armed with muskets, nor did you protest when they were sent to the campgrounds and trained for war. You did not rebel when the adolescents were sent to die in Africa.'[123]

In a similar spirit a woman harangued those women who were 'guardians

---

119 Letter to Moro, signed by Cino and Ciro, 30 January 1945 (IG, *BG*, 07850).
120 'Parole alla classe media', *L'Italia del popolo*, 22 January 1944.
121 Editorial in *Per un'Italia nuova*, 27 May 1944.
122 *Un sabotatore: Giorgio Labò*, with a preface by Lionello Venturi, Milan 1946, p. 9 (the passage is dated *ferragosto*, a holiday on and around 15 August, probably from 1940).
123 'Appello alle donne italiane', in *Bandiera Rossa*, 26 December 1943.

and vestals' of the hearth: What are you safeguarding 'in that closed circle of the kitchen and the saucepans imposed on us for centuries by the arrogance of men', and what if the war should put an end to all that?[124]

A friend told Franco Calamandrei how his father 'trapped' him into enlisting into the RSI: 'He's mortified, exasperated – but doesn't feel he can break with his family. And seeing that I consider this fact to be extremely grave makes him even more depressed.'[125] *Avanti!* noted with regret: 'There are a good number who, seeing their parents' tears, have crossed the thresholds of the Fascist barracks.'[126]

The family, wrote another of the minor papers, was corroded by the same selfishness that was the ruin of society: the fact that what is involved was 'dilated selfishness' does not makes things essentially any different; on the contrary it means that the interest of the ruling classes springs from the coalition of this broader selfishness. If the revolutionary does not succeed in re-educating his own family (the 'felicitous' solution) or at least in being tolerated by them (the 'peaceable' solution), he has no choice but to 'abandon his family and seek another family among his comrades of faith and struggle' (the 'hard' solution). This declaration concludes with an argument that reinforces the invective recorded above:

> It is strange that that affection which everybody talks about was not manifested to prevent the young from participating in an infinitely more murderous war than any political action: one is led to suspect that this is because it is more convenient to have a combatant and perhaps even a 'fallen hero' in the family than a deserter or a conspirator.[127]

This sarcasm, aimed at combating 'the hypocrisy of social customs', and what, in a different context, would be called 'amoral familism',[128] could nevertheless end up, on the plane of proposals, in requests that were not really radical, such as 'the abolition of prostitution, the protection of young women, the repression of adultery, the granting of divorce'.[129]

---

124 'Rivendicazione', *La Fiamma*, March 1945.

125 Calamandrei, *La vita indivisibile*, pp. 143–4 (8 March 1944). Recall, here, the scene in Luigi Comencini's film *Tutti a casa* (1960), in which the father (Eduardo De Filippo) advises his son (Alberto Sordi) to present himself to the Fascist authorities.

126 'Il problema dei giovani', in the Rome edition of 16 March 1944.

127 'Famiglia e libertà', in *La Voce del Popolo*, 20 October 1944 (probably written by Delfino Insolera).

128 On the use of this category, see E. C. Banfield, *The Moral Basis of a Backward Society*, Glencoe, IL: Free Press, 1958.

129 'Dichiarazione fondamentale', by the Italian Labour Party, whose organ was *La Voce del Popolo* (see *Partito italiano del lavoro – 'Popolo e Libertà'*, p. 18).

The shelving of programmes for restructuring the age-old institution of the family may be seen as the application of the 'the two-stage policy' – first let's think about winning the war of liberation, and the reforms we'll think about later – even to a field in which it was more than ever uncertain when the second stage would occur. But it is also true that a particular form of nostalgia for family life certainly helped encourage this postponement. Those who fought in the Fascist war had felt that 'a gust of wind is taking us away from that family that we loved so much'.[130] For the *resistenti*, being cut off from one's family was more often than not experienced, with simplicity, as a sad unavoidable fact, as a parenthesis accepted, because of the exceptional circumstances, which left intact the nucleus, both real and ideal, of family ties. 'In a situation of ferocious laceration' the importance of the family could even assume towering proportions, and 'the drama of the families ... multiplied the dramas that each person had to live day by day'.[131] 'It's incredible, but what torments them is fear of alarming their families. The fact that the Germans will very soon be returning fire bothers them less', wrote Pesce of a group of young Gappists of the Olona valley out on their first action.[132] The same 'breadth of female solidarity around the partisan movement'[133] was coloured by family solidarity, whose reality and warmth it evoked, as when in relations with the population there appeared the '"maternal" figures of women'.[134]

At the same time, so great was the force of the family model that it bestowed reality on the mannered formula of the band as being 'like a family', which I have already mentioned. The solidarity and fraternity that were established between those who participated together in risky exploits became a sort of surrogate way of satisfying needs that are normally met by family life but that Fascism had frustrated, fostering fractures and distrust within the very bosom of families.[135] 'It's the struggle that unites', remarked a woman partisan about an elderly couple,

---

130 Letter from a soldier to his brother – also under arms – 29 August 1940 (in Rizzi, *Lo sguardo del potere*, p. 119).

131 As recalled by Italo Calvino in *Tante storie che abbiamo dimenticato*.

132 Pesce, *Senza tregua*, p. 272. However, on another occasion, Pesce told his men: 'We must behave like a family faced with a fire that is destroying their home' (ibid., pp. 174–5).

133 Here I use the words of O. Prati in 'Le donne ravennati nell'antifascismo e nella Resistenza', in the volume of the same title published by the Istituto per la storia della resistenza di Ravenna, Ravenna: Edizioni del Girasole, 1977, p. 35.

134 Portelli, *Biografia di una città*, pp. 276–7.

135 'Think what reaction is, what point it reached, in dividing father from son, brother from brother, in the same family. You didn't trust, I didn't trust my brothers; my father did not trust me.' Testimony of Arnaldo Lippi (ibid., p. 231). He is presumably the same A.L., a former worker, who elsewhere speaks of the family as a place 'which manages to hold together at once the pressures towards individualism and those towards solidarity' (Portelli, *Assolutamente niente*, p. 137).

comrades of hers, who resembled two young people in love. Still more significantly, another woman partisan lived the life of the band so intensely 'like a
family' that, when a partisan fell in love with her but waited for the war to end
before making ardent declarations, she started crying, 'because they seemed like
incest to me'.[136]

It was 'partisan marriages' that marked the re-establishment, within the
bosom of the band and with its blessing, of what was well and truly a family
nucleus, but one freed from the customary civil and ecclesiastical procedures.
An episode recounted by Franco Calamandrei shows how timeworn, though
ineluctable, the latter might appear. Comrade E. had got married in church
in order to content his wife's relations, and was ashamed to confess it: 'But I
thought – he told me – that the Fascist registrar would have been no better than
the priest: he too would have represented a falsehood. And this comforted me
in my decision ... And what does it matter, anyhow! The important thing is that
he's happy, with a gleam of liberty on his face, and an unusual confidence'.[137]

The non-existence, for the time being, of morally valid positive laws was
stated by a civil delegate of the 6th Langhe Garibaldi brigade who, celebrating
a marriage in liberated Alba on 28 October 1944, reminded the newly-weds of
'the duties deriving from the laws of nature and the customs of peoples fixed in
the civil laws, and which in the case of Italy will be established in the laws that
our people will give themselves when the *patria* is liberated from the foreign
invader'.[138] Another partisan official delivered the following address to all those
present, 'after having spoken separately with the couple':

> Not knowing what the partisan rite by which you want to marry involves (you are
> the first to make such a request to the Command), I believe that all this public cer-
> emony need do is announce the fact that you are husband and wife, besides the fact,
> which is already known, that you love one another. Carry on as you are, and when
> this situation has changed, you can, if you want, legalise this union of yours which
> rests on your consent, on love and mutual esteem.[139]

---

136 Testimonies of di Anna Cinanni and of Tersilla Fenoglio Oppedisano, in
Bruzzone and Farina, eds, *La Resistenza taciuta*, pp. 100, 159. Fenoglio recalls a partisan
who told him: 'This is like a family, and you are a little sister' (p. 160).

137 Calamandrei, *La vita indivisibile*, p. 140 (6 March 1944).

138 Bruzzone and Farina, eds, *La Resistenza taciuta*, p. 85, n. 1.

139 Repport from the Command of the 1st Gramsci Division to the Command of the
Valsesia, Ossola, Cusio, Verbano divisions-group, 12 December 1944. The celebrant was
labelled the 'Rev.mo Cap/no Bruno', playing on the two possible extensions of the abbre-
viation (i.e. cap/no could represent either *cappellano*, chaplain, or *capitano*, captain). On
a political commissar who held wedding ceremonies in the Oltrepò Pavese, see 'Rapporto
informativo e osservazioni per il comitato federale', signed by the inspector Medici,
10 August 1944.

And a GL partisan spoke of his marriage to a comrade as being 'an enchant-
ing ceremony'.[140]

If, then, few traces remain of how the *resistenti* conceived of family morality,
still more tenuous and hard to interpret are those concerning sexual morality. One can just about seek to identify the poles between which not so much
conduct as the few sufficiently explicit declarations move.

In the first place we find a rigoristic pole, which follows a well-known trend
of the revolutionary tradition, and was made more demanding here by the
promiscuity to which life in the bands often compelled one. An Italian soldier
related how the men and women Slovene partisans generally slept in separate
bunkers, and that in any case relations between them 'never went beyond the
limits of rigid "partisan correctness"'.[141] 'My chiefs', an Italian woman partisan
recalls, 'had an exaggerated puritan rigour, a truly extremist prudery', so much
so that they sent her fiancé into another, distant formation. As for herself, 'I
calmly accepted it when they said I was acting like a whore. But I have lived as
a Catholic.'[142]

Demands for seriousness addressed to partisans of both sexes mirrored this.[143] A male partisan was 'tied to a stake for an hour in punishment
for having spoken indecorously to a woman'.[144] In the Communists this rigour
was reinforced by the party ethic. 'Communist women must set an example',
one female partisan recalled having heard Gramsci say to settle a question
of morals.[145] Another woman partisan, Anna Cinanni, narrates: 'There was
great respect, the maximum respect, between women and men: I can say that
I slept together with partisans, he on one side, I on the other.' This partisan
based her conduct on words that her brother had said to her: 'Remember that
you're not a woman: you're a Communist, and you're fighting in the Resistance.'
Years later, Cinanni remarked: 'Perhaps, if I had felt the sentiment of love more
than the fighting sentiment, my life would have been different.'[146] It has been

140 Letter from Alberto Bianco, in the Valle Grana, to Gino Marchese, in the
Langhe, 4 January 1945 (*Formazioni GL*, pp. 292–3).

141 Parri (Spartaco), *Otto mesi coi partigiani di Tito*, p. 92.

142 Testimony of Tersilla Fenoglio Oppedisano (Bruzzone and Farina, *La Resistenza
taciuta*, p. 152).

143 See, for example, the circular sent by the Command of the Belluno Division to
all commanders and commissars, 10 December 1944 (*Le Brigate Garibaldi*, vol. III, p. 51).

144 The news of this punishment was reported in their wall-newspaper (Lazagna,
Ponte rotto, p. 225).

145 Testimony of Albina Caviglione Lusso (Bruzzone and Farina, *La Resistenza
taciuta*, p. 65).

146 Paolo Cinanni responded to his Calabrian mother, who reproached him for
having cast his sister 'into the arms of boys', 'Look, Anna is not a woman … She is a
Communist, and she is not viewed as a woman.' Later the mother, too, would become
a Communist (ibid., pp. 94, 105).

justly written, by way of comment on the declarations of a woman worker about her brothers' severity towards her when she was young: "'Severità' corresponds in the women's accounts to workers' 'serietà' in the men's accounts.'[147]

It is hard to make out how much conformism to ancient codes lay hidden in this puritan rigour. Eugenio Curiel guessed as much when he rebuked the Calabrese Paolo Cinanni, mentioned above, for seeing in Anna not so much a Communist as a sister, and not a woman.[148] But sometimes it was simply a question of countering the vulgarity of certain clumsy attempts to be humorous, which used 'the witty quips of pornographic rags or those of the humorous papers that come out under a Fascist regime'.[149]

Rigour motivated not by reasons of principle, but in the name of the needs for security imposed by clandestinity and the partisan struggle at once takes us onto a higher plane. Here, ancient fears could emerge, which saw women as being fragile to the point of betrayal, and made it seem in any case risky to have relations with them. There were those who felt 'a sense of disgust at seeing certain goings-on of partisans with peasant wenches, which are dangerous'.[150] Even where a more indulgent view was taken, concern often tempered the paternalism with which the gallant exploits of the partisans were looked upon. The 'women who have too soft a spot for the Garibaldini' and the women dispatch-riders who got tongues wagging were seen as a danger.[151] In the view of some, 'it is still thought that women are not to be trusted'[152] or, worse, that women were more likely to become morally degenerate and be spies.[153] The reproaches meted out to those who gave way to this way of seeing things are therefore important. Taking the use of weapons as a symbol of equality, the SAP Command's reply to the above-mentioned report urged the abandonment of 'preconceptions that women are weak creatures incapable of using

147 Portelli, *Biografia di una città*, p. 99. Note (ibid., pp. 175–7) the case of the Fascist who had a Communist banished and then 'took his sister for a ride' for some seventeen years. After the Liberation, the brother clobbered the Fascist seducer, and his sister told him, '*Bravo*, my treasure, you did the right thing!'

148 Bruzzone and Farina, *La Resistenza taciuta*, p. 107.

149 See the critiques directed against the papers *Tre Vedette*, *Il Partigiano* and *La Saetta garibaldina* by the commissariat of the Valle di Susa divisions-group. This letter, from 17 December 1944, began by making clear: 'We are not puritans' (*Le Brigate Garibaldi*, vol. III, pp. 102–4).

150 Quazza, *Un diario partigiano*, pp. 174–5 (26 March 1944).

151 See the letter from the Command of the Biella area divisions-group to the Piedmont Delegation, 22 February 1945 (*Le Brigate Garibaldi*, vol. III, p. 385).

152 'Relazione sulla situazione politica e militare della nostra provincia', Terni, 1 February 1944 (IG, *Archivio PCI*).

153 Monthly report by Costa, military organiser responsible for the Marconcini SAP brigade (*Le Brigate Garibaldi*, vol III, p. 293).

weapons. Such preconceptions are the fruit of our social conventions and of our backwardness.'[154]

Nelia Benissone Costa, a Communist partisan, recognised that the GAPs often died 'because however much prudence was recommended, they were young, possibly they got involved with some girl who talked, who was not serious'; but with proud firmness she asserted: 'It is as well to say that of all the women who fell into the hands of the Fascists not one spoke. They were marvellous.'[155]

Many complaints emerge from the Communist sources about the fact that 'thanks to the comrades who sabotage them' the women are still badly organised and are absent from the governing organisms where they ought instead to be admitted, freeing them from 'purely technical work'.[156] Writing to Dr Anna Marengo ('Fiamma'), who had been put in charge of the cultural section of the 12th division, the commander Moranino remarked: 'Life among the men is so hard since it involves uprooting a whole baggage of prejudices that these lads still have about women.'[157]

In Bergamo 'no one has ever given any thought to the work women should be doing, through the usual incomprehension', and if anything the *ceto medio* had been approached, not the factories or country areas.[158] In Padua, to support his appeal 'to put a stop to bourgeois and Fascist prejudices' against women, a party envoy felt compelled to recall that women are gifted with 'admirable reserves of energy' and constitute '50 percent of the human race'.[159] Another leader urged: '*Compagne*, react against the Social Democratic tendencies of some of your comrades who still can't conceive that Italian women are worth as much as the women of the Soviet Union and the Balkans.'[160]

'I don't do woman's work', was how a Communist answered a woman comrade who had asked him to wash the dishes: 'Gina was saying to him, "From now on you can stop calling yourself commander because you don't deserve it", when I, a member of the ferocious bourgeoisie, turned up and did the job for her.'

---

154 See ibid., p. 294, n. 2.

155 Bruzzone and Farina, eds, *La Resistenza taciuta*, pp. 38, 52.

156 'Informazioni da Milano', 22 April 1945, which also reports that in the Pavan works, 'the men do not back the group for the defence of women, and thus it cannot go forward', and the report by Oreste on the federation for Venice, 7 March 1945 (*Le Brigate Garibaldi*, vol. III, pp. 669, 450).

157 Quoted in Dellavalle, *Operai*, p. 205 (letter from 30 March 1945).

158 'Rapporto sul lavoro di partito', 29 December 1943 (*Le Brigate Garibaldi*, vol. I, p. 192).

159 Transcript of the meeting of Party representatives in several Padua factories, 18 March 1945.

160 Letter from the 'Comando Raggruppamento Brigate 400 Matteotti, 520 Puecher, 550 Rosselli' (Valtellina) addressed to 'Care compagne' ('Dear women comrades') (IG, *Archivio PCI*).

Artom, who was there on the scene, declared his sympathy for Gina, even if he was keen to make it clear that 'she has the fanatical mentality common to women who busy themselves with politics'. Nevertheless, Artom was at least scrupulous enough to ask himself whether this view of his stemmed from misogyny or anti-Communism.[161]

Rarely then was there coherence between the solemn declarations of women's rights[162] and relations between the sexes as they were actually practised. At times a simple adjustment to common practice prevailed, which an Umbrian partisan has expressed in the following words: 'What can you do, do you want to check every man? If one wants to go about nitpicking ... '[163] The old practice of transposing into play what rigour denied in principle could moreover show its face again. The rigid Tersilla Fenoglio tells of the game, played with the 'boys', of 'rape trials. What wild laughter there was!' Once, when, in the clutches of a 'colossal Lombard', she was screaming 'he's raping me!', in came the political commissar, who, when informed about what was going on, 'ruled *omnia munda mundis* [to the pure all things are pure] and went off like an old priest'.[164]

But there were also relations between men and women inspired by a higher morality which repudiated both asceticism and laxity, and gave a glimpse of the conquest of love as a choice freely made. Anna Cinanni has spoken of the discussions about free love made in the 'Fronte della gioventù' during the period of clandestinity.[165] There is some indication of this in the letter in which 'an Italian woman' accuses Fascism of having reduced her to 'an instrument of procreation', and in the condemnation of 'bourgeois prejudices that would have the woman either as a beast of burden or a lapdog'.[166] A similar formula – woman as 'an instrument of pleasure or an instrument of luxury' – is stigmatised in the manifesto of one of the minor parties.[167]

In the Resistance there were also traces of that tradition of the rebel woman which, although broken after the Paris Commune had, at least partly, acquired a new lease on life among the women factory workers.[168] The struggles waged by

---

161 Artom, *Diari*, pp. 113, 93 (10 December and 28 November 1943).

162 See the articles 'Le donne e la lotta del popolo italiano' (*L'Unità*, northern edition, 4 June 1944) and 'Dalla doppia schiavitù alla liberazione femminile' (*La voce della donna. Mensile delle italiane in Svizzera*, of Communist inspiration, December 1944).

163 Testimony of Bruno Zenoni (Portelli, *Biografia di una città*, p. 291).

164 Bruzzone and Farina, eds, *La Resistenza taciuta*, p. 157.

165 Ibid., p. 106. They read texts by Lenin and Clara Zetkin.

166 See 'Corrispondenza coi lettori', *L'Unità* Rome edition, 6 January 1944, and 'Verbale di una riunione di partito dei comunisti della 30 divisione Aliotta' (Oltrepò Pavese), 1 April 1945 (*Le Brigate Garibaldi*, vol. III, p. 563).

167 'Dichiarazione fondamentale', by the Italian Labour Party, paragraph 3.

168 Note the remarks to this effect by Luisa Passerini, in De Grazia and Passerini, *Alle origini della cultura di massa*, p. 22.

women workers since before Fascism may in fact be seen as a connecting link with the Resistance struggles.[169] And these struggles were interpreted even by a partisan commander as 'an act of rebellion against national tradition and the moralistic mentality of our country'[170] – a tradition and a mentality which had a death camp survivor compelled to hear these words addressed to her by her husband and nephew: 'If you hadn't got yourself involved in certain things no one would have come to get you', and 'You asked for it; if you'd stayed at home knitting ...'.[171]

On one point sexual morality and political morality came face to face: that of how women who had relations with the enemy were to be judged, not only in the sense of sexual relations but also in the other sense that any contact they had with the enemy was to be classed as both treason and impurity.

Attitudes varied widely here. An enlightened Gappist, Elio Cicchetti, prevented two girls from being executed only because they flirted with the Germans (though later they were executed because they were found to be spies): 'Certainly they deserved to be given a thick ear as a lesson in dignity, but we didn't want our mission to sink to the level of moralistic exercises, which seemed rather more the task of the vice squad than of a formation of combatants.'[172]

An Action Party pamphlet said: 'For women who keep accompany with Germans, unworthy of the name either of woman or of Italian – contempt and humiliating, exemplary punishments.'[173] *La Voce delle donne*, organ of the 'Gruppi di difesa della donna' denounced the 'brazen females who sink so low as to fall into the hands of our tyrants ... Does it not occur to these wretches that the hands that caress them are still stained with Italian blood?'[174]

The enemy's women could only be whores – this was a view widely held by partisans and Fascists alike. A Garibaldino document speaks of an 'ardent Fascist ... notorious also for her private conduct, who denounced people in the *questura*'.[175]

The partisans often associated sexual corruption with Nazi-Fascist ferocity. When Rosanna Rolando was arrested and taken to the Sitea hotel in Turin, headquarters of the RAU (Reparto arditi ufficiali), she recalls that 'in front of my

169 See Prati, *Le donne ravennati nell'antifascismo e nella Resistenza*, pp. 33–4. See also Guidetti Serra, *Compagne*.

170 Bernardo, *Il momento buono*, p. 150.

171 Testimony of the woman worker Margherita Bergesio Coccalotto (Bravo and Jalla, *La vita offesa*, p. 341).

172 Cicchetti, *Il campo giusto*, p. 228.

173 *La guerra di liberazione*, p. 15.

174 'Disprezzo ed odio ai tedeschi', in the 26 January 1945 edition.

175 'Relazione sugli avvenimenti di Montegrazia del 13–14 dicembre 1943' (Imperia) (*Le Brigate Garibaldi*, vol. I, p. 169).

bedroom there was the night-club; they were up until two in the morning drinking and dancing with their mistresses'.[176]

Head-shaving became the act that symbolically summed up the punishment to be inflicted on the woman enemy. There was nothing new about this practice. The paratroopers of the Royal Army had adopted it for the young men they regarded as draft-dodgers, in order to emphasise and humiliate their effeminacy.[177] The RSI Fascists did no less: they shaved the head of a girl who had danced with the partisan 'Pillo' (Paolo Spriano).[178] There seem to have been cases of girls shaved twice – first by the Germans, then by the partisans.[179] Quazza recalls the head-shaving inflicted on four female spies (given the accusation, a mild enough punishment) and on four young men and four women 'for having relations with the Germans'.[180] Two Veneto parish priests justified, as ' harsh lessons', the complete head-shaving of women who had gone to bed with Germans.[181] As early as 15 December 1943 the Rome edition of *L'Unità* was announcing that the few women who kept company with the Germans were coming to the North with their heads shaven down to nothing.[182] In the days of the insurrection mass head-shaving became a practice above all against the women auxiliaries of the Fascist army. *L'Unità* published two photographs side by side with the caption: 'Our combatant comrades and the so-called auxiliaries', also defined as 'ausiliarie-spie'.[183]

Attitudes towards sexual morals also indicate a more general way of living the Resistance experience, revealing as they do profound and differentiated tendencies.

At a meeting of Communists at the 3rd Lombardia Aliotta division, a trial was improvised against Italo, who frequented 'the house of a certain "mamma" with girls'. His prosecutors were the elderly and rigid militant Riccardo and the neophyte intellectual Albero. Albero warned: 'The Communists must give an example concerning everything, and therefore *dongiovannismo* [Don Giovanni-ism] as well. If we set a bad example, how will we be able to reprimand the

---

176 Bruzzone and Farina, *La Resistenza taciuta*, p. 25.

177 An episode of this kind, which took place in Rome's Grande Italia café on 11 May 1943, is discussed in Di Giovanni, laureate thesis, on the basis of a *questura* report held in the Archivio Centrale dello Stato.

178 Gobetti, *Diario partigiano*, p. 251 (8 December 1944).

179 Intervention by Giovanni De Luna in a debate on 'Ethics and Politics' at Turin's Centro Gobetti, 28 April 1980. De Luna referred to an oral testimony collected during the seminar on 'Women and Politics' held at the Turin Facoltà di Magistero (teaching faculty) in 1979–80.

180 Quazza, *Un diario partigiano*, pp. 212 and 239 (26 September 1944 and 31 March 1945).

181 See Tramontin, *Contadini e movimento partigiano*, p. 303.

182 In the article, 'Isolare il nemico'.

183 Northern edition, 29 April 1945.

Garibaldini?' Italo was backed by Piero, according to whom, 'when the men are off duty it doesn't do to be excessively moralistic'. Italo was accused of being too light-hearted and flippant, and on this point his defence was: 'I don't take the mickey, but I have fun; life should be taken merrily', to which another who was present, Mascheroni, retorted: 'Being merry is often the cause of inconclusiveness at meetings. One needs to be serious.' But Italo was not to be beaten: 'Even at meetings you can joke and laugh. And besides, I'm not the only one.'[184]

This expostulation and reply gives some idea of the relationship between *severità* and *allegria*, whatever might have prompted the latter, in a situation that permitted no slackening of tension. The commissar Michele reprimanded commanders who participated in dances and 'little parties'.[185] Alongside the appeal to reasons of security, there appears at times, in these reproaches, the tendency to involve in the condemnation of rich people who were living it up in the midst of tragedy, those who, among the partisans, did not seem equal to their role. At work in these cases is the memory, in a new guise, of the age-old conviction that the poor have been deprived even of the possibility of enjoying life: this fact should be a cause for pride at a time when they were struggling to reverse this state of affairs. Witness the contempt with which what was going on in the hotels of Madesimo was denounced, where 'the pleasure-seeking folk of Milanese and local high society had got together, and, in utter disregard of the sufferings of the population, were living it up.'[186]

Also linked to the question of the personal dignity of those invested with a noble mission was the reproof of 'ferocious bickering even over access to drinking water', of down-market bravado, of useless 'multi-coloured ribbons and frills', of personal dirtiness, inadmissible 'even if one's clothes are in tatters and one's feet are bare'.[187]

'It is not dirtiness and slovenliness', says another document 'that distinguishes the partisan – a conscientious combatant of the people and of liberty – from the Fascist mercenary, but the care and propriety of his person, even in the difficult situation he is in, which attracts prestige and general respect.'[188]

All the same, it would be mistaken to conclude that the ideal of the perfect partisan was embodied in a type of human being rigid and severe to the point of

184 Transcript of the 21 March 1945 meeting (IG, *BG*, 01933)

185 Letter from the commissar of the 1st Gramsci Division to the commissar of the Volante Loss Brigade, Santino, 20 January 1945, and associated notes (*Le Brigate Garibaldi*, vol. III, pp. 254–7).

186 Order of the day no. 2 of the Command of the 90th Elio Zampiero brigade, 25 February 1945 (IG, *BG*, 01023).

187 Extract of a letter from the office of the political commissar of the unified command (Sesia Division – Ossola Division), sent to the commissar of the Volante Loss Brigade, undated but from winter 1944–45 (IG, *BG*, 06560).

188 Letter from 'C.F.' (federal committee?) to the Spartaco Lavagnini Detachment, undated (IG, *BG*, 011659).

surliness. What I have in mind here are not the numerous and well-documented somewhat mannered invitations to be good-humoured, which smack rather too much of the 'santa allegria' of Catholic moralism. Nor do I mean to stress the gap (a hallmark of the Communists, but present in the Actionists as well) between the man of today – the severe and inflexible militant – and the man of tomorrow, who alone will be allowed to enjoy a life in joyous expansion. My purpose, rather, is to recall the theme of the 'Resistance for man's happiness' (the formula that Simone de Beauvoir, in *The Mandarins*, puts into the mouth of one of her characters) – a happiness that can be partially anticipated insofar as the cost of conquering it is in itself a bearer of hope and even of gaiety. 'I wish to make it known that there is no melancholy among the partisans' – these words appear written on a mural newspaper.[189]

Roberto Battaglia, in his book of memoirs, put this point well. On the eve of his wedding, a partisan blows up a factory commandeered by the Germans. His reply to the question 'Why did you do it?' is: 'Just like that ... for fun ... I was about to get married.' Battaglia speaks of the 'light-hearted and jokey wind of folly' that was rustling through the partisans, and remarks: 'Almost as if the Italian need to reacquire, after so much indifference or meanness or selfishness, a mobile and light childlike spirit before reality so as to know how to live and die without emphasis.'[190]

The literature about the free zones has brought to light how a sudden and almost incredulous *joie de vivre* broke forth in those zones. In the precocious zone of Visso, in the Marche, Battaglia found an inebriating atmosphere; he felt 'cheered by the environment', invested with a 'new warm-heartedness'.[191] Ada Gobetti, during the first occupation of the Val Germanasca, was caught up in a climate of *allegra complicità*, almost holiday-like and almost playful, a climate of normality and serenity.[192] In the Republic of Montefiorino, the Catholic Gorrieri was struck by the excessive number of dances and of women, which seemed to him to be dangerous phenomena, comparable to the 'flaunting of red'.[193] In the

---

189 See Lazagna, *Ponte rotto*, p. 225. Here referring to a formation operating in the Ligurian Appennines, the author of these words perhaps had in mind the lyrics of a popular song, according to which 'there is no melancholy among the Genovese'. Whoever 'arrived among the partisans, however tired and sad', was lifted up again 'in the soul and in the heart' ('I nuovi e i vecchi compagni. Mie impressioni', report by Ramis on the Nino Franchi Detachment, 5 November 1944: INSMLI, *CLNAI*, envelope 8, folder 2, subfolder 12).

190 Battaglia, *Un uomo*, pp. 218–19, 227, 231.

191 Ibid., p. 35.

192 Gobetti, *Diario partigiano*, pp. 93–100 (March 1944). He had the same impression in Val Chisone the following June (p. 140). However, after the Nazi-Fascists reoccupied, he could read 'a stunned, disoriented sadness' on the faces of the valley's inhabitants (p. 104).

193 Gorrieri, *La Repubblica di Montefiorino*, pp. 370–4.

free zone of Cascia (February 1944) the festivities that were taking place inspired a Dutch colonel who had taken refuge there to remark: 'This is how we should live, given what is befalling us.' Portelli observed (though his comment cannot be taken as generally applicable): 'A liberated zone, like a festivity, is a protected space where new relations flourish; an upside-down world where workers and peasants feel they have power (and the fear that it is precarious only reinforces its festive connotation).'

A partisan fighting in the same zone remarks in turn: 'We can't always be thinking in terms of shooting'; merry-making is necessary 'especially for the young, to soothe their spirits ... otherwise one might go barmy'. Before the indecision of the inhabitants of Leonessa, another small town which had been liberated, Portelli's observation is this: 'The very gap between the facts and the version we are given of them gives voice to the dream of the free zone as a fragment of a future already achieved.'[194]

3. RELATIONS BETWEEN THE GENERATIONS

The *resistenti* experienced their connection both with anti-Fascism and with Fascism as a relationship between generations.

'There are short generations and long generations', Marc Bloch has written, 'and only observation enables us to identify the points at which the curve changes direction'. 'Generation', in this sense, should be seen as meaning a historical–cultural fact, and not just a question of people's literal dates of birth. It derives from a 'shared imprint' created by a 'shared age' or, as has also been written, by a fusion between 'personal time' and 'social time', due to 'great historical events' lived through together between their twenties and their thirties by people 'who have associated their age not with fashion but with history'.[1]

H. Stuart Hughes endorses this view in the following comment on Bloch's words: 'individuals who have participated in psychologically decisive events in company with people fifteen years their seniors may feel closer to these latter than they do to individuals only slightly younger than themselves who just

194 Portelli, *Biografia di una città*, pp. 273–6. See, too, the section 'Esodo', pp. 253–8, in Portelli's *Assolutamente niente*.

1 M. Bloch, 'Apologie pour l'histoire ou métier d'historien', *Cahiers des Annales*, Paris, 1949, and P. Abrams, 'Rites of passage: The Conflict of Generations in Industrial Society', in *Journal of Contemporary History* 5: I (1970), pp. 175–90 – the whole issue is devoted to 'Generations in Conflict'. In its elaboration of the historical–sociological concept of 'generation', K. Mannheim's 'The Problem of Generations' (in *Essays on the Sociology of Knowledge*, New York: Oxford University Press, 1952) remains of fundamental significance.

missed this great experience: the generations of the two world wars are a case in point'.[2]

However, there may also be a generational overlap, given the different dates and durations of the formative processes experienced by those involved, and the dissimilar effects that the very same great, and in so many respects unifying, experiences, like the two world wars, may nevertheless have. Thus the opposition between Fascists and anti-Fascists should be seen above all as a clash between two long generations, which intertwine in different ways with the natural generations. The Fascist generation was a long one. On the eve of its fall the regime had made an effort to weld the young people that it had itself forged (of whom Aldo Vidussoni, the twenty-eight-year-old penultimate party secretary, was to be the emblem) to the comrades of the early days, like the last secretary, Carlo Scorza, who did not intend to give up the fight. During the Social Republic this long generation attempted to rediscover its identity in the myth of the return to origins and in re-proposing the 'irresistibile ebrezza' ('irresistible inebriation') of risk to 'young men who are not such only because the registry office has them filed as the representatives of the last drafts'.[3] Mussolini himself recognised that the only men on whom the Republican Fascist Party could rely were the veterans and the very young.[4] And a long generation too was that born of the encounter between the anti-Fascists of the *ventennio* and the young *resistenti* of various backgrounds and inspirations.

The middle generation remained, by contrast, a short generation. Its liveliest members joined either the Fascist generation or the anti-Fascist one. Not even the generation of the Second World War, oppressed by the burden of defeat, managed to establish itself as a long generation. In spite of the tendencies towards ex-servicemen's solidarity that surfaced after 25 July and after 8 September, that generation was rent by the civil war. A powerful majority of it converged into the anti-Fascist generation; a more restricted minority sank into the Fascist one.

Within the anti-Fascist long generation, the younger ones had specific accounts to settle with the veterans. They reproached them for the errors they

---

2 H. S. Hughes, *Consciousness and Society*, New Brunswick: Transaction, 2002 [1958], p. 18.

3 On the first point, see D. Fossa, 'Il Partito e le Generazioni', and G. Pini, 'I nostri giovani', in *Gerarchia* XXI: 2 (February 1942), pp. 59–62, and XXII: 6 (June 1943), pp. 192–3. The latter piece resolved the question with a peremptory claim that 'there is no young people's question'. On the second point, see the 2 March 1944 *Il Regime fascista*.

4 Amicucci, *I seicento giorni*, p. 68. From research concerning one Emilian village – too restricted in scope to allow for generalisations (there being only 2,000 inhabitants) – it emerges that it was primarily men under twenty-four or over forty years of age who signed up for the Partito Fascista Repubblicano, thus missing out the age group that had the greatest presence in the Second World War. D. Gagliani, 'Ma chi erano i fascisti repubblicani?', in *Protagonisti* X: 34 (January–March 1989), pp. 28–32.

had committed and undertook not to repeat them. It is no accident that the creation of the long generation was more successful among the Communists and members of the Action Party and GL – that is, in the movements which in their pre-Resistance activities had already succeeded in presenting themselves as new.

The break with the defeated anti-Fascists was created more by the defeat than by age. In a previous chapter, I recorded Filippo Turati and Claudio Treves's bitter reflections during their Paris exile. After 25 July 1943, during the Resistance, and then during the days of the Liberation, irritation and often contempt for the revenants are evident.

Ada Gobetti, who was actually no longer that young, presents the two vice-mayors, the Socialist (Domenico Chiaramello) and the Christian Democrat (Giacchino Quarello), designated for Turin, as follows: 'Tranquil and satisfied like heirs finally coming into possession of an inheritance to which they had a right and of whose possession there was no longer any doubt.'[5] Franco Calamandrei is crueller than this when he describes his encounter in Rome with two Socialists: 'The older one is afflicted by a slight stutter, the younger one is slightly cross-eyed. From their persons, their manner, the vanity of their plans, I get a sense of discomfort, and am almost embarrassed for them because of their incompetence and evident inferiority complex.'[6]

The reproaches levelled at older people, and particularly parents, for having been Fascists was so painful and profound that the very connotation of the word 'Fascist' was at times watered down. There was the withering accusation of not having told the truth, of having hidden their pre-Fascist past even when it was part of their biography, of having exhorted them to play safe, of having in short betrayed their mission as educators:

The oldies know how to defend themselves well, and what a huge lie they tell to defend themselves! ... On the one hand, they say that they are indeed conscious that liberty is the best of things, and on the other hand they deny it in saying that they are old, and have a family and so many other moral ties that can't be dissolved. The paradox is this ... And they believe they love us and that they are doing right by giving us this advice, which fundamentally we could call selfish advice

This is how a young man was writing as early as 1934.[7]

---

5 Chiaramello sarcastically remarked on 'the revolutionary ideas our Ada has got into her head', on account of her discussion of internees, prisoners, the homeless, schools and the families of those victimised because of their politics (Gobetti, *Diario partigiano*, pp. 342–3: 14 April 1945).

6 Calamandrei, *La vita indivisibile*, p. 158 (24 March 1944).

7 Letter from Marcello Frullini to Aligi Barducci, Florence, 5 July 1934. Note the preceding letter, 24 May. The formation of an example of what Mannheim terms 'generational units' shines through in the comments Barducci, doing his military service

The son of the secretary of the pre-Fascist internal commission of the Galileo works in Florence has recounted how he never 'heard *babbo* [father] utter a word of political orientation for me to become this or that, never'; and he tries to explain that his parents

> loving us as they did, knowing how much they themselves had suffered, did not wish us to take the road they had taken ... Possibly in their heart of political hearts they would have been happier if we had done so, yet they were afraid of being responsible for guiding us along a road that might lead us to jail ... or worse.[8]

Nuto Revelli does not hesitate to reproach fathers who did not speak out in time.[9] When Piero D'Angiolini, a law student, read the newspapers of 1924–25 in the library, he became indignant with his father, a divisional chief in the Ministry of Finance, who had never spoken to him about the murder of Matteotti.[10] Artom writes of a young partisan that 'he feels the abyss separating fathers and sons and knows that it cannot be bridged. The abyss opened by the partiality of parents' opinions and by the shame that prevented their children from revealing the transformations that have come about in them, a more yawning abyss than ever, now that centuries seem to have passed between one generation and another.'

As far as he personally was concerned, Artom presented his youth as a reason for elitist pride: on 30 July 1943 he went to a GL meeting, and 'it galled them a bit when I said that of all those present I was the only one who had never shouted: viva il Duce'.[11] Without mincing words, a GL newspaper wrote: 'If the previous generation had had the courage to brave death in order to conserve liberty, today we wouldn't have needed to fight this war.'[12]

At times the confrontation took the form of tit-for-tat exchanges between the young and the old. An 'Appeal to the Young' by the Youth Front contains a curt declaration: 'Nothing can be expected from the old generations. Only we

---

in Messina, made to Frullini: 'It is with pleasure that I hear that you have discovered a *counterpart* of ours' (2 August 1934; the letters are in G. and E. Varlecchi, *Potente*, pp. 118, 114, 123). When the present author, then a second lieutenant, reached a border guard unit in 1941, an anti-fascist officer, Carlo Martinenghi, said to this *counterpart* of his – even before any exchange of their secret political views – 'One of our own has arrived'.

8 Giovanni Contini interviewing Bruno Banchelli, a Communist cadre in the Florence Pignone plant, 29 April 1980. G. Contini, 'Operaismo e innovazione. Militanza politica e alfabetizzazione imperfetta', in *Problemi del socialismo* 2–3 (1988), pp. 212–13.

9 Revelli, *La guerra dei poveri*, p. 124.

10 D'Angiolini's testimony, in conversation with the author.

11 Artom, *Diari*, p. 176 (23 February 1944) and p. 59.

12 'Ai partigiani' editorial of *Lungo il Tanaro*, newssheet of the 10th GL Alpine Division, April 1945.

young people can make the new Italy.' To which comes the crude rebuke: 'Death and deportation do not respect age.'[13]

In taking youth as the highway to salvation, there was the risk of making people slip towards the position of those who made invocations identical to those of the RSI in their attempt to distance themselves from decisions made on behalf of it. We young people, they wrote in one of their newspapers which came in for a rough time from the Fascist authorities, 'tomorrow, however things turn out, will have to impose our will on the country. Old men and old systems continue to dominate more or less everywhere: it is with this stale garbage that we have to make a clean break if we are to present ourselves as free and rejuvenated in the post-war fray'; but such was the fracture created by the civil war that the same newspaper invoked firing-squad executions to avenge comrades killed by the partisans.[14]

The intellectuals were called to account particularly heavily: 'We can shout at them that they didn't educate us' – and, besides, what did one encounter in the Italian literary tradition? In Manzoni there was the 'hidden hypocrisy ... midway between the priest and the bourgeois', in Carducci and D'Annunzio 'the rhetorical bombast of the mixture of a classical formalism and an oratorical and popular low romanticism'.[15]

There were invocations, together with warnings, not to betray a second, and irremediable, time. Bewildered, and anxious to find in the professors 'not only masters of knowledge, but men, defenders of that honour and that humanity which were the pride of the free school of Italy' is how the students declared themselves when they implored the professors not to take the oath to the Social Republic. 'If we have been given the task of paying for the errors of a past that we refuse to recognise as our own, it is for you to offer us your doleful experience, so that youth is not betrayed once again.' Emphatic, diplomatic and menacing words: whoever swears the oath 'will be expelled from teaching after the war'.[16]

---

13 Appeal published in *Virtù e Lavoro* (in the municipality of San Vito al Tagliamento). Comrade Sante's reply is from 20 March 1945 (IZDG, envelope 272, folder IV/A).

14 The Modena Fascist paper *Valanga repubblicana*, 8 October 1944, quoted in Gorrieri, *La Repubblica di Montefiorino*, p. 201. One issue of the paper was seized from the newsstands, and its director, the young officer Rino Lavini, relieved of his duties.

15 'Umanità e cultura', initialed 'L.N.' in *Chiarezza* ('Notebooks of political discussion among the youth, free voice of the Associazione universitaria studentesca'), July–August 1944 (a typescript in my possession). One young woman (Franca Gronda, from Milan), though approving of the substance of the text containing this and other statements, noted in the margin 'The style is too extravagant for any sincerity to come through!'

16 Appeals of the 'Comitato studentesco di agitazione' ('Student agitation committee') and 'Comitato di difesa degli insegnanti aderente al Fronte della gioventù' ('Committee in defence of teachers attached to the Youth Front') – notable, here, that

Weighing heavily on the young was the inheritance of the Fascist-style slogans 'Make way for the young' and of 'Giovinezza! Giovinezza!' Repudiating one's elders might have been a way of getting out of a tight corner. A clandestine Catholic newspaper spoke of Fascism as a 'gerontocracy of the generation who wanted the war'[17] – so vivid was the memory in certain Catholic circles of the papal condemnation of 'useless slaughter', which in other respects, like democratic belligerence, formed, by contrast, one of the fundamental elements of the long wave of secular anti-Fascism.

'Make way for the young?' wrote a newspaper of the Italian Students' Union for Liberty, but the young people worth their salt would in any case come forward, while it was as well for the others to stay where they were.[18] Actually, in that context the very word *goliardica* (university student) rang a bit false, though it was adopted also by a newspaper of the Youth Front[19] 'Trovarsi smarriti' ('Finding yourself at a loss') is the title of an article that appeared in a Young Socialists' newspaper. The article describes the bewilderment provoked in the young by the youth-obsessed Fascist mottos, and immediately adds: 'And anyway how can we be blamed for it?':

> Ours has been the story first of men's reprobation, then of doubt and the all too easy burial of a faith. Now it is of disgust, of hatred for those who gulled us, of regret at having lost our bearings, of the tormenting desire to do something, to be finally worthy of the Patria, of the older people who did not deflect, of the masters who here and there illuminate the shadowy regions we have traversed. And we've become anti-Fascists with so enraged and overwhelming an anti-Fascism that alone, politically, it is no longer enough for us, now that the crimes of the neo-Fascists are so gross as to make [our anti-Fascism] merge with a general front against criminality.[20]

In the same paper, 'l'anziano di turno' (that day's older contributor) offered his reply. He seemed to be frightened by so much fury, and, before the claim that what the future demanded did not mean adhesion to a party programme, was ready to offer the reassuring picture of the 'inevitable destiny of socialism,

---

just like women and peasants, university professors had to be 'defended', and at that by students (*Attività clandestina*, pp. 11–12).

17 Box 'Ai giovani', signed 'faber', *Il Segno*, 1 March 1944.

18 See 'Il nostro posto', in *Libertà* (Rome), 1 May 1944. Another article, 'Vent'anni di ineducazione', was very critical as regards bad educators, professors, men of culture etc. *L'Unione*, which said it had emerged on 25 May 1943 – in memory of the Unione Goliardica born on 23 March 1924 – 'supported the Partito liberale'.

19 *Nuova Goliardia*, organ of the students of the Fronte della gioventù, Genoa, 1 October 1944 (*Saggio bibliografico*, n. 2839).

20 *Avanguardia*, 'Paper of the Socialist youth', June 1944 (the article is signed by 'a young man').

a supreme good lying at the end, not far-off by now, towards which mankind is being driven' – a description in heartfelt tones that could well have been found in a newspaper at the turn of the century.

Outbursts of hatred against the Fascists, based on the generation factor, were frequent:

> And really it must be said that this generation's hatred, the hatred we young people have for Fascism is, in its intensity and insatiability, something altogether particular. We have hated Fascism as those who have never known anything else; not with the passion of the political adversary, which is itself a source of life, but with anxiety that it might be identified with our very destiny.[21]

Books like Ruggero Zangrandi's pioneering work,[22] and prominent personalities like Pietro Ingrao, have attributed to the 'long journeys' of the young, primarily students, from so-called left-wing Fascism to anti-Fascism (and Communism above all) a more important role than they actually had. Significant, though, on the issue of generations, is the regret expressed by a Fascist paper, mentioned earlier, that the young had found themselves on opposite sides of the barricades.[23]

If we shift our sights to the older people, by and large we find that, the less engaged they had been in militant anti-Fascism and the less they were now engaged in the active Resistance, the more severe they were in their attitude to the young – a severity mitigated only by paternalism. While the anti-Fascist survivors of jail, internment, exile, did have doubts and prejudices about the young who had been born and educated under Fascism, they were also, witnessing their commitment, ready to overcome these.[24] For their part, the young, above all with regard to the survivors of exile, felt admiration and respect, though fear too that the latter had lost contact with the real state of affairs in Italy. This applied not just to the political plane but to social customs too: it was hard for even the best-intentioned veteran to understand certain changes that had come about in those who had lived 'legally' in the years of Fascism. 'Oh! Una capocellula che

---

21 Rome edition of *Avanti!*, 30 December 1943, with a page devoted to the killing of Mario Fioretti by a Fascist ('La figura del caduto').

22 I refer, here, to R. Zangrandi, *Il lungo viaggio attraverso il fascismo*, Milan: Feltrinelli, 1962 (a more succinct first edition was published in 1947).

23 This type of passage from Fascism to anti-Fascism is judged harshly in the article 'Peccatori contro lo spirito', appearing in the liberal Piedmont paper *L'Opinione*, 14 January 1945. On the Fascist left's early hints at a rapprochement with socialism – mainly among students – see the letter from Lucio Luzzatto to Giuseppe Faravelli, November 1936 (in Merli, *La ricostruzione*, pp. 743–4).

24 One fine example is the obituary that Eugenio Colorni – soon before himself being killed – wrote of Giuseppe Lopresti, shot at the Fosse Ardeatine (copy in the author's possession).

balla!' ('Oh! A woman partisan leader dancing!'), exclaimed a horrified older comrade about a former partisan; and the latter explained: 'We already had a different vision of life ... We had seen nuns taking part in the Resistance!'[25]

As I have said, it was the revenants of various shades who proved, at least initially, to be least sympathetic towards the young, almost as if, paradoxically, they had assimilated one of the aspirations of aggressive nationalism – the substitution of the class struggle with the generational struggle.[26]

'Old and new democracy', an article possibly penned by Ivanoe Bonomi, derided those who blamed the advent of Fascism on the old institutions and the older men: the culprits were either the young, ill-educated by Fascism, or older men who failed, at the opportune time, to give their leaders the support that would have enabled the latter to 'react in quite another way'.[27] Those who spoke in terms of the 'ruins of the Aventino' met with a contemptuous reply: 'The young who, if only out of necessity, up until 25 July kept that party membership card "from which the ruins of the Aventino, and not just they, remained immune, and above all kept their anti-Fascist sentiments locked in their breasts, should wait a bit before seeking the limelight. Certain infections require a period of quarantine."'[28]

To complete the reassurance, the youth paper of the same 'Party of Democracy and Labour' trembled with indignation against those who were going around saying that 'the young don't feel the need for authority, for order, for control'.[29]

Before extremist positions of this sort there shone the good sense of those wise and well-balanced young people who recognised that it was not easy to free oneself from Fascism, which had penetrated into their brains, but added that this was no less applicable to the old than to the young.[30] More often than not the elderly assumed indulgent tones, shading into blandishments. The Liberal Paolo Serini, having described as confused and suspicious the young people who had believed in Fascism 'with the fideistic abandon typical of their age', concluded: 'We want to draw near them in order to help them.'[31] The 'New Year's message

---

25 Testimony of Teresa Cirio (Bruzzone and Farina, *La Resistenza taciuta*, p. 30). On the novelties in the lives of young people in the 1930s, see the food for thought given by Victoria de Grazia in her aforementioned discussion with Luisa Passerini (p. 24), as well as the same author's *The Culture of Consent: Mass Organization and Leisure in Fascist Italy*, New York: Cambridge University Press, 1981). On the differences among the older and younger generations of incarcerated women, see Mariani, *Quelle dell'idea*.

26 See Mosse, *Masses and Man*.

27 *Azione democratica*, 31 January 1944.

28 'Note in margin', *ibid*.

29 'Autorità e abulia', *Rinascita giovanile*, 24 May 1944.

30 'Pregi e difetti della nostra generazione', *L'Azione*, 10 November 1943.

31 See the pamphlet *Orientamenti programmatici*, p. 12 (*Quaderni del Risorgimento liberale*, 4).

to the young' of the Italian Socialist Party of Proletarian Unity (PSIUP) spoke of young people who had been duped and betrayed, and invoked an 'obscure sentiment of pity for yourselves and your vanished illusions'.[32]

The Catholics swung between the most diverse positions. There were young people who claimed to have 'gone over spiritually to anti-Fascism even if, out of a false formal conscience, they did not dare enter into contact with the anti-Fascist organisation'. Therefore, they added, there was no sense in the accusations of incoherence levelled at the young by the old: 'Shouldn't they perhaps accuse the more mature generations instead?'[33]

But there were also young Catholics who, acknowledging themselves to be 'miseducated and bewildered', seemed to step aside respectfully to make way for their elders,[34] and older people glad to acknowledge that 'the best young people' understood that 'it was natural that the helm of the ship of the nation should be taken up again by the "first men"'.[35] Still in April 1946, Attilio Piccioni, a former member of the Italian Popular Party would accuse the young, 'used to the wicked climate' of Fascism, of having derived from it 'aridity of heart, careerism and contempt for any dedication consisting of humility', thereby attracting this pitiless reply from the young Carlo Donat Cattin: 'The experience of our contact with the anti-Fascist political class is a bitter one and only adds to the experience of Fascism, which it would be absurd to deny'.[36]

In political terms, the problem was that of the relationship between the Italian Popular Party and the Christian Democrat party. If experience had taught that 'making way for the young' demanded caution, entrenchment in 'making way for the old' was no less advisable. It is no accident that Alcide De Gasperi explicitly made himself the promoter of an intergenerational line, quite different from the model of the 'long generation', the equivalent rather of the inter-class policy. In an article that appeared in the clandestine edition of *Il Popolo*, he wrote: 'We are younger and older people who have given each other a hand to build a bridge between two generations, between whom Fascism had attempted

---

32 *Avanti!*, Rome edition, 12 January 1944.

33 'La Generazione vittima', article signed by 'Stilcone', *Il Segno*, 18 May 1944. Ronconi also suggests reading the differences among the upper and lower clergy in generational terms, in *Note sui rapporti fra il clero toscano, la Repubblica sociale italiana e le autorità d'occupazione tedesche*, p. 137.

34 'I giovani parlano ai vecchi', signed 'Uno del '22' (i.e. born in 1922) in *Il Popolo*, Rome edition, 23 January 1944. It is probably a response to 'Posizioni di giovani', an article published in the 12 December 1943 edition signed 'Uno del '19', which raised the alarm over the fact that 'young people view the men of the pre-Fascist period – no use denying it – with little trust'.

35 'La Democrazia Cristiana ai giovani', poster printed in Bologna just after Liberation (MRB, Raccolta Adversi).

36 Open letter to Piccioni, 'Il problema dei giovani', in *Il Popolo nuovo*, 14 April 1946.

to dig an abyss': namely, the First World War generation, who later 'experienced the turbid social struggles' and tried in vain to oppose Fascism, and the generation who had lived through Fascism 'without getting contaminated'.[37]

Elsewhere we have seen how, for the Communists, the conflict between generations sometimes figured as being between the old guard, more or less *bordighista* in origin, but whose roots also lay in the temperamentally fence-sitting attitude of 'neither adhere nor sabotage', and the lively fighting spirit of the young. Those of the Communist leaders who preferred the latter attitude did however denounce, realistically but with pedagogic indulgence, certain features that the Garibaldini had inherited from Fascism: 'Certainly one cannot ignore the fact that our volunteers are all young men who have undergone twenty years of Fascist rule and who therefore are in need of intense and continuous explanation, clarification and persuasion', says one report.[38] And another blames the difficulties that the partisans sometimes had in their relations with the population on the 'evil consequences of Fascist miseducation, which cannot be wiped out just like that in young twenty-year-olds brimming over with life and energy'.[39] The instructions of one Command are inspired by undisguised pedagogy:

Very often, rather than gathering more comrades, pretend to be interested in a possibly stupid conversation and then gently let things slide into subjects that interest us more. Having got the discussion going like this, it's sometimes better to pretend to withdraw from it and let the comrades chew over the subject, otherwise you would very often end up giving a monologue, given how much better informed you are than the comrades listening. If you hear cock-eyed things don't interrupt immediately; let them get into the habit of putting forward a concept, way out though it might be, then, with very simple words and reasoning, correct them. Speak with the greatest simplicity, in such a way that the comrade is not nonplussed by reasoning

---

37 Demofilo, 'La parola dei democratici cristiani', in the 12 December 1943 issue. The article was then republished as a pamphlet in January 1944, which can now be found, under the title 'Rinascita della Democrazia cristiana. 1.' in A. De Gasperi, *I cattolici dall'opposizione al governo*, Laterza, Bari 1955, pp. 477–91. In the early post-war years, a group of young Catholic intellectuals set up the magazine *Terza Generazione*, their number including Gianni Baget-Bozzo, Barto Ciccardini (its director), Leopoldo Elia and Baldo Scassellati. The name 'Third Generation' meant the generation of the editors themselves, after the 'first', pre-Fascist generation and the 'second' generation, the anti-Fascists. See, too, G. Tassani, *La terza generazione. Da Dossetti a De Gasperi, tra Stato e rivoluzione*, Edizioni Lavoro, Rome 1988, in particular Chapter 10, 'Fuori dalle parti: "Terza Generazione"'.

38 'Relazione generale' of the 4th Daniele Manin Brigade (Piedmont), 5 November 1944 (IG, BG, 04456).

39 'Relazione di Antonio su una ispezione a Monforte', 18 December 1944 (*Le Brigate Garibaldi*, vol. III, pp. 107–8).

that is too difficult for him; in short, make sure that when comrades talk to you or anyhow when they take part in a discussion, they don't immediately feel the commissar's presence, but rather the accessible reasoning of a comrade who is also having his 'say'. In any case, examples are more important than anything else.[40]

This was a far cry from the behaviour of those Communists, exiles for years in the USSR, who addressed the Italian prisoners 'in the wrong tone, in committee-room jargon, which was mostly incomprehensible, and with inquisitorial and illogical questions like: "Why have you come? Why didn't you rebel? Why didn't you desert?"'.[41] In the case of the Communists, too, it was the most prestigious leader who assumed responsibility for ensuring that the manner adopted towards the young was consistent with the general line of the 'partito nuovo'. Togliatti made numerous approaches to the young, even, as we have seen, to those fighting on the opposite side in the civil war.[42]

Interwoven with the generational problem within the Communist party was the other, more complex, one of the partial 'succession' of the PCI to the PSI. This phenomenon occurred at times within the same family nucleus, precisely as if it were something being handed over by one generation to another.

'Was your dad a Socialist?' – 'Yes, in those days he was a Socialist because the Communists weren't around yet', is the answer a Turinese worker born in 1904 recently gave to her interviewer.[43] 'Here's to the young partisan recruits and their parents!' said a Romagnolo poster that intended to thank the parents for having persuaded their children to join the Garibaldini.[44] By contrast, 'a seventy-year-old man, who had stuck to the pre-1914 war positions', called the Communists 'figliol prodighi' ('prodigal sons'), and interpreted the contemplated fusion between the two parties as a wish to 'return to the fold'.[45]

I myself personally remember various episodes of the initiation into Communism within traditionally Socialist family circles. Here I have to add

---

40 Extract of a letter from the office of the political commissar of the unified command (Sesia Division – Ossola Division), sent to the commissar of the Volante Loss Brigade, undated but from winter 1944–45 (IG, BG, 06560).

41 Gambetti, 'L' Alba', giornale dei prigionieri italiani in URSS, p. 340.

42 Refer back, here, to the text 'Ai giovani', published in the July 1944 La Rinascita, where young people – on whom 'it is too easy to lay ... blame that is not theirs' – were called 'victims' and 'made a mockery of' by fascism (Togliatti, Opere, vol. V, pp. 52–4). See, too, the report to the cadres of the Naples Communist organisation, 11 April 1945 (ibid., p. 35).

43 Passerini, Torino operaia, p. 19. On these movements within working-class families, see Guidetti Serra, Compagne, passim, and A voi cari compagni.

44 See Casali, Il movimento di liberazione a Ravenna, I, p. 51 (this undated poster is probably from January 1944).

45 'The kind of thing that gives you goose bumps', the Communist who recounted the episode commented, on 21 April 1945 (quoted in Gibelli, Genova operaia, p. 294).

that, on numerous occasions, the Communists showed intolerance towards the human and political dotage of the Socialists, and we have already seen some examples of this; 'they've remained stuck in the same old positions of 1920–21'; their activism is scant, but they enjoy 'a certain amount of sympathy among the older workers'; they are 'survivors'.[46] Then again, their claim, as in Modena, to invoke the relations sanctioned by the 1921 election appears absurd.[47] It is evident that, in judgments of this kind, no account is taken of the minority young people's wing of the PSIUP, originating from the MUP (Movement of Proletarian Unity), whom the Communists suspected of 'leftism'.[48]

But, leaving aside the competitive dislikes and fears on the left, the Communists were capable of lucid foresight. Thus, at a 'meeting of PCI representatives in several Padua plants', to combat the opinion that 'the Socialists didn't exist', this was said: 'Tomorrow at the polling-stations you will see how many folk who are today singing the praises of the Soviet Union and Communism will be more willing to give their vote to the Socialist Party than to the Communist Party'.[49]

The Action Party too had put itself forward as the bearer of a new and ideologically up-to-date socialist message, to succeed the old PSI. The Action Party,

---

46 Giovanni's report from Turin, 22–24 August 1943; an anonymous, undated report from Brescia (December 1943?); a report by 'comrade Silvio' on the provinces of Terni and Perugia, 25 June 1944 (all in IG, *Archivio PCI*; the former is partially reproduced in Secchia, *Il PCI e la guerra di liberazione*, pp. 90–2, and the latter in the 23 June 1964 *Rinascita*). A member of the Rome military organisation of the PSIUP, a FATME worker whose thirtieth birthday had been and gone, asked the present author – being the young man that he was – how on earth he had gone along with the Socialists and not the Communists. His face bore an amazed, distressed and stern expression.

47 Letter from the PCI federation to the PSIUP federation, 21 October 1944 (ISHR, *Archivio del triumvirato insurrezionale dell'Emilia-Romagna*). In 1919, the PSI had won some 60 percent of votes in Modena province, but in 1947 received 26 percent as against 44.2 percent for the PCI (see Gorrieri, *La Repubblica di Montefiorino*, p. 701).

48 On 23 March 1945, in a letter to Pertini, Basso showed his pride in having been able to substitute the old members of the Party with young people (see Salvati, *Il Psiup Alta Italia*, p. 84). In December 1937, the Socialists' 'internal centre', in correspondence with the Austrian party, described its illegal groups as being formed of 'the young and very young', above all intellectuals, while 'working-class elements are generally of more advanced years' and 'the old guard of the Party ... is not activist, with some exceptions'. See, too, the report from Erba to the national council, 3 December 1938, and the letter from Curiel to the PCI leadership of 15 May 1938, in which he displayed his respect for the tired old members (see Merli, *La ricostruzione*, pp. 790, 810–12, 800).

49 Report on the meeting of 18 March 1945 (*Le Brigate Garibaldi*, vol. III, p. 494). In the constituent assembly votes of June 1946, the Socialists obtained 4,758,129 votes (20.72 percent) and the Communists 4,356,686 (18.6 percent). See C. Ghini, *L'Italia che cambia. Il voto degli italiani 1946–1976*, Rome: L'Unità – Editori Riuniti, 1976, p. 34.

it was claimed, 'is the Socialist Party of the new generation'.[50] This conviction was shared by many of the party's leaders, from Parri to Calogero and Foa. That things did not turn out like this is an issue that goes beyond that of different generations.[51]

4. RECKONING WITH THE PAST

If the Resistance was anything it was an attempt to settle accounts with the past.

'Il miserabile crollo dello Stato fascista fa sì che oggi tutti i nodi vengano al pettine', said *L'Italia Libera*[1] – a declaration which might be translated as follows: 'The wretched collapse of the Fascist state means that today no one will escape a whipping'. Here *tutti* should be interpreted in a sense that goes beyond the problem of the state and power, the one immediately posed by the Action Party newspaper. Many threads of my argument so far are in fact connected by a series of questions: How responsible were the Italian people for the birth, advent and dominion of Fascism? How was it possible to transform the sense of guilt, the desire for expiation, the proclamations of innocence into a project for the future? Not the social, economic, institutional and political programmes, elaborated and achieved to a greater or lesser extent, that were put forward at the time, but fundamental aspirations and the desire that that exceptional historical opportunity should not be missed. Nor, as far as the past is concerned, do I mean to examine the historiographic validity of the theses formulated at the time, even if some points of view of the *resistenti* have inspired the historians' subsequent arguments to various degrees. What I wish to do, rather, is seek to glean some features that distil the experience lived at the time – an experience which was later bracketed, to a greater or lesser extent in manipulated and distorted form, among the different facets of the shared collective version of things. It should never be forgotten that the victory of the *resistenti* was 'the work of a minority – the work of a large minority, but still in no sense the achievement of the whole Italian people'.[2]

---

50 Motion by the Milan section, just after Liberation (ISRT, *Partito d'Azione*, envelope 15, folder 4, Stampa, subfolder *Non Mollare*). See, too, the 'Presentazione' in *Giovani*, Rome, 1 March 1944.

51 See De Luna, *Storia del Partito d'Azione*, in particular p. 41. Again on 14 July 1946, Tristano Codignola, in a letter to Enzo Enriques Agnoletti, lamented the fact that the Action Party had not seized the reins of the Socialist Party, towards which it showed a blunt disrespect (ISRT, *Carte Enzo Enriques Agnoletti*, envelope 1, folder 13, subfolder *Carteggi vari*).

1 Editorial, 'Dopo il congresso di Bari. Il problema del potere', in the 18 February 1944 Lombardy edition.

2 Hughes, *United States and Italy*, p. 135.

But nor should it be forgotten that the intensity of the experience of that large minority, who truly wanted to settle accounts with the past, was to reverberate throughout the entire Italian people, who absorbed, though partly debased, its achievements. Rosario Romeo, the last great Italian liberal historian, has formulated a fundamentally correct judgment on this point:

> The Resistance, valued in terms of an albeit hypothetical 'second Risorgimento', allowed ... solid connections to be established with the more prestigious national tradition. In this way accounts with the Fascist past were settled in Italy extremely rapidly with the general forgetting of all responsibilities and of all the sins committed, which were soon absolved by one and all as being venial.[3]

Early on, a poet and essayist warned, with one of his paradoxical proposals, against the consequences of this attitude: 'As from 1 January of the year 2000 no politician or political party or similar movement will be able to declare themselves not responsible for their errors, nor expect a diminution of public blame by pleading that there was Fascism.'[4]

There is one aspect of Italy's responsibility which more or less all the documents and testimonies of the Resistance period choose to keep quiet about, and which clearly exemplifies what has just been said: the question of responsibility in the persecution against the Jews. The racial campaign, when it is spoken about, is blamed exclusively on the more fanatical of the Fascists, and even then insofar as they were dominated by the Nazis. Rather than becoming a stimulus for a critical examination of the forms that anti-Semitism had assumed in a country such as Catholic Italy, the way in which the racial campaign had been conducted and the resistance it had encountered, that resistance became a source of self-congratulation for being better than the Germans, whose treatment of the Jews in Russia was denounced at times in the Resistance press.[5] As is well known, the far from transparent attitude taken at the time and later towards the persecution of the Jews was paraded by the Catholic Church as proof of its extraneousness to Nazi-Fascism. When the newspaper of the Catholic Communists wished to indicate what was most despicable about anti-Semitism, it made the following gaffe: 'To attack men for what they cannot *liberate* themselves from.' The self-criticism of many Italians, both secular and religious, for their personal responsibility towards the Jews took the form of concrete action, offering them help and refuge, even if other Italians behaved ignobly.[6]

---

3 R. Romeo, *Nazione*, in *Enciclopedia del Novecento*, IV, 1979, p. 632.

4 'Articolo primo della confederazione italiana', *Gazzetta del Nord*, 5 August 1946.

5 See *Il Risorgimento Liberale*, Rome edition, 15 April 1944.

6 The quote (my italics) is taken from 'Cattolici ed Ebrei', *Voce Operaia*, 26 October 1943. Apart from what I have already cited in previous pages, see also G. Miccoli, 'Santa

The debate about the foundations, breadth and results of the post-war anti-Fascist purging lies at the junction between a past that had to be repudiated and punished, but also understood, and a future to be safeguarded against any new risk of a Fascist nature. The condemnation of Fascist conduct, even of decisions to support the Social Republic, had to give due consideration to the need to live with certain results of that behaviour and those decisions that could not be eliminated. All would depend on the clarity of ideas and the moral and political strength that one succeeded in bringing into play. Togliatti went so far as to say that the doors of the Communist Party should not be closed even to those who, out of necessity, had sworn allegiance to the Social Republic[7] – and that the party was a voluntary association, not a necessary one, as the state was. When Mauro Scoccimarro, the high commissioner for the *epurazione* (the anti-Fascist purging process), accelerated the crisis of Bonomi's first government by giving an interview in which he demanded greater punitive vigour, at party headquarters he was severely reprimanded by Togliatti, who was echoed by Giuseppe Di Vittorio: 'The purging has made us appear ... as elements who wanted to ruthlessly punish all those, and there are millions of them, who have in one way or another performed Fascist activities. We have failed to maintain the imprint that was ours in the long years of national unitary political action.'

Ermete (Agostino Novella) sealed this position by urging a 'stronger reaction against the orientation of the party rank-and-file', who were demanding greater rigour.[8]

Very rarely during the Resistance were blanket condemnations or absolutions of the Italian people pronounced. Judgments about collective responsibility were immediately splintered and diversified, passing at times from one side to another. Nevertheless, even though not everyone spoke about it, weighing on one and all was the shadow of the suspicion that Fascism had been, as Gobetti had said, the autobiography of the Italians – the hallmark of a historical inferiority that began at least with the sad triumph of 'Guicciardini's man', the prototype of the Italian who only thinks of his own interests, referred to by De Sanctis.[9] A

Sede e Chiesa italiana di fronte alle leggi antiebraiche del 1938', in *La legislazione antiebraica in Italia e in Europa*, acts of the conference held upon the fiftieth anniversary of the Racial Laws (Rome, 17–18 October 1988), pp. 163–274, and S. Zuccotti, *L'Olocausto in Italia*, Milan: Mondadori, 1987. Also, more generally, R. De Felice, *Storia degli ebrei italiani sotto il fascismo*, Turin: Einaudi, 1972.

7 P. Togliatti, 'I compiti del partito nella situazione attuale', speech in Florence, 3 October 1944 (*Opere*, vol. V, p. 105).

8 The interview with Scoccimarro appeared in the 10 November *Avanti!*. On the hostility towards Scoccimarro, above all from the quarter of the Liberal treasury minister, Soleri, and Admiral De Courten, minister of the navy, see Flores, *L'epurazione*, pp. 425–6. The transcript of the leadership meeting, 16–18 December 1944, is in IG, *Archivio PCI*. Only Grieco took Scoccimarro's side.

9 Four works, which could be brought together under the title 'De antiquissima

book about the reconstruction of Italy published in England in 1941 had already sought to combat this defeatist pessimism, which was indeed greatly fanned by comparison with the English model, noting that Italy had 'erroneously' been deemed 'more inclined than other western nations to throw herself into the arms of a dictator'.[10] In his last letter to his brother Luigi, Giaime Pintor made a severe remark about the Italian people, 'flabby, profoundly corrupted by her recent history, always on the point of giving in to an act of cowardice or a weakness', but expressed faith in the revolutionary minorities which Italy possessed and in the fact that 'today all the possibilities of the Risorgimento are once again open to the Italians'.[11]

An article that appeared in the clandestine edition of *Avanti!*, and which was certainly penned by an old pre-Fascist, juxtaposed, as was often the case in these acts of self-flagellation, a drastic condemnation, an invitation to keep quiet out of charity for the *patria*, and finally an obligatory optimism: 'That the wretched twenty-year business has laid bare the political acerbity and spiritual inadequacy of a whole people, is, unhappily, a truth which it is as well not repeat to others or to ourselves'; but this does not mean that 'the Italian people are the constitutional village idiot'.[12]

At least two roads diverged from the recognition of the people's misdeeds and weaknesses. The first finished by taking the reverse turn of indemnity for one and all. The second attempted a more carefully considered judgment. Both contained elements of realism, in the sense that they called into question the consolatory image of a civil people instinctively hostile to tyranny.

The first position is formulated particularly clearly in several Liberal Party writings, chiefly from the Roman area, aimed at encouraging the emergence of the very few and uncorrupted elect to lead the cowardly and compromised majority. This line had been taken early on in a pamphlet by Niccolò Carandini,[13] and was then repeated and developed in various ways. *Il Risorgimento Liberale* wrote: 'It was the fault of one and all, with the due exception of the few superior spirits

Italorum insipientia', and which had significant distribution after Liberation, consecrated this viewpoint: G. Fenoaltea, *Storia degli italieschi dalle origini ai giorni nostri*, Florence: G. Barbèra, 1945; G. A. Borgese, *Golia. Marcia del fascismo*, Milan: Mondadori, 1946 (the first edition, in English, was published by Viking Press in the USA in 1937–38 as *Goliath: The March of Fascism*); G. Colamarino, *Il fantasma liberale*, Milan: Bompiani, (undated, but 1945); F. Cusin, *Antistoria d'Italia*, Turin: Einaudi, 1948.

10 PENTAD, *The Remaking of Italy*, p. 262.

11 Pintor, *Il sangue d'Europa*, pp. 245–8.

12 'Scherziamo', 8 November 1943 (no indication as to the edition).

13 Movimento Liberale Italiano, *Primi chiarimenti*, 1 May 1943. The pamphlet commenting on 25 July, subsequent to this one, again the work of Carandino, toned down this haughtiness somewhat, but reminded readers that 'a people is not redeemed in just one night' (*Realtà*, 15 August 1943, p. 6). On the attribution of these Liberal pamphlets, see E. Camurani, *Bibliografia del PLI*, pp. 33–4.

who knew how to steer clear of all these errors.'[14] With rhetorical élan, Medici Tornaquinci was to say: 'To purge ourselves of twenty years of tyranny which the whole nation was responsible for having accepted and tolerated … it was necessary for the nation to suffer, fight, bleed.'[15]

The most cultivated formulation of this attitude was given by Benedetto Croce in the famous passage in which, after sketching a scornful portrait of Mussolini, he adds:

> But he, called to answer for the damage and shame into which he has cast Italy with his words and actions and with all his arts of oppression and corruption, could reply to the Italians as that wretched demagogue of Florence, spoken of by Giovanni Villani, replied to his fellow exiles who rebuked him for having led them to the disaster of Montaperti: 'Why then did you believe in me?'[16]

Actually, these words suggest a distinction between the active responsibility of the leader and the passive responsibility of the people, and, though the ruling class is placed in parenthesis, this distinction is less simplistic than Churchill's pragmatic formula of 'one man, one man alone', being responsible for Italy's misfortunes. Taddeo Orlandi, General Commander of the *carabinieri*, took his cue instead, without further ado, from this *lectio facilior* (facile reading) when, saying he was convinced that he was speaking for the 'best Roman circles', he hoped that the Allies would understand that 'Italy is paying for the misdeeds of one man', and had already paid enough.[17]

In the Catholic press the problem of the responsibility of everyone, of only a few, or of just one[18] acquired notable intensity, but contradictory slants as well. De Gasperi, the candidate for the 'succession', sought to grasp the lifeline thrown by Churchill and to give it greater solidity. He wrote that

---

14 'Alibi', in the 18 August 1943 Rome edition. More balanced was the judgment in the northern edition, which noted the 'political neurasthenia' of Italians, the same people in the same town-squares having shifted from red to black in the years 1919–22; but it deemed the behaviour of the masses 'admirable, as a whole'. However, the paper also invited readers to 'recognise also the courageous conduct of at least part of the ruling classes' ('Carattere', in the 1 February 1944 issue).

15 Speech of 24 September 1944 to the first assembly of the Florence section of the Liberal Party (printed in a pamphlet, 'La Sezione di Firenze del Partito liberale italiano', in ISRT, *Archivio Medici Tornaquinci*, envelope 10, 1, no. 1).

16 B. Croce, *Scritti e discorsi politici*, Bari: Laterza, 1973, pp. 217–18 (under the date 2 December 1944).

17 Report from the general Taddeo Orlando to the Ministries of the Interior and of War, 10 August 1944, 'Notizie varie sulla capitale' (held at the Archivio Centrale dello Stato, quoted in Aga-Rossi, *La situazione politica ed economica*, pp. 109–10).

18 For *La Voce Repubblicana*, the one man responsible, even more than the Duce, was the king. See 'Come si imbroglia il popolo', 30 January 1944.

the Italian people, 'as English and American statesmen have solemnly admitted, are not to be held responsible for Mussolini's bids for conquest'.[19] But less than a couple of months earlier, in the same newspaper, a quivering piece of invective had appeared against 'the vast majority of Italians ... who were jointly responsible for the appalling disaster' and against 'the tendency to obliterate past offences in order to look only to the future. A convenient expedient to evade individual and collective responsibilities; but a dreadful beginning for a radical renewal of national life which the utter ruin of the country demands'.[20]

The fire animating this article (which – and this was quite something for a Catholic broadsheet – even succeeds in mentioning Guernica)[21] smacks of a young person's pen, as does an article that appeared soon after De Gasperi's, quoted above: 'Let's face facts: the great majority of the people have been emasculated ... And enough with the myth of Rome, with the millenary tradition of the race, of imperial destiny, the cradle of art, of Christianity. Only babies sleep in cradles'.[22]

An article in *La Punta*, organ of the young Christian Democrats, presented an exemplary sequence of arguments. The article began by affirming that 'no *truly* civil people' would have tolerated Fascism: the few banished and exiled do not change this sad reality. Therefore,

We should not lull ourselves in the cosy but melancholy reflection that we have been victims of one man and one regime, because, if this was enough to tranquilise our consciences, there really would be reason to despair, since it would mean that we would feel incapable of shaking off the torpor which once already was fatal for us. So let us beat our breasts and shamelessly cry our *mea culpa*.

From this point on the article slid towards a total distrust in the Italian people's capacity for self-redemption – 'are the Italians really ready *intellectually* to understand what liberty is?' – and, therefore, to indicating pedagogic instruction as the sole path to salvation: 'Educate! Educate! That is the real mission. Indeed, *re-educate* the thousands and thousands of young people led astray and bewildered.' The article ended by reversing the initial position with an appeal more or less to wait on events: 'Abandon the stolid propaganda of retaliation and

19 'La parola dei democratici cristiani', signed 'Demofilo', in the 12 December 1943 Rome edition of *Il Popolo*. See too Lanaro, *Società civile*, p. 34, which brings to light the more advanced positions of a document produced by the Venetian Christian Democrats.

20 'Rinnovamento', in the 23 October 1943 issue.

21 Note the campaign in favour of Franco waged by the Italian Catholic press during the Civil War. See the collection in *La guerra di Spagna*.

22 'Carattere degli italiani', 31 December 1943. Demofilo had even spoken of civilisation in the third millennium, etc.

recrimination over the German and republican-Fascist acts of baseness. Cease from inciting hatred. Ignore the recent past. Because the present and the future are what count for us.'[23]

The condemnation of the Italian people and their misdeeds, in whatever ideological context it was found, could assume widely diverse tones: forthright and hard-bitten, if those crying it were the young; flaccid and self-absolving if it was being preached by older folk. In the Catholics, moreover, the path of intransigence ran up against the thorny question of the relations between the Church and the regime. However noble the appeals to 'shift the problem of responsibility onto us and begin the work of redemption from ourselves, from our innermost conscience, to lead it to the light of social life,'[24] the problem nevertheless remained. And it could not be dodged by unconsidered assertions like this one which appeared, during the Badoglio period, in L'Italia, the Milanese Catholic newspaper: 'Catholics have bent their backs less than anyone else,'[25] nor by the other, still more facile one according to which Pius XI had come to an accord with Mussolini, who had however deceived him, out of excessive love for Italy and because he had taken the class collaboration preached by Fascism seriously. This misapprehension had lasted, continued the journalist, prefiguring a successful historiographical thesis, until racism and the alliance with Nazism came along to set the record straight.[26]

On the left as well there was a mixture, albeit of a different kind, between the desire for moral clarity, realism and pragmatism. The left showed itself sensitive to the duty of safeguarding the good name of the Italian people abroad. An elaborate top-level document, like the pact of unity of action between the PCI and the PSIUP of October 1943, solemnly affirmed that the two parties were deciding to 'join forces in the international field against any direct attempt to put the blame on the Italian people for the Fascist regime, against which the popular avant-garde has waged a heroic struggle for twenty years.'[27] The appeal to the avant-gardes' struggle was de rigueur; but the relationship between the latter and the people remained a doctrinaire postulate. In the same days in October L'Unità took a less all-absolving stance, distinguishing between Communists and the working class on the one hand, and the rest of the Italian people on the other. A people, it was explained, which 'by washing away its grave responsibility for its participation in the odious

23 'Libertà cosciente', in La Punta, 2 February 1944. A group of young secular anti-Fascists had termed 'youth and the people' not yet 'led astray, lost', however 'stunned and aggrieved' ('Ai migliori degli Italiani', August 1942, an appeal published in the Bollettino Popolo e Libertà, 1 June 1943, pp. 5–7).

24 'Posizione', in Il Segno, 1 March 1944.

25 L'Italia, August 1943 (cited in Webster, The Fasces and the Cross, p. 202).

26 'Fascismo e cattolicesimo', initialed 'e.m.g.' in La Punta, 23 February 1944.

27 See the text of the pact in the Rome edition of Avanti!, 19 October 1943.

Fascist war of aggression, regains the right to the collaboration and aid of free peoples.[28]

These acknowledgments of popular responsibility were gradually to disappear, or almost so, from the Communist press, committed as it was to presenting a people marvellously in unison with its avant-gardes. Those with any doubts about this were reproached. Thus a commissar who had attributed 'the errors of the past' to the 'widespread, ignorant superficiality and *pecorinismo* [sheep-like, or poor-spirited, character] congenital to Italians', received a reprimand intended as a real history lesson: it was not the people's fault if all the anti-Fascist parties, save one, capitulated; if at times the people had wavered, this was due to those capitulations; in 1919–20 the people fought for power 'alone against everybody and against its own party'; then there were the people's Arditi, the events in Parma, 'true' anti-Fascism, Spain, the 1943 strikes. So energetic was this indignant harangue that the conclusion contradicted the initial assumption: deficiencies in the people, if they existed, stemmed only from those of the avant-garde.[29]

In its newspaper *Virtù e Lavoro*, the Fronte della gioventù (Youth Front) of San Vito al Tagliamento had declared:

> At present the average person's conscience is depraved. It must be raised. The man in the street, in short the *popolo*, must be made honest. He must be educated, educated and then instructed. And the plebs, *who will no longer be plebs*, will be able to converse with the noble *who will no longer be noble*, because being at an equal level of education and instruction he will be subject to the elimination of every social distance.

The local Communist Party leaders did not take kindly to so much pedagogic zeal, smacking as it did of anarchy:

> You may say that they are not educated, but you must on all accounts say that they are honest. The honesty you are looking for you will find in the corns on their feet and in their sweat. When we say that our heroic partisans are the best sons of the people we are saying that they are the sons of this people ... Fascism hasn't managed to corrupt the popular masses.[30]

---

28 'In Corsica, Venezia Giulia, a Napoli gli italiani sono al posto di combattimento a fianco dei popoli liberi', in the 12 October 1943 Northern edition.

29 Letter from the commander of the 1st Zone of Liguria, Simon, to the commissar of the 2nd Cascione Division, 23 November 1944. The critique concerned a 3 November circular (*Le Brigate Garibaldi*, vol. II, pp. 624–8).

30 The critique of the (former?) comrade Sante, 20 March 1945, is directed against the article 'Formare la coscienza', 20 February 1945 (IZDG, envelope 272b, folder IV/A).

Obviously, behind these stances was the view of Fascism as being the work of capitalism or, to revert to the well-known Third Internationalist formula, of the more aggressive and reactionary forces of finance capitalism. This view of things made it possible to project onto the entire people (once the capitalists, and not even all of them, had been separated from it) the anti-Fascist purity of the working class and its avant-garde, skipping the changes of position and nuances which, in their more carefully thought-out documents, the Communists themselves had sought to analyse.[31]

The pragmatic value and expansive force of this position are evident. Detached from its ideological presuppositions, it can be found in minority groups, such as the Armata garibaldina di Roma and the Ligurian-Piedmontese Unitarian Movement for Italian Renewal (MURI).[32] An echo of this can be gleaned also in an article that appeared in the newspaper of the young Christian Democrats, which was highly polemical against those who claimed that the Italian people would never be capable of governing by themselves, and was bitterly critical of the royal and Badoglian manoeuvre bent on ensuring that 'the paternal and commodious dictatorship of consortiums, monopolies and financings could continue, for all one knew with a general in charge.'[33]

The more strictly working-class tradition jibbed at this tendency to dissolve class differences in the general idea of the people, in order to redeem it, thereby throwing out a lifeline to the bourgeoisie. Let the bourgeoisie make no mistake, wrote *Avanti!*: 'It is too late', let it be made clear, 'to make amends, to redeem oneself. A clean sweep must be made, once and for all, of the whole ruling class, and not just its Fascist vanguard.'[34] Before 25 July a nascent youth movement had written that the people, who had 'at the very least endured Fascism and the war against liberty' should not be flattered and urged to disclaim all responsibility. Later that same group was to absolve the people, who had however to be subjected to re-education, because they had been dragged into error by trickery, while 'the young have no need for justification and absolution': in fact 'it is the ruling class, taken as a whole, that is responsible for this state of affairs.'[35]

---

31 It is enough to recall here Togliatti's *Lezioni sul fascismo* (1936), a 1970 reprint of which was edited by E. Ragionieri, Rome: Riuniti.

32 See the article 'La nostra guerra' (which was 'not an opportunistic improvisation') in *L' Azione*, 1 November 1943, and, on the MURI, which 'declare[d] itself in full harmony with Catholicism', the pamphlet 'Laws and History of the Movement', published in Genoa immediately after Liberation (held at the INSMLI): the Italian people could 'not be mixed up in the blame for this war, which is, rather, limited to a usurper class' (p. 12).

33 'Maturità politica', *La Punta*, 29 March 1944.

34 'La Prova', in the 10 October 1943 Rome edition.

35 'Orientamenti', in *Bollettino Popolo e Libertà*, July 1943, 2, p. 38, and the 'Dichiarazione fondamentale' of the Italian Labour Party, paragraph 2.

It is in some Action Party writings that the greatest efforts were made to marry historical and moral condemnation, the elitist spirit and faith in the people. GL and Action Party political thought prided itself on having been quick to recognise the importance and originality of Fascism, and this pride was nourished by that of a group which felt itself to be a ruling class in the making, in contrast to the one that had had so gravely failed.[36] The Actionists were keen to present the result of their analysis of things as true realism, to be inseminated with determination. The root of this attitude lay in the fact that the Action Party, as Rodolfo Morandi had already polemically written about GL, assumed the form of 'absolute anti-Fascism'.[37] This view was similar to the one that Altiero Spinelli expressed while a prisoner at Ventotene, when he remarked that 'perhaps only the democrats of Giustizia e Libertà were direct adversaries of Fascism': for Communists and anarchists, 'Fascism had, so to speak, concealed the real adversary'.[38] The truth of these claims thus explains the rapid disappearance of the Action Party, as it does the way that the 'spirito azionista' has persisted down to our own times.[39]

Soul-searching as to one's own personal relationship with Fascism meant asking oneself a similar question about anti-Fascism and its claim to represent the true Italy.[40] The link between anti-Fascism and the struggle taking place at the time was obviously taken for granted;[41] but this recognition concealed widely diverse positions, just as it concealed the affirmation, which was also very widespread, that it was not possible to return to pre-Fascism. 'Fascism is intimately linked with the past: breaking with Fascism therefore means breaking with the past', wrote Emilio Lussu.[42]

---

36 See for example the editorial 'Responsibilità' in the Rome edition of *L'Italia Libera*, 11 November 1943, reproduced 'from the Turin organ of the Action Party'.

37 See Morandi's unpublished response to an article by Magrini (Aldo Garosci), written for a magazine produced among German Socialist émigrés in Prague (undated, but after 1934, thus after the end of the Concentrazione antifascista) in Merli, *La ricostruzione*, pp. 615–17.

38 Spinelli, *Io, Ulisse*, p. 268.

39 The persistence of the *spirito azionista* is one of the polemical targets of Catholic neo-fundamentalism: I refer in particular to the theses advanced by Augusto Del Noce, which appear in different forms in both historiography and political debate.

40 Think of the analogous ambitions of German émigrés, as expressed by Thomas Mann in a letter to René Schickele: that they 'must do our jobs very well; then some day people will say that during this period we were the real Germany' (*Letters of Thomas Mann, 1889–1955*, Berkeley: University of California Press, 1975, p. 188).

41 This theme was developed in many of the reports written after Liberation on the CLNs, partisan formations, and local situations. See, for example, the report 'on the partisan and conspiratorial movement in Ostiglia', authored by the Socialist Paride Mantovani (INSMLI, *CLNAI*, envelope 6, folder 2, subfolder 4, old cataloguing).

42 Lussu, *La ricostruzione dello Stato*, p. 4.

The thesis of 'Fascism as a parenthesis' circulated more as a simplistic commonplace, nostalgia for less harrowing times, than as a fully-fledged stance.
Even the 'Guizots of an Italian restoration'[43] presented themselves in the form
of novelty. A Liberal pamphlet said that the PLI was 'in certain respects a new
party ... it is not a simple continuation of the liberal currents of the first twenty
years of the century. We don't refuse to acknowledge the value of the past but we
don't feel nostalgia for it.'[44]

The refusal to return to 1922 could signify two very different things. It could
contain an invitation not to revert to the 'reformist and bureaucratic tendency'
and not to let oneself be attracted by 'pseudo-revolutionary maximalism'[45] –
these words, written by a Liberal, might however just as easily have appeared
in the Communist press, due care being taken to conceal their origin. But this
refusal could also be a warning against the 'haunting and unjustified fear of
Bolshevism',[46] as well as a severe admonition 'to those who appeal to the positions of 1922, an absurd and anti-historical principle that would reward those
very people who in these twenty years have done nothing'.[47] Here there is an eye
to the power relations between the anti-Fascist parties, in the hope that they will
mirror the intensity of the commitment given to combating Fascism.

At the same time, the 'lesson' imparted by Fascism came in for different
readings as well. The old idea of Fascism as a destroyer of the illusions placed
in bourgeois democracy and reformism could never again be advanced, except
by the historic left-wing dissident groups. Polemicising with the 'Centro interno
socialista', Angelo Tasca had written early on: 'The "great illusion" is precisely
that of a Fascism as destroyer of democratic "illusions", a simplifier of our tasks,
an accelerator of the revolutionary process, the matrix of our socialism.'[48] In
some manifestations of Resistance socialist maximalism, this illusion took the
form of an objective prediction: capitalism, after having inevitably led to war,
was 'marching rapidly towards its ruin everywhere and in Italy in particular'.[49]

---

43   Deakin, *Brutal Friendship*, p. 241, defined thusly the survivals of the Liberals,
Populars and Socialists like Romita, re-emerging in Spring 1943.

44   Serini, *Orientamenti programmatici*, p. 3.

45   'Libertà sociale', *Risorgimento liberale*, Rome edition, 5 May 1944.

46   'Saldezza del fronte antifascista', editorial in *La Riscossa italiana*, January–
February 1944.

47   'Direttive politiche per l'insurrezione nazionale, n. 11', 25 October 1944 (*Le
Brigate Garibaldi*, vol. II, p. 489).

48   Letter of 4 June 1935 from Angelo Tasca to Giuseppe Faravelli, in Merli, *La
ricostruzione*, p. 677.

49   Declaration of the central committee, announcing the fusion of the PSI, MUP
and Unione Proletaria Italiana, in the 22 August 1943 *Avanti!*. In the Northern edition of
Avanti!, 10 January 1944, the editorial 'Timori in sagrestia' read: 'The 1915–18 war heralded the crisis of the capitalist system, and this war now concluding marks its end.
Truly, another history is beginning ... The socialist revolution appears out of irreparable

The prospect of the collapse of capitalism was so fully incorporated in the Third Internationalist line that the PCI scarcely felt the need to mention it again explicitly: it constituted the presupposition of the conviction that history would carry the final game into Communist hands.

Settling accounts with Fascism in one way or another, and at the same time with the various anti-Fascist currents, implied the question as to whether anti-Fascism would survive Fascism. During the Resistance, this problem was rarely formulated explicitly. Anti-Fascism was making ready to enjoy its victory and to experience it as the natural assumption of every different current within it.[50] To foresee its own demise along with that of the defeated enemy seemed tantamount to putting itself almost on the same plane, even if in this fear anti-Fascism as a political subject and anti-Fascism as the *humus* of new Italian democracy became confused. Those who thought that the defeat of Fascism was not the be-all and end-all felt it their duty to keep their eyes peeled against the rebirth, in whatever form, of that barbarous phenomenon, which was always a possibility as long as its roots were not completely severed. But the greater the originality granted to Fascism as a phenomenon that had had its day, the more powerful was the tendency to consider that it would not be long before anti-Fascism became a thing of the past as well. Historic anti-Fascism might thus die together with Fascism, but survive it as a field of imprescriptible values. It is no accident that this tendency appeared precisely in the most intrinsically anti-Fascist of the parties, the Action Party. Foa clearly envisaged that the Fascism/anti-Fascism antithesis would be superseded.[51] Aldo Capitini expressed a similar view, with just one word of caution: '*Antifascista* might one day become a useless and tiresome word in people's memories, like *fascista*. Save in the case of one thing happening – that the residues of Fascism reappeared alongside or within the new political alignments.'[52]

The need to put the Fascism/anti-Fascism antithesis behind one was vehemently emphasised by some young people who had lived through the Fascist period. Giaime Pintor had noted in his diary: 'The Fascism/anti-Fascism antithesis and its transcendence allowed us to establish an extremely wide range of values, and in that field we were well and truly more mature than the others.'[53]

---

necessity' for both the victors and the defeated.

50 See the essays in the collection *Fascismo e antifascismo negli anni della Repubblica* (*Problemi del socialismo*, January–April 1986, new series no. 7).

51 See, above all, Inverni (V. Foa), *I partiti*, pp. 68–71. Many years later, Foa would write with reference to the 1933–35 period, 'Perhaps so as not to be dependent on fascism, not even in rejecting it, we refused to call ourselves anti-Fascists' (P. Marcenaro and V. Foa, *Riprendere tempo*, Turin: Einaudi, 1982, p. 102).

52 A. Capitini, *Prime idee di orientamento*, Perugia: Centro di Orientamento Sociale, 1944, p. 9.

53 Pintor, *Doppio diario*, p. 115. In writing 'we', Pintor was referring to the young

Another youth, Raimondo Musatti, had written more angrily that the young could not help being revolutionary because they had learned from Fascism 'the sense of the "totalitarity" of life', only to turn it against Fascism, reinvigorated by the 'primacy of human liberty':

> We have learned that there can be no absenteeism before any aspect of life ... We now know that political struggle is part of the struggle for life itself, an essential element of it ... To be no more than anti-Fascist is of hardly any concern to us. The very word 'anti-Fascism' smacks of sectarianism, which disenchants us; it seems to us to drag with it a weight from the past, which is not relevant to us. Our field of action ... is above all to remake the Italians, starting with ourselves.[54]

The desire to liberate oneself from the past and its protractions could take the form, in those who were not Communist, of an aspiration to take the 'terza via' (the 'third way') between Liberalism and Socialism, between capitalism and Communism. This amounted to taking up the challenge of Fascism, which had itself wished to present itself as a third way and which, by claiming to do so, had fed the high moments of its international prestige, attracting political fringes which would subsequently be encountered among the collaborationist movements of the various countries. There was consequently a powerful commitment, not just in Italy, to sketch out a democratic and anti-Fascist third way. A French underground newspaper wrote, shortly after the defeat of France:

---

people who had adopted the point of view that 'to absent oneself, from birth, is little less than suicide, and thus we all found ourselves mixed up – some more than others – in contemporary life, and were ready to reap its fruits. This position, though very dangerous in that it could easily confuse the weakest souls, was, however, the most productive one: it meant the definitive overcoming of the Fascism/anti-Fascism antithesis, and, with the outbreak of the war, posed us with a praxis that we instinctively felt to be more urgent and wider in scope than that for a long time ... sought by those planning an eventual restoration. They were incapable of finding the *point d'issue*; we, and perhaps not through our own merit, were already stronger, because we showed ourselves at the right moment' (pp. 118–19).

54 Anonymous, undated note in CSPG, *Fondo Calosso*, no. 4. Musatti, having recently fled Italy, had written an article in the January issue of *Mondo* entitled 'Lotta, non rivincita', which aroused 'animated discussions' among anti-Fascists. In the June issue, Musatti had published another article, 'Crepuscolo dei tamburi', from which this note cited the words quoted in the text above. It was probably referring to *Il Mondo (The World)*, 'A Monthly Forum for Unfettered Italian Opinion on World Events', edited by Umberto Gualtieri, published in New York from 1938 (but the January 1939 issue, the only one it was possible to consult did not include the article referred to in the note). My thanks to Luciano Boccalatte for giving me this information.

Indeed, on the one hand capitalism could barely survive, on the other hand the proletariat was not capable of being its 'gravedigger' and replacing it. It is a phenomenon of the reciprocal decline of the role of the two antagonistic classes that gave birth to social evolution.[55]

Several versions of the third way were given in the anti-Fascist camp. The first was dynamic and aggressive; it had behind it Carlo Rosselli's theoretical elaboration and the experience of GL, and was incarnated, in the Action Party, in the prospect of 'democratic revolution' as the only alternative to a return to the pre-Fascist status quo, new reactionary exploits and the Communist and totalitarian way out of the European crisis. Without indulging in a pat anti-Communism, Foa stated that the PCI had not understood Fascism well and that the only serious criticism of Communism was the political line of the Action Party.[56] The liberal socialism of Guido Calogero, so disliked by Benedetto Croce, was in its turn a formulation of the third way.[57]

The quest for a third way wholly within the socialist and classist tradition, and consequently never called by that name, was that attempted by the groups headed by Rodolfo Morandi and Lelio Basso, who were committed to getting beyond both the old reformism and the old maximalism. Albeit with their mutual differences and suspicions, the two groups aimed at the rebirth of a Socialist party that was different from the pre-Fascist one and capable of absorbing the novelties brought by Communism, yet still remaining distinct from it: thus, if the fusion of the two parties was to come about, from it a truly new body would be born.[58]

But the third way also lent itself to interpretation not as an ambitious innovative project but rather as conciliation and a middle way within the existing one, as a smoothing out of its contradictions. In this sense, whatever the formulae adopted, it ended up becoming an honourable watchword of middle and moderate anti-Fascism. As early as April 1943, *Ricostruzione* was writing:

---

55 'Projet de programme pour la Révolution Nationale' – a national revolution different from that of the Vichy régime – in *La Révolution Française. Bulletin pour un mouvement national révolutionnaire français*, September–October 1940, 1.

56 Inverni (V. Foa), *I partiti*, pp. 45–7. On the Action Party's perspective of an anti-totalitarian socialism, see De Luna, *Storia del Partito d'Azione*, p. 201.

57 See the articles collected in G. Calogero, *Difesa del liberalsocialismo*, Rome: Atlantica, 1945. Calogero distinguished the 'third way' from the 'third force': for a discussion on this point, see C. Pavone, 'Terza forza e terza via', in *La Cittadella* III: 5–6 (15–30 March 1948), p. 4.

58 I refer here to the studies of Gaetano Arfé and Stefano Merli, already quoted in part above. On the 'fusionism' which sought to make two parties into one new body, 'without however leaving out dissident minorities', see in particular Arfé, *La politica del gruppo dirigente socialista*, p. 27.

Pure laissez-faire and integral collectivism are abstract ideals and hypotheses. Reality is always a combination of individual initiative and state intervention. [Wilhelm] Röpke announces the third way. The Fascists respond: 'We're the ones who found it!' No, the regime has combined the defects of the two systems, it has not eliminated them in a synthesis that supersedes them. Only a new, anti-Fascist order, which has a profound sense of the values of justice and liberty, will be able to do that.[59]

The prospect of a tranquilising and safe third way, imbued with nostalgia for the past, belonged to that vast area of Catholic society that reverted to the corporatism of the Christian Socialist school, which insisted on its difference from the Fascist brand.[60]

In what I earlier called the non-Communist Resistance *senso comune* (but many Communists also participated in it), the idea of a socialisation of the economy that differed from nationalisation and bureaucratisation was widely current. This theme had traversed the entire history of the workers' movement from the First to the Second International, and then to the 'second and a half'; in Italy alone, from Andrea Costa[61] and Antonio Labriola. It is no accident that a long quotation from the latter appeared in a Liberal pamphlet:

We need to insist on the expression of democratic socialisation of the means of production because the other form, collective ownership, besides containing a certain theoretical error insofar as it takes the juridical exponent for the real state of the economy, gets confused in many people's minds with the increase of monopolies, with the growing stratification of public services and with all the other phantasmagoria of eternally renascent state socialism, whose secret is to increase the economic means of oppression in the hands of the class of the oppressors.[62]

---

59 'Economia del lavoro'.

60 Apart from the abundant degree of corporativism in the *Idee ricostruttive della Democrazia cristiana*, see, among others, the defence of corporativism against the way it had been mystified by Fascism, in the article 'La liquidazione del sindacalismo fascista', signed 'Il sindacalista', *Il Popolo*, Rome edition, 28 November 1943; the section 'Tornare al corporativismo genuino' of the programme expounded in *Il Lavoratore*, organ of the Friuli Christian Democrat union movement, in September 1944; and the definition of the Fascist corporations as 'pseudo-corporations' in the undated poster directed by the Movimento guelfo d'azioni, 'To Italians Worthy of Freedom' ('Agli italiani degni della libertà', INSMLI, *CLNAI*, envelope 8, folder 9).

61 See, for example, his report from the 1877 Gand Congress and the famous 27 July 1879 letter 'Ai miei amici di Romagna', in the 3 August *La Plebe*. See A. Romano, *Storia del movimento socialista in Italia*, vol. III, Laterza: Bari, 1967, pp. 435–40, 447–53, and A. De Clementi, 'Costa Andrea', in *Dizionario Biografico degli Italiani* 30 (1984), pp. 128–44.

62 *Gli scambi internazionali, la nazionalizzazione delle imprese ed i piani economici*, printed in Rome by the Movimento Liberale Italiano in June 1944 (though it is dated 15

The author of the pamphlet, Guido Carli, deduced from this that, whatever formulae and stratagems were used, collective ownership would inevitably fall into the hands of the state, when it was, on the contrary, the state's task to ensure the correct functioning of the free market. A lot of journalism, intent on differentiating itself from both Communism and Fascism, made every effort to give concrete form to the socialising but not nationalising third way. PENTAD (five anonymous authors) had already spoken of the 'transference of the ownership of the means of production to the workers (not to the state)' and of a 'system of non-bureaucratic planning'.[63] In France the exile Silvio Trentin's newspaper *Libérer et Fédérer* had echoed this, from the Proudhonian comments, mentioned earlier, which pleaded the case for 'fédérations de services' aimed at bringing together all the 'communautés de producteurs', and the expropriation of the large enterprises in favour of the 'communautés de travail': these measures should, it was explained, be implemented in the ambit of a planned economy.[64] But how that plan, the autonomy of the community of producers and the market could combine was a point that remained obscure in all the expressions of this inspiration (nor, for that matter, would things be made any clearer by the historical experience of the ensuing decades).

The Actionist Giorgio Diena declared that 'a classless society would certainly be the best guarantee of liberty', and that the enormous power of the 'state as manager of the economy' need not 'necessarily be handled in bureaucratic forms'. But he was equally convinced that, when it came down to it, things would end up being anti-libertarian: 'Stalin is therefore the logic of the revolution and is its saviour.'[65] Another Actionist, Leo Aldi (Franco Venturi), shifted the discourse to the terrain of political institutions: 'an economic critique of socialism' he wrote, 'leaves this central problem unanswered', and does not succeed in being truly anti-totalitarian.[66]

On several occasions *Avanti!* polemicised against those who saw the socialist state as necessarily centralising, despotic and bureaucratic: on the contrary, the socialist state would allow a vast range of solutions, from nationalisation to

---

January) and reprinted in Milan in 1945 by the Upper Italy Delegation of the PLI. The Labriola quote (p. 19 of the Milan edition) is taken from *Primo Saggio*, p. 476, n. 1. See F. Sbarberi, *Ordinamento politico e società nel marxismo di Antonio Labriola*, Milan: Franco Angeli, Milan 1986. Sbarberi holds that in his Marxism, Labriola was always opposed to a statist development of the future society, which, significantly, was conceived of as the 'self-government of labour' (see pp. 13–60, 120–61).

63 PENTAD, *Remaking of Italy*, p. 268.

64 'Notre programme d'action', in the first issue of *Libérer et Fédérer*, 14 July 1942.

65 Diena, *La rivoluzione minimalista*, pp. 15–17.

66 See 'Aldi' (F. Venturi), *Socialismo di oggi e di domani*; 'Pan't' (A. Spinelli), 'Alcune osservazioni a proposito di "Socialismo di oggi e di domani" di Leo Aldi', in *Nuovi Quaderni di Giustizia e Libertà*, May–June 1944, 1, pp. 62–6; and L.A., 'Postilla', on pp. 67–9 of the same issue.

cooperatives, to small family ownership, especially in agriculture.[67] In many texts cooperatives are indicated as the most valid institution for achieving the difficult goal of squaring the circle. The Actionists rejoiced when they found some 'Communist but not governmentalist', in other words a champion of cooperatives.[68] A Tuscan Action Party document spoke of cooperatives as the rule, from which nationalised and individual firms should be only the exceptions: thus the factory would become the 'autonomous cell of public life'.[69] Even the 'extremists' of the Communist Movement of Italy demanded the transfer to the state of all means of production, and in order to achieve this to 'cooperatives or other collective associations'.[70] In presenting his decrees on the occupation of uncultivated land, the Communist minister of agriculture, Fausto Gallo, who probably did find himself not isolated within his own party on this point alone, spoke of 'collective forms of managing the land', namely cooperatives, the 'cell of future organisation'.[71] The flowering immediately after the war of many cooperatives, which were soon to wither, should be seen in relation to this aspiration, albeit vague, among workers, often ex partisans, to 'run things by themselves',[72] to do it themselves, with neither private nor public masters.[73]

There are clear connections between the polemic against, or even quite simply distrust of, state-controlled running of the economy and the stances taken against totalitarianism. Certainly, this category was to enjoy wide circulation above all in the years of the Cold War, and the Communists or Communist-oriented left-wing factions would look on it with suspicion. But the idea was very much present among the *resistenti*, to the extent that anti-totalitarianism could be regarded as an essential feature of the Resistance throughout Europe.[74] A brake was, however, put on the explicit and generalised use of the opposing couple totalitarianism–anti-totalitarianism by the presence of the USSR among the major Allies, and by the fundamental contribution that the Communists

---

67 'Che vuol dire Stato socialista', in the 12 January 1944 Rome edition.

68 See, for example, a report by Raffaello Ramat on a visit to Figline Valdarno, 9 October 1944 (ISRT, *Carte Enzo Enriques Agnoletti*, folder 10, subfolder *PdA provincia*).

69 See paragraph 13 of the *Direttive programmatiche* of the Action Party, Tuscan section, June 1944 (*Quaderni dell'Italia Libera*, 3).

70 'Nella società socialista', in *Bandiera Rossa*, 22 October 1943.

71 See Rossi-Doria, *Il ministro e i contadini*, p. 106.

72 Such was the request of the Teramo National Transport Institute, dissolved by the Allies, to the local CLN, which (according to its 7 August 1944 minutes), in agreement with the prefect, approved its being constituted as a cooperative (AS Teramo, CLN, envelope 1, folder 4/A).

73 The spontaneous cooperativist drive of the immediate post-war years gets little coverage in the large volume edited by F. Fabbri on cooperativism, *Il movimento cooperativo nella storia d'Italia*, Milan: Lega Nazionale Cooperative e Mutue and the Fondazione Feltrinelli, 1979.

74 A judgment expressed by H. Michel, *The Shadow World*.

made to the Resistance movements. To reduce the democratic significance of this contribution to a fallacy, or worse still a deception, would be not so much to oversimplify as to parody history. From 22 June 1941, just as the USSR kept mum about the capitalistic nature of Great Britain and the USA, so the two Anglo-Saxon countries did likewise about the totalitarian nature of the Soviet state. In the shadow of this mutual discretion, the Communists of the individual countries enjoyed remarkable autonomy, which should be identified more in the profound significance acquired by their conduct than in their clearly expressed ideological dissent from the leading state.

Within this general scenario explicit stances were taken against totalitarianism as such, and not all of these were expressed with the delicacy that Ettore Passerin d'Entrèves was to use in 1965 when, speaking of the Resistance as an 'anti-totalitarian revolution', he added: 'even if many germs of totalitarianism are still fermenting on the banks of various rivers'.[75] *Il Risorgimento Liberale* undoubtedly considered Communism a new version of totalitarianism, though conceding that Russia was 'run by an enlightened dictatorship'.[76] The Catholics, some from excessive insouciance, some out of genuine democratic sentiments, played down the seeds of 'Christian totalitarianism' present in their political culture,[77] but eagerly spoke out against totalitarianism 'of any leaning'. The radical and explicit anti-totalitarianism of the Action Party was neither restorative, like the Liberal version, nor ambiguous, like the Catholic one. The 'democratic revolution' could not be other than anti-totalitarian as well. Foa spoke of the 'totalitarianism innate in every exclusivistic approach to the proletarian initiative'.[78] The document written by the Action Party of the North on the Salerno 'turning-point' says: 'Certainly we are not turning a blind eye to the totalitarian aspects of modern mass tendencies'; it was therefore necessary to overcome 'the Marxist class concept of politics, anarchism, and bureaucratic reformism', in order to achieve an 'anti-totalitarian socialism'.[79]

An argument not frequently encountered occurs in another Action Party pamphlet, clearly written with the memory of the consequences of the First World War still fresh in the author's mind: namely that 'the economics of war, the very technique of war have a profound tendency to drive even those forces that least want it down the road of totalitarianism'.[80] This was a realistic appeal

75 Passerin D'Entrèves, *Un recente saggio sui problemi di storia della Resistenza*, p. 93.

76 Editorial 'Liberalismo e assolutismo', in the April 1944 Piedmont edition.

77 R. Moro, *La formazione della classe dirigente cattolica (1929–1937)*, Bologna: Il Mulino, 1979, pp. 470–2, with reference to the FUCI and Laureati cattolici.

78 Inverni (V. Foa), *I partiti*, pp. 68–9, 46.

79 A defaced copy of the document is held in INSMLI, *CLNAI*, envelope 8, folder 12.

80 T. Ruoti, *La lotta per la libertà*, October 1943, p. 6.

to guard against the structural drives making for totalitarianism that were set in motion by war itself – even by that war which was being won against it.

And it is perhaps in the alarm against that fragmentation of man which foreshadows his authoritarian recomposition, whatever weight is given to its economic structures, that we should seek the intrinsically anti-totalitarian motif which, in different forms, to different degrees and at different levels of awareness, traverses much of the shared mentality of the Resistance, regardless of the political or military side one belonged to.

5. THE SENSE OF THE FUTURE

On receiving the news of the Liberation of Paris, Ada Gobetti recalled the suffering experienced four years before at the time of the fall of the city, but was tormented by the thought that the world that collapsed then would never again be reborn:

> What will Paris be like, or rather what will the world that will come out of the torment of today be? I fear this tomorrow that will be so different, so hostile possibly to too many things I have believed in. I realise that that is how it must be; I am ready to give my life to ensure that it will be like that; but will I have the strength to live in it, in this 'new order' of tomorrow?[1]

The use of the formula 'new order' – the very same one that the Nazis used to designate the Europe they wanted – bespeaks a profound anxiety, and prompts the confident optimism manifested on so many occasions by Gobetti to reckon with that culture of crisis that had had one of its centres precisely in Paris, and in which the radical criticism of the existing era contained a thread of nostalgia for at least certain aspects of the past. Fascism, by freezing some elements of that culture, had kept Italy outside a full awareness of the crisis, precipitating it rather into the flaccid optimism of which events had duly demonstrated the utter vacuity. Anti-Fascism was thus, by and large, insensitive to the ambiguities of twentieth-century culture, even if some of its exponents sensed its disquieting presence.[2] The anti-Fascists had before them, at least initially, an enemy with clear and well-marked features. The 'tension that anti-Fascism introduced into moral life'[3] concealed the ambiguities of the culture of crisis,

---

1 Gobetti, *Diario partigiano*, pp. 190–1 (23 August 1944).

2 For example, the spell that certain aspects of this culture held over Pavese can help us better to grasp this writer's attitude towards anti-Fascism and the Resistance, around which a polemic – rarely of a high standard – lit up after the publication of some of the pages from his diary, edited by Lorenzo Mondo, in *La Stampa* of 8 August 1990.

3 I take these words from a typescript by Giampiero Carocci, first draft of a work in progress.

and bestowed nobility on certain archaic features that belonged to anti-Fascism itself. By blaming all, or almost all, of the disasters brought about by contemporary society on Fascism, the anti-Fascists and the *resistenti*, on the one hand, were held back from analysing the society from which the crisis had sprung, and on the other bequeathed to post-Fascist society a faith – perhaps a trifle ingenuous, but certainly solid – in the future of democracy. This process was favoured by the fact that, to bring oneself finally to the level of the advanced countries, whose image was optimistically simplified, was considered an objective worthy of a long, hard and all-absorbing commitment by the whole Italian people. As often happens with 'latecomers', the future as the present of others held back the planning of the future as a radical innovation.[4]

The Catholics had their own specific position on this point. In them one encounters a bipolarity between their adoption as an apologetic argument of the culture of crisis and prophecies of the collapse of civilisation and a realism that sketches out the future by making itself the interpreter of the average situations and aspirations of the present. Since the nineteenth century, the Jesuit fathers had preached that those who have sown the wind shall reap the whirlwind. Now that the whirlwind, provoked by the de-Christianisation of society – or better, by its turning away from the teaching of the Catholic Church – had well and truly been unleashed, all that remained was to take stock of its consequences and seek to govern them, without ever tiring of denouncing their causes. This appeared the only way to 'contend with the Communists for the future city'; otherwise all that would remain would be black 'pessimism about the future'.[5] The tragedy that had befallen the modern world could thus be resolved in the triumph of the truth improvidently violated and 'in the design to elaborate a genuinely "Catholic solution"' to the crisis of civilisation.[6]

'Without needing to appeal to the apocalyptic and woolly Spengler, we consider that in this century we are witnessing the end of a cycle of civilisation': hence, wrote a Catholic broadsheet of the Resistance period, 'the religious duty, the obligation of conscience' to unite in a party, to organise oneself politically in order to impose an honest political order on the country.[7] While the Church was guaranteeing the essential and final fruits of the 'Catholic solution', a wide

---

4 The future as 'the present of another: of another individual, of another group, of another civilisation: is the first and exact meaning of the word "future", and it is almost always the last we think of' (G. Noventa, *Futuro*, in *Opere complete*, vol. IV, '*Dio è con noi*' *e altri scritti*, Venice: Marsilio, 1989, p. 338).

5 The first of the two expressions is from Lanaro, the second from Miccoli: these, in my view, have a common root (see *Società rurale*, pp. 199–200).

6 See, on these themes, Moro's *La formazione*, chapter 'Il dibattito sulla crisi della civiltà' (in particular p. 413).

7 'La nostra ora', signed Guittone, in *Il Segno*, 1 March 1944.

space was opening up for immediate action by Catholics present in society and engaged in the political struggle. The triumphant apocalyptics and the re-emergent empiricists thus protected each other, both fronts reiterating Catholic 'diversity'. The realism of the politicians, their supple adherence to the creases and contradictions of Italian society, were favoured by the fact that it was not so much a question of changing society as of 'saving it' by continuing the work of re-conquest that had been proceeding since 1929 under the protective wing of the Fascist regime.

In 1897 Gaetano Salvemini had identified the strength of the 'neo-Guelph' party as lying in the fact that it knew how to stamp the hallmark of 'order' on its criticism of liberal and capitalistic society.[8] In 1933 Sergio Paronetto, one of the interlocutors to whom De Gasperi paid most heed, spoke critically of the New Deal and the dangers that it involved, and predicted its failure if it were not detached from the optimistic–rationalistic model of the lay democracies and did not assimilate the model of 'Latin equilibrium and measure, and still more of the primacy of the spirit and of Christian realism'.[9]

The capacity of the soaring spirit to coexist with a realism that observes and mingles with the world was to be the basis of the political success of the Italian Catholics, who were ready to proclaim the maximum faith in man but at the same time never to lose sight of the weaknesses and depths of human nature that bore the wound of original sin. The soaring flight rediscovered man's equality before God; the low-flying one observed, to quote Il Popolo, 'the social distinctions and qualifications of wealth, work and culture', attributing to them a 'trivial importance before simple humanity', and thus reducing them to a 'purely technical value'.[10]

In order to put a brake on aspirations to 'make it all new', Don Moretti, the priest who organised the Osoppo formations, said that he preferred 'the new patch to the old suit':[11] it was after all a suit you reckoned to know well, and whose durability you could vouch for. Thus, having kept the Utopian aspiration as it were suspended, it was possible to get down to programmes with no Utopia, at times irritating those Catholic resistenti who, engaged in action and even criti-cal of the maximalism of the young men reared in Catholic Action, considered the programmatic preoccupations of the Christian Democrat politicians as often mistaken or less useful to immediate ends.[12] A like degree of irritation was prob-ably kindled in the Catholic partisans, for its one-sidedness, by the thanks given to providence for having sent 'this period of inner preparation, of concentration,

---

8 Letter to Carlo Placci, from Faenza, 31 May 1897, in G. Salvemini, Carteggi, I, 1895–1911, ed. E. Gencarelli, Milan: Feltrinelli, 1968, pp. 55–8.

9 Quoted in Moro, La formazione, p. 468.

10 'Il sentimento democratico', in Il Popolo, Rome edition, 20 February 1944.

11 See Fogar, Le brigate Osoppo-Friuli, p. 294.

12 See Gorrieri, La Repubblica di Montefiorino, esp. pp. 634–5.

of whetting one's energies for tomorrow's activity.[13] 'Faith in man' and 'acting in the real world ... for Christian civilisation' were the two central exhortations of another article in *Il Popolo*.[14] The objection raised to the Communists' project for the unitary organisation of the young (the 'Youth Front') is telling: the proposal did not seem to the Christian Democrats to 'correspond with the reality of things'.[15] The ductility of this realism did not exclude the unity represented by the CLN;[16] indeed it bent it to its own ends, and at the same time paved the way for that degree of innovation that would have come about in any case, being, to a considerable extent, the work of those who had felt its allure and urgency least intensely.

Those who did not enjoy the reassuring mediation offered by the Catholic Church saw the tension between desire for the future – the alteration of oneself and of the world – and the impact with reality more dramatically. Luciano Bolis was to speak of 'this Liberation of ours' having cost a 'heap of values, in blood, terror and expectations'.[17] Sounding the memory of a now old and sick partisan, Alessandro Portelli later had the impression that he was listening to a 'tale permeated with dream and desire'.[18] The recognition that, in the action of the *resistenti*, rationality regarding value did not always coincide with instrumental rationality[19] meant acknowledging a Utopian dimension to the Resistance, which was quite another thing from attributing to it illusions that history would then rightly have belied:

> Seeking the flashes of Utopia where they manage to shine, the historian inevitably encounters the fragments of Utopia too, the shattered dreams. As befits it, does not the Utopian imagination perhaps reproduce the historic future from which it emerges and by which it is swallowed up? ... In the shadow cast by the representations of the transparent City, is not the power of the dream perhaps placed at the

13 'Prepararsi', in *Il Popolo*, Rome edition, 23 January 1944.

14 'Sugli indirizzi della Democrazia cristiana', *Il Popolo*, Northern edition, 20 August 1944.

15 'La Democrazia cristiana e il Fronte della gioventù' and 'I gruppi democristiani confermano l'astensione dal Fronte della gioventù', *Il Popolo*, Northern edition, 31 May and 10 June 1945.

16 'The most far-sighted policy of the party, which will reap further fruits for us, too, is the policy which, for the moment, prescinds from the party and transcends it; the policy of the freedom of the Italian people, the policy of unity for the complete emancipation of this martyred people.' Togliatti could not have put it better, except perhaps for the word 'martyred' (see the article 'Il comandamento dell'ora', in *Democrazia*, organ of the Lombard Christian Democracy, 9, undated, but after the establishment of the second Bonomi government, quoted in Bianchi, *I cattolici*, p. 266).

17 Bolis, *Il mio granello di sabbia*, p. 4.

18 Portelli, *Biografia di una città*, p. 289.

19 See Weber, *Economy and Society*, I, p. 26.

service of the machine of power, and the energy of this dream converted into the heavy inertia of a discourse of oppression?[20]

It might be said that the *resistenti* had the sentiment but not the theory of liberty.[21] There thus germinated in them a 'maximalism' of consciences, an admirable occurrence in a people in whom almost everyone wants to mediate and few commit themselves to constructing, risking the things the very things mediated. At times that maximalism expressed its desires and its needs in the form of prediction, thereby exposing itself to the all-to-easy irony of the 'realists'. One protagonist has said:

> If someone recounts an event differently from the way it actually occurred, perhaps unconsciously he has actually aimed to do so; it was a desire that he had and in which he has actually operated, probably. If, then, it has not come about as a historical fact, because it has not been achieved materially, you can nevertheless be sure that he who recounts it aspired to it.[22]

The living of the future as if it were the present, the entrusting to predictions and hopes of the process of unification, which the systemisation of empirical experiences was no longer able to guarantee,[23] are features characterising the Resistance. In some way they stand in, as it were, in the absence of economic, political and institutional planning, as if the vagueness of content was compensated for by the intensity of aspiration. One Catholic-Liberal historian has recalled, with specific reference to the Resistance, that 'in great struggles and popular uprisings, sentiments count more than well-defined projects, "politico-juridical planning" of structural, economico-social forms etc.'.[24] To this one might add that what was involved was the intertwining of sentiments with ethical demands, sketches for theoretical formulations, demands for existential guarantees. Faith in some form of palingenesis helped exorcise a death, to be inflicted or suffered which events showed to be always very, very close.

'A thousand signs herald the fullness of the times', wrote a Garibaldino newspaper, transforming its expectations into biblical form.[25] 'In that epoch

20 B. Baczko *Lumière de l'utopie*, Paris: Payot & Rivages, 1978.

21 Constant spoke thusly with regard to Rousseau: see *Discours de M. Benjamin Constant à la Chambre des Députés*, I, Pinard, Paris 1827, p. 211. My thanks to Franco Sbarberi for making me aware of this passage.

22 Testimony of Mario Conti, in Portelli, *Biografia di una città*, p. 18.

23 A paraphrase of one of the concepts used in Koselleck, *Futures Past*. See also G. Ambrosino, 'Koselleck: quando la politica ha pretese di verità', interview in *Il manifesto*, 5 February 1987.

24 Passerin d'Entrèves, *Un recente saggio sui problemi di storia della Resistenza*, replying to Cotta, *Lineamenti di storia della Resistenza italiana*, p. 96.

25 '1945, anno della vittoria', in *Stella garibaldina*, paper published by the 1st Piedmont

we thought, we believed, that we could turn things upside-down, that we were overturning things';[26] 'I'd say that folk expected so profound a change that they seemed to want everything.'[27] Possibly these words, recorded after 1968, are resonant with the echo of 'vogliamo tutto' ('we want everything'); but the contamination is significant.

There was also the projection of the future into an already mythicised past: 'Remember, Lupo di Vecchio, what we chattered about through the woods ... and you wanted to know how primitive society developed, when men hadn't yet learned to hate one another and lived in communion with one another.'[28]

At times exploitation was interpreted as the ultimate form of man's dominion over man.[29] A commissar serving in the very same zone of the eastern frontier from which the above quotation comes wrote: 'We had an ambitious vision of the future of our country', and we did not want to end up at Caprera like Garibaldi.[30]

A Jewish teacher, Giuliana Tedeschi, returned from deportation animated by the 'need to put everything back on its feet, the whole world', by the 'need to make the world be reborn'; and she was frustrated 'because the world was never in the right shape ... And so why did a war occur, to what purpose so many victims, if we were going back to square one?'[31] Others attempt to forestall frustrations, but what they actually do is reinforce their presuppositions by taking their aspirations as having been fulfilled: witness a GL paper that speaks of a 'radical transformation that has come about in the mentality, customs and will of the Italians'.[32] On the other hand, these transformations had come about so rapidly that it seemed legitimate to expect the rhythm not to slow down.[33]

Division, 15 January 1945. Pointing to the examples of the Soviet and Yugoslav partisans, the paper called on readers to emulate their 'virtue'.

26 Testimony of Mario Filipponi, in Portelli, *Biografia di una città*, p. 297.

27 Testimony of the trade unionist Emilio Guglielmino, born 1911, in *A voi cari compagni*, p. 27. Soon before, Guglielmino recalled 'There was a need to know, but also be to protagonists in some way, and above all to change ourselves and all society'.

28 Report on the activities of the Potente (Arno) Division, written by the political commissar Alessandro Pieri (ISRT, *CVL*, Comando militare toscano, envelope 5, folder 7). Pieri was a carpenter, a long-time Communist, jailed during the Fascist period (see Francovich, *La Resistenza a Firenze*, p. 330).

29 See the text of the fifteenth lesson of the commissars' course organised by the 1st Garibaldi-Osoppo Division (IZDG, envelope 272b, folder A/I).

30 Padoan (Vanni), *Abbiamo lottato insieme*, p. 145.

31 Testimony of Giuliana Fiorentino Tedeschi, in Bravo and Jalla, *La vita offesa*, pp. 363–4.

32 Editorial 'La vittoria del popolo', in *Giustizia e Libertà*, Cuneo, 30 April 1945 (quoted in Giovana, *Storia di una formazione partigiana*, pp. 379–80).

33 On how confident expectations of great transformations clouds perceptions of those really under way, see Contini, *Operaismo e innovazione*.

This Resistance utopianism assumed a curious form, almost as if it were a last-minute attempt to keep the respective inheritances of Romanticism and of the Enlightenment united, in manifestations of a *concretismo* (concreteness) interwoven with a need to be most fully alive. I have already recalled how Manlio Rossi-Doria, the last great expert on the problems of Southern Italy, spoke of the need to pass back from science to Utopia. Ferruccio Parri, with a 'minimalism' fed by his polemic against the political schemers in Rome, said: 'And I naively believed that, if anything, the liberation would have brought a greater sensitivity to certain social problems, such as that regarding the supply of provisions.'[34]

The partisans' hope in the future was at times so strong, but at the same time so vague in terms of content, as to coexist with a scant interest in becoming familiar with more precise analyses and programmes, especially when these were offered in the form of indoctrination. We have already seen how complaints about the scant enthusiasm aroused in the Garibaldi brigades by the *ora politica* (the hour of political education) were not infrequent. A party leader declared that it was 'not viable because the Garibaldini get tired'. A partisan from Terni recalls that his comrades fled (that was 'il sòno della campana sorda' – 'the sound of the deaf bell').[35] But another commissar, after speaking out very severely against the political ignorance of the Garibaldini ('It's quite clear, they grew up under the past regime') acknowledged that they 'were still enthusiastic about future liberty' because they 'were still rebels' – though the commissar seemed anything but satisfied about this fact.[36] Possibly the rejection pointed out in this and similar documents helps explain why an English officer could write that the vast majority of partisans who declared themselves to be Communists actually 'thought along the lines of the Conservatives in England'.[37]

Requests to receive some political education did come from the rank-and-file.[38] But the most besetting requests regarded the final goals, rather than how

---

34 'Intervista sulla guerra partigiana', interview given to L. La Malfa Calogero and M. V. de Filippis. See Rossi-Doris pamphlet *Il problema politico italiano e il partito d'azione* (*Quaderni dell'Italia libera*, July 1944, 6). On the 'revolutionary conception, but only in the ethical sense of the word' subordinate to the 'slow, empirical reformism' of Parri, see Valiani, *Tutte le strade*, p. 119.

35 Letter from Albero to the Lombardy triumvirate, on the Aliotta Division, 13 February 1945 (*Le Brigate Garibaldi*, vol. III, p. 355); testimony of Vero Zagaglioni (Portelli, *Biografia di una città*, pp. 266–7).

36 Report by the commander Ninel on the situation in Val Nure, Milan, 25 January 1945 (*Le Brigate Garibaldi*, vol. III, pp. 284–5).

37 Report by the general P. Neame, having escaped from an Italian prison camp, quoted in Absalom, *Ex prigionieri alleati*, p. 465.

38 Apart from what has already been mentioned in previous pages, see the report by Paolo 'for the Communist Federation of Savona', 1 November 1944. (INSMLI, *CLNAI*, envelope 8, folder 2, subfolder 12).

to set about achieving those goals. Giovanni Pesce relates how, after their first action a group of Gappists, mostly peasants, 'want to know, and with desperate tenacity, what future prospects will be, after the defeat of the Germans and Fascists. What might happen tomorrow? They want to get straight in their minds not only who they are fighting against, but why they are fighting ... What is the final objective of the struggle?'

Pesce's answers do not appear to be aimed at placating all this anxiety: they centre, rather, on the need to behave 'like a family before the fire which is about to destroy their house', leaving the rest for later. This seems rather like a request for a promissory note, to be honoured even with one's very life. However, since there was a Catholic among his interlocutors, on that occasion Pesce added that one was fighting in order that the Fifth Commandment would finally be fully put into effect, 'and the Slaughter of the Innocents therefore finish'.[39]

In a fable written after the war, Maarbale says to Hannibal: 'Every war is like this ... Every war. Because it puts everything off until later, when it's over. And, while there's the war, it's like being suspended in mid-air, outside time. Time will get going again an hour later, but war is already the sum of all the hours lost.'[40]

Pietro Secchia explained clearly that 'the combatants of the partisan war want to know that they are fighting for a new and better Italy' – but then added 'putting together programmes is not what is needed at the moment'.[41]

In fact, in the PCI, or to be more precise among its leaders, the reign of final ends was on the one hand assured, once and for all, by doctrine, and on the other hand embedded and hidden in the organisation. Faith in the rightness of the line to follow and in the party's capacity to put it into practice was to give sufficient support to action as the priority choice. This helps explain the PCI's particular commitment, already mentioned, to militarising the bands, and also the type of guarantee that the party implicitly offered the militants: do your duty, and the rest will be given you in addition. A report by Giordano Pratolongo on the Venice federation took its leaders to task for being too practical and for not bothering to do their homework on what was being discussed by the party's leaders, but in the same breath recommended that the young be rallied to act, without wasting time over the preliminaries of theoretical elucidation – 'If theory is the right word for it, since I consider it the fruit of opportunism'.[42]

---

39 Pesce, *Senza tregua*, pp. 174–6.

40 V. Ciaffi, 'Colloquio davanti alla città (Annibale era 'alle porte')', in *Sempre Avanti!*, 11 July 1948, cited in G. Quazza, 'Tra cultura e politica: un latinista nel 1945–48', in *Rivista di storia contemporanea* XII (1983), p. 438.

41 Comment piece on the conference of the insurrectionary triumvirates held in November 1944, published in the 15 November 1944 northern edition of *L'Unità*, under the title 'Serrare le file e vincere ogni difficoltà per la vittoria della insurrezione nazionale'.

42 Report of 7 March 1945 (*Le Brigate Garibaldi*, vol. III, pp. 452–3).

This attitude could result in 'too euphoric and contrived a tone', criticised a Roman Gappist,[43] a tone that aimed at reinforcing the exhortation by presenting it as a statement of fact: not 'Italians, fight!', but 'All Italians are fighting.' Compared with *Avanti!* and *L'Italia Libera*, but also with *Il Popolo* and *Il Risorgimento Liberale*, the underground edition of *L'Unità* in fact appears more tied to contingency and less rich in attempts to bring about the problematic reign of ends.[44]

One gets a better idea of future hopes and expectations not so much in closely argued positions as quite simply in the way people behaved. Some cases see the loftiest principles of Communism being translated into prescriptions for the needs of the immediate present. One Command made the following recommendation: 'Incidentally, we say that it is not always a good thing to distribute into equal parts: when a political commissar knows his men thoroughly, he will distribute more fairly according to the needs of each man.'[45]

Solidarity and dignity were requested and were willingly paired with each other. The waiters, like those of Petrograd described by John Reed in *Ten Days that Shook the World*, and like the barbers of Barcelona in the first weeks of the Spanish Civil War, no longer wanted to feel themselves despised by the workers, nor be considered 'ever ready to sink to the worst sort of bowing and scraping in order to obtain a tip'; they no longer wanted to see themselves treated as 'floor mats' by the *padroni* who used them as 'mudguards' against the complaints of the customer, who, then, 'moved to pity and wishing to show indulgence, pardons, and gives a few coins' worth of tip, the humiliating alms'.[46]

In the Action Party, too, or at least in one of its wings, there was strong activist commitment, the legacy of GL. But the need to assert their identity as a new party led the Actionists, who unlike the Communists had no solid doctrinaire references to appeal to, on the one hand to engage as far as was possible also in refining their ideological position and formulating a programme, and on the other hand to arguing that action was not just an instrument used with a view to the future but in some way already anticipated it. Referring to the GL years, and rejecting 'the fateful time of transition', Vittorio Foa would later write that

---

43 Letter from Giovanni to 'Dear G.', undated but soon after the Liberation of Rome (IG, *Archivio PCI*).

44 On the Florence press, see Francovich, *La Resistenza a Firenze*, pp. 166, 182–4, 198–9.

45 Circular from the Command of the 28th GAP brigade Mario Gordini, 15 July 1944, on the 'functions of a political commissar' ('Funzioni del commissario politico', IG, BG, 02309-12).

46 'Colleghi della mensa, sveglia!' and 'Lottare per la nostra dignità', *Il Lavoratore della mensa*, Turin, 22 December 1944. I base my remarks on the Barcelona barbers determined to smash the capitalist yoke on a conversation with Aldo Garosci.

'liberation lay within the struggle. The future had to be lived immediately.'[47] A somewhat forced exegesis of this grass-roots version of the 'democratic revolution' pursued by the Action Party was given by the GL partisan Mario Giovana:

> We even refused to stop and meditate about political issues and to read the newspapers that came up to us from the plain. Running through us were anarchist tremors (even when we believed ourselves to be indeed legitimists), in revolt against an infinite number of things from our past without the slightest notion of possible remedies, nor the wish to waste our time analysing prospects for the future. What good would that do?[48]

The 'Gobettian seriousness', summed up in the formula 'for this generation no leave is granted',[49] was likewise a way of calmly affirming faith in the future. It can be descried in this stance, which has its touch of rhetoric, against political professionalism and thus in favour of politics as the duty of everybody:

> Let us return home with simplicity, after twenty months of struggle and distance: we shall find the warmth of family affection, we shall find Mamma aged, poor blessed Mamma. Read, study in the newspapers about political problems which are problems that concern us, our well-being, our existence. Take the thought and not the form seriously, the work and not the chatter ... Don't trust the politicos: someone who wants to make a living from politics is above all an idler and always ready to sell himself into the bargain. Political activity comes at the end of the working day.[50]

At the source of a faith in a politically better future was faith in life and humanity. This was a characteristic feature of all the Resistance movements. 'Hoping in life I go forth to death', wrote a German woman worker before being beheaded; and a Frenchman, on the eve of being shot: 'I wanted all humanity to be happy.' A condemned Belgian woman believed that 'after this war a life of happiness will begin'; and another Frenchman, who was sixteen years old, asked for 'a free France and happy French people. Not a proud France, the top nation in the world, but a hard-working, industrious and honest France. That the French be happy, that's the essential thing.'[51]

---

47 Marcenaro and Foa, *Riprendere tempo*, p. 103.

48 See the exchange of letters between Giovana and Valiani, published in *Il Movimento di liberazione in Italia* 89 (October–December 1967), p. 126.

49 These words appear in the Cuneo area GL proclamation of 29 April 1945; and see Bianco, *Guerra partigiana*, p. 147.

50 'Prima di separaci', in *Lungo il Tanaro*, newssheet of the 10th Alpine GL Division, May 1945 (quoted in De Luna, *Storia del Partito d'Azione*, pp. 299–300).

51 Letters by Elli Voigt, 8 December 1944; Félicien Joly, 4 December 1941; Fernande Vorral, guillotined on 7 August 1944; and Henri Fertet, shot on 26 September 1943 (*LRE*, pp. 409, 289, 104, 318).

Paraphrasing an old anarchists' song, an elderly Italian Communist said this to his children: 'Love your motherland, but remember that one's true *patria* is the whole world, and wherever your fellow-men are, they are your brothers.'[52] 'The world will improve, you can be sure of that', wrote one of the members of the CMRP (the Piedmontese regional military command) with serene faith, before being shot on 5 April 1944 at the Martinetto rifle-range in Turin.[53]

Writing about the letters of those awaiting execution, Thomas Mann condemned the 'infantile thought' he had nourished between 1914 and 1918 that after the war 'a life of happiness' would begin: 'Happiness and morality too are not, in fact, of this earth.'[54] And at times it is the priority to be given to justice that seems to call into question the possibility of being happy: 'But with peace it will be difficult for well-being and joy to return ... Above all justice needs to be done.'[55]

Doubts and contradictions arose about seeing happiness as being the essence of the future. Not many *resistenti*, actually, belonged to that category, defined by Sorel, of those 'optimistic, idealistic and sensitive' types who 'showed themselves to be the more unyielding the greater their desire for universal happiness.'[56] Weighing on one and all was the accumulation of sufferings which drove a Catholic to invoke divine protection for his father, for 'Italy, the world, the poor sad world as we have known it, and I especially'.[57] It is the memory of so many fallen comrades and 'the effort imposed on our nerves and our hearts to master sorrow' which has 'perhaps withered for ever our capacity for joy'. This is the doubt besetting Ada Gobetti, who tries to free herself from it by appealing to the intrinsic force of life: 'Or maybe it won't be like this, because life goes on inexorably and is stronger than anything. New creatures are born to replace those that have been lost and affirm the eternity of life.'[58]

This elementary appeal left all roads open, from the most dynamic to the most tranquilising, and each had its share of truth. After lacerating and prolonged collective upheavals, the tension involved in the effort to keep awake

---

52 Letter by Pietro Benedetti, shot by Polizia Africa Italiana firing squad at Rome's Forte Bravetta on 29 April 1944. The PAI was one of many police squads in the service of the Italian Social Republic (*LRE*, pp. 515–16).

53 Letter by Paolo Braccini, GL (*LRI*, p. 55).

54 See T. Mann's preface to *LRE*, p. xiv.

55 Poster of the Piedmont regional union of the Action Party, directed 'to the valorous partisans of the CVL', undated but 'after twenty months of bloody struggle' (INSMLI, *CLNAI*, envelope 8, folder 12).

56 G. Sorel, *Reflections on Violence*, p. 10.

57 Letter by the university student Carlo Pizzorno, shot by the Fascists in Turin on 22 September 1944 (*LRI*, p. 186).

58 The diary passage closes by recounting the visit made to Annalisa Rizzini (Anna Foa), the daughter born to Lisetta Giua and Vittorio Foa (*Diario partigiano*, p. 257, 25 December 1944).

the need for change and the desire for security and peace which allow wounds to be assuaged may coexist far better than in so-called 'normal' periods, when security degenerates into conformity and tension gives way to boredom. Thus, the minority who have actively resisted and the majority of a population that has been sorely tested find themselves once again living in a climate of expectations – different, and at times conflicting, though they may be in terms of their contents and the formulae used to express them: from the Gobettian 'generation to whom no leave is granted' and 'à da veni' Baffone' ('Stalin is coming'), to the saying of the war veteran Gennaro Jovine in Eduardo di Filippo's 1945 play *Napoli Milionaria*: 'à da passà' 'a nuttata' ('this night must first pass').

6. THE RETURN

Even for those who had not chosen to flee for home immediately, the hour of return arrived. This return has to be measured according to how high people's aspirations were, and how deep the doubts accompanying them. The sense of an action not altogether completed wormed its way into satisfaction at the victory and the rediscovery of the full joy of living. 'I felt uneasy, as if I didn't really have the right to rejoice', wrote one protagonist whose anxiety was permeated with 'irritating streaks of tranquility'.[1] It was an underlying joy, but one marred by shadows dense to the point of grief. The dispute, which was to drag on for a long time, between the disillusioned and the satisfied who had fought in the Resistance should take this elementary fact as its starting point. If the great utopian dream of the Resistance had been to succeed in slipping the grip that the twentieth century seemed to have prepared for man, to many *resistenti* it seemed that things had gone off course.[2]

Even before the Liberation, alarmed stances had been taken against a future demobilisation of people's minds that might accompany that of the military formations. This included those, already mentioned, who were urged to go on being always, in every field, the best – 'to be the first to do what they will have to demand of others',[3] to remember their 'duty and obligation to be the first tomorrow in the no less important battle for reconstruction'.[4]

'When it is all over with the Fascists and Germans', asked Dante Di Nanni, 'will we be truly free?' And, in this possibly imaginary conversation, this was the

---

1 Meneghello, *Bau-sète*, pp. 28, 14.

2 On the use of this image see Hirschman, *Shifting Involvements* p. 104. Note Falaschi's comparison between the conclusions of the memoirs of Martini Mauri, Lazagna and Revelli in *La Resistenza armata*, pp. 32ff.

3 Letter by Ulisse (the lawyer Plinio Corti) to 'Dear Tom', 22 December 1944 (INSMLI, *CVL*, envelope 93, folder 5, subfolder a).

4 'Rubrica Gapista', in *Audacia*, Modena, 28 March 1945.

698   A CIVIL WAR

answer Giovanni Pesce gave: 'We shall be free to resume the struggle for true liberty, which exists only when every man is valued for what he is.'[5] Likewise, in France a newspaper of the Francs-Tireurs Partisans Français had written that 'our task does not start on day X and does not finish with it but will continue after the victory'; and still earlier than this, in its introductory leading article, another newspaper had announced: 'We have understood that our union could not just limit itself to the duration of the war.'[6]

At the beginning of 1945, the commissar 'Eros' (Didimo Ferrari) had urged people to remain strong 'so as to be at the breach tomorrow, determined to repress the reactionary forces that might attempt to impede the rebirth of Italy'.[7] In the days of the Liberation, a GL newspaper wrote:

A thousand signs tell us that the forces of reaction are not dead. All around us we sense regret for the parades, the rhetoric, the big business deals, which all complement each other. If we could read into the hearts of many generals, prefects, industrialists, we would read the word Fascism. It will be up to us to defeat these forces.[8]

The unified Command of the partisan forces of the Maira valley, which was also strongly GL, told the demobbed partisans of the need to keep 'ever ready to hasten back into the ranks the moment your job becomes necessary again'.[9]

The attitude of many Garibaldini is expressed in this warning: 'As in Aesop's Fables ... Lads, eyes wide open! Dear comrades, if we needed only two eyes for the Germans, now we need four.'[10] The men of the Gordini brigade declared themselves 'ready to take up arms again in defence of the interest of the people and of Italian Democracy'; and meanwhile they gave the narrowest of interpretations to the handing over of arms, hanging on to 'berets, tunics, red scarves,

---

5 Pesce, *Senza tregua*, p. 135.

6 *France d'abord*, 1 June 1944 (quoted in Michel, *Shadow War*, p. 319); *Libérer et Fédérer*, 14 July 1942.

7 'La popolazione deve essere con noi' ('The population must be with us'), a document drawn up by Eros, general commissar of the Unified Command of the Garibaldi and Fiamme Verdi brigades in Reggio Emilia, 26 January 1945 (*Le Brigate Garibaldi*, vol. III, p. 291). See the rich portrait of Eros in Battaglia, *Un uomo*, pp. 98–9.

8 'Ai Partigiani', editorial of *Lungo il Tanaro*, April 1945.

9 Circular of 3 May 1945, quoted in Giovana, *Storia di una formazione partigiana*, p. 378, which adds that 'reread today, this passage seems to have been crowbarred into the document as a pre-emptive attempt at appeasing the men'. See the passage from the fourth issue of *Giustizia e Libertà*, June 1944, cited in ibid., p. 102.

10 Testimony of a partisan in Venezia Giulia (*Le Brigate Garibaldi*, vol. III, p. 723). 'Attenzione alla Guardia Bianca!' ('Beware the White Guard') was a recurring motto, from as early as the clandestine *Democrazia Internazionale*, Rome, 3, undated.

trousers, overcoats, trench coats, kit-bags, and cartridge pouches'.[11] More explicitly, a Terni partisan made sure that the consignment of weapons to the British took place in the most orderly fashion, so as to show 'that on that occasion we were only handing over weapons, not, to be sure, our ability to reorganise and rearm'[12] – an assertion of proud collective identity that was more liable to arouse the distrust than the admiration of those who were in receipt of those weapons. Some Communists had entertained the idea of 'conserving this force for the defence of the party when the struggle to drive the Germans out and liquidate Fascism is behind us'.[13]

Hand in hand with the exuberance of red belligerence, there was in fact distrust of what was still after all a bourgeois state, internationally located in the imperialist camp. Doubt as to the complete legality of the post-Liberation period had been rife even among the Communist leadership. 'We mustn't imagine that with the English the situation will be altogether legal [*legalissima*] ; it may well not be like that', Pietro Secchia had written at the end of 1943.[14] Distrust of Rome, which does not bear any distinct ideological mark, had surfaced among the Actionists. Ferruccio Parri was to recall this, while Vittorio Foa had shown irritation towards the comrades of central and southern Italy who were expecting everything from what was then to be called 'il vento del nord' ('the north wind').[15] The concealing of arms, a 'subterfuge' authorised *sotto voce* by several Communist partisan chiefs of the North,[16] was the most immediate way in which the mixture of suspicions and hopes expressed itself.[17]

---

11 'Verbale del collettivo dei comandanti e commissari tenutosi in Codevigo alle ore 21 dell'8 maggio 1945', on the demobilisation of the Gordini Brigade (ISRR, catalogue 2, CXXVI, e, 25).

12 Testimony of Bruno Zenoni, in Portelli, *Biografia di una città*, p. 288.

13 'Relazione sulle formazioni e azioni dei guastatori', signed 'Gino', Vicenza zone, undated (September 1944?) (IG, *BG*, 09322).

14 Letter from the Milan centre to the Rome centre, 10 December 1943 (IG, *Archivio PCI*).

15 For Parri, see *Intervista sulla guerra partigiana*, the above-cited interview given to L. La Malfa Calogero and M. V. de Filippis; for Foa, see 'Commento al programma del partito d'azione'(commenting on the Action Party's 'sixteen points') in Carocci, *La Resistenza italiana*, p. 186.

16 Quazza, *Resistenza e storia d'Italia*, p. 339.

17 Quazza (ibid., p. 342), making reference to the works of Kogan and Delzell, speaks of an arms consignment that was only 60 percent complete. The large quantity of weapons abducted from the Allies by the end of September – '215,000 rifles, 12,000 sub-machine-guns, 5,000 machine-guns, 760 anti-tank weapons, 217 cannon, twelve armoured cars, but only 5,000 pistols' – has been taken as a measure of the strength the Resistance achieved (Ginsborg, *A History of Contemporary Italy*, p. 70, drawing on the figures supplied in C. R. S. Harris, *Allied Military Administration of Italy 1943–45*, H.M. Stationery Office, London 1957, p. 358). L. Meneghello described the matter of his own sten-gun as indicative of the post-war climate (*Bau-sète*, pp. 49–50). According to some

'Throughout the Fifties', one partisan has recalled, 'there was the conviction that the war of liberation was not over'.[18] The return to the mountains where – an extreme prospect – 'we shall fight among ourselves'[19] was the alternative contemplated here and there, until the unsuccessful and innocuous attempts of August 1946 put paid to it forever.[20]

Hopes placed in hidden weapons were at least as great as repugnance for the openly displayed weapons to be used in the regular units – above all those responsible for public safety, where the partisans had hoped to find a place for themselves after the war.[21] Once the prospect of a radical democratic renewal involving the military and police institutions had come to nothing, a future as professional soldiers or policemen could not have warmed the hearts of the partisans, leaving aside growing government distrust about their presence in such delicate sectors of the state machinery. Those who had repudiated the Royal Army and had reasoned like the partisan Condor ('Then wars finish and you're worse off than before. But this time those *signori*, the king's officers, aren't here to command us'[22]) were doomed to disappointment.

An ex-deportee, who enlisted in the police, recalled: 'It was mortifying finding myself again in a military milieu'; and in fact this was not the way to redress the 'inertia, the indifference that we found in Italy, which has wounded us far more than German hatred wounded us'.[23] The PCI urged its most trusted militants to enlist, and a certain number undoubtedly obeyed. But, whatever the underlying political purpose of that invitation, a militant could find himself in situations like this one recounted by a Terni partisan:

---

of the testimonies collected by Portelli in *Biografia di una città*, the prudent silence of the early years was replaced with an arrogant claim of right. Mario Filipponi spoke, for example, of the 'tonnes' of arms that had been hidden, speaking of a federation secretary who says, 'It will not be today, but within a year, five years, we will have to take up arms' (p. 299). The most energetic points of the reaction to the attempt on Togliatti's life – Genoa, Piombino – were also seen in this light.

18 Testimony of Valente Tognarini, in R. Pincelli, K. Sonetti and S. Taccola, 'Coscienza e soggettività dentro una città fabbrica: Piombino 1944–1956', in C. Bermani and F. Coggiola, eds, *Memoria operaia e nuova composizione di classe*, Milan: Istituto Ernesto de Martino, 1986, p. 240.

19 See 'Relazione politica del Comando della Sezione Tremezzina al Comando della 520 brigata Clerici', 13 May 1945 (IG, *BG*, 01115).

20 On those who went back to the mountains, see E. Piscitelli, *Da Parri a De Gasperi*, Milan: Feltrinelli, 1975, pp. 168–75.

21 On the Allies' perspectives with regard to enrolling people into the Italian armed forces 'within the agreed limits', see 'Piano per I patrioti del N.O. dell'Italia', drawn up by the Local Government Subcommission of the Civil Affairs Section of the Allied Commission HQ, 7 April (INSMLI, *CVL*, envelope 94, folder 7).

22 See Lazagna, *Ponte rotto*, p. 156.

23 Testimony of Liborio Dottore, in Bravo and Jalla, *La vita offesa*, p. 364. In the *Lager*, this deportee had thought of 'Italy with a capital I'.

Then an order came – the party was urging us to join the police ... But at the last minute I pulled out, because I heard the reasoning of a policeman, who while explaining how a light machine-gun worked – which in any case we knew better than they did – was saying: 'OK, now on the church tower, when all the scum are up there yelling, let 'em have it, with machine-gun volleys ...' It was then I realised what it was all about. What I say is steer clear of it, or things will come to a sorry pass.[24]

Thus the end of the Resistance saw the reappearance of the conflict, which the process of militarisation had sought to resolve, between 'the Communard spirit that any movement of rebellion, linked to the people, instils in the masses of the disinherited'[25] and the requirements of an institutionalisation that was moreover felt to be old and politically untrustworthy. Solidarity taken as having been acquired once and for all was rapidly being belied. In Bologna, shortly after the liberation of the city, Elio Cicchetti found himself by mistake in a partisan headquarters different from the one he was looking for:

'Sorry, comrades'. 'We're not comrades,' one of them explained, 'we're partisans, but not comrades'. 'Pardon me, sorry again,' I repeated, a trifle resentfully. I didn't know you could offend someone by calling a partisan a comrade. I really didn't know. Of everyone I had known during the struggle, no one had ever taken it out on me for hearing themselves called comrade. At the time I didn't think too much about that distinction, but I vaguely sensed that it must have its own particular importance if they had been so keen to draw my attention to it. I went down the steps again shaking my head. I had better things to do than try to understand certain nuances of language. In the years that followed, thinking back on that small incident, I came to understand better and better its significance.[26]

A partisan diehard spirit, then, hovered over Italy.[27] In contrast with the demoralised ex-combatants of 1940–43 and the doubly defeated men of the Social Republic, the partisans were the only ones for whom the fact of having fought constituted an undeniable badge of nobility. But it became clear at once, and would become still clearer in the immediately ensuing Cold War years, that it was a badge that didn't get you far in practical terms, and that it could also be turned on its head; and we know how underrated or indeed unacknowledged glory is a breeding ground for veterans' resentment.

---

24 Testimony of Claudio Locci, in Portelli, *Biografia di una città*, p. 304.

25 Bernardo, *Il momento buono*, p. 108.

26 Cicchetti, *Il campo giusto*, p. 264.

27 See G. Grassi, 'Les Archives de la Résistance italienne: sources documentaires et histoire', in *La mémoire de la seconde guerre mondiale*, pp. 5–21; Pavone, *Appunti sul problema dei reduci*; A. Bistarelli, 'Sconfitti due volte. Le associazioni dei reduci di Salò', in Legnani and Vendramini, *Guerra, guerra di liberazione, guerra civile*, pp. 391–400.

There had been partisans who had declared that they 'disdained any preference and any privilege over other workers by virtue of this past of theirs'.[28] But this austere attitude could exacerbate the discomfort indicated in a book of memoirs: 'With our victory, with our descent into the cities, our partisans' morale undoubtedly underwent its most severe trial.'[29] And the author of another book of memoirs, with a rage that the years have done nothing to placate: 'Never has a national movement been betrayed in the twinkling of an eye by the bourgeois pack of hounds of the cities.'[30]

The prediction of the ever level-headed Emanuele Artom had been: 'The government will never be able to abandon the partisans. In looking after the ex-combatants, which it cannot avoid doing, we will have to come first.'[31] A certain Major Barni seems to have gone so far as to dream that 'in the future republican state only those who participated in the war of liberation will have full rights.'[32] Lelio Basso, with the 'soviets of workers, peasants and soldiers' in mind, thought, not only for the partisans, of 'Veterans' Councils', to set alongside those for factories and farms.[33] Dante Livio Bianco had noted alarming symptoms of *trincerismo* (a diehard trench mentality) in the apolitical partisans.[34]

And it was indeed the politicisation of the bands, which at the day of reckoning strongly insisted on their militarisation and still more on their final unification under an exclusively military sign, that prevented a partisan diehard veteran's mentality from thriving. Massimo Mila grasped this fact when, warning against the birth of a 'partisan belligerence', he considered 'the partisans going their various ways into different parties and the liquefaction of "unification" a good thing': the partisans, he said, ought to let their voices be heard through their parties.[35] One might also add that those who had more or less candidly professed themselves to be apolitical had chosen their parties too. This is borne out by the fact that while the ex-'regular' servicemen were to conserve a single

---

28 'Verbale del collettivo dei comandanti e commissari tenutosi in Codevigo alle ore 21 dell'8 maggio 1945', (ISRR, catalogue 2, CXXVI, e, 25)

29 Lazagna, *Ponte rotto*, p. 291.

30 Bernardo, *Il momento buono*, p. 275.

31 Artom, *Diari*, p. 124 (16 December 1943).

32 The lawyer Franco Bartoli Avveduti, active with the Garibaldi Brigades in the Barge area. See ibid., p. 92 (28 November 1943).

33 See his report 'to the PSIUP secretariat for central/northern Italy', June 1944, cited Salvati, *Il Psiup Alta Italia*, p. 65.

34 Bianco, *Guerra partigiana*, p. 65. Bianco was evidently referring to the 'Trenchocracy' of which Mussolini had spoken in 'Trincerocrazia', *Il Popolo d'Italia*, back on 15 December 1917, in which he had argued that the veterans of the trenches would be the aristocracy of tomorrow (see R. De Felice, *Mussolini il rivoluzionario*, Turin: Einaudi, 1965, p. 403).

35 Mila, *Bilancio della guerra partigiana*, p. 418.

association – the 'The National Association of Combatants and Veterans of All Wars' – the partisans were to group themselves very quickly according to the major political and ideological tendencies.[36]

But the memory of the Resistance is not exhausted in the partisans' associations. An adequate study still has to be made of the post-war process that presents two apparently contradictory faces. On the one hand, there was the demobilisation not only of the armed partisans but of all 'resistance society', only a small part of which would enter 'political society'. For the women, this withdrawal often came to seem like expulsion at the very moment when the long wave of the Resistance was bringing them the vote. On the other hand, Italy witnessed the persistence of a memory that, for all the distrust and official celebrations and alternating waves of political preferences, came to constitute a subtle and intricate thread of a fairly broad part of collective consciousness – that in which 'the memory of the wounded, the capacity for endurance, and the refusal of the unacceptable are deposited'.[37] Like all great historical events, the Resistance also influenced those who had not taken part in it, though in a less triumphant way than the *resistenti* would have wished.[38] Recalling the quotation with which this book began, we might observe that those who had seen only the hazards in the two years that had just passed tried to repress the memory of it; those who had experienced it as an opportunity, and who emerged from it transformed, had to strike a difficult balance between the processing of memory and the processing of a project that on no account was to become just a mere scrap of memory.

What one had proved to oneself about oneself became inscribed in the legacy of one's own personal identity: 'Certainly it was a mark of character if you were capable of committing yourself so completely; certainly it was a precious thing to have this secular faith in humanity which unfortunately many of us lack or which is so tinged with practical scepticism.'[39] Burying one's machine-gun became the symbol of the interment of a road towards the future, which might

---

36 Associazione Nazionale Partigiani d'Italia (Communist in tendency), Federazione Italiana Associazioni Partigiane (secular third force), Federazione Volontari della Libertà (Catholic).

37 Calvino, *Tante storie che abbiamo dimenticato*.

38 It has been written, with reference to the whole European Resistance experience, that 'the Resistance marked domestic, national life more than international relations, more the resistants themselves than the politics of their countries' (Michel, 'Gli Alleati e la Resistenza in Europa', p. 94). Note also an English historian's remarks concerning Italy: 'It was the Resistance, more than Fascism, that decisively weakened some of the constitutive elements of Italy's *ancien régime*'. T. Mason, 'Moderno, modernità, modernizzazione: un montaggio', in *Movimento operaio e socialista*, new series X: 1–2 (January–August 1987), p. 55.

39 Augustinus (Paolo Faraggiana), 'Seppellisco i ricordi', in *La Verità* II (24 June 1946), p. 13.

nevertheless be trodden once again: 'Given that for the time being there was no longer anything for them to do, they returned home and buried their machineguns. But engraved within them there remained that great dream that they had yearned for up in the mountains: the honest and unique dream of social renewal.'[40]

In his memoirs, a Fascist was keen to equate the *odi et amo* complex of the *resistenti* regarding the outcome of their experience with the hopelessness of the Fascist catastrophe: 'Among them as well there was by now an air of having been liquidated', he wrote; and he quotes a Fascist prisoner as saying: 'You see, they've screwed you as well.'[41]

Perhaps this Fascist longed to find common ground with those who had beaten him in the cultivation of a new myth of the 'mutilated victory'. Standing out in contrast to this consolatory and transformist advance is the chasteness of the position taken by the French Fascist Drieu La Rochelle: 'Be faithful to the pride of the Resistance, as I am faithful to the pride of the Collaborators. Do not cheat me any more than I am cheating you. Sentence me to death.'[42]

The welding together of the generation of the active anti-Fascists of the *ventennio* and that of the *resistenti* gave birth, as I said earlier, to a long generation, favoured by the fact that the same thing happened in the Resistance as, it has been said, happens in revolutions: namely that thirty- to forty-year-old people 'who believed themselves young'[43] found themselves in positions of command. The generation of the adversities remained a short generation and, in this sense, the post-war period came to an end earlier for them, not without several advantages, before it did for those who felt committed to keeping open the season of the great opportunities. The long generation may be said to have ended only in 1968 (with some initial symptoms in 1956), when, in an Italy where, by virtue of its very longevity, it had been incapable of perceiving all that was new, a new generation appeared on the scene, eager to take up again the task of widening the field of possibility. Up to that moment the generation of anti-Fascism and of the Resistance had been able to grow old without having to face new rites of passage. These appeared in 1968 and were to be extremely demanding; for many of the older generation they were to prove insuperable. But the polemics against

---

40 'Questi partigiani' (unsigned), *La Verità* II (24 June 1946), p. 13.

41 Mazzantini, *A cercar la bella morte*, pp. 298–9.

42 P. Drieu La Rochelle, *Secret Journal and other Writings*, New York: Howard Fertig, New York, 1973, p. 72.

43 Abrams, 'Rites de passage', p. 179. As regards left-wing circles, Basso and La Malfa were born in 1903, Lombardi in 1901, Longo in 1900, Morandi in 1902, Pajetta in 1911, Rossi-Doria in 1905, Secchia in 1903, and Sereni in 1907. The main leaders were not much older: Nenni was born in 1891, Parri in 1890 and Togliatti in 1893. These chiefs' relative youth was probably one of the causes of the slow turnover of political and trade union leaderships.

the Resistance as a failed revolution of one's fathers and the subsequent salvage operations ('the Resistance is red, it is not Christian Democrat') are perhaps less significant, from the point of view of passages between generations, than the auroral and truly *resistenziale* atmosphere recalled some years later by a *sessantottotino* (sixty-eighter):

> I still have the memory of a profound euphoria, an experience of happiness, of great faith in ourselves and in others. The extraordinary thing was above all seeing in a very brief space of time the transformations that took place in people. Young people who until the day before I had seen as moderates and totally indifferent to social problems changing their attitude completely, as if the discovery of new tools of communication made it possible to draw out of the unconscious of each what until that moment had lain buried.[44]

When Parri had been crushed 'between the two theological and cardinalitial faces of the two illustrious leaders of the left and the right [Togliatti and De Gasperi] and by the symmetrical glinting of their spectacles', and the faces of the ushers of the Viminale glowed with satisfaction that the intruders had been driven out,[45] something was already over:

> In the history of post-war Italy, Prime Minister Parri emerges as an appealing and tragic figure. A man of unquestioned integrity, of lofty aspirations and a conscience tempered through long suffering, he had a Lincolnian grandeur. But the very lack of political and administrative experience that made him so attractive as a symbol of a new and better Italy was also his ruin.[46]

For many, that was the beginning of the end of the post-war era, and they heaved a sigh of relief. Some were delighted, and were even more delighted on 18 April 1948, that the danger had been avoided. Others seized the opportunity to turn their backs on the terrible recent past without deeply engaging their passions, if passions they had. Others still concentrated on the effort for survival, which required work, food and home, as well as the rediscovery of the capacity simply to have fun. This is what Colonel Stevens failed to grasp when, from the microphones of Radio London, he contrasted with a Europe hard at work on the job of reconstruction an Italy where – what are they doing? – 'In Italy they're dancing.'[47]

---

44 Pietro Marcenaro in Marcenaro and Foa, *Riprendere tempo*, p. 85.

45 C. Levi, *L'Orologio*, Turin: Einaudi, 1950, p. 167. This is the description of the press conference Parri held at the Viminale after the resignation of his government.

46 Hughes, *United States and Italy*, p. 139.

47 I keenly remember this, but have not been able to locate the text of the broadcast in the BBC's Written Archives.

Perhaps nobody expected years that might have seemed, as Calvino said, a new *belle époque*. When these years came, they came as a surprise above all to those who had seen the moral catastrophe suffered by mankind at Auschwitz as foreshadowing the final catastrophe of the entire species, which Hiroshima, also a product of man, showed to be possible[48] – and to those who had at that same time placed their trust in new struggles and newly attainable concord to rescue and redeem the future.

48 On the Auschwitz–Hiroshima link, see the series of reflections, collected under the title 'La fine del mondo come gesto tecnico della mano dell'uomo', in E. de Martino, *La fine del mondo*, Turin: Einaudi, 1977, p. 236 (see also pp. 475–6, 630, 638).

Chronology

1918: First World War ends; implementation of the Treaty of London (1915) denied by Wilson; myth of the 'mutilated victory' born.

1919 (23 March): Mussolini convenes the *Fasci di combattimento* in Piazza San Sepolcro in Milan.

1919–1922: Fascist violence in cities and countryside.

1921 (January): Formation of the PCI (Communist Party of Italy) in Livorno.

1922 (October): Mussolini threatens to 'March on Rome'.

1922 (28 October): King Victor Emmanuel III invites Mussolini to form a government.

1923: Fascist *squadristi* transformed into MVSN (Voluntary Militia for National Security).

1924 (May–June): Reform socialist deputy Giacomo Matteotti denounces Fascist electoral fraud and violence; his assassination precipitates the 'Matteotti crisis' and the Aventine Secession.

1925 (3 January): In a speech before the Chamber of Deputies, Mussolini takes full responsibility for the Matteotti affair and challenges his opponents to remove him from office; King Victor Emmanuel III refuses to ask for his resignation; 'Matteotti crisis' is overcome; beginnings of full dictatorship. *Fuorusciti* begin life in exile.

1926: Promulgation of Exceptional Laws (outlawing freedom of the press, association, political parties) effectively ends liberal parliamentary system in Italy and destroys the legal anti-Fascist opposition. Regime inaugurates the Special Tribunal for the Defence of the State and OVRA (secret police).

1929 (August): Justice and Liberty founded in Paris by Carlo Rosselli; establishes cells in northern and central Italy.

1935–36: Ethiopian War.

1936–39: Italian Fascist and anti-Fascist intervention in the Spanish Civil War.

1937 (27 April): Antonio Gramsci dies after years of jail; (9 June) Rosselli brothers assassinated in France.

1939 (September): Nazi Germany invades Poland; Second World War begins; Mussolini delays joining his Axis partner.

1940 (10 June): With the fall of France imminent on the anniversary of Matteotti assassination, Mussolini declares war on France and Britain.

1940–43: Military debacles in Greece, Albania, North Africa, Russia.

1943–45: Civil war in Italy.

1943 (9–10 July): Allied troops land in Sicily.

1943 (25 July): Fascist Grand Council votes 'no confidence' in Mussolini, who is removed from office by the king; Marshal Pietro Badoglio is named prime minister and announces via radio that 'the war continues'.

1943 (8 September): Marshal Badoglio announces via radio that General Castellano, representing Italy in Cassibile, Sicily, has signed an armistice with the Allies who will thereafter accept the country as a 'co-belligerent'; the next day the CLN is formed. German divisions pour into Italy via the Brenner Pass. Hitler, outraged by Italy's 'betrayal', demands the country be treated as occupied territory.

      Anglo-American troops approach Salerno and Taranto. German Field Marshall Rommel is charged with occupying Italy and disarming the Italian Army in the north. Field Marshall Kesselring is responsible for the central and southern part of Italy; he quickly controls the area around Rome and is charged with halting the Allied advance at Salerno.

1943 (12 September): Benito Mussolini, arrested by Badoglio government and imprisoned first on the island of Ventotene, is freed without resistance from a makeshift prison on the Gran Sasso in Abruzzo by German paratroopers. In Germany, he is charged by Hitler with creating the Repubblica Sociale Italiana (RSI), in effect a puppet regime, located near Salò, hence the name Salò Republic.

1943 (19 September): First military encounters between partisans and Germans. The village of Boves in the province of Cuneo is burned to the ground by the Germans. The mayor and parish priest, along with dozens of others, are burned alive. A week later there is a massacre of Jews at Meina on Lake Maggiore. The two events signal the beginning of Nazi terror on Italian soil.

1943 (27 September): Outbreak of the so-called 'Four Days of Naples' (the first civilian uprising against Nazi occupation in Europe.) Allies establish a beachhead at Salerno while Kesselring retreats slightly to Montecassino. At the private residence of Mussolini in Rocca delle Caminate in the province of Forlì, the first meeting of the new fascist government. Rodolfo Graziani is named minister of defence.

1943 (9 November): A draft notice appears in all newspapers for four years of conscripts. Approximately a minority of 50,000 answers the call, most are sent to Germany for labour (with men captured after 8 September) or enrolled in four divisions under German command.

1943 (20 November): Workers' demonstrations in Turin; Fiat factory workers on strike. Germans name General Zimmerman to stamp out the demonstrations.

1944 (8 January): Verona Trial: Count Galeazzo Ciano (Mussolini's son-in-law and former foreign minister) is charged with treason for having voted against the Duce in July 1943. He and others are sentenced to death.

1944 (24 March): Fosse Ardeatine massacre.

1944 (2 April): Trial in Turin against General Giuseppe Perotti and his colleagues in the partisan Piedmontese Military Command captured by the Fascists. Condemned to death, they are shot at Martinetto. Period of greatest repression against the anti-Fascist Resistance. Nazi-Fascist terror against wide swaths of population in northern and central Italy.

Palmiro Togliatti, recently returned from the Soviet Union, in an interview in *L'Unità*, the organ of the PCI, issues the so-called 'svolta di Salerno', a call for national unity and the expulsion of the Germans and the defeat of the Fascists before any political revolution or institutional reform.

1944 (23 April): Partisans kill philosopher Giovanni Gentile (former minister of education in the Fascist regime) in Florence.

1944 (4 June): Allies enter Rome. While there is general jubilation and the Allies are greeted warmly, there is no popular insurrection against the Germans. The Holy See urges restraint and counsels against a popular uprising.

1944 (8 June): Political crisis forces Badoglio to resign; he is replaced by the moderate socialist Ivanoe Bonomi.

1944 (16 July): Battle for Florence begins; city is liberated on 10 August. The retreating Germans destroy all bridges over the Arno River, except the Ponte Vecchio.

1944 (15 August): The Allies land in southern France, forcing the Germans to defend the north-west part of the country. Partisans fight Germans fiercely for control of the Alpine passes. In retreat from Tuscany, German Wehrmacht and SS engage in scorched-earth policy; in Marzabotto they execute 1,830 civilians.

1944 (8 September): Partisans liberate Domodossola and form one of the first short-lived independent republics.

1944 (13 November): General Alexander of the Allies issues a radio message to the partisans declaring the summer offensive over and ordering them to return home for the winter of 1944–45. Luigi Longo of the PCI, speaking on behalf of the Corp Volontari della Libertà, responds that the partisans will remain at their posts in the mountains and will continue to fight.

1944 (6 December): Mussolini returns to Milan for his last public speech, while a German offensive in France briefly raises Fascist hopes. But the Allies regroup and advance, and a final battle for Milan begins.

1945 (21 February): Mussolini dismisses Guido Buffarini Guidi, a diehard fanatical Fascist, as minister of the interior in the RSI: a cynical attempt to mitigate the worst aspects of Fascism in order to attract moderate and conservative political elements.

1945 (22 March): RSI announces the immediate socialisation of all industry and companies. Fiat workers respond by forming the factory councils. Germans begin first desperate negotiations for surrender with Allies.

1945 (18 April): Mussolini leaves Gargnano and establishes final outpost in Milan.

1945 (21 April): The German line is broken; city of Bologna liberated.

1945 (25 April): CVL issues orders for general uprising; partisan formations enter Italy's largest cities. In Milan, Mussolini has a last meeting with representatives of the CLN, who demand unconditional surrender. Mussolini departs Milan that evening towards Swiss border.

1945 (28 April): Mussolini and mistress Clara Petacci are arrested near Lake Como and are executed along with RSI functionaries. The corpses are taken to a petrol station in Piazzale Loreto in Milan, where they are displayed to the crowds. CLNAI assumes provisional power.

1945 (19 June): Ferruccio Parri of the Action Party named prime minister.

1945 (24 November): Parri government falls.

1946 (2 June): First political elections: in the referendum between monarchy and republic the latter wins, and a Constituent Assembly is elected to draft a new Constitution.

1948 (1 January): The new Constitution takes effect.

Adapted from Giorgio Bocca, *Storia popolare della Resistenza*, Bari: Laterza, 1978, p. 115, and Stanislao G. Pugliese, *Fascism, Anti-Fascism and the Resistance in Italy*, Lanham, MD; Rowman & Littlefield, 2004, p. xvii–xviii.

List of Abbreviations

AMG	Allied Military Government
CIL	Corpo italiano di liberazione (Italian Corps of Liberation)
CLN	Comitato di liberazione nazionale (Committee of National Liberation)
CLNAI	Comitato di liberazione nazionale Alta Italia (Committee of National Liberation Northern Italy)
CMRP	Comando militare regionale piemontese (Regional Piedmontese Military Command)
CTLN	Comitato toscano di liberazione nazionale (Tuscan Committee of National Liberation)
CUMER	Comando unico militare Emilia-Romagna (Single Military Command for Emilia-Romagna)
CVL	Corpo volontari di libertà (Volunteer Corps for Freedom)
DC	Democrazia cristiana (Christian Democracy)
FFI	Forces françaises de l'Intérieur (French Forces of the Interior)
FTPF	Franc-tireurs partisans français (French Partisan Sharpshooters)
GAG	Gruppi d'azione giovanile (Youth Action Groups)
GAP	Gruppi d'azione patriottica (Patriotic Action Groups)
GL	Giustizia e Libertà (Justice and Liberty)
GNR	Guardia nazionale repubblicana (National Republican Guard)
MUP	Movimento di unità proletaria (Movement of Proletarian Unity)
MVSN	Militia volontaria per la sicurezza nazionale (Voluntary Militia for National Security)
ONARMO	Opera nazionale assistenza religiosa e morale agli operai (National Organisation for Religious and Moral Assistance for Workers)
OSCAR	Organizzazione del soccorso cattolico agli antifascisti ricercati (Catholic Relief Organisation for Persecuted Antifascists)
OSS	Office of Strategic Services
PCI	Partito comunista italiano (Halian Communist Party)
PdA	Partito d'azione (Action Party)
PFR	Partito fascista repubblicano (Fascist Republican Party)
PIL	Partito italiano del lavoro (Italian Labor Party)
PLI	Partito liberale italiano (Italian Liberal Party)
PNF	Partito nazionale fascista (National Fascist Party)

PRI	Partito repubblicano italiano (Italian Republican Party)
PSI	Partito socialista italiano (Italian Socialist Party)
PSIUP	Partito socialista italiano di unità proletaria (Italian Socialist Party of Proletarian Unity)
RAU	Reparto arditi ufficiali (Department of Arditi Officers)
RSI	Repubblica sociale italiana (Italian Social Republic)
SAP	Squadre d'azione patriottica (Patriotic Action Squads)
SIM	Servizio informazioni militari (Military Intelligence Service)
SOE	Special Operations Executive

Glossary

Arditi/arditismo (lit.: 'the daring ones'): Italian shock troops during the First World War, many were later followers of D'Annunzio and Mussolini.

Attesismo/attesistico: the stance of waiting to see which way the wind was blowing before deciding on a course of action.

Autonomi: 'autonomous' brigades, often politically tied to the Christian Democrats.

Avanti!: daily newspaper of the Italian Socialist Party.

Aventino (from the hill in Rome where the *plebei* withdrew against the *patrizi* in the third to fifth centuries BC, the first time with Menenio Agrippa): summer 1924 secession of Parliament in protest over the assassination of the Socialist Deputy Giacomo Matteotti.

Azionismo: The political philosophy of the Action Party; left-wing but non-Marxist.

Badogliani-comunisti: term of contempt used by the Germans when referring to the partisans, conveniently grouping together disparate political elements. The Nazis and Fascists also referred to the partisans as 'terroristi'.

Baffone/Barbisun (lit.: 'big moustache' or 'big whiskers'): colloquial name for Stalin.

biennio rosso: two red years of 1919–20 of intense political agitation in Italy in aftermath of the First World War.

Bordighista: follower of Amadeo Bordiga, a founder of the PCI.

Camicie nere (also 'squadristi', lit.: 'black shirts'): Mussolini's followers, often perpetrators of arson, physical assaults and assassination of political opponents.

Caporetto: First World War battle of October–November 1917; Italy's worst military defeat, when the very nation appeared on the brink of surrender; instead, Italy rallied on to victory with the Vittorio Veneto offensive of October–November 1918.

CLN/CLNAI (Committee of National Liberation/Committee of National Liberation for Northern Italy): the political arm of the armed Resistance. Formally convened in September 1943 and comprising five parties: Liberal, Christian Democrat, Socialist, Communist and Action.

confino: the practice of internal or domestic exile, often to one of the penal islands such as Ustica or Lipari, or a remote village in the Mezzogiorno.

Democrazia Cristiana (DC, Christian Democracy): Catholic Political Party
founded in 1943 by Alcide De Gasperi as heir to the Partito Popolare Haliano
(PPI) of Don Luigi Stunzo, founded 1919. With the fall of the Parri government, De Gasperi became prime minister in December 1945.

Fasci di combattimento: the first groups of fascists organised on 23 March 1919
in Milan's Piazza San Sepolcro.

Fiat (Fabbrica Italiana Automobili Torino): the automobile factory works in
Turin owned by the Agnelli family; site of the largest communist workers'
organisation and strikes against the regime in 1943–45.

federale: provincial Fascist party secretary.

Fosse Ardeatine: cave outside Rome where, on 24 March 1944, Nazis executed
335 men and boys in retaliation for a partisan attack.

fuorusciti: anti-fascist political exiles, ranging from monarchists and Liberals to
Socialists, Communists and members of Justice and Liberty/Action Party.

Gappista (GAP, Gruppi di Azione Patriottica): armed anti-fascist communists engaged in guerrilla actions against Fascists and Nazis; often termed
'bandits' or 'outlaws' by the Fascist and Nazi authorities.

Garibaldino: Member of the Garibaldi (Communist) anti-Fascist partisan
brigades.

gerarca/gerarchi (lit.: 'hierarchs'): high-ranking leaders of the Partito Nazionale
Fascista.

GL: Giustizia e Libertà (Justice and Liberty), movement founded in 1929 by
Carlo Rosselli, whose followers were often referred to as *giellisti* from the
first letters of the name. Rejected Marxism and espoused liberal socialism.

Gruppo di Riconstruzione Liberale (Liberal Reconstruction Group): founded
late 1942 by Liberals, liberal Catholics and some reform socialists.

Italia Libera: daily newspaper of the Action Party.

L'Unità: daily newspaper of the Italian Communist Party.

manganello (lit.: 'little club'): a favourite weapon of the fascist *squadristi* and
camicie nere in their street fights against political opponents.

Matteotti, Giacomo: reform socialist deputy assassinated June 1924; anti-Fascist
Matteotti Brigades named in his memory.

Il Messaggero: daily newspaper of Rome.

Movimento d'Unità Proletaria (MUP, Movement of Proletarian Unity):
founded 10 January 1943 in an attempt to renew traditional Italian socialism.
Strong in the regions of Piedmont, Lombardy, Emilia-Romagna, and Lazio.

MSI (Movimento Sociale Italiano): a neo-fascist party formed in December 1946
by former Fascist officials of the RSI.

'Mutilated Victory': rhetorical and political myth that Italy's 'victory' in
WWI was "mutilated" by Woodrow Wilson, the Entente and the Treaty of
Versailles, denying Italy of her just rewards and spurring the formation of
Fascism.

MVSN (Milizia Volontaria per la Sicurezza Nazionale): Voluntary Militia for National Security, formed 1 February 1923 in an attempt to bring the *squadristi* under the control of the new fascist state.

naja: military service in vernacular.

Ordinovisti: members of the *Ordine Nuovo* journal and movement in Turin, followers of Antonio Gramsci's wing of the PCI.

OVRA (Opera Vigilianza per la Repressione Antifascista): special police organisation established in 1927 to discover and imprison anti-Fascists.

paracadutisti: paratroopers.

Partito Comunista Italiano (Italian Communist Party): founded in Livorno in January 1921 after split from PSI; first as PCDd'I then PCI (1943), by Antonio Gramsci, Armadeo Bordiga, Palmiro Togliatti, Iognazio Silone and others. Outlawed by fascist regime in 1926, led the armed Resistance and emerged from war as the largest communist party in Western Europe.

Partito d'Azione (PdA, Action Party): founded July 1942 by the political heirs of Carlo and Nello Rosselli, founders of Giustizia e Libertà, assassinated June 1937, based on liberal socialism and rejecting Marxist determinism. Largest and most influential political movement in the Resistance after the PCI.

Partito Socialista Italiano (PSI, Italian Socialist Party): founded in Genoa in 1892, externally split between its reformist and revolutionary factions, still played a major role in the Resistance.

passo romano (lit.: 'Roman step'): introduced into the Italian military after the Rome–Berlin Axis and similar to the Nazi goose-step.

podestà: local fascist government official who usurped the powers and responsibilities of the more traditional (and autonomous) *sindaco* (mayor), *consiglio comunale* (communal council) and *giunta comunale*.

quadri (mil): cadres.

quadrumviri: four fascists appointed by Mussolini to direct the 'March on Rome': Emilio De Bono, Cesare Maria De Vecchi di Val Cismon, Italo Balbo, and Michele Bianchi; later members of the Fascist Grand Council.

questore: police commissioner.

ras (word of Ethiopic origin): local paramilitary fascist officials; often responsible for 'punitive expeditions' against anti-fascists, especially in the countryside.

Regina Coeli (lit.: 'Queen of Heaven'): notorious prison in Rome.

repubblichino: derogatory term for a follower of the RSI.

resistenti: 'resisters'; used here often in place of *partigiani*.

Risorgimento: the movement for national unification in nineteenth-century Italy.

Il Risorgimento Liberale: daily newspaper of the Liberal Party (1943–48).

Romanità (lit.: 'Roman-ness'): the cultural policy in Fascist Italy of portraying contemporary Fascist Italy as the heir to ancient Rome; classicism corrupted for the Fascist political programme.

RSI (Repubblica Sociale Italiana): the Italian Social Republic (September 1943–April 1945) established with Hitler's assistance after 8 September. Controversy still rages over whether the RSI was a legitimate form of government, worthy of the loyalty of patriotic Italians, or a puppet regime controlled by a foreign power (the Nazis). Also known as the Salò Republic.

squadristi/squadrismo: *see* camicie nere.

svolta di Salerno: Palmiro Togliatti's (leader of the PCI) abrupt reversal of long-standing Communist Party platform urging revolution. Instead, in April 1944, Togliatti returned to Naples from Moscow and announced a new policy: the PCI would work with other parties to expel the Germans from Italy, defeat the Fascists and put off questions and debate regarding fundamental institutional reforms.

trinceristi/trincerismo (lit.: 'those from the trenches'): veterans of the First World War who found it difficult to return to civilian life and who were often attracted to the military ethos and lifestyle of Fascism.

uomo qualunque/qualunquista: 'everyman' movement (1944) and subsequent political party (1946) with Fascist echoes and post-Fascist character.

ventennio (lit.: 'twenty years'): the two decades of Fascist rule.

via Rasella: site of a communist partisan attack against German military unit which killed thirty-three soldiers; in retaliation, Hitler ordered ten Italians shot for each German. *See also* Fosse Ardeatine.

via Tasso: headquarters of the Nazi Gestapo and SS in Rome; notorious for the torture and executions of soldiers, anti-Fascists, and civilians that took place there.

Index

see also collapse of Fascist regime (July 1943)
Mussolini, Vittorio 275–6
Muti brigades 160, 552, 559, 562
Muti, Ettore 275, 359
MVSN (Milizia Volontaria per la Sicurezza Nazionale)/Blackshirts 13, 109–10, 277
mythology
    goodness of the Italians 107–8, 123–4, 209
    of Resistance xxi–xxiii
    of the USSR 483–6, 489–90, 492–3

naja 121, 131, 153
Nanni, Roberto 71
Naples 165, 241, 533
Nation Collapses, A: The Italian Surrender of September 1943 (Aga Rossi) xiii, xxii
National Guard 175–6, 288, 322
national identity
    borders and colonies 247–50
    and civil war 271
    and the collapse of the Fascist state 205–8
    crisis of xii
    and occupation by two foreign armies 214–17
    and the partisan movement 209–10
    post-war 245–7, 250–1
    restored by Resistance 91, 624
    and the Risorgimento 217–21
    see also patria
national unity 145, 147, 318–19, 376, 435, 450, 602–3
Natisone division 128, 225, 235, 467–8, 473, 595–6
    see also Ferdinando Mautino; Giovanni Padoan
Natta, Alessandro 87
Nazione (Romeo) 669
Nazioni Unite 365
Nazism 32–3, 80, 84, 221, 257–60, 364–5, 370–1
    see also Germany; Hitler
negotiation
    with Fascists and Germans 327–32, 404–6, 575
    with industrialists 404, 412–13
    with RSI authorities 333–6
Nembo paratroops 43, 47
Nenni, Pietro 79–80, 80–1, 219, 223, 357, 373

neo-Fascism xviii–xix, 274, 275, 371, 610, 634
neo-Guelphism 219–20, 688
Nicoletta, Giulio 106
Nicoletti, Italo ('Andreis') 189, 372
Nogara, Giuseppe 344–5
Nolte, Ernst 363, 570
noms de guerre 224–6, 471–2, 534
Non abbiamo bisogno 63
normalisation 295–6
Nuovo Avanti! 80
Nuovo Risorgimento Italiano 220

oaths of allegiance
    to the king and the Duce 60–4, 71–2, 125, 301–2
    and the Resistance 66–70
    to the RSI 61, 64–6, 660
officers
    attitude to 113–14, 118–22, 125–31, 141–2
    code of values 105
    and the collapse of armed forces 19–20
    competence 122–4
    election and selection 155–7
    oaths of allegiance 61–2
    of the RSI 137–40
Oliva, Elsa 527–8, 530
Olivelli, Teresio 28, 361, 622, 637
Oltrepò 166
    see also Pavese Oltrepò Garibaldini
'Omero antimilitarista' (Calvino) 5
Omodeo, Adolfo 109, 116, 365
Opera Nazionale Assistenza Religiosa e Morale agli Operai (ONARMO) 356
Opere (Togliatti) 270–1, 310
Operti, Raffaello 123–4, 195
O'Regan, Patrick ('Chape') 372
Orlandi, Taddeo 672
OSCAR (Organizzazione del Soccorso Cattolico agli Antifascisti Ricercati) 356–7
Osoppo brigades
    and the Alpini 134
    Catholic influence 119, 187, 344, 345, 532, 580, 640–1
    conflict between bands 190–1
    and ex-army officers 127
    military style 151–2
    Pai Nestris Fogolârs 165
    politics 316, 379, 486, 617